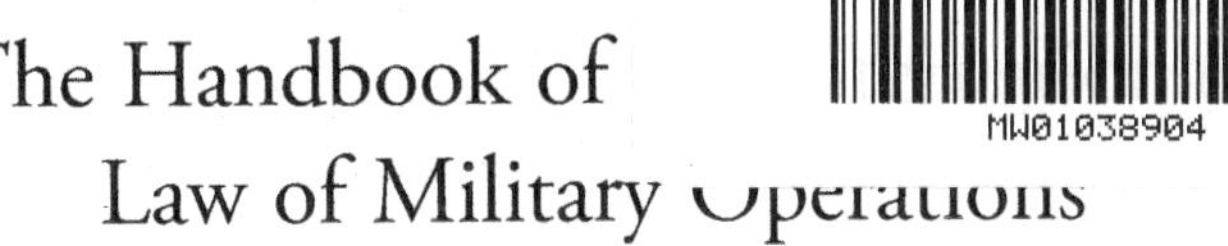

The Handbook of Law of Military Operations

SECOND EDITION

The Handbook of the International Law of Military Operations

SECOND EDITION

Edited by

TERRY D. GILL AND DIETER FLECK

In collaboration with

Hans F.R. Boddens Hosang, William H. Boothby, Patrick C. Cammaert, Blaise Cathcart, Paul A.L. Ducheine, William J. Fenrick, Martin D. Fink, Charles H.B. Garraway, Gloria Gaggioli Gasteyger, Wolff Heintschel von Heinegg, Ben F. Klappe, Jann K. Kleffner, Boris Kondoch, William K. Lietzau, Timothy McCormack, Nils Melzer, Eric P.J. Myjer, Bruce M. Oswald, A.P.V. Rogers†, Joseph A. Rutigliano Jr, Michael N. Schmitt, Darren M. Stewart, Nigel D. White, and Marten Zwanenburg

OXFORD
UNIVERSITY PRESS

OXFORD
UNIVERSITY PRESS

Great Clarendon Street, Oxford, OX2 6DP,
United Kingdom

Oxford University Press is a department of the University of Oxford. It furthers the University's objective of excellence in research, scholarship, and education by publishing worldwide. Oxford is a registered trade mark of Oxford University Press in the UK and in certain other countries

First published 2015
First published in paperback 2017

Published in the United States of America by Oxford University Press
198 Madison Avenue, New York, NY 10016, United States of America

British Library Cataloguing in Publication Data
Data available

Library of Congress Cataloging in Publication Data
Data available

ISBN 978–0–19–874462–7 (Hbk.)
ISBN 978–0–19–881364–4 (Pbk.)

Contents

PART II MILITARY OPERATIONS WITHIN THE CONTEXT OF THE UN COLLECTIVE SECURITY SYSTEM

PART IV CAPITA SELECTA OF INTERNATIONAL MILITARY OPERATIONAL LAW

Preface

This Handbook, first published in 2010, was well received by students and practitioners. It responds to a growing need to interpret and implement principles and rules of law regulating military operations in context. The present revised edition considers developments in State practice and research during the last five years. It also significantly benefits from teaching experience.

This revised edition builds upon the previous one and is intended to provide a single comprehensive guide to the various areas of international law which regulate and influence the planning and conduct of contemporary international military operations by States and by international organizations. It is aimed at practitioners, scholars, and students alike and is meant to assist senior civilian and military policy makers and their legal advisors in identifying the relevant law and in drawing up legal and policy guidelines and regulations for a whole range of military operations. It is also intended to serve as a research and teaching tool for scholars, instructors, and students at universities, military staff colleges, and other institutions where attention is devoted to all or some of the areas of international law covered.

The present edition has maintained the same structure and perspective as its predecessor and new developments, such as cyber warfare and additional areas of relevant law, such as weapons law, together with recent practice and decisions by international organizations and adjudicatory bodies have been included alongside the existing material. Several new contributors have joined the original group of authors to help with this update and expansion and bring in their own expertise and views alongside those of the original group of authors. As with the previous edition, the commentary in the chapters by the contributors represents the views of the author(s) of that chapter, while the 'black letter rules' represent a consensus between the contributors and between the contributors and editors. The role of the editors has been to maintain the overall cohesion and structure of the book as a whole. The present edition again represents a collective effort in every sense and the editors would like to express their sincere appreciation and thanks to all the contributors for the effort all have put into the project. It should be added that the views expressed by all contributors are the personal views of the participants and do not represent the official views of any institution, organization, or government which they presently work for or have worked for in the past.

This project forms part of a joint research project of the Amsterdam Center for International Law and the Netherlands Defence Academy entitled 'The Role of Law in Armed Conflict & Peace Operations'. The editors would like to express their sincere thanks to the support by both institutions.

The support and understanding from the publishers throughout this project has been outstanding and the editors would like to express their sincere thanks to

Oxford University Press, in particular to Mr John Louth, Ms Merel Alstein, and Ms Emma Endean for helping make this project possible.

This book is intended hopefully to serve as both a practical guide for legal practitioners involved in the planning and conduct of military operations, as well as an educational tool and academic reference. It is only fitting, therefore, that it be dedicated to legal advisors in the armed forces on operational deployment, who are charged with interpreting and applying the law under the most difficult and challenging circumstances any international legal practitioner can face.

Utrecht and Cologne, April 2015
Terry Gill Dieter Fleck

List of Contributors

Hans F.R. Boddens Hosang, Senior Legal Advisor and Head of International Affairs Department Netherlands Ministry of Defence. Mr Boddens Hosang has represented the Netherlands MoD at numerous international conferences and working groups on issues of international and operational law and has overall responsibility for the rules of engagement for the Netherlands armed forces on operational deployment. He is currently in an advanced stage of PhD research on the relationship of international and (comparative) national criminal law with rules of engagement and is a Guest Lecturer at the University of Amsterdam and the Netherlands Defence Academy (*Chapter 24*).

Air Commodore (ret.) Dr **William H. Boothby** served in the Royal Air Force Legal Branch for 30 years, retiring in 2011 as Deputy Director of the RAF Legal Service. He served in a wide range of home and overseas assignments during his military career. He obtained his doctorate in 2009 and has published a monograph on the Law of Weapons in 2009 and another on the Law of Targeting in 2012 through OUP. He participated in the preparation of the HPCR Manual on Air and Missile Warfare and the *Tallinn Manual on Cyber Warfare* under the auspices of NATO CCDCOE. He is presently an Associate Fellow at the Geneva Centre for Security Policy (*Chapter 18*).

Major General (ret.) **Patrick C. Cammaert**, Member of the Board of the European Centre for Conflict Prevention and former senior fellow at the Netherlands Defence Academy (2008–2011); formerly Royal Netherlands Marine Corps; served in United Nations operations in Cambodia (UNTAC), Bosnia/Herzegovina (UNPROFOR), Eritrea (UNMEE), and the Democratic Republic of Congo (MONUC), as Force Commander in the latter two missions. He also served as Military Advisor to the United Nations Department of Peacekeeping Operations (DPKO) (*sub-Chapters 6.4* and *6.5*).

Major General **Blaise Cathcart**, Judge Advocate General Canadian Forces. He is a member of the bar of Nova Scotia and has served in a range of functions within the Office of the Judge Advocate General at home and on deployment overseas, including Deputy Judge Advocate General for Operations, Senior Legal Advisor to the Commander Canadian Task Force SFOR, and to Joint Task Force 2, Special Operations and Counter-Terrorism. He graduated with distinction from the LLM Programme of the LSE (2004) and was awarded the Lauterpacht-Higgins Prize for top student in the LLM Programme and the Blackstone Prize for top legal dissertation in his year (*sub-Chapter 5.4; Chapters 10, 15, and 22*).

Brigadier General Dr **Paul A.L. Ducheine**, Legal Advisor in the Netherlands Army Legal Service; Professor Cyber Operations at the Netherlands Defence Academy; and Adjunct Professor Law of Military Cyber Operations and Cyber Security at the University of Amsterdam. He is a graduate of the Royal Military Academy (civil engineering), Public Administration (Free University of Amsterdam), and Constitutional and International Law (Utrecht University). He defended his doctorate in 2008 at the University of Amsterdam on the role of the armed forces in counter-terrorism operations (*Chapters 12, 23,* and *Glossary of Terms*).

Professor (Emeritus) **William J. Fenrick**, Dalhousie University Law School in Halifax, Canada; formerly Senior Legal Advisor with the Office of the Prosecutor for the International Criminal Tribunal for the former Yugoslavia (1994–2004); naval officer and legal officer in the Office of the Judge Advocate General Canadian Forces where he held a number of positions, including Director of International Law, Director of Legal Training and Director of Operational Law (*Chapter 29*).

Lt Commander **Martin D. Fink**, Royal Netherlands Navy Legal and Logistical Service; Assistant Professor of International and Operational Law, Netherlands Defence Academy; PhD candidate University of Amsterdam on the Law of Maritime Interception. Lt Commander Fink has served as Legal Advisor at NATO Allied Joint Force Command (Naples), and as Legal Advisor in Libya, Somalia, and Iraq and is currently deployed at the UN Mission South Sudan (UNMISS). He received his LLM in 2001 (Leiden University) (*Chapter 21*).

Dr **Dieter Fleck**, formerly Director International Agreements & Policy of the German Ministry of Defence; Honorary President of the International Society for Military Law and the Law of War; Member Advisory Board, Amsterdam Center for International Law; editor and co-author of the *Handbook of International Humanitarian Law* and *The Handbook of the Law of Visiting Forces* (*Chapter 1, sub-Chapters 5.2 and 6.2, Chapters 9, 28,* and *32*).

Dr **Gloria Gaggioli Gasteyger**, Legal Advisor International Committee of the Red Cross. Dr Gaggioli organized an ICRC Expert Meeting on the Interplay between the Paradigms of Hostilities and Law Enforcement in 2012 and currently conducts research and prepares reports on the protection of victims in armed conflict. She was previously associated with the University of Geneva and the Geneva Academy for Human Rights and Humanitarian Law, following her PhD *summa cum laude* in 2011 (*Chapter 4*).

Colonel (ret.) Professor **Charles H.B. Garraway**, Fellow Human Rights Centre, University of Essex; Associate Fellow (International Security Programme) Royal Institute of International Affairs (Chatham House); former Legal Advisor, British Red Cross; formerly member of the Army Legal Service of the United Kingdom with 30 years' service in military criminal law, international law, and operational law; Charles H. Stockton Visiting Chair of International Law at the United States Naval War College, Newport, RI (*sub-Chapter 5.5* and *Chapter 11*).

Professor Dr **Terry D. Gill**, Professor of Military Law, University of Amsterdam; Professor Military Law and Head of the Military Law Section within the Faculty of Military Sciences, Netherlands Defence Academy; Chairman, Research Program on the 'Role of Law in Armed Conflict & Military Operations' within the Amsterdam Centre for International Law; Member of Expert Group which prepared the *Tallinn Manual on Cyber Warfare*; Member Advisory Council to the Netherlands Government and Parliament on Matters of Public International Law; General Editor *Yearbook of International Humanitarian Law*; Chairman Study Group of the International Law Association on the Conduct of Hostilities in the 21st Century; formerly member of faculty, Institute of Public International Law, Utrecht University (1985–2013) (*Chapter 1, sub-Chapters 5.1, 5.3, 6.1, 6.3, Chapters 8, 12, 13, 14, 28,* and *32*).

Professor Dr **Wolff Heintschel von Heinegg**, Professor of Public Law in particular Public International Law and former Dean of the Faculty of Law of the Europa-Universität Viadrina Frankfurt (Oder) from 2004–2008 and former Vice President of that University from 2008–2012; Member of the Council of the International Institute of Humanitarian Law, San Remo; Vice President of the International Society for Military Law & the Law of War; Member of the expert groups on 'The Law of Armed Conflict at Sea' established by the San Remo Institute of International Humanitarian Law, 'The Law of Air and Missile Warfare' established by the Harvard Program on Humanitarian Policy and Conflict Research and the *Tallinn Manual on Cyber Warfare* under the auspices of NATO CCDCOE; Co-Chair of the Lieber Society within the American Society of International Law; formerly, two-time Charles H. Stockton Visiting Chair of International Law at the United States Naval War College, Newport, RI (*Chapters 20* and *21*).

Colonel **Ben F. Klappe**, *Director Administrative Law Department, Ministry of Defence, the Netherlands;* visiting lecturer at the Netherlands Defence Academy; *formerly* Military Judge and Judge in the Criminal Law Department of the District Court of Arnhem, the Netherlands; Special Assistant to the Military Advisor, Department of Peacekeeping Operations, United Nations Headquarters, New York (*sub-Chapters 6.4 and 6.5, Chapter 27*).

Professor Dr **Jann K. Kleffner**, Head of the International Law Centre, Swedish National Defence College, Stockholm; Member Advisory Board International Law Studies U.S. Naval War College, Newport, RI; Member Reading Committee ICRC Project to Update Commentaries to the Geneva Conventions and their Additional Protocols (*Chapter 3, sub-Chapter 5.5, Chapters 11* and *26*).

Boris Kondoch, Professor Far East University, Chungbuk Korea Director of the Asia Center for Peace and Security Studies in Seoul; Editor-in-Chief of the *Journal of International Peacekeeping*; Member of the Advisory Council, East Asia Integration Studies (*Chapter 30*).

Colonel (ret.) **William K. Lietzau,** Former Deputy Assistant Secretary of Defense Rule of Law and Detainee Policy (2011–2013); Deputy Legal Counsel, National Security Council at the White House 2009–2010; United States Marine Corps Judge Advocate with 27 years' service (*Chapter 2*).

Professor **Timothy McCormack**, Professor of Law at the Melbourne University Law School, Melbourne Australia; Foundation Director of the Asia Pacific Centre for Military Law established by the Melbourne Law School and The Australian Defence Force Legal Service; Adjunct Professor of Law at the University of Tasmania Law School; Special Advisor to the Prosecutor, International Criminal Court, The Hague; Editor Correspondent's Reports and former General Editor *Yearbook of International Humanitarian Law*; former Australian Red Cross Professor of International Humanitarian Law at Melbourne University Law School and Former Vice President Australian Red Cross (*Chapter 25*).

Dr **Nils Melzer**, Senior Adviser at the Swiss Federal Department of Foreign Affairs; former Senior Fellow Geneva Centre for Security Policy (2012–2014); former member of the Legal Division, International Committee of the Red Cross; author of ICRC *Interpretive Guidance on the Notion of Direct Participation in Hostilities* (2009) and of his award winning doctoral dissertation *Targeted Killing* (2008) (*Chapters 4* and *17*).

Professor Dr **Eric P.J. Myjer**, Professor of Conflict and Security Law and Associate Professor Public International Law, Utrecht University; Director Centre for Conflict and Security Law Co-Editor in Chief, *Journal of Conflict and Security Law*; Judge (locum) at Utrecht District Court and The Hague Court of Appeal (*Chapter 7*).

Bruce (Ossie) M. Oswald, CSC, Associate Professor, University of Melbourne; Director Asia Pacific Centre for Military Law, Melbourne Law School in cooperation with the Australian Defence Forces; formerly legal officer of the Australian Army, Legal Advisor, Deployable Joint Force Headquarters, Headquarters Australian Theatre, Strategic Command and Directorate of Operations and International Law, has served in Rwanda, the Former Yugoslavia, East Timor, and Iraq; presently reserve officer in ADF (*Chapter 25*).

Major General (ret.) **A.P.V. Rogers**†, OBE, Former Yorke Distinguished Visiting Fellow of the Faculty of Law, University of Cambridge (2004–2009) and Senior Fellow of the Lauterpacht Centre for International Law in Cambridge (1999–2011); formerly Director of Army Legal Services of the United Kingdom; and Vice-President of the International Fact-Finding Commission; author of *Law on the Battlefield* (*Chapter 31*).

Mr **Joseph A. Rutigliano** Jr, Civilian Deputy Branch Head, International and Operational Law Branch/Special Assistant on Law of War for the United States Marine Corps; formerly US Marine Corps Judge Advocate (*Chapter 2*).

Professor **Michael N. Schmitt**, Chair of Public International Law, Exeter University; Charles H. Stockton Professor and Director Stockton Center for International Law, US Naval War College; Senior Fellow at NATO Cooperative Cyber Defence Centre of Excellence, Tallinn; General Editor *Tallinn Manual on the Application of International Law to Cyber Warfare*; formerly Professor of Public International Law, Durham University, former Dean of the George C. Marshall European Center for Security Studies, Garmisch-Partenkirchen, Germany; Charles H. Stockton Visiting Chair of International Law at the United States Naval War College, Newport, RI; Sir Ninian Stephen Visiting Scholar at Melbourne University; Visiting Scholar at Yale Law School; retired officer, United States Air Force (*Chapters 16* and *19*).

Colonel **Darren Stewart**, Army Legal Service of the United Kingdom; Assistant Director Administrative Law, Army Legal Service; former Head of the Military Department, International Institute of Humanitarian Law, San Remo; formerly Legal Advisor at Headquarters Allied Command Europe Rapid Reaction Corps; member of the Australian Army Legal Corps; has served in Afghanistan (*Chapter 31*).

Professor **Nigel D. White**, Dean of the Faculty of Law and Professor Public International Law, Nottingham University; formerly Director of the Law in Its International Context Research Cluster, University of London; formerly Professor of Public International Law, University of Sheffield and Professor International Organisations, University of Nottingham; co-editor-in-chief *Journal of Conflict and Security Law* (*Chapter 7*).

Dr **Marten Zwanenburg**, Legal Counsel and Advisor, Netherlands Ministry of Foreign Affairs; formerly Legal Advisor, Directorate of Legal Affairs Netherlands Ministry of Defence; Visiting Lecturer Leiden University; PhD Leiden University; member of the editorial board of *Leiden Journal of International Law*; author of *Accountability of Peace Support Operations* (ICRC Paul Reuter Prize 2006) (*Chapter 30*).

Table of Abbreviations

ACO	Allied Command Operations (NATO)
ADIZ	Air Defence Identification Zones
AFDI	*Annuaire français de droit international*
AfrCHPR	African [Banjul] Charter on Human and Peoples Rights of 27 June 1981
AJIL	*American Journal of International Law*
ANC	African National Congress
AOO	Area of operations
AP I	Protocol I of 8 June 1977, Additional to the Geneva Conventions of 12 August 1949, and Relating to the Protection of Victims of International Armed Conflicts
AP II	Protocol II of 8 June 1977, Additional to the Geneva Conventions of 12 August 1949, and Relating to the Protection of Victims of Non-International Armed Conflicts
ARSIWA	Draft Articles on the Responsibility of States
AU	African Union
BPUFF	UN Basic Principles on the Use of Force and Firearms by Law Enforcement Officials, adopted by the 8th UN Congress on the Prevention of Crime and the Treatment of Offenders (1990)
BYBIL	*British Yearbook of International Law*
C2	Command and control
CAT	Convention Against Torture an Other Cruel, Inhuman or Degrading Treatment or Punishment of 10 December 1984
CCD COE	NATO Cooperative Cyber Defence Centre of Excellence Tallinn
CCLEO	UN Code of Conduct for Law Enforcement Officials, adopted by UN GA Res 34/169 (17 December 1979)
CCW	Convention on Prohibitions or Restrictions on the Use of Certain Conventional Weapons Which May be Deemed to be Excessively Injurious or to Have Indiscriminate Effects of 10 October 1980, amended on 20 December 2001, with Protocols I, II (revised on 3 May 1996), III, IV (13 October 1995), and V (28 November 2003)
CEDAW	Convention on the Elimination of All Forms of Discrimination Against Women of 18 December 1979
CERD	International Convention on the Elimination of All Forms of Racial Discrimination of 7 March 1966
CIHL	J.-M. Henckaerts/L. Doswald-Beck (eds), *Customary International Humanitarian Law, Vol. I* (Cambridge: Cambridge University Press, 2006)
CIMIC	Civil–military cooperation

CMCO	Civil–military coordination
CRC	Convention on the Rights of the Child of 20 November 1989
CWC	Convention on the Prohibition of the Development, Production, Stockpiling and Use of Chemical Weapons and on their Destruction of 13 January 1993
DARIO	Draft Articles on the Responsibility of International Organizations
DoD	US Department of Defense
DoS	denial of service
DPKO	UN Department of Peacekeeping Operations
EBAO	Effects-based approach to operations
ECHR	European Convention for the Protection of Human Rights and Fundamental Freedoms of 4 November 1950
ECiHR	European Commission on Human Rights
ECOSOC	Economic and Social Council
ECOWAS	Economic Community of West African States
ECtHR	European Court of Human Rights
EEZ	Exclusive Economic Zone
EJIL	*European Journal of International Law*
ENMOD	Convention on the Prohibition of Military or Any Other Hostile Use of Environmental Modification Techniques of 2 September 1976
ERW Protocol	Protocol on Explosive Remnants of War of 28 November 2003
ESDP	European Security and Defence Policy
EU	European Union
GC I	First Geneva Convention of 12 August 1949 for the Amelioration of the Condition of Wounded and Sick in Armed Forces in the Field
GC II	Second Geneva Convention of 12 August 1949 for the Amelioration of the Wounded, Sick and Shipwrecked Members of Armed Forces at Sea
GC III	Third Geneva Convention of 12 August 1949 relative to the Treatment of Prisoners of War
GC IV	Fourth Geneva Convention of 12 August 1949 relative to the Protection of Civilian Persons in Time of War
HagueReg	Regulations respecting the Laws and Customs of War on Land, annexed to Hague Convention (IV) of 18 October 1907
HOM	Head of Mission
HOMC	Head of Military Component
HOPC	Head of Police Component
HPCR	Harvard University's Program on Humanitarian Policy and Conflict Research
HRQ	*Human Rights Quarterly*
HuV-I	*Humanitäres Völkerrecht-Informationsschriften*, now the *Journal of International Law of Peace and Armed Conflict*

IACHR	Inter-American Convention on Human Rights of 22 November 1969
IACiHR	Inter-American Commission on Human Rights
IACtHR	Inter-American Court of Human Rights
ICAO	International Civil Aviation Organization
ICC	International Criminal Court
ICCPR	International Covenant on Civil and Political Rights of 19 December 1966
ICESCR	International Covenant on Economic, Social and Cultural Rights of 19 December 1966
ICJ	International Court of Justice
ICLQ	*International and Comparative Law Quarterly*
ICoC	International Code of Conduct for Private Security Providers
ICRC	International Committee of the Red Cross
ICTR	International Criminal Tribunal on Rwanda
ICTY	International Criminal Tribunal for the former Yugoslavia
IFOR	Implementation Force (Bosnia-Herzegovina and Croatia)
IHL	International humanitarian law
ILA	International Law Association
ILC	International Law Commission
ILM	*International Legal Materials*
IMS	International Military Staff (NATO)
IMT	International Military Tribunal Nuremberg
INTERFET	International Force for East Timor
IO	Information operation
IRRC	*International Review of the Red Cross*
ISAF	International Security Assistance Force (Afghanistan)
ITC	International Telecommunication Convention of 6 June 1982
ITU	International Telecommunication Union
JAG	Judge Advocate General
JCSL	*Journal of Conflict and Security Law*
JTF	Joint task force
KFOR	Kosovo Force
LOAC	Law of armed conflict
MC	Military Committee (NATO)
MCO	Military Cyber Operations
MILREP	Military representatives
MINUSTAH	Mission des Nations Unies pour la stabilisation en Haïti
MIO	Maritime interception operation
MNF	Multinational Force (Iraq)
MoD	Ministry of Defence
MONUC	Mission de l'Organisation des Nations Unies en République Démocratique du Congo
MONUSCO	United Nations Stabilization Mission in the Democratic Republic of the Congo
MOU	Memorandum of understanding
MPA	Maritime patrol aircraft

MPEPIL	*Max Planck Encyclopedia of Public International Law*
NAC	North Atlantic Council
NATO	North Atlantic Treaty Organization
NATO SOFA	Agreement between the Parties to the North Atlantic Treaty Regarding the Status of their Forces of 19 June 1951
NJIL	*Netherlands Journal of International Law*
NOTAM	Notice to airmen
NOTMAR	Notice to mariners
NPG	Nuclear Planning Group (NATO)
OAS	Organization of American States
OCHA	UN Office for the Coordination of Humanitarian Affairs
ONUC	Opérations des Nations Unies au Congo
OPCOM	Operational command
OPCON	Operational control
OPLAN	Operational plan
OSCE	Organization for Security and Cooperation in Europe
PfP SOFA	Agreement Among the States Parties to the North Atlantic Treaty and the Other States Participating in the Partnership for Peace Regarding the Status of their Forces of 19 June 1995
PMSC	Private military and security company
PRT	Provincial reconstruction team
PSI	Proliferation Security Initiative
RdC	*Recueils des Cours de l'Académie de droit international de la Haye*
RDMilG	*Revue de Droit Militaire et de Droit de la Guerre*
Res.	Resolution
ROE	Rules of engagement
ROEAUTH	ROE authorization
ROEIMP	ROE implementation
SACEUR	Supreme Allied Commander Europe (NATO)
SACT	Supreme Allied Commander Transformation (NATO)
SC	Security Council
SFOR	Stabilization Force (Bosnia-Herzegovina and Croatia)
SG	Secretary General
SHAPE	Supreme Headquarters Allied Powers Europe (NATO)
SOF	Special operations forces
SOFA	Status-of-forces agreement
SOMA	Status-of-mission agreement
SSR	Secondary Surveillance Radar
SUA	Convention for the Suppression of Unlawful Acts against the Safety of Maritime Navigation of 10 March 1988
TA	Technical Arrangement
TACOM	Tactical Command
TCC	Troop contributing country
TEU	Treaty on European Union of 7 February 1992
TF	Task force
TOA	Transfer of authority agreement

UAV	Unmanned aerial vehicle
UCAV	Unmanned combat air vehicle
UDHR	Universal Declaration of Human Rights of 10 December 1948
UN	United Nations
UN Charter	Charter of the United Nations of 26 June 1945, as amended on 17 December 1963, 20 December 1965, and 20 December 1971
UNAMA	United Nations Assistance Mission in Afghanistan
UNAMET	United Nations Mission in East Timor
UNAMI	United Nations Assistance Mission for Iraq
UNAMID	African Union-United Nations Hybrid Operation in Darfur
UNAMSIL	United Nations Mission in Sierra Leone
UNCLOS	United Nations Convention on the Law of the Sea of 30 April 1982
UNEF I & II	United Nations Emergency Force (Egypt and Israel)
UNFICYP	United Nations Force in Cyprus
UNGA	United Nations General Assembly
UNHRC	UN Human Rights Committee
UNIFIL	United Nations Interim Force in Lebanon
UNITAR	United Nations Institute for Training and Research
UNMEE	United Nations Mission in Ethiopia and Eritrea
UNMIK	United Nations Mission in Kosovo
UNOCI	United Nations Operation in Côte d'Ivoire
UNPROFOR	United Nations Protection Force (Bosnia-Herzegovina and Croatia)
UNTS	*United Nations Treaty Series*
USG	Under Secretary General
YIHL	*Yearbook of International Humanitarian Law*

Table of Treaties and Other International Instruments

Treaties

Other International Instruments

Table of Judgments

African Commission on Human and Peoples' Rights

European Commission of Human Rights

European Court of Human Rights

European Court of Justice

Inter-American Commission of Human Rights

Inter-American Court of Human Rights

International Court of Justice

International Criminal Court

International Criminal Tribunal for Rwanda

International Criminal Tribunal for the former Yugoslavia

Nuremberg and Tokyo Trials

Permanent Court of Arbitration

Permanent Court of International Justice

Special Court for Sierra Leone

UN Human Rights Committee

National Courts

Belgium

Israel

Netherlands

United Kingdom

United States

PART I

GENERAL ISSUES

Chapter 1

CONCEPT AND SOURCES OF THE INTERNATIONAL LAW OF MILITARY OPERATIONS

The International Law of Military Operations comprises all areas of public international law which relate to: 1.01

- **the provision of a legal basis for any type of military operation in an international context;**
- **the command and control of such operations;**
- **the deployment of forces from the State(s) participating in the operation to and within the mission area (and vice versa) through the transit of international sea and airspace, and through the territory of third States;**
- **the use and regulation of force for the conduct of hostilities and law enforcement operations, the maintenance of public order, and the treatment of persons captured or detained within the context of the conduct of the operation;**
- **the status of the forces throughout the duration of the operation; and**
- **the legal responsibility of States, of international organizations, and of individual members of the forces and all other entities participating in the operation for any violations of international law and contravention of relevant international regulations in force for the operation.**

1. *General.* The term 'International Law of Military Operations' is perhaps not (yet) a generally used term of art as is, for example, 'international humanitarian law', 'international human rights law' or 'the law of the sea'. It therefore calls for some explanation. 'Military operational law' is a term in general use in a growing number of armed forces, but it is relatively new, only having come into use in the past two decades to describe the various bodies of national and international law which are applicable to and regulate the planning and conduct of military operations. These include traditional areas or branches of international law, such as the law governing the use of force (the *jus ad bellum*), international humanitarian law (or as it more often referred to within many armed forces, the law of armed conflict), the law of the sea, and military use of airspace; as well as various branches or types of national

TERRY D. GILL AND DIETER FLECK

1.01 law of any given country involved in military operations, such as military criminal justice and disciplinary regulations. It has also come to include hybrid areas of law and regulation, such as the 'rules of engagement' drawn up for a particular operation and status-of-forces arrangements for troops deployed on another State's territory, either in the form of formal treaties (status-of-forces agreements), or more informal ad hoc arrangements, combining both areas of international and national law and regulation. However, with the increase in both the density and importance of international rights and obligations to most military operations, there is a need to identify which areas of international law and the rules contained within them are most relevant to military operations.

2. *Definition of Terms*. Specific information will be appropriate on some terms used in this Handbook for specific forms of military operations. While the conceptual distinction between 'conduct of hostilities' and 'law enforcement operations' follows generally accepted principles relating respectively to the application of the means and methods of warfare within the context of an armed conflict on the one hand and the exercise of authority over persons or territory and maintenance of public order on the other hand as explained and discussed in Chapter 4, certain military operations are often referred to in different terms, so that more specific definitions had to be developed for this book. This for example is the case for the term 'peace operation' which is often used as comprising all operations that are conducted under the authority of the UN or conducted by regional organizations and alliances or by ad hoc (non-standing) coalitions of States that were sanctioned by the UN or authorized by a UN Security Council resolution, with stated intention to: '(a) serve as an instrument to facilitate the implementation of peace agreements already in place, (b) support a peace process, or (c) assist conflict-prevention or peacebuilding efforts'.[1] For the purposes of this Handbook such a wide approach appeared not specific enough as it includes aspects of enforcement, peace enforcement, and peace support for which different legal parameters have to be observed. Hence we define 'enforcement operations' as action which can be characterized as sustained full-scale combat operations authorized by the Security Council against a State to maintain or restore international peace and security under Chapter VII of the UN Charter and qualifying as an international armed conflict under international humanitarian law; 'peace enforcement operations' as action authorized by the Security Council under Chapter VII to maintain or restore international peace and security, which—while potentially involving combat—will not entail the application of full-scale hostilities on a sustained basis against a State, and which fall conceptually and in terms of their objectives and the intensity of the use of force between enforcement operations and traditional peacekeeping; and 'peace operations' as military operations—enforcement and peace enforcement operations excluded—to establish or maintain peace, which have their legal basis

[1] Stockholm International Peace Research Institute (ed.), *SIPRI Yearbook 2009: Armaments, Disarmament and International Security* (Oxford: Oxford University Press, 2009), 126.

in the general powers of the Security Council, of the General Assembly, and of regional organizations, and which require the consent of the Receiving State(s), considering that peace operations are governed further by the underlying principles of consent of all relevant parties, impartiality, and use of force restricted to defence of the peacekeepers and their mandate. These more specific definitions are used throughout this Handbook and commented on in the relevant chapters. The Glossary of Terms in the Annex will facilitate information and transparency. 1.01

3. *Sources.* Contemporary military operations conducted by States, or by or under the authority of international organizations such as the UN, NATO, or the European Union and the African Union, are increasingly complex in character and more often than not involve a large number of States and other international actors, bringing the participating States and their armed forces into contact with a variety of different areas of international legal regulation, ranging from the more traditional areas of international law named above to rules governing specific types of operations. More generally, international human rights law has increasingly become regarded as complementing the rules and principles of international humanitarian law in certain aspects of military operations and the rules relating to accountability and (criminal) responsibility for breaches have become of operational concern, which civilian and military policy makers, planners, commanders, and legal advisors must have a knowledge of and be able to apply in the planning and conduct of military operations. Moreover, this relevance and applicability of various areas of international law usually takes place in a complex and dynamic environment in which at one moment traditional war fighting can occur, while simultaneously or immediately afterwards, the same troops can be involved in maintaining public order, in law enforcement, or in providing humanitarian assistance. This complexity, in both the nature of contemporary operations and in the branches and subdivisions of international law relevant and applicable to military operations, has led to the gradual development of what may be considered a new sub-discipline of international law, referred to as 'International Law of Military Operations'. It is defined or described in the 'black letter' text of Section 1.01 and is intended to cover all areas of public international law, both traditional and more recent in terms of concern to the armed forces, which are of relevance throughout the planning and execution of any military operation, especially, but not limited to, those conducted across State borders or involving any outside actor.

4. *A New Perspective.* The International Law of Military Operations (ILMO) consists of various existing branches of international law. What is new is the way and extent to which these various areas of the law interact with each other and influence and regulate and shape the way in which contemporary military operations are planned and conducted. Whether 'ILMO' qualifies as a distinct sub-discipline of international law or is a combination of existing areas or sub-disciplines of international law which apply to military operations, is to a large extent a question of how one defines the notion of legal sub-discipline and is probably less important than the function it has in bringing together the rules and principles of

1.01 international law relating to the planning and conduct of a military operation and applying these in a systematic manner to promote coherence, consistency, and compliance with legal obligations. There are, of course, numerous sources in which the relevant international legal rules and regulations can be found, but these are scattered across a huge array of documents, treaties, and academic references, which makes it an extremely challenging, if not almost impossible, undertaking to locate, identify, and apply the many rules which are relevant to contemporary military operations. There are numerous manuals and handbooks issued by the armed forces of various nations, which describe and comment upon various branches of international and national law relevant for their armed forces.[2] However, none is completely devoted to and specifically designed to bring all areas of international law of relevance into focus, and most include large bodies of national law of relevance only to that particular nation's forces (which is one reason why we have not attempted to include national law within this Handbook beyond noting where it interacts with international law) and are moreover, generally 'service-specific'; that is, specifically aimed at one branch of the armed forces (army, air force, or navy) or one generic type of operation (e.g. naval operations, counterinsurgency, or peace operations). Despite the large number of sources available, there is no single source which offers a complete overview of the different rules and guidelines contained in various areas and sub-disciplines of international law which are relevant to contemporary military operations.

5. This Handbook is an attempt to fill this gap by providing as comprehensive an overview as possible of all areas of international law relevant to all types of operations; ranging from traditional combat operations to peace operations and devoting attention to a wide variety of areas of specific interest and importance within the context of contemporary military operations. While it is impossible to cover every single aspect of international law of potential interest and area of concern, we have tried to make the book as comprehensive as possible in terms of scope and coverage, while still keeping it readable and usable as both a training tool and as an academic reference. This also indicates the dual purpose underlying the book: it is firstly intended to serve as a comprehensive, but usable guide to policy officials, commanders, and their legal advisors at both the national and international level for the planning and conduct of any military operation, and as a general training tool which complements other existing resources, such as military manuals, internal guidelines and regulations, and other similar materials. The planning and conduct of any military operation has become increasingly intertwined with knowledge of and correct application of international law in its various manifestations to promote compliance with the law as a matter of both policy and principle, as a means of contributing to the mission's success and legitimacy, and to assist in maintaining political and public support for the mission and cohesion and

[2] See e.g. The Judge Advocate General's Legal Center & School, International and Operational Law Department, Charlottesville, Virginia 22903, *Operational Law Handbook 2014*.

cooperation between allies, and between participating States and international organizations with host governments and their populations. Secondly, the Handbook is also intended to serve as an academic reference for students and scholars engaged in teaching and research in one or more areas of international law which are covered in the book. Such research and teaching is conducted at a variety of institutions including military staff colleges, defence academies, universities, and international institutions, organizations and similar bodies engaged in developing and applying international law in both a traditional academic sense and in a more practical sense, such as in training courses for senior personnel or in research projects relating to one or more areas of international law addressed in this Handbook. We have attempted to maintain a balance throughout in terms of these dual purposes and intended audiences, but with an emphasis on the former over the latter wherever a choice became necessary. That means that while we have paid attention and given due recognition to areas of controversy relating to certain aspects and applications of international law, we have emphasized clarity and usability over lengthy investigations and discussions of certain rules and practices which are subject to differing interpretations and controversies. We have also aimed at maintaining this balance in terms of the background and perspective of the contributors to this Handbook, which is a collective effort on the part of contributors from differing backgrounds, perspectives, and nationalities. Many of the contributors are serving or recently retired military legal advisors with extensive practical experience, while others are professional academics or (former) policy officials engaged in researching and teaching one or more areas of international law covered in this Handbook; and a few of the contributors combine both of these backgrounds and perspectives. As such, this Handbook is unique in attempting to bring together both a professional and academic perspective and including persons from differing regions and experience. **1.01**

6. *General Organization of the Handbook.* This Handbook is organized along the lines of an annotated manual and follows the general style and approach used in such works, particularly the companion volumes addressing international humanitarian law[3] and the law of visiting forces[4] under the editorship of one of the editors of this work and issued by the same publisher. The book is divided into five parts and into (sub-)chapters, sections (in bold 'black letter' type), and numbered paragraphs containing commentary. The sections are consecutively numbered per chapter and together form a Manual, which is intended as an easy reference tool for practical use and which appears integrally as an annex to the complete work. Part I addresses certain issues of general importance. It is divided into four chapters and serves as a general introduction to the work. Parts II and III are organized along the general theme of the relevant international legal basis for any given type of

[3] D. Fleck (ed.), *The Handbook of International Humanitarian Law*, 3rd edn (Oxford: Oxford University Press, paperback 2014).

[4] D. Fleck (ed.), *The Handbook of the Law of Visiting Forces* (Oxford: Oxford University Press, 2001).

1.01 operation, with Part II addressing operations conducted within the context of the UN Collective Security System in a broad sense and Part III addressing operations conducted on the basis of individual or collective exercise of national self-defence, or another possible legal basis under international law. These two parts are respectively divided into three and seven chapters, with two of those within Part II (Chapters 5 and 6) further subdivided into sub-chapters. In both these parts, the approach has been to address the relevant legal basis, the regulation and use of force, command and control, and the status of forces respectively. Separate attention is given to some of these issues in relation to specific legal bases, in Part IV, where 16 chapters address areas of particular concern and interest covering a wide range of topics and specific issues. Two of these chapters (20 and 22) are also further subdivided into sub-chapters. We have attempted to provide as broad a coverage as possible and address issues of topical or special concern and which are of both practical and academic importance. These can play a role in any of the types of operation covered in Parts II and III, but are specific enough to warrant separate coverage. Part V containing two chapters is a synthesis and conclusion to the Handbook, addressing the role of the military legal advisor in contemporary military operations and providing general conclusions.

1.02 **As such, the International Law of Military Operations includes rules embedded in:**

- **the UN Charter and customary international law relating to the use of force and the maintenance and restoration of international peace and security,**
- **international humanitarian law,**
- **international human rights law,**
- **other areas of conventional and customary international law relevant to international military operations such as international law relative to the status of forces and the exercise of criminal jurisdiction, the international law of the sea and air law, the law of international responsibility and international criminal law, international environmental law, and the law of international organizations.**

It is supplemented by national constitutions, laws, and regulations. While the conduct of hostilities in armed conflict is regulated by international humanitarian law as *lex specialis,* law enforcement operations undertaken outside the context of armed conflict must follow human rights law. Where authority is exercised over persons or territory within the context of an armed conflict, both bodies of law are applicable and should be applied in accordance with established rules of legal interpretation and methodology to ensure compliance with all applicable legal obligations and resolve any conflict between rules from different bodies of law which may arise.

1. As with any branch of public international law, the International Law of Military Operations is governed by the traditional sources of international law contained in Article 38 of the Statute of the International Court of Justice, which is generally recognized as containing an authoritative but incomplete listing of the sources of international legal obligation. Alongside treaties and international customary law as primary sources, these include general principles of law recognized in all legal systems, judicial decisions, authoritative publications, and decisions of international organizations (the last of which does not appear in Article 38). The first two are the most important in terms of setting out primary legal obligations, while the other sources are generally used in a more supportive role to supplement and interpret the obligations contained in the primary sources of treaty law and customary law. Since the International Law of Military Operations is in some respects a hybrid body of law (as are most areas of military law) it is largely governed by treaties, customary law, and the other sources governing various other branches and sub-disciplines of international law such as, for example, those relating to the use of force, international humanitarian law, international human rights law, or the law of the sea and air law. The most important of these other areas of international law are contained in the 'black letter' text of Section 1.02 immediately above. It is obvious that the number of treaties and customary rules from so many different branches of international law are far too numerous to name or even to attempt to list separately. However, all rules and commentary contained in this Handbook contain full references in the footnotes indicating the sources of legal obligation and their interpretation in academic and official publications. Three branches of international law mentioned earlier call for some brief comments in terms of our approach and the way they have been applied within this Handbook. **1.02**

2. *Regulation of the Use of Force.* It is self-evident that any international military operation must have a legal basis under international law for it to be in compliance with international law. We have taken the approach that any international military operation must comply with these rules; that the only recognized exceptions to the Charter prohibition of the use of force in international relations are those contained in the Charter itself, or are otherwise generally recognized in international law and that therefore any use of force which is not in compliance with these, will be *prima facie* illegal. We have stated clearly where there are areas of controversy and set out a legal position on what to us seems to be the most reasonable and persuasive position, without attempting to provide a definitive interpretation or ignore points of contention. Likewise, we have avoided pronouncing judgment on the legality or lack thereof of any specific military operation, which is not the purpose of a Handbook such as this. Possible uses of force which have not been gone into extensively, such as armed reprisals, preventive war, national liberation wars and so forth, were considered to be either clearly lacking in any recognized legal basis or irrelevant for the purposes of this Handbook, or both.

3. *International Humanitarian Law.* As regards the other branch of international law most associated with military operations, international humanitarian law, it is axiomatic that it will apply equally to any and all parties to an armed conflict,

1.02 irrespective of whether that party is acting in compliance with or in breach of the law governing the use of force. Moreover, it can be applied as a set of guiding principles without prejudice to legal obligations arising from any other applicable body of law in any military operation not constituting an armed conflict, whether international or non-international in character. In the context of the conduct of hostilities, the treatment of specific categories of protected persons such as prisoners of war, the wounded, sick or shipwrecked and in certain other areas, such as the law of belligerent occupation, it will operate as the primary international legal regime in determining the legality or lack thereof of any particular action or omission carried out by a party to an armed conflict. In its relationship to international human rights law, it will have the status of *lex specialis* in the abovementioned situations.

4. *Human Rights Law*. With respect to international human rights law we have taken the approach that it is applicable in principle to all military operations, including situations of armed conflict, wherever and whenever individuals are under the jurisdiction or territorial control of any given State or international organization, or are in the physical custody of any State or other subject of international law. It will depend on the actor involved (State or international organization) and the scope of treaty obligations, whether it applies as conventional or customary law. In situations of armed conflict it will complement the provisions of international humanitarian law to the extent there is either territorial or personal jurisdiction over persons affected. In the situations referred to in the previous paragraph international humanitarian law will have the status of *lex specialis* in the event of any conflict of obligation. In situations of belligerent occupation and operational detention it will complement and act alongside the obligations contained in international humanitarian law and other relevant legal considerations. In the context of law enforcement and maintenance of public order outside the abovementioned situations it will serve as the sole or primary governing legal paradigm.

5. *National Law*. These and other relevant areas of the International Law of Military Operations are supplemented by national constitutions, laws, and regulations. These can include the rules relating to the use of force which are governed by national criminal law (such as personal self-defence addressed in Chapter 24), national caveats in multinational operations relating to specific activities, law enforcement, certain aspects relative to the status of forces, and other areas. These have received attention in this Handbook to the extent this was felt essential to provide a complete picture and analysis. However, in keeping with the title and purpose of this work, we have avoided dealing with national law in detail, instead indicating where the demarcation between national and international law lies wherever the two come into contact. It would be impossible to do justice to the complexity and depth of domestic legal regulation of any State or selection of States, much less all States, alongside the various branches of international law which are dealt with in this Handbook. Moreover, national legal rules and regulations are dealt with in specific directives and publications issued by individual nations and are better left to other publications to comment specifically upon.

Alongside rules of positive international law of either a conventional or customary nature, international military operational law is also influenced and to a significant extent regulated by rules and practices which are not of a legal nature, but which are part of the policy of States and international organizations. International cooperation has led to accepted standards and best practice, even in the absence of treaty or established customary obligations. However, while States and international organizations may adopt further going restrictions on the employment of force or allow for more favourable treatment of persons who have been detained for any lawful reason, they may never exceed what is allowed by the relevant binding international legal obligations applicable in a given situation. 1.03

1. We have included, where necessary, rules and practices which are not strictly of a legal nature. These include hybrid constructions such as 'rules of engagement', which combine legal, policy, and operational considerations and 'memoranda of understanding' relating to various topics such as, for example, status-of-forces arrangements outside of a formal treaty relationship. We have also included so-called 'best practice', where appropriate, as guidelines on how to conduct certain types of activity, not governed by legal rules, or as a complement to legal rules, where these are relevant and have gained a large degree of acceptance. Whenever such non-legally binding rules are used they are indicated by the use of 'should' or similar language to denote their non-legal character, rather than the use of terms such as 'shall', which denote a binding legal obligation. These practices serve a useful, indeed in some cases, a vital role in supplementing and complementing binding legal obligations.

2. While such non-binding practices can provide a useful supplement to existing legal obligations, they may never exceed what is allowed under any binding legal obligation which is applicable to a given situation. For example, many States will apply international humanitarian law relating to the treatment of prisoners of war as a guideline for the detention of persons outside the context of an armed conflict, since it provides for a comprehensive set of standards, which is familiar to members of the armed forces. However, this is without prejudice to the obligations arising from international human rights law which are applicable to the detention of persons and which are applicable to the State in question.

In applying rules from different branches of international law, all applicable rules must be taken into account and interpreted and applied with a view to giving them the fullest possible effect. This follows both from the obligations the parties have undertaken and are bound by and from the fact that international law is an integrated system of rights and obligations which is governed by established rules of interpretation and legal methodology. 1.04

1.04 1. The fact that rules from different legal instruments arising from a single branch of international law, or rules arising from different branches of international law may apply to a given situation has the consequence that they must be applied with a view to meeting all legal obligations and giving all relevant obligations the fullest possible effect. A State can be bound by different legal instruments or sources of obligation arising from a single branch or sub-discipline of international law such as two or more treaties from, for example, international humanitarian law, which are both applicable in a given situation. It will also often be the case that rules from different branches of international law can be applicable to a given situation such as, for example, when both international humanitarian law and international human rights law apply to a particular situation, or when a Security Council mandate permitting the use of force or detention of persons for a particular purpose must be applied in accordance with relevant obligations arising from international humanitarian law and or international human rights law.

2. In such cases, the established rules and principles of interpretation and legal methodology will provide guidance in how such obligations can be applied in a coherent fashion and in resolving any conflicts between specific rules which may arise. The first step in this will be determining which legal sources and obligations apply to a given situation. Once this has been established, the next step will be to ascertain to which extent the obligations arising from them are mutually compatible and to identify any potential conflicting obligations. The third step is to interpret and apply all relevant legal instruments and obligations in context, both in relation to each other, and in relation to the relevant factual situation. The guiding principle here will be to apply them in such a way that they complement each other to the maximum extent possible, thereby contributing to the fulfillment of obligations to which the State is bound. Finally, any potential conflicts between rules and obligations must be resolved using the established principles of legal methodology. These include the application of principles relating to any hierarchy between instruments or other sources of obligation alongside other principles relating to the precedence of rules, including, but not limited to the aforementioned principle of *lex specialis*, whereby a rule or set of related rules specifically enacted for a particular subject or situation will be given precedence to the extent necessary to resolve any conflict of obligation, while taking account of the obligations contained in another legal instrument to the extent they are compatible with the rule with a *lex specialis* character. For example, the rules relating to the conduct of hostilities will act as *lex specialis* in the context of an armed conflict when hostilities occur to which the State in question is a party, but this will not affect the applicability of other rules from other legal regimes in so far as they do not collide with the former. Hence, there is no reason why rules from, for example, international human rights law would not continue to apply to the extent they were applicable in other contexts.[5]

[5] For extensive discussion in depth of the problems arising from the application of rules from different legal regimes within international law and the function of principles of legal methodology,

The International Law of Military Operations is therefore more than a mere collection of rules from different legal sub-disciplines. It can serve as an instrument which is aimed at harmonizing obligations arising from different legal sub-disciplines and translating such obligations from the abstract level of treaty and customary law to operational directives aimed at applying these obligations in the practical context of military operations. 1.05

1. The International Law of Military Operations serves a dual purpose. The first is 'horizontal' in nature, which it can fulfil by bringing together and applying in context the relevant rules of international law from different sources and legal regimes which are relevant to the planning and conduct of military operations; it can assist in providing guidance and promoting coherence between these legal regimes and their respective obligations. The second is 'vertical' in nature which it can achieve by integrating legal obligations and considerations into operational planning and directives, which aim to apply often abstract and broadly formulated rules and principles of treaty and customary law in an operational context.

2. In this context, if done correctly, legal and military considerations will be interwoven and integrated in such a way as to promote mission accomplishment while ensuring compliance with the law. This is a task which falls primarily upon the shoulders of the military legal advisor, alongside policy makers and military commanders. The International Law of Military Operations can therefore be seen as a sort of 'language' in which legal obligations and considerations are communicated to the responsible political and military leadership and are fully integrated into the planning and conduct of a military operation. It therefore serves a purpose as not only being a specialized area of international law, but also an instrument to promote compliance with the law in a special context, that of a military operation. As such it may well qualify as a distinct sub-discipline of international law and is, in any case, more than a mere collection of rules.

see 'Fragmentation of International Law' Report of the Study Group of the International Law Commission Finalized by Martti Koskienniemi, A/CN.4/L.682, 13 April 2006.

Chapter 2

HISTORY AND DEVELOPMENT OF THE INTERNATIONAL LAW OF MILITARY OPERATIONS

2.01 **The International Law of Military Operations has developed in both theory and practice in response to the development of:**
(a) the nature of warfare;
(b) the use of military forces; and
(c) underlying international norms.

I. Overview—The Transcendent Nature of Change

Silent enim leges inter arma.
Cicero

1. In Cicero's day, his aphorism may have been accurate. But few would find much value in the antiquated maxim today. Indeed, not only is the law an ever present consideration for modern military forces, it is also in a constant state of flux, meaning that legal advisors must make an effort to keep themselves current. And when crisis comes—an almost requisite constituent in the development of twenty-first-century armed conflict—lawyers must be ready with an understanding of the law that comprehends its historical context. In such crises, military legal advisors are charged to identify, apply, and distinguish norms relevant to the situation and the potential responses thereto. Such norms are frequently of long-standing pedigree, their principles having been established in code and treaty, developed over decades through critical assessment and practical application. In many cases, these norms are susceptible either to direct application or incremental honing to render them germane to the matter at hand. On rare occasions, however, the lawyer's skill must be exercised not only in the interpretation and application of extant law in the immediate term, but also in the conception and establishment of new law.

2. By way of example, we can look to the circumstances that yielded today's most notable conflict. In the days, weeks, and months that followed 9/11, the global community of nations joined the United States in mourning the deaths of innocent citizens, the destruction of renowned landmarks, and the demise of its aura of inviolable

safety and security. Despite the passage of years and notwithstanding the tangible evidence of recovery, rebuilding, and to some extent, progress, a more important consequence of the 9/11 attacks—the imperative to develop a legal regime to govern a war on terror—has not so readily matured. The first principle challenging the practitioner of the International Law of Military Operations is that the law of yesterday is unlikely to fit neatly the conflict of today. Warfare has always been the most extreme bearer of change; and we should not be surprised to find that the very law that attempts to regulate use of the military instrument is not immune from warfare's effects. But we must also ensure that the law does not become warfare's victim. **2.01**

3. The law of war is in transition—perhaps to a degree evoking the era of post-Westphalian peace[1] and the new world order emerging from the chaos of World War II. It goes without saying that lawyers should consciously and conscientiously seek to impact this change. A failure to participate thoughtfully and deliberately in fashioning the legal norms that are being developed—norms that will guide the global community for the next century—would constitute a missed opportunity of substantial moment. That current norms ill fit current circumstances should not surprise. Rarely has mankind accurately predicted tomorrow's challenge with yesterday's law. As Oliver Wendell Holmes so aptly noted, '[t]he life of the law has not been logic but experience'.[2]

4. This introductory chapter reviews the historical development of the use of military legal advisors. That history highlights the challenges legal advisors have faced over time in providing legal advice for present and future operations based on rules formulated for a past conflict.

II. Development of *Jus ad Bellum* and *Jus in Bello*—When and How Military Force is Used—and its Impact on the Practice of Operational Law

The law spoke too softly to be heard in such a noise of war.
Plutarch[3]

One of the reasons the practice of law regarding military operations has become so complex is the plethora of missions assigned to today's military forces. These

[1] Treaty of Westphalia, Peace Treaty between the Holy Roman Emperor and the King of France and their Respective Allies, 24 October 1648, available at <http://www.yale.edu/lawweb/avalon/westphal.htm>. Ending the Eighty Years' War between Spain and the Dutch, and the German phase of the Thirty Years' War, the Peace of Westphalia recognized the full territorial sovereignty of the member States of the Holy Roman Empire, rendering the princes of the empire absolute sovereigns in their own dominions. See *Encyclopedia Britannica*, 2002.

[2] *Lecture 1—Early Forms of Liability*, in O.W. Holmes Jr, *The Common Law* (Boston: Little, Brown & Co., 1881).

[3] Life of Caius Marius, quoted in John Bartlett (1820–1905) *Familiar Quotations* (Boston: Little, Brown, 1980), 8782.

2.01 missions range from civil support operations during humanitarian crises, to establishing the rule of law in a failed State, to the enforcement of a Security Council resolution, to force-on-force combat. The law of war and the laws related to the deployment of armed forces change in relation to the evolution of means and methods of warfare and the politico-military environment that gives rise to a use of military force. Any discussion of this evolution naturally must begin with a discussion of the development of *jus ad bellum*—the law that applies to when and under what circumstances the military instrument may be used. In the earliest days of the history of warfare, *jus ad bellum* was arguably the only body of law at issue. Although that is no longer the case, it is nevertheless the appropriate starting point for any review of the International Law of Military Operations.

Not only does *jus ad bellum* constitute an important component of the International Law of Military Operations, it is inextricably linked to the other bodies of law that may come into play. The first task of a legal advisor during a military operation is defining what legal authority justifies the operation itself. This is important both to confirm the legality of the operation and to provide a framework under which other legal determinations are made. For example, if the legal authority for a particular deployment is the consent of a Receiving State, and the mission is assisting that State's law enforcement forces, human rights law and the Receiving State's local criminal law are likely critical to fashioning the procedures that will govern the capture and detention of a hostile individual. But if the deployment involves armed conflict with another State premised on the right to self-defence, the law of war as it relates to prisoners of war (the Third Geneva Convention) is likely to be the appropriate place from which to draw the guiding principles. All subsequent determinations begin with, and flow from, the first component of the International Law of Military Operations—the authority to use military force.

Today, the Charter of the United Nations provides the legal regime governing the use of force among nations (*jus ad bellum*). The Charter essentially outlaws the use of force, authorizing it only pursuant to a Security Council resolution issued under Chapter VII, while preserving and recognizing in Article 51 the inherent right to self-defence, including collective self-defence. Prior to the establishment of the UN Charter, international law recognized a variety of legal bases permitting a nation's resort to the use of force against another nation. In fact, some form of *jus ad bellum* has existed for as long as has war,[4] although it was largely municipal in nature—applicable only to the specific civilizations that adopted them.

Over the centuries, transcendent norms have emerged that give form to what now constitutes *jus ad bellum* for the modern age. The narrative that led us to this era has been punctuated by distinctive events and periods that warrant mention.

[4] For an excellent discussion of the history of *jus ad bellum*, see L. Friedman, *The Law of War—A Documentary History*, Vol. 1 (New York: Random House, 1972).

Part III of this Handbook provides an in-depth discussion of the legal bases for the use of force in various types of military operations. 2.01

1. Jus ad Bellum

The period from approximately 335 BC, to AD 1800, is generally referred to as 'The Just War Period'.[5] The governing philosophy during this period was rooted in the writings of Aristotle and demanded a just cause for engaging in war.[6] The most important modern event affecting the 'just war' period was the 1648 Treaty of Westphalia that ended the Thirty Years' War and attempted to bring about a period of peace grounded in public law and the 'Balance of Power'.[7] These two prongs of nation-state relations would sustain Europe until 1914 and the outbreak of World War I.

In a similar vein, this period from the Peace of Westphalia to the French Revolution saw warfare that was limited in nature and aimed at maintaining a balance of power.[8] Over this 150-year period, concepts of a sovereign nation-state and nationalism were only beginning to mature. The customs of warfare adhered to by European States in this period were influenced by both the medieval code of chivalry and the Enlightenment—influences that tended to mitigate the effects of warfare. The rules governing warfare had a hospitable environment within which to develop, moving many toward positivism, which, by the nineteenth century, would become the predominant view.[9]

The positivist, or 'war as fact', theory can be traced as far back as the writings of Niccolo Machiavelli. It posited that international law could not proscribe sovereign States from waging war; war simply existed, and the only question worth considering was the rights and duties that accompanied it. Clausewitz reflected the conventional wisdom of the Positivist period (1800–1919), articulating his belief that war was merely the extension of politics.[10] Accompanying this political thought, burgeoning industrialization—like railway transportation and its concomitant application to military purposes—and the emergence of conscription on the European continent, impacted military strategy and increased the lethality of warfare. Positivism had the consequence of focusing effort on developing the *jus in bello* to mitigate the negative effects of war.

[5] See J. Moore, F. Tipson, and R. Turner, *National Security Law* (Durham: Carolina Academic Press, 1990), 51, hereinafter, '*National Security Law*'.

[6] See ibid. 56.

[7] See I. Brownlie, *International Law and The Use of Force by States* (Oxford: Clarendon Press; Oxford University Press, 1963), hereinafter, 'Brownlie, *International Law and the Use of Force*' at 14.

[8] See M.E. Howard, *War in European History* (Oxford: Oxford University Press, 1976), chapter 4.

[9] See ibid. 16.

[10] See C. von Clausewitz, *On War,* M. Howard and P. Paret, (eds) and translators (Princeton: Princeton University Press, 1976), 610. <http://www.clausewitz.com/readings/OnWar1873/TOC.htm>, accessed on 1 August 2015.

2.01 During the period, as dynastic wars fuelled by the 'just war' doctrine waned, constitutional forms of government and democratic principles spread, and widespread access to newspapers promoted public debate. Reacting to increased public scrutiny, States took care to articulate reasons of necessity and justness associated with the use of force with a view to securing and maintaining public support.[11] The then-unprecedented death and widespread destruction visited by World War I led to a re-evaluation of the positivist view. After World War I, several treaties manifested the desire of statesmen to expand the reach of the law in order to prevent wars of aggression.[12] One of the central components of the Treaty of Versailles, which ended World War I, was the Covenant of the League of Nations.[13] The parties agreed that, '[i]n order to promote international co-operation and to achieve international peace and security' they would accept 'obligations not to resort to war' and submit disputes to arbitration or judicial settlement, or to review by the League's Council.[14] Implicit in its provisions, however, the Covenant recognized the long-held customary international law right of States to resort to war to settle their disputes.[15] The League of Nations effectively made the resort to war illegal if it was waged in violation of the Covenant.[16]

The Kellogg-Briand Pact,[17] joined by virtually all nations of the world including Germany, Italy, and Japan, renounced war as an instrument of national policy, rejecting outright the positivist school. No longer was the focus on whether war was 'just' or whether certain procedural rules had been followed in advance of war. The focus shifted to whether the use of force was aggressive (unlawful) or defensive (lawful).[18] In 1932, the US Secretary of State, Henry Stimson,[19] stated that aggressive war 'is no longer to be the source and subject of rights'.[20] The Kellogg-Briand treaty, however, lacked an enforcement mechanism, and ultimately would prove ineffective in preventing the outbreak of World War II.

Notwithstanding the efforts of these legal regimes to control the waging of war, the outbreak of World War II appears inevitable in retrospect; the magnitude of the

[11] See Brownlie, *International Law and The Use of Force*, 26.

[12] See R.H. Jackson, Opening Address for the United States, Nuremberg Trials (found at <http://avalon.law.yale.edu/subject_menus/imt.asp>), hereinafter, 'Jackson Opening Address'.

[13] See Treaty of Versailles, <http://www.firstworldwar.com/source/versailles.htm>.

[14] The Covenant of the League of Nations, Preamble.

[15] See Brownlie, *International Law and The Use of Force*, 56, fn 5.

[16] See *National Security Law*, 66 ('The famous "gap" in the Covenant is that, although the Covenant clearly prohibited resort to war, it did so only if such action was taken prior to or without submission of the dispute to the League's procedures and principles').

[17] See The Treaty between the United States and other Powers Providing for the Renunciation of War as an Instrument of National Policy, signed 27 August 1928; see also *National Security Law*, 68 ('It reflected a fundamental shift in the history of the international law of conflict management that may have been the single most important intellectual leap in that history').

[18] See *National Security Law*, 68.

[19] Henry Stimson (1867–1950), was US Secretary of State (1929–33), and Secretary of War (1911–13; 1940–45).

[20] See Jackson Opening Address.

destruction it wrought far exceeded anything that had gone before. New regimes were needed to address both prongs of the law of war, *jus ad bellum* and *jus in bello*. With respect to the former, the creation of the UN Charter was seminal. Significantly for purposes of this Handbook, the Charter imposed on *jus ad bellum* a more universally acknowledged structure that finally brought it into the realm of legal practitioners below the national level. Whereas previously the legal issues associated with a resort to force were more often than not matters of custom or various bilateral agreements, which were addressed primarily at the national level, the UN Charter more simply and consistently requires any use of force to be justified by one of the two legal bases. This gave military lawyers a common lexicon and necessitated their understanding of the legal underpinnings for every military operation. **2.01**

Widely recognized as one of the most important achievements of the post-World War II period, the fundamental purpose of the UN Charter is the maintenance of international peace and security.[21] It prohibits the use of force between nations and requires all Member States to 'settle their international disputes by peaceful means in such a manner that international peace and security are not endangered'.[22] And the UN Charter is equally firm in its recognition of the sovereignty of the nation-state. Article 2(4) reads, in pertinent part: 'All members shall refrain in their international relations from the threat or use of force against the territorial integrity or political independence of any state'.

Notwithstanding this proscription, the UN Charter was formulated by nations that had just participated in the bloodiest war in human history. The authors were sufficiently pragmatic to recognize that there would be occasions when the resort to force would be required.[23] Accordingly, they codified in the UN Charter two bases upon which a nation could resort to the use of force. The primary basis was a refinement of the League of Nations' collective security arrangement—a nation could employ force when authorized or directed by the Security Council (usually communicated through an SC resolution issued under Chapter VII of the UN Charter). The second occasion authorizing the use of force is reflected in Article 51—when responding in self-defence, including collective self-defence.

The precise boundaries established by Article 51 are the subject of some controversy in the international community and are discussed more thoroughly in Chapter 8 of this Handbook. Those who tend towards a more expansive view read the 'inherent right' language as incorporating customary international law

[21] Art. 1(1) UN Charter; see also Ruth B. Russell, *A History of the United Nations, the role of the United States 1940–1945*, 964 (Jeannette E. Muther, asst, Washington DC: The Brookings Institution, 1958) (providing an in-depth description of the formation of the Charter).

[22] See Art. 2(3) UN Charter.

[23] Not all architects of the post-war period were sold on the efficacy of the UN Charter. For example, Dean Acheson considered the UN Charter 'impracticable' and the United Nations itself an example of a misguided Wilsonian 'faith in the perfectibility of man and the advent of universal peace and law'. For Acheson, support for the UN was nothing more than 'an aid to diplomacy'. See R. Kagan, *Of Paradise and Power* (New York: Vintage Books, 2003, 2004), 79, quoting J. Chace, *The Secretary of State Who Created the American World* (New York: Simon & Schuster, 1998), 107, 108.

2.01 principles of 'anticipatory self-defence' and clarifying that the right is not elucidated in the UN Charter itself, but is preexisting and unaffected by the Charter regime. Others focus on the 'if an armed attack occurs' language, viewing the same as limiting any self-defence right to actual incursions into State territory. In between the two extremes are various opinions as to what extent the inherent right of self-defence allows a nation to strike first in order to defend itself against an imminent attack.[24] Most at some point reflect on language from the 1837 *Caroline* case—now most famous for US Secretary of State Daniel Webster's articulation of a standard for anticipatory self-defence:[25] there must be 'an instant and overwhelming necessity for self-defense, leaving no choice of means, and no moment for deliberation'.[26]

Modern conflicts involving transnational terrorist groups and the potential for use of weapons of mass destruction have severely pressured traditional understandings regarding the limits of *jus ad bellum* as it relates to self-defence,[27] and the last chapter regarding this component of the law of military operations clearly has not been written.

In contradistinction to self-defence under Article 51, Chapter VII, the UN Charter's primary mechanism for recognizing legal authority for use of military force has been used only once in the first 40 years of the UN's existence. In June 1950, North Korea attacked the Republic of South Korea. In an ill-conceived decision to boycott the UN, the Soviet Union was absent for the vote,[28] and on 27 June 1950, the Security Council (SC) authorized the use of force to remove the North Koreans from South Korea and recommended that Member States 'furnish such assistance to the Republic of Korea as may be necessary to repel the armed attack and to restore international peace and security in the area'.[29] The next time the SC would authorize Member States to conduct military operations to restore peace and security would be in 1990, after Iraq invaded Kuwait. Sub-Chapter 5.1 of this Handbook addresses in detail SC-sanctioned enforcement operations.

[24] See Y. Dinstein, *War, Aggression and Self-Defense* (Cambridge: Cambridge University Press, 1988), 169–72 ('While some commentators believe that customary international law permits self-defense only after an armed attack occurs, the more common view is that customary right of self-defense is also accorded to States as a preventive measure.'). But see A. Randelzhofer, 'Article 51, 10' in B. Simma (ed.), *The Charter of the United Nations: A Commentary*, 3rd edn (Oxford: Oxford University Press, 2012), (contending that the appropriate debate is whether Article 51's 'inherent' language recognizes that the right exists with respect to non-UN Members as well; it is not intended to evince 'a right of self-defense existing independently from the Charter under natural Law').

[25] The Caroline (exchange of diplomatic notes between Great Britain and the United States, 1842), 2 J. Moore, *Digest of International Law* (1906), 409, 412.

[26] See Letter from Daniel Webster, US Secretary of State, to Henry Fox, British Minister in Washington (24 April 1841), in 29 British and Foreign State Papers 1840–1841, 1138 (1857).

[27] W. Lietzau, *Old Laws, New Wars:* 'Jus ad Bellum in an Age of Terrorism', Vol. 8, Number 1, *Max Planck Year Book of the United Nations Law* (2004), 383, 384, hereinafter, '*Old Laws*'.

[28] See SC Res. 82 (25 June 1950). The vote was 9-0, with one abstention (Yugoslavia). The USSR representative was not present for the vote.

[29] See SC Res. 83 (27 June 1950). The vote was 7–1, with Yugoslavia voting against. Again, the USSR representative was not present for the vote. Egypt and India did not participate in the vote.

The UN Charter requires the affirmative vote of nine Members of the SC, including the concurring votes of the Permanent Members, for action on all matters other than procedural ones.[30] Effectively a veto power of the Permanent Members: China, France, Russia, the United Kingdom, and the United States,[31] this provision, created contemporaneously with the advent of the Cold War, resulted in the so-called 'P-5' often finding themselves at odds as to how the United Nations should address various threats, breaches of the peace, or acts of aggression associated with the Cold War. Hence, the UN Charter's collective security scheme never operated as originally intended. The result was not only a resort to self-defence that was more extensive than what may have been envisioned, but also the establishment of a new way of using armed forces that was more amenable to the compromises necessary to secure Security Council decisions during the Cold War peacekeeping. **2.01**

UN peacekeeping efforts, discussed in sub-Chapter 6.1, are international uses of the military instrument, but with a mission and authority that is limited in nature, such as maintaining ceasefires and stabilizing conditions in order to allow diplomatic efforts to resolve the conflict peaceably.[32] UN peacekeeping usually involves the use of military observers and lightly armed monitors who are responsible to monitor, report, and provide a confidence-building presence in support of ceasefires and limited peace agreements.[33] Over time there has been substantial development in the variety of peacekeeping missions and the legal authority to use force accorded them.

The geopolitical shift of the post-Cold War period has required the UN Department of Peacekeeping Operations (DPKO) both to expand and to shift its operations away from a strictly military model, to a more complex 'multidimensional' approach in order to facilitate the implementation of comprehensive peace agreements and assist in laying the foundations for sustainable peace. 'Today's peacekeepers undertake a wide variety of complex tasks, from helping to build sustainable institutions of governance, to human rights monitoring, to security sector reform, to the disarmament, demobilization and reintegration of former combatants.'[34] The military still plays an essential role in peacekeeping operations, but more often than not, lawyers, law enforcement professionals, economists, administrators, electoral observers, and human rights monitors will join the military to perform essential peacekeeping functions.[35]

[30] See Art. 27 UN Charter. [31] See Art. 23(1) UN Charter.

[32] See UN Department of Peacekeeping Operations website (hereinafter, 'UN DPKO website') (<http://www.unrol.org/article.aspx?n=dpko>).

[33] Ibid. [34] Ibid.

[35] Ibid. See, generally, Harry A. Almond and James A. Burger (eds), *The History and Future of Warfare. Selections from Professional Readings in Military Strategy Published by the Strategic Studies Institute of the US Army War College* (The Hague, London, Boston: Kluwer, 1999); see, in particular, the contribution by D.M. Snow, 'Peacekeeping, Peace-making and Peace Enforcement: The US Role in the New International Order', 882–915.

2.01 Further complicating matters is the changing nature of conflict. Originally, UN peacekeeping operations were designed to address State-on-State conflict. More frequently today and premised on an expanded Security Council view of what constitutes a threat to international peace and security, UN peacekeeping operations are used to address intrastate conflicts and civil wars, as well as to protect ethnic minorities. Re-establishing order and a functioning government in places and under conditions in which the warring factions are divided on ethnic or religious grounds is a complex task requiring the efforts of a multi-disciplinary team of peacekeepers. Such missions also involve bodies of law far more complex than those applicable in the time of Hugo Grotius.

For the legal advisor, the key lesson here is that any military deployment associated with a UN mission likely derives its authority from the Security Council mandate. Understanding that mandate, the legal authority it provides for the use of force and its characterization of the mission, are absolutely critical to understanding the legal framework under which peacekeepers may operate.

Related to this development, some would find an emerging caveat to our previous claim that today's *jus ad bellum* is reflected completely in the UN Charter: the belief that a return to some form of 'just war' doctrine is warranted by the ascendance of a need for humanitarian intervention. Whether humanitarian intervention may independently justify military action even in circumstances in which the SC has not authorized the use of force under Chapter VII is a matter of significant debate in the international community. This issue is discussed more thoroughly in Chapter 13, but for purposes of this overview, we simply highlight the most prominent example of the nascent doctrine of humanitarian intervention: Operation Allied Force.[36]

The Kosovo intervention represents the quintessential example of why legal advisors still must be concerned with *jus ad bellum*. While the NATO intervention in Kosovo had the laudable goal of protecting an ethnic minority, the controlling SC Resolution 1199 (1998) did not authorize the use of force. Post-conflict legal apologists have set forth justifications ranging from a claim of consistency with other portions of the UN Charter,[37] to the theory that intervention was necessary as a matter of collective self-defence given the potential for the continued flow of

[36] Allied Force was not the first reliance upon the doctrine. In 1991, the United Kingdom and France relied on the principle of humanitarian intervention to intercede in northern Iraq, citing concerns over the severe plight of Kurdish refugees. The United States, a partner in the Kurdish refugee relief operation, Operation Provide Comfort, did not justify its actions on the principle of humanitarian intervention, however. Rather, the United States relied upon standing SC resolutions that authorized the use of force in Iraq. Long concerned with the doctrine's open-ended character and the opportunity for its misuse by other powers to justify misguided interventions (see *Factors that may be Cited in Support of NATO Action in Kosovo*, dated 7 October 1998 (on file with the authors)), the United States has deliberately and consistently declined to adopt the doctrine of humanitarian intervention, under which one State is entitled to use force to prevent or terminate a humanitarian catastrophe in another.

[37] UN Charter Preamble (reciting humanitarian purposes of Charter).

refugees to destabilize the region.[38] Prime Minister Tony Blair provided perhaps the most celebrated explanation in his April 1999 speech to the Chicago Economic Club;[39] he essentially argued for the adoption of a new values-based 'just war' doctrine, reflecting a notion of 'international community'.[40] But again we see that the last chapter on humanitarian intervention is not yet written. Today's operational lawyer needs to be able to track trends in *jus ad bellum* that depart from UN Charter text. **2.01**

While not necessarily indicative of major changes in *jus ad bellum*, operations 'Enduring Freedom' and 'Iraqi Freedom' also provide examples of the import to national interests of adherence to the international law of military operations generally and the continuing import of *jus ad bellum* more specifically. With respect to the former, there has been relatively little debate regarding the authority to intervene under international law, but there has been substantial discussion regarding the proper characterization of the conflict and therefore the legal regime that attends constituent military actions. Conversely, the United States' invasion of Iraq was seen by all to be an international armed conflict, making clear the propriety of *jus in bello* as the *lex specialis* of the conflict. But there has been substantial controversy regarding the application of *jus ad bellum*, i.e. the legal authority to intervene in the first place.

Legal and political debate regarding operations 'Enduring Freedom' and 'Iraqi Freedom' has been ubiquitous and need not be summarized here, but suffice it to say that the disparate reactions to the military operations in Afghanistan and Iraq demonstrate the continuing importance of *jus ad bellum* in the international law of military operations. Failing to comprehend how legal authorities will be perceived could affect a nation's foreign relations for years to come. While major structural changes to the *jus ad bellum* regime are not evident on the perceivable horizon, minor course adjustments are a certainty. For example, a definition of the crime of aggression was added to the corpus of International Criminal Court offences.[41] And the advent of transnational terrorist groups, coupled with their increasing capability and desire to secure weapons of mass destruction, will undoubtedly pressure fundamental tenets of self-defence law. As tomorrow's legal advisors prepare to

[38] See Henry H. Perritt, 'Kosovo: Internal Conflict, International Law', 144 *Chicago Daily Law Bulletin* 2 (24 July 1998); Guy Dinmore, 'New Kosovo Massacre May Spur NATO to Act', *Washington Post*, 30 September 1998, at A1 (asserting that the massive refugee flows from Kosovo into the neighbouring countries of Albania and Macedonia arguably posed a 'threat to international peace and security' and did so long before NATO's bombing campaign).

[39] See Prime Minister Tony Blair's Address at the Chicago Economic Club (24 April 1999) (hereinafter, Blair Speech to Chicago Club). See also Tony Blair, 'A Military Alliance, and More', *New York Times*, 24 April 1999, at A19; Tony Blair, 'A New Moral Crusade', *Newsweek*, 14 June 1999, at 35 ('We are succeeding in Kosovo because this was a moral cause . . . ').

[40] The speech does not actually use the term, 'just war'. But see C. Abbott and J. Sloboda, *The 'Blair Doctrine' and After: Five Years of Humanitarian Intervention* (22 April 2004), available at <https://www.opendemocracy.net/globalization-institutions_government/article_1857.jsp> (characterizing the Blair speech as introducing a 'just war' doctrine).

[41] Arts 8*bis*, 15*bis*, and 15*ter* ICC Statute, as adopted in Kampala, 11 June 2010.

2.01 navigate the yet unknown course ahead, they should do so with a clear understanding of the mistakes of the past and the enduring principles upon which we have built the present.

2. *Jus in Bello*

If the legal regime regarding *jus ad bellum* is fundamental to determining the legality of the military operation itself and the legal framework that will provide its regulation, *jus in bello*—the *lex specialis* for the conduct of hostilities—is the most significant legal regime impacting the international law of military operations. The pedigree of *jus in bello* also hails from ancient history, but unlike *jus ad bellum*, its tenets are more a function of the means and methods of warfare of the time as opposed to the more recurrent themes of *jus ad bellum*.

As with *jus ad bellum*, fundamental principles of the law of armed conflict were originally principles complied with as a matter of policy to affect the political ends of the conflict—or they manifested chivalrous behaviour that may have been deemed to be self-rewarding in a religious sense. Post-Westphalian treaty making, however, has moved *jus in bello* into the realm of 'harder' law, described more thoroughly in a companion volume to this book.[42] Today, *jus in bello* is divided generally into two major categories, which are oriented toward their animating conventions and can be referred to as the 'Law of The Hague', and the 'Law of Geneva'. The Law of The Hague had its roots in the American Civil War's Lieber Code and is primarily concerned with regulating the means and methods of warfare.

Contemporaneously with the Law of The Hague, the Law of Geneva was developed in response to the terrible suffering wrought upon civilians and other victims of war. Particularly noteworthy in its development was Jean Henri Dunant's book, *A Memory of Solferino*, which described the carnage he witnessed in the Second Italian War of Independence. Dunant's work inspired the first Geneva Convention (1864)[43] and the founding of the International Committee of the Red Cross. Ultimately, he inspired the Geneva Conventions of 1949, and their subsequent Protocols.[44] The existence of the varied and numerous law of war treaties requires military legal advisors not only to understand their terms, limitations, and proscriptions, but also to be able to discern current trends in international law and attitudes of allies and coalition partners. In recognition of this need, many nations have developed the distinct legal discipline of Operational Law, with a robust, professional cadre of specialized military legal advisors.

[42] D. Fleck (ed.), *The Handbook of International Humanitarian Law*, 2nd edn (Oxford: Oxford University Press, 2008).

[43] Geneva Convention for the Amelioration of the Condition of the Wounded in Armies in the Field, Geneva, 22 August 1864.

[44] See The Geneva Conventions of 12 August 1949, International Committee of the Red Cross, Geneva, 23–50.

III. Development of the Use of Legal Advisors 2.01

For by wise counsel thou shalt make thy war: and in multitude of counsellors there is safety.
Proverbs 24:6

Although nations have for centuries enacted codes and regulations to govern the conduct of their armed forces, the historical record reflecting the assignment of lawyers to advise and assist commanders is of a more recent vintage. For the United States, the first military code was modelled on the British Articles of War of 1661 and adopted in 1775 by the Continental Congress.[45] In 1776, the Rules for the Regulation of the Navy of the United Colonies were enacted.[46] These rules were rudimentary in nature and focused primarily on maintaining good order and discipline among the members of a unit. Nevertheless, they represented a rubric for internal discipline that included proscriptions on the violation of the laws and customs of war.[47] As such, they reflected an early attempt to apply the international law of military operations at a level below that of the nation-state.

Indeed, one of the requirements of the Geneva Conventions is that States disseminate the norms found therein. In many ways, dissemination through military manuals represents the quintessential method for actualizing and implementing a norm that otherwise might be discarded in the heat of battle.[48] In addition to ensuring that the norm is understood by those in a position to implement it, such dissemination may substantially raise the cost of later choosing to violate the norm; disregarding training or altering standard operating procedures so as to countenance violations of the laws and customs of war is more difficult to do in the heat of battle when those charged with implementation and obedience have been socialized to do the opposite.

The movement to embed legal advisors with military forces came to fruition at a much later time—initially to facilitate domestic law mandates regarding the preservation of good order and discipline. On 29 July 1775, General George

[45] See Burke and Gibbons, *The Articles of War—1749* (<https://www.prismnet.com/gibbonsb/articles.html>, see also R.A. McDonald, *Canada's Military Lawyers* 2 (Office of the Judge Advocate General, 2002). *The Articles* were first implemented in 1661 and subsequently amended in 1749 and again in 1757.

[46] The Rules for the Regulation of the Navy, enacted in 1776, were amended, in 1862, to the Articles for the Government of the Navy, commonly called, 'Rocks and Shoals'. See G.D. Solis, *Marines and Military Law in Vietnam: Trial by Fire* 3 (Washington: History and Museums Division, Headquarters, US Marine Corps, 1989) (hereinafter, 'Solis, *Trial by Fire*'). The Navy and Marine Corps continued to operate under the same Articles for the Government of the Navy until 1950, with the passage of the Uniform Code of Military Justice. Ibid. 5.

[47] See Art. 9, UK's Articles of War of 1749 ('If any ship or vessel be taken as prize, none of the officers, mariners, or other persons on board her, shall be stripped of their clothes, or in any sort pillaged, beaten, or evil-intreated, upon the pain that the person or persons so offending, shall be liable to such punishment as a court martial shall think fit to inflict.').

[48] See M. Reisman and W. Lietzau, 'Moving International Law From Theory to Practice: The Role of Military Manuals in Effectuating the Law of Armed Conflict', in H. Robertson, Jr (ed.), *The Law of Naval Operations, 64 International Law Studies* (Newport, RI: Naval War College, 1991).

2.01 Washington appointed William Tudor as the Judge Advocate of the Continental Army, and on 10 August 1776, Tudor was appointed the first Judge Advocate General.[49] But the advisory capacity of the office certainly did not reach down to the operational level. In 1865, the US Congress established the position of Solicitor and Naval Judge Advocate General, which it then abolished after the incumbent passed away. Later, in 1880, Congress enacted legislation creating the Office of the Judge Advocate General of the Navy. A US Marine Corps captain was appointed by President Hayes to serve as the Navy's first Judge Advocate General. He was to serve in the rank of Colonel, and did so for the next 12 years.[50] This early recognition of the important role of legal leadership can only be understood in the context of the time. For example, in World War I, the Navy Judge Advocate General's Office was proud of the fact that not a single lawyer served on its staff. In fact, it was not until 1950 that the Navy Judge Advocate General was required to be trained and credentialled as a lawyer.[51]

While other States used legal advisors as well, the United States is highlighted here as an example, due in major part to the authors' greater familiarity with US military service. That aside, the United States also was one of the first States to incorporate legal advisors in the field as a regular part of military practice. In fact, the US Army had been assigning judge advocates to the headquarters of every field army since 1862. During World War II, Marine Corps officers with law degrees were assigned only to the Atlantic and Pacific Fleet headquarters, and Headquarters, Marine Corps in Washington, DC. It was not until 1942 that a staff legal advisor position was created for each Marine division. This position was to be filled by a captain. The US Army, on the other hand, by this time had assigned a three-officer judge advocate section to each of its divisions. The section was manned by a lieutenant colonel, a captain, and a warrant officer, and was supported by two enlisted clerks.[52]

Up to the Vietnam War, the primary role of the military lawyer was to assist commanders in maintaining good order and discipline. But the US military experience in Vietnam led to a substantial expansion in the role of military lawyers. As a result, military lawyers would be called upon to assist actively in the planning and conduct of actual military operations. The watershed event triggering this transformation was the massacre at My Lai.

Before Vietnam, training in the law of war (LOW), now more commonly referred to as the law of armed conflict (LOAC) or international humanitarian law (IHL),[53] emphasized the rights of US military personnel upon capture, rather than the obligations imposed by LOAC on members of the US armed forces with

[49] See <http://www.history.army.mil/books/R&H/R&H-JAG.htm>; see also <http://www.famousamericans.net/william tudor/>.

[50] See Solis, *Trial by Fire*, 3. [51] See ibid. 4. [52] See ibid.

[53] The US Department of Defense defines the law of war as follows: 'That part of international law that regulates the conduct of armed hostilities. It is often called the "law of armed conflict". The law of war encompasses all international law for the conduct of hostilities binding on the United States or its individual citizens, including treaties and international agreements to which the United States is a party,

regard to the treatment of enemy captives.[54] Further, the fact that one aspect of the Vietnam conflict was a counterinsurgency mandated, as a practical matter, some emphasis on the treatment to be provided to civilians. This emphasis on the treatment of enemy combatants and civilians was not concerted, however, and it depended on the personality of the unit's commander. If a commander thought it important, LOAC training was emphasized and judge advocates provided it. But the training was of inconsistent quality at best.[55] In May of 1968, two months after My Lai, but well before the incident came to light, the Chief of Staff of the US Army complained about recurring reports of US forces mistreating captured enemy personnel. The response attributed part of the blame to the characterization of LOAC training provided by judge advocates as 'abstract and academic, rather than concrete and practical'.[56] **2.01**

Also, before and even during Vietnam, the primary role of judge advocates was the prosecution of those who violated the law. Most frequently, the judge advocate's traditional role in punishing violators was emphasized in lieu of training service members to avoid violations.[57] As early as 1961, certain Army lawyers expanded their practice to include the investigation of alleged LOAC violations. Several US military advisors who had been captured by the Viet Cong later escaped and subsequently, at the behest of Lieutenant Colonel (LTC) George C. Eblen, US Army JAGC, detailed in tape-recorded interviews evidence of their mistreatment while in captivity. The impact of LTC Eblen's interviews led to a new policy requiring judge advocate participation in all interviews involving allegations of LOAC violations. Ultimately, the Army promulgated a directive that required the reporting and investigation of all alleged violations of LOAC—one of the first recorded examples of the significant impact that legal advisors could have on traditionally 'non-legal' operational concerns.[58]

In November 1964, Army Colonel (COL) George S. Prugh became the staff judge advocate (SJA) of Military Assistance Command, Vietnam (MACV). Shortly after arriving in country, COL Prugh identified three areas—all of which fell outside the traditional judge advocate's practice—that required the involvement of military legal advisors: the status and treatment of captured enemy personnel; the investigation and reporting of war crimes; and the provision of assistance to the South Vietnamese in matters of resource control. 'Each [of these areas] would take Army lawyers into uncharted waters.'[59]

and applicable customary international law.' See DoD Directive 2311.01E, *DoD Law of War Program*, 9 May 2006.

[54] See W. Hays Parks, *The United States Military and the Law of War: Inculcating an Ethos—International Justice, War Crimes, and Terrorism: The US Record* (2002) (<http://findarticles.com/p/articles/mi_m2267/is_4_69/ai_97756588/>).

[55] Ibid. [56] Ibid. [57] Ibid.

[58] See F.L. Borch, *Judge Advocates in Combat: Army Lawyers in Military Operations from Vietnam to Haiti* (Washington: Office of the Judge Advocate General and Center of Military History, US Army, 2001) (hereinafter, 'Borch, *Judge Advocates in Combat*'), 8.

[59] Ibid. 10–11.

2.01 COL Prugh became aware that both the Viet Cong and South Vietnamese routinely executed their prisoners. The South Vietnamese justified their actions on the grounds that the Geneva Conventions did not apply to civil insurrections.[60] The Viet Cong also did not view the Geneva Conventions as applicable. The Viet Cong initially reserved execution for the South Vietnamese prisoners only, but this changed when the South Vietnamese publicly executed a number of captured Viet Cong. In response, the Viet Cong executed a number of captured US advisors.[61]

Prugh diligently attempted to persuade the South Vietnamese Director of Military Justice to require his forces to treat captured Viet Cong as prisoners of war under the Geneva Conventions, reasoning that humane treatment of captured Viet Cong could prompt reciprocity in the Viet Cong's treatment of captured American and South Vietnamese personnel. Despite staunch support for Prugh's efforts on both the military and diplomatic fronts, South Vietnam did not respond favourably until mid-1966 when it first constructed appropriate facilities in which to detain prisoners of war. The increasingly humane treatment afforded by the South Vietnamese appears to have pressured the Viet Cong and North Vietnamese, albeit informally, to treat US personnel more humanely; an increasing number of American personnel survived captivity during this period. At the core of this positive development was COL Prugh's active effort to apply international law to an operational issue once solely the province of military commanders.[62]

COL Prugh also impacted the investigations of alleged war crimes. When he first arrived in Vietnam, there was no policy addressing the reporting and investigation of alleged war crimes. In early 1965, COL Prugh drafted a directive requiring that allegations of LOAC violations be reported to the SJA for investigation. By the middle of 1965, Army judge advocates were advising, assisting, and reviewing all investigations of LOAC violations in Vietnam, a trend that would continue through the end of that conflict and inaugurate a long-standing tradition that continues to the present day.[63]

United States judge advocates had broken new ground in the Vietnam conflict, but their new roles were still ill-defined and implemented in an ad hoc manner. It would take the My Lai incident to propel the Army judge advocate community towards wholesale change in its approach to providing legal services and support during military operations. Other US military services' judge advocate communities would follow suit. The watershed of My Lai would revolutionize the way the US judge advocate community approached its role.

On 16 March 1968, members of US Army's Company C, 1st Battalion, 20th Infantry, an element of the Americal Division, murdered approximately 350 civilians in the Vietnamese village of My Lai. The killings did not come to light until April 1969, when a veteran who had learned of the massacre brought it to the

[60] Indeed, the Conventions presume a state of armed conflict between two or more sovereign States, each fielding a regular army fighting on a readily identifiable battlefront—classic conditions that did not exist in the early stages of the Vietnam conflict.

[61] Borch, *Judge Advocates in Combat*, 11. [62] Ibid. 12. [63] Ibid. 12–13.

attention of the Army Chief of Staff, General Westmoreland. The Army Criminal Investigation Division (CID) conducted an investigation and identified Army 1st Lieutenant William L. Calley and 12 other men as the likely perpetrators. Of the 13 soldiers charged, only Calley would be convicted; charges against six men were dropped for lack of evidence and the others were acquitted by courts-martial.[64] **2.01**

Although Calley could have been charged with war crimes and tried either by military commission—a forum that had not been used since World War II—or by court-martial, which had technically been granted jurisdiction over war crimes (a jurisdictional option that has never been tested), Calley was ultimately tried and convicted at court-martial of the non-LOAC offence of pre-meditated murder. On 29 March 1971, he was sentenced to life in prison. Post-trial action resulted in the reduction of his sentence, initially to 20 years, then later to only 10 years of confinement. In November 1974, Calley was granted parole.[65]

In addition to the Army CID investigation, an independent investigation, known as the Peers Inquiry,[66] identified 30 individuals involved in either the actual My Lai murders or the subsequent cover-up of the massacre. More importantly, the Peers Inquiry also assessed the root causes of the incident. One finding was that Calley's unit had not received adequate LOAC training, particularly with regard to the treatment of civilians and the responsibility to report war crimes.[67]

In May 1970, the JAG Corps responded to this disturbing finding by revising its LOAC regulation to require soldiers to receive more thorough instruction on the Geneva and Hague Conventions, and to mandate that the instruction be presented by judge advocates, together with officers who had command experience, preferably in combat. This requirement ensured that the training was supported by actual, practical experience, which contributed to its credibility, and further drove home the lesson that commanders bore ultimate responsibility for compliance with LOAC, and hence should participate actively in its instruction.[68]

More significantly, in 1972, retired Army Colonel W.A. Solf undertook an initiative to persuade the Department of Defense (DoD) to create a DoD-level LOAC programme. The Judge Advocate General of the Army, now Major General Prugh, fully supported this proposal. As a result of Solf's initiative, on 5 November 1974 the Secretary of Defense signed DoD Directive 5100.77 establishing the DoD Law of War Program.[69] This Directive required a uniform approach among all of the armed services for LOAC training, reporting, and investigating, and further established the Army's JAG Corps as the lead organization for implementing the DoD LOAC programme.[70]

64 Ibid. 29. 65 Ibid. 30.

66 The Peers Inquiry was named after the lead investigator, Lt Gen. William R. Peers.

67 See Borch, *Judge Advocates in Combat*, 30. 68 Ibid.

69 DoD Directive 5100.77, *DoD Program for Implementation of the Law of War* (Washington: US Government Printing Office, 5 November 1974). This Directive has been revised and updated over the years. It is currently DoD Directive 2311.01E, *DoD Law of War Program*, 9 May 2006.

70 See Borch, *Judge Advocates in Combat*, 30.

2.01 Although the Army and its JAG Corps focused almost exclusively on enhancing the Army's compliance with US LOAC obligations, this DoD Directive would play a significant role in the future development of what is now referred to as Operational Law.[71] For example, in addition to mandating that extensive LOAC training be provided to armed forces personnel, the DoD Directive also required legal reviews of all weapons, weapon systems, and munitions being procured by the armed services. This requirement pre-dated by three years the requirement set forth in Additional Protocol I.[72]

Probably the most significant change instituted in the DoD Directive was the requirement that military lawyers be involved in the development and review of operational plans in order to ensure their compliance with LOAC. 'This latter requirement was of particular significance, as it represented the first institutionally mandated involvement of military attorneys in the operational planning process.'[73] Judge advocates were required to communicate directly with military commanders and their staffs throughout the planning process; for the first time, military lawyers would, by regulation, be involved in the planning and conduct of military operations, even at the operational level.

My Lai changed substantially the traditional role of military lawyers in the planning and execution phases of military operations. And it professionalized a new area of law—Operational Law—thus fostering its further development. It was not until the US operation in Grenada (Operation Urgent Fury) in 1983, however, that the Army judge advocate community would recognize the need to institutionalize the training of its judge advocates in the newly forged discipline of Operational Law.[74]

The DoD Law of War Program requiring judge advocate review of operational plans had been in place for more than nine years when US forces entered Grenada. Judge advocates were focused on the international and operational legal issues that potentially could arise during a military operation to a much greater degree than in any previous conflict. During 'Operation Urgent Fury', judge advocates were involved in assessing and resolving an expanded issue set that impacted almost every aspect of mission success. These issues included developing rules of engagement (ROE), advising on the proper handling of prisoners of war, establishing

[71] See D.E. Graham, 'My Lai and Beyond: The Evolution of Operational Law', in J.N. Moore and R.F. Turner (eds), *The Real Lessons of the Vietnam War: Reflections Twenty-Five Years After the Fall of Saigon* (Carolina Academic Press, 2002), 365 (hereinafter, 'Graham, My Lai and Beyond').

[72] Art. 36 AP I: 'In the study, development, acquisition or adoption of a new weapon, means or method of warfare, a High Contracting Party is under an obligation to determine whether its employment would, in some or all circumstances, be prohibited by this Protocol or by any other rule of international law applicable to the High Contracting Party.' Ironically, although there are 168 States parties to AP I, there are less than a dozen countries that are actually complying with this provision. Today, the requirement for the US military to conduct legal reviews is found in DoD Directive 5000.01, *The Defense Acquisition System*, 12 May 2003, and DoD Directive 3000.3, *Policy for Non-Lethal Weapons*, 9 July 1996.

[73] Graham, 'My Lai and Beyond', 366; see also Borch, *Judge Advocates in Combat*, 31.

[74] Graham, 'My Lai and Beyond', 366; see also Borch, *Judge Advocates in Combat*, 31.

policy on war trophies, and assisting the US State Department in negotiating a status-of-forces agreement. Judge advocates adjudicated claims for damaged and seized property, provided advice to the Government of Grenada regarding the drafting of domestic law, and served as liaisons with various US Government agencies and international organizations, to include the International Committee of the Red Cross.[75] 2.01

The brevity of 'Operation Urgent Fury'[76]—and the associated movement from the law of peace to the law of war and back again in very short order—also taught the judge advocate community that it must be prepared to address operational law issues that fell outside the traditional practice areas of *jus ad bellum* and *jus in bello.* Several years later, the invasion of Panama, 'Operation Just Cause', reinforced this lesson; military operations involved both armed conflict and a law enforcement component related to bringing an indicted drug dealer to justice. The plethora of legal issues associated with such a complex operation—beginning with the highly criticized *jus ad bellum* justification for the intervention and ending with the trial of Manuel Noriega at the confluence of two disparate legal regimes: domestic law enforcement and LOAC—clearly brought the field of operational law into its own. No longer would military lawyers be left back in the nation's capital to draft rules and derive *ex post facto* esoteric legal justifications. Legal advisors now practised the International Law of Military Operations at the strategic, operational, and even tactical levels.

Recognizing this trend, the Army's Judge Advocate General's School (JAG School)[77] began to apportion legal assets to revitalize legal community training. The JAG School set out to define 'Operational Law', craft a curriculum, and publish an Operational Law Handbook for use by deployed judge advocates that outlined the wide variety of legal issues likely to arise in the context of military operations. The Handbook noted sagely:

> [t]hese issues cannot be neatly segregated, but instead transcend most of the legal disciplines of military law. That is, the [judge advocate] will confront international law, administrative law, civil law (to include contract, fiscal, and environmental law), and claims issues that arise from and impact on the manner in which military activities are conducted and supported across the operational spectrum.[78]

[75] See D.E. Graham, 'Operational Law', in *National Security Law* (John Norton Moore and Robert F. Turner (eds), Carolina Academic Press, 2005), 373, 376 (hereinafter, Graham, 'Operational Law').

[76] US troops, together with forces from Antigua, Barbados, Dominica, Jamaica, St Lucia, and St Vincent, landed on Grenada on 25 October 1983, and the hostilities were declared at an end on 2 November 1983. See Paul Seabury and Walter A. McDougall (eds), *The Grenada Papers*, 12 (Institute for Contemporary Studies, San Francisco, CA, 1984); see also *'Grenada, Operation Urgent Fury (23 October–21 November 1983)'*, adapted from: Berry, William et al., 'Ten Days of Urgent Fury', *All Hands* 807 (May 1984), 19–27, Department of the Navy Historical Center (<http://www.history.navy.mil/research/library/online-reading-room/title-list-alphabetically/g/grenada-operation-urgent-fury.html>).

[77] Today, the school is part of the Judge Advocate General's Legal Center and School.

[78] Graham, 'Operational Law', 377.

2.01 In 1987, an article published in *The Army Lawyer* introduced the concept of Operational Law to the military legal community as a whole.[79] The article would serve as the forcing mechanism that, over the ensuing years, would lead to the broad-based acceptance of Operational Law as a distinct discipline. In 1987, the Army JAG School began offering a Master of Laws (LL.M.) degree in Military Law. Students may specialize in the area of international and operational law.[80] Foreign students from allied militaries regularly attend the courses taught by and for US judge advocates, and many other countries have initiated training in the Operational Law discipline as well. Finally, in 1990, the Army JAG School conducted the first Operational Law symposium, which was offered to military lawyers in all of the US armed services as well as to civilian attorneys of the Department of Defense and other US Government agencies. The value and applicability of the Operational Law construct is undeniable, and in short order the legal schoolhouses of the other armed services established international law divisions. Service headquarters also all launched operational law cells and departments.[81]

2.02 **The International Law of Military Operations is further developing in a reactive manner challenging the military legal advisor to stay current and to anticipate future developments in law and practice.**

1. Throughout history, international law, and the law of war in particular, has evolved in response to new developments in warfare. But that evolution has not always equated to 'progress'. It is often asserted that Generals—charged to prepare for the war to come—prepare, in fact, for the war just past. So too, those who conceive, negotiate, and articulate the law of war too often do so through the 20/20 lens of hindsight. The most successful Field Marshals take lessons from historic battles and apply them analogously to future conflicts, all the while maintaining a clear perspective on present realities. Similarly, the authors of the law that will govern tomorrow's military operations must adapt that which is useful and appropriate from the law forged by conflicts past and merge those concepts with fledgling norms and customs that anticipate future challenges. In the present time, in which the law already has repeatedly proven itself a most critical element of world order, we ignore this mandate at our peril.

2. In recent years we have seen military forces become involved in illegal drug interdiction operations, humanitarian relief efforts, and a multitude of increasingly nuanced peacekeeping and peace enforcement and nation-building operations.[82]

[79] See D.E. Graham, 'Operational Law (OPLAW) – A Concept Comes of Age', *Army Lawyer* 10 (July 1987).

[80] See Title 10 United States Code § 4315; see also Correspondence (email) between D.E. Graham and J. A. Rutigliano Jr, dated 15 October 2009 (on file with the authors).

[81] See Graham, 'Operational Law', 377.

[82] To assist military legal advisors in these widely disparate operations, several handbooks have been published by the US military. For example, see *Rule of Law Handbook, A Practitioner's Guide for Judge Advocates* (US Army's Center for Law and Military Operations 2009).

Many times, the first to deploy in novel circumstances are faced with applying a body of law they are only beginning to identify. For instance, although LOAC is considered *lex specialis* as regards armed conflict, the hybrid nature of today's conflicts sometimes calls into question whether LOAC or human rights law is more properly applied. One prominent practitioner and scholar has noted: **2.02**

> At a minimum, some types of armed conflicts, including occupation, internal armed conflicts and the contemporary 'war on terror', inevitably require an assessment of the interface between humanitarian law governing armed conflict and human rights law which applies to law enforcement situations.[83]

But even that author concedes that applying human rights law in these hybrid situations can be problematic. For instance, were the November 2004 operation in Fallujah, Iraq, viewed as having taken place during the occupation phase of the armed conflict, it would have proven difficult to apply a human rights standard to the level of violence that far exceeded anything contemplated under any law enforcement model.[84]

3. Divining tomorrow's war may be impossible, but history informs our presumption that it will be different from what has gone before. That such change will involve disciplines across the spectrum of both international and domestic jurisprudence seems clear. Tacking from the law of peace to the law of war and returning again to peace—but lacking the clear demarcations that have signalled such transitions in past conflicts—change will impact both *jus ad bellum* and *jus in bello* and extend to those domestic statutes that implement international norms.[85] All of these bodies of law are undergoing transformation likely to continue in the days, months, and years to come; all present interesting challenges for attorneys and leaders; all are susceptible to contouring, if not direct alteration; and all require substantial, informed colloquy—a colloquy furthered in Chapter 31, 'The Role of the Military Legal Advisor'.

4. Today's reform of the legal landscape involves change different from and more profound than that of the recent past. The most controversial area of debate in recent conflicts—at least those involving the United States—was grounded in the realm of *jus ad bellum*: the first legal issue addressed in analysing a use of the military

[83] See K. Watkin, 'Assessing Proportionality: Moral Complexity and Legal Rules', 8 *YIHL* (2005), 35, citing L. Moir, 'Law and the Inter-American Human Rights System', 25 *HRQ* (2003), 182, and K. Watkin, 'Controlling the Use of Force: A Role for Human Rights Norms in Contemporary Armed Conflict', 98 *AJIL* (2004), 24–30.

[84] See K. Watkin, 'Controlling the Use of Force', who points out that were '540 air strikes and 14,000 artillery shells and mortar shells fired, as well as 2,500 tank main gun rounds', during the battle for Fallujah.

[85] See e.g. Uniting and Strengthening America by Providing Appropriate Tools Required to Intercept and Obstruct Terrorism (USA PATRIOT) Act of 2001, Pub. L. No. 107-56, 115 Stat. 272; USA PATRIOT Improvement and Reauthorization Act of 2005, Pub. L. No. 109-177, 120 Stat. 192 (2006); USA PATRIOT Act Additional Reauthorizing Amendments of 2006, Pub. L. No. 109-178, 120 Stat. 278 (2006).

2.02 instrument likely will be the authority for the use of force itself. The relevant restraining norm is that of the inviolability of State sovereignty; that norm will continue to be pressured as the risk increases that a devastating initial attack could come from another State or even a transnational armed group.[86] But the *jus ad bellum* debate is soon relegated to the academic as conflicts progress and *jus in bello* concerns assume prominence. *Jus in bello* too is in the throes of change as new norms are being conceived and old norms are questioned. Indeed, the war against al Qaeda has unleashed a torrent of debate, accusations, and litigation regarding the legality of the conduct of hostilities—*jus in bello*—opening international rifts that strain even our most long-standing alliances.[87] The result of this controversy is that challenging, probing questions have arisen regarding what the applicable legal norms are or should be and how they should be applied. There are no ready responses to some of these questions. Thus military lawyers, the most steadfast practitioners of the International Law of Military Operations, can be assured steady employment for the foreseeable future.

5. We have future wars to win, but they will never be won by devolution to the maxim of *inter arma enim silent leges*.[88] Unflagging belief in the rule of law is one of the core principles for which so many have been willing to fight and die. We must demonstrate our respect for that law, both by adhering to it, and by developing norms—laws—that make sense for the context in which they will be applied. We must strive to win both the war and the peace and establish an international rule of law capable of guiding us into the future.

[86] Art. 2(4) UN Charter ('All members shall refrain in their international relations from the threat or use of force against the territorial integrity or political independence of any state . . . ').

[87] See e.g. Letter from Brad Davis, Executive Director, Asia Division, Human Rights Watch, to the Secretary General of the North Atlantic Treaty Organization (NATO), 29 November 2006, see <http://www.state.gov/documents/organization/176589.pdf> (asserting that substantial disagreements between Members of NATO regarding detention policies in Afghanistan are the consequence of the United States' failure to comply with international legal standards).

[88] In 2004, Justice Antonin Scalia used this phrase to decry the plurality decision in *Hamdi v Rumsfeld*. Scalia argued passionately: 'Many think it not only inevitable but entirely proper that liberty give way to security in times of national crisis that, at the extremes of military exigency, *inter arma silent leges*. Whatever the general merits of the view that war silences law or modulates its voice, that view has no place in the interpretation and application of a Constitution designed precisely to confront war and, in a manner that accords with democratic principles, to accommodate it.' *Hamdi v Rumsfeld*, 542 US 507, 630 (2004).

Chapter 3

HUMAN RIGHTS AND INTERNATIONAL HUMANITARIAN LAW

General Issues

Introductory Remarks

Human rights and international humanitarian law are two pivotal components of the International Law of Military Operations (cf. generally Section 1.02). The two fields of law are closely intertwined. That close relationship has been confirmed and developed by decisions of international and domestic courts on a number of occasions.[1] It chiefly emanates from the shared purpose of human rights law and international humanitarian law to protect individual and human dignity, which also explains the substantial material overlap between the two fields.[2] However, while one can witness a certain approximation and cross-fertilization, human rights law and international humanitarian law remain distinct areas of international law. Significant differences remain, not only as regards their historical roots and evolution, normative frameworks, and enforcement mechanisms,[3] but also concerning their respective applicability *ratione materiae, personae, temporis,* and *loci.*

In military operations amounting to an armed conflict, international humanitarian law applies. Human rights law is generally considered to apply to the extent that individuals are subject to the jurisdiction of a State or international organization. **3.01**

[1] See e.g. ICJ, *Legality of the Threat or Use of Nuclear Weapons*, Advisory Opinion of 8 July 1996, ICJ Reports 1996, 226, 35 *ILM* (1996), 809, para. 25; *Legal Consequences of the Construction of a Wall in the Occupied Palestinian Territory*, Advisory Opinion of 9 July 2004, ICJ Reports 2004, 43 *ILM* (2004), 1009, paras 102–142, at 106; *Case Concerning Armed Activities on the Territory of the Congo (Democratic Republic of the Congo v Uganda)*, Judgment of 19 December 2005, paras 216–221. Israel, Supreme Court, sitting as the High Court of Justice, *Marab et al. v Israeli Defence Force Commander*, Final Decision of 5 February 2003, HCJ 3239/02; ILDC 15 (IL 2003), paras 19–21, 25–29, 41–42.

[2] R.E. Vinuesa, 'Interface, Correspondence and Convergence of Human Rights and International Humanitarian Law', 1 *YIHL* (1998), 69–110, at 70–6.

[3] For a detailed analysis, see R. Provost, *International Human Rights and Humanitarian Law* (Cambridge: Cambridge University Press, 2002).

JANN K. KLEFFNER

3.01 1. *International Humanitarian Law: Applicability* Ratione Materiae. International humanitarian law regulates, and as a rule applies in times of, armed conflicts.[4] More particularly, international humanitarian law seeks to limit the effects of armed conflicts by protecting persons who are not or no longer participating in the hostilities and by restricting the means and methods of warfare, that parties to an armed conflict may use in their quest to overcome the adversary. Underlying international humanitarian law as a whole is a balance between considerations of humanity and military necessity in times of armed conflict. In this sense, humanity and military necessity are the primary principles of international humanitarian law that inform this body of law in its entirety.

2. *Principles of International Humanitarian Law.* The balance between humanitarian concerns and military necessity as primary principles gives rise to a number of general principles of international humanitarian law. First, it is a cardinal principle that parties to an armed conflict have to distinguish between members of the armed forces of a party to an armed conflict, civilians directly participating in hostilities and military objectives, on the one hand, and civilians and civilian objects, on the other hand. While attacks may be directed against the former, it is prohibited to direct attacks against the latter.[5] Second, international humanitarian law prohibits launching an attack which may be expected to cause incidental loss of civilian life, injury to civilians, damage to civilian objects, or a combination thereof, which would be excessive in relation to the concrete and direct military advantage anticipated.[6] While this principle of proportionality recognizes that it will not always be possible to spare civilians and civilian objects in the process of attacking military objectives, it restricts the extent of permissible incidental harm to that which is proportionate to the concrete and direct military advantage anticipated. Third, international humanitarian law rests on the principle that those in the power of a party to an armed conflict must be protected and respected and are entitled to humane treatment without any adverse distinction.[7] A fourth principle of international humanitarian law that flows from the basic tenet that the right of parties to an armed conflict to choose methods and means of warfare is not unlimited, seeks to protect members of the armed forces from superfluous injury and unnecessary suffering.[8] The aforementioned principles of distinction, proportionality, and protection as well as the principle that prohibits causing superfluous injury and

[4] As an exception to the rule that IHL applies in times of armed conflicts, some rules, such as those relating to dissemination are applicable in peacetime as well. For these exceptions, see e.g. Arts 23, 44, 47 GC I; 127 GC III; 144 GC IV; 6(1), 83(1) AP I; 7 AP III.

[5] See amongst others, Rule 1 CLS, Arts 48, 51(2) and 52(2) AP I, 13(2) AP II.

[6] Cf. J.-M. Henckaerts and L. Doswald-Beck (eds), *Customary International Humanitarian Law* (Cambridge: Cambridge University Press, 2005), *Vol. I* (hereinafter, 'CIHL'), Rule 14 CIHL, Arts 51 (5)(b) and 57 AP I.

[7] Cf. Arts 12 GC I & II; 16 GC III; 27 GC IV; 75(1) AP I; Common Art. 3(1) GC I–IV; Arts 2(1) and 4(1) AP II.

[8] See amongst others, Rule 70 CIHL, Art. 35(2) AP I; Preamble of the CCW, Art. 6(2) of Protocol II to the CCW, Art. 3(3) of Amended Protocol II to the CCW.

unnecessary suffering in turn translate into more detailed rules of international humanitarian law. 3.01

3. *Separation Between* jus ad bellum *and* jus in bello. The legality or illegality of an armed conflict under the law regulating the recourse to the use of armed force is irrelevant for the applicability and interpretation of international humanitarian law. International humanitarian law applies equally to all parties to an armed conflict, irrespective of whether an armed conflict is waged in compliance with, or in violation of, the general prohibition of the use of force embodied in the UN Charter[9] and in customary international law or any of the recognized exceptions to that prohibition, i.e. the right to use force in self-defence against an armed attack[10] and the right to use force with authorization of the Security Council acting under Chapter VII of the Charter.[11] Acts of members of the armed forces participating in an illegal use of armed force are subject to the same constraints under international humanitarian law as those of their opponents. Although international law is agnostic as regards the legality of the use of force *within*—as opposed to *between*—States, the separation between the cause for initiating an armed conflict and the applicable rules of international humanitarian law applies *mutatis mutandis* in non-international armed conflicts.[12]

4. *Reciprocity.* Conventional humanitarian law is, as a rule, only binding between those States which are parties to the respective treaties, but remains applicable between those parties in their mutual relations even if another party to the conflict has not become a party to the respective treaty.[13] However, once the applicability of international humanitarian law has been determined, the obligation to respect and ensure respect for international humanitarian law does not depend on reciprocity.[14]

5. *International and Non-International Armed Conflicts.* One can generically distinguish between, on the one hand, armed conflicts of an international character, including belligerent occupations, and, on the other hand, armed conflicts not of an international character. The two situations are subject to distinct sets of rules of international humanitarian law: the law of international armed conflicts,[15] including the law of belligerent occupation,[16] and the law of non-international armed conflicts.[17]

[9] Cf. Art. 2(4) UN Charter. [10] Cf. Art. 51 UN Charter. [11] Cf. Art. 42 UN Charter.

[12] M. Sassòli, '*Ius ad Bellum* and *Ius in Bello*—The Separation between the Legality of the Use of Force and Humanitarian Rules to Be Respected in Warfare: Crucial or Outdated?' in Schmitt and Pejic (eds), *International Law and Armed Conflict: Exploring the Faultlines. Essays in Honour of Yoram Dinstein* (Leiden, Boston: Nijhoff, 2007), 241–64, at 254–7.

[13] Cf. Common Art 2(3) GC I–IV. [14] Rule 140 CIHL.

[15] Chiefly comprising the 1907 Hague Regulations on Land Warfare, the Four 1949 Geneva Conventions (except Common Art. 3), the 1977 Additional Protocol I, and a significant number of treaties pertaining to more specific issues, as well as customary international law.

[16] In the main comprising Arts 42–56 HagueReg 1907; Arts 47–78 GC IV; and customary international law.

[17] Most important treaty rules are Common Art. 3 GC I–IV and AP II. Furthermore, rules of customary international humanitarian law apply.

3.01 6. *International Armed Conflicts.* In the words of the Geneva Conventions, the law of *international armed conflict* applies to 'all cases of declared war or of any other armed conflict which may arise between two or more of the High Contracting Parties, even if the state of war is not recognized by one of them'.[18] The ICRC Commentary further explains that 'any difference arising between two states and leading to the intervention of members of the armed forces is an armed conflict'.[19] Similarly, the ICTY has held that an international armed conflict exists whenever there is 'resort to armed force between States'.[20] These views adhere to the so-called 'first-shot' theory, according to which the law of international armed conflict applies from the first moment that force is used by one State against another State. It is irrelevant, according to that view, what form that force takes or what its intensity or duration is.[21] It may be obvious, however, that a minor incursion by the armed forces of one State into another State, for instance, will not bring into operation the whole plethora of rules of international humanitarian law. Rather, the factual circumstances of a military operation amounting to an international armed conflict will determine which of the rules are practically relevant and, as a consequence, the extent to which the law applies. If, during such an operation, no member of the opposing armed forces is captured the law pertaining to prisoners of war is not applicable. Pivotal in that regard is, however, that the reason for the inapplicability is purely *factual* rather than *legal*, namely that the facts are such that the preconditions for the applicability of the law pertaining to prisoners of war are absent. As soon as a member of the opposing armed forces falls into the power of the enemy, s/he becomes a prisoner of war entitled to the full protection that international humanitarian law grants to that category of persons.

7. *Irrelevance of Formal Acknowledgment of Existence of an Armed Conflict.* The existence of an international armed conflict, and hence the applicability of international humanitarian law pertaining to that type of armed conflict, is independent of the subjective views of the parties to it. In contradistinction to the period prior to the adoption of the four 1949 Geneva Conventions, the facts on the ground—i.e. resort to armed force between States—are decisive. A formal acknowledgment of the existence of a state of armed conflict or war is not required. Nor is a formal declaration of war. This is notwithstanding the possibility that international humanitarian law may also be rendered applicable through a formal declaration of war in the absence of any resort to armed force between the State declaring war, on the one hand, and the State against whom war is being declared, on the other hand.[22] Such a

[18] Common Art. 2 GC I–IV.

[19] J. Pictet (ed.), *Commentary to the First Geneva Convention for the Amelioration of the Condition of the Wounded and the Sick in Armed Forces in the Field* (Geneva: ICRC, 1952), 32.

[20] Cf. *Prosecutor v Tadić*, Decision on the Defence Motion for Interlocutory Appeal on Jurisdiction, IT-94-1, Appeals Chamber (2 October 1995), para. 70.

[21] Pictet (ed.), *Commentary to the First Geneva Convention*, 32.

[22] For historical examples, see Dinstein, *War, Aggression and Self-Defence*, 5th edn (Cambridge: Cambridge University Press, 2011), 9.

declaration would trigger those parts of the law of international humanitarian law that **3.01**
are not directly concerned with, or dependent on, the conduct of hostilities. Examples of these parts are the rules on the treatment of aliens in the territory of a party to the conflict[23] and those governing the treatment of internees.[24] Be that as it may, the possibility of a formal declaration of war without the occurrence of actual hostilities today seems remote, not the least because States today generally abstain from making formal declarations of war.

8. *Wars of National Liberation.* According to Article 1(4) of AP I (1977), armed conflicts 'in which peoples are fighting against colonial domination and alien occupation and against racist regimes in the exercise of their right to self-determination' trigger the applicability of the law of international armed conflict.

9. *Belligerent Occupation.* As part of the law of international armed conflict, the law of *belligerent occupation* applies to situations in which territory of one State is placed under the authority of a hostile army.[25] The occupation extends only to the territory where such authority has been established and can be exercised.[26] Once the aforementioned conditions are fulfilled, the law of belligerent occupation applies, whether or not the occupation meets with resistance.[27] As in the case of determining whether an international armed conflict exists by virtue of the fact that there is 'resort to armed force between States', the determination of a given situation as amounting to belligerent occupation is exclusively governed by the facts on the ground. The evidence must be sufficient to demonstrate that the said authority was in fact established and exercised by the intervening State in the areas in question.[28] Relevant indicative factors in making that determination include the ability of the Occupying Power to substitute its own authority for that of the occupied authorities, which must have been rendered incapable of functioning publicly; the surrender, defeat, or withdrawal of enemy forces; the presence of a sufficient force, or the capacity to send troops within a reasonable time to make the authority of the Occupying Power felt; the establishment of a temporary administration over the territory; and the issuance and enforcement of directions to the civilian population.[29] It follows from the foregoing that battle areas may not be considered as occupied territory.[30]

10. *Non-International Armed Conflicts.* The law of non-international armed conflicts applies to situations of 'protracted armed violence between governmental authorities and organized armed groups or between such groups within a State'.[31]

23 Cf. Arts 35–46 GC IV. 24 Cf. Arts 79–135 GC IV.

25 Cf. Art. 42 HagueReg (1907). As to the customary status of Art. 42, see ICJ, *Legal Consequences of the Construction of a Wall in the Occupied Palestinian Territory*, Advisory Opinion, ICJ Reports 2004, 167, paras 78 and 172, para. 89; ICJ, *Case Concerning Armed Activities on the Territory of the Congo (Democratic Republic of the Congo v Uganda)*, Judgment of 19 December 2005, para. 172.

26 Art. 42 HagueReg (1907). 27 Cf. Common Art. 2(2) GC I–IV.

28 ICJ, DR *Congo v Uganda*, para. 173.

29 Cf. ICTY, *Prosecutor v Naletilić and Martinović*, Trial Chamber Judgment, 31 March 2003, para. 217.

30 Ibid. 31 Cf. *Prosecutor v Tadić*, para. 70.

3.01 Two basic requirements flow from this definition of a non-international armed conflict: the armed violence must be of sufficient intensity and the parties must be sufficiently organized. The following are indicative factors in assessing whether the requirement of intensity is satisfied: the number, duration, and intensity of individual confrontations; the type of weapons and other military equipment used; the number and calibre of munitions fired; the number of persons and type of forces partaking in the fighting; the number of casualties; the extent of material destruction; and the number of civilians fleeing combat zones. The involvement of the Security Council may also be a reflection of the intensity of a conflict.[32] As far as the requirement of organization is concerned, the following factors are relevant: the existence of a command structure and disciplinary rules and mechanisms within the group; the existence of a headquarters; the fact that the group controls a certain territory; the ability of the group to gain access to weapons, other military equipment, recruits, and military training; its ability to plan, coordinate, and carry out military operations, including troop movements and logistics; its ability to define a unified military strategy and use military tactics; and its ability to speak with one voice and negotiate and conclude agreements such as cease-fire or peace accords.[33] The aforementioned factors for determining the intensity of the armed violence and the organization of the parties to it must not be understood as a conclusive check-list, however. Rather they are guidelines in distinguishing non-international armed conflicts from situations in which violence occurs that does not rise beyond internal disturbances and tensions, such as riots, isolated and sporadic acts of violence, and other acts of a similar nature.[34] Such instances of lesser violence are not considered armed conflicts. This is notwithstanding the fact that non-international armed conflicts are often preceded by a period of internal disturbances and tensions. It will then be necessary to determine at what point in time such disturbances and tensions reach the threshold of intensity, and the parties to it the required degree of organization, for the situation to be governed also by international humanitarian law rather than exclusively by human rights law and national law. While there is thus a need to distinguish non-international armed conflicts from internal disturbances and tensions on the lower end of the spectrum, non-international armed conflicts on the higher end of the spectrum may reach the threshold for the applicability of AP II. This is the case when the armed conflict:

> take[s] place in the territory of a High Contracting Party between its armed forces and dissident armed forces or other organized armed groups which, under responsible command, exercise such control over a part of its territory as to enable them to carry out sustained and concerted military operations and to implement this Protocol.[35]

[32] ICTY, *Prosecutor v Ramush Haradinaj, Idriz Balaj and Lahi Brahimaj*, Case no. IT-04-84-T, Judgment of 3 April 2008, para. 49.

[33] Ibid. para. 60.

[34] Cf. Art. 1(2) AP II, Art. 8(2)(d) and (f) ICC Statute.

[35] Cf. Art. 1(1) AP II.

This latter requirement of territorial control distinguishes non-international armed conflicts under AP II from other non-international armed conflicts. Furthermore, AP II does not apply to non-international armed conflicts in which organized armed groups are pitted against each other, without the State being a party to the armed conflict. **3.01**

11. *Relevance of Distinction Between International and Non-International Armed Conflicts.* The relevance of distinguishing between international and non-international armed conflicts is being diminished to an extent due to a tangible *approximation between the law of international and non-international armed conflicts.* A considerable body of treaty rules and customary international humanitarian law has evolved which applies in both types of armed conflicts.[36] However, important differences remain. One pivotal example of these differences is the absence of combatant status in non-international armed conflicts, which entails the right to participate directly in hostilities[37] and is the precondition for the status of prisoner of war.[38] Another example is the law of occupation, which exclusively applies in international armed conflicts. Moreover, the applicability in non-international armed conflicts of a number of rules regulating methods and means of combat, i.e. tactics and weapons, is uncertain according to the ICRC Customary Law Study.[39] Some other findings of the ICRC Customary Law Study on methods and means of warfare in non-international armed conflicts have also given rise to a critical response from the US Government and academics.[40]

12. *Determining the Nature of an Armed Conflict.* The foregoing suggests that it may still be necessary to determine the nature of the armed conflict. In certain instances, however, it may be difficult to establish whether an armed conflict is international or non-international. The following are examples and guidelines as to how to approach the characterization of armed conflicts in these situations.

13. *Involvement of a State, Groups of States, or an International Organization in a Prima Facie Non-International Armed Conflict.* A *prima facie* non-international

[36] See D. Fleck (ed.), *The Handbook of International Humanitarian Law*, 3rd edn (Oxford: Oxford University Press, 2013), Sections 1207–1212. For customary international humanitarian law, see CIHL, concluding that of the 161 Rules that were found, 159 apply in international armed conflicts and 148 apply in non-international armed conflicts.

[37] Cf. Art. 43(2) AP I. [38] Cf. Art. 44(1) AP I.

[39] See the findings of the Study on the prohibition of the improper use of the flags or military emblems, insignia, or uniforms of the adversary, applicable in international armed conflicts, but only 'arguably' so in non-international armed conflicts. Cf. CIHL, Rules 62 and 63.

[40] See e.g. J.B. Bellinger III and W.J. Haynes II, 'A US Government Response to the International Committee of the Red Cross Study on Customary International Humanitarian Law', 866 *IRRC* (2007), 443–71, at 460, 465; Y. Dinstein, 'The ICRC Customary International Humanitarian Law Study', 36 *Israel Yearbook of Human Rights* (2006), 1–15; D. Turns, 'Weapons in the ICRC Study on Customary International Humanitarian Law', 11 *JCSL* (2006), 201–37. For a response to the first two of the aforementioned criticisms, see J.-M. Henckaerts, 'Customary International Humanitarian Law: a response to US comments', 866 *IRRC* (2007), 473–88; and 'The ICRC Customary International Humanitarian Law Study—A Rejoinder to Professor Dinstein', 37 *Israel Yearbook of Human Rights* (2007), 259.

3.01 armed conflict in State A will have to be treated as an international armed conflict by virtue of the fact that State B exercises control over an organized armed group which fights against the government of State A. The level of control required for such internationalization is a matter of dispute. The International Court of Justice requires 'effective control' that needs to be exercised, or the instructions of State B need to be given, in respect of each operation rather than generally in respect of the overall actions taken by the persons or groups of persons in question.[41] That level of control thus requires control on the tactical level. In contrast, the ICTY has held that 'overall control' would be sufficient for purposes of determining the nature of an armed conflict. Accordingly, it would not be required to prove that each operation of an organized armed group is being carried out on the instructions, or under the effective control, of State B.[42] While such control must go beyond the mere provision of financial assistance or military equipment or training, the ICTY has held that it is not necessary:

> that the controlling authorities should plan all the operations of the units dependent on them, choose their targets, or give specific instructions concerning the conduct of military operations [. . .]. The control required by international law may be deemed to exist when a State (or, in the context of an armed conflict, the Party to the conflict) has a role in organising, coordinating or planning the military actions of the military group, in addition to financing, training and equipping or providing operational support to that group.[43]

When third States or an international organization partake in hostilities in the context of a non-international armed conflict upon invitation of a government that finds itself in a non-international armed conflict against an organized armed group, the armed conflict is not, without more, thereby rendered international. Decisive for the characterization of an armed conflict as international is that the violent confrontation is one between two or more States. If one side of the armed conflict consists of an organized armed group whose actions cannot be attributed to another State in the way suggested above (see previous paragraph), the armed conflict remains of a non-international nature.

14. *Parallel Existence of a Non-International and an International Armed Conflict.* The existence of a non-international armed conflict in the territory of one State does not preclude the parallel existence of an international armed conflict between that latter State and other States or an international organization. The fact alone that there is an international armed conflict between one State and (an)other State(s) or an international organization does not automatically internationalize a non-international armed conflict between the former State and an organized armed

[41] ICJ, *Military and Paramilitary Activities in and against Nicaragua (Nicaragua v United States of America)*, ICJ Reports, 1986, 65; *Case Concerning the Application of the Convention on the Prevention and Punishment of the Crime of Genocide (Bosnia and Herzegovina v Serbia and Montenegro)* Judgment of 26 February 2007, General List no. 91, paras 399–400.

[42] ICTY, *Prosecutor v Tadić*, Judgment of the ICTY Appeals Chamber in the *Tadić* Case (IT-94-1-A, Judgment, 15 July 1999), para. 122.

[43] Ibid. para. 137.

group. This is the case to the extent that any operational synergy between the organized armed group pitted against the State in the context of the non-international armed conflict, on the one hand, and the States or an international organization confronting that same State, on the other hand, is such that it fails to reach the threshold of control (see above, para. 13).[44] 3.01

15. *Transnational Armed Conflicts.* It is not uncommon that contemporary armed conflicts bear both international and non-international traits in as much as the parties to it are one or more organized armed groups, on the one side, and a State or other organized armed group(s), on the other side, but the geographical dimension of that armed conflict is not limited to the territory of a single State (see also later on the applicability *ratione loci* of international humanitarian law). These transnational armed conflicts vary greatly and may involve, for instance, operations of the armed forces of the State party to the armed conflict against an organized armed group on the territory of another State, or an organized armed group engaged in protracted armed violence with a State in the form of repeated cross-border incursions from a neighbouring State. While it is relatively uncontroversial that Common Article 3 and the general principles of international humanitarian law apply as a minimum, it is a matter of dispute whether the law of international or of non-international armed conflicts applies to transnational armed conflicts. It is sometimes suggested that the notion of non-international armed conflict functions as a catch-all category for all armed conflicts other than those in which two or more States resort to armed force against one another.[45] Others have called for the development of a body of rules that takes due account of the hybrid nature of transnational armed conflicts by drawing from both sets of rules.[46] However, the better view seems to be to approach the problem more casuistically than in the abstract. The following parameters may be of assistance in determining whether the law of international or of non-international armed conflict is more adequate. In light of the fact that international humanitarian law does not provide clear answers to the question, these parameters should be understood as policy guidelines rather than legal requirements.

16. *Consent.* One factor in the equation as to whether a transnational armed conflict should be regarded as international or non-international is whether or not the territorial State has consented to the military operation. As a general guideline, in case such consent has been given, the situation resembles more closely that of a non-international armed conflict in as much as the territorial State allies itself with the other State in the latter's fight against an organized armed group. Such an alliance does not necessarily have to manifest itself in military support by

[44] ICJ, *Nicaragua*, Merits (1986), para. 219. See also the position taken by Germany, for instance, on the characterization of NATO's use of armed force against Yugoslavia, on the one hand, and the armed conflict between the KLA and the Yugoslav Government, on the other hand, S.R. Lüder and G. Schotten, Correspondents' Reports (Germany), 2 *YIHL* (1999), 364.

[45] US Supreme Court, *Hamdan v Rumsfeld et al.*, 548 US 67 (2006).

[46] See e.g. G.S. Corn, 'Hamdan, Lebanon, and the Regulation of Hostilities: the Need to Recognize a Hybrid Category of Armed Conflict', 40 *Vanderbilt Journal of Transnational Law* (2007), 295–355.

3.01 the territorial State, but can consist of the mere permission to let the other State operate on its territory. The opposite is true when the consent of the territorial State is not forthcoming. Even if there is no military activity of the territorial State in support of the organized armed group, an invasion by one State into another State's territory should thus be seen as triggering the law of international armed conflict. This approach also finds support in the recognition that pacific occupation triggers the law of belligerent occupation.[47]

17. *The Nature of the Operation.* A further parameter in determining the applicable law in a transnational armed conflict is the nature of the military operation that is being contemplated or carried out. When the armed forces of a State party to a non-international armed conflict temporarily pursue an organized armed group into the territory of a neighbouring State in the course of an uninterrupted military operation which commenced in the territory of the former State, it is submitted that the applicable law does not change by the mere fact that an international border is being crossed in the process. This is different in a situation where State armed forces conduct sustained operations on another State's territory without the consent of the territorial State. Furthermore, if and to the extent that the nature of the operation is such that it is not limited to engaging the organized armed group, but is also directed against the armed forces and/or infrastructure of the territorial State, the law of international armed conflict applies.

18. *Protection of non-Combatants.* In the course of a transnational armed conflict, non-combatants who find themselves in the hands of a party to the conflict of which they are not nationals should be treated as protected persons in accordance with the Fourth Geneva Convention,[48] notwithstanding the fact that the armed conflict takes place between a State and an organized armed group. Accordingly, they must not only be respected and protected under all circumstances and be treated humanely, but their internment and transfer, for instance, is subject to the same regulatory framework as the one applicable in international armed conflicts.

19. *Applicability of International Humanitarian Law in Military Operations.* It is readily apparent from the earlier discussion that the question whether a given military operation is governed by international humanitarian law or not, and if applicable, by the law of international or non-international armed conflicts, depends on the nature of the operation and the facts on the ground. As a rule, international humanitarian law is applicable to enforcement operations and those self-defence operations rising to the level of an armed conflict due to the nature of these operations (see Sections 5.01 and 11.01). In contrast, its applicability to peace enforcement and peace operations (see Sections 5.01 and 6.02) will have to be determined on a case-by-case basis in light of the factual environment and the

[47] See Common Art. 2(2) GC I–IV. In this vein, see also T. Gill, *The 11th of September and the International Law of Military Operations* (Amsterdam: Vossiuspers Universiteit van Amsterdam, 2002), 25.

[48] Cf. Art. 4 GC IV.

operationalization of the mandate for the operation in question within that environment. Relevant factors in making that determination therefore include, *inter alia*, the relevant Security Council resolutions for the operation, the specific operational mandates, the role and practices actually adopted by the peacekeeping mission during the particular conflict, their rules of engagement and operational orders, the nature of the arms and equipment used by the peace enforcement or peacekeeping force, the interaction between that force and the parties involved in the conflict, any use of force between the peace enforcement or peacekeeping force and the parties in an armed conflict, the nature and frequency of such force, and the conduct of the alleged victim(s) and their fellow personnel.[49] **3.01**

20. *Applying International Humanitarian Law beyond the Legally Required Minimum.* The foregoing is notwithstanding the possibility to render (parts of) the law of international armed conflict applicable *de jure* in non-international armed conflicts[50] or in armed conflicts whose nature cannot easily be determined. Parties to an armed conflict may also wish to go beyond the legally required minimum as a matter of policy and render (parts of) the law of international armed conflict applicable *de facto*. In contrast, such choices are not available when the situation at hand is not amounting to an armed conflict and governed by more stringent rules. International humanitarian law allows certain actions, such as the rendering *hors de combat* of members of the armed forces of a party to an armed conflict, and civilians directly participating in hostilities, and the destruction or damage of military objectives, while the wounding and killing of persons and the destruction or damage of property is subject to more rigid rules during peacetime. States and international organizations do not have the choice of replacing the legal obligations under the more stringent legal framework applicable during peacetime for the more permissive rules of international humanitarian law. In short, parties to an armed conflict have the possibility to go beyond the minimum legally required under international humanitarian law, but those conducting military operations are not allowed to apply the permissive aspects of international humanitarian law in the absence of an armed conflict to the extent that these are incompatible with more stringent rules of international law (in particular human rights law).

21. *International Humanitarian Law: Applicability* Ratione Personae. International humanitarian law first and foremost binds parties to an armed conflict. These parties may be States, international organizations, or organized armed groups. Furthermore, international humanitarian law is one of the few branches of international law that directly binds individuals.

[49] Cf. *mutatis mutandis* Special Court for Sierra Leone, *Prosecutor v Sesay, Kallon and Gbao*, Trial Chamber Judgment, 2 March 2009, para. 234.

[50] Cf. also Common Art. 3(3) GC I–IV, which encourages parties to a non-international armed conflict 'to bring into force, by means of special agreements, all or part of the other provisions of the [Geneva Conventions]'. In a similar vein, parties to an armed conflict can do so unilaterally without however thereby binding other parties.

3.01 22. *States.* As primary and original international legal subjects, States are bound by those treaties of international humanitarian law to which they have consented, as well as the rules of customary international humanitarian law to which they have not persistently objected. Likewise, States are equally bound by those principles of international humanitarian law that amount to general principles of law in the sense of Article 38(1)(c) of the ICJ Statute. Furthermore, applicable binding resolutions of inter-governmental organizations may be the source for obligations of States under international humanitarian law, regardless of whether or not the rule in question applies to the respective State by virtue of its being embodied in a treaty binding upon that State, in the corpus of customary international humanitarian law or in the body of general principles of law in the sense of Article 38(1)(c).[51]

23. *International Organizations.* As a rule, international humanitarian law treaties do not provide for the possibility of international organizations to become parties. However, by virtue of their international legal personality,[52] international organizations are bound by customary international humanitarian law when they are a party to an armed conflict.[53] The binding force of international humanitarian law on UN forces under that condition is also confirmed by a number of other instruments.[54] The determination whether or not, and for what time, international

[51] Although the SC has not acted, through the exercise of its Chapter VII powers, as legislator in the field of international humanitarian law thus far, that possibility cannot be excluded. See G. Nolte, 'The Different Functions of the Security Council with Respect to Humanitarian Law', in V. Lowe, A. Roberts, J. Welsh, and D. Zaum (eds), *The United Nations Security Council and War—The Evolution of Thought and Practice since 1945* (Oxford: Oxford University Press, 2008), 519–34, at 532.

[52] For the UN, see ICJ, *Reparation for Injuries Suffered in the Services of the United Nations,* Advisory Opinion (1949), p. 179. Whether all international organizations possess international legal personality is largely a definitional question. However, in the following, use will be made of the definition of an international organization as expounded in the Draft Articles on Responsibility of International Organizations. Draft Art. 2(a) defines an international organization as 'an organization established by a treaty or other instrument governed by international law and possessing its own international legal personality'. Cf. ILC Report on the work of its sixty-third session (UN Doc. A/66/10, para. 87). For the commentary to this article, see Official Records of the General Assembly, Fifty-eighth Session, Supplement no. 10 (A/58/10), 38–45.

[53] See amongst many others, C. Greenwood, 'International Humanitarian Law and United Nations Military Operations', 1 *YIHL* (1998), 3–34, at 16; D. Shraga, 'The United Nations as an Actor Bound by International Humanitarian Law', 5 *International Peacekeeping* (1998), 64–81, at 65. For parallel arguments vis-à-vis the European Union, see M. Zwanenburg, 'Toward a More Mature ESDP: Responsibility for violations of International Humanitarian Law by EU Crisis Management Operations', in S. Blockmans (ed.), *The European Union and Crisis Management* (The Hague: TMC Asser Press, 2008), 395–415, at 400–1. See also ECJ, *Racke* (Case C-162/96) [1998] ECR I-3655, para. 45; *Poulsen and Diva Navigation* (Case C-286/90) [1992] ECR I-6019, para. 9, confirming that the EC is required to comply with the rules of (customary) international law in the exercise of its powers.

[54] See e.g. Arts 2(2) and 20 of the 1994 Convention on the Safety of United Nations and Associated Personnel: 'Convention shall not apply to a United Nations operation authorized by the Security Council as an enforcement action under Chapter VII of the Charter of the United Nations *in which any of the personnel are engaged as combatants against organized armed forces and to which the law of international armed conflict applies.*' 'Nothing in this Convention shall affect: (a) The applicability of international humanitarian law and universally recognized standards of human rights as contained in international instruments in relation to the protection of United Nations operations and United Nations and associated personnel *or the responsibility of such personnel to respect such law and standards*'

organizations are to be considered 'a party to an armed conflict' may involve complex issues of fact and law and is subject to controversy.[55] As a general rule, this will be the case once, and for such time as, members of an international organization take direct part in hostilities during a preexisting armed conflict on behalf of a party to that armed conflict, provided its actions are related to the conduct of hostilities in the context of that preexisting conflict,[56] or when their actions reach the threshold of an international or non-international armed conflict in its own right.[57] In any event, such actions need to be distinguished, however, from the situation in which military personnel of an international organization exercise their right to individual self-defence. It has also been suggested that the threshold of direct participation is equally not reached by the fact alone that such personnel use force in self-defence in the discharge of their mandate, provided that it is limited to such use.[58] **3.01**

24. *Organized Armed Groups*. It is generally accepted that international humanitarian law, and in particular the law of non-international armed conflicts, binds organized armed groups. This is not only evident from the wording of Common Article 3, which is addressed to 'each Party to the conflict', and some other instruments applicable in non-international armed conflicts,[59] but also confirmed by various resolutions and decisions of international bodies[60] as well as the ICRC. Beyond this general acceptance, however, the conceptual basis for the binding force of international humanitarian law on organized armed groups is far from settled. Some hold that the binding force emanates from the fact that the respective 'parent' State (i.e. the State of nationality of members of the organized armed group) has accepted a given rule of international law. Having the capacity to

[emphases added]; UN Secretary General's Bulletin: *Observance by United Nations Forces of International Humanitarian Law*, 6 August 1999. ST/SGB/1999/13; UN DPKO Department of Field Support, 'United Nations Peacekeeping Operations—Principles and Guidelines' (*Capstone Doctrine*) January 2008, 15.

[55] See for further analysis, e.g. T. Ferraro, 'The Applicability and Application of International Humanitarian Law to Multinational Forces', 95(891/892) *IRRC* (2014) 561–612, 575–87.

[56] For this so-called 'support-based approach', see T. Ferraro, 'Applicability and Application', 583–7.

[57] See also Section 5.27 and commentary. For discussion of when IHL ceases to apply in such situations, see T. Ferraro, 'Applicability and Application', 604–7.

[58] Cf. Special Court for Sierra Leone, *Prosecutor v Sesay, Kallon and Gbao*, Trial Chamber Judgment, 2 March 2009, para. 233. For further discussion as to when and under what conditions the use of force in self-defence can render a multinational force a party to an armed conflict, see T. Ferraro, 'Applicability and Application', 577–9.

[59] Cf. e.g. Arts 7 and 8 of the 1999 Second Hague Protocol, both equally addressed to 'each Party' or 'Parties to the conflict'; ICC Statute, Art. 8(2)(e)(vii): 'conscripting or enlisting children ... into armed forces or groups ... ', and Art. (2)(e)(xi): 'subjecting persons who are in the power of another party to the conflict to physical mutilation ... '.

[60] See for recent examples e.g. SC Res. 1868 (2009), Preamble (Afghanistan); 1863 (2009) para. 15 (Somalia); 1856 (2008), para. 23 (DR Congo); all calling upon, or demanding that *all* parties to the respective armed conflicts comply with international humanitarian law; Special Court for Sierra Leone, *Prosecutor v Kallon and Kamara*, Appeals Chamber Decision on Challenge to Jurisdiction: Lomé Accord Amnesty (13 March 2004), para. 45.

3.01 legislate for all its nationals, the State thereby imposes obligations upon them, even if those individuals take up arms to fight that State or other organized armed groups within it.[61] A related though distinct alternative possible basis is that international humanitarian law binds individuals regardless of whether they are members of State armed forces, members of the armed forces of an organized armed group or, indeed, civilians (see further the next section). It has also been suggested that organized armed groups are bound by international humanitarian law because of their exercising *de facto* governmental functions[62] or because of their international legal personality.[63] Finally, a further conceptual basis for their being bound is the consent of these groups themselves, as contemplated by Common Article 3 to the Geneva Conventions in the form of 'special agreements' and the possibility to unilaterally accept certain rules of international humanitarian law.[64] All of the aforementioned approaches have their merits and flaws, a discussion of which is beyond the purview of the present Handbook.[65] Suffice it to say that the ambiguity surrounding the conceptual bases for the binding force of international humanitarian law upon organized armed groups has not put into question the general acceptance that organized armed groups are, as a matter of law, subject to obligations under this body of international law.

25. *Individuals*. The binding force of international humanitarian law on individuals has been recognized for a long time. Ever since individuals have been punished for transgressions of the law it is clear that individuals bear duties under international humanitarian law.[66] Such duties do not only extend to the individual combatant but to members of organized armed groups as much as to civilians.[67]

[61] L. Moir, *The Law of Internal Armed Conflict* (Cambridge: Cambridge University Press, 2002), 53–4, with references to the writings of Pictet, Baxter, Schindler, Elder, Greenspan, and Draper as authors taking that view. See also S. Sivakumaran, 'Binding Armed Opposition Groups', 55 *ICLQ* (2006), 369–94, 381–93.

[62] J. Pictet (ed.), *Commentary to the Fourth Geneva Convention Relative to the Protection of Civilian Persons in Time of War* (Geneva: ICRC, 1958), 37. See also L. Moir, *The Law of Internal Armed Conflict*, 55

[63] Darfur Commission of Inquiry, para. 172. See also Ph. Alston, 'The Darfur Commission as a Model for Future Responses to Crisis Situations', 3-3 *Journal of International Criminal Justice* (2005), 600–7.

[64] As to the latter, see e.g. the so-called 'Deeds of Commitment' to ban anti-personnel landmines made under the auspices of the NGO 'Geneva Call'. Information available at <http://www.genevacall.org/home.htm>.

[65] See generally, J.K. Kleffner, *The Applicability of International Humanitarian Law to Organized Armed Groups*, 93 *IRRC* (2011), 443–61.

[66] For an early example, see e.g. the *Henfield's Case*, 11 F. Cas. 1099 (C. C. D. Pa. 1793)(no. 6,360), reproduced in J. Paust, M.C. Bassiouni, M. Scharf et al. (eds), *International Criminal Law, Cases and Materials*, 2nd edn (Durham: Carolina Academic Press, 2000), 232–8.

[67] C. Greenwood in Fleck (ed.), *Handbook of International Humanitarian Law*, 2nd edn (Oxford: Oxford University Press, 2008), 39. For the criminal responsibility of civilians for war crimes, see amongst many others, *Trial of Alfried Felix Alwyn Krupp and Eleven Others*, United States Military Tribunal, Nuremberg 17 November 1947–30 June 1948. Law Reports of Trials of War Criminals, Vol. X, p. 150. For a useful summary of other case law, including criminal trials of civilians for war crimes, see R. Provost, *International Human Rights Law and Humanitarian Law* (Cambridge: Cambridge University Press, 2002), 75–102. For a recent restatement, see *Prosecutor v Akayesu*, ICTR-96-4-T, Judgment, Appeals Chamber, 1 June 2001, paras 443–4.

International humanitarian law imposes such duties upon individuals directly on the international plane, i.e. without requiring the inter-position of a rule of domestic law for establishing individual criminal responsibility. **3.01**

26. *International Humanitarian Law: Passive Personal Scope.* In international armed conflicts, international humanitarian law formally recognizes and defines distinct categories of 'protected persons'. These are the wounded, sick and shipwrecked,[68] prisoners of war,[69] and civilians.[70] While no *formal* categories of 'protected persons' exist in non-international armed conflict, the applicable international humanitarian law nevertheless grants material protection to those who do not or no longer actively participate in hostilities. In addition, combatants in international armed conflicts and fighters in non-international armed conflicts enjoy a number of protections through some rules on methods and means of warfare, such as the prohibition of certain weapons deemed to inflict superfluous injury and/or unnecessary suffering and of those that actually do.

27. *International Humanitarian Law: Applicability* Ratione Temporis. International humanitarian law begins to apply with the start of an armed conflict. The beginning of the applicability *ratione temporis* thus coincides with the moment at which an international or non-international armed conflict exists (see earlier applicability *ratione materiae*).[71] As much as the beginning of the applicability of international humanitarian law, the end of that applicability is essentially a matter of fact. As far as international armed conflicts are concerned, the law ceases to apply 'on the general close of military operations'.[72] This is different in situations of belligerent occupation. Art. 6(3) GC IV stipulates that in such a case, the Convention ceases to apply 'one year after the general close of military operations' except for certain rules which apply for the duration of the occupation and 'to the extent that [an Occupying Power] exercises the functions of government in [occupied] territory'. AP I differs to some extent from GC IV in as much as it extends the applicability of the entire law of belligerent occupation until the 'termination of the occupation'.[73] Regardless of whether or not there is a general close of military operations or a termination of the occupation, persons for whom the final release, repatriation, or re-establishment is pending continue to benefit from the relevant rules of international humanitarian law.[74] In case of a non-international armed conflict, international humanitarian law ceases to apply with the 'end of the armed conflict', with a similar exception as regards those deprived of their liberty or whose liberty is restricted for reasons related to that conflict. They continue to benefit from a limited number of protections, regardless of whether they are so deprived or restricted during or after the conflict.[75]

[68] Cf. Arts 13 of GC I and II respectively, and Art. 8(a) and (b) AP I.

[69] Cf. Art. 4 GC III and Arts 43 and 44(1) AP I.

[70] Cf. Art. 4 GC IV and Art. 50 AP I.

[71] For limited exceptions, see e.g. Arts 23, 44, 47 GC I; 127 GC III; 144 GC IV; 6(1), 83(1) AP I; 7 AP III.

[72] Cf. Art. 6(2) GC IV and Art. 3(b) AP I.

[73] Cf. Art. 3(b) AP I.

[74] Cf. Arts 5 GC I, 5(1) GC III, Art. 6(4) GC IV, 3(b) AP I.

[75] Cf. Art. 2(2) AP II.

3.01 28. *Objective Test.* Although these rules governing the end of the applicability *ratione temporis* of international humanitarian law are clear in the abstract, it may at times be difficult to precisely determine the point at which there is a 'general close of military operations', an occupation is 'terminated', and a non-international armed conflict has ended. It needs to be re-emphasized, however, that the determination whether or not the conditions for an end of the applicability of international humanitarian law are fulfilled, much as assessing whether the law begins to apply, has to be made on the basis of the facts on the ground. The subjective views of the parties to the armed conflict or of the Occupying Power are immaterial if contradicted by the facts. It is also neither necessary nor determinative that a peace agreement has been reached by the parties to an armed conflict. Such an agreement may be indicative of the intentions of the parties to an armed conflict to end hostilities and move from a time of armed conflict to peace. However, if and when these intentions are not followed by actual conduct, it is that actual conduct which is determinative.

29. *International Humanitarian Law: Applicability* Ratione Loci. The law of international armed conflict applies in the territory of the belligerent States, including any occupied territories. It also applies in any area other than the territory of the belligerent States, such as the high seas, to the extent that actual hostilities occur. The territorial applicability of the law of non-international armed conflict extends to the entire territory of the State concerned.[76] In both international and non-international armed conflicts, the territorial reach of international humanitarian law as a whole is thus not limited to areas of actual combat or their vicinity. While some rules, for instance those governing the conduct of hostilities, are practically relevant first and foremost in those areas where such hostilities actually occur, other rules apply throughout the territory irrespective of whether or not combat takes place.[77]

30. *International Human Rights Law: Applicability* Ratione Materiae. International human rights law is chiefly concerned with the regulation of the exercise of a State's power vis-à-vis individuals. In regulating that exercise, international human rights law provides for civil and political, as well as economic, social, and cultural rights, as expressed in the International Bill of Rights, consisting of the Universal Declaration of Human Rights, and the 1966 International Covenants on Civil and Political Rights and on Economic, Social and Cultural Rights, respectively. A number of individual human rights, such as the prohibition of torture, of slavery, of racial discrimination and the human rights of specially vulnerable groups, such as women and children, are also subject to specific instruments. More recently, human rights of the third generation, such as the right to development, to peace, and to a clean environment have evolved.

31. *Nature of Human Rights Obligations.* While international human rights are generally held to be interrelated, interdependent, and indivisible, the nature of the

[76] ICTR, *Akayesu*, paras 635–636.

[77] ICTY, *Tadić* Interlocutory Appeal, para. 68.

obligations flowing from human rights differs. Broadly speaking, States assume three dimensions of human rights obligations, namely to respect, to protect, and to fulfil human rights. The obligation to *respect* requires States to refrain from interfering directly or indirectly with the enjoyment of the respective right. The obligation to *protect* requires them to take measures that prevent third parties from interfering with the enjoyment of that right. The obligation to *fulfil* includes the obligations to provide, facilitate, and promote that right by adopting appropriate legislative, administrative, budgetary, judicial, and other measures to ensure its full realization.[78] It is often said that civil and political rights, such as the right to life, freedom from torture, and freedom from arbitrary arrest and detention, first and foremost entail negative obligations 'of conduct' of States to refrain from certain behaviour,[79] while economic, social, and cultural rights, such as the right to work, to social security, and to the enjoyment of the highest attainable standard of physical and mental health, contain, as a rule, positive obligations 'of result' of States to take the necessary steps towards achieving progressively their full realization.[80] That distinction between civil and political rights as negative obligations of conduct, on the one hand, and economic, social, and cultural rights as positive obligations of result, on the other hand, is not absolute, however. Civil and political rights also impose certain obligations on States to take positive measures to secure them, for instance to take adequate measures to protect the right to life of individuals subject to their jurisdiction;[81] and economic, social, and cultural rights entail limited obligations of conduct.[82] It is readily apparent from the different categories of human rights that international law regulates the exercise of State power in its various forms. It is immaterial what form the exercise of that power takes. The exercise of executive power, including by means of military operations, thus squarely falls into the reach of international human rights law *ratione materiae*.[83] **3.01**

32. *International Human Rights Law: Applicability* Ratione Personae. The primary addressees of international human rights law, whether emanating from treaty, custom, or general principles of law, are *States*.

33. *International Organizations.* Conventional international human rights law, much as international humanitarian law treaties, does not provide for the possibility

[78] On these three dimensions, see Office of the High Commissioner for Human Rights, 'What are Human Rights?' available at <http://www.ohchr.org/EN/Issues/Pages/WhatareHumanRights.aspx>.

[79] On the distinction between obligations of conduct and obligations of result, see I. Brownlie, *System of Law of Nations: State Responsibility* (Oxford: Oxford University Press, 1983), 244–5.

[80] Cf. Art. 2(1) ICESCR.

[81] Human Rights Committee, *Burrell v Jamaica*, Communication no. 546/1993, views of 18 July 1995, at 3.6; IACtHR, *Velasquez Rodriguez*, Judgment of 29 July 1988, Series C, no. 4 (1998), paras 166–167; ECtHR, *Kaya v Turkey*, Applications nos 158/1996/777/978, Judgment of 19 February 1998.

[82] CESCR, General Comment no. 3, The nature of States parties' obligations (Art. 2, para.1) 14/12/90. UN Doc. E/1991/23, paras 1, 2, 9, and 10.

[83] See e.g. Human Rights Committee, General Comment no. 31: Nature of the General Legal Obligation on States Parties to the Covenant, UN Doc. CCPR/C/21/Rev.1/Add.13 (2004), 4.

3.01 of *international organizations* to become parties to the relevant treaties. Nevertheless, international organizations are bound by customary international human rights law by virtue of their international legal personality, to the extent that they exercise functions in a way that can be equated with the exercise of jurisdiction by a State (on the notion of 'jurisdiction', see further, later in this chapter: Applicability *Ratione Loci*).[84] In addition, the binding force of international human rights law upon international organizations can at times be construed on the basis of, or further strengthened by, their constituent treaties, internal rules, and practice.[85]

34. *Organized Armed Groups.* In contrast to international humanitarian law, the applicability of international human rights law to *organized armed groups* is hotly contested.[86] While some evidence suggests that organized armed groups are gradually brought into the reach of international human rights law by virtue of a process of international customary law formation,[87] the better view is that such evidence currently is insufficient to conclude that such a customary process has already reached the point of crystallizing into a firm rule.[88]

[84] See on international organizations as parties to an armed conflict, earlier in this chapter (para. 23 above).

[85] For the UN, see in particular the reference to the promotion and encouragement of respect for human rights as one of its purposes (Art. 1(3) UN Charter), but also Decision no. 2005/24 of the Secretary General's Policy Committee on Human Rights in Integrated Missions, which directs that human rights be fully integrated into peace operations and all human rights functions coordinated by one component. See also *Capstone Doctrine*, 14, 27. For the EU, see Art. 6 TE, general principles of EU law etc.

[86] For critical examination of the different positions taken, see J.K. Kleffner, *The Applicability of the Law of Armed Conflict and Human Rights Law to Organised Armed Groups*, in E. de Wet and J.K. Kleffner (eds), *Convergence and Conflicts of Human Rights and International Humanitarian Law in Military Operations* (Pretoria University Law Press, 2014), 49–64.

[87] That customary process consists, amongst others, of instances in which UN organs and other bodies have addressed organized armed groups in monitoring human rights and/or condemning human rights violations. See e.g. Commission on Human Rights, UN Doc. E/CN.4/2005/3 (7 May 2004), Sixty-first Session, Item 4, Situation of Human Rights in the Darfur Region of the Sudan, where the Human Rights Commission stated that '[t]he rebel forces also appear to violate human rights and humanitarian law'; UN Doc. E/CN.4/2006/53/Add.5 (27 March 2006) Report of the Special Rapporteur, Philip Alston, Addendum, 'Mission to Sri Lanka' (28 November to 6 December 2005) especially paras 24–27 and accompanying footnotes. For the Security Council, see e.g. SC Res. 1814 (15 May 2008) on the situation in Somalia, para. 16, addressed to 'all parties in Somalia'; SC Res. 1778 (25 September 2007) on the situation in Chad, the Central African Republic, and the subregion, Preamble ('activities of armed groups and other attacks in eastern Chad, the north-eastern Central African Republic and western Sudan which threaten the security of the civilian population, the conduct of humanitarian operations in those areas and the stability of those countries, and which result in serious violations of human rights and international humanitarian law'). For further relevant resolutions of the Security Council and the General Assembly pertaining to violations of human rights (as well as humanitarian law) committed in the former Yugoslavia, Afghanistan, The Sudan, Sierra Leone, Ivory Coast, The Congo, Angola, Liberia, and Somalia, and further discussion, see C. Tomuschat, 'The Applicability of Human Rights Law to Insurgent Movements', in H. Fischer, U. Froissart, W. Heintschel von Heinegg, and C. Raap (eds), *Krisensicherung und Humanitärer Schutz—Crisis Management and Humanitarian Protection, Festschrift für Dieter Fleck* (Berlin: Berliner Wissenschafts-Verlag, 2004), 577–85.

[88] For contrary practice that supports that conclusion, see L. Zegveld, *Accountability of Armed Opposition Groups in International Law* (Cambridge: Cambridge University Press, 2002), 39–46.

35. *International Human Rights Law: Applicability* Ratione Temporis. International human rights law differs from international humanitarian law in as much as the temporal scope of its applicability is not limited to any particular time. International human rights law applies at all times. This is subject to the exception that States are allowed to derogate from certain rights in time of public emergency which threatens the life of the nation.[89] That right of derogation is, however, subject to a number of substantive and procedural restraints. First, certain human rights are non-derogable.[90] Second, measures derogating from derogable rights must be limited to the extent strictly required by the exigencies of the situation. Third, derogation measures must not be discriminatory on the ground of race, colour, sex, language, religion, or social origin. Fourth, such measures must be consistent with the State party's other obligations under international law. One such set of 'other obligations' derive from international humanitarian law when the 'time of public emergency which threatens the life of the nation' constitutes an armed conflict. Fifth, certain procedural safeguards apply. This includes that the State party must have officially proclaimed a state of emergency and complies with a regime of international notification. The latter includes informing other States parties to the relevant human rights treaty about the start and end of derogation measures, the human rights provision(s) affected by them, and the reasons for taking them.[91] **3.01**

36. *International Human Rights Law: Applicability* Ratione Loci. It is uncontroversial that human rights apply, as a rule, in the territory of the State bound by the respective treaty or customary rule of human rights. Nevertheless, parts of that State's territory may find themselves under the control of an organized armed group in the course of a non-international armed conflict. While evidence exists to suggest that the State retains, as a rule, its obligation to protect individuals from such groups,[92] the obligation is temporarily inoperative in such a scenario of a lack of territorial control on behalf of the State.[93] This is namely the case if, to the extent, and for such time, that such lack of territorial control meets the criteria for invoking *force majeure* as a ground precluding the wrongfulness of breaching its human rights

[89] Cf. Art. 4(1) ICCPR; ECHR; IACHR. In contrast, the ICESCR does not contain a derogation clause.

[90] Art. 4(2) ICCPR. On the question whether and to what extent all rights under the ICCPR not expressly mentioned as non-derogable can indeed be derogated from, see Human Rights Committee, General Comment no. 29, States of Emergency (Art. 4), UN Doc. CCPR/C/21/Rev.1/Add.11 (2001), paras 11–16.

[91] Art. 4(3) ICCPR.

[92] On that evidence in the form of findings of international human rights bodies, see Zegveld *Accountability*, 166–73.

[93] See e.g. ECtHR, *Ilascu and others v Moldova and Russia*, Judgment 8 July 2004, paras 312 and 330. Note, however, that the Court nevertheless held (at para. 331) that the positive obligation under Art. 1 ECHR 'to take the diplomatic, economic, judicial or other measures *that are in a State Party's power* and in accordance with international law to secure to individuals the rights guaranteed by the Convention' (emphasis added).

3.01 obligations under the law of State responsibility.[94] Under the same condition, a State may be temporarily absolved from its human rights obligations on territory under the control of another State[95] or an international organization.

37. *Applicability to Measures Having Extraterritorial Effect.* In addition, several human rights bodies have recognized that human rights obligations extend to measures within a State's territory that have an extraterritorial effect. Thus, when a State party to the respective human rights treaty deports or expels an individual within its territory or subject to its jurisdiction to another State where there is a real risk that that individual would fall victim of violations of human rights, such deportation of expulsion may violate the State's human rights obligations.[96]

38. *Extraterritorial Applicability.* In the words of the ICCPR, States parties have to respect and ensure civil and political rights 'to all individuals within [their] territory and subject to [their] jurisdiction'.[97] This wording differs in some respects from regional instruments,[98] while an indication as to the territorial reach is absent from the ICESCR. These divergences have led to deviating jurisprudence and a considerable debate about the extraterritorial applicability of human rights.

39. *Human Rights Committee.* The Human Rights Committee has interpreted Article 2(1) of the ICCPR to mean that a State party:

> must respect and ensure the rights laid down in the Covenant to anyone within the power or effective control of that State Party, even if not situated within the territory of the State Party . . . This principle also applies to those within the power or effective control of the forces of a State Party acting outside its territory, regardless of the circumstances in which such power or effective control was obtained, such as forces constituting a national contingent of a State Party assigned to an international peace-keeping or peace-enforcement operation.[99]

[94] Cf. Art. 23 ASR, which defines *force majeure* as 'the occurrence of an irresistible force or of an unforeseen event, beyond the control of the State, making it materially impossible in the circumstances to perform the obligation', and excludes the plea of *force majeure* if 'the situation of *force majeure* is due, either alone or in combination with other factors, to the conduct of the State invoking it; or the State has assumed the risk of that situation occurring'.

[95] Human Rights Committee, Concluding Observations on Cyprus (1998) UN Doc. CCPR/C/79/Add.88, at 3; Concluding observations on Lebanon (1997) UN Doc. CCPR/C/79/Add.78, paras 4–5; ECtHR *Loizidou v Turkey* (preliminary objections), Judgment of 23 March 1995, Series A, no. 310, and *Cyprus v Turkey*, paras 76–80.

[96] ECtHR: *Soering v the United Kingdom*, 14038/88 [1989] ECHR 14 (7 July 1989); following that jurisprudence, HRC: *Ng v Canada*, UN Doc. A/49/40, vol. II, 189 (1993); *Kindler v Canada*, UN Doc. A/48/50, 189 (1993); *Cox v Canada*, UN Doc. A/50/40, vol. II, 105 (1994); IACiHR, *Haitian Centre for Human Rights v US*, IACiHR Report no. 51/96, Case no. 10.675, 13 March 1997.

[97] Cf. Art. 2(1) ICCPR.

[98] Art. 1 ECHR ('to everyone within their jurisdiction'); Art. 1(1) IACHR ('to all persons subject to their jurisdiction').

[99] HRC, General Comment no. 31: Nature of the General Legal Obligation on States Parties to the Covenant, UN Doc. CCPR/C/21/Rev.1/Add.13 (2004), 10.

That interpretation, although contested by a limited number of States,[100] finds further support in other findings of the Human Rights Committee,[101] endorsed by the International Court of Justice's jurisprudence,[102] and in some judgments of domestic courts.[103] Examples of situations in which persons have been found to find themselves 'within the power or effective control' of a State party include extraterritorial detention by a State party to the ICCPR,[104] and belligerent occupation.[105] 3.01

40. *European Court of Human Rights.* In its case law, the European Court of Human Rights has held on various occasions that the European Convention applies extraterritorially if and when a State party acts abroad so as to bring the person concerned into its 'jurisdiction' in the sense of Article 1 of the ECHR. This is the case, for instance:

> when as a consequence of military action—whether lawful or unlawful—it exercises effective control of an area outside its national territory. The obligation to secure, in such an area, the rights and freedoms set out in the Convention derives from the fact of such control whether it be exercised directly, through its armed forces, or through a subordinate local administration.[106]

As to the level of 'effective control' required to satisfy the threshold for the applicability *ratione loci* of the European Convention, the Court further specified that '[i]t is not necessary to determine whether [the State concerned] actually exercises detailed control over the policies and actions' of the authorities in question. Rather, 'effective overall control' is sufficient.[107] The Court has further clarified the extraterritorial reach of obligations under the European Convention by determining that aerial bombardment is, without more, insufficient to bring persons affected by such bombardments into the 'jurisdiction' of States parties to the Convention that carry out the bombardments.[108] In contrast, a person that finds themselves in the hands of State organs abroad, for instance by virtue of being

[100] See e.g. the positions taken by the Netherlands, Israel, United Kingdom, and the USA before the Human Rights Committee, referred to in C. Droege, 'The Interplay between International Humanitarian Law and International Human Rights Law in Situations of Armed Conflict', 40 *Israel Law Review* (2007), 310–55, at 326 (fn 64). For a critique of the position taken by the Human Rights Committee, see M.J. Dennis, 'Application of Human Rights Treaties Extraterritorially in Times of Armed Conflict and Military Occupation', 99 *AJIL* (2005), 119–41.

[101] See in particular for observations on military occupation or control by a State party, D. McGoldrick, in F. Coomans and M.T. Kamminga (eds), *Extraterritorial Application of Human Rights Treaties* (Antwerp and Oxford: Intersentia, 2004), 63–6.

[102] ICJ, *The Wall*, paras 108–111; *Armed Activities (DRC Congo v Uganda)*, para. 216.

[103] For an overview, see C. Droege, 'The Interplay', 325–7.

[104] See e.g. HRC, *Lopez Burgos v Uruguay*, para. 12.1.

[105] HRC, Concluding Observations on Israel, UN Doc. CCPR/C/79/Add.93, para. 10 (1998); Concluding Observations on Israel, UN Doc. CCPR/CO/78/ISR (2003), para. 11.

[106] ECtHR, *Loizidou*, Preliminary objections, para. 62; Merits, para. 52.

[107] ECtHR, *Loizidou*, Merits, para. 56. Confirmed in *Cyprus v Turkey*, para. 77; *Ilascu v Moldova and Russia*.

[108] ECtHR, *Banković*, paras 75–80.

3.01 detained, finds themselves in the 'jurisdiction' of that State.[109] The Court has once restricted the reach of the extraterritorial application of the Convention to contracting States, holding that it operated in 'an essentially regional context and notably in the legal space (*espace juridique*) of the Contracting States'.[110] However, that restriction has been abandoned in subsequent case law of the European Court of Human Rights.[111] The Court also seems to have nuanced its previous position that the rights and freedoms defined in the Convention cannot be divided and tailored[112] in favour of an approach that allows for the division and tailoring of Convention rights in the sense that, 'whenever the State, through its agents, exercises control and authority over an individual, and thus jurisdiction, the State is under an obligation under Article 1 to secure to that individual the rights and freedoms under Section I of the Convention that are relevant to the situation of that individual'.[113]

41. *Inter-American Court and Commission on Human Rights.* The Inter-American Court and Commission on Human Rights have also held the human rights instruments of the Inter-American system to be applicable outside the territory of the States parties. Thus, in the words of the Commission, the obligation to uphold the protected rights of any person subject to the jurisdiction of a State:

> may, under given circumstances, refer to conduct with an extraterritorial locus where the person concerned is present in the territory of one state, but subject to the control of another state—usually through the acts of the latter's agents abroad. In principle, the inquiry turns not on the presumed victim's nationality or presence within a particular geographic area, but on whether, under the specific circumstances, the state observed the rights of a person subject to its authority and control.[114]

Cases of 'authority and control', according to the Commission's findings, do not only comprise extraterritorial detention,[115] but also military operations conducted by a State outside its territory,[116] including—and in contrast to the findings of the

[109] ECtHR, *Ocalan v Turkey*, Application no. 46221/99, Judgment of 12 May 2005, para. 91; *Issa and others v Turkey*, Application no. 31821/96, Judgment of 16 November 2004, para. 71 ('under the former State's authority and control through its agents operating—whether lawfully or unlawfully—in the latter State').

[110] ECtHR, *Banković*, para. 80.

[111] See e.g. ECtHR, *Ocalan v Turkey*, Application no. 46221/99, Judgment of 12 May 2005, para. 91 (Grand Chamber) concerning actions of Turkish officials in Kenya; *Issa and others v Turkey*, Application no. 31821/96, Judgment of 16 November 2004, para. 71 concerning military operations of Turkish armed forces in Iraq; *Al-Skeini and others v UK*, Application no. 55721/07, Judgment of 7 July 2011 (Grand Chamber), para. 142 (with references to further case law of the EctHR).

[112] ECtHR, *Banković*, para. 75.

[113] ECtHR, *Al-Skeini*, para. 137.

[114] IACiHR, *Coard et al. v United States*, Case no. 10.951, Report no. 109/99, 29 September 1999, para. 37.

[115] IACiHR, *Request for Precautionary Measures Concerning the Detainees at Guantánamo Bay*, 12 March 2002, 41 *ILM* (2002), 532.

[116] IACiHR, *Salas v United States*, Case no 10.573 (1994), para. 6 ('use of military force [that] has resulted in non-combatant deaths, personal injury, and property loss' as falling within the territorial reach of a State's human rights obligations).

European Court of Human Rights in *Banković*[117]—military air operations in international airspace.[118] 3.01

42. *International Court of Justice.* The ICJ has held the International Covenant on Economic, Social and Cultural Rights to also apply extraterritorially. It endorsed the views of the Committee on Economic, Social and Cultural Rights that the obligations of States under the Covenant extend to all territories and populations under their effective control.[119]

When applicable simultaneously, international humanitarian law and human rights law are complementary. In case of collision between a norm of international humanitarian law and a norm of human rights law, the more specific norm prevails in principle. 3.02

1. *Situations of Simultaneous Application.* It is readily apparent from the foregoing that international humanitarian and human rights law may apply simultaneously in a number of situations. That is the case, for instance, when a non-international armed conflict occurs on a State's territory. In such a situation, the State pitted against an organized armed group is bound by the international humanitarian law applicable to such conflicts and by human rights to the extent that the State retains territorial control.[120] Another situation of simultaneous application is belligerent occupation, where the Occupying Power is bound by the law of belligerent occupation as well as by human rights law.[121] Furthermore, international humanitarian law and human rights law apply simultaneously when, in times of armed conflict, persons are being detained.[122] Whether and to what extent the two bodies of law apply simultaneously to military operations beyond the aforementioned situations is less certain. While the applicability of international humanitarian law to a given military operation is dependent on the existence of an armed conflict, especially the findings of the Inter-American Commission and the European Court of Human Rights differ as to when a person finds themselves within, or is subject to, 'the jurisdiction' of a State. The former adopts a broader approach to the extraterritorial applicability of human rights than the latter.

2. *Complementarity.* In cases of simultaneous application, the relationship between international humanitarian law and human rights law is often referred to as 'complementary'.[123] The actual meaning and content of such complementarity

[117] ECtHR, *Banković*, para. 82.

[118] IACiHR, *Armando Alejandre Jr et al. v Cuba* ('Brothers to the Rescue'), Report no. 86/99, Case no. 11.589, 29 September 1999, para. 23.

[119] ICJ, *The Wall*, paras 111–112.

[120] See L. Zegveld, *Accountability of Armed Opposition Groups in International Law* (Cambridge: Cambridge University Press, 2002), 39–46.

[121] See e.g. Art. 2(1) ICCPR.

[122] See e.g. HRC, General Comment no. 31, 10.

[123] See e.g. HRC, General Comment no. 31, 11; ICRC, 'IHL in brief—What is the difference between humanitarian law and human rights law?' (2002) available at <http://www.icrc.org/Web/Eng/siteeng0.nsf/html/5KZMUY>. Note that far less frequently the relationship between international

3.02 between the two fields of law is, however, regularly left unexplained.[124] Generally speaking, matters or things are described as being 'complementary' if and when they are 'completing something else' or 'making a pair or a whole'. 'Complementarity', in turn, refers to a relation of different parts and denotes the condition of things that complement one another, while a 'complement' is generally understood as something that completes or perfects something else or supplies the other's deficiencies or as something that, together with other things, forms a unit.[125] By describing the relationship between human rights law and international humanitarian law as 'complementary', the two fields are thus regarded to be mutually reinforcing in as much as they complete and perfect each other. That mutual reinforcement can manifest itself in a number of ways, which depend on whether (a) a given question is regulated exclusively by humanitarian law; (b) a given question is regulated exclusively by human rights law; and (c) a given question is regulated by both humanitarian law and human rights law.[126] In the *first* situation, the mutual reinforcement takes the form of international humanitarian law filling the gaps left by human rights law. The use of the red cross, red crescent, and red crystal emblem may serve as an illustration of such an area unregulated by human rights law. The pertinent rules of international humanitarian law then apply exclusively.[127] In the *second* situation, the reverse is true: for instance, since only human rights law regulates rights such as freedom of expression and freedom of assembly, international humanitarian law is irrelevant to the issue. Answers to questions pertaining to such rights thus fall into the exclusive province of human rights law.[128] In the *third* situation where a matter is regulated by international humanitarian law and human rights law, however, the applicable law will have to be determined by recourse to the general rule that priority should be given to the norm that is more specific (*lex specialis derogat legi generali*).

3. *Lex Specialis.* The maxim of *lex specialis derogat legi generali* is a technique of interpreting legal rules and a means to resolve conflicts between legal norms. The maxim can be conceived in two ways. Either the specific rule is to be read and

humanitarian law and human rights law is described as mutual exclusion so that human rights law ceases to apply in times of armed conflict. This is the position taken by the USA in certain instances, for which see P. Alston, J. Morgan-Foster, and W. Abresch, 'The Competence of the UN Human Rights Council and its Special Procedures in relation to Armed Conflicts: Extrajudicial Executions in the "War on Terror"', 19(1) *EJIL* (2008), 183–209, at 191–7.

[124] In this vein, on the practice of international bodies, see J. Tobin, 'Seeking Clarity in Relation to the Principle of Complementarity: Reflections on the Recent Contributions of some International Bodies', 8(2) *Melbourne Journal of International Law* (2007), 356.

[125] Cf. *Oxford English Dictionary*.

[126] On these three possible situations, see also ICJ, *The Wall*, para. 106; *Armed Activities on the Territory of the Congo (Democratic Republic of the Congo v Uganda)*, para. 216.

[127] For this and other pertinent examples, see M. Sassòli, 'Le droit internationale humanitaire, une *lex specialis* par rapport aux droits humains?', in Auer, Flückiger, and Hottelier (eds), *Les droits de l'homme et la constitution, Études en l'honneur du Professeur Giorgio Malinverni* (Geneva: Schulthess, 2007), 375–95, at 386.

[128] Ibid. 393–5.

understood within the confines or against the background of the general rule, as an elaboration, updating, or specification of the latter.[129] Or the specific rule is applied instead of, and as an exception to, the general rule.[130] Whether a rule is seen as an 'application', 'modification', or 'exception' to another rule depends on how those rules are viewed in the environment in which they are applied, including their object and purpose.[131] The maxim of *lex specialis derogat legi generali* functions in the aforementioned ways also in the relationship between international humanitarian law and human rights law. **3.02**

4. *Lex Specialis as Technique of Interpretation.* As a *technique of interpretation*, international humanitarian law informs the interpretation of human rights law if and when the former is more specific. This is the approach adopted by the ICJ in its *Nuclear Weapons* Advisory Opinion when discussing the right not arbitrarily to be deprived of one's life in times of armed conflict. In the words of the Court, '[t]he test of what is an arbitrary deprivation of life [. . .] falls to be determined by the applicable *lex specialis*, namely, the law applicable in armed conflict which is designed to regulate the conduct of hostilities'.[132] However, when applying the maxim of *lex specialis derogat legi generali* as a technique of interpretation, the more specific norm may also derive from human rights law, which then informs a more general rule of international humanitarian law. When Common Article 3 prohibits, for instance, 'the passing of sentences and the carrying out of executions without previous judgment pronounced by a regularly constituted court, affording all the judicial guarantees which are recognized as indispensable by civilized peoples', the notions of 'regularly constituted court' and 'judicial guarantees' will have to be determined by reference to human rights law, which is more specific on these matters.[133] The maxim of *lex specialis* as a means of interpretation finds its limits in reconciling clearly incompatible norms, contrary to what seems to have been suggested at times.[134] Instead, the maxim as a means to resolve norm conflicts enters the equation in such situations.

5. *Lex Specialis as Means to Resolve Conflict.* As a *means to resolve conflicts between legal norms*, the maxim of *lex specialis derogat legi generali* suggests that, in times of armed conflicts, a rule of international humanitarian law will often prevail over an incompatible norm of human rights law. This is so because international humanitarian law is specifically devised to regulate situations of armed conflicts. For example, when international humanitarian law stipulates that prisoners of war may, as a rule, be detained until the cessation of active hostilities[135] without having

[129] International Law Commission, Fifty-eighth Session (1 May–9 June and 3 July–11 August 2006), Fragmentation of International Law: Difficulties arising from the Diversification and Expansion of International Law, Report of the Study Group of the International Law Commission, Finalized by Martti Koskenniemi, UN Doc. A/CN.4/L.682, para. 56.

[130] Ibid. para. 57.

[131] Ibid. para. 97.

[132] ICJ, *Nuclear Weapons*, para. 25.

[133] Cf. CIHL.

[134] EctHR, *Hassan v UK*, Application no. 29750/09, Judgment of 16 September 2014 (Grand Chamber), para. 104.

[135] Cf. Arts 21 and 118 GC III.

3.02 the right to legally challenge that detention, while human rights law provides for a right of everyone to make such challenges,[136] the latter right is set aside as far as prisoners of war are concerned. Similarly, when human rights law prohibits imposing the death penalty on persons under the age of 18 when committing the crime, and carrying out the death penalty on pregnant women,[137] while several rules of international humanitarian law are more restrictive in several respects[138] or fall short of them in some limited respects,[139] the applicable international humanitarian law prevails over the incompatible human rights norms. However, the rule that international humanitarian law functions in the aforementioned way as *lex specialis* to human rights law in times of armed conflicts is not absolute. In certain areas, human rights law supplies the more specific standards even in times of armed conflict. This is notably the case in situations that, while occurring during an armed conflict, closely resemble those for which human rights standards have been developed. Examples include the use of force in relatively calm situations of occupation for the purpose of maintaining public order and safety[140] or in areas under the firm control of State authorities in times of non-international armed conflicts.[141]

3.03 **In the event of a conflict between, on the one hand, applicable international humanitarian law and human rights law, and, on the other hand, obligations of States under the United Nations Charter, the latter prevails.**

1. *Article 103 UN Charter.* Article 103 of the UN Charter provides that '[i]n the event of a conflict between the obligations of the Members of the United Nations under the present Charter and their obligations under any other international agreement, their obligations under the present Charter shall prevail'. It is generally accepted that the scope of that provision extends not only to the Articles of the Charter but also to binding decisions made by United Nations organs such as the

[136] Arts 9(4) ICCPR; 5(4) ECHR; 7(6) IACHR.

[137] Arts 6(5) ICCPR; 4(5) IACHR (also prohibiting imposition of the death penalty on persons over 70 years of age).

[138] Cf. Arts 100–101 GC III, Arts 68 and 75 GC IV; Art. 76(3) AP I; and Art. 6(4) AP II (extending prohibition on carrying out death penalty to 'mothers of young children').

[139] Art. 77(5) AP I (only prohibiting the execution of, but not to impose, the death penalty for an offence related to the armed conflict on persons under the age of eighteen at the time the offence was committed).

[140] Cf. University Centre for International Humanitarian Law, Expert Meeting on the Right to Life in Armed Conflicts and Situations of Occupation (2005), available at <http://www.adh-geneve.ch/pdfs/3rapport_droit_vie.pdf>, p. 23, discussing in particular whether and to what extent human rights law also governs the use of force in calm situations of occupation for other purposes remains subject to divergent opinions amongst experts.

[141] M. Sassòli and L. Olson, 'The Relationship between International Humanitarian and Human Rights Law where it Matters: Admissible Killing and Internment of Fighters in Non-International Armed Conflicts', 90 (871) *IRRC* (2008), 599–627, at 613–14.

Security Council.[142] Furthermore, such obligations under the Charter may also prevail over inconsistent customary international law.[143] The practice of the UN and Member States suggests that the rule of Article 103 applies not only to 'obligations' in the strict sense, i.e. mandatory measures, but also to action authorized under Articles 40–42.[144] **3.03**

2. *Applicability of Article 103 UN Charter.* In order for Article 103 of the UN Charter to be applicable, there must be a *conflict* between, on the one hand, a measure required or authorized under the Charter and, on the other hand, another rule of international law. Article 103 thus does not govern situations in which the Security Council, granting a general mandate to States under Chapter VII to take certain measures which it deems necessary to maintain or restore international peace and security, when these measures can be taken in conformity with a State's international obligations. For example, when a general mandate given to States under Chapter VII empowers States to intern persons for reasons of security, without however departing from applicable international law, such an authorization does not *conflict* with a State's international obligations that govern internments. Contrary to what has sometimes been suggested,[145] Article 103 of the UN Charter does not free States from their international obligations under applicable international law, if actions authorized by Chapter VII can be taken in a manner that conforms to these obligations.[146]

3. *Examples of Conflicts with International Humanitarian Law and Human Rights Law.* Much as from other areas of international law, obligations conflicting with those under the UN Charter may stem from international humanitarian law or human rights law. SC Resolution 1483 (2003) on the situation in Iraq, adopted under Chapter VII of the UN Charter, for instance, provided for several abrogations from the law of belligerent occupation by granting the Occupying Powers (US and UK) several specific rights and imposing on them certain responsibilities which conflicted with the rights and obligations of an Occupying Power under the law of

[142] ICJ, *Case concerning Questions of Interpretation and Application of the 1971 Montreal Convention arising from the Aerial Incident at Lockerbie* (*Libyan Arab Jamahiriya v United States of America*) (Provisional Measures) ICJ Reports, 1998, para. 42; and *Case concerning Questions of Interpretation and Application of the 1971 Montreal Convention arising from the Aerial Incident at Lockerbie* (*Libyan Arab Jamahiriya v the United Kingdom*) (Provisional Measures) ICJ Reports, 1992, paras 39–40.

[143] ILC, Conclusions of the work of the Study Group on the Fragmentation of International Law: Difficulties arising from the Diversification and Expansion of International Law (2006) adopted by the International Law Commission at its Fifty-eighth Session, in 2006, and submitted to the General Assembly as a part of the Commission's report covering the work of that session (A/61/10, para. 251), para. 35.

[144] J.A. Frowein and N. Krisch, 'Article 40', 'Article 41', and 'Article 42' in B. Simma (ed.), *The Charter of the United Nations: A Commentary*, 2nd edn (Oxford: Oxford University Press, 2002), 729; ECtHR, *Behrami*, paras 147–149.

[145] House of Lords, *R (on the application of Al-Jedda) (FC) (Appellant) v Secretary of State for Defence (Respondent)*, especially paras 34, 151–152.

[146] EctHR, *Al-Jedda v UK*, Application no. 27021/08, Judgment of 7 July 2011 (Grand Chamber), para. 105.

3.03 belligerent occupation as enshrined in the Hague Regulations (1907), the Fourth Geneva Convention, and customary international humanitarian law.[147] In such a case, the addressees of the relevant binding Security Council resolutions must give precedence to their obligations under the resolution on the basis of Article 103 of the UN Charter.

4. *Constraints on the Power of the Security Council.* The Security Council possesses a wide discretion in exercising its powers under Chapter VII of the UN Charter to determine the existence of any threat to the peace, breach of the peace, or act of aggression and the measures that are necessary to maintain or restore international peace and security. That discretion is nevertheless subject to some constraints.

5. *UN Charter.* A first set of such constraints emanate from the UN Charter itself. More specifically, the underlying situation at hand must indeed amount to a threat to the peace, breach of the peace, or act of aggression; the mandatory or authorized measures must be *necessary* to maintain or restore international peace and security; and in taking such measures, the Security Council must act 'in accordance with the Purposes and Principles of the United Nations'.[148]

6. *Jus Cogens.* Secondly, the Security Council remains bound by, and is legally barred from authorizing measures inconsistent with, norms of *jus cogens.*[149] If it were nevertheless to authorize or oblige Member States to act contrary to such norms, States would be under no obligation to act in accordance with that authorization or obligation. While there is some uncertainty as to exactly which norms of international law have the character of *jus cogens,* the basic rules of international humanitarian law and some human rights, including the prohibition of torture and the right to self-determination, are widely held to fall into that category.[150]

[147] For discussion, see D. Scheffer, 'The Security Council and International Law on Military Occupations', in Lowe, Roberts, Welsh, and Zaum (eds), *The United Nations Security Council,* 596–605.

[148] On the latter, cf. Art. 24(2) UN Charter; E. de Wet, *The Chapter VII Powers of the United Nations Security Council* (Oxford: Hart Publishing, 2004), 191–215. See J.A. Frowein and N. Krisch 'Article 40', 'Article 41', and 'Article 42', and more generally on constraints of the Chapter VII powers of the Security Council, R. Bernhardt, 'Article 103' in B. Simma (ed), *The Charter of the United Nations: A Commentary,* 2nd edn (Oxford: Oxford University Press, 2002), 1295–302.

[149] See amongst many others, E. de Wet, *The Chapter VII Powers,* 187–91, with further references. Also note that the purposes and principles of the United Nations include norms of *jus cogens*: International Law Commission, Conclusions on Fragmentation of International Law (A/61/10, 2006), para. 40.

[150] ILC, ibid. 33, with further references.

Chapter 4

CONCEPTUAL DISTINCTION AND OVERLAPS BETWEEN LAW ENFORCEMENT AND THE CONDUCT OF HOSTILITIES

Forces involved in contemporary military operations are often called upon to assume functions both of law enforcement and of hostilities, each of which are governed by different legal standards. It is therefore important to distinguish between these two concepts, identify potential overlaps between them, and determine how the respective legal paradigms governing each type of operation interrelate. 4.01

The generic concept of law enforcement can be defined for the purposes of operational law as comprising all territorial and extraterritorial measures taken by a State or other collective entity to maintain or restore public security, law and order or to otherwise exercise its authority or power over individuals, objects, or territory. The rules and principles of international law governing the conduct of law enforcement activities form the legal paradigm of law enforcement. 4.02

1. *Law Enforcement as a Generic Concept Based on Function.* The concept of law enforcement is not defined in international law. However, useful guidance for the interpretation of the term can be derived from its use in 'soft law' instruments issued by multilateral organizations.[1] For example, according to the UN Code of Conduct for Law Enforcement Officials (CCLEO)[2] and the UN Basic Principles

[1] Instruments of 'soft law', such as declarations, recommendations, or reports expressing a general expectation with regard to conduct, constitute neither treaty law, nor customary law, nor general principles of law within the meaning of Art. 38 ICJ Statute and, therefore, do not formally qualify as sources of international law. However, instruments of 'soft law' do represent facts, and often even 'subsequent practice' within the meaning of Art. 31(3)(b) Vienna Treaty Convention that may be taken into account when interpreting treaty law. It would certainly be difficult for States to reject in good faith the interpretation of treaty law in the light of a non-binding instrument the creation of which they supported in the framework of their participation in the issuing international organization. Moreover, particularly in the field of international law, the role of 'soft law' as a consensus-building precursor to binding norms should not be underestimated.

[2] UN Code of Conduct for Law Enforcement Officials, adopted by UN GA 34/169 of 17 December 1979.

4.02 on the Use of Force and Firearms (BPUFF),[3] the term law enforcement refers to the exercise by State agents of police powers, especially the powers of arrest or detention. Where police powers are exercised by military authorities, whether uniformed or not, or by State security forces, they are regarded as law enforcement officials.[4] While the exact scope of police powers may vary according to national legislation, the CCLEO describes the core duty of law enforcement officials as 'serving the community' and 'protecting all persons against illegal acts'.[5]

2. Similarly, the European Code of Police Ethics (2001),[6] applies to 'traditional public police forces or police services, or to other publicly authorized and/or controlled bodies with the primary objectives of maintaining law and order in civil society, and who are empowered by the State to use force and/or special powers for these purposes'.[7] The Code applies to such forces regardless of how they are organized; whether centralized or locally oriented, whether structured in a civilian or military manner, whether labelled as services or forces, or whether they are accountable to the State, to regional or local authorities, or to a wider public.[8] According to the European Code, the main purposes of the police are to maintain public tranquillity and law and order; to protect and respect the individual's fundamental rights and freedoms; to detect, prevent, and combat crime; and to provide assistance and service functions to the public.[9]

3. Thus, both the UN instruments and the European Code adopt a primarily functional definition of police and law enforcement officials, describing them as those persons whom a State authorizes to vertically impose public security, law, and order on its behalf, regardless of military or civilian status.[10] The concept of law enforcement could thus be said to comprise all measures taken by civilian or military State agents to maintain, restore, or impose public security, law, and order or to otherwise exercise its authority or power over individuals, objects, or territory.

[3] UN Basic Principles on the Use of Force and Firearms by Law Enforcement Officials, adopted by the 8th UN Congress on the Prevention of Crime and the Treatment of Offenders (1990).

[4] See commentary Art. 1 CCLEO and, synonymously, preambular note to the BPUFF. Numerous other UN documents use the term without providing a definition (e.g. *Principles on the Effective Prevention and Investigation of Extra-legal, Arbitrary and Summary Executions*, annex to UN ECOSOC Res. 1989/65 of 24 May 1989, endorsed by UN GA Res. 44/162 of 15 December 1989).

[5] Art. 1 CCLEO.

[6] European Code of Police Ethics, Appendix to Recommendation (2001) 10, adopted by the Committee of Ministers of the Council of Europe on 19 September 2001.

[7] See: Definition of the Scope of the Code, European Code of Police Ethics.

[8] Commentary (Scope), European Code of Police Ethics.

[9] Art. 1 European Code of Police Ethics.

[10] Other criteria, such as the democratic legitimacy of an authority and the characterization of its police as a public body (Art. 2 European Code of Police Ethics) may be indispensable for the legality and legitimacy of police activities in democratic societies but are less relevant for a functional definition of law enforcement.

4. In the practice of contemporary military operations, military forces are often called upon to carry out law enforcement and maintenance of order functions.[11] For instance, military forces can be involved in quelling riots; searching for or arresting narco-traffickers, pirates, or other criminals; or guarding detainees and carrying out activities aiming to maintain, restore, or otherwise impose public security, law, and order. It should be emphasized that law enforcement for the purposes of operational law does not necessarily correspond to the understanding of that term in domestic settings. In particular, it does not only involve the suppression of criminal activity *stricto sensu* but involves broader activities such as the maintenance of order (e.g. in a peace operation or in the context of belligerent occupation), the control of access to persons or goods (e.g. in the context of manning a checkpoint or enforcing an embargo at sea), or the guarding of persons deprived of their liberty (e.g. prisoners of war, civilian security internees, or persons detained in a non-international armed conflict for reasons related to the conflict as well as persons detained for their criminal activity). **4.02**

5. In principle, the functional understanding of law enforcement would even include military operations conducted for the suppression of a rebellion or insurgency in non-international armed conflict,[12] or of armed resistance against belligerent occupation.[13] This is not to say that these military operations will be legally governed by the law enforcement paradigm (as further defined later). They may well be (and will generally be) governed by the paradigm of hostilities as *lex specialis* even if they aim at restoring public security, law, and order (and thus fall within the generic concept of law enforcement). The subtle distinction between the generic concept of law enforcement on one hand, and the governing paradigm of law enforcement on the other hand, deserves to be noted as States may be tempted to wrongly deny the applicability of the paradigm of hostilities (and thus the applicability of IHL) to situations such as insurgencies based on the argument that their military operations simply aim at restoring public security, law, and order (and thus fall within the generic concept of law enforcement). As a matter of generic concept, therefore, law enforcement and military hostilities are not mutually exclusive, but may overlap considerably.[14] While the generic concept of law enforcement is useful to understand the mindset in which police and military forces operate when conducting law enforcement activities, it does not suffice to draw the dividing line between law enforcement and military hostilities in terms of the applicable legal paradigm. It will therefore be important to determine how the distinct legal

[11] For a very broad understanding of the maintenance of law and order in military operations, see Chapter 25.

[12] See e.g. the reference in Art. 2(2) ECHR to 'action lawfully taken for the purpose of quelling a riot or insurrection' as a justification for the resort by States to lethal force against individuals 'within their jurisdiction' (Art. 1 ECHR).

[13] For the *de facto* duty of the Occupying Power 'to restore, and ensure, as far as possible, public order and safety', see Art. 43 of the 1907 Hague Regulations.

[14] See Sections 4.03 and 4.04.

4.02 standards, which govern law enforcement and the conduct of hostilities, interrelate with regard to operations falling within the area of overlap between the two concepts.[15] The distinction between law enforcement and the conduct of hostilities is particularly important in the context of the use of lethal force because, as will be seen, the legal rules and standards governing the use of force differ under the two legal paradigms.[16]

6. *Territorial and Personal Scope of the Concept of Law Enforcement.* In practice, law enforcement presupposes an authority stable and strong enough to impose public security, law, and order. Therefore, law enforcement operations usually take place within the jurisdiction of a State. The latter is given not only on the national territory of the State, but also in situations where the State (or an international organization such as the UN) exercises sufficient territorial control abroad, such as in the case of a military occupation or of a territory under transitional authority (such as in Kosovo and East Timor). However, jurisdiction is not necessarily territorially defined. To the extent that a State actually exercises authority or power over individuals, the latter come within the personal jurisdiction of that State even if the operation in question is conducted outside its territorial control.[17] For example, the exercise of a State's jurisdiction over captured military personnel in an armed conflict,[18] or over pirates on the high seas,[19] does not presuppose the existence of territorial jurisdiction but merely the actual exercise of authority or power. Thus, while territorial considerations may be relevant for the international

[15] On the dividing line, see Sections 4.04 and 4.05.

[16] G. Gaggioli, *The Use of Force in Armed Conflicts: Interplay between the Conduct of Hostilities and Law Enforcement Paradigms* (Geneva: ICRC, 2013) (hereinafter, 'Gaggioli, ICRC Use of Force Report').

[17] See e.g. UNHRC, General Comment no. 31 (2004), para. 10; UNHRC, *Sergio Euben Lopez Burgos v Uruguay,* Communication no. R.12/52, UN Doc. Supp. no. 40 (A/36/40), 29 July 1981, paras. 12.1–12.3. (extraterritorial abduction); UNHRC, *Lilian Celiberti de Casariego v Uruguay,* Communication no. R.13/56, UN Doc. Supp. no. 40 (A/36/40), 29 July 1981, para. 10.3. IACiHR, *Report on the Situation of Human Rights in Chile,* 9 September 1985, chapter III, paras 29 *et seq.*, 81–91 (extraterritorial assassination); IACiHR, *Alejandre et al. v Cuba,* Case no. 11.589, Report no. 86/99, 29 September 1999, paras 23–25 (shooting down of private airplanes in international airspace); ECiHR, *G v the United Kingdom and Ireland,* Application no. 9837/82, Decision of 7 March 1985, para. 25; ECtHR, *Issa and others v Turkey,* Application no. 31821/96, Judgment of 16 November 2004, paras 69 and 71 (extraterritorial incursion); ECtHR, *Öcalan v Turkey,* Application no. 46221/99, Judgment of 12 March 2003 (Chamber), para. 88 and *Öcalan v Turkey,* Application no. 46221/99, Judgment of 12 May 2005 (Grand Chamber), para. 85 (extraterritorial arrest). But see also ECtHR, *Bankovic and others v Belgium and 16 other Contracting States,* Application no. 52207/99, Admissibility Decision of 12 December 2001, paras 71, 75, and 80, rejecting the existence of jurisdiction in a case of international air warfare. See also ICJ, *Advisory Opinion on the Legality of the Threat or Use of Nuclear Weapons,* 8 July 1996, para. 25, confirming that the permissibility of the (presumably extraterritorial) use of nuclear weapons would remain subject to Art. 6 ICCPR (right to life) complemented by international humanitarian law. Affirmative also T. Meron, 'Extraterritoriality of Human Rights Treaties, Extraterritoriality of Human Rights Treaties', 89 *AJIL* (1995), 78, at 81; F. Hampson, 'Using International Human Rights Machinery to enforce the Law of Armed Conflict', XXXI-1 *RDMilG* (1992), 118, at 121 *et seq.*; O. Ben-Naftali/Y. Shany, 'Living in Denial. The Application of Human Rights in the Occupied Territories', 37-1 *Israel Law Review* (2003–2004), 17–118, at 62 *et seq.*

[18] See e.g. Arts 12 GC I; 12 GC II; 13 GC III and 27 GC IV.

[19] Art. 105 UNCLOS.

lawfulness of a State's exercise of jurisdiction, they are not decisive for its *generic categorization* as law enforcement. In sum, for the purposes of operational law, the generic concept of law enforcement can be widely construed as comprising all territorial and extraterritorial measures taken by a State to maintain or restore public security, law, and order or to otherwise exercise its authority or power over individuals, objects, or territory. **4.02**

7. *Law Enforcement by Non-State Entities.* In this functional sense, law enforcement operations can be conducted not only by States but, in exceptional circumstances, even by other collective entities capable of having obligations under international law. Most notably, to the extent that they are in a position to exercise the requisite power and control, even multilateral organizations[20] and non-State parties to an armed conflict[21] may be in a position to conduct law enforcement activities.[22]

8. *The Legal Basis for Law Enforcement Operations.* When law enforcement operations are conducted on the relevant State's territory, their legal basis is to be found firstly in domestic law. States have the 'monopoly of the legitimate use of physical force'[23] in order to maintain or restore law and order on their territory, to the exclusion of other entities; be they non-State actors or other States. International law may even require States to adopt a number of law enforcement measures within their jurisdiction—such as criminalizing and prosecuting international crimes,[24] or preventing the use of their territory for terrorist activities against other States.[25,26]

[20] For example, the administration of territories by the United Nations Organization under the authority of the UN Security Council regularly involves the exercise of law enforcement functions.

[21] For example, in a non-international armed conflict, AP II imposes a wide range of obligations on dissident armed forces and other organized armed groups towards persons finding themselves within territory under their control. For similar, but less developed obligations, see also Art. 3 common to the Geneva Conventions.

[22] Note, however, that the precise international obligations of non-State entities may differ from those of States, because they strongly depend on the extent to which they are bound by the relevant legal instruments. In particular, non-State actors are not directly bound by human rights treaties (although they may have human rights responsibilities if they exercise *de facto* control over territory and State-like functions). See: ICRC, International Humanitarian Law and the Challenges of Contemporary Armed Conflicts (31IC/11/5.1.2, October 2011), p. 15.
Moreover, in the case of insurgents, the obligation to comply with international law enforcement standards in certain situations does not give rise to a corresponding 'right' to exercise law enforcement authority in contravention of domestic law.

[23] Max Weber, *Politics as a Vocation*, 1919. <http://www.sscnet.ucla.edu/polisci/ethos/Weber-vocation.pdf>.

[24] On war crimes, see: Art. 49 GC I; Art. 50 GC II; Art. 129 GC III; Art. 146 GC IV; Art. 85 AP I; J.-M. Henckaerts and L. Doswald-Beck (eds), *Customary International Humanitarian Law* (Cambridge: Cambridge University Press, 2005), Rules 156–158; Art. 8 of the Rome Statute. On genocide, see Art. 1 of the Convention on the Prevention and Punishment of the Crime of Genocide in 1948. For torture, see: Art. 2(1) Convention against Torture and Other Cruel, Inhuman or Degrading Treatment or Punishment of 10 December 1984. On piracy, see Art. 100 of the UN Convention on the Law of the Sea in 1982. On slavery: Art. 2 of the Convention to Suppress the Slave Trade and Slavery of 25 September 1926.

[25] UN GA Res. 2625 (1970) 'Friendly Relations', Principle 3(2).

[26] See Chapter 25.

4.02 9. *Extraterritorial Law Enforcement as an Exception.* While domestic law may have an extraterritorial reach, the enforcement of the relevant national provisions through extraterritorial law enforcement measures will be limited by the sovereignty of other States. As prominently stated already in the *Lotus* judgment of the Permanent Court of International Justice:

> the first and foremost restriction imposed by international law upon a State is that—failing the existence of a permissive rule to the contrary—it may not exercise its power in any form in the territory of another State. In this sense jurisdiction is certainly territorial; it cannot be exercised by a State outside its territory except by virtue of a permissive rule derived from international custom or from a convention.[27]

As a general rule, therefore, international law does not authorize police or military forces to maintain or restore law and order abroad. There are, however, a number of exceptions to this rule. Of course, any territorial State remains free to express its genuine consent to and, thereby, provide a legal basis for law enforcement operations by other States within its territory. Also, the Security Council may decide to authorize States, or to mandate peace operations to maintain or restore law and order in a given territory.[28] Moreover, in the context of an armed conflict, extraterritorial law enforcement activities may also find an international legal basis in IHL. Most notably, where an armed conflict results in a situation of belligerent occupation, the Occupying Power is obliged to maintain law and order as the *de facto* authority of that territory.[29] Similarly, the Geneva Conventions oblige belligerent States to ensure safety, law, and order within detention facilities for both combatants and civilians, which they may establish outside their own territory as a result of the war. Less straightforward is the question of whether a State affected by hostile action originating from non-state actors based in another State may be entitled to resort to force extraterritorially against the perpetrators based on its inherent right of self-defence.[30] Assuming, for the sake of the argument, that this would be considered as lawful, there would be no reason why the said State could not use extraterritorial law enforcement measures (instead of acts of hostilities) in response to an armed attack when such measures would be deemed sufficient and appropriate.

[27] PCIJ, 'Lotus' case, *France v Turkey* (1927), Judgment, § 45: 'Now the first and foremost restriction imposed by international law upon a State is that—failing the existence of a permissive rule to the contrary—it may not exercise its power in any form in the territory of another State. In this sense jurisdiction is certainly territorial; it cannot be exercised by a State outside its territory except by virtue of a permissive rule derived from international custom or from a convention' (para 45).

[28] See, e.g. S/RES/1264 (1999), § 3; S/RES/1833 (2008), preamble. For more examples, see Chapter 24 in this book, commentary to Section 24.05.

[29] Art. 43 of the 1907 Hague Regulations.

[30] On the possibility of resorting to the right of self-defence when an armed attack originates from non-state actors, see Chapter 8 in this book, Section 8.03. The ICJ in its Advisory Opinion on the construction of a wall in occupied Palestinian Territory recognized the existence of an inherent right of self-defence only in the case of armed attack by one State against another State. This restrictive interpretation was, however, the subject of vigorous dissent within the Court. See: ICJ Reports 2004, 194, para. 139 and note 20 in Chapter 8 in this book.

10. *The Legal Paradigm of Law Enforcement.* As far as international law is concerned, the legal standards which govern the conduct of law enforcement operations are derived primarily from human rights law and, in times of armed conflict, also from international humanitarian law. Additionally, numerous soft law instruments issued by the United Nations and regional organizations have contributed significantly to the relevant practice and legal opinion of States.[31] Although human rights law generally remains applicable during armed conflict, the precise content of the individual rights may have to be determined by reference to the *lex specialis* of international humanitarian law.[32] In addition to human rights law and IHL, there are a number of principles regulating law enforcement activities which are common to virtually all legal systems around the world and which, therefore, can be termed general principles of law. These principles would continue to apply even if, in a particular case, the applicability of human rights law and/or IHL may be questionable. In conjunction, the totality of all rules and principles of human rights law, humanitarian law, and general international law that regulate the conduct of law enforcement operations form the international legal paradigm of law enforcement.[33] **4.02**

11. Given the large range of possible law enforcement activities, the relevant specific rights and obligations will vary from one situation to another. When it comes to the use of lethal (or potentially lethal) force, the most directly affected human right is the right to life,[34] which is protected in every general human rights treaty[35] and under customary law.[36] Human rights case law and non-binding

[31] See, most notably, the UN Code of Conduct for Law Enforcement Officials, the UN Basic Principles on the Use of Force and Firearms, the UN Principles on the Effective Prevention and Investigation of Extra-legal, Arbitrary and Summary Executions, the European Code of Police Ethics, and the UN Standard Minimum Rules for the Treatment of Prisoners, adopted by the 1st UN Congress on the Prevention of Crime and the Treatment of Offenders (Geneva, 1955), approved in ECOSOC Resolutions 663 C (XXIV) of 31 July 1957 and 2076 (LXII) of 13 May 1977.

[32] On the interrelation between human rights law and international humanitarian law, see also Chapter 3, 'Human Rights and International Humanitarian Law. General Issues'.

[33] The proposed paradigms of law enforcement and hostilities (see Section 4.03) are termed *legal* rather than *moral* or *ethical* paradigms because they comprise the rules and principles of international law that govern the conduct of hostilities and, respectively, of law enforcement operations. They are termed *paradigms* rather than *frameworks* because they bring together rules and principles from several existing normative frameworks under a paradigm designed to govern a type of situation that may be relevant under each of the contributing frameworks.

[34] It is not the only relevant right however. For instance, when it comes to the destruction of objects (rather than the killing of persons), the right to property or to private and family life may be relevant as well.

[35] See: International Covenant on Civil and Political Rights (ICCPR), Art. 6; European Convention on Human Rights (ECHR), Art. 2; American Convention on Human Rights (ACHR), Art. 4; African Charter on Human and Peoples' Rights (ACHPR), Art. 4.

[36] Article 6 of the ICCPR qualifies the right to life as 'inherent', which serves to indicate its customary nature. On the customary, or even *jus cogens* nature of the right to life, see among many others: N. Melzer, *Targeted Killing under International Law* (Oxford University Press, 2008), 177–220; M. Nowak, *U.N. Covenant on Civil and Political Rights: CCPR Commentary* (Kehl/Strasbourg/Arlington: N. P. Engel, 2005), 122; T. Desch, 'The Concept and Dimensions of the Right to Life (as Defined in International Standards and in International and Comparative Jurisprudence)' 36:1/2 *Österreichische Zeitschrift für öffentliches Recht und Völkerrecht* (1985), 79; B. G. Ramcharan, 'The Right to Life' 30:3

4.02 standards, such as the UN Code of Conduct for Law Enforcement Officials[37] and the UN Basic Principles on the Use of Force and Firearms by Law Enforcement Officials[38] have helped to specify the standards that have to be complied with when force is used in law enforcement operations.[39]

12. In substantive terms, any operation subject to the law enforcement paradigm must be planned, prepared, and conducted so as to minimize, to the greatest extent possible, the recourse to lethal force (*precaution*). Potentially lethal force may only be used in self-defence or defence of others against the imminent threat of death or serious injury, to prevent the perpetration of a particularly serious crime involving grave threat to life, to arrest a person presenting such a danger and resisting their authority, or to prevent his or her escape (*proportionality*), and only when less extreme means are insufficient to achieve these objectives (*necessity*). The use of force with the actual intent to kill is only permissible when strictly unavoidable to protect life.

4.03 **The generic concept of hostilities refers to the resort to means and methods of warfare between parties to an armed conflict. Strictly speaking, the actual 'conduct' of hostilities corresponds to the sum total of all hostile acts carried out by individuals directly participating in hostilities. The rules and principles of international law governing the conduct of hostilities form the legal paradigm of hostilities.**

1. *Resort to Means and Methods of Warfare*. The concept of hostilities—like the concept of law enforcement—is not expressly defined in international law. However, where treaty law uses the term, it is intrinsically linked to armed confrontations occurring between parties to an international or non-international armed conflict.[40] Hostilities within the meaning of international law cannot occur outside

Netherlands International Law Review (1983), 299; Y. Dinstein, 'The Right to Life, Physical Integrity, and Liberty', in L. Henkin (ed.), *The International Bill of Rights: The Covenant on Civil and Political Rights* (New York: Columbia University Press, 1981), 114–15. See also UNHRC, General Comment no. 24: *Issues relating to reservations made upon ratification or accession to the Covenant or the Optional Protocols thereto, or in relation to declarations under article 41 of the Covenant*, 11 April 1994, UN Doc. CCPR/C/21/Rev.1/Add.6, para. 8.

[37] UN Code of Conduct for Law Enforcement Officials, adopted by UN GA 34/169 of 17 December 1979.

[38] UN Basic Principles on the Use of Force and Firearms by Law Enforcement Officials, adopted by the 8th UN Congress on the Prevention of Crime and the Treatment of Offenders (1990).

[39] N. Melzer, *Targeted Killing under International Law* (Oxford: Oxford University Press, 2008), 177–220.

[40] The notion of hostilities is frequently used in treaties regulating situations of international and non-international armed conflict, for example in the following contexts: opening of hostilities, conduct of hostilities, acts of hostility, persons (not) taking part in hostilities, effects of hostilities, suspension of hostilities, end of hostilities. See Title and Art. 1 of Hague Convention III; Title Section II HagueReg; Art. 3(1) GC I–IV; Art. 17 GC I; Art. 33 GC II; Title Section II and Arts 21(3), 67, 118, 119 GC III; Arts 49(2), 130, 133, 134, 135 GC IV; Arts 33, 34, 40, 43(2), 45, 47, 51(3), 59, 60 AP I and Title Part IV, Section I AP I; Arts 4 and 13(3) AP II; Arts 3(1)–(3); and 4 ERW Protocol.

situations of armed conflict, such as during internal disturbances and tensions, including riots, isolated and sporadic acts of violence, and other acts of a similar nature.[41] But even in situations of armed conflict, not all forcible measures are necessarily part of the hostilities. On the contrary, a wide range of activities occurring in situations of armed conflict are governed exclusively by the law enforcement paradigm, such as the exercise of administrative, disciplinary, and judicial authority over occupied territory, the civilian population, and persons deprived of their liberty.[42] The primary purpose of hostilities is 'to weaken the military forces of the enemy'[43] and, ultimately, to achieve 'the complete or partial submission of the enemy at the earliest possible moment with the minimum expenditure of life and resources'.[44] In the very general terms used in treaty law, the concept of hostilities could be said to refer to the resort by parties to an armed conflict to means and methods of 'warfare'[45] or, more accurately, of 'injuring the enemy'.[46] **4.03**

2. *Requirement of Direct Causation of Harm.* But the notion of hostilities is narrower still. Not all activities which aim to 'injure' (harm or defeat) the enemy are necessarily part of the hostilities. During armed conflicts, the civilian population often significantly contributes to the general war effort without getting involved in the actual conduct of hostilities, for example through industrial and agricultural production, or political, administrative, and financial support.[47] Thus, whether a specific operation is part of the actual conduct of hostilities depends not only on its contribution to the war effort, but also on its causal proximity to the actual

[41] According to Art. 1(2) AP II, such situations fall below the threshold of armed conflicts.

[42] Thus, international humanitarian law provides a specific legal basis for the exercise of law enforcement authority by States over prisoners of war, internees, and protected persons in occupied territory (Arts 8, 43 HagueReg; Art. 82 GC III; Arts 27(4), 64, 66, 68, 76, 117 GC IV), and arguably even by insurgent parties to a non-international armed conflict over persons and within territory having fallen into their power (Art. 3 GC I–IV, Arts 4–6 AP II).

[43] According to the St Petersburg Declaration (1868), this is 'the only legitimate object which States should endeavour to accomplish during war'.

[44] According to the UK LOAC Manual (2004), this is 'the legitimate purpose of the conflict'. See United Kingdom: Ministry of Defence, *The Manual of the Law of Armed Conflict* (Oxford: Oxford University Press, 2004), Section 2.2 (Military Necessity). For similar formulations as to the object to be achieved during the conduct of hostilities see, for example, the definition of military necessity in NATO: *Glossary of Terms and Definitions (AAP-6V)*, p. 2-M-5; United States: Department of the Army, *Field Manual 27-10* (1956), para. 3; US Department of the Navy, *The Commander's Handbook on the Law of Naval Operations, NWP 1–14M/MCWP 5–12-1/COMDTPUB P5800.7A* (2007), para. 5.3.1, p. 5-2; France: Ministry of Defence, *Manuel de Droit des Conflits Armés* (2001), 86 *et seq.*; Germany: Federal Ministry of Defense, *Triservice Manual ZDv 15/2: Humanitarian Law in Armed Conflicts* (May 2013), para. 141; Switzerland: Swiss Army, *Regulations 51.007/IV, Bases légales du comportement à l'engagement* (2005), para. 160.

[45] See Art. 35(1) AP I. [46] See Art. 22 HagueReg.

[47] See N. Melzer, *Interpretive Guidance on the Notion of Direct Participation in Hostilities under International Humanitarian Law* (Geneva: ICRC, 2009), 51–2; Sandoz et al. (eds), *Commentary on the Additional Protocols of 8 June 1977 to the Geneva Conventions of 12 August 1949* (Geneva: ICRC, 1987), paras 1679, 1945. Affirmative also ICTY, *Prosecutor v Strugar*, Case no. IT-01-42-A, Judgment of 17 July 2008, paras 175–176. See also the distinction between 'taking part in hostilities' and 'work of a military character' in Art. 15(1)(b) GC IV.

4.03 infliction of harm on the enemy.[48] Accordingly, as far as specific activities are concerned, international humanitarian law distinguishes between 'direct' and 'indirect' participation in hostilities,[49] a distinction which essentially corresponds to that between 'direct' and 'indirect' causation of harm to the enemy.[50] Strictly speaking, the actual 'conduct' of hostilities includes only activities amounting to 'direct participation' in such hostilities (i.e. which are designed to directly cause harm to the enemy). This is precisely the reason why civilians directly participating in hostilities may be lawfully attacked as if they were combatants, whereas civilians only indirectly participating in hostilities remain protected against direct attack. In short, the concept of hostilities corresponds to the sum total of all hostile acts carried out by individuals directly participating in hostilities.[51]

3. Treaty law does not define direct participation in hostilities, nor does a clear interpretation of the notion emerge from State practice or international jurisprudence. The notion must therefore be interpreted in good faith in accordance with the ordinary meaning to be given to its constituent terms in their context and in light of the object and purpose of international humanitarian law.[52] In its Interpretive Guidance on the notion, the International Committee of the Red Cross

[48] According to the Sandoz et al. (eds), *Commentary on the Additional Protocols*, paras 1679, 1944, 4788, the notion of hostilities should be interpreted to refer to 'acts of war which are intended by their nature or purpose to hit specifically the personnel or *matériel* of the armed forces of the adverse Party'. Compare Fleck (ed.), *The Handbook of International Humanitarian Law*, 2nd edn (Oxford: Oxford University Press, 2008), Section 212: 'Acts of war are all measures of force which one party, using military instruments of power, implements against another party in an international armed conflict. These comprise combat actions designed to eliminate opposing armed forces and other military objectives.'

[49] The notion of direct participation in hostilities has evolved from the phrase 'taking no active part in the hostilities' used in Art. 3 GC I–IV. Although the English texts of the Geneva Conventions and Additional Protocols use the words 'active' (Art. 3 GC I–IV) and 'direct' (Arts 43(2) AP I; 45(1) and (83) AP I; 51(3) AP I; 67(1)(e) AP I; 13(3) AP II), respectively, the consistent use of the phrase 'participent directement' in the equally authentic French texts demonstrate that the terms 'direct' and 'active' refer to the same quality and degree of individual participation in hostilities. See also ICTR, *Prosecutor v Jean-Paul Akayesu*, Case no. ICTR-96-4-T, Judgment of 2 September 1998 (Trial Chamber), para. 629.

[50] On the element of direct causation, see the ICRC's Recommendation V.2 and accompanying commentary at: Melzer, *Interpretive Guidance*, 51–8. See also Chapter 16 'Targeting in Operational Law'.

[51] This is also the official view of the ICRC. See Melzer, *Interpretive Guidance*, 44. According to Sandoz et al. (eds), *Commentary on the Additional Protocols*, para. 1943: 'It seems that the word "hostilities" covers not only the time that the civilian actually makes use of a weapon, but also, for example, the time that he is carrying it, as well as situations in which he undertakes hostile acts without using a weapon.' The notion of 'hostile act', in turn, is defined as 'acts which by their nature and purpose are intended to cause actual harm to the personnel and equipment of the armed forces' (Sandoz et al. (Art. 51 AP I) paras 1942 *et seq.*). Furthermore, see P. Verri, *Dictionary of the International Law of Armed Conflict* (Geneva: ICRC, 1992), 57, who defines hostilities as: 'acts of violence by a belligerent against an enemy in order to put an end to his resistance and impose obedience', and J. Salmon, *Dictionnaire de droit international public* (Bruxelles: Bruylant, 2001), 550 (*hostilités*): 'Ensemble des actes offensifs ou défensifs et des opérations militaires accomplis par un belligérant dans le cadre d'un conflit armé'. See also the use of the term 'hostile act' in Arts 41(2) and 42(2) AP I.

[52] Art. 31(1) Vienna Convention on the Law of Treaties.

defines direct participation in hostilities essentially as all conduct which is specifically designed to support a party to an armed conflict against another (*belligerent nexus*), either by directly adversely affecting its military operations or military capacity or by directly inflicting death, injury, or destruction on protected persons or objects (*threshold of harm and direct causation*).[53] Arguably, therefore, the notion of hostilities is approximately equivalent to actual combat action, including preparatory measures, deployments, and withdrawals constituting an integral part of combat operations; indirect participation, on the other hand, refers to support activities which contribute to, and may even be indispensable for, the general war effort, but which are not part of the actual conduct of hostilities.[54] Nevertheless, even indirect participation in hostilities may trigger certain rights and duties under the law governing the conduct of hostilities.[55] **4.03**

4. *Specific Activities Amounting to Hostilities.* In practical terms, the conduct of hostilities certainly includes all attacks, that is to say, offensive or defensive operations involving the use of violence against the adversary,[56] whether (lawfully) directed against legitimate military targets or (unlawfully) against protected persons or objects.[57] It includes not only open combat, but also the placing of explosive devices, sabotage, and computer network attacks. Also part of the hostilities are military operations preparatory to specific attacks, geographic deployments to and withdrawals from attacks, as well as unarmed activities supporting a party to the conflict by directly harming another, such as transmitting tactical intelligence, directing combat operations, interrupting the power supply to military facilities, interference with military communications, and the construction of roadblocks

[53] See the ICRC's Recommendation V and accompanying commentary at: Melzer, *Interpretive Guidance*, 46–64. According to the ICRC, acts amounting to direct participation in hostilities must meet three cumulative requirements: (1) a threshold regarding the harm likely to result from the act, (2) a relationship of direct causation between the act and the expected harm, and (3) a belligerent nexus between the act and the hostilities conducted between parties to an armed conflict. But see also Chapter 16 'Targeting in Operational Law'.

[54] See the ICRC's Recommendation V.2 and accompanying commentary at: Melzer, *Interpretive Guidance*, 51–4. During the Diplomatic Conference of 1974 to 1977, several delegations indicated that 'hostilities' included *preparations for combat* and *return from combat*. See Sandoz et al. (eds), *Commentary on the Additional Protocols*, paras 1679, 1943, 4788. Arguably, the fact that it was deemed necessary to clarify this point indicates that the notion of hostilities was generally interpreted as approximately equivalent to actual combat.

[55] For example, even persons not or only indirectly participating in hostilities may have obligations in relation to the study, development, acquisition, or adoption of new weapons (Art. 36 AP I), as well as with regard to the protection of the civilian population, individual civilians, and civilian objects under their control from the effects of enemy attacks (Art. 58 AP I).

[56] See the definition of 'attacks' as 'acts of violence against the adversary, whether in offence or in defence' in Art. 49(1) AP I. According to Sandoz et al. (eds), *Commentary on the Additional Protocols*, para. 1882, the term attack '... refers simply to the use of armed force to carry out a military operation at the beginning or during the course of armed conflict'.

[57] See the use of the term 'attack' in Arts 85(3)(a) to (e) and (4)(d) AP I (grave breaches) and related Arts 12(1); 41(1); 42(1); 51(2), (4) to (6), 52(1); 54(2); 55(2); 56(1); 59(1) AP I. See also Sandoz et al. (eds), *Commentary on the Additional Protocols*, para. 1877. For a confirmation in national case law, see Israel High Court of Justice, *PCATI v Israel* (HCJ 769/02), Judgment of 13 December 2006, para. 33.

4.03 impeding military deployments.[58] Conversely, activities such as financing, recruiting and training, or the production and smuggling of weapons and equipment may build up the military capacity of a party to the conflict, but do not employ that capacity to directly inflict harm on its enemy and, therefore, fall short of the actual conduct of hostilities. Also, as a matter of specific design, and as further developed later,[59] the use of force in exercise of authority or power over persons, objects, or territory under effective control, violent civil unrest against such authority, as well as the use of necessary and proportionate force in individual self-defence against unlawful attack do not aim to weaken or defeat the enemy militarily and, therefore, would not qualify as hostilities.[60]

5. In sum, for the purposes of operational law, the concept of hostilities is best understood as comprising all activities that are specifically designed to support one party to an armed conflict against another, either by directly inflicting death, injury, or destruction, or by directly adversely affecting its military operations or military capacity.

6. *The Legal Paradigm of Hostilities.* The primary international legal framework governing the conduct of hostilities in both international and non-international armed conflict is international humanitarian law.[61] While human rights law generally remains applicable during armed conflict, its role in regulating the conduct of hostilities is limited because, in this respect, it is generally superseded by the *lex specialis* of humanitarian law.[62] Where humanitarian law does not provide a

[58] According to the ICRC's Commentary, 'the word "hostilities" covers not only the time that the civilian actually makes use of a weapon, but also, for example, the time that he is carrying it, as well as situations in which he undertakes hostile acts without using a weapon' (Sandoz et al. (eds), *Commentary on the Additional Protocols*, para. 1943). For a comprehensive analysis with numerous examples see the ICRC's Recommendations IV–VI and accompanying commentary at Melzer, *Interpretive Guidance*, 41–68.

[59] See Section 4.04, paras 3–10.

[60] On the requirement of belligerent nexus, see the ICRC's Recommendation V.3. and accompanying commentary at Melzer, *Interpretive Guidance*, 58–64.

[61] The most recent and complete codification of the IHL governing the conduct of hostilities can be found in the First Additional Protocol of 1977 to the Geneva Conventions of 1949 (AP I) applicable in situations of *international armed conflict.* Other instruments, such as the Hague Regulations (1907), the various instruments prohibiting, restricting, or regulating the use of certain weapons, as well as individual provisions of the four Geneva Conventions are also part of the law of hostilities. While treaty IHL contains only few provisions on the conduct of hostilities in *non-international armed conflict*, most of the basic rules applicable in international armed conflict have by now become part of customary IHL applicable also in non-international armed conflict.

[62] For international judicial and quasi-judicial practice applying the *lex specialis* principle to the interrelation between IHL and human rights law see ICJ, *Advisory Opinion on the legal consequences of the construction of a wall in the occupied Palestinian territory*, 9 July 2004, para. 106; ICJ, *Case concerning Armed Activities on the Territory of the Congo (Democratic Republic of the Congo v Uganda)*, Judgment of 19 December 2005, para. 216; UNHRC, General Comments no. 31 (2004), para. 11, no. 29 (2001), para. 3; IACiHR, *Abella v Argentina (La Tablada)*, Case no. 11.137, Report no. 55/97, 18 November 1997, para. 159; IACiHR, *Third Report on the Situation of Human Rights in Colombia*, 26 February 1999, chapter IV, paras 11, 151; IACiHR, *Coard et al. v United States*, Case no. 10.951, Report no. 109/99, 29 September 1999, para. 42; IACiHR, *Precautionary Measures in Guantanamo Bay, Cuba*, Decision of 13 March 2002. More specifically with regard to the right to life in armed conflict, see: ICJ,

sufficiently clear or precise answer to a specific question arising during the conduct of hostilities, its rules have to be clarified primarily through the usual means of treaty interpretation and by reference to the general principles of military necessity and humanity underlying and informing international humanitarian law as a whole. 4.03

7. In substantive terms, and particularly when it comes to the use of lethal (or potentially lethal) force, the paradigm of hostilities requires that use of means and methods of warfare: (a) be directed against a person or object subject to lawful attack; (b) be planned and conducted so as to avoid erroneous targeting of, as well as to avoid, and in any event to minimize, incidental harm to, protected persons or objects; (c) not be expected to cause incidental harm to protected persons or objects that would be excessive in relation to the concrete and direct military advantage anticipated; (d) be suspended when the targeted persons surrender or otherwise fall *hors de combat*; and (e) not otherwise be conducted by resort to means or methods specifically prohibited by international humanitarian law. Even where not prohibited under the above standards (a–e), the use of lethal force is not necessarily automatically permissible, but still remains governed by the basic principles of military necessity and humanity underlying and informing international humanitarian law as a whole. Arguably, therefore, lethal force should not be resorted to where the threat posed by the targeted person can manifestly be neutralized through capture or other non-lethal means without additional risk to the operating forces or the surrounding civilian population.[63]

Within the context of an armed conflict, the paradigms of law enforcement and of hostilities can apply in parallel to different persons and objects at the same time and location. The legal paradigm of law enforcement continues to govern all exercise by parties to the conflict of their authority or power outside the conduct of hostilities. The resort to means and methods of warfare between parties to an armed conflict is governed by the legal paradigm of hostilities even if the ultimate purpose of its military operations is to maintain, restore, or otherwise impose public security, law, and order. 4.04

1. *Applicability 'by Default' of the Law Enforcement Paradigm.* Not all military operations carried out for reasons related to an armed conflict are necessarily governed by the legal paradigm of hostilities. As previously noted, considerable portions of international humanitarian law do not regulate the conduct of hostilities, but the exercise of authority or power over persons, objects, and territory, that

Nuclear Weapons Opinion, para. 25; IACiHR, *La Tablada Case*, above, para. 161; IACiHR, *Report Colombia 1999*, above, chapter IV, paras 152–154, 169. On the interrelation between human rights law and international humanitarian law, see also Chapter 4.

[63] For a more detailed discussion of the standards governing the use of force against individuals under the paradigm of hostilities, see Section 17.04.

4.04 is to say, typical law enforcement situations.[64] In doing so, international humanitarian law essentially protects persons not, or no longer, directly participating in hostilities against various forms of abuse of authority or power including, *inter alia*, violence to life and person, torture, cruel, humiliating and degrading treatment, collective punishment, hostage-taking, acts of terrorism, forced displacement, and the expropriation and destruction of property.[65] Moreover, international humanitarian law goes into great detail in regulating the treatment and protection of various categories of persons, most notably those interned, detained, or otherwise deprived of their liberty; the population under belligerent occupation; or enemy nationals within the territory of a party to the conflict. The rules and principles of international humanitarian law regulating the exercise of authority or power outside the conduct of hostilities are complemented and reinforced by applicable human rights law.[66] While human rights law creates obligations for States only, humanitarian law binds even non-State actors. Therefore, to the extent that non-State actors *de facto* exercise authority or power over persons, objects, or territory for reasons related to an armed conflict they, too, must comply with the law enforcement paradigm, albeit derived exclusively from international humanitarian law. Overall, in regulating the exercise by belligerents of authority or power outside the conduct of hostilities, international humanitarian law significantly contributes to the shape and content of the law enforcement paradigm in situations of armed conflict and even expands the legal basis for the exercise of law enforcement authority beyond what would be permitted in peacetime.

2. *Precedence of the Hostilities Paradigm.* In situations of armed conflict, the standards governing the exercise of authority or power under the law enforcement paradigm are supplemented by the special rules of the paradigm of hostilities. While the concept of law enforcement comprises, in essence, all measures aiming to maintain, restore, or otherwise impose public security, law, and order, the concept of hostilities comprises those aiming to directly bring about, or defend against, the military weakening or defeat of a party to an armed conflict. The two concepts may overlap significantly, especially when States conduct hostilities within territory under their effective control.[67] For example, for a governmental authority or Occupying Power, armed confrontations with insurgents or organized resistance movements will generally not only constitute a military threat, but at the same time

[64] See e.g. Arts 8, 43 HagueReg; Art. 82 GC III; Arts 27(4), 64, 66, 68, 76, 117 GC IV, and arguably also Art. 3 GC I–IV, Arts 4–6 AP II.

[65] See e.g. Arts 46, 47, 50 HagueReg; Article 12 GC I and II; Arts 13–14, 102 GC II; Arts 27–28, 49, 53, 71 GC IV; Art. 3(1) GC I–IV; Arts 4–6 AP II.

[66] On the interrelation between human rights law and international humanitarian law, see also Chapter 3.

[67] It is precisely in recognition of the difficult interrelation between a State's law enforcement authority and its role as a party to an armed conflict that Art. 3(1) AP II states: 'Nothing in this Protocol shall be invoked for the purpose of affecting the sovereignty of a State or the responsibility of the government, by all legitimate means, to maintain or re-establish law and order in the State or to defend the national unity and territorial integrity of the State.'

also a threat to public security, law, and order.[68] While the State's military operations aiming to weaken or defeat the insurgency or armed resistance are part of the hostilities, the ultimate purpose of the State's conduct of hostilities is to restore public security, law, and order. This raises the question as to the interrelation between the two paradigms. Overall, the interaction between the two legal paradigms is governed by the *lex specialis* maxim.[69] In this context, this means that whenever a party to an armed conflict engages in the conduct of hostilities, the paradigm of hostilities takes precedence over the paradigm of law enforcement—even if the ultimate aim is to maintain, restore, or otherwise impose public security, law, and order. The ultimate aim of an operation is thus not necessarily decisive for determining the prevailing paradigm. **4.04**

3. *Specific Interrelation Regarding the Use of Lethal (or Potentially Lethal) Force Against Persons* (hereafter: the use of force). The use of force is an area in which it is essential to draw a clear dividing line between the legal paradigms of law enforcement and of hostilities. This is so because the standards governing the use of force under the two paradigms differ significantly. Even though they share common principles—such as the principles of necessity, proportionality, and precautions—these principles operate differently under each paradigm. Four main differences shall be highlighted here.[70] First, the paradigm of hostilities does not prohibit the targeting of persons considered as legitimate targets under IHL, provided that, among others, the IHL principles of proportionality and precautions are fulfilled. In other words, the military necessity to use force against legitimate targets is presumed to exist. In contrast, the paradigm of law enforcement demands that persons suspected of a crime be arrested and prohibits the resort to lethal force against persons, unless they pose an imminent threat to life. This derives from the principle of 'absolute necessity' according to which the use of force must be the last resort for achieving a legitimate purpose, which, in the extreme, would justify the destruction of life. In addition, this principle requires using the smallest amount of

[68] See e.g. ECtHR, *Isayeva v Russia*, Application no. 57950/00, Judgment of 24 February 2005, para. 180, where the European Court of Human Rights used the term 'law enforcement bodies' to describe Russian armed forces resorting to combat weapons, including military aviation and artillery, against armed Chechen insurgents.

[69] The maxim *lex specialis generalibus derogat* was cited in the *travaux préparatoires* of Article 38 ICJ Statute as a general principle of law (see reference in B. Cheng, *General Principles of Law as Applied by International Courts and Tribunals* (Cambridge: Cambridge University Press, 2006), 25 *et seq.*). Affirmative also Y. Dinstein, *The International Law of Belligerent Occupation* (Cambridge: Cambridge University Press, 2009), 99–101.

[70] For a comparison of the principles of necessity, proportionality and precautions, see, Gaggioli, ICRC Use of Force Report, from which the following paras are inspired. See also Melzer, *Targeted Killing*, 423–9; and D. Fleck, 'Law Enforcement and the Conduct of Hostilities: Two Supplementing or Mutually Excluding Legal Paradigms?', in A. Fischer-Lescano, H.-P. Gasser, T. Marauhn, and N. Ronzitti (eds), *Frieden in Freiheit. Peace in liberty. Paix en liberté. Festschrift für Michael Bothe zum 70. Geburtstag* (Baden-Baden: Nomos, Zürich: DIKE, 2008), 391–407, at 401–5; N. Lubell, 'Challenges in Applying Human Rights Law to Armed Conflict', 87:860 *International Review of the Red Cross* (2005), 745–6; G. Gaggioli, *L'influence mutuelle entre les droits de l'homme et le droit international humanitaire à la lumière du droit à la vie* (Paris: Pedone, 2013), 353–7.

4.04 force necessary and applying force in a graduated manner (i.e. 'escalation of force procedure'). Second, under the paradigm of hostilities, the principle of proportionality prohibits the causation of incidental harm to civilians or civilian objects which would be excessive in relation to the military advantage pursued, whereas the principle of proportionality under the paradigm of law enforcement (as developed in human rights case law) more broadly requires that the harm expected to result from the use of force—not only to uninvolved bystanders, but also to the targeted perpetrator himself—be justified in view of the importance and urgency of the legitimate aim pursued.[71] As a general rule, the paradigm of hostilities tolerates significantly greater incidental harm than the law enforcement paradigm, both in terms of scope and of intensity. Third, under the paradigm of hostilities, the principle of precaution requires belligerents to take constant care to spare the civilian population, civilians, and civilian objects; whereas under the paradigm of law enforcement, all precautions must be taken to avoid, as far as possible, the use of force as such, and not merely incidental civilian death or injury or damage to civilian objects.[72] Fourth, there are important differences in terms of planning and investigation between the two paradigms. For instance, contrary to the paradigm of hostilities, the paradigm of law enforcement requires the training of law enforcement officials in non-lethal methods of arrest, the provision of self-defensive equipment and alternative means to firearms. The paradigm of law enforcement also obliges States to investigate each allegation of a violation of the right to life. By contrast, the paradigm of hostilities requires an investigation only in case of alleged war crimes. These substantial differences indicate that the determination of the appropriate paradigm may have a crucial impact on the scope and intensity of harm that may be expected to result from a particular operation.

[71] But note that, even under human rights law, the incidental causation of death or injury to bystanders does not necessarily violate the right to life as long as the use of force was absolutely necessary and strictly proportionate. See e.g. ECtHR, *Finogenov and others v Russia* (Applications nos 18299/03 and 27311/03), Judgment of 20 December 2011, para. 236; ECtHR, *Andronicou and Constantinou v Cyprus*, Application no. 25052/94, Judgment of 9 October 1997, para. 194; ECtHR, *Kerimova and others v Russia*, Application no. 17170/04 et al., Judgment of 3 May 2011, para. 246.

[72] The 'principle of precaution' in human rights law does not appear explicitly in the treaty provisions pertaining to the right to life. It has been mainly developed through human rights case law. The ECtHR was the first to develop the concept, borrowing in part from IHL. See ECtHR, *McCann and others v United Kingdom*, Application no. 18984/91, 27 September 1995, paras 150 and 194; ECtHR, *Ergi v Turkey*, Application no. 23818/94, 28 July 1998, para. 79. On the influence of IHL on human rights law for the introduction of the principle of precaution in human rights law, see A. Reidy, 'The Approach of the European Commission and Court of Human Rights to International Humanitarian Law', 38:324 *International Review of the Red Cross* (1998), 526. The Inter-American Court of Human Rights (IACtHR) has followed the jurisprudence of the ECtHR. See IACtHR, *Neira Alegria et al. v Peru*, 19 January 1995, para. 62; IACtHR, *Montero-Aranguren et al. v Venezuela*, 5 July 2006, para. 82; IACtHR, *Zambrano Velez et al. v Ecuador*, 4 July 2007, para. 89. Some human rights bodies refer more generally to the obligation to 'prevent' violations of the right to life: UNHRC, General Comment no. 6 (1982), para. 3; UNHRC, *Burrell v Jamaica*, Communication no. 546/1993, UN Doc. CCPR/C/53/D/546/1993, 18 July 1996, para. 9.5; African Commission on Human and Peoples' Rights (ACommHPR), *Commission Nationale des Droits de l'Homme et des Libertés v Chad*, Communication no. 74/92, 11 October 1995, para. 21.

4. Given these differences and the parallel applicability of both paradigms in armed conflicts, a crucial question for belligerent armed forces in particular is how to determine which paradigm to apply in a given situation in order to act in conformity with international law. International law does not provide a clear-cut answer to this question. The ICRC has attempted a clarification exercise in this field and published a Report in 2013 on 'The Use of Force in Armed Conflicts: Interplay between the Conduct of Hostilities and Law Enforcement Paradigms'.[73] The Report does not provide ICRC's position but rather a summary and analysis of the discussions that were held during an ICRC expert meeting that was convened in Geneva in 2012. Five practical case studies were discussed during the meeting. They portrayed different use-of-force situations taking place in a traditional non-international armed conflict opposing governmental armed forces to an organized non-State armed group on its own territory.[74] Moreover, the cases were analysed from a State perspective since human rights law, and thus an important part of the rules to be found in the paradigm of law enforcement, is binding *de jure* only for States.[75] For each of the five case studies, experts had to determine whether the use of force falls within the paradigm of hostilities or within that of law enforcement.[76] **4.04**

5. The discussions of these various cases showed that, for many experts, 'the main (if not the only) legal criterion for determining whether a situation is covered by the conduct of hostilities or law enforcement paradigms is the status, function or conduct of the person against whom force may be used'.[77] In other words, when belligerents are confronted with a person considered as a legitimate target under IHL, the paradigm of hostilities would generally prevail as the normative framework governing their response. A person is a legitimate target under IHL if he or she belongs to one of the three following categories:

(1) The person is a combatant and is therefore a potential target because of his/her *status* under IHL applicable in international armed conflicts.[78]

[73] Gaggioli, ICRC Use of Force Report.

[74] The choice of a traditional NIAC by the ICRC was commended by different considerations. First, the situations where the issue of interplay between the paradigms of hostilities and law enforcement take place are mainly non-international armed conflicts and situations of occupation. Second, in a traditional NIAC taking place on the territory of the belligerent State, the controversial issue of the extraterritorial application of human rights law does not arise.

[75] See ICRC, International Humanitarian Law and the Challenges of Contemporary Armed Conflicts (31IC/11/5.1.2, October 2011), p. 15.

[76] The case studies dealt with the following specific situations: (1) Use of force by governmental armed forces against a fighter sleeping at home with his family in a part of the territory controlled by the government (isolated sleeping fighter example); (2) Riot situation where civilians and fighters are intermingled; (3) Use of force by governmental armed forces against common criminals who operate in the same area as fighters and who entertain close links with fighters; (4) Escape attempts by former fighters and riots in detention; (5) Checkpoint scenario where a suspicious car arrives at high speed and does not stop when ordered to do so.

[77] Gaggioli, ICRC Use of Force Report, 59.

[78] For the definition of persons having the combatant status, see Articles 4 of the Third Geneva Convention and 43 of Additional Protocol I. The status of combatant is given to members of regular armed forces as well as to irregular armed forces, such as militias, volunteer corps, or resistance

4.04 (2) The person is a 'fighter', i.e. he/she lacks formal combatant status, but assumes a continuous combat function for the fighting forces of a belligerent State or a belligerent non-State armed group.[79]

(3) The person is a civilian directly participating in hostilities and, due to this conduct, loses protection against attack for the duration of each hostile act.

In contrast, in situations where belligerents are not confronted with legitimate targets, such as in cases of civilian unrest or the fight against common criminality (e.g. drug lords not organized as a belligerent force and not directly participating in hostilities), the paradigm of law enforcement is to be applied.[80] In the context of operations that are directed against legitimate military targets, including those likely to cause proportionate incidental harm to protected persons and objects, the paradigm of hostilities prevails as *lex specialis*.[81] Any forcible measures directed against persons or objects protected against direct attack under IHL, however, must comply with the stricter standards of the law enforcement paradigm, even if they occur during the conduct of hostilities.[82]

6. Additional possible factors—other than the status, function, or conduct of the person against whom force may be used—to draw the dividing line between the paradigms of hostilities and law enforcement have been suggested and were discussed at the ICRC expert meeting.[83] Two sets of factors were mentioned in

movements belonging to a party to the conflict and fulfilling certain criteria. It shall be noted that while membership in regular armed forces of a State is regulated by domestic law, this is not always the case for irregular State armed forces. In such a case, membership can only be reliably determined on the basis of functional criteria, such as those applying to organized armed groups in non-international armed conflict. See Melzer, *Interpretive Guidance*, 25.

[79] Ibid. 25 and 27.

[80] There is generally a genuine agreement that civilian unrest has to be dealt with under the paradigm of law enforcement even in armed conflicts. Human rights case law is consistent with this conclusion. See e.g. ECtHR, *Güleç v Turkey*, Application no. 54/1997/838/1044, 27 July 1998; ECtHR, *Simsek et al. v Turkey*, Application no. 35072/97 and 37194/97, 26 July 2005. Another situation that is generally considered as governed by the law enforcement paradigm is the use of force to maintain law and order in detention settings and to avoid escapes. This remains true even if the person deprived of his/her liberty is a prisoner of war for instance. See e.g. Article 42 of the Third Geneva Convention which provides that the use of weapons against prisoners of war trying to escape is considered as the last resort and warnings have to be made, just as required by the law enforcement paradigm. On this issue, see Gaggioli, ICRC Use of Force Report, 33–8.

[81] It should be noted however that if a civilian, for instance, uses force against an enemy soldier in self-defence (e.g. to prevent him from killing members of his family), this use of force does not fall under the paradigm of hostilities because the act lacks any belligerent nexus. See Melzer, *Interpretive Guidance*, 61. In other words, for the paradigm of hostilities to prevail, the use of force must not only be directed against a legitimate target but it must also have a belligerent nexus.

[82] This principle stands in contrast to the causation of *incidental* (i.e. *not deliberate*) harm to protected persons and objects, the permissibility and proportionality of which is governed by the paradigm of hostilities.

[83] Gaggioli, ICRC Use of Force Report, 17–19; T. Ferraro, *Occupation and Other Forms of Administration of Foreign Territory, Third Meeting of Experts: The Use of Force in Occupied Territory* (Geneva; ICRC, 2012) at 129; University Centre for International Humanitarian Law, *The Right to Life in Armed Conflicts and Situations of Occupation*, Geneva, Switzerland, 1–2 September 2005, p. 19. Available at <http://www.geneva-academy.ch/docs/expert-meetings/2005/3rapport_droit_vie.pdf>

particular. The first factor was the location of the potential target, i.e. whether the person against whom force may be used is inside or outside the conflict zone. The notion of conflict zone is derived from an interrogation in relation to the geographical scope of application of IHL, and more specifically of the paradigm of hostilities.[84] It has been argued that the geographical scope of application of the paradigm of hostilities is limited to the 'conflict zone', i.e. the area where active hostilities are taking place. According to this view, outside the conflict zone, the paradigm of hostilities would not apply (or, at least, would not prevail over the paradigm of law enforcement).[85] Another distinct set of criteria that was discussed comprised the intensity of violence and degree of control over the area/circumstances.[86] The underlying idea would be that the paradigm of hostilities would prevail only in operations directed against legitimate targets, and only when the intensity of violence is high and there is a lack of control over the area and circumstances. On the other hand, the higher the control over the area and circumstances, and the lower the intensity of violence in the area, the more likely the law enforcement paradigm would prevail and impose its rationale of avoiding the resort to lethal force to the maximum extent possible. Most experts at the meeting, however, did not see these factors as decisive legal criteria.[87] They were seen as 'too subjective, too open **4.04**

(Last accessed on 30 September 2013); UNHRC, *Outcome of the Expert Consultation on the Issue of Protecting the Human Rights in Armed Conflicts: Reports of the United Nations High Commissioner for Human Rights*, Eleventh session, 4 June 2009, UN Doc. A/HRC/11/31, para. 14.

[84] The notion of 'conflict zone' is neither defined nor used in IHL treaties. It is, however, frequently used, in practice, to describe an area where active hostilities are taking place.

[85] See ICTY, *Prosecutor v D. Tadić*, Appeals Chamber, Decision of 2 October 1995, Case IT-94-1-AR72, paras 68–69: 'Although the Geneva Conventions are silent as to the geographical scope of international "armed conflicts," the provisions suggest that at least some of the provisions of the Conventions apply to the entire territory of the Parties to the conflict, not just to the vicinity of actual hostilities. *Certainly, some of the provisions are clearly bound up with the hostilities and the geographical scope of those provisions should be so limited* (emphasis added). Others, particularly those relating to the protection of prisoners of war and civilians, are not so limited. [. . .] The geographical and temporal frame of reference for internal armed conflicts is similarly broad. This conception is reflected in the fact that beneficiaries of common Article 3 of the Geneva Conventions are those taking no active part (or no longer taking active part) in the hostilities. This indicates that the rules contained in Article 3 also apply outside the narrow geographical context of the actual theatre of combat operations.' On the basis of the italicized sentence of this quotation, it could be argued that the geographical scope of application of the paradigm of hostilities is limited to the 'conflict zone'.

[86] Some experts and legal scholars developed these notions of intensity of violence and degree of control on the basis notably of the fact that some human rights bodies have applied a law enforcement rationale in some particular circumstances where force was used against persons who would be considered as a legitimate target under IHL. See para. 5 in this Section.

[87] Gaggioli, ICRC Use of Force Report, 22: '[F]or the vast majority of experts, whether favouring the conduct of hostilities paradigm or the law enforcement paradigm, the factor of the conflict zone should not be seen as a relevant additional criterion from a purely legal point of view. Introducing such an additional criterion for determining the applicable paradigm was regarded as dangerous and not workable. The conflict zone criterion was seen as being too subjective, too open to debate and misinterpretation or disagreement. It raised a number of issues such as: Who decides what is the immediate theatre of operations? Would that imply that an encampment of fighters outside the conflict zone could not be targeted? Would that not constitute an incitement for fighters to operate from outside the conflict zone? If a fighter is targeted in a zone where there are no hostilities, does that zone become a conflict zone? What if a civilian is directly participating in hostilities in an area where there are no

4.04 to debate and misinterpretation or disagreement',[88] adding undesirable complexity to the analysis. It was stressed that, in order to be realistic and fair for combatants who need to make split-second decisions, the rules regulating the use of force must be clear and simple.

7. Although this approach may seem fair and adequate as a general rule, its application to specific cases may prove at times more problematic. Take the example of an isolated fighter sleeping at home with his family in the context of a non-international armed conflict and in a part of the territory controlled by the government.[89] In such circumstances, his capture by the governmental armed forces would appear to be realistic and feasible, whereas a shoot to kill operation would be disturbing not only from the perspective of the governing principles of military necessity and of humanity underlying and inspiring IHL as a whole, but also from a purely humanitarian and ethical perspective. Given this unease, various experts and legal scholars provide different answers.[90] On one side of the spectrum, some contend that the solution is not to be found in the law but in policy.[91] A reasonable commander would most probably decide—for policy reasons—in such a situation a capture operation, especially if it does not imply additional risks for its own forces. On the other side of the spectrum, others consider that, in such a situation, the paradigm of law enforcement should prevail.[92] For instance, Kretzmer, Ben-Yehuda, and Furth derive this conclusion from the fundamental difference between international and non-international armed conflicts.[93] While an isolated sleeping soldier in an international armed conflict might be targeted and killed,[94] as this derives from his/her status, the situation would be different in non-international armed conflicts because there is no such status and because, according to these authors, the permissive rules pertaining to the conduct of hostilities are unclear under Common Article 3, Additional Protocol II, and customary law.[95] In non-international armed conflicts, the paradigm of law enforcement would thus remain the default applicable paradigm except 'in those concrete situations in which the scope and level of organized armed violence are such that a policing, law-enforcement model of law is clearly inappropriate'.[96] Still others are of the view

confrontations at all? Would this area be considered as a conflict zone? Experts made fewer comments on the control and intensity of violence factors. Overall, however, these factors were criticized as being too context-dependent. It was stressed in particular that the factor of control is often difficult to assess.'

[88] Ibid. [89] Ibid.. 13–23 (case study 1: isolated sleeping fighter scenario).

[90] See e.g. *Webinar on the Use of Force in Armed Conflicts: Interplay between the Conduct of Hostilities and Law Enforcement Paradigms*, 25 November 2014. Available at: <https://www.icrc.org/eng/resources/documents/event/2014/webinar-use-of-force.htm>.

[91] Gaggioli, ICRC Use of Force Report, 23.

[92] Ibid. 20–2.

[93] D. Kretzmer, A. Ben-Yehuda, and M. Furth, '"Thou Shalt Not Kill": The Use of Lethal Force in Non-International Armed Conflicts' 47:02 *Israel Law Review* (2014), 191–224.

[94] *Contra*: R. Goodman, 'The Power to Kill or Capture Enemy Combatants' 24 *European Journal of International Law* (2013) 819.

[95] Kretzmer, Ben-Yehuda and Furth , 'Though Shalt Not Kill', 199, 223–4.

[96] Ibid. 195.

that, in specific cases, the paradigm of law enforcement may be the *lex specialis* and may prevail over the paradigm of hostilities depending on the particular facts of the case. In order to determine the *lex specialis*, one should thus identify the rules having the 'greatest common contact surface area' with those facts.[97] Some human rights bodies have applied in practice the law enforcement paradigm regarding the use of force against legitimate targets,[98] but it is true that they did not explicitly address the issue of the interplay between the paradigm of hostilities and law enforcement. The direct relevance of such case law has therefore been questioned.[99] **4.04**

8. It is submitted by the present authors that policy is not sufficient to protect individuals from attacks that are simply unnecessary to reach the goals of the armed conflict. The answer must be found in the law. It is also submitted that, although the hostilities paradigm derived from IHL supports the presumption that legitimate targets may be attacked and killed at any time, there may be circumstances where the principles of military necessity and humanity impose a legal duty on belligerents to consider the appropriateness of the use of lethal force even against legitimate targets. The emblematic case is the isolated sleeping fighter whose capture poses no additional risk to the operating forces.[100] While under the law enforcement paradigm the use of lethal force is presumably unlawful and can only be justified in exceptional cases of strict necessity and proportionality, the killing of legitimate targets in the conduct of hostilities is generally presumed to be lawful, and a duty to use non-lethal means arises only when there manifestly is no necessity for the use of lethal force. As far as legitimate targets are concerned, the presumption as to the lawfulness of lethal force is thus reversed compared to the paradigm of law enforcement.[101] While the arguments for applying the law enforcement paradigm as the default legal paradigm or as *lex specialis* in a case like the isolated sleeping fighter scenario are original and seductive from a purely humanitarian perspective,

[97] Gaggioli, ICRC Use of Force Report, 20.

[98] UNHRC, *Camargo and Suarez de Guerrero v Colombia*, Communication no. 45/1979, UN Doc. CCPR/C/15/D/45/1979, 31 March 1982; UNHRC, *Concluding Observations: Israel*, UN Doc. CCPR/CO/78/ISR, 21 August 2003, para. 15; UNHRC, *Concluding Observations: Israel*, UN Doc. CCPR/C/ISR/CO/3, 29 July 2010, para. 10; *Report of the Special Rapporteur on the Extrajudicial, Summary and Arbitrary Executions, Philip Alston: Mission to the United States of America*, UN Doc. A/HRC/11/2/Add.5, 28 May 2009, paras 71–73; ECtHR, *Gül v Turkey*, Application no. 22676/93, 14 December 2000; ECtHR, *Oğur v Turkey*, Application no. 21594/93, 20 May 1999; ECtHR, *Hamiyet Kaplan and others v Turkey*, Application no. 36749/97, 13 September 2005; ECtHR, *Mansuroglu v Turkey*, Application no. 43443/98, 26 February 2008. See also: Israel High Court of Justice, *PCATI v Israel* (HCJ 769/02), Judgment of 13 December 2006, para. 40. Although the Court applied a conduct of hostilities reasoning when dealing with the targeting of civilians directly participating in hostilities, it ultimately held—in conformity with the law enforcement paradigm—that 'if a terrorist taking a direct part in hostilities can be arrested, interrogated, and tried, those are the means which should be employed'. On these cases, see: Gaggioli, ICRC Use of Force Report, 14–16 and G. Gaggioli and R. Kolb, 'A Right to Life in Armed Conflicts? The Contribution of the European Court of Human Rights' 37 *Israel Yearbook on Human Rights* (2007), 115–63.

[99] Gaggioli, ICRC Use of Force Report, 22 and the written statement by Françoise Hampson in Appendix 3 of the Report.

[100] Ibid., at 16–17; Melzer, *Interpretive Guidance*, 78 *et seq.*

[101] Melzer, *Interpretive Guidance*, 78 *et seq.*

4.04 their legal basis remains questionable and the specific legal criteria for determining when exactly the paradigm of hostilities takes over remain to be identified. This is especially so if the factors of conflict zone, control, and intensity are not regarded as legitimate additional legal criteria, as was the case for the majority of the participants in the ICRC expert meeting.[102] In any case, nothing would impede belligerents from applying, for policy or other reasons, the more protective paradigm of law enforcement in a situation like case study 1.

9. Other difficult situations from a practical perspective are cases where civilian unrest/common criminality concurs with actual hostilities, the typical example being a riot situation, in which fighters take advantage of the crowd to conduct an attack against the soldiers facing the riot.[103] In accordance with what has been suggested earlier[104] a 'parallel approach' could be applied to such cases.[105] This means that the paradigm of hostilities would prevail regarding action taken against legitimate targets (such as fighters in the crowd) while the potential use of force against violent civilians (not directly participating in hostilities) would still be governed by the paradigm of law enforcement. It goes without saying that an attack against a legitimate target in the riot situation just described would be feasible under the paradigm of hostilities only if the IHL principles of proportionality and precautions can be respected. This might be the case if a sniper could precisely target and kill the fighter in the middle of the crowd without excessively endangering the surrounding civilians. In the operational practice of any situation of civil unrest, however, the use of lethal force would almost always be associated with great risks of error, arbitrariness, and unwanted escalation. Despite its value for the clarification and distinction of theoretical concepts, therefore, the 'parallel approach' may prove to be of limited practical value to operators and it may be preferable to revert to well-trained escalation of force procedures in line with the law enforcement character of the overall situation.

10. Finally, questions arise in relation to situations of doubt as to the status, function, or conduct of a person seemingly posing a threat. For instance, at a checkpoint, how should a soldier react if a suspicious car arrives at high speed and does not stop when ordered to do so?[106] The starting point to answer this question is to be found in the IHL rule that provides that in case of doubt, a person is

[102] Although experts discarded the factors of conflict zone, control, and intensity to determine the dividing line between the paradigm of hostilities and law enforcement paradigms and provided valid arguments for doing so, they recognized that they were important factors in military operations. A deeper reflection on the impact of these factors in military operations and on the interpretation and application of IHL principles pertaining to the conduct of hostilities notably would be needed.

[103] Gaggioli, ICRC Use of Force Report, 24–9 (case study 2: riots in armed conflict situations). For a case law on the fight against common criminality, see Gaggioli, ICRC Use of Force Report, 29–33 (case study 3: fight against criminality).

[104] Paragraphs 5–6 in this Section.

[105] Gaggioli, ICRC Use of Force Report, 24.

[106] Gaggioli, ICRC Use of Force Report, 39–42 (case study 5: lack of respect for military orders: the example of checkpoints).

presumed to be a civilian.[107] Since civilians cannot be directly attacked, it would seem logical and consistent with the approach developed earlier in the chapter to apply the law enforcement paradigm.[108] As a consequence, lethal (or potentially lethal) force may be used only as a last resort when other means are ineffective or without any promise of achieving the intended result and an escalation of force procedure needs to be applied.[109] During the ICRC expert meeting, there was a broad consensus among experts that an escalation of force procedure must be applied in case of doubt.[110] However, some experts interestingly reached that conclusion on the basis of the paradigm of hostilities. They read an obligation to do so through the precautionary rule, which requires doing everything feasible to verify that the objectives to be attacked are not civilians/civilian objects.[111] In other words, the escalation of force procedure would be a feasible measure to determine whether the person seemingly posing a threat is a legitimate target or not. Lastly, some experts were of the view that the escalation of force procedure to be applied in the checkpoint scenario derived neither from the paradigm of hostilities nor from the paradigm of law enforcement, but rather from the concept of 'self-defence' as encompassed in many States' rules of engagement.[112] **4.04**

11. *Self-defence and the Interplay between the Paradigms of Hostilities and of Law Enforcement.* The previous checkpoint example raises a related issue that was not directly addressed at the ICRC expert meeting and that requires additional research and analysis:[113] What is the role/place of self-defence in the interplay between the paradigms of hostilities and law enforcement?[114] The concept of self-defence is multifaceted (or multilayered) and its exact contour lacks clarity. Even its characterization (as a right, obligation, exception, justification, excuse, and circumstance

[107] Art. 50(1) AP I. Further, the ICRC *DPH Guidance* (Melzer, *Interpretive Guidance*, 74), includes as a recommendation that 'all feasible precautions must be taken in determining whether a person is a civilian and, if so, whether that civilian is directly participating in hostilities. In case of doubt, the person must be presumed to be protected against direct attack.'

[108] M. Sassòli, 'Legislation and Maintenance of Public Order and Civil Life by Occupying Powers', 16 *EJIL* (2005), 661–94, at 665 *et seq*.

[109] See, in this sense: ECtHR, *Kakoulli v Turkey,* Application no. 38595/97, 22 November 2005 (shooting of a Greek Cypriot allegedly carrying a weapon by Turkish soldiers in the buffer zone inside the territory of northern Cyprus). This does not deal with a checkpoint scenario but is relevant to the extent that it deals with the use of force in case of doubt and when there is a lack of respect for military orders.

[110] Gaggioli, ICRC Use of Force Report, 41.

[111] Art. 57(2)(a)(i) of AP I. This rule is considered as customary for international armed conflicts as well as for non-international armed conflicts. See J.-M. Henckaerts and L. Doswald-Beck, *Customary International Humanitarian Law*, Rule 16.

[112] Gaggioli, ICRC Use of Force Report, 41. In a checkpoint scenario that was submitted before the ECtHR, the Dutch serviceman who had fired at the vehicle arriving at the checkpoint in Iraq invoked self-defence. The ECtHR did not however deal with the use of force as such in this case but only with the obligation to investigate that derives from Article 2 of the European Convention on Human Rights. See ECtHR, *Jaloud v Netherlands*, Application no. 47708/08, 20 November 2014.

[113] Gaggioli, ICRC Use of Force Report, 11–12: 'It was suggested that clarification of the notion of "self-defence" might be useful but would go beyond the realm of this expert meeting.'

[114] On the concept of personal self-defence, see in this book sub-Chapter 5.4, and Chapters 10 and 24.

4.04 precluding wrongfulness) is open to debate.[115] At the domestic level, the definitions provided vary considerably. For instance, while in some States force can be lawfully used in defence of property, in others it can only be resorted to in order to protect life or limb from an attack or imminent attack.[116] At the international level, a key distinction needs to be made between inter-State self-defence in the realm of the United Nations Charter[117] and personal self-defence by State agents as an 'exception' to the right to life.[118] The notion of personal self-defence is further governed by domestic criminal law, which must comply with human rights law rules and standards. The concept of inter-State self-defence as derived from the United Nations Charter should not be considered as having any direct impact on IHL rules pertaining to the conduct of hostilities. This flows from the basic distinction to be made between *jus ad bellum* and *jus in bello*.[119] In the same way, the concept of inter-State self-defence enshrined in the United Nations Charter does not have any direct impact on the rules and principles shaping the paradigm of law enforcement as far as the standards governing the use of force are concerned.[120] Instead, personal self-defence by State agents as an exception to the prohibition on the use of lethal force is eminently relevant in the context of the paradigm of law enforcement. It is one of the legitimate objectives for which the use of lethal force by State agents may be lawful. This aspect of self-defence is thus an integral part of the paradigm of law enforcement. It is more restrictive than the broader concept of law enforcement as it allows the use of lethal force only in case of imminent threat of death or serious injury.[121] For State

[115] L. Cameron and V. Chetail, *Privatizing War: Private Military and Security Companies under Public International Law* (Cambridge: Cambridge University Press, 2013), 457.

[116] See the contribution of Blaise Cathcart in this Handbook, para. 6 of the commentary to Section 10.03. See also: Cameron and Chetail, *Privatizing War*, 463 (footnote 265); Gaggioli, ICRC Use of Force Report, 12.

[117] Article 51 of the United Nations Charter.

[118] Article 2, paragraph 2 (a), of the European Convention on Human Rights (ECHR) does indeed explicitly refer to the use of force by State agents 'which is no more than absolutely necessary in defence of any person from unlawful violence' as an exception to the right to life. Outside of the ECHR framework, it is also widely accepted that a use of force in self-defence is not an 'arbitrary deprivation of life'. See e.g. M. Nowak, *U.N. Covenant on Civil and Political Rights: CCPR Commentary* (Strasbourg: N.P. Engel, 2005), 128. See also the UN Basic Principles on the Use of Force and Firearms, principle 9. The concept of self-defence is also used in the context of international criminal law as a ground for excluding criminal responsibility. See e.g. Art. 31(1)(c) of the Rome Statute of the International Criminal Court. It has however intentionally been left out of this contribution to avoid complexity and because of space constraints.

[119] On this distinction, see Preamble of Protocol I. For legal writings, see among many others: C. Greenwood, 'The Relationship between jus ad bellum and jus in bello', 9 *Review of International Studies* (1983), 221–34; R. Kolb, 'Sur l'origine du couple terminologique *ius ad bellum – ius in bello*', 827 *International Review of the Red Cross* (1997), 593–602. See also Chapter 2 in this book.

[120] This is not however the approach taken by the United States of America, which has developed a special doctrine of self-defence encompassing *jus ad bellum* considerations as well as a domestic law definition of self-defence that is derived from law enforcement standards. See Chairman of the Joint Chiefs of Staff Instruction (CJCSI) 3121.01B—Standing Rules of Engagement/Standing Rules for the Use of Force, 13 June 2005.

[121] See the UN Basic Principles on the Use of Force and Firearms, principle 9, which provides that self-defence is one amongst four exceptions to the use of firearms (and more broadly to the use of lethal or potentially lethal force) by law enforcement officials.

agents, therefore, the concept of self-defence cannot be seen as a separate and additional basis for the use of force because, from an international law perspective, this notion is already part and parcel of the paradigm of law enforcement. Domestic concepts of self-defence may not go beyond what is already authorized under the international paradigm of law enforcement. For non-state actors, which are not directly bound by human rights law,[122] self-defence as derived from domestic law may play an important complementary role to international humanitarian law in armed conflict situations and, as an inherent right of individual self-preservation, may even be regarded as a general principle of law. 4.04

The legal paradigm of hostilities imposes special restrictions on certain means and methods of warfare, such as riot control agents, expanding bullets, or undercover operations and other forms of deception, although very similar means and methods are widely used by law enforcement officials in peacetime. 4.05

1. *Special Restrictions on Means and Methods.* In situations of armed conflict, the legal paradigm of hostilities imposes special restrictions on means and methods that are widely used by law enforcement officials in peacetime, such as riot control agents, expanding bullets, or undercover operations and other forms of deception. This raises the question as to the permissibility of such means and methods in territorial law enforcement and arrest operations against enemy personnel, particularly when they are not, at the time, engaged in hostile operations.

2. *Riot Control Agents.* The Chemical Weapons Convention (1993) prohibits the use of riot control agents as a method of warfare.[123] Riot control agents are defined as any chemicals 'which can produce rapidly in humans sensory irritation or disabling physical effects which disappear within a short time following termination of exposure', such as OC (pepper spray) or CS gas (tear gas).[124] However, the Convention expressly permits the use of such chemicals for 'law enforcement including domestic riot control purposes'.[125] Therefore, the use of riot control agents in response to riots, violent demonstrations, and other forms of civil unrest is not prohibited, even if they are politically linked to a situation of armed conflict or occupation.[126] The same principle presumably applies if armed insurgents or resistance fighters intermingle with the protesting crowd and participate in the violence without, however, engaging in actual combat against the authorities. Arguably, as long as riot control agents are not directed against enemies engaged in combat, and as long as they are used in strict compliance with the principles governing the use of force under the law enforcement paradigm, they should not be

[122] See ICRC, International Humanitarian Law and the Challenges of Contemporary Armed Conflicts (31IC/11/5.1.2, October 2011), p. 15.

[123] Art. 1(5) CWC. [124] Art. 2(7) CWC. [125] Arts 2(9)(d) and 6(1) CWC.

[126] Affirmative also Dinstein, *The International Law of Belligerent Occupation* (Cambridge: Cambridge University Press, 2009), 98–9.

4.05 considered as a 'method of warfare' within the meaning of the Chemical Weapons Convention.[127] Analytically, such operations could be said to lack 'belligerent nexus' inherent in the notion of hostilities, because their specific design remains the restoration of law and order, and not the infliction of harm on the enemy.[128] As suggested in the case discussed earlier, the analysis may become more complicated when resistance fighters intermingling with rioting civilians engage in actual combat.[129] However, as long as the situation is predominantly a situation of civil unrest and riot control agents are used to respond to that situation with a view to restoring law and order, the use of riot control agents should not be considered as prohibited simply because some of the affected persons happen to qualify as legitimate targets under IHL.[130]

3. *Expanding Bullets.* In the conduct of hostilities it is prohibited to resort to 'expanding bullets', that is to say, bullets which expand or flatten easily in the human body.[131] Expanding bullets cause more severe injuries and increase the chance of incapacitating or killing the targeted person with immediate effect. The prohibition of expanding bullets is an early concretization of the customary prohibition on the use of means and methods of warfare of a nature to cause superfluous injury or unnecessary suffering to combatants.[132] International law does not prohibit the use of expanding bullets in peacetime or otherwise outside the conduct of hostilities. The practical advantage of using expanding bullets in law

[127] In operational practice, a similar question arose, for example, when Russian Special Forces tasked to liberate hundreds of hostages held by Chechen rebels in a Moscow theatre in October 2002 pumped an incapacitating gas into the building's ventilation system and raided it, causing numerous deaths among hostage-takers and hostages. See J. Miller and W. Broad, 'Hostage drama in Moscow: the toxic agent', *New York Times*, 29 October 2002 (<http://www.nytimes.com>). It should be noted however that this gas did not constitute a 'riot control agent' as per the definition provided by the Chemical Weapons Convention. On the difference between incapacitating gas and riot control agents as well as on the ICRC position that the use of toxic chemicals as weapons for law enforcement purposes should be limited exclusively to riot control agents (and thus not extended to incapacitating gas), see <https://www.icrc.org/eng/resources/documents/legal-fact-sheet/2013-02-06-toxic-chemicals-weapons-law-enforcement.htm>. On the Moscow theatre case, see also ECtHR, *Finogenov and others v Russia*, Application no. 18299/03 and 27311/03, 20 December 2011. For a critical analysis of this case notably, see V. Gowlland-Debbas and G. Gaggioli, 'The Relationship between International Human Rights and Humanitarian Law: an Overview', in R. Kolb and G. Gaggioli (eds), *Research Handbook on Human Rights and Humanitarian Law* (Cheltenham UK [etc.]: Edward Elgar Publishing, 2013), 91.

[128] See Melzer, *Interpretive Guidance*, 46–64.

[129] See Section 4.04, para. 8.

[130] See also in this sense the intervention of Colonel Juan Carlos Gomez Ramirez in the context of the ICRC Webinar on the Use of Force in Armed Conflicts, when discussing case study 2. This expert highlighted that the use of riot control agents in such cases allows reducing or avoiding the use of lethal force.

[131] Hague Declaration concerning Expanding Bullets (1899); Art. 8(2)(b)(xix) ICC Statute. The prohibition is also contained in Section 6.2 of the 1999 UN Secretary General's Bulletin. Affirming the customary nature of this prohibition in international and non-international armed conflict: J.-M. Henckaerts and L. Doswald-Beck (eds), *Customary International Humanitarian Law*, Rule 77.

[132] Art. 35(2) AP I; Art. 23(e) HagueReg. See also the determination of the International Court of Justice that the prohibition on the use of means and methods of warfare of a nature to cause unnecessary suffering to combatants constitutes an intransgressible principle of international customary law and a cardinal principle of IHL (ICJ, *Nuclear Weapons Opinion*, 8 July 1996, para. 78).

enforcement operations is that they are less likely to break up upon impact and tend to remain inside the body of the targeted person, thus presenting a much lower risk to bystanders. At the same time, expanding bullets used in law enforcement are generally fired from pistols and deposit only a fraction of the energy carried by rifle bullets, thus causing much less severe wounds than the classic 'dumdum' bullets, which triggered the prohibition. **4.05**

4. In operational practice, the prohibition of expanding bullets in the conduct of hostilities must be interpreted in line with its original purpose, namely to avoid the 'employment of arms which uselessly aggravate the sufferings of disabled men, or render their death inevitable'.[133] If expanding pistol bullets, which do not have the effect prescribed in the Hague Declaration, are not considered as 'contrary to the laws of humanity'[134] when used in law enforcement operations against persons entitled to protection against direct attack, their use outside the conduct of hostilities should not be considered a war crime simply because the targeted person happens to qualify as a legitimate military target. Consistent with the same logic, of course, any use of low-energy expanding bullets in law enforcement operations, even against persons qualifying as legitimate military targets, would have to comply with the stricter use of force standards imposed by the law enforcement paradigm. For example, in the course of a hostage rescue operation against insurgents, the use of expanding bullets likely to put the lives of the hostage takers in danger would be permissible only where absolutely necessary to save the lives of the hostages or the operating forces and only if other means remain ineffective or without any promise of achieving the intended result.[135] As soon as the operation is conducted under more permissive rules of engagement, however, the prohibition of expanding bullets would have to be respected.

5. *Undercover Operations*. In the conduct of hostilities, it is prohibited to kill, injure, or capture an adversary by resort to perfidy, such as by feigning of civilian, non-combatant status.[136] In contrast to the prohibition of riot control agents and expanding bullets, which aims to prevent unnecessary suffering and superfluous injury, the prohibition of perfidy safeguards the adversary's good faith in the

[133] St Petersburg Declaration (1868). The Hague Declaration of 1899 on expanding bullets is '[i]nspired by the sentiments which found expression in the Declaration of St Petersburg'.

[134] Ibid.

[135] To the extent that the use of expanding bullets may be, in certain cases (e.g. expanding rifle bullets), considered as intentional lethal use of firearms, it may only be made when 'strictly unavoidable in order to protect life'. See UN Basic Principles on the Use of Force and Firearms, principle 9, *in fine*.

[136] Art. 37(1)(c) AP I. In contrast to the prohibition of perfidy in Art. 37 AP I, the prohibition on treachery in Art. 23(b) HagueReg refers only to 'killing' and 'injuring', but not to 'capture'. According to the ICRC, the prohibition of perfidy as expressed in Art. 37 AP I has attained customary nature in both international and non-international armed conflict (J.-M. Henckaerts and L. Doswald-Beck (eds), *Customary International Humanitarian Law*, Rule 65). See also ICTY, *Prosecutor v Dusko Tadić*, Case no. IT-94-A, Decision on the Defence Motion for Interlocutory Appeal on Jurisdiction of 2 October 1995 (Appeals Chamber), para. 125, confirming the customary nature of the prohibition of perfidy in non-international armed conflict.

4.05 protection of international humanitarian law. More specifically, perfidy involves acts which invite the adversary's confidence that he either must accord, or is entitled to, protection under international humanitarian law, with the intent to betray that confidence.[137]

6. Employing plain-clothed commandos to kill, injure, or capture an adversary almost always amounts to the feigning of civilian, non-combatant status, thus falling under the prohibition of perfidy.[138] Perfidious undercover operations severely jeopardize the protection of peaceful civilians and, when involving the killing or injury of an adversary, amount to war crimes both in international and non-international armed conflict.[139] Not prohibited are ruses of war intended to mislead an adversary or to induce him to act recklessly (e.g. camouflage, decoys, mock operations, and misinformation),[140] or operations that depend upon the element of surprise (e.g. uniformed commando raids), as long as there is no attempt to invite the confidence of an adversary with respect to protection under international humanitarian law.[141] Nor would the prohibition of perfidy seem to prevent the mere gathering of targeting intelligence by undercover units for later use in separate operations by uniformed personnel,[142] or the infiltration of insurgent groups by undercover agents, as long as their operations do not involve the capture, injuring, or killing of insurgents.[143]

[137] Sandoz et al. (eds) *Commentary on the Additional Protocols*, paras 1483, 1497; M. Schmitt, 'State-Sponsored Assassination in International and Domestic Law', 17 *Yale Journal of International Law* (1992), 609–85, at 633; F. Kalshoven and L. Zegveld, *Constraints on the Waging of War* (Geneva: ICRC, 2001), 93.

[138] Art. 37(1)(c) AP I. Affirmative Middle East Watch/Human Rights Watch, 'License to Kill, Israeli Undercover Operations A License to Kill, Israeli Undercover Operations Against "Wanted" and Masked Palestinians', July 1993, 39; Schmitt, 'State-Sponsored Assassination', 635; J.B. Kelly, 'Assassination in War Time', 30 *Military Law Review* (1965), 101–11, at 104; S.R. David, *Fatal Choices: Israels's Policy of Targeted Killing* (Bar-Ilan University: Begin-Sadat Center for Strategic Studies, 2002), 16; N.J. Kendall, 'Israeli Counter-Terrorism: "Targeted Killings" Under International Law', 80 *North Carolina Law Review* (2002), 1069–88, at 1077; T. Ruys, 'License to Kill? State-Sponsored Assassination under International Law', 44/1–2 *Military Law and Law of War Review* (2005), 13–49, at 35; P. Zengel, 'Assassination and the Law of Armed Conflict', 134 *Military Law Review* (1991), 123–55, 132 *et seq*. Undecided apparently W.H. Parks, 'Executive Order 12333 and Assassination, Memorandum of Law' (Department of the Army, Office of the Judge Advocate General, Washington DC), 5, who merely concedes that 'a question remains regarding the donning of civilian clothing by conventional forces personnel for the purpose of killing enemy combatants'.

[139] Arts 8(2)(b)(xi) and 8(2)(e)(ix) ICC Statute. The ICC Statute does not criminalize capture by resort to perfidy.

[140] Art. 37(2) AP I.

[141] Parks, 'Memorandum EO 12333', 5; Schmitt, 'State-Sponsored Assassination', 634; Ruys, 'License to Kill?', 25 *et seq*.

[142] However, if captured in an international armed conflict, such personnel could be treated as spies.

[143] The infiltration of the insurgent military wing by undercover State agents posing as insurgent combatants would no longer be an issue of perfidy, but may raise the question of improper use of enemy uniforms and insignia in non-international armed conflict. According to State practice in situations of international armed conflict, such use outside combat situations generally would not be regarded as prohibited (J.-M. Henckaerts and L. Doswald-Beck (eds), *Customary International Humanitarian Law*), Vol. I, 215–17.

7. The original prohibition of treachery in the Hague Regulations banned the killing and wounding—but not the capture—of any individual 'belonging to the hostile nation or army',[144] thus suggesting that the term 'adversary' in the modern prohibition of perfidy includes both civilians and combatants.[145] While the application of this criterion is fairly straightforward in traditional international armed conflicts with clear frontlines, the nature of non-international armed conflicts can make it very difficult to reliably determine who, apart from the respective fighting forces and political leaderships, 'belongs to' each party to the conflict.[146] Moreover, in conjunction with the contemporary extension of the prohibition beyond killing and injuring in order to also include capture by resort to perfidy, a wide interpretation of the 'belonging to' criterion would almost automatically make it unlawful to use undercover agents (or any other civilian police officers) to arrest (i.e. capture) persons affiliated to, or supportive of, an insurgency, even within territory firmly under governmental control. This outcome certainly would not correspond to the aim of this provision. While there currently is no straightforward legal solution to the dilemma surrounding the prohibition particularly of capture through perfidy, teleological considerations would seem to point towards a compromise which may serve as a viable basis for best practice and, perhaps, a potential future clarification or development of the law. **4.05**

8. First, it should be recalled that the prohibition of perfidy applies only during the conduct of hostilities,[147] and was never envisaged to prevent States from employing undercover agents or civilian police officers for law enforcement operations outside the conduct of hostilities. Second, the exercise of authority over persons finding themselves in the power of a party to the conflict traditionally is not regarded as part of the hostilities. Generally speaking, persons are considered to be in the power of a party to the conflict not only when they are in physical custody, but also when they are present inside territory effectively controlled and administered by that party, always provided that they do not, at the time, directly participate in hostilities. Third, it would nevertheless go too far to regard all combatants present within the territorial power of the adversary as '*hors de combat*' and thus protected against attack, provided only that they do not, at the time, directly participate in hostilities.

[144] Art. 23(b) HagueReg.

[145] Affirmative J.-M. Henckaerts and L. Doswald-Beck (eds) *Customary International Humanitarian Law*, Vol. I, 226.

[146] This may also explain the general limitation of the war crime of perfidy to acts directed against a 'combatant' adversary, which is specific to situations of non-international armed conflicts, in Art. 8(2)(e)(ix) ICC Statute.

[147] According to Sandoz et al. (eds) *Commentary on the Additional Protocols*, para. 1484, 'The title of this article, "Prohibition of perfidy", as well as the definition of perfidy given in the article, should not give rise to confusion. The article is concerned only with acts that take place in combat, as is clear from the scope of this Part, as well as this Section. Thus this prohibition is formulated with reference to those participating in hostilities, and the present article only aims to provide for that aspect of the problem.' In treaty law, this view is supported by the systematic position of Art. 37 AP I and Art. 23(b) HagueReg in the respective treaty sections on the conduct of hostilities and by the list of examples provided in Art. 37 AP I.

4.05 9. By way of compromise between these two seemingly contradictory observations, the 'non-hostile' presence of a combatant within enemy controlled territory could be recognized as removing the prohibition of perfidy during operations conducted under the stricter use of force standards of the law enforcement paradigm. This would allow the territorial authorities to benefit from the advantages of undercover operations while at the same time obliging them to minimize, to the greatest extent possible, the resort to lethal force. On the other hand, mere 'non-hostile' presence within enemy controlled territory would not entail protection against direct attack and would still permit military targeting unless capture is feasible without unduly increasing the risk to the operating forces. Thus, arguably, while a commando operation behind enemy lines aiming to capture an insurgent commander would automatically constitute part of the hostilities subject to the prohibition of perfidy, the arrest of the same insurgent commander during a clandestine family visit inside government controlled territory would not necessarily do so, regardless of the fact that he has not formally regained protection against direct attack. As soon as insurgents present within government controlled territory engage in combat operations, however, any military response would have to comply with the paradigm of hostilities, including the prohibition of perfidy.

PART II

MILITARY OPERATIONS WITHIN THE CONTEXT OF THE UN COLLECTIVE SECURITY SYSTEM

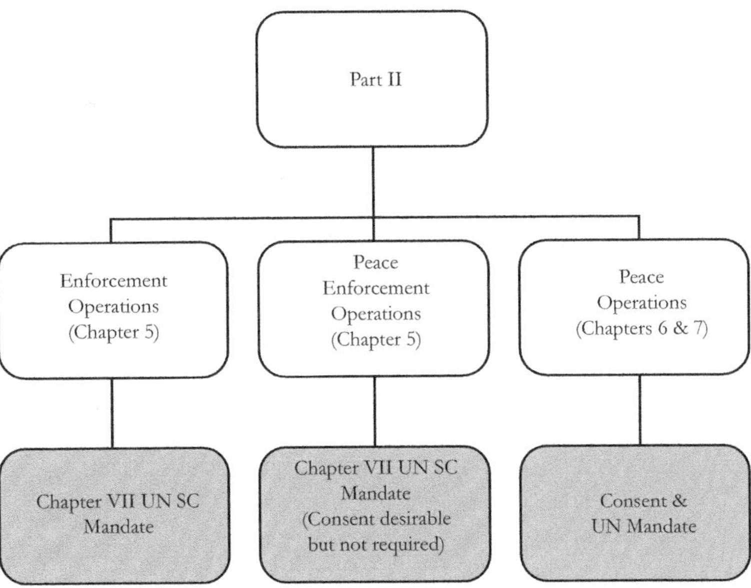

Figure 1

Chapter 5

ENFORCEMENT AND PEACE ENFORCEMENT OPERATIONS

5.1 Legal Characterization and Basis for Enforcement Operations and Peace Enforcement Operations under the Charter

Enforcement Action taken or authorized by the Security Council of a military nature can be conceptually subdivided into two broad categories: *enforcement operations*, which can be characterized as sustained full-scale combat operations directed against a State authorized by the Security Council to maintain or restore international peace and security, and *peace enforcement operations*, which, while potentially involving combat, will not amount to full-scale warfare on a sustained basis against a State, and which fall conceptually and in terms of their objectives and the intensity of the use of force between enforcement operations and traditional peacekeeping (see Section 5.21 below). 5.01

1. The Charter itself provides no clear definition of what constitutes military enforcement action and still less any subdivision of such action into (sub)categories with specific characteristics and objectives. Nonetheless, it is clear from UN practice that there are in fact important, if not always clear, distinctions between various types of enforcement action involving the threat or use of force outside the context of self-defence.[1] These distinctions relate to both the objectives and purposes underlying the particular action and to the factual and military situations and means of implementation.

2. The differences in both a conceptual and in a practical sense between collectively authorized action which has as its purpose the defeat of the opposing party and the imposition of the will of the international community on the one hand, and on the

[1] See e.g. the contrast in the mandates issued to halt the invasion of Korea and end the occupation of Kuwait on the one hand (SC Res. 83 (1950) and 678 (1990) and other resolutions of the Council under Chapter VII authorizing force for more limited purposes. For a clear treatment of the distinction between enforcement (referred to here as military enforcement operations) and peace enforcement see T. Findlay, *The Use of Force in UN Peace Operations* (Oxford: Oxford University Press, 2002), 6–7.

5.01 other hand, action under Chapter VII of an enforcement nature, which, while including the use of proactive (non-defensive) force when strictly necessary, is primarily designed to create a stable environment and promote the conditions necessary to facilitate a peaceful solution, are important enough to justify a subdivision of enforcement action involving the use or threat of force into two distinct categories which will be respectively referred to as enforcement operations and peace enforcement operations in this Handbook. These designations are often used elsewhere and will be used here to distinguish between collectively authorized traditional war fighting directed against a State constituting an international armed conflict under international humanitarian law and which are conducted with the purpose of defeating the opposing party and imposing a collectively sanctioned solution to a particular situation and operations conducted under a Chapter VII mandate of the Council, which while not dependent upon the consent of the parties or restricted to defensive force, do not involve protracted full-scale combat against a State and for purposes of application of international humanitarian law may or may not constitute participation as a party to a non-international armed conflict and do not have the intention of militarily defeating an opposing force.[2] To date, there have been only two unambiguous examples of enforcement operations of the first category referred to here: Korea (1950–3)[3] and the UN-authorized military operation to drive Iraqi forces out of Kuwait (Operation Desert Storm 1991).[4] A third example, which is more controversial, was the NATO led intervention in the Libyan Civil War in 2011 against the government of then President Gaddafi under a Security Council mandate which authorized the use of 'all necessary measures' to enforce a no-fly zone and provide protection to the civilian population.[5] Peace enforcement operations, on the other hand, have been more numerous and have included in addition to the UN Operation in the Congo (ONUC)[6] between 1961 and 1963, such operations as the stabilization and implementation forces in post-conflict Bosnia (SFOR and IFOR) and Kosovo (KFOR)[7]

[2] Ibid. 7.

[3] See SC Res. 82 of 25 June 1950; SC Res. 83 of 27 June 1950; GA Res. 377 (V) of 3 November 1950; GA Res. 498 (V) of 1 February 1950 and GA Res. 500 (V) of 18 May 1951.

[4] See *The United Nations and the Iraq-Kuwait Conflict 1990–1996*, The United Nations Blue Book Series, Vol. IX (New York: Department of Public Information, United Nations, 1996).

[5] Under SC Res. 1973 of 17 March 2011, the use of force was authorized to enforce the no-fly zone and protect civilians. Some Member States interpreted the Resolution broadly and in the context of protecting civilians provided air support to rebel forces under the National Transitional Council (NTC) and attacked the command and control structure of the Libyan armed forces to help bring about a conclusion of the conflict. While opinions differ as to whether the mandate was stretched or exceeded, there is little doubt that the division within the Security Council, especially among its permanent members, has done much to greatly complicate any repetition of such action within the foreseeable future, as is evidenced by the inability of the Council to effectively address the even more serious situation in Syria. See e.g. N.D. White, 'Libya and the Lessons from Iraq: International Law and the Use of Force by the United Kingdom' in *NYIL* (2011), 215 *et seq*.

[6] ONUC, while *de jure* a peacekeeping operation, 'crossed the line' into *de facto* peace enforcement in suppressing the rebellion in Katanga, see Findlay, *The Use of Force*, 71 *et seq*.

[7] For a comprehensive treatment of more recent peace enforcement operations see Findlay, *The Use of Force*, 374–81.

and more recent operations such as the stabilization forces in Iraq (MNFI)[8] and Afghanistan (ISAF).[9] Two even more recent examples are the extension of the mandate of the African Union stabilization force in Somalia (AMISOM) from February 2012 to include peace enforcement tasks in support of the Federal Somali Government, along with the deployment of an intervention brigade to Eastern Congo in the context of the UN's MONUSCO mission to conduct peace enforcement in support of the DRC Government.[10] The latter was the first time a UN Force had been given a peace enforcement mandate since the ONUC operation in the Congo in the 1960s. 5.01

Both enforcement and peace enforcement operations have the overriding purpose of the maintenance or restoration of international peace and security through the employment of the degree of force which is necessary and required under the circumstances to suppress breaches of the peace and acts of aggression and/or to respond to threats to the peace. Consequently, enforcement and peace enforcement operations are by their nature proactive, coercive, and directed against a particular State or entity which has been deemed by the Security Council as a threat to or in breach of international peace and security. 5.02

1. The maintenance of international peace and security is one of the primary purposes of the UN and the Charter provides for a comprehensive legal basis and system designed to achieve that objective.[11] The source of authority for the achievement of this primary objective and the means for carrying it out are set out throughout the Charter, specifically in Articles 1(1), 2, 24, 27, and in Chapters VII and VIII, as well as being proclaimed in declaratory and aspirational form in the Preamble to the Charter. Article 1(1) identifies the maintenance of international peace and security through the implementation of effective collective measures as the first and most important of the UN Organization's primary purposes and identifies three situations in which this is relevant and applicable; namely, the prevention and removal of threats to the peace, and the suppression of breaches of the peace and acts of aggression.[12]

[8] MNFI was established under SC Res. 1511 (2003).

[9] ISAF was established under SC Res. 1386 (2001).

[10] AMISOM was first established as a UN-authorized peacekeeping mission conducted by the AU under SC Res. 1744 (2007). Its mandate was periodically renewed and gradually expanded and became a peace enforcement mandate under SC Res. 2036 (2012). The MONUSCO intervention brigade was established under SC Res. 2098 (2013).

[11] R. Wolfrum, 'Preamble', in B. Simma (ed.), *The Charter of the United Nations: A Commentary*, 3rd edn (Oxford: Oxford University Press, 2012), Vol. 1, 101–6; L.M. Goodrich, E. Hambro, and A.P. Simons, *Charter of the United Nations*, 3rd rev. edn (New York: Columbia University Press, 1969), 25–9.

[12] See also Art. 39.

5.02 2. The notion of collective security which the Charter envisages to achieve this overriding purpose has two complementary sides to it.[13] On the one hand, the prohibition of force, except in the context of collective measures aimed at maintaining and restoring international peace and in self-defence. This is collective security *stricto sensu* and the use of collectively authorized force for this purpose is what is referred to in Article 1(1) of the Charter. On the other hand, collective security in a broader sense includes the encouragement of the peaceful settlement of disputes in accordance with international law and justice and the promotion of international cooperation, self-determination, and respect for human rights, which are set out in the remaining paragraphs of Article 1 of the Charter.[14] Article 2 of the Charter reinforces this objective by setting out the core principles by which both the UN Organization and its Member States are expected to abide and are legally bound,[15] including the well-known prohibition of the use or threat of force by States in their international relations.[16]

3. Article 24 provides the Security Council with primary responsibility in the realm of the maintenance and restoration of international peace and security and further stipulates that in carrying out this responsibility it acts on behalf of the UN Organization and all Member States. It also lays down the 'constitutional limits' to the acts of the Council by stipulating that they must be in conformity with the Purposes and Principles of the UN Organization.[17] It is generally agreed that the Council possesses a wide mandate, including not only the specific powers enumerated in Article 24(2), but those general powers necessary to carry out its responsibilities, including, in particular, those related to its primary function of the maintenance and restoration of international peace and security. However, this is not to say that the power of the Security Council is limitless or that the Council

[13] Simma et al., *The Charter of the United Nations*, 109–11.

[14] Ibid.

[15] Ibid. 121 *et seq.*; Goodrich et al., *Charter of the United Nations*, 36 *et seq.*

[16] Art. 2(4) of the Charter reads as follows: 'All Members shall refrain in their international relations from the threat of use of force against the territorial integrity or political independence of any State, or in any other manner inconsistent with the Purposes of the United Nations.' For authoritative interpretation of this core provision see, *inter alia*, Simma et al., *The Charter of the United Nations*, 200 *et seq.*; Goodrich et al., *Charter of the United Nations*, 48 *et seq.*; Y. Dinstein, *War Aggression and Self-Defence*, 4th edn (Cambridge: Cambridge University Press, 2005), 85–97. I. Brownlie, *International Law and the Use of Force between States* (Oxford: Oxford University Press, 1963 repr. 2002), 112–22; C.H.M. Waldock, 'The Regulation of the Use of Force by Individual States in International Law' 81 *RdC* (1952) 455, 487–9; C. Gray, *International Law and the Use of Force* (Oxford: Oxford University Press, 2004), 29–31; and D.W. Bowett, *Self Defence in International Law* (Manchester: Manchester University Press, 1958), 3–25, to name but some of the most well known. While there are widely contending views concerning the scope of the prohibition and the legality of certain specific grounds for using force, there is general agreement relating to the central importance and peremptory *jus cogens* nature of this provision as a rule of both Charter and customary international law.

[17] For commentary relating to the interpretation of Article 24 see Simma et al., *The Charter of the United Nations*, 764 *et seq.* and Goodrich et al. *Charter of the United Nations*, 202–7. On the constitutional limitations to the Council's power under this provision, see in addition to these sources, *inter alia*, T.D. Gill, 'Legal and Some Political Limitations to the Power of the UN Security Council to Exercise its Enforcement Powers under Chapter VII of the Charter', 26 *Netherlands Yearbook of International Law* (1995), 33, at 68 *et seq.*

can act arbitrarily or without due regard for fundamental principles of international law and it would seem to be axiomatic that the Council is bound by fundamental principles of a peremptory or *jus cogens* character, in carrying out its functions and responsibilities, although there is no universal agreement as to which principles this would include.[18] **5.02**

4. Within the context of the maintenance of international peace and security, including the authorization or use of collective force, the Council possesses, as stated, a very broad mandate and wide discretionary powers to determine that a particular situation constitutes a threat to the peace, or that a breach of the peace or act of aggression has occurred which requires the taking of measures of either a non-forceful nature, or, in the event these measures have proven to be insufficient, or the Council deems they would be inadequate under the particular circumstances to restore and prevent a further aggravation of the situation, the authorization or taking of measures involving the threat or use of force with the object of maintaining or restoring international peace and security. Such measures are generally referred to in the relevant literature and in UN practice as 'enforcement action' or 'enforcement measures'.[19] They have their basis in Chapter VII of the Charter; specifically in Articles 39, 40, 41, and 42, although the Council rarely refers to specific provisions of the Charter in carrying out its function.

5. Enforcement action does not require the consent or cooperation of the State or entity against which it is directed and will by its nature impact upon, restrict, or suspend the rights which States and other subjects of international law normally enjoy under specific treaties and under general international law within the limitations of Article 24 of the Charter. Clearly, sanctions of an economic or diplomatic nature will inevitably limit the rights of States to engage in normal economic and diplomatic relations, while military measures authorized or carried out by the Council will necessarily have an even greater impact upon a State's sovereignty and citizens; this is inherent to the nature of such measures and to the system of collective security as has been built into the Charter.[20] In so far as enforcement action is not of a military character, it is also binding upon all Member States within the United Nations.[21] However, in the absence of any agreements between Member States and the Organization for the provision of armed forces to the UN, the Council is dependent upon the voluntary cooperation of Member States and regional organizations and arrangements in the form of contributing armed

[18] Gill, 'Legal and Some Political Limitations', 72–90. See also Goodrich et al., *Charter of the United Nations*, 205–7.

[19] See, *inter alia*, Simma et al., *The Charter of the United Nations*, Vol. 2, 1294–6; Goodrich et al., *Charter of the United Nations*, 301–17.

[20] Goodrich et al., *Charter of the United Nations*, 290 *et seq.*; Simma et al., *The Charter of the United Nations*, 1310–11 and 1344.

[21] Goodrich et al., *Charter of the United Nations*, 311–12; Simma et al., *The Charter of the United Nations*, 1310–11.

5.02 forces and other military assets and support for the carrying out of any type of military action, including military enforcement action of any nature.[22]

6. Enforcement action, including military enforcement action undertaken or authorized by the Council, differs fundamentally in concept and its objectives from other forms of action undertaken by the Council or any other organ of the UN in that it does not require the consent of the target State or entity, and need not be impartial, reactive, or restricted to self-defence measures.[23] Enforcement operations involving the use of force will, in particular, be directed against a particular State or entity and can include measures of a proactive and offensive nature, including full-scale combat in the air, on land, or at sea, aimed at suppressing a breach of the peace or act of aggression or removing an ongoing threat to peace and security if the situation calls for this according to the Council's determination. Proactive and offensive in this context means that operations can be carried out with the object of destroying or reducing the target State's or entity's political, economic, and military capability to continue to pose a threat to or to otherwise violate international peace and security and impose the will of the Council upon the target State or entity with the object of restoring the situation. Such action by its nature will not be impartial or neutral and can include far-reaching impingements upon the target State's sovereignty, including, in principle, the removal of its government and imposition of a transitional authority if the Council deems this necessary for the restoration of maintenance of international peace and security.[24]

7. Enforcement action, including authorizations to take military action as a response to a particular situation which the Council has deemed as constituting a threat to the peace or as a breach of the peace or act of aggression, can be directed against a State or States or against any other entity the Council has determined to be responsible for the situation. This can include a government or armed group in control of a territory, which may or may not constitute a State, a rebel or insurgent movement, or even a criminal group or organization. A few examples should suffice to illustrate this point: the Council recommended and authorized the use of force against North Korea as its first use of collective measures in the 1950s, imposed sanctions, and authorized their enforcement at sea against the white minority government of Southern Rhodesia in the 1960s. It was far from clear in both these instances whether either North Korea or Southern Rhodesia were 'States' at the time those measures were taken. More recently, the Council has implemented enforcement measures, including, in some cases, the authorization of military action, *inter alia*, against the rebel UNITA movement in Angola, against Bosnian Serb militias in the former Yugoslavia, against the Taliban government of

[22] T. Franck, *Recourse to Force* (Cambridge: Cambridge University Press, 2002), 20 *et seq.*; Simma et al., *The Charter of the United Nations*, 1335–7; Dinstein, *War Aggression*, 310–15.

[23] Simma et al., *The Charter of the United Nations*, 1344, Dinstein, *War Aggression*, 279–89, and D.W. Bowett, *United Nations Forces* (New York: Frederick A. Praeger, 1964), 266–7.

[24] Bowett, *United Nations Forces*, 412–13 and 485. See also Dinstein, *War Aggression*, 283–9, and Gill, 'Legal and Some Political Limitations', 52.

Afghanistan, and against warlords and pirates in Somalia. In short, enforcement action, including military enforcement measures, can be directed against any entity or organized (armed) group in control of territory or even against criminal organizations in addition to being directed at a recognized State whenever the Council deems this necessary in the context of international peace and security.[25] 5.02

While both enforcement operations and peace enforcement operations share certain common characteristics of not requiring the consent of the Host State and not requiring impartiality or restricting the use of force to self-defence, they can differ significantly in their objectives and in the degree, intensity, and duration of the force they are required to employ in order to carry out their respective mandates. 5.03

1. As such, peace enforcement, as referred to here and elsewhere, falls conceptually between enforcement and peacekeeping and other peace operations of an essentially consensual nature which are restricted to the defensive use of force, even if self-defence is sometimes given a broader definition, in principle, if not always in practice, than is usually meant in relation to the term 'defensive force'.[26] (For descriptive analysis of peace operations of a non-enforcement character, see Sections 6.01–6.03.) Enforcement and peace enforcement operations differ from peacekeeping and other peace support operations (referred to in this Handbook as peace operations) in that they share the characteristics of not requiring consent of the parties and the capability, both legally and militarily, of using force proactively and offensively as referred to in the commentary to the previous Section (see para. 6 of the commentary to the previous section). However, peace enforcement differs from enforcement in that it is not designed to impose a 'classic' military solution by engaging a State in hostilities but rather will use or threaten force, sometimes rising to the level of participation in a non-international armed conflict in support of a government when this is necessary to achieve a particular objective or objectives such as disarmament or withdrawal of parties to a conflict, support governmental agencies in the imposition of a stable and peaceful environment, the suppression of unlawful activities and threats to the civilian population by armed groups, or the forceful apprehension of persons and groups suspected of engaging in such

[25] The following Security Council resolutions are pertinent in this respect: SC Res. 80 and 83 (1950), Korea; SC Res. 217 (1965), SC Res. 221 (1966) Rhodesia; SC Res. 1127 (1997) UNITA/Angola; 88, SC Res. 836 (1994), SC Res. 998 (1995) Bosnian Serbs; SC Res. 1267 (1999) Taliban; SC Res. 794 (1992) Somalia, a SC Res. 1851 (2008) piracy off Somali coast and SC Res. 2098 (2013) armed groups in Eastern DRC. These are illustrative and not intended to comprise an exhaustive list of measures aimed at or affecting non-State entities or individuals.

[26] Self-defence in the context of UN peacekeeping operations (referred to in this Handbook as 'peace operations') has evolved over the years from a fairly restrictive notion of self-defence related more to personal or individual self-defence of persons who were reacting to prior illegal use of force to a much broader notion—at least in theory—of movement, protection of UN personnel and installations, and even of civilians in so far as the situation allows. This goes considerably beyond what is normally understood as self-defence within the context of domestic criminal law. See, *inter alia*, Findlay, *The Use of Force*, 87 *et seq.* and Sections 6.08, 24.05, and 24.06.

5.03 activities. This list is meant to be illustrative not exhaustive, but it should assist in distinguishing peace enforcement from enforcement on the one hand, and peacekeeping and other forms of peace support (peacemaking and peacebuilding operations) on the other side of the conceptual scale.[27]

2. Peace enforcement also differs from both enforcement operations and from peace operations in relation to the element of consent. While enforcement operations and peace enforcement operations are both based on Chapter VII of the Charter and consequently do not require consent as a legal condition for their deployment, there are marked differences between them in this respect. Enforcement operations will anticipate and encounter resistance to their entry from the outset of their deployment and will seek to overcome such resistance by offensive force and, as such, consent is militarily as well as legally irrelevant to their presence.[28] Peace enforcement operations, however, while not requiring consent from a strictly legal perspective, will normally have the consent of the government in so far as one exists and will whenever feasible seek and attempt to achieve and maintain consent, or at least acquiescence, from the relevant parties whenever possible and will not normally have to 'fight their way into' their area of deployment and operation as would be the case in relation to a military enforcement operation.[29] Since most peace enforcement operations act in support of a (transitional) government in order to establish a stable environment, the consent of the government can in such situations be presumed and is often referred to in the mandates issued by the Security Council. When that government is engaged in a non-international armed conflict against one or more organized armed groups, the peace enforcement mission will normally not have the consent of the opposing party or parties and may itself become party to that conflict if the material conditions for participation as a party are met and the mandate so authorizes.[30]

3. Other probable differences between enforcement operations and peace enforcement operations would normally include such questions as the nature and objectives of their respective mandates, the relation to a possible host government, the applicability of the humanitarian law of armed conflict (in enforcement operations it will be *ipso facto* fully applicable, while in peace enforcement it will only apply to the extent there is an armed conflict to which the peace enforcement force is party), the composition and size of the forces concerned, and questions related to the command

[27] For a typology of various types of UN (authorized) peace operations ranging from enforcement to classical peacekeeping see in addition to Findlay, *The Use of Force*, 3–7, N.D. White, *Keeping the Peace: The United Nations and the Maintenance of International Peace and Security* (Manchester: Manchester University Press, 1993), 199 *et seq.* The official UN typology can be found in the Secretary General Reports 'An Agenda for Peace' (A/5/277-S/24111) 31 January 1992 and 'Supplement to an Agenda for Peace' (A/50/60-S/1995/1) of 3 January 1995.

[28] See Section 5.01 and accompanying commentary.

[29] Findlay, *The Use of Force*, 376.

[30] The applicability of international humanitarian law to enforcement and peace enforcement operations is dealt with in more detail in sub-Chapter 5.5.

and control of the forces.[31] For example, should forces engaged in a peace enforcement operation become involved in hostilities rising to the level of armed conflict against organized armed opposition by an armed group of insurgents, international humanitarian law of both a conventional and customary nature relating to non-international armed conflict would apply to the conduct of such hostilities and treatment of persons for the duration of the conflict. However, this will depend upon whether the factual conditions for being considered as a party to such a non-international armed conflict are fulfilled and continue to be met. Likewise, if hostilities were confined to a specific region or zone of operations within the State where the operation was being conducted, there would be no need, in principle, to conduct hostilities outside that region, notwithstanding the applicability of humanitarian law throughout the territory of the State where the conflict was in progress. **5.03**

4. By the same token, notwithstanding certain similarities and overlaps between peace enforcement and certain types of more robust peacekeeping and other peace operations, they will differ both conceptually and practically from each other as much as peace enforcement differs from enforcement in relation to most, if not all, of the aspects referred to in the immediately preceding paragraph. For example, a mandate for a peace operation would not necessarily be based upon Chapter VII of the Charter. It would then require the consent of the government of the State where it was deployed and would aim for the consent, or at least acquiescence, of all other parties. As the Force conducting a peace operation would not normally be willing or capable of engaging in sustained high intensity combat, even if forcibly opposed, it would not normally fall within the framework of international humanitarian law other than in the exceptional case it became party to a non-international armed conflict and would normally have a very different force composition and relationship to all relevant parties, unlike either an enforcement operation or peace enforcement operation.[32]

In addition to enforcement and peace enforcement operations as described above in Sections 5.01, 5.02, and 5.03, the Security Council has the power to implement sanctions not involving the use of force, such as, but not limited to the interruption of land, sea and air communications, and/or the selective or comprehensive interruption of trade and commerce in designated goods or services and to authorize the effective implementation and enforcement of such non-military sanctions. To the extent such measures of implementation called for the threat or use of limited force to ensure compliance, they would qualify as military enforcement measures for that specific purpose. Such measures will not be designated as enforcement or peace enforcement operations as described above, in order to avoid possible confusion. **5.04**

[31] See Section 5.10 in relation to command and control issues arising from enforcement operations.
[32] See Chapter 6 in relation to peace operations.

5.04 1. Under Article 41 of the Charter, the Security Council is empowered to take enforcement measures not involving the use of force in conjunction with Article 39 of the Charter whereby a particular situation is deemed by the Council to constitute a threat to or breach of the peace, or an act of aggression. Such non-forceful enforcement measures can include the partial or total interruption of land, air, or maritime communications, the imposition of trade or financial sanctions and so forth. On occasion, the Council has authorized measures involving the use of limited force or coercive action which are specifically related to the enforcement of such embargoes and fall under Chapter VII of the Charter. Such measures which are aimed at the effective enforcement of non-military sanctions can fall within specific types of military operations. Notwithstanding the enforcement nature in a legal sense, they are not designated in this Handbook as enforcement or peace enforcement operations, in order to avoid possible confusion. While falling conceptually broadly within the scope of peace enforcement, they differ from it in that they are restricted to the specific purpose of enforcement of the embargo or interception of communications that the Council has imposed and do not purport to carry out other objectives or tasks normally associated with peace enforcement operations of the type referred to in the previous section.[33]

2. The type of force authorized in the enforcement of trade embargoes is usually related to the interruption of maritime communications and would involve such measures as the use of warning or disabling shots and the carrying out of non-consensual boarding and inspection operations against vessels attempting to violate or suspected of violating the embargo restrictions imposed by the Council. An example of such a specific authorization to ensure compliance with an embargo imposed by the Council under Chapter VII of the Charter was SC Resolution 665 of August 1990 whereby the forces of States with naval units operating in the Persian Gulf/Arabian Sea area were authorized to take measures strictly aimed at ensuring compliance with the maritime embargo against Iraq which had been imposed earlier by the Council. These measures will be dealt with separately in the context of this Handbook (see Sections 18.07 and 20.03). They will not be referred to as enforcement or peace enforcement operations in order to avoid possible confusion.

3. A graphic description and glossary of terms for the different military operations discussed in this Handbook is provided in the Annex.

5.05 **Enforcement operations and peace enforcement operations are taken pursuant to a Security Council determination under Chapter VII of the Charter that there is a threat to international peace and security, or that a breach of international peace or act of aggression has occurred.**

[33] See para. 1 of the commentary to Section 5.03. See also Findlay, *The Use of Force*, 275–381.

1. Enforcement operations of any type are dependent upon a decision of the Council in which force is authorized in relation to a situation which has been deemed to constitute a threat to or a breach of the peace or an act of aggression as referred to previously in Section 5.02.[34] 5.05

In practice, the Council has taken a broad view of what constitutes a threat to the peace to include internal conflicts, large-scale violations of human rights and humanitarian law, the proliferation of weapons of mass destruction, and acts of international terrorism. The Council's authority and discretion within the context of making such determinations can be characterized as being extremely broad and in practice only limited by the Council's ability to reach such a determination and by the Purposes and Principles of the UN Charter. 5.06

1. As stated previously, the Council possesses a very broad mandate to determine that a particular situation poses a threat to international peace or constitutes an act of aggression. These can include large-scale internal conflicts, or breakdowns of authority or violations of human rights or humanitarian law with or without (potential) spill-over effects within a particular region. The Council is not limited in this respect to reacting to situations involving classic cross-border aggression, although such situations would normally rank among the most serious violations and would be most likely to trigger a robust response by the Council.[35]

2. This broad mandate is legally and practically only limited by the Council's ability to reach the necessary majority to reach a decision (under Article 27 of the Charter this requires two-thirds of the Members of the Council voting affirmatively with no negative votes by one of the Permanent Members of the Council),[36] and by the Purposes and Principles of the Charter under Article 24 of the Charter. As stated previously, it would appear to be axiomatic that these would include fundamental rules and principles of international law of a peremptory nature (*jus cogens*), even though there is less than complete agreement as to which rules and principles of international law would be included in this category. Likely examples of such rules in this context would include in any case fundamental rules of human rights and humanitarian law such as the right to not deprive a person arbitrarily of life, freedom from torture or inhumane treatment, the prohibition of deliberately

[34] See paras 4 and 5 of the commentary to Section 5.02. See also Simma et al., *The Charter of the United Nations*, 1294–5.

[35] See paras 3 and 4 of the commentary to Section 5.02. See also Simma et al., *The Charter of the United Nations*, 1277–8.

[36] Specifically Art. 27(3) of the Charter requires the affirmative vote of nine members including the concurring votes of the Permanent Members. For authoritative commentary see Simma et al., *The Charter of the United Nations*, 911 *et seq*. In practice, this has come to mean that an abstention by a Permanent Member on a non-procedural question will not stand in the way of the Council reaching a decision, provided the necessary two-thirds majority votes in favour of the question. A negative vote by a Permanent Member is the 'veto' which precludes a decision being reached.

5.06 attacking civilians not directly participating in hostilities, as such, or the employment of prohibited means and methods of combat and fundamental guarantees of impartial and fair adjudication of persons suspected of violations of international law which form the core of international human rights and humanitarian law.[37] These fundamental rules forming part of the Purposes and Principles apply to decisions and measures taken by the Council, but do not affect its discretionary competence to determine when a situation constitutes a threat or breach of the peace or aggression under Article 39.

5.07 **While the Security Council is empowered under Article 42 of the Charter to take such action by air, sea, or land forces as may be necessary to maintain or restore international peace and security, in the absence of agreements with Member States under Article 43, which were originally intended to provide the Council with independent military capacity, the Council is in fact dependent upon the voluntary participation of Member States to carry out enforcement and peace enforcement operations. The practice of the Council is to authorize such States or international organizations as are willing to participate in a given enforcement or peace enforcement operation with the legal authority to do so by use of the phrase 'all necessary means', or similar terminology, on a case-by-case basis.**

1. As stated previously, in the absence of the special agreement under Article 43 envisaged by the drafters of the Charter, the Council is dependent upon the voluntary cooperation of Member States in the form of the provision of forces necessary to carry out any type of enforcement operation involving the threat or use of force.[38] Nevertheless, while no State is obliged to participate in the carrying out of enforcement measures involving the use of force, all Member States are under an obligation to not engage in any action which would interfere with or obstruct the execution of such measures and are required to comply with any Council decision under Chapter VII of the Charter.[39]

5.08 **The mandate provided by the Council, including the specific authorization to use the necessary force to carry it out, is a legal requirement for the deployment of forces onto a State's territory in the absence of that State's consent and for any use of force going beyond self-defence. While a mandate from the Council authorizing deployment and the use of force will obviate the need for the consent of the State where the operation is conducted, wherever appropriate or feasible,**

[37] See para. 3 of the commentary to Section 5.02.

[38] See para. 5 of the commentary to Section 5.02. See also Simma et al., *The Charter of the United Nations*, 1354–6; Franck, *Recourse to Force*, 22–6, and N. Blokker and N. Schrijver (eds), *The Security Council and the Use of Force* (Leiden: Nijhoff, 2005), 13–14 and 28–9.

[39] See Simma et al., *The Charter of the United Nations*, 1341–4.

such consent will be sought as providing a useful and desirable complement to the Council's authority to act under Chapter VII of the Charter. 5.08

1. Under the Charter and general international law, there are only three legal grounds whereby the forces of one or more States can be deployed onto or operate within the territory of another State. These are:

(a) a mandate of the Council under Chapter VII to carry out enforcement measures;
(b) an act of self-defence (individual or collective) in response to an armed attack or imminent threat of attack against another State's territory, vessels, or aircraft, or citizens in conformity with Article 51 of the Charter and customary international law; and
(c) the consent of the other State's lawful government.

We are concerned with the first of these at present; the other two will be dealt with in subsequent chapters of this Handbook. (See Chapters 6, 8, and 14.) For the differing role of consent in relation to enforcement operations involving sustained full-scale hostilities and peace enforcement operations see para. 2 of the commentary to Section 5.03.

While the Security Council provides the legal authority for enforcement and peace enforcement operations through the provision of a mandate and retains overall political control, the actual conduct of these operations may be delegated to the participating State(s) or international organization. 5.09

Military operations requiring and reaching the level of full-scale hostilities against a State are normally entrusted to a lead nation or nations providing the bulk of the forces employed in the operation. Forces established and controlled by the UN for the conduct of enforcement action have remained an exception. 5.10

1. The question of the provision of a mandate forming the legal basis for any enforcement operation and the question of command and control over the forces engaged in carrying out the mandate are distinct.[40] While only the Council is legally empowered to undertake enforcement action and determine the overall objectives of any military operation undertaken under Chapter VII of the Charter,

[40] The original intent laid down in the Charter was that in cases of military enforcement action mandated by the Council under Art. 42, command and control would be exercised by the Military Staff Committee under Arts 46 and 47 of the Charter. However, the Military Staff Committee has never exercised any command function due to lack of agreement between the Permanent Members, unwillingness on the part of other Member States to put forces at its disposal, and the failure of Art. 43 to be carried out. See Simma et al., *The Charter of the United Nations*, 1366 *et seq.*

5.10 the actual command and control of the operation can be delegated to one or more States, or to a (regional) organization or arrangement operating under the Council's authority and within the terms of the given mandate.

2. Generally speaking, the larger the forces employed and the more ambitious the objectives of the mandated operation are, the more likely it is that actual military command and control will be delegated to one or more of the participating States, or to a (regional) organization or arrangement. While specific command arrangements have differed from operation to operation, this is the general pattern due primarily to the fact that the UN (both the Council and the Secretariat) does not possess the capacity to direct and conduct large-scale sustained combat operations. An additional reason is the reluctance of most Member States to relinquish command over their forces in such situations. However, there is no legal obstacle to prevent the UN carrying out an operation which involved participation in an armed conflict and the UN has in fact elected to do so on at least one recent occasion, to wit, in the Eastern Congo. Moreover, if Member States are willing to provide the necessary troops and equipment, the UN is capable of mounting a peace enforcement operation if the political will to do so and the conditions for doing so are present, although it would still not be capable of conducting an enforcement operation against a State involving full-scale hostilities. The deployment of an intervention brigade to engage various non-state organized armed groups in Eastern Congo is an indication that the UN's position and capacity may be changing with regard to peace enforcement. It remains to be seen whether this operation portends a more proactive role of the UN in peace enforcement than hitherto has been the case.

3. In both of the earlier enforcement operations which involved full-scale hostilities (Korea and Operation Desert Storm), the Council delegated command to a lead nation (the US in both cases) while retaining overall political authority over those operations. In the Libya operation of 2011 it delegated command to NATO. In most peace enforcement operations, with the exception of the Congo operation of the early 1960s, and most notably in the ongoing stabilization operation in Eastern Congo the Council has exercised political control of either a more general or a more specific nature while entrusting the military command to one or more 'lead' nations, or to a (regional) organization or arrangement. For example, in Bosnia following the Dayton Agreement of 1995, and in Kosovo following the NATO aerial campaign of 1999 and subsequent (imposed) consent by the Yugoslav Government to the deployment of UN mandated peace enforcement forces onto those respective territories, political authority was exercised by the UN, while military command was delegated to NATO, which provided the bulk of forces comprising IFOR and KFOR, respectively.[41] In short, the Council can, legally speaking, employ any type of command arrangement it feels is expedient in carrying

[41] See Dinstein, *War Aggression*, 313–214; Findlay, *The Use of Force*, 381.

out its decisions and objectives. In Afghanistan, the Council has provided ISAF with the necessary mandate to carry out operations in cooperation with the Afghan Government, while military command has been exercised first by individual NATO Member States and subsequently by NATO itself.[42] 5.10

In situations where the Security Council has mandated a particular State, group of States, or regional or other organization to carry out an enforcement or peace enforcement operation, it will retain overall authority over and responsibility for the operation, notwithstanding any delegation of command and control which may be decided upon. 5.11

1. Notwithstanding any command arrangement or delegation the Council chooses to employ in consultation and cooperation with the States participating in a specific enforcement operation of any type, it is the Security Council which retains and exercises overall political control over the operation and its objectives. Consequently, Member States or other organizations exercise their command functions on behalf of the Council and under its overall direction.

[42] See the provision of ISAF's mandate in SC Res. 1386 (2001) which has been extended and modified in subsequent resolutions.

5.2 Status of Forces in Enforcement and Peace Enforcement Operations

5.12 **Forces participating in an enforcement or peace enforcement operation enjoy immunity vis-à-vis the Receiving State and any Transit State, as a matter of customary international law. Status-of-forces agreements entered into with any Receiving State(s) or third States may specify the rights and obligations of the forces participating in the operation.**

1. *General.* The term 'status of forces', as used here and throughout all relevant sections of this Handbook, is a term of art referring to matters pertaining to immunity from, and respect for, the law of the Receiving State, Transit States, and any third States. Status-of-forces rules include provisions on jurisdiction, entry and exit modalities, force protection, freedom of movement, weapons and ammunition, communications, host nation support, tax and duty exemptions, and other issues relevant for an unimpeded performance of the particular mission.[1] Regulation of such matters does not affect issues of combatant status under international humanitarian law of regular armed forces engaged in hostilities, neither should it prejudge legal issues of protection of civilians in an armed conflict. The general status of a foreign force is not determined by the specific type of the enforcement operation, peace enforcement operation, or sanction (see Sections 5.01 and 5.04), in which it is involved. It should also be considered that classification of enforcement operations versus peace operations may be difficult, as many missions can transform from a hostile situation to a less hostile one and vice versa. However, in the case of pure enforcement operations as part of an international or non-international armed conflict, international humanitarian law fully applies and this would make the status of participating forces similar to that of forces engaged in self-defence operations (see Chapter 9). While different modes of operation may change very quickly for peacekeepers in a post-conflict situation, their status derives from general principles of international authority and State sovereignty and will remain essentially the same in any situation of enforcement, peace enforcement, and peace support.

2. *Respect for UN Operations.* States participating in operations that are performed under United Nations authority deserve respect for the execution of their mission.[2] They must have unimpeded access to the area of operations. This includes entry by their participating military units and civilian personnel in that area, the use of transport routes, and a general readiness of the Receiving State to arrange for support. It does not exclude, however, regulations of the Receiving State concerning

[1] See D. Fleck (ed.), *The Handbook of The Law of Visiting Forces* (Oxford: Oxford University Press, 2001).

[2] See Fleck, 'The Legal Status of Personnel Involved in United Nations Peace Operations', 95 (891/892) *IRRC* (2013), 613–36.

their right of carrying arms, use of communications, wearing of uniforms, acceptance of permits and licences for vehicles and aircraft, use of identity cards, or even subjection to tax and customs procedures of the State in which they are located. Where there are no specific rules regulating the conditions of support, all goods and services may be charged by the State rendering such support. The terms and conditions of support by the Receiving State, Transit States, and any third States remain a matter of negotiation. Third States may even deny transit, a position which was taken by Iran, Jordan, and some other States during Desert Storm which was respected by the Coalition without any adverse comment from either States participating in this enforcement operation or the UN. Yet all UN Member States are under an obligation not to interfere with operations authorized by the Security Council, irrespective whether they are serving enforcement, peace enforcement, or peace support purposes. 5.12

3. *Immunity under Customary Law.* Under customary international law military and civilian personnel participating in (peace) enforcement operations have a special legal status. As organs of their Sending State they are protected by the sovereign immunity of the latter and accordingly they enjoy privileges and immunities in the Receiving State and any Transit State. Two types of immunity are to be considered in this context: immunity *ratione personae* (which is normally limited to Heads of State, Heads of Government, and Ministers of Foreign Affairs during their term of office) and immunity *ratione materiae.* Both types of immunity have functional elements in common, since the protection afforded to persons who enjoy immunity is ultimately granted to these persons by virtue of the functions or tasks that each of them performs. Yet it is mostly in relation to immunity *ratione materiae* that the functional nature of immunity is referred to. The application of immunity *ratione materiae* to military forces of a foreign State is generally recognized. It ensures an unimpeded cooperation between sovereign States in protecting the official functions of the personnel involved.

While arguments against unlimited applications of immunity rules might be derived from international human rights law and international criminal law,[3] the immunity of organs of a Sending State in the Receiving State may not be disregarded without jeopardizing the particular mission itself. It must also be considered that the purpose of privileges and immunities is not to benefit individuals in private affairs but rather to ensure an unimpeded performance of their official functions. In the absence of full diplomatic status such personnel thus have 'functional immunity' and they may rely on it in the performance of their operations in the Receiving State and any Transit State. Unless agreed otherwise and stated in explicit treaty provisions, the principle of immunity applies to members of

[3] R. van Alebeek, *Immunities of States and Their Officials in International Criminal Law and International Human Rights Law* (Oxford: Oxford University Press, 2008); H. Fox and Ph. Webb, *The Law of State Immunity*, 3rd edn (Oxford: Oxford University Press, 2013); A. Peters, E. Lagrange, S. Oeter, and C. Tomuschat (eds), *Immunities in the Age of Global Constitutionalism* (The Hague, Brill/Nijhoff, 2014).

5.12 foreign armed forces. This principle is fully accepted in State practice and legal doctrine. There is consistent practice of Receiving States respecting the immunity of Sending States forces for acts performed in an official capacity. Sinclair has provided abundant material which reveals that there is no single criminal case where a Receiving State had claimed criminal jurisdiction over a member of visiting forces outside agreed treaty provisions.[4] Brownlie has observed that '[r]ecent writers emphasize that there is a trend in the practice of states towards [a] restrictive doctrine of immunity but avoid firm and precise prescriptions as to the present state of the law'.[5] In no case so far has a member of a foreign visiting force been prosecuted by the courts of a Receiving State unless the exercise of jurisdiction was specifically accorded in an agreement with the Sending State.[6]

The immunity of members of foreign armed forces is the result of a balance between the law of the flag and host nation law. This implies two general restrictions: the requirement to have immunity for acts *iure imperii* does not extend to acts of private law character *iure gestionis*, and the immunity is limited to procedural matters. Hence a foreign force may not be considered free to disregard the constitutional, penal, or other law of a Receiving State, but the latter is bound not to exercise jurisdiction where this would affect the performance of official duties of the foreign force.[7]

The status of a force (*jus in praesentia*) does not depend upon any permission granted by a Receiving State or Transit State (*jus ad praesentiam*). As State immunity follows from State sovereignty, it is not 'granted' by any other State, but exists per se. Hence forces, State aircraft, and warships present in a foreign country share the immunity status of their flag State even in the absence of any agreement with the Host State (see also Sections 19.11 and 20.11). Such agreement may, however, confirm the immunity status and also provide limits for it, which would then apply by mutual consent. The issue whether the immunity status of foreign forces might be denied in extreme situations with the argument that such forces had conducted unlawful operations unauthorized by the 'Host' State,[8] is more difficult

[4] I. Sinclair, 'The Law of Sovereign Immunity: Recent Developments', Hague Academy of International Law (ed.), 162 *Collected Courses* (1980), 113–284, at 216–17.

[5] I. Brownlie, *Principles of Public International Law*, 5th edn (Oxford: Oxford University Press, 1998), 325–48, and 371–83.

[6] Fleck, 'Are Foreign Military Personnel Exempt from International Criminal Jurisdiction under Status of Forces Agreements?', 1 *Journal of International Criminal Justice* (2003), 651–70.

[7] See Fleck (ed.), *Handbook of The Law of Visiting Forces*, 3–6.

[8] There is neither accepted State practice nor case law on this issue. The *Rainbow Warrior* dispute between France and New Zealand, often referred to in this context, is not fully relevant here, as it is comprised partly of mediation and partly of arbitration. The underlying facts are the prosecution in New Zealand of two French military officers, agents of the French Directorate General of External Security (DGSE) for acts committed in covert action by order of the French Government, which later offered its apologies for these acts and readiness to pay compensation to New Zealand for the damage suffered, but also declared that criminal prosecution of its two officials in New Zealand was not justified. The resulting custody of both officers in French Polynesia was based on a bilateral agreement which did, however, not imply any recognition or acceptance of New Zealand's exercise of jurisdiction in this case; see *Rainbow Warrior, Ruling of 6 July 1986 by the Secretary-General of the United Nations, Reports of*

to solve. Unlawful operations, if committed on behalf of a Sending State or as part of an official mission, may provoke disputable reactions. Yet in peace operations the situation is quite different: peacekeepers are operating with the consent of the Receiving State, and that consent has been formally notified or declared by the Security Council under Chapter VII with binding force for the Receiving State. For armed forces participating in self-defence operations amounting to an armed conflict international humanitarian law applies (see Chapter 9). **5.12**

Immunity does not imply impunity for any crimes or any exclusion of claims in the event of wrongful acts committed by members of a mission: Should a member of a foreign armed force be suspected of having committed a crime, he or she may be indicted before a competent national court of his or her Sending State or an international court exercising jurisdiction over the case. While immunity may be invoked in criminal procedures conducted in a foreign State, this would not apply to proceedings before the International Criminal Court in so far as it had jurisdiction on genocide, crimes against humanity, war crimes, or the crime of aggression on the basis of its Statute. Article 27 of the Rome Statute expressly provides that official capacity shall not exempt a person from criminal responsibility and immunities shall not bar the Court from exercising its jurisdiction. Efforts towards a removal of immunity from proceedings in national courts as one way by which effective reparation for the commission of international crimes—i.e. serious crimes under international law such as genocide, crimes against humanity, torture, and war crimes—may be achieved, have led to the adoption by the *Institut de Droit International* of a resolution[9] which confirms that immunities are conferred to ensure an orderly allocation and exercise of jurisdiction in accordance with international law, to respect the sovereign equality of States, and to permit the effective performance of the functions of persons who act on behalf of States. The Resolution stipulates that immunities should not constitute an obstacle to the appropriate reparation to which victims of international crimes are entitled. It further stipulates that States should consider waiving immunity where international crimes are allegedly committed by their agents. As to desired limitations of immunities, however, the adopted text does not go further than stipulating that no immunity from jurisdiction 'other than personal immunity in accordance with international law' applies with regard to international crimes, a statement that would hardly affect existing rules on functional immunity of State organs. The Resolution confirms that the provisions proposed are without prejudice to the issue whether and when a State enjoys immunity from jurisdiction before the national courts of another State in civil proceedings relating to an international crime committed by an agent of the former State. The Resolution also refrains from stipulating limitations of immunity

International Arbitral Awards (*RIAA*) Vol. xix, pp. 199–221; Decision of the Arbitral Tribunal (30 April 1990), *RIAA*, Vol. xx, pp. 215–84; C. Hoss and J. Morgan-Foster, 'The Rainbow Warrior', *MPEPIL*.

[9] *Institut de Droit International*, Session de Naples (10 September 2009): International Crimes and Immunities from jurisdiction of States and their agents, available at <http://www.idi-iil.org/idiE/resolutionsE/2009_naples_01_en.pdf>.

5.12 of international organizations. Even under these principles, Receiving States and Transit States will not be in a position to prosecute members of foreign visiting forces. Such action would be for Sending States to take. As far as settlement of claims is concerned, these should be settled in negotiations with the United Nations and/or the Sending State, and in contentious cases they may be brought to competent national courts of the Sending State (see Chapter 30 'International Responsibility and Military Operations').

4. *Sources for Immunity in Conventional Law.* There are various treaty provisions regulating the immunities of personnel participating in UN operations without, however, referring to the special requirements of enforcement operations or peace enforcement operations:

(a) For representatives of the Members of the United Nations and officials of the Organization Article 105(2) of the UN Charter stipulates that they shall 'enjoy such privileges and immunities as are necessary for the independent exercise of their functions in connection with the Organization'.

(b) UN representatives serving at a specific and temporary mission including military observers and members of UN peace missions are protected under Article VI of the 1946 UN Convention on the Privileges and Immunities of the United Nations. The latter provision calls for special protection of UN officials[10] as well as of 'experts on missions for the United Nations',[11] a formula that has been used by States to also describe the status of peacekeepers,[12] even if this has not officially been confirmed by the United Nations.[13] In 1989 the ICJ noted without objections that experts on mission within the meaning of Article VI of the 1946 Convention participated 'in certain peacekeeping forces, technical assistance

[10] On the application of this provision to UN personnel participating in peace operations see A.J. Miller, 'Privileges and Immunities of United Nations Officials', *International Organizations Law Review* (2007), 169–257.

[11] For details concerning the notion of experts on mission see A.J. Miller, 'United Nations Experts on Mission and their Privileges and Immunities', *International Organizations Law Review* (2007), 11–56.

[12] See e.g. M. Gerster and D. Rotenberg, 'Art. 105, 29' in B. Simma (ed.), *The Charter of the United Nations. A Commentary*, 3rd edn (Oxford: Oxford University Press, 2012); S.J. Lepper, 'The Legal Status of Military Personnel in United Nations Peace Operations. One Delegate's Analysis', 18 *Houston Journal of International Law* (1995–96), 359–464, at 365–9; Fleck, 'Securing Status and Protection of Peacekeepers', in R. Arnold and G.-J.A. Knoops (eds), *Practice and Policies of Modern Peace Support Operations Under International Law* (Ardsley, NY: Transnational Publishers, 2006), 141–56, at 146.

[13] See Regulations Governing the Status, Basic Rights and Duties of Officials other than Secretariat Officials and Experts on Mission, adopted as UN GA Res. 56/280 of 27 March 2002, promulgated with commentary as Secretary General's Bulletin ST/SGB/2002/9 of 18 June 2002. Personnel participating in peace operations are not expressly referred to in this document. However, a study prepared by the Secretariat for the International Law Commission on *The Practice of the United Nations, the Specialized Agencies and the International Atomic Energy Agency concerning their Status, Privileges and Immunities*, UN Doc. A/CN.4/L.118 and Add. 1, 1967 Yearbook of the International Law Commission Vol. II, Sales no. E.86.V.9, 284–5 (para. 341) noted that, by the mid-1960s, it was clearly established that, in peacekeeping missions, military observers and officers serving as part of the Force Commander's Headquarters staff were classified by status-of-forces agreements as experts on mission.

work, and a multitude of other activities'.[14] There are no specific examples for peace enforcement operations carried out by the UN itself, where the applicability of the 1946 Convention would have been confirmed. The Security Council has for a long time refrained from addressing status issues in its resolutions, although these are relevant for any military deployment and have practical consequences for Receiving States.[15] Hence the status of personnel engaged in enforcement, peace enforcement, and peace operations generally derives from customary law. As will be discussed later,[16] ONUC took place in an era before doctrine and practice relating to peace missions had fully developed. It remains an isolated case of the UN engaging in peace enforcement instead of leaving this task to be performed by an authorized regional arrangement or group of States. The United Nations Protection Force (UNPROFOR) was an example of a peace mission which received additional tasks and responsibilities of a peace enforcement nature for which it was not equipped or which it was not capable of carrying out and for which until the very end phase there was no political will on the part of the participating States to engage in enforcement type operations involving the risk of direct confrontation or the use of offensive force. While the 1946 Convention applies to personnel participating in a peace enforcement operation conducted by the UN, this is not necessarily the case for peace enforcement operations conducted by a group of States authorized under Article 48(2) of the Charter, such as IFOR, SFOR, KFOR, or ISAF, much less to an enforcement operation like Desert Storm or the Korean conflict. In any case, forces acting under a UN mandate must be treated differently from forces performing exclusively national missions. 5.12

(c) Under the 1994 UN Convention on the Safety of United Nations and Associated Personnel States parties shall take appropriate measures to ensure the safety and security of personnel engaged in United Nations operations. The Convention entered into force on 15 January 1999 and by now has 91 parties,[17] many of them troop contributors to UN peace enforcement and peace operations. Its 2005 Optional Protocol expands the scope of legal protection. But both instruments regrettably miss their main objective to a large extent: so far hardly any States that have become Receiver States of a peace enforcement or peace operation on their territory are parties to the Convention, let alone the Optional Protocol.[18] There are also unfortunate limits to the Convention's scope of application: pursuant to Article 2(1) the Convention applies to UN operations which are defined in Article 1(c) as

[14] ICJ, Applicability of Article VI, Section 22 of the Convention on the Privileges and Immunities of the UN, Advisory Opinion of 15 December 1989 [Mazilu], ICJ Reports, 1989, 177, at 193–4 (para. 48).

[15] More recently, this practice was changed, to decide that the Model Status-of-Forces Agreement for Peacekeeping Operations (UN Model SOFA) shall apply provisionally, pending the conclusion of a specific SOFA, see Section 6.06, commentary para. 3.

[16] See para. 5 below.

[17] See <https://treaties.un.org/Pages/ViewDetails.aspx?src=IND&mtdsg_no=XVIII-8&chapter=18&lang=en>.

[18] Of the 16 current operations listed by DPKO <http://www.un.org/en/peacekeeping/operations/current.shtml>, no more than five (Côte d'Ivoire, Cyprus, Liberia, Lebanon, and Mali) are parties to the Convention. Haiti had signed it in 1994, but did not ratify.

5.12 operations 'conducted under United Nations authority and control'. Operations authorized by the United Nations Security Council but operated under the command and control of regional organizations or Sending States, a situation that quite frequently occurs in practice, regrettably remained out of the focus of negotiations. Furthermore, Article 2(2) of the Convention expressly provides that:

> [it] shall not apply to a United Nations operation authorized by the Security Council as an enforcement action under Chapter VII of the Charter of the United Nations in which any of the personnel are engaged as combatants against organized armed forces and to which the law of international armed conflict applies.

It is unlikely that the drafters of the Convention intended it not to be applicable in any operation authorized by the Security Council but operated under the command and control of Sending States. Neither should it be assumed that application of the 1994 Convention, if it is really excluded in any case of enforcement operation, should also cease in a peace enforcement operation as soon as there was any fighting, however low-level. Such interpretation would, indeed, reduce the scope of the Convention to almost nothing.[19] Yet the text itself stands against any broader interpretation. Thus the Convention regrettably leaves room for misconceptions with respect to safety and security of United Nations operations in practice. For enforcement and peace enforcement missions and even all other forms of robust peacekeeping the Convention fails to make a clear difference between parties to an armed conflict and forces engaged in the maintenance or restoration of peace and security. While it would not be acceptable to interpret the Convention in a manner limiting the role and protection of personnel engaged in such missions, its provisions should be clarified to underline that UN mandates must be respected and supported without any exception.[20]

(d) The International Law Commission (ILC) has included the topic 'Immunity of State officials from foreign criminal jurisdiction' in its programme of work, which is still in progress. Three draft articles, together with commentaries thereto were adopted at its sixty-sixth session in 2014, confirming, *inter alia*, that 'State officials acting as such enjoy immunity *ratione materiae* from the exercise of foreign criminal jurisdiction'[21] and that '"State official" means any individual who represents the State or who exercises State functions'.[22] It remains to be seen whether and to what extent the ILC will specifically deal with the situation of members of the armed forces as State officials.

[19] See C. Greenwood in Fleck (ed.), *The Handbook of International Humanitarian Law,* 2nd edn (Oxford: Oxford University Press, 2008), Section 208, para. 4.

[20] See E.T. Bloom, 'Protecting Peacekeepers: The Convention on the Safety of United Nations and Associated Personnel', 89 *AJIL* (1995), 621–31; A. Bouvier, '"Convention on the Safety of United Nations and Associated Personnel": Presentation and Analysis', 309 *IRRC* (1995), 638–66; Fleck, 'The Legal Status of Personnel Involved', 621–9.

[21] Draft article 5 (Persons enjoying immunity *ratione materiae*), Official Records of the General Assembly, Sixty-ninth Session, Supplement no. 10 (A/69/10), Chapter IX, 236–7.

[22] Draft article 2 (Definitions), sub-paragraph (e), Official Records of the General Assembly, Sixty-ninth Session, Supplement no. 10 (A/69/10), Chapter IX, 231–6.

5. *United Nations Practice*. In many peace enforcement operations security and safety of personnel involved was severely challenged by States and armed opposition groups. The Security Council was not, and is not today, always in a position to respond to such challenges by taking action under Chapter VII. As expressed in the guidelines issued by Secretary General Kurt Waldheim for UNEF II, peacekeeping operations were first based on principles of consent and non-use of force except in self-defence.[23] An early exception was the UN Congo Operation (1960–4) when the Security Council authorized ONUC to take 'all appropriate measures to prevent the occurrence of civil war in the Congo, including . . . the use of force, if necessary, in the last resort'.[24] Such strong reaction has still not become general practice today. In the Croatian war of independence (1992–5), when UN Protected Areas (UNPAs) were attacked by the Croatian Army, the Security Council, this time verbally acting under Chapter VII, used more ambiguous language. It authorized UNPROFOR, 'in carrying out its mandate . . . , acting in self-defence, to take the necessary measures, including the use of force, to ensure its security and its freedom of movement'.[25] Rather than resorting to clear military sanctions against those who deliberately attacked UN forces, UNPROFOR, while numbering nearly 40,000 troops, 'remained configured for peacekeeping: lightly equipped, widely dispersed, its logistic support vulnerable, with troop contributors manifestly unwilling to let their contingents be drawn into fighting'.[26] Any use of force was limited to self-defence, thus accepting an armed conflict type situation in which UN forces were vested with no other rights than those of the warring parties. Mission defence and enforcement activities were not part of the mandate. Several years later, the Brahimi Report, providing an independent review and recommendations for reform of UN peace operations including peace enforcement operations, pleaded for clear, credible, and achievable mandates based on a preliminary site survey in the prospective mission area and carried out with robust rules of engagement against those who renege on their commitments to a peace accord or otherwise seek to undermine it by violence, thus ensuring unity of effort under a clear chain of command.[27] While these recommendations have strongly influenced current doctrine[28] **5.12**

[23] UN Doc. 42/22.10.73 (26 October 1973), para. 3.

[24] SC Res. 161 A (1961) of 21 February 1961, para. 1.

[25] SC Res. 871 (1993) of 4 October 1993, para. 9.

[26] M. Berdal, 'The Security Council and Peacekeeping', in V. Lowe, A. Roberts, J. Welsh, and D. Zaum, *The United Nations Security Council and War. The Evolution of Thought and Practice since 1945* (Oxford: Oxford University Press, 2008), 175–204, at 194.

[27] *Report of the Panel on United Nations Peace Operations* (Brahimi Report, October 2000), UN Doc. A/55/305 – S/2000/809, <http://www.un.org/documents/ga/docs/55/a55305.pdf>, Chapter II.

[28] See *United Nations Peacekeeping Operations: Principles and Guidelines*: DPKO International Publications, UN Secretariat, March 2008, <http://www.un.org/en/peacekeeping/operations/principles.shtml>, at 79; The Secretary General, Safety and Security of Humanitarian Personnel and Protection of United Nations Personnel, delivered to the General Assembly, UN Doc. A/60/223 (12 August 2005), <http://www.un.org/News/Press/docs/2005/ga10420.doc.htm>; Report of the Secretary General on

5.12 and practice,[29] problems of security and safety of personnel involved in United Nations operations remain a continuing challenge to the success of their mission.

6. *Practice in Missions Not Under UN Command and Control.* For peace enforcement operations conducted outside the chain of command of the United Nations, such as the larger operations in former Yugoslavia, Afghanistan, and Chad, States have preferred to set up clear regulations rather than applying general principles.[30] This may have been influenced by the normal practice within NATO, to conclude status-of-forces agreements (SOFAs) for peacetime deployments. For the purposes of the EU mission model SOFAs and SOMAs (status-of-mission agreements) have been developed.[31]

7. *The Situation in Afghanistan since 2001.* While the conflict in Afghanistan which has persisted in various forms since 1979 is significant for the development of Security Council policy,[32] it also provides distinct examples of specific status regulations for the three very different forms of international presence in the country since 2001.

Strengthened and Unified Security Management System for the United Nations, delivered to the General Assembly, UN Doc. A/59/365 (11 October 2004); Report of the Secretary General on Strengthening the Security and Safety of United Nations Operations, Staff and Premises, delivered to the General Assembly, UN Doc. A/58/756 (5 April 2004); United Nations, Peacekeeping Best Practice Unit, Handbook on United Nations Multidimensional Peacekeeping Operations (December 2003), <http://pbpu.unlb.org/Pbps/library/Handbook%20on%20UN%20PKOs.pdf>; Report of the Independent Panel on Safety and Security of UN Personnel in Iraq (20 October 2003), <http://www.un.org/News/dh/iraq/safety-security-un-personnel-iraq.pdf>.

[29] See e.g. the Intervention Brigade in the Democratic Republic of the Congo, which is mandated under SC Res. 2098, Preamble, para. 9, op. paras 12–16, to protect civilians, neutralize armed groups, monitor the implementation of the arms embargo and provide support to national and international judicial processes, without, however, deviating from the fundamental principles of consent of the Host State, impartiality, and non-use of force except in self-defence or defence of the mandate.

[30] See the two similar SOFAs for SFOR, concluded between the North Atlantic Treaty Organization (NATO) on the one side and the Republic of Croatia and the Republic of Bosnia and Herzegovina on the other side, Dayton Accords, Appendix B to Annex 1-A (23 November 1955), 35 *ILM* 1 (1996), 102; Military Technical Agreement between the International Security Force ('KFOR') and the Government of the Federal Republic of Yugoslavia and the Republic of Serbia (4 June 1999), UNMIK/KFOR Joint Declaration (17 August 2000) and UNMIK Regulation no. 2000/47 On the Status, Privileges and Immunities of KFOR and UNMIK and their Personnel in Kosovo (18 August 2000), all reprinted in Fleck (ed.), *Handbook of The Law of Visiting Forces*, Annexes D and E. The military bridging operation EUFOR Tchad/RCA in eastern Chad and the north-east of the Central African Republic was launched on 28 January 2008 in accordance with the mandate set out in SC Res. 1778 (2007). The SOFA with the Central African Republic was not yet ready, but the Central African Republic has made a unilateral declaration on status of EU-led forces, to cover the interim. The SOFA with Tchad was signed on 26 March 2008. The Operation came to an end in March 2009.

[31] Draft Model Agreement on the status of the European Union-led forces between the European Union and a Host State, 11894/07 (20 July 2007) and Corr. 1 (5 September 2007), <http://register.consilium.europa.eu/pdf/en/07/st11/st11894.en07.pdf>.
Draft Model Agreement on the Status of the European Union Civilian Crisis Management Mission in a Host State (SOMA), 17141/08 (15 December 2008), <http://register.consilium.europa.eu/pdf/en/08/st17/st17141.en08.pdf>.

[32] For a critical review of this practice see e.g. G. Dorronsoro, 'The Security Council and the Afghan Conflict', in V. Lowe, A. Roberts, J. Welsh, and D. Zaum (eds), *The United Nations Security Council and War. The Evolution of Thought and Practice since 1945* (Oxford: Oxford University Press, 2008), 452–65.

These examples may well illustrate similarities in the status of peace enforcement operations, peace operations, and even self-defence operations: **5.12**

(a) The International Security Assistance Force (ISAF) was tasked in December 2001 'to assist the Afghan Interim Authority in the maintenance of security in Kabul and its surrounding areas, so that the Afghan Interim Authority as well as the personnel of the United Nations can operate in a secure environment'.[33] Its area of operations was gradually expanded and the status of participating personnel specified in a Military Technical Agreement confirming full immunity of ISAF personnel in Afghanistan.[34]

(b) The United Nations Assistance Mission in Afghanistan (UNAMA), mandated to support the government in improving governance and the rule of law and fight corruption, as well as to facilitate the delivery of humanitarian assistance,[35] is a non-military political mission, comparable to other UN presences in Afghanistan.[36] UNAMA is administered by the Department of Peacekeeping Operations (DPKO) and has eight regional offices and 12 provincial offices in the country. The status of UNAMA personnel, who also have the right to investigate human rights violations and, where necessary, recommend corrective action,[37] follows general rules for privileges and immunities of UN missions (see earlier, paragraph 4, and later, sub-Chapter 6.2).

(c) For the US-led Operation 'Enduring Freedom', which was operating in Afghanistan on a mandate recognized by the Security Council,[38] to address the threat to the security and stability of Afghanistan posed by the Taliban, al Qaeda, other extremist groups, and criminal activities, an agreement between the US and Afghan Governments applies, according military and civilian personnel of the US Department of Defense present in Afghanistan 'a status equivalent to that accorded to the administrative and technical staff' of the US Embassy under the Vienna Convention on Diplomatic Relations of 1961.[39] There are no specific

[33] SC Res. 1386 (2001), para. 1.

[34] Military Technical Agreement Between the International Security Assistance Force (ISAF) and the Interim Administration of Afghanistan (4 January 2002), <http://www.operations.mod.uk/fingal/isafmta.pdf>, Annex A. See also Draft Technical Agreement Between the Government of Afghanistan and the North Atlantic Treaty Organization as a Framework to Improve Methods and Procedures for the Prosecution of the Global War on Terrorism to Ensure Our Joint Success (10 January 2009), <http://thecable.foreignpolicy.com/posts/2009/02/24/afghanistan_seeking_sofa _lite#sofa_docs>.

[35] See Agreement on Provisional Arrangements in Afghanistan Pending the Re-establishment of Permanent Government Institutions (Bonn Agreement) of 5 December 2001, Annex II; SC Res. 1662 (2006), 1746 (2007), 1776 (2007), 1806 (2008), 1817 (2008), 1833 (2008), and 1868 (2009).

[36] UN Good Offices Mission in Afghanistan and Pakistan (UNGOMAP) from 1988–90, UN Special Mission to Afghanistan (UNSMA, former OSGA) from 1994–2000, UN Office for the Coordination of Humanitarian and Economic Assistance Programmes in Afghanistan (UNOCA) from 1988, with revised mandate restricted to humanitarian assistance (UNOCHA) since 1993.

[37] Agreement on Provisional Arrangements in Afghanistan Pending the Re-establishment of Permanent Government Institutions (Bonn Agreement) of 5 December 2001, Annex II, para. 6.

[38] See SC Res. 1746 (2007), para. 25.

[39] T.I.A.S. Exchange of Notes 26 September and 12 December 2002 and 28 May 2003, entered into force on 28 May 2003; see R.C. Mason, CRS Report for Congress, *Status of Forces Agreement*

5.12 accords relating to the status of non-US personnel participating in Operation 'Enduring Freedom'. For details see Chapter 9 'Status of Forces in Self-Defence Operations'.

(d) For the NATO-led operation following ISAF after 2014, a status-of-forces agreement was signed in Kabul on 30 September 2014 and ratified by the Afghan Parliament on 27 November 2014. It again confirms that members of the force and members of the civilian component are under the exclusive jurisdiction of the State of which the person is a national, while Afghanistan maintains the right to exercise jurisdiction over NATO Contractors and NATO Contractor Employees.[40]

8. *The Special Case of Iraq 2003–2010.* The legal significance of the armed conflict in Iraq in 2003 is not limited to the *jus ad bellum* and the *jus in bello*;[41] important post-conflict developments have opened new issues also on the law of visiting forces and challenged discussions on its further development:[42]

(a) *The presence of coalition forces.* The Security Council explicitly recognized the presence of the United States and the United Kingdom as Occupying Powers under unified command in Iraq,[43] supporting at the same time the formation, by the people of Iraq, with the help of the Occupying Powers and working with the Special Representative of the Secretary General, of Iraqi interim administration as a transitional administration run by Iraqis.[44] The Security Council has thus modified obligations Occupying Powers generally have to respect the laws in force.[45] Authorizing the deployment of a Multinational Force (MNF) in Iraq,[46] it determined that the temporary nature of the exercise by the Coalition Provisional Authority of the specific responsibilities, authorities, and obligations under applicable international law will cease when an internationally recognized, representative government established by the people of Iraq is sworn in and assumes the responsibilities of the Authority.[47] On 8 June 2004 the Security Council endorsed the formation of a sovereign Interim Government of Iraq, as presented on 1 June 2004, and determined that by 30 June 2004 the occupation would end and the Coalition

(SOFA): What Is It, and How Might One Be Utilized In Iraq? (16 June 2008), <http://www.fas.org/sgp/crs/natsec/RL34568.pdf>, 8.

[40] Agreement between the North Atlantic Treaty Organization and the Islamic Republic of Afghanistan on the Status of NATO Forces and NATO personnel conducting mutually agreed NATO-led activities in Afghanistan of 30 September 2014, <http://www.nato.int/cps/en/natohq/official_texts_116072.htm?selectedLocale=en>, Art. 11.

[41] See e.g. P. Shiner and A. Williams (eds), *The Iraq War and International Law* (Oxford and Portland, Oregon: Hart Publishing, 2008).

[42] See M.J. Matheson, 'Status of Forces Agreements and UN Mandates: What Authorities and Protections Do They Provide to US Personnel?' (Statement before the House of Representatives Committee on Foreign Affairs Subcommittee on International Organizations, Human Rights, and Oversight, 28 February 2008), <http://psm.du.edu/media/documents/congressional_comm/house_foreign_affairs/us_house_foreign_affairs_hearing_feb_28_2008.pdf>.

[43] SC Res. 1483 (2003), Preamble, para. 13.

[44] Ibid. operative para. 9.

[45] See Art. 43 HagueReg and Art. 64 GC IV.

[46] SC Res. 1511 (2003), para. 13.

[47] Ibid. para. 1.

Provisional Authority would cease to exist, and that Iraq would reassert its full **5.12** sovereignty.[48] At the same time the Security Council, noting the request of the incoming Interim Government for a continued presence of the Multinational Force in Iraq, reaffirmed the authority of the Multinational Force under unified command, as specified in the letters addressed to the President of the Security Council by the Prime Minister of the Interim Government of Iraq Dr Ayad Allawi and United States Secretary of State Colin L. Powell.[49] The rights and obligations of any Sending State were defined in SC Resolution 1546 (2004) which welcomed and approved arrangements being put in place to establish a security partnership between the Government of Iraq and the Multinational Force.[50] The status of the MNF is regulated in accordance with its task to contribute to the maintenance of security in Iraq, to protect its territory, and to help the Iraqi people to complete the political transition. As stated in Secretary Powell's letter and confirmed by SC Resolution 1546 (2004), the MNF and its personnel enjoy a 'status that they need to accomplish their mission, and in which the contributing states have responsibility for exercising jurisdiction over their personnel and which will ensure arrangements for, and use of assets by, the MNF'.[51] The Resolution not only excludes any exercise of jurisdiction over personnel of the MNF by the Receiving State, but also by any third State. Resolution 1546 (2004) thus provides for a setting that is customary for peacekeeping and peace enforcement operations. The status provisions enshrined in SC Resolution 1546 (2004) are part of an established practice for peacekeeping and peace enforcement operations. While exclusive jurisdiction of the particular Sending State does not preclude a close cooperation with the competent authorities of other States involved, with a view to ensure an effective investigation and provide for a convincing settlement under the rule of law including reparation of any wrongful act, criminal jurisdiction of the Receiving State and any third State is effectively excluded by these arrangements. In the absence of a specific SOFA, jurisdiction on members of the MNF is regulated by customary international law, as applicable under the framework of the Resolution. As a result of difficult negotiations in which also a model on sharing jurisdiction was worked out,[52] a SOFA was signed on 17 November 2008[53] along with a Strategic Framework Agreement. Yet parliamentary approval in Iraq was delayed on the issue of legal immunity for US

[48] SC Res. 1546 (2004), paras 1 and 2.

[49] Ibid. paras 9 to 14, and the letters by Prime Minister Dr Ayad Allawi and Secretary of State Colin L. Powell annexed to this resolution.

[50] Ibid. para. 11.

[51] Ibid. Secretary Powell's letter, para. 6.

[52] See H. Fürtig, 'Das "Status of Forces Agreement" zwischen den USA und Irak: kein bequemes SOFA', Nr. 10/2008 *GIGA* Focus *Nahost*, 1–8, <http://www.giga-hamburg.de/dl/download.php?d=/content/publikationen/pdf/gf_nahost_0810.pdf>; see also T.A. Rush, 'Don't Call It a SOFA! An Overview of the New US-Iraq Security Agreement', 34 *Army Lawyer* (May 2009), 34–60.

[53] Agreement between the United States of America and the Republic of Iraq on the Withdrawal of United States Forces from Iraq and the Organization of Their Activities during their Temporary Presence in Iraq of 17 November 2008, <http://www.cfr.org/publication/17880>.

5.12 troops and dates for a full withdrawal.[54] Consequently, the Mission was withdrawn from Iraq on 31 December 2011 when its mandate expired and agreement on a SOFA could not be reached. As of December 2014, a new Iraqi request to NATO for defence capacity building support is being reviewed by the North Atlantic Council.

(b) *UN civilian presence in Iraq.* To facilitate the political process in Iraq in a manner as inclusive and transparent as possible, the Council established the United Nations Assistance Mission for Iraq (UNAMI),[55] a civilian mission which was based on the existing UN presence in the country for the 'oil-for-food' programme,[56] and extended until the end of 2008.[57] Even when UNAMI was closed, the Council affirmed that the United Nations should continue to play a leading role in supporting the efforts of the Iraqi Government to strengthen institutions for representative government, promote political dialogue and national reconciliation, engage neighbouring countries, assist vulnerable groups, including refugees and internally displaced persons, and promote the protection of human rights and judicial and legal reform,[58] activities that include export controls,[59] and the exercise of economic sanctions,[60] and would require an extended presence of UN officials and experts in the country.

9. *Conclusion.* Adequate solutions for existing problems of personnel involved in enforcement and peace enforcement operations must be sought in clear and unequivocal determinations of their status, efficient protection of that status, and convincing activities to ensure that privileges and immunities would not result in impunity for any violation of existing obligations by peacekeepers themselves. For each operation the status of military and civilian personnel should be expressly addressed in the mandate and in other relevant instruments and agreements flowing from the mandate. A consistent procedure for handling questions of immunity and determining what constitutes official duty including necessary legal controls of any such determination should be introduced.[61] In so far as a particular (peace) enforcement mission is conducted directly by the United Nations under the direction of the Department of Peacekeeping Operations (DPKO), no court proceedings may be initiated in a Receiving State against a foreign member of the mission without first promptly informing the Head of Mission and allowing him or her to certify whether the proceeding is related to official duties. Only on acts clearly committed outside official duties would the possibility arise that the Receiving State

[54] The SOFA provides in Art. 34(1) that all US Forces shall withdraw from all Iraqi territory no later than 31 December 2011. During 2008 the US Forces have left many of their Forward Operating Bases (FOBs) in Iraq and also reduced the number of Joint Security Stations (JSS).

[55] SC Res. 1500 (2003), para. 2. [56] SC Res. 986 (1995).

[57] SC Res. 1546 (2004), 1557 (2005), 1619 (2005), 1700 (2006), and 1790 (2007).

[58] SC Res. 1859 (2008), para. 1.

[59] SC Res. 1483 (2003), and 1546 (2004), para. 20.

[60] SC Res. 1770 (2007) and 1830 (2008).

[61] Concurrent F. Rawski, 'To Waive or not to Waive: Immunity and Accountability in UN Peacekeeping Operations', 18 (1) *Connecticut Journal of International Law* (2002), 103–32, at 131.

could exercise jurisdiction.[62] In (peace) enforcement operations conducted by regional organizations or by coalitions of participating States acting under a United Nations Security Council mandate, the practice hitherto is to base the status upon agreements between the organization (or States conducting the operation) and the Receiving State. These agreements will usually confirm functional immunity for the Sending State's forces. In the absence of specific determinations, status issues continue to be deduced from general principles and rules. In (peace) enforcement operations involving the sustained conduct of hostilities, international humanitarian law would be fully applicable. However, attacks against peacekeepers cannot be legally accepted and their legal status should be considered as an important argument for taking criminal action against offenders. In case of any crimes, human rights violations, or breaches of other relevant obligations which may be committed by members of forces participating in a (peace) enforcement operation themselves, transparent measures of investigation, prosecution, and evaluation of lessons learned should be secured. 5.12

The responsibility of the Sending State extends to all acts performed by its forces on its behalf. This includes acts committed in excess of authority or in contravention of instructions (see below, sub-Chapter 6.2 and Chapter 30). 5.13

1. *General.* Forces participating in peace enforcement or enforcement operations have obligations deriving from international law, including international humanitarian law and human rights law, as well as the law of their Sending State.[63] They are liable for breaches under the rules of State responsibility. State responsibility has been reaffirmed and further developed by the International Law Commission's Articles on the Responsibility of States for Internationally Wrongful Acts (ARSIWA),[64] without affecting the *lex specialis* character of relevant provisions of international humanitarian law.[65] Sending States are obliged to make reparations in case of wrongful acts (see Chapter 30 'International Responsibility and Military Operations').

[62] This legal situation deriving from the principle of functional immunity is confirmed in Sections 47 and 49 of the Model Status of Forces Agreement for Peacekeeping Operations, UN Doc. A/45/594 (9 October 1990), reprinted in B. Oswald, H. Durham, and A. Bates (eds), *Documents on the Law of UN Peace Operations* (Oxford: Oxford University Press, 2010), 39–50, and Fleck (ed.), *Handbook of the Law of Visiting Forces*, Annex F.

[63] C. Greenwood, 'International Humanitarian Law and United Nations Military Operations', 1 *YIHL* (1998), 3–34, at 17.

[64] Articles on Responsibility of States for Internationally Wrongful Acts (ARSIWA), Annex to General Assembly resolution 56/83 of 12 December 2001, and corrected by document A/56/49(Vol. I)/Corr.4; *Yearbook of the International Law Commission 2001*, Vol. II Part Two, Chapter IV; J. Crawford, A. Pellet, and S. Olleson (eds), *The Law of International Responsibility* (Oxford: Oxford University Press, 2010).

[65] See Art. 55 ARSIWA.

5.13 2. *State Responsibility and International Responsibility*. When the Security Council authorizes States to take necessary measures of enforcement or peace enforcement, participating States act on behalf of the World Organization. Hence, the conduct of participating forces may not be exclusively attributable to Sending States, but at least partially to the United Nations, depending on the degree of authority and control of the latter (see Section 5.14). The current ILC work on Draft Articles on Responsibility of International Organizations[66] has addressed the responsibility of organs placed at the disposal of an international organization by a State, considering as a relevant criterion whether the organization exercises effective control over the conduct of the particular State organ.[67] That criterion may not be sufficient for attribution of the conduct of peacekeepers to the organization in question, as their Sending States normally retain significant control.[68] A convincing decision will depend on a sound operational assessment which in practice, e.g. in Afghanistan and Kosovo, has often led to a shared responsibility of Sending States and international organizations involved.[69] In any event the nature and effectiveness of command and control exercised by the United Nations will be a relevant factor for attributing a degree of shared responsibility to the United Nations. Nevertheless, the responsibility of the Sending State will hardly vanish altogether, and this is most important for the settlement of claims. The responsibility of the Sending State extends to all acts performed by peacekeepers on its behalf. It includes acts committed in excess of authority or in contravention of instructions. Responsibility of States also prevails in joint operations within a regional organization, or NATO,[70] as the latter, although they have legal personality and may exercise a

[66] Draft Articles on Responsibility of International Organizations (DARIO), UN Doc. A/66/10 (August 2011), Chapter V.

[67] DARIO, Article 6 '*General rule on attribution of conduct to an international organization.* (1) The conduct of an organ or agent of an international organization in the performance of functions of that organ or agent shall be considered as an act of that organization under international law whatever position the organ or agent holds in respect of the organization. (2) Rules of the Organization shall apply to the determination of the functions of its organs and agents.'
Article 7 '*Conduct of organs placed at the disposal of an international organization by a State or another international organization.* The conduct of an organ of a State or an international organization that is placed at the disposal of another international organization for the exercise of one of that organization's functions shall be considered under international law an act of the latter organization to the extent that the organization exercises effective control over the conduct of the organ.'

[68] C. Leck, 'International Responsibility in United Nations Peacekeeping Operations: Command and Control Arrangements and the Attribution of Conduct', 10 *Melbourne Journal of International Law* (2009), 346–64, at 361–4, <http://www.mjil.law.unimelb.edu.au/issues/archive/2009(1)/16Leck.pdf>.

[69] F. Sanfelice di Monteforte, 'Operational Command versus Organic Command: Who is in charge?' in International Institute of Humanitarian Law (ed.), *International Humanitarian Law, Human Rights and Peace Operations.* 31st Round Table on Current Problems of International Humanitarian Law, San Remo, 4–6 September, 2008, 246–8; T. Gill, 'Legal Aspects of the Transfer of Authority in UN Peace Operations', 42 *Netherlands Yearbook of International Law* (2011), 37–68; A. Sari and R.A. Wessel, 'International Responsibility for EU Military Operations: Finding the EU's Place in the Global Accountability Regime', in B. Van Vooren, S. Blockmans, and J. Wouters, *The EU's Role in Global Governance. The Legal Dimension* (Oxford: Oxford University Press, 2013), 126–41.

[70] T. Stein, 'Kosovo and the International Community. The Attribution of Possible Internationally Wrongful Acts: Responsibility of NATO or of its Member States?'; *contra*: A. Pellet, 'L'imputabilité

coordinating role including operational command, generally do not have full legal authority and competence for the conduct of operations and consequently depend on sovereign decisions taken by their Member States.[71] In many cases international organizations lack the budget and organizational means to process claims. When the Security Council authorizes enforcement or peace enforcement operations of States acting outside a United Nations chain of command the accountability of the United Nations may be at the vanishing point and it will be difficult for claimants to identify exact responsibilities among participating States. Agreed legal principles may also be tacitly amended by practice. Under the Dayton SOFAs claims for damage or injury caused by SFOR were to be submitted through governmental authorities 'to the designated NATO Representatives'.[72] But in fact such claims have been processed and settled by the respective national contingents; NATO as an organization was not involved except in a capacity of supporting coordination between these national contingents.[73] For further consideration see commentaries to Sections 5.14 (para. 2), 6.07 (para. 3), and 30.01 (para. 2). **5.13**

3. *Responsibility and Jurisdiction.* The responsibility of States and international organizations is distinct from 'jurisdiction' in the sense of Article 2(1) ICCPR. The latter provision limits a State's extraterritorial human rights obligations to persons 'subject to its jurisdiction', thus forming primary rules in taking care of objective difficulties which might impede the implementation of the Covenant outside its territory.[74] The former defines the secondary rules of State responsibility, i.e. 'the general conditions under international law for the State to be

d'éventuels actes illicites—Responsabilité de l'OTAN ou des Etats membres', both in C. Tomuschat (ed.), *Kosovo and the International Community* (The Hague/London/New York: Kluwer, 2002), 181–92 and 193–202.

[71] S.R. Lüder, *Völkerrechtliche Verantwortlichkeit bei Teilnahme an 'Peace-Keeping'-Missionen der Vereinten Natione* (Berlin: BWV Berliner Wissenschafts-Verlag, 2004), 37 *et seq.*, 165 *et seq.*, 200–4. A different view is taken by M. Zwanenburg, *Accountability of Peace Support Operations*, International Humanitarian Law Series, Vol. 9 (Leiden/Boston: Nijhoff, 2005), 51 *et seq.*, 338–40, based on a more general notion of international legal personality of the organization concerned, but not excluding concurrent or secondary responsibility of States.

[72] See the two similar SOFAs for SFOR, concluded between the North Atlantic Treaty Organization (NATO) on the one side and the Republic of Croatia and the Republic of Bosnia and Herzegovina on the other side, Dayton Accords, Appendix B to Annex 1-A (23 November 1955), 35 *ILM* 1 (1996), 102, para. 15. See also Military Technical Agreement between the International Security Force ('KFOR') and the Government of the Federal Republic of Yugoslavia and the Republic of Serbia (4 June 1999), UNMIK/KFOR Joint Declaration (17 August 2000) and UNMIK Regulation no. 2000/47 on the Status, Privileges and Immunities of KFOR and UNMIK and their Personnel in Kosovo (18 August 2000), all reprinted in Fleck, *Handbook of The Law of Visiting Forces*, Annexes D and E; Military Technical Agreement Between the International Security Assistance Force (ISAF) and the Interim Administration of Afghanistan (4 January 2002), <http://www.operations.mod.uk/isafmta.doc>, Annex A.

[73] J.M. Prescott, in Fleck, *Handbook of The Law of Visiting Forces*, 177–80.

[74] Similar provision may be found e.g. in Art. 2(1) of the UN Torture Convention, Art. 2(1) of the Child Convention, and Art. 1 ECHR. For further discussion, see Fleck, 'Extraterritorial Implementation of Human Rights Obligations. A Challenge for Peacekeepers, Sending States and International Organisations', in G.H. Gornig et al. (eds), *Iustitia et Pax. Gedächtnisschrift für Dieter Blumenwitz* (Berlin: Duncker & Humblot, 2008), 365–82.

5.13 considered responsible for wrongful acts and omissions, and the legal consequences which flow therefrom'.[75] To the extent this responsibility arises from a breach of human rights obligations, it may depend from 'jurisdiction' in the sense of the relevant human rights treaty. For further considerations on this issue, see Section 3.01.

4. *Accountability and the Efficacy of Remedies.* Accountability of States flows from their responsibility and will not be affected by their immunity against foreign court procedures. States may be interested to settle claims for any wrongful acts or omissions as part of their peace-building efforts. Even if they are reluctant to do so, they may find themselves as addressees of political demands that may be legally convincing irrespective of any argument related to sovereign immunity. Yet for individual claimants the efficacy of remedies available will be the most relevant problem.

5.14 **The responsibility of the United Nations Organization for acts committed in an enforcement or peace enforcement operation is limited to acts committed under UN command and control.**

1. *General.* The rules concerning the responsibility of international organizations are fully applicable to all United Nations operations (see Chapter 30). International organizations involved in such operations bear a coordinate responsibility together with troop contributing States for ensuring compliance with the applicable rules of international law in operations conducted under their control or authority. This principle is generally accepted.[76] It has been confirmed and further developed in the International Law Commission's Draft Articles on the Responsibility of International Organizations.[77]

2. *The Reach of UN Responsibility.* The responsibility of the United Nations Organization for acts committed in a UN peace operation is generally accepted.[78] The same should apply as a starting consideration for UN peace enforcement operations. As discussed in Section 5.13, para. 2, it will, however, be limited to acts committed under UN command and control, and 'the decisive question in relation to attribution of a given conduct appears to be who has effective control

[75] ARSIWA, General Commentary, para. 1.

[76] See Final Report of the Committee on Accountability of International Organisations, Recommended Rules and Practices on Liability/Responsibility of International Organisations (RRPs), Section IV (peacekeeping and peace enforcement activities), in The International Law Association, Report of the Seventy-first Conference, held in Berlin, 16–21 August 2004 (London: ILA, 2004), 164–241, at 195.

[77] DARIO, UN Doc. A/66/10 (August 2011).

[78] 'As a subsidiary organ of the United Nations, an act of a peacekeeping force is, in principle, imputable to the Organization, and if committed in violation of an international obligation entails the international responsibility of the Organization and its liability in compensation.' Cited in the 2004 Report of the International Law Commission, at 112 from an unpublished letter of 3 February 2004 by the United Nations Legal Counsel to the Director of the Codification Division. See also Report of the Secretary General on financing of United Nations peacekeeping operations (A/51/389), paras 7–8, 4.

over the conduct in question'.[79] Within such limits UN responsibility includes acts committed in excess of authority or in contravention of instructions. 5.14

3. *Accountability and the Efficacy of Remedies.* Judicial control has been difficult in the case of UN-led operations. There is no competent international court to decide on the legality of United Nations operations and its compliance with norms of international law including human rights standards;[80] yet an expansion of municipal jurisdiction on acts falling under international command and control would hardly provide convincing solutions.[81] The European Court of Human Rights has declared itself not to be competent to judge on issues falling under the responsibility of the United Nations,[82] thus leaving unexamined a case of cluster ammunition causing the death of playing children in Kosovo 2000,[83] operational detentions for more than seven months in 2001,[84] and a claim to respect private property rights over five years until 2004.[85] This jurisprudence has been convincingly criticized,[86] as it assumed a United Nations responsibility for acts and omissions falling outside UN command and control,[87] thus shadowing the responsibility of Sending States. In so far as the UN bears responsibility for enforcement and peace enforcement operations, there is a lack of judicial control which has not been closed so far.

[79] 2004 Report of the International Law Commission, 113.

[80] M. Singer, 'Jurisdictional Immunity of International Organizations: Human Rights and Functional Necessity Concerns', 36 *Virginia Journal of International Law* (1995), 53–165.

[81] C.H. Brower, II, 'International Immunities: Some Dissident views on the Role of Municipal Courts', 41 *Virginia Journal of International Law* (2000), 1–92.

[82] See ECtHR, *Behrami and Behrami v France*, Application no. 71412/01 and *Saramati v France, Germany and Norway*, Application no. 78166/01, Judgment of 31 May 2007; *Gajic v Germany*, Application no. 31446/02, Judgment of 28 August 2007.

[83] *Behrami and Behrami v France*, Application no. 71412/01.

[84] *Saramati v France, Germany and Norway*, Application no. 78166/01, Judgment of 31 May 2007.

[85] *Gajic v Germany*, Application no. 31446/02, Judgment of 28 August 2007.

[86] See H. Krieger, 'A Credibility Gap: The Behrami and Saramati Decision of the European Court of Human Rights', 13 *Journal of International Peacekeeping* (2009), 159–80.

[87] An authorization under Chapter VII of the UN Charter does not generally exclude State responsibility for forces participating in a mission. The Court's assumption that the Security Council had retained 'ultimate authority and control' and for this reason only delegated 'operational command' (*Behrami and Saramati*, paras 133–5) has missed the fact that military leadership of KFOR lay not with the UN, that only Sending States as owners of full command were in a position to delegate 'operational command' or 'operational control', and that the Security Council exercising 'ultimate authority and control' cannot be expected to deal with individual claims. Even if the arguments of participating States pretending that acts and omissions falling under the 'unified command and control' of COMKFOR are excluded from the responsibility of participating individual States (see *Behrami and Saramati*, para. 98) were to be accepted, this would not necessarily lead to establishing responsibility of the United Nations, as the latter had no influence on the implementation of the KFOR mandate.

5.3 Legal Parameters for the Use of Force in the Context of the UN Collective Security System

5.15 **The UN collective security system requires express authorization of any use of force other than in self-defence.**

5.16 **Such authorization should also be provided for law enforcement operations including detentions (see Chapters 25 and 26).**

5.17 **The UN Charter and customary international law prohibit the use of force in international relations outside the maintenance or restoration of international peace and security within the context of the UN collective security system or in the exercise of the right of self-defence.**

1. The UN Charter and customary international law of a peremptory (*jus cogens*) nature prohibit the threat or use of force in international relations in any situation or for any purpose other than in self-defence, or in the maintenance and restoration of international peace and security within the context of the UN Collective Security System.[1] Consequently, any use of force which is undertaken in the absence of consent by a Host Government other than in the context of self-defence requires the express authorization of the UN Security Council through a decision in the form of a resolution authorizing the use or threat of force which is based upon Chapter VII (or in the case of authorization to a regional organization or arrangement upon Chapter VIII) of the Charter.

2. In addition to the above, a State may consent to the deployment of foreign military forces within its territory and authorize the use of force for the purpose of assisting it in the maintenance of law and order or acting against threats to its civilian population, and in restoring a stable environment. While such consent is not strictly speaking an exception to the abovementioned prohibition of the use of force, it does provide a sufficient legal basis for the deployment of foreign military forces and the use of force for purposes not otherwise prohibited under international law.[2] Such consent must be freely given by the lawful government of the State requesting assistance and can provide an additional legal basis alongside an authorization by the UN Security Council under Chapter VII of the Charter. In case of deployment by the UN or a regional organization of troops or police units onto the territory of a State within the context of a peace operation of a non-enforcement

[1] See, *inter alia*, Simma et al., *The Charter of the United Nations* (sub-Chapter 5.1) at 208 *et seq*., and Dinstein, *War Aggression*, 85 *et seq*.

[2] 'Consent' is generally acknowledged as a circumstance precluding wrongfulness under the law of (State) responsibility. See, in this context, Art. 20 of the Draft Articles on Responsibility of States for Internationally Wrongful Acts (DARS); Report of the International Law Commission, Fifty-third session, 43 (2001) at 48. See Chapter 14.

character, such Host State consent forms a strict legal requirement as referred to elsewhere in this Handbook.[3] 5.17

3. In the absence of such Host State or express authorization by the Security Council, any force used outside the context of self-defence will be in violation of the prohibition of the use of force and constitute an illegal act under international law. The use of force for purposes of law enforcement outside areas where a State exercises territorial or functional jurisdiction, or otherwise is permitted under international law, such as in relation to vessels and aircraft of its nationality in international sea or airspace or in the combating of piracy in international waters, will equally require express authorization by the Security Council. This applies both in relation to law enforcement conducted upon another State's territory and in relation to areas not subject to any State's jurisdiction.[4]

Any force used in enforcement and peace enforcement operations, other than in self-defence, requires specific authorization provided for by the Security Council within the mandate to be worked out under the specific Operational Plan (OPLAN) and Rules of Engagement (ROE) for the operation. The OPLAN and ROE may under no circumstances exceed the level or objective of the force provided for in the mandate. In addition, the general principles of necessity and proportionality relating to any use of force are likewise relevant to the employment of force within the context of enforcement and peace enforcement operations. 5.18

The nature and purpose of both enforcement and peace enforcement operations (referred to in Section 5.01) signifies that the use of force within the context of such operations need not be restricted to reactive and defensive responses to counter overt hostile acts or intent. On the contrary, the force necessary to carry out the mandate, within the limitations posed by mandate, articulated through the OPLAN and the ROE, and the principles of necessity and proportionality, is legally permitted. Where circumstances require, this can include the use of offensive and proactive force and threat of force necessary for mission accomplishment and to carry out the mandate. 5.19

[3] See Section 6.01 and supporting commentary.

[4] Under international law, the exercise of enforcement jurisdiction outside State territory requires a general attribution of enforcement jurisdiction or a specific authorization. Such general attribution is provided in the UN Law of the Sea Convention of 1982 in relation to maritime areas falling under the functional jurisdiction of coastal States (e.g. the contiguous zone, the exclusive economic zone, and the continental shelf) and in relation to vessels flying the State's flag and in relation to piracy outside the territorial waters of another State. However, in relation to law enforcement elsewhere, a specific authorization is required. An example of such authorization is SC Res. 1851 of 16 December 2008 which authorizes law enforcement measures directed towards combating piracy off the coast of Somalia in Somali territory and territorial waters.

5.19 1. The necessary authorization for the use of force or threat of force beyond self-defence will be formulated within the terms of a mandate issued by the Security Council. The mandate is given in the form of a resolution issued by the Security Council, acting under Chapter VII of the Charter, in which the Council sets out the general purposes and objectives of a particular mission and authorizes a State or group of States, a regional organization or arrangement, or a particular UN or regional peace enforcement mission to utilize force to achieve those objectives. This authorization will be worked out in an OPLAN and in ROE which are drawn up by the UN or relevant regional organization, or by the lead nation, in accordance with the terms of the mandate. The terms of the mandate may under no circumstances be exceeded in the OPLAN or ROE.[5]

2. As stated previously (see Sections 5.01 and 5.02 with supporting commentary), the use of force in the context of enforcement and peace enforcement operations is not restricted to self-defence and may include offensive measures of a proactive nature designed to impose particular conditions or terms of settlement determined by the Council, within the overall terms of its mandate, upon a particular State or other group or entity. As a rule, the broader the terms of the mandate and authorization are, the more force may be employed to carry it out. However, the principles of necessity and proportionality relating to the use of force (not to be confused with their counterparts within the context of the humanitarian law of armed conflict in so far as it is applicable to the situation) are relevant to all situations in which force is employed including UN (authorized) enforcement measures. Consequently, force beyond what is required under the circumstances to achieve the objectives and purposes of the mandate would be unnecessary and/or disproportionate and hence illegal. The reason for this is that the Security Council as an organ of the United Nations is bound by the Purposes and Principles of the UN Organization under Article 24(2) of the Charter. These include the core rules principles of international law of a peremptory nature to which the principles of necessity and proportionality belong.[6]

5.20 **Wherever and whenever circumstances do not require the use of force to secure the mission objectives or maintain force protection or where the use of force would be counterproductive, the principles of necessity and proportionality would prohibit the use of force. Likewise, where a lesser degree or duration of the use of force**

[5] The legal basis for the operation and the use of force is provided in the mandate issued by the Security Council or other issuing authority. The Operational Plan and Rules of Engagement are instruments to implement the mandate and consequently may never exceed the mandate. See Simma et al., *The Charter of the United Nations*, 1183–5 and *Capstone Doctrine* (see sub-Chapter 5.2), 16 and 54–5. For general comment on the relationship between legal, policy, and operational considerations in the context of ROE, see sub-Chapter 5.4.

[6] See para. 3 of the commentary to Section 5.02. Necessity and proportionality are core principles relating to any use of force to which the Security Council is bound and considers itself bound by. See *Capstone Doctrine*, 51.

would suffice to secure the mission objectives and maintain force protection, the use of force in excess of what was required would be unnecessary and/or disproportionate, and consequently illegal. 5.20

Peace enforcement operations lie conceptually between military enforcement operations and traditional peacekeeping. While sharing the characteristics of possessing a Security Council mandate under Chapter VII of the Charter and the ability to operate proactively and coercively outside the context of self-defence, they will not involve the conduct of hostilities against a State and may or may not involve participation of the Peace Enforcement Force as a party to a non-international armed conflict in support of a government, depending on whether the material conditions for the existence of such a conflict and the participation of the Peace Enforcement Force as a party thereto are met. Consequently, force will be applied on a case-by-case basis and may not necessarily include the use of high intensity force on a protracted and systematic basis as will be the case with military enforcement operations which are synonymous with full-scale warfare. Where at all feasible, they will require the cooperation and consent of the Host State government and other relevant parties. Consequently, the use of force parameters must be strictly and judiciously tailored to what is required to achieve the mission objective and maintain such consent and cooperation without prejudice to the inherent right of self-defence. 5.21

1. The distinction between enforcement and peace enforcement operations has been set out previously (see Sections 5.01 and 5.02 and supporting commentary) and need not be repeated here. Suffice it to say in this context that while consent is not legally required for either type of operation (and would be irrelevant within the context of a 'pure' military enforcement operation such as Korea or Desert Storm), it can be both desirable and necessary from a more practical, political, and operational perspective within the context of a peace enforcement operation which is deployed to assist a government or internationally mandated transitional authority to provide a stable environment. Since such operations do not necessarily aim to impose a military solution or usually involve sustained high intensity combat operations over an extended period of time, they will only use force when the situation objectively requires this to carry out the mandate. Moreover, even where they are actively engaged as parties to a non-international armed conflict in support of a government, policy considerations aimed at maintaining support of the government and population may often militate in favour of restraint in the use of force to avoid collateral civilian casualties to a greater extent than is required under the humanitarian law of armed conflict. Consequently, the use of force must be carefully and judiciously applied with a view to maintaining the maximum consent, or at least acquiescence, possible under the circumstances in order to facilitate and promote mission accomplishment. This can mean that policy and operational

5.21 restrictions can be imposed upon the tactics and means and methods of force employment through the OPLAN and ROE which go beyond what would be required under the relevant rules of the humanitarian law of armed conflict.[7] For example, the Peace Enforcement Mission in Afghanistan (ISAF) acted under a Chapter VII mandate in an environment in which large parts of that country were and remain highly unstable, and are (or have been) operating within the context of a non-international armed conflict between the Afghan Government supported by ISAF on one side, and Opposing Militant Forces (OMF) consisting of organized elements of the former Taliban regime and assorted local allies and foreign volunteers on the other. In those areas of that country where hostilities were conducted, the rules of the humanitarian law of armed conflict relating to the conduct of hostilities applicable to non-international armed conflict were legally applicable and the existence of a Chapter VII mandate provides a legal basis for the mission. Such rules permit the use of force against OMF fighters and military objectives and do not rule out the occurrence of collateral civilian casualties and damage which is not excessive in relation to the concrete military advantage anticipated from a particular engagement.[8] However, the main objective of the ISAF mission was to support the Afghan Government in its efforts to create a stable environment and constitutional order and was not primarily aimed at imposing a 'classical' military solution by defeating the adversary, notwithstanding frequent engagements with OMF where those occurred. Moreover, the effort was primarily aimed at increasing the Afghan Government's authority and winning and maintaining the support of the civilian population and not inflicting as much damage upon the adversary as was legally permitted. Hence, while offensive force was sometimes necessary within the overall objective of the mission, it was considered to be counterproductive to the objectives of the mission to employ force in many situations to the maximum extent allowed under the law of armed conflict where this would have undermined the consent of the Afghan Government and civil population.[9] Similar considerations apply to most other peace enforcement missions.

[7] Ibid.

[8] Under IHL/LOAC the law prohibits an 'attack' (which is synonymous with a combat engagement) which is expected to cause excessive death, injury, or damage to civilians and their property in relation to the concrete military advantage anticipated from the attack. See Section 16.06. Consequently an attack which caused significant collateral death, damage, or injury would not be illegal if the military advantage anticipated was substantial. But, notwithstanding these fairly permissive legal parameters, most ISAF actions, particularly in the latter phase of deployment, were aimed at avoiding collateral effects altogether in view of the mission objectives and the need to maintain support from the Afghan government and population.

[9] This was both stated NATO policy and was apparent from the numerous reports relating to civilian casualties released by the UN Assistance Mission in Afghanistan (UNAMA), NGOs—such as Human Rights Watch and Amnesty International—and independent journalists and scholars. There were repeated requests by the Afghan Government to NATO during the ISAF Mission to use caution and restraint in operations conducted against OMF elements to avoid civilian casualties and maintain support for ISAF's mission.

5.4 Force Application in Enforcement and Peace Enforcement Operations

Controlling the use of force by United Nations (UN) or Troop Contributing Countries (TCCs) is both an operational command responsibility and legal imperative. Rules of Engagement (ROE) are accepted by the UN and TCCs as the most common and effective framework in which to control the use of force by military forces. The ROE framework ensures that political direction and objectives as well as legal, diplomatic, policy and operational considerations are coherently conveyed in military orders or directives. This is to make sure the level of force authorized for UN or TCCs forces contributes towards mission accomplishment. 5.22

1. As discussed in sub-Chapter 5.1 and elaborated further in this Section, the collective security structure envisaged by the UN Charter did not fully develop. Rather than having armed forces at its disposal, pursuant to 'Article 43 Agreements' and commanding them through the Military Staff Committee, the Security Council has instead authorized enforcement action by 'coalitions of the willing' or 'regional agencies', which have retained authority for planning as well as strategic direction. The current practice is for the Security Council to authorize Member States to carry out enforcement or peace enforcement operations against target States or entities by way of resolutions issued under the authority of Chapter VII of the UN Charter.[1]

2. Whenever a UN mandated (peace) enforcement operation is conducted, the use of force by UN forces or TCCs forces is controlled in order to ensure discipline and to protect persons from unnecessary injury and property from unnecessary damage. International and domestic (i.e. host nation and/or Sending State) law prescribes the boundaries of force that may be used by UN or TCCs forces on operations. For example, depending upon the type of international operation, one or more of the various legal regimes identified in this Handbook, such as international humanitarian law (IHL) also referred to as law of armed conflict (LOAC), international human rights law, law of the sea, air law, and Security Council Resolutions (SC Res.) will be relevant. Additionally members of the force are at all times individually legally responsible for their actions and are subject to their own national legislation, such as their military disciplinary law and domestic criminal law. The law may also delineate the methods and means by which that force may be applied. In all circumstances, military commanders and subordinates have a responsibility to ensure compliance with the rule of law.

[1] For details on the nature and scope of 'enforcement' and 'peace' operations see sub-Chapter 5.1 'Legal Characterization and Basis for Enforcement Operations and Peace Operations under the Charter'.

5.22 3. ROE are an indispensable instrument of command and control (C2) for ordering and controlling the use of force during military operations. ROE are orders or directives issued by military authority that define the circumstances, conditions, degree, manner, and limitations within which force, or actions which might be construed as provocative, may be applied to achieve military objectives in accordance with national policy and the law.[2] Notably, ROE are not normally used to assign missions or tasks nor are they used to give tactical instructions. It is important to note that ROE are not simply a statement of the legal parameters within which force may be used. ROE are an authorization to use or threaten force within defined legal, policy, diplomatic, and operational factors.[3] These factors are generally described as follows:

(a) *Legal considerations*. Use of force by military forces shall comply with international and applicable national law and, where appropriate, host nation law. The applicable legal regimes will delineate the framework within which UN and TCC planners may develop ROE for approval. In addition to the authority to use force found in SC Res. under Chapter VII or during armed conflict, international law may also delineate the methods and means by which that force may be used. During times of armed conflict this would include customary and treaty law of armed conflict (LOAC) or international humanitarian law (IHL), including various weapons treaties such as the Ottawa Convention on Anti-Personnel Mines,[4] the Convention on Certain Conventional Weapons,[5] and the Chemical Weapons

[2] Many States have ROE and use of force doctrine and processes but most are classified and unavailable publicly. Those States and organizations that have portions of their ROE and use of force doctrine public have generally defined 'ROE' as defined here. For example see, Canadian Forces (CF) Pub B-GJ-005-501/FP-001, *CFJP-5.1 Use of Force for CF Operations*, August 2008 (issued under the authority of the Chief the Defence Staff) at 2–3; US CJCS Joint Publication 1-02, *Dictionary of Military and Associated Terms*, 8 November 2011 (as amended through 15 December 2014) which defines ROE as 'Directives issued by competent military authority that delineate the circumstances and limitations under which United States forces will initiate and/or continue combat engagement with other forces encountered'. The *NATO Allied Joint Publication AAP-6* (NATO Standardization Agency, 2013), at 2-R-10 defines 'ROE' as 'directives issued by competent military authority which specify the circumstances and limitations under which forces will initiate and/or continue combat engagement with other forces encountered'. The UN *Glossary of UN Peacekeeping Terms,* defines 'ROE' as 'Directives issued by DPKO that specify the way how units in PKO's have to act with hostile parties and the population'. For general overview of ROE sources and doctrine see A.J. Roach, 'Rules of Engagement', vol. 36, no. 1, *Naval War College Review* (January/February 1983) and W.H. Parks, 'Righting the Rules of Engagement', vol. 115, no. 5, *U.S. Naval Institute Proceedings* (May 1989).

[3] See CF Publication B-GJ-005-501/FP-001, *CFJP-5.1 Use of Force for CF Operations*; the UK MoD Joint Warfare Publication 3-00 (JWP 3-00), March 2004, *Joint Operations Execution* (2nd edn) 2D-6; the US Army *Operational Law Handbook 2014* (Charlottesville, VA: The Judge Advocate General's Legal Center & School, International and Operational Law Department), 79–80.

[4] Convention on the Prohibition of the Use, Stockpiling, Production, and Transfer of Anti-Personnel Mines and on Their Destruction (18 September 1997), 2056 U.N.T.S. 211, (APM Convention).

[5] Convention on Prohibitions or Restrictions on the Use of Certain Conventional Weapons Which May Be Deemed to Be Excessively Injurious or to Have Indiscriminate Effects of 10 October 1980, 1342 UNTS 137 (CCW), with Protocols I, II (revised on 3 May 1996), III, IV (13 October 1995), and V (28 November 2003).

Convention.[6] During other international operations not amounting to an armed 5.22
conflict, it is often the policy of military forces to apply the spirit and principles of IHL.[7] The application of international human rights law will also be a significant consideration in ROE development. At times, depending upon the nature of the operation, other international legal regimes may influence the ROE. This may not always be restricted to issues relating to the level and intensity of force to be used but may rather impact on the geographic parameters of the operations should regimes such as law of the sea, air, or space law be applicable. Any set of ROE will, in part, be defined by the applicable international law, national law, and/or host nation law. Often, more then one source or law will be relevant. It is important to identify all legal sources which may be relevant for a particular operation and to ensure that any ROE comply with the rule of law.

(b) *Political and policy considerations.* To secure and protect national interests at home and abroad, the UN and each TCC establishes policies, goals, and strategic objectives. The use of military force is one means to meet the UN's and TCCs' policies and objectives. Other methods include economic, social, cultural, diplomatic, and technological instruments. Military forces are instruments of national policy and power.[8] Military planners must take into consideration UN and TCCs policies and strategic objectives, as applicable, when developing ROE for a specific international military operation.

(c) *Diplomatic considerations.* During international operations and, in particular, during combined or coalition operations, the authority to use force reflects the collective objectives of the UN or coalition.

(d) *Operational considerations.* The use of force will also depend on current and future operational considerations (e.g. the use of force may be restricted in designated circumstances to avoid friendly fire incidents or the destruction of specified lines of communications). Further the authority to use force set out in the ROE will often reflect the unique capability of weapon systems.

4. A number of ROE systems have been developed by individual nations, alliances, coalitions, and services within various military forces. Generally (peace) enforcement operations under a Chapter VII mandate will use multinational alliance (e.g. NATO) or coalition ROE.[9]

[6] Convention on the Prohibition of the Development, Production, Stockpiling and Use of Chemical Weapons and on Their Destruction 1974 UNTS 45 (CWC).

[7] For example, see Canadian Forces publication B-GJ-005-104/FP-021 *Law of Armed Conflict at the Operational and Tactical Levels*, c. 17, para. 3; B-GJ-005-104/FP-023 *Code of Conduct for Canadian Forces Personnel*, C. 1, para.10.

[8] Canadian Forces publication B-GJ-005-501/FP-001, *CFJP-5.1 Use of Force for CF Operations*, at 1-1.

[9] For example, the NATO ROE are referred to as 'NATO MC 362', see NATO Legal Deskbook (2nd edn) 2010. EUFOR has ROE for its mission in Bosnia-Herzegovina as noted at the EUFOR website: <http://www.euforbih.org/index.php?option=com content&view=article&id+15:eufor-fact-sheet&catid=185:about-eufor&Itemid=134>. See also US Army *Operational Law Handbook 2009*, 518, p. 83.

5.22 5. Alliances, such as NATO, are designed to incorporate force specific (naval, army, air force, and marines) and joint ROE doctrines and architectures which each Alliance Member has agreed to comply with during multinational allied operations. Therefore, when conducting such operations, the applicable alliance ROE doctrine and system will normally be used. Commanders must be aware that there are both significant and subtle differences between the various alliance ROE doctrines and architectures, and great care must be taken to ensure that the underlying concepts and applications are not confused between systems.

6. Generally during a coalition operation there is no standard reference for ROE, ROE principles, concepts, and measures because of the often ad hoc nature of such operations. A coalition force may operate under the same coalition ROE or each TCC may operate under its own national ROE. In the latter case, every effort must be made to avoid divergent or contradictory ROE. As with alliance ROE, commanders must also be aware that there are often subtle yet important differences between the ROE systems of various nations. Many nations share the same basic concepts but interpret and apply these concepts in significantly different ways. Usually, once an enforcement or peace enforcement operation has been completed, the coalition is normally disbanded and the applicable ROE are cancelled.

7. Importantly, it must be noted that the military forces (alliance or coalition) of nations participating in (peace) enforcement operations will adhere to their own national laws and policies. They are not obliged to execute tasks or operations that would constitute a breach of these national laws and policies. Therefore, it must be recognized that nations may issue restrictions and/or amplifying instructions (e.g. regarding the concepts of unit and personal self-defence, defence of property, and handling of detainees) in order to ensure compliance. Such restrictions or amplifications are often referred to as 'national caveats' and commanders of enforcement operations must be aware of every national caveat of each TCC in order to properly employ and task such forces.[10]

5.23 **Generally, ROE are defined as orders or directives that are intended to ensure commanders and their subordinates use only such force or other measures as are necessary, appropriate and authorized by higher command. ROE are an essential instrument of command and control for ordering, directing and controlling the use of force during military operations. ROE are orders or directives (i.e. lawful commands) issued by a competent military authority, which define**

[10] For example, see Canadian Forces Publication B-GJ-005-501/FP-001, *CFJP-5.1 Use of Force for CF Operations*, August 2008, 4–3. NATO ROE MC 362/1 states: 'Nations must inform the NAC/DPC and the Strategic Commander of any inconsistencies [i.e. caveats], as early as possible.' See also B. Lombardi, 'All Politics is Local: Germany, the Bundeswehr, and Afghanistan', Annual John W. Holmes Issue on Canadian Foreign Policy: Canada-Germany Relations: Essays in Honour of Robert Spencer, 63 *Int'l J.* (2007–2008), 587.

the circumstances, conditions, degree, manner and limitations within which force may be applied to achieve military objectives in furtherance of the UN mandate. Mission specific ROE are tailored to meet the requirements of each operation. 5.23

1. ROE are often defined as 'orders' or 'directives' that are intended to ensure that commanders and their subordinates do not use force or other measures beyond that authorized by higher command. The terms 'orders' or 'directives' should not be interpreted as an *obligation* to use force, but, rather, a confirmation as to the level of force that commanders or individuals *may* legitimately employ in support of their military mission.

2. As already noted, (peace) enforcement operations usually involve the forces of more than one nation acting together to accomplish a single mission. In such operations, the use of force, and in particular, the authority to use deadly force by military members to accomplish a mission, receives detailed scrutiny and attention by the senior leadership of the UN and/or of the TCCs' forces. Every member of the UN or TCC force who may be required to use force in self-defence or to accomplish a mission must have a reasonable level of knowledge and understanding of the ROE and supporting law and doctrine.

3. The command and control structure (C2) of a multinational (peace) enforcement operation is a crucial element in the development of ROE and in controlling the use of force by each member of the TCC. Depending on the scope of the mission, naval, land, air forces, and marines, as well as logistics and communications support, may all be included in a multinational operation. Nations will typically contribute to the multinational allied or coalition force headquarters staff and operational components in accordance with alliance arrangements or as agreed at meetings of TCCs. The commander of the multinational (peace) enforcement operation is usually an officer of the nation contributing the largest number of forces to the operation. The other TCCs often create individual national Task Forces (TF) which are placed under the operational command (OPCOM) or control (OPCON) of the Force Commander for the duration of the (peace) enforcement operation.[11] As a function of the exercise of command, the supporting operational staff of the Force Commander normally leads the ROE and targeting development process.[12]

4. ROE and targeting development should be accomplished through an effective dialogue between the Force Commander, the commander's staff and the commanders of each TCC TF. Usually, the Force Commander establishes a ROE team that

[11] For further details on command and control in military operations see Chapter 15 'Command and Control in Military Operations'.

[12] See Canadian Forces Publication B-GJ-005-501/FP-001, *CFJP-5.1 Use of Force for CF Operations* and US Army *Operational Law Handbook 2014*.

5.23 will develop the ROE and will coordinate with the staffs that are developing the targeting process.[13]

5. The ROE team is normally comprised of key staff officers and representatives of the operational commanders, representatives of the applicable staff (i.e. navy, army, air, and marines), representatives of TCCs TFs, policy and legal advisors. In order to assist the operational team (at the strategic, operational, and tactical levels) and ensure that legal requirements are satisfied, military doctrine often requires that legal officers are involved in the ROE planning process from the outset.[14]

6. There are number of key documents that are required before the Force Commander and the TCCs can properly develop the ROE. Such documents include, but are not limited to: the legal basis for the mission (e.g. UNSCR);[15] a clear mandate and mission;[16] the political and diplomatic objectives of the mission; the military objectives for the mission; an accurate threat assessment; the Force Commander's mission analysis, estimate and concept of operations with clearly defined tasks; the Force Commander's initial ROE request often referred to as the 'ROEREQ'; the force structure and weapons; targeting process and products, if applicable; and other ROE used by the TCCs.

7. The primary goal of any use of force doctrine and ROE architecture is to provide direction on the use of force, which is clear, concise, comprehensive, and in compliance with the rule of law. Such direction is generally issued by the Force Commander through the ROE Authorization (ROEAUTH) message.[17]

[13] For details on the law of targeting see Chapter 16 'Targeting in Operational Law'.

[14] See Canadian Forces Publication B-GJ-005-501/FP-001, *CFJP-5.1 Use of Force for CF Operations*, 2–6; US Army *Operational Law Handbook 2014*, 83–6; and UK MoD Joint Doctrine Publication 3-46 (JDP 3-46), *Legal Support To Joint Operations* (2nd edn) August 2010, 1–11.

[15] As noted in sub-Chapter 5.1 'Legal Characterization and Basis for Enforcement Operations and Peace Operations under the Charter', and sub-Chapter 6.1, 'Characterization and Legal Basis for Peace Operations', peace enforcement and peacekeeping are separate concepts and it is important not to confuse them. UN peacekeeping has traditionally been based on the consent of the opposing parties and involves the deployment of peacekeepers to implement agreements approved by those parties. In the case of enforcement action, the Security Council normally provides Member States with the authority pursuant to Chapter VII to take all necessary measures to achieve a stated objective or to enforce the mandate. Consent of the parties is not necessarily required.

[16] Generally, Chapter VII resolutions do not provide detailed and precise authorizations on the exact parameters within which Member States may use force. This is not surprising given the often complex subject matter and the fact that normally the substance of a resolution is based primarily on political or diplomatic considerations rather than strictly legal ones. The existence of ambiguous resolutions leads inevitably to differing interpretations of the mandate and the limits on the use of force. For example, see SC Res. 688 (1991) which some have interpreted as implying the authorization for the use of force to create 'no-fly zones' in Iraq; SC Res. 1160 (1998), 1199 (1998), 1203 (1998), and 1239 (1999) which have been interpreted as implying the authorization for the use of force by NATO in its Kosovo air campaign; and SC Res. 1441 (2002) on Iraq which has been interpreted as implying the authorization for the use of force by Member States for Iraq's failure to comply with UN weapons inspectors.

[17] States may vary on who approves ROE. For example, in the US the Secretary of Defense approves ROE, see US Army *Operational Law Handbook 2014*, 80; in Canada it is the Chief of the Defence Staff, see Canadian Forces Publication B-GJ-005-501/FP-001, *CFJP-5.1 Use of Force for CF Operations*, 2–4; in NATO it is the North Atlantic Council (NAC). Nonetheless, it is common practice to use the term

8. The ROEAUTH message is a concise method of authorizing and issuing mission specific numbered ROE for an operation. It requires that each commander and other member of the Force is well versed and trained in the use of force, ROE architecture, definitions, principles, and concepts on self-defence. **5.23**

9. The normal procedure for requesting, authorizing, and implementing ROE follows a chain of command between the Force Commander, senior representatives of TCCs, and all subordinate commanders within the operation. Usually, the Force Commander authorizes ROE, and subordinate commanders implement the ROE (i.e. disseminate ROE to subordinate commanders and troops). This is usually referred to as a 'ROEIMP' message.[18] Commanders may withhold implementation of all or part of the ROE without the Force Commander's approval. However, they must inform the Force Commander that they have done so. Subordinate commanders must not assume a ROE has been authorized to them or their forces until they receive a ROE implementation message from their immediate commander. ROEAUTH and ROEIMP messages are vital and necessary command and control tools in (peace) enforcement operations and are considered to be orders or directives issued by the competent military authority.[19]

10. Of note, *in extremis* during (peace) enforcement operations, if command, control, and communications systems become impaired or if timely communication with the Force Commander is impossible, subordinate commanders may need to implement ROE without prior Force Commander approval. In such extraordinary circumstances, commanders may do so if, in their judgement, an emergency arises where the delay in obtaining authorization of ROE would jeopardize their forces or the mission. Any ROE, which are implemented in this fashion, shall comply with the authorized mandate of the operation and the Force Commander is to be informed at the earliest opportunity.[20]

11. Commanders at all levels in an enforcement or peace enforcement operation must ensure their subordinates are trained on the meaning and application of the ROE for assigned missions, and on any subsequent changes. In addition, commanders at all levels must ensure their subordinate commanders take the following steps to ensure that the authorized level of force is properly applied: (a) read, understand, appropriately interpret, and disseminate the ROE; (b) seek additional guidance or direction through the commander should the situation change, or if the existing ROE are insufficient or a particular situation is not adequately covered by the ROE; and (c) seek clarification if there is any perceived discrepancy within the ROE in effect, or if the role and the ROE have diverged and are no longer compatible.

'ROEAUTH' to describe the formal process by which military commanders and subordinates are advised of what ROE have been approved.

[18] See Canadian Forces Publication B-GJ-005-501/FP-001, *CFJP-5.1 Use of Force for CF Operations*, 2–9.

[19] Ibid. 2–3. [20] Ibid. 2–9.

5.23 12. Accountability and responsibility for the use of force in enforcement operations must always be monitored and enforced at all levels of the chain of command. While subordinates can always be held accountable for their own actions, commanders are responsible for the actions of their subordinates and for ensuring that all operations are conducted in accordance with orders and applicable legal prescriptions. Although commanders may delegate the authority for operations, they are still responsible for the conduct of their forces even if their forces are under someone else's operational or tactical control.[21]

5.24 **ROE should be established for each military operation, including enforcement and peace enforcement operations. Generally, ROE in (peace) enforcement operations are restrictive whereas in self-defence they are permissive. ROE must not permit the use of force that exceeds existing legal limitations and may further limit the use of force. The right of self-defence (individual and national) must be respected (see below, Sections 6.09, 8.01–4, and 23.01). The right of self-defence is closely linked to ROE but may not necessarily be expressed as a ROE. The exercise of the use of force in personal self-defence may be the subject of further military direction (e.g. types of weapons authorized for use or hold fire orders).**

1. ROE are applicable throughout the entire spectrum of conflict. Generally ROE in (peace) enforcement operations are primarily restrictive whereas in self-defence they are permissive. The reason for this is based on the nature of the Chapter VII mandate that authorizes the (peace) enforcement operation.

2. As noted in this section, during (peace) enforcement operations the Security Council authorizes Member States under Chapter VII to enforce a mandate using up to and including 'all necessary means' or 'all measures necessary'. It is the authorization of 'all necessary means' or some variation thereof, that usually provides international legal authority for a coalition or regional agency to use force beyond that required for self-defence. In practice, the authorization of 'all means necessary' during (peace) enforcement operations has resulted in the use of force which can rise to the level of full-scale combat operations or armed conflict.[22]

[21] For more on 'command responsibility' see Chapter 29 'The Prosecution of International Crimes in Relation to the Conduct of Military Operations'.

[22] Art. 42 UN Charter authorizes 'action . . . as may be necessary to maintain or restore international peace and security'. The action may include 'operations by air, sea, or land forces'. Accordingly, Art. 42 is a legal basis upon which the SC can authorize Member States to use force against a State or other entity. Such force is often viewed as 'coercive' in that it is applied without the specific consent of the target State or entity and is not limited to self-defence. Force that is 'necessary to maintain or restore international peace and security' is authorized. For example, many Member States have conducted major (peace) enforcment operations under SC mandates in Iraq, Arabian Sea and Gulf Region, the Former Yugoslavia, Kosovo, East Timor, Haiti, Somalia, Afghanistan, Sudan, and the Congo. The enforcement operations carried out in Korea and in Kuwait constituted full-scale international armed conflicts.

3. There is a fundamental difference between the laws governing the use of force in peacetime and those applicable to the use of force during armed conflict. During peacetime, and unless acting in self-defence, the use of force by the military is generally prohibited unless specifically authorized. When authorized, only minimum force may generally be used in peacetime after all reasonable non-force options have been exhausted, and the application of such force must cease once the objective has been met. In peacetime the use of force is generally regulated by, and reflective of, international human rights law and States' domestic laws. **5.24**

4. Conversely, during (peace) enforcement operations that rise to the level of armed conflict, the use of force during armed conflict is regulated by IHL or LOAC.[23] When full-scale hostilities occur, a commander must be able to seek out, engage and defeat the hostile entity in accordance with the principles of armed conflict, IHL, and the assigned mission. Nonetheless, the UN or TCCs may wish to impose specific restraints or prohibitions on the military commander for political or diplomatic reasons and senior commanders may wish to do the same for operational requirements. Therefore, the structure for armed conflict ROE is usually the opposite of peacetime ROE. The reason for this structure is two-fold: the use of force during (peace) enforcement operations rising to the level of armed conflict will be controlled and regulated by IHL or LOAC; and a commander may have to be restricted from exercising the full spectrum of force options available under international law based on the UN mandate, national political, diplomatic, or operational imperatives.

5. Consequently, when relying upon a Chapter VII mandate to deploy a multinational force for the purposes of enforcing a SC mandate, military commanders and legal advisors must study the relevant resolution(s) to determine who is authorized to do what, against whom, and with what level of force.

6. In any operation, including (peace) enforcement operations, the concept of (unit and personal) self-defence applies and must be clearly understood by commanders

[23] In a situation of armed conflict, human rights obligations are not displaced but the relevant human rights principles can only be interpreted by reference to the law applicable in armed conflict, the specialized law of IHL. In the event of an apparent inconsistency regarding the content of the two areas of law, the more specific provisions should prevail. See C. Greenwood, 'Rights at the Frontier-Protecting the Individual in Time of War', in *Law at the Centre-The Institute of Advanced Legal Studies at Fifty* (The Hague: Kluwer, 1999), 227–93; *Legality of the Threat or Use of Nuclear Weapons*, Advisory Opinion [1996], ICJ Reports; *Legal Consequences of The Construction of a Wall in the Occupied Palestinian Territory* [2004]; *Loizidou v Turkey* (Jurisdiction) (1995) 20 EHRR 99, para. 57; *Hassan v UK*, Application no. 29750/09, ECHR (2009) paras 103 and 107 at <http://hudoc.echr.coe.int/sites/eng/pages/search.aspx?i=001-146501>; *Abella v Argentina*, IACHR Report 55/97 (1997), paras 158 and 159 and the Provisional Measures Decision, note 55, 730; and HRC General Comment no. 31 on Art. 2 ICCPR (29 March 2004), at <http://www.unhchr.ch/tbs/doc.nsf/(Symbol)/c92ce711179ccab1c1256c480038394a?Opendocument>. In complex operational and security environments, where there may be multiple legal bases and mandates, there will not always be a clear delineation between when IHL or human rights law applies. The use of force during a self-defence operation, like the use of force in an armed conflict, is not unlimited, and the principles of IHL, and/or, as appropriate, human rights law, must be adhered to. Therefore, military forces must display operational and legal awareness, flexibility, and agility.

5.24 and members of all forces. This is even more crucial when there are differences in national interpretations as to what constitutes 'self-defence'. Some nations specifically authorize the exercise of self-defence in ROE while others note that the concept of self-defence is closely linked, but separate from, authorized ROE.[24]

7. The authorized military responses under the right of personal, unit, or force self-defence vary from nation to nation. Some nations allow for much greater discretion in the use of force in self-defence than other nations. Furthermore, nations have differing interpretations of what constitutes a hostile act or hostile intent and consequently the timing and manner of response may differ.

8. Such differences in doctrine are understandable and unavoidable from the perspective of national legislation, but do provide significant challenges to a combined or coalition force and its commanders. Commanders must know how the forces under their command or control will respond to a given situation and their goal will be to ensure unity of response. It remains the responsibility of commanders at all levels to determine the reactions and responses that their forces will or will not take in self-defence.

9. In using force, including force in self-defence, during (peace) enforcement operations, there are often key definitions and concepts that must be fully understood by commanders and their forces. These include the concepts of 'non-deadly force', 'deadly force', 'minimum force', 'hostile act', and 'hostile intent'.

10. Broadly, 'non-deadly' force is that force not intended or likely to cause death, or serious injury resulting in death.[25] This is usually through the use of physical force short of the use of firearms or other deadly force. 'Deadly force' is that force intended or likely to cause death, or serious injury resulting in death.[26]

11. The concept of minimum force is related to both the use of non-deadly and deadly force. It is the minimum degree of authorized force which is necessary and reasonable in the circumstances. Depending on the circumstances, particularly those existing in (peace) enforcement operations, minimum force may include deadly force.[27]

12. Generally, 'hostile acts' against a State consist of an attack or other actions that threaten the security of the State, its forces, citizens, territory, or property. A response by military forces to hostile acts against their State will normally be initiated by government direction.[28]

[24] For example, see US Army *Operational Law Handbook 2014*, 80–1; Canadian Forces Publication B-GJ-005-501/FP-001, *CFJP-5.1 Use of Force for CF Operations*, 2-2.

[25] *NATO Allied Joint Publication AAP-6 (2013)*, 2-N-4; Canadian Forces Publication B-GJ-005-501/FP-001, *CFJP-5.1 Use of Force for CF Operations*, GL-4.

[26] Ibid. [27] Ibid.

[28] US Army *Operational Law Handbook 2014*, 81; Canadian Forces Publication B-GJ-005-501/FP-001, *CFJP-5.1 Use of Force for CF Operations*, GL-2.

13. Usually, 'hostile acts' against military personnel, units, or forces consist of an attack or other use of force against military personnel where there is a reasonable apprehension that death or serious injury will be the likely result. An immediate response to attacks on military personnel, units, or forces is often authorized in self-defence.[29] **5.24**

14. 'Hostile intent' against a State normally consists of the threat of an attack or other actions which threaten the security of the State, its forces, citizens, territory, or property. A response by military forces to hostile intent against their State will usually be initiated by government direction.[30]

15. Similarly, 'hostile intent' against military personnel, units, or forces consists of the threat of an attack or other use of force against military personnel where there is a reasonable apprehension that death or serious injury will be the likely result. An immediate response to hostile intent towards military personnel, units, or forces is often authorized in self-defence.[31]

16. Although it is relatively easy to establish precise criteria for identifying hostile acts, it is much more difficult to recognize hostile intent. Therefore, mission specific hostile intent criteria should be issued during self-defence operations. Practice has shown that two basic decision indicators should be satisfied in order to constitute hostile intent against a State or against military personnel, units, or forces. These are: capability and preparedness to use force, and evidence and intelligence information.[32]

17. Evidence indicating an intention to attack, in addition to capability and preparedness is enhanced by political policy guidance, increasing indications of the hostile entity's mobilization and warlike gestures revealed by intelligence sources. The weight of evidence and intelligence indicating an intention to attack must usually be compelling.[33]

18. In general terms, both international law and national laws recognize the authority to use appropriate force in self-defence, up to and including deadly force. Without further written or oral direction most military personnel are entitled to use force in self-defence to protect: oneself; other members of their national forces; and non-national military personnel who are attached or seconded to their forces against a hostile act or hostile intent.

19. Importantly, however, there may be extraordinary circumstances where the TCCs, in support of higher national interests, may direct their forces to take all necessary action *except for* the use of deadly force when facing hostile intent. Such

[29] Ibid. [30] Ibid. [31] Ibid.

[32] Canadian Forces Publication B-GJ-005-501/FP-001, *CFJP-5.1 Use of Force for CF Operations*, 1-8; US CJCS Joint Publication 1-02, *Department of Defense Dictionary of Military and Associated Terms*, 8 November 2011 (as amended through 15 December 2014), 111.

[33] Canadian Forces Publication B-GJ-005-501/FP-001, *CFJP-5.1 Use of Force for CF Operations*, 2-2; US Army *Operational Law Handbook 2014*, 81.

5.24 direction would be exceptional and under constant review by the chain of command. The purpose of such direction would normally be to limit the escalation of a situation. This in no way limits the ability of an individual or commander to use minimum force in self-defence in response to a hostile act.

20. The authority to restrict the response to hostile intent also exists within the military chain of command. In exceptional circumstances, and only when there is a clear need to de-escalate a situation with no other alternative, a commander could restrict subordinates in their right to respond to hostile intent. Such direction would be exceptional and the chain of command will inform the Force Commander by the quickest means available that such an order has been given to military personnel. This is a controversial issue and it is often the subject of national caveats during enforcement operations. Such caveats usually indicate that no non-national commander can direct such a restriction on national forces without the TCC's approval.[34]

21. Such restriction on a response to hostile intent should not be confused with an order to hold fire which an on-scene commander may give to gain a tactical advantage prior to engaging or disengaging a hostile entity. Normally, hold-fire orders are not considered to be a restriction or limitation of the right of personal, unit, or force self-defence.[35]

22. Clearly, in (peace) enforcement operations, the Force Commander has many challenges in understanding the differing TCCs' views of the concepts of self-defence, defence of others, and defence of property. Frequently, in order to meet differing interpretations of these concepts, the Force Commander will use the ROE to reconcile and harmonize the differences.

23. When operating with forces of other nations in enforcement operations, the definition of self-defence is normally expanded, through ROE authorization, to include all individuals or units who comprise the force.[36] In multinational international military operations, there is also the challenge of understanding each State's interpretation of the concepts of self-defence. Frequently, in order to meet differing interpretations of these concepts, the Force Commander will use the ROE architecture with national caveats to reconcile and harmonize the differences. In multinational operations, where there may not be a common set of ROE, specific ROE authorization is normally promulgated and implemented for all TCCs' forces to permit the defence of all forces' personnel or units that are attacked or threatened.

[34] Canadian Forces Publication B-GJ-005-501/FP-001, *CFJP-5.1 Use of Force for CF Operations*, 2–3; US Army *Operational Law Handbook 2014*, 80–3.

[35] Canadian Forces Publication B-GJ-005-501/FP-001, *CFJP-5.1 Use of Force for CF Operations*, 2–3.

[36] Canadian Forces Publication B-GJ-005-501/FP-001, *CFJP-5.1 Use of Force for CF Operations*, 4–3; see also US Army *Operational Law Handbook 2014*, 448 which highlights that NATO employs the concept of 'extended self-defence' to 'defend other NATO/NATO-led forces and personnel in the vicinity from attack or imminent attack'.

24. Moreover, ROE are also used to reconcile and harmonize possible national differences regarding other key operational issues such as defence of civilians, defence of international community personnel, defence of property,[37] the prevention of serious crimes, the authority to stop and search, detention of persons, protection of detainees, entry into territory, territorial waters or airspace, harassment, weapon systems restrictions, and blockades. **5.24**

25. It is important to note the distinction between the uses of the term 'self-defence', particularly when dealing with the concept of the exercise of State self-defence under international law. However, as indicated in the preceding paragraphs, the issue of unit or individual self-defence exists in all types of military operations, including international (peace) enforcement military operations. As highlighted earlier, the use of military force in (peace) enforcement operations can rise to the level of armed conflict. In such circumstances, the *lex specialis* of IHL permits a more robust use of force than do peacetime or international human rights rules. This means that some of the concepts noted earlier, such as 'minimum force', 'hostile act', or 'hostile intent', which are largely based on peacetime or human rights norms, are either not applicable in armed conflict operations or are modified. For example, in armed conflict combat operations under IHL, the mere fact that a person is a member of the enemy forces, or has otherwise taken a direct part in hostilities, makes the person a lawful military objective who could be targeted at any time.

26. Nonetheless, in modern international military operations, including (peace) enforcement operations, it is quite possible to have a mixture of missions or tasks depending on applicable legal bases and mandates. Such operations have been described in various ways in the past. Of particular note was the use of the term '3 Block War'.[38] Currently, the most common descriptor is 'Stability Operations'.[39] Frequently, the transition through the spectrum of stability operations

[37] See US Army *Operational Law Handbook 2014*, 455, which notes that self-defence rules in relation to protection of property often differ very significantly amongst nations. British and Canadian forces are not permitted to use lethal force to defend property unless the loss of or damage to that property will result in an immediate threat to life. Canadian Forces Publication B-GJ-005-501/FP-001, *CFJP-5.1 Use of Force for CF Operations*, 4–3, indicates that specific ROE must be authorized before members of the CF may use force to defend property and supplies. The level of force authorized to defend property will be based upon the legal basis and mandate for the operation. Should deadly force to defend property be authorized, it will not be all-inclusive and will generally be restricted to property with designated special status.

[38] The term '3 Block War' is generally attributed to General Charles Krulak, USMC, in the late 1990s. It was used to describe complex operational and security environments in which military forces would have to conduct a spectrum of opertations including combat, humanitarian assistance, and peacekeeping, often simultaneously, in the same theatre of operations. See General C. Krulak, 'The Strategic Corporal: Leadership in the Three Block War', *Marines Magazine* (January 1999), available at <http://www.au.af.mil/au/awc/awcgate/usmc/strategic_corporal.htm>.

[39] Generally 'stability operations' are viewed as encompassing international military missions, tasks, and activities conducted by military forces in coordination with other instruments of national/international power to maintain or re-establish a safe and secure environment, provide essential

5.24 will be seamless and rapid, often with no clear line of demarcation between various tasks. Such complex operational and security environments give rise to complex legal and interoperability issues when it comes time to determine which legal framework governs the use of force and authorizing ROE. Therefore, military commanders, subordinates, and legal advisors will need to remain vigilant in recognizing the facts and law (i.e. IHL, human rights law, SC resolutions, and/or domestic law as appropriate) throughout the spectrum of operations during international enforcement missions.

governmental services, emergency infrastructure reconstruction, and humanitarian relief. See US CJCS Publication 3-0 *Joint Operations* (11 August 2011), GL-25 and US Army Field Manual FM 3-07, '*Stability*', (June 2014). available at <http://armypubs.army.mil/doctrine/DR_pubs/dr_a/pdf/fm3_07.pdf>.

5.5 Applicability and Application of International Humanitarian Law to Enforcement, Peace Enforcement, and Peace Operations

Where peace enforcement operations fall below the threshold of armed conflict, international humanitarian law will not apply; the Force will be subject to relevant international and national law, including that applicable to law enforcement operations as defined above (see Section 3.01). Peace enforcement operations which do not reach the threshold of an armed conflict must adhere to law enforcement principles and follow the mandate issued by the Security Council. Whenever the Force has become a party to an armed conflict or is in belligerent occupation of foreign territory, international humanitarian law applies. 5.25

1. Where the level of violence does not amount to an armed conflict, international humanitarian law will not apply. However, this does not mean that there is no international law governing the operation. Human rights law which applies primarily in peacetime continues to apply in emergencies subject to any relevant derogation provisions.[1] The use of force provisions under human rights law are based on the requirements necessary for law enforcement, essentially the minimum force required to counter the threat posed. The treaty provisions are supported by a number of 'soft law provisions' such as the Basic Principles on the Use of Force and Firearms by Law Enforcement Officials.[2] Armed forces will remain subject to their own domestic law and, depending on any status-of-forces arrangements, subject also to the domestic law of the host nation (see also sub-Chapter 5.2 'Status of Forces in Enforcement and Peace Enforcement Operations'). The 'legal paradigm' of law enforcement is dealt with in greater detail in Chapter 4, 'Conceptual Distinction and Overlaps between Law Enforcement and the Conduct of Hostilities'.

2. Any force will also be subject to the mandate issued by the Security Council. Even when the Council includes a provision permitting the Force to use 'all necessary means' or similar wording, this cannot be interpreted as granting powers beyond those permitted under international law. Article 103 of the United Nations Charter provides that '[i]n the event of a conflict between the obligations of the Members of the United Nations under the present Charter and their obligations under any other international agreement, their obligations under the present Charter shall prevail'. However, there is no *obligation* to use 'all necessary means'

[1] Art. 4(1) ICCPR, Art. 15(1) ECHR, Art. 27(1) ACHR. The African (Banjul) Charter on Human and Peoples' Rights and the UN Covenant on Economic, Social and Cultural Rights do not allow for derogations.

[2] Basic Principles on the Use of Force and Firearms by Law Enforcement Officials, adopted by the Eighth United Nations Congress on the Prevention of Crime and the Treatment of Offenders, Havana, Cuba, 27 August to 7 September 1990.

5.25 as this is a permission. When the Council grants such a permission, it is subject to law and must be read as 'all necessary legal means'. At the same time, the mandate provides for the outer bounds of permissible 'necessary means'. Actions that may otherwise be permissible under applicable general rules of international law (most pertinently international human rights and humanitarian law) may be precluded if and to the extent that they are not necessary to fulfil the Security Council mandate. Issues of applicability should be distinguished from those of State responsibility.[3] See also Section 4.04 and the commentary thereto.

3. As soon as the level of violence amounts to an armed conflict, the relevant law of armed conflict will apply.[4] This will include situations of occupation. The law of occupation applies even where the occupation 'meets with no armed resistance'.[5] This does not mean that human rights law ceases to apply as has been made clear by the International Court of Justice.[6] For the interrelationship between international humanitarian law and human rights law in such situations, see Section 4.02 and the commentary thereto.

4. United Nations Forces are subject to the UN Secretary General's Bulletin *Observance by United Nations Forces of International Humanitarian Law.*[7] Its 'field of application' section applies the Bulletin:

> to United Nations Forces when in situations of armed conflict they are actively engaged therein as combatants, to the extent and for the duration of their engagement. [The Bulletin] is accordingly applicable in enforcement actions, or in peacekeeping operations when the use of force is permitted in self-defence.[8]

Whilst there is some doubt as to the meaning of this last sentence, the better view is that it applies when the Force is acting as 'combatants', using the term in its generic sense, i.e. when they have become themselves party to a conflict. This would include situations where the United Nations Force was subject to the laws of occupation. It does not apply to those situations falling below the threshold of armed conflict even though the Force is permitted to use force in self-defence.

[3] ECtHR, *Behrami v France*, Application no. 71412/01, *Saramati v France, Germany and Norway*, Application no. 78166/01, Admissibility Decision of 31 May 2007, 45 EHRR SE10, <http://hudoc.echr.coe.int/eng?i=001-80830"{"itemid":["001-80830"]}>. *Jaloud v The Netherlands*, Application no. 47708/08, Grand Chamber Judgment of 20 November 2014, <http://hudoc.echr.coe.int/sites/eng/pages/search.aspx?i=001-148367>.

[4] See also Section 4.01.

[5] Art. 2(2), Geneva Convention Relative to the Protection of Civilian Persons in Time of War, 12 August 1949, 6 U.S.T. 3516, 75 U.N.T.S. 287.

[6] ICJ, *Legal Consequences of the Construction of a Wall in the Occupied Palestinian Territory*, Advisory Opinion of 9 July 2004, ICJ Reports, 2004, 43 *ILM* (2004), 1009, at para. 106.

[7] Secretary General's Bulletin: *Observance by United Nations Forces of International Humanitarian Law*, ST/SGB/1999/13 (1999), <http://www.un.org/peace/st_sgb_1999_13.pdf>; reprinted in ICRC Manual, Chapter 20, 155–60; A. Roberts and R. Guelff (eds), 721; Vol. 5 (4–5) *International Peacekeeping* (1999), 160.

[8] Secretary General's Bulletin: *Observance by United Nations Forces of International Humanitarian Law*, Section 1(1).

In enforcement operations involving the authorized use of force against a State amounting to an armed conflict, the full body of international humanitarian law relevant to international armed conflicts will apply. The State(s) participating in the operation will be governed by the provisions of any conventions and protocols thereto in the realm of international humanitarian law to which they are a party, as well as by the rules and principles of customary international humanitarian law. **5.26**

1. In all cases where operations are conducted against another States' armed forces, including organized military or paramilitary units or formations acting on behalf of a State and/or involving the non-consensual occupation of (part of) another State's territory, international humanitarian law relevant to international armed conflicts applies.

2. The term 'armed conflict' is undefined in treaty texts. However, the Appeals Chamber of the International Criminal Tribunal for the Former Yugoslavia has adopted the following definition:

> [A]n armed conflict exists whenever there is a resort to armed force between States or protracted armed violence between governmental authorities and organized armed groups within a State. International humanitarian law applies from the initiation of such armed conflicts and extends beyond the cessation of hostilities until a general conclusion of peace is reached; or, in the case of internal conflicts, a peaceful settlement is achieved. Until that moment, international humanitarian law continues to apply in the whole territory of the warring States or, in the case of internal conflicts, the whole territory under the control of a party, whether or not actual combat takes place there.[9]

See also Section 3.01 and the commentary thereto.

3. The United Nations and other multinational bodies are not themselves parties to any international humanitarian law treaties. However, the States providing the military contingents are parties and the contingents are thus subject to all treaties and other international agreements to which the relevant State is bound. Similarly, the forces of States are bound by customary law in exactly the same way as if they were engaged in operations in their own right. Any doubt as to the customary status of a particular rule or principle should be resolved in favour of its full applicability unless the State concerned has consistently and unequivocally maintained a position at variance with that particular rule to the extent allowed by international law. No derogations or deviation from a rule or principle of peremptory character is permissible under any circumstances.

4. This applicability would include situations where a United Nations (authorized) Force was subject to the laws of occupation. This may occur in any situation subject

[9] ICTY, *The Prosecutor v Dusko Tadić*, IT-94-1-A, Decision on the Defence Motion for Interlocutory Appeal on Jurisdiction, 2 October 1995, 105 ILR 419, 488.

5.26 to the laws of occupation where a UN (authorized) force exercises authority over an area and/or with respect to any persons under its physical control or custody. In such cases, dependent upon the scope of applicable treaties, customary international law and the mandate authorized by the UN, international human rights law will apply alongside humanitarian law.

5. United Nations Forces will also be bound by the provisions of the Secretary General's Bulletin *Observance by United Nations Forces of International Humanitarian Law.*[10]

6. This general rule is subject to a caveat that arises from the interplay between United Nations law and international humanitarian law. In cases where forces are acting under a United Nations mandate under Chapter VII of the United Nations Charter, there may be a conflict between the terms of the relevant Security Council resolution and the obligations of States under international humanitarian law. A pertinent example from past UN-authorized operations stems from Iraq where the Security Council overrode provisions of the law of occupation by binding resolutions adopted in 2003–4.[11] See also Section 3.04 and the commentary thereto.

5.27 **Where a UN or UN-authorized force is acting on behalf of a State engaged in a non-international armed conflict and becomes involved in the conduct of operations against a non-State actor participating in that conflict, or becomes a party to a non-international armed conflict in its own right, the international humanitarian law relating to non-international armed conflicts will apply.**

1. Where a State is involved in a non-international armed conflict, both the State and the non-State actors involved will be bound by the international humanitarian law relating to non-international armed conflicts. Any United Nations or United Nations-authorized force that acts on behalf of the State forces will be bound by the applicable rule of international humanitarian law relating to non-international armed conflicts. This will include both treaty and customary law. If the UN or UN-authorized force intervenes in a preexisting non-international armed conflict and acts on behalf of the State party to that armed conflict, the law of non-international armed conflict becomes applicable to that force from the moment it acts on behalf of the State party, provided its actions are related to the conduct of hostilities in the context of that preexisting conflict.[12] See also Section 3.01 and the commentary thereto.

2. Besides the case in which a UN or UN-authorized force acts on behalf of the State forces in an ongoing non-international armed conflict, a UN or UN-

[10] Secretary General's Bulletin: *Observance by United Nations Forces of International Humanitarian Law.*

[11] See SC Res. 1483 (2003), 1511 (2003), and 1546 (2004).

[12] For this so-called 'support-based approach', see T. Ferraro, 'The Applicability and Application of International Humanitarian Law to Multinational Forces', 95 *International Review of the Red Cross* 891/892 (2014), 561–612, 583–7.

authorized force can also become a party to a non-international armed conflict in 5.27
its own right.[13] This is the case where the confrontations between the UN or UN-authorized force, acting on its own behalf, on the one hand, and a sufficiently organized armed group on the other, reach the threshold of intensity that a situation of non-international armed conflict requires.[14] In cases where the UN or UN-authorized force becomes a party to a non-international armed conflict in its own right, the situation is governed by the law that regulates this type of armed conflict.

3. The United Nations may give instructions to the Force on issues relating to the application of international humanitarian law. Where those instructions are contained in a binding Security Council resolution, the States participating in the operation will be bound by those instructions whether or not they are bound by the relevant provision of international humanitarian law. In other cases, the binding nature of the instructions will depend upon the agreement between the UN and the State concerned. Such instructions may go further than the law itself though, subject to Article 103 of the UN Charter, such instructions cannot seek to derogate from any legal obligation that already binds a participating State. For Article 103, see Section 4.03. For example, as there is no combatant status in non-international armed conflict, the provisions of the Secretary General's Bulletin may not strictly apply. However, the Secretary General may seek to apply it to United Nations forces in such circumstances.

Without prejudice to more restrictive applicable rules of international law, States participating in a UN or UN-authorized operation may require their forces to comply with the principles of international humanitarian law as a matter of policy, regardless of its applicability as a matter of law. 5.28

1. Where operations fall below the threshold of armed conflict, international humanitarian law will not apply as a matter of law and, dependent upon the mandate issued by the Security Council, the Force will be subject to relevant international and national law, including that applicable to law enforcement

[13] On the question who is to be considered the 'party to the armed conflict' in this case—the UN, troop contributing countries, or both—see T. Ferraro, 'The Applicability and Application', 588–95. See also O. Engdahl, 'Multinational Peace Operations Forces involved in Armed Conflict: Who Are the Parties', in Gro Nystuen, Kjetil Mujezinović Larsen, and Camilla Guldahl Cooper (eds), *Searching for a 'Principle of Humanity' in International Humanitarian Law* (Cambridge: Cambridge University Press, 2012), 233–71.

[14] For discussion of the question whether the criteria for determining the existence of an armed conflict in a situation where a UN force is involved depart from the classic criteria under international humanitarian law, and arguments in support of an answer in the negative, see T. Ferraro, 'The Applicability and Application', 580–3.

5.28 operations.[15] States may require their forces to apply higher standards than are required by international law by seeking to apply the principles of international humanitarian law.[16] However, they may not seek to derogate from any legal obligation that already binds a participating State. This in particular relates to the application of human rights law. Where international humanitarian law does not apply as a matter of law, the principle of *lex specialis* will not set aside any obligations upon the State arising from any other body of law.

2. In addition, States may also agree to apply provisions of international humanitarian law that are not strictly binding upon them as a matter of law, even where international humanitarian law itself in general applies. Thus, for example, they may agree to abide by the prohibition on the use of incendiary weapons contained in Section 6.2 of the Secretary General's Bulletin even though there is no such prohibition contained in either treaty or customary law.

[15] For a more detailed account of the law relating to the maintenance of law and order within the context of international military operations, see Chapter 25.

[16] For an account of the general principles of international humanitarian law, see A.P.V. Rogers, *Law on the Battlefield*, 3rd edn (Manchester: Manchester University Press, 2012), 1–27.

Chapter 6

PEACE OPERATIONS

6.1 Characterization and Legal Basis for Peace Operations

While a strict division between peacekeeping and peace enforcement has often proven to be difficult or even impossible to achieve and maintain in practice, there are clear distinctions in legal concept and in the resulting applicable legal regime between peace enforcement falling short of traditional war-fighting operations on the one hand, and other peace operations which are essentially consensual in nature, on the other. 6.01

1. The UN Charter makes no reference to any kind of military operation other than enforcement operations under Chapter VII, which were dealt with in the previous chapter (see sub-Chapter 5.1). Nevertheless, the concept and practice of UN operations have emerged and developed over the years into one of the major tools the UN possesses and utilizes in the maintenance of international peace and security.[1] UN peacekeeping and what is now referred to as 'peace operations' in UN parlance and within the context of this Handbook are conceptually and legally distinct from enforcement measures under Chapter VII of the Charter, even though it is not always possible to maintain a strict distinction in practice between peace enforcement and certain aspects of peace operations from a practical perspective. Enforcement measures involving the use of force, as set out in the previous chapter, are characterized by lack of the need of consent and by the (possibility of) the use of proactive (offensive) force to carry out the mandate provided by the Security Council and impose the will of the international community, and have their legal basis in Chapter VII of the Charter. As stated previously, they can be conceptually subdivided into 'enforcement operations' involving full-scale and protracted hostilities directed against a State which are aimed at imposing a solution and 'peace enforcement operations', which operate under a Chapter VII authorization to employ force beyond self-defence, and will usually be undertaken in support of a government or transitional authority with the aim of providing a stable environment and may in some cases be or become engaged as parties to a non-international

[1] M. Bothe, 'Peace-keeping' in B. Simma, (ed.). *The Charter of the United Nations: A Commentary*, 2nd edn, 2 vols (Oxford: Oxford University Press, 2002), 1171 *et seq.*; N.D. White, *Keeping the Peace: The United Nations and the Maintenance of International Peace and Security* (Manchester, New York: Manchester University Press; 1993), 199–206.

TERRY D. GILL

6.01 armed conflict in support of a government if the material conditions for the existence of such a conflict and their participation as a party to that conflict are fulfilled. Even when this is not the case, their operations will not be legally dependent upon the consent of the relevant parties and their use of force, while tailored to fulfilling the mandate with as much restraint as possible, will not be restricted to self-defence.[2]

2. In contrast, UN peace operations are not conceptually based upon Chapter VII of the Charter and consequently legally require the consent of the Host State in order to be able to deploy and operate on that State's territory and are additionally subject to the principles of impartiality and restricted to the use of force in self-defence.[3] In addition to the legal requirement of Host State consent, peace operations are also dependent upon the consent, or at the least acquiescence, of all the parties to the conflict or dispute, in order to function and carry out their mandate, and are not intended or usually organized and equipped to engage in protracted hostilities or impose a solution militarily. Their primary purpose is to act in support of efforts aimed at promoting disengagement of the parties to a particular conflict and of achieving a diplomatic solution.[4] Traditionally, the role and function of peacekeeping operations during the first decades of UN Peacekeeping, in the 1950s and 1960s, was to act as a buffer between opposing forces after a ceasefire agreement had been reached and oversee and facilitate the carrying out of the terms of such agreements through monitoring, interposition, and persuasion. Since the end of the Cold War, these traditional tasks have been progressively expanded to include in many cases the promotion of a stable environment, the maintenance of public order, the provision of humanitarian assistance in cooperation with civilian governmental and non-governmental agencies, and the protection of civilians from violations of humanitarian and human rights law to the extent possible within the terms of their mandate and their operational capabilities.[5] This has sometimes resulted in the blurring of the distinction between 'peace enforcement' and 'peacekeeping', to some extent from a practical perspective, but even so, the legal basis and operational capabilities of peace enforcement operations and peacekeeping and other consent-based peace operations are quite distinct and remain highly relevant, notwithstanding the fact that many recent peacekeeping operations operate in

[2] See Sections 5.01 and 5.02 with supporting commentary.

[3] *United Nations Peacekeeping Operations: Principles and Guidelines*, DPKO International Publication, UN Secretariat, March 2008, available online at <http://www.un.org/en/peacekeeping/operations/principles.shtml> (hereinafter, cited as *Capstone Doctrine*). See for discussion of the basic principles and distinction between enforcement and peacekeeping chapter 3, at 31 *et seq*. See also T. Findlay, *The Use of Force in UN Peace Operations* (Oxford: Oxford University Press, 2002), 3–7. Recent practice of the UN has seen the blurring of the lines between expanded 'wider' or 'robust' peacekeeping and peace enforcement. For commentary see Findlay, *The Use of Force*, 5–6.

[4] *Capstone Doctrine*, chapter 2, 'The Evolving Role of United Nations Peacekeeping Operations', 17–29; Findlay, *The Use of Force*, 4.

[5] *Capstone Doctrine*, 24. See also SC Res. 1674 (2006) on the protection of civilians in armed conflict.

unstable environments against the background of often complex intrastate conflicts involving multiple actors and tenuous consent (of some) of the parties to the conflict and sometimes are provided with mandates under Chapter VII of the Charter as an additional means of inducing compliance of the parties and signalling the resolve of the international community.[6] **6.01**

3. Essentially, despite the existence of undeniable 'grey areas' and a certain degree of overlap between more 'robust' forms of peacekeeping operations on the one hand and peace enforcement operations on the other, the essential difference between the two lies in the elements of consent, impartiality, and the use of coercion. Peace enforcement may strive for the maximum degree of consent feasible under the particular circumstances, but is not legally or operationally dependent upon it. Likewise, impartiality, while sometimes possible, is not required or always feasible or even desirable within the context of peace enforcement. Finally, and as a consequence of the foregoing, peace enforcement operations will be mandated, organized, and equipped to employ coercion and use force to a far greater degree than peacekeeping or other consent-based peace operations would normally be.[7] By contrast, peacekeeping or other consent-based peace operations, whether conducted by the UN or by a regional organization or arrangement, are governed by and subject to the principles of consent of the parties, impartiality, and restricted to the use of force in self-defence, which in contemporary UN doctrine includes defence of the mandate (see Chapter 24 'Force Protection, Unit Self-Defence, and Personal Self-Defence: Their Relationship to Rules of Engagement').[8] Consequently, while contemporary peace operations are undeniably multifaceted and multidimensional, there are clear distinctions between enforcement measures including peace enforcement operations which are essentially non-consensual and coercive and peacekeeping and other consensual peace operations, which are bound by these core principles and are primarily an instrument in support of a broader political solution to a particular conflict or situation.[9]

Enforcement operations and peace enforcement operations have their legal basis in Chapter VII of the Charter and are not subject to the consent of the Host State where they are deployed, nor to considerations of impartiality in the conduct of their operations. (See sub-Chapters 5.1 and 5.3 above.) By contrast, peace operations other than enforcement and peace enforcement operations are subject to the consent of the Receiving State and are governed by the principles of impartiality and restricted to the use of force in self-defence. These operations will be referred to subsequently as peace operations. **6.02**

See commentary to Section 6.01.

[6] Ibid. 14. [7] Ibid. 18–19; Findlay, *The Use of Force*, 5–6 and 375–81.
[8] Findlay, *The Use of Force*, 14–19; *Capstone Doctrine*, 34–5.
[9] See commentary para. 2 to this Section. See also Sections 5.01 and 5.02.

6.03 **Peace operations have their legal basis in the general powers of the Security Council, of the General Assembly, and of regional organizations. The authorization of such operations with the consent of the Receiving State has emerged in UN practice as a means of support for diplomatic efforts to establish and maintain peace. Notwithstanding the absence of a specific provision in the UN Charter which refers to such operations, they have become an established and generally accepted instrument in the maintenance of peace.**

1. As stated previously, the Charter makes no specific reference to peacekeeping or peace operations and the instrument of peacekeeping has emerged in UN practice, starting with the first observer missions in the years immediately following the coming into force of the Charter and continuing up to the present day.[10] They were initially a pragmatic solution to the failure of the UN collective security system to function as it was originally intended due to Cold War tensions and the inability of the Permanent Members of the Council to reach agreement on the employment of enforcement measures and filled a gap left by the political stalemate that characterized international relations over the first four decades of the UN's history. Since the end of the Cold War, they have developed into a multifaceted instrument of UN policy to not only contain traditional inter-State conflicts but to assist broader efforts by the UN, by regional organizations, and by other actors, which are directed towards promoting the overall settlement of intrastate conflicts and restoration of stability following breakdowns of authority, preventing large-scale violations of human rights, and assisting in post-conflict efforts aimed at conflict prevention and the (re)establishment of democratic self-governance.[11]

2. The legal basis for peace operations is to be found in the general powers of the UN Security Council to promote peaceful settlement of disputes and to maintain and restore international peace and security. These find their bases in Article 1(1) and in Chapters VI and VII of the Charter respectively.[12] Former UN Secretary General Dag Hammarskjöld referred to them as being 'Chapter VI and a half' measures, and prior to the end of the Cold War, all peace operations of a non-enforcement character were undertaken on the basis of a Chapter VI mandate of the Council, or in some cases of the General Assembly.[13] The involvement of the latter organ was a direct result of the Cold War political situation referred to immediately above and resulted in a major controversy regarding the legality of the General

[10] Bothe, 'Peace-keeping' in Simma et al., *The Charter of the United Nations*, 1171 *et seq.*; White, *Keeping the Peace*, 199–206.

[11] *Capstone Doctrine*, chapter 2, 'The Evolving Role of United Nations Peacekeeping Operations', at 17 *et seq.*

[12] Simma et al., *The Charter of the United Nations*, 1185–7 . See also D.W. Bowett, *United Nations Forces* (New York: Frederick A. Praeger, 1964), 274 *et seq.* and White, *Keeping the Peace*, 199 *et seq.*

[13] Simma et al., *The Charter of the United Nations*, 1174 *et seq.*; White, *Keeping the Peace*, 199–206. *Capstone Doctrine*, 13–14. It should be pointed out that while peacekeeping has been traditionally associated with Chapter VI, the Council's practice is not to refer to specific provisions of the Charter and no mandate has ever been explicitly based on Chapter VI.

Assembly's role in peace operations and in a crisis within the UN which led to vehement opposition by two Permanent Members of the Council to UN peace operations set up by the General Assembly in the Suez and Congo crises of the 1950s and 1960s and their refusal to pay contributions for the UN Emergency Force (UNEF) and UN Organisation in the Congo (ONUC) missions.[14] Although the International Court of Justice determined in its 1962 Advisory Opinion on *Certain Expenses* that the General Assembly had the power to make specific recommendations of a non-mandatory character related to international peace and security, including the establishment of missions such as those in Suez and the Congo, and that the expenses involved in the conduct of such operations constituted expenses of the UN organization to which all Member States were required to contribute financially,[15] this controversy and ensuing crisis, together with shifts in the membership and influence of the various groupings of States within the General Assembly and the political situation in general, has led to the reasserting of the predominant role of the Security Council in conducting peace operations and all such operations since the early 1960s have been exclusively mandated and politically controlled through the Council.[16] Hence, while the General Assembly is theoretically capable of setting up a peace operation through its general powers of recommendation, the practice over the past near half century has been that the Security Council has paramount authority to authorize and conduct peace operations of both an enforcement and a more consensual character and the Assembly's role has been largely ancillary and supportive to that of the Council in this context.[17] **6.03**

3. Under Chapter VIII of the Charter, regional organizations and arrangements have the power to conduct peace operations of a non-enforcement character within the context of the maintenance of regional peace and security and the settlement of regional disputes and conflicts (see Chapter 7 for further elaboration). The Council has taken a flexible approach to what constitutes a regional organization and has been generally supportive of the efforts of such organizations in the conducting of various types of peace operations, irrespective of whether such organizations technically qualify, or even view themselves as 'regional organizations' within the

[14] L. Goodrich, E. Hambro, and A.P. Simons, *Charter of the United Nations* 3rd rev. edn (New York: Columbia University Press, 1969), 157–65.

[15] The 'Uniting for Peace Resolution', GA Res. 377 (V) 3-11-1950 was originally intended by the then predominant Western States within the General Assembly to serve as a basis for enforcement action. Although this was largely abortive, it did play a role in the establishment of several early peacekeeping operations, notably those in Suez (UNEF I) and the Congo (ONUC), leading to the abovementioned constitutional and financial crisis and commented upon in the sources cited in the previous note. The ICJ's Advisory Opinion on *Certain Expenses* (ICJ Reports, 1962, 155 *et seq.*) determined that both the Suez and Congo operations were not enforcement operations and were not 'unconstitutional'. However, the solution was found in the political compromise referred to earlier whereby the Security Council reasserted its predominant role. See also Simma et al., *The Charter of the United Nations*, 1176–7.

[16] See also White, *Keeping the Peace*, 127–35.

[17] See Simma et al., *The Charter of the United Nations*, 1174 *et seq.*; White, *Keeping the Peace*, 199–206. *Capstone Doctrine*, 13–14.

6.03 context of Chapter VIII of the Charter. Such regionally initiated peace support operations are subject to the consent of the Receiving State's government and the consent or acquiescence of other relevant partners in the same way UN-initiated peace support operations are and follow the same basic principles of impartiality and defensive force as their UN counterparts. As such, they do not require UN authorization in order for them to be carried out. In practice, however, the UN Security Council has been generally supportive of such regional efforts and has often provided them with political endorsement and on request a degree of logistical and material support.[18] These should not be confused with peace enforcement operations undertaken by regional organizations which do require Security Council authorization under Article 53(1) of the Charter.[19]

6.04 **Political control, exercised by the Security Council, by regional organizations, and by States is the predominant factor for the regulation of such operations, alongside any conditions posed by the Receiving State which have been accepted by the Security Council or other authorizing entity such as a regional organization. This regulation is further subject to the abovementioned principles of consent, impartiality, and the restriction of force to self-defence. These existing legal restraints are worked out into multinational and national rules of engagement (ROE) which often contain additional restraints of an operational or policy nature.**

1. The political control by the Security Council or by the appropriate organ of a regional organization through the provision and supervision of the execution of the mandate provides the overall parameters and legal basis for any peace support operation alongside the consent of and any conditions imposed by the Receiving State. These are further governed by the abovementioned basic principles of impartiality and the restriction of force to self-defence and mission accomplishment.

2. The operational planning and regulation of a peace operation will be worked out in an Operations Plan (OPLAN) and rules of engagement (ROE) within the overall framework of the mandate and subject to the political control of the Security Council or other mandating authority. The drawing up of the OPLAN and ROE for the particular mission will normally be entrusted to the relevant designated body or authority within the organization charged with the administrative and operational direction and supervision of such operations. Within the UN, this is the Department of Peacekeeping Operations (DPKO), which forms part of the UN Secretariat under

[18] For example, the DPKO has worked, and still works closely with, *inter alia*, the African Union, the European Union, NATO, the Organization for Security and Cooperation in Europe (OSCE), and the Organization of American States in a variety of missions and has been instrumental in helping to set up the African Standby Force and works closely with the AU in Sudan and Somalia. For facts and figures see <http://www.unrol.org/article.aspx?n=dpko>.

[19] See e.g. Simma et al., *The Charter of the United Nations*, 1484–7 and Goodrich et al., *Charter of the United Nations*, 364–7.

overall direction of the UN Secretary General and which is under the direction of the Under-Secretary General for Peacekeeping Affairs. Within DPKO, the Office of Operations and the Office of Military Affairs would be primarily responsible for the formation of the relevant OPLAN and the drawing up of mission-specific ROE, based upon the UN model ROE and taking into account the restrictions imposed by individual Troop Contributing Countries (TCCs) upon specific types of operations (these are often referred to as 'national caveats').[20] While it is the policy of the UN to discourage the imposition of such caveats, it is nevertheless a common practice that TCCs will often insist upon certain restrictions on the operational deployment of the forces they contribute to a particular mission as a condition of their participation in the mission. (An example of such a caveat could be that the troops provided by a particular TCC will not be used for crowd and riot control duties since they may not be trained or authorized to carry out such tasks.) **6.04**

3. Once the OPLAN and ROE have been drawn up in consultation with the TCCs providing forces and other personnel and equipment for the mission in question, and the voluntary contribution of the troops by the participating States has been agreed, the forces provided will be transferred to the operational command and control of the UN or regional organization which has mandated and is carrying out the mission through a 'Transfer of Authority Agreement' (TOA) between the relevant organization such as the UN and the individual TCCs contributing forces to the mission.[21] For further specifics concerning the command and control arrangements in UN peace operations, see sub-Chapter 6.5 'Authority, Command, and Control in United Nations-led Peace Operations'.

4. The Security Council or relevant organ within a regional organization carrying out a specific peace support operation will retain overall political control and authority over the mission, while the actual conduct of the mission falls under the responsibility of the UN Secretary General and his delegated officials for UN peace support operations, or the counterpart organ, agency, and officials within the context of a regional peace support operation.

While all consent-based peace operations share the abovementioned general characteristics which define their legal status and which differentiate them from enforcement and peace enforcement operations, their mandates and objectives, the challenges they face, and their resulting practices will differ (widely) from case to case. In cases where peacekeeping forces become involved in hostilities, the principles and rules of international humanitarian law will be applicable to them for the duration of their participation as parties. 6.05

[20] *Capstone Doctrine*, Part II: Planning United Nations Peacekeeping Operations, 47 *et seq*. See also sub-Chapters 6.4 and 6.5 in this Handbook, relating to ROE and the Application of Force and Authority, Command, and Control in UN Peace Operations.

[21] Ibid.

6.05 1. As stated previously (see Sections 5.01, 5.02, and 6.01 with supporting commentary), peace operations differ conceptually and in the nature of their objectives, legal basis, and in many of their operational aspects from enforcement operations, including peace enforcement operations. Nevertheless, modern UN peacekeeping is multifaceted and often faces complex challenges. These can include the use of force in the context of self-defence and mission accomplishment, sometimes in exceptional cases even reaching the threshold of participation as parties within the context of a (non-international) armed conflict. If the conditions for this are met, international humanitarian law will apply as law to them for as long as they remain parties. In such cases, UN forces are bound by the principles of humanitarian law as set out in the Secretary General's Bulletin on the *Observance by United Nations Forces of International Humanitarian Law*,[22] as well as by humanitarian law rules contained in treaties and in customary law to which individual TCCs are bound. Whenever force is employed, even within a relatively localized and temporary context, which rises to the level of conducting hostilities, these humanitarian principles and rules would be applicable. In all other situations, short of hostilities and whenever UN forces exercise jurisdiction over persons or a geographical area, human rights standards and rules would be applicable to UN forces as customary law.

[22] Of 6 August 1999 (ST/SGB/1999/13).

6.2 Status of Forces in Peace Operations

Forces participating in peace operations enjoy immunity vis-à-vis the Receiving State and any other (Transit) State as a matter of customary international law. Their rights and obligations may be specified in status-of-forces agreements (SOFAs). 6.06

1. *General.* The status of foreign armed forces participating in peace operations derives from both their immunity as organs of their Sending States and the international mission they are authorized to perform (see sub-Chapter 5.2). There are no fundamental status differences between forces participating in peace operations and those participating in enforcement and peace enforcement operations. In practical terms, status regulation for personnel participating in peace operations falls into three different categories: the general status and protection; special regulations under specific agreements distributing also tasks and responsibilities between the Sending State and the Receiving State; and a regime against impunity to be secured primarily by the Sending State.[1]

2. *Conventional Specifications.* While the status of military and civilian personnel participating in UN operations is addressed in Article VI of the 1946 UN Convention on the Privileges and Immunities of the United Nations and the 1994 UN Convention on the Safety of United Nations and Associated Personnel, their immunity in the Receiving State and any Transit State derives from customary international law (see Section 5.12, commentary paras 3 and 4). The rights and duties of such personnel should be further regulated for each peace operation in a status-of-forces agreement (SOFA) or status-of-mission agreement (SOMA). The advisability of such agreements, even where they may be not legally necessary, was stressed from the beginning of the UN peacekeeping practice,[2] yet often factual developments lagged behind for lack of time for negotiations which would be necessary for that purpose, lack of expertise by the States involved, and a preference for *modus vivendi* solutions where treaty implementation and the implied administrative efforts appeared too complicated and unreliable. To the extent that SOFAs and SOMAs affect the legislative order of the participating States, they will be subject to ratification, another barrier that may be difficult to overcome. Decades ago, upon request of the UN General Assembly a Model Status-of-Forces Agreement for

[1] See O. Engdahl, 'The legal status of United Nations and associated personnel in peace operations and the legal regime protecting them', International Institute of Humanitarian Law (ed.), *International Humanitarian Law, Human Rights and Peace Operations.* 31st Round Table on Current Problems of International Humanitarian Law, San Remo, 4–6 September, 2008, 113–17, at 113; same author, *Protection of Personnel in Peace Operations: The Role of the 'Safety Convention' against the Background of General International Law* (Stockholm University, 2005, republished in Leiden: Brill, 2006).

[2] See D.W. Bowett et al., *United Nations Forces: A Legal Study of United Nations Practice* (London: Stevens & Sons, 1964), chapter 13 'Agreements with Host States', 428–67.

6.06 Peacekeeping Operations (UN Model SOFA),[3] and also a Model Agreement between the United Nations and Member States Contributing Personnel and Equipment to United Nations Peace-Keeping Operations[4] were prepared with great care by the Secretary General. While modifications are not excluded, both texts may be considered as influential guidance in practice.[5] In addition, issues of mutual cooperation may be settled by Memoranda of Understanding (MOU), Technical Arrangements (TA), or similar instruments. Different requirements for military and civilian components of a force, private companies, and humanitarian workers could be addressed in such arrangements. But in the absence of such agreements and arrangements participants must rely on general principles and rules as deriving from existing conventions and customary law (see Section 5.12, para. 3). The provisions of NATO SOFA and its extension to the new partners of the Alliance, the PfP (Partnership for Peace) SOFA,[6] were prepared for purposes different from peace operations. The close cooperation between Sending States and Receiving States within NATO and its Partnership for Peace programme includes sharing responsibilities, e.g. for the exercise of jurisdiction and also for the settlement of claims, which in the case of peace operations may be impossible or even unacceptable. In contrast to allied training exercises, a Receiving State should not be accorded concurring jurisdiction on members of a peace operation and in most cases it will also be unable to participate in the settlement of claims.

(a) *Armed forces* as organs of their Sending States enjoy immunity in the Receiving State irrespective of any special agreement. This principle fully applies to individual soldiers as members of the Sending State's mission. SOFAs or SOMAs might limit that immunity in offering the Receiving State's rights vis-à-vis the Sending State's forces that otherwise would not exist. They may also confirm obligations of the Sending State's forces under international law (see Section 6.07), underline the respect for and application of the law of the Receiving State, and regulate its mode of application.

(b) *Civilian personnel including police.* The immunity of personnel participating in a peace operation also applies to civilian members of the foreign armed force and to police personnel on mission in a Receiving State. The 1990 UN Model SOFA provides that military observers, UN civilian police, and civilian personnel other than UN officials shall be considered as experts on mission within the meaning of

[3] UN Doc. A/45/594 (9 October 1990), reprinted in B. Oswald, H. Durham, and A. Bates, *Documents on the Law of Peace Operations* (Oxford: Oxford University Press, 2010), 34–50, and D. Fleck (ed.), *The Handbook of the Law of Visiting Forces* (Oxford: Oxford University Press, 2001), Annex F.

[4] UN Doc. A/51/967, Annex, reprinted in Oswald et al., *Documents on the Law of Peace Operations*, 51–66.

[5] See Fleck, 'Securing Status and Protection of Peacekeepers', in R. Arnold and G.-J.A. Knoops (eds), *Practice and Policies of Modern Peace Support Operations Under International Law* (Ardsley, NY: Transnational Publishers, 2006), 141–56, at 150.

[6] Agreement Among the States Parties to the North Atlantic Treaty and the Other States Participating in the Partnership for Peace Regarding the Status of their Forces (PfP SOFA) of 19 June 1995, reprinted in Fleck (ed.), *Handbook of the Law of Visiting Forces*, Annex B.

Article VI of the 1946 Convention, while military personnel of national contingents of a UN peacekeeping operation 'shall have the privileges and immunities specifically provided for in the present Agreement'.[7] The latter distinction remains of course subject to the conclusion of a SOFA which may be missing in the actual case (see later, para. 3). It does not exclude that both groups, military and civilian members of a peace contingent, may be considered as experts on mission, as described above (Section 5.12, para. 4 b). The same applies to foreign *police* personnel involved in peace operations: operating under the control of their Sending States, police officers also enjoy immunity in the Receiving State. 6.06

(c) *Private companies* may be hired by Sending State's military or police forces. As they do not enjoy immunity absent agreement, their status may be that of foreign workers in the Receiving State, unless otherwise agreed. Private companies should be limited to a strictly civilian function. Their manpower management must observe that certain activities are inherently governmental and remain military in nature.[8] Best practice activities should aim at ensuring better supervision and accountability.[9] The regulatory regime of such companies remains unsatisfactory when the legislation of the Sending State does not apply to their performance abroad and the Receiving State does not provide sufficient regulation.[10] It should be in the interest of both the Receiving State and the Sending State to address these aspects in the SOFA and provide for cooperative solutions of any contentious issue in this respect. For further discussion see Chapter 28 'Private Contractors and Security Companies'.

(d) *Humanitarian workers* will often have no opportunity to be included in status agreements before entering an area of operations in a foreign State. In international and non-international armed conflicts humanitarian relief personnel as well as objects used for humanitarian relief operations must be respected and protected under customary international humanitarian law.[11] In territories under foreign occupation they may point to the rule stated in Article 59 of the Fourth Geneva Convention which provides that '[i]f the whole or part of the population of an occupied territory is inadequately supplied, the Occupying Power shall agree to relief schemes on behalf of the said population, and shall facilitate them by all the means at its disposal'. For humanitarian assistance in Kosovo 1999, the Security

[7] See UN Model SOFA, Sections 26 and 27.

[8] See e.g. US Department of Defense Instruction 3020.41 USD (AT&L) of 3 October 2005 'Contractor Personnel Authorized to Accompany the US Armed Forces' and US Department of Defense Instruction 1100.22 USC (P&R) of 7 September 2006 'Guidance for Determining Workforce Mix'.

[9] Montreux Document on pertinent international legal obligations and good practices for States related to operations of private military and security companies during armed conflict of 17 September 2008, UN GA Doc. A/63/467 and UN SC Doc. S/2008/636 (6 October 2008), <https://www.icrc.org/eng/assets/files/other/icrc_002_0996.pdf>.

[10] See O. Quirico, 'National Regulatory Models for PMSCs and Implications for Future International Regulation', European University Institute Working Papers MWP 2009/25, Max Weber Programme, <http://cadmus.eui.eu/dspace/bitstream/1814/11759/1/MWP_2009_25.pdf>.

[11] Rules 31–32 CIHL.

6.06 Council referred to the right of access of humanitarian organizations to the theatre in the following terms:

> *Bearing in mind* the provisions of the Charter of the United Nations and guided by the Universal Declaration of Human Rights, the international covenants and conventions on human rights, the Conventions and Protocol relating to the Status of Refugees, the Geneva Conventions of 1949 and the Additional Procols thereto of 1977, as well as other instruments of international humanitarian law . . .
>
> *Calls for* access for United Nations and all other humanitarian personnel operating in Kosovo and other parts of the Federal Republic of Yugoslavia.[12]

3. *Practice in UN Peace Operations.* In the past many UN peace operations have been initiated and conducted without specific status agreement, although since the mid-1990s the UN has sought to negotiate such agreements for each mission. Recent Security Council resolutions establishing a peace operation often provide that the UN Model SOFA[13] shall apply provisionally, pending the conclusion of a specific SOFA.[14] This may work as a provisional solution, but should be followed by SOFA negotiations with the Receiving State. For military and civilian personnel in current peace operations SOFAs and SOMAs are more widely available,[15] but the state of their implementation is uncertain. In no case has agreement on a SOFA been considered as a condition for deployment. In fact, many SOFAs were prepared months after the beginning of the deployment[16] or not at all. Even after conclusion of such agreements their legal validity under the law of the Receiving State may be questionable absent parliamentary approval. SOFAs should include provisions on jurisdiction (criminal and civil), entry and exit modalities, force protection, freedom of movement in the area of operations, licences and permits, weapons and ammunition, communications, host nation support, exemptions from import restrictions,

[12] SC Res. 1239 (1999), 14 May 1999; see also SC Res. 1653 (2006), 27 January 2006, on the situation in the Great Lakes region.

[13] See UN Doc. A/45/594 (9 October 1990), reprinted in Oswald et al., *Documents on the Law of Peace Operations.*

[14] Examples include SC Res. 1320 (2000), para. 6, in respect of the UN mission in Ethiopia and Eritrea (UNMEE), and SC Res. 2043 (2012), para. 7, noting the agreement between the Syrian Government and the UN in respect to the UN Supervision Mission in Syria (UNSMIS), to be established under the command of a Chief Military Observer. Some of these decisions were taken under Chapter VII of the UN Charter, see SC Res. 1990 (2011), para. 4, to apply the SOFA for the UN Mission in Sudan (UNMIS) *mutatis mutandis* to the UN Interim Security Force for Abyei (UNISFA); SC Res. 1996 (2011), para. 26, to apply the UN Model SOFA *mutatis mutandis* to the UN Mission in the Republic of South Sudan (UNMISS).

[15] For many operations currently conducted by the UN or by the EU, NATO, AU, ECOWAS, and OAS (for an inventory of such operations see <http://www.sipri.org/databases/pko>), SOFAs or SOMAs are publicly accessible. Implementing legislation is not available.

[16] For the United Nations Mission in Liberia (UNMIL) which started on 1 October 2003 a SOFA was concluded on 6 November 2003. For the African Union–United Nations Hybrid Operation in Darfur (UNAMID) comprising more than 19,000 troops from 40 States which started on 31 October 2007, a SOFA was signed by Joint Special Representative Adada and Sudanese Foreign Minister Deng Alor on 10 February 2008.

and exemption from taxation by the Receiving State.[17] Yet many Receiving States are unable or unwilling to deal with these issues in a forthcoming and effective manner. The Security Council has occasionally drawn attention to the need of a SOFA for peace operations. In 1993 the Government of Georgia was called upon to conclude expeditiously a SOFA with the United Nations to facilitate deployment of the UN Observer Mission in Georgia (UNOMIG).[18] For the UN Mission in Ethiopia and Eritrea (UNMEE), the Security Council requested both governments to conclude, 'as necessary', SOFAs within 30 days; pending conclusion the Model SOFA of 9 October 1990 should apply provisionally.[19] Ethiopia did conclude a SOFA, but Eritrea did not.[20] Similar requests were made with respect to other missions, e.g. the UN Missions in Sierra Leone (UNAMSIL)[21] and the Democratic Republic of Congo (MONUC).[22] The language used in these resolutions shows certain interesting deviations between the English[23] and the French[24] texts. But it appears that in practice it does not make much difference whether the UN Model SOFA 'should' or 'will' or even 'shall' apply. Yet it is essential to have clear provisions implemented and for this purpose sustained efforts should be undertaken by responsible authorities. For UNMEE the Lessons Learned Report recorded a requirement to negotiate SOFAs as early as possible to secure the mission's full legal rights and protection, even recognizing that political exigencies may militate against such negotiations. The Report underlines that: **6.06**

> whether there be a specific agreement with the host country or the imposition of the Model SOFA, it is suggested that greater efforts could be made to ensure that there is a meeting of minds between the host country and the mission on the legal rights and protection to be afforded to the mission and its staff.[25]

This reveals that the conclusion and joint implementation of SOFAs, although they may not be considered 'necessary', could have facilitated operations and improved cooperation with competent authorities of the host country. For effective peace

[17] For details see A.P.V. Rogers, 'Visiting Forces in an Operational Context', in Fleck (ed.), *Handbook of the Law of Visiting Forces*, 533–57 (with checklist for lawyers involved in pre-deployment negotiations, at 554–7; see also P.J. Conderman, 'Status of Armed Forces on Foreign Territory Agreements (SOFA)', in *Max Planck Encyclopedia of Public International Law (MPEPIL)*, <http://opil.ouplaw.com/home/EPIL>.

[18] SC Res. 858 (1993), 24 August 1993, para. 8.

[19] SC Res. 1320 (2000), 15 September 2000, para. 6.

[20] R. Zacklin, 'United Nations Management of Legal Issues', in J. Howard and B. Oswald (eds), *The Rule of Law on Peace Operations. A Challenge of Peace Operations' Project Conference* (Melbourne: Asia-Pacific Centre for Military Law, 2003), 115–26, at 119.

[21] SC Res. 1270 (1999), 22 October 1999, para. 16.

[22] SC Res. 1291 (2000), 24 February 2000, para. 10.

[23] '. . . pending the conclusion of such an agreement the model status-of-forces agreement dated 9 October 1990 (A/45/594) should apply provisionally'.

[24] '. . . c'est le modèle d'accord sur le statut des forces en date du 9 octobre 1990 (A/45/594) qui s'appliquera provisoirement'.

[25] United Nations Mission in Ethiopia and Eritrea (UNMEE) Lessons Learned Interim Report: Updated Plan of Action (24 November 2004), 36. For general information see <http://unmee.unmissions.org>.

6.06 operations the immunity of military and civilian personnel deployed in the Receiving State and the exclusive jurisdiction of their respective Sending State on any act committed by peacekeepers remains essential. In any case, peacekeepers must remain exempt from jurisdiction of the Receiving State.[26]

4. *Security and Safety of Peace Operations*. Devastating bomb attacks against the UN Headquarters in Baghdad[27] on 19 August and 22 September 2003 were investigated by an independent panel which also submitted proposals for a new security strategy for the UN system as a whole, including the use of professional assessment tools for the collection of information on potential threats, clear guidance by and clear responsibilities of the United Nations to ensure the security of its staff, a robust security management system with adequate disciplinary measures to counter non-compliance, and significant increases in resources to develop and maintain the necessary security infrastructure.[28] Following the appointment in 2005 of an Under-Secretary General for Safety and Security, the issue is under continuous review of the General Assembly,[29] which expressed its deep concern that, 'over the past decade, threats and attacks against the safety and security of humanitarian personnel and United Nations and associated personnel have escalated dramatically and that perpetrators of acts of violence seemingly operate with impunity',[30] and recommended that:

> the Secretary-General continue to seek the inclusion of, and that host countries include, key provisions of the Convention on the Safety of United Nations and Associated Personnel, among others, those regarding the prevention of attacks against members of the operation, the establishment of such attacks as crimes punishable by law and the prosecution or extradition of offenders, in future as well as, if necessary, in existing status-of-forces, status-of-mission, host country and other related agreements negotiated between the United Nations and those countries, mindful of the importance of the timely conclusion of such agreements.[31]

These issues are of increasing relevance. The Security Council has tasked the Secretary General in January 2013 'to take all measures deemed necessary to strengthen United Nations field security arrangements and improve the safety and security of all military contingents, police officers, military observers and, especially, unarmed personnel'.[32]

[26] See Model Status-of-Forces Agreement for Peacekeeping Operations, UN Doc. A/45/594 (9 October 1990), Sections 7, 15, 24–31, and 46–9.

[27] See Section 5.2, para. 8b.

[28] Report of The Independent Panel on the Safety and Security of UN Personnel in Iraq of 20 October 2003, <http://www.un.org/News/dh/iraq/safety-security-un-personnel-iraq.pdf>.

[29] A/RES/62/95 of 17 December 2007; *Safety and security of United Nations personnel*. Report of the Secretary General, UN Doc. A/63/305 (18 August 2008), <http://reliefweb.int/report/world/safety-and-security-humanitarian-personnel-and-protection-un-personnel-report-secreta-0>.

[30] A/RES/63/138 of 5 March 2009, para. 9.

[31] Ibid. para. 15; see also para. 14.

[32] SC Res. 2086 (2013), para. 20.

5. *Training*. Professional training of the personnel engaged in relevant missions should include implementation of existing rights and obligations with respect to the mandate of the mission, the status of military and civilian personnel, and security management.[33] Ideally, such training would also involve competent authorities of the Receiving State to develop confidence-building and ensure effective cooperation. **6.06**

6. *Conclusions*. The status of personnel participating in peace operations is essentially the same as in enforcement and peace enforcement operations. While it largely derives from established custom, the United Nations and regional organizations, as well as Sending States and Receiving States should make further efforts to ensure that relevant rules and provisions are specified in treaty law, considering that this will facilitate and support cooperation with local authorities which is essential for the success of the mission. For each peace operation a SOFA or SOMA should be concluded, making full use of international experience and responding to requirements at local level.

Forces participating in peace operations shall observe their obligations under international law, in particular human rights law. They shall also respect the laws applicable in the Receiving State and any Transit State. Local institutions and individuals should be given appropriate access to independent review mechanisms to control and ensure these obligations. **6.07**

1. *General*. The obligations of foreign armed forces and civilian personnel participating in peace operations derive from international law, in particular human rights law, a general obligation to respect the law of the Receiving State and any Transit State,[34] and the law of the Sending State. For the applicability of human rights law, see Chapter 3. These obligations apply irrespective of the status of the personnel involved.

2. *Specific Standards*. The extent to which forces participating in peace operations may enjoy rights and must fulfil obligations under international law may be specified in agreements between participating States. Yet their immunity in the Receiving State and any Transit State will not be affected.

3. *Responsibilities*. For the responsibility of Sending States and international organizations, see Chapter 30, 'International Responsibility and Military Operations'. This responsibility includes acts committed in excess of authority or in contravention of instructions.

[33] On the latter see *Towards a Culture of Security and Accountability*. The Report of the Independent Panel on Safety and Security of UN Personnel and Premises Worldwide (9 June 2008), <http://www.alnap.org/resource/11168> as well as <http://www.un.org/News/dh/infocus/terrorism/PanelOnSafetyReport.pdf>.

[34] There may be diverging views on the practical consequences of that respect. Respect, for the aims and purposes of the law of the Receiving State, does not necessarily include its procedural requirements. See R. Batstone in Fleck (ed.), *Handbook of the Law of Visiting Forces*, 61–7.

6.07 (a) The responsibility of the United Nations Organization for acts committed in a UN peace operation is limited to acts committed under UN command and control (see Section 5.14, para. 2 a).

(b) The responsibility of the Sending State extends to all acts performed by peacekeepers on its behalf.

6.3 Legal Parameters for the Use of Force within the Context of Peace Operations

The conduct of peace operations with the consent of the Receiving State excludes any use of force other than in self-defence. According to UN doctrine, this includes any force which is authorized and necessary for mission accomplishment and the protection of civilians (see Chapter 22). In cases of such authorization, self-defence may extend beyond mere reaction to direct threat of force against the peacekeeping forces and can include reactions in response to armed threats against the integrity of the mission and the protection of civilians accompanying the mission and of the civilian population of the Receiving State within the capability of the mission. 6.08

1. The UN doctrine of self-defence has evolved over the years from a strictly personal level of self-defence in response to acts directed against individual peacekeepers into a significantly broader concept of self-defence which allows for the use of force in response to armed actions directed against UN personnel, equipment, installations, and to the extent possible within the capabilities of the mission in the protection of civilians and the execution of the mandate.[1] This concept of self-defence has its legal basis in the UN's powers in the realm of maintaining international peace and security and in the terms of the mandate.

2. For a more detailed discussion relating to the application of force in the context of UN Peace Operations and the UN doctrine of self-defence see sub-Chapter 6.1 'Characterization and Legal Basis for Peace Operations', sub-Chapter 6.4 'Application of Force and Rules of Engagement in Peace Operations', and Chapter 24 'Force Protection, Unit Self-Defence, and Personal Self-Defence: Their Relationship to Rules of Engagement'.

[1] See Findlay, *The Use of Force*, 87 *et seq.*, especially at 89–93. See also Section 24.05 and supporting commentary.

6.4 Application of Force and Rules of Engagement in Peace Operations

6.09 **Rules of engagement should be established for each peace operation. They may limit the use of force, but must not exceed existing legal limitations. The inherent right of personal self-defence must be respected (see above, Section 5.24, and below, Sections 10.02–10.03). Where hostilities take place, the rules of humanitarian law will be applicable (see Section 5.25 above).**

1. When analysing the mandate and drafting a concept of operations for a peace operation, the commander and his planning staff will make an assessment of the participating components (sea, air, land), the type and number of units, and weapon systems necessary to conduct the mission. Simultaneously, planners will develop a set of tailor-made rules of engagement based on the missions' mandate, political guidance, and the concept of operations, taking into consideration limitations based on law. Rules of engagement for peace operations would normally contain a description of principles applicable to the use of force under all circumstances referring to international humanitarian law as a guiding parameter for any use of force irrespective of whether the situation qualifies *de jure* as an armed conflict. These principles include distinction, proportionality, humanity, and military necessity.

2. Specific rules are developed for the various components, based upon a generic set of rules of engagement (United Nations and African Union-led operations) or are based on a detailed catalogue containing numbered rules (NATO and European Union led operations). Self-defence must be addressed in detail to ensure that soldiers are clear as to what sort of actions against oneself or one's unit would authorize the use of force. Although rules of engagement traditionally are developed for military personnel, nowadays police units are also using rules of engagement or similar directives for the use of force. Private (military) contractors are gradually becoming more involved during peace operations and under certain circumstances contractors are authorized to carry weapons. In these situations, rules on the use of force (mainly based on the principle of self-defence) should be available and personnel should be thoroughly familiar with the application of the rules.

6.10 **While remaining predominantly defensive in nature, the ROE allow for the potential need for offensive action if necessary, in order to ensure the implementation of the tasks assigned. The ROE contain definitions for the circumstances under which the use of force may be justified. Whenever the operational situation permits, every reasonable effort must be made to resolve any hostile confrontation by means other than the use of force. Any force used must be limited in its intensity and duration to what is strictly necessary to achieve the objective.**

1. In peace operations, force, defined as the use of physical means to achieve a legitimate objective, should be used only as a means of last resort. Although the presence of the mission in the area of operations is based on an international mandate, usually a Security Council resolution, and consent of the host country, the relationship between a foreign force and the population is not self-evident. Although ongoing hearts-and-minds projects will help build a strong relationship between the two, use of force incidents involving the unintended killing of civilians may jeopardize the relationship overnight. All efforts should be aimed at avoiding casualties within the civilian population in order not to lose the necessary respect and support of those whom the peacekeepers came to protect in the first place. **6.10**

2. Rules of engagement may therefore limit the use of force when the target is in the proximity of the civilian population. Although under international law this would be a regular precaution, rules of engagement may add extra precautionary measures, not required under treaty law. Such measures could include the obligation to deploy forward observers in case of indirect fires (mortars, artillery) or fire only after visual verification of the target. Rules may also contain operational considerations of importance to the commander and may limit the use of force in such a way that it will be used in a manner consistent with the overall military and mission objective. This may include the prohibition on destroying critical infrastructure, communication facilities, and other potential military targets, whilst allowing the disabling or disruption of such objects.

3. Limitations may also regulate command involvement in battle by vesting authority in a commander or subordinate commander to authorize pre-planned strikes, or the use of certain weapon systems, weapons, types of fires, and aircraft. For example, use of heavy weapons such as long-range artillery, may have a high risk of escalation and senior commanders with their additional staff capacity are normally better suited to oversee all consequences of employing those weapons. Whenever appropriate, commanders will consider the use of unarmed force instead of the use of armed force, for example deception, psychological methods, or negotiation. Stop, search, and apprehension of opponents using at most physical restraint can be qualified as unarmed force, even if weapons are on the scene or at hand.

4. If unarmed force is inappropriate, a gradual escalation of force will be considered. Two distinct levels of armed force can be applied: deadly force or non-deadly force. Non-deadly force is the level of force which is neither intended nor likely to cause death, regardless of whether death actually results.[1] It entails the use of non-lethal weapons, including batons, teargas, and other means of crowd and riot control and the use of firearms firing warning shots or shots aimed at lower body parts. Non-deadly force would be appropriate if the opponent is not carrying

[1] Standard Generic Rules of Engagement, United Nations, Department of Peacekeeping Operations, Military Division, May 2002, on file with authors.

6.10 firearms and poses a non-deadly threat to peacekeepers or to those under their protection. The ultimate degree of force of peacekeepers would be deadly force, the level of force intended or likely to cause death, regardless of whether death actually results.[2] This generally will be applied if no other means or methods are available to react to a hostile act or hostile intent of armed opponents.

5. One of the most controversial issues is the use of armed force (including and up to deadly force) against unarmed civilians. Such a situation occurred between 15 and 20 January 2006 in Côte d'Ivoire when a group known as the Young Patriots organized violent demonstrations against the Government and the United Nations peacekeeping operation in Abidjan and in western areas of the country.[3] The UNOCI headquarters in Abidjan, the French Embassy, and the 43rd French marine infantry battalion were besieged and repeatedly attacked for several days by crowds of the Young Patriots.[4]

During the siege, United Nations property suffered extensive damage. In Guiglo, groups of people incited by hate media attacked UNOCI troops, forcing them to use their rules of engagement to ensure their own safety. On at least one occasion a UN compound with peacekeepers was overrun as a result of the absence of sufficient means of riot control, no adequate fence, and the unwillingness to use deadly force against the violent demonstrators climbing over fences. Those same groups pillaged and burned the offices of humanitarian agencies and non-governmental organizations, while their staff were molested and chased from their houses, which were also vandalized. The direct threats to United Nations personnel led to a temporary relocation to safe havens of staff based in the west and in Abidjan.[5] In such a situation peacekeepers are authorized to use force, including deadly force, in self-defence. Whether or not soldiers will actually use force in such a situation is a matter of culture, training, and leadership. It depends also on how the commander on the scene assesses the situation. Especially in a rapidly deteriorating situation, the commander, with or without the assistance of his staff, should be able to quickly review his possible courses of action and make a decision and communicate it to everyone. What if he orders the use of firearms? Are his troops adequately trained to handle such situations? Will a few warning shots or aimed shots de-escalate or have

[2] Ibid. 5.

[3] Eighth Report of the Secretary General on the United Nations Operation in Côte d'Ivoire, UN Doc. S/2006/222, dated 11 April 2006.

[4] Ibid. 3. The anti-United Nations propaganda and incitement to violence, especially on the Radio Télévision Ivoirienne (RTI) and local radio networks, resulted in the extensive looting and destruction of assets and property of United Nations and humanitarian agencies in the western towns of Daloa and San-Pédro, and most seriously in Guiglo.

[5] As a result of the violent demonstrations organized by the Young Patriots, the security situation in Côte d'Ivoire deteriorated sharply at the beginning of the year. There were serious obstructions to the freedom of movement of the impartial forces, interruption of socio-economic activities and rampant insecurity in Abidjan, as well as in various parts of Government-controlled areas. Humanitarian activities came to a standstill as a result of the destruction by protesters of the offices of the United Nations and those of other humanitarian agencies, their relief supplies, warehouses, communications, and other equipment. UN Doc. S/2006/222 dated 11 April 2006, para. 18, at 4.

the opposite effect? It may be clear from the example that a thorough understanding of the applicable rules of engagement alongside such principles as distinction and proportionality is necessary; while the required de-escalation of the situation is also a matter of training, experience, and soldiers' fortune. 6.10

In some circumstances operational urgency may dictate the immediate use of deadly force. The use of force must be commensurate with the level of the threat and all necessary measures are to be taken to avoid collateral damage. During peace operations, use of force beyond personal self-defence may only be used in the circumstances as specified in the ROE. 6.11

1. The United Nations generic Rules of Engagement authorize under certain circumstances the use of force up to deadly force in situations where there is a hostile act. Hostile act is defined as: '[a]n attack or other use of force, intended to cause death, bodily harm or destruction'.[6] As most mandates nowadays explicitly include as a duty of the peacekeeping force 'to protect civilians under imminent threat of physical violence', no hesitation should exist on the part of commanders and soldiers in using up to deadly force if civilians are attacked or are about to be attacked and time does not allow for negotiation or the use of non-lethal means. It should be clearly understood at all levels that this is the *raison d'être* of peacekeeping: if peacekeepers are unable, unwilling, or not authorized, then what is their role in the first place? Attention should be paid to the precise wording of the mandate. It raises questions whether there is any difference in the execution of the mission when the relevant passage reads: 'to protect',[7] 'to ensure protection',[8] or 'to contribute to the protection'.[9] If discussions in the Security Council do not result in clarity, then answers should be found in the mission implementation plan, the operational plans, and orders for military and police components. An independent study recently examined the creation, interpretation, and implementation of mandates for United Nations peacekeeping missions to protect civilians. The study contains insights and recommendations for the entire range of UN protection actors, including the Security Council, troop and police contributing countries, the Secretariat, and the peacekeeping operations implementing protection of civilians' mandates.[10]

[6] See Standard Generic Rules of Engagement, United Nations, Department of Peacekeeping Operations, Military Division, May 2002, 7.

[7] SC Res. 1542 (2005) of 30 April 2005 (MINUSTAH, Haiti): to protect civilians under imminent threat of physical violence, within its capabilities and areas of deployment.

[8] SC Res. 1565 (2004) of 1 October 2004 (MONUC, Democratic Republic of Congo): to ensure the protection of civilians, including humanitarian personnel, under imminent threat of physical violence.

[9] UNAMID, Darfur, SC Res. 1769, 2007: to contribute to the protection of civilian populations under imminent threat of physical violence and prevent attacks against civilians, within its capability and areas of deployment, without prejudice to the responsibility of the Government of the Sudan.

[10] Victoria Holt and Glyn Taylor, Independent study commissioned jointly by the UN Office for the Coordination of Humanitarian Affairs (OCHA) and the UN Department of Peacekeeping Operations (DPKO), 17 November 2009.

6.11 2. Having witnessed confusion on mandates in the past (Rwanda 1994, Srebrenica 1995), a contemporary example of differing views related to the interpretation of the mandate and the ensuing Rules of Engagement which occurred at the end of May 2004 with the UN Mission in the Democratic Republic of Congo (MONUC) serves as an illustration of the possible repercussions. Nkunda, a former ANC commander refusing to adhere to the cease-fire agreement, marched from North-Kivu with ex-ANC soldiers to join Mutebutsi north of Bukavu, a city of 600,000 inhabitants. He was reinforced along the route and his force increased to about 2,000 men. MONUC, led by the deputy Force Commander, was planning to disarm Mutebutsi's units and use attack-helicopters to canalize Nkunda's troops along the shore of Lake Kivu, preventing Nkunda from seizing Bukavu. Tactics were to warn Nkunda verbally, followed, if necessary, by warning shots and finally, if Nkunda still did not stop, to attack his advance units. HQ MONUC Kinshasa then decided that in the given situation deadly force was prohibited. Nkunda passed Bukavu airport and headed for Bukavu. Subsequently, MONUC troops blocked the road and delayed the attack for 18 hours. The next day, Nkunda's troops reached Bukavu and spread out across the city. Houses and shops were looted and citizens robbed. Summary executions and widespread rape occurred and many lives were lost and many citizens injured. UN HQ New York had expected MONUC and the Kivu-brigade to use force and did not share the views of HQ MONUC Kinshasa on taking a neutral position in Bukavu. The Bukavu crisis influenced the peace process seriously and delayed it politically and militarily for more than five months. When Nkunda arrived in Bukavu demonstrations started in all major cities in the DRC. The UN was blamed for not stopping Mutebutsi and Nkunda. HQ MONUC, under pressure from severe attacks on UN establishments in Kinshasa, prepared for evacuation and UN property was destroyed.[11]

3. Decisions to use force will often have to be taken at the lowest tactical level, sometimes by individual soldiers. It is for that reason that soldiers should be aware of all possible scenarios. During pre-deployment exercises individual soldiers should have gone through extensive shoot or no-shoot scenarios, providing the clarity needed once they are confronted with real-life situations. An imminent attack on property necessitates a more sophisticated approach when circumstances such as limited numbers of troops or limited (air) mobility dictate the concentration of scarce means to protect mission-essential assets or designated infrastructure. In addition, troop contributing countries using caveats may have excluded the use of deadly force to defend property, based on national legislation. Hostile intent has been defined in UN Rules of Engagement[12] as: '[t]he threat of imminent use of force, which is demonstrated through an action which appears to be preparatory to a

[11] Excerpt from 'Experiences from UN Military Peace Enforcement Operations in the DRC April 2003–January 2005', Brigadier General Jan Isberg, Former Deputy Force Commander and Brigade Commander MONUC, on file with authors.

[12] See Standard Generic Rules of Engagement, United Nations, Department of Peacekeeping Operations, Military Division, May 2002, 7.

hostile act'. In case of hostile intent, Rules of Engagement will authorize an incremental escalation of force to counter the threat. The remainder of the definition, 'only a reasonable belief in the hostile intent is required, before the use of force is authorized' will provide back-up for a soldier or the on-scene commander if he has chosen to use force. Whether or not hostile intent is being demonstrated must be judged on the basis of one or a combination of factors, including: the capability and preparedness of the threat, the available evidence which indicates an intention to attack, and the historical precedent within the mission's area of responsibility. **6.11**

4. In sum, the phrase: 'use of force beyond self-defense may only used be in the circumstances as specified in the ROE' suggests a severe limitation on the use of force, while on the contrary the phrase 'only a reasonable belief in the hostile intent is required before the use of force is authorized' suggests a free hand leaving the decisions to use force to the discretion of the soldier or commander-on-scene. The often suggested limitation in UN ROE, referred to as 'peacekeepers with arms tied behind their backs', seems not to be correct.

5. In March 2013 the UN Security Council adopted Resolution 2098,[13] creating on an exceptional basis, a specialized 'Intervention Brigade' within the MONUSCO's[14] existing 19,815 strong force. The Force consists, *inter alia*, of three infantry battalions, one artillery and one Special force and Reconnaissance company. The Resolution strongly condemned M23, the Democratic Forces for the Liberation of Rwanda (FDLR), the Lord's Resistance Army (LRA) 'and all other armed groups and their continuing violence and abuses of human rights'.[15]

The resolution authorized the brigade to carry out targeted offensive operations either unilaterally or jointly with the FARDC, in a robust, highly mobile and versatile manner and in strict compliance with international law, including international humanitarian law and with the human rights due diligence policy on UN support to non-UN forces (HRDDP). The aim is to prevent the expansion of all armed groups, neutralize these groups, and to disarm them in order to contribute to the objective of reducing the threat posed by armed groups on state authority and civilian security in eastern DRC and to make space for stabilization activities.[16]

Between July and November 2013, the brigade engaged by various means (artillery, aerial attacks, snipers etc.) alongside FARDC units that were leading the pushback against DRC's then strongest armed group. The offensive led to an unexpectedly quick win on the side of FARDC/FIB. The primary reason for this was the use of well-trained and disciplined FARDC units (mostly Unités de

[13] SC Res. 2098 (2013), March 2013.

[14] United Nations Organization Stabilization Mission in the Democratic Republic of the Congo.

[15] See Standard Generic Rules of Engagement, United Nations, Department of Peacekeeping Operations, Military Division, May 2002, para. 8.

[16] Ibid. para. 9.

6.11 Réaction Rapide) that benefitted from functioning supply chains for equipment, logistics, and food in conjunction with massive FIB support.[17]

As early as December 2013 and again in May 2014, MONUSCO announced the start of anti-FDLR operations. This operation failed due to the persistence of certain FARDC-FDLR networks at the local level, but also reluctance within the FIB.[18] Ever since, it remains unclear if and when anti-FDLR operations will begin. While not prescribed by MONUSCO's current mandate, the mission is clear on the fact that the FIB will not start unilateral operations without the consent of the DRC Government. Amongst DRC elites (political and military) the FDLR question is highly controversial. Within the FIB, similar political thinking is at play. Various stakeholders have independently confirmed that as of now Tanzanian and South African troops do not have clearance to engage in fighting with the FDLR—leaving the Malawian battalion as the only force that could engage.[19]

The mandate and in particular the phrase 'neutralize' rebel groups has drawn attention from scholars. One report[20] states that the brigade's mandate appears to go beyond all three of the basic principles of UN peacekeeping—consent, impartiality, and non-use of force except in self-defence. The report analyses the legal issues and states, *inter alia*, that the UN's peacekeeping mission as a whole—not just the Intervention Brigade component—is a party to the conflict under international law, concluding that all military members of MONUSCO no longer enjoy legal protection[21] from attacks.

This conclusion, however, dismisses the official UN position as promulgated in the SG Bulletin:[22] the fundamental principles and rules of international humanitarian law are applicable to United Nations forces when in situations of armed conflict they are actively engaged therein as combatants. The examples of earlier actions by the Intervention Brigade illustrate the relatively small footprint and temporary scope and scale of operations, having hardly any tangible impact on operations outside the area of responsibility of the brigade. However, the question of whether MONUSCO as a whole or the FIB has become party to a non-international armed conflict would depend upon whether the material conditions for the applicability of IHL to all or part of the Force had been met.[23]

The report furthermore concludes that MONUSCO premises and bases can be categorized as a military objective under IHL, and UN civilian staff may become

[17] Christoph Vogel, DRC: Assessing the performance of MONUSCO's Force Intervention Brigade, posted on 14 July 2014, African Arguments Editor.

[18] Ibid. [19] Ibid.

[20] Scott Sheeran and Stephanie Case, 'The Intervention Brigade: Legal Issues for the UN in the Democratic Republic of the Congo', International Peace Institute, Policy Paper, 20 November 2014.

[21] Afforded to them under international humanitarian law [IHL], the Convention on the Safety of United Nations and Associated Personnel through the status of forces agreement (SOFA), and the Rome Statute of the International Criminal Court.

[22] *Observance by United Nations Forces of International Humanitarian Law*, ST/SGB/1999/13, 6 August 1999.

[23] See sub-Chapter 5.5.

collateral damage in an attack. The Intervention Brigade's mandate is likely to lead to more instances of detention or internment by MONUSCO. This may generate IHL and international human rights law concerns, including the UN's practical capacity to meet obligations of treatment, transfer of detainees to national forces, and legal authority for sustained detention or internment.[24] **6.11**

The discussion on the use of force by UN peacekeepers has been going on for decades, however most UNSC resolutions today authorize the use of 'all necessary means' to protect civilians under imminent threat of physical violence.[25] This robust legal framework has resulted in successful operations against armed groups in various missions, occasionally leading to the dispersal or neutralization of armed groups. At the same time, the 'all necessary means' mandates have resulted in miscommunication and misinterpretation of the mandate by both Troop Contributing Countries and Senior Mission Leadership when developing courses of action in order to protect civilians. Despite the robust mandate, oftentimes troops were neither prepared nor equipped to launch offensive operations against armed group, whilst Force Commanders, eager to take action, have faced serious disagreement with their subordinate commanders interpreting and construing 'imminent threat'.

What is new is that the explicit wording in the mandate may create expectations by all actors involved. Just the name of the brigade suggests an agile, mobile, and offensive posture leaving no uncertainty about the purpose of the unit. The composition of infantry battalions, artillery, and special forces is another indication that the brigade is armed to the teeth and ready to fight. Lastly, the order to neutralize and disarm is explicit language making it clear that the armed groups pose a threat to stability and security in any case, dismissing the necessary nexus of 'imminent threat'.

MONUSCO's pre-existing 'protection of civilians' mandate provided the ability to use force against the main armed groups in the DRC. The addition of the Intervention Brigade's mandate may reflect deficiencies of political will and capacity, more than it does the legal authority to use force. The Intervention Brigade may therefore risk undercutting the legal interpretation of MONUSCO's and other missions' long-standing mandates for the protection of civilians.

The implementation of the ROE is a command responsibility. The ROE are normally addressed to the Force Commander, who is then responsible for issuing them to all subordinate commanders. All commanders have an obligation to seek clarification, if the authorized ROE are considered to be unclear or inappropriate for the military situation. 6.12

1. Rules of engagement are issued once they are approved by the competent authority. For UN-led operations, the Military Advisor will propose Rules to the

[24] See SC Res. 1565 (2004) of 1 October 2004 (MONUC, Democratic Republic of Congo).
[25] See SC Res. 1542, 1565, and 1769.

6.12 Under-Secretary General for Peace Operations who is the executive authority on behalf of the UN Secretary General for peace operations and is the approval authority for the Integrated Mission Plan, including the Operation Plan and the rules of engagement. For NATO-led missions, SACEUR will propose Rules to the Defence Planning Committee of the North Atlantic Council (NAC DPC) through the NATO Military Committee.

2. The Rules are issued to the Force Commander or to the Head of the Police Component if applicable. The Force Commander subsequently passes the ROE to subordinate unit commanders whom may seek additional guidance if necessary. Subordinate commanders are not authorized to alter the ROE. They may propose changes to the existing rules if they believe such is necessary for the adequate execution of their tasks. Proposals for change are reviewed by the Force Commander and if he concurs, approval will be sought from the competent authorities. It is the responsibility of the commanders of all national contingents to ensure that all those under their command understand these ROE. To assist in this process, they must issue a ROE aide-memoire or pocket card, translated into the language(s) appropriate for their own contingent, to each individual.

6.13 **Rules of engagement will determine under what circumstances search, apprehension, and detention operations may take place. Minimum principles must be observed during all search procedures: the purpose of the search must be clearly stated in the orders and to the individuals to be searched; searchers are not to humiliate, nor embarrass persons being searched; the search procedure must take into account gender and be sensitive to other factors such as race, religion, etc.**

1. Search, apprehending, and detaining an individual is authorized when acting in self-defence or in case of hostile act or hostile intent. In such cases use of up to deadly force is authorized taking into consideration common principles of humanity and proportionality. Non-lethal means must have priority here.

2. Other situations that may involve search, apprehension, and detention include third parties crossing roadblocks set up by the Force or when individuals enter restricted areas. Warning signs and information in the local language should be available and explain the procedure and rights of the individuals. All soldiers should be familiar with search and apprehension procedures and should have received adequate training.

6.14 **Detainees must not be subjected to torture, to cruel, inhuman or degrading treatment or punishment, or to intimidation, deprivation, humiliation, mistreatment, or any form of abuse (see below Chapter 25). Full respect is to be shown for their gender, race, and religious beliefs and for the customs and practices of the group to which they belong. Particular care is to be taken to ensure the**

protection and wellbeing of women and children. Detainees must be protected against all acts or threats of violence, insults, and public curiosity. Detainees are to be given rations, shelter, and access to medical care. 6.14

1. Before apprehension and detention, suspects must be searched. Ideally, the search is to be conducted in the presence of at least one witness, and should be conducted by a person of the same gender. The on-scene commander must ensure that all confiscated items are recorded properly. Persons may not be apprehended other than in accordance with the authorization given in the ROE. All apprehended persons are to be handed over to appropriate local authorities as soon as possible. Until hand-over takes place, such individuals may be detained. Regular peacekeeping forces are usually neither trained nor programmed to deal with civilian detainees. Therefore, straightforward procedures should be established to act rapidly and hand over to units and levels that are better equipped and prepared to guarantee safety of the unit and the detained individual. Strict adherence to ROE and detention procedures based on accepted human rights norms and standards[26] applied by peacekeeping forces should guarantee a minimum standard for detained individuals.

2. Wherever possible, detainees are to be informed of the reason for their apprehension or detention. This rule, based on the Universal Declaration and various human rights treaties[27] can be applied readily, provided that language assistants or interpreters are available. If such is not the case, peacekeepers should anticipate such circumstances by preparing translated written statements including the caution and detention grounds referring to language derived from the ROE. A ground for detention could be (attempted) use of armed force against a peacekeeper. Peace operations personnel are fully responsible for the safety and wellbeing of persons whom they apprehend or detain, as long as those persons are in their charge.

3. The authority to detain and the subsequent hand-over to appropriate national authorities is usually based on an agreement with the Host State and based on the notion that the Host State itself is not always in a position to apprehend and detain individuals whenever there may be a need. A recent phenomenon is the attention and sensitivity related to the responsibility of peacekeepers for detainees once they are handed over to appropriate national authorities. Claims based on violations of human rights obligations may be brought against peacekeepers by relatives or next of kin of a detained person if that person disappears or dies after hand-over.

4. Sometimes an agreement is concluded between troop contributing States and the Host State to stress the mutual obligation to respect basic standards of

[26] An example is the Professional Training Series no. 5/Add.3, Human Rights Standards and Practice for the Police, Geneva/New York 2004, <http://www.ohchr.org/Documents/Publications/training5Add3en.pdf>.

[27] Universal Declaration of Human Rights, Art. 9; ICCPR, Art. 9.

6.14 international humanitarian law, human rights law, and national law such as the right to life, to a fair trial, and the protection against torture. The agreement may include an obligation for the Host State to allow full access to detainees after their transferral to the Host State by representatives of a national human rights commission, the ICRC, or relevant human rights institutions within the UN system. The agreement may also include the responsibility for keeping an accurate account of all persons transferred to national authorities, making records available upon request, notifying the transferring State prior to the initiation of legal proceedings involving individuals, and prohibiting detainees being subjected to the death penalty.

5. Detainees must not be subjected to torture, to cruel, inhuman or degrading treatment or punishment, or to intimidation, deprivation, humiliation, mistreatment or any form of abuse. At no time in history has the treatment of detainees been more scrutinized by the international community based on photographs taken by perpetrators. It is therefore necessary to avoid ambiguity about the applicable rules or their interpretation. Mixed messages are not well understood or not understood at all by soldiers on the ground.

6.5 Authority, Command, and Control in United Nations-led Peace Operations

The Security Council provides the legal authority, high-level strategic direction, and political guidance for all UN peace operations, and it vests the operational authority for directing these operations in the Secretary General of the United Nations. The Under-Secretary General for Peacekeeping Operations (USG DPKO) has been delegated responsibility from the Secretary General for the administration of, and provision of executive direction for, all UN peace support operations. 6.15

1. The management of a peacekeeping operation at UN Headquarters in New York is considered to be the strategic level of authority, command, and control. The USG DPKO directs and controls UN peacekeeping operations and formulates policies and develops operational guidelines based on Security Council resolutions. In addition, the Under-Secretary General for Management has financial authority and the Under-Secretary General for Safety and Security is responsible for the safety and security of UN staff, responsibilities which affect UN peacekeeping operations. The Under-Secretary General for Field Support is responsible for delivering dedicated support to the field operations, including on personnel, finance, procurement, logistics, communications, information technology, and other administrative and general management issues.[1]

United Nations Member States may transfer authority to the United Nations to use the operational capabilities of their national military contingents, units, and/or uniformed personnel to undertake mandated missions and tasks. Operational authority over such forces and personnel is vested in the Secretary General, under the authority of the Security Council. Contributing Member States that provide uniformed personnel to United Nations peace operations retain full and exclusive strategic level command and control of their personnel and equipment. 6.16

1. Contributing Member States that provide military and police personnel to United Nations peacekeeping operations retain full and exclusive strategic level command and control of their personnel and equipment. Contributing Member States may assign these personnel and assets to serve under the authority of the Secretary General of the United Nations and under the operational control of the Head of the Military Component of a UN peacekeeping operation for a specified

[1] The text which follows is partly based on the contribution of the authors to the approved intern policy document on Authority, Command, and Control in UN Peacekeeping Operations, Department of Peacekeeping Operations, 15 February 2008, on file with authors.

6.16 period and purposes as agreed in the MOU with UN HQ. Administrative control is exercised by a senior national officer of a contributed military contingent within a mission area. The authority is limited to administrative matters such as personnel management, supply, and services and must not adversely influence the management and conduct of UN operations within a mission area. A UN report[2] revealed a persistent pattern of peacekeeping operations not intervening with force when civilians are under attack, partly as a result of a *de facto* dual line of command involving mission leadership and troop contributing countries that regulates the use of force by missions.[3]

Interviewees from Member States, troop contributing countries, the Secretariat, and throughout the civil and military pillars of missions consistently highlighted that some troop contributing countries imposed written and unwritten 'national caveats' on their contingents, effectively ruling out the use of force. This was generally interpreted as a lack of willingness on the part of troop contributing countries to put troops in danger. Interviewees also stated that commanders in the field routinely reported and sought advice from their capitals when commands were issued within the mission and acted on that advice even if it conflicted with that of the mission Force Commander or a Brigade Commander.[4]

The report states that the chain linking the intent of the Security Council to the actions of the Secretariat, troop and police contributing countries and peacekeeping missions themselves remains broken in relation to the use of force. Recommendations include a requirement for frank dialogue on the issue within the peacekeeping partnership of troop, police, and finance contributing countries, host governments, the Security Council, the Secretariat, and other parties. In addition, operational control of the United Nations over contingents needs to improve and situations in which contingents are hesitant or do not carry out duly issued orders from the mission military structure should be reported.[5]

Member States may withdraw their military and police personnel and the operational control of those personnel from the United Nations through formal communication with United Nations Headquarters.[6]

2. UN Operational Authority involves the authority to issue operational directives within the limits of: (1) a specific mandate of the Security Council; (2) an agreed period of time, with the stipulation that an earlier withdrawal of a contingent would require the contributing country to provide adequate prior notification; and (3) a specific geographic area (the mission as a whole). UN Operational Authority does not include any responsibility for certain personnel matters of individual members of military contingents and formed police units, such as pay, allowances, promotions and so on. These functions remain a national responsibility. With regard to

[2] UN Doc. A/68/787 of 7 March 2014, Office of Internal Oversight Services, Evaluation of the implementation and results of protection of civilians mandates in UN peacekeeping operations, <https://oios.un.org/resources/ga_report/a-68-787-dpko.pdf>.

[3] See also para. 30 of this Report for a detailed analysis of effective control over national contingents.

[4] Ibid. para. 35. [5] Ibid. para. 90. [6] Ibid. para. 7.

disciplinary matters it should be noted that while the discipline and administration of military justice of military personnel remain the responsibility of the troop contributing countries; the UN may take administrative steps in relation to misconduct including the repatriation of military contingent members and staff officers. **6.16**

The Head of Mission is the senior UN Representative and has overall authority over the activities of the United Nations in the mission area. He leads and directs the heads of all mission components and ensures unity of effort and coherence among all UN entities in the mission area. The Head of Military Component exercises operational control over all military personnel, including military observers and in the mission. The Head of Police Component exercises operational control over all members of the police component of the mission. **6.17**

1. The field-based management of a peacekeeping operation at Mission Headquarters is considered to be the operational level, while Head of Mission, Head of Military Component, Head of Police Component, Deputy Special Representative of the Secretary General, and the Director of Mission Support hold operational level authority, command, and control responsibilities.[7] The Head of Mission of a multidimensional peacekeeping operation is generally the Special Representative of the Secretary General.[8] He reports to the Secretary General through the USG DPKO. The Head of Mission has overall authority over the activities of the United Nations in the mission area. The Head of Mission (HOM) represents the Secretary General, leads UN political engagement, and speaks on behalf of the UN within the mission area. The HOM leads and directs the heads of all mission components and ensures unity of effort and coherence among all UN entities in the mission area, in accordance with the UN Integrated Strategic Framework. The HOM provides political guidance for mandate implementation and sets mission-wide operational direction including decisions on resource allocation in case of competing priorities. The HOM delegates the operational and technical aspects of mandate implementation to the heads of all components of the mission.[9]

2. The Head of Military Component (HOMC) reports to the HOM.[10] The HOMC exercises operational control over all military personnel, including Military Observers, in the mission. United Nations Operational Control is defined as the authority granted by Member States to a Military Commander in a United Nations peacekeeping operation to direct forces assigned so that the Commander may accomplish specific missions or tasks which are usually limited by function, time, or location (or a combination), to deploy units concerned and/or military personnel, and to retain or assign tactical command or control of those units/personnel.[11]

[7] Ibid. para. 7.

[8] For an excellent insight on the work of a Head of Mission see 'On Being a Special Representative of the Secretary-General', UNITAR, 2004.

[9] Ibid. 7. [10] Ibid. 8. [11] Ibid. 11.

6.17 The HOMC may establish subordinate Sector Commands, as appropriate. In doing so, the HOMC places military units under the tactical control of military commanders in the operational chain of command. The HOMC maintains a technical reporting and communication link with the DPKO Military Advisor in UN Headquarters. The technical reporting link must not circumvent or substitute the command chain between USG DPKO and the HOM, nor should it interfere with decisions taken by the HOM.

3. The Head of Police Component (HOPC) reports to the Head of Mission, exercises operational control, and provides direction to all members of the police component of the mission.[12] This includes all UN police officers (including all members of formed police units) and relevant civilian staff serving in the police component. The HOPC shall determine the police chain of command in the mission. The HOPC shall also determine appropriate succession arrangements within the police component to ensure effective command and control in his/her absence. The HOPC maintains a technical reporting and communication link with the DPKO Police Advisor in UN Headquarters. The technical reporting link must not circumvent or substitute the command chain between USG DPKO and the HOM, nor should it interfere with decisions taken by the HOM.[13]

4. The management of military, police, and civilian operations below the level of Mission Headquarters is considered to be at the tactical level and is exercised at various levels by subordinate commanders of respective components and designated civilian heads at levels below the Mission Headquarters. For military components, the tactical level includes all subordinate command levels established within the military command frameworks (for example Brigade, Regional, and Sector Command). Tactical level commanders report directly to their respective operational commanders.

5. The HOMC is accountable and responsible to the HOM for the supervision and technical management of the military component with particular responsibility to ensure effective and efficient mandate implementation and strict compliance with UN policies and procedures. Decisions on major operations or re-deployment of troops should result from consultations between the HOM and HOMC and must have HOM's concurrence.[14] This is clearly different in non-UN led operations such as operations led by NATO, where Force Commanders supported by political advisors or senior representatives have decision-making authority in the field and report directly to senior military commanders located at strategic headquarters outside the mission area.

[12] Ibid. 9. [13] Ibid. 9. [14] Ibid. 11.

Chapter 7

PEACE OPERATIONS CONDUCTED BY REGIONAL ORGANIZATIONS AND ARRANGEMENTS

The UN Charter does not preclude regional organizations from addressing matters of regional peace and security 'as are appropriate for regional action' (Article 52 of the UN Charter). Subject to the requirements of its constituent treaty a regional organization is competent under international law to authorize a peace operation with the consent of the Receiving State (this can be implied from Article 52). Subject to the requirements of its constituent treaty, a regional organization is competent to authorize peace enforcement and enforcement operations but only with authority from the Security Council (this is an express requirement under the terms of Article 53). 7.01

For peace operations based on consent, operating with impartiality, and restricted to defensive force, Security Council authorization need not be sought but is desirable. Regional organizations should report on the activities of any military operations undertaken under its authority to the Security Council (Article 54 of the UN Charter). 7.02

1. *General.* Chapter VIII of the UN Charter is devoted to actions of what can be termed regional organizations. It considers in three Articles—Articles 52, 53, and 54—regional organizations and arrangements with regard to the maintenance of peace and security. This, therefore, corresponds with the subject matter covered in Chapter VI (the peaceful settlement of disputes) and Chapter VII (actions with respect to threats to the peace, breaches of the peace, and acts of aggression). This part of the commentary is about the competences of regional organizations that perform peace support operations given the UN Charter rules and principles, specifically those within Chapter VIII. Firstly, this raises the question of what is meant by regional organizations and which organizations view themselves as regional organizations, or can be regarded as such. Is acting within the context of Chapter VIII the *raison d'être* of these organizations (the reason why this organization or arrangement has been brought into being), or is the main focus of these organizations totally different, and does it concern a mere additional activity? For instance, is the main focus of such an organization on economic and social issues of a regional nature, and is it that the organization merely wants to include issues of

ERIC P.J. MYJER AND NIGEL D. WHITE

7.02 dispute settlement or enforcement action within the region because it is conducive to its primary purpose? And if so, how far does its competence extend, both according to the general rules and principles of the UN Charter and according to its own constitution? Furthermore, how are these criteria applied in practice? Given the nature of this Handbook, the primary focus will be on organizations that may involve themselves with (peace) enforcement operations and peace operations that may include the use of military force.

The commentary to Sections 7.01 and 7.02, therefore, will consist of legal analyses of the concept of regional organizations (origin, criteria, region, dispute settlement, conformity with UN purposes and principles), concrete examples of organizations that can be regarded as regional organizations, and the legal basis of their actions in the constitutive instrument of the regional organization, if there is one, for this type of peace support operation. With regard to the different possible types of operations (whether there is an enforcement mandate from the Security Council or not) the commentary will include recent practice. There the focus will in particular be on the North Atlantic Treaty Organization (NATO), the European Union (EU), the Economic Community of West African States (ECOWAS), the Organization of American States (OAS), and the African Union (AU). The theory and practice of these organizations raise important questions with regard to the subordinate character of regional organizations to the UN Security Council and whether regional organizations have, or have developed, a competence to independently authorize the use of military force.

2. *The Features of Regional Organizations.*[1] Chapter VIII of the UN Charter refers to 'regional arrangements or agencies'. In practice nowadays it is common usage to refer to *regional organizations.* This indicates that a certain level of organization at the regional level is expected. It may be an international organization at a defined regional level with a constituent treaty. Such regional organizations would normally have legal personality,[2] although lesser forms of organization and even informal forms of organization by States at a regional level might suffice. First, there should be clarity as to what constitutes a *regional* organization. Article 52 does not contain a definition but, on the contrary, 'contains the most important treaty terms of an indefinite nature'.[3] This is the result of the compromise between the universalists

[1] On regional organizations see W. Hummer and M. Schweitzer in B. Simma (ed.), *The Charter of the United Nations. A Commentary,* 3rd edn (Oxford: Oxford University Press, 2012), chapter VIII 'Regional Arrangements'; L.M. Goodrich, E. Hambro, and A.P. Simons, *Charter of the United Nations. Commentary and Documents,* 3rd rev. edn (New York: Columbia University Press, 1969), 182–8; Hans Kelsen, *The Law of the United Nations* (London: Stevens & Sons, 1950), 319–28; D. Sarooshi, *The United Nations and the Development of Collective Security. The Delegation by the UN Security Council of its Chapter VII Powers* (Oxford: Clarendon Press, 1999), 247–84; C. Gray, *International Law and the Use of Force,* 3rd edn (Oxford: Oxford University Press, 2008), 370–428; E. Abass, *Regional Organisations and the Development of Collective Security* (Oxford: Hart, 2004).

[2] See for a discussion on legal personality N.D. White, *The Law of International Organizations,* 2nd edn (Manchester: Manchester University Press, 2005), 30–69.

[3] Walter in Simma et al., *The Charter of the United Nations,* commentary on Article 52.

and the regionalists[4] when the UN Charter was adopted in 1945.[5] However, some criteria can be established, both from the negotiating history of the Charter and from subsequent practice. From the qualifying words after 'regional arrangement or agency' in Article 53 UN Charter and from the place in the Charter, it seems to follow that such arrangements or agencies will be concerned with the matters covered by Chapters VI and VII.[6] Chapter VIII does not create new modes of settlement of disputes. In so far as the possible use of force is concerned, Chapter VII allows, alongside self-defence, an exception to the ban on the use of force, by empowering the Security Council to authorize military enforcement action under Article 42 of the UN Charter.[7] In so far as regional organizations have competence under their own constituent treaties to authorize military action,[8] such competence is subject to gaining the authorization of the Security Council under Article 53 of the UN Charter. According to the Charter, the competence of regional organizations to take military action without the consent of the Host State is lawful, if, and only if, such action falls within that other exception to the ban on the use of force relating to the maintenance of peace and security. There are no formal criteria or tests to determine whether a given organization qualifies as a regional organization; a material test suffices. For that purpose the following elements should be considered: **7.02**

(a) *The meaning of 'regional arrangement or agency'.* Given the formulation in Article 52 of regional 'arrangements' or 'agencies', some argue that these terms are synonymous, and some that they are alternatives.[9] Hummer and Schweitzer prefer the latter, although they admit that such theoretical distinction is of little practical significance.[10] 'Arrangement' does not necessarily point to a treaty[11] but might be an informal arrangement. 'Agency', however, appears to indicate something more structural, such as acting via an organ.[12] This may be on the basis of a bilateral or multilateral treaty between States, or on the basis of a treaty, whereby specifically an international organization is created. In the latter case that treaty would be the 'constitution' of that particular international organization. A regional arrangement that coincides with an international organization of a regional character has apparent

[4] See on this also C. Schreuer, 'Regionalism V. Universalism', 6 *EJIL* (1995), 477–99.

[5] Walter, in Simma et al., *The Charter of the United Nations*, commentary on Article 52.

[6] Goodrich et al., *Charter of the United Nations*, 183.

[7] See also D. Sarooshi, 'The Security Council's Authorization of Regional Arrangements to Use Force: The Case of NATO' in V. Lowe, A. Roberts, J. Welsh, and D. Zaum, *The United Nations Security Council and War: The Evolution of Thought and Practice since 1945* (Oxford: Oxford University Press, 2008), 226–47, at 229.

[8] See e.g. Art. 29 of the OAS Charter: 'If the inviolability or the integrity of the territory or the sovereignty or political independence of any American State should be affected by an armed attack or by an act of aggression that is not an armed attack, or by an extra continental conflict, or by a conflict between two or more American States, or by any other fact or situation that might endanger the peace of America, the American States, in furtherance of the principles of continental solidarity or collective self-defence, shall apply the measures and procedures established in the special treaties on the subject.'

[9] Walter, in Simma et al., *The Charter of the United Nations*, commentary on Article 52.

[10] Ibid. [11] Ibid. [12] Ibid.

7.02 advantages. It may be more flexible and amenable to changing circumstances, with its constitution providing clarity into what the regional arrangement could contribute to, not only with regard to the peaceful settlement of disputes, but also with regard to peace enforcement or peace operations. A more regulated structure of this nature could furthermore clarify issues such as command and control, responsibility, and accountability. It appears clear from the negotiating history of the Charter that the type of regional arrangements or agencies that were debated in 1945 tended to be of a more permanent nature. This may explain why it is common usage to refer to regional organizations. This also appears to follow from the proposal of the Egyptian delegation at the time of the establishment of the UN to include a definition of regional arrangements in Chapter VIII, as quoted by Goodrich and Hambro:

> There shall be considered as regional arrangements *organizations of a permanent nature* grouping in a given geographical area several countries which, by reason of their proximity, community of interests or cultural, linguistic, historical or spiritual affinities, make themselves jointly responsible for the peaceful settlement of any disputes which may arise between them and for the maintenance of peace and security in their region, as well as for the safeguarding of their interests and the development of their economic and cultural relations.[13]

Such a definition was, however, rejected since it failed to include all the situations which might be covered by the regional arrangements.[14] What was left is the present formulation in Article 52. From this it can also be concluded that a constitution is not necessary. A looser arrangement between States might well serve the purpose. Two elements, however, appear to be central: the *regional* element and the element of *peaceful settlement of disputes*.

(b) *The meaning of 'regional'*. Region should not be taken solely in a geographical sense, since there is no generally agreed concept of region.[15] In the constitution of a (regional) international organization, States parties could define a certain area as a region. Consequently, it then could be held that membership of that particular international organization is restricted to States within that region, which would make it a closed international organization. In the North Atlantic Treaty establishing the collective self-defence organization NATO, there is an explicit reference to a region. Article 6[16] defines the wider region besides Europe or North America,[17] as mentioned in Article 5, thereby clarifying the (collective) self-defence commitment of its Member States ex Article 5. This is an interesting clause for its object is to

[13] Goodrich et al., *Charter of the United Nations*, 184 (emphasis added). [14] Ibid.

[15] Walter in Simma et al., *The Charter of the United Nations*, commentary on Article 52.

[16] Art. 6 North Atlantic Treaty (1949), as amended by Art. 2 of the Protocol to the North Atlantic Treaty on the accession of Greece and Turkey: 'For the purposes of Article 5 an armed attack on one or more of the Parties is deemed to include an armed attack: (1) on the territory of any of the Parties in Europe or North America, on the Algerian Departments of France, on the territory of Turkey or on the islands under the jurisdiction of any of the Parties in the North Atlantic area north of the Tropic of Cancer; (2) . . .'

[17] 'The parties agree that an armed attack against one or more of them in Europe or North America . . .' (Art. 5 North Atlantic Treaty 1949).

restrict the activities of an international organization (a collective self-defence organization) to a specific area, namely the region in which NATO might be active. For that reason, it certainly is an element in the 'out of area' discussion. Beckett, in discussing the regional or non-regional character of the North Atlantic Treaty, comes to the clear conclusion: 7.02

> Therefore, in so far as there is a regional character at all in the North Atlantic Treaty, it lies in a common interest in the peace and security of a certain area, and not necessarily the possession of territory within a certain area.[18]

The term 'region' in Chapter VIII involves a certain measure of proximity, but there is no strict definition of this term and in any event it is important to look for the purpose of the regulation.[19] At the insistence of certain delegations at the San Francisco Conference, particularly the Latin American States, the recognition of then already existing, regional organizations within the UN system of collective security was debated. As a result thereof, Chapter VIII was inserted in the UN Charter, for it was felt that especially with regard to dispute settlement, the effectiveness of dispute settlement would gain by involving where possible local 'organizations' in solving local disputes.[20] Article 52(1) reflects this localization by restricting regional organizations to 'such matters relating to the maintenance of international peace and security as are appropriate for regional action'. Not surprisingly we see this also reflected in Chapter VI (Pacific Settlement of Disputes) of the UN Charter where there is an explicit reference to the role of regional agencies or arrangements in Article 33. Given this purpose of introducing regional organizations in the UN Charter, it is logical that the availability of a certain structure for facilitating the settlement of disputes is an element in determining whether there is a regional organization.

(c) *Peaceful settlement of disputes within the region (criteria ex Art. 52(2) Charter).* 'Regional and local' therefore are closely linked with the purpose and suitability of the arrangement for peaceful settlement within the territory of the participating States. This reference to peaceful settlement of disputes is to be interpreted in relation to Article 33 of Chapter VI (Pacific Settlement of Disputes). This, however,

[18] E. Beckett, *The North Atlantic Treaty, The Brussels Treaty and the Charter of the United Nations* (London: Stevens & Sons, 1950). He develops an interesting argument regarding NATO, at 30: '. . . It is called the North Atlantic Treaty. Perhaps you could say that States whose shores are washed by the North Atlantic and its contiguous seas and bays are in a geographical region, though it is, of course, a very wide one. But not all the parties to the Treaty have shores washed by the North Atlantic Ocean. Italy certainly has not. It is perhaps only by a stretch of the imagination that we consider the North Sea and Arctic Ocean which washes Norway part of the North Atlantic. Moreover, when we come to Article 10 we shall see that any European State may be invited to accede to the Treaty if it is thought to be in a position to contribute to the security of the North Atlantic area. There is nothing to say that such a State should have territory bordering on the Atlantic.'

[19] Walter in Simma et al., *The Charter of the United Nations*, commentary on Article 52.

[20] Ibid. 'The purpose of Chapter VIII is to grant certain international organizations—by modifying the general and immediate jurisdiction of the UN powers to resolve local disputes [. . .] within their own jurisdiction and on a local basis, and to serve thereby the purpose of the maintenance of international peace and security.'

7.02 does not mean that any association of States that is conducive to the settlement of disputes is also a regional organization that could be utilized by the Security Council for enforcement action under Article 53 UN Charter. The Council of Europe, an organization of general competence[21] with its European Court of Human Rights as a central dispute settlement body in the area of human rights and within a very wide region—spanning 47 Member States—is not an appropriate agency in the sense of Article 53 UN Charter for enforcement purposes since it does not take on any military role and likewise has no military capacity. The European Union on the other hand seems perfectly suited for such a role, contributing both to the peaceful settlement of disputes within its area and using the different modes of dispute settlement as in Article 33 of the UN Charter, and a possible enforcement task which it is intent on further developing.[22] It has already demonstrated a capacity to perform both civilian and military functions and thereby to be an actor in peace operations under the mandate of the UN. Examples are the civilian EULEX[23] Mission, or the military EU-led operation EUFOR Althea,[24] or EU operation Atalanta against piracy off the coast of Somalia. This also involves NATO's operation Allied Protector and Ocean Shield.[25] Also the European Union training mission in Somalia should be mentioned.[26] Besides the European Union,[27] other clear examples of regional organizations can be mentioned that fulfil the criteria discussed previously, such as the AU,[28] ECOWAS, the OAS, the Southern African

[21] See P. Sands and P. Klein (eds), *Bowett's Law of International Institutions*, 6th edn (London: Sweet & Maxwell, 2009), 162.

[22] Compare the Treaty on European Union provisions on a Common Foreign and Security Policy (Title V) and its Preamble (1993) and the 2007 Treaty of Lisbon amending the Treaty on European Union and the Treaty establishing the European Community, in particular the Preamble and Title V. Illustrative are: 'The common security and defence policy shall be an integral part of the common foreign and security policy. It shall provide the Union with an operational capacity drawing on civilian and military assets. The Union may use them on missions outside the Union for peace-keeping, conflict prevention and strengthening international security in accordance with the principles of the United Nations Charter. The performance of these tasks shall be undertaken using capabilities provided by the member States (Article 42, paragraph 1)' and 'The tasks referred to in Article 42 (1), in the course of which the Union may use civilian and military means, shall include joint disarmament operations, humanitarian and rescue tasks, military advice and assistance tasks, conflict prevention and peace-keeping tasks, tasks of combat forces in crisis management, including peace-making and post-conflict stabilisation. All these tasks may contribute to the fight against terrorism, including by supporting third countries in combating terrorism in their territories (Article 43 paragraph 1).' See for an analysis S. Blockmans and R. Wessel, 'The European Union and Crisis Management: Will the Lisbon Treaty Make the EU more effective?', 14 *JCSL* (2009), 265–308.

[23] Council Joint Action 2008/124/CFSP of 4 February 2008, referring to SC Res. 1244 (1999) and SC Res. 1674 (2006).

[24] Based on SC Res. 1575 (2004).

[25] See SC Res. (2010); SC Res. (2011); SC Res. (2012); SC Res. (2013); SC Res. (2014).

[26] SC Res. (2011); SC Res. (2012)

[27] See N.D. White, 'The EU as a Regional Security Actor within the International Legal Order' in M. Trybus and N.D. White (eds), *European Security Law* (Oxford: Oxford University Press, 2007), 333–5.

[28] Until 2001: *Organization of African Unity (OAU).* On the African Union see Yves G. Muhire, *The African Union's Right of intervention and the UN system of collective security* (Academic PhD Dissertation, Utrecht University 2013), in particular chapter II.

Development Community Organ on Politics, Defence and Security Cooperation (SADC Organ), the League of Arab States,[29] or the Organization for Security and Cooperation in Europe (OSCE).[30] NATO, which was established as a collective self-defence alliance, denied being a regional organization at the time of its incorporation,[31] but has come to be regarded as a regional organization when it acts outside its collective self-defence role.[32] It was only in 2001 that NATO invoked Article 5 of its treaty embodying the defence pact, in response to the terrorist attacks on the USA of 11 September.[33] In other NATO operations, in Bosnia in the 1990s, and in Afghanistan after the overthrow of the Taliban, NATO has undertaken enforcement action under the authority of the Security Council.[34] Of historic significance was Resolution 1973 (2011), building on Resolution 1970 (2011), on Libya in which a Security Council Chapter VII mandate was given to Member States to use all necessary measures 'acting nationally or through regional organizations or arrangements'.[35] This led to the involvement of NATO with Operation Unified Protector controlling a no-fly zone, and using significant levels of force by means of air strikes to protect civilians under threat. 7.02

However, in 1999, NATO undertook enforcement action against the Federal Republic of Yugoslavia without any clear authority from the Security Council.[36] Peace operations by regional organizations operate within or between Member States of the regional organization, with the agreement of the Member State or States in question. Regional organizations may exceptionally deploy peace support operations in or between non-Member States, with the consent of the State or States in question. Regional military operations undertaking any type of enforcement action require authorization from the Security Council (Article 53 of the UN Charter).

(d) *Peacekeeping by regional organizations.* Regional organizations have competence to authorize and deploy peacekeeping forces that are based on the key principles of peacekeeping—impartiality, consent, and limited use of force, since these respect the basic principles of international law—respecting the sovereignty of the State, non-intervention in the internal affairs of States, and non-aggression against the territorial integrity or political independence of States. In such consensual

[29] Organization of general competence, Sands and Klein, *Bowett's*, 241.

[30] Organization of limited competence, Sands and Klein, *Bowett's*, 202.

[31] See I.F. Dekker and E.P.J. Myjer, 'Air Strikes on Bosnian Positions: Is NATO also Legally the Proper Instrument of the UN?', 9 *LJIL* (1996), 411–16; N. Blokker and S. Muller, 'NATO as the UN Security Council's Instrument: Question Marks From the Perspective of International Law', 9 *LJIL* (1996), 417–21; A.L. Goodhart, 'The North Atlantic Treaty', 79-2 *RdC* (1951), 220; 464 Hansard 2018; for the Netherlands parliamentary proceedings 1948–1949 Handelingen Kamer II, Bijlagen no. 1237, no. 3, at 6; Bijlagen no. 1237, no. 6, at 6 and 422–4.

[32] White, 'The EU as a Regional Security Actor', 333.

[33] NATO's response to terrorism, statement issued at the Ministerial Meeting of the North Atlantic Council, 6 December 2001, M-NAC-2 (2001) 159.

[34] SC Res. 1386 (2001) mandated ISAF to provide security in and around Kabul.

[35] This mandate was terminated by SC Res. 2016 (2011) after the death of Muammar Qadhafi on 20 October 2011: '[...] Decides that the provisions of paragraphs 4 and 5 of resolution 1973 (2011) shall be terminated from 23.59 Libyan local time on 31 October 2011'.

[36] SC Res. 1199 (1998); SC Res. 1203 (1998).

7.02 operations key principles of the UN Charter, embodied in Articles 2(1), 2(4), and 2(7), are not called into question. If the regional organization wishes to conduct an operation of an enforcement character, then it will have to act within the exceptions to Article 2(4) and 2(7), under Chapter VII and VIII, requiring the authorization of the Security Council. Simply labelling a military operation as fulfilling a 'peacekeeping' role does not exonerate a regional organization from the limitations of the UN Charter and international law, if it violates one of the key principles governing consensual peacekeeping. American regional practice illustrates some of these problems. In 1965 the US claimed that its intervention in the Dominican Republic was carried out to protect American citizens caught in internal strife.[37] In fact the US intervention altered the course of the civil war in favour of the right wing faction. Once this was achieved the US force was replaced by an OAS force emplaced after a cease-fire at the request of the various factions. The US claimed that the Force was impartial and was there to facilitate the restoration of democracy,[38] but a number of States on the Security Council saw the OAS force as a continuation of the illegal US intervention.[39] In any case the involvement of the OAS could not somehow retrospectively legalize the initial illegal intervention by the US which went beyond an operation to rescue nationals, and was not clearly undertaken at the request of the legitimate government.[40]

3. *The Security Council as Supervisor of the Regional Organization.* The central role of the UN Security Council in issues of peace and security under the Charter is clear. Under Article 24 the Security Council has the 'primary responsibility for the maintenance of international peace and security', whereas in Chapter VII under Article 42 the Security Council is in fact given the monopoly on the use of military force, beyond individual or collective self-defence undertaken by States under Article 51. Both are exceptions to the central Charter prohibition on the use of force in Article 2(4), which is one of the few generally recognized peremptory (*jus cogens*) norms. It is for this very reason that in case the Security Council either authorizes individual States directly under Chapter VII, or a regional organization under Chapter VIII with enforcement powers it remains the ultimate guardian, exercising 'overall control and authority'.[41] This supervision of its delegated power under Chapter VII is clearly expressed with regard to Chapter VIII authorization in Article 53 where it says that enforcement action, i.e. possible use of military force, shall take place 'under its authority'. More indirect is the authority and control that follows from Article 54 that the Security Council shall at all times be kept fully

[37] UN Doc. S/6310 (1965). [38] SC 1202nd meeting (1965).

[39] SC 1221st meeting (1965).

[40] M. Akehurst, 'Enforcement Action by Regional Organisations with Special Reference to the Organisation of American States' 42 *BYIL* (1967), 175, at 213.

[41] Sarooshi, 'The Security Council's Authorization', 229: 'The fact that these powers are being exercised through the mechanisms of a regional arrangement does not alter the legal position that the Council must ensure that it can exercise overall control authority and control over the use of its delegated powers.'

informed of activities undertaken or in contemplation by regional organizations for the maintenance of international peace and security. This is about the Security Council's primary responsibility for the maintenance of peace and security. It apparently refers to any activity by a regional organization with regard to peace and security, both those of a non-military character and preparatory ones (i.e. the disposition of troops) with regard to a possible future military operation for which an Article 53 authorization is necessary. The authority and control is indirect since the Security Council would have to take the initiative if it was of the opinion that the activity of the regional organization was detrimental to the preservation of international peace and security and would have to take a mandatory decision to reverse such activity. 7.02

Any regional organization conducting military operations that have or exercise enforcement elements must obtain the authority of the Security Council under Chapter VIII (Article 53 of the UN Charter). 7.03

1. Looking at the growing body of recent UN Security Council resolutions there appears to be a growing awareness of the role regional and subregional organizations can play. In that context the explicit reference to Chapter VIII is notable in SC Resolution 1935 (2010) on Sudan, which referred to the importance of the partnership between the United Nations and the African Union.[42] Also SC Resolution 2033 (2012) on cooperation between the United Nations and regional and subregional organizations in maintaining international peace and security that made reference to the African Union and concerned the relationship between the Security Council and the African Union in general, but it concerned more generally cooperation between the UN and regional and subregional organizations in maintaining international peace and security. It stressed:

> the importance of developing effective partnerships between the United Nations and regional organizations, in particular the African Union, in accordance with the Charter of the United Nations and the relevant statutes of regional and subregional organizations.[43]

Furthermore in an explicit reference to Chapter VIII:

> [r]eiterating that cooperation with regional and subregional organizations in matters relating to the maintenance of peace and security and consistent with Chapter VIII of the Charter of the United Nations, can improve collective security,[44]

the resolution stressed the need for regional and subregional organizations to act in accordance with Article 54 UN Charter at all times in order to keep the Security Council fully informed of its efforts to settle conflicts.

[42] 'Underlining, without prejudice to the Security Council's primary responsibility for the maintenance of international peace and security, the importance of the partnership between the United Nations and the African Union (AU), consistent with Chapter VIII of the UN Charter, with regard to the maintenance of peace and security in Africa, particularly in Sudan'—SC Res. 1935 (2010).

[43] Preambular, para. 1.

[44] Preambular, para. 3.

7.03 2. In general there is frequent (repeated) reference to involvement of the African Union and ECOWAS in Security Council resolutions for instance with regard to the African Union Mission to Somalia (AMISOM),[45] or with regard to Côte d'Ivoire.[46] Another instance is a Chapter VII mandate for an EU operation in the Central African Republic.[47]

Another rare explicit reference to Chapter VIII is found in SC Resolution 2086 (2013),[48] on UN peacekeeping operations and SC Resolution 2151 of 28 April 2014 on the maintenance of international peace and security. A further prominent reference to Chapter VIII is found in SC Resolution 2167 (2014) on UN peacekeeping operations, the first preambular paragraph of which refers to Chapter VIII.[49] It then enumerates the different regional and subregional organizations by explicitly welcoming 'the initiatives taken by regional and subregional organizations in the maintenance of international peace and security including the African Union, the European Union, the Economic Community of Central African States (ECCAS), and the Economic Community of West African States (ECOWAS), the Southern African Development Community (SADC) and the Eastern African Community (EAC), the Organization of American States (OAS), the Union of South American Nations (UNASUR), the Community of Latin America and Carribbean States (CELAC), the Caribbean Community and Common Market (CARICOM), the Collective Security Treaty Organization (CSTO), the League of Arab States (LAS), the Association of Southeast Asian Nations (ASEAN) and the Arbab Maghreb Union (UMA)'. In this list, a reference to NATO is notably lacking, most likely for political reasons. In addition, SC Resolution 1271 (2014) in its operational paragraphs refers to Chapter VIII.[50]

The following comments outline the competences of regional organizations and explain why, for those organizations that claim military enforcement competence, the authority of the Security Council is a prerequisite. This limitation is made clear if consideration is given to the broad range of competences regional organizations may claim to have in the field of collective security.

3. *The Competences of Regional Organizations.* The competence of a regional arrangement will follow from the instrument whereby the regional organization has been established (constitutional restrictions or internal competence) and by the

[45] SC Res. 2011 (2011); SC Res. 2037 (2012); SC Res. 2060 (2012); SC Res. 2072 (2012); SC Res. 2093 (2013); SC Res. 2103 (2013); SC Res. 2111 (2013); SC Res. 2124 (2013); SC Res. 2142 (2014); SC Res. 2159 (2014); SC Res. 2182 (2014).

[46] SC Res. 1980 (2011); SC Res. 2000 (2011); SC Res. 2045 (2012); SC Res. 2101 (2013); SC Res. 2112 (2013); SC Res. 2153 (2014); SC Res. 2162 (2014).

[47] SC Res. 2134 (2014) as extended by SC Res. 2181 (2014).

[48] Para. 18 underlines the importance of partnership and cooperation with regional and subregional arrangements and organizations, in accordance with Chapter VIII of the United Nations Charter, in supporting peacekeeping and peacebuilding activities as well as forging greater regional and national ownership.

[49] '[R]ecalling Chapter VIII of the Charter of the United Nations'. It also recalls previous resolutions such as UN SC Res. 2033 (2012).

[50] See operational paras 21 and 22. See also SC Res. 2173 (2014) on Sudan.

rules and principles of the Charter of the United Nations. The latter will include the Charter principles in Article 2 and those that can be found in Chapters VI, VII, and VIII. Also rules of customary law may play a role (restrictions on its external competence). 7.03

4. *Rules and Principles in the Charter.* What regional organizations are competent to do will primarily be determined by the UN Charter rules of Chapter VIII and by general rules and principles of public international law. More particularly, Article 52 stipulates that actions by regional organizations should be in conformity with the Purposes and Principles of the UN Charter. Complications may arise because of emerging customary law, treaties concluded by States agreeing on more powers for regional organizations than foreseen in Chapter VIII as appears to be the case with the AU, or by similar constitutional developments of regional organizations.

It is clear from Chapter VIII that two types of activities are foreseen for regional organizations, namely peaceful settlement of disputes as in Article 52 and enforcement action as in Article 53 Charter. With regard to both types of activities the competences flow from Chapter VI and Chapter VII respectively. Chapter VIII does not foresee forms of peaceful settlement beyond Chapter VI, or enforcement measures beyond Chapter VII. The crux of Chapter VIII is that it is about the competence of the Security Council to delegate its Chapter VII powers to a regional organization.[51]

While a strict division between peacekeeping and peace enforcement has often proven to be difficult or even impossible to achieve and maintain in practice, there are clear distinctions at the legal conceptual level and in the resulting applicable legal regime between enforcement operations, including operations falling short of traditional war-fighting operations on the one hand, and other peace operations which are not based upon Chapter VII of the Charter on the other hand (see Sections 6.01–6.05).

Generally, peace support operations or peacekeeping operations have been defined in various operational, political, and legal ways. Central to any legal definition are three legal characteristics or prerequisites: the consent of the States involved, the limitation of the use of force by peacekeepers to situations of self-defence, and impartiality. Fundamentally, the traditional legal basis for peacekeeping rests on the consent of the parties to a conflict, in particular the Host State, to the creation and presence of a peacekeeping force within its territory. This consent to allow a peacekeeping force to supervise a peace agreement may be facilitated by the General Assembly, the Security Council, other organs of the UN, or by regional organizations and arrangements. Customary international law, based on State consent and agreement, can also support a peace operation without reliance on the UN Charter.

In most cases, peace operations have their legal basis in the general powers of the Security Council pursuant to Chapters VI and VII of the Charter. The Security

[51] See also Sarooshi, 'The Security Council's Authorization', 228.

7.03 Council can specifically authorize such operations to be undertaken by regional organizations under Chapter VIII of the Charter though UN practice reveals this has rarely been done. Peace operations by regional organizations can be legally and operationally complex and it is important to be aware of the parameters of action permitted under the applicable legal basis or bases. This is particularly so in cases where forces of regional organizations are deployed under dual authorities (Host State consent and a UN Chapter VI, VII, or VIII mandate).

For status issues reference may be made to sub-Chapter 6.2, considering the absence of diverging practice in peace operations conducted by regional organizations. The advantages of regional organizations becoming involved in peace operations is that they 'often enjoy a special legitimacy amongst local actors', they will be 'more familiar with local conditions', and in some ways they 'have a greater incentive to stay the course and implement long-term conflict prevention and monitoring strategies'.[52] However, they may be dominated by regional Powers that will push them towards higher levels of enforcement than may be necessary (for example Nigeria's domination of ECOWAS). Alternatively, some organizations (for example the AU) may not have the resources to mount an effective peace operation of any sort, and civilians are left unprotected despite the expectations created by Article 4 of the AU Treaty. A better approach would be to develop 'an interlocking system of peacekeeping capacities that will enable the United Nations to work with relevant regional organisations',[53] drawing upon NATO or the EU if the level of coercion needed is significant.

(a) *Chapter VI competences.* The peaceful settlement of disputes clearly is included (Article 52 UN Charter) in the general competence of a regional organization. Although a regional organization may contribute to the peaceful settlement by applying one of the methods of Article 33 of the Charter, interestingly 'resort to regional agencies or arrangements' is then introduced as a separate method of pacific settlement of disputes. While this somewhat circular notion is of no particular consequence, it does, however, illustrate the core premise that regional organizations are primarily related to the peaceful settlement of disputes within the Charter framework. All of the other methods mentioned—like negotiation, enquiry, mediation, conciliation, arbitration, and judicial settlement—need the consent of the State receiving help. Non-coercive (consensual) peacekeeping falls under the 'other peaceful means of their own choice' mentioned in Article 33. This clearly comes within the regional organization's competence. This would also relate to a peacekeeping operation, where the peacekeepers are armed, when these arms are strictly for personal self-defence and this is clearly reflected in rules of engagement.

(b) *Chapter VII competences.* Peacekeeping operations, with a so-called robust mandate allowing for use of force beyond personal protection but to protect the

[52] J. Cockayne and D. Malone, 'United Nations Peace Operations: Then and Now', 9 *Yearbook of International Peace Operations* (2005), 1–26, at 11.

[53] *In larger freedom: towards development, security and human rights for all.* Report of the Secretary General, UN Doc. A/59/2005 (21 March 2005), para. 115.

peacekeeping mission itself, obviously falls outside the realm of the pacific settlement of disputes of Chapter VI. Increasingly, after the Brahimi Report of 2000, peace operations under UN authority have been given a mandate that includes a Chapter VII injunction to use necessary measures to deal with 'spoilers' (those who would undermine the peace agreement) and to protect civilians under threat within their areas of deployment.[54] This raises the possibility of an application of military force which goes beyond personal self-defence. This concerns the ban on the use of force under Article 2(4) of the UN Charter, a peremptory norm of public international law, and clearly concerns the monopoly on the use of force of the UN Security Council under Article 2(4) in conjunction with Chapter VII. Any regional peacekeeping operation with such enforcement mandate, in which combat is permitted against a State or State-backed organized armed group, therefore needs to be authorized by the UN Security Council. There appears, however, to be a trend towards the acceptance of robust peacekeeping when it is undertaken with the consent of the host government in case the coercive action is not directed against the State but in support of it, i.e. against internal spoilers in the maintenance and restoration of law and order; which does not violate the ban on the use of force, and is (arguably) interpreted as not constituting enforcement within the terms of Article 53.[55] Such an instance, however, should be viewed as an exception within clearly defined boundaries given that robust peacekeeping as a mater of principle needs a Security Council mandate in view of the Security Council's primary responsibility in this area. For that reason a blanket prior consent by the host government as a member of a regional organization towards their regional organization to decide on the use of such force when the case arises, is unacceptable. Such 'blanket prior consent' would need to be complemented by consent by the lawful government for each specific mission at the time the operation is undertaken. **7.03**

5. Without any UN authority a NATO or other regional organization peace support operation with a coercive protection mandate will be in conflict with the UN Charter provisions, but if force is used against spoilers and not the government then the prohibition on the use of force in Article 2(4) arguably is not being violated, since the use of force is not directed against the State. However, the requirement that enforcement action be authorized by the Security Council is violated by unauthorized regional action, given that coercive military action must come within the notion of enforcement action.

[54] N.D. White, 'Empowering Peace Operations to Protect Civilians: Form over Substance' 13(3–4) *Journal of International Peacekeeping* (2009), 327–55, at 346.

[55] Supported by the advisory opinion of the International Court of Justice in *Certain Expenses of the United Nations*, ICJ Reports, 1962, 151 at 177, where the Court stated: 'but it can be said that the operations of ONUC did not include a use of armed force against a State which the Security Council, under Article 39, determined to have committed an act of aggression or to have breached the peace. The armed forces which were utilized in the Congo were not authorized to take military action against any State. The operation did not involve "preventive or enforcement measures" against any State under Chapter VII and therefore did not constitute "action" as that term is used in Article 11'.

7.03 No consent of the Receiving State, or a failed State, is necessary where the UN Security Council utilizes the regional organization for enforcement action under its authority (Article 53 UN Charter). Alternatively, a regional organization might decide of its own accord that enforcement action is necessary and seek UN Security Council approval. In both cases the regional organization would act as a subsidiary organ of the UN.[56] It is therefore clear that the width of the powers of the UN Security Council is similar to those under Chapter VII and in conformity with Article 24 UN Charter. In general, enforcement action has been narrowly interpreted to mean use of military force, although it could be argued that also non-military binding enforcement decisions by the UN Security Council fall under Article 53. This also appears to follow from the *travaux préparatoires* of the UN. However, from the Security Council debates with regard to OAS measures against the Dominican Republic (1960: breaking of diplomatic relations and a partial economic boycott) and Cuba (1962, expulsion from the OAS and quarantine) it appears that the majority of the membership does not view non-military sanction as enforcement action.[57] Some argue that at least '. . . the precise nature of the relationship between the UN and regional organizations on non-forcible measures has not been fully developed'.[58]

This leaves actions by regional organizations involving use of military force. These may be either traditional peacekeeping operations, with consent, or peace enforcement operations under Chapter VII. A third category would be peacekeeping operations of a non-enforcement nature, that operate with military force and that have been established by a regional organization, but without the Receiving State's consent. Furthermore, there can be mixed operations, with a mixed mandate.

6. What if such regional military enforcement action is directed against States that are not members of that regional organization? Is such action compatible with Article 52?[59] Arguably the Security Council can authorize such out-of-area regional operations on the basis that it has the competence to authorize a coalition of willing States to do so under Chapter VII and, therefore, it should be able to so authorize a regional organization. Another much debated question is whether Security Council authorization should be explicit, or whether it can also be inferred. Although it has been argued that retroactive authorization is also possible, this appears to be a *contradictio in terminis*. The more correct approach would be to argue that under certain circumstances, by explicit or implicit approval of the Security Council, an operation involving the use of force is lawful but only prospectively from the point of approval, unless the Security Council explicitly makes the approval retrospective. Although in such case of explicit retrospective approval the acts performed until the permissive (authorizing) Security Council decision remain illegal as a breach of the *jus ad bellum* norm forbidding unilateral use of force outside the Charter exceptions,

[56] Walter in Simma et al., *The Charter of the United Nations*, commentary on Article 52.
[57] Ibid. [58] N.D. White, 'The EU as a Regional Security Actor', 341.
[59] Walter in Simma et al., *The Charter of the United Nations*, commentary on Article 53.

the adoption by the Security Council of this decision may lead to mitigating the consequences in terms of State responsibility or individual responsibility under international criminal law.[60] Given that such a case concerns breach of the *jus cogens* norm of Article 2(4) of the Charter, it is important to note that Article 26 of the Articles on State Responsibility makes clear that the wrongfulness of these acts will not be precluded, for '[n]othing in this chapter precludes the wrongfulness of any act of a State which is not in conformity with an obligation arising under a peremptory norm of general international law'.[61] As far as mitigating circumstances are concerned one could compare in this context the civil law principle, whereby although a breach of the criminal law norm has been established, no punishment has to follow in cases of clear emergency, necessity, or self-defence. The requirement of explicit retrospective approval is essential if we are to avoid self-serving attempts by States to read in retrospective approval of what would have otherwise been aggressive action. **7.03**

7. For all practical purposes the Security Council's prior authorization should be explicit, for implied authorization is always more difficult to prove. Furthermore, authorization will be an element in establishing responsibility. A clear example of such authorization was the UN Security Council's broadly phrased authorization to NATO in the case of Bosnia[62] in Resolution 836, para. 10:[63]

> [d]ecides that, notwithstanding paragraph 1 of resolution 816 (1993), Member States, acting nationally or through regional organizations or arrangements, may take, under the authority of the Security Council and subject to close coordination with the Secretary-General and the Force, all necessary measures, through the use of air power, in and around the safe areas in Bosnia and Herzegovina, to support the Force in the performance of its mandate set out in paragraphs 5 and 9 above.

This Resolution was about the protection of the six safe areas in Bosnia that the Security Council has designated and that if need be were to be protected by air power. From the whole setting it is obvious that the wording of this Resolution is careful by referring to 'acting nationally or through regional organizations or arrangements' and not directly to the regional organization as foreseen. It was, however, clear from the debate on the Vance/Owen plan that NATO was the

[60] Crime against the peace as defined in Art. 6 Charter of the International Military Tribunal (8 August 1945) and VI(a) Principles of International Law Recognized in the Charter of the Nuremberg Tribunal and in the Judgment of the Tribunal, adopted by the International Law Commission (1950). The crime against aggression figures as one of the crimes in Art. 5(1)(d) Rome Statute of the International Criminal Court (ICC Statute, 1998); this Article applies once the States parties to the Rome Statute will have reached agreement on the definition of the crime of aggression. See W.A. Schabas, *An Introduction to the International Criminal Court*, 4th edn (Cambridge: Cambridge University Press, 2011), 34–9.

[61] Articles on Responsibility of States for Internationally Wrongful Acts (ARS) adopted by the International Law Commission at its fifty-third session (2001), promulgated by UN GA Res. 56/83 (28 January 2002).

[62] On this case see in general D. Sarooshi, 'The Security Council's Authorization', 232–41.

[63] SC Res. 836 (1993).

7.03 regional organization referred to. Interestingly we find scarce reference to NATO in the Security Council debate[64] on this Resolution. One finds only a single reference, namely after the vote by the British representative.[65] From the Report by the UN Secretary General pursuant to Resolution 836, however, there is no mistaking that NATO is the regional organization which may be asked for air support.[66] It is therefore inconsistent with the Charter system of collective security that the Security Council in Resolution 836 only referred to Chapter VII as a legal basis, and not also to Chapter VIII. The same applies to Resolution 844 of 18 June 1993 in which the Secretary General's Report of 14 June 1993 is confirmed and paragraph 10 (as quoted above) of Resolution 836 is confirmed and Member States are encouraged 'acting nationally or through regional organizations or arrangements, to coordinate closely with the Secretary-General in this regard'.[67] In practice there was a cumbersome chain of command before air support could be granted. As a reaction to the Srebrenica debacle the Secretary General's Special representative 'delegated the necessary authority to the Force Commander who was authorized to delegate further to the Commander' of UNPROFOR. This led to the transfer of military force away from the UN and towards NATO.[68] Sarooshi views this as one of the key institutional lessons from the operation of the UN–NATO relationship in the former Yugoslavia: '. . . once the Security Council decides to delegate its military enforcement powers then the decision to use these powers should be left solely to NATO,[69] notwithstanding that the Security Council always remains the final arbiter'.[70]

[64] See SC Debate, reproduced in D. Bethlehem and M. Weller, *The 'Yugoslav' Crisis in International Law: General Issues, Part I* (Cambridge: Grotius Publications/Cambridge University Press, 1997), 284–98.

[65] D. Hannay (UK), in Bethlehem and Weller, *The 'Yugoslav' Crisis*, 297: '. . . The aim [of Resolution 836] is to provide further help to large concentrations of the civilian population, most of whom are Muslims. A new element is that we, with France and the United States, probably acting in a NATO framework, are prepared, once authorized by this resolution, to make available air power in response to calls for assistance from United Nations forces in and around the "safe areas".'

[66] Report of the Secretary General pursuant to Security Council Resolution 836 (1993) (UN Doc. S 25939, 14 June 1993), 625–7: 'I have asked the North Atlantic Treaty Organisation (NATO), which is already assisting the United Nations in the implementation of several earlier Security Council resolutions, to prepare plans for provision of the necessary air support capacity, in close coordination with me and my Special Representative for the former Yugoslavia. In a letter dated 11 June 1993 from its Deputy Secretary-General, NATO confirmed its willingness to offer protective air power in case of attack against UNPROFOR in the performance of its overall mandate, if it so requests.' And also: 'As the analysis above indicates, the implementation of Resolution 836 (1993) will require the deployment of additional troop resources on the ground as well as the provisions of air support. I have initiated contacts with Member States to solicit contributions in both respects and have invited NATO to coordinate with me the use of air power in support of UNPROFOR. It is of course understood that the first decision to initiate the use of air resources in this context will be taken by the Secretary-General in consultation with the members of the Security Council.'

[67] SC Res. 844 (1993), para. 4.

[68] Sarooshi, 'The Security Council's Authorization', 236.

[69] Ibid. 247: 'The dual-key arrangements that were used in relation to the so-called "safe areas" in Bosnia saw prevarication by the UN with fatal consequences. The UN as an organization—specifically the Office of the Secretary-General—is simply not well-suited to make decisions relating to the use of force and this points to a greater role for regional arrangements acting on behalf of the UN.'

[70] Ibid.

8. The UN's Special Committee on Peacekeeping has recognized the significant contribution that regional organizations can make to peacekeeping, but has stressed that this must be in accordance with Chapter VIII of the UN Charter. The Committee put particular emphasis on Article 53 of the UN Charter which states that enforcement action undertaken by regional organizations requires the authorization of the Security Council.[71] The High Level Panel endorsed this in 2004, and because of the propensity of modern peace operations to use force more widely, stated that all regional peace operations, including those undertaken by NATO, must have the authority of the Council, except in urgent situations when it could be sought after the operation had started.[72] This unacceptable concept of retrospective authorization utilized in the past in relation to ECOWAS clearly presents difficulties if the Security Council is deadlocked. Arguably in these cases authority should be sought from the General Assembly under its exceptional competence for peace and security. **7.03**

Peace operations by regional organizations should be conducted under the authority, command, and control of the regional organization. Even to the extent they are commanded by TCCs, they remain under the control of the regional organization. **7.04**

1. While 'blue-helmeted' UN forces act under UN authority, command, and control, coalitions of the willing acting under Chapter VII simply have the authority of the Security Council, and are commanded and controlled by the TCNs. With modern peace operations often possessing enforcement elements within their mandates, it would clearly be desirable for the regional organization to exercise control as well as authority over an operation undertaken under a regional mandate.

2. Furthermore, in attributing (wrongful) acts of a regional organization, international law stipulates that there must be effective control exercised by the regional organization over the acts in question.[73] Given that a peace support operation acting under the authority of a regional organization consists of contingents from TCNs as State organs, Article 5 of the ILC's Articles on the Responsibility of International Organizations 2011 provides that the 'conduct of an organ of a State or an organ or agent of an international organization that is placed at the disposal of another international organization shall be considered under international law an act of the latter organization if the organization exercises effective control over that conduct'.[74]

3. The AU force sent to Darfur in Sudan in 2004—the African Union Mission in Sudan (AMIS)—to try and halt the violence there consisted of troops drawn from

[71] Special Committee on Peacekeeping, UN Doc. A/56/767 (28 March 2003), paras 161–162.

[72] High Level Panel Report on Threats, Challenges and Change, UN Doc. A/59/565 (2 December 2004), paras 272–273.

[73] *Case Concerning Military and Paramilitary Activities in and Against Nicaragua (Nicaragua v United States)*, Judgment, ICJ Reports, 1986, 14, at 62–4; Art. 8 of the Articles on State Responsibility 2001.

[74] ILC, Report of the Sixtieth Session, UN Doc. A/63/10 (2008), para. 164.

7.04 Nigeria, Rwanda, Senegal, Kenya, Gambia, and South Africa. In 2005 its force strength was about 7,000. Subsequently though the AU and the UN have cooperated and coordinated their efforts in response to the crisis in Darfur caused by the crimes against humanity being committed there since 2003; the hybrid UN/AU force mandated in 2007[75] had only deployed 7,000 troops by January 2008, far short of the 26,000 required, thus restricting the impact of UNAMID on preventing attacks on civilians. However, by the end of 2008, UNAMID had increased in size to 15,000 and in 2015 remains at that level. Despite this, there has been precious little evidence of it carrying out its mandate which explicitly includes the protection of civilians within its areas of deployment.[76] In February 2009 the Secretary General reported that the security situation had deteriorated and that UNAMID 'will continue its efforts to systematically monitor, report and investigate attacks in accordance with its mandate', noting a number of attacks against civilians that had occurred. The Secretary General appealed for the promised troops from a number of countries to be deployed which 'would constitute a significant increase in the mission's troop strength and thus its protection capability and ability to implement its core mandated tasks'.[77]

4. Peace operations by regional organizations that operate alongside UN peace operations should cooperate with the UN Force Commander under an agreement to be arrived at by the UN and the regional organization. Regional organizations may provide convincing representation of the States concerned and offer specific knowledge of the region. At the same time their success may be limited by opposing interests of neighbouring States and the lack of facilities.

7.05 **For peace operations regional organizations should seek encouragement and support by the Security Council and will require the consent of the Receiving State. Whenever a peace enforcement operation is undertaken in the absence of such consent, the operation will require the authorization of the Security Council. Such authorization can take various forms and modalities, but may not be dispensed with under any circumstances.**

The following comments review the issue of autonomous regional competence in undertaking enforcement action of a military nature. While regional organizations may undertake such action with the consent of the legitimate government of the

[75] SC Res. 1769 (2007). See R.P. Barnidge, 'The United Nations and the African Union: Assessing a Partnership for Peace in Darfur', 14 *JCSL* (2009), 93; A. Bashua, 'Challenges and Prospects of AU-UN Hybrid Operations: The UNAMID Experience', 18 *Journal of International Peacekeeping* (2014), 92.

[76] SC Res. 1769 (2007), para. 15. See also SC Res. 2113 (2013), in which the Security Council underlined the need for UNAMID to make full use of its capabilities and prioritize the protection of civilians; safe, timely and unhindered humanitarian access; and emphasized UNAMID's Chapter VII mandate to deliver its core task to protect civilians.

[77] Report of the Secretary General on the deployment of the African Union-United Nations Hybrid Operation, UN Doc. S/2009/83 (10 February 2009), paras 10, 31, and 44. See further UN Doc. S/2014/852 (26 November 2014).

Host State under the customary law principles,[78] the Charter rules do not permit such a use of force against the will of the Host State without the agreement of the government of that State. 7.05

1. *Regional Organizations Performing Enforcement Operations without Prior Security Council Mandate.* What if the regional organization undertakes an enforcement action without prior authorization from the Security Council?[79] The regional organization may decide to act without a Security Council authorization because it is evident that the Security Council will not give any authorization to use force because of a threatened veto by one of the veto powers, as with Russia and China in the case of Kosovo prior to the NATO action using unauthorized force in 1999. The regional organization may, however, also decide to act without authorization because it does not want to see any prior restrictions placed on actions in which it uses military force. A third possibility is that the regional organization in the final instance regards its regional system of security as superior to the UN system of collective security. This appears to be the case with the system foreseen by the AU. Finally, it may be that the regional organization is of the opinion that any one of these options finds support in customary international law.

The position taken here is that none of these options finds support either in conventional or customary international law. The formulation of Article 53 of the Charter is pertinent. The regional organization needs to ask prior UN Security Council authorization before any enforcement action involving the use of force is undertaken. The expectation that a veto is forthcoming from one or more Security Council Members is no ground for an exception, since the veto is an element of the system of collective security.[80] Depending on differing perspectives of a situation it may be regretted that certain powers may make use of their power to veto, but that is the way the UN system of collective security is constructed. As a rule the same argument applies whether one labels the action as a necessary humanitarian intervention, or as one caused by a duty flowing from the responsibility to protect. More generally these restrictions not only flow from Article 52 of the Charter, but also from Articles 2(4), 24, 25, and from Chapter VII.

UN Member States are furthermore bound by Article 103 of the Charter from which it follows that in case of conflict between obligations under the Charter and obligations under any other international agreement, their obligations under the present Charter shall prevail. Applying this for instance to the case of the African Union's Peace and Security Council[81] it is evident that the UN Charter takes

[78] L. Doswald-Beck, 'The Legal Validity of Military Intervention by Invitation of the Government', 56 *BYBIL* (1985), 189.

[79] See E. De Wet, 'The Evolving Role of ECOWAS and SADC in Peace Operations: A Challenge to the Primacy of the UN Security Council in Matters and Peace and Security?' 27 *LJIL* (2014), 353.

[80] Walter in Simma et al., *The Charter of the United Nations*, commentary on Article 53.

[81] J.I. Levitt, 'The Peace and Security Council of the African Union and the United Nations Security Council: The Case of Darfur, Sudan', in N. Blokker and N. Schrijver (eds), *The Security Council and the Use of Force* (Leiden/Boston: Martinus Nijhoff/Brill, 2005), 213–51.

7.05 precedence. The African Union adopted in 2002 a Protocol establishing The Peace and Security Council of the African Union.[82] The Peace and Security Council is established by Article 5(2) of the Constitutive Act of the African Union as a separate organ on which the Assembly of the African Union may decide. This Council was created in order to establish 'an operational structure for the effective implementation of the decisions taken in the areas of conflict prevention, peace-making, peace support operations and intervention, as well as peace-building and post-conflict reconstruction'.[83] Objectives that are specifically mentioned are: promote peace, security, and stability in Africa (Article 3 a); anticipate and prevent conflicts (Article 3 b); and develop a common defence policy for the Union (Article 3 e). The Peace and Security Council shall thereby be guided by a number of principles which are listed in Article 4 and are 'enshrined in the Constitutive Act, the Charter of the United Nations and the Universal Declaration of Human Rights'. Most pertinent for our subject matter are the following principles:

> [...] j. the right of the Union to intervene in a Member State pursuant to a decision of the Assembly in respect of grave circumstances, namely war crimes, genocide and crimes against humanity, in accordance with Article 4(h) of the Constitutive Act;
>
> k. the right of Member States to request intervention from the Union in order to restore peace and security, in accordance with Article 4(j) of the Constitutive Act.[84]

With regard to the functions of the Peace and Security Council Article 6 illustrates the wide area in which, according to this Protocol, this organ of the African Union may perform functions, namely:

a) promotion of peace, security, and stability in Africa;
b) early warning and preventive diplomacy;
c) peacemaking, including the use of good offices, mediation, conciliation, and enquiry;
d) peace support operation and intervention, pursuant to article 4(h) and (j) of the Constitutive act;
e) peace-building and post-conflict reconstruction;
f) humanitarian action and disaster management.

With regard to intervention according to Article 7 the Peace and Security Council shall:

> (7.1e): recommend to the Assembly, pursuant to Article 4 h) of the Constitutive Act, intervention, on behalf of the Union, in a Member State in respect of grave circumstances, namely war crimes, genocide and crimes against humanity, as defined in relevant international conventions and instruments.

Furthermore, after the Assembly has so decided it shall:

> (7.1f): approve the modalities for intervention by the Union in a Member State, following a decision by the Assembly, pursuant to Article 4 (j) of the Constitutive Act.

[82] Protocol Relating to the Establishment of the Peace and Security Council of the African Union, adopted on 9 July 2002 by the 1st Ordinary Session of the Assembly of the African Union.
[83] Ibid. 3. [84] Ibid.

Especially with regard to interventions which involve the use of force it is clear that neither the Peace and Security Council nor the Assembly of the African Union is allowed to decide on such use of force, given the UN Charter in general and Article 53 read in conjunction with Article 2(4) of the UN Charter in particular. This appears to be the case even if one were to argue that this Protocol should be viewed as a collection of separate prior invitations by its Member States to come to its assistance possibly using military force, if the case would arise. Such blanket invitations would go against the very purposes and principles of the UN Charter. That these should guide its decisions is clear from both the wording of the Constitutive Act of the African Union and from the Protocol relating to the establishment of the Peace and Security Council of the African Union.[85] The very tension between its goal and the principles was exposed at a meeting of the Heads of State and Government of 25 May 2004, where the Peace and Security Council was ceremoniously launched,[86] when it was expressed that 'the authority vested in the Peace and Security Council is fairly and proactively exercised' and that 'no conflict on our continent will be considered to be out of bounds for the African Union'. However, it was also stressed 'bearing in mind that the UN Security Council has the primary responsibility for the maintenance of global peace and security, and Africa is part of that international community'. 7.05

Also the subregional organization ECOWAS in a Protocol Relating to the Mechanism for Conflict Prevention, Management, Resolution, Peacekeeping and Security appears to claim these far-reaching competences such as 'authorize all forms of intervention and decide particularly on the deployment of political and military missions'.[87] This Protocol was adopted in the wake of the ECOWAS interventions in Liberia and Sierra Leone,[88] and more pointedly after the NATO operation in Kosovo, as will be discussed later when discussing possible customary law developments. At the time it was argued that:

> [t]o the extent that it incorporates the doctrine of humanitarian intervention and provides extensively for an early warning system, the Mechanism probably is the most ambitious instrument on the regulation of collective security ever attempted to date, not only by ECOWAS but by any regional Organization for that matter.[89]

The ECOWAS Protocol seems to have been a model for the more elaborate African Union Protocol. These appear the only regional organizations that explicitly claim to be able to decide themselves on the use of military force. Neither NATO nor the European Union claims such competence.

[85] The Constitutive Act of the African Union, Art. 3; Protocol, Preambular Art. 4.

[86] See Statement of Commitment to Peace and Security in Africa, issued by the Heads of State and Government of Member States of the Peace and Security Council of the African Union, PSC/AHG/ST(X).

[87] Art. 10 ECOWAS Protocol Relating to the Mechanism for Conflict Prevention, Management, Resolution, Peacekeeping and Security (1 December 1999).

[88] J. Levitt, 'Humanitarian Intervention by Regional Actors in Internal Conflicts: The Cases of ECOWAS in Liberia and Sierra Leone', 12 *Temple International and Comparative Law Journal* (1998), 333–75.

[89] Ibid.

7.05 2. *Regional Organizations Performing Enforcement Operations without Prior Security Council Mandate: Customary Law Developments?* Having established that under conventional law, in particular the rules of the UN Charter, a regional organization needs prior UN Security Council authorization, this leaves us with the question as to whether there perhaps exists a customary law exemption allowing a regional organization to decide of its own accord to use military force in case the Security Council is blocked by a veto. In other words, has customary law developed allowing States, or States operating via regional organizations to perform under certain circumstances enforcement operations without prior Security Council mandate? Those who argue in favour refer to the ECOWAS case in Liberia, both between 1990 and 1998 and in 2003 and Sierra Leone,[90] the NATO operation in Kosovo, or contested concepts such as the right to humanitarian intervention, or the Responsibility to Protect Doctrine (R2P).

With regard to the Liberia, Sierra Leone, or Kosovo cases both the debate in the UN and that by scholars make clear that these States view these instances not as developing State practice, whereby authorization by the UN Security Council is no longer necessary for enforcement action to be lawful, but on the contrary as instances whereby such authorization is necessary but may be granted retroactively. The UN sent military observers and took over ECOMOG's peacekeeping responsibilities in Sierra Leone by 2000.[91] There does not appear to be uniform State practice, nor *opinio juris*, to claim emerging customary law to that effect. Also it cannot be held that in as far as both ECOWAS and the African Union claim such right regionally this *opinio juris* is uncontested. Furthermore, the larger question remains how to view the commitments under these Protocols in relation to Article 103 Charter.

The Responsibility to Protect Doctrine was devised by the International Commission on Intervention and State Sovereignty (ICISS)[92] in its 2001 report. In as far as the World Summit Outcome document as adopted by the General Assembly appears to endorse this doctrine it still is in the realm of soft law, and does not contain obligations for States. This doctrine is 'essentially focussed on the question of humanitarian intervention'.[93] There are no R2P obligations for States, and there is no countervailing right to humanitarian intervention for States, and for that matter for regional organizations. Humanitarian intervention (in the strict sense) is:

> the threat or use of force by one or more states, whether not in the context of an international organisation, on the territory of another state:

[90] See A. Adebajo, 'The Security Council and Three Wars in West Africa' in Lowe et al. (eds), *The United Nations Security Council and War: The Evolution of Thought and Practice since 1945* (Oxford: Oxford University Press, 2008), 466–93.

[91] Ibid. 466–7.

[92] Available at <http://www.responsibilitytoprotect.org>.

[93] Both on this relationship and on the R2P doctrine in general see C. Focarelli, 'The Responsibility to Protect Doctrine and Humanitarian Intervention: Too Many Ambiguities for a Working Doctrine', 13 *JCSL* (2008), 191–213, at 209.

in order to end existing or prevent imminent grave, large-scale violations of fundamental human rights, particularly individuals' right to life, irrespective of their nationality; — without the prior authorisation of the Security Council and without the consent of the legitimate government of the state on whose territory the intervention takes place . . .[94] 7.05

Under customary law no such right to humanitarian intervention has developed. There is no uniform State practice nor *opinio juris*. In discussing this question with regard to a possible emerging regional *opinio juris*, two Dutch Governmental Advisory Committees pointed out that 'the fundamental question remains whether such a development of customary law is possible if it conflicts with peremptory (*ius cogens*) rules such as the ban on the use or threat of force, unless that exception is deemed to form an integral part of the said *ius cogens* rules'.[95] The Dutch Governmental Advisory Committees then concluded that 'there is no sufficient legal basis for humanitarian intervention without a Security Council mandate, but also that there is no clear evidence of such a legal basis emerging'.[96] This notwithstanding, the Committees then proceeded by remarking that '[a]t the same time [. . .] it is no longer possible to ignore the increasingly perceived need to intervene in situations where fundamental human rights are being or are likely to be violated on a large scale, even if the Security Council is taking no action'.[97] Then one starts talking about justifications of otherwise *contra legem* behaviour. This commentary, however, is not the place to extensively debate these exceptional circumstances and possible defences. In such extreme cases what at a minimum should be aimed for is the involvement of the UN General Assembly to help 'to generate maximum legitimacy for humanitarian intervention without Security Council authorisation'.[98]

Arguably in exceptional circumstances, where the regional organization has authorized the use of force to prevent genocide, crimes against humanity, or widespread violations of humanitarian law, the Security Council can endorse such an operation after it has been deployed but before it has completed its task. It is doubtful though whether such endorsement, unless it is clear, can cure the original illegality, but it does provide the operation with legality going forward. Peace support operations may use force in self-defence, and (arguably) in defence of civilians within their areas of deployment, without Security Council authority. A regional military operation that uses non-defensive force against a sovereign State without authorization from the Security Council is violating the UN Charter (Article 53) and also the *jus cogens* prohibition on the use of force (Article 2(4)).

[94] Humanitarian Intervention, Report by the Netherlands Advisory Council on International Affairs and the Advisory Committee on Issues of Public International Law, no. 13 April 2000, at 7. See Chapter 13 in relation to humanitarian intervention.

[95] Ibid. 23. [96] Ibid. 23. [97] Ibid. 34.

[98] Ibid. 27 and 35 on the competence of the General Assembly to recommend military measures to be taken when the Security Council has failed to exercise its primary responsibility for collective security. For a general discussion of humanitarian intervention undertaken without a Security Council authorization, see Chapter 13 'Humanitarian Intervention'.

7.05 3. *Constitutional Restrictions.* What effect do constitutional restrictions of a regional organization—in cases where there is a constitution—have on external operations? This concerns what was referred to earlier as the internal competence of regional organizations. It may be that, as is the case with the NATO Treaty, a clear and delimited area in which the organization may operate is described in the constitution of the regional organization. Does this then impose any restrictions for 'out-of-area' activities for the regional organization in question?

Could an international organization like NATO, that at the time of its incorporation (and later), has denied being a regional organization, still act as such?[99] If a regional organization has a constitution which so stipulates,[100] or it clearly follows from the *travaux préparatoires*, there may be an issue from the point of view of the organization, for it calls into question whether it has the internal competence to act as such. From the point of view of the UN Security Council, however, if such organization fulfils all other criteria, there appears to be nothing against being utilized by the UN Security Council to act as a regional organization in the sense of Chapter VIII.[101] Such constitutional issues, therefore, are an internal matter and any such possible constitutional restrictions that are identified will have to be dealt with within the regional organization, but do not form an impediment against action. The issue of internal competence clearly has to be distinguished from the question of external restrictions, like those flowing from UN Charter rules and principles such as that contained in Article 2(7) concerning domestic jurisdiction. Clear State consent then is needed. This situation of course is different where the UN Security Council utilizes such regional organization for enforcement action under Article 53.

The 'last minute' insertion of Article 51, preserving the right of individual and collective self-defence, into the UN Charter at San Francisco in 1945, at the insistence of regional bodies such as the American organization, led to a conceptual distinction between self-defence organizations (such as NATO) based on Article 51, which did not require any prior Security Council approval to respond to an armed attack against any one of its Members, and regional organizations such as the OAS, which were seen as potentially enforcers of the peace and thereby subject to the strictures of Article 53. In fact the Latin American States, pushing for Article 51, were to form a regional organization with a defensive Pact (the Rio Treaty of 1947) built in, thus undermining the idea that there is a clear distinction between defensive pacts and regional organizations. Indeed, the Lisbon Treaty of the EU

[99] See Dekker and Myjer, 'Air Strikes'; Blokker and Muller, 'NATO as the UN Security Council's Instrument'; Goodhart, 'The North Atlantic Treaty'.

[100] See Art. 1 OAS Charter: '. . . [w]ithin the United Nations, the Organization of American States is a regional agency'.

[101] Sarooshi, 'The Security Council's Authorization', 231: 'From the perspective of the UN Charter, however, the internal constraints on a regional arrangement being able to exercise delegated Chapter VII powers do not affect the lawfulness of the delegation or the exercise of delegated powers by the arrangement.'

has a defensive pact built into an already elaborate regional organization.[102] NATO was defined under Article 51 early in the Cold War when it was realized that the UN would not be able to provide active collective security. In fact NATO changed with the end of the Cold War, claiming in its 1999 Strategic Concept document, as well as acting in collective self-defence under Article 5 of the NATO Treaty, that it should also be able to undertake 'non-Article 5 crisis response operations'.[103] Similar in idea to the so-called 'Petersberg tasks' of the EU, which include 'humanitarian and rescue tasks and tasks of combat forces in crisis management including peacemaking',[104] neither NATO nor the EU defer to Security Council authority, but the above analysis shows that such authorization is necessary for any 'non-Article 5' or 'Petersberg tasks' taking the form of non-consensual military enforcement action for such action to be compliant with the UN Charter and basic concepts of international law governing the use of force. 7.05

[102] See Art. 42 TEU.
[103] NATO Doc. NAC-s(99) 65, para. 41 (24 April 1999).
[104] Art. 17(2) TEU.

PART III

MILITARY OPERATIONS WITHIN THE CONTEXT OF THE RIGHT OF SELF-DEFENCE AND OTHER POSSIBLE LEGAL BASES FOR THE USE OF FORCE

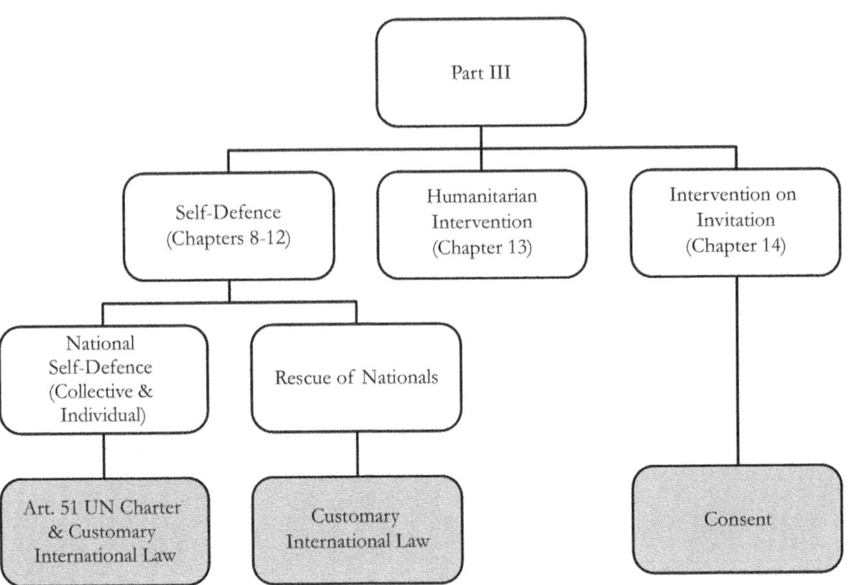

Figure 2

Chapter 8

LEGAL BASIS OF THE RIGHT OF SELF-DEFENCE UNDER THE UN CHARTER AND UNDER CUSTOMARY INTERNATIONAL LAW

The right of self-defence is used within different contexts (i.e. national or State self-defence, unit self-defence, and individual or personal self-defence) and can relate to different applicable legal regimes (e.g. international law, national criminal law, etc.). While these different manifestations of the right of self-defence share certain characteristics, in particular the notion that self-defence denotes the lawful use of force in response to a prior or impending illegal use of force, they are governed by different and distinct legal criteria and considerations. For the sake of clarity, the term self-defence as used in Part III of this Handbook will be used to denote the right of a State under international law to respond individually or collectively to an illegal armed attack directed against its territory, citizens, military vessels, aircraft, or installations, abroad or located in international sea or airspace, and subject to the legal criteria and conditions laid down in the UN Charter and in customary international law. These international legal criteria and conditions can be supplemented by other considerations of a policy or domestic legal nature, but those are separate and distinct and should not be confused with the legal regime governing the exercise of self-defence under international law. **8.01**

1. Self-defence under international law refers tó the right of a State (or States) to forcibly respond to an armed attack originating or controlled and directed from outside its territory against its territory, citizens, vessels, aircraft or military personnel stationed abroad, or which are situated in international sea or airspace.[1] It shares

[1] On the legal character of the right of self-defence and its relationship to related but distinct notions such as self-help and self-preservation see *inter alia*, D.W. Bowett, *Self Defence in International Law* (Cew York: Praeger, 1958), 3–25; I. Brownlie, *International Law and the Use of Force by States* (Oxford: Clarendon Press, 1963), 251 *et seq.*, Y. Dinstein, *War, Aggression and Self-Defence*, 5th edn (Cambridge: Cambridge University Press, 2011), 187 *et seq.* and C.H.M. Waldock, 'The Regulation of the Use of Force by Individual States in International Law', in 41 *RdC* (1952), 455–68.

TERRY D. GILL

8.01 a common legal origin with other manifestations of self-defence, such as the right of personal self-defence under national criminal law, both of which trace their origins to the natural law doctrine of the just war tradition. But under modern positive law, national self-defence is a separate legal regime which is relevant only to States and is governed solely by international law criteria and conditions contained in the UN Charter and in customary international law. Consequently, it should not be confused with other manifestations of self-defence referred to and covered elsewhere in this Handbook.[2]

2. Under contemporary international law the use or threat of force is prohibited except in the context of the UN collective security system or in exercise of the right of self-defence.[3] Consequently, the right of self-defence is an exception to the prohibition of the use of force which provides for a recognized legal basis for the use of transboundary force in response to a prior or impending illegal use of force originating or directed from abroad with the aim and purpose of halting the attack and forestalling the occurrence of further attacks in the immediate future from the same source.[4] It follows that self-defence only relates to a forcible response to an illegal use of force. In short, there is no right of self-defence against the lawful use of force, whether this is in the form of a lawful exercise of self-defence by another State or the exercise by the UN Security Council of its enforcement powers under the Charter.[5]

8.02 **The right of self-defence under international law is directed towards and possessed by States and is governed firstly by the provisions of the UN Charter relating to the use of force in general and the exercise of that right in particular. The relevant provision (Article 51) refers to the right as being 'inherent' in nature. This reference is generally accepted as a reference to the continuing relevance of customary international law which provides an additional legal basis and criteria for the exercise of this right, alongside those contained in Article 51 and other relevant provisions of the UN Charter. Consequently, the international right of self-defence has a dual legal basis: Article 51 of the UN Charter and customary international law, and both are**

[2] See sub-Chapter 5.3 and Chapters 22 and 23.

[3] On the prohibition of force under contemporary international law see Section 5.02 with supporting notes and commentary.

[4] The purpose of forestalling future repeated attacks from a given source once an attack has been launched or is imminent should not be confused with the notion of 'preventive self-defence', in advance of any clear and manifest threat of an armed attack in the immediate future. See in this respect, T.D. Gill, 'The Temporal Dimension of Self-Defence; Anticipation, Pre-emption, Prevention and Immediacy', in M.N. Schmitt and J. Pejic (eds), *International Law and Armed Conflict: Exploring the Faultlines* (Leiden and Boston, Nijhoff, 2007), 113. This precision will make later references more transparent.

[5] Dinstein, *War, Aggression and Self-Defence*, 190 quoting the decision by a US Military Tribunal in the 1949 *Ministries* case (*USA v von Weizsäcker et al.*, Nuremberg), 1949, 14 NMT 314, 329.

relevant in determining the legality and the modalities of the exercise of this right. They should be applied in a complementary fashion which fully takes into account the criteria and conditions for the exercise of this right which are laid down in both of these legal sources, as well as taking into account all relevant factual considerations which are available at the time in question. 8.02

1. The dual legal basis of the right of self-defence is generally recognized and acknowledged as being Article 51 of the UN Charter and customary international law, which is indirectly referred to in that provision by use of the term 'inherent' in relation to the nature of the right of self-defence.[6] Notwithstanding the general acknowledgement of the dual legal basis of the right in both Charter and customary law, there is nevertheless a considerable degree of legal disagreement and controversy relating to the scope of the right under customary international law between those States and authors who support a more restrictive approach and those which take a more liberal attitude as to what is permitted under customary law.[7] In keeping with the intention and purpose of a work such as this Handbook, it is not felt necessary to reproduce this doctrinal debate and controversy at any length here. The approach taken here is that Article 51 provides the starting point for an examination of the scope and purpose of the right of self-defence and is complemented by customary international law to the extent that this is not incompatible with Article 51 and the overall purpose of the Charter's legal framework governing the use of force and the primacy of the Security Council in the maintenance and restoration of international peace and security. Consequently, the lawful exercise of self-defence must meet both the conditions set out in Article 51 and other relevant provisions of the Charter, and those provided for under customary international law, which complement the Charter legal framework, such as necessity, proportionality, and immediacy.

[6] *Case Concerning Military and Paramilitary Activities in and against Nicaragua* (Merits), ICJ Reports 1986, 14, 94 (hereinafter, referred to as the *Nicaragua* case/decision/judgment).

[7] It is dangerous to try to label the opinions of authors or court decisions as 'permissive' or 'restrictive'. However, it is fair to say that, at least generally speaking, most authorities tend towards one basic view or another. Amongst those who are generally 'restrictive' in their approach towards self-defence are authors such as Brownlie, *International Law*, 25 *et seq*.; C. Gray, *International Law and the Use of Force* (Oxford: Oxford University Press, 2000), 86 *et seq*. and the majority of the Court in the *Nicaragua* decision of 1986 (ICJ Reports 1986, 14; 98–106). Among those who take a somewhat wider view of self-defence and the role of customary international law therein are Bowett, *Self Defence*, 269 *et seq*.; T.M. Franck, *Recourse to Force State Action against Threats and Armed Attacks* (2003), 45 *et seq*. and the dissenting judges in the *Nicaragua* judgment. In reality, these and other authorities' viewpoints are often too complex and nuanced to be able to be fit neatly into a given 'school', but there is a divide between those who emphasize the literal text of Article 51 and rely heavily upon certain General Assembly resolutions and on condemnations by the Security Council of specific invocations of self-defence as support for the general position that customary law has little specific separate content from the relevant Charter provisions, and those who take the position that custom continues to exist alongside the Charter and has specific legal content which must be taken into account in interpreting the relevant Charter provisions.

8.02 2. The application of the legal criteria referred to in the previous paragraph must also take account of the relevant factual circumstances and conditions pertaining at the time a self-defence action is undertaken. Principles such as necessity, proportionality, and immediacy, while capable of a general legal definition, only take on meaning in the light of relevant circumstances such as the nature, gravity, and scope of the attack; the likelihood of further attacks in the immediate future; the availability of effective and feasible alternatives; the factual evidence relating to the source of the attack; the availability and likeliness of possible outside assistance; the state of readiness and capabilities of the defending State's armed forces, and so forth.[8] This list is indicative, and not meant to be exhaustive, but it does serve to illustrate that the legal criteria governing the exercise of self-defence cannot be seen in isolation from other relevant considerations. Whether a particular action taken in the context of self-defence is, for example, proportionate will depend on the seriousness of the attack and the likelihood of further attacks and can only be reasonably assessed on the basis of the information readily available at the time, not on what may come to light weeks, months, or even years later.[9]

8.03 **The exercise of self-defence under Article 51 of the Charter is predicated upon the occurrence of an armed attack. Under customary international law, the possibility is not ruled out that a State may respond to a clear and manifest danger of an impending armed attack when the danger of such an impending attack is supported by convincing factual evidence and no other alternatives are reasonably available. An armed attack can be carried out either directly by a foreign State's armed forces, or indirectly by a State acting through organized armed groups which are under a foreign State's control or are subject to significant involvement and influence from a foreign State. Additionally, an armed attack can be carried out by an organized armed group which is capable of mounting an armed attack, which is comparable in its scale and effect to a conventional armed attack carried out by a State. An 'armed attack' denotes a reasonably significant use of force originating or directed from abroad, or a series of smaller related armed incidents which have the common purpose of destabilizing the victim State or exacting political concessions from it.**

[8] See further e.g. O. Schachter, *International Law in Theory and Practice* (Dordrecht: M. Nijhoff, 1991), 152–4 and 167–9.

[9] For example, the UN Security Council unanimously condemned an Israeli air strike against an Iraqi nuclear reactor in 1981 as essentially not meeting the criteria of necessity at the time. When evidence emerged later in the 1990s of Iraq's efforts to obtain nuclear weapons, some States and authors reconsidered their position in hindsight. However, this is not acceptable as a legal proposition; the question of whether a particular act was necessary can only be assessed on the basis of available evidence.

1. The notion of an 'armed attack' is a generally recognized prerequisite for the exercise of the right of self-defence as is provided for in the text of Article 51 of the Charter.[10] The Charter does not define or clarify what is meant by the term; for this recourse must be had to customary international law and the interpretations thereof by the International Court of Justice, the Security Council, and other competent organs of international organizations, as well as to legal literature. **8.03**

2. On the basis of these indications and interpretations it is clear that an 'armed attack' denotes a reasonably significant use of force which rises above the level of an ordinary criminal act, an isolated frontier incident, or an expression of purely verbal or material support for the acts of an organized armed group acting independently of another State's control.[11] Such acts, while 'unfriendly' or even 'hostile' would not rise to the level of an 'armed attack', even when they were otherwise illegal under national or international law. The question of purely material support for an insurgency or other armed group is somewhat controversial[12] in this respect. The *Nicaragua* decision of the ICJ would seem to rule out the possibility that purely material support (of a non-humanitarian character) such as the provision of weapons, training, and military equipment to an insurgent or other organized armed group would qualify as an 'armed attack'. However, this interpretation has been the subject of a considerable amount of criticism and commentary.[13] It is fair to assume as a general proposition that purely material support for an insurgency or other organized armed activity will not normally qualify as an 'armed attack'; but if the level of support is significant and includes more than mere material assistance (such as logistical support, training, intelligence and so forth), it could so qualify once it reached the level of 'substantial involvement'.[14]

3. The modality of an armed attack can vary in terms of authorship. A direct armed attack is carried out by the armed forces or other State organs against another State. This is the type of armed attack which the framers of the Charter had in mind when Article 51 was drafted and such attacks usually pose few difficulties in terms of establishing which State is responsible for carrying out the attack.[15] An indirect attack is one whereby a State conducts an attack through an organized armed group over which it exercises control, instead of through official organs of the attacking State.

[10] The term 'armed attack' is used in the English version of Art. 51. The Spanish, Russian, and Chinese texts are a direct translation of the English. However, the equally authoritative French text uses the term *agression armée* which is generally considered to be a somewhat wider notion. See e.g. Dinstein, *War, Aggression and Self-Defence*, 196–7.

[11] *Nicaragua* decision, para. 195, 103–4.

[12] Some of these would violate the principle of non-intervention or non-use of force without necessarily rising to the level of an armed attack, at least on the basis of the ICJ's interpretation in the *Nicaragua* decision.

[13] See, in this respect, the vigorous dissents by Judges Jennings and Schwebel to the *Nicaragua* decision in ICJ Reports, 1986, 347–450 (Schwebel) and 542–4 (Jennings).

[14] In this, the position of the two disserting judges referred to in the previous note appears to me to be more realistic and persuasive.

[15] This is clear from an examination of the drafting history of Art. 51. See in this respect Bowett, *Self Defence*, 182 *et seq.* and Franck, *Recourse to Force State Action*, 45–51.

8.03 International courts and tribunals have expressed somewhat different viewpoints regarding the requisite degree of control necessary to be able to attribute such an attack to the supporting State.[16] In any case once an organization comes under the effective control of a State, or the level of a State's involvement in providing the armed groups with training, equipment, supplies, sanctuary, and other possible forms of assistance can be qualified as 'substantial', there is general agreement that an attack launched by such an armed organization or group can be attributed to the controlling or supporting State.[17] However, in such cases, it will often be more difficult for the target State to provide sufficient factual evidence of the suspected attacking State's degree of involvement and control which may be necessary to convince a court or the international community at large of the necessity of taking self-defence measures against the supporting State. There is no generally recognized standard of proof which has been accepted in this regard.[18] It will depend upon a number of factors; including the seriousness of the attack, the degree of objectively recognizable involvement or control linking the (suspected) supporting State to the armed organization, and the 'reputation' of the States concerned, to name but several of the more important considerations. Certainly, mere allegations of outside support for an attack carried out by an armed group or organization will not suffice and should not be regarded as sufficient to justify measures against the alleged supporting State. However, it would likewise be unrealistic to expect a State which has been the target of repeated attack by an armed group or organization which it has reasonable grounds to believe is under the control of another State, or which receives a substantial degree of support from another State enabling that organization to carry out its activities, to forgo the taking of necessary and proportional measures of self-defence against both the organization and the source of support or control, provided it has the means to do so and there was reasonable evidence to establish the relationship of dependence or substantial involvement.

4. A third modality for the authorship of an armed attack is that of an attack being conducted by an armed group or organization which is capable of launching an

[16] In its *Nicaragua* decision, the ICJ characterized the necessary level of control as 'effective', (see ICJ Reports, 1986, 65) while the ICTY determined that 'overall control' was sufficient to impute the acts of an armed group to a supporting State in the decision of the Appeals Chamber in the *Tadić* case (see ICTY Case no. 94-I-A, Appeals Chamber 1999 reproduced in 38 *ILM* (1999), 1518, 1540 *et seq.*).

[17] In *Nicaragua*, the Court determined that 'substantial involvement' on the part of a State in the acts of an armed group (rebels, terrorists, mercenaries, etc.) was a form of indirect attack on the basis of UN GA Res. 3314 'Definition of Aggression' (XXIX) 1974. However, the Court made little effort to determine what would constitute 'substantial involvement'; a point which was criticized by both Judges Jennings and Schwebel in their respective dissents referred to earlier in the chapter.

[18] The ICJ has generally required a high level of proof, as for example in the *Oil Platforms* case reproduced in 42 *ILM* (2003), 1334. See in this respect, the Court's pronouncements on the requisite burden of proof in relation to the existence of an armed attack on a reflagged tanker and a US warship in paras 53–61 and 69–71. The Court indicated that the evidence was respectively 'suggestive' and 'highly suggestive' in relation to those two incidents, but insufficient to establish Iranian involvement. This and other aspects of the judgment were vigorously criticized by a number of judges in their individual opinions. See e.g. Judge Higgins at 1384–6, Kooijmans at 1396–7, Buergenthal at 1413–16 and Owada at 1424–5.

attack autonomously and on its own initiative without the substantial involvement of another State.[19] There is nothing in either the provisions of the UN Charter or in customary international law which rules out this possibility or restricts the right of self-defence to reactions to State launched or controlled armed attacks, notwithstanding certain pronouncements to the contrary. Recent practice indicates that this possibility has been recognized and customary law has long acknowledged this possibility.[20] In cases where an armed group or organization carries out an armed attack against a State, it will either be carried out with the knowledge and support of another State, or it will be capable of operating independently from another State's territory, but without that State's support or control over its activities.[21] This will usually be a consequence of the incapacity of the State from where the attack is carried out to effectively control its territory and halt the activities of the armed organization. This could be the result of a (partial) breakdown in the State's authority over its territory, the remoteness of the area from where the organization operates, or a degree of sympathy with the activities of the armed organization without necessarily being significantly involved in them or exercising control over the organization. **8.03**

5. The modalities discussed earlier have consequences for the courses of action open to the defending State. Obviously, a direct attack by a State upon another State will justify measures of defence directed against the attacking State itself. Likewise, an 'indirect armed attack' which is carried out by an armed group or organization which is under the effective control or with the substantial involvement of another State would justify defensive measures aimed at both the armed group and its source of control or substantial support. In such a case, the defensive measures aimed at the controlling or supporting State would be directed at countering the organization's attacks and disrupting the links between it and its supporting State. Finally, in the event an organization was capable of mounting an attack from another State's territory, but independent of any control or substantial degree of support by that State, this would justify defensive measures directed against the armed group or organization, but not against (the organs of) the State

[19] See e.g. Dinstein, *War, Aggression and Self-Defence*, 224–230, Franck, *Recourse to Force State Action*, 64–8.

[20] The ICJ in its Advisory Opinion on the construction of a wall in occupied Palestinian Territory inferred that self-defence was restricted to situations where an armed attack is carried out by a State against another State. This came in for vigorous criticism by a number of judges in their individual opinions. See ICJ Reports, 2004, 194, para. 139 for the Court's pronouncement on this issue. For the contrary opinion see, for example, Judge Higgins' separate opinion at 215. See also SC Res. 1368 and 1373 UNSC (2001), which refer to the right of self-defence in relation to the attacks on the WTC and Pentagon, which were carried out by non-State agents. The well-known *Caroline* incident of 1837 related to the support of private US citizens for an insurgency in Canada and is often referred to as the *locus classicus* for assessing the customary right of self-defence. See Gill, 'The Temporal Dimension', 125–8.

[21] An example of the former situation would be that of al Qaeda operating from the territory of Afghanistan in and prior to 2001, and of the latter, the operations conducted by the PKK from the territory of Northern Iraq in recent years.

8.03 from where it operated if no other means were available to the defending State. In such a situation, the State from where the attack was being conducted would be under an obligation to not forcibly oppose the defensive measures undertaken.[22]

6. The temporal dimension of the right of self-defence relates both to the question when an 'armed attack' can be said to have occurred and the timeframe within which it is permissible for the target State to take action in self-defence.[23] In particular, the question whether a State has the right to institute self-defence measures in response to an impending and imminent threat of an attack has received a considerable amount of attention in both State practice and in legal literature, especially in recent years.[24] The literal text of Article 51 has given rise to one school of opinion that self-defence is only permissible once an armed attack 'occurs', which to some implies that an attack must have been initiated before self-defence measures may be taken. However, there is another body of opinion and interpretation which takes the position that self-defence measures may be taken in response to a manifest threat of an impending armed attack, when this is based on clear indications and no other feasible alternatives are available to forestall an attack being launched.[25] This approach refers to the recognition of this possibility in customary international law and to the dual legal basis of self-defence in both customary and Charter (-based) law.[26] On balance, it would appear that a reasonable interpretation of the right to self-defence would allow for the possibility of taking action in self-defence in response to a clear and manifest threat of an impending (threat of an) attack if the indications are convincing and no alternatives are available. This interpretation takes into account both the complementary nature of the Charter and customary law and the basic intention underlying the concept of self-defence as a legal right. Any other interpretation results in the consequence that either target State would have to suffer a possibly devastating first strike before being

[22] This is a consequence of the fact that there is 'no self-defence against self-defence' (as set out in Dinstein, *War, Aggression and Self-Defence*, 190) and the failure of the State whence the attack originated to exercise the requisite due diligence to prevent its territory being used as a base of operations by an armed group to carry out attacks against another State, due to either incapacity or unwillingness. This duty of due diligence has long been recognized in legal doctrine and in jurisprudence. See e.g. the *Corfu Channel* case, ICJ Reports, 1949, 4 at 22.

[23] See, *inter alia*, Gill, 'The Temporal Dimension', 151–4.

[24] This refers to the ongoing controversy relating to the permissibility of 'anticipatory' or 'pre-emptive' self-defence. See in addition to the sources cited earlier the ongoing debate in legal journals, especially in the aftermath of the '9/11' attacks and the invocation by the Bush Administration of a wider right of pre-emptive and even preventive self-defence in its national security strategy of 2003. It should be pointed out that this proposed wider right went well beyond the more generally accepted *Caroline* criteria of an immediate threat of attack and met with vigorous criticism from many States and in legal doctrine.

[25] Examples of authors opposing anticipatory or 'interceptive' self-defence as it is sometimes referred to include those cited as 'restrictive', while those categorized as belonging to the more 'permissive' school are in favour of such a right within the confines of the *Caroline* criteria.

[26] Anticipatory self-defence is generally derived from the famous *Caroline* incident of 1837 as evidence of its recognition under customary law. For an extensive treatment of this incident and its legal significance, see R. Jennings, 'The Caroline and McLeod Case' in 32 *AJIL* (1938), 82 *et seq*. See also Gill, 'The Temporal Dimension', 125–8.

allowed to respond; or in the expansion of self-defence beyond its legal boundaries and essential underlying purpose, with the consequence of undermining the legal framework regulating the use of force.[27] 8.03

In addition to the occurrence of an armed attack, or the clear and manifest danger of an impending attack, the Charter requires that any action undertaken in self-defence be reported forthwith to the Security Council and gives the Council primacy in determining what further measures may be necessary in order to restore international peace and security. Under customary international law, the requirements of necessity, proportionality, and immediacy are well established as complementing the requirements provided in the Charter in relation to the exercise of self-defence. Necessity relates to the existence of an ongoing armed attack or clear threat of repeated attack within the near future, as well as the absence of feasible alternatives including measures undertaken by the Security Council which have the effect of restoring the situation pertaining prior to the attack and ending the threat of further attacks. Proportionality in this context refers to the requirement that the measures taken in self-defence must be roughly commensurate with the scale and effect of the attack and are directed towards ending the attack and neutralizing the danger of further attack. Immediacy refers to the requirement that measures of self-defence must be taken within a reasonable period, taking into account the relevant factual circumstances. 8.04

1. In addition to the requirement of an 'armed attack', action taken in self-defence must meet the other requirements for the exercise of this right which are set out in the Charter and which are well established in customary law. The Charter provides for a duty to report self-defence action as soon as possible to the Security Council and establishes the Council's primacy in the relationship between the exercise of its enforcement powers under Chapter VII and the right of self-defence.[28]

2. The duty to report to the Security Council is not to be confused with a requirement of prior authorization. The defending State has the right to initiate measures of self-defence once an armed attack has occurred, or is imminent. However, once defensive action has been initiated, the primacy of the Council signifies that it has the final authority to endorse, take note of, or reject the reporting State's invocation of self-defence. If the Council succeeds in taking measures which have the effect of restoring the situation, the defending State's

[27] Gill, 'The Temporal Dimension', 145–55.

[28] This primacy is evident from both the terms of Article 51 and the underlying purpose and object of the Charter. See in this respect for example, Dinstein, *War, Aggression and Self-Defence*, 234, R. Higgins, *Problems and Process: International Law and How We Use It* (Oxford: Clarendon Press 1994), 239–40 and Waldock, 'Regulation of the Use of Force', 487–8.

8.04 right of self-defence will cease to be operative. The Council can also decide to take measures which complement the defensive action of the attacked State in which self-defence measures will mutually reinforce each other and operate side by side until the situation has been restored, or the Council determines otherwise. Finally, the Council can determine that the invocation of self-defence is no longer necessary or is unjustified and order both parties to a conflict to cease and desist from further action.[29] In short, while self-defence is an autonomous right of every State, it is subject to the Council's final authority and is part of the overall Charter's legal framework regulating the use of force.

3. Alongside the abovementioned Charter framework, the exercise of self-defence is also subject to the well-established conditions of necessity, proportionality, and immediacy which are part of the customary law relating to self-defence and which complement the provisions of Article 51 of the Charter.[30] The terms 'necessity', 'proportionality', and 'immediacy' have a specific connotation within the customary law relating to self-defence and should not be confused with their counterparts in other branches of international law, such as, for example, the law of armed conflict, where similar or identical terms are in use to express related but distinct concepts.[31]

4. Within the context of self-defence, necessity signifies the existence of an ongoing attack or the clear and manifest threat of an imminent threat of an armed attack or of further attack. It also relates to the absence of feasible alternative courses of action open to the defending State under the prevailing circumstances. These can include the implementation of collective measures by the Security Council which have the effect of restoring the situation, the agreement by the attacking State to terminate its actions by means of accepting a cease-fire and accepting conditions aimed at ensuring compliance and preventing the recurrence of further attacks, or the realistic alternative of terminating or forestalling attack through measures other than self-defence, such as law enforcement measures or cooperation by the authorities of the State from where the attack originated without its knowledge or assistance.[32]

[29] These possibilities and alternative courses of action open to the Security Council are set out and analysed in Dinstein, *War, Aggression and Self-Defence*, 236–9. The effect of Security Council action upon a State's right to exercise self-defence should be seen in context. If the Security Council takes note of, or explicitly or implicitly endorses, a State's invocation of self-defence, the right will continue to operate alongside any measures taken by the Council in the exercise of collective security as was the case in SC Res. 678 (1990) and in SC Res. 1373 (2001). However, if the Council orders a State to refrain from further action in self-defence as it did in SC Res. 598 (1987) in the context of the Iran/Iraq War, the right of self-defence will be terminated unless one of the parties continues with military action in violation of the Council's cease and desist order.

[30] This is universally accepted in both legal doctrine and State practice. See e.g. ICJ Reports, 1980, 103.

[31] See in this respect J. Gardam, *Necessity, Proportionality and the Use of Force by States* (Cambridge: Cambridge University Press, 2004), 10 *et seq.*

[32] See e.g. Schachter, *International Law*, 152–5, Dinstein, *War, Aggression and Self-Defence*, 262–7, and Gardam, *Necessity*, 148–53 on necessity and proportionality in general. Self-defence specifically in relation to non-State controlled or conducted terrorist acts is a measure of last resort, which can only

5. Proportionality in the context of self-defence refers to the requirement that the measures taken in self-defence must be roughly comparable in scale and effects to that of the armed attack and the overall threat of attack posed by the attacking State or entity. Proportionality means the measures taken must be aimed and geared towards terminating the attack or continuation of attack and not exceed what is required for this purpose. If an attack is relatively limited in scope and duration, the measures taken in self-defence must correspondingly be limited to repelling that attack and not seek to widen the conflict. On the other hand, a large-scale offensive by an attacking State aimed at subjecting the target State or inflicting large-scale casualties or dismembering its territory would justify a defensive war conducted by the defending State and its possible allies to defeat the attacking State or entity's forces and prevent the occurrence of further aggression. Proportionality can be measured against a single larger scale attack, or a series of related and successive smaller scale attacks carried out by the same author over a period of time. In the latter situation, the defending State would be justified in undertaking measures of self-defence on a larger scale than the individual actions forming what is in essence a phased armed attack.[33] **8.04**

6. Immediacy in this context signifies that action taken in self-defence must be taken within a reasonable timeframe in relation to the occurrence of the attack. The notion of reasonableness allows for the necessary flexibility in this respect in taking the relevant circumstances into account. These include such factors as the necessity of providing the evidence of responsibility for an attack when this is not otherwise clear, the geographical location of an attack, the time required to deploy or mobilize forces to repel the attack and so forth. The essential notion underlying this requirement is that measures taken in self-defence must be taken within a reasonable period and aimed at terminating the attack rather than being essentially punitive in nature.[34]

Self-defence may be exercised either individually by a State which has been subjected to an attack, or collectively by one or more States which have been subjected to an attack originating from a common source, or by one or more States which at the request of a State which has been subjected to an attack, elect to come to that State's assistance. Such a request for assistance may be based on a pre-existing **8.05**

be exercised when the act rises to the level of an armed attack and the logical alternative course of action in the form of law enforcement is either unavailable or would clearly not suffice to counter the threat posed.

[33] See the sources cited in the previous note in relation to the general content of proportionality *ad bellum*. For the question of proportionality in relation to a phased armed attack, see the Report by Roberto Ago in his capacity as Special Rapporteur to the International Law Commission in 'Addendum to the Eighth Report on State Responsibility', 1980 II (1) *Yearbook of the International Law Commission* 13, 69–70.

[34] Ibid. See also Gill, 'The Temporal Dimension', 151–4.

8.05 **commitment to provide assistance in the event of an attack, or be made on an ad hoc basis once an attack has been mounted or is imminent.**

1. Collective self-defence is recognized in both the Charter provisions and in customary international law and provides both for a right of more than one State to mount a joint defence against an attack or series of attacks which is aimed at all of them, or for one or more States to come to the assistance of a State which has been subjected to an attack at the request of that State's government.[35] Such a request may be made in the form of a pre-existing commitment through a treaty of alliance or other agreement or on an ad hoc basis in response to an attack or threat of imminent attack. An example of the former would be the provision in the NATO Treaty providing for a commitment of mutual assistance in the event of an attack, while an example of the latter can be seen in the request by the Kuwaiti Government in exile to the United States and United Kingdom to come to its assistance after the invasion and occupation by Iraq in August 1990.[36]

2. In addition to such a request any action taken in collective self-defence is subject to all the requirements relating to self-defence provided for in both Charter law and in customary international law referred to in Sections 8.01–8.04.

[35] Article 51 refers to 'the inherent right of individual or collective self-defence' and the ICJ recognized the customary nature of collective self-defence in paras 196–199 of its 1986 *Nicaragua* decision, ICJ Reports, 1986, 104–5.

[36] Article 5 of the North Atlantic Treaty, 1949, 34 *UNTS* 243, 246. On Kuwait's request for military assistance see D. Hiro, *Desert Shield to Desert Storm: The Second Gulf War* (Bloomington, IN: iUniverse, 1992), 102–6.

Chapter 9

STATUS OF FORCES IN SELF-DEFENCE OPERATIONS

Regular armed forces participating in a self-defence operation in an international armed conflict are combatants in relation to the opposing State. They enjoy immunity in the assisted Receiving State and any Transit State as a matter of customary international law. 9.01

Regular armed forces participating in a self-defence operation amounting to a non-international armed conflict enjoy immunity in the assisted Receiving State and any Transit State as a matter of customary international law. Armed opposition fighters in non-international armed conflicts do not enjoy the combatant privilege under international humanitarian law. However, this does not preclude agreements or unilateral conferral of such status or amnesty from prosecution under national law for participation in hostilities which does not constitute a violation of international humanitarian law. 9.02

1. *General.* When armed forces become involved in self-defence operations, status issues as discussed previously (sub-Chapters 5.2 and 6.2) may be looked at as being put aside by rules of combatant status under international humanitarian law. This will definitely be the case where the qualification of the situation as an armed conflict is no longer a matter of dispute. Yet specific issues pertaining to status are to be considered nevertheless. As soon as a third State becomes involved and comes to the assistance of the defending State, this will bring status issues into play. The Sending State could conclude a status-of-forces agreement with the State it is assisting, and also with Transit States, in order to facilitate deployment of troops and equipment on their territory.[1] There could also be third State military forces already stationed on the defending State's territory on the basis of preexisting agreement, thus raising the question of wartime applicability of the latter.[2] The relevance of such issues is not limited to self-defence operations between States. It may occur in internal conflicts as well. While in an international armed conflict

[1] See Exchange of Notes between the US and UK Governments dated 27 July 1942, *Hansard*, HC (series 5) Vol. 382, col. 877 (4 August 1942); P. Rowe, 'Visiting Forces During World War II', in D. Fleck (ed.), *The Handbook of the Law of Visiting Forces* (Oxford: Oxford University Press, 2001), 15–18.

[2] See Art. XV NATO SOFA; Fleck, 'Applicability during Crisis or War', in *Visiting Forces*, 255–6.

DIETER FLECK

9.02 regular armed forces are combatants and—if detained by the enemy—are protected under the Third Geneva Convention, this is not the case in non-international armed conflicts. In internal disturbances, such as riots, isolated and sporadic acts of violence, or other acts of a similar nature international humanitarian law formally does not apply at all, yet fundamental human rights protections must be observed in all conflict situations.[3] The question of which status the various groups of fighters have in different situations remains of practical importance and the answer to be given will depend upon the specific circumstances in each case.

2. *Armed Forces.* The status of regular armed forces participating in self-defence operations depends upon the nature of the conflict:

(a) In an *international armed conflict* all self-defence operations will be part of that conflict with the result that members of regular armed forces enjoy combatant status and upon detention by an adversary State all persons meeting the requirements of Article 4 GC III and Articles 43–44 AP I are protected as prisoners of war. In relation to the Receiving State and any Transit State they enjoy immunity under customary international law.
(b) In *non-international armed conflicts* regular armed forces operating on the territory of their own State have essentially the same status as in peacetime. Allied forces operating in the Receiving State by invitation of its government enjoy immunity as a matter of customary international law. The same applies in Transit States. For the conduct of hostilities the law of non-international armed conflict applies. Armed opposition fighters in non-international armed conflicts do not enjoy the combatant privilege under international humanitarian law. However, this does not preclude special agreements pursuant to Article 3(3) Common to the Geneva Conventions; or unilateral conferral of such status; or amnesty in accordance with Article 6(5) AP II from prosecution under national law for participation in hostilities which does not constitute a violation of international humanitarian law.
(c) During *peacetime* (including internal disturbances below the threshold of an armed conflict) the status of armed forces follows the national law of their State for all operations within its boundaries; but for operations abroad essentially international law applies, as deriving from customary rules on State immunity and existing status-of-forces agreements. A visiting force coming to the assistance of the government of the Receiving State will rely on these rules in its relation to that State. With respect to opposition groups it may share rights and obligations of the Receiving State and is bound to existing human rights obligations.

3. *Police.* The status of police forces engaged in self-defence situations follows the national law of their State and—for operations abroad—pertinent rules of international law. Police forces may be deployed in a peace operation which gets under

[3] Fleck (ed.), *The Handbook of International Humanitarian Law*, 3rd edn (Oxford: Oxford University Press, 2013), Sections 704–706, 1205, and 1215.

attack by warring parties, thus becoming involved in a self-defence operation amounting to an international armed conflict. Even in such extreme cases the members of the police are civilians, unless they are incorporated by their particular State into the armed forces in conformity with Article 43, paragraph 3, AP I. 9.02

4. *Private Companies* hired by military or police forces may also become involved in situations of individual self-defence. As they must be limited to a strictly civilian function (see Section 6.06, para. 2 c, and Chapter 27), their status remains that of civilians even when a larger self-defence operation amounts to an international armed conflict.

5. *Armed Opposition Groups.* Non-State fighters in internal conflicts do not enjoy any special status. Yet they bear rights and responsibilities under human rights law,[4] and the law of non-international armed conflict applies for the conduct of hostilities.

6. *Responsibilities.* For the responsibility of Sending States and international organizations see Chapter 30. This responsibility includes acts committed in excess of authority or in contravention of instructions.

[4] Fundamental rights are summarized in Art. 75 AP I. For obligations of non-State actors under international law see A. Clapham, *Human Rights Obligations of Non-State Actors* (Oxford: Oxford University Press, 2006), 271–316; Fleck, 'Humanitarian Protection Against Non-State Actors', in J.A. Frowein et al. (eds), *Verhandeln für den Frieden/Negotiating for Peace. Liber Amicorum Tono Eitel* (Berlin: Springer, 2003), 69–94; C. Tomuschat, 'The Applicability of Human Rights Law to Insurgent Movements', in H. Fischer et al. (eds), *Krisensicherung und Humanitärer Schutz—Crisis Management and Humanitarian Protection* (Berlin: Berliner Wissenschafts-Verlag, 2004), 573–91.

Chapter 10

APPLICATION OF FORCE AND RULES OF ENGAGEMENT IN SELF-DEFENCE OPERATIONS

10.01 **Controlling the use of force by military forces is both an operational command responsibility and legal imperative. Rules of Engagement (ROE) are accepted by military forces as the most common and effective framework in which to control the use of force. The ROE framework ensures that political direction and objectives as well as legal, diplomatic, policy and operational considerations are coherently conveyed in military orders or directives. This is to make sure the level of force authorized for military forces contributes towards mission accomplishment.**

1. The concept of individual and collective State self-defence under public international law is comprised of both treaty law and customary international law. The right of self-defence is one of the express exemptions found in Article 51 of the UN Charter to the general prohibition on the use of force. Moreover, the right of individual and collective self-defence in customary international law operates and is separate from Article 51 and from international treaty law.[1]

2. Generally, the use of force by States in national self defence, whether at home or abroad, requires authorization from the government of the State. National self-defence includes the defence of the State, the State's citizens, and the State's territory and property from hostile acts or hostile intent (for further discussion of national self-defence see Sections 8.01 and 8.02 in Chapter 8). For example, depending on the circumstances, the rescue of a State's nationals abroad to remove its citizens from a state undergoing civil unrest could be based on the exercise of national self-defence (see Chapter 12 'Rescue of Nationals').

3. Similarly, States may use force in collective self-defence of another State. When a State or its citizens are subjected to an armed attack or are confronted with the immediate and impending threat of attack, it may request other States to assist in its defence. NATO and the Canada-US North American Aerospace Defence Command

[1] For details see Chapter 8, 'Legal Basis of the Right of Self-Defence under the UN Charter and under Customary International Law'.

BLAISE CATHCART

(NORAD) are two examples of regional arrangements which facilitate the collective implementation of self-defence. Coalition Operations in Kuwait in 1991 and Afghanistan in 2001 were examples of the exercise of the collective right of self-defence in conjunction with a Security Council mandate authorizing 'all necessary means' in the context of the UN Collective Security System. **10.01**

4. Whenever a military operation, including one in national or collective self-defence, is conducted, the use of force by military forces is controlled in order to ensure discipline and to protect persons from unnecessary injury and property from unnecessary damage. International and domestic (i.e. host nation and/or Sending State) law prescribe the boundaries of force that may be used by military forces on self-defence operations. For example, depending upon the type of self-defence operation, one or more of the various legal regimes identified in this Handbook, such as IHL (or LOAC), international human rights law, law of the sea, air law, and Security Council resolutions (SC Res.) will be relevant. Additionally, members of the Force are at all times individually legally responsible for their actions and are subject to their own national legislation, such as their military disciplinary law and domestic criminal law. The law may also delineate the methods and means by which that force may be applied. In all circumstances, military commanders and subordinates have a responsibility to ensure compliance with the rule of law.

5. The conditions for the exercise of the right of self-defence under international law are set out comprehensively under Sections 8.01–8.04 in Chapter 8 of this Handbook. It is crucial that States incorporate these conditions into the ROE, and other operational documents, which regulate the use of force and the conduct of military operations during self-defence missions.

6. Unlike the use of force during enforcement operations, the use of force in the exercise of the right of self-defence is not dependent upon authorization by the UN, specifically the Security Council. However, on occasion, a situation may arise when the legal authority for self-defence exists and the Security Council simultaneously issues one or more resolutions dealing with the same situation. At this moment, the complexity of the legal framework authorizing the use of force multiplies. An immediate question will be whether the Security Council has triggered the 'until clause' and has taken sufficient 'measures necessary' pursuant to Article 51 to override and extinguish the exercise of self-defence.[2] In such circumstances, the

[2] Article 51 recognizes the right of a State to act in self-defence 'until the Security Council has taken measures necessary to maintain international peace and security'. Debate exists regarding the effect of this limitation, particularly in circumstances where self-defence is being exercised and the Security Council has issued resolutions on the matter. In these situations, such as the 1991 Gulf War and the post 9/11 'Campaign Against Terrorism' (primarily in Afghanistan), it is not clear whether the SC measures would have had to effectively eliminate the threat in order for the 'until clause' to have applied. See C. Greenwood, 'New World Order or Old' 55 *Military Law Review* (1992), 153; M. Halberstam, 'The Right to Self-Defence once the Security Council Takes Action', 17 *Michigan Journal of International Law* (1995–6), 229; Y. Dinstein, *War, Aggression and Self-Defence,* 4th edn (Cambridge: Cambridge University Press, 2006), 189; C. Gray, *International Law and the Use of Force*, 2nd edn

10.01 resolution(s) will have to be scrutinized in order to determine precisely whether the Security Council has permitted the continued exercise of the right of self-defence. Clearly, the determination of the effect of the Security Council Resolution(s) on the exercise of self-defence will have a direct and immediate impact on the use of force and ROE used in national and collective self-defence operations, perhaps to the extent that the ROE will have to be cancelled and/or revised to comply with the resolution(s). Generally speaking, a termination of the right of a State to exercise self-defence in the event of an imminent or ongoing armed attack will have to be explicitly stated in the operative paragraphs of such a Security Council resolution. If doubt should arise, the nature of the measures undertaken by the Council, viewed in the context of the object and purpose of the resolution and the negotiations leading to its adoption will provide guidance as to whether the right of self-defence has been terminated or should be adopted to take account of any measures the Council may have determined.

7. A number of ROE systems have been developed by individual nations, alliances, coalitions, and services within various military forces. Generally, self-defence operations under Article 51 or customary international law will use national, alliance (e.g. NATO), or coalition ROE.[3]

8. Alliances, such as NATO, are designed to incorporate service specific (i.e. navy, army, air force, and marines) and joint ROE doctrines and architectures to which each alliance member has agreed to comply with during combined alliance operations. Therefore, when conducting such alliance self-defence operations, the applicable alliance ROE reference and system will normally be used. Commanders must be aware that there are both significant and subtle differences between the various alliance ROE doctrines and architectures, and great care must be taken to ensure the underlying concepts and applications are not confused between systems.

9. Generally during a multinational international military self-defence operation undertaken outside a formal alliance structure there is no standard reference for ROE, ROE principles, concepts and measures because of the often ad hoc nature of such operations. A coalition force may operate under one common set of ROE or each troop contributing country (TCC) may operate under its own national ROE. In the latter case, every effort must be made to avoid divergent or contradictory ROE. As with alliance ROE, coalition commanders must also be aware that there are often subtle yet important differences between the ROE systems of various nations. Many nations share the same basic concepts but may interpret and apply these concepts in vastly different ways. Usually, once a self-defence operation has been completed, the coalition is normally disbanded and the applicable ROE are cancelled.

(Oxford: Oxford University Press, 2004), 104–5; and E. Rostow, 'Until What? Enforcement Action or Collective Self-Defence?', 85 *AJIL* (1991), 506.

[3] See sub-Chapter 5.4 'Force Application in Enforcement and Peace Enforcement Operations'.

10. Importantly, it must be noted that the military forces (e.g. alliance or coalition) of nations participating in self-defence operations will adhere to their own national laws and policies. They are not obliged to execute tasks or operations that would constitute a breach of these national laws and policies. Therefore, it must be recognized that nations may issue restrictions and/or amplifying instructions (e.g. regarding the concepts of personal self-defence or defence of property in so far as these are relevant) in order to ensure compliance. Such restrictions or amplifications are often referred to as 'national caveats' and commanders of enforcement operations must be aware of every national caveat of each TCC in order to properly employ and task such forces.[4] In any case, such caveats may not exceed the limits posed by international law. 10.01

Generally, ROE are defined as orders or directives intended to ensure (see above, Sections 5.23–5.24) commanders and their subordinates do not use force or other measures beyond that authorized by higher command. ROE are an essential instrument of command and control for ordering, directing and controlling the use of force during military operations. ROE are orders or directives (i.e. lawful commands) issued by a competent military authority, which define the circumstances, conditions, degree, manner, and limitations within which force may be applied to achieve military objectives in furtherance of the national or collective self-defence mission. ROE, therefore, regulate the use of force by military forces during operations in peacetime, periods of tension, and armed conflicts. 10.02

1. The command and control (C2) structure of a self-defence operation is a crucial element in the development of ROE and in controlling the use of force by each member of the military force. Depending on the scope of the mission, naval, land, air forces, and marines, as well as logistics and communications support, may all be included in a national or multinational operation.

2. Generally, if the self-defence operation is a single State, national operation, the State will use its own C2 structure and ROE.[5] These will certainly vary from State to State. However, the practice of modern militaries is to have all their environmental elements (i.e. naval, land, air, and special forces) operate as a unified force. Usually such forces conduct operations with elements of at least two environments. When elements of two or more environments of a force are required to operate in the same theatre or area of operations in support of the same national strategic

[4] For example, see Canadian Forces Publication B-GJ-005-501/FP-001, *CFJP-5.1 Use of Force for CF Operations*, August 2008, 4–3. NATO ROE MC 362/1 states: 'Nations must inform the NAC/DPC and the Strategic Commander of any inconsistencies [i.e. caveats], as early as possible.'.

[5] See Canadian Forces Publication B-GJ-005-501/FP-001, *CFJP-5.1 Use of Force for CF Operations*, August 2008 (issued under the authority of the Chief the Defence Staff), 2-2; US Army *Operational Law Handbook 2014* (Charlottesville, Virginia: The Judge Advocate General's Legal Center & School, International and Operational Law Department), 80.

10.02 objective, they will operate under a national *joint* structure using internationally recognized joint terminology. Normally, States will create and deploy a multi-element Joint Task Force (JTF) to conduct national and collective self-defence operations. The JTF will be issued with national ROE either specifically tailored to the mission or standing ROE (SROE) which existed prior to the mission. Every member of the national force who may be required to use force in self-defence or to accomplish a mission must have a reasonable level of knowledge and understanding of the ROE and supporting law and doctrine.

3. Similarly, collective self-defence operations usually involve the forces of more than one nation acting together to accomplish a single mission. Such an operation is referred to under military doctrine as a 'combined operation'. Nations will contribute to the combined force headquarters staff and operational components in accordance with alliance arrangements or as agreed at meetings of TCCs. The commander of the enforcement operation is usually an officer of the nation contributing the largest number of forces to the operation. The other TCCs often create individual national Task Forces (TF) which are placed under the operational command (OPCOM) or control (OPCON) of the Force Commander for the duration of the operation.[6] As a function of the exercise of command, the supporting operational staff of the Force Commander leads the ROE and targeting development process.[7]

10.03 **ROE should be established for each military operation, including national or collective self-defence operations. ROE may limit the use of force, and must not permit a use of force that exceeds existing legal limitations. The right of individual (personal) self-defence must be respected in so far as it is relevant (see above, Sections 5.22 and 6.09). The right of self-defence is closely linked to ROE but may not necessarily be expressed as a ROE. The exercise of the use of force in individual self-defence may be the subject of further military direction (e.g. types of weapons authorized for use or hold fire orders).**

1. Generally, ROE in national or collective self-defence operations are often framed in a restrictive architecture. The reason for this is based on the law of self-defence which provides the legal basis for the operation.

2. As noted in this section, the law of self-defence operations permits States to use force in the exercise of national or collective defence. However, the law does not specifically describe the nature and scope of the force which a State can use. There

[6] For further details on command and control in military operations see Chapter 15 'Command and Control in Military Operations'.

[7] See Section 5.23 in sub-Chapter 5.4 'Force Application in Enforcement and Peace Enforcement Operations' of this Handbook for further details on development of ROE and targeting. The same principles apply in the development of ROE and targeting in self-defence operations.

is, of course, always the general obligation to ensure that the use of force in self-defence is restricted to that which is *necessary and proportional* to meet the lawful objective of removing the threat or defending against the attack. Absent a Security Council resolution that may restrict the nature and scope of the use of force, the law of self-defence permits the use of force which could rise to the level of full-scale combat operations or armed conflict. **10.03**

3. Unlike peacetime ROE, which are expressed as authorizations, self-defence operations ROE are usually expressed as prohibitions or restrictions. The reason for this structure is two-fold: the use of force during self-defence operations rising to the level of armed conflict will be controlled and regulated by IHL; and a commander may have to be restricted from exercising the full spectrum of force options available under international law based on national political, diplomatic, or operational imperatives or if the Security Council intervenes.

4. Consequently, when relying upon the international law of self-defence to deploy a national or multinational military force for the purpose of meeting the lawful objective of removing the threat or defending against the attack, military commanders and legal advisors must know the law and, if applicable, any relevant Security Council resolution(s), to determine who is authorized to do what, against whom, and with what level of force.

5. In any operation, including national and collective self-defence operations, the concept of self-defence, including personal, unit, or force self-defence, must be clearly understood by commanders and members of all forces. This is even more crucial when there are differences in national interpretations as to what constitutes 'self-defence'. Some nations specifically authorize the exercise of personal, unit, or force self-defence in ROE while others note that the concept of self-defence is closely linked, but separate from, authorized ROE.[8]

6. The authorized military responses under the right of personal, unit, or force self-defence vary from nation to nation. Some nations allow for much greater discretion in the use of force in (personal) self-defence and force protection than other nations. Furthermore, nations have differing interpretations of what constitutes hostile act or hostile intent and consequently the timing and manner of response may differ.

[8] For example, see *US Army Operational Law Handbook 2014*, 80; Canadian Forces Publication B-GJ-005-501/FP-001, *CFJP-5.1 Use of Force for CF Operations*, 2-2. Generally, 'national self-defence' operations are combat operations in the context of an armed conflict. Accordingly, there are no 'national' legal concepts relating to the international right of self-defence of States. This is governed wholly by international law. However, it must be noted that even within a 'national self-defence' operation, a military force may, depending on circumstances, still have to exercise 'personal or unit self-defence'. For example, a military force may have to defend its camp not only from enemy forces, but also from local criminals who have no connection to the enemy. In such situations, the use of force to defend against criminal threats is most likely limited by national definitions or interpretations of 'personal or unit self-defence' which are less robust than the use of force permitted in the context of an armed conflict.

10.03 7. Such differences in doctrine are understandable and unavoidable from the perspective of national legislation, but do provide significant challenges to a combined or coalition force and its commanders. Commanders must know how the forces under their command or control will respond to a given situation and their goal will be to ensure unity of response. It remains the responsibility of commanders at all levels to determine the reactions and responses that their forces will or will not take in self-defence (see Chapter 24).

8. In using force and developing ROE, there are often key definitions and concepts that must be fully understood by commanders and their forces. These include the concepts of 'non-deadly force', 'deadly force', 'minimum force', 'hostile act', and 'hostile intent'.[9]

9. In general terms, both international law and national laws recognize the authority to use appropriate force in personal self-defence and force protection, up to and including deadly force. Therefore, during self-defence operations, without further written or oral direction most military personnel are entitled to use force in self-defence to protect themselves; other members of their national forces; and non-national military personnel who are attached or seconded to their forces against a hostile act or hostile intent.[10]

10. During self-defence operations there may be extraordinary circumstances where States, in support of higher national interests, may direct their forces to take all necessary action *except for* the use of deadly force when facing hostile intent. Such direction would be exceptional and under constant review by the chain of command. The purpose of such direction would normally be to limit the escalation of a situation. This in no way limits the ability of an individual or commander to use force in personal or unit self-defence in response to a hostile act.[11]

11. Clearly, in self-defence operations, the Force Commander has many challenges in understanding the differing concepts of national, collective, personal, unit, and force self-defence, defence of others and defence of property. In multinational international military operations, there is also the challenge of understanding each State's interpretation of the concepts of self-defence. Frequently, in order to meet differing interpretations of these concepts, the Force Commander will use the ROE architecture with national caveats to reconcile and harmonize the differences. For example, when operating with forces of other nations in self-defence operations, the definition of self-defence is normally expanded, through ROE authorization, to

[9] See sub-Chapter 5.4 of this Handbook, 'Force Application in Enforcement and Peace Enforcement Operations', Section 5.24, paras 10–17 for details on these concepts.

[10] Canadian Forces Publication B-GJ-005-501/FP-001, *CFJP-5.1 Use of Force for CF Operations*, 2-2; US Army *Operational Law Handbook 2014*, 81.

[11] See sub-Chapter 5.4 of this Handbook, 'Force Application in Enforcement and Peace Enforcement Operations', Section 5.24, paras 19–21 for details on restricting self-defence.

include all individuals or units who comprise the force.[12] In multinational operations, where there may not be a common set of ROE, specific ROE authorization is normally promulgated and implemented for all TCCs' forces to permit the defence of all forces' personnel or units that are attacked or threatened. **10.03**

12. It is important to note the distinction between the uses of the term 'self-defence'. This section is dealing primarily with the concept of the exercise of State self-defence under international law. However, as indicated in the preceding paragraphs, the issue of unit or individual self-defence exists in all types of military operations, including international State self-defence military operations. As highlighted earlier, the use of military force in State self-defence operations often rises to the level of armed conflict. In such circumstances, the *lex specialis* of IHL permits a more robust use of force than do peacetime or IHRL rules. This means that some of the concepts noted previously, such as 'minimum force', 'hostile act', or 'hostile intent', which are largely based on peacetime or human rights norms, are either not applicable in armed conflict operations or are modified. For example, in armed conflict combat operations under IHL, the mere fact that a person is a member of the enemy forces, or has otherwise taken a direct part in hostilities, makes the person a lawful military objective who could be targeted at any time.

13. Nonetheless, in modern international military operations, including State self-defence operations, it is quite possible to have a mixture of missions or tasks depending on applicable legal bases and mandates. Therefore, military commanders, subordinates, and legal advisors will need to remain vigilant in recognizing the facts and law (i.e. IHL, human rights law, Security Council resolutions, and/or domestic law as appropriate) throughout the spectrum of operations during international self-defence operations.

[12] Canadian Forces Publication B-GJ-005-501/FP-001, *CFJP-5.1 Use of Force for CF Operations*, 4–3. See also US Army *Operational Law Handbook 2009*, 519, which highlights that NATO employs the concept of 'extended self-defence' to 'defend other NATO/NATO-led forces and personnel in the vicinity from attack or imminent attack'.

Chapter 11

INTERNATIONAL HUMANITARIAN LAW IN SELF-DEFENCE OPERATIONS

11.01 **In so far as self-defence operations amount to armed conflict, international humanitarian law is fully applicable in such operations (see above, Sections 5.24–5.26).**

1. The causes of the conflict are irrelevant to the applicability of the international humanitarian law of armed conflict.[1] The sole question in relation to the applicability of international humanitarian law therefore is whether or not there is an 'armed conflict' to which the relevant international humanitarian law applies, which will always be the case in self-defence operations, except perhaps in cases of isolated small-scale border clashes and aerial and naval incidents.[2] If there is an armed conflict, then Sections 5.25–5.28 will apply as appropriate.

2. The application of international humanitarian law is not based on any requirement of reciprocity.[3] Common Article 1 to the four Geneva Conventions of 1949 requires States 'to respect and to ensure respect for [the Conventions] in all circumstances'. This reflected the decision in the *Von Leeb (The High Command Trial)* case before the United States Military Tribunal at Nuremberg[4] and subsequently the International Court of Justice[5] and the International Criminal Tribunal for the Former Yugoslavia[6] have confirmed that legal obligations of a humanitarian nature cannot be dependent on reciprocity.

11.02 **The applicable international humanitarian law will depend on the nature of the conflict. Unless and until it is determined that the conflict is non-international, the law applicable to international**

[1] Preambular paragraph 5 to Protocol Additional to the Geneva Conventions of 12 August 1949, and Relating to the Protection of Victims of International Armed Conflicts of 8 June 1977 (AP I).

[2] See J. Kleffner in D. Fleck (ed.), *The Handbook of International Humanitarian Law*, 3rd edn (Oxford: Oxford University Press, 2013), Section 202, para. 1, pp. 44–5.

[3] See Rule 140, J.-M. Henckaerts and L. Doswald-Beck (eds), *Customary International Humanitarian Law* (Cambridge: Cambridge University Press, 2005) (CIHL).

[4] US Military Tribunal at Nuremberg, *Von Leeb (The High Command Trial)* case, Judgment, 30 December 1947–8, WCR, Vol. XII, 1949 1, at p. 64.

[5] See *Legal Consequences for States of the Continued Presence of South Africa in Namibia (South West Africa) notwithstanding SC Res. 276* (1970), Advisory Opinion of 21 June 1971 (*Namibia* case) ICJ Reports, 1969, 16, at para. 96.

[6] See ICTY, *Prosecutor v Zoran Kupreškić et al.*, Case no. IT-95-16-T, Judgment, 14 January 2000, at paras 515–518.

armed conflict should generally apply. Once the nature of the conflict is determined, all the law relevant to that type of conflict and binding on the individual parties will apply. 11.02

1. Whenever the use of armed force involves armed clashes between two or more States, or occupation, however temporary, by one State of all or part of another State's territory, the conflict will be international in nature, even when a State is engaging in self-defence against another State. This will apply to any use of armed force between States including small-scale border clashes between State armed forces, although in such situations the applicability of international humanitarian law may be limited in duration and material scope. If armed force is employed in self-defence in response to an armed attack conducted by an organized armed group, the applicable regime within international humanitarian law will depend upon a number of factors. These include whether the armed group is under the control or substantial influence of a State, the ability and willingness of the State whence the attack originated to prevent the organized armed group from operating from its territory, and possible consent, or lack thereof, by the State where the organized armed group is operating to the exercise of self-defence measures by the victim State directed against the armed group.

2. The law distinguishes generically between armed conflicts of an international armed character, including belligerent occupations, and armed conflicts not of an international character. However, this distinction is often not as clear cut as might appear. For example, there may be separate conflicts taking place alongside each other and there may be difficulty in ascertaining whether they are indeed separate or whether they have merged into a single conflict. In Afghanistan in 2001, there was already a long-standing non-international armed conflict between the Taliban and the Northern Alliance taking place before the intervention by the American-led Coalition following the attacks by al Qaeda on targets in the United States on 11 September 2001. In such circumstances, it may be that the two conflicts merge into a single international armed conflict or they may retain their own distinctive nature, thus being subject to separate legal paradigms.

3. Furthermore, a conflict that begins as a conflict not of an international character may evolve into an international armed conflict due to outside factors such as the intervention of a foreign State in the conflict on behalf of the non-State actors. However, this does not necessarily mean that the whole of the conflict will be classed as international. In the *Nicaragua* case, the International Court of Justice stated:

> The conflict between the contras' forces and those of the Government of Nicaragua is an armed conflict which is 'not of an international character'. The acts of the contras towards the Nicaraguan Government are therefore governed by the law applicable to conflicts of that character; whereas the actions of the United States in and against Nicaragua fall under the legal rules relating to international conflicts.[7]

[7] *Case Concerning Military and Paramilitary Activities in and against Nicaragua (Merits)* ICJ Reports, 1986, 14, at 114.

11.02 4. In the case of the former Yugoslavia, the situation was different again in that a State, subject to internal divisions amounting to an armed conflict of a non-international conflict, imploded and fragmented into a number of independent States. In that case, the situation was further complicated by internal conflict even within the new States. Bosnia-Herzegovina was subject to both internal conflict and intervention by neighbouring States. For a more detailed account of the distinction between international armed conflicts and those not of an international character, see Section 3.01 and the commentary thereto.

5. With the changing nature of conflict, it is not always clear as to the exact nature of a conflict or even whether there is a conflict at all. A number of States now require their forces as a matter of national policy to comply with the rules of international humanitarian law in the conduct of military operations, regardless of the nature of any conflict.[8] If there is doubt as to the nature of the conflict, then the highest standards should be applied, namely those applicable to international armed conflict as this is likely best to serve both humanitarian interests and operational requirements. Whilst it is accepted that there remain important differences between various types of conflict, the principles that underlie international humanitarian law are applicable across the board. Thus, even if detainees in a non-international armed conflict are not entitled to the status of prisoners of war, they are still entitled to humane treatment and in terms of practical treatment, this will amount to much the same.

6. In addition to restraints arising from rules of international humanitarian law, it should be pointed out that the law relating to the exercise of self-defence may itself pose additional restraints on targeting individuals or objects constituting lawful military objectives under international humanitarian law and upon the geographical and temporal scope of targeting law in general. For example, if self-defence is exercised in response to a small-scale localized armed attack, although international humanitarian law is applicable to the entire territory of the States participating in the conflict, the principles of necessity and proportionality governing the exercise of self-defence (not to be confused with their counterparts in international humanitarian law) may preclude extending the application of force beyond the area of the original armed attack. Likewise, while certain industrial and leadership targets may constitute lawful military objectives under international humanitarian law, it may not be lawful under the law relating to the exercise of self-defence to target them, if this is not required to respond proportionately to the attack. An example of this was in the Falkands/Malvinas War of 1982, when the UK (and Argentina) restricted their operations to the disputed islands and surrounding sea and airspace. This made sense from a policy standpoint in terms of limiting the conflict and was moreover in accordance with the principles of necessity and proportionality relating to self-defence, in that under the circumstances it was neither necessary, nor

[8] Fleck (ed.), *Handbook of International Humanitarian Law*, Sections 209, 1216, commentary at 605.

proportionate from an *ad bellum* perspective, to extend operations beyond this area, or to attack targets on the mainland, such as the Argentinean leadership or munitions plants which may well have qualified as lawful military objectives from the perspective of international humanitarian law.[9] 11.02

11.03 **Necessity cannot be used to justify actions prohibited by international humanitarian law. Military necessity is fully incorporated into international humanitarian law which reflects a balance between military and humanitarian considerations in all of its provisions.**

1. One of the principles on which international humanitarian law is based is military necessity. International humanitarian law is designed as a balance between humanity and military necessity. The Lieber Code defined military necessity as 'those measures which are indispensable for securing the ends of war and which are lawful according to the modern law and usages of war'.[10] This was confirmed in some of the earliest decisions in war crimes trials such as the *Peleus Trial*[11] and *The Hostage Case*.[12]

2. International humanitarian law incorporates military necessity.[13] Hence it is also a fundamental principle of international humanitarian law that military necessity 'cannot be used to justify actions prohibited by law'.[14] A doctrine of *Kriegsraison*[15] has no place in international law. On the contrary, the principle of necessity can operate as an additional level of restraint in that acts which might otherwise be legal under international humanitarian law may be prohibited if they are not necessary for the pursuance of legitimate goals.[16] Put simply, just because something is legal, it does not mean that it has to be done. International humanitarian law is frequently a reflection of military common sense in that if something is not necessary, then it would probably breach the military maxim of 'economy of effort' to attempt it.

[9] See e.g. C. Greenwood, 'The Relationship of the Ius ad Bellum and the Ius in Bello', 9 *Review of International Studies* (1983), 221–34; 'Self-Defence and the Conduct of International Armed Conflict', in Y. Dinstein (ed.), *International Law at a Time of Perplexity: Essays in Honour of Shabtai Rosenne* (Dordrecht: Martinus Nijhoff Publishers, 1989), 273–88. See additionally, T.D. Gill, 'Some Considerations Concerning the Role of the ius ad bellum in Targeting', in P. Ducheine, M. Schmitt, and F. Osinga (eds), *Targeting: The Challenges of Modern Warfare* (Springer/TMC Asser Publishers, forthcoming in 2015).

[10] Art. 14, Lieber Code.

[11] The Peleus Trial, 1948, <http://www.loc.gov/rr/frd/Military_Law/pdf/Law-Reports_Vol-1.pdf>.

[12] *The Hostage Case* (*USA v List et al.*) American Military Tribunal, Nuremburg, 1948, 11 NMT 1230.

[13] See the list in W.A. Solf and J.A. Roach (eds), *Index of International Humanitarian Law* (Geneva: ICRC, 1987), 152.

[14] UK Ministry of Defence, *The Manual of the Law of Armed Conflict* (Oxford: Oxford University Press, 2004), para. 2.3, 23.

[15] 'Kriegsraison geht vor Kriegsmanier' ('necessity in war overrides the laws of war', or 'necessity knows no law', slogans used in World War I to marginalize international legal obligations).

[16] D. Fleck (ed.), *Handbook of International Humanitarian Law*, Section 134, commentary, at 37.

Chapter 12

RESCUE OF NATIONALS

12.01 **States may rescue their nationals when their lives or physical safety are directly threatened and the State in which this occurs is either directly responsible, or is unable or unwilling to provide security. Rescue of nationals is generally referred to as 'non-combatant evacuation' in military doctrine.**

12.02 **Action undertaken in this context must be directly aimed at ending the threat to the safety of the victims and evacuating them as quickly as possible from the State where they are located with the force strictly necessary to achieve these objectives. It is not prohibited under such circumstances to additionally evacuate the nationals of third States when their lives or safety are also directly threatened and circumstances allow for their evacuation along with the rescuing State's nationals, in so far as they wish to be evacuated.**

1. The right of States to protect their nationals abroad in situations where their lives or physical safety are directly threatened was well established as part of the customary right of self-defence before the Second World War.[1] Rescue of nationals requires a genuine link of nationality between the persons to be rescued and the rescuing State which has been conferred in accordance with international law. It does not allow for military action based solely on common ethnicity, language, race, or religion in the absence of established grounds for the granting of nationality. However, there is no reason why a State conducting an operation to rescue its own nationals may not evacuate the nationals of a third State possibly at that State's request if the circumstances objectively require this and the nationals of that State wish to be evacuated. It should be stressed that such rescue and evacuation operations, when undertaken in the absence of the consent of the State where the nationals are located, may only be undertaken when there is a clear and direct threat to their lives or physical safety and when other means of providing for the safe exit of foreign nationals are no longer feasible.

[1] In this context see D.W. Bowett, *Self-Defence in International Law* (New York: Praeger, 1958), 87 *et seq.*, where he cites numerous arbitral awards, State practice, and the position taken in international law writings of the nineteenth and early twentieth centuries in support of this position. See also S. Alexandrov, *Self-Defense Against the Use of Force in International Law* (The Hague: Kluwer International, 1996), 189.

TERRY D. GILL AND PAUL A.L. DUCHEINE

2. Since the introduction of the Charter regime governing the use of force, the legal basis of this right has been the subject of vigorous legal debate and contending views amongst States. One body of opinion takes the position that this right still forms part of the customary right to self-defence, subject to the conditions of necessity, proportionality, and immediacy, while another position held by a substantial number of States and by legal scholars adhering to a more restrictive interpretation of self-defence, is that such action is no longer legal under contemporary international law. The reasons underlying this position vary, but one of the most frequently cited is the fact that the exercise of this right is subject to abuse and in fact has been abused on a number of occasions since 1945. Finally, there is a middle position, which while denying that the rescue of nationals (still) forms part of the right of self-defence, holds that such rescue can be justified under strict limitations within the context of 'necessity' as a general ground for precluding wrongfulness, or even as a separate exception to the prohibition of force under customary international law.[2] **12.02**

3. While not wishing to ignore the complexity of the doctrinal debate surrounding this issue, the position taken here is that the rescue of nationals under the conditions already stated is justifiable under international law and that the most logical and coherent legal basis for this justification is that it forms part of the right of self-defence under customary international law. The reasons underlying this position are briefly the following. Firstly, that, as stated, the protection of nationals was well established under the customary law relating to self-defence prior to the adoption of the Charter. Secondly, that nothing in the terms of either the relevant provisions of the Charter, or the preparatory work leading to the adoption of the Charter excludes such actions as no longer falling within the ambit of self-defence. Thirdly, that States have frequently continued to carry out such action since the Charter came into force, sometimes justifiably and sometimes not; but that the fact that the right has been undeniably abused on certain occasions does not, in and of itself, vitiate the existence of such a right *in abstracto*, notwithstanding the undeniable illegality of certain actions put forward under the guise of protection of

[2] The opinion in support of protection of nationals as part of the right to self-defence includes Bowett, *Self-Defence* and in 'The Use of Force to Protect Nationals Abroad' in A. Cassese (ed.), *The Current Legal Regulation of the Use of Force* (Dordrecht: M. Nijhoff, 1986), 231 *et seq*.; T.M. Franck, *Recourse to Force: State Action against Threats and Armed Attacks* (Cambridge: Cambridge University Press, 2002), 76 *et seq*.; and C.H.M. Waldock, 'The Regulation of the Use of Force by Individual States in International Law', 81 *RdC* (1952), 455 at 462–4 and 503. For the contrary opinion see I. Brownlie, *International Law and the Use of Force by States* (Oxford: Clarendon Press, 1963 reprinted 2003), 298–301; C. Gray, *International Law and the Use of Force* (Oxford: Oxford University Press, 2000), 108–11. The 'middle position' is represented by Alexandrov, *Self-Defence Against the Use of Force*, 203–4; N. Ronzitti, *Rescuing Nationals Abroad Through Military Coercion and Intervention on Grounds of Humanity* (Dordrecht: M. Nijhoff, 1985), 69 *et seq*., with some authors taking a more ambiguous (or nuanced) position, deeming some actions as possibly falling within the context of self-defence, while others would belong to 'necessity' as a general ground for precluding wrongfulness; e.g. O. Schachter, *International Law in Theory and Practice* (Dordrecht: M. Nijhoff, 1991), 166–7 and 169 *et seq*.

12.02 nationals.[3] Fourthly, despite the numerous occasions on which the issue has come before the Security Council and to a lesser extent before the International Court of Justice, neither organ has ever taken the position as a general statement of the law, that the right has ceased to exist, or even condemned a specific invocation of the right as being illegal.[4] Fifthly, and finally:

(i) since an attack against a State's nationals with a view to obtaining concessions from a State or affecting its policy can credibly be seen as an attack upon a State and its interests;
(ii) the vast majority of incidents relating to the protection of nationals in post-1945 State practice have been justified on the basis of self-defence, irrespective of whether such actions were or were not justifiable under the specific circumstances; and
(iii) the Charter legal regime relating to the use of force logically permits only two recognized exceptions to the prohibition of the use of force (aside from consent) and that the other 'candidates' for a legal basis for rescuing nationals look on balance to be neither persuasive, nor would they logically fit into the system without opening the door to other pretended exceptions, thereby undermining the Charter legal regime relating to the use of force.[5]

4. Consequently, the most logical and persuasive legal position is that action taken by a State to protect its nationals against a clear and immediate threat to their lives or physical safety can only be justified on the basis of self-defence, or the consent of the State where the threat occurs, in which case no violation of the prohibition of force or of the State's sovereignty would occur and any action undertaken with consent of the State where the nationals were located would have to conform to the conditions posed by that State. In any situation where consent was not forthcoming from the State where the nationals were located, the conditions of necessity, proportionality, and immediacy which are part of the right of self-defence would require that there was a clear and unequivocal threat to the lives and safety of the intervening State's citizens, that the State where the threat occurred was either complicit or directly involved, or was unable to take the necessary action to end the threat and meet its responsibility under international law vis-à-vis foreign nationals and their parent States. A justification of necessity could conceivably be invoked in situations where the State where the nationals were located was in no way involved

[3] Brownlie, *International Law and the Use of Force*, 299–301 and others rightly point out that the right is subject to abuse and it has both historically and more recently been abused on numerous occasions. So for that matter have many other rights, including self-defence in general, without that leading to the vitiation of the right.

[4] See Franck, *Recourse to Force*, 96 in analysing the practice of the Security Council and Alexandrov, *Self-Defence Against the Use of Force*, 197–8 in relation to the ICJ's pronouncements on the failed US rescue attempt of its diplomats held hostage in Teheran in 1980.

[5] See Sections 5.02 and 8.01 with supporting commentary. The point here is one of logical consistency of the legal regime relating to the use of force. Additional exceptions to the *jus cogens* prohibition of the use of force are not lightly to be presumed without overwhelming evidence in favour of their general acceptance.

in any threat to the safety of foreign nationals and where as a result of a general breakdown in law and order, it was not able to either provide protection or grant consent to any parent State to evacuate its nationals and a serious threat to their safety existed which could not be addressed by any other means.[6] In either case, conditions of necessity, proportionality, and immediacy would require that any action undertaken either in self-defence, or under the justification of necessity would be limited in scale and duration to what was strictly required to end the direct threat to the safety of the intervening State's nationals and bring about their safe and speedy evacuation, with as little possible collateral effect upon the State where the incident took place.[7] As a final remark, it is obvious that a clear, unambiguous, and genuine link of nationality is required between the persons threatened and the intervening State in order for there to be a legitimate claim of self-defence, or necessity by the intervening State on their and its own behalf. However, it would be spurious to conclude that this would preclude the evacuation of third State nationals in an emergency situation if their safety were also threatened, as a side effect of the evacuation of the State's own nationals, if this were possible under the circumstances and if they wished to be taken out. **12.02**

[6] Necessity is an exceptional plea of disculpation under international law and is subject to a number of strict conditions. It presupposes that there is a grave and imminent peril to an essential State interest, that there are no feasible alternatives to the taking of a particular course of action, that the State against which necessity is invoked is in no way complicit or responsible for the existence of the grave and imminent peril, that the action undertaken does not compromise an equally or more essential interest of the State against which necessity is invoked or those of any other State or the international community as a whole 'in other words the interest relied on must outweigh all other considerations, not merely from the point of view of the acting State but on a reasonable assessment of the competing interests, whether these are individual or collective', 2(2) *Yearbook of the International Law Commission* (2001), 83–4.

[7] This is in fact a paraphrase of the *Caroline* criteria relating to self-defence, tailored to the issue of rescue of nationals, as put forward by Waldock in his still influential and authoritative Hague Academy course of 1952 ('The Regulation of the Use of Force', 467). These were: (1) an imminent threat of injury to nationals; (2) a failure or inability on the part of the territorial sovereign to protect them; and (3) measures of protection strictly confined to the object of protecting them.

Chapter 13

HUMANITARIAN INTERVENTION

13.01 **In cases of large-scale, systematic, and acute violations of fundamental human rights, especially of the right to life, which result either from a government deliberately targeting (a significant part of) its population, or through a general breakdown in governmental authority, the Security Council should take all necessary and feasible measures, including whenever necessary, the authorization of military enforcement measures with the purpose of ending the ongoing violations and preventing further violations, and restoring a secure and stable environment. In the event the Security Council issues a mandate under Chapter VII of the Charter to halt the violations, the operation undertaken will have a recognized legal basis and will constitute a (peace) enforcement operation within the context of the UN Collective Security System (see Chapter 5, above).**

1. The Security Council, as the organ of the international community entrusted with the primary responsibility for the maintenance of peace and security, has both the legal authority and the responsibility to undertake any necessary measures to halt and prevent large-scale violations of fundamental human rights, including the undertaking of enforcement measures of a military character, either under its own auspices, or through the authorization of Member States or a regional organization under Chapter VII, with the purpose of ending such violations and restoring a stable and secure environment. Experience has shown on numerous occasions that such large-scale and systematic human rights violations very often lead to regional and even wider destabilization and aggravation of international tension, in addition to constituting violations of fundamental *jus cogens* norms and qualifying as international crimes in their own right.[1] The Security Council's powers and functions under the Charter provide it with the necessary authority and responsibility to either undertake or to authorize enforcement measures, including military enforcement measures aimed at halting widespread and systematic human rights violations as part of a wider effort to restore a stable and secure environment and maintain

[1] The examples of the former Yugoslavia, Somalia, and Rwanda are but several which illustrate the long-term spill-over effects of gross human rights violations in the region where they occurred. Such human rights violations can constitute genocide, crimes against humanity, or war crimes, depending upon the context in which they occurred and these are punishable as international crimes under the Rome Statute of the International Criminal Court. See e.g. 'Lessons from Rwanda: The United Nations and the Prevention of Genocide' adopted in UN GA Res. A/RES/60/225 of 22 March 2006.

TERRY D. GILL

international peace and security. This is the case irrespective of whether such violations are the result of deliberate governmental policy and actions, or are caused by a breakdown of governmental authority or inability to prevent such violations.[2] 13.01

2. While a State's sovereignty and territorial inviolability are fundamental rights under the UN Charter and under general international law, they are not wholly unconditional. Article 2(7) of the Charter, which provides for the duty of the UN organization to refrain from intervening in the domestic affairs of Member States, explicitly does not preclude the Council from taking enforcement measures of either a non-military or of a military nature in response to any situation which it deems as posing a threat to international peace and security and the practice of the Council over many years has demonstrated that it has viewed such large-scale violations of human rights as a threat to the peace on repeated occasions.[3]

3. The concept of 'Responsibility to Protect', which has emerged in recent years, has underlined and reinforced the Council's and the wider international community's responsibility to undertake and support measures of protection, including where necessary and feasible, military enforcement measures of a coercive nature in response to large-scale and systematic human rights violations as part of a wider effort to protect populations from violations of their fundamental human rights, and promote stability and the creation of conditions aimed at preventing further such violations.[4] The notion of 'Responsibility to Protect', although not in any way amending the existing legal rights and obligations of States or of UN organs under the Charter or under general international law, reinforces and emphasizes the political, moral, and legal authority of the Security Council and competent international organizations acting in conjunction with the Council, to address such violations and to take the measures necessary aimed at ending ongoing violations and preventing their recurrence. It also serves as a clear indication that a State cannot use its sovereignty as a cover for the perpetration of atrocities against its citizens, and that such acts cannot be seen as a wholly internal matter falling outside the scope of international law or the concern of the international community. It also places some pressure on the Members of the Security Council and upon the

[2] On the discretion of the Security Council to determine the existence of a 'threat to the peace' see Section 5.02. For further literature see Y. Dinstein, *War Aggression and Self-Defence*, 4th edn (Cambridge: Cambridge University Press, 2005), 85–97.

[3] E.g. in relation to Somalia, SC Res. 733 (1992), Rwanda, SC Res. 1556 (2004).

[4] The Report of the International Commission on Intervention and State Sovereignty, *The Responsibility to Protect* (December 2001), <http://www.responsibilitytoprotect.org/>, put forward what was termed as a 'new approach to sovereignty' specifically in relation to human rights violations. The UN Secretary General at the time adopted and approved this approach in his report relating to reform of the UN entitled 'In Larger Freedom' A/59/2005 of 21 March 2005. The concept was also elaborated upon in relation to the UN Collective Security System in the Report of the High Level Panel on Threats, Challenges and Change entitled 'A More Secure World: Our Shared Responsibility' as GA Res. A/59/565 of 2 December 2004. It should be stressed that these reports and documents do not constitute binding interpretations of, or amendments to, the UN Charter or any other international instrument, but are rather authoritative policy statements by the UN Secretary General and by experts in the form of recommendations to the UN Member States.

13.01 international community in general to support, or at least not to frustrate, efforts aimed at addressing and halting such violations. This principle was explicitly referred to in the case of Libya in 2011 and in that situation, the Council was able to adopt measures constituting a collectively authorized intervention for the purpose of ending large-scale indiscriminate violence directed against the civilian population. Nevertheless, there is no guarantee that the Council will invariably be able to come to a decision to undertake measures which are likely to end such violations. The necessity of a two-thirds majority and the possibility of a veto by a Permanent Member of the Council can still impede or even preclude the taking of effective collective measures and has done so on a number of occasions, even when those were clearly called for and probably feasible under the circumstances.[5] However, it is also not always possible or desirable to undertake military action in response to human rights violations, when it is likely that such action would be unsuccessful, or would result in a significant aggravation of international tension, or even threaten more serious international consequences.[6]

4. To the extent the Security Council is able and willing to undertake or authorize enforcement measures aimed at halting or preventing large-scale and systematic human rights violations within the legal framework of its enforcement powers, it will have a clearly recognized and established legal basis under international law to take any measures it deems necessary, including military enforcement measures of a coercive nature, to halt such violations and prevent their recurrence. Such measures would qualify as 'enforcement action' under Articles 39 and 42 of the UN Charter and would not require any additional legal basis under the guise of humanitarian intervention. However, such measures are often referred to as 'collective humanitarian intervention' in policy statements and legal literature to distinguish them from military action undertaken by individual States, coalitions of States, or regional organizations which have not been authorized under Chapter VII of the Charter.[7] To the extent military intervention is undertaken by an individual State, a group of States acting in conjunction, or by a regional organization or arrangement

[5] A clear example of this was the failure of the international community, and the Security Council in particular, to respond to the genocide in Rwanda, despite it being a case where action could have probably resulted in preventing or at least reducing the scale of the atrocities. See OAU Report, 'The Preventable Genocide' reproduced in 40 *ILM* (2001), 141. The Security Council has since then equally been unable to achieve agreement concerning the taking of effective measures to halt the humanitarian crisis in Syria. For a discussion of the Responsibility to Protect principle and its relationship to humanitarian intervention in the Libyan and Syrian crises see T.D. Gill, 'The Responsibility to Protect and the Security Council' in G. Zyberi (ed.), *An Institutional Approach to the Responsibility to Protect* (Cambridge: Cambridge University Press, 2013), 83.

[6] The consideration that humanitarian intervention must not result in 'more harm than good' is expressed by a variety of authors and reflects what one authority refers to as 'tactical realism', see e.g. T.M. Franck, *Recourse to Force* (Cambridge: Cambridge University Press, 2002), 189.

[7] Ibid. 136–7. For comprehensive treatment and analysis of UN Security Council action and authorization to Member States in response to large-scale violations of human rights see S. Chesterman, *Just War or Just Peace: Humanitarian Intervention and International Law* (Oxford: Oxford University Press, 2001), 112 *et seq.*

without the authorization of the Security Council, such intervention cannot be considered as 'enforcement action' within the framework of the UN Collective Security System. Military intervention aimed at halting or preventing a large-scale violation of human rights of the inhabitants of a State who are not nationals of the intervening State(s) and which has not received the authorization of the Security Council is generally referred to as 'humanitarian intervention' in policy statements and in legal literature and this definition will be utilized in this Handbook to denote military intervention which is aimed at halting large-scale human rights violations of non-nationals and which is carried out without the authorization of the UN Security Council.[8] 13.01

Humanitarian intervention defined as military intervention, which is undertaken without the authorization of the UN Security Council by one or more States, or by a regional organization, with the purpose of halting or preventing large-scale systematic and acute violations of fundamental human rights of persons who are not nationals of the intervening State(s), falls outside of either of the two generally recognized exceptions to the prohibition on the use of force contained in the UN Charter and in customary international law. As such, it is in contravention of the prohibition on the use of force and the closely related principle of non-intervention and is *prima facie* illegal under contemporary international law. Nevertheless, such intervention can be legitimized and wholly or partially justified under strict legal, moral, and policy conditions, provided it meets certain requirements which have increasingly come to be recognized by a wide segment of the international community, by the public conscience, and by leading authorities and publicists. While this has not yet resulted in creating a new generally recognized exception to the prohibition on the use of force of a customary or conventional nature, it can be seen as grounds for partial or complete mitigation of responsibility for otherwise illegal conduct on the part of the intervening State(s). 13.02

To qualify for legitimization resulting in complete or partial mitigation of responsibility under international law humanitarian intervention must meet the requirements of necessity, proportionality, and immediacy governing the use of force and must additionally fully comply with relevant humanitarian and human rights rules and principles. It must, additionally, not pose a greater threat to international peace and security than the situation it purports to address. Legitimization and mitigation of responsibility in no way affect the 13.03

[8] This is a definition used by, *inter alia*, W. Verwey, 'Humanitarian Intervention', in A. Cassese (ed.), *The Current Legal Regulation of the Use of Force* (Dordrecht: Nijhoff, 1986), 57 *et seq.* at 59.

13.03 **legal status of the prohibition on the use of force under international law, or the primacy of the UN Security Council in the maintenance and restoration of international peace and security.**

1. The criteria for undertaking a humanitarian intervention have been frequently discussed in legal literature and policy statements.[9] The starting point is that humanitarian intervention may only be undertaken in response to an acute, large-scale violation of fundamental human rights, in particular the right to life, of a significant portion of a State's inhabitants, which result either from deliberate governmental action aimed at the persons who are affected, or which are the result of a government's inaction or inability to prevent such violations.

2. Humanitarian intervention may only be undertaken when it has become abundantly clear that the Security Council has failed to reach a decision or is unwilling to authorize the necessary enforcement action under Chapter VII of the Charter to prevent or halt the violations of fundamental human rights in the State where they are occurring. Such inaction on the part of the Security Council will not affect its primacy in the maintenance of international peace and security, or its legal authority to take such action as it may deem necessary and is capable of agreeing upon to restore and maintain international peace and security and preventing a further aggravation of the situation. No humanitarian intervention should be undertaken whenever it is likely that this would result in a threat to international peace and security which would exceed the threat posed by the situation it is intended to address.

3. Humanitarian intervention must conform to the general requirements governing the use of force under international law of necessity, proportionality, and immediacy. Within this context, these principles require that any forceful measures undertaken must be in response to an immediate and ongoing violation of fundamental human rights on a significant scale or a grave and impending threat of such violations, must be primarily directed at halting their occurrence and preventing

[9] The legal status of humanitarian intervention has triggered a very large number of books and articles on the topic, far too many to attempt to name here. Essentially, the opinions of practically all authors can be categorized as follows. A minority of authors take the position that humanitarian intervention does not violate Article 2(4) of the Charter, or alternatively, that it is part of customary law. Writers from a legal perspective adhering to this view include, *inter alia*, F. Teson, *Humanitarian Intervention: An Inquiry into Law and Morality*, 2nd edn (Dobbs Ferry, NY: Transnational, 1997) and R.B. Lillich, 'Humanitarian Intervention: A Reply to Ian Brownlie and a Plea for Constructive Alternatives', in J.N. Moore (ed.), *Law and Civil War in the Modern World* (London and Baltimore: Johns Hopkins University Press, 1974), 229 *et seq*. However, the majority view among publicists is that humanitarian intervention conflicts with the Art. 2(4) prohibition on the use of force, but can be morally and/or politically justified and condoned or excused from a legal perspective, provided it meets criteria similar to those set out earlier in the chapter. Among this group of writers are, *inter alia*, I. Brownlie, 'Thoughts on a Kind-hearted Gunmen' in Moore, *Law and Civil War*, 139 *et seq*.; O. Schachter, *International Law in Theory and Practice* (The Hague, Boston, London: Nijhoff, 1991), 123–6; Franck, *Recourse to Force*, 189 *et seq*., and J.L. Holzgrefe and R.O. Keohane (eds), *Humanitarian Intervention, Ethical, Legal, and Political Dilemmas* (Cambridge: Cambridge University Press, 2003).

their recurrence, should not exceed what is strictly required to achieve that objective, and should provide the greatest possible degree of protection and security to the affected population. 13.03

4. In addition to the abovementioned criteria relating to the use of force which are of an *ad bellum* character, the use of force and treatment of persons must additionally and fully conform to any and all relevant rules and principles of the humanitarian law of armed conflict and with human rights standards relating to the conduct of any hostilities and to the treatment of any persons who find themselves in the custody, or under the control, of the intervening State(s).

5. The humanitarian intervention must not last longer than is necessary to halt the violations and should provide the groundwork for the creation of as stable and secure an environment as is possible under the relevant circumstances. The government(s) and armed forces of the intervening State(s) must cooperate fully with the United Nations Security Council and all other authorized organs and agencies of the UN in providing a full account of its/their actions and transferring responsibility to the UN or its designated representatives and bodies as soon as this can be carried out in an orderly fashion. If the UN is unwilling or unable to assume responsibility for the situation, the intervening State(s) should remain in the State where the intervention took place for as long as is necessary to prevent further outbreaks of violence, until such time as the UN or another designated authority is able to assume responsibility for the situation and for the security of the affected population, or the situation clearly no longer warrants their presence.

To the extent a humanitarian intervention fully conforms to the abovementioned criteria laid down in Section 13.03 and the commentary thereto, it should qualify for far-reaching mitigation of responsibility and legitimization. To the extent it falls short of meeting these criteria, the intervention will not (fully) qualify for mitigation of responsibility and the intervention will incur any consequences determined by the Security Council, by other competent organs of the United Nations, and by the international community at large. 13.04

1. Mitigation of responsibility is a recognized general principle of (international) law[10] and is relevant to humanitarian intervention since such intervention, when carried out without the authorization of the Security Council, neither fits into one

[10] Franck, *Recourse to Force*, makes out a coherent case for the existence of mitigation of responsibility as a principle of law and its applicability to humanitarian intervention. The present author expressed a similar approach in an article published in 2001; T.D. Gill, 'Humanitaire Interventie: Rechtmatigheid, Rechtvaardigheid en Legitimiteit', in 94 *Militair Rechtelijk Tijdschrift* 6 (2001), 221–41, which was translated and updated as 'Humanitarian Intervention: Legality, Justice and Legitimacy', in I *The Global Community Yearbook of International Law and Jurisprudence* (2005), 51–76.

13.04 of the recognized exceptions to the prohibition of the use of force and the related principle of non-intervention, nor falls within the scope of any of the circumstances precluding wrongfulness under the law of State responsibility.[11] It is based on the consideration that there are degrees of wrongfulness relating to an illegal act and that the actions and motivations of the party committing a violation of any legal rule or principle should be taken into account in determining the consequences of such unlawful conduct. Such actions and motivations relating to unlawful conduct can either aggravate or mitigate the degree of unlawfulness and the consequences, if any, which attach to the unlawful conduct. The concept of mitigation of responsibility is common to all legal systems, and relates both to public or private acts and is further related to notions of fairness, equity, and reasonableness.

2. The notion that there are degrees of unlawfulness attached to a violation of a legal rule or norm and the principle of mitigation of responsibility are generally recognized in legal literature and in case law and have been widely recognized as being relevant to humanitarian interventions, in particular by a significant body of legal opinion. While there is not complete unanimity of views relating to the legality of humanitarian intervention, there is widespread support for the proposition that military intervention which is undertaken in conformity with the criteria set out in the previous section and commentary thereto (or similar criteria) should not be equated with aggression or other serious violations of the Charter *jus ad bellum* and that any consequences of such formally unlawful conduct should be limited or even nominal.[12]

3. However, it is equally clear that such interventions have not as yet gained the widespread consistent and representative support in the form of *opinio juris* which is required to establish a new rule of customary international law as a third exception to the prohibition of the use of force. As such, humanitarian intervention (outside

[11] The application of the doctrine of necessity in relation to humanitarian intervention was expressly excluded by the International Law Commission: see J. Crawford, *The International Law Commission's Articles on State Responsibility* (Cambridge: Cambridge University Press, 2002), 185 and accompanying note 434. It is self-evident that none of the other circumstances precluding wrongfulness contained in the ILC Article would be relevant to a case of humanitarian intervention.

[12] See para. 1 above. An example of how mitigating circumstances were applied by an international tribunal can be found in the decision of the International Court of Justice in the *Corfu Channel* case, where the Court determined by a large majority that the UK's conduct in violating Albania's sovereignty in the context of a minesweeping operation was a violation of the principle of non-intervention, and while reaffirming that principle, went on to determine that Albania's conduct in allowing the mines to be deployed was a violation of the elementary principle of humanity and determined that Albania was liable to pay compensation for its illegal conduct and limited the consequences of the UK's action to a purely verbal reaffirmation of the law. While this did not concern a question of humanitarian intervention, it is analogous to it in several important respects; not least of which are the reaffirmation of non-intervention as a cardinal principle of international law, while taking the relevant circumstances fully into account and mitigating the UK's unlawful, but under the circumstances, at least to some extent, excusable conduct. This not only illustrates that degrees of unlawful conduct and mitigation of responsibility are part of international law, but that it is perfectly possible to apply these concepts in an objective way which distinguishes between degrees of unlawfulness and is at the same time supportive of the underlying norm. See ICJ Reports, 1949, 4, at 35.

the context of the UN Collective Security System) remains controversial and constitutes *prima facie* illegal conduct which must be assessed on a case-by-case basis and in light of all relevant circumstances, including in particular the degree of conformity by the intervening State(s) with the criteria set out previously and elsewhere in legal literature and policy statements such as the doctrine of 'Responsibility to Protect'. **13.04**

TERRY D. GILL

Chapter 14

MILITARY INTERVENTION WITH THE CONSENT OR AT THE INVITATION OF A GOVERNMENT

14.01 **Consent of a government for a military intervention can form either a separate or an additional legal basis for the deployment of forces onto its territory and can include permission to conduct operations, either alongside and in conjunction with the consenting State's forces or independently. In the absence of any other legal basis, consent is a strict requirement for the deployment of armed forces or the conduct of any type of military operations on another State's territory.**

1. Consent is generally recognized as a ground for precluding the wrongfulness of an act which would otherwise be illegal under international law.[1] This also applies to military intervention, which in the absence of any other recognized legal basis in the form of a Security Council mandate or in the lawful existence of the right of self-defence, would constitute a violation of the prohibition of the use of force and the principle of non-intervention, which are core principles under both the UN Charter and under customary international law.[2]

2. Consent can act either as an independent legal basis for the deployment of military forces within the territory of another State, or can function alongside another legal basis as an additional justification for the deployment of forces and conduct of operations on another State's territory.

3. When intervention is undertaken solely on the basis of the consent of a government or at its invitation, the intervention will be subject to any conditions posed by the consenting State, either in the form of a formal agreement, or conditions of a more informal nature. Such agreement is always subject to amendment. This is a natural consequence of the independence and sovereignty of every State in relation to its territory and of other relevant rules and principles of international law.[3]

[1] J. Crawford, *The International Law Commission's Articles on State Responsibility* (2002), 163–5. Article 20 of the Articles on State Responsibility lays down the generally accepted conditions for the granting of valid consent, which are discussed in para. 1 of the commentary to Section 14.02. See 2(2) *Yearbook of the International Law Commission,* (2001), 72–4.

[2] See Sections 5.02 and 8.01 and supporting commentary.

[3] This is a paraphrase of a classic rule of international law that a State possesses exclusive jurisdiction over its territory, which was set out in the arbitral decision of the *Island of Palma's Awards* (RIAA),

4. Wherever forces are stationed on another State's territory with the agreement of the Receiving State's government, they would require additional consent to conduct any type of operations not covered by the stationing agreement, or which were carried out in the context of the lawful exercise of self-defence.[4] 14.01

Any consent granted must be freely given and issued by the lawful authority of the consenting State which is recognized under international law and the national law of the consenting State as authorized to act on behalf of that State. 14.02

1. For consent to be valid, it must be freely obtained or granted without any compulsion in the form of a threat or use of force or through coercion of the consenting State's leadership or representatives.[5] It must, moreover, be forthcoming from the recognized government of the consenting State by State officials who have the authority under international law and the national law of the consenting State to grant such consent on behalf of that State. There have been numerous examples in State practice of interventions undertaken on the basis of invalid or dubious consent, which consequently would not qualify as lawful interventions.[6]

2. In addition to meeting the abovementioned conditions of valid consent, any operations which were carried out would also have to comply with human rights and, if relevant, humanitarian law rules and principles which were applicable. The consent of a government in no way affects or diminishes the applicability of other relevant rules and principles of international law, including, in particular, those of a humanitarian or otherwise peremptory character. This is a logical consequence of the fact that a State's government may not grant more authority than it itself possesses under international law.[7]

To the extent the intervention has another legal basis in the form of either a Security Council mandate under Chapter VII of the Charter, or the lawful exercise of the right of self-defence, the consent of the 14.03

4 April 1928, Vol. II, 829 at 838. Other relevant rules of international law would include the principle of non-intervention, the prohibition of the use of force, and the right to self-determination. For a restatement of these rules see, *inter alia*, GA Res. 2625 (XXV) (1970).

[4] If attacked, forces which were stationed on another State's territory could obviously defend themselves; see para. 3 of the commentary to Section 14.03 for further explanation of this question.

[5] See Crawford, *International Law Commission's Articles*, 164–5 (part 4 of his commentary to Article 20 of the Articles on State Responsibility).

[6] Examples which readily spring to mind include, but are not limited to, the German and Soviet invasions of Czechoslovakia in 1938 and 1968 respectively, the Soviet intervention in Afghanistan in 1979, and the United States intervention in Grenada in 1983, the last of which was partly justified by an alleged invitation by the Governor General, whose authority to issue such consent was subject to doubt. For a general treatment of the question see L. Doswald-Beck, 'The Legal Validity of Military Intervention by Invitation of the Government', 56 *BYBIL* (1985), 189.

[7] This is a general principle of law contained in the Roman law maxim '*Nemo plus iuris ad alium transferre potest, quam ipse habet*' in J.E. Spruit, *Textus Iuris Romani* (Deventer: Kluwer, 1977), para. 462 at 198.

14.03 **State where the intervention is conducted would not be required from a strictly legal perspective. However, such consent would provide an additional legal basis alongside the primary one and would be welcome from a political and operational perspective. In such cases, the conduct of operations should conform to any conditions put forward by the consenting State's government in so far as these do not clash with the legal requirements and conditions which form part of the primary legal basis for the intervention. In the event of any conflict between the two, the requirements and conditions relating to the primary legal basis will prevail.**[8]

1. In the event that an intervention is carried out with a mandate of the UN Security Council under Chapter VII of the Charter in the form of a peace enforcement operation, no additional legal basis for the operation would be required from a purely legal perspective since the Council has the necessary legal authority to undertake such an operation, with or without the consent of the government of the State where the operation was conducted. However, as has been pointed out earlier, the consent of the State where the operation is conducted can provide a useful and desirable complement to the Council's mandate from a political and an operational perspective.[9]

2. The Council's mandate would prevail over any conditions put forward by the consenting State's government in the event of any clash between the two. However, the related Operational Plan (OPLAN) and rules of engagement (ROE) should be adjusted and tailored as far as possible within the terms of the mandate and the requirements of mission accomplishment to maintain the Host State's support and consent. This will in turn normally contribute to the successful conduct of the operation and would help limit the effect of the operation upon the Host State's legal order and authority to the maximum extent possible.[10]

3. With respect to the relationship between consent and self-defence, the situation is somewhat more complex. Firstly, consent would be completely out of place in a situation of classic self-defence whereby one State (State A) initiates an armed attack against another State (State B). State B in such a situation would neither seek nor require the consent of State A to conduct operations against State A directed towards repelling the attack and forestalling further attacks. In such a case, consent would be obviously irrelevant since State A was the author of the attack. However, it might be a case of collective self-defence, in which a State which was the object of an armed attack (State B) by another State (State A) called for or was offered military

[8] On the basis of, *inter alia*, Articles 103 and 24 of the Charter in relation to a Security Council mandate and the right of a State to defend itself within the terms of the Charter and customary law relating to self-defence with regard to the concurrent applicability of consent and self-defence; see para. 3 of the commentary to this Section for further elaboration.

[9] See Section 5.03 with supporting commentary.

[10] Ibid. See also Section 5.08 with supporting commentary.

assistance by or from a third State (State C) to help it repel the attack. In such a situation, the request by the attacked State, or in any case its consent to assistance from a third State, would be a strict requirement for the lawful provision of military assistance on the part of State C.[11] **14.03**

There is also a third possible scenario; namely a situation whereby a State (State A) responds to an attack against its territory, nationals, military, vessels, aircraft, or installations which were located either in international sea or airspace, or were stationed on the territory of the State where the attack originated (State B) but without the active involvement of that State's government or armed forces. In such a situation the author of the attack would not be State B itself, but an armed organized group of a non-State character (Group X) which was capable of mounting an armed attack in its own right, without acting in any way on behalf of or under the control of the State where the attack originated from. Self-defence would only be relevant within such a context to the extent that State B were neither willing nor capable of carrying out either law enforcement or other measures directed against the armed organization or group which had carried out the attack, and did not consent to measures by the State which had been subjected to attack.[12] In such a case, the target State of the attack (State A) would be justified in taking measures in self-defence in conformity with the Charter and customary requirements governing the exercise of self-defence which were directed against the organization responsible for the attack, even in the absence of consent by the State where the organization was located and conducting its operation from. Although this position is not wholly uncontroversial, it does seem to best reflect considerable (recent) State practice and best conform to the legal structure relating to the use of force, as well as with contemporary realities in which States are not the only actors capable of conducting an armed attack and do not always exercise effective control or a monopoly over armed force on their territory.[13]

[11] See Section 8.05 and supporting commentary. The requirement of a request (or clear consent) in relation to collective self-defence was stated clearly in the ICJ decision in the *Nicaragua* case; ICJ Reports, 1986, 14, at 104.

[12] See Section 8.03 and supporting commentary.

[13] Ibid. para. 5 of the commentary. An alternative aside from self-defence for possible justification of military action directed against a non-State entity which acts upon its own initiative without the substantial involvement of a State includes 'state of necessity'. However, it is a less satisfactory ground in view of the ILC's consistent position that it could not be invoked to justify military intervention. See Crawford, *International Law Commission's Articles*, 185.

PART IV

CAPITA SELECTA OF INTERNATIONAL MILITARY OPERATIONAL LAW

Chapter 15

COMMAND AND CONTROL IN MILITARY OPERATIONS

Generally, in multinational and coalition force operations, including UN (peace) enforcement operations, command authority, in the form of operational command (OPCOM) or operational control (OPCON), over military members and units will be assigned from Sending States or troop contributing countries (TCCs) to a multinational allied or coalition force. However, Sending States or TCCs will normally retain full command over their units and members when they are assigned to a coalition or allied force. 15.01

1. Generally, if a State deploys its military forces on a mission it will use its own command and control (C2) structure and rules of engagement (ROE). These will certainly vary from State to State. However, the practice of modern military forces is to have all their elements (i.e. naval, land, air, marines, and special forces) operate as a unified force. Usually such forces conduct operations with elements of at least two environments. When elements of two or more environments of a force are required to operate in the same theatre or area of operations (AOO) in support of the same national strategic objective, they will operate under a national joint structure using internationally recognized joint terminology.[1] Normally, States will create and deploy a multi-element joint task force (JTF) to conduct national operations.

2. Similarly, multinational international military operations usually involve the forces of more than one nation acting together to accomplish a single mission. Doctrinally, international military operations conducted by two or more nations are usually termed 'multinational' or 'combined' operations.[2] These may be subdivided into those undertaken within the structure of an alliance and those undertaken by

[1] Most States and military alliances have developed C2 doctrine, including joint C2 doctrine for national and international operations. For example, see Canadian Forces Publication B-GJ-005-300/FP-000 *Canadian Forces Operations*, Change 2 (15 August 2005); US Joint Chiefs of Staff Publication 3-0, *Joint Operations* (17 September 2006, Incorporating Change 1 of 13 February 2008); USJCS Publication 3-16 *Multinational Operations* (7 March 2007); UK MoD *Joint Doctrine Publication 01 Campaigning* (2nd edn, December 2008); NATO AJP-01 *Allied Joint Doctrine*, and AJP-3 *Allied Joint Operations*. For the UN see *United Nations Peacekeeping Operations Principles and Guidelines* 2008, Department of Peacekeeping Operations, Department of Field Support, available at <http://pbpu.unlb.org/pbps/Library/Capstone_Doctrine_ENG.pdf>.

[2] Ibid.

15.01 a coalition. Generally, an 'alliance' is a relationship that results from a formal agreement, such as a treaty, between two or more nations for shared strategic objectives that further the common interests of the members while a 'coalition' is often an ad hoc arrangement between two or more nations for common action, commonly termed 'a coalition of the willing'.[3] States participating in multinational operations have to strike a balance between their own national strategic objectives and those of the coalition or alliance. Often it is viewed that multinational operations provide three advantages: increased political influence and enhanced legitimacy across the international community; shared risk and cost; and increased military power and effectiveness.[4]

3. C2 structures provide the framework within which military resources drawn from different States can operate together effectively to accomplish a common international military operation. Command relationships in multinational operations usually involve both national and multinational C2 structures and doctrines. Most States will normally retain full national command in multinational operations.[5] However, any multinational C2 structure must be sufficiently flexible, agile, and responsive to changing circumstances in order to ensure mission success. Operational, policy, and legal issues often arise from command and control (C2) structures and doctrines, particularly when military forces are involved in multinational allied or coalition operations, including UN enforcement and peace enforcement operations.[6] Consequently, it is important to be aware of the C2 structure and terminology of such forces.

15.02 **Many key operational and legal issues arise from command and control (C2) matters, particularly when military forces are involved in multinational coalition or allied operations. When working in a coalition or allied force operation, it is important to be aware of the command structure and terminology of the coalition or allied forces. While military forces may use the same terms, such as 'full command', 'operational command', 'operational control', and 'tactical control', these may have different meanings. This could have significant operational and legal consequences, particularly in areas such as issuing orders and taskings (especially as related to command responsibility); requesting, authorizing, and implementing ROE; identifying decision-making authority in targeting, disciplinary, and**

[3] UK MoD *Joint Doctrine Publication 01 Campaigning.* [4] Ibid.

[5] See *United Nations Peacekeeping Operations Principles and Guidelines* 2008, Department of Peacekeeping Operations, Department of Field Support, available at <http://pbpu.unlb.org/pbps/Library/Capstone_Doctrine_ENG.pdf>.

[6] This chapter addresses authority, command, and control in the context of multinational international enforcment or self-defence operations. While some of the terminology and concepts are applicable in UN peace operations, the authority, command, and control issues arising from UN peace operations are addressed in detail in sub-Chapter 6.5 'Authority, Command, and Control in United Nations-led Peace Operations'.

policing jurisdiction; identifying signing authority for agreements, contracts, leases, and Memoranda of Understanding (MOUs); and controlling movement of personnel and equipment. 15.02

1. While military forces may use the same terms, such as 'full command', 'operational command', 'operational control', and 'tactical control', they may have different meanings. This could have significant operational and legal consequences, particularly in areas such as issuing orders and taskings (this is especially important for the concept of 'command responsibility');[7] requesting, authorizing, and implementing ROE; identifying decision-making authority in targeting; use of weapon systems; disciplinary and police jurisdiction; identifying signing authority for agreements, contracts, leases, and MOUs; and controlling movement of personnel and equipment.

2. C2 doctrine provides the framework within which military resources drawn from different nations and organizations can operate together effectively to accomplish a common mission. This framework must be flexible and responsive to changing circumstances, especially during complex enforcement operations. Fundamental to understanding any C2 structure is the requirement to use agreed terms. This is a real challenge in combined or coalition operations. The following are some of the most crucial concepts and definitions:[8]

(a) *Command.* The authority vested in an individual of the armed forces for the direction, coordination, and control of military forces. Command is further generally defined in terms of two important levels: full command and operational command.
(b) *Full command.* The military authority and responsibility of a commander to issue orders to subordinates. It covers every aspect of military operations and administration and exists only within national services. Note: The term 'command' as used internationally implies a lesser degree of authority than when it is used in a purely national sense. No NATO or coalition commander has full command over the forces assigned to him since, in assigning forces to NATO, nations will delegate only operational command (OPCOM) or operational control (OPCON).
(c) *National command.* A command that is organized by, and functions under the authority of, a specific nation. It may or may not be placed under a NATO or coalition commander.
(d) *OPCOM.* The authority granted to a commander to assign missions or tasks to subordinate commanders, to deploy units, to reassign forces, and to retain or

[7] For more on 'command responsibility' see Chapter 29 'The Prosecution of International Crimes in Relation to the Conduct of Military Operations' and Chapter 30 'International Responsibility and Military Operations'.

[8] The concepts and defintions are based largely on *NATO Allied Joint Publication AAP-6* (NATO Standardization Agency, 2009). While different States and organizations may have variations on these concepts and definitions, the NATO publication represents a strong consensus and standardization amongst major military forces.

15.02 delegate operational and/or tactical control (OPCON and/or TACON) as the commander deems necessary. Note: It does not include responsibility for administration and military discipline.

(e) *Tactical command (TACOM).* The authority delegated to a commander to assign tasks to forces under his command for the accomplishment of the mission assigned by higher authority.
(f) *Control.* That authority exercised by a commander over part of the activities of subordinate organizations, or other organizations not normally under his command, which encompasses the responsibility for implementing orders or directives. All or part of this authority may be transferred or delegated.
(g) *Operational control (OPCON).* The authority delegated to a commander to direct forces assigned so that the commander may accomplish specific missions or tasks which are usually limited by function, time, or location; to deploy units concerned; and to retain or assign tactical control of those units. It does not include authority to assign separate employment of components of the units concerned. Neither does it, of itself, include administrative or logistic control.
(h) *Tactical control (TACON).* The detailed and, usually, local direction and control of movements or manoeuvres necessary to accomplish missions or tasks assigned.

3. It is also important to identify the broad levels of command used by most military forces. The three main levels of command are as follows:[9]

(a) *Strategic level of command.* The level of command through which control of an operation is exercised at the strategic level. This includes the overall direction and coordination of assigned military forces and the provision of advice to and from political authorities at the national and international level.
(b) *Operational level of command.* The level of command which employs forces to attain strategic objectives in a theatre or area of operations through the design, organization, and conduct of campaigns and major operations. At the operational level, naval, land, and air activity must be conceived and conducted as one single concentrated effort. Activities at this level link strategy and tactics.
(c) *Tactical level of command.* The level of command which directs the specific use of military forces in operations. Such operations are designed to implement the operational level plan.

These levels of command, combined with the above-noted definitions, form the basic framework of C2 arrangements of most military operations, including enforcement operations.

[9] The concepts and defintions are based largely on Canadian Forces Publication B-GJ-005-300/FP-000 *Canadian Forces Operations* (Change 2, 15 August 2005). While different States and organizations may have variations on these concepts and definitions, the following represent a standard view shared by most major military forces.

4. The C2 structure of a multinational international military operation is a crucial element to achieving mission success. C2 arrangements have a direct impact on the development of ROE and other key operational issues such as command responsibility. Depending on the scope of the mission, naval, land, and air forces, as well as logistics and communications support, may all be included in a multinational operation. Nations will contribute to the multinational force headquarters staff and operational components in accordance with alliance arrangements or as agreed at meetings of troop contributing countries (TCCs). The commander of a (peace) enforcement operation is usually an officer of the nation contributing the largest number of forces to the operation. The other TCCs often create individual national Task Forces (TF) which are placed under the operational command or control of the Force Commander for the duration of the (peace) enforcement operation. TCCs will normally retain full command over their assigned forces in order to ensure national governments maintain final decisions regarding the employment and actions of the forces. **15.02**

5. Currently, the best-known example of a multinational alliance or coalition, with a defined and well developed C2 structure, that has been involved in international enforcement and self-defence operations is the North Atlantic Treaty Organization (NATO).[10] It has no operational forces of its own other than those assigned to it by member countries or contributed by partner countries for the purpose of carrying a specific operation.[11] Nonetheless, NATO has developed a number of structures and processes to ensure efficient functioning and mission success. In particular, it has military structure that combines the functions of a multinational force planning organization with an alliance-wide system of command and control of the military forces assigned to it. Essentially, under the command of NATO's strategic commanders, it provides for the joint planning, exercising, and operational deployment of forces provided by the Member States in accordance with a commonly agreed force planning process.[12]

[10] NATO is currently an alliance of 28 countries from North America and Europe committed to fulfilling the goals of the North Atlantic Treaty signed in Washington on 4 April 1949. The Alliance is committed to defending its Member States against aggression or the threat of aggression and to the principle that an attack against one or several members would be considered as an attack against all (Art. 5 of the North Atlantic Treaty). It also has undertaken peacekeeping tasks in areas of conflict outside the Alliance, opening the way for a lead role in multinational crisis-management operations and extensive cooperative arrangements with other organizations (see *NATO Handbook*, Public Diplomacy Division NATO (2006) at <http://www.nato.int/docu/handbook/2006/hb-en-2006.pdf>). Since its first military intervention in 1995 (Bosnia-Herzegovina), NATO has been engaged in an increasingly diverse array of operations. Today, roughly 70,000 military personnel are engaged in NATO missions around the world, successfully managing complex ground, air, and naval operations in all types of environment. These forces are currently operating in Afghanistan (ISAF), Kosovo (KFOR), Iraq (NATO Training Mission in Iraq (NTM-I), the Mediterranean (Operation Active Endeavour in support of counter-terrorism initiatives), off the Horn of Africa and in Somalia (Operation Allied Protector counter-piracy operations). For details see NATO website at <http://www.nato.int/cps/en/natolive/topics_52060.htm#current>.

[11] *Nato Handbook* (2006), 15–16. [12] Ibid.

15.02 6. NATO is structured as follows:

(a) NATO Headquarters (Brussels) is the home to national delegations of member countries and to liaison offices or diplomatic missions of partner countries. The work of these delegations and missions is supported by NATO's International Staff and International Military Staff, which are also located within the Headquarters. Each member country is represented on the North Atlantic Council (NAC), the most important political decision-making body within NATO, by an Ambassador (or Permanent Representative). The Secretary General of NATO is nominated by Member States and chairs the NAC, the Defence Planning Group (DPC), and the Nuclear Planning Group (NPG). The Secretary General also directs the International Staff, which is drawn from member nations and acts as the principal spokesperson for the Alliance.[13]

(b) The Military Committee (MC) is the senior military authority in NATO, providing NATO's civilian decision-making bodies—the NAC, the DPC, and the Nuclear Planning Group—with advice on military matters. The Military Committee is composed of senior military officers from the NATO Member States who serve as their country's Military Representatives (MILREPs) to NATO, representing their Chief of Defence.[14]

(c) The International Military Staff (IMS) is the executive support staff to the MC. It is responsible for the preparation of assessments, studies, and other papers on NATO military matters. Importantly, the IMS ensures that decisions and policies on military matters are implemented by the appropriate NATO military bodies. Accordingly, it is the essential link between NATO's political decision-making bodies and its Strategic Military Commanders (Supreme Allied Commander Europe (SACEUR) and Supreme Allied Commander Transformation (SACT)) and their staffs.[15]

(d) Allied Command Operations (ACO) is one of NATO's two strategic military commands, the other being the Allied Command Transformation (ACT). Both commands are responsible to the MC. The ACO is based at Supreme Headquarters Allied Powers Europe (SHAPE), near Mons, Belgium. It is responsible for all Alliance operations wherever it may be required.[16]

The command structure is based on functionality rather than geography. There are three levels of command: strategic, operational, and tactical. The strategic level is commanded by Supreme Allied Commander Europe (SACEUR). SACEUR is dual-hatted as the commander of the US European Command, which shares many of the same geographical responsibilities.[17] The recently established NATO Special Operations Forces (SOF) Coordination Centre (NSCC) reports to SACEUR.[18]

[13] See NATO website at <http://www.nato.int/cps/en/natolive/topics_49205.htm>.
[14] Ibid. [15] Ibid. [16] Ibid. [17] Ibid.
[18] For more details on the NSCC see sub-Chapter 22.1 'Legal Dimensions of Special Operations'.

The operational level consists of two standing Joint Force Commands (JFCs): one in Brunssum, Netherlands and one in Naples, Italy. Both can conduct operations from their static locations or provide a land-based Combined Joint Task Force (CJTF) headquarters. There is also a robust but more limited standing joint headquarters in Lisbon, Portugal, from which a deployable sea-based CJTF headquarters capability can be drawn.[19] **15.02**

The tactical level consists of six Joint Force Component Commands (JFCCs), which provide service-specific land, maritime, or air capabilities and support to the operational level. Although these tactical commands are available for use in any operation, they are subordinated to one of the Joint Force Commanders. For the Joint Force Command in Brunssum, there will be an Air Component Command at Ramstein, Germany, a Maritime Component Command at Northwood in the United Kingdom, and a Land Component Command at Heidelberg, Germany. For the Joint Force Command in Naples, there is an Air Component Command at Izmir, Turkey, a Maritime Component Command in Naples, and a Land Component Command at Madrid, Spain. In addition to these tactical commands, there are four static Combined Air Operations Centres (CAOCs)—in Uedem, Germany; Finderup, Denmark; Poggio Renatico, Italy; and Larissa, Greece, and two deployable CAOCs—in Uedem and Poggio Renatico.[20]

(e) Allied Command Transformation (ACT) is the NATO strategic command level responsible for the transformation of NATO's military structure, forces, capabilities, and doctrine. It is enhancing training, particularly of commanders and staffs, conducting experiments to assess new concepts, and promoting interoperability throughout the Alliance. Headquarters, Supreme Allied Commander Transformation (HQ SACT), based at Norfolk, Virginia, is home to the Supreme Allied Commander Transformation (SACT), the command structure of ACT. HQ SACT directs ACT's various subordinate commands including the Joint Warfare Centre in Norway, the Joint Forces Training Centre in Poland, the NATO Undersea Research Centre in Italy, the Joint Analysis and Lessons Learned Centre in Greece, various NATO schools, and Centres of Excellence (COE). The recently established NATO Cooperative Cyber Defence Centre of Excellence (CCD COE) in Tallinn, Estonia reports to SACT. The CCD COE mission is to enhance the capability, cooperation, and information sharing among NATO, NATO Member States, and partners in cyber defence by virtue of education, research and development, lessons learned, and consultation. The CCD COE vision is to be the main source of expertise in the field of cooperative cyber defence by accumulating, creating, and disseminating knowledge in related matters within NATO, NATO Member States, and partners.[21]

19 See NATO website at <http://www.nato.int/cps/en/natolive/topics_49205.htm>.

20 Ibid.

21 See CCD COE website at <http://www.ccdcoe.org/> and for more details on information operations generally see sub-Chapter 22.2 'Legal Dimensions of Information Operations'.

15.02 7. Effective implementation of alliance military strategy and orders depends upon the delegation of an appropriate level of command authority to NATO commanders and on an effective deployable command structure supported by fast, secure, and reliable communications and information systems. A NATO Combined Joint Task Force Commander (CJTF) is generally delegated operational control over assigned Member States' forces. However, as previously stated, most Member States will retain full national command over forces assigned to NATO.

8. NATO military forces may be required to conduct operations in coalition with forces of other organizations or nations. In this case, C2 would be exercised through a coordination, control, communications, and integration centre which would link the NATO force headquarters with other headquarters.[22] Political control and guidance of an enforcement or peace enforcement operation is exercised by the NAC, in consultation with the UN Security Council and Member States' capitals. C2 within the NATO command structure highlights the complexity of multinational allied and coalition operations. The C2 structure has its challenges but, in practice, has shown it can function efficiently.

9. While this general C2 structure, as reflected in the current NATO command structure, has worked well in (peace) enforcement operations, it presents many challenges for an allied or coalition Force Commander in all aspects of operations. Interoperability issues and challenges may arise because the various allied or coalition members may have different national legal and policy obligations. For example, interoperability issues often arise in the following areas:

(a) Each TCC will undoubtedly maintain jurisdiction over its forces for military justice and disciplinary purposes. Jurisdiction over TCC personnel suspected of committing criminal offences is normally decided on a case-by-case basis in accordance with applicable international agreements with host nation authorities (often via status-of-forces agreements (SOFAs)).[23] It is generally the policy of most TCCs to retain jurisdiction in all criminal cases to the fullest extent possible during multinational operations. Usually, foreign military commanders exercising operational (OPCON) or tactical control

[22] For example in Afghanistan, NATO ISAF forces operated from August 2003 to December 2014 under a UN mandate (SC Res. 1386 (2001)) with other nations and worked with forces involved in counter-terrorism operations under the US-led Operation Enduring Freedom (OEF). ISAF and OEF operated under separate mandates and missions. ISAF focused on its stabilization and security mission while OEF focused on counter-terrorism. Clear command arrangements coordinated and, where necessary, deconflicted efforts within the two missions as agreed under the auspices of the ISAF and OEF Operational Plans (OPLANs). While support for the continued development of the Afghan security forces and institutions and wider cooperation with Afghanistan continue, Afghans assumed full responsibility for security at the end of 2014, see NATO website at <http://www.nato.int/cps/en/natohq/69772.htm>.

[23] For more detail on SOFAs see sub-Chapters 5.2 'Status of Forces in Enforcement and Peace Enforcement Operations' and 6.2 'Status of Forces in Peace Operations'.

(TACON) over other TCC forces do not administer discipline over the members of the TCCs.[24] **15.02**

(b) Each TCC will normally have its own ROE or, at least, national caveats on the ROE used by the allied or coalition force. In particular, each TCC will likely have its own interpretation of (unit and personal) self-defence (including notions of extended self-defence to protect others outside the Force) and the use of deadly force in the defence of property.[25]

(c) Each TCC will have its own targeting process and interpretation of a military objective.[26]

(d) Each TCC will have its own policy for the detention of persons and the treatment of detainees. In support of the operational or security objectives of an international operation, multinational forces may be required to detain persons for a variety of reasons. Thus, it is vital for commanders, troops, and legal advisors to understand the legal bases to detain and the legal standards of treatment and, possibly, transfer of detainees.[27]

(e) Each TCC may have differing treaty obligations or differing interpretations of treaty obligations.[28]

[24] See Canadian Forces Publication B-GG-005-027/AF-011, *Military Justice at the Summary Trial Level* (updated 15 February 2006), chapter 3; US Army *Operational Law Handbook 2014* (Charlottesville, Virginia: The Judge Advocate General's Legal Center & School, International and Operational Law Department), 93.

[25] For more details on multinational international military operations ROE and caveats see sub--Chapter 5.4 'Force Application in Enforcement and Peace Enforcement Operations' and Chapter 10 'Application of Force and Rules of Engagement in Self-Defence Operations'; US Army *Operational Law Handbook 2014* (Charlottesville, Virginia: The Judge Advocate General's Legal Center & School, International and Operational Law Department), 455.

[26] For more details on multinational international military operations targeting see sub-Chapter 5.4 'Force Application in Enforcement and Peace Enforcement Operations', Chapter 10 'Application of Force and Rules of Engagement in Self-Defence Operations', and Chapter 16 'Targeting in Operational Law'. See also US Army *Operational Law Handbook 2014*, 481.

[27] For more details on detention during operations see Chapter 26 'Operational Detention and the Treatment of Detainees'. See also US Army *Operational Law Handbook 2014*, 453, Canadian Forces (CF) Pub B-GJ-005-501/FP-001, *CFJP-5.1 Use of Force for CF Operations*, August 2008 (issued under the authority of the Chief the Defence Staff), 4–4.

[28] See e.g. the Convention on the Prohibition of the Use, Stockpiling, Production, and Transfer of Anti-Personnel Mines and on Their Destruction of 3 December 1997, which prohibits developing, producing, acquiring, stockpiling, retaining, or transferring anti-personnel mines, either directly or indirectly, and assisting, encouraging, or inducing any of these activities. During multinational operations, it is crucial to understand the limits of these prohibitions for a particular multinational partner; the Convention on Prohibitions or Restrictions on the Use of Certain Conventional Weapons Which May Be Deemed to Be Excessively Injurious or to Have Indiscriminate Effects of 10 October 1980, with Protocols I, II (revised on 3 May 1996), III, IV (13 October 1995), and V (28 November 2003). One area under this Convention which may impact multinational operation is the use of hollow or soft point ammunition during armed conflict operations. The Convention on the Prohibition of the Development, Production, Stockpiling and Use of Chemical Weapons and on Their Destruction of 13 January 1993 prohibits the use of Riot Control Agents (RCAs) 'as a method of warfare'. However, it does permit RCA use for law enforcement operations. The interpretation of the use of RCAs in armed conflict operations may cause challenges in multinational operations. The same may be true for the recently created Convention on Cluster Munitions (Dublin, 30 May 2008). Article 21 of this Convention permits States parties, their military personnel, or nationals, to engage in 'military

15.02 (f) Each TCC will have its own intelligence and information gathering/sharing rules and policies.[29]
(g) Each TCC will have its own civil claims and settlement process.[30]
(h) Each TCC will have its own fiscal law rules and policies.[31]
(i) Each TCC will have its own environmental law rules and policies.[32]

Considerable differences in national interests will have significant influence on the way that a coalition member operates.

10. Moreover, the resources, or lack thereof, that are available to a coalition or allied member may also have a significant impact upon the C2 structure and the ability of the Force Commander to exercise effective command. It is far easier for a Force Commander to employ and control a well-equipped and trained force than one that is not.

11. Nonetheless, an effective, efficient, clear, and practical C2 structure will be able to overcome differing national interests and interoperability issues during enforcement operations. Accordingly, a solid understanding of the multinational force C2 structure in international military enforcement operations is essential. All commanders, subordinates, and legal advisors need to remain alert to the potential legal, operational, and policy challenges that can arise from C2 issues and be prepared to effectively address them. This will promote clarity in C2 and in identifying which lawful authorities a commander may exercise. This, in turn, will substantially contribute to the achievement of mission success.

cooperation and operations' with States not party to this Convention that might engage in activities prohibited to a State party.

[29] For more details on Information Operations see sub-Chapter 22.2 'Legal Dimensions of Information Operations'. See also US Army *Operational Law Handbook 2014*, chapter 6 'Intelligence Law and Interrogation Operations' and Canadian Forces Publication B-GJ-005-200/FP-000, *Joint Intelligence Doctrine* (21 May 2003).

[30] See e.g. US Army *Operational Law Handbook 2014*, chapter 18 'Foreign and Deployment Claims'.

[31] For example, US Army *Operational Law Handbook 2014*, chapter 14 'Fiscal Law'.

[32] For example, US Army *Operational Law Handbook 2014*, chapter 19 'Environmental Law in Operations'.

Chapter 16

TARGETING IN OPERATIONAL LAW

The general rules governing targeting apply equally in land, air, sea, space, and cyberspace. Specialized rules may apply in particular types of operations, such as peace operations or naval warfare. 16.01

1. The material contained in this chapter should be read in conjunction with that in Chapter 4 'Conceptual Distinction and Overlaps between Law Enforcement and the Conduct of Hostilities' and Chapter 17 'Targeted Killings in Operational Law Perspectives'. [1]

2. The basic norms governing targeting are derived from the principle of distinction (see Section 16.02). While certain of the rules set forth in this Section have been codified in treaty law, they generally reflect extant customary international humanitarian law.[2]

3. The core treaty that addresses targeting, Additional Protocol I to the 1949 Geneva Conventions (AP I), provides that its provisions on general protection against effects of hostilities (including rules governing targeting):

> apply to any land, air or sea warfare which may affect the civilian population, individual civilians or civilian objects on land. They further apply to all attacks from the sea or from the air against objectives on land but do not otherwise affect the rules of international law applicable in armed conflict at sea or in the air.[3]

According to the ICRC Commentary, the provision limits applicability of the Protocol to attacks against land targets or those that would affect the civilian population on land.[4] Nevertheless, State practice establishes that the customary international humanitarian law rules of targeting are equally applicable in land, air, and naval warfare, although certain additional rules apply to the case of targeting at sea (see Chapter 20).

[1] For an excellent survey of this body of law, see D. Fleck (ed.), *The Handbook of International Humanitarian Law*, 3rd edn (Oxford: Oxford University Press, 2013).

[2] See e.g. J.-M. Henckaerts and L. Doswald-Beck (eds), *Customary International Humanitarian Law* (Cambridge: Cambridge University Press, 2005) (hereinafter CIHL), Part I; M. Schmitt, C. Garraway, and Y. Dinstein, 'Manual on the Law of Non-International Armed Conflict', 36 *Israel Yearbook of Human Rights* (2006), Special Supplement (hereinafter NIAC Manual), chapter 2.

[3] Art. 49(3) AP I.

[4] Y. Sandoz, C. Swinarski, and B. Zimmermann (eds), *Commentary on the Additional Protocols of 8 June 1977* (Geneva: ICRC, 1987) (hereinafter ICRC Commentary), paras 1893–1899.

MICHAEL N. SCHMITT

16.01 4. Although no armed conflict has to date occurred in space, it is well accepted that should such a conflict occur, the rules of international humanitarian law, in particular those bearing on the principle of distinction, would apply. To begin with, there is no indication that the drafters of Additional Protocol I intended to exclude space from the *land, air, or sea* phraseology. Rather, the most reasonable interpretation is that the Protocol encompasses space-based attacks against land targets. It also logically extends to attacks against space-based assets (whatever the source) that if damaged, destroyed, or neutralized would affect the civilian population (for instance, by interfering with emergency response communications). Customary international humanitarian law principles certainly govern warfare to, through, and from space, since general consensus exists that the customary principles of targeting apply regardless of the *situs* of battle. There is little reason to distinguish their extension to space warfare from applicability to other forms of combat for which there are few written norms (e.g. air-to-air, air-to-sea, sea-to-sea, and sea-to-air).[5]

5. The case of cyber operations (see Chapter 23) presents greater difficulties.[6] Although it is well accepted that the law applicable to targeting governs non-kinetic attacks, two major controversies continue to dominate the discussion of the applicability of key rules of targeting law to cyber operations. The first is whether the rules regarding targeting apply to all cyber operations or only some of them.[7] The crux of the debate centres on the term 'attacks', which lies at the heart of most express targeting rules. Additional Protocol I defines attacks as 'acts of violence, whether in offence or defence'.[8] There are two primary schools of thought. The first interprets the notion broadly, relying on the requirement in Article 48 of the Protocol that parties 'direct their operations only against military objectives'.[9] By this interpretation, any 'cyber operation' targeting civilians, the civilian population, or civilian objects is forbidden.[10] An alternative approach focuses on the reference to violence in the Protocol's definition of attack. By it, a cyber operation qualifies as an attack subject to the various prohibitions and restrictions of humanitarian law if it results in, or was intended to result in, injury or death of civilians or damage or destruction of civilian objects. Thus, a cyber operation intended merely to inconvenience the civilian population, for instance by temporarily interfering with access to the Internet, would not qualify as an attack to which the rules governing targeting apply.[11] This approach was developed further

[5] See M. Schmitt, 'International Law and Military Operations in Space', 10 *Max Planck Yearbook of United Nations Law* (2006), 89.

[6] On this law, see M. Schmitt (gen. ed.), *The Tallinn Manual on the International Law Applicable to Cyber Warfare* (Cambridge: Cambridge University Press, 2013), chapters 4 and 5.

[7] Ibid. Commentary accompanying Rule 30.

[8] Art. 49(1) AP I. See also NIAC Manual, para. 1.1.6.

[9] Art. 48 AP I.

[10] See e.g. K. Dörmann, 'Applicability of the Additional Protocols to Computer Network Attacks', online article, <https://www.icrc.org/eng/resources/documents/misc/68lg92.htm>, 4.

[11] M. Schmitt, 'Wired Warfare: Computer Network Attack and International Law' 84(846) *International Review of the Red Cross* (June 2002), 365–99.

during the so-called Tallinn Manual process, with a majority of the 'International Group of Experts' interpreting 'damage' as extending to cyber operations that affected the 'functionality' of cyber infrastructure and equipment. Within the group, there were nuances. Some experts took the position that such an interpretation was only appropriate when the cyber operation necessitated repair of the cyber infrastructure and equipment involved. Others were willing to include operations that required reload of the operating system or of data upon which operation of the system relied.[12] Despite the difference of opinion, it is clear that the scope of the targeting rules of international humanitarian law when applied in the cyber context depends, at least in part, on the scope of the term attack. **16.01**

6. The second major controversy involving application of international humanitarian law rules governing targeting to cyber operations surrounds the meaning of the term 'object' in the customary law and Additional Protocol I's prohibition on attacking civilian 'objects' (see the discussion which follows).[13] During the Tallinn Manual process, the majority of the International Group of Experts rejected interpretation of the term as including data, in part (but only in part) based on the ICRC's Additional Protocols Commentary observation that an object is something 'tangible and visible'.[14] Therefore, a cyber operation directed at data does not run afoul of the prohibition on directly targeting civilian objects. Others opined that the term had evolved in light of extensive reliance on data in modern societies and it was accordingly reasonable to read the term object as including data, such that the destruction or alteration of civilian data is prohibited.[15]

7. The formal applicability of the law of targeting to peace operations (Chapters 6 and 7) depends on whether the operation in question qualifies as an international or non-international armed conflict to which the peace operations forces are party. If so, there is no doubt that their activities would be governed by the said rules. Peace force operations that do not take place in armed conflicts of this nature are technically not governed by humanitarian law rules, although they are commonly applied as a matter of policy.[16] For instance, the 1999 Secretary General's Bulletin provides:

> The fundamental principles and rules of international humanitarian law set out in the present bulletin are applicable to United Nations forces when in situations of armed conflict they are actively engaged as combatants, to the extent and for the duration of their engagement. They are accordingly applicable in enforcement actions or in peacekeeping operations when the use of force is permitted in self-defence.[17]

[12] M. Schmitt (ed.), *Tallinn Manual on the International Law to Cyber Warfare* (Cambridge: Cambridge University Press, 2013), 108–9.

[13] Art. 52(1) AP I. [14] Additional Protocols Commentary, para. 2008.

[15] Tallinn Manual, 127.

[16] See, generally, Chapter 4 'Conceptual Distinction and Overlaps Between Law Enforcement and the Conduct of Hostilities'.

[17] Secretary General's Bulletin: *Observance by United Nations Forces of International Humanitarian Law* (6 August 1999), 38 *ILM* (1999) 456, para. 1.1.

16.01 It further provides that 'the United Nations force shall respect the rules prohibiting or restricting the use of certain weapons and methods of combat under the relevant instruments of international humanitarian law'.[18] Similarly, the United States requires its forces to 'comply with the law of armed conflict during all armed conflict, however such conflicts are characterized, and in all other military operations'.[19]

8. The applicability of the rules of targeting to counter-terrorist operations unconnected to an ongoing armed conflict remains uncertain because of controversy over the legal character of such operations. However, it is clear that to the extent they qualify as an armed conflict of any kind, the general principles, especially that of distinction, would apply. This is without prejudice to any other rules, such as those of international human rights law, which might apply as a matter of law.

16.02 **The parties to the conflict must distinguish between civilians and combatants. Attacks must not be directed against civilians unless, and for such time as, they directly participate in hostilities. Acts or threats of violence the primary purpose of which is to spread terror among the civilian population are prohibited.**

1. The principle of distinction is the foundational principle governing the conduct of hostilities during an armed conflict. In its *Nuclear Weapons Advisory Opinion*, the International Court of Justice cited it as one of the two 'cardinal' principles of international humanitarian law (the other being unnecessary suffering).[20] The principle, first codified in the 1868 St Petersburg Declaration,[21] finds its modern expression in Article 48 of AP I:

> In order to ensure respect for and protection of the civilian population and civilian objects, the parties to the conflict shall at all times distinguish between the civilian population and combatants and between civilian objects and military objectives and accordingly shall direct their operations only against military objectives.

2. Section 16.02 focuses on the distinction between civilians and combatants. Combatants are all members of the armed forces except for medical and religious personnel.[22] The armed forces comprise a State's officially organized military forces, as well as any other organized armed groups or units which are under a command that is responsible to a party to the conflict for the conduct of its subordinates.[23] For example, during the 1991 and 2003 international armed conflicts in Iraq, members

[18] Ibid. para. 6.2.

[19] Department of Defense, Law of War Program (DoD Directive 2311.01E, 9 May 2006), para. 4.1; US Navy, US Marine Corps, US Coast Guard, *The Commander's Handbook on the Law of Naval Operations* (NWP 1-14M, MCWP 5-12.1, COMDTPUB P5800.7A), para. 6.1.2 (June 2007).

[20] ICJ, *Legality of the Threat or Use of Nuclear Weapons*, Advisory Opinion (1996), para. 78.

[21] St Petersburg Declaration Renouncing the Use, in Time of War of Explosive Projectiles Under 400 Grammes Weight (11 December 1868), Preamble.

[22] CIHL, Rule 3; Art. 43(2) AP I; Art. 3 of the 1907 Hague Regulations.

[23] CIHL, Rules 3 and 4.

of the uniformed armed forces of Iraq and of all the Coalition States qualified as combatants on this basis. Under customary international humanitarian law, as codified in Article 1 of the 1907 Hague Regulations and Article 4 of the Third 1949 Geneva Convention, to qualify as combatants (and thereby be entitled to prisoner-of-war status and belligerent immunity), the individuals concerned must wear clothing or accoutrements which distinguish them from the civilian population, carry their weapons openly, and generally conduct their operations in compliance with the laws and customs of war.[24] These requirements have been relaxed in Article 44(3) AP I, a provision which is highly controversial and generally may not be deemed to be reflective of customary law. In terms of targeting, however, the distinction is not critical, for despite failure to comply with the requirements said individuals would usually be targetable as members of an organized armed group directly participating in the conflict. **16.02**

3. In addition to members of a State's formal military units, international humanitarian law envisages the incorporation of paramilitary or other armed law enforcement agencies into the armed forces, such that its members become combatants. Pursuant to Additional Protocol I, incorporation must be notified to the other parties to a conflict.[25] The Italian *Carabineri* or Afghan National Police are good examples of such forces. With regard to targeting, however, such notification is irrelevant, for, even absent notification, the member of such groups would be targetable as belonging to an organized armed group directly participating in hostilities.

4. Although the notion of combatancy technically applies only in international armed conflict, for the purposes of targeting law, both members of a State's armed forces and rebel groups are treated as combatants, i.e. an attack on them does not violate international humanitarian law (although an attack on a State's forces will violate domestic law).

5. A civilian is a person who is not a member of the armed forces as already defined.[26] The status of those who are not members of the armed forces, but who nevertheless participate in hostilities, is controversial. By one interpretation, they have forfeited their civilian status and are so-called 'unlawful combatants'.[27] As such, they both lose the protections to which civilians are entitled, such as those bearing on detention, and lack the benefits of combatant status, most notably belligerent immunity from prosecution for lawful combat activities. By the alternative view, such individuals lose their immunity from attack, but nevertheless retain civilian status and its attendant entitlements. For the purposes of the law

[24] On their face, these Article 4 preconditions for prisoner-of-war status apply only to 'irregular' armed forces such as members of militia, volunteer corps, and resistance movements. However, State practice arguably establishes that the cumulative conditions also bind the regular armed forces.

[25] Art. 43(3) AP I.

[26] See CIHL Rule 5; Art. 50(1) AP I.

[27] Y. Dinstein, *Conduct of Hostilities under the Law of International Armed Conflict*, 2nd edn (Cambridge: Cambridge University Press, 2010), chapter 2.

16.02 governing targeting, however, all experts agree that they do not enjoy protection from attack for such time as they are directly participating in hostilities (Article 51(3) AP I and 13(3) of AP II).

6. The express prohibition on attacking civilians is codified for international armed conflict in Article 51(2) of AP I: 'The civilian population as such, as well as individual civilians, shall not be the object of attack.' Article 13(2) of AP II sets forth an analogous prohibition in the context of non-international armed conflict. These prohibitions undoubtedly reflect customary international law.[28]

7. The prohibition on attacking civilians applies only to direct attacks. It does not prohibit attacks against the armed forces that incidentally result in harm to civilians. Rather, such attacks are governed by the principle of proportionality and the requirement to take feasible precautions in attack (see Section 16.07). It should be noted that the prohibition on attacking civilians applies even if the eventual attack proves unsuccessful. In other words, it is the intent to attack the civilians that is the *sine qua non* of the rule, not the fact that civilians are actually harmed.

8. In the event of doubt as to whether a person to be attacked is a civilian or combatant, he or she shall be assumed to be a civilian.[29] Although there is agreement that the principle reflects customary international humanitarian law, concern has been expressed as to how it might be interpreted. It is clear that it does not refer to situations in which an attacker harbours slight doubt, for doubt often pervades armed conflict. Accordingly, at the time of ratification of Additional Protocol I, some States expressed their understanding that the presumption of civilian status did not override a commander's duty to protect his forces.[30] The United States, in its *Commander's Handbook on the Law of Naval Operations*, notes that 'combatants in the field must make an honest determination as to whether a particular person is or is not taking a direct part in hostilities based on that person's behavior, location and attire, and other information available at the time'.[31] In this regard, it is essential to recall that attackers are obligated to do everything feasible to confirm that targets are in fact military objectives (see Section 16.07).

9. 'Attacks' are defined in Article 49(1) of AP I as 'acts of violence against the adversary, whether in offence or in defence'. In other words, the key is the application of violence against the enemy, not the purpose, or even the legality,

[28] CIHL, Rule 6, NIAC Manual, para 2.1.1.1; NWP 1-14M, para. 8.3. For additional codifications of the principle, see Art. 25 HagueReg; Convention on Conventional Weapons (CCW) Protocol II, Art. 3(2); CCW Protocol II Amended, Art. 3(7); CCW Protocol III, Art. 2(1). Amended Art. 1 CCW extends the application of the Convention and its protocols to situations of non-international armed conflicts. See also Art. 8(2)(b)(i) ICC Statute.

[29] Art. 50(1) AP I.

[30] See e.g. United Kingdom, Statement Made upon Ratification, in A. Roberts and R. Guelff, *Documents on the Law of War*, 3rd edn (Oxford University Press, 2000), 511 (hereinafter UK Statement).

[31] NWP 1-14M, para. 8.2.2.

of such use. As noted previously (see commentary accompanying Section 16.01), controversy exists over whether the notion includes non-kinetic operations that cause neither harm to, nor death of, individuals.[32] Those who argue that it does not would exclude, for instance, cyber attacks designed to cause the civilian population inconvenience, from the reach of the prohibition on attacking civilians. Beyond this issue, it is well accepted that psychological operations against the civilian population (e.g. 'psyop' television and radio broadcasts or leaflet dropping) do not amount to attacks.[33] **16.02**

10. Despite the prohibition on attacking civilians, those who directly participate in hostilities may be attacked for such time as they do so. Codified in Article 51(3) of AP I and Article 13(3) of AP II, this principle reflects customary international humanitarian law in both international and non-international armed conflicts.[34] Notwithstanding universal acceptance of the rule itself, uncertainty pervades its application. The first question is the scope of the participation that qualifies as 'direct'. For instance, whereas all would agree that attacking a combatant qualifies, there is disagreement over whether financing insurgent groups does. Following a multi-year study conducted by a group of international experts, the ICRC issued its *Interpretive Guidance on the Notion of Direct Participation in Hostilities* in 2009.[35] Although not formally binding, the guidance provides useful, albeit somewhat controversial, criteria for assessing acts of hostility.[36]

11. Pursuant to the guidance, an act will constitute direct participation if it fulfils three cumulative criteria (constitutive elements).[37] First, the act must be 'likely to adversely affect the military operations or military capacity of a party to an armed conflict or, alternatively, to inflict death, injury, or destruction on persons or objects protected against direct attack' (threshold of harm). Second, there must be a 'direct causal link between the act and the harm likely to result either from that act, or from a coordinated military operation of which that act constitutes an integral part' (direct causation). Finally, the act must be 'specifically designed to directly cause the required threshold of harm in support of a party to the conflict and to the detriment of another' (belligerent nexus). Application of these criteria is designed to distinguish between acts constituting direct participation, and thereby subjecting the actor to attack, and those that, although taking place in the context of hostilities, do not remove the immunity from attack that civilians enjoy. It must be noted that

[32] See Dörmann, 'Applicability of the Additional Protocols to Computer Network Attacks' and Schmitt, 'Wired Warfare'.

[33] See sub-Chapter 22.2 'Legal Dimensions of Information Operations'.

[34] CIHL, Rule 6; NIAC Manual, para. 2.1.1.2.

[35] N. Melzer, *Interpretive Guidance on the Notion of Direct Participation in Hostilities under International Humanitarian Law* (Geneva: ICRC, 2009), (hereinafter *Interpretive Guidance*).

[36] On the targeting of specific individuals, see Chapter 17 'Targeted Killings in Operational Law Perspectives'. See also N. Melzer, *Targeted Killings in International Law* (Oxford: Oxford University Press, 2008).

[37] Ibid. 46–64.

16.02 disagreement exists over the sufficiency of the constitutive elements. For instance, some experts argue that limiting the threshold element to harm is under inclusive in the sense that it fails to account for acts that enhance a party's military capacity or operations.[38]

12. A point of uncertainty regarding the standard surrounds the concept of 'for such time'. Controversy exists over when the direct participation is deemed to begin and cease. The *Interpretive Guidance* takes the position that it commences with 'measures preparatory to the execution of a specific act of direct participation in hostilities, as well as the deployment to and the return from the location of its execution'. Examples of general participation not amounting to direct participation would include 'purchase, production, smuggling and hiding of weapons; general recruitment and training of personnel; and financial, administrative or political support to armed actors'.[39] A broader interpretation suggests that direct participation extends as far as a definitive causal nexus exists. Thus, for instance, acquiring the materials that are to be used to build an improvised explosive device, or assembling one for imminent use, begins the participation. Obviously, though, a remote or contrived causal link would not suffice.

13. A related dispute involves the individual who repeatedly directly participates, albeit in separate incidents—the so-called 'revolving door' phenomenon. Most commentators would agree that an individual who is a member of an organized armed group loses civilian status and, thereby, protection against direct attack throughout his or her membership, although some would limit the notion of 'membership' in such groups to individuals who have a continuous combat function within the group. The ICRC *Interpretive Guidance* adopts this qualification.[40] However, as to individuals who participate in hostilities without being members of an armed group, a restrictive school of interpretation, and the *Interpretive Guidance*, aver that each act must be treated separately.[41] Once the direct participant desists from participation as to a specific incident, he or she reacquires immunity from attack. It is only upon commencement of a subsequent operation that the participant becomes targetable again; hence, there is a 'revolving door' through which the individual passes into and out of liability to attack. The alternative interpretation holds that such individuals remain subject to attack throughout their activities, only regaining immunity upon unambiguously withdrawing from participation. It should be noted that this approach risks treating an individual who has in fact decided to desist from further participation, but whose decision is not apparent, as if he had not done so. However, since this individual chose to directly participate in the first place, it is arguably more appropriate for him to bear the risk of mistake

[38] A collection of essays by Kenneth Watkins, Hays Parks, William Boothby, and Michael Schmitt, setting forth various concerns with the Interpretive Guidance, as well as a response by Nils Melzer of the ICRC, can be found at 42:3 *New York University Journal of International Law and Politics* (2010).

[39] *Interpretive Guidance*, 65–8. [40] Ibid. 71–3. [41] Ibid. 72.

than combatants whom he might attack as a direct participant if he has not withdrawn. **16.02**

14. In the direct participation context, controversy also exists over human shielding. The weight of authority is that involuntary human shields retain their status as civilians at all times for the purpose of international humanitarian law. Thus, for instance, they must be factored into proportionality calculations (see Section 16.06). The ICRC *Interpretive Guidance* suggests that voluntary human shields that are not physically impeding attack are equally to be treated as civilians.[42] Many commentators counter that voluntary human shields are in fact direct participants who, therefore, need not be considered during such calculations.[43] This position would suggest that, having lost their civilian immunity from attack, they could be attacked directly. In any case, however, there would be little practical purpose in doing so, since the target they are shielding is the military objective to be attacked.

15. The prohibition on terrorizing the civilian population is based on Article 51(2) of AP I for international armed conflicts and Article 13(2) of AP II for non-international armed conflicts; it is undoubtedly reflective of customary international humanitarian law.[44] The prohibition is not limited to 'attacks', as defined above. Rather, it extends to any acts intended to terrorize the civilian population. Thus, radio or television broadcasts, although presenting no risk of physically harming the civilian population, would violate the prohibition if intended to terrorize, for instance by falsely claiming the population had been subjected to a biological attack.

16. It must be noted that the prohibition does not apply to attacks that have an incidental effect of terrorizing civilians. Many attacks will in fact terrify the civilian population; however, attacks that do so are only prohibited under that provision if terrorizing civilians was the intended purpose thereof.

Parties to a conflict must distinguish between civilian objects and military objectives. Attacks may only be directed against military objectives. Military objectives are those objects which by their nature, location, purpose, or use make an effective contribution to military action and whose partial or total destruction, capture, or neutralization, in the circumstances ruling at the time, offers a definite military advantage. Civilian objects are all objects that are not military objectives. **16.03**

[42] Ibid. 56–7.

[43] M. Schmitt, 'Human Shields in International Humanitarian Law', 47 *Columbia Journal of Transnational Law* (2009), 292, at 324–7.

[44] CIHL, Rule 2; NIAC Manual, para. 2.3.9. Note that Art. 4(2)(d) AP II also prohibits acts of terrorism. See also NWP 1-14M, para. 8.9.1.2. The Fourth Geneva Convention's prohibition on 'all measures of intimidation or of terrorism' (Art. 33 GC IV) provides further support for the prohibition.

16.03 1. This rule derives from the general principle of distinction, and is the counterpart to the prohibition on attacking civilians (see discussion at Section 16.02). It is codified most prominently in Article 52 of AP I.[45] Although Additional Protocol II does not contain an analogous rule for non-international armed conflicts, the notion of military objective appears in both the Conventional Weapons Convention and the Second Protocol to the Hague Cultural Property Convention.[46] There is no doubt that the prohibition reflects customary international humanitarian law in both international and non-international armed conflicts.[47]

2. Since civilian objects comprise all objects that are not military objectives,[48] the key to the prohibition lies in the definition of military objectives.[49] The term was first used in the 1923 Hague Rules of Air Warfare.[50] Article 52(2) of AP I provides the template for the rule as set forth in Section 16.03.

3. The definition consists of two cumulative criteria. First, the object in question must make an effective contribution to the enemy's military action. Most obvious in this regard is military equipment. The requirement of effectiveness is meant only to exclude contributions that are insignificant or otherwise inconsequential; there is no requirement that the contribution be particularly significant. Second, even if an object makes an effective contribution, its destruction, capture, or neutralization must offer an attacker a definite military advantage. A definite military advantage is one that is not merely potential or indeterminate.[51] As with 'effective', 'definite' does not imply that the advantage need be great. Despite the existence of two cumulative criteria, it is unlikely that either would appear in isolation of the other. In other words, it will typically be the case that an object which makes an effective contribution to the enemy's military action is also one the destruction of which will yield the enemy a definite military advantage—and vice versa. Reduced to basics, the first criterion addresses the issue from the perspective of a defender, whereas the second does so from the attacker's perspective.

4. The term 'military advantage' should not be exaggerated. Although advantage is not to be understood merely as ground gained or enemy killed,[52] it is limited to advantage that is military in nature. Political, psychological, economic, or other

[45] See also CCW Protocol II Amended, Art. 3(7); CCW Protocol III, Art. 2(1); Art. 8(2)(b)(ii) ICC Statute.

[46] CCW Protocol II Amended, Art. 3(8); CCW Protocol III, Art. 2(2). On the definition of military objectives, see CCW Protocol II Amended, Art. 2(6); CCW Protocol III, Art. 1(3); Hague Cultural Property Convention, Protocol II, Art. 1(f); Art. 8(2)(e)(iii). ICC Statute.

[47] CIHL, Rules 7, 8, and 9; NIAC Manual, para. 2.1.1.1; NWP 1-14M, para. 8.2.

[48] Art. 52(1) AP I; CIHL, Rule 9. See also CCW Protocol II, Art. 2(5); CCW Protocol II Amended, Art. 2(7); CCW Protocol III, Art. 1(4).

[49] Regarding the definition of military objectives, see AP I, Art. 52(2); CCW Protocol II, Art. 2(4); CCW Protocol II Amended, Art. 2(6); CCW Protocol III, Art. 1(3); Hague Cultural Property Convention, Protocol II, Art. 1(f).

[50] 1923 Hague Draft Rules of Air Warfare, Art. 24.

[51] ICRC Commentary, para. 2024. [52] Ibid. 2218.

forms of advantage are not the sort contemplated by the rule. Even forcing the enemy to the negotiating table is not 'military' advantage in the sense of the rule. Rather, military advantage is that which exhibits some direct nexus to military operations. The extent of nexus is important. The US *Commander's Handbook on the Law of Naval Operations* suggests that military objectives include not only war fighting (e.g. military equipment) and war supporting objects (e.g. armament factories), but also those which are war sustaining.[53] Supporters of this approach would, for example, take the position that it is lawful to target the Afghan poppy crop because of the substantial funding the Afghan Taliban derives from opium production and trade. The weight of opinion on this issue, however, is that the advantage resulting from an attack on war sustaining objects is too remote to qualify as military advantage. **16.03**

5. In assessing military advantage, it is necessary to consider the advantage accruing from the attack as a whole, not merely that from isolated or particular aspects of the attack.[54] In other words, the attack must be considered in the context of the ongoing campaign. The classic example involves an attack constituting a ruse intended to cause the enemy to believe an operation is to take place at other than its intended location. Since the operation is to be mounted elsewhere, the immediate military advantage of the destruction of the target is minimal. However, if the enemy is fooled as to where the operation will actually be launched, the military advantage of the attack can prove significant. Additionally, military advantage is not considered in hindsight. Rather, the determinative factor is the degree of military advantage that the attacker expected to attain at the time the attack was planned, approved, or executed.

6. Objects qualify as making an effective contribution to military action on one of four bases.[55] 'Nature' refers to the intrinsic character of an object. Military equipment, for example, is always of a 'military nature' and thus by definition makes an effective contribution to the enemy's military actions. This is true of any enemy military equipment not just that used for combat purposes.

7. An object may become also a military objective by 'location'. For instance, an area of heavy vegetation that might be used to mask the enemy's activities may be cleared to deny its use to the enemy. In Afghanistan, certain mountain passes are well-known smuggling routes for organized armed groups like the Taliban. Targeting the passes in order to block or degrade their usefulness would be permissible based upon their location.

8. The 'purpose' criterion refers to future use of an object. By this criterion, the conversion of a civilian object to military purposes need not be complete before it becomes a targetable military objective. To take a simple example, a civilian aircraft which is being fitted out to carry troops or military equipment is a military object

[53] NWP 1.14M, para. 8.2. [54] See UK Statement.

[55] For an explanation of the four criteria, see ICRC Commentary, paras 2020–2024.

16.03 and may be attacked as soon as the intent of the enemy to so use it becomes clear. In Gaza, tunnels are regularly built to smuggle in civilian supplies and/or military armament such as rockets. As soon as reliable intelligence exists that a tunnel being built, or one presently employed only for civilian smuggling, will be used to arm organized armed groups in Gaza, it becomes a military objective that may be attacked subject to the proportionality rule and the requirement to take precautions in attack (a tunnel built solely for military purposes, such as those from Gaza into Israel, is a military objective by nature). It must be cautioned that mere speculation that a civilian object will be converted to military use is insufficient to qualify it as a military objective. Rather, there must be a reasonable degree of certainty, typically based on reliable intelligence, that it is in fact going to be converted.

9. Finally, the 'use' criterion refers to an object's present function. Through use by the enemy, an object that is civilian may become a military objective, as in the case of a civilian apartment building used to billet troops or residences that serve as command centres or in which arms are stored. Despite the fact that they are meant for civilian purposes, religious sites, schools, and hospitals are now often used by insurgent forces for weapons and ammunition storage or as sites from which to conduct attacks. Such use renders them subject to lawful targeting.

10. Some objects are used for both military and civilian purposes. These 'dual use' facilities, such as an airfield employed for military and civilian flights, qualify fully as military objectives. Their civilian aspects are considered during proportionality calculations (see Section 16.06). This application of the rules governing qualification of objects as military objectives is particularly important in the cyber context because of the extensive use by both civilians and the military of certain cyber infrastructure.

11. Should doubt exist as to whether an object normally dedicated to civilian purposes is a military objective through use, it is to be presumed to be so used; the object may only be attacked if, based on all the readily available information, a reasonable attacker would conclude that it is being used militarily.[56] The key is that the object in question be normally dedicated to civilian use, that is, not be used for military purposes with any regularity. Consider railroad container cars. While primarily used for civilian purposes, they also regularly transport military equipment and troops. The strict presumption of civilian character does not apply to them. Instead, as with other objects, an attacker would assess the surrounding circumstances to determine whether it was more or less likely that the container cars in question were carrying, or were designated to carry, military supplies, equipment, or troops. Similarly, the frequent use of abandoned residences, as distinct from occupied ones, in Afghanistan as production factories for homemade explosives relieves an attacker of any obligation to apply a rebuttable presumption of civilian status. However, it does not relieve that attacker of the requirement to reasonably

[56] Art. 52(3) AP I.

conclude in the circumstances that the abandoned residence is being used militarily before attacking it. For example, insurgents frequently change locations to avoid detection by Coalition and Afghan forces. This is one key fact that an attacker must consider before attacking such buildings. **16.03**

12. This rebuttable presumption does not preclude attack in the face of any doubt, for combat is replete with doubt. Instead, the presumption merely implies that when evaluating doubt to determine whether it is reasonable in the circumstances to attack, the fact that the object is normally used for civilian purposes must be taken into consideration.

Indiscriminate attacks are prohibited. Indiscriminate attacks are those which are not directed at a specific military objective, employ a method or means of combat which cannot be directed at a specific military objective, or employ a method or means of combat the effects of which cannot be limited as required by international humanitarian law, and consequently are of a nature to strike military objectives and civilians or civilian objects without distinction. **16.04**

1. Derived from the general principle of distinction, the prohibition on indiscriminate attacks, codified in Article 51(4) of Additional Protocol I, reflects customary international humanitarian law in both international and non-international armed conflict.[57] Whether an attack is indiscriminate typically depends on the specific circumstances attendant to the attacks. However, the essence of the prohibition is that an indiscriminate attack is one in which the attacker either does not, or cannot, adequately distinguish combatants or military objects from civilians or civilian objects; this may occur because the weapon employed is indiscriminate or because a discriminate weapon is being used in an indiscriminate fashion. The rule sets forth three situations that constitute indiscriminate attacks.

2. The first form of indiscriminate attack involves one during which the attacker makes no effort to distinguish lawful targets from civilian objects or civilians. The weapon used can be aimed, but is not; a discriminate weapon is being used indiscriminately. For instance, insurgent forces may operate from an urban area. This fact does not justify blindly shelling or bombing the area without making an effort to aim at military objectives. The use of SCUD missiles by Iraqi forces during the First Gulf Conflict in 1990–1 exemplifies violation of the prohibition as does the use of rockets by Hamas and Hezbollah against Israel. Although capable of being directed against certain military objectives, such as Coalition tanks or troops in the uninhabited areas of Iraq, the weapons were indiscriminately fired into population centres.

[57] CIHL, Rules 11, 12, and 71; CCW Protocol II, Art. 3(3); CCW Protocol II Amended, Art. 3(8); NIAC Manual, paras 2.1.1.3, 2.2.1.1; NWP 1-14M, paras 5.3.2, 9.1.2.

16.04 3. The second type of indiscriminate attack involves use of a weapon (means of warfare) or tactic (method of warfare) that is incapable of distinguishing lawful targets from those that are not. With regard to weapons, this implies that the weapon is by nature incapable of being directed against a military objective; in other words, it cannot be aimed reliably and, as a result, is as likely to hit civilians and civilian objects as combatants and military objectives. The paradigmatic historical example is the Japanese use of balloon-borne bombs against the United States and Canada during World War II. The weapons were entirely dependent on the flow of air currents, thereby rendering them uncontrollable. Similarly, the aiming mechanism on the German V-2 rocket in World War II was so inaccurate that any attempt to use it to attack a particular military objective, including large objectives such as military installations, would likely fail; successful attack was essentially the product of luck. To some extent, the prohibition continually evolves over time in that advances in guidance technology affect expectations as to the sufficiency of a weapon's ability to be aimed. For example, the increasingly accurate targeting capabilities of armed unmanned weapon systems (so-called drones), as well as their contribution to increasingly accurate attacks by manned aircraft, will continue to raise expectations regarding the requisite precision of attacks. Similarly, there is presently much discussion in the humanitarian law community as to whether the tactic of returning artillery or mortar fire into heavily populated areas violates the prohibition on indiscriminate tactics.

4. Not only does the prohibition prohibit weapons that cannot be aimed, but it also disallows weapons and tactics that have uncontrollable effects likely to harm the civilian population or civilian objects. This third form of indiscriminate attack involves using a weapon or tactic that can be directed at a military objective, but which has effects that cannot be adequately limited. For example, setting fires in order to block the enemy's advance or deprive its forces of cover would be indiscriminate if the terrain, wind conditions, or the dryness would make it difficult to keep the blaze from spreading uncontrollably into populated areas. In the contemporary context, certain computer viruses and other malware designed to spread randomly throughout networks might violate the norm. Consider a virus developed to exploit a particular vulnerability in a military cyber system. If such systems are networked with civilian cyber infrastructure, and the virus is likely to spread into those systems and cause injury or damage, the malware violates the prohibition on weapons with indiscriminate effects.

16.05 **Attacks that treat as a single military objective a number of clearly separated and distinct military objectives located in a city, town, village, or other area containing a similar concentration of civilians or civilian objects are prohibited.**

1. Section 16.05 is based on Article 51(5 lit. a) of AP I, and constitutes a restatement of a customary international humanitarian law norm applicable in

MICHAEL N. SCHMITT

both international and non-international armed conflict.[58] It is designed to address situations in which multiple military objectives are collocated with civilians and civilian objectives. The rule depends on the attacker's capability to strike those targets separately, an ability determined by such factors as the nature of the commingling, weapons capabilities, and the accuracy of intelligence and other information. If an attacker is capable of mounting separate attacks, it must do so, as long as militarily feasible. 16.05

2. It should be noted that this prohibition does not necessarily bar so-called carpet-bombing and other area targeting methods. Such tactics are not prohibited when separate targeting is not feasible in the circumstances. Instead, area targeting would be permissible so long as other provisions of international humanitarian law, especially the rule of proportionality and requirement to take precautions in attack, are observed.

Ordering or executing an attack which may be expected to cause incidental loss of civilian life, injury to civilians, damage to civilian objects, or a combination thereof, which would be excessive in relation to the concrete and direct military advantage anticipated is prohibited. 16.06

1. The principle of proportionality is codified in Article 51(5 lit. b) of AP I. It is also found, in the context of precautions in attack (see Section 16.07), in Article 57(2). Although no explicit reference to the principle of proportionality is found in Additional Protocol II, it is widely viewed as customary international humanitarian law in both international and non-international armed conflict.[59]

2. In essence, the principle of proportionality is a recognition that harm to civilians (incidental injury) and civilian property (collateral damage) is often an unavoidable incident of attack on a military objective. Therefore, it is an explicit effort to achieve balance between the military necessity and humanitarian requirements.[60] However, proportionality does not require a strict mathematical comparison, nor does it, as is often mistakenly believed, call for a balancing test with the scales resting at equilibrium; rather, likely collateral damage only precludes attack when it is 'excessive'—that is, where there is a significant imbalance between the military advantage anticipated and the expected collateral damage. Civilians who directly participate in hostilities (see Section 16.02) are not factored into proportionality calculations; to the extent they lose immunity from attack, they obviously do not enjoy the lesser protection provided by the principle of proportionality.

[58] See also CIHL, Rule 13; CCW Protocol II Amended, Art. 3(9); NWP 1-14M, para. 5.3.2.

[59] CIHL, Rules 14, 19; CCW Protocol II, Art. 3(3)(c); CCW Protocol II Amended, Art. 3(8)(c); Hague Cultural Property Convention, Protocol II, Art. 7; Art. 8(2)(b)(iv) ICC Statute; NIAC Manual, para. 2.1.1.4; NWP 1-14M, para. 8.3.1.

[60] This balance was first articulated in the St Petersburg Declaration of 1868.

16.06 3. It is important to fully grasp each of the qualifiers found in the rule. Significantly, it does not envision hindsight examination of the incidental harm caused to civilians and civilian property, nor of the military advantage that resulted from an attack. Rather, the rule applies as of the time an attack is planned, approved, executed (depending on who has the ability to perform such functions), for the standard is one of 'expected' harm and 'anticipated' advantage. It is assessed by reference to a reasonable combatant in the same or similar circumstances. In other words, what degree of harm or advantage would a reasonable planner, commander, or combatant in the field have concluded was likely? This standard is objective in that the attacker will be charged with the knowledge that he should have possessed had he taken reasonable steps to make the assessment. It is subjective in that it is conducted in light of the information available at the time.[61] Although the precise degree of requisite expectation or anticipation cannot be quantified, a workable standard is that of more likely than not—that is, probable.

4. Equally essential in understanding proportionality is the term 'excessive'. It is sometimes mistakenly asserted that the rule prohibits severe losses or extensive damage.[62] It does not. Rather it is a relative standard that considers civilian harm vis-à-vis the military advantage accruing from the attack in question. Consider, for example, the targeting of Taliban leaders in Afghanistan. In many instances, attacks are launched at night while the targeted individual is in a residence, presumably sleeping; family members may also be present. For operational reasons, it is often not feasible to attack at other times or places. When considering whether to proceed, those deciding on the operation must first identify the anticipated military advantage of eliminating the individual based upon his prior actions and function in the organization. They then estimate the expected loss of civilian life or damage to civilian property. In some instances, the leader may not be of sufficient stature to merit any significant loss of civilian life and the operation will be prohibited as a matter of law. In others, the balance may weigh in favour of targeting the leader, even though civilian deaths will result. Thus, even slight harm may be prohibited when the anticipated military advantage is low, while great civilian harm may be justified in cases involving exceptional military advantage. The key is that an attack will be prohibited when there is no proportionality at all between expected harm to civilians and anticipated military advantage.

5. Military advantage that is 'concrete and direct' is that which is identifiable and clearly discernable. The advantage must be 'substantial and relatively close' and 'advantages which are hardly perceptible and those which would only appear in the long term should be disregarded'.[63] There is no requirement that the advantage be great; rather, the phrase is typically interpreted in the negative as excluding advantage that is purely speculative.

[61] See UK Statement. [62] ICRC Commentary, para. 2218.
[63] ICRC Commentary, para. 2209.

6. The civilian harm that must be considered when performing proportionality calculations includes both the direct and indirect effects of an attack. Direct effects are those resulting during the attack itself; in the case of a bomb, for instance, direct effects are those caused directly by the blast and fragmentation of the weapon. Indirect effects include those with a causal link to the attack, but which are not immediately caused by it. For instance, an attack on an electrical grid will disrupt activities reliant on its electricity. Any damage or injury to civilian objects or civilians that results from shutting them down must be considered when doing the respective proportionality calculation. Only indirect effects that an attacker was, or should reasonably have been, aware of are relevant in assessing whether an attack complied with the principle of proportionality. The key is foreseeability. **16.06**

7. As discussed earlier (see Section 16.03), proportionality is evaluated in the context of the operation as a whole, not vis-à-vis individual aspects thereof.[64] The example of a ruse attack in which the relevant military advantage derives from the ruse's success rather than destruction of the military objective attacked was cited to illustrate the point. It should be noted, however, that the advantage to be considered when assessing proportionality does not extend to the entire conflict. In other words, there must be some nexus between the attack and the advantage that is to be factored into the proportionality calculation. An attack may not be justified on the grounds that the harm to civilians and civilian property was 'not excessive' relative to the ultimate war aims.

8. There are several points of controversy surrounding specific application of the rule. First, experts are divided over whether civilians who are voluntarily within a military objective count as such when conducting proportionality calculations. An example would include civilians within a military installation and workers in a munitions factory.[65] The majority opinion is that such individuals count fully as civilian incidental injury when assessing whether harm to civilians is excessive relative to the military advantage likely to result from the attack.

9. A second point of contention involves human shields (see Section 16.02). As discussed, the effect of human shielding on proportionality calculations depends on whether the shields are acting voluntarily or being forced to shield a military objective. As to the former, many experts believe voluntary shielding constitutes direct participation in hostilities, such that the shields do not count in any proportionality calculations. Others argue that voluntary human shields, so long as they are not physically impeding an attack (e.g. blocking a bridge over which troops are to pass), retain the protection of civilian status, which includes that provided by the principle of proportionality. As to involuntary shields, there is near universal consensus that they retain their civilian immunity from attack and, therefore, any injury to them is a factor in proportionality analysis.

[64] This is the standard adopted in Art. 8(2)(b)(iv) ICC Statute.
[65] Dinstein, *Conduct of Hostilities*, 136–7.

16.06 It should be noted that Article 51(8) of AP I provides that a violation of, *inter alia*, the prohibition on human shielding 'shall not release Parties to a conflict from their legal obligations with respect to the civilian population and civilians'. However, some experts suggest that the enemy's violation of international humanitarian law must nevertheless be taken into account when doing the proportionality assessment, such that greater harm to civilians is necessary before an attack will be deemed excessive than would be the case if the enemy had acted lawfully.[66]

16.07 **Constant care is required to spare the civilian population, civilians, and civilian objects. All feasible precautions must be taken to avoid, and in any event to minimize, incidental injury to civilians or collateral damage to civilian objects. In particular, an attacker must do everything feasible to confirm that targets are in fact military objectives and to assess the proportionality of a planned attack. When the available options yield a similar military advantage, methods and means of warfare, as well as targets, must be selected with a view to minimizing incidental injury to civilians and collateral damage to civilian objects.**

1. The requirement to take precautions in attack in order to minimize harm to civilians is codified in Article 57 of AP I.[67] It reflects customary international law applicable in international armed conflict.[68] Particular care must be taken when attacking works and installations containing dangerous forces, namely dams, dykes, and nuclear electrical generating stations.[69] As to non-international armed conflict, the ICRC's Customary International Humanitarian Law study notes that while most of the text set forth in Section 16.07 is customary law, that relating to selection of targets only 'arguably' rises to the customary level.[70]

2. The concept of feasibility lies at the heart of the precautions in attack requirement. 'Feasible' means that which is practicable or practically possible, taking into account all circumstances prevailing at the time, including humanitarian and military considerations.[71] In other words, it is a contextual determination. Factors which determine feasibility include, for instance, the availability of weapon systems and sensors, the placement of the military objective relative to civilians and civilian property, enemy defences, available countermeasures to enemy defences, weather, time of day, and force protection. Moreover, feasibility is temporally contextual in

66 See discussion in Schmitt, 'Human Shields', 323–33.

67 See also CCW Protocol II Amended, Art. 3(10); Hague Cultural Property Convention, Protocol II, Arts 6, 7.

68 CIHL, Rules 15, 16, 17, 18, and 21.

69 Ibid. Rule 42.

70 Ibid. Vol. I, 65.

71 See Declarations made by States at the time of ratification, in Roberts and Guelff, *Documents* 498–512. See also CCW Protocol II Amended, Art. 3(10).

that it is judged by the circumstances at the time the attack was decided upon and executed. Ultimately, feasibility is a 'matter of common sense and good faith'.[72] 16.07

3. The requirement to take feasible precautions in attack includes efforts to verify the target and to assess the likely incidental harm to civilians. An attacker must similarly take feasible precautions to determine whether the target benefits from special protection under international humanitarian law, as would be the case, for instance, with a hospital or cultural property. Requisite measures include timely collection, analysis, and dissemination of intelligence to those planning, approving, and executing attacks. Intelligence, surveillance, and reconnaissance assets must be employed to the extent necessary and militarily feasible in the circumstances. As an example, when a reconnaissance drone can contribute to the verification of a target, one must be used if available. However, the feasibility of its use will depend on factors such as present competing demands for the system's use and target area threats to the system from air defences considered in light of future probable uses.

4. The intent of the requirement is to provide sufficient information to permit an attack to be conducted with reasonable certainty that the target is a military objective and that the attack will comply with the principle of proportionality. The requirement varies depending on the stage of the attack. For instance, processed intelligence may be available to an air attack planner, but not to the aircrew executing an attack. Similarly, the aircrew may be able to visually identify a target and identify potential collateral damage, while the planner could not. Thus, the extent and nature of the verification requirement varies depending on the role of the individual concerned. Each individual must do whatever is feasible. Finally, the timeliness requirements regarding a potential attack are relevant. Greater efforts to verify a target and determine potential collateral damage and incidental injury may be called for in a pre-planned attack against a fixed target, than during a time sensitive attack against a valuable fleeting target.

5. In addition to measures of verification, an attacker must consider militarily feasible weapons (means) and tactics (methods) options. Use of a precision weapon may be required if likely to result in less harm to civilians or civilian property than an unguided weapon, assuming, of course, that the attacker possesses such precision weapons and their use in the circumstances makes sense from a military perspective (for instance, the commander may wish to preserve them for later urban operations where the risk to civilians will be higher). If not, the attack may or may not be unlawful depending upon the criteria of proportionality, but in any case, all the considerations laid out previously relating to precautions, indiscriminate attack, and proportionality will apply just as they would for an attacker who did have access to precision weapons.

6. Similarly, attack planners must consider options regarding tactics, including both ground tactics and the manner in which a bomb is dropped during an air-to-ground

[72] ICRC Commentary, para. 2208.

16.07 attack, in an effort to minimize collateral damage and incidental injury. For example, techniques to mitigate the effects of a bomb include, among others, delay fuzing or 'bomb burial',[73] variable time fuzing or 'air burst',[74] delivery heading,[75] and aimpoint offset.[76] It must be understood that the viability of options is determined in the context of military feasibility. As an example, tactics that can minimize civilian harm sometimes so significantly increase the risk to an attacker that they are militarily impractical.

7. Beyond weapons and tactics choices, attackers must consider the full range of potential targets that can be struck to achieve their military aim. This is a particularly important requirement in light of the near universal understanding that contemporary targeting is typically designed to achieve particular effects (effects-based warfare), as distinct from simply destroying enemy forces (attrition warfare). By this aspect of the requirement to take precautions in attack rule, if striking a target other than the initially intended one would cause less collateral damage and incidental injury without sacrificing military advantage, that option must be selected. Consider an attack designed to disrupt electrical supply to an enemy command and control facility. Attacking the electrical generating station might effectively cut electricity to the facility, but would also likely disrupt civilian systems that also rely on the generating station, thereby risking harm to civilians and civilian objects. In such a case, it might be militarily feasible to attack a substation of the system, or even the electrical lines carrying electricity to the facility, rather than the electrical generating station itself. Along the same lines, an attack designed to disrupt rail traffic might risk fewer civilian casualties and less damage to civilian property if conducted against a bridge on the rail line rather than against the central railroad station. It must be remembered, though, that the military advantage attained must be similar. Thus, in the cases cited, the relative ability of the enemy to repair the targets would be a factor in assessing the options. The determination would depend on whether the military aim was merely to temporarily disrupt a function or to permanently destroy the enemy's capability. Equally

[73] Delay fuzing occurs when the fuze of a bomb is set, either manually or through electronic fuses, which allows pilots to make changes in-flight, to delay detonation until a short period after a bomb hits in order to mitigate the effects of bomb blast or fragments. For instance, a bomb can be delayed several milliseconds until it has pierced the roof of a building so that the effects of the explosion are generally contained within the building.

[74] Variable time fuzing, or air burst, occurs when a fuze is set to detonate a short period of time before the bomb hits its target. For example, if combatants are using the roof of an apartment building, a variable time fuze could be used to detonate the bomb before it penetrated the roof of the apartment building, thereby still having the desired effect on the combatants while minimizing potential harm to civilians inside the apartment building.

[75] Dropping a bomb using a particular delivery heading can mitigate collateral damage effects by influencing the direction of the blast, weapons fragments, and debris. Delivery angle can therefore serve to direct effects away from vulnerable civilians and civilian objects.

[76] In aimpoint offset the desired point of detonation is offset from the centre of the target to alter the area encompassed in the blast or fragmentation radius. For instance, offsetting the point of detonation a few feet the centre of the military objective, it may be possible to minimize collateral damage to nearby residences, while still achieving the desired effect of the attack.

relevant is the military feasibility of an attack. An attacker need not target a heavily defended alternative military objective merely because the attack would minimize collateral damage and incidental injury. 16.07

Persons performing certain functions enjoy special protection under international humanitarian law. Medical, religious, civil defence, and humanitarian relief personnel may not be attacked unless they commit, outside their humanitarian functions, acts harmful to the enemy. Civilian journalists performing professional functions may not be attacked unless they directly participate in hostilities. Forces participating in a UN mission may not be attacked so long as they are entitled to protection, in the circumstances, as civilians. **16.08**

1. International humanitarian law singles out certain persons for special protection because of either the humanitarian functions they perform or because they are particularly liable to be harmed. Technically, they enjoy no greater protection than ordinary civilians, who enjoy immunity from attack and benefit from the requirement to take feasible precautions in attack and the principle of proportionality. Thus, Section 16.08 serves primarily to highlight the fact that they also enjoy protection and emphasize the need to take care to avoid harming them. When such persons take a direct part in hostilities, they lose the protection from attack—just as ordinary civilians do. Similarly, it is lawful to conduct an attack against a military objective even if these protected persons will be harmed, so long as the attack has complied with the requirement to take feasible precautions in attack and is proportional.

2. The obligation to respect and protect military medical personnel is based on Articles 24–26 of the First Geneva Convention of 1949 and Article 36 of the Second Convention. The protection is extended to civilian medical and religious personnel in Article 15 of AP I. Such provisions reflect customary international humanitarian law in both international and non-international armed conflict.[77]

3. The term medical personnel includes not only individuals directly involved in providing care to the sick and wounded, but also personnel tasked with searching for, collecting, and transporting them, as well as those involved in the administration of medical units. They may be military or civilian medical personnel of a party to the conflict; medical personnel of National Red Cross or Red Crescent Societies and other voluntary aid societies recognized by a party to the conflict, including the ICRC; medical personnel made available for humanitarian purposes by a neutral or other State which is not a party to the conflict (or recognized aid society of such a State); or medical personnel provided by an impartial humanitarian organization.[78] While those permanently assigned to such duties enjoy the protection at all times,

[77] CIHL, Rules 25 and 27; NIAC Manual, para. 3.2.
[78] Art. 8(c) AP I.

16.08 individuals temporarily assigned to medical tasks benefit from the protections only for such time as they are so engaged. Religious personnel are those individuals engaged in a religious ministry, whether assigned permanently or temporarily to such duties. Individuals who are not assigned to medical or religious duties are not protected by the rule even if acting in that capacity. For instance, soldiers who provide immediate medical care on the battlefield to wounded comrades do not qualify as medical personnel.[79]

4. Civil defence personnel are likewise protected. The concept of civil defence personnel includes both those who are actually members of civil defence organizations, and members of the armed forces and military units who are assigned to civil defence organizations. Such protection, set forth in Articles 62 and 67 of AP I, is generally deemed customary international humanitarian law. Although no specific treaty protection exists for such personnel in non-international armed conflict, those that are civilians would nevertheless be entitled to full protections to which civilians are entitled.

5. While civilian organizations that perform such functions need not be solely dedicated to civil defence (and thus enjoy the special protection only while they perform the functions), military forces enjoy the protection only if they are permanently and exclusively tasked with civil defence duties. They are prohibited from performing any military functions.

6. Humanitarian relief personnel are protected pursuant to Article 71(2) of AP I. However, it is generally agreed that such personnel enjoy protection as a matter of customary international humanitarian law in both international and non-international armed conflict.[80] Humanitarian relief personnel may perform the functions on behalf of a party to the conflict, a national relief society, a neutral State, a non-governmental organization, or an international organization. Whatever their affiliation, they are entitled to protection while providing humanitarian assistance. Military personnel of a party to the conflict performing humanitarian relief activities do not qualify as humanitarian relief personnel and are subject to attack as combatants. It should be noted that the humanitarian mission may be conditioned on the consent of the party on whose territory the activities occur and compliance with technical arrangements, such as the route and schedule of delivery. Violation of the conditions will deprive the mission of its special protection, although any civilians performing it would continue to benefit from civilian protections so long as they did nothing that would amount to direct participation in hostilities.

7. Article 79 of AP I extends special protection to journalists. The protection is generally deemed applicable in both international and non-international armed

[79] Depending on the circumstances, they might qualify as auxiliary medical personnel pursuant to Art. 25 GC I, and would therefore be protected from attack whilst performing medical duties.
[80] CIHL, Rule 31; NIAC Manual, para. 3.3.

conflict.[81] It includes periods when the journalists are accompanying military units, although, like civilians, they risk being harmed incidentally during attacks on military objectives. 16.08

8. UN personnel engaged in a peacekeeping or humanitarian relief mission are entitled to special protection as civilians, even though they may be members of a military, so long as the Force does not become a party to the conflict and the individuals concerned refrain from directly participating in hostilities.[82] This protection, codified for States parties in the 1994 United Nations Convention on the Safety of UN and Associated Personnel, extends to military forces, police units, and UN civilian organizations, as well as to officials of, and experts on mission for, the United Nations. Should the UN Force become a party to the conflict, its military personnel would become combatants.[83] However, should individual members of the Force or specific units thereof directly participate in hostilities the remainder of the Force would continue to enjoy protection as civilians. Further, acts of individual or unit self-defence, including self-defence in the performance of their mandate, in the face of unlawful attacks would not deprive them of protected status.[84]

Certain objects and facilities enjoy special protection under international humanitarian law. They may not be attacked unless they become military objectives. These include medical facilities and units; areas specially established as civilian protective zones and for the care of wounded and sick; humanitarian relief facilities, supplies, and transports; peacekeeping equipment and facilities; cultural property; works and installations containing dangerous forces, such as dams, dykes, and nuclear electrical generating stations; the natural environment; and objects indispensable to the survival of the civilian population. Designated protective emblems are used to make certain of these objects and facilities. 16.09

1. International humanitarian law singles out certain objects and facilities for special protection either because of the humanitarian functions they perform or because an attack on them would prove especially harmful to the civilian population.[85] Generally, they enjoy no greater protection than ordinary civilian objects, which enjoy immunity from attack and benefit from the requirement to take feasible precautions in attack and the principle of proportionality. Thus, Section 16.09 serves primarily to highlight the fact that they also enjoy such protection and emphasize the need to take care not to damage or destroy them.

[81] CIHL, Rule 34; NIAC Manual, para. 3.10.

[82] CIHL, Rule 33, NIAC Manual, para. 3.3.

[83] 1994 UN Safety Convention, Art. 2.

[84] See Section 6.08 and Chapter 24 'Force Protection, Unit Self-Defence, and Personal Self-Defence: Their Relationship to Rules of Engagement'.

[85] CIHL, Rules 28, 29, 30, 32, 33, 35, 38, 39, 42–45, 54, and 55.

16.09 Should such objects or facilities be used for military purposes, they would lose their protection from attack during the period of such use.

2. While the enumerated objects are entitled to special protection, special protective regimes, that is, particular rules addressing their protection, exist as to a number of them.

3. The requirement to protect and respect medical units appears in multiple provisions of the 1949 Geneva Conventions and Additional Protocol I. They extend to fixed and mobile medical units,[86] civilian hospitals,[87] and medical transports for the sick and wounded on land, at sea, and in the air.[88] Treaty-based protection for such objects extends to non-international armed conflict.[89] The provisions generally reflect customary international humanitarian law in both international and non-international armed conflict.[90] For a discussion of the rules governing attacks on medical aircraft, see Sections 19.18 and 19.19.

4. The parties to a conflict may establish special zones designed as sanctuary for civilians or for the sick and wounded.[91] Such protected zones have been established in a number of international and non-international armed conflicts. Agreement between the parties to the conflict is necessary for the creation of such zones, which may be established on land or at sea, as well as in the airspace above them. Generally, they are demilitarized, that is, no combatants, weapons, military equipment, or military installations may be present, no hostile actions may emanate from the zone, and all military activities within the zone must have ceased. Should these conditions be breached, the zone loses its special protection, although persons and objects otherwise entitled to protection, such as civilians and civilian objects, retain their protection under international humanitarian law.

5. Humanitarian relief facilities, supplies, and transports are civilian objects entitled to protection as such. Their special protection derives from the obligation to allow and facilitate humanitarian aid codified in Articles 55 and 59 of the Fourth Geneva Convention, Articles 69 and 70 of AP I, Article 18(2) of AP II, and customary international humanitarian law applicable in both international and non-international armed conflict.[92] Military equipment and facilities used for such purposes are nevertheless military objectives; the humanitarian items therein would be considered civilian objects factored into proportionality calculations.

6. As with peacekeepers themselves (see Section 16.01), the equipment and facilities they employ are entitled to special protection. In this regard, Article 7 of the 1994 Convention on the Safety of United Nations and Associated Personnel, which provides that such equipment and premises 'shall not be the object of attack', is of

[86] Art. 19 GC I; Art. 12(1) AP I. [87] Art. 18 GC IV; Art. 12(2) AP I.
[88] Art. 35 GC I; Art. 21 GC IV; Arts 21, 22, 24 AP I. [89] Art. 11(1) AP II.
[90] CIHL, Rules 28 and 29; NIAC Manual, para. 4.2.1.
[91] See Art. 23 GC I; Arts 14 and 15 GC IV; Art. 60 AP I; CIHL, chapter 11.
[92] CIHL, chapter 8; NIAC Manual, para. 5.1.

particular relevance. Should the forces become combatants or should individual peacekeepers or units directly participate in hostilities, their associated equipment and facilities would lose protection from attack. **16.09**

7. Cultural property is the subject of the 1954 Cultural Property Convention and its 1999 Second Protocol. Article 53 of AP I and Article 16 of AP II also protect it. Certain of the protections are customary international humanitarian law in both international and non-international armed conflicts.[93] However, the regime is complex, and particular reference must be made to the applicable treaty provisions to fully grasp the nature and limits of the attendant protections.

8. As a general matter, parties to a conflict may not use cultural property or its immediate surroundings for military purposes except in cases of imperative military necessity. Cultural property must be marked with the internationally recognized distinctive emblem identifying it as such. Should imperative military necessity require its use, the emblem must be removed. Further, the enemy should be notified of the location of cultural property. Failure to appropriately mark cultural property or notify the enemy of its location does not deprive it of its special protection when identified as such. Every effort should be made to avoid locating military objectives near cultural property and movable cultural property should be removed from the vicinity of military objectives.[94] Cultural property, like other civilian objects, may not be made the subject of attack and an attacker must take feasible precautions in attack to avoid damaging it. Should cultural property become a military objective through use, the decision to attack it should be taken by a high echelon of command.

9. Articles 35(3) and 55 of AP I, the 1977 Environmental Modification Convention, and Article 2(4) of Protocol III to the 1980 Conventional Weapons Convention provide special protection to the natural environment. No consensus exists as to the definition of 'natural environment'. However, it is agreed that it does not extend to man-made components of the environment and always extends to natural ecosystems. Similarly, no consensus exists regarding the threshold of prohibited harm set forth in Articles 35(3) and 55 of AP I as 'widespread, long-term and severe damage'.[95]

10. It is agreed that the natural environment comprises a civilian object in the context of international humanitarian law.[96] Thus, the environment as such may

[93] CIHL, chapter 12; NIAC Manual, para. 4.2.2.

[94] In a paradigmatic example, Saddam Hussein violated this principle during the Persian Gulf War of 1991 when he deliberately located several MiG fighter jets near the Ziggurat of Ur, a 4,000-year-old cultural site.

[95] The United States opposed these AP I provisions. For a discussion of US opposition, see M. Matheson, 'The United States Position on the Relation of Customary International Law to the 1977 Protocols Additional to the 1949 Geneva Conventions', 2 *American University Journal of International Law and Policy* (1987), 419.

[96] CIHL, Rules 43–45; NIAC Manual, para. 4.2.4.

16.09 not be attacked unless it has become a military objective (e.g. through location); feasible precautions must be taken to avoid harming the environment during an attack, and an attack's impact on the environment must be considered when performing proportionality calculations.

11. Works and installations containing dangerous forces which, if released, would place the civilian population at particular risk of severe losses are subject to special safeguards pursuant to Article 56 of AP I for States parties. The Article applies to dams, dykes, and nuclear electrical generating stations. The provisions set forth in Article 56 do not reflect customary international humanitarian law.[97] Nevertheless, it is generally agreed that in both international and non-international armed conflict special care must be taken when attacking such facilities because of the risks they pose to the civilian population.[98]

12. The obligation to grant protection to objects indispensable to the survival of the civilian population is found for States parties in Article 54 of AP I and Article 14 of AP II. It is generally customary international humanitarian law in both international and non-international armed conflict.[99] It prohibits intentional starvation of the civilian population as a method of warfare. Starvation includes not only the deprivation of food, but also drinking water or other essential supplies. The prohibition does not ban lawful methods of warfare—such as siege warfare, blockade, or embargoes—that have a military purpose, but which incidentally cause the civilian population to be deprived of such goods. Rather, such methods would be governed by the principle of proportionality and the general requirement to allow humanitarian relief to the civilian population.

13. The specific prohibition set forth in Section 16.09 applies to attacking, destroying, removing, or rendering useless objects that are indispensable to the civilian population's survival for the specific purpose of denying the population their use. Examples include food supplies, agricultural areas, livestock, drinking water facilities, irrigation works and, in adverse conditions, shelter and clothing. The prohibition does not apply when deprivation of the items is merely incidental to lawful military purposes. It is also inapplicable to such objects when they are used by the enemy as sustenance solely for members of its armed forces or, if not used as sustenance, in direct support of military operations, as when an agricultural area is being used by the enemy for cover. In the latter case, no action expected to result in the starvation of the civilian population or force its movement away from the area can be taken against such objects.

16.10 **Combatants who are *hors de combat* because they have surrendered, are prisoners, or are wounded or shipwrecked may not be attacked.**

[97] See Matheson, 'The United States Position', 419.
[98] CIHL, Rule 42; NIAC Manual, para. 4.2.3.
[99] CIHL, Rule 54; NIAC Manual, para. 2.3.10 (starvation).

Persons parachuting from an aircraft in distress may not be attacked during their descent and must be afforded an opportunity to surrender upon landing. Parlementaires may not be attacked while performing their functions. **16.10**

1. The provision prohibiting attacks on those who are *hors de combat* derives from Article 23(c) of the 1907 Hague Regulations, Common Article 3 to the 1949 Geneva Conventions, and Articles 40 and 41 of AP I. In non-international armed conflict, Article 4(1) of AP II prohibits attacks on persons 'who have ceased to take a direct part in hostilities'. Common Article 3 also applies in such conflicts. The prohibition in Section 16.10 reflects customary international humanitarian law applicable in both international and non-international armed conflict.[100]

2. This provision reflects the traditional prohibition on ordering that no quarter be given to the enemy, that is, that survivors not be taken.[101] Both combatants and those who directly participate in hostilities are protected by this rule. The first category of persons *hors de combat* consists of those who have surrendered. Surrender is effective when the intent to surrender is communicated in a clear manner to the enemy, the individual surrendering is taking no further hostile actions, and no attempt is made to evade capture.[102] Merely being defenceless in the face of the enemy does not constitute surrender. For instance, even an unarmed combatant can be attacked until he or she surrenders.

3. A person is *hors de combat* if as a result of wounds or sickness he is no longer able to continue to fight. Merely being wounded is insufficient, for many wounded combatants can and do continue fighting. The key, therefore, is that the individual concerned be unconscious or otherwise incapacitated. The incapacitation does not have to result from hostile action. Combatants who are ill may also be incapacitated.

4. Shipwrecked individuals who are not fighting must be afforded the opportunity of rescue to the extent militarily and practically feasible. In any event, they may not be attacked unless they engage in hostile action while shipwrecked or otherwise evidence an intention to harm the enemy. Combatants who are shipwrecked as a result of a crash of an aircraft or after bailing out of a damaged aircraft at sea are encompassed by the rule.

5. A person descending from a disabled aircraft, whether over land or at sea, is treated in the same fashion as one who is *hors de combat.*[103] Upon landing, he must be afforded an opportunity to surrender. Should he not do so, he is subject to attack. This prohibition covers both the crew of the aircraft and passengers, although airborne troops are not included. Of course, if airborne troops evidence

[100] CIHL, chapter 15; NIAC Manual, paras 2.3.1, 2.3.2, and 2.3.3; NWP 1-14M, para. 6.2.6.
[101] Art. 23(d) HR.
[102] See e.g. UK Ministry of Defence, *The Manual on the Law of Armed Conflict* (Oxford: Oxford University Press, 2004), para. 5.6.
[103] Art. 42 AP I; NWP 1-14M, para. 8.2.3.1.; CIHL, Rule 48.

61.10 an intention to surrender and comply with the other criteria for effective surrender, they are *hors de combat*.

6. Parlementaires are individuals designated to negotiate with the enemy over such matters as surrender, cease-fire, and casualty collection. Pursuant to Article 32 of the 1907 Hague Regulations, they may not be attacked.

16.11 **Perfidious attacks are prohibited. In a perfidious attack, the attacker feigns protected status in order to kill, injure, or capture the enemy. Examples include feigning: an intent to negotiate under a flag of truce or of surrender; incapacitation by wounds or sickness; civilian, non-combatant status; or protected status by the use of signs, emblems, or uniforms of the United Nations or of neutral or other States not parties to the conflict.**

1. The concept of perfidy is based in traditional international humanitarian law prohibitions on treachery, notably those found in Articles 23(b) and 34 of the 1907 Hague Regulations. The term 'perfidy' was introduced in Article 37 of AP I. It is a customary IHL norm in both international and non-international armed conflict.[104]

2. Perfidy comprises killing or injuring the enemy through the use of acts that invite its forces to conclude that the attacker is entitled to protection under international humanitarian law, with the intent to betray that conclusion. The classic example is a false surrender that causes the enemy to come forward to accept said surrender only to be fired on; other examples are set forth in Section 16.11. Perfidy must be distinguished from ruses, which are lawful acts of deception not involving protected status.[105] For instance, camouflaging military equipment or transmitting false military signals are lawful ruses.

3. It is essential to note that Section 16.11 mirrors Article 37 of AP I in that it includes capture as one of the purposes that can underpin perfidy. States party to the Protocol are unquestionably prohibited from feigning protected status in order to capture the enemy whenever involved in a conflict to which AP I applies. Whether the capture provision reflects customary international law is a controversial question. While Rule 65 of the Study on Customary International Humanitarian Law[106] includes capture as a purpose, capture did not appear in Article 23(b) of the 1907 Hague Regulations, nor was it included in Article 8(2)(b)(xi) of the ICC Statute.[107]

4. For perfidy to occur there must be intent to mislead in order to kill or wound. As an example, whereas it is not perfidious to fight in civilian clothing, wearing civilian

[104] CIHL, Rule 65; NWP 1-14M, para. 12.1.2; NIAC Manual, para. 2.3.6.
[105] Art. 24 HR; Art. 37(2) AP I; CIHL, Rule 57. [106] CIHL, Rule 65.
[107] Both instruments deal with the notion of 'treachery', which includes, but is somewhat broader than, the act of feigning protected status.

clothes in order to get close enough to the enemy to effectively mount an attack would be perfidious and violate the norm. 16.11

5. International humanitarian law sets forth numerous other prohibitions on deception that require no perfidious intent. For instance, it is prohibited to improperly use the Red Cross, Red Crescent, or Red Crystal, or other distinctive emblems, signs, or signals provided for in IHL;[108] misuse the flag of truce;[109] use the distinctive emblem of the United Nations except when authorized by the organization;[110] use flags or military emblems, insignia, or uniforms of neutrals;[111] or use the flags or military emblems, insignia, or uniforms of the enemy in combat operations.[112] If such unlawful use occurs in an effort to kill or wound the enemy, the conduct would also violate the prohibition on perfidy. Note that unlike land and aerial warfare, naval warfare permits the use of false flags or military emblems.[113]

An attack involving use of means and methods of warfare which are of a nature to cause superfluous injury or unnecessary suffering or which are by nature indiscriminate is prohibited. 16.12

1. The prohibition on weapons that cause superfluous injury or unnecessary suffering stretches back to the 1868 St Petersburg Declaration's prohibition on arms that 'uselessly aggravate the suffering of disabled men, or render their death inevitable'. In 1899, the Hague Regulations, in Article 23(e), prohibited weapons causing 'superfluous injury'. Its 1907 counterpart, in the non-binding English translation, referenced 'unnecessary suffering'. Article 35(2) of AP I combined the two phrases in 'superfluous suffering or unnecessary suffering', the format adopted in Section 16.12 and by the Customary International Humanitarian Law Study in Rule 70.[114] Article 35 also expands the prohibition beyond means of warfare (weapons) to methods of warfare.[115] The principle was recognized by the International Court of Justice as one of two 'cardinal principles' of international humanitarian law in its 1996 Advisory Opinion on *Legality of the Threat or Use of*

[108] Art. 23(f) HR; Art. 38(1) AP I; CIHL, Rules 59 and 61; NIAC Manual, para. 2.3.4; NWP 1-1-4M, para. 8.5.1.6.

[109] Art. 23(f) HR; Art. 38(1) AP I; CIHL, Rule 58; NIAC Manual, para. 2.3.3.

[110] Art. 38(2) AP I; CIHL, Rule 60; NIAC Manual, para. 2.3.4.

[111] Art 39(1) AP I; CIHLS, Rule 63; NWP 1-14M, para. 12.3.2.

[112] Art. 39(2) AP I; Art. 23(f) HR; CIHL, Rule 62; NWP 1-14M, para. 12.5. Note that AP I extends the prohibition to acts designed to shield, favour, protect, or impede military operations. This provision is not deemed reflective of customary IHL. Therefore, the text of Section 16.11 is limited to the generally accepted restrictions on such use during combat.

[113] Art. 39(3) AP I; NWP 1-14M, para. 12.5.1.

[114] The same format was adopted in the Preamble to the 1980 Convention on Conventional Weapons.

[115] An example would be conducting hostilities on the basis that there would be no survivors, as otherwise prohibited in Art. 40 AP I.

16.12 *Nuclear Weapons.*[116] It constitutes customary international humanitarian law in both international and non-international armed conflict.[117]

2. Understanding the context of the prohibition is essential. It is one designed to protect combatants, not civilians, for civilians are already immune from attack; in other words, the superfluous injury and unnecessary suffering rule applies based on the presumption that an attack will occur against lawful targets. The underlying premise of the rule is that it is usually sufficient to attain one's military aims by rendering the enemy *hors de combat*.

3. The prohibition has been plagued by a debate—driven by various textual formulae in the early treaty law—over whether it applies to weapons that by nature cause such wounding or only to those designed to do so.[118] Section 16.12 adopts the former approach, tracking that of Additional Protocol I and other contemporary treaty formulations.[119] Thus, it is generally accepted that even if a weapon was not intended to cause such injuries, it will violate the prohibition if they are the result of its normal usage. It will unquestionably violate the prohibition if intended to cause superfluous injury or unnecessary suffering. As an example, modifying a weapon to exacerbate wounding is unlawful, as in the case of a bullet dipped in an irritant.

4. Although there is no agreed upon definition of unnecessary suffering and superfluous injury, the prohibition bars weapons that, when employed for their intended purpose, foreseeably cause injuries which serve no military purpose. Often, this will be a matter of the availability of other weapons that achieve an intended effect (military purpose) with less suffering. In this regard, two questions are critical: (1) are other less injurious weapons available, and (2) do those weapons effectively meet the intended military purpose? If so, the weapon is prohibited.

5. Unnecessary suffering and superfluous injury are not necessarily analogous to severe suffering. Depending on the circumstances, severe suffering may result from use of a necessary weapon (e.g. an incendiary weapon used against a chemical factory to ensure the chemicals do not spread). However, even light suffering may breach the standard (e.g. use of certain non-lethal riot control weapons when other less harmful non-lethal weapons might suffice). Superfluous injury and unnecessary suffering are presently interpreted as including both physical and psychological suffering.

6. Indiscriminate weapons are discussed in the commentary accompanying Section 16.04.

[116] Advisory Opinion on *Legality of the Threat or Use of Nuclear Weapons*, para. 78.
[117] CIHL, Rule 70; NIAC Manual, para. 2.2.1.3; NWP 1-14M, para. 9.1.1.
[118] For instance, the 1899 Hague Regulations employed the phrase 'of a nature to cause', whereas the 1907 variant used 'calculated to cause' (Art. 23(e) in both instruments).
[119] See CCW, Preamble; Art. 8(2)(b)(xx) ICC Statute.

The rules governing targeting apply to the employment of all weapons and weapon systems, including unmanned, autonomous and cyber weapon systems, during an armed conflict. 16.13

1. No weapons or weapon systems are excluded from application of the rules set forth in this chapter. In particular, the fact that a weapon or weapon system did not exist at the time a particular treaty rule of international humanitarian law came into force or customary international law norm crystallized into binding law does not preclude application of the rules. This is self-evident from, *inter alia*, the requirement under Article 36 of AP I to conduct a review of new methods and means of warfare.

2. Of particular note in this regard are two categories of weapon systems that have drawn widespread public attention—unmanned armed systems such as the Predator and Reaper remotely piloted aircraft (drones) and so-called 'man out of the loop' autonomous systems. The fact that a weapon system is unmanned or operates autonomously at the time of engagement does not relieve those who plan, approve, or control engagements of their responsibility to ensure the employment of the system comports with international humanitarian law in the circumstances. Of course, unmanned and autonomous weapon systems that serve as delivery platforms may only employ lawful weapons.

3. 'Unmanned' weapon systems are those that are operated remotely. They include systems used on land, at sea, in the air, and in space. Although the means of complying with the applicable rules of international humanitarian law may differ as a result of the fact that the operator is not co-located with the system, the rules themselves apply fully. For instance, the operator of a remotely piloted aircraft must be able to verify that the target is a military objective to a reasonable level of certainty in the circumstances before conducting an attack. That operator may do so by relying upon information provided by onboard sensors, sensors aboard other aircraft, or friendly personnel in the target area, but may not engage the target if doubt as to its status as a military objective would cause a reasonable attacker to hesitate in the circumstances; these are the same standards that apply to pilots and weapon systems operators in manned aircraft. Similarly, the fact that a weapon system is unmanned does not relieve those who plan, decide upon, and execute attacks from the obligation to fully consider collateral damage in assessing the proportionality of an attack.

4. Of particular note with respect to attacks by unmanned systems is the requirement to take precautions in attack (Section 16.07). The sensors on the systems and their ability to stay aloft or afloat for extended periods are often useful in providing persistent coverage of a particular target in order to enhance verification or to avoid striking the target when in the proximity of civilians or civilian objects. Additionally, the fact that they can operate in high threat environments without placing their operators at risk further enhances the opportunity to verify the target and avoid collateral damage. To the extent that such systems are available and their use is

16.13 militarily feasible, international humanitarian law requires their employment in lieu of manned systems if such use would likely result in less harm to civilians and civilian objects. It must be cautioned in this regard that military considerations influence the feasibility of an unmanned system's use. For example, there may be competing demands for the systems. Similarly, some of the present unmanned systems are relatively vulnerable to enemy defences and the military commander may deem it preferable not to employ them in high threat environments when their use later in the conflict is probable.

5. Much of the controversy over the use of unmanned systems is less a matter of international humanitarian law's rules on the conduct of hostilities than it is of either the issue of conflict classification or the *jus ad bellum*. As to the former, the classification of the conflict will determine which law applies to an operation conducted by means of the unmanned system. In the absence of an armed conflict, whether international or non-international in character, human rights norms and domestic law will govern the operation, not international humanitarian law (Chapter 3). The issue most relevant in the *jus ad bellum* context is whether or not a remotely piloted aircraft may conduct strikes extraterritorially pursuant to the right of self-defence (Chapter 8). Although this is arguably an unsettled area of law, there is no difference between applications of the relevant law to unmanned or manned systems.[120]

6. Weapon systems are sometime labelled 'man in the loop', 'man on the loop', and 'man out of the loop' systems. In the first, a human locates the target and makes the decision to attack with the weapon system. The second involves a weapon system that can locate and engage targets, but that is monitored by a human who can take control or terminate the engagement. The third term refers to systems that locate and attack targets without any human intervention or monitoring; they are autonomous. It is this third category that has been the source of much public controversy. Note that the debates do not involve point defence autonomous weapon systems, such as the Close in Weapon System (CWIS) used to defend warships against incoming missiles. Rather, they focus on autonomous systems that hunt for and attack targets.[121]

7. The fact that a weapon operates autonomously does not alone render it 'indiscriminate', as that term is understood in international humanitarian law. On the contrary, it is likely that the technology making up such systems in the future will make them highly discriminate. For instance, with present-day technology, an autonomous system could be programmed to identify and attack military vehicles, aircraft, and warships without significant risk of mistakenly striking their civilian counterparts. Additionally, it is always necessary to consider the environment for

[120] On these and related issues, see M. Schmitt, 'Extraterritorial Lethal Targeting: Deconstructing the Logic of International Law', 52 *Columbia Journal of Transnational Law* (2013), 77.

[121] On the issues, see M. Schmitt and J. Thurnher, '"Out of the Loop": Autonomous Weapon Systems and the Law of Armed Conflict', 4 *Harvard National Security Journal* (2013), 231.

which a weapon system is designed when determining whether it is indiscriminate per se. To take a simple example, an autonomous weapon system incapable of distinguishing between civilians and combatants that is intended for use in an urban setting would clearly be indiscriminate by nature. But a system meant for employment in environments where civilians were unlikely to be present, such as remote areas on land or regions of the high seas not used for civilian shipping, would not be indiscriminate as such. Simply put, an autonomous weapon system, like every other weapon and weapon system, must be capable of distinguishing between civilians and combatants, and civilian objects and military objectives, when both are likely to be present in its intended target area. Of course, even though not indiscriminate per se, an autonomous weapon system can be used indiscriminately. **16.13**

8. The obligations to assess proportionality and take precautions in attack to minimize harm to civilians and civilian objects are continuous. Therefore, autonomous systems must be capable of adjusting to changes in the target area, both in terms of risk to civilians and civilian objects and with respect to the military advantage of engagement. The first of these requirements is achievable. Using current technology, for example, sensors of weapon systems can determine that humans are in the target area or that a vehicle has entered it. An autonomous weapon system equipped with such sensors could be programmed not to engage when it identifies individuals or vehicles not fitting the engagement parameters. As technology advances, such capabilities are likely to become highly refined.

9. More problematic is the question of how autonomous systems will be able to assess military advantage, which can change very quickly during military operations. As an example, an autonomous weapon system could be programmed to only engage a tank when there are no more then six individuals in the target area. However, as the flow of battle shifts in favour of the party using the system, the military advantage that accrues by destroying an enemy tank may drop, such that six is no longer a lawful level of collateral damage. For the foreseeable future, autonomous weapon systems cannot assess military advantage and therefore cannot make proportionality decisions autonomously. They will have to be limited in terms of both geographical area of coverage and time spent in the target area, lest the military situation shift so significantly that pre-programmed proportionality calculations violate the rule of proportionality. Another control method would be to tether the system such that an operator could remotely adjust the proportionality threshold or recall the system if the situation changes dramatically. But to be employed lawfully, the party employing an autonomous weapon system must be sensitive to the fact that proportionality thresholds programmed into the system can be perishable.

10. As with unmanned weapon systems, autonomous systems may not be employed when the use of other systems is militarily feasible in the circumstances and would result in fewer civilian deaths or injuries or less damage to civilian objects. Similarly, their use is required if militarily feasible and such use would minimize civilian harm.

MICHAEL N. SCHMITT

16.14 **The use of poison, chemical, or biological weapons is generally prohibited, although riot-control agents and herbicides may be used in certain limited circumstances. Small arms projectiles that are designed to explode within the human body, certain types of booby-traps, laser weapons designed to blind, and weapons the primary effect of which is to injure by fragments that escape detection by X-ray are prohibited, as are, during periods of international armed conflict, bullets that flatten upon impact. Specific treaty prohibitions or limitations apply, for States party to the instruments, to the use of anti-personnel land mines, incendiary weapons, and cluster munitions. There is no absolute obligation to use precision weapons. Rather, their use is governed by the feasible precautions in attack requirements (see Section 16.07).**

1. The legal regime applicable to specific weapons is a complex web of treaty restrictions and customary international humanitarian law (see Chapter 18). In assessing whether particular weapons are lawful and whether specific restrictions apply to their use, it is essential to refer to the relevant treaties and the party status of the States fielding and employing them.

2. Use of poison weapons is prohibited in customary international humanitarian law for both international and non-international armed conflict.[122] They are prohibited by treaty law in Article 23(a) of the 1907 Hague Regulations. Poisons are substances (either chemical or toxins) that harm human beings through a chemical reaction on or in the body.

3. Chemical weapon use is likewise prohibited in customary international humanitarian law applicable in international and non-international armed conflict.[123] Their use was first prohibited in the 1899 Hague Declaration (IV, 2) Concerning Asphyxiating Gases. Subsequent treaty prohibitions included the 1925 Gas Protocol and the 1993 Chemical Weapons Convention. Uncertainty surrounds the precise scope of the prohibition. The Chemical Weapons Convention bans the use of 'riot control agents as a method of warfare', but fails to effectively define what is meant by a 'method of warfare'.[124] Most experts agree that certain uses, such as controlling rioting prisoners, is not a method of warfare, nor is the use of such agents to control a civil disturbance (see commentary to Section 4.01). However, disagreement persists over certain uses, such as employment during rescue missions to protect downed aircrew members from hostile civilians.[125] Also unsettled is the prohibition's applicability to herbicides. The Chemical Weapons Convention only mentions such agents in its Preamble. Some States argue that their use is nevertheless banned in armed conflict. Others contend they may be used for certain

[122] CIHL, Rule 72; NIAC Manual, para. 2.2.2.
[123] CIHL, chapter 24; NIAC Manual, para. 2.2.2; NWP 1-14M, para. 10.3.
[124] 1993 Chemical Weapons Convention, Art. I (5).
[125] US, Executive Order 11,850 (1975); NWP 1-14M, para. 10.3.2.1.

purposes, such as 'control of vegetation within . . . bases and installations or around their immediate defensive perimeters'.[126] **16.14**

4. Far less controversy surrounds biological weapons; there is universal agreement that their use would violate customary international humanitarian law in both international and non-international armed conflict.[127] The 1925 Gas Protocol forbids the use of 'bacteriological methods of warfare', while the 1972 Biological Weapons Convention implicitly prohibits their use through a ban on developing, producing, stockpiling, or otherwise acquiring or retaining 'microbial or other bacteriological agents, or toxins', as well as weapons, equipment, or means of delivery for their use.[128]

5. Small arms projectiles designed to explode on impact or within the human body were first prohibited in the 1868 St Petersburg Declaration. State practice has established the prohibition as customary international humanitarian law in both international and non-international armed conflict.[129]

6. Despite specific treaty restrictions on their use for States party to Protocol II and Amended Protocol II to the Convention on Certain Conventional Weapons, booby traps are not prohibited as such in customary international humanitarian law. Nevertheless, there is general agreement that it is prohibited to attach or associate them with objects or persons entitled to special protection under international humanitarian law (e.g. bodies, the wounded or sick, medical facilities) or to objects that are likely to attract civilians (e.g. children's toys).[130]

7. Laser weapons are prohibited in customary international humanitarian law for international and non-international armed conflict if they are specifically designed to cause permanent blindness to unenhanced vision.[131] Unenhanced vision refers to the naked eye or the eye with corrective lenses. In treaty law, the prohibition is found in Protocol IV to the Conventional Weapons Convention. The limitations of the prohibition are significant. The weapon must be specifically designed to cause permanent blindness as its combat function. Weapon systems that may incidentally cause such blindness are not prohibited. Thus, for example, a laser range finder that risks causing the permanent blindness of those in the vicinity of its use is not prohibited. Additionally, the blindness must be permanent. A laser weapon, even one for anti-personnel use, which causes only temporary blindness, such as a dazzling laser system used for perimeter defence, is lawful.

8. Weapons the primary effect of which is to injure by fragments that escape detection by X-ray are prohibited in customary international humanitarian law

[126] US, Executive Order 11,850 (1975); NWP 1-14M, para. 10.3.3.
[127] CIHL, Rule 73; NIAC Manual, para. 2.2.2; NWP 1-14M, para. 10.4.
[128] 1972 Biological Weapons Convention, Art. 1.
[129] CIHL, Rule 78; NIAC Manual, para. 2.2.2.
[130] CIHL, Rule 80; NIAC Manual, para. 2.2.3.1; NWP 1-14M, para. 9–6.
[131] CIHL, Rule 86; NIAC Manual, para. 2.2.2.

16.14 applicable in international and non-international armed conflict.[132] The treaty law counterpart to the customary norm is found in Protocol I of the Conventional Weapons Convention. The prohibition is based on the premise that it serves no military purpose to use such weapons, as they merely exacerbate the treatment of the wounded combatant. Thus, the suffering is superfluous. It should be noted that some weapons employ components that would be difficult to detect by X-rays. For instance, they may consist in part of non-metallic components in order to reduce weight. Such weapons are not prohibited because the non-metallic fragments that would result are not intended to comprise the primary means of injury.

9. Bullets that expand or flatten upon impact have been prohibited since the 1899 Hague Declaration IV, 3 concerning Expanding Bullets. The prohibition is based on the notion that a non-expanding bullet would suffice to render a combatant *hors de combat*; thus, they constitute weapons that cause superfluous injury and unnecessary suffering, since by flattening upon impact they more grievously injure those they strike than is necessary to disable. All experts agree that their use during international armed conflict as a means of warfare is prohibited as a matter of customary international humanitarian law.[133] However, recent State practice suggests that the prohibition does not extend to non-international armed conflict or to law enforcement situations during international armed conflict.[134] Hollow point and similar bullets have proven highly effective because of their ability to instantaneously incapacitate those against whom they are used. This characteristic renders them indispensable in certain situations, such as freeing hostages or stopping suicide bombers, when delay in incapacitation might prove disastrous (see commentary to Section 4.01).

10. Certain weapons, the use of which is generally lawful under customary international humanitarian law, are the subject of specific treaty regimes that either prohibit or restrict their employment. Noteworthy in this regard are anti-personnel land mines,[135] incendiary weapons,[136] and cluster munitions.[137] States party to such instruments are bound by the provisions thereof, whereas others are governed by the general principles of international humanitarian law, especially the prohibition of indiscriminate attack, the requirement to take feasible precautions in attack, and the principle of proportionality.

11. No express requirement exists in treaty or customary international humanitarian law to employ precision munitions. Rather, the requirement only arises in the context of the requirement to take feasible precautions in attack (see Section 16.07 and accompanying commentary).

132 CIHL, Rule 79; NIAC Manual, para. 2.2.2.
133 CIHL, Rule 77.
134 But see CIHL, Commentary to Rule 77.
135 CCW Protocol II and Protocol II Amended; 1997 Ottawa Treaty on Anti-Personnel Mines.
136 CCW Protocol III.
137 2008 Dublin Convention on Cluster Munitions of 30 May 2008.

Parties to a conflict who are subject to attack shall, to the extent feasible, endeavour to remove civilians and other protected persons and objects under their control from the vicinity of military objectives, avoid locating military objectives within or near protected persons or objects, and take other measures that are necessary to protect civilians and civilian objects under their control against the dangers resulting from military operations. 16.15

1. Section 16.15 is based on Article 58 of AP I. It is a general rule requiring passive precautions, that is, precautions taken by the party to the conflict that is subject to attack. In addition to the general rule, specific rules mandating passive precautions exist for certain objects, such as densely populated areas.[138]

2. The removal of civilians would typically be accomplished through either general evacuation or evacuation of a particularly vulnerable portion of the population, such as children, the elderly, or the infirm. It must be noted that although Article 49 of the 1949 Fourth Geneva Convention limits the right of Occupying Powers to transfer the population, such an evacuation is permissible when conducted for its safety or for reasons of imperative military necessity.

3. With regard to the requirement to avoid locating military objects in the vicinity of protected persons and objects, note that the requirement attaches 'to the extent feasible'. Many military facilities located in urban areas pre-date the requirement; others need to be located in or near particular locations, such as a key line of communication or the seat of government. In such cases, it may not be feasible to relocate the facilities or base them elsewhere.

4. Other measures necessary to protect the civilian population might include, for instance, the construction of air raid shelters or establishing an attack warning system.

5. Under no circumstances may the presence or movements of the civilians or other protected persons be used to shield combatants or military, or to otherwise enhance friendly operations or impede the enemy's.[139]

Except as noted, the basic international humanitarian law rules of targeting set forth above apply equally in both international and non-international armed conflict. 16.16

1. In *Tadić*, the International Criminal Tribunal for the former Yugoslavia's Appeals Chamber stated:

> it cannot be denied that customary rules have developed to govern internal strife. These rules . . . cover such areas as protection of civilians from hostilities, in particular from indiscriminate attacks, protection of civilian objects, in particular cultural property,

[138] Art. 58(b) AP I. [139] Art. 51(7) AP I; NWP 1-14M, para. 8.3.2.

16.16 protection of all those who do not (or no longer) take active part in hostilities, as well as prohibition of means of warfare proscribed in international armed conflicts and ban of certain methods of conducting hostilities.[140]

2. Although the Tribunal's assertion was somewhat controversial at the time it was made, today it is widely accepted that the core rules governing the conduct of hostilities during an international armed conflict, especially the prohibitions on attacking civilians and civilian objects, the rule of proportionality, and the requirement to take precautions in attack, are applicable also in non-international armed conflicts as a matter of customary international law. This was the position taken by the International Committee of the Red Cross in its *Customary International Humanitarian Law* study[141] and by the expert groups that prepared the San Remo *Manual on the Law of Non-international Armed Conflict*,[142] the Harvard *Air and Missile Warfare Manual*,[143] and the Tallinn Manual[144] on cyber warfare. The prohibition on attacking civilians during a non-international armed conflict is reflected in Article 13(1) of AP I and the ICRC commentary to the provision acknowledge its customary law status.[145]

3. Human rights law and domestic law govern targeting during operations in situations not qualifying as an armed conflict (Chapter 3). In particular, lethal targeting of individuals is prohibited during operations in situations not qualifying as an armed conflict except in self-defence or defence of others against the imminent threat of death or serious injury, to prevent the perpetration of a particularly serious crime involving grace threat to life, to arrest a person presenting such a danger, or to prevent his or her escape. The use of lethal means is only permissible when less extreme means of addressing the situation are insufficient. The targeting of individuals based solely on their status (status-based targeting) is prohibited during such operations.[146]

4. Targeting conducted extraterritorially, whether during an armed conflict or not, must account for the sovereignty of the state into which the operation is mounted.[147]

[140] International Criminal Tribunal for the former Yugoslavia, *Prosecutor v Tadic*, Decision on Defence Motion for Interlocutory Appeal on Jurisdiction, Appeals Chamber, Case IT-94-1, (2 October 1995), para. 127.

[141] CIHL, chapters 1–5.

[142] NIAC Manual, chapter 2.

[143] Harvard Program on Humanitarian Policy and Conflict Research, *Manual in International Law Applicable to Air and Missile Warfare* (Cambridge: Cambridge University Press, 2013), Sections D and G.

[144] Tallinn Manual, chapter 4.

[145] ICRC Commentary, para. 4761.

[146] On the rules generally deemed applicable to 'targeting' pursuant to human rights law, see Eighth UN Congress on the Prevention of Crime and the Treatment of Offenders, Havana, Cuba, 27 August–7 September 1990, UN Doc. A/CONF.144/28/Rev.1, at 110–16 (1991) (reporting on the basic principles on the use of force by law enforcement officials).

[147] For a discussion of this issue, see Schmitt, 'Extraterritorial'.

Chapter 17

TARGETED KILLINGS IN OPERATIONAL LAW PERSPECTIVE

For the purposes of this Handbook, the term 'targeted killing' refers to military operations involving the use of lethal force with the aim of killing individually selected persons who are not in the physical custody of those targeting them. 17.01

1. *A Method of Employing Lethal Force.* In international law, 'targeted killing' is not a defined term of art, but has been used in a variety of different contexts and meanings.[1] From a military practitioner's perspective, targeted killing should be understood as a tactical method characterized by objective elements rather than subjective or political considerations. For the purposes of this Handbook, the term 'targeted killing' refers to military operations characterized by four cumulative elements:[2] First, targeted killing is a method of employing lethal force against human beings. While targeted killings almost invariably involve the use of some sort of weapon, the notion of lethal force includes any forcible measure capable of causing the death of a human being, regardless of the means employed.

2. *Intent, Premeditation, and Deliberation to Kill* (dolus directus). Second, targeted killings always involve the intent, premeditation, and deliberation to kill. The intent to kill distinguishes targeted killings from unintentional, accidental, negligent, or reckless use of lethal force. The premeditation to kill requires that the intent to kill be based on a conscious choice, as opposed to voluntary acts driven by impulse or passion. The deliberation to kill requires that the death of the targeted person be the actual purpose of the operation, as opposed to deprivations of life which, although intentional and premeditated, remain the incidental result of an operation pursuing other aims. While logic requires a certain lapse of time between the decision to carry out a targeted killing and the actual application of lethal force, the relevant decision can in practice be taken in a split second, thus rendering the significance of the temporal requirement merely theoretical.

[1] For an overview, see Melzer, *Targeted Killing in International Law* (Oxford: Oxford University Press, 2008), 6–8. The definition proposed here has also been adopted in: Report of the Special Rapporteur on Extrajudicial, Summary or Arbitrary Executions, Philip Alston, Addendum, Study on Targeted Killings, UN Doc. A/HRC/14/24/Add.6, (28 May 2010).

[2] See also Melzer, *Targeted Killing*, 3–5.

NILS MELZER

17.01 3. *Targeting of Individually Selected Persons.* Third, the requirement of targeting individually selected persons distinguishes targeted killings from operations directed against collective, unspecified, or random targets.

4. *Lack of Physical Custody.* Fourth, at the time of their killing, the targeted persons are not in the physical custody of those targeting them. This element distinguishes targeted killings from judicial and extra-judicial executions, both of which presuppose the existence of physical custody.

17.02 **The international lawfulness of targeted killing is regulated primarily by human rights law and, in situations of armed conflict, international humanitarian law. To the extent that targeted killings attributable to a State also interfere with the sovereignty of another State, their international lawfulness additionally depends on international law governing the use of inter-State force.**

1. The primary international legal frameworks regulating the use of lethal force against individuals are human rights law and, in situations of an armed conflict, international humanitarian law. To the extent that targeted killings interfere with the sphere of sovereignty of another State, their international lawfulness additionally depends on the law governing the use of inter-State force. While all three regimes can simultaneously apply to the same targeted killing, each of them regulates the use of force from a different perspective. In essence, human rights law and humanitarian law determine the lawfulness of force with respect to the injured individual, whereas the law of inter-State force determines the lawfulness of force with respect to the injured State. Targeted killings involving inter-State force are internationally lawful only when they are justified with respect to both, the injured State and the injured person.

2. *Prohibition of Inter-State Force.* In principle, any targeted killing carried out by a State within the sphere of sovereignty of another State comes under the prohibition of inter-State force expressed in Article 2(4) of the UN Charter and, therefore, must be justified based on an exculpatory circumstance recognized in international law. In operational practice, the most relevant justifications for the use of force within the sphere of sovereignty of third States are the inherent right of self-defence, consent given by the territorial State, and UN Security Council authorization.[3] Where the use of inter-State force cannot be justified based on a recognized exculpatory clause, even a single targeted killing would amount to a violation of the UN Charter and customary international law and may qualify as an act of aggression.[4]

[3] Strictly speaking, UN Security Council authorization is not an independent exculpatory clause but is based on the prior consent given by all UN Member States to the Organization's Charter, which defines the extent and purposes of the powers bestowed upon the Security Council. More controversial is the question whether the use of inter-State force could also be justified by a State of necessity, for the protection of nationals abroad, or as part of a humanitarian intervention.

[4] See, most notably, SC Res. 611 of 25 April 1988 condemning the assassination by Israel of Abu Jihad in Tunis as an act of aggression. On the prohibition of inter-State force see also sub-Chapter 5.1

3. On the other hand, even the existence of a circumstance justifying the use of inter-State force does not necessarily entail the international lawfulness of a particular targeted killing. It is conceivable, for instance, that a targeted killing carried out in self-defence or with the consent of the territorial State is permissible under the law of inter-State force, but that neither human rights law nor international humanitarian law allow the deliberate killing of the targeted individual. In such cases, it is possible that the latter frameworks permit alternative measures, such as capture and arrest. It is also conceivable that the pursuit and targeted killing of an opposing rebel commander across an international border is lawful under international humanitarian law and human rights law but does not fulfil the requirements for the lawful use of force with respect to the injured State. Therefore, the prohibition of targeted killings as a form of inter-State force and their exceptional permissibility based on justifications such as consent or self-defence is relevant exclusively with regard to the question as to whether a particular targeted killing violates the rights of another State, most notably under Article 2(4) of the UN Charter. The answer to this question has no influence on the permissibility of the same targeted killing with regard to the targeted individual. This second question requires a separate determination based on human rights law and international humanitarian law. **17.02**

4. *Human Rights Law and International Humanitarian Law.* The primary frameworks of international law regulating the use of lethal force against individuals are human rights law and international humanitarian law. Although both frameworks find their common basis and *raison d'être* in the protection of human dignity,[5] they do not have the same scope of applicability. While the applicability of humanitarian law presupposes the existence of an international or non-international armed conflict, human rights treaties generally require the existence of jurisdiction. Arguably, some human rights obligations, including the duty to respect the right to life, have also become part of general international law and are applicable wherever individuals are exposed to the exercise of authority or power by States.[6]

5. Today, it is widely recognized that situations of armed conflict trigger the applicability of international humanitarian law without necessarily suspending the applicability of human rights law.[7] This raises the practical question as to how

'Legal Characterization and Basis for Enforcement Operations and Peace Enforcement Operations under the Charter', in particular Section 5.01, commentary para. 2.

[5] Confirmed, for instance, in ICTY, *Prosecutor v Furundzija*, Case no. IT-95-17/1-T, Judgment of 10 December 1998 (Trial Chamber), para. 183; IACiHR, *Abella v Argentina (La Tablada)*, Case no. 11.137, Report no. 55/97, 18 November 1997, para. 158.

[6] For a detailed analysis into the contemporary scope and status of the non-conventional right to life, see Melzer, *Targeted Killing*, 177–221.

[7] The continued applicability of human rights law during armed conflicts is confirmed in major human rights treaties (Arts 27(1) ACHR, 15(1) ECHR and, implicitly, 4(1) ICCPR), international humanitarian law (Preamble AP II, Arts 51(1) and 72 AP I), and the practice of the Inter-American Commission on Human Rights (e.g. *Coard et al. v United States*, Case 10.951, Report no. 109/99, 29 September 1999, para. 39; *La Tablada Case*, para. 158), the UN Human Rights Committee (General

17.02 human rights law and international humanitarian law interrelate specifically with regard to targeted killings. As a general rule, the use of lethal force outside the conduct of hostilities, for instance against looters, hostage-takers, and other common criminals, or in suppressing riots and other forms of civil unrest, is governed by law enforcement standards derived from both human rights law and international humanitarian law. While human rights law generally provides more detailed standards for the use of force in law enforcement operations, it is complemented by humanitarian law in aspects more specific to situations of armed conflict. Thus, international humanitarian law provides a more extensive legal basis for the exercise of law enforcement authority over persons and territory in situations of armed conflict[8] and protects persons taking no active part in hostilities against violence to life and person, murder, wilful killing, extrajudicial executions, collective punishment, and acts of terrorism.[9] The lawfulness of lethal force used during the conduct of hostilities, on the other hand, depends primarily on the more specific rules of international humanitarian law regulating the resort to means and methods of warfare.[10]

6. In case of contradiction between obligations arising under human rights law and international humanitarian law with regard to the same military operation, the *lex specialis* principle generally entails that the international humanitarian law takes precedence over human rights law. Where international humanitarian law is not sufficiently clear or precise to determine the lawfulness of a specific killing during

Comments no. 29 (2001), para. 3; no. 31 (2004), para. 11), the International Court of Justice (*Advisory Opinion on the Legality of the Threat or Use of Nuclear Weapons*, 8 July 1996, para. 25; *Advisory Opinion on the legal consequences of the construction of a wall in the occupied Palestinian territory*, 9 July 2004, paras 105 *et seq.*; *Case concerning Armed Activities on the Territory of the Congo (Democratic Republic of the Congo v Uganda)*, Judgment of 19 December 2005, para. 216), the UN General Assembly (Res. 2252 of 4 July 1967; 2444 of 19 December 1968; 2675 of 9 December 1970; 58/96 of 9 December 2003, paras 3, 5; 58/99 of 9 December 2003, paras 2, 5), and the UN Security Council (Res. 237 of 14 June 1967; 1041 of 29 January 1996; Presidential Statement of 12 February 1999 (UN Doc. S/PRST/1999/6), paras 2 and 7). See also para. 10 of the Proclamation of Teheran (1968) and, *pars pro toto*, T. Meron, 'Humanization of Humanitarian Law', 94–2 *AJIL* (2000), 239–78, at 267 *et seq.*; H.-J. Heintze, 'The European Court of Human Rights and the Implementation of Human Rights Standards During Armed Conflicts', 45 *German Yearbook of International Law* (2002), 60–77, at 62 *et seq.*; O. Ben-Naftali and Y. Shany, 'Living in Denial. The Application of Human Rights in the Occupied Territories', 37–1 *Israel Law Review* (2003–2004), 17–118, at 101 *et seq.*; O. Ben-Naftali and K. Michaeli, 'We Must Not Make a Scarecrow of the Law. A Legal Analysis of the Israeli Policy of Targeted Killings', 36 *Cornell International Law Journal* (2003), 233, at 264; Y. Dinstein, 'The Right to Life, Physical Integrity and Liberty', in L. Henkin et al. (eds), *The International Bill of Rights* (New York: Columbia University, 1981), 114–37, at 136.

[8] For instance, international humanitarian law provides a special legal basis for the exercise of law enforcement authority by States over prisoners of war (Arts 82 GC III; 8 H IV R) and internees or other protected persons in occupied territory (Art. 43 HagueReg; Arts 27(4), 64, 66, 68, 76, 117 GC IV), and arguably even by insurgent parties to a non-international armed conflict over persons and within territory having fallen into their power (Art. 3 GC I–IV, Arts 4–6 AP II).

[9] See e.g. Art. 12 GC I and II; Arts 13–14, 102 GC II; Arts 27–28, 71 GC IV, Arts 31–34; Art. 3(1) GC I–IV; Arts 4–6 AP II.

[10] Affirmative, for example, Heintze, 'The European Court', 64; Ben-Naftali and Shany, 'Living in Denial', particularly at 103; Ben-Naftali and Michaeli, 'We Must Not Make a Scarecrow', 289.

the conduct of hostilities, its rules have to be clarified primarily through the usual means of treaty interpretation and by reference to the general principles of military necessity and humanity underlying and informing international humanitarian law as a whole. Only where humanitarian law specifically designed to regulate the conduct of hostilities is silent, and no guidance can be derived from the general principles underlying that law, should clarification be sought in the more general rules and principles of human rights law.[11] **17.02**

Outside the conduct of hostilities in armed conflict, a targeted killing can be permissible only in very exceptional circumstances, namely where it, cumulatively: (a) aims at preventing an unlawful attack by the targeted person on human life; (b) is absolutely necessary for the achievement of this purpose; (c) is the result of an operation which is planned, prepared and conducted so as to minimize, to the greatest extent possible, the recourse to lethal force. States have a duty to regulate the use of lethal force by their agents in accordance with these standards. 17.03

1. States have a basic right and duty to take all measures necessary to uphold law and order within their jurisdiction. This includes the duty to respect and protect the life of all individuals under their authority or directly exposed to their conduct. While the negative aspect of this obligation prohibits that life be taken arbitrarily, its positive aspect may even require, *in extremis*, the use of lethal force in order to protect individual life from being unlawfully taken. In regulating the use of lethal force for situations other than the conduct of hostilities, both human rights law and international humanitarian law provide a practically uniform set of conditions and modalities that are here referred to as the 'law enforcement paradigm'.

2. *Scope of Applicability of the Law Enforcement Paradigm.* Inspired by human rights treaties, the exercise of 'jurisdiction' is often regarded as a prerequisite for the applicability of the law enforcement paradigm to operations involving the use of lethal force.[12] However, the obligation to respect—that is to say, not to interfere with—individual life is also widely recognized as a norm of general international law binding upon all States at all times and in all places, regardless of their treaty obligations.[13] Thus, the discussion of the extraterritorial scope of human rights

[11] Affirmative, for example, ICJ, *Legal Consequences of a Wall Opinion*, para. 106; ICJ, *Congo Case*, para. 216; UNHRC, General Comments no. 31 (2004), para. 11, no. 29 (2001), para. 3. More specifically with regard to the right to life in armed conflict, see ICJ, *Nuclear Weapons Opinion*, para. 25; IACiHR, *La Tablada Case*, para. 161. On the interrelation between human rights law and international humanitarian law, see also Chapter 3. 'Human Rights and International Humanitarian Law: General Issues'.

[12] Except for the African Charter all major human rights treaties restrict their applicability to individuals that are subject to the 'jurisdiction' of the acting State (Art. 2(1) ICCPR; Art. 1(1) ACHR; Art. 1 ECHR).

[13] The right to life has been expressly recognized a non-derogable rule of *jus cogens* by the UN Human Rights Committee (General Comments no. 24 (1994), para. 10, and no. 29 (2001), para. 11),

17.03 treaties is much more relevant for the determination of the jurisdiction of treaty-based human rights bodies than for the determination of the legal standards governing targeted killings. In essence, all targeted killings except those directed against a legitimate military target in a situation of armed conflict remain subject to the legal paradigm of law enforcement.

3. When applying the law enforcement paradigm to specific targeted killings, the conditions and modalities governing the use of lethal force must be interpreted in good faith and in accordance with the prevailing circumstances, including the level of control that can actually be exercised over the targeted individual. Nevertheless, however limited the control of a State over a particular territory or individual may be, flexibility in interpretation must not be confused with flexibility in application. For instance, depending on the circumstances, the requirements of necessity, proportionality, and precaution may be open to restrictive or extensive interpretation, but they can in no case be derogated from so as to allow the use of lethal force which is not necessary, which is likely to cause harm that is disproportionate to the expected benefit, or which could have been avoided by taking precautions that were objectively feasible. Similarly, the choice of legitimate purposes for the use of lethal force requires interpretation, but is not open to modification or extension. For example, even in armed conflict, the lawfulness of a deprivation of life for punitive purposes is inconceivable 'without previous judgment pronounced by a regularly constituted court affording all the judicial guarantees which are recognized as indispensable by civilized peoples'.[14]

4. In operational practice, targeted killings are often conducted outside the territorial control of the operating State or in situations where the applicability of the more liberal standards governing the conduct of hostilities is uncertain, either because it is not clear whether the targeted individual is a legitimate military target, or because it is doubtful whether there is a situation of armed conflict in the first place. It is therefore important to note that any targeted killing not directed against

and the Inter-American Commission on Human Rights (IACtHR, *Villagran Morales et al. v Guatemala (the 'Street Children' Case)*, Judgment of 19 November 1999, Series C, no. 63, 1999, para. 139). Moreover, by interpreting Art. 3 GC I–IV as reflecting 'elementary considerations of humanity', the International Court of Justice has derived a universal prohibition of murder and extrajudicial execution directly from general principles of law (ICJ, *Case concerning Military and Paramilitary Activities in and Against Nicaragua (Nicaragua v United States of America)*, Judgment of 27 June 1986 (Merits), para. 218). Arguably, being 'even more exacting in peace than in war' (ICJ, *Corfu Channel Case (United Kingdom v Albania)*, Judgment of 9 April 1949 (Merits), ICJ Reports, 1949, 22.), this prohibition is binding even outside situations of armed conflict and may not be derogated from 'at any time and in any place whatsoever' (Art. 3 GC I–IV). In situations of armed conflict, the prohibition of murder and extrajudicial execution expressed in Art. 3 GC I–IV and various other provisions of treaty IHL are considered to have become part of customary international law, see J.-M. Henckaerts and L. Doswald-Beck (eds), *Customary International Humanitarian Law*, Vol. 1 (Cambridge: Cambridge University Press, 2005), Rules 89 and 100. For detailed references to the discussion of the customary or peremptory nature of the right to life in the legal doctrine, see Melzer, *Targeted Killing*, 189, n. 66 and, respectively, 229, n. 231.

[14] Art. 3(1) GC I–IV.

a legitimate military target within the meaning of international humanitarian law must—'by default' and regardless of temporal or territorial considerations—comply with universally binding law enforcement standards, namely the requirements of strict necessity, proportionality, precaution, and legality. **17.03**

5. *The Requirement of Strict Necessity.* Outside the conduct of hostilities, the use of lethal force must not exceed what is strictly necessary to maintain, restore, or otherwise impose law and order in the concrete circumstances.[15] The requirement of necessity has a qualitative, a quantitative, and a temporal aspect. First, the use of potentially lethal force must be 'strictly unavoidable' in the sense that less harmful means remain ineffective or without any promise of achieving the purpose of the operation (qualitative necessity). A targeted killing cannot be qualitatively necessary if the desired purpose could also be achieved by means other than the use of potentially lethal force.

6. Second, even if the use of potentially lethal force is strictly unavoidable (i.e. qualitatively necessary), State agents must endeavour to minimize damage and injury to human life (quantitative necessity). Targeted killings can only be quantitatively necessary for the achievement of the desired purpose where it is not sufficient to merely incapacitate the targeted individual by the use of potentially lethal force. Instead, it must be objectively indispensable for the success of the operation to intentionally kill the targeted individual.[16]

7. Third, the use of lethal force is unlawful if, at the very moment of its application, it is not yet or no longer absolutely necessary to achieve the desired purpose

[15] See Art. 2(2) ECHR, Art. 3 (and Commentary para. a) to the UN Code of Conduct for Law Enforcement Officials (CCLEO), adopted by UN GA 34/169 of 17 December 1979, Principles 4, 9, 13–14 UN Basic Principles on the Use of Force and Firearms by Law Enforcement Officials (BPUFF), adopted by the 8th UN Congress on the Prevention of Crime and the Treatment of Offenders (1990). Confirmed, for example, in UNHRC, *Suarez de Guerrero v Colombia,* Communication no. R.11/45 of 31 March 1982, UN Doc. Supp. no. 40 (A/37/40), paras 13.1–13.3; ECtHR, *McCann and others v the United Kingdom,* Application no. 18984/91, Judgment of 27 September 1995, paras 132, 149, 196 *et seq.*, 212; ECtHR, *Andronicou and Constantinou v Cyprus,* Application no. 25052/94, Judgment of 9 October 1997, para. 171; ECtHR, *McKerr v the United Kingdom,* Application no. 28883/95, Judgment of 4 May 2001, para. 110; ECtHR, *Gül v Turkey,* Application no. 22676/93, Judgment of 14 December 2000, para. 77; ECtHR, *Nachova and others v Bulgaria,* Application no. 43577/98 and 43579/98, Judgment of 6 July 2005, paras 94, 108; ECtHR, *Handyside v the United Kingdom,* Application no. 5493/72, Judgment of 7 December 1976, para. 48; IACiHR, *Alejandre et al. v Cuba,* Case no. 11.589, Report no. 86/99, 29 September 1999, paras 37, 42; IACiHR, *Report Guatemala 2001,* para. 50; IACiHR, *Report on Terrorism and Human Rights,* 22 October 2002 (OEA/Ser.L/V/II.116 Doc. 5 Rev. 1 Corr.), paras 87–88, 90–92; IACiHR, *Chumbivilcas v Peru,* Case no. 10.559, Report no. 1/96, 1 March 1996; IACtHR, *Neira Alegria et al. v Peru,* Judgment of 19 January 1995 (Series C, no. 21, 1995); ACiHPR, *Ouédraogo v Burkina Faso,* Communication no. 204/97, Decision of 1 May 2001, 29th Ordinary Session, April/May 2001, para. 4. With regard to prisoners of war, see Art. 42 GC III.

[16] The element of quantitative necessity is sometimes described as requiring that the use of lethal force be 'strictly proportionate' to what is necessary to achieve the desired purpose. It is important, however, not to confuse the requirement of *quantitative* necessity with that of proportionality, which involves a value judgement independent from considerations of necessity.

17.03 (temporal necessity). If the circumstances of a case evolve so as to permit the achievement of the desired purpose without necessarily killing the targeted individual, that killing may no longer lawfully be intended. Where the use of potentially lethal force becomes unnecessary altogether, such force may no longer lawfully be used. As a consequence, the law enforcement paradigm requires that any operation of targeted killing be constantly reassessed as to its continued necessity to achieve the desired purpose.

8. In sum, while the requirement of strict necessity does not categorically exclude the permissibility of targeted killing as a method of law enforcement, it does require that such operations comply with exceptionally strict standards of necessity in qualitative, quantitative, and temporal terms.

9. *The Requirement of Proportionality.* The requirement of proportionality always involves a value judgement independent from, and additional to, considerations of necessity. Even if the use of lethal force is strictly necessary for the removal of a concrete threat to law and order, it would not be permissible if the harm expected to result from such force must be regarded as disproportionate compared to the gravity of the threat or offence to be removed by it.[17]

10. A separate proportionality assessment must be made in light of the circumstances of each case. As a general rule, potentially lethal force should not be used except to: (1) defend any person against the imminent threat of death or serious injury, (2) prevent the perpetration of a particularly serious crime involving grave threat to life, or (3) arrest a person presenting such a danger and resisting arrest, or to prevent his or her escape.[18] Thus, even the aim of lawful arrest cannot justify the use of potentially lethal force against a suspect who does not pose a concrete threat to human life or limb and is not suspected of having committed a violent crime.[19] In such cases, the risk of the suspect escaping arrest is to be preferred over the risk of causing his death. Nevertheless, in situations of armed conflict, the military threat posed by the escape of captured combatants is generally regarded as sufficient to justify the use of potentially lethal force against fugitives.[20] Targeted killing, that is

[17] Confirmed, for example, in ECiHR, *Kelly v the United Kingdom*, Application no. 17579/90, Admissibility Decision of 13 January 1993; ECiHR, *Aytekin v Turkey*, Application no. 22880/93, Report of 18 September 1997, para. 95; ECtHR, *McCann Case*, 15, paras 192 *et seq.*; ECtHR, *Gül Case*, para. 82; ECtHR, *Streletz, Kessler and Krenz v Germany*, Applications nos 34044/96, 35532/97, and 44801/98, Judgment of 22 March 2001, paras 87, 96, and 102; ECtHR, *Makaratzis v Greece*, Application no. 50385/99, Judgment of 20 December 2004, paras 64 to 66; ECtHR, *Nachova Case*, para. 95. UNHRC, *de Guerrero Case*, paras 13.1–13.3; IACtHR, *Neira Alegria Case*, paras 43, 69, and 72; IACiHR, *Alejandre Case*, paras 37, 42, 45; IACiHR, *Report Guatemala 2001*, para. 50; IACiHR, *Report Terrorism and Human Rights*, paras 87 and 92; IACiHR, *Report Colombia 1999*, Chapter IV, para. 169.

[18] Strictly speaking, it is therefore an expression of the requirement of proportionality when Art. 2(2) ECHR limits the purposes which may potentially justify the resort to lethal force to (a) defending any person from unlawful violence, (b) effecting a lawful arrest or preventing the escape of a person lawfully detained, and (c) lawfully quelling a riot or insurrection. See also Commentary (c) to Art. 3 CCLEO.

[19] ECtHR, *Nachova Case*, paras 95, 103, and 107.

[20] Art. 42 GC III.

to say, the use of lethal force with the intention to kill ('shoot-to-kill') is an even more extreme measure and has been regarded as proportionate only where strictly unavoidable for the protection of human life from unlawful attack.[21] **17.03**

11. In sum, outside the conduct of hostilities, the targeted killing of an individual can never become an end in itself, but must remain a means for the achievement of a different, legitimate purpose. More specifically, the requirement of proportionality prohibits the resort to targeted killing as a method of law enforcement except where strictly indispensable to save human life from unlawful attack. While considerations of proportionality may permit the use of potentially lethal force to secure the incapacitation or arrest of a person whose past conduct indicates that he or she continues to pose a potential but unspecified threat to human life also for the future, the intentional killing of an individual can only be justified by the protection of human life from a concrete and specific threat.

12. *The Requirement of Precaution.* All military operations conducted in situations other than hostilities must be planned, organized, and controlled so as to minimize, to the greatest extent possible, the use of lethal force.[22] The duty of precaution applies in all organizational and operational stages and binds not only commanding officers, but each individual potentially involved in the use of lethal force. Consequently, superior orders do not absolve the shooter from the duty to make an individual assessment of the situation, provided that such an assessment can reasonably be expected from him in the prevailing circumstances.

13. When military forces are called upon to carry out law enforcement functions, they must be provided with all appropriate equipment to fulfil their duties, including non-lethal weapons.[23] Moreover, in the planning and conduct of specific operations, the determination of whether the circumstances justify the resort to lethal force must be made with the greatest care. As law enforcement activities, and especially counter-terrorist operations, often have to be conducted on the basis of incomplete intelligence and hypotheses, particular precautions must be taken to avoid the use of lethal force based on erroneous assumptions.[24] Therefore, any previous determination that a situation absolutely requires the use of lethal force must remain subject to constant scrutiny. Also, outside the conduct of hostilities, the use of lethal force must, in principle, be preceded by a clear warning with sufficient time for the warning to be observed. This duty can only be deviated from in circumstances where warnings would be clearly inappropriate or pointless or

[21] Principle 9 BPUFF.

[22] See, for example, Commentary (c) to Art. 3 CCLEO. Confirmed, for example, in: ECiHR, *Wolfgram v Germany,* Application no. 11257/84, Admissibility Decision of 6 October 1986; ECiHR, *Aytekin Case,* para. 97; ECtHR, *McCann Case,* paras 150, 194, and 205; ECtHR, *Andronicou and Constantinou Case,* para. 171; ECtHR, *Gülec v Turkey,* Application no. 21593/93, Judgment of 27 July 1998, para. 71; ECtHR, *Gül Case,* para. 84; ECtHR, *Nachova Case,* para. 93.

[23] Principles 2 and 3 BPUFF.

[24] ECtHR, *McCann Case,* paras 193 and 211.

17.03 would unduly place the agents themselves or other persons at risk of death or serious harm.[25] Last but not least, during and after operations likely to involve the use of lethal force, every effort must be made to ensure that assistance and medical aid is provided to any injured or otherwise affected persons at the earliest possible moment.[26]

14. The required standard of precaution cannot impose an unrealistic burden on the authorities but must always relate to what is reasonably achievable in the circumstances.[27] For example, while it clearly is not permissible to use lethal force based on the mere suspicion that the targeted individual may be involved in a particularly serious crime or otherwise constitute a grave threat, a deprivation of life is not necessarily unlawful if it is carried out based on a honest but mistaken belief that all requirements for the use of lethal force are fulfilled. The distinctive criterion between 'mere suspicion' and 'honest but mistaken belief' is not only the degree of subjective conviction or doubt actually held by the operating personnel, but also the objective reasonableness of that subjective conviction in view of the circumstances prevailing at the time.[28]

15. In sum, outside the conduct of hostilities, the requirement of precaution aims not only at minimizing the incidental effects of military operations on uninvolved bystanders, but also at minimizing the recourse to lethal force against the targeted individuals themselves. Thus, the requirement of precaution is diametrically opposed to the basic idea underlying the method of targeted killing, which actually aims at depriving the targeted individuals of their life. Outside the conduct of hostilities, therefore, the killing of a person cannot be the actual purpose of a military operation; the use of lethal force cannot be an end in itself but must always remain the means to a different, legitimate end. Operational practice has shown that, where States resort to targeted killing as a method of law enforcement, insufficient precautions entail a great risk of erroneous or arbitrary deprivations of life in violation of international law.[29]

[25] See Principle 10 BPUFF; Art. 42 GC III. Confirmed, for example, in UNHRC, *de Guerrero Case*, paras 13.1–13.3; IACiHR, *Alejandre Case*, para. 42.

[26] Principle 5 UN Force and Firearms Principles.

[27] ECtHR, *McCann Case*, para. 200; ECtHR, *Andronicou and Constantinou Case*, paras 183, 192; ECtHR, *McKerr Case*, para. 116; ECtHR, *Kelly and others v the United Kingdom*, Application no. 30054/96, Judgment of 4 May 2001, para. 99; ECtHR, *Hugh Jordan v the United Kingdom*, Application no. 24746/94, Judgment of 4 May 2001, para. 110; ECtHR, *Gül Case*, para. 78; ECtHR, *Makaratzis Case*, paras 66, 69.

[28] UNHRC, *de Guerrero Case*, paras 13.1–13.3; ECtHR, *McCann Case*, para. 200. Confirmed, *inter alia*, in ECtHR, *Andronicou and Constantinou Case*, para. 192; ECtHR, *McKerr Case*, para. 116; ECtHR, *Kelly and others Case*, para. 99; ECtHR, *Jordan Case*, para. 110; ECtHR, *Gül Case*, para. 78; ECtHR, *Makaratzis Case*, para. 66.

[29] The *McCann Case* is the classic case where the failure of the operating authorities to take sufficient precautionary measures led to the unlawfulness of a targeted killing, although the shooting operatives were exculpated based on their honest but mistaken belief that it was absolutely necessary and proportionate to use intentional lethal force against the suspects in question. More cases of targeted killing giving rise to similar concerns are the killing of Jean-Charles de Menezes by the UK Police

16. *The Requirement of Legal Basis.* National law governing the conduct of law enforcement operations must strictly control and limit the use of lethal force so as to comply with the applicable human rights law and, in situations of armed conflict, international humanitarian law. In doing so, national law must make the recourse to lethal force dependent on a careful assessment of the surrounding circumstances, including both the nature of the offence committed and the threat posed by the suspect or fugitive. The requirement of a sufficient legal basis has important implications for current State practice with regard to targeted killing in law enforcement operations. National laws and doctrines, rules of engagement and other legislative or executive instruments authorizing the resort to targeted killing in domestic or extraterritorial police, military, counterinsurgency, counter-terrorism, or counter-piracy operations must strictly align with the law enforcement paradigm, except where such operations are directed against legitimate military targets in an armed conflict.[30] In operational practice, failure of domestic law to regulate and control the use of lethal force in accordance with internationally binding standards is likely to provoke arbitrary deprivations of life and, at least as far as territory under its jurisdiction is concerned, may amount to a violation of the State's positive duty to protect the right to life even before lethal force has actually been used.[31] **17.03**

17. *Summary.* The preceding analysis leads to the conclusion that any State-sponsored targeted killing, except those directed against legitimate military targets in an armed conflict, is governed by the law enforcement paradigm derived from human rights law and international humanitarian law. These standards do not categorically prohibit, but impose extensive restraints on the use of lethal force. Accordingly, outside the conduct of hostilities, a targeted killing can be permissible only in very exceptional circumstances, namely where it: (a) aims at preventing an unlawful attack by the targeted person on human life, and (b) is absolutely necessary for the achievement of this purpose, and (c) is the result of an operation which is planned, prepared, and conducted so as to minimize, to the greatest extent possible, the recourse to lethal force. States have an international obligation to regulate the use of lethal force by their agents in accordance with these standards.

In a situation of armed conflict, a targeted killing can be permissible only where it cumulatively: (a) is directed against a person subject to lawful attack; (b) is planned and conducted so as to avoid erroneous targeting, as well as to avoid, and in any event to minimize, incidental civilian harm; (c) is not expected to cause incidental civilian harm that would be excessive in relation to the concrete and direct military **17.04**

(2005); of Rigoberto Alpizar by US Air Marshals (2005); and of Ewald K. by the Swiss Police (2000). For a more detailed discussion of these cases, see Melzer, *Targeted Killing*, 236–9.

[30] For an overview of the policies and practices adopted in Germany, Israel, Switzerland, the UK, and the US with regard to targeted killing outside the conduct of hostilities, see Melzer, *Targeted Killing*, 9–43.

[31] See e.g. ECtHR, *Streletz Case*; UNHRC, *de Guerrero Case*; ECtHR, *Makaratzis Case*.

17.04 **advantage anticipated; (d) is suspended when the targeted person surrenders or otherwise falls *hors de combat*; and (e) is not otherwise conducted by resort to prohibited means or methods of warfare. Even where not expressly prohibited under the above standards, targeted killings may not be resorted to where the threat posed by the targeted person can manifestly be neutralized through capture or other non-lethal means without additional risk to the operating forces or the civilian population.**

1. States resorting to the method of targeted killing often argue that the targeted individuals are legitimate military targets and, thereby, seek justification in international legal standards designed to govern the conduct of hostilities in situations of armed conflict (hereafter: 'paradigm of hostilities'). Comprising the conditions and modalities which govern the resort to means and methods of warfare, the paradigm of hostilities is derived primarily from international humanitarian law but, to a certain extent, may also be complemented by applicable human rights law.

2. *Applicability of the Paradigm of Hostilities.* The first prerequisite for the applicability of the legal paradigm of hostilities to a particular targeted killing is the existence of a situation of international or non-international armed conflict. Even in armed conflicts, however, the paradigm of hostilities supersedes that of law enforcement only where force is resorted to as part of the conduct of hostilities. As far as targeted killings are concerned, the legal paradigm of hostilities determines whether an individual is subject to lawful attack and, if so, provides the standards governing the use of force against legitimate military targets. While persons protected against direct attack may be exposed to incidental harm arising from military operations against legitimate targets, lethal force specifically directed against protected persons, even for reasons related to the conduct of hostilities, must always comply with the law enforcement paradigm.

3. *The Requirement of Distinction.* According to the fundamental principle of distinction, all those involved in the conduct of hostilities must distinguish between persons who do and those who do not constitute legitimate military targets and may direct their operations only against the former.[32] Both in international and in non-international armed conflict, the category of persons protected from direct attack includes peaceful civilians, medical and religious personnel, and persons *hors de combat.*[33] Lethal force specifically directed against individuals belonging to these

[32] See, for example, Art. 48 AP I. This rule has attained customary nature in both international and non-international armed conflict (Henckaerts and Doswald-Beck (eds), *Customary International*, Vol. I, Rule 1).

[33] International armed conflict: Art. 23(c) HagueReg; Art. 24 GC I; Art. 36 GC II;. Arts 12(1), 41(1) and (2), 51, 67(1) AP I; Art. 8(2)(b)(xxiv) ICC Statute. Non-international armed conflict: Arts 7(1), 9(1), 13 AP II; Art. 8(2)(e)(i) and (ii) ICC Statute and, implicitly, Art. 3 GC I–IV. On the customary nature of these rules in both international and non-international armed conflict see Henckaerts and Doswald-Beck (eds), *Customary International*, Vol. I, Rules 1, 25, 27, 47.

categories must in all circumstances comply with the law enforcement paradigm. The category of persons who do not benefit from immunity against direct attack, on the other hand, includes members of organized armed forces or groups belonging to a State or non-State party to the conflict, medical and religious personnel, or persons *hors de combat* who commit 'hostile' or 'harmful' acts despite the special protection afforded to them, as well as civilians 'taking a direct part in hostilities'.[34] Most significant for the lawfulness of targeted killings is the fact that, in contrast to civilians (who directly participate in hostilities on a merely spontaneous, sporadic, or unorganized basis), members of organized armed forces or groups belonging to a State or non-State party to an armed conflict do not regain their protection in the interval between specific combat operations, but remain subject to direct attack for the entire duration of their membership.[35] **17.04**

4. In situations of international armed conflict, the targeted killing of leading members of the opposing armed forces rarely gives rise to significant concern under the requirement of distinction. For example, the lawfulness under the requirement of distinction of the 'decapitation strikes' attempted at the outset of the joint US-British invasion of Iraq in 2003 against Iraqi President Saddam Hussein was not seriously questioned. Well-known historical examples of this category of operation are the targeted killing by the United States of Japanese Admiral Yamamoto Isoroku (1943) and the unsuccessful British commando raid against German Field Marshal Erwin Rommel (1941).

5. The determination of whether a targeted person represents a legitimate military target becomes more difficult in occupied territories or non-international armed conflict. Organized resistance movements, as well as non-State parties, are often composed of insufficiently distinguishable armed and political wings and may engage not only in hostilities, but also in social and humanitarian activities for the benefit of that segment of the population which is supporting them. Their fighting personnel may directly participate in hostilities on a permanent, regular, temporary, or punctual basis and, depending on the circumstances, may have a deliberate policy of intermingling with the peaceful civilian population. Additionally, such groups are regularly accompanied or supported by informants, collaborators, weapons smugglers, bomb manufacturers, and other civilian providers of goods, services, and finances. This intermingling poses enormous practical difficulties for a reliable distinction between combatants and civilians on the one hand, and

[34] International armed conflict: Art. 21 GC I; Arts 41(2), 48, 51(3), 67(1)(e) AP I. Non-international armed conflict: Arts 11(2), 13(3) AP II and, implicitly, Art. 3 GC I–IV. See also: Sandoz et al. (eds), *Commentary on the Additional Protocols of 8 June 1977 to the Geneva Conventions of 12 August 1949* (Geneva: ICRC, 1987), para. 4789. On the customary nature of these rules in both international and non-international armed conflict see Henckaerts and Doswald-Beck (eds), *Customary International*, Vol. I, Rules 6, 25, 27, 47.

[35] This view is affirmed by the ICRC in its *Interpretive Guidance on the Notion of Direct Participation in Hostilities under International Humanitarian Law* (Geneva: ICRC, 2009), Recommendation VII and accompanying Commentary.

17.04 between peaceful civilians and civilians directly participating in hostilities on the other. These difficulties may provoke ill-considered simplifications, such as authorizing targeted killings based on excessively wide interpretations of 'self-defence', 'hostile act', and 'hostile intent' or, more generally, against any person known to be, or suspected of being, a 'terrorist'—a juridically undefined notion strictly irrelevant for the principle of distinction. Thus, if erroneous and arbitrary targeting is to be avoided in operational practice, targeting decisions must be based on criteria derived from those branches of international law that have actually been designed to govern the conduct of hostilities in situations of armed conflict. Moreover, in many armed conflicts, informants, collaborators, factions, and gangs may be tempted to provide false intelligence to operating forces in order to provoke an attack against a rival group or individual, sometimes for reasons completely unrelated to the conflict. It is therefore of utmost importance that, in practice, no targeted killing be carried out before all feasible precautions have been taken to rule out erroneous or arbitrary targeting.[36]

6. Requirement of Precaution. States planning and conducting operations of targeted killing must take all feasible precautions to avoid, and in any event to minimize, incidental loss of civilian life, injury to civilians, and damage to civilian objects.[37] Therefore, those who plan and decide upon targeted killings must: do everything feasible to verify that the targeted individuals are legitimate military targets and that international humanitarian law does not otherwise prohibit attacks against them; take all feasible precautions in the choice of the means and methods to be used with a view to avoiding, and in any event to minimizing, incidental civilian harm; and refrain from launching a planned operation of targeted killing which may be expected to cause excessive incidental harm.[38] Moreover, once an operation of targeted killing has commenced, those responsible for its conduct must do everything feasible to cancel or suspend the operation if it becomes apparent that the targeted person is not, or is no longer, a legitimate military target or that the attack may be expected to cause excessive incidental harm.[39] In practice, targeted killings must be cancelled or suspended not only when a person was mistakenly considered a legitimate military target, but also when a civilian ceases to directly participate in hostilities, when a combatant surrenders or falls *hors de combat*, as well as when it becomes apparent that the incidental harm will be more significant or the

[36] On manipulations of the targeting process occurring during the Phoenix program in Vietnam see, for example, P.B. Heymann and J.N. Kayyem, *Protecting Liberty in an Age of Terror* (Cambridge, MA: The MIT Press, 2005), 66 *et seq*. See also ICRC/Asser Institute, Report on the Expert Meeting 'Direct Participation in Hostilities' (2005), 42.

[37] Art. 57(1) AP I. On the customary nature of this rule in international and non-international armed conflict see Henckaerts and Doswald-Beck (eds), *Customary International*, Vol. I, Rule 15.

[38] Arts. 57(2)(a)(i), (ii) and (iii) AP I. On the customary nature of this rule in international and non-international armed conflict see Henckaerts and Doswald-Beck (eds), *Customary International*, Vol. I, Rules 16–18.

[39] Art. 57(2)(b) AP I. On the customary nature of this rule in international and non-international armed conflict see Henckaerts and Doswald-Beck (eds), *Customary International*, Vol. I, Rule 19.

military advantage less important than anticipated and that, therefore, the overall ratio would have to be regarded as disproportionate. 17.04

7. 'Feasible' precautions are those precautions which are practicable or practically possible taking into account all circumstances ruling at the time, including humanitarian and military considerations.[40] In practice, the extent to which precautionary measures are feasible will depend on factors such as the availability of intelligence on the targeted persons and their surroundings, the level of control exercised over the territory where the targeted killing is to take place, the choice and sophistication of available weapons, the urgency of the operation, and the additional security risk which precautionary measures may entail for the operating forces or the civilian population. As a general rule, more can be expected, for instance, from an Occupying Power confronted with sporadic resistance within territory under its effective control than from an invading force involved in major combat operations, more from a State disposing of air supremacy, satellite reconnaissance, and modern weapon systems than from a low-tech force equipped with unsophisticated weaponry and lacking precise intelligence, more also from a rebel force well acquainted with the local circumstances than from an alien invasion force without knowledge of the terrain. Obviously, however, the flexibility of the notion of 'feasibility' cannot be construed as justifying the violation of express prohibitions of international humanitarian law.

8. Whether a particular targeted killing is permissible under international humanitarian law must in each case be determined in good faith by those planning, deciding, and conducting the operation. In view of the often extreme circumstances of armed conflict, there must be a measure of tolerance for error, provided that the required assessment has been made 'within the limits of honest judgment on the basis of the conditions prevailing at the time'.[41] Where all feasible precautions do not succeed in clarifying whether an individual is subject to direct attack both juridical logic and elementary considerations of humanity require that the presumption be in favour of protection.[42] In no case does the paradigm of hostilities permit the targeting of selected individuals based on mere suspicion that they may be a legitimate target.[43] Just as under the law enforcement paradigm, the distinctive

[40] Art. 3(4) CCW Protocol II (1980); Art. 1(5) CCW Protocol III (1980); Art. 3(10) CCW Amended Protocol II (1996). Affirmative also Henckaerts and Doswald-Beck (eds), *Customary International*, Vol. I, Rule 15, p. 54, with reference to State practice contained in Vol. II, 357 *et seq*. See also Sandoz et al. (eds), *Commentary on the Additional Protocols*, para. 2198, with certain reservations regarding the taking into account of military considerations. See also the French text of Art. 57 AP I ('faire tout ce qui est pratiquement possible').

[41] UNWCC, *USA v Wilhelm List and others (The Hostages Case)*, Nuremberg, 8 July 1947 to 19 February 1948, Law Reports of Trials of War Criminals, Vol. VIII, Case no. 47 (London: HM Stationery Office, 1949), 69.

[42] Art. 50(1) AP I. A general presumtion of protection in case of doubt is affirmed also by the ICRC in its Interpretive Guidance, Recommendation VIII and accompanying Commentary.

[43] Affirmative also M. Kremnitzer, 'Präventives Töten [Preventive Killings]', in D. Fleck (ed.), *Rechtsfragen der Terrorismusbekämpfung durch Streitkräfte* (Baden-Baden: Nomos, 2005), 201–22;

17.04 criterion between 'mere suspicion' and erroneous 'honest judgement' is not only the degree of subjective conviction or doubt actually held by the acting State agent, but also the objective reasonableness of that subjective conviction in view of the circumstances prevailing at the time.

9. If operations of targeted killing are to have any chance of success, they must be planned and organized with pinpoint accuracy and based on excellent intelligence. Compared to major military confrontations involving a multitude of personnel, equipment, and unpredictable factors on both sides, operations of targeted killing have very little tolerance for improvisation, and even minor unexpected events may lead to failure, erroneous targeting, or excessive incidental harm. Therefore, decisions to target pre-selected individuals in the conduct of hostilities are not typically taken under the time pressure of immediate combat operations. On the contrary, targeted individuals are often tracked for several days or weeks before the attack is carried out. Therefore, in the case of targeted killings, the 'heat of battle' will rarely be a valid justification for failure to take extensive precautionary measures already during the planning and decision phase of an operation. Consequently, the requirement to take all feasible precautions merits particularly strict and literal interpretation in relation to operations of targeted killing.[44]

10. *The Requirement of Proportionality.* Targeted killings directed against a legitimate military target are subject to the requirement of proportionality. In contrast to the law enforcement paradigm, the focus of the proportionality assessment under the paradigm of hostilities is not the harm caused to the targeted persons themselves, but the incidental harm inflicted on peaceful bystanders. Under the paradigm of hostilities, the principle of proportionality prohibits the targeted killing of a person subject to lawful attack if the expected incidental harm would be excessive in relation to the concrete and direct military advantage anticipated from the death of the targeted individual.[45] The proportionality of incidental harm caused by a targeted killing does not depend on the achievement of a strict numerical balance of some sort, but on the relative military importance of a target, its 'military target

T. Ruys, 'License to Kill? State-Sponsored Assassination Under International Law', XLIV-1-2 *Military Law and Law of War Review* (2005), 13–49, at 22 *et seq.*

[44] In developing guidelines for the lawfulness for targeted killing against civilians directly participating in hostilities, the Israeli High Court of Justice formulated the requirement of precaution as follows: '[F]irst, well based information is needed before categorizing a civilian as falling into one of the discussed categories. Innocent civilians are not to be harmed [. . .]. Information which has been most thoroughly verified is needed regarding the identity and activity of the civilian who is allegedly taking part in the hostilities [. . .]. [. . .] The burden of proof on the attacking army is heavy [. . .]. In the case of doubt, careful verification is needed before an attack is made' (Israeli High Court of Justice, *The Public Committee Against Torture et al. v The Government of Israel et al.* (HCJ 769/02), Judgment of 13 December 2006, para. 40).

[45] Art. 51(5)(b) AP I. On the customary nature of the principle both in international and non-international armed conflict see Henckaerts and Doswald-Beck (eds), *Customary International,* Vol. I, Rule 14; ICTY, *Prosecutor v Kupreskić et al.*, Case no. IT-95-16-T-14, Judgment of 14 January 2000 (Trial Chamber), para. 524. See also ICJ, *Nuclear Weapons Opinion*, (Dissenting Opinion of Judge Higgins), para. 20.

value'. While any person subject to direct attack may, in principle, be targeted, 'high value' targets will justify a greater incidental harm than 'low value' targets. The military target value of individuals depends on factors such as their rank, operational function, and momentary tactical position and may be subject to change. For example, especially capable military leaders and highly specialized technical personnel are likely to be high value targets as long as their special skills are effectively employed in the conduct of hostilities, but may become low value targets when removed from their influential position. Ultimately, no single set of objective criteria is likely to lead to satisfactory conclusions in all situations. Therefore, the requirement of proportionality will always remain a delicate issue to be determined in good faith and on a case-by-case basis. **17.04**

11. In operational reality, the resort to targeted killing as a method of individualized warfare regularly results in incidental civilian death and injury. For example, the Israeli policy of targeted killing having been officially operational since November 2000, it is now possible to make an approximate long-term evaluation of the method from the perspective of proportionality. Thus, according to available statistical data covering the period from 2000 to 2007, the Israeli policy would have caused an approximate overall average of six incidental casualties (one death and five injuries) for every two targeted killings.[46] While this ratio may be acceptable on an exceptional basis, it can hardly be regarded as proportionate if institutionalized in the long term. Thus, although targeted killing is usually portrayed as a method of surgical warfare,[47] there may arguably be a risk of disproportion in a

[46] According to statistics provided by B'Tselem, between 9 November 2000 and 1 June 2007, the Israeli policy of targeted killings caused the death of 364 persons, of whom 216 were killed intentionally and 148 incidentally (statistics: B'Tselem, available at <http://www.btselem.org>). Apparently less cautious, the statistics of PCATI provide similar numbers already for the period from November 2000 until May 2004, namely a total of 362 deaths caused by targeted killings, 237 of whom were intended and 125 incidental. In addition, PCATI counts 585 persons who were injured during these attacks, stating that only seven of them were intended victims (PCATI, Press Release of 17 February 2005, available at <http://www.stoptorture.org>). Before the Israeli High Court of Justice, the petitioners (PCATI and LAW) claimed that, between November 2000 and the end of 2005, Israeli operations killed approximately 300 targeted persons and 150 bystanders, wounded hundreds of others and failed more than 30 times (see Israel HCJ, *PCATI v Israel*, § 2). Israeli air force commander Elyezer Shkedy claimed that the ratio between incidental and intended deaths in targeted air strikes had improved significantly from 1:1 until 2003, to 1:12 in 2004 and to 1:28 in 2005: Amos Harel, *Probe: Air force didn't fully survey Gaza strike scene*, Haaretz, 8 March 2006, available at <http://www.haaretz.com>.

[47] See, for example, S.R. David, *Fatal Choices: Israel's Policy of Targeted Killing*, Mideast Security and Policy Studies no. 51 (Bar-Ilan University: Begin-Sadat Center for Security Studies, 2002), 17; J.N. Kendall, '"Targeted Killings" Under International Law', 80 *North Carolina Law Review* (2002), 1069, at 1087; J. Ulrich, 'The Gloves Were Never On: Defining the President's Authority to Order Targeted Killing in the War Against Terrorism', 45 *Virginia Journal of International Law* (2005), 1029–63, at 1054. Critical, however, O. Ben-Naftali and K.R. Michaeli, '"We Must Not Make a Scarecrow of the Law": A Legal Analysis of the Israeli Policy of Targeted Killings', 36 *Cornell International Law Journal* (2003), 233–92, at 250, who doubt the pinpoint character of targeted killings. D. Kretzmer, 'Targeted Killing of Suspected Terrorists: Extra-Judicial Executions or Legitimate Means of Defence?', 16 *EJIL* (2005), 171–212, at 200 *et seq.*, demands a particularly strict proportionality test for targeted killings.

17.04 long-term military strategy which essentially reduces the conduct of hostilities to the 'decapitation' of the adverse forces without a realistic prospect of bringing about a permanent military solution to the conflict.[48] After all, the concrete and direct military advantage obtained from targeted killings must be evaluated from the perspective of the only legitimate purpose of the conduct of hostilities, which is to weaken and overcome the military forces of the enemy.

12. In conclusion, targeted killings are neither inherently disproportionate nor inherently proportionate. Instead, a separate proportionality assessment will have to be made for each operation. Nevertheless, States resorting to this method should not lose from sight that the targeted killing of an enemy is not a purpose in itself but must be undertaken with a view to progressing the military effort against the adverse party and, ultimately, to ending the conflict. Strategies which are calculated to contain a conflict on a low level of intensity while sacrificing a substantial number of peaceful civilians for each targeted combatant therefore appear to be in disaccord with the fundamental principle of proportionality underlying the paradigm of hostilities.

13. *The Prohibition of Denial of Quarter*. The purpose of the conduct of hostilities is not to kill combatants, but to defeat the enemy, even if it should be necessary to kill his combatants to achieve that goal. Therefore, it is prohibited to order that there shall be no survivors or to conduct hostilities on that basis, to refuse to accept an enemy's surrender, or to kill those who are *hors de combat*.[49] Whether or not the circumstances permit the capture and evacuation of adversaries who are *hors de combat* is immaterial. The method of targeted killing is problematic under this rule because it aims specifically at the killing of the targeted person. In view of the prohibition of denial of quarter, any order of targeted killing, or to 'capture or kill', which excludes the option of suspending the attack when the targeted person falls *hors de combat*, constitutes a serious violation of international humanitarian law.[50] The same principle applies to the practice of offering a price for the 'liquidation' of an individual or for his or her capture 'dead or alive'.[51]

14. The prohibition of denial of quarter may pose significant operational problems where small commando units tasked with carrying out a targeted killing behind enemy lines are confronted with a surrendering or wounded target. However, the

[48] While the Israeli head of the air force, Lt Gen. Dan Halutz, stated that targeted killing 'is the most important method of fighting terror', the standard of proportionality to be applied in such operations appears to remain controversial among those responsible for the implementation of the Israeli policy of targeted killing. See, as a whole, L. Blumenfeld, 'In Israel, a Divisive Struggle Over Targeted Killing', *Washington Post*, 27 August 2006, available at <http://www.washingtonpost.com>.

[49] Art. 40 AP I. See also Art. 23(1)(d) HagueReg and, for non-international armed conflict, Art. 4(1) AP II. On the customary nature of this rule in both international and non-international armed conflict see Henckaerts and Doswald-Beck (eds), *Customary International*, Vol. I, Rule 46.

[50] Art. 8(2)(b)(xii) ICC Statute.

[51] Henckaerts and Doswald-Beck (eds), *Customary International*, Vol. I, Rule 65, pp. 225 *et seq.*, with references to State practice contained in Vol. II, 1380 *et seq.* (paras 938 *et seq.*).

law of hostilities tolerates no deviation whatsoever from the duty to give quarter and to respect persons *hors de combat*. Where the targeted person indicates an intention to surrender or is otherwise placed *hors de combat*, he or she must be captured or, if capture and evacuation are not feasible, may be disarmed but must be released without further harm.[52] **17.04**

15. Of course, targeted killings do not always involve direct fire delivered by commando units, but may also be carried out by way of manned or unmanned aircraft, clandestinely planted explosive devices, or otherwise in a manner which does not give the targeted victim a realistic opportunity to surrender. This does not per se suggest a violation of the denial of quarter. It is inherent in the conduct of hostilities that individuals who are liable to direct attack run the risk of being individually targeted and that the circumstances may not at every moment permit them to surrender to the adversary. With regard to targeted killings, the prohibition of denial of quarter simply requires that the operating forces remain receptive to a declaration of surrender should the opportunity arise and that they must imperatively suspend any attack against persons who have fallen *hors de combat*, even if the chosen means and methods or other circumstances do not permit their capture and evacuation. Thus, it is always prohibited to declare that the adversary is outside the law, and to treat him as such on the battlefield.[53]

16. The Prohibition of Perfidy. During the conduct of hostilities, it is prohibited to kill, injure, or capture an adversary by resort to perfidy. Perfidy is understood to comprise any act inviting the confidence of an adversary to lead him to believe that he is entitled to, or is obliged to accord, protection under international humanitarian law, carried out with the intent to betray that confidence.[54] Not prohibited are ruses of war, that is to say, acts which are intended to mislead an adversary or to induce him to act recklessly but which neither invite the confidence of an adversary with respect to legal protection nor otherwise violate the law.[55] The prohibition of perfidy applies only during the conduct of hostilities and not to operations governed by the law enforcement paradigm.[56]

17. The practical relevance of the prohibition of perfidy for the method of targeted killing is considerable, and there is no lack of examples where it has been violated.

[52] Art. 41(3) AP I.

[53] Sandoz et al. (eds), *Commentary on the Additional Protocols*, para. 1600.

[54] Art. 37(1) AP I. See also Art. 23(b) HagueReg, which prohibits treacherous killing and injuring, but not capturing. According to the ICRC, the rule expressed in Art. 37 AP I has attained customary nature in both international and non-international armed conflict, see Henckaerts and Doswald-Beck (eds), *Customary International*, Vol. I, Rule 65. See also ICTY, *Prosecutor v Dusko Tadić*, Case no. IT-94-A, Decision on the Defence Motion for Interlocutory Appeal on Jurisdiction of 2 October 1995 (Appeals Chamber), para. 125. On the prohibition of perfidy see also Section 3.06, commentary para. 5, and Section 16.11, commentary para. 3.

[55] Art. 37(2) AP I.

[56] See also Chapter 4 'Conceptual Distinction and Overlaps Between Law Enforcement and the Conduct of Hostilities'.

17.04 Most notably, States operating in a hostile environment or in the territory of a third, neutral State have regularly relied on undercover forces in order to maintain the element of surprise. Although an apparently frequent practice, it must be emphasized that the use of plain clothes operatives to carry out targeted killings will almost always amount to the feigning of civilian, non-combatant status for the purpose of killing an adversary. Such operations severely jeopardize the protection of peaceful civilians and not only fall under the prohibition of perfidy, but also amount to war crimes in international and non-international armed conflict.[57]

18. While the use of undercover forces is the aspect of perfidy most likely to become relevant in connection with State-sponsored targeted killings, other conceivable examples may include the feigning of protected status through the use of protective emblems, flags of truce, or ambulances. Conversely, the prohibition of perfidy does not prevent States from carrying out targeted killings that depend upon the element of surprise, such as uniformed commando raids, the placing of explosive devices behind enemy lines, and attacks from camouflaged positions or properly marked military aircraft, as long as there is no attempt to invite the confidence of an adversary with respect to protection under international humanitarian law. Nor would the prohibition of perfidy prevent the mere gathering by undercover units of target intelligence for later use in separate operations by uniformed personnel.[58] Furthermore, since the prohibition of perfidy applies only to the conduct of hostilities, States are not prevented from employing undercover forces for operations governed by, and complying with, the law enforcement paradigm.

19. *Prohibition or Restriction of Certain Weapons.* Modern international humanitarian law includes an extensive body of rules prohibiting or regulating the use of certain weapons. Of particular operational relevance for the method of targeted killing are the restraints imposed by international humanitarian law on the use of poison, expanding bullets, and booby-traps including remote or timer controlled devices. Other prohibited weapons, such as bacteriological and chemical agents, explosive bullets, and ammunition producing non-detectable fragments, could conceivably be employed to target selected individuals but are not separately addressed here.

20. *Poison or Poisonous Weapons.* The resort to poison or poisonous weapons in the conduct of hostilities is prohibited in absolute terms.[59] Poison is silent, invisible, and extremely difficult to remedy without the corresponding antidote and, therefore, represents a tempting weapon for targeted killings. Indeed, despite

[57] See Arts 8(2)(b)(xi) and 8(2)(e)(ix) ICC Statute.

[58] In situations of international armed conflict, if caught in the act, such personnel could be prosecuted for espionage under domestic law.

[59] See, for example, Art. 23(a) HagueReg and Art. 8(2)(b)(xvii) ICC Statute. On the customary nature of this rule in international and non-international armed conflict see Henckaerts and Doswald-Beck (eds), *Customary International*, Vol. I, Rule 72.

the prohibition on the use of poison or poisonous weapons in the conduct of **17.04** hostilities, poison has actually been used for targeted killings to eliminate individual adversaries in situations of armed conflict.[60]

21. *Expanding Bullets.* In the conduct of hostilities it is prohibited to resort to 'expanding bullets', that is to say, bullets which expand or flatten easily in the human body.[61] Expanding bullets cause more severe injuries and increase the chance of incapacitating or killing the targeted person with immediate effect. With regard to the method of targeted killing, this gives rise to the seemingly contradictory situation where an operation specifically aiming to kill a selected individual may not resort to ammunition which would significantly increase the probability of success. Properly understood, however, the prohibition of expanding bullets, like the prohibition of denial of quarter, illustrates that the purpose of the conduct of hostilities is not to kill enemy combatants, but to defeat the opposing party to the conflict and that, to this end, it may be sufficient to disable them without rendering their death inevitable.[62] While it would go too far to interpret the prohibition of expanding bullets as suggesting a general prohibition of operations specifically aiming to kill an adversary, it does indicate a certain tension between the logic of targeted killings and the fundamental principles underlying the normative paradigm of hostilities. It would appear that the method of targeted killing, although of minimal quantitative effect, must be located at the extreme end of what the law of armed conflict permits as a matter of concept and principle.

22. The fact that expanding bullets are permissible in situations of law enforcement but not in the conduct of hostilities may be explained, *inter alia*, by the fact that expanding bullets do not pass through the body of the targeted person and, therefore, are less likely to cause incidental injury to innocent bystanders. Although not perfectly balanced, this approach accurately reflects the fact that the tolerance for incidental harm is significantly greater in the conduct of hostilities than it is under the law enforcement paradigm. Moreover, since expanding bullets used by law enforcement personnel are generally fired from pistols, they deposit much less energy and cause less severe wounds than rifle bullets. To the knowledge of the author, expanding bullets have been used for targeted killings only in situations governed by the law enforcement paradigm.[63]

[60] For example, on or around 19 March 2002, in a secret service operation for which the Russian State has officially assumed responsibility, a poisoned letter killed Chechen rebel leader Khattab a few seconds after he opened the envelope. Further, on 25 September 1997, two plain clothes Mossad agents attempted to kill the political leader of Hamas, Khalid Mashal, in Amman, Jordan, by injecting a toxic substance into his ear. The agents were subsequently apprehended by the Jordanian authorities and, upon pressure by King Hussein, Israel was forced to hand over the antidote required to save Mashal's life. For a more detailed description of these cases, see also Melzer, *Targeted Killing*, 437–8.

[61] See Hague Declaration concerning Expanding Bullets (1899); Art. 8(2)(b)(xix) ICC Statute. On the customary nature of this prohibition in international and non-international armed conflict see Henckaerts and Doswald-Beck (eds), *Customary International*, Vol. I, Rule 77.

[62] See St Petersburg Declaration (1868).

[63] An example in this respect is the case of Ewald K., which occurred in Chur, Switzerland, in 2000. In this case, although there was no risk to innocent bystanders, Swiss police snipers deliberately used

17.04 23. *Booby-Traps including Remote or Timer Controlled Devices.* In the conduct of hostilities, it is prohibited to resort to booby-traps[64] and other, remote or timer controlled devices,[65] which are in any way attached to or associated with objects or persons entitled to special protection under international humanitarian law or with objects that are likely to attract civilians. Prohibited is also the prefabrication of booby-traps or other devices in the form of apparently harmless portable objects. Of course, in accordance with the principle of distinction, such devices may not be used indiscriminately or directly against persons protected against direct attack.[66]

24. In operational practice, numerous targeted killings have been carried out through booby-traps and other devices.[67] It is clear, for example, that the booby-trapping of a public phone and, depending on the circumstances, also of a mobile phone or letter would probably have to be regarded as 'indiscriminate', unless sufficient precautions are taken to exclude unintended civilian casualties. Therefore, in practice, the lawfulness of such devices would almost always require a manual detonation by remote control. Of course, apart from the permissibility under international humanitarian law of the employed explosive device as such, the lawfulness of each of these operations depends on additional factors. Thus, it may be questioned whether all of the targeted persons could actually be regarded as legitimate military objectives at the time of attack, whether their killing was actually militarily necessary and, where applicable, whether the resulting 'incidental harm' was excessive.

25. *Operational Relevance of Considerations of Military Necessity and Humanity.* In regulating the use of force against legitimate military targets, international humanitarian law neither provides an express 'right to kill' (akin to a State's right to execute a lawfully pronounced death sentence), nor does it impose a general obligation to 'capture rather than kill' (as would be the case under the law enforcement paradigm). Instead, international humanitarian law simply refrains from providing certain categories of persons with protection against attacks, that is to say, against 'acts of violence against the adversary, whether in offence or in defence'.[68] The fact alone that a person is not protected against acts of violence, however, is not

expanding rifle bullets in order to ensure that Ewald K. had no opportunity to return fire but would be killed instantly. This motivation was accepted by the Cantonal Court as sufficient to justify the use of expanding rifle bullets. For a more detailed case description see Melzer, *Targeted Killing*, 437–8.

[64] 'Booby-trap' means any device or material which is designed, constructed, or adapted to kill or injure and which functions unexpectedly when a person disturbs or approaches an apparently harmless object or performs an apparently safe act (Art. 2(2) CCW Protocol II and Art. 2(4) CCW Amended Protocol II).

[65] 'Other devices' means manually-emplaced munitions and devices including improvised explosive devices designed to kill, injure, or damage and which are actuated manually, by remote control or automatically after a lapse of time (Art. 2(5) CCW Amended Protocol II and, without the phrases in brackets, Art. 2(3) CCW Protocol II).

[66] Art. 3(2)–(4) CCW Protocol II; Art. 3(7), (8), and (10) CCW Amended Protocol II.

[67] For examples, see Melzer, *Targeted Killing*, 417–18.

[68] Art. 41(1) AP I.

equivalent to a legal entitlement of the adversary to kill that person without any further considerations. Rather, even in the conduct of hostilities, elementary considerations of humanity require that no more death, injury, or destruction be caused than is actually necessary to accomplish a legitimate purpose. **17.04**

26. The restrictive function of considerations of humanity can be based on three distinct theoretical arguments. First, in situations where operating forces exercise sufficient territorial control to carry out an arrest, the parallel applicability of human rights law arguably influences international humanitarian law regulating the conduct of hostilities so as to impose considerations of humanity even in the execution of direct attacks on legitimate targets.[69] Second, a similar argument can be made based on a wider proportionality requirement, which would constitute a general principle of international law.[70] In contrast to the specific proportionality test stipulated by international humanitarian law for the conduct of hostilities, this general principle of proportionality would balance the military advantage expected to result from an attack not only against expected incidental harm, but also against the harm likely to be inflicted on the targeted persons themselves.[71] The third approach is to derive the restrictive function of considerations of humanity directly from the fundamental principles of military necessity and humanity underlying and informing the entire normative framework of international humanitarian law.[72]

27. In the conduct of hostilities, the strict requirement of 'absolute necessity', which governs the use of lethal force against persons under the law enforcement paradigm, is replaced by the more widely conceived requirement of 'military necessity', which no longer refers to the removal of an imminent threat or the prevention of a serious crime, but to the achievement of a legitimate military

[69] See, for example, the expert discussions recorded in: ICRC, Report DPH 2006, 78 ff., annexed to: ICRC, Interpretive Guidance.

[70] This argument has been made by the Israeli High Court of Justice in its judgments on a particular section of the West Bank Barrier (2004) and on the Israeli policy of targeted killing (2006). In Israeli High Court of Justice, *Beit Sourik Village Council v The Government of Israel et al.* (HCJ 2056/04), Judgment of 30 June 2004, para. 37 the Court held: 'Proportionality is recognized today as a general principle of international law. [. . .] From the foregoing principle springs the Principle of Humanitarian Law (or that of the law of war): Belligerents shall not inflict harm on their adversaries out of proportion with the object of warfare, which is to destroy or weaken the strength of the enemy.' Furthermore, in Israeli High Court of Justice, *The Public Committee Against Torture et al. v The Government of Israel et al.* (HCJ 769/02), Judgment of 13 December 2006, para. 40, the Court held that 'a civilian taking a direct part in hostilities cannot be attacked at such time as he is doing so, if a less harmful means can be employed. In our domestic law, that rule is called for by the principle of proportionality. Indeed, among the military means, one must choose the means whose harm to the human rights of the harmed person is smallest. Thus, if a terrorist taking a direct part in hostilities can be arrested, interrogated, and tried, those are the means which should be employed [. . .]. Trial is preferable to use of force. A rule-of-law State employs, to the extent possible, procedures of law and not procedures of force.'

[71] For a more detailed discussion of this approach see: Melzer, 'Targeted Killing or Less Harmful Means?—Israel's High Court Judgment on Targeted Killing and the Restrictive Function of Military Necessity', 9 *Yearbook of International Humanitarian Law* (2006), 87–113.

[72] This is the view taken by the ICRC in its Interpretive Guidance, Recommendation IX and accompanying Commentary.

17.04 purpose. Today, the principle of military necessity is generally recognized to permit 'only that degree and kind of force, not otherwise prohibited by the law of armed conflict, that is required in order to achieve the legitimate purpose of the conflict, namely the complete or partial submission of the enemy at the earliest possible moment with the minimum expenditure of life and resources'.[73] Complementing the principle of military necessity is the principle of humanity, which 'forbids the infliction of suffering, injury or destruction not actually necessary for the accomplishment of legitimate military purposes'.[74] In conjunction, the principles of military necessity and of humanity could be said to reduce the sum total of permissible military action from that which international humanitarian law does not expressly prohibit to that which is actually necessary for the accomplishment of a legitimate military purpose in the prevailing circumstances.[75]

28. In operational practice, the kind and degree of force to be used against legitimate military targets obviously cannot be pre-determined for all conceivable military operations, but must be determined by the operating forces based on the totality of the circumstances prevailing at the relevant time and place. As a general rule, circumstances which would allow an attempt at capture or the issuing of a warning prior to the use of lethal force are more likely to arise in territory over which the operating forces exercise effective control. This may be the case, for example, where an unarmed adversary or civilian is observed while transmitting targeting information, marking targets on the ground, transporting ammunition to

[73] United Kingdom: Ministry of Defence, *The Manual of the Law of Armed Conflict* (Oxford: Oxford University Press, 2004), Section 2.2 (Military Necessity). Similar interpretations are provided in numerous other contemporary military manuals and glossaries. See, for example, NATO: *Glossary of Terms and Definitions (AAP-6V)*, p. 2-M-5; United States: Department of the Army, *Field Manual 27-10* (1956), para. 3; US Department of the Navy, *The Commander's Handbook on the Law of Naval Operations, NWP 1–14M/MCWP 5–12-1/COMDTPUB P5800.7A* (2007), para. 5.3.1, p. 5–2.; France: Ministry of Defence, *Manuel de Droit des Conflits Armés* (2001), 86 *et seq*.; Germany: Federal Ministry of Defence, *Triservice Manual ZDv 15/2: Humanitarian Law in Armed Conflicts* (August 1992) § 130; Switzerland: Swiss Army, *Regulations 51.007/IV, Bases légales du comportement à l'engagement* (2005), § 160. Historically, the modern notion of 'military necessity' has been strongly influenced by the definition provided in Art. 14 of the Lieber Code (United States: *Adjutant General's Office, General Orders No. 100*, 24 April 1863).

[74] United Kingdom, *Manual of the Law of Armed Conflict*, Section 2.4 (Humanity). Although no longer in force, see also the formulation provided in: United States: Department of the Air Force, *Air Force Pamphlet, AFP 110–31* (1976), para. 1–3 (2), p. 1–6. Thus, as far as they aim to limit death, injury, or destruction to what is actually necessary for legitimate military purposes, the principles of military necessity and of humanity do not oppose, but mutually reinforce, each other. Only once military action can reasonably be regarded as necessary for the accomplishment of a legitimate military purpose, do the principles of military necessity and humanity become opposing considerations which must be balanced against each other as expressed in the specific provisions of international humanitarian law.

[75] Affirmative also the ICRC in its Interpretive Guidance, Recommendation IX and accompanying Commentary. See Sandoz et al. (eds), *Commentary on the Additional Protocols*, § 1395. See also the determination of the International Court of Justice that the prohibition on the use of means and methods of warfare of a nature to cause unnecessary suffering to combatants constitutes an intransgressible principle of international customary law and a cardinal principle of IHL, which outlaws the causation of 'harm greater than that unavoidable to achieve legitimate military objectives'. See ICJ, *Nuclear Weapons Opinion*, § 78.

a firing position, or sabotaging military installations, always provided that the circumstances are such that the persons in question could be confronted and arrested without additional risk to the operating forces or the surrounding civilian population.[76] In sum, while military forces certainly cannot be required to take additional risks for themselves or the surrounding civilian population in order to capture an armed adversary alive, it would defy basic notions of humanity to shoot to kill an adversary or to refrain from giving him or her an opportunity to surrender where the circumstances are such that there manifestly is no necessity for the application of lethal force. **17.04**

29. During a series of expert meetings conducted by the ICRC, the proposition that the kind and degree of force permissible against legitimate targets is subject not only to express restrictions imposed on specific means and method of warfare, but also to a general requirement of necessity, remained highly controversial. While one group of experts held that the use of lethal force against persons constituting legitimate military targets is permissible only where capture is not possible without additional risk for the operating forces, another group of experts insisted that, under international humanitarian law, there is no legal obligation to capture rather than kill.[77] Throughout the discussions, however, it was neither claimed that there was an obligation to assume increased risks in order to protect the life of an adversary not entitled to protection against direct attack, nor that such a person could lawfully be killed in a situation where there manifestly is no military necessity to do so.[78]

[76] See also the expert discussions recorded in ICRC, Report DPH 2006, 65, annexed to ICRC, Interpretive Gudiance.

[77] For the official position taken by the International Committee of the Red Cross in this respect, see ICRC, Interpretive Guidance DPH, Section IX. For four critiques of the ICRC's position, and the organization's official response, see NYU/JILP, Forum on 'Direct Participation in Hostilities', pp. 637–916. See also Israeli High Court of Justice, *The Public Committee against Torture et al. v The Government of Israel et al.* (HCJ 769/02), Judgment of 13 December 2006, para. 40. For a detailed discussion see Melzer, 'Targeted Killing or Less Harmful Means?', 87–113.

[78] For an overview of the relevant discussions see: ICRC, Report DPH 2004, 17 *et seq.*; ICRC, Report DPH 2005, 31 *et seq.*, 44 *et seq.*, 50, 56 *et seq.*, 67; ICRC, Report DPH 2006, 74–79; ICRC, Report DPH 2008, 7-32, annexed to ICRC, Interpretive Guidance.

Chapter 18

WEAPONS UNDER THE LAW OF MILITARY OPERATIONS

Introduction

This chapter addresses the law of military operations rules that regulate the possession and use of weapons. It therefore sets forth the rules that apply during both international and non-international armed conflict, and during situations that do not constitute an armed conflict.

Much of the relevant law is based on treaties, some of which are, as will be explained, reflective of customary law and thus bind all States. Some legal rules prohibit certain weapons altogether, while other rules limit the circumstances in which particular weapons may lawfully be used.

The chapter starts by considering the rules that apply during armed conflict. Section 18.01(a) and (b) explains the two customary principles of weapons law, namely the superfluous injury/unnecessary suffering and indiscriminate weapons principles. Section 18.01(c) addresses a customary and two conventional law rules relating to the natural environment. In Section 18.01(d) the IHL rules that prohibit particular weapons technologies are related while in the following section we discuss such rules as restrict the circumstances in which particular weapons technologies may be employed. Section 18.02 briefly addresses non-lethal weapons and Section 18.03 notes the law in relation to the use of nuclear weapons. In Section 18.04 we discuss the rules as to the legal review of new weapons and Section 18.05 analyses the extent to which the rules that apply during non-international armed conflicts differ from those applying to armed conflict between States. The discussion concludes in Section 18.06 with an assessment of the fundamentally different legal arrangements that apply to weapons procurement and use when the situation falls below or does not reach the armed conflict threshold. Some of the law relating to particular weapons is complex, intricate, and detailed. What follows is of necessity a brief summary of the core principles and rules.

The terms 'weapon', 'means of warfare', and 'method of warfare' are not defined in the law of armed conflict. The idea of a 'weapon'[1] is critically linked

[1] See W.H. Boothby, *Weapons and the Law of Armed Conflict* (Oxford: Oxford University Press, 2009), 4 and J. McClelland, 'The Review of Weapons in Accordance with Article 36 of Additional Protocol I', 850 *IRRC* (2003), 397. Weapons are described in the Air and Missile Warfare Manual as 'a means of warfare used in combat operations, including a gun, missile, bomb or other munitions, that is

WILLIAM H. BOOTHBY

to the use,[2] intended use,[3] or design purpose[4] of the relevant capability. It can therefore be defined as an offensive capability that is applied, or that is intended or designed to be applied, to an adversary. A destructive, damaging, or injurious effect of the weapon will usually result from physical impact, but the offensive capability need not be kinetic.[5] 'Means of warfare' are weapons, weapon systems,[6] or platforms employed for the purposes of attack. 'Methods of warfare' are activities designed adversely to affect the enemy's military operations or military capacity,[7] so 'means of warfare' can be regarded as the equipment used to cause harm to the enemy while 'methods of warfare' are the ways in which hostilities are conducted.

18.1 The Conventional and Customary Principles of Weapons Law Applying in Armed Conflict

The right to choose methods or means of warfare is not unlimited. **18.01**

1. Acknowledged in 1874 by the authors of the Brussels Declaration,[8] the notion that '[t]he laws of war do not recognize in belligerents an unlimited power in the adoption of means of injuring the enemy' was adopted in treaty form in the Hague Regulations of 1899 and 1907[9] and in Article 35(1) of AP I. The principles and rules considered in the following Sections of this part of the chapter define the limitation to which reference is made here. The precise terms in which these principles and rules are expressed are important as they define the extent of the prohibitions and restrictions that States have accepted.

capable of causing either (i) injury to, or death of, persons; or (ii) damage to, or destruction of, objects', AMW Manual, Rule 1(ff).

[2] The decision, for example, to use a rock to cause injury to an adversary converts an inoffensive natural object into a weapon by virtue of use.

[3] The collection of a number of rocks with the intention of using them in the future to cause injury to an adversary similarly converts those objects into weapons in advance of their actual use.

[4] Designing an object so as to be used to cause injury or damage in the course of an armed conflict will render that object a weapon, for example when a flint is shaped into an arrowhead.

[5] So, for example, a cyber tool may be capable of causing damaging or injurious effects to an adversary and thus may be capable of constituting a weapon. It will only actually be a weapon, however, if the cyber tool, or a system of which it is an integral part, is used, intended or designed to deliver an offensive capability against the adversary in the course of an armed conflict; Consider for example Commentary to AMW Manual Rule 1(ff), at para. 1.

[6] Y. Dinstein, 'The Conduct of Hostilities under the Law of International Armed Conflict', 2nd edn (Cambridge: Cambridge University Press, 2010), 1.

[7] AMW Manual, Rule 1(v).

[8] Project of an International Declaration concerning the Laws and Customs of War, Brussels, 27 August 1874 (Brussels Declaration), Art. 12.

[9] Regulations Respecting the Laws and Customs of War on Land annexed, respectively, to Hague Convention II of 29 July 1899 and Hague Convention IV of 18 October 1907, Art. 22.

18.01 (a) It is prohibited to employ weapons, projectiles and material and methods of warfare of a nature to cause superfluous injury or unnecessary suffering.

1. This cardinal principle of IHL[10] and thus of the law of weaponry is based on language in AP I[11] and is a customary rule that binds all States in relation to international and non-international armed conflicts.[12] The rule was reflected in the Preamble to the St Petersburg Declaration of 1868 and in Article 23 of the Hague Regulations of 1899 and 1907.[13]

2. The words 'superfluous' and 'unnecessary' reflect the comparative element that is core to the principle. The terms of the principle require that the wounding effect, the injury, and other suffering consequent on the use of the weapon shall be considered in this comparison process, but the terms of the principle do not specify with what they are to be compared. It is evident that weapons are used in order to achieve a military advantage or purpose in connection with an armed conflict. Accordingly, '[t]he legitimacy of a weapon, by reference to the superfluous injury and unnecessary suffering principle, must be determined by comparing the nature and scale of the generic military advantage to be anticipated from the weapon in the application for which it is designed to be used, with the pattern of injury and suffering associated with the normal intended use of the weapon.'[14]

3. The meaning of the superfluous injury and unnecessary suffering principle has not been clarified or defined by agreement between States. Moreover, although succinctly expressed, the principle involves the assessment of phenomena such as suffering, injury, and military utility that are hard to measure and difficult to compare. A weapon is not however rendered unlawful merely because it causes severe injury, suffering, or loss of life. It is the injury or suffering inevitably caused by the weapon in its normal or designed circumstances of use that must be disproportionate to its military purpose or utility for the rule to be broken. Due account must be taken of comparable lawful weapons in current use when making that assessment.[15]

[10] ICJ Nuclear Weapons Advisory Opinion paras 74–87.

[11] AP I, Art. 35(2) and for corresponding language in the Rome Statute of the International Criminal Court, Rome, 17 July 1998, see Art. 8(2)(b)(xx).

[12] ICRC Customary Law Study Report, vol. 1, 237, Rule 70.

[13] St Petersburg Declaration, 11 December 1868, preambular paras 3–6; Brussels Declaration, Art. 13(e) and Hague Regulations 1899 and 1907, Art. 23(e). See also G.D. Solis, The Law of Armed Conflict (Cambridge: Cambridge University Press, 2011), 269–72.

[14] Boothby, *Weapons*, 63 and see W.J. Fenrick, 'The Conventional Weapons Convention: A modest but useful treaty', 279 *IRRC* (1990), 498, at 500: 'A weapon causes unnecessary suffering when in practice it inevitably causes injury or suffering disproportionate to its military effectiveness. In determining the military effectiveness of a weapon, one looks at the primary purpose for which it was designed.' See also W. Hays 'Parks, Means and Methods of Warfare, Symposium issued in Honour of Edward R Cummings', 38 *George Washington International Law Review* (2006), 511, 536 at note 25 where the formulation of the test for the purposes of the United States Department of Defense Weapons Review Directive, prepared by E.R. Cummings, W.A. Solf, and H. Almond, is given.

[15] See US DoD Weapons Review Directive, n. 14.

4. The principle is reflected in the title of the Conventional Weapons Convention.[16] It should, however, be noted that the terms of that Convention do not presuppose that the use of weapons technologies addressed by Protocols made under the Convention necessarily breached the superfluous injury principle. States have made no such determination, and the 'which may be deemed to be' language in the title to the Convention is significant in that regard. Examples of weapons that may be expected to breach the rule include lances or spears with barbed heads, serrated edge bayonets, explosive anti-personnel bullets, and projectiles smeared with substances that inflame wounds.[17] **18.01**

5. The superfluous injury and unnecessary suffering principle should therefore be considered when conducting a weapon review of a new weapon, or method of warfare as referred to in Section 18.01(a).

(b) It is prohibited to employ weapons that are of a nature to be indiscriminate.

1. The principle of distinction obliges parties to the conflict at all times to distinguish between combatants and civilians and between military objectives and civilian objects and only to direct their military operations against combatants and military objectives.[18] The notion that indiscriminate attacks should be unlawful is reflected in Article 24(3) of the Hague Draft Rules of Aerial Warfare.[19] It was, however, some 50 years later, in 1977, that a treaty-based rule prohibiting indiscriminate attacks and indiscriminate weapons first appeared.

2. Article 51(4) of AP I prohibits indiscriminate attacks, which are defined in the same paragraph of the treaty as including:

(b) those which employ a method or means of combat which cannot be directed at a specific military objective; or
(c) those which employ a method or means of combat the effects of which cannot be limited as required by th[e] Protocol;
and [which], consequently, in each such case, are of a nature to strike military objectives and civilians or civilian objects without distinction.[20]

[16] Convention on Prohibitions or Restrictions on the Use of Certain Conventional Weapons Which may be Deemed to be Excessively Injurious or to Have Indiscriminate Effects, Geneva, 10 October 1980 (CCW).

[17] See, for example, ICRC Customary Law Study Report, vol. 1 at pp. 243–4.

[18] See F. Lieber, Instructions for the Government of Armies of the United States in the Field, 24 April 1863 (The Lieber Code), Arts 14, 15, and 22; the Preamble to the St Petersburg Declaration; Brussels Declaration, Arts 12, 13, 15, and 17; and Hague Regulations, 1907, Arts 23(g), 25, and 27. The modern formulation of the principle of distinction is to be found in AP I, Arts 48, 51, and 52.

[19] Rules of Aerial Warfare, The Hague, 1923. The rules were never formally adopted by States and do not therefore have the status of a source of international law. Article 24(3) asserted that in cases where objectives cannot be bombarded without the indiscriminate bombardment of the civilian population, 'the aircraft must abstain from bombardment'.

[20] The discrimination rule in Art. 51(4) of AP I is an important element in compliance with the principle of distinction.

18.01 3. The effect of sub-paragraphs (b) and (c) is to prohibit weapons which, either because they cannot be directed at a military objective or because their effects cannot be limited, essentially do not distinguish as required by the principle of distinction.[21] When applying the rule, however, the focus must be on whether the weapon, when used in its normal or designed circumstances, will inevitably be indiscriminate in the sense discussed in the present paragraph. Any weapon is capable of being used indiscriminately. The present rule is concerned with the inherent characteristics of the weapon, as opposed to the particular activities of its user.

4. The rule is customary and therefore binds all States, including those not party to AP I. The rule applies in both international and non-international armed conflicts.[22]

5. The principle is reflected in the title of CCW. It should, however, be noted that the terms of that Convention do not presuppose that the use of weapons technologies addressed by Protocols made under the Convention necessarily breached the indiscriminate weapons principle. States have made no such determination, and the 'which may be deemed to be' language in the title to the Convention is significant in that regard. The V2 rockets used to attack the south of England commencing in September 1944, their predecessor the V1 rocket, and certain Scud missiles would be examples of weapons that would breach this rule.

(c) Customary law requires all States to have due regard to the natural environment and provides that, as a civilian object, the natural environment may not be made the object of attack and may not be subjected to wanton destruction.

1. This Rule is concerned with direct damage to the natural environment, whether as the intended or as the incidental outcome of a military operation.[23] The destruction of the natural environment, carried out wantonly, is prohibited to all States as a matter of customary law; indeed, the natural environment is a civilian object and, thus, is entitled to general protection from the results of military operations.[24] As a result, when planning and carrying out military operations and, by extension, when procuring weapons, all States are obliged to have due

[21] Consider *Advisory Opinion on Legality of the Threat or Use of Nuclear Weapons*, ICJ Reports, 1996, 226, at 257: 'States must never make civilians the object of attack and must consequently never use weapons that are incapable of distinguishing between civilian and military targets.'

[22] ICRC Customary Law Study, vol. 1, Rule 71 at p. 244. See also, in relation to international armed conflicts, Rome Statute, Art. 8(2)(b)(xx).

[23] Dinstein, 'Conduct of Hostilities', 209–12 and A.P.V. Rogers, *Law on the Battlefield*, 3rd edn (Manchester: Manchester University Press, 2012), 218–20, where it is observed that ENMOD applies to damage caused in another State whereas Arts 35(3) and 55 of AP I can apply to damage in one's own State, on the high seas or in Antarctica; that ENMOD appears to be absolute whereas for the AP I rule to apply, the consequences must have been intended or foreseen; and that ENMOD applies to any hostile use whereas AP I applies only in armed conflicts and hostile occupations. For the application of the environment rules to particular weapons technologies, see Rogers, *Law on the Battlefield*, 221–5.

[24] ICRC Customary Law Study, vol. 1 Rule 43, p. 143, AMW Manual, Rule 88, and Tallinn Manual, Rule 83(a).

regard to the impact that such weapons may be expected to have on the natural environment.[25] 18.01

2. Additional Protocol I (AP I) binds the overwhelming majority of States and Article 35(3) prohibits the use of 'methods or means of warfare which are intended or may be expected to cause widespread, long-term and severe damage to the natural environment' while Article 55 prohibits such methods or means that thereby 'prejudice the health or survival of the population'.[26] There is a division of informed opinion as to the customary status of these rules. A number of States and experts consider that these rules as expressed in the treaty are customary and thus bind all States.[27] Other States and experts, of which the author is one, do not consider that these AP I rules have yet achieved customary status.

3. The terms 'widespread, long-term and severe' apply cumulatively, so if any one of the criteria is absent, the treaty provision will not have been breached. AP I contains no definition of 'widespread, long-term and severe', but only the most serious of damage will breach the rule.[28] A number of States when ratifying AP I made statements in relation to nuclear weapons which are relevant to the present rule and as to which see Section 18.03 and the associated commentary.

4. States party to the UN Environmental Modification Convention must not engage in military or any other hostile use of environmental modification techniques having widespread, long-lasting, or severe effects as the means of destruction, damage, or injury to any other State party to that Convention.[29] This treaty prohibition only applies if environmental modification techniques[30] having the specified effects are used as the method of causing destruction, damage, or injury to another State that is also party to the Convention. The treaty rule will therefore

[25] AMW Manual, Rule 89.

[26] AP I, Art. 55(1).

[27] Note in particular the ICRC Customary Humanitarian Law Study, Rule 45 and the associated Commentary.

[28] 'The time or duration required (i.e. long-term) was considered by some to be measured in decades. References to twenty or thirty years were made by some representatives as being a minimum. Others referred to battlefield destruction in France in the First World War as being outside the scope of the prohibition... It appeared to be a widely shared assumption that battlefield damage incidental to conventional warfare would not normally be proscribed by this provision. What the article is primarily directed to is thus such damage as would be likely to prejudice, over a long term, the continued survival of the civilian population or would risk causing it major health problems', Rapporteur's Report CDDH/215/Rev.1 para. 27, reported in ICRC Commentary, para. 1454.

[29] Convention on the Prohibition of Military or any Other Hostile Use of Environmental Modification Techniques, Geneva, 2 September 1976 (ENMOD), Art. I.

[30] The term 'environmental modification techniques' refers to 'any technique for changing—through the deliberate manipulation of natural processes—the dynamics, composition or structure of the Earth, including its biota, lithosphere, hydrosphere and atmosphere, or of outer space'; ENMOD, Art. II. The term 'widespread' has been interpreted as 'encompassing an area on the scale of several hundred square kilometres', while 'long-lasting' would involve 'lasting for a period of months, or approximately a season' and effects are 'severe' if they involves 'serious or significant disruption or harm to human life, natural and economic resources or other assets'. Conference Understanding relating to Article I, available at the ICRC treaty database at <http://www.icrc.org>.

18.01 only usually apply during international armed conflicts and essentially addresses the use of the natural environment as a weapon with which to cause injury or damage to the enemy State. An activity would involve environmental modification if, for example, it consisted of an attempt to modify the weather by either increasing or reducing rainfall in an area in order to bring about floods or drought.[31] A Conference Understanding indicates that possible results of environmental modification techniques could include earthquakes, tsunamis, a disturbance in the ecological balance of a region, changes in weather and climate patterns.[32]

(d) It is prohibited to use the following weapons or weapon technologies:

The use of some of the weapons listed below is prohibited to all States as a matter of customary law, irrespective of their participation in a particular, relevant treaty. Some weapons prohibitions apply only to States that are party to a relevant treaty, and this is noted below where applicable.

(1) poison or poisoned weapons;

1. This prohibition dates from the late Middle Ages. The Lieber Code notes that '[m]ilitary necessity does not permit of... the use of poison in any way...'.[33] The Brussels Declaration and Oxford Manual record similar prohibitions.[34] The prohibition was reflected in treaty law in the Hague Regulations of 1899 and 1907.[35]

2. The term 'poison or poisoned weapons' has been interpreted in the practice of States in its ordinary sense as covering weapons whose primary, or even exclusive, effect is to poison or asphyxiate.[36] The ICRC, in the Customary Law Study report, notes the position of certain States that the Rule does not apply to substances that could incidentally poison, but that poisoning must be the intended injuring mechanism. The Rule seems therefore to apply, for example, to smearing arrows to prevent recovery from injury, to using any substance to aggravate a wound and to the poisoning of wells, pumps, and rivers from which the enemy draws water supplies.[37]

(2) asphyxiating, poisonous or other gases, all analogous liquids, materials or devices and bacteriological methods of warfare;

1. Hague Declaration 2 of 1899 prohibited the use of projectiles the sole object of which was the diffusion of asphyxiating or deleterious gases. Following extensive use

[31] P.J. Rowe, *Defence, the Legal Implications* (London: Brassey's, 1987), 117.

[32] Conference Understanding relating to Article II, available at the ICRC treaty database at <www.icrc.org>.

[33] Lieber Code, Art. 16.

[34] Brussels Declaration, Art. 12 and Oxford Manual, Art. 8(a).

[35] Hague Regulations 1907, Art. 23(a).

[36] ICJ, *Nuclear Weapons*, Advisory Opinion, para. 111.

[37] H. Lauterpacht (ed.), *Oppenheim's International Law*, Vol. II (Reissue of 1952 edn, Longmans 1955) 340; ICRC Customary Law Study, vol. 1, 253 and AP I Commentary, para. 1419.

of asphyxiating gas during World War I, the 1925 Geneva Gas Protocol,[38] adopted by an international conference convened by the Council of The League of Nations, prohibited the use in war of asphyxiating, poisonous or other gases, and of all analogous liquids, materials, or devices. The prohibition also extended to the use of bacteriological methods of warfare. A number of States, including the UK, US, and France, ratified the Protocol on the basis that they would only remain bound by the prohibitions so long as the adverse party in an armed conflict did not use the prohibited weapons.[39] These 'no first use' arrangements have since been overtaken by the adoption of the Chemical Weapons Convention and of the Biological Weapons Convention.[40] **18.01**

2. The prohibition binds all States in relation to both international and non-international armed conflicts.

(3) the use of expanding bullets in armed conflict;

1. The Hague Declaration 3 of 1899[41] prohibits 'the use of bullets which expand or flatten easily in the human body, such as bullets with a hard envelope which does not entirely cover the core or is pierced with incisions'. This treaty prohibition applies as a matter of customary law to all States in relation to the conduct of hostilities in international armed conflicts.

2. In non-international armed conflicts, the application of a similar customary rule recognizes that difficult situations may arise, such as when a hostage-taker may need to be instantly disabled to protect civilians or when the risk of ricochet may render use of a normal high velocity round inappropriate. In such relatively limited non-international armed conflict situations, the use of expanding ammunition may yield an additional military utility by facilitating compliance with distinction and discrimination, would not therefore occasion superfluous injury/unnecessary suffering, and would not therefore breach the customary law rule.[42]

(4) exploding bullets intended for anti-personnel use;

1. The St Petersburg Declaration prohibited the employment during international armed conflict of projectiles below 400 grammes weight that are either explosive or

[38] Geneva Protocol for the Prohibition of the Use in War of Asphyxiating, Poisonous or Other Gases, and of Bacteriological Methods of Warfare, 1925.

[39] The precise texts of the statements were not always identical, but the general import remained broadly the same.

[40] The 'no first use' reservations have in practice been withdrawn by States as they have become party to the Chemical Weapons Convention 1993 and to the Biological Weapons Convention 1972.

[41] Declaration Concerning Expanding Bullets, The Hague, 29 July 1899.

[42] UK Manual, para. 6.9 and note 32. Note the Resolution adopted on 10 June 2010 by the Kampala Review Conference for the Rome Statute of the International Criminal Court, RC/Res. 5 adopted at the 12th Plenary Meeting, which makes it clear the crime of using expanding bullets in a non-international armed conflict is only committed 'if the perpetrator employs the bullets to uselessly aggravate suffering or the wounding effect upon the target of such bullets, as reflected in customary international law', preambular para. 9. See also the discussion in Chapter 4.

18.01 charged with fulminating or inflammable substances.[43] The 400 gramme limit was rendered somewhat obsolete by subsequent technical developments, as reflected in the 1923 draft Hague Rules of Aerial Warfare.[44]

2. State practice indicates that explosive or incendiary bullets designed solely for use against personnel are prohibited under customary law. This seems to be because a solid round would achieve the relevant military purpose, with the evident implication that using the explosive round in such circumstances will cause injury for which there is no corresponding military utility.[45]

(5) certain conventional weapons prohibited under CCW Protocols to which the relevant State is party;

1. In 1980 a Conference convened pursuant to a UN General Assembly resolution[46] adopted the CCW. It is essentially an enabling Convention under which Protocols have been negotiated which address particular types of weapon.

2. Protocol I provides that 'it is prohibited to use any weapon the primary effect of which is to injure by fragments which in the human body escape detection by x-rays';[47]

3. Protocol II[48] and Amended Protocol II[49] are concerned with the use in armed conflict of mines,[50] booby-traps and other devices.[51]

4. Article 1 of Protocol II defined booby-traps as 'any device or material which is designed, constructed or adapted to kill or injure and which functions unexpectedly when a person disturbs or approaches an apparently harmless object or performs an apparently safe act'.[52] Article 6 of the Protocol prohibits the use of booby-traps in the form of apparently harmless portable objects if they are specifically designed and constructed to contain explosive material and to detonate when they are disturbed

[43] Declaration Renouncing the Use, in Time of War, of Explosive Projectiles Under 400 Grammes Weight, St Petersburg, 11 December 1868.

[44] Draft Hague Rules of Aerial Warfare, 1923, Art. 18(2).

[45] See UK Manual, para. 6.10.1. This implies that the prohibition is based on the customary superfluous injury and unnecessary suffering principle as opposed to the treaty rule.

[46] A/RES/34/82, dated 11 December 1979.

[47] Protocol on Non-Detectable Fragments, Geneva, 10 October 1980.

[48] Adopted in Geneva on 10 October 1980.

[49] Adopted in Geneva on 3 May 1996.

[50] Protocol II, Art. 2(1): 'Mine means any munition placed under, on or near the ground or other surface area and designed to be detonated or exploded by the presence, proximity or contact of a person or vehicle.' There are minor and relatively inconsequential amendments to the equivalent definition in Amended Protocol II, Art. 2(1).

[51] Protocol II, Art. 1(3): 'Other devices means manually-emplaced munitions and devices designed to kill, injure or damage and which are actuated by remote control or automatically after a lapse of time.' The Amended Protocol II, Art. 2(5) definition of 'other devices' is 'Other devices means manually-emplaced munitions and devices including improvised explosive devices designed to kill, injure or damage and which are actuated manually, by remote control or automatically after a lapse of time.'

[52] Protocol II, Art. 1(2).

or approached.[53] Protocol II also prohibits the use of booby-traps in any way attached to or associated with: **18.01**

(a) internationally recognised protective emblems, signs or signals;
(b) sick, wounded or dead persons;
(c) burial or cremation sites or graves;
(d) medical facilities, medical equipment, medical supplies, or medical transportation;
(e) children's toys or other portable objects or products specially designed for the feeding, health, hygiene, clothing, or education of children;
(f) food or drink;
(g) kitchen utensils or appliances except in military establishments, military locations or military supply depots;
(h) objects clearly of a religious nature;
(i) historic monuments, works of art or places of worship which constitute the cultural or spiritual heritage of peoples;
(j) animals or their carcasses.[54]

5. Amended Protocol II specifically prohibits: 'mines, booby-traps or other devices which employ a mechanism or device specifically designed to detonate the munition by the presence of commonly available mine detectors as a result of their magnetic or other non-contact influence during normal use in detection operations';[55]

'a self-deactivating mine equipped with an anti-handling device that is designed in such a manner that the anti-handling device is capable of functioning after the mine has ceased to be capable of functioning';[56]

anti-personnel mines that do not incorporate in their construction a material or device that enables the mine to be detected by commonly available technical mine detection equipment and that provides a response signal equivalent to a signal from 8 grammes or more of iron in a single coherent mass;[57]

remotely delivered[58] anti-personnel mines which do not comply with certain self-destruction and self-deactivation requirements;[59]

certain remotely-delivered mines other than anti-personnel mines;[60]

[53] Protocol II, Art. 6(1)(a).

[54] Protocol II, Art. 6(1), Amended Protocol II, Art. 7(1).

[55] Amended Protocol II, Art. 3(5). [56] Amended Protocol II, Art. 3(6).

[57] Amended Protocol II, Art. 4 and Technical Annex, para. 2(a). This restriction applies to anti-personnel mines produced after 1 January 1997. Mines produced before that date must either incorporate into their construction or have attached prior to their emplacement in a manner that is not easily removable a material or device with identical characteristics; Amended Protocol II, Technical Annex para. 2(b).

[58] For the definition of 'remotely-delivered', see Amended Protocol II, Art. 2(1).

[59] Amended Protocol II, Art. 6(2). For the requirements, see Amended Protocol II, Technical Annex, para. 3(a) taken with (b).

[60] Amended Protocol II, Art. 6(3).

18.01 booby-traps or other devices in the form of apparently harmless portable objects which are specifically designed and constructed to contain explosive material.[61]

6. Protocol IV stipulates that it is prohibited 'to employ laser-weapons specifically designed, as their sole combat function or as one of their combat functions, to cause permanent blindness to unenhanced vision, that is, to the naked eye or to the eye with corrective eyesight devices'.[62]

(6) for States party to the Ottawa Convention, anti-personnel mines;

1. An anti-personnel mine for these purposes is a mine designed to be exploded by the presence, proximity, or contact of a person and that will incapacitate, injure, or kill one or more persons. Mines designed to be detonated by the presence, proximity, or contact of a vehicle as opposed to a person and that are equipped with anti-handling devices, are not considered anti-personnel mines as a result of being so equipped.[63]

2. The Convention is an arms control treaty under which States parties must never use, develop, produce, otherwise acquire, stockpile, retain, or transfer anti-personnel mines or assist, encourage, or induce, in any way, anyone to do so. It includes detailed provisions as to the destruction of anti-personnel mines in stockpiles and in mined areas and limits the retention of anti-personnel mines for training purposes. It also includes an extensive compliance regime.[64]

3. The Ottawa Convention applies in connection with international and non-international armed conflicts; its provisions do not yet reflect customary law.

(7) chemical weapons;

1. The Geneva Gas Protocol 1925 did not prohibit the possession of Chemical Weapons. The Chemical Weapons Convention 1993[65] is an arms control treaty in the sense that it prohibits the use, development, production, acquisition, stockpiling, or retention of chemical weapons or their direct or indirect transfer to anyone. States parties must not prepare to use them or assist, encourage, or induce anyone to do any of these things.[66]

[61] Amended Protocol II, Art. 7(2).

[62] CCW, Protocol IV, Art. 1. Blinding as an incidental or collateral effect of the legitimate use of laser systems is not prohibited; Art. 3. Laser systems that are not specifically designed to cause permanent blindness are not prohibited by this provision. Permanent blindness means irreversible and uncorrectable loss of vision which is seriously disabling with no prospect of recovery. Serious disability is equivalent to visual acuity of less than 20/200 Snellen measured using both eyes; Protocol IV, Art. 4.

[63] Ottawa Convention, Art. 2(1).

[64] See Ottawa Convention 1997, Art. 8.

[65] Convention on the Prohibition of the Development, Production, Stockpiling and Use of Chemical Weapons and on Their Destruction, Paris, 13 January 1993.

[66] Chemical Weapons Convention, Art. I(1).

2. 'Chemical weapons' means, essentially, toxic chemicals and their precursors and equipment and munitions connected with their use. The term does not include such substances intended for purposes not prohibited under the Convention, provided that the types and quantities are consistent with such purposes.[67] **18.01**

3. A toxic chemical is any chemical whatever its origin and however or wherever produced which, through its chemical action on life processes can cause death, temporary incapacitation, or permanent harm to humans or animals.[68] A 'precursor' is any chemical reactant which takes part, at any stage, in the production, by whatever method, of a toxic chemical.[69]

4. Purposes which are not prohibited under the Convention are industrial, agricultural, research, medical, pharmaceutical, or other peaceful purposes; protective purposes, namely those purposes directly related to protection against toxic chemicals and to protection against chemical weapons; military purposes not connected with the use of chemical weapons and not dependent on the use of the toxic properties of chemicals as a method of warfare; and law enforcement, including domestic riot control purposes.[70] 'Law enforcement' in this context would seem to mean the enforcement of domestic law.[71]

5. The Convention is widely ratified and applies in non-international as well as international armed conflicts. The Convention includes an important verification annex.[72] The prohibitions specified in the Convention as to use and possession of chemical weapons are now customary[73] and thus bind all States, irrespective of their participation in the Convention, in relation to both classes of armed conflict.

(8) riot control agents, if used as a method of warfare;

1. Riot control agents are defined by the Chemical Weapons Convention as 'chemicals not listed in a Schedule to the Treaty which can produce rapidly in humans sensory irritation or disabling physical effects which disappear within a short time following termination of exposure'.[74] It is lawful to use such weapons during an armed conflict for law enforcement, including domestic riot control purposes. It is, however, prohibited to use them as a method of warfare.

(9) bacteriological or biological weapons; and

[67] For the precise definition see Chemical Weapons Convention, Art. II(1).
[68] Chemical Weapons Convention, Art. II(2).
[69] Chemical Weapons Convention, Art. II(3).
[70] Chemical Weapons Convention, Art. II(9).
[71] D.P. Fidler, 'The Meaning of Moscow: 'Non-Lethal' Weapons and International Law in the 21st Century', 859 *IRRC* (2005), 525, at 540–4.
[72] The Chemical Weapons Convention Annex on Implementation and Verification includes complex provisions as to national declarations and verification arrangements.
[73] Boothby, *Weapons*, 137.
[74] Chemical Weapons Convention, 1993, Art. II(7).

18.01 1. Article I of the Biological Weapons Convention[75] prohibits the development, production, stockpiling, acquisition, or retention of microbial or other biological agents or toxins whatever their origin or method of production, of types and in quantities that have no justification for prophylactic, protective, or other peaceful purposes, and weapons or equipment for their use for hostile purposes or in armed conflict.[76] The Fourth Review Conference in 1996 agreed this has the effect of also prohibiting the use of such weapons.[77]

2. This is another arms control treaty the prohibitions of which apply to both international and non-international armed conflict. The Convention is widely ratified including by almost all militarily significant States. This and the consistent practice of States shows that the prohibitions on possession and use of such weapons, and probably the other prohibitions set forth in the Convention, are now customary and therefore bind all States in relation to both international and non-international armed conflicts. It is therefore unlawful for any State, whether it is party to the Biological Weapons Convention or not, to plan, prepare for, equip itself for, or undertake a biological attack. There is no verification mechanism for the Convention.

(10) for States party to the Cluster Munitions Convention, cluster munitions.

1. The Cluster Munitions Convention[78] is a treaty that requires States parties never to use, develop, produce, otherwise acquire, stockpile, retain, or transfer cluster munitions or to assist, encourage, or induce anyone to do any of these things.[79]

2. A cluster munition is 'a conventional munition that is designed to disperse or release explosive sub-munitions each weighing less than 20 kilograms and includes those explosive sub-munitions'. The definition excludes: munitions or sub-munitions designed to dispense flares, smoke, pyrotechnics, or chaff; munitions designed exclusively for an air defence role; munitions or sub-munitions designed to produce electrical or electronic effects; munitions that, in order to avoid indiscriminate area effects and the risks posed by unexploded sub-munitions, contain fewer than 10 explosive sub-munitions each of which weighs more than 4 kilograms, is designed to detect and engage a single target object, is equipped with an electronic self-destruction mechanism and is equipped with an electronic self-deactivating feature.[80] Explosive sub-munitions consist of conventional munitions which, in order to perform their task, are dispersed or released by a cluster munition and are

[75] The Convention on the Prohibition of the Development, Production and Stockpiling of Bacteriological (Biological) and Toxin Weapons and on their Destruction 1972 was opened for signature on 10 April 1972 (Biological Weapons Convention).

[76] Biological Weapons Convention, Art. I.

[77] UK Manual, 104, Note 8.

[78] Convention on Cluster Munitions, Dublin, 30 May 2008.

[79] Cluster Munitions Convention, Art. 1(1).

[80] Cluster Munitions Convention, Art. 2(2).

designed to function by detonating an explosive charge prior to, on, or after impact.[81] 18.01

3. Interoperability issues are addressed in Article 21 of the Convention, which requires States parties to encourage States that are not party to participate in the Convention, obliges a State that is party to notify the governments of States that are not party of its Convention obligations but explicitly permits States parties or their military personnel or nationals to 'engage in military cooperation and operations with States not party to this Convention that might engage in activities prohibited to a State party'.[82] This provision does not permit a State party itself to acquire, transfer, or use cluster munitions, neither may the State party specifically request the use of cluster munitions where the choice of munitions used is within its exclusive control.[83]

4. It is therefore lawful for a military planner from a State party to the Convention to allocate targets to a State contributing to the operation that is not party to the Convention knowing that that State will, in all likelihood, engage those targets using cluster munitions. It is, however, unlawful for military personnel from a State party to the Convention actively to participate in the use of such cluster munitions.

(e) The use of certain weapons is subject to treaty law restrictions.

1. Protocol II and Amended Protocol II to CCW both restrict the use of mines, booby-traps, and other devices. Some restrictions simply restate general targeting rules and will not be repeated here. The following restrictions under Protocol II reflect established doctrine and are probably customary in nature. The Amended Protocol II restrictions only bind States that are party to that treaty.

2. Protocol II, Article 4, prohibits the use of mines other than remotely delivered mines, booby-traps, and other devices in any city, town, village, or other area containing a similar concentration of civilians in which combat between ground forces is not taking place or does not appear to be imminent unless either they are placed on or in the close vicinity of the military objective belonging to or under the control of an adverse party, or measures are taken to protect civilians from their effects such as, for example, the posting of warning signs, the posting of sentries, the issue of warnings, or the provision of fences.[84]

3. Article 5 of Protocol II limits the use of remotely delivered mines to areas that are or contain military objectives and requires that their location can be accurately recorded and that an effective neutralizing or remotely controlled mechanism is used on each such mine.[85]

[81] Cluster Munitions Convention, Art. 2(3). The treaty defines the notions of self-destruction and self-deactivation.

[82] Cluster Munitions Convention, Art. 21(3).

[83] Cluster Munitions Convention, Art. 21(4).

[84] 'Remotely-delivered mines' means, for the purposes of Protocol II, any mine delivered by artillery, rocket, mortar, or similar means or dropped from an aircraft.

[85] See Protocol II to CCW, Art. 5(1).

18.01 4. Article 7 of Protocol II requires that parties to the conflict record the location of all pre-planned minefields that they lay and of all areas in which they have made large-scale and pre-planned use of booby-traps.

5. Article 3 of Amended Protocol II makes a party to the conflict that employs mines, booby-traps, or other devices responsible to clear, remove, destroy, or maintain them as specified later in the treaty. Practical precautions must be taken.[86]

6. Article 5 of AP II prohibits use of anti-personnel mines other than remotely delivered mines[87] if they are not designed and constructed according to criteria set forth in the treaty.[88] Weapons that do not comply with those requirements may nevertheless be used by a State party to Amended Protocol II if the treaty's conditions as to use and subsequent action are met.[89]

7. Some weapons of this sort are excluded from the restrictions referred to in the previous paragraph. This exclusion applies to weapons which propel fragments in a horizontal arc of less than 90° and which are placed on or above the ground. The maximum permitted use of such weapons is 72 hours, they must be located in immediate proximity to the military unit that emplaced them, and the area must be monitored by military personnel to ensure the effective exclusion of civilians.[90]

8. Remotely delivered mines may only be used if they are recorded in accordance with the Technical Annex and remotely delivered mines other than Anti-Personnel Mines must, to the extent feasible, be equipped with an effective self-destruction or self-neutralization mechanism and have a back-up self-deactivation feature which is designed so that the mine will no longer function as a mine when the mine no longer serves the military purposes for which it was placed in position.

9. *Booby-traps*. Amended Protocol II prohibits the use of booby-traps or other devices in any town, village, or other area containing a similar concentration of civilians and in which combat between ground forces is not taking place or does not appear to be imminent, unless either they are placed on or in the close vicinity of a military objective; or, measures are taken to protect civilians from their effects, for example, by the posting of warning sentries, the issuing of warnings, or the provision of fences.[91]

10. *Laser Weapons*. Protocol IV to CCW[92] restricts the use of certain weapons that are not specifically prohibited under Article 1.[93]

[86] As to the factors to consider, see Amended Protocol II, Art. 3(10).
[87] 'Remotely-delivered mine' is defined in Art. 2(2), Amended Protocol II.
[88] See Amended Protocol II, Technical Annex, para. 3(a) and (b).
[89] For these requirements, see Amended Protocol II, Art. 5(2).
[90] Amended Protocol II, Art. 5(6).
[91] Amended Protocol II, Art. 7(3).
[92] See in particular Article 2 of Protocol IV to CCW which addresses the risk of blindness caused by laser weapons that do not come within Article 1 by requiring States parties to take all feasible precautions to avoid the incidence of permanent blindness to unenhanced vision.
[93] See the commentary to Section 18.02.

11. *Incendiary Weapons*. Protocol III[94] defines incendiary weapons as 'any weapon or munition which is primarily designed to set fire to objects or to cause burn injury to persons through the action of flame, heat, or a combination thereof, produced by a chemical reaction of a substance delivered on the target'.[95] **18.01**

12. Under the Protocol it is prohibited 'in all circumstances to make any military objective located within a concentration of civilians[96] the object of attack by air-delivered incendiary weapons'.[97] It is also prohibited to make military objectives located within a concentration of civilians the object of attack using incendiary weapons other than air-delivered incendiary weapons 'except when such military objective is clearly separated from the concentration of civilians and all feasible precautions are taken with a view to limiting the incendiary effects to the military objective and to avoiding, and in any event to minimizing, incidental loss of civilian life, injury to civilians and damage to civilian objects'.[98]

13. It is in addition prohibited to make forests or other kinds of plant cover the object of attack using incendiary weapons except when such natural elements are used to cover, conceal, or camouflage combatants or other military objectives, or have themselves become military objectives.[99]

The application of weapons law does not discriminate between weapons exclusively on the basis of their intended non-lethal character. **18.02**

1. A convenient definition of non-lethal weapons (NLW) is:

Non-lethal weapons are weapons which are explicitly designed and developed to incapacitate or repel personnel, with a low probability of fatality or permanent injury, or to disable equipment with minimal undesired damage or impact on the environment.[100]

2. NLW are not required to have zero lethality; indeed, lethality will inevitably in part depend on how the weapon is used. Nevertheless, fatal or permanent injury should generally be less frequent than is to be expected from the use of conventional lethal weapons.

3. When undertaking a weapon review as referred to in Section 18.04, the same legal criteria must be applied to non-lethal weapons as to lethal weaponry and the non-lethal character of a weapon will not alone exclude it from the effect of an otherwise applicable prohibition or restriction in weapons law.

[94] Protocol on Prohibitions or Restrictions on the Use of Incendiary Weapons (Protocol III), Geneva, 10 October 1980.

[95] Protocol III, Art. 1(1). The definition notes that such weapons can take a variety of forms, but excludes munitions with incidental incendiary effects, such as tracers or illuminants, smoke or signalling systems, and combined effects munitions in which the incendiary effect is designed to be used against objects not persons.

[96] A 'concentration of civilians' may be permanent or temporary, and can include inhabited parts of cities, towns, villages, camps, columns of refugees, or groups of nomads; Protocol III, Art. 1(2).

[97] Protocol III, Art. 2(2). [98] Protocol III, Art. 2(3). [99] Protocol III, Art. 2(4).

[100] NATO Policy on Non-Lethal Weapons dated 27 September 1999.

18.03 **International law neither specifically prohibits nor explicitly permits the use of, or a threat to use, nuclear weapons. Any use, or threat to use, nuclear weapons is unlawful unless it complies with the general principles of international law, including the law applicable to armed conflict.**

1. In July 1996 the International Court of Justice delivered a comprehensive opinion as to the legality of the threat or use of nuclear weapons. The Court concluded that there is in neither customary nor conventional international law any specific authorization of the threat or use of nuclear weapons and that there is in neither customary nor conventional international law any comprehensive and universal prohibition of the threat or use of nuclear weapons as such.

2. The ICJ Advisory Opinion notes that a threat to use, or use of, nuclear force that is contrary to Article 2(4) of the UN Charter and that fails to meet the requirements of Article 51 is unlawful and that such a threat or use should be compatible with the law of armed conflict and with treaties and other undertakings dealing expressly with nuclear weapons. So while a threat or use of nuclear weapons would generally be contrary to the law of armed conflict, the Court could not 'conclude definitively whether the threat or use of nuclear weapons would be lawful or unlawful in an extreme circumstance of self defence, in which the very survival of a state would be at stake'.[101]

3. While this non liquet judgment of the Court has attracted considerable debate,[102] it represents the currently available statement of the Court's position on the matter and will continue to apply unless and until the issue is further litigated. It would seem to follow from the Court's judgment that the possession of nuclear weapons does not breach any specific rule under the law of armed conflict. States party to the Nuclear Non-Proliferation Treaty are bound to act in conformity with that treaty in relation to the development, deployment, or proliferation of nuclear weapons.

4. It should, moreover, be recalled that numerous States ratified AP I on a basis that excluded the application of its new rules to nuclear weapons.[103] The declarations did not explicitly state which rules were considered for these purposes to be 'new', but they would seem to include the environmental protection rules in

[101] ICJ, *Nuclear Weapons Case*, Advisory Opinion 18 July 1996, ICJ Reports, 226.

[102] See, for example, T.L.H. McCormack, 'A non liquet on Nuclear Weapons—The ICJ avoids the application of general principles of international humanitarian law', 316 *IRRC* (1997), 76, but also see C. Greenwood, 'The Advisory Opinion on Nuclear Weapons and the Contribution of the International Court to International Humanitarian Law', 316 *IRRC* (1997), 65, 73.

[103] See, for example, statement (a) made by the UK on ratification of AP I on 28 January 1998, first statement made by Belgium on ratification of AP I on 20 May 1986, first statement by Italy on ratification of AP I on 27 February 1986, and statement 2 made by France on ratification of AP I on 11 April 2001.

Articles 35(3) and 55, the prohibition on taking reprisals against civilians and civilian objects, the elaboration of the principle of proportionality and, arguably, the indiscriminate weapons principle.[104] In the opinion of the author, the principles of proportionality and discrimination are applicable to any use of nuclear weapons but there is no evidence that the relevant States have resiled from their declarations as they apply to the environmental protection and indiscriminate weapons rules. The lawfulness of the reprisal action addressed in AP I will depend on the position taken by the relevant State when ratifying AP I. **18.03**

5. While the possession of nuclear weapons is not generally prohibited, Article I of the Non-Proliferation Treaty prohibits nuclear weapons States from transferring nuclear weapons or explosive devices or control over nuclear weapons to any non-nuclear weapons State, or to assist a non-nuclear weapons State in the manufacture or acquisition of nuclear weapons or explosive devices or control over them. Under Article II of the Non-Proliferation Treaty non-nuclear weapons States are bound not to receive the transfer from any transferor whatsoever of nuclear weapons or nuclear explosive devices or of control over them, and not to seek or receive any assistance in the manufacture of such weapons or explosive devices.[105]

All States are required legally to review new weapons to determine whether their employment would in some or all circumstances breach the rules of international law applicable to that State. **18.04**

1. With regard to the suggested customary rule, consider the 1868 St Petersburg Declaration,[106] Article 1 of Hague Convention II of 1899, and Article 1 of Hague Convention IV of 1907 which require States parties to issue instructions to their armed land forces 'in conformity with the Regulations' annexed to those instruments.[107] Moreover, States that are party to AP I are required '[i]n the study, development, acquisition or adoption of a new weapon, means or method of warfare [. . .] to determine whether its employment would, in some or all circumstances, be prohibited by th[e] Protocol or by any other rule of international law applicable to the High Contracting Party'.[108] The ICRC suggests that '[t]he requirement that the legality of all new weapons, means and methods of warfare

[104] F. Kalshoven, 'Arms, Armaments and International Law', 191 *RdC* (1985-II), 183–341, at 236 and 287.

[105] Treaty on the Non-Proliferation of Nuclear Weapons, 1 July 1968.

[106] Note in particular the final paragraph of the St Petersburg Declaration, 1868.

[107] Consider e.g. W. Hays Parks, 'Conventional Weapons and Weapons Reviews', 8 *Yearbook of International Humanitarian Law* (2005), 55, at 55–7 and note that an important State not party to AP I, the United States, legally reviews the new weapons that it acquires.

[108] AP I, Art. 36.

18.04 be systematically assessed is arguably one that applies to *all* States, regardless of whether or not they are party to Additional Protocol 1'.[109]

2. So far as is known, relatively few States have systematic administrative arrangements to ensure that all weapons are subjected to review in accordance with these Rules.[110] It is nevertheless suggested that customary law obliges all States to conduct such a review in relation to all new weapons. The law that should be applied consists of the rules of international law that bind the State in question, consisting of the customary principles and rules supplemented by rules set forth in treaties to which the State is party.

3. The second, treaty-based, obligation to review the lawfulness of a weapon, means, or method of warfare first arises with its study. 'Study' would seem to include the first consideration or evaluation of particular kinds of weaponization of a technology.[111]

4. 'Development' would include forming a weapon and improving, refining, or testing it[112] while 'acquisition' and 'adoption' involve procuring weapons from commercial undertakings and/or from other States; 'adoption', in relation to methods of warfare, would involve a State or its armed forces deciding to use a particular weapon or method of warfare in military operations. For the meanings of 'weapon', 'method of warfare', and 'means of warfare', see the introductory paragraphs to the present chapter.

5. A State that undertakes such a review should assess the general circumstances in which it is intended to use the weapon, means, or method of warfare and should determine whether the existing rules of law applicable to that State prohibit or restrict those general intended circumstances of use. If this is the case, the document that is issued at the conclusion of the review should make this clear.

6. Neither customary nor treaty law is prescriptive as to the form that a weapon review must take, nor as to the procedure to be adopted in preparing it. Advice to an appropriate commander may, depending on the circumstances, be sufficient.[113]

[109] K. Lawand, 'A Guide to the Legal Review of New Weapons, Means and Methods of Warfare: Measures to Implement Article 36 of Additional Protocol I of 1977', *ICRC* (2006), 4 and see AMW Manual, Rule 9, Tallinn Manual, Rule 48(a), the Commentary to which cites Common Article 1 of the Geneva Conventions of 1949. See also the UK Manual, paras 6.20–6.20.1, the *United States Naval Commanders' Handbook on the Conduct of Naval Operations*, NWP 1-14, para. 5.3.4, the Canadian Manual, para. 530 and the new German Manual, Section 405.

[110] K. Lawand, 'A Guide to the Legal Review', 5.

[111] Boothby, *Weapons*, 345.

[112] Consider I. Daoust, R. Coupland, and R. Ishoey, 'New Wars, New Weapons? The Obligation of States to Assess the Legality of Means and Methods of Warfare', 846 *IRRC* (2002), 345, 348.

[113] Tallinn Manual, Commentary accompanying Rule 48, para. 3.

There are similarities and differences in the weapons law rules that apply respectively to international and non-international armed conflicts. 18.05

1. The CCW was amended in 2001[114] so as to provide that the Convention and its annexed Protocols with their prohibitions and restrictions apply to 'situations referred to in Article 3 common to the Geneva Conventions of 12 August 1949'.[115] This application of the Convention and its Protocols to non-international armed conflicts applies to States that ratify that extending provision.[116] Amended Protocol II has always applied to such conflicts.[117]

2. The Biological Weapons Convention, the Chemical Weapons Convention, the Ottawa Convention, and the Cluster Munitions Convention all apply to international and non-international armed conflicts.

3. Similarly, the customary law prohibitions relating to biological weapons, chemical weapons, weapons that are of a nature to cause superfluous injury or unnecessary suffering, weapons that are indiscriminate by nature, poisons and poisoned weapons, and exploding bullets intended for anti-personnel purposes apply equally to international and non-international armed conflicts.

4. The treaty prohibition of expanding bullets only relates to international armed conflicts and makes no reference to superfluous injury or unnecessary suffering, whereas the rule is only broken in relation to non-international armed conflicts if the expanding ammunition is employed uselessly to aggravate an injury or to cause unnecessary suffering.[118]

5. ENMOD applies if the destruction, damage, or injury is caused by one State party to another, which will generally not be the case in non-international armed conflicts. Articles 35(3) and 55 of AP I only apply to States parties in relation to international armed conflicts.

6. The weapons law rules that apply in non-international armed conflicts do not differentiate between conflicts to which only Common Article 3 applies and those also regulated by Additional Protocol II.

[114] CCW Review Conference, December 2001.

[115] CCW, Art. 1(2) as amended.

[116] At the time of writing 102 States have ratified the extension, <https://www.icrc.org/applic/ihl/ihl.nsf/Treaty.xsp?documentId=82CF2C7C75E37C5AC12563FB006181B4&action=openDocument>.

[117] CCW, Amended Protocol II, Art. 1(2).

[118] The Preamble to the Kampala Review Conference Resolution, Resolution RC/Res. 5, Advance Version, dated 16 June 2010 preambular para. 9, states: 'Considering that the crime proposed in article 8, paragraph 2(c)(xv) (employing bullets which expand or flatten easily in the human body), is also a serious violation of the laws applicable in armed conflict not of an international character, and understanding that the crime is committed only if the perpetrator employs the bullets to uselessly aggravate suffering or the wounding effect upon the target of such bullets, as reflected in customary international law.'

18.2 Rules Applying in Situations Other than Armed Conflict

18.06 **Domestic and human rights law determine the weapons that may lawfully be used, and the weapon options that should be available, in dealing with law enforcement situations both inside and outside the territory of the user irrespective of whether in the context of an armed conflict or otherwise.**

1. If a situation does not reach the armed conflict threshold, fundamentally different legal rules apply to the use of weapons. Those rules derive from domestic law of the relevant State as supplemented by human rights law. The weapons that a State issues to its internal security personnel, including the police force and any armed forces or militia forces deployed to deal with law enforcement situations, must enable those forces to comply with human rights law obligations, in particular those relating to the right to life. The precise terms of relevant human rights norms will depend on the applicable human rights Convention and/or customary human rights rules.

2. Limitations on the right to life should be construed narrowly.[119] Lethal force can only lawfully be used if it is absolutely necessary. Such use must be strictly proportionate[120] to the achievement of its self-defence purpose[121] and planning must be undertaken with great care[122] taking into account the foreseeable consequences of a planned operation. Loss of life resulting from the use by the State authorities of disproportionate force in an unplanned operation is likely to constitute a breach of the right to life.[123]

3. Accordingly, the weapons that are deployed for use in addressing foreseeable situations of the sort referred to in the rule must provide the security personnel with a suitable range of response options so that lethal force can in practice be limited to circumstances of absolute necessity. This suggests that, when deployed to address

[119] *Andronicou and Constantinou v Cyprus*, European Court of Human Rights, Application no. 25052/94, Judgment of 9 October 1997.

[120] D.J. Harris, M. O'Boyle, and C. Warbrick et al., *Law of the European Convention on Human Rights*, 2nd edn (Oxford: Oxford University Press, 2009), 62.

[121] See *McCann and others v UK*, Application no. 18984/91, Judgment of 27 September 1995; 21 EHRR 97, para. 212; *Isayeva, Yusupova and Bazayeva v Russia*, 41 EHRR 847 (2005) at paras 190, 191, and 200; see also D.J. Harris et al., *Law of the European Convention*, 61–4.

[122] See *Andronicou and Constantinou v Cyprus*, European Court of Human Rights, Application no. 25052/94, Judgment of 9 October 1997, para. 183. As to the circumstances when a use of lethal force to disperse demonstrators was not found to be absolutely necessary, see *Gülec v Turkey*, European Court of Human Rights, Application no. 21593/93, Judgment of 27 July 1998. Note *Gül v Turkey*, European Court of Human Rights, Application no. 22676/93, Judgment of 14 December 2000.

[123] Note the UN Basic Principles on the Use of Force and Firearms by Law Enforcement Officials adopted by the 9th UN Congress on the Prevention of Crime and Treatment of Offenders, Havana, 27 August–7 September 1990, UN Doc. A/CONF.144/28/Rev.1 at 112 (1990), Arts 9 and 10, which limit the circumstances in which officers exercising police powers may use firearms.

such situations, the security forces ought, in addition to appropriate lethal options, to be equipped for example with some or all of batons or truncheons, shields, CS or tear gas, water cannon, rubber bullets, and other non-lethal technologies. **18.06**

4. Similar considerations apply to the deployment of a peace force if the activities of the parties to a former conflict fall below the armed conflict threshold. A peace enforcement operation may, however, take place in circumstances of ongoing armed conflict. If the peacekeeping force remains uninvolved in the armed conflict, it will be bound to comply with applicable domestic law and human rights law norms, save to the extent that a relevant UN Security Council resolution explicitly requires otherwise,[124] and should be equipped with weapons accordingly.

5. It should be noted that the use of certain weapons, prohibited in relation to an armed conflict, may be lawful in relation to an internal security or law enforcement situation of the sort discussed in the present Rule. Thus, riot control agents that cannot be used as a method of warfare become options that should actively be considered as an alternative to the use of lethal force. Furthermore, expanding bullets may be the option of choice to deal, for example, with a situation in which terrorists are holding hostages or in which terrorists are threatening to detonate a munition and thereby cause mass civilian casualties. Provided that the requirements as to proportionality, planning, absolute necessity, and limitation and control of the use of force are met, the use of such ammunition would per se not breach human rights law.

[124] M. Sassoli, 'The Role of Human Rights and International Humanitarian Law in New Types of Armed Conflicts', in O. Ben-Naftali (ed.), *International Humanitarian Law and International Human Rights Law* (Oxford: Oxford University Press, 2011), 34, at 66–7.

Chapter 19

AIR LAW AND MILITARY OPERATIONS

The rules that follow are applicable in both peace time and during armed conflict, except as otherwise noted or as apparent from context. Although no treaty specifically addresses air warfare, the 1923 Hague Rules of Air Warfare informally drawn up by a Commission of Jurists have greatly influenced the development of customary international humanitarian law (IHL) applicable in air warfare. Dramatic changes in the nature and scope of air warfare since then have transformed the content and interpretation of this body of law. Therefore, special attention should be paid to the *Manual on International Law in Air and Missile Warfare* produced by an international group of experts under the auspices of the Harvard University's Program on Humanitarian Policy and Conflict Research (HPCR).[1] The rules that follow draw heavily on the authoritative work of that group.

19.01 **Airspace is classified as either national or international. National airspace lies over the land, internal waters, archipelagic waters, and territorial seas of a State. International airspace is that over contiguous zones, exclusive economic zones, the high seas, and territory not subject to the sovereignty of any nation, such as Antarctica and the Arctic.**

1. *Airspace* is defined in Section 19.02. The terms 'national' and 'international waters', although not formally international law terms of art, are commonly used to distinguish the operational rights and obligations of States in various waters and airspace.[2] In international airspace, States enjoy the right of overflight. All waters seaward of the territorial sea constitute international waters, which are subadjacent to international airspace. There is no general right of overflight over national waters (see Section 19.03).

2. *Maritime Zones* and the airspace over them are determined from baselines. Baselines usually follow the low water line along a coast as marked on large-scale charts, although technical rules apply in a variety of cases, such as in the treatment of harbours, bays, and deeply indented coastlines.[3]

[1] Harvard Program on Humanitarian Policy and Conflict Research, *Manual in International Law Applicable to Air and Missile Warfare* (Cambridge: Cambridge University Press, 2013) (HPCR Manual).

[2] See e.g. US Navy, US Marine Corps, US Coast Guard, *The Commander's Handbook on the Law of Naval Operations* (NWP 1-14M, MCWP 5-12.1, COMDTPUB P5800.7A), para. 2.7 (June 2007).

[3] See generally Arts 5–14 of the 1982 United Nations Convention on the Law of the Sea (UNCLOS). On maritime zones, see Chapter 20 'The Law of Military Operations at Sea'.

MICHAEL N. SCHMITT

3. *Land* begins at the baseline, that is, the low water point. Internal waters are 19.01
those which are landward of the baseline, such as rivers and lakes.[4] Archipelagic States are those consisting entirely of one or more groups of islands.[5] In such cases, straight baselines are drawn from the outmost points of their outermost islands, provided the baselines meet certain land–water ratio requirements. Waters contained within these baselines are archipelagic waters. The territorial sea consists of waters, depending on the claim of the coastal State, seaward up to 12 nautical miles from the baseline.[6]

4. *Contiguous Zones* may begin at the outer limit of the territorial sea. States may claim a contiguous zone that extends to a distance seaward from the baseline up to 24 nautical miles.[7] Coastal States enjoy the right in a contiguous zone to exercise the control necessary to address certain customs, fiscal, immigration, and health laws and regulations infringements that might occur within its territory. Exclusive economic zones claimed by a coastal State may extend seaward no more than 200 nautical miles from the baseline.[8] Within the zone, coastal States enjoy certain resource-related rights (such as those relating to fishing). The high sea consists of all waters seaward of the exclusive economic zone.[9]

5. The waters and icepack of the Arctic region other than lawfully claimed territorial waters of States in the region constitute international waters and cannot be claimed by any State. Thus, the airspace lying above them constitutes international airspace. Although a number of States have made claims to portions of Antarctica, most experts deem the area to be beyond the sovereignty of any State. As a result, the airspace above it is international airspace.[10] It should be noted that the 1959 Antarctic Treaty preserves the region for 'peaceful purposes' and that, therefore, it prohibits 'any measure of a military nature, such as the establishment of military bases and fortifications, the carrying out of military manoeuvres, as well as the testing of any type of weapon'.[11]

Airspace extends vertically to space. Although not authoritatively 19.02
defined in international law, space is generally understood as beginning at the point at which artificial satellites can be placed in orbit without free-falling to earth.

1. The distinction between airspace and space is important because States may not exercise sovereign rights in space, as they may in national airspace, and unimpeded

[4] Art. 8 UNCLOS; NWP 1-14M, para. 1.3.1.

[5] Art. 46 UNCLOS; NWP 1-14M, para. 1.5.4.

[6] Art. 2 UNCLOS; NWP 1-14M, para. 1.3.2. Coastal States may choose to claim less than the 12 nautical mile limit; other circumstances, such as States which face each other across a strait of less than 24 nautical miles, may limit the breadth of the territorial sea.

[7] Art. 33 UNCLOS; NWP 1-14M, para. 1.3.3.

[8] Arts. 56 and 86 UNCLOS; NWP 1-14M, para. 1.3.4.

[9] Art. 86 UNCLOS; NWP 1-14M, para. 1.3.5.

[10] NWP 1-14M, para. 2.6.5.1 and 2.6.5.2.

[11] Art. 1 Antarctic Treaty.

19.02 overflight of national territory and territorial waters is permitted through space. Airspace is generally viewed as that area in which aircraft can fly by deriving support through their reaction with air. By contrast, space is that area in which satellites can sustain orbit without descending into the atmosphere. Although no precise distance has been agreed upon, airspace is usually said to extend to roughly 100 km above ground level.

19.03 **Each State enjoys complete and exclusive sovereignty over its national airspace and may deny entry to it, subject to the right of transit passage through international straits and archipelagic sea lane passage. There is no right of innocent passage through the airspace above the territorial sea. Except as agreed to by treaty, the aircraft of all nations are free to operate in international airspace. All States enjoy equal access to space; no State may exercise sovereignty over space or claim its exclusive use.**

1. States control the airspace over their land territory and territorial sea and have the right to deny entry into or passage through it.[12] Unlike ships in territorial waters, aircraft do not enjoy a right of innocent passage through airspace over territorial waters. Neither do aircraft have any such rights in or over archipelagic waters. Thus, States have the right to regulate and prohibit flights within national airspace, subject to any international agreements to which they are party. Aircraft that wish to enter national airspace must identify themselves according to the requirements of the respective State and secure entry permission. Conditions, such as altitude and flight path, may be set as a condition of entry.

2. Exceptions to the rule of absolute sovereignty over airspace exist with regard to international straits and archipelagic waters. An international strait is a strait used for international navigation through national waters (of one or more States) that connects one area of international waters with another. An archipelagic sea lane passes through archipelagic waters in an analogous manner. All aircraft, including military aircraft, enjoy the right of transit passage over international straits and archipelagic passage over archipelagic sea lanes. The passage must be continuous and expeditious and no actions may be taken that threaten the coastal or archipelagic State. During armed conflicts, belligerent aircraft may exercise these rights.[13] So too may the missiles, such as cruise missiles, of a party to the conflict. However, military aircraft of one party to the conflict are subject to attack by the other party should they pass over the national waters of either's territory.

[12] Arts 1–2 of the 1944 ICAO Convention (Chicago Convention); Art. 2 UNCLOS; NWP 1-14M, para. 1.9.

[13] San Remo Manual: International Institute of Humanitarian Law (L. Doswald-Beck, ed.), *San Remo Manual on International Law Applicable to Armed Conflicts at Sea, Prepared by a Group of International Lawyers and Naval Experts* (Cambridge: Cambridge University Press, 1994), <http://www.icrc.org/ihl.nsf/FULL/560?OpenDocument>, para. 27.

3. Outer space is not subject to the sovereignty of any State.[14] 19.03

When necessitated by *force majeure* or distress, foreign aircraft may enter a State's national airspace; in such cases, every effort must be made to coordinate entry with the concerned authorities. Foreign aircraft may also enter national airspace in 'assistance entry' to render emergency assistance to those in distress at sea. They must depart upon request once the coastal State is providing rescue services. The right of assistance entry only applies in situations where the location of the distress is known; there is no right to enter national airspace to conduct a search absent the consent of the coastal State. 19.04

1. Aircraft in distress or at risk for other reasons beyond their control (such as weather) must be allowed entry for the purpose of emergency landing, and allowed to depart once the emergency has been addressed.[15] However, during an international armed conflict, the aircraft and crew of a belligerent aircraft that lands in neutral territory, for whatever reason, must be interned.

2. Ships and aircraft have a duty to render assistance to those in danger of being lost at sea.[16] Therefore, they may enter airspace over the territorial sea to conduct a rescue. The location of the individual(s) to be rescued must be reasonably certain, for there is no right to conduct search incident to the right of assistance entry.

States may declare a temporary closure or warning area on or over the high seas to conduct hazardous activities such as missile testing, gunnery exercises, and space vehicle recovery operations. Although ships and aircraft are not required to remain outside a declared closure or warning area, they must not directly interfere with activities within them; by entering the area, such ships and aircraft place themselves at risk from the hazardous activities. 19.05

1. States are entitled to establish zones over national airspace incident to their absolute sovereignty over such airspace. However, in international airspace, the right of States to use an area is subject to the rights of other States to also transit through and conduct activities in the area. Thus, there is no right in international law to definitively close international airspace to flight, and it is common for aircraft of other States to monitor such activities.

2. Section 19.05 seeks to balance such competing rights by establishing a requirement to place aircraft on notice that hazardous activities are underway. A 'notice to mariners' (NOTMAR) and/or a 'notice to airmen' (NOTAM) should be promulgated in advance of the activities to provide adequate notice of the areas affected and set forth general information such as temporary airspace restrictions; continuous

[14] NWP 1-14M, para. 1.10. [15] NWP 1-14M, para. 2.7.1.
[16] Regarding ships, see Art. 98 UNCLOS.

19.05 listening channel frequencies; weather-avoidance radar and identification modes and codes; altitude, course, and speed restrictions; radio response procedures; and likely military response in the event that non-compliance with the NOTAM is deemed threatening.

3. These procedures may be employed during armed conflict, although reasons of operational security may preclude issuing notices. In such cases, all reasonable steps should be made to ensure the safety of civilian and neutral flights in the vicinity of hazardous activities.

19.06 **Some States have established Air Defence Identification Zones (ADIZ) in international airspace adjacent to their national airspace. In an ADIZ, a foreign aircraft can be required to identify itself and provide position reports as a condition for entry into national airspace.**

1. Although based in international airspace, international law does not prohibit States from establishing an ADIZ in international airspace adjacent to their territory to ensure their security. The legal basis for the ADIZ is the right of a State to set conditions on entry into its national airspace.[17]

2. There is no legal basis for applying ADIZ procedures to aircraft not intending to enter national airspace. In such cases, compliance with ADIZ requirements is optional. The sole permissible consequence for failure to comply with ADIZ requirements is denial of permission to enter national airspace. It is the policy of some States, such as the United States, to refuse to comply with ADIZ procedures when its State aircraft do not seek entry.

19.07 **In peacetime, no-fly zones, or other restrictions on flight, may be established by UN Security Council resolution(s). The relevant mandates govern permissible enforcement activities within the zone. In the absence of a Security Council mandate, such zones are unlawful except within an establishing State's national airspace.**

1. In peacetime, all States enjoy unimpeded access to international airspace on the one hand and enjoy a near absolute right to control national airspace on the other. Thus, States may bar access to national airspace, but enjoy no right to do so with regard to international airspace.

2. However, the Security Council, operating pursuant to its power under Chapter VII of the UN Charter, may take steps necessary to maintain or restore international peace and security, to include authorizing the use of force. It does so through the adoption of Chapter VII resolutions containing mandates to take specified actions to achieve a defined purpose. Measures may include establishing

[17] See e.g. Art. 11 UNCLOS.

a zone within which aircraft may not fly or within which other flight restrictions apply. Such zones are lawful even though they limit the right of a State's aircraft to fly within its own airspace or the right of aircraft to operate in international airspace. The respective resolution may authorize the use of force to enforce the no-fly zone or other restrictions. Establishment of an aerial zone by the Security Council may occur during peacetime or in connection with an ongoing conflict. As an example, in 1992 the Security Council banned military aircraft flights over Bosnia-Herzegovina in order to protect the delivery of humanitarian assistance.[18] When military flights nevertheless continued, the Council banned all flights except those authorized by the United Nations Protection Force (UNPROFOR); it further authorized the use of force to enforce the ban.[19] 19.07

Most States are a party to the 1944 Convention on International Civil Aviation (Chicago Convention). The Convention established the International Civil Aviation Organization (ICAO) to enhance flight safety by developing international air navigation principles and procedures. In particular, ICAO has established Flight Information Regions (FIR) in national and international airspace to provide flight information and alerting services. The Convention does not apply to 'State aircraft' (including military aircraft). Although such aircraft may follow ICAO flight procedures as a matter of policy, certain operational missions (such as classified missions, politically sensitive missions, or routine aircraft carrier operations) may require non-compliance with them. In such cases, the aircraft involved must fly pursuant to the 'due regard' standard. 19.08

1. The Chicago Convention applies, by Article 3(a), only to civil aircraft, and expressly not to State aircraft. Nevertheless, to enhance the safety of all aircraft, military aircraft commonly follow ICAO procedures unless doing so would have negative operational consequences. Even when they do not follow ICAO principles, they must fly with 'due regard' to the safety of other aircraft. In other words, safety must be a consideration in all flight operations and military aircraft should do nothing endangering other aircraft.

2. Flight Information Regions are established by ICAO to enhance the safety of civil aircraft in both national and international airspace. Although some States purport to require military aircraft to comply with FIR procedures in international airspace, most experts agree that they are not entitled to do so as a matter of international law.[20] Only if a military aircraft intends to enter national airspace must it comply with the requirements established by the territorial State.

[18] SC Res. 781 (1992).

[19] SC Res. 816 (1993).

[20] This is the position taken by the United States. See DoD Directive 4540.1, Use of Airspace by US Military Aircraft and Firings Over the High Seas (13 January 1981).

19.09 **The legal rights and obligations of aircraft, and the duties owed them by others, depend in great part on their status. There are two broad categories of aircraft, 'State' and 'civil'. Although the term 'State' aircraft is not defined in international law, it is understood to mean any aircraft owned or used by a State for exclusively non-commercial purposes. The category includes military, police, and customs aircraft. All other aircraft are 'civil' aircraft. For the purposes of international humanitarian law, it is necessary to further subdivide aircraft into 'cartel aircraft', 'civilian aircraft' (including the subcategory 'civilian airliners'), 'medical aircraft', and 'military aircraft'.**

1. The term *aircraft* includes unmanned aerial vehicles (UAVs). State aircraft are those used by the State for military, customs, or law enforcement purposes.[21] Law enforcement aircraft include those of the police, as well as any other agency tasked with law enforcement functions. State aircraft used for other purposes, such as weather monitoring and research, are assimilated to civil aircraft in the substantive rules that follow.

2. *Cartel Aircraft* are aircraft granted safe conduct for any specific purpose, although historically they have been used for the transport of prisoners or parlementaires (those who negotiate on behalf of a belligerent). To acquire cartel status, the belligerents must agree that the respective aircraft shall have such status; typically they also agree on a wide range of other conditions, such as route, altitude, period of flight, and so forth. Violation of the agreement will cause the cartel aircraft to lose its special status. Both State and civil aircraft may serve as cartel aircraft.

3. *Civil Aircraft* comprise all aircraft other than State aircraft. Civilian airliners are civilian aircraft identifiable as such and engaged in carrying civilian passengers, whether in scheduled or non-scheduled service.[22] Civilian airliners are entitled to special protective measures during peacetime pursuant to Article 3*bis* of the Chicago Convention. However, the protection does not apply in armed conflict, during which all civilian aircraft are instead protected by the rules on targeting (see Chapter 16 'Targeting in Operational Law').

4. *Medical Aircraft* are aircraft permanently or temporarily assigned by a belligerent exclusively to transportation or treatment of the wounded or sick, or to the transport of medical or religious personnel, supplies, or equipment.[23] They may be State or civil aircraft, and may be operated by belligerents, neutrals, or impartial non-governmental organizations, such as the International Committee of the Red

[21] Art. 3(b) Chicago Convention; see the historical basis for the distinction at Articles 2, 4, and 5 of the 1923 Hague Rules of Air Warfare.

[22] International Institute of Humanitarian Law (L. Doswald-Beck, ed.), *San Remo Manual on International Law Applicable to Armed Conflicts at Sea, Prepared by a Group of International Lawyers and Naval Experts* (Cambridge: Cambridge University Press, 1994), <http://www.icrc.org/ihl.nsf/FULL/560?OpenDocument>, para. 13(m).

[23] Art. 39 GC II; Art. 8(g), (f), and (j) AP I.

Cross or Doctors without Borders. Should an aircraft carry combatants, military equipment, or otherwise be assigned other than the aforementioned duties, it would not qualify as a medical aircraft even if it did transport, for instance, some wounded personnel. Search and rescue aircraft are not medical aircraft. 19.09

5. *Military Aircraft* are discussed in Section 19.11.

6. The category of '*auxiliary aircraft*', referred to in the San Remo Manual and the US Navy's *Commander's Handbook on the Law of Naval Operations* is a concept applicable primarily in naval warfare. It has not been used in this Handbook because aircraft which might qualify are adequately encompassed in the term 'State aircraft'.[24]

Aircraft must have a national identity, unless representing an intergovernmental organization, such as the United Nations, vested with an international legal personality. 19.10

1. The Chicago Convention provides that civilian aircraft possess the nationality of the State of registration.[25] They may be registered in only one State and must display nationality and registration markings.[26] Military aircraft must be marked to indicate nationality and military character (see discussion accompanying Section 19.11).

Military aircraft are those operated under the command of members of the armed forces and marked as such, as well as unmanned aerial vehicles operated by the military. As 'State aircraft', they enjoy sovereign immunity from foreign search and inspection and foreign officials may not board them without the aircraft commander's authorization. However, if the aircraft commander fails to certify compliance with local customs, immigration, or quarantine requirements, the aircraft may be directed to leave immediately. 19.11

1. Military aircraft are those operated by the armed forces of a State; bearing the markings of that State; commanded by a member of the armed forces; and controlled or manned by a crew subject to regular armed forces discipline.[27] It is prohibited to mark military aircraft as neutral or enemy aircraft. The aircraft need not be owned by the military, so long as operated by the armed forces. For instance, an aircraft leased for use by the military would qualify if the aforementioned conditions were met. UAVs may qualify as military aircraft, whether armed or not, despite the fact that they are operated remotely. Only military aircraft may exercise belligerent rights, especially that of conducting attacks against lawful targets.[28]

[24] San Remo Manual, para. 63; NWP 1-14M, para. 2.4.3.

[25] Art. 17 Chicago Convention. [26] Arts 18 and 20 Chicago Convention.

[27] Adopted from Arts 3, 7, and 14 of the 1923 Hague Rules of Air Warfare; see also NWP 1-14M, para. 2.4.1; San Remo Manual, para. 13(j).

[28] 1923 Hague Rules of Air Warfare, Arts 13 and 16(1).

19.11 2. Military aircraft must bear both nationality marking and marking as a military aircraft, although the two can be combined into a distinctive single mark.[29] The markings should be sufficiently visible from multiple angles to distinguish the military aircraft from other State aircraft and from civil aircraft. They may also bear other appropriate markings, such as that of an international organization like NATO. Despite the requirement that markings be visible, a number of States employ subdued or other low-visibility markings, particularly on special operations aircraft. State practice evidences no serious objection to such markings.

3. A military aircraft must be 'commanded' by a member of the armed forces who exercises control over the aircraft.[30] On manned aircraft, the commander must be aboard the aircraft, although he or she need not be the pilot. Unmanned aircraft may be controlled remotely by members of the armed forces. Despite the requirement that the aircraft be crewed by personnel subject to armed forces discipline, it is not necessary that the entire crew be military, a fact apparent from the 1949 Third Geneva Convention's Article 4A(4) reference to 'civilian members of military aircraft crews'. Aircraft operated by civilian contractors, including private military companies, are 'civilian aircraft', which may not exercise belligerent rights.

4. All State aircraft, including military aircraft, enjoy sovereign immunity and, as such, are exempt from boarding by officials of other States without the consent of the commander. However, they must depart if the commander fails to certify compliance with local law and regulations.[31]

19.12 **Civilian aircraft flying in the vicinity of ongoing military operations should file flight plans with the relevant air traffic control service that include such information as route, registration, destination, passengers, cargo, and identification codes and modes. They may not leave a designated air traffic service route or deviate from their flight plan without air traffic control clearance. In the case of unforeseen situations involving safety of the aircraft or its occupants, such aircraft must immediately notify civil and military authorities.**

1. Section 19.12 draws directly on the work of the HPCR *Manual on International Law Applicable to Air and Missile Warfare*[32] and on Rule 76 of the 1994 San Remo Manual. As a general matter, civilian aircraft flying in the vicinity of military operations need not file a flight plan with the servicing air traffic control service, but doing so enhances safety in flight and is highly encouraged. The HPCR group of experts believed the requirement was obligatory during armed conflict. It also emphasized the criticality of the relevant air traffic control service making advance

[29] On marking, see 1923 Hague Rules of Air Warfare, Arts 3 and 7; NWP 1-14M, para. 2.4.1.
[30] San Remo Manual, para. 13(j). [31] NWP 1-14M, para. 2.4.2.
[32] HPCR Manual.

information on the flight plans, emergency communication channels, and identification modes and codes of civilian aircraft available to military forces. 19.12

2. As a general matter, aircraft other than military aircraft ought to avoid areas of potentially hazardous military activities.[33] For reasons of safety in flight, they should always comply with the instructions of military authorities. Although failure to do so does not cause a civilian aircraft to lose its character, non-compliance will be a factor in the military commander's determination as to whether the civilian aircraft represents a threat which must be defended against. This is especially so in light of the possibility of an aircraft, including a hijacked aircraft, being used as a weapon.

3. To enhance the safety of non-military flights in the vicinity of military operations, belligerents should, when militarily feasible in the circumstances, issue a NOTAM providing information on military operations that might place such aircraft at risk.[34] Such NOTAMs should include, *inter alia*, any temporary restrictions on flights imposed by the military forces, frequencies which the aircraft should continually monitor, instructions regarding continuous operation of identification modes and codes, procedures by which the aircraft can communicate with military forces, and cautionary information on how the military forces might respond should they deem the aircraft to be a threat.

All States providing air traffic control service should establish procedures that permit military forces to be aware of designated routes assigned to, or flight plans filed by, civilian aircraft in the area of military operations. Supplemental data should include, but not necessarily be limited to, communication channels frequencies, identification modes and codes, flight destination, and passengers and cargo. 19.13

1. The purpose of Section 19.13 is to enhance the safety of civil aircraft operating in the vicinity of military operations. This is especially important in light of the fact that aerial engagements can occur beyond visual range, that is, without the attacking pilot actually seeing his target. The provision encourages the dissemination of information which might assist military forces to identify civil aircraft and communicate with them. Tragic incidents, such as the Soviet downing of Korean Airlines Flight 007 in 1983 and the 1988 shooting down of Iranian Air Flight 655 by the USS *Vincennes*, highlight the need to ensure the transparency of civilian flight activities.

2. Such measures are particularly imperative during armed conflicts.[35] They should be complied with by all States, including neutrals.

[33] San Remo Manual, para. 72.
[34] San Remo Manual, para. 75.
[35] See e.g. San Remo Manual, para. 74.

19.14 **Only military aircraft may engage in attacks. All enemy military aircraft constitute military objectives, unless they enjoy specific protection. Other enemy aircraft may acquire the status of military objectives through their use or purpose (see Section 16.03).**

1. Military aircraft alone are entitled to exercise belligerent rights such as attack, interception, and blockade enforcement.[36] Other State aircraft can engage in activities involving the use of force so long as such activities are not strictly belligerent rights. Examples include criminal law enforcement and customs and border control. Aircraft operated by private military companies, even if under contract to the military, are not military aircraft and may not engage in attacks except in self-defence. If paramilitary or other armed law enforcement agencies are incorporated into the armed forces (see discussion accompanying Section 16.02), their members become combatants. The aircraft of the organization could then be converted into military aircraft through compliance with the conditions for qualifying as military aircraft, such as being appropriately marked (see Section 19.10).

2. All military aircraft, except medical aircraft or aircraft designated temporarily for cartel duties, are military objectives.[37] This is so regardless of their function. For instance, a military aircraft tasked with carrying civilian officials is nevertheless a military aircraft, although the presence of civilians aboard the aircraft would be relevant when making a proportionality calculation (see Section 16.06). Military aircraft are military objectives at all times. Their character as military aircraft means they qualify on the basis of 'nature'. Further, their inherent mobility means their destruction, damage, or neutralization will always offer a definite military advantage. For a discussion of the requirements for qualifying as a military objective, see Section 16.03.

3. Other aircraft may become military objectives through use or purpose. Examples of use include engaging in acts of war on behalf of the enemy, transporting troops or military material and equipment, and being incorporated into the enemy's intelligence gathering system. A civilian aircraft which is being fitted out to transport troops would illustrate the purpose criterion, as would the activation of a reserve fleet of civil aircraft (such as the US Civil Reserve Air Fleet) for military purposes. Once such aircraft begin carrying troops, they would qualify as military objectives through use.

4. During an attack on an aircraft that constitutes a military objective, the principle of proportionality (see Section 16.06) and the requirement to take all feasible precautions in attack (see Section 16.07) apply. Although some experts suggest that civilians within a military objective are not factored into a proportionality analysis, the weight of opinion is that they do.[38] This is a particularly relevant

[36] 1923 Hague Rules of Air Warfare, Arts 13 and 16.

[37] San Remo Manual, para. 65.

[38] See discussion accompanying Section 16.06.

consideration in the case of civil aircraft, such as a hijacked airliner, which has become a military objective through use. **19.14**

5. The taking of feasible precautions is especially important in aerial warfare because combat is fast-paced and often conducted from beyond visual range. Therefore, the need to adequately verify that a potential target is in fact a military objective is paramount. In this regard, considerations include, but are not limited to, visual identification; responses to radio warnings; infrared, radar, and electronic signatures; identification modes and codes; number and formation of aircraft; altitude, speed, track, profile, and other flight characteristics; and pre-flight and in-flight air traffic control information.

During armed conflict, the establishment of an exclusion or no-fly zone is governed by international humanitarian law and other applicable rules of international law. The extent, location, and duration of the zone, and enforcement measures, are limited to those required by military necessity or the need to safeguard protected persons and objects. A zone may not include neutral airspace. The party establishing such a zone must provide full notification of its establishment, location, duration, and conditions. Aircraft, other than enemy belligerent aircraft, approaching the zone must be appropriately notified and warned away. **19.15**

1. Exclusion and no-fly zones are employed during armed conflicts. An exclusion zone restricts the freedom of aerial navigation over international airspace, whereas a no-fly zone does so over a State's own territory or in enemy airspace.[39] Such zones may not be established in neutral airspace, as the law of neutrality prohibits belligerent actions in neutral territory. The concept of exclusion zones does not apply in non-international armed conflict.

2. Whether in an exclusion or a no-fly zone, belligerents continue to be bound by norms of international humanitarian law. For instance, civilian aircraft which enter such zones may not be attacked once identified as such. Rather, entry into the properly identified and announced zone by an aircraft merely creates a presumption that it is engaged in non-innocent activities. Exclusion and no-fly zones are not 'free fire' zones in which air warfare is unrestricted; such zones are unlawful whether on land, at sea, or in the air.

3. Exclusion and no-fly zones should not be confused with the right of belligerents to control civil aviation, including neutral aviation, in the vicinity of hostilities, whether on land, at sea, or in the air. A belligerent is entitled, for purposes of military necessity, to prohibit the operation of aircraft in the vicinity of his

[39] The legality of no-fly zones is generally accepted. State practice has demonstrated that exclusion zones are now permissible. See e.g. NWP 1-14M, paras 7–9; UK Manual, paras 12.58, 13.77, San Remo Manual, paras 105–108.

19.15 operations or prescribe set routes for passage.[40] Similarly, they are not warning zones, which are force protection measures that merely serve to warn off aircraft approaching the vicinity of military operations or facilities.

4. An exclusion zone may be established to defend high-value military assets or safeguard protected persons and objects, such as concentrations of civilians. It may also be established to contain the geographic area of hostilities, for instance by generally excluding areas beyond the zone from belligerent action. Since they represent impediments to unimpeded navigation in international airspace, exclusion zones should be limited in nature and scope. In particular, the extent, location, and duration of the zone must be justifiable on the basis of military necessity, and notification of such features must be made to all those who might be affected thereby. An exclusion zone may not be established in neutral airspace, nor may it bar access to such airspace (although blocking a particular route is permissible if viable alternative routes exist).[41]

5. As they are not established in international airspace, the establishment of no-fly zones by a belligerent over its own or enemy territory is relatively uncontroversial. As with exclusion zones, the duration, location, and extent of a no-fly zone must be appropriately notified to all affected civil aviation, whether enemy, own, or neutral, typically through issuance of a NOTAM. No notification need be made to enemy military aircraft, for they are subject to attack. Although aircraft entering a no-fly zone without proper authorization may be attacked without warning, the international humanitarian law regarding attacks nevertheless continues to apply. Thus, civil aircraft which have been identified as such retain their immunity from attack. The no-fly zone simply creates a rebuttable presumption that the aircraft is engaging in activities that are non-innocent and subject it to attack.

19.16 **During armed conflict, aircraft and their crews are entitled to surrender. However, as there is no accepted means for doing so, a military force accepting surrender of an aircraft may establish reasonable procedures for doing so. Non-compliance may subject the aircraft to attack. Aircrew of the surrendering aircraft should do everything possible to communicate their intention to surrender.**

1. Since there is no generally accepted means of surrender of an aircraft, and because surrender is only effective when communicated to the enemy, aircrew should do everything feasible to indicate their desire to surrender. For instance, they should notify enemy forces on common radio channels, such as the distress channel. Other means that may indicate a desire to surrender, although not formally recognized as such, include rocking the wings, lowering the landing gear,

[40] See 1923 Hague Rules of Air Warfare, Art. 30; NWP 1-14M, paras 7.8 and 7.9; San Remo Manual, para. 108.

[41] Neutral territory, including airspace, is inviolable. See 1907 Hague Conventions V and XIII; 1923 Hague Rules of Air Warfare, Arts 39–40.

flashing navigational signals, and jettisoning weapons. However, since there may be other reasons for taking such actions they may not be viewed in the circumstances as a sufficient indication of surrender by the enemy. Ultimately, the aircrew may have to bail out to effect a surrender. While descending they may not be attacked and upon landing they must be afforded the opportunity to surrender (see Sections 16.10 and 19.17). 19.16

2. Belligerents may establish means of surrender for enemy aircraft, for instance flying at a set altitude on a specific course at a given airspeed towards a particular airfield. Failure to comply with the prescribed procedures for surrender creates a rebuttable presumption that the aircraft is not surrendering.

Persons parachuting from an aircraft in distress may not be attacked during their descent. They should be given an opportunity to surrender upon landing. Those who continue fighting (for example, by firing a weapon) may be attacked in the air or upon landing. Airborne troops, including Special Forces and others who intend to perform military activities upon reaching the ground, may be attacked while in the air. 19.17

1. See Section 16.10 and accompanying discussion.

As a general rule, medical aircraft may not be attacked. 19.18

1. A special regime applies to medical aircraft.[42] When flying over land physically controlled by friendly forces or over sea areas not controlled by the enemy, they are entitled to the full protection and may not be attacked. However, when over areas either controlled by the enemy or where the opposing forces are in contact, the protection is only fully effective when prior consent to their operation has been granted by the enemy. If they are identified as medical aircraft, they should be diverted or ordered to land. Search and rescue aircraft used to recover wounded or stranded combatants enjoy no special protection.

2. Medical aircraft must be marked with the protective emblem (Red Cross, Red Crescent, or Red Crystal) and national colours.[43] Other means of identification as a medical aircraft may be used when feasible.[44] Examples include a flashing blue light and distinctive signals. Belligerents may also execute agreements regarding the means of identifying medical aircraft. Temporary medical aircraft which cannot be marked with the protective emblem should employ the most effective means of identification available. Note that protective emblems do not, of themselves, confer protected status; rather, they are intended only to facilitate identification as a protected medical aircraft.

[42] See specific rules in Arts 25–27 AP I.
[43] Art. 36(2) GC I; Art. 18(4) AP I; San Remo Manual, para. 175.
[44] Art. 18(5) AP I, and Annex I.

19.19 Medical aircraft performing military activities harmful to the enemy become military objectives subject to attack.

1. A medical aircraft which engages in activities that are militarily harmful to the enemy becomes a military objective by virtue of the use criterion (see Section 16.03). This is so even if they are also engaged in medical activities. Thus, for instance, a medical aircraft which is also carrying combatants is a military objective. That said, the presence of medical personnel, civilians, or those who are *hors de combat* on board must be taken into consideration during proportionality calculations and when assessing possible feasible precautions in attack.

2. Although medical aircraft may be equipped with encrypted communications equipment for navigation, identification, and communication in order to perform their medical functions, they may not be equipped with intelligence collection or transmission equipment.[45] Medical aircraft may be equipped with deflective defensive equipment (such as chaff or flares). Personnel on board may carry light weapons necessary to protect the aircraft, the medical personnel, and the wounded, sick, or shipwrecked on board. Carrying the individual weapons of the wounded, sick, or shipwrecked during their evacuation does not entail loss of protection.[46]

19.20 Aircraft conducting military search-and-rescue operations do not enjoy special protection, unless pursuant to prior consent of the enemy.

1. Aircraft used to search for and rescue combatants on land are not protected aircraft, since combatants remained lawful targets subject to attack unless they are wounded, sick, or shipwrecked (or indicate an intention to surrender). Civil aircraft used for search and rescue of such combatants are engaging in hostile activities and therefore become military objectives through the use criterion. Medical aircraft are likewise barred from engaging in such activities.

2. International humanitarian law specifically prohibits medical aircraft from searching even for wounded, sick, and shipwrecked combatants without prior agreement with the opposing belligerent.[47] To the extent this is so, the same restriction would apply to civil aircraft.

19.21 Aircraft involved in civil defence functions, humanitarian relief, or UN activities (other than those which qualify them as a party to an armed conflict) are entitled to special protection. In particular, a party to the conflict should agree to relief flights to aid a civilian population under its control if in need of food, medical supplies, and other items indispensable to its survival. The party may set reasonable conditions, such as search of aircraft involved, incident to the

[45] Art. 28(2) AP I. [46] Art. 28(3) AP I. [47] Art. 28(4) AP I.

delivery of the items. Relief efforts must be conducted impartially. Occupiers of an occupied territory are required to agree to humanitarian relief activities in such circumstances. 19.21

1. On the general protection of civil defence, humanitarian relief, and UN personnel, see Section 16.08.

2. When the civilian population of an area under control of a belligerent, including occupied territory, is in need of supplies essential to survival, humanitarian and impartial relief actions conducted without adverse distinction can be mounted. Agreement of the parties is required, and in the case of occupied territories it is obligatory to give such consent as necessary to satisfy the requirements of the civilian population.[48] The relief activities may be conducted either by States (especially neutral States) or impartial humanitarian organizations such as the International Committee of the Red Cross.

3. In light of the possibility of abuse, technical arrangements may be included in the relevant agreement to ensure the relief effort is purely humanitarian in nature and is not harmful to the belligerent. However, they may not be so onerous as to seriously impede the relief effort, thereby placing the civilian population at risk. Non-compliance with the agreement or with the general condition of impartiality can result in termination of the agreement.

4. Aircraft may be used for a variety of purposes to facilitate the relief effort. Examples include transporting relief supplies and personnel, determining the viability of overland relief routes, and airdropping relief supplies to isolated locations.

Civilian airliners are entitled to special protection, as well as the general protections to which civilian objects are entitled by international humanitarian law. Absent reliable information to the contrary, civilian airliners are presumed to be carrying civilian passengers. 19.22

1. In the aftermath of multiple shoot-downs of civilian airliners, the 1944 Chicago Convention was amended to add Article 3*bis*, which provides that States must refrain from the use of weapons against civil aircraft in flight. The Chicago Convention applies only in peacetime.

2. The HPCR group of experts concluded that civilian airliners are now also entitled to special protection during armed conflict as a matter of customary law based in State practice. In doing so, they followed the lead of the experts responsible for drafting the *San Remo Manual on the Law of Naval Warfare*.[49] The unique status

[48] See esp. Arts 55, 59 GC IV; Arts 69–70 AP I.
[49] See also San Remo Manual, para. 53(c).

19.22 of airliners derives from the large number of civilians aboard and the importance of the domestic and international air travel.

3. Civilian airliners already enjoy the protection of international humanitarian law to which civilian objects are entitled, such as immunity from attack. As such, they may only be attacked if they are believed to have become a military objective, most likely through use for military purposes. Therefore, there are two keys to the enhanced protection. First, there would appear to be a higher threshold for concluding that a civilian airliner has become a military objective. Second, even if it is determined that the airliner has become a military objective, the presumption that it is transporting civilian passengers would affect the proportionality calculation (see Section 16.06).

4. Despite the enhanced protection, it must be emphasized that the protection of airliners is not absolute. A civilian airliner may become a military objective by virtue of its use or purpose (see Section 16.03). Examples include situations in which the enemy intends to use it to carry military troops or military supplies and equipment, or in which it is doing so; being used to gather intelligence for the enemy; or being hijacked and used as a weapon. Before attacking a civilian airliner in such circumstances, an attempt should be made to divert it for landing, visit, and search. Attack is permissible only if no other means to exert control over the airliner exists and the harm to passengers will not be excessive relative to the military advantage anticipated from its attack (see Section 16.06). Decisions to attack civilian airliners should be taken at the highest feasible level of authority. In case of doubt, a civilian airliner shall be presumed not to be engaged in activities harmful to the enemy.

5. Although they should not enter exclusion or no-fly zones or areas in which potentially hazardous military activities are underway, they retain their protected status if they do. On such zones, see Section 19.15 and accompanying discussion.

19.23 **Belligerent military aircraft may intercept and inspect civilian aircraft to determine their identity, cargo, and nature of use.**

1. Section 19.23 is based on the right of belligerents to conduct a visit and search of ships and aircraft.[50] These activities may be conducted to determine whether the aircraft is of neutral or enemy character. In the latter case it may be subject to the law of capture.[51] Interception and inspection may also be conducted to determine whether the aircraft is transporting contraband (see Section 19.26). Finally, such actions are appropriate in order to determine the activities of a civilian aircraft, in particular whether it is engaging in activities beneficial to enemy military actions. Reasonable grounds must exist for conducting the interception and inspection. The airfield to which the aircraft is directed must be reasonably accessible, safe, and suitable for landing and takeoff for the type of aircraft being intercepted. In the

[50] NWP 1-14M, para. 7.6.
[51] On the capture of enemy aircraft, see the HPCR Manual.

event an appropriate airfield is unavailable, the aircraft may be diverted from its intended destination.[52] **19.23**

Parties to a conflict may agree to grant aircraft safe conduct. However, such aircraft lose protection if they seriously violate the terms of the agreement or act in a manner that makes them a military objective. **19.24**

1. Belligerents may always execute agreements that aircraft performing certain actions or functions are exempt from attack. The agreement will set forth the conditions for the exemption, which may include such matters as altitude, route, and timing of flight and means of communication. Cartel aircraft (see Section 19.09) typically operate pursuant to such agreements.

Neutral airspace is inviolable, except for the right of transit passage through an international strait or archipelagic sea lanes passage. Belligerents are prohibited from conducting any military activities in neutral territory, including airspace. Neutrals may not permit such use and must use all means available, including the use of force if necessary, to preclude it. If possible, offending belligerent military or auxiliary aircraft should be forced to land and the aircraft and crew interned for the remainder of the armed conflict. Should a serious violation of the neutral's territory nevertheless continue because of the inability or unwillingness of the neutral to end it, the opposing belligerent may, in the absence of non-forceful alternatives, use such force as is required to terminate its opponent's unlawful activities. **19.25**

1. As a matter of customary law, the conduct of hostilities by belligerents is not permitted on the territory, territorial sea, or in the national airspace of a neutral State. Neutral airspace is inviolable; overflight by belligerent aircraft or missiles is prohibited.[53] Military aircraft in distress may enter neutral airspace, but the neutral is required to intern the aircraft and its crew.[54] Belligerent warships may pass through the territorial waters of a neutral State in innocent passage, but while doing so may not launch or recover aircraft. There is no prohibition on conducting military activities in the airspace over the exclusive economic zone, although in its conduct a belligerent must pay due regard to the right of the coastal State in the area. Military aircraft and missiles, including those embarking on or returning from combat missions, may transit international straits and engage in archipelagic sea lane passage.[55] Their passage must be 'continuous and expeditious', in 'normal

[52] San Remo Manual, para. 125.

[53] 1907 Hague Convention V, Art. 1; 1907 Hague Convention XIII, Art. 1; 1923 Hague Rules of Air Warfare, Art. 39; NWP 1-14M, para. 7.3.9.

[54] NWP 1-14M, para. 7.3.9.

[55] NWP 1-14M, paras 7.3.6, 7.3.9, 7.7; San Remo Manual, para. 23.

19.25 mode' (i.e. the normal mode of operations), and no acts of hostility may be engaged in while in transit, unless necessary to defend themselves or naval forces in transit through the passage. Since warships are entitled to proceed in 'normal mode', they may launch and recover aircraft during such passage.

2. An exception exists in the case of military medical aircraft, which may, with prior notice, overfly neutral territory, land there in case of necessity, and use neutral airfields as ports of call. They must comply with all requirements imposed by the neutral State as conditions for doing so.[56] The consent of the opposing belligerent to such arrangements is not required. Should a medical aircraft enter neutral airspace without permission or through navigational error, it may be required to land for inspection. If the inspection determines the aircraft is a valid medical aircraft, it must be allowed to continue its flight.[57]

3. A neutral State is required to take reasonable steps to identify and prevent violations of its airspace by belligerent aircraft, including the use of force, and to intern captured aircrew and aircraft for the duration of the conflict.[58] The requirement to survey airspace to ensure it is not being violated by belligerents is derived from Article 25 of the 1907 Hague Convention XIII. A customary law requirement, it is also found in Articles 42 and 47 of the non-binding 1923 Hague Rules of Air Warfare. The requirement to force violating belligerent aircraft to land and to intern the crew and aircraft is customary in nature, and set forth in non-binding form in Article 42 of the Rules of Air Warfare.[59]

4. Should a neutral fail to meet its obligation to ensure its territory is free of belligerent action, the opposing belligerent may take actions necessary to put an end to serious violations endangering its security, even if doing so requires the use of force within neutral territory.[60] However, before taking such steps, the aggrieved belligerent must issue a warning and afford the neutral an opportunity to comply. Only upon non-compliance by the neutral may the belligerent take remedial action. Such action is limited to that necessary to end the violation.

5. The case of Security Council enforcement action under Chapter VII of the UN Charter poses a special case with regard to neutrality. Should the Council take such measures, no State may, on the basis that it is a neutral, engage in conduct inconsistent with the mandate. Pursuant to Article 25 of the Charter, decisions of the Security Council are binding and, therefore, supersede any neutral rights or obligations. Additionally, Article 103 provides that the Charter prevails over treaties. Therefore, the provisions of treaties bearing on neutral rights and obligations, such as the 1907 Hague Conventions V and XIII, do not apply to the extent they are inconsistent with obligations set forth in a Security Council resolution.

[56] See Art. 31(1) AP I. [57] San Remo Manual, para. 182.
[58] 1923 Hague Rules of Air Warfare, Art. 42.
[59] See also NWP 1-14M, para. 7.3.1.
[60] NWP 1-14M, para. 7.3; see also San Remo Manual, para. 22.

When a Security Council resolution mandates the use of force, States not participating may do nothing to impede fulfilment of the mandate and should generally act to ensure its fulfilment. For instance, they should allow overflight of military aircraft executing the mandate despite the principle of impartiality in neutrality law, and may not intern aircrew members who find themselves on their territory. 19.25

Neutral aircraft may not be attacked unless they become military objectives. 19.26

1. Neutral military aircraft are immune from attack because they are not belligerent aircraft. Neutral State and civil aircraft are immune from attack because they qualify as civilian objects. As an exception, a neutral aircraft that breaches a lawfully declared and enforced blockade may be intercepted and forced to land. Should it fail to comply with instructions to do so or otherwise resist enforcement of the blockade, it may be attacked.

2. Despite their immunity from attack, neutral aircraft which become involved in the hostilities lose their protected status and are liable to be diverted, forced to land, or attacked while so engaged. This rule is consistent with those providing that civilians who directly participate in hostilities (see discussion accompanying Section 16.02) and civilian objects used for military purposes may be attacked.

3. Neutral aircraft may not carry contraband to a belligerent. Contraband comprises goods which may be used by belligerents in the armed conflict and which are ultimately destined for enemy, or enemy controlled, territory.[61] Such goods may include weapons, munitions, military equipment, and other items destined for use by a belligerent force, such as uniforms and food. During an international armed conflict, belligerents are entitled to publish lists to place neutrals on notice as to the goods they consider, and do not consider, to be contraband. Should a belligerent reasonably suspect a neutral civilian aircraft is carrying contraband, it may order it to divert or to land to be searched. Failure to comply with the demands will subject the aircraft to attack. A neutral civilian aircraft escorted by a neutral military aircraft is exempt from interception and inspection if the military aircraft certifies that the civilian aircraft is not carrying contraband and provides requested information as to the character and cargo of the civilian aircraft.[62] Aircraft which otherwise reasonably appear to be contributing to an enemy's military action may also be intercepted and ordered to divert, desist, or land and be searched.

4. In certain cases, the contribution of a neutral aircraft to an enemy's military action is so direct that it effectively constitutes participation in the conflict. Examples include situations in which the aircraft engages in hostile acts, conducts intelligence gathering, or otherwise directly facilitates enemy military actions.

[61] NWP 1-14M, para. 7.4.1.

[62] NWP 1-14M, para. 7.6.3.

19.26 Aircraft engaging in such activities become military objectives and may be attacked without warning (see Section 16.03).

19.27 **A State remains responsible for the actions of its aircraft engaged in coalition operations, regardless of the nationality of the commander or any other command and control relationships.**

1. Section 19.27 sets forth the rule that States and their armed forces engaged in coalition or other combined operations, whether as part of a permanent alliance such as NATO or in an ad hoc coalition, continue to be bound by the State's legal obligations, in particular those found in international humanitarian law. It matters not whether the forces are commanded by a State's own personnel or those of another State. The only exception to this general rule occurs when a UN Security Council resolution sets forth a mandate inconsistent with pre-existing obligations. In such a case the resolution prevails (see discussion accompanying Section 19.07).

2. There is no prohibition on operating in concert with forces who shoulder different legal obligations.[63] However, a commander of a coalition force retains the legal obligations incident to his nationality. Thus, he may not order an action that would by the law binding on his State be unlawful, even if conducted by forces for which the action would not be unlawful. When the legal obligations of coalition partners differ, the most expedient and effective means of achieving unity of effort among the forces is through common rules of engagement (see also sub-Chapter 5.4 and Chapter 10).

[63] See e.g. Dublin Convention on Cluster Munitions, Art. 21.

Chapter 20

THE LAW OF MILITARY OPERATIONS AT SEA

1. This chapter exclusively deals with situations of international armed conflicts at sea.

2. The law of naval warfare does not apply to non-international armed conflicts. Parties to a non-international armed conflict are not entitled to interfere with the navigation and aviation of foreign States—the only exception applying to the respective government that may subject international navigation to certain restrictions within the territorial sea and close the national airspace for international aviation. This does not exclude an application of those principles and rules that limit the rights of the parties to the conflict and that are equally binding in international and non-international armed conflicts (e.g. principle of distinction, definition of military objective). Still, the law of naval warfare is not applicable in non-international armed conflict. Otherwise, the parties to such conflicts would be entitled to interfere with international navigation and aviation in areas beyond the territorial sovereignty of the respective State. Such conduct has not been recognized as in accordance with international law. For instance, during the Algerian War, France subjected international shipping to far-reaching control measures in the Mediterranean. The French measures triggered strong protests by the international community.[1]

3. Moreover, the law of belligerency at sea does not apply to military operations that do not qualify as an international armed conflict (e.g. counter-terrorism, counter-piracy, counter-proliferation, or other maritime interception/interdiction operations). Accordingly, the legal bases for interference with foreign navigation and aviation applicable to such operations do not stem from the law of naval warfare but from other parts of public international law, such as decisions of the UN Security Council under Chapter VII of the UN Charter, the law of the sea, or other multilateral or bilateral treaties. Those maritime security operations are dealt with in Chapter 21 of this Handbook.

4. Despite the non-applicability of the law of naval warfare it may not be left out of consideration that a number of States have ordered their armed forces to comply

[1] See J. Bernigaud, 'Les aspects maritimes de la guerre d'Algérie', *Revue de Défense Nationale* (Octobre 1968), 1496–502; L. Lucchini, 'Actes de contrainte exercés par la France en Haute Mer au cours des opérations en Algérie', 12 *AFDI* (1966), 805–21.

WOLFF HEINTSCHEL VON HEINEGG

with that law in situations other than international armed conflicts. However, that conduct is not expressive of an *opinio juris* that armed forces engaged in such maritime operations are legally bound by the law of naval warfare. Rather, the decision to apply the law of naval warfare has been guided by operational and political considerations only.

20.1 The Area of Naval Operations and Navigational Rights

20.01 **Without prejudice to the powers of the UN Security Council under Chapter VII of the UN Charter or to special agreements, the area of naval operations is to be determined in accordance with the international law of the sea.**

1. In view of its powers under Chapter VII of the UN Charter the UN Security Council is entitled to authorize the conduct of naval operations within the internal waters and the territorial sea of a State. This, of course, presupposes that the Security Council has acted under Chapter VII, i.e. that the Council has determined a threat to the peace, a breach of the peace, or an act of aggression, and that it has delivered a decision as distinguished from a recommendation.[2] It may not be left out of consideration, however, that if Member States choose to heed a Council's recommendation, as distinguished from a decision, authorizing them to take measures predicated on a binding determination concerning the existence of a threat to the peace, etc., those measures must be regarded as lawful notwithstanding their permissive character.[3] Hence, Member States acting on the basis of such a recommendation will not be in violation of the territorial sovereignty of the target State.

2. It is generally recognized that an authorization of the use of force decided upon by the Security Council does not only serve as a legal basis for the resort to armed force for those States willing to take action. Such authorization also imposes obligations on States refraining from taking part in military actions. This has been proven by State practice, e.g. during the 1991 Iraq War. Accordingly, States not participating in the hostilities may not hamper or otherwise impede the measures taken in accordance with the authorization. They are not entitled to rely upon the principle of impartiality or to intern members of the armed forces acting on the basis of the authorization.

3. The Security Council may decide either on enforcement or on preventive measures. The former are taken with a view to the removal of threats to the

[2] According to Article 25 UN Charter only decisions are binding upon the UN Member States.

[3] Y. Dinstein, *War, Agression and Self-Defence*, 5th edn (Cambridge: Cambridge University Press, 2011), 306.

peace, breaches of the peace, or acts of aggression. The latter are taken in anticipation of a future breach of the peace. The Council's entitlement to act preventively is derived not only from Chapter VII but also from Article 1(1) of the UN Charter. Accordingly, as made clear in the introductory sentence, the area of naval operations is not to be determined in light of the international law of the sea or of the law of naval warfare if the UN Security Council has exercised its powers under Chapter VII of the UN Charter. The Council's resolution will prevail over the law of the sea and the law of naval warfare. It is important to stress that if the UN Security Council has authorized the conduct of naval operations in foreign internal waters and territorial sea areas exact knowledge of the wording of the UN Security Council's resolution is crucial. Commanders should not leave that to their legal advisors but should know which measures have been authorized by the respective resolution. **20.01**

4. Under the principle of territorial sovereignty, it is an exclusive right of coastal States to exercise jurisdiction within their internal waters and their respective territorial sea. Hence, naval operations—as distinguished from a mere exercise of passage rights—conducted in foreign internal waters and territorial sea areas will be in violation of the principle of territorial sovereignty and the international law of the sea. Of course, coastal States may consent to naval operations within their territorial waters. This is also made clear in the introductory part of Section 20.01. It may be recalled that it is not necessary that such consent is given by way of a—multilateral or bilateral—treaty. Any consent, implicit or explicit, will suffice. Again, exact knowledge of the scope of the coastal State's consent is crucial.

5. The main objective of Section 20.01 is to emphasize that the area of naval operations is to be determined in accordance with the international law of the sea. This does not necessarily mean that the international law of the sea applies technically to situations of international armed conflict. It may be recalled that the 1982 United Nations Convention of the Law of the Sea (UNCLOS)[4] is a peacetime instrument. However, as evidenced by military manuals,[5] the San Remo Manual,[6] and the ILA Helsinki Principles,[7] UNCLOS has had a considerable

[4] United Nations Convention on the Law of the Sea of 10 December 1982; entry into force on 16 November 1994. See also the Agreement relating to the Implementation of Part XI of the Convention, UN Doc. A/RES/48/263 of 17 August 1994; entry into force on 28 July 1994.

[5] UK Ministry of Defence, *The Manual of the Law of Armed Conflict*, 2004; *The Commander's Handbook on the Law of Naval Operations*, NWP 1-14M; German Federal Ministry of Defence, *Humanitarian Law in Armed Conflicts—Manual*, 1992. See also the German Navy's *Commander's Handbook on the Law of Naval Operations*.

[6] International Institute of International Humanitarian Law, San Remo Manual on International Law applicable to Armed Conflicts at Sea. See also the Explanations to the Manual in L. Doswald-Beck (ed.), *San Remo Manual on International Law Applicable to Armed Conflicts at Sea* (Cambridge: Cambridge University Press, 1995).

[7] Helsinki Principles on the Law of Maritime Neutrality, Final Report of the Committee on Maritime Neutrality, International Law Association, Report of the 68th Conference, Taipei, 1998, 496 *et seq*.

20.01 impact on the law of naval warfare and maritime neutrality. Its most extensive impact was on the rules defining the regions of operations, i.e. the area where the parties to an international armed conflict are entitled to take belligerent measures, including prize measures.[8]

6. It needs to be stressed that the international law of the sea as codified in the UNCLOS has merely contributed to a modification of the geographic scope of the area of naval operations and to a specification of passage rights. There is no prohibition on conducting naval warfare in the high seas. Despite allegations to the contrary,[9] neither the peaceful uses clauses of the Convention nor State practice have contributed to the emergence of a rule of international law restricting the parties to an international armed conflict at sea to their respective internal waters and territorial sea areas. In the course of the negotiations of the Third United Nations Conference on the Law of the Sea the use of littoral waters, the territorial sea, and the EEZ by foreign warships was as controversial as the demilitarization of the world's oceans—an approach sponsored by the then socialist countries and by a number of developing countries. If those States had succeeded in outlawing military uses of the seas manoeuvres, weapons exercises, weapons tests, and military marine (scientific) research would have been banned from all high seas areas. Hence, those efforts met with strong opposition by the predominantly Western sea powers.[10] Eventually, no consensus was achieved on the issue of military uses of the seas. Articles 88 and 301 UNCLOS are typical compromise formulations. Seemingly, therefore, both sides could claim they have ultimately prevailed.[11] However, already the wording of the third sentence of Article 87(1) UNCLOS—*inter alia*—reveals that the list of high seas freedoms in lit. a) to f) is far from being exhaustive. Accordingly, the freedom of the high seas also comprises other uses. Moreover, it is emphasized in the second sentence that the freedom of the high seas is to be exercised not only 'under the conditions laid down by this Convention' but also 'by other rules of international law'. Hence, the admissibility of, for example,

[8] San Remo Manual, paras 112 *et seq.*; W. Heintschel von Heinegg, 'Visit, Search, Diversion and Capture in Naval Warfare—Conditions of Applicability: Part II, Developments since 1945', XXX *Canadian Yearbook of International Law* (1992), 89–136.

[9] Based on the concept of 'limited war' especially O'Connell took the position that belligerents are restricted to their respective territorial sea areas, D.P. O'Connell, 'International Law and Contemporary Naval Operations', XLIV *BYBIL* (1970), 19–85.

[10] For further details see R.R. Churchill and A.V. Lowe, *The Law of the Sea*, 3rd edn (Manchester: Manchester University Press, 1999), 426; R. Wolfrum, 'Restricting the Use of the Sea to Peaceful Purposes, Demilitarization in Being?', 24 *German Yearbook of International Law* (1981), 200–41: T. Treves, 'La notion d'utilisation des espaces marines à fins exclusivement pacifiques dans le nouveau droit de la mer', 26 *AFDI* (1980), 687–99, at 687 *et seq.*

[11] Ch.E. Pirtle, 'Military Uses of Ocean Space and the Law of the Sea', 31 *Ocean Development and International Law* (2000) 7–45, at 9; Churchill and Lowe, *The Law of the Sea*, 421; E. Rauch, 'Military Uses of the Ocean', 28 *German Yearbook of International Law* (1985), 227–67, at 238 *et seq.*; R.L. Friedheim and R.E. Bowen, 'Neglected Issues at the Third UN Law of the Sea Conference', in J. King Gamble, Jr (ed.), *Law of the Sea: Neglected Issues* (Honolulu: University of Hawaii Press, 1979), 2–39.

nuclear tests is to be judged in the light of the Seabed Treaty of 11 February 1971.[12] The legality and admissibility of other military uses follows from either the law of naval warfare and neutrality at sea[13] or from other rules and principles of customary international law. Since naval exercises and maritime weapons tests as well as other military activities (especially marine scientific research for military purposes) have long since been generally recognized uses of the high seas, they are covered by the freedom of the high seas under customary international law.[14] Of course, during each deployment of warships (and of military aircraft) due regard has to be paid to the legitimate interests of other States and to the safety of international navigation and aviation.[15] **20.01**

Belligerent measures may be taken in the following sea areas: **20.02**
— belligerent internal waters,
— where applicable, belligerent archipelagic waters,
— belligerent territorial seas, and
— sea areas where the high seas freedoms apply.

1. Section 20.02 is declaratory of the customary rule that belligerent measures are permissible in those sea areas where the belligerent States enjoy sovereignty.[16] The term 'belligerent measures' is to be understood as comprising the use of methods and means of (naval) warfare against the enemy or against persons and objects qualifying as legitimate military targets/objectives as well as prize measures against neutral vessels and aircraft.

2. As already stated, the development of the law initiated by the UNCLOS has had a considerable impact on the geographical scope of the area of naval operations. However, the principle according to which that area is, in a first step, to be determined in view of the extent of the belligerent's territorial sovereignty has remained intact. Accordingly, the extension of the breadth of the territorial sea

[12] Wolfrum, 'Restricting the Use', 220–4; H.S. Levie, *Mine Warfare at Sea* (Dordrecht, etc.: Nijhoff, 1992), 38.

[13] For an analysis of that law see G.P. Politakis, *Modern Aspects of the Laws of Naval Warfare and Maritime Neutrality* (London, New York: Kegan Paul International, 1998); W. Heintschel von Heinegg, *Seekriegsrecht und Neutralität im Seekrieg* (Berlin: Duncker & Humblot, 1995).

[14] For an in-depth assessment of the customary character see U. Jenisch, *Das Recht zur Vornahme militärischer Übungen und Versuche auf Hoher See in Friedenszeiten* (Hamburg: Forschungsstelle für Völkerrecht und ausländisches öffentliches Recht, 1970), 75 *et seq.*; Heintschel von Heinegg, *Seekriegsrecht*, 255 *et seq.*

[15] See Art. 87(2) UNCLOS; E. Rauch, 'Militärische Aspekte der Seerechtsentwicklung', in W. Graf Vitzthum (ed.), *Aspekte der Seerechtsentwicklung, Arbeitshefte Staat und Wirtschaft* (München: Universitat der Bundeswehr, 1980), 75–121, at 80 *et seq.*; R. Wolfrum, 'Military Activities on the High Seas: What are the impacts of the U.N. Convention on the Law of the Sea' in M.N. Schmitt and L.C. Green (eds), *The Law of Armed Conflict: Into the Next Millennium* (Newport, RI: Naval War College, 1998), 501–13, at 504.

[16] For a detailed analysis of the area of naval warfare see, *inter alia*, H.B. Robertson Jr, *The 'New' Law of the Sea and the Law of Armed Conflict at Sea*, Newport Paper no. 3 (Newport, RI: Naval War College, 1992).

20.02 from three to 12 nautical miles[17] as well as the recognition of straight baselines[18] have contributed to a considerable extension of the area of naval operations. The same holds true for archipelagic waters.[19]

3. Again, as stated earlier, belligerents are not prevented from taking belligerent measures in the high seas.[20] The same holds true for all other sea areas where the high seas freedoms apply. Accordingly, belligerent measures are permissible in (and above) sea areas beyond the territorial sovereignty of third/neutral States. This means that there is no prohibition on taking such measures within the exclusive economic zone or on the continental shelf of third/neutral States.[21] Note, however, that, as emphasized in Sections 20.03 and 20.04, due regard must be paid to the legitimate uses of those sea areas by other States.

4. It may be recalled that belligerent measures may be prohibited in certain sea areas. For example, Antarctica is subject to a special legal regime that prohibits 'any measure of a belligerent nature'.[22]

20.03 **Belligerent measures are strictly forbidden in those sea areas in which third/neutral States enjoy territorial sovereignty. In sea areas in which third/neutral States enjoy sovereign rights—EEZ, continental shelf, fishery zones—belligerent measures are not prohibited. However, due regard must be paid to the sovereign rights enjoyed by the (neutral) coastal States.**

1. The first sentence of Section 20.03 re-emphasizes the customary principle of the inviolability of neutral territory and neutral waters. Belligerents are prohibited from taking belligerent measures within neutral sea areas or using them as a base of operations or as a sanctuary.[23] Should a belligerent warship or military aircraft be in violation of the regime of neutral waters and neutral airspace, the neutral State is under an obligation to take the measures necessary to terminate that violation including, if necessary, by the use of force.[24]

2. For the purposes of this Handbook the term 'neutral' applies to States not parties to an international armed conflict. Accordingly, the status of a State as 'neutral' does not depend upon a declaration of neutrality nor is it to be judged in the light of the various positions taken by States on the traditional law of neutrality,

[17] Art. 3 UNCLOS. [18] Art. 7 UNCLOS. See also Art. 10 (Bays).
[19] Art. 46 *et seq.* UNCLOS. [20] San Remo Manual, para. 36.
[21] Ibid. paras 34 *et seq.*
[22] Art. I(1) of the Antarctic Treaty of 1 December 1959 provides: '1. Antarctica shall be used for peaceful purposes only. There shall be prohibited, inter alia, any measure of a military nature, such as the establishment of military bases and fortifications, the carrying out of military manoeuvres, as well as the testing of any type of weapon.'
[23] Hague Convention No. XIII Concerning the Rights and Duties of Neutral Powers in Naval War, 18 October 1907, Articles 1, 2, and 5; San Remo Manual, paras 14 *et seq.*; Helsinki Principles, paras 1.4 and 2.1.
[24] San Remo Manual, para. 22.

especially that reflected in the 1907 Hague Conventions V and XIII.[25] Rather, the present Handbook is guided by the object and purpose of the rules and principles of customary international law governing the relationship between the belligerents and States not taking part in the armed hostilities that emerged from post-1945 State practice.[26] While the international armed conflicts that occurred after the end of the Second World War (e.g. the conflicts between Israel and Egypt, India and Pakistan, Great Britain and Argentina, or Iraq and Iran) cast doubts on the applicability of the traditional law of neutrality, they give sufficient evidence of some core principles and rules recognized to apply during every international armed conflict.[27] Those rules and principles can be summarized as serving a double protective purpose: on the one hand, they are to protect States not parties to an international armed conflict and their nationals against the harmful effects of the ongoing hostilities. On the other hand, they aim at the protection of belligerent interests against any interference of neutrals and their nationals to the benefit of one belligerent party and to the detriment of the other. Thus, the said rules and principles aim at preventing an escalation of an ongoing international armed conflict. Accordingly, belligerent parties are obliged to respect the inviolability of States not parties to the international armed conflict. States not parties to the conflict are under an obligation of strict impartiality and of defending their neutral status. While neutral aviation and navigation may proceed they are liable to belligerent interference if they contribute to the war-fighting or war-sustaining effort of either side. It is to be emphasized, however, that the concept of neutrality applies neither in non-international armed conflicts nor to naval operations authorized by the Security Council in exercise of its powers under Chapter VII of the UN Charter. **20.03**

3. Neutral waters consist of the internal waters, territorial sea, and, where applicable, the archipelagic waters, of neutral States as defined by the UNCLOS and by the respective rules of customary international law.[28] Neutral States may, if they consider this essential for their security or for the safety of navigation, close their neutral waters for belligerent warships and auxiliary vessels. Other than in times of peace this closure may comprise the neutral State's entire territorial sea and may last for the duration of the international armed conflict. The only restriction the neutral State has to observe vis-à-vis the parties to the conflict is the principle of impartiality.[29]

[25] Hague Convention No. XIII, Articles 1, 2, and 5; San Remo Manual, paras 14 *et seq.*; Helsinki Principles, paras 1.4 and 2.1; Hague Convention No. V Respecting the Rights and Duties of Neutral Powers and Persons in Case of War on Land, 18 October 1907.

[26] For the continuing validity of the essentials of the law of neutrality see W. Heintschel von Heinegg, '"Benevolent" Third States in International Armed Conflict: The Myth of the Irrelevance of the Law of Neutrality', in M.N. Schmitt and J. Pejic (eds), *International Law and Armed Conflict: Exploring the Faultlines* (Leiden: Nijhoff, 2007), 543–68.

[27] Accordingly, the same approach underlies the San Remo Manual on International Law Applicable to Armed Conflicts at Sea. See the explanation on the San Remo Manual, para. 13 lit. (d).

[28] Ibid.

[29] San Remo Manual, para. 19: 'Subject to paragraphs 29 and 33, a neutral State may, on a nondiscriminatory basis, condition, restrict or prohibit the entrance to or passage through its neutral waters by belligerent warships and auxiliary vessels.' See also Helsinki Principles, para. 2.3.

20.03 If, however, neutral waters are part of an international strait or of an archipelagic sea lane, the neutral State is not allowed to prohibit belligerent warships, auxiliary vessels, and military aircraft from transiting those waters.[30] The same holds true for the non-suspendable right of innocent passage within certain straits.[31]

4. It follows from the second sentence that belligerent measures are permissible within those sea areas where third/neutral States do not enjoy territorial sovereignty but only certain limited sovereign rights. Accordingly, the exclusive economic zone, fisheries zones, and the continental shelf of third/neutral States are not excluded from the area of naval operations during an international armed conflict.[32]

5. However, as stressed in the third sentence, belligerent measures in those areas may not be taken in total disregard of the rights of coastal States. Rather, under customary international law, belligerents are obliged to pay due regard to installations and other structures third/neutral States have established in accordance with the respective rules of the law of the sea.[33]

6. The 'due regard' principle is a concept of the law of the sea and therefore established in international law. In the relation between belligerents and third/neutral States the law of the sea, in principle, continues to apply. Therefore, and in view of the fact that the law of armed conflict principle of proportionality is inapplicable vis-à-vis neutral States, the obligation of belligerents to pay due regard to the rights enjoyed by third/neutral States under the law of the sea and general international law is the only legal principle limiting belligerent operations in such areas.[34] It needs to be stressed that the 'due regard' principle imposes no absolute and affirmative obligation. Rather, according to that principle, belligerent parties are held to balance the military advantages anticipated with the negative impact on neutral States' rights in the respective airspace and sea areas.

7. It may be recalled that the prohibition of Section 20.03 is without prejudice to navigational rights belligerents continue to enjoy in neutral waters. Of course, a third/neutral State may, on a non-discriminatory basis, condition, restrict, or prohibit the entrance to or passage through its neutral waters by belligerent warships.[35] However, belligerent warships continue to enjoy the rights of transit passage and, where applicable, of archipelagic sea lanes passage.[36] Under the 1907 Hague Convention XIII and customary international law,[37] neutral States are free

[30] San Remo Manual, paras 23–30; Helsinki Principles, para. 2.4. Further Heintschel von Heinegg, 'Straits and the Law of Naval Warfare', in M.N. Schmitt and L.C. Green (eds), *The Law of Armed Conflict*, 263–92.

[31] Art. 45(2) UNCLOS provides that there 'shall be no suspension of innocent passage' through straits that are '(a) excluded from the application of the regime of transit passage under article 38, paragraph 1; or (b) between a part of the high seas or an exclusive economic zone and the territorial sea of a foreign State'.

[32] San Remo Manual, paras 34 *et seq*.

[33] See e.g. UK Manual, para. 13.21; San Remo Manual, para. 34.

[34] See San Remo Manual, paras 12, 34, 35, and 36.

[35] San Remo Manual, para. 19. [36] Ibid. paras 27–30. [37] Ibid. para. 20.

to permit the following acts by belligerent warships within their internal waters and their territorial sea: (1) passage through the territorial sea (Article 10); (2) replenishment of food, water, and fuel to reach an own or allied port (Article 18); and (3) repairs found necessary by the neutral State to make them seaworthy, provided that such repairs do not restore or increase their fighting strength (Article 17). The latter issue arose in the case of the *Graf Spee*. However, a belligerent warship may not extend the duration of its passage through neutral waters, or its presence in those waters, for longer than 24 hours unless unavoidable on account of damage or stress of weather.[38] The 24-hour limitation does not apply to innocent passage through archipelagic waters, to transit passage through international straits, or archipelagic sea lanes passage if the time ordinarily needed for such passage is more than 24 hours.[39] 20.03

8. For the inviolability of neutral airspace see Section 19.25 and the accompanying commentary.

In the high seas due regard must be given to the high seas freedoms enjoyed by third/neutral States. **20.04**

1. In view of the special legal status of the Area and in view of the rights neutral States continue to enjoy in the high seas, belligerents are, however, obliged to pay due regard to these aspects and to refrain from interference if that is feasible and reasonable.[40]

2. As to the meaning of the 'due regard principle' see the commentary to Section 20.03.

Vis-à-vis third States belligerents may suspend the right of innocent passage. However, the rights of transit passage and, where applicable, of archipelagic sea lanes passage may neither be suspended nor impeded. **20.05**

1. Since the relations between belligerents and third/neutral States continue to be governed, *inter alia*, by the international law of the sea, belligerents are entitled to exercise their right, under Article 25(3) UNCLOS, to suspend, 'without discrimination in form or in fact among foreign ships, [. . .] the innocent passage of foreign ships if such suspension is essential for the protection of its security'. While Article 25 UNCLOS merely mentions 'weapons exercises', this is not exclusive. Therefore, the term 'security' is to be understood as also comprising other interests, including the closure of the territorial sea for the navigation of third/neutral States.

[38] Art. 12 of the 1907 Hague Convention XIII; San Remo Manual, para. 21; Helsinki Principles, para. 2.2.

[39] Helsinki Principles, para. 2.4; San Remo Manual, para. 21.

[40] San Remo Manual, para. 10 lit. (b) and para. 36: 'Hostile actions on the high seas shall be conducted with due regard for the exercise by neutral States of rights of exploration and exploitation of the natural resources of the seabed, and ocean floor, and the subsoil thereof, beyond national jurisdiction.' See also Helsinki Principles, para. 3.1.

20.05 2. It may not be left out of consideration that the right of suspending innocent passage, according to Article 52(2) UNCLOS, also applies to archipelagic waters.

3. Any suspension of the right of innocent passage shall take effect only after having been duly published.[41] Such publication may be effected by a Notice to Mariners (NOTMAR) or by use of diplomatic channels.

4. It is an unsettled matter, whether such suspension is subject to the limitations of Articles 25(3) and 52(2) UNCLOS, i.e. whether it may only be suspended temporarily in specified areas of the territorial sea or of the archipelagic waters. It is here, where the impact of UNCLOS on the law of naval warfare and of maritime neutrality is not as far-reaching as it is on other aspects of the area of naval operations. Therefore, there are good reasons to assume that during an international armed conflict, belligerents are entitled to suspend the right of innocent passage in their entire territorial sea. In view of a lack of State practice it is, however, unclear whether this would also hold true for the right of innocent passage in archipelagic waters.

5. Although belligerent security interests are to be recognized with a view to the territorial sea, the rights of transit passage and of archipelagic sea lanes passage enjoyed by the navigation and aviation of third/neutral States may neither be suspended nor hampered by the belligerents.[42] Hence, vessels and aircraft of third/neutral States may continue to use belligerent straits and archipelagic sea lanes in 'normal mode'. This, *inter alia*, means that neutral submarines are entitled to transit a belligerent's international strait submerged although the respective belligerent will most probably consider any submarine contact a severe threat to its military operations.

6. It is to be emphasized that, according to Article 35(c) UNCLOS, the right of transit passage does not apply to straits in which passage is regulated in whole or in part by long-standing international conventions in force specifically relating to such straits. Accordingly, the right of transit passage does not apply to the Turkish Straits,[43] the Strait of Magellan,[44] nor, probably, to the Danish Straits.[45] It must be added that, in Article V(2) of the Egyptian-Israeli Peace Treaty of 26 March 1979,[46] the two States have agreed as follows:

[41] Art. 25, para. 3 and Art. 52, para. 2 UNCLOS.

[42] San Remo Manual, para. 27; Heintschel von Heinegg, 'Straits', 264 *et seq.*

[43] Montreux Convention of 20 July 1936 (173 LNTS 213, 219), printed in N. Ronzitti (ed.), *The Law of Naval Warfare* (Dordrecht: Nijhoff, 1988), 437 *et seq.*

[44] Boundary Treaty between Argentina and Chile of 23 July 1881, printed in Martens, *Nouveau Receuil Général*, série I, tome XVI, 491 (Göttingen, 1887). See also the Treaty between Argentina and Chile of Peace and Amity of 18 October 1984, printed in *Law of the Sea Bulletin* 50–72 (no. 4, February 1985).

[45] Treaty on the Redemption of Sound Dues of 14 March 1857, printed in Martens, *Nouveau Receuil Général*, série I, tome XVI, partie II, 345 *et seq.*; US–Danish Convention on Discontinuance of Sound Dues; 11 Stat. 719, T.S. 67.

[46] Printed in R. Lapidoth and M. Hirsch (eds), *The Arab-Israel Conflict and Its Resolution: Selected Documents* (Dordrecht: Nijhoff, 1992), 218 *et seq.*

The Parties consider the Strait of Tiran and the Gulf of Aqaba to be international waterways open to all nations for unimpeded and non-suspendable freedom of navigation and overflight. The Parties will respect each other's right to navigation and overflight for access to either country through the Strait of Tiran and the Gulf of Aqaba. **20.05**

While, in view of the date of signature, that treaty will hardly qualify as a 'long-standing international convention', it is declaratory for the right of transit passage as laid down in the UNCLOS.[47] As regards the Strait of Gibraltar, passage of ships—not overflight by aircraft—is the subject of a number of agreements between France, Spain, and the UK of 1904, 1907, and 1912.[48] There is, however, no indication in those treaties that the parties also intended to either guarantee or exclude passage by ships of third States.[49] When those treaties were concluded any area of the high seas—hence also the high seas corridor between Gibraltar and North Africa—could not be made subject to bi- or multilateral international treaties. Nevertheless, Spain has repeatedly maintained that the Strait of Gibraltar is regulated by the Declaration of 1904 and, therefore, exempted from at least the right of overflight.[50] It is interesting to note that during the Yom Kippur War (1973) US military aircraft on their flights from the Azores to Israel scrupulously kept within the airspace above the high seas corridor between the former three nautical miles territorial waters of Spain and Morocco.[51] But in 1973 the regime of

[47] See R. Lapidoth, The Strait of Tiran, the Gulf of Aqaba, and the 1979 Treaty of Peace between Egypt and Israel, 77 *AJIL* (1983), 84–108, at 99 *et seq*. A more cautious view is taken by L.M. Alexander, 'International Straits', in H.B. Robertson Jr (ed.), *The Law of Naval Operations* (Newport: Naval War College, 1991), 91–108, at 102. See also J.E. Fink, 'The Gulf of Aqaba and the Strait of Tiran: The Practice of "Freedom of Navigation" after the Egyptian-Israeli Peace Treaty', 42 *Naval Law Review* (1995), 121–44.

[48] Art. VII of the London Declaration by France and the UK concerning Egypt and Morocco of 8 April 1904; printed in Martens, *Nouveau Receuil Général* XXXII, 18 (Leipzig, 1905). Spain acceded on 3 October 1904. Franco-Spanish Declaration of Mutual Assistance in Mediterranean Affairs of 16 May 1907, 204 Parry's T.S. 353. Anglo-Spanish Declaration of Mutual Assistance in Mediterranean Affairs of 16 May 1907; 204 Parry's T.S. 179. Art. 6 of the Franco-Spanish Accord concerning Morocco of 27 November 1912, 217 Parry's T.S. 288. Sometimes also the Treaty of Utrecht of 13 July 1713, by which Philip V had ceded Gibraltar to England, is referred to. However, Art. 10 does not regulate the high seas corridor between Gibraltar and North Africa. Still, Spain maintains that the provisions of UNCLOS on straits do not apply to that sea area. Upon signature Spain declared: 'The Spanish Government, upon signing this Convention, declares that this act cannot be interpreted as recognition of any rights or situations relating to the maritime spaces of Gibraltar which are not included in article 10 of the Treaty of Utrecht of 13 July 1713 between the Spanish and British Crowns.'

[49] See S.C. Truver, *The Strait of Gibraltar and the Mediterranean* (Alphen a.d. Rijn: Sijthoff & Noordhoff, 1980), 179; J.A. Roach and R.W. Smith, *Excessive Maritime Claims*, 2nd edn (Newport: Naval War College, 1996), 185 *et seq*.

[50] See the references in L.M. Alexander, 'International Straits', 102. See also M. Saenz de Santa and A.M. Paz, 'Spain and the Law of the Sea—Selected Problems', 32 *Archiv des Völkerrechts* (1994), 202–19. When signing the UNCLOS Spain declared: 'It is the Spanish Government's interpretation that the regime established in part III of the Convention is compatible with the right of the coastal State to issue and apply its own air regulations in the air space of the straits used for international navigation so long as this does not impede the transit passage of aircraft.' According to the Spanish position this recognition of the right of overflight is without prejudice to the legal status of the Strait of Gibraltar because Spain has made clear that its signature does not affect 'the maritime spaces of Gibraltar'.

[51] L.M. Alexander, 'International Straits', 102.

20.05 transit passage was still unknown. Four years after the adoption of UNCLOS, US military aircraft that had come from the UK to attack targets in Libya flew over the Strait of Gibraltar. The US justified the overflight with the right of transit passage laid down in the UNCLOS.[52] Hence, neither the treaties referred to nor State practice allows the conclusion that the Strait of Gibraltar is a strait within the meaning of Article 35 lit. (c) UNCLOS. So far, only Spain has taken a view to the contrary. Since it did not protest the overflight by US military aircraft in 1986, the Spanish position has had no influence on the legal characterization of the Strait of Gibraltar.

7. Finally, it is important to note that, according to Article 45 UNCLOS, there exists a non-suspendable right of innocent passage in straits 'excluded from the applications of the regime of transit passage under Article 38, paragraph 1; or... between a part of the high seas or an exclusive economic zone and the territorial sea of a foreign State'. This special right of innocent passage must also be respected by belligerents.[53]

20.06 **In any case, due regard should be given to rare and fragile marine ecosystems.**

1. Section 20.06 repeats San Remo Manual, para. 11(a), which reflects Article 194(5) UNCLOS. It is obvious that this rule does not impose an absolute obligation on belligerents to protect such ecosystems. It merely encourages them to take the fragility of such ecosystems into account when taking belligerent measures at sea. For the meaning of 'due regard' see the commentary on Section 20.03.

2. It needs to be recalled that despite the uncertainties existing with regard to the exact meaning and scope of the term 'natural environment' the natural environment will generally qualify as a civilian object. Accordingly, a wanton destruction of the natural environment is prohibited.[54] Direct attacks on the natural environment that is not a lawful military objective will be illegal under the law of armed conflict. Attacks causing, or expected to cause, collateral damage on the natural environment which is excessive in relation to the concrete and direct military advantage anticipated, are prohibited. Moreover, belligerent parties must take all feasible precautions to spare the 'natural environment' under the precautionary principle.

20.2 Warships and Other Platforms

20.07 **'Warship' means a ship belonging to the armed forces of a State bearing the external marks distinguishing such ships of its nationality, under the command of an officer duly commissioned by the government of a State and whose name appears in the appropriate**

[52] Ibid. [53] San Remo Manual, para. 33. [54] NWP 1-14M, para. 8.4.

service list or its equivalent, and manned by a crew which is under regular armed forces discipline. 20.07

1. While many commentators refer to the 1907 Hague Convention VII as the first international treaty specifying the conditions a ship must fulfil in order to qualify as a warship, it may not be left out of consideration that the definition's elements are closely linked to the prohibition of privateering under the 1856 Paris Declaration.[55] Since the adoption of the Paris Declaration the right of visit, search, and capture, under the law of prize as well as the right of harming the enemy have been limited to warships.[56] Most of the elements contained in Articles 1 to 4 of the 1907 Hague Convention VII[57] have found their way into Article 8(2) of the 1958 Geneva Convention on the High Seas[58] which defines a 'warship' as:

> a ship belonging to the naval forces of a State and bearing the external marks distinguishing warships of its nationality, under the command of an officer duly commissioned by the government and whose name appears in the Navy List, and manned by a crew who are under regular naval discipline.

The 1982 UNCLOS, in Article 29, provides a similar definition subject, however, to the following modifications. First, the ship must belong to 'the armed forces of a State' not to the naval forces. Second, the commanding officer's name must appear in the 'appropriate service list or its equivalent', not in the Navy List. Third, the crew must be 'under regular armed forces discipline', not under regular naval discipline. These modifications are due to the fact that many States operate government ships for military and related purposes that do not belong to their respective naval forces. In some cases States do not dispose of naval forces at all but still operate State ships other than police vessels for military or security purposes. Although the scope of applicability of the above treaty definitions is limited to 'the purposes of these articles' (1958) or to the 'purposes of this Convention' (1982) there is today general agreement that all ships meeting the requirements of Article 29 UNCLOS qualify as warships under international law.[59] Hence, it has also been incorporated into the military manuals of the US,[60] the UK,[61] Germany,[62] and of other States as well as the San Remo Manual.[63]

2. As to the particulars of the definition it needs to be emphasized from the outset that it covers all seagoing vessels—surface or subsurface—irrespective of their size, design, construction, propulsion, or equipment. Accordingly, not only traditional

[55] Declaration Respecting Maritime Law, Paris, 16 April 1856.

[56] R.W. Tucker, *The Law of War and Neutrality at Sea* (Washington DC: US Naval War College, 1957), 40 *et seq*.

[57] Hague Convention No. VII Relating to the Conversion of Merchant Ships into War-Ships of 18 October 1907.

[58] Convention on the High Seas, Geneva 29 April 1958, (1963) 450 UNTS 11-167.

[59] Tucker, *The Law of War*, 38; C.J. Colombos, *The International Law of the Sea*, 6th rev. edn (London: Longmans, 1967), 259.

[60] NWP 1-14M, para. 2.2.1.

[61] UK Manual, para. 13.5.

[62] German Manual, para. 1002.

[63] San Remo Manual, para. 13 lit. (g).

20.07 warships—like frigates, destroyers, or submarines—qualify as warships but also small speed boats, transport ships, and tankers if they meet the specifications. In particular, there is no need for any kind of armament or other military equipment. With regard to submarines it may be recalled that the efforts during the beginning of the twentieth century to outlaw the use of submarines were in vain.[64] Hence, submarines are warships as long as they meet the requirements of the definition.

3. *Belonging to the Armed Forces.* While there is, today, no longer a need to distinguish between naval and other services of the armed forces, it is essential that warships belong to the regular armed forces of a State. Whether forces qualify as armed forces of a State is subject to the respective State's domestic law and to the law of international armed conflict. Accordingly, all organized armed groups which are either incorporated into a State's armed forces or which are entitled to perform military operations qualify as armed forces in the sense of the definition. Hence, US Coast Guard vessels designated 'USCGC' under the command of a commissioned officer are also warships under international law.[65] Ships belonging to the French *Gendarmerie*, the Spanish *Guardia Civil*, or to the Italian *Carabinieri* also qualify as warships if under command of a commissioned officer. Some doubts remain as to the status of ships belonging to other paramilitary units, such as, for example, the small speed boats of the Iranian *Pasdaran*. If considered a unit distinct from the Iranian armed forces and if they cannot be equated with the paramilitary units just mentioned they must be considered State ships but may not be considered warships proper. 'Belonging to' does not mean property. It suffices if the ship is under the exclusive control of the armed forces and employed for genuinely military purposes. However, ships performing auxiliary functions, even if owned by or under the exclusive control of the armed forces, do not qualify as warships. Auxiliary vessels[66] are State ships but not warships and, thus, they are not entitled to conduct operations that, under international law, are strictly limited to warships (e.g. prize measures during an international armed conflict).

4. *Marks.* The requirement of 'bearing the external marks' is closely linked with the powers warships enjoy under international law. Since many of such powers are exclusively reserved to warships they are under an affirmative obligation to distinguish themselves from other State ships and to identify their nationality. Ships not bearing such external marks do not qualify as warships and are not allowed to perform any of the acts reserved for such ships. This obligation applies in times of peace and in times of war. Of course, electronic means enable modern warships, aircraft etc. to detect and identify objects over considerable distances, i.e. from beyond visual range. Still, there is a continuing necessity for visible marks. On the one hand, not all States dispose of a sophisticated (military) technology. On the other hand, warships are not exclusively entrusted with genuinely war-fighting

[64] W.T. Mallison Jr, *Submarines in General and Limited Wars* (Washington DC: US Naval War College, 1968), 32 *et seq.*

[65] NWP 1-14M, para. 2.2.1.

[66] NWP 1-14M, para. 2.3.1.

tasks. If, for example, engaged in maritime interdiction operations the merchant vessels affected must be sufficiently certain that the intercepting ship is a warship. Finally and most importantly, warships as sovereign immune platforms enjoy certain privileges and respect by other States presupposes that they clearly distinguish themselves from other State or merchant vessels. 20.07

5. *Military Command and Discipline*. As regards the requirement of being under command of an officer the term 'duly commissioned' could be interpreted in a strict sense. For example, in the US the term is well established and covers only officers holding presidential commissions and who are confirmed at their ranks by the Senate. Accordingly, the commanding officer of a warship must hold, by commission, a rank of second lieutenant or ensign or above. This is, however, peculiar to the US and some other States. Therefore, the different national practices regarding the term 'officer duly commissioned' must be taken account of. In view of these practices it does not exclude warrant officers and other senior petty officers as commanders of a warship.[67] The criterion of a 'crew under military discipline' does not rule out the use of civilian mariners or of private contractors on board a warship. There is no requirement under international customary or treaty law that the crew consists of members of the armed forces only. Therefore, no problems arise if civilian mariners or private contractors on board a warship are otherwise subjected to military discipline, e.g. by assimilating them to reservists. However, if the entire crew consists of civilian mariners not under military discipline the ship no longer qualifies as a warship under international law. Whether this also holds true if only one part of the crew belongs to the regular armed forces but the other part consists of civilian mariners is a matter of dispute. It should, however, not be left out of consideration that the definition of warships does not envisage the entire crew to be subjected to military discipline. It suffices if the warship is manned by *a* crew fulfilling that requirement. The use of the indefinite article is of importance in view of the different wording of Article 4 of the 1907 Hague Convention (VII) which provides that *the* crew of a converted merchant vessel 'must be subject to military discipline'. The use here of the definite article is logical in view of the fact that the ship concerned used to be a merchant vessel and is now to be used as a warship. No such necessity exists in cases of ships that have from the outset been designed, constructed, and employed as warships. Of course, there is no final answer to the question about the exact percentage of crew members who need to be under military discipline. In any event, the presence of civilians on board a warship does not alter that ship's status under international law.[68]

6. *Unmanned Vehicles*. Many naval forces of the world dispose of and operate unmanned seagoing vehicles—surface and subsurface. Such craft are either autonomous or remotely navigated and may be launched from surface, subsurface, or

[67] M.H. Nordquist (ed.), *United Nations Convention on the Law of the Sea 1982. A Commentary*, Vol. II (Dordrecht. Nijhoff, 1993), 252.

[68] NWP 1-14M, para. 2.2.1.

20.07 aviation platforms.[69] In case they are remotely navigated, in particular when controlled by a warship, they could be considered an integral part of the controlling platform and, thus, they would share the platform's legal status. However, if they navigate autonomously they can hardly share the legal status of another platform. Moreover, they are not 'manned by a crew which is under regular armed forces discipline' and may not qualify as warships *stricto sensu*. However, the definition does not necessarily mean that all warships must be manned. The object and purpose of that requirement is to limit the exercise of belligerent rights to members of the regular armed forces responsible to the flag State. Accordingly, unmanned seagoing vehicles could be considered warships if the persons remotely operating, controlling, or having pre-programmed them are subjected to regular armed forces discipline. Only if the definition were interpreted as requiring the presence of persons on board would unmanned seagoing vehicles not qualify as warships. Such an interpretation would, however, be without prejudice to their legal status under general international law and to the rights such unmanned vehicles enjoy under the law of the sea or of naval warfare. If they belong to the armed forces and if they are engaged exclusively in non-commercial government services they may not qualify as warships; still, they will have to be considered State ships or State craft enjoying sovereign immunity (see Section 19.10).

20.08 **'Military aircraft' means an aircraft operated by commissioned units of the armed forces of a State having the military marks of that State, commanded by a member of the armed forces, and manned by a crew subject to regular armed forces discipline.**

1. This definition is based on Articles 3, 7, and 14 of the 1923 Hague Rules that, as evidenced by military manuals,[70] are declaratory for customary international law. The definition has been adopted in the San Remo Manual[71] as well, although with a slightly different wording.

2. A 'military aircraft' must be operated by the armed forces of a State. It is not necessary that it is 'operated by commissioned units of the armed forces of a State'.[72] Nor must the aircraft belong to the armed forces.[73] Today, property is irrelevant because aircraft may remain the property of a private entity as is the case for example when the aircraft have been leased. The term 'armed forces' is not limited to the air forces and comprises all services of the armed forces of a State.

[69] NWP 1-14M, paras 2.3.4, 2.3.5.

[70] UK Manual, para. 12.10; NWP 1-14M, para. 2.2.1; Australia, Defence Force Manual, para. 804; German Manual, para. 1007.

[71] San Remo Manual, para. 13(j): '"Military aircraft" means an aircraft operated by commissioned units of the armed forces of a State having the military marks of that State, commanded by a member of the armed forces and manned by a crew subject to regular armed forces discipline.'

[72] Ibid. [73] See, however, German Manual, para. 1007.

3. An aircraft need not be specially designed or built for the performance of genuinely military purposes. Hence, as recognized by Article 9 of the 1923 Hague Rules, another State aircraft or a civilian aircraft may be converted into a military aircraft.[74] Of course, a converted aircraft must meet the conditions of the present definition. Military aircraft need not be armed. **20.08**

4. The obligation of 'bearing the military markings of that State' is based upon Article 3 of the 1923 Hague Rules.[75] See also Section 19.10 and the accompanying commentary. There is no necessity of two marks, one for the nationality and one for the military character. In some air forces, the same marking indicates both nationality and military character.[76] In order to be clearly distinguishable from other State aircraft, i.e. from police or customs aircraft, the marking must indicate that the aircraft is employed for military purposes.[77] It may be added that regular military aircraft are on a special military register. Sometimes they are identified as military in a civil register.[78] The requirement of markings indicating their nationality is to secure that a military aircraft has the nationality of one State. A military aircraft may not possess two or more nationalities. This, however, is without prejudice to the right of bearing additional markings indicating an international grouping, such as NATO, provided that modifications of that nature are promptly notified to all other States.[79]

5. Aircraft not bearing the military markings of a belligerent party do not qualify as military aircraft and are therefore not entitled to exercise belligerent rights, including attack (see Sections 19.14 and 20.09). The crux of this requirement is the marking itself. It is now common for States to use subdued or otherwise low-visibility markings on military aircraft. The absence of any objection to this widespread practice evidences its lawfulness.

6. A 'military aircraft' must be 'commanded by a member of the armed forces'. It is not necessary that the aircraft is under the command 'of a person duly commissioned or enlisted in the military service' of the State.[80] While in most cases members of the armed forces of a State will be enlisted there is no absolute obligation to that effect. The system of commissioning is specific to States like the US and not demanded by customary international law. The object and purpose of being under command of a member of the armed forces is to secure that belligerent measures are taken by combatants only. The term 'command' as used in this Section refers to the individual aboard the aircraft (or controlling it remotely)

[74] Note, however, that, according to that provision, the conversion must be effected within the jurisdiction of the belligerent State and not on the high seas.

[75] 'A military aircraft shall bear an external mark indicating its nationality and military character.' According to Article 7 of the 1923 Hague Rules the 'external marks . . . shall be so affixed that they cannot be altered in flight. They shall be as large as practicable and shall be visible from above, from below and from each side.'

[76] UK Manual, para. 12.10.4.

[77] NWP 1-14M, para. 2.2.1.

[78] See EUROCONTROL, Decision of the Provisional Council of 12 July 2001, Principle 1.

[79] UK Manual, para. 12.10.4.

[80] See, however, Article 14 of the 1923 Hague Rules.

20.08 who exercises authority over that aircraft. It is to be distinguished from the more general 'command' over a military unit or organization.

7. If a military aircraft is manned by a crew the members of the crew must be 'subject to regular armed forces discipline'. This, however, does not mean that the entire crew must consist of members of the armed forces. It follows from Article 4A(4) Geneva Convention III that the crew of military aircraft may also comprise civilian members. The presence of such civilian crew members on board military aircraft does not alter the aircraft's legal status.

8. The requirement of a crew under military discipline does not mean that all military aircraft must be manned by a crew. Today, unmanned aerial vehicles (UAV/UCAVs) also qualify as 'military aircraft' if the persons remotely controlling them are subject to regular armed forces discipline. The same applies to autonomously operating UAVs. The object and purpose of the two preceding requirements may be explained as follows:

> Operations of war involve the responsibility of the state. Units of the fighting forces must, therefore, be under the direct control of persons responsible to the state. For the same reason the crew must be exclusively military in order that they may be subject to military discipline.[81]

9. Aircraft operated by private security companies or other private contractors are civilian. Once a military aircraft is operated or commanded by PMSCs, it loses its status as a military aircraft and may no longer engage in attacks.

10. The members of the crew of military aircraft who are combatants must be accorded prisoner-of-war status when captured. According to Article 4A(4) Geneva Convention III captured civilian members of military aircraft crews are entitled to prisoner-of-war status as well.

20.09 **Only warships and military aircraft are entitled to perform belligerent acts at sea.**

1. As regards ships, it is a well-established rule of customary law that the exercise of belligerent rights is reserved to the 'lawfully commissioned cruisers of a belligerent nation'.[82] Accordingly, only warships are entitled to employ methods and means of naval warfare, i.e. to attack military objectives, to maintain and enforce blockades, or to visit, search, and capture enemy or neutral merchant vessels. Other State ships, such as auxiliary vessels, as well as merchant vessels are at all times prohibited from engaging in acts harmful to the enemy or to neutrals. These principles were affirmed by the 1856 Paris Declaration and by the 1907 Hague Convention VII and are, today, customary in character.[83]

[81] Commission of Jurists To Consider and Report upon the Revision of the Rules of Warfare, General Report, 32 *AJIL* (1938), 18.

[82] Lord Stowell in the case of *The Maria* (1799) 1 C. Rob. 340.

[83] See e.g. German Manual, para. 1015; San Remo Manual, para. 118.

2. As regards aircraft, the same rule applies (see also Sections 19.14, 19.23, and accompanying commentary). Accordingly, the exercise of belligerent rights is reserved to military aircraft. This rule is based on Articles 13 and 16 of the 1923 Hague Rules on Air Warfare and also recognized as customary in character.[84] As in the case of warships, State aircraft other than military aircraft, e.g. aircraft used for police or customs functions, are not entitled to exercise belligerent rights. **20.09**

3. Belligerent warships and military aircraft are lawful military objectives because by their nature they make an effective contribution to military action and their total or partial destruction, capture, or neutralization will always offer a definite military advantage. Accordingly, they may be attacked as long as they are encountered outside neutral waters or neutral airspace. Therefore, the sinking of the *General Belgrano*, during the 1982 Falklands/Malvinas conflict, was in accordance with the law of naval warfare although the *Belgrano* had been encountered outside the British Total Exclusion Zone.

4. If belligerent warships or military aircraft are captured by enemy forces property passes *uno actu* to the captor State as booty of war.[85] A prior decision by a prize court is not necessary. The captured warship or military aircraft may be either destroyed or incorporated into the armed forces of the captor State.

5. It follows from Section 20.09 that other State ships and aircraft, such as auxiliary vessels and aircraft and ships performing police or customs functions, are prohibited from exercising belligerent rights, unless, for example, the police forces have been incorporated into the regular armed forces by national regulation. It may be added in this context that the category of auxiliaries exclusively applies to vessels. It is true that the San Remo Manual and the UK Manual[86] recognize a special category of 'auxiliary aircraft'. However, in State practice such a distinct category has not become generally recognized. Therefore, such aircraft are to be considered State aircraft that are not entitled to exercise belligerent rights. The prohibition on an exercise of belligerent rights by State ships and aircraft other than warships and military aircraft is limited to the exercise of belligerent rights proper, i.e. to those rights the exercise of which is reserved for warships and military aircraft, such as conducting an attack. Accordingly, other State ships and aircraft may continue to perform their genuine law enforcement functions. Of course, in practice it will be most difficult to clearly establish whether, for example, the boarding of a merchant vessel or the interception of a civil aircraft constitutes an exercise of belligerent rights or whether it qualifies as law enforcement.

[84] See e.g. UK Manual, para. 12.34.

[85] Y. Dinstein, 'Booty of War', in R. Wolfrum (ed.), *Max Planck Encyclopedia of Public International Law*, <http://www.mpepil.com>.

[86] San Remo Manual, para. 13(k); UK Manual, para. 12.5.

20.10 **Warships and military aircraft enjoy sovereign immunity. This also applies to unmanned (surface, subsurface, or aerial) vehicles whether operating autonomously or not.**

1. The legal status of warships flows from the sovereignty of the State whose flag they fly. However, they may not any longer be considered as 'floating territory' of the State.[87] That doctrine was, *inter alia*, rejected by Lord Atkins in the Chung Chi Cheung case.[88] Rather, warships are platforms operated by a State exclusively for non-commercial government purposes thus sharing the flag State's sovereign immunity. The same applies to military aircraft. Still, an act of violence against a foreign warship or military aircraft is not only a violation of the prohibition of the use of force under the UN Charter but also an armed attack in the sense of Article 51 UN Charter triggering the flag State's right of self-defence.

2. The principle of sovereign immunity applies to all ships and aircraft qualifying as warships or as military aircraft in the sense of Sections 20.07 and 20.08.[89] Accordingly, unmanned vehicles—whether aerial or seagoing—belonging to the armed forces of a State enjoy that status independently from other platforms. So far, sovereign immunity of unmanned vehicles has been expressly recognized only in the US Navy's Handbook.[90] However, in view of the fact that unmanned vehicles belonging to the armed forces will only be operated in governmental and military services they by necessity participate in the respective State's sovereignty. It is, therefore, a logical and necessary consequence that such vehicles enjoy sovereign immunity.

3. Sovereign immunity is to be distinguished from the flag State principle according to which States acquire authority over the ships flying their respective flags. The flag State principle alone does not confer sovereign immunity upon ships. Whereas the applicability of the flag State's domestic law to the ships flying its flag is not absolute in character[91] warships are immune from any exercise of another State's jurisdiction, especially from arrest or search, whether in national or international waters. They are also immune from foreign taxation, exempt from any foreign State regulation requiring flying the flag of such foreign State either in its ports or while passing through its territorial sea, and are entitled to exclusive control over persons onboard such vessels with respect to acts performed on board. The privilege of sovereign immunity includes protecting the identity of personnel, stores, weapons, or other property on board the vessel.[92] In times of peace the immunity of warships ceases if the crew has mutinied, taken control of the ship, and if it has committed acts of piracy. Then, according to Article 102 UNCLOS the ship is assimilated to a pirate ship that, according to Article 105 UNCLOS, is subject to seizure by every State.

[87] That was the position taken by the PCIJ in the case of *The Lotus*, PCIJ Series A no. 10 (1927).
[88] *Chung Chi Cheung v The King* [1939] AC 160 (PC).
[89] NWP 1-14M, paras 2.2.2, 2.4.2.
[90] NWP 1-14M, paras 2.3.6, 2.4.4.
[91] Colombos, *The International Law of the Sea*, 296 *et seq.*
[92] NWP 1-14M, para. 2.1.1; Colombos, *The International Law of the Sea*, 260, 262 *et seq.*

4. The aforementioned rules and principles apply *mutatis mutandis* to military aircraft. It may not be left out of consideration, however, that there is no equivalent to the right of innocent passage of aircraft. Still, a military aircraft continues to enjoy sovereign immunity if it is on foreign territory. This especially holds true for cases of distress landing. **20.10**

5. It is important to note that sovereign immunity is without prejudice to the well-established belligerent right to treat captured enemy warships and military aircraft as booty of war.[93] If a belligerent warship (or military aircraft) is captured by enemy forces property passes *uno actu* to the captor State. A prior decision by a prize court is not necessary. The captured warship (or military aircraft) may be either destroyed or incorporated into the armed forces of the captor State. For example, during the 1956 Sinai Campaign the Egyptian destroyer Ibrahim I, after it had been disabled by battle damage, was boarded by Israeli sailors and brought to Haifa. After repair it was integrated into the Israeli navy and became the INF Haifa.

6. It needs to be emphasized that sovereign immunity remains applicable to sunken warships that have not been captured. The destruction of an enemy warship during an international armed conflict 'does not, in itself, give the destroying power any rights over the enemy's vessel'.[94] Rather, the acquisition of rights over a foreign warship necessarily presupposes a capture to have occurred. Such capture may be exercised with or without prior battle damage. If, however, a warship is not captured but merely sunk and if the flag State has not abandoned the ship it remains that State's property. Neither the title of ownership nor the special legal status of sovereign immunity becomes extinct. Moreover, 'such warships are frequently the final resting place of deceased military personnel and disturbance of such vessels for the purpose of salvage is not generally deemed proper'.[95] The fact that a sunken warship has been lying on the ocean floor for a longer period of time does not result in an extinction of the title to ownership or of the ship's sovereign immunity. For example, HMS Birkenhead had been sunk in 1852, the Confederate Ship CSS Alabama in 1864, the Spanish warship Juno in 1802.[96] The US, Singapore, and Norway recognized the German title to ownership of German warships sunk during the two World Wars.[97] Sunken warships on the ocean floor either on the continental shelf or within the exclusive economic zone of another State are to be treated as if in high seas areas. In its commentary on the draft convention on the continental shelf the International Law Commission made clear that 'the rights in question do not cover objects such as wrecked ships and their cargoes (including bullion) lying on the seabed or covered by the bed of the subsoil'.[98] Therefore, the sovereign rights coastal States enjoy with regard to the natural resources of the

[93] See H.A. Smith, 'Booty of War', 23 *BYBIL* (1946), 227–39.

[94] US Dept. of State File no. P81 0004-0338.

[95] 60 *BYBIL* (1990), 672.

[96] 94 *AJIL* (2000), 678 *et seq.*

[97] See the references in Heintschel von Heinegg, *HuV-I* (1994), 23.

[98] UN Doc. A/3159 at 42.

20.10 continental shelf or their exclusive economic zone do not include foreign sunken warships whose sovereign immunity and special status as war graves must be respected at all times. While most States seem to agree that the flag States of sunken warships retain their rights of property it is a matter of controversy whether coastal States are obliged to respect the sovereign immunity of sunken warships when such ships are located within their respective territorial sea. Still, they remain to be specially protected under international law as war graves thus precluding the coastal State from any unilateral action aimed at their salvage or exploration.

20.3 General Principles of the Law of Naval Warfare

20.11 **In naval warfare, the general rules of the law of armed conflict apply.**

1. The law of naval warfare provides a special regime for naval operations during an international armed conflict. This becomes evident by a considerable number of treaties specially designed to regulate the conduct of naval forces in times of war.[99] Despite the fact that modern operations will in most cases be joint there still is, therefore, a branch of the law of international armed conflict that is to be distinguished from land warfare and from aerial warfare. This has been reaffirmed by the San Remo Manual and by the ILA Helsinki Principles. However, the existence of that special legal regime does not mean that that regime is absolutely autonomous and not influenced by the general law of international armed conflict. For those States parties to the 1977 AP I[100] it follows from Article 49(3) that the Protocol's rules on methods and means of warfare, including the basic rules in Article 35 AP I, apply to naval warfare even if naval operations do not affect the civilian population, individual civilians, or civilian objects on land. Moreover, States not parties to AP I also recognize that the general principles of the law of international armed conflict apply in naval warfare. For example, NWP 1-14M provides:

> The law of armed conflict seeks to minimize unnecessary suffering and destruction by controlling and mitigating the harmful effects of hostilities through standards of protection to be accorded to combatants, non-combatants, civilians and civilian property. [...] To

[99] See, *inter alia*, Hague Conventions of 18 October 1907: No. VI Relating to the Status of Enemy Merchant Ships at the Outbreak of Hostilities; No. VIII Relative to the Laying of Automatic Submarine Contact Mines; No. IX Concerning Bombardment by Naval Forces in Time of War; No. XI Relative to Certain Restrictions with Regard to the Exercise of the Right of Capture in Naval War; Procès-verbal relating to the Rules of Submarine Warfare Set Forth in Part IV of the Treaty of London of 22 April 1930, London, 6 November 1936; Geneva Convention for the Amelioration of the Conditions of Wounded, Sick and Shipwrecked Members of Armed Forces at Sea, 12 August 1949. Mention must also be made of the Declaration of London Concerning the Laws of Naval War, signed on 26 February 1909 which did not however enter into force because it was not ratified by any signatory. See also The Laws of Naval War Governing the Relations between Belligerents, Manual adopted by the Institute of International Law, Oxford, 6 November 1913.

[100] Protocol Additional to the Geneva Conventions of 12 August 1949, and Relating to the Protection of Victims of International Armed Conflict (Protocol I), 8 June 1977.

achieve this goal, the law of armed conflict is based on four general principles: military necessity, unnecessary suffering, distinction, and proportionality.[101] **20.11**

The customary character of the basic principles and their applicability to naval warfare have been reaffirmed by the San Remo Manual.[102] Moreover, their applicability to naval operations in times of war is recognized in other military manuals as well.[103]

2. The general principles of the law of international armed conflict applicable to naval warfare may be summarized by quoting the respective rules of the San Remo Manual:

(a) 'In any armed conflict the right of the parties to the conflict to choose methods or means of warfare is not unlimited.'[104] Of course, this principle is far too general and abstract to allow concrete conclusions as to the legal limits that apply to the conduct of naval operations. Still, it remains important as it emphasizes that methods and means of naval warfare may not be applied in disregard of the more specific principles and other rules of the law of international armed conflict—especially of those rules prohibiting the use of certain methods and means of naval warfare. Accordingly, considerations of military necessity alone will not suffice to render the use of a given method or means legal. Rather, military necessity may only be relied upon if an applicable rule expressly provides for an exception to that effect.

(b) 'Parties to the conflict shall at all times distinguish between civilians or other protected persons and combatants and between civilian or exempt objects and military objectives.'[105] The principle of distinction, as formulated in the San Remo Manual, implies a duty of naval commanders to always distinguish military objectives from civilians and civilian objects before launching an attack. This imposes a clear obligation on naval commanders to take all feasible measures to identify whether a person or an object may be targeted and to comply with the further obligations following from the precautionary principle. Moreover, the principle of distinction prohibits indiscriminate attacks.[106]

(c) It may not be left out of consideration, however, that the principle of distinction also means that armed forces must distinguish themselves from civilians and from civilian objects. In land warfare, combatants are obliged to wear uniforms or other distinctive signs and to carry their arms openly. In naval warfare, which predominantly focuses on objects rather than on persons, this aspect of the principle of distinction means that warships and military aircraft must be identifiable as such, i.e. they must bear marks that give sufficient evidence that they are entitled to exercise belligerent rights.[107]

[101] NWP 1-14M, para. 5.3. [102] San Remo Manual, paras 38 *et seq.*

[103] See e.g. UK Manual, paras 13.24 *et seq.*; German Manual, para. 1017. See also Heintschel von Heinegg in D. Fleck (ed.), *The Handbook of International Humanitarian Law*, 3rd edn (Oxford: Oxford University Press, 2013), Section 1017.

[104] San Remo Manual, para. 38. [105] San Remo Manual, para. 39.

[106] NWP 1-14M, para. 5.3.2; German Manual, para. 1017; UK Manual, para. 13.25.

[107] San Remo Manual, para. 39, and explanation thereto.

20.11 (d) 'Attacks shall be limited strictly to military objectives. Merchant vessels and civil aircraft are civilian objects unless they are military objectives [...].'[108] This is but a specification of the general principle of distinction obliging belligerents at sea to limit their attacks to objectives fulfilling the definition of military objectives laid down in Section 20.15.[109]

(e) 'In addition to any specific prohibitions binding upon the parties to a conflict, it is forbidden to employ methods and means of warfare which: (a) are of a nature to cause superfluous injury or unnecessary suffering; or (b) are indiscriminate, in that (i) they are not, or cannot be, directed against a specific military objective; or (ii) their effects cannot be limited as required by international law [...].'[110] The prohibition of superfluous injury or unnecessary suffering[111] is difficult to apply in practice. In principle, it will therefore become operable only if the use of a certain weapon is prohibited or restricted by treaty. However, the existing treaty prohibitions (e.g. under the 1980 UN Weapons Convention) only have a minor impact on naval warfare because, in principle, methods and means of naval warfare are directed against objects and not against individuals.

(f) The prohibition of indiscriminate attacks is of special relevance to naval operations when it comes to attacks by naval forces against targets on land. Accordingly, attacks that are not, or cannot be, directed at a specific military objective—e.g. because several distinct military objectives are treated as a single military objective—are prohibited. The effects cannot be limited as required by lit. (b)(ii) if the use of methods and means causes collateral damage or casualties which would be excessive in relation to the concrete military advantage anticipated.[112] Hence, the prohibition of indiscriminate attacks is closely linked to the principle of proportionality.

(g) With regard to sea-to-sea, sea-to-air, and air-to sea operations the prohibition on indiscriminate effects is of less practical importance. Most of the contemporary means of naval warfare are very precise and their use will rarely result in indiscriminate effects. This especially holds true for missiles and torpedoes but also for naval guns. The only means of naval warfare whose use might result in indiscriminate effects is the naval mine. It is, in theory, conceivable than an extensive minefield results in damage to military and civilian objects alike. It may not be left out of consideration, however, that according to the 1907 Hague Convention VIII and customary international law belligerents laying naval mines are obliged to comply with the principles of effective surveillance, of risk control, and of warning.[113] Only if belligerents act in disregard of these obligations may a minefield be considered an indiscriminate attack.

(h) 'It is prohibited to order that there shall be no survivors, to threaten an adversary therewith or to conduct hostilities on that basis.'[114]

[108] San Remo Manual, para. 4.
[109] See also UK Manual, para. 13.27.
[110] San Remo Manual, para. 42.
[111] See also UK Manual, para. 13.28; NWP 1-14M, para. 5.3.4.
[112] See also NWP 1-14M, paras 5.3.2 and 5.3.3; UK Manual, para. 13.28.
[113] German Manual, para. 1040.
[114] San Remo Manual, para. 43. See also UK Manual, para. 13.29.

(i) 'Methods and means of warfare should be employed with due regard for the natural environment taking into account the relevant rules of international law. Damage to or destruction of the natural environment not justified by military necessity and carried out wantonly is prohibited.'[115] Despite the fact that the natural environment is protected by Articles 35(3) and 55 AP I, and by the 1976 ENMOD Convention,[116] there is no generally recognized definition of the term 'natural environment'. Still, there is general agreement that the 'natural environment' will generally qualify as a civilian objective. Moreover, State practice provides sufficient evidence that considerations of environmental protection have become part of operational planning.[117] If feasible, and if the respective operation is not jeopardized, existing regimes of environmental protection, such as regional treaty systems on the protection of the marine environment, should be taken into consideration. Military manuals provide sufficient evidence for the customary character of the prohibition on wanton destruction of the 'natural environment'.[118] Moreover, the prohibition on wanton destruction of objects not constituting lawful military objectives has been affirmed by Article 23 lit. (g) of the 1907 Hague Regulations and by Article 147 of the 1949 Geneva Convention IV. 'Wanton' means that the destruction is the consequence of a deliberate action taken without motive or provocation, or one that is malicious. In other words, it is an action that cannot be justified by considerations of military necessity. Accordingly, the destruction of an entire ecosystem, like the Baltic Sea, will by definition always constitute a violation of the law. However, destruction of individual parts of the natural environment, like some fish, will ordinarily not be contrary to the law of naval warfare. **20.11**

(j) 'Surface ships, submarines and aircraft are bound by the same principles and rules.'[119] This rule reflects the 1936 Submarine Protocol[120] and the judgment of the Nuremberg Tribunal in the case of Admiral Dönitz. It is, therefore, declaratory for customary international law. Since the law of naval warfare does not provide for exceptions applicable to submarines their employment is governed by the general principles of the law of naval warfare, especially by the principle of distinction. However, modern submarines are equipped with a variety of sophisticated sensors and other electronic devices which enable them to positively identify legitimate military objectives. Torpedoes, in particular, are highly discriminating weapons whose use will regularly not result in a violation of the principle of discrimination or

[115] San Remo Manual, para. 44.

[116] Convention on the Prohibition of Military or Any Other Hostile Use of Environmental Modification Techniques of 2 September 1976.

[117] See e.g. NWP 1-14M, para. 8.4.

[118] NWP 1/14M, para. 8.4: 'Destruction of the natural environment not necessitated by mission accomplishment and carried out wantonly is prohibited.' UK Manual, paras 12.26 lit. (f) and 5.29; German Manual, para. 401.

[119] San Remo Manual, para. 45.

[120] Procès-verbal relating to the Rules of Submarine Warfare Set Forth in Part IV of the Treaty of London of 22 April 1930, London, 6 November 1936.

20.11 of other rules of the law of armed conflict.[121] The same holds true for submarine launched cruise missiles (TLAMs and TASMs) and other missiles provided they are equipped with sensors or are employed in conjunction with external sources of targeting data that are sufficient to ensure effective target discrimination.[122] Hence, the main task of attack submarines during armed conflict—neutralization of enemy surface and subsurface forces—while governed by the general principles of target discrimination, will in most cases not be prevented by the rule.

It was a contentious issue whether submarines could be employed for exercising prize measures, i.e. visit and search of merchant vessels at sea. If submarines are used for such purposes[123] the rules of the 1936 London Protocol will apply. This means that '[i]n their action with regard to merchant ships, submarines must conform to the rules of International Law to which surface vessels are subject'.[124] It must be emphasized, however, that the London Protocol only deals with prize measures taken against enemy or neutral merchant vessels. Accordingly, the limitations of the Protocol applying to the sinking of merchant vessels, i.e. placing passengers, crew, and the ship's papers in a place of safety, are applicable only to those cases in which a merchant vessel is destroyed as prize. Such destruction must be clearly distinguished from attacks against merchant vessels that have become legitimate military objectives.[125]

Two situations in which a merchant vessel becomes a legitimate military objective are explicitly provided for in the Protocol itself: persistent refusal to stop on being duly summoned or active resistance to visit and search. Moreover, already in 1922, after the negotiations of the Submarine Treaty, the Italian delegate stated that the term 'merchant ship' was to be understood as referring to 'unarmed merchant vessels' only.[126] During the 1930 London Naval Conference a commission of lawyers made abundantly clear that 'the expression "merchant vessel", where it is employed in the declaration, is not to be understood as including a merchant vessel which is at the moment participating in hostilities in such a manner as to cause her to lose her right to the immunities of a merchant vessel'.[127] Finally, the Nuremberg Tribunal, in the case against Admiral Dönitz, was 'not prepared to hold Dönitz guilty for his conduct of submarine warfare against British armed merchant ships'.[128] The Tribunal also explicitly referred to the British convoy system, to the integration of 'merchant vessels into the warning network of naval intelligence',

[121] According to the San Remo Manual, para. 79, torpedoes must 'sink or otherwise become harmless when they have completed their run'. See also UK Manual, para. 13.51; NWP 1-14M, para. 9.4.

[122] NWP 1-14M, para. 9.10; UK Manual, para. 13.50.

[123] While modern submarines will in most cases be employed for genuinely military purposes many navies continue to envisage their use also against enemy and neutral trade.

[124] Rule 1 of the 1936 London Protocol. See also UK Manual, para. 13.31.

[125] See the Explanations to paras 139 of the San Remo Manual in Doswald-Beck (ed.), *San Remo Manual*, 209 *et seq*.

[126] See the references in Mallison, *Submarines*, 42, fn 84.

[127] Documents of the London Naval Conference 1930 (London, 1930), 443.

[128] 1 *IMT* 312.

and to the announcement of the British Admiralty of 1 October 1939 'that British merchant ships had been ordered to ram U-boats if possible'.[129] Accordingly, submarines may very well be employed in a 'commerce raider' role if enemy or neutral merchant vessels are to be considered legitimate military objectives. If, however, merchant vessels continue to enjoy their protection against attack (not against capture as prize!) submarines will only in exceptional circumstances be in a position to make use of the right to destroy a captured merchant vessel as prize. **20.11**

Apart from the strategic submarines most of the submarines currently in use by the naval armed forces will not be in a position to place passengers, crews, and ship's papers into a place of safety because they are simply too small to take on board passengers. Moreover, they will, in order to comply with their obligations under the 1936 London Protocol, have to surface and will thus become extremely vulnerable to enemy attacks. Therefore, it is more than doubtful whether submarines will be employed for the purpose of visiting, searching, or capturing enemy or neutral merchant vessels.

Finally, the obligation to rescue may constitute an insurmountable problem for submarines in view of the limited space on board. As regards the obligation to rescue it has to be kept in mind that there exist two separate legal bases. On the one hand, there is Article 18 of Geneva Convention II. On the other hand, a duty to rescue is contained in the 1936 London Protocol. To start with the latter, it needs to be emphasized that the obligation to place passengers, crew, and ship's papers in a place of safety must be complied with only before a captured merchant vessel is destroyed as prize. Article 18 Geneva Convention II provides: 'After each engagement, Parties to the conflict shall, without delay, take all possible measures to search for and collect the shipwrecked, wounded and sick, to protect them against pillage and ill-treatment, to ensure their adequate care, and to search for the dead and prevent their being despoiled.' It follows from Article 13 Geneva Convention II that this obligation is not owed to members of enemy armed forces only. It also applies, *inter alia*, to persons accompanying the armed forces, e.g. civilian contractors on board a warship, and to the members of the crews, including masters, of merchant vessels.[130] Therefore, it makes no difference whether an enemy warship or an enemy (or neutral) merchant vessel has been sunk.[131] However, Article 18 may not be interpreted as obliging naval commanders to search for and rescue survivors 'at all times'. Such an obligation only exists for land warfare.[132] In naval warfare the obligation comes into operation 'after each engagement' only. The duration of such an engagement will depend upon the circumstances ruling at the time but it is quite obvious that an engagement is not necessarily terminated as soon as a vessel has been sunk. Moreover, belligerents are obliged only to take all

[129] Ibid.

[130] For the historical background see J.S. Pictet, *Commentary on the II Geneva Convention* (Geneva: ICRC, 1960), 98 *et seq.*

[131] Ibid. 131.

[132] Art. 15(1) GC I provides: 'At all times, and particularly after an engagement [. . .].'

20.11 'possible' measures. While it is clear that submarine commanders are not obliged to engage in search and rescue operations if that would imply an unreasonable risk for the ship, this does not mean that they are relieved of any obligation whatsoever. If available the survivors must be provided with the means necessary to enable them to await rescue or to reach the coast.[133]

(k) As regards the precautionary principle the San Remo Manual provides:

> With respect to attacks, the following precautions shall be taken: (a) those who plan, decide upon or execute an attack must take all feasible measures to gather information which will assist in determining whether or not objects which are not military objectives are present in the area of attack; (b) in the light of the information available to them, those who plan, decide upon or execute an attack shall do everything feasible to ensure that attacks are limited to military objectives; (c) they shall furthermore take all feasible precautions in the choice of methods and means in order to avoid or minimise collateral casualties or damage; and (d) an attack shall not be launched if it may be expected to cause collateral casualties or damage which would be excessive in relation to the concrete and direct military advantage anticipated from the attack as a whole; an attack shall be cancelled or suspended as soon as it becomes apparent that the collateral casualties or damage would be excessive.[134]

While the above obligations under the precautionary principle may be considered declaratory of customary international law,[135] it is difficult to give guidance that would be more specific than the respective rule of the San Remo Manual. Eventually, it will depend upon the circumstances of each single case which precautionary measures naval commanders are obliged to take prior to or during an attack. There is, however, widespread agreement on the meaning of the term 'feasible'. 'Feasible' means that which is practicable or practically possible, taking into account all circumstances prevailing at the time, including humanitarian and military considerations. This definition is based upon declarations made by States at the time of ratification of AP I, with respect to Articles 41, 56, 57, 58, 78, and 86. A similar definition is given in the second sentence of Article 3(10) of Protocol II to the 1980 Conventional Weapons Convention, as amended in 1996.[136] The term 'feasible' appears in several provisions and could have different practical meaning when the context is different. With regard to, for instance, verification of military objectives, what is feasible will depend on the availability of technical means for observation. This is supported in the ICRC Commentary.[137] With regard to the removal of the civilian population from the vicinity of military objectives, the feasibility will

[133] Pictet, *Commentary*, 131. [134] San Remo Manual, para. 46.

[135] See e.g. UK Manual, para. 13.32.

[136] Protocol on Prohibitions or Restrictions on the Use of Mines, Booby-Traps and other Devices, annexed to the 1980 Convention on Prohibitions or Restrictions on the Use of Certain Conventional Weapons Which May Be Deemed to be Excessively Injurious or to Have Indiscriminate Effects (Protocol amended in 1996), Art. 3: '(10) All feasible precautions shall be taken to protect civilians from the effects of weapons to which this Article applies. Feasible precautions are those precautions which are practicable or practically possible taking into account all circumstances ruling at the time, including humanitarian and military considerations...'

[137] ICRC Commentary, Art. 57 AP I, 682.

depend on the availability of means of transportation and alternative housing. The term 'at the time' is to emphasize that any judgment on feasibility is to be taken at the time at which attacks are decided upon or executed. This is a clear rejection of any 'hindsight rule'. For example, Australia, upon ratification of AP I, declared that 'military commanders and others responsible for planning, deciding upon or executing attacks, necessarily have to reach their decisions on the basis of their assessment of the information from all sources, which is available to them at the relevant time'.[138] As made clear in the last part of this definition, feasibility is to be determined by taking into account both humanitarian and military considerations. Hence, neither the former nor the latter prevail *ab initio.* Military commanders may, therefore, take into account the circumstances relevant to the success of an attack or of the overall military operation, including the survival of military aircraft and their crews. However, the factoring in of such military consideration may not result in a neglect of humanitarian obligations under the law of armed conflict. This means that a particular course of action might be considered not feasible if it would entail excessive risks to the aircraft and crews. Some risks would, however, have to be accepted. Finally, it needs to be stressed that the determination of feasibility 'will be a matter of common sense and good faith'[139] and there are no absolute standards applicable to any judgment on feasibility. 20.11

(l) 'Perfidy is prohibited'.[140] This statement in the San Remo Manual is far too wide to reflect customary international law. Rather, the provision should read: 'It is prohibited to kill, injure or capture an adversary by resort to perfidy'.[141]

20.4 Specially Protected Enemy Vessels and Aircraft

The following classes of enemy vessels are exempt from attack: 20.12

- **hospital ships; small craft used for coastal rescue operations and other medical transports;**
- **vessels granted safe conduct by agreement between the belligerents;**
- **vessels engaged in transporting cultural property under special protection;**
- **passenger vessels when engaged only in carrying civilian passengers;**
- **vessels charged with religious, non-military scientific, or philanthropic missions, and vessels collecting scientific data of likely military applications are not protected;**

138 Declaration relating to Articles 51 to 58 made upon ratification on 21 June 1986.

139 ICRC Commentary, Art. 57 AP I, 682.

140 San Remo Manual, para. 111.

141 Art. 37(1) AP I; UK Manual, para. 13.83. For examples of acts that constitute a violation of the prohibition of perfidy see Heintschel von Heinegg in Fleck (ed.), *The Handbook of International Humanitarian Law*, Sections 1018 and 1019.

20.12 **— small coastal fishing vessels and small boats engaged in local coastal trade, but they are subject to the regulations of a belligerent naval commander operating in the area and to inspection;**
— vessels designed or adapted exclusively for responding to pollution incidents in the marine environment;
— vessels which have surrendered;
— life rafts and life boats.

1. The exemption from attacks of the vessels listed in Section 20.12 is based on the 1907 Hague Convention XI,[142] the San Remo Manual,[143] and on customary international law as reflected in military manuals.[144]

2. For the different categories of vessels protected under the present Section see Heintschel von Heinegg in Fleck (ed.), *The Handbook of International Humanitarian Law*, Commentary to Section 1034.

3. It may be recalled that hospital ships remain to be protected against attack if they communicate via satellites, i.e. by using encryption. Although Article 34(2) of the Second Geneva Convention of 1949 provides that 'hospital ships may not possess or use a secret code for their wireless or other means of communication',[145] there is widespread agreement today that the prohibition of Article 34(2) GC II has become obsolete by derogation through subsequent State practice. The same holds true for the prohibition on arming hospital ships if and in so far as hospital ships are equipped with deflective means like chaff and flares.[146]

4. As regards the exemption from attacks of ships that have surrendered, it is important to stress that the traditional sign indicating a warship's intent to surrender (i.e. hoisting the flag) will in most cases not be taken notice of in practice. However, State practice has not contributed to the formation of another form of surrender that would be operable in a modern battlefield environment. Therefore, the commander who wishes to surrender must use all feasible means to inform the enemy of his intention, including radio transmissions. Still, in view of the lack of a generally recognized sign different from hoisting the warship's flag he cannot expect the enemy to cancel or suspend an attack until visual contact is established. For the surrender of military aircraft see Section 19.16 and accompanying commentary.

20.13 **The following classes of enemy aircraft are exempt from attack:**
— medical aircraft;

[142] Convention No. XI Relative to Certain Restrictions with Regard to the Exercise of the Right of Capture in Naval War.
[143] San Remo Manual, para. 47.
[144] German Manual, para. 1034; UK Manual, para. 13.33; NWP 1-14M, para. 8.6.3.
[145] The French text of Art. 34(2) is concurrent: '... les navires-hôpitaux ne pourront posséder ni utiliser de code secret pour leurs émissions par T.S.F. ou par tout autre moyen de communication'.
[146] San Remo Manual, para. 170.

— **aircraft granted safe conduct by agreement between the belligerents; and** 20.13
— **civil airliners.**

1. According to Article 24 AP I medical aircraft are entitled to protection against attack (see also Section 19.18 and accompanying commentary). Moreover, they shall be respected and protected. Despite the wording of Section 20.13 it is important to observe that the protection of medical aircraft will differ depending on the location of the aircraft. Accordingly, in and over land areas physically controlled by friendly forces, or in sea areas not physically controlled by the enemy, the special protection of medical aircraft is not dependent on the consent of the enemy.[147] However, they must be recognizable as such and they may not perform acts that are contrary to the conditions of their exemption according to Section 19.19. If operating in and over areas physically controlled by the enemy as well as in and over the so-called contact zone the protection of medical aircraft is dependent upon prior consent by the enemy.[148] While flying over those areas, medical aircraft may be ordered to land or to alight on water to permit inspection. Medical aircraft are obliged to obey any such order.[149] For aircraft conducting military SAR operations see Section 19.20 and accompanying commentary. For other aircraft entitled to special protection see Section 19.21 and accompanying commentary.

2. The second category of aircraft exempt from attack under Section 20.13 (and under Section 19.24) is generally called 'cartel aircraft'.[150] By agreement between the belligerents any aircraft—military or civil—may be granted safe conduct for performing whatever function the belligerents agree upon. It is important, however, that the agreement reached by the belligerents contains the details about the flight and the activities carried out by the aircraft. Aircraft granted safe conduct may be identified through the filing of a detailed flight plan and through the use of Secondary Surveillance Radar (SSR) modes and codes for civilian aircraft. However, it may not use medical aircraft identification. ICRC aircraft—one type of aircraft that may be granted safe conduct—constitute an exception in this respect: ICRC aircraft may use the same means of identification as medical aircraft, even though they operate under a safe conduct.

3. Although recognized as specially protected in the San Remo Manual, in military manuals,[151] and in Section 19.22 of this Handbook, it is not settled whether civil airliners are to be considered a distinct category of protected aircraft or whether they simply belong to the category of civilian aircraft. It is maintained here, however, that civil airliners are in fact specially protected under the law of armed conflict in view of their worldwide employment in carrying civilian passengers in international

[147] Art. 25 AP I. [148] Arts. 26(1) and 27(1) AP I.
[149] Art. 30(1) AP I. See also San Remo Manual, para. 180.
[150] San Remo Manual, para. 53(b); UK Manual, para. 12.30.
[151] San Remo Manual, para. 53 (c); UK Manual, para. 12.28.

20.13 air navigation and the potential risks to innocent passengers in areas of armed conflict. However, the special protection of civil airliners presupposes that they are identifiable as such and that they are engaged only in carrying civilian passengers in scheduled or non-scheduled service. Accordingly, in order to benefit from the special protection, the civilian passengers must actually be on board the aircraft, whether in flight or while the aircraft is on the ground. Civil airliners will usually be identifiable as such because belligerents and neutrals provide regular air traffic services within their respective flight information region in accordance with ICAO regulations and procedures. Their protected status, however, does not depend on whether the flight in question is scheduled. Similarly, it is immaterial whether the flight takes place along Air Traffic Service Routes. Civil airliners, like all civil aircraft, should avoid areas of potentially hazardous military activity,[152] especially areas in the immediate vicinity of (naval) operations. However, the mere fact that they have entered such areas does not deprive them of their specially protected status. It is important to stress that civil airliners are not exempt from interception and inspection. Hence, if there are reasonable grounds for suspicion that a civil airliner is engaged in activities inconsistent with its status (e.g. by carrying contraband) it is subject to inspection in an airfield that is safe for this type of aircraft and reasonably accessible. Moreover, enemy civilian airliners are subject to capture at all times, provided that the safety of the passengers can be guaranteed and that the aircraft's papers are preserved.

20.14 **Vessels and aircraft listed in Sections 20.12 and 20.13**
- **must be innocently employed in their normal role;**
- **must submit to identification and inspection when required; and**
- **must not intentionally hamper the movement of combatants and obey orders to stop or move out of the way when required.**

1. In view of the fact that exemption from attack of the vessels and aircraft listed in Sections 20.12 and 20.13 is granted owing to the special functions they are performing it is evident that they lose their specially protected status as soon as they are no longer employed in their normal role.[153] For example, if such vessels (or aircraft) are employed for the transport of arms destined to the enemy's armed forces they are no longer employed in their innocent role. It is, however, important to distinguish between conduct that results in a loss of special protection and conduct rendering a vessel a legitimate military objective. The present Section only deals with the conditions that must be fulfilled in order to render the vessels concerned exempt from attack, i.e. granting them a specially protected status under the law of naval warfare. Accordingly, any conduct that must be considered as not in compliance with the specially protected function will result in a loss of protection. For example, a cartel vessel granted safe conduct for the purpose of transporting parlamentaires is no longer specially protected if it also transports other persons or goods not necessary for the

[152] San Remo Manual, para. 72.
[153] See also San Remo Manual, para. 48; UK Manual, para. 13.34.

performance of the respective function. That conduct, however, will not necessarily render the vessel a legitimate military objective. Therefore, the conditions of exemption are wider than those rendering vessels legitimate military objectives. For the conduct rendering vessels legitimate military objectives see the commentary on Section 20.15. 20.14

2. Although the vessels and aircraft listed in Sections 20.12 and 20.13 are to be considered as specially protected under the law of naval warfare, the enemy continues to be entitled to verify whether they are indeed employed in their innocent role. Hence, those vessels are at all times obliged to submit to identification and inspection. Any effort to conceal their identity or to escape inspection by enemy warships and military aircraft will, therefore, result in a loss of the specially protected status.

3. As regards the third condition of exemption it is important to observe that belligerents are entitled to prevent vessels and aircraft from navigating in the immediate vicinity of naval operations.[154] In particular, vessels and aircraft may be ordered to move out of the vicinity of naval operations. Any non-compliance with such legitimate orders will necessarily lead to a loss of the specially protected status. Again, it needs to be emphasized that such loss of protection does not necessarily render the respective vessel a legitimate military objective.

20.5 Legitimate Military Targets at Sea

In so far as objects are concerned, military objectives are limited to those objects which by their nature, location, purpose, or use make an effective contribution to military action and whose total or partial destruction, capture, or neutralization, in the circumstances ruling at the time, offers a definite military advantage. 20.15

1. This definition is based on Article 52(2) AP I and constitutes customary international law.[155]

2. For lawful targets in naval warfare see Heintschel von Heinegg in Fleck (ed.), *The Handbook of International Humanitarian Law*, Commentary to Sections 1021 and 1015.

3. There is a division of opinion whether a contribution to the enemy's war-sustaining effort—as distinguished from the war-fighting effort—may also render an object a legitimate military objective. This approach is taken in NWP 1-14M.[156]

[154] See e.g. NWP 1-14M, para. 7.8; San Remo Manual, para. 108.

[155] San Remo Manual, para. 40; NWP 1-14M, para. 8.2; German Manual, para. 1017; UK Manual, para. 13.26.

[156] Ibid.

20.15 If accepted it would mean that an activity like the exports of certain goods, such as oil, could render a vessel a military objective because the enemy could, by the revenues, continue the war-fighting effort. However, so far, this approach has been adopted only by the US. The overwhelming majority of States do not recognize the contribution to the war-sustaining effort to be part of the definition of military objectives. According to their view exports may only be interfered with by establishing a blockade that complies with the requirements under the law of armed conflict.

4. Objects qualifying as military objectives by nature are all warships, military aircraft, and other military equipment. Their neutralization will always constitute a definite military advantage. Therefore, the sinking of an enemy warship will always be in accordance with the law of naval warfare. They may be attacked as long as they are encountered outside neutral waters. Therefore, the sinking of the *General Belgrano*, during the 1982 Falklands/Malvinas conflict, was in accordance with the law of naval warfare although the *Belgrano* had been encountered outside the British Total Exclusion Zone.

5. Other vessels and aircraft may only be considered as legitimate military objectives if, by their location, use, or purpose, they make an effective contribution to the enemy's military effort. Under customary international law,[157] *inter alia*, the following activities render merchant vessels military objectives:

— engaging in belligerent acts on behalf of the enemy, e.g. laying mines, minesweeping, engaging in visit and search or attacking other merchant vessels;
— acting as an auxiliary to an enemy's armed forces, e.g. carrying troops or replenishing warships;
— being incorporated into or assisting the enemy's intelligence gathering system, e.g. engaging in reconnaissance, early warning, surveillance, or command, control and communications missions;
— sailing under convoy of enemy warships or military aircraft;
— refusing an order to stop or actively resisting visit, search or capture; being armed to an extent that they could inflict damage to a warship; this excludes light individual weapons for the defence of personnel, e.g. against pirates, and purely deflective systems such as chaff.

Enemy civil aircraft[158] as well as neutral merchant vessels[159] and neutral civil aircraft[160] are liable to attack if they are engaged in similar activities. See also Section 19.26 and accompanying commentary.

[157] San Remo Manual, para. 60; UK Manual, para. 13.41; German Manual, para. 1025; NWP 1-14M, paras 8.6.2.2, 8.7.1.
[158] San Remo Manual, para. 63; UK Manual, para. 12.37; NWP 1-14M, para. 8.8.
[159] San Remo Manual, para. 67; UK Manual, para. 13.47; NWP 1-14M, para. 7.5.1.
[160] San Remo Manual, para. 70; UK Manual, para. 12.43.1; NWP 1-14M, para. 7.5.1.

20.6 Methods and Means of Naval Warfare

Means of naval warfare, such as missiles, torpedoes, and mines, shall be used in conformity with the principles of target discrimination and the prohibition on unnecessary suffering and superfluous injury. 20.16

1. It is important to emphasize that the employment of naval mines and of torpedoes is regulated by the 1907 Hague Convention VIII.[161] Of course, in view of the date of its adoption most of the provisions of Hague Convention VIII no longer reflect subsequent technological developments. Therefore, the present section has been formulated in a more generic way. It is to emphasize that means of warfare may only be used if the basic principles and rules referred to in Section 20.11 are observed. This means that missiles, mines, and torpedoes may only be used against objects qualifying as legitimate military objectives. Any use of such means of naval warfare may not result in indiscriminate attacks and must be in compliance with the precautionary principle and with the principle of proportionality.[162] Their use may neither result in inflicting unnecessary suffering nor superfluous injury.

2. In most cases, means of naval warfare will be in compliance with these principles because they are highly discriminating and exact. For example, a torpedo, especially when wire-guided in the first stage of attack, will regularly only hit the target it was designed to attack. The same holds true for missiles and for sophisticated naval mines reacting to pre-programmed signatures.

3. However, naval mines are not necessarily discriminating weapons. In particular, naval mines, like the automatic contact mine, will regularly explode on the physical contact of any object, including merchant vessels and protected vessels. Still, the use of such mines will generally not be contrary to the law of naval warfare. It must be kept in mind that very often naval mines are not primarily used to hit certain targets but to modify the geography: minefields are established in order to deny the enemy the use of certain sea areas. Even though the mines used may explode on any impact that would not render their use illegal if and in so far as the principles of surveillance, risk control, and warning are observed. Hence, if the location of the minefield is notified to international navigation, if the respective belligerent is in a position to prevent vessels in distress from running into a mine, and if safe channels are provided for the passage of innocent navigation, even the laying of 'indiscriminate' mines will be in accordance with the law of naval warfare. The most appropriate way of notifying a minefield is by use of a Notice to Mariners (NOTMAR). It is important to stress that the mine-laying belligerent is under an obligation to provide safeguards for vessels that might navigate into the minefield because of a navigation error or due to distress.

[161] Convention No. VIII Relative to the Laying of Automatic Submarine Contact Mines.
[162] See, *inter alia*, NWP 1-14M, para. 8.1.

20.16 4. For an in-depth analysis of mine warfare at sea see Heintschel von Heinegg in Fleck (ed.), *The Handbook of International Humanitarian Law*, Preliminary Remarks and Commentary to Sections 1039–1043.

20.17 **(a) Blockade is a method of naval warfare aimed at preventing all vessels and/or aircraft from entering or exiting specified ports, air-fields, or coastal areas belonging to, occupied by, or under the control of an enemy nation.**
(b) A blockade must be effective. It may be enforced and maintained by a combination of legitimate methods and means of warfare. A blockade must not bar access to ports and coasts of third/neutral States.
(c) Due regard must be paid to the humanitarian needs of the civilian population of the blockaded area.

1. The definition of blockade in lit. (a) is generally considered as customary in character.[163] Today, there is widespread agreement that such a blockade may be maintained by military aircraft including unmanned aerial vehicles (UAVs) and unmanned combat air vehicles (UCAVs) and enforced against aircraft as well. State practice, e.g. the blockade established by Israel in 2006, gives sufficient evidence for the correctness of that finding. A blockade must also be enforced against UAVs and UCAVs even though they do not transport personnel or goods to and from the blockaded area.

2. The primary purpose of establishing a blockade, whether naval or aerial, is to deny the enemy the benefit of the use of enemy and neutral aircraft or vessels to transport personnel and goods to or from enemy, or enemy controlled, territory. That purpose may be achieved by the use of a variety of lawful means of warfare.

3. A blockade must be declared and notified to all States. This rule is based on Article 8 of the 1909 London Declaration, according to which a blockade, in order to be binding for neutral aviation (and navigation), 'must be declared in accordance with Article 9, and notified in accordance with Articles 11 and 16'. The declaration is the act of the blockading State (or of the competent commander) stating that a blockade is, or is about to be, established. The declaration of a strategic blockade is reserved to the blockading State's government. A strategic blockade will be of a considerable extent and duration. A local blockade may be declared by the competent commander and is of limited extent and duration (e.g. in preparation of an operation). The notification is the means by which that fact is brought to the knowledge of neutrals or, in case of a local blockade, of the authorities in the blockaded area or of individual vessels (or aircraft). The declaration must specify the commencement, duration, location, and extent of the blockade and the period in which neutral vessels (and aircraft) may leave the blockaded area. A lack of

[163] NWP 1-14M, para. 7.7.1.

specificity may render a blockade void.[164] The same obligation applies to the cessation, temporary lifting, re-establishment, extension, or other alteration of a blockade.[165] **20.17**

4. The principle of effectiveness is based on rule 4 of the 1856 Paris Declaration and on Articles 2 and 3 of the 1909 London Declaration. Its object and purpose is to rule out so-called 'paper blockades', i.e. blockades which have been merely declared and which are enforced randomly. No abstract rule can be laid down as to the strength or position of the blockading force. All depends on matters of fact and geographical circumstances. Hence, effectiveness is to be judged on the merits of each case—ultimately by the competent judicial authority. It should be recalled, however, that according to the 1856 Paris Declaration and Article 2 of the 1909 London Declaration a blockade is effective only if it is 'maintained by a force sufficient really to prevent access to the coast of the enemy'. This does not mean that all vessels (and aircraft) must in fact be prevented from either entering or leaving the blockaded area. Rather, it is sufficient if the maintaining force is of a strength or nature that there is a high probability that ingress to and egress from the blockaded area will be detected and prevented by the blockading power. In other words: a blockade is to be considered effective if any attempt to leave or enter the blockaded area proves to be a dangerous undertaking. Accordingly, for a blockade to be effective, it is not necessary that warships and/or military aircraft are in the area or in the air on a permanent basis. Rather, the area may be monitored by electronic means of surveillance and/or by the use of UAVs. If, thus, the blockading power is in a position to immediately respond to an attempted breach of blockade the blockade remains effective.

5. A blockade need not be enforced by warships alone. The blockading power is entitled to make use of any means of warfare not prohibited under the law of international armed conflict. Therefore, a blockade may be maintained and enforced by military aircraft, including UAVs, missiles (AAM, SAM), mines, or by a combination thereof. While none of these means is prohibited it needs to be observed that the blockading force, under certain circumstances, may be obliged to allow entry into and egress from the blockaded area. For example, vessels (and aircraft) in distress must be permitted to enter the blockaded area.[166] Moreover, the blockading party or the competent commander may give permission to neutral warships (or military aircraft) to enter or leave the blockaded area[167] or to allow

[164] Art. 10 of the 1909 London Declaration.

[165] Arts 12 and 13 of the 1909 London Declaration.

[166] Under Art. 7 of the 1909 London Declaration, in 'circumstances of distress, acknowledged by an authority of the blockading force, a neutral vessel may enter a place under blockade and subsequently leave it, provided that she has neither discharged nor shipped any cargo there'. Moreover, there is an affirmative obligation under both customary and treaty law to render assistance to those who are in distress in the high seas. See Art. 98 UNCLOS.

[167] According to Art. 6 of the 1909 London Declaration the 'commander of a blockading force may give permission to a warship to enter, and subsequently to leave, a blockaded port'.

20.17 relief consignments for the civilian population of the blockaded area. Accordingly, the means employed for maintaining and enforcing a blockade may not render passage of such vessels (or aircraft) impossible.

6. The prohibition to bar access to neutral territory is based on Article 18 of the 1909 London Declaration that, in view of the inviolability of neutral territory and neutral airspace, is declaratory of customary international law. Since blockade is a method of warfare directed against the enemy State it may not have the effect of preventing access to and egress from neutral territory (and airspace). A neutral State continues to enjoy its right of using its territory and national airspace for the purpose of gaining access to international sea areas and airspace. Hence, the blockading party is under an obligation to provide free passage to and from neutral territory if the blockade is established and maintained in the vicinity of neutral neighbouring States.

7. Lit. (c) is a necessary specification of the principle of humanity. Accordingly:

> [the] declaration or establishment of a blockade is prohibited if (a) it has the sole purpose of starving the civilian population or denying it other objects essential for its survival; or (b) the damage to the civilian population is, or may be expected to be, excessive in relation to the concrete and direct military advantage anticipated from the blockade.[168]

Under customary international law starvation of civilians as a method of warfare is prohibited. This prohibition has been reaffirmed by Article 54(1) AP I which, according to Article 49(3) AP I, applies to 'any land, sea or air warfare which may affect the civilian population, individual civilians or civilian object on land'. A blockade will regularly affect the civilian population of the blockaded area which will be under an increasing risk of being deprived of objects essential for its survival and, ultimately, of starvation. Still, the blockade would, in such cases, not become of itself illegal. It is made clear by the wording ('sole purpose') that a blockade remains legal if denying the population objects essential for its survival is but a mere side effect pursued by the blockading power. Therefore, a blockade which has been established for the unlawful purpose of denying the civilian population objects essential for its survival is not illegal per se if it simultaneously serves a lawful military purpose. In any event, it will be difficult to ascertain that the subjective purpose of the blockading party is exclusively or primarily aimed at such effects on the civilian population. The second prohibition applies to situations in which the blockade, after its legal establishment, results in increasing losses among the civilian population due to a deprivation of objects essential for its survival. However, a small number of civilian losses due to starvation will not suffice to render a blockade illegal. This will be the case only if the blockading power does not act in accordance with its obligation to allow relief consignments and if the civilian losses due to starvation reach a number that is excessive in relation to the lawful military purpose. Moreover, if the civilian population of the blockaded area is

[168] San Remo Manual, para. 102.

inadequately provided with food and other objects essential for its survival, the blockading power: **20.17**

> must provide for free passage of such foodstuffs and other essential supplies, subject to: (a) the right to prescribe the technical arrangements, including search, under which such passage is permitted; and (b) the condition that the distribution of such supplies shall be made under the local supervision of a Protecting Power or a humanitarian organisation which offers guarantees of impartiality, such as the International Committee of the Red Cross.[169]

Under customary international humanitarian law a belligerent party is obliged to provide the civilian population with food, drinking water, and other objects essential for survival if that belligerent party controls the respective area and if the civilian population is not adequately supplied with such objects. If the belligerent party in control of the area is not in a position to provide the civilian population with those indispensable objects it must allow free passage of such supplies. This obligation has been reaffirmed by Article 70 AP I. For the purpose of securing the safe passage of relief consignments, the blockading power may designate a specified route—'humanitarian corridor' (as in the 2006 Israel–Lebanon conflict)—on which vessels or other means of transport can enter and leave the blockaded area. The obligation to provide for free passage of relief consignments is not absolute in character. It is important to stress that consent by the blockading power is essential. Since relief consignments could be abused for military or other harmful purposes the blockading power is entitled to verify whether they in fact are of a nature to only provide the civilian population with indispensable objects. Moreover, the blockading power may limit the transport of relief consignments to certain quantities, times, routes, or means of transport in order to prevent both infringements on the blockade's effectiveness and diversions of the relief consignments to the enemy armed forces. If there are reasonable grounds for suspicion that relief consignments will be abused the blockading power is entitled to withhold them (for the purpose of verifying their innocent character) or to prohibit them altogether. Supervision by a Protecting Power or by an impartial humanitarian organization is a safeguard the blockading power may claim to be observed because the supplies are meant to provide only the civilian population with objects essential for its survival, not the enemy armed forces. It may be added that the blockading power must also allow the passage of medical supplies for the civilian population or for the wounded and sick members of armed forces, subject to the right to prescribe technical arrangements, including search, under which such passage is permitted. The fact that medical supplies are dealt with separately is due to the fact that—other than relief consignments that are destined for the civilian population only—medical supplies, according to the 1949 Geneva Conventions, are to be provided to the civilian population and to the wounded and sick members of the enemy armed forces or to prisoners of war who may be held in custody in the blockaded area.

[169] San Remo Manual, para. 103.

20.17 8. For the law of blockade see Heintschel von Heinegg in Fleck (ed.), *The Handbook of International Humanitarian Law*, Commentary to Sections 1051–1053.

20.18 **Special zones may be established for the purpose of, *inter alia*:**

— defending objects and installations of high military value;

— containing the geographic area of military operations;

— subjecting civil navigation and/or aviation to restrictions or contraband control; or

— safeguarding:

- **protected persons,**
- **works and installations containing dangerous forces,**
- **objects and installations for the medical treatment of wounded and sick civilians or combatants, or**
- **objects protected under the law of armed conflict such as cultural property.**

1. The term 'zone' is used for various, and often unrelated, operational concepts: safety zones, security zones, protection zones, danger zones, warning zones, air defence identification zones, operational zones, etc. For the purposes of the present manual it is important to distinguish between exclusion zones and no-fly zones.[170] An 'exclusion zone' is a three-dimensional area/space beyond the territorial sovereignty of any State in which a belligerent claims to be relieved from certain rules of the law of international armed conflict or where that belligerent party purports to be entitled to restrict the freedom of navigation (or aviation) of other States. A 'no-fly zone' is a three-dimensional area/space established in a belligerent party's national airspace by which the belligerent restricts or prohibits aviation in its own or in enemy national airspace.

2. Whereas the legality of 'no-fly zones' has not been seriously questioned (see Section 19.15 and the accompanying commentary) the legality of exclusion zones, in view of twentieth-century State practice, especially during the two World Wars and during the 1980–8 Iran–Iraq War, was a matter of dispute. Indeed, the majority of 'zones' ('war zones', 'barred areas', etc.) established and enforced during international armed conflicts of the past were in violation of the law of international armed conflict because they resulted in unrestricted warfare. However, since the 1990s, exclusion zones have become a reality and they have been recognized as a lawful method of warfare in military manuals and elsewhere.[171]

3. 'Exclusion zones' and 'no-fly zones' must be clearly distinguished from blockades. A blockade, according to Section 20.17(a) of this Handbook, is a belligerent operation to prevent aircraft (including UAVs/UCAVs) from entering or exiting specified airfields

[170] For a distinction between zones in international and zones in national airspace see UK Manual, para. 12.58.

[171] NWP 1-14M, para. 7.9; UK Manual, paras 12.58, 13.77; German Manual, paras 1048 *et seq.*; San Remo Manual, paras 105 *et seq.*

or coastal areas belonging to, occupied by, or under the control of the enemy. With blockades the focus lies on the horizontal line (or rather: 'curtain') marking the outer limits of the blockaded area. The area/space within that line is of minor interest. In contrast, the focal point of 'exclusion zones' and of 'no-fly zones' is the three-dimensional area/space within the declared borderline. An exclusion or no-fly zone may not be established for the purpose of interfering with enemy experts, although the practical effect of the establishment of such zones may be to do so. The only lawful method of warfare for the purpose of preventing enemy exports is an enemy blockade. **20.18**

4. Moreover, zones must be distinguished from the rights enjoyed by belligerents in the immediate vicinity of (naval) operations and for the purpose of force protection. For the concept of 'immediate vicinity of military operations' see the commentary to Section 20.20. It is a generally recognized belligerent right to take measures of force protection.[172] Such measures may include the establishment and enforcement of warning zones around naval units ('defence bubbles') or around military units stationed on the ground and other measures the responsible commander considers necessary in view of a given threat. Such warning zones merely serve to warn others off. They may never result in attacks without prior warning. However, aircraft approaching a warning zone may become liable to attack if, after warning, they continue on their course and the risk for the protected units becomes unbearable.

5. Many of the uncertainties regarding the legality of exclusion zones are due to a lack of specificity as to the lawful purposes such zones may serve. While State practice has contributed to some clarification, it is impossible to enumerate in an exhaustive manner the purposes that may lawfully be pursued with the establishment and enforcement of an exclusion zone. It is, therefore, made clear by the use of '*inter alia*' that Section 20.18 is not to be understood as exhaustively specifying them.

6. The defence of high-value targets reflects State practice (e.g. during the 2003 Iraq War). Especially in situations of asymmetric threats an exclusion zone will very often be the only means of effectively protecting such objects. The value of the respective object is to be determined in the light of the circumstances of each case. The second purpose (containing the area of hostilities) gives an option for limiting the region of hostilities. Such limitation may be all embracing or confined to specific methods and means of warfare. It must be kept in mind, however, that the establishment of a zone would exclude belligerent measures outside the zone only if the declaring belligerent has made it abundantly clear that it will not, for example, attack enemy military objectives outside the zone. Therefore, the attack on the Argentine warship *General Belgrano*, during the 1982 Falklands/Malvinas War, was not illegal because the British proclamation of the total exclusion zone (TEZ) could not be interpreted as a binding self-restriction of the UK to attack Argentine military objectives only within the TEZ. If there is no binding statement to the contrary the belligerent party having established an exclusion zone continues

172 NWP 1-14M, para. 7.8.

20.18 to be entitled to attack all enemy military objectives whether they are within or outside the exclusion zone. This especially holds true for objects that by their nature make an effective contribution to the enemy's military action, e.g. enemy military aircraft and warships. The third purpose is similar to the second but restricted to visit, search, diversion, and capture. Again, the respective declaration must be very specific that the belligerent establishing the zone indeed intends to limit the exercise of prize measures to the respective geographic area. A further purpose an exclusion zone may lawfully serve is the safeguarding of persons and objects protected under the law of international armed conflict. Such an exclusion zone serving humanitarian aims may not be confused with 'humanitarian zones' established under an agreement between the belligerents. An exclusion zone serving humanitarian purposes is a method unilaterally taken and enforced by the declaring belligerent party. The opposing belligerent party is not obliged to refrain from conducting hostilities within the zone as long as the rules of the law of international armed conflict on protected persons and objects are observed.

20.19 **(a) Should a belligerent party establish a special ('no-fly') zone outside its territory, in principle, the same rules of the law of armed conflict will apply both inside and outside the exclusion ('no-fly') zone.**

(b) The extent, location, and duration of the ('no-fly') zone and the measures imposed shall not exceed what is reasonably required by military necessity or by the need to safeguard protected persons and objects.

(c) The commencement, duration, location, and extent of the ('no-fly') zone, as well as the restrictions imposed, shall be appropriately notified to all concerned.

(d) In principle, the establishment of a ('no-fly') zone may not affect neutral territory or airspace.

1. Section 20.19 specifies the criteria that are constitutive for the legality of a zone. These preconditions must be fulfilled cumulatively.[173] It must be added in this context that the term 'international airspace' in the chapeau may not be interpreted as covering the airspace above Antarctica.

2. Lit. (a) re-emphasizes the general rule that a belligerent, by establishing a zone, neither acquires additional rights nor becomes absolved from its obligations under the law of international armed conflict. It must be kept in mind, however, that a belligerent may, as a matter of policy, decide to limit the hostilities to the area covered by the zone. However, the distinction between 'exclusion zones' and 'no-fly zones' may not be disregarded. It is recognized that a belligerent is entitled to establish and enforce far-reaching flight restrictions in its own or in the enemy's

[173] See also Heintschel von Heinegg in Fleck (ed.), *The Handbook of International Humanitarian Law*, Commentary to Sections 1049 and 1050.

national airspace.[174] Accordingly, all aircraft entering a no-fly zone without prior special permission are liable to attack. This does not mean that, by their mere presence within the zone, they are at all times to be considered lawful military objectives by location. Accordingly, as emphasized in the UK Manual, 'attacks on ostensibly civil aircraft should only be carried out as a last resort when there is reason to believe that it is itself deployed on an attack'.[175] Of course, any attack is subject to the principles of the basic rules and principles. **20.19**

3. Lit. (c) applies to exclusion zones and to no-fly zones alike. A belligerent cannot expect navigation and aviation to observe the restrictions imposed if vessels and aircraft are unaware of the zone, its location, extent, and duration. Therefore, under lit. (c), the belligerent establishing a zone is obliged to publicize these details as well as the restrictive measures it has decided to apply and enforce within the zone. The term 'notify' is to be understood in a non-technical manner. It is not necessary to communicate the information via diplomatic channels. In most cases it will be appropriate to make use of a 'Notice to Mariners' (NOTMAR) or of a 'Notice to Airmen' (NOTAM).

4. Lit. (d) aims at preserving the rights of neutral States. Neutral territory, including neutral airspace, is inviolable under the law of international armed conflict. Moreover, the existence of an international armed conflict does not deprive a neutral State of its right to use its national airspace for all lawful purposes, such as egress from and entry into high seas areas and international airspace, as well as military exercises and operations. According to lit. (d), belligerents are under an affirmative obligation to respect these neutral rights. One ought to distinguish between what is impermissible, i.e. encompassing neutral airspace within the zone, and what is permissible, i.e. establishing the zone in areas of the high seas, provided that appropriate access/exit routes are established. While a zone encompassing neutral territory and airspace will always be illegal, the mere fact that access on certain routes is no longer possible or has become restricted is not sufficient to render a zone illegal. It needs to be emphasized, however, that a partial barring of access to neutral territory and airspace may be a violation of the neutral State's rights if other access routes of similar safety are unavailable.

The right to establish and maintain special ('no-fly') zones is without prejudice to the customary right of a belligerent to control merchant shipping and civil aviation in the immediate vicinity of military operations. **20.20**

1. It may be recalled that Article 30 of the 1923 Hague Rules provides:

> In case a belligerent commanding officer considers that the presence of aircraft is likely to prejudice the success of the operations in which he is engaged at the moment, he may prohibit the passing of neutral aircraft in the immediate vicinity of his forces or may oblige them to follow a particular route. A neutral aircraft which does not conform to such directions, of which it has had a notice issued by the belligerent commanding officer, may be fired upon.

[174] UK Manual, para. 12.58. [175] UK Manual, para. 12.58.2.

20.20 In order to prevent neutral vessels (and aircraft) from jeopardizing the military operations by their presence or by communicating with others a belligerent may establish special restrictions upon their activities (e.g. by controlling or neutralizing their communications) or prohibit them from entering the area.[176]

20.7 Economic Warfare at Sea

20.21 **Belligerent warships and military aircraft have a right to visit and search merchant vessels and civil aircraft where there are reasonable grounds for suspicion that they are subject to capture.**

1. On the one hand, Section 20.21 recognizes the well-established belligerent right to visit and search neutral merchant vessels and civil aircraft.[177] On the other hand, it emphasizes that only warships and military aircraft are entitled to exercise these rights.

2. The rights of visit and search are to enable belligerents to verify the true character of merchant vessels and civil aircraft or whether they are employed in their innocent role. However, interference with neutral navigation and aviation may not be exercised on an arbitrary basis because, under the applicable law, there is no prohibition for neutral vessels and aircraft to continue to pursue their commercial tasks. Moreover, an interception of an aircraft in flight always implies dangers for the aircraft and the people on board. Hence, the visit and search of neutral merchant vessels and interception (and inspection) of civil aircraft is subject to the existence of reasonable grounds of suspicion that they are engaged in activities rendering them liable to capture. Such reasonable grounds exist if the intercepting belligerent disposes of information that, if verified, would render the aircraft liable to capture. The sources of such information are immaterial.

3. On economic warfare at sea see Heintschel von Heinegg in Fleck (ed.), *The Handbook of International Humanitarian Law*, Commentary to Sections 1023, 1026–1033, 1121–1122, and 1138–1147.

20.22 **Specially protected enemy merchant vessels and civil aircraft may not be captured, unless they:**
— are not employed in their normal role;
— commit acts harmful to the enemy;
— do not immediately submit to identification and inspection when required; or
— intentionally hamper the movement.

[176] UK Manual, para. 12.58; NWP 1-14M, paras 7.8 and 7.9. See also San Remo Manual, para. 108.

[177] San Remo Manual, paras 118, 125. See also Art. 49 of the 1923 Hague Rules on Aerial Warfare.

1. Section 20.22 reflects customary law according to which enemy merchant vessels and civil aircraft 'are liable to capture in all circumstances'.[178] The rationale of this rule is to entitle belligerents to deprive the enemy of its merchant vessels and civilian aircraft and thus to interfere with the enemy's trade and lines of commercial communication. There is no need for a link to the enemy's military action or of a prior exercise of visit and search. It suffices that the vessel or aircraft concerned is of enemy character. 20.22

2. However, enemy merchant vessels and civil aircraft that enjoy a specially protected status may not be captured if they comply with the conditions laid down in Section 19.22. The enemy vessels and aircraft listed in the San Remo Manual are exempt from capture under international treaty and customary law.[179]

Neutral merchant vessels and civil aircraft are subject to capture if they: 20.23
- **are carrying contraband;**
- **are on a voyage especially undertaken with a view to the transport of individual passengers who are embodied in the armed forces of the enemy;**
- **are operating directly under enemy control, orders, charter, employment, or direction;**
- **present irregular or fraudulent documents, lack necessary documents, or destroy, deface or conceal documents;**
- **are violating regulations established by a belligerent within the immediate area of military operations; or**
- **are breaching or attempting to breach a blockade.**

1. Capture is a belligerent act and may therefore not be exercised within neutral waters or neutral airspace. Moreover, it must be observed that the determination of the conditions rendering a neutral merchant vessel or civil aircraft liable to capture may be based not only on visit and search but also on other means. Hence, the captor may dispose of intelligence or other information. As long as the information thus gained is sufficient to establish one of the conditions laid down in Section 20.23 there is no need for a prior exercise of visit and search. If, however, the source of the information cannot be disclosed the vessel or aircraft should be inspected in order to enable the prize court to adjudicate on the legality of capture.

2. As regards the cargo on board neutral merchant vessels and civil aircraft it needs to be emphasized that neutral merchant vessels and civil aircraft, during an international armed conflict, continue to enjoy the rights of pursuing their commercial activities, including the transportation of goods, be they of neutral or be they of enemy character. However, they are prohibited from transporting contraband.

[178] Art. 52 of the 1923 Hague Rules of Aerial Warfare; San Remo Manual, paras 135, 141.
[179] San Remo Manual, paras 136, 142.

20.23 'Contraband' means goods which are ultimately destined for territory under the control of an enemy belligerent and which are susceptible to use in international armed conflict. Hence, ownership—be it enemy or neutral—is irrelevant. The traditional distinction between absolute and conditional contraband has become obsolete. Moreover, it is not necessary that the goods considered contraband are contained in a contraband list. It is sufficient if it can be established that the goods are susceptible to belligerent use and that they are ultimately destined to enemy territory. However, for reasons of legal clarity, belligerents should publish a contraband list prior to the exercise of prize measures. The fact that the goods in question must be 'ultimately destined for territory under the control' of the enemy is a recognition of the doctrine of continuous voyage. Hence the goods may, according to the vessel's or aircraft's papers, be destined for neutral territory, but the intercepting belligerent may dispose of information according to which the goods are then to be transported from neutral territory to the enemy's territory. In such cases the initial destination is irrelevant. It needs to be emphasized that the concept of contraband is limited to goods destined to enemy territory and that it does not apply to exports from enemy territory.

3. In most cases neutral merchant vessels and civil aircraft 'operating directly under enemy control, orders, charter, employment or direction' will lose their neutral character. If that is the case they may be considered enemy merchant vessels or enemy civil aircraft that are always liable to capture. If enemy character cannot be presumed the vessel or aircraft, under customary international law, is liable to capture.[180]

4. The presentation of false documents and the lack of documents are also considered sufficient to render neutral merchant vessels and civil aircraft liable to capture.[181] The lack of papers or the presentation of irregular or fraudulent papers is sufficient ground for suspicion that the vessel or aircraft has in fact enemy character and that it thus is subject to capture. According to Article 54 of the 1923 Hague Rules:

> [the] papers of a private aircraft will be regarded as insufficient or irregular if they do not establish the nationality of the aircraft and indicate the names and nationality of the crew and passengers, the points of departure and destination of the flight, together with the particulars of the cargo and the conditions under which it is transported. The logs must also be included.

5. Violation of belligerent regulations within the immediate vicinity of military operations is derived from the San Remo Manual[182] and from Article 53(b) of the 1923 Hague Rules. It needs to be stressed that, generally, neutral merchant vessels and civil aircraft are not obliged to avoid certain areas. However, in the immediate area of military operations (see Section 20.20) belligerents enjoy the right to prevent

[180] San Remo Manual, paras 146(c), 153(c).
[181] San Remo Manual, paras 146(d), 153(d). See also Art. 53(f) of the 1923 Hague Rules.
[182] San Remo Manual, paras 146(e), 153(e).

the passing of neutral merchant vessels and aircraft if their presence is 'likely to prejudice the success of the operations'.[183] Neutral merchant vessels and civil aircraft not complying with such legitimate belligerent orders are liable to attack and, *a fortiori*, to capture. **20.23**

6. According to customary international law,[184] breach of blockade renders neutral merchant vessels and civil aircraft liable to capture. If a belligerent has established a blockade and if that blockade meets the requirement of effectiveness, that belligerent is entitled to prevent all vessels and aircraft from entering or leaving the blockaded area.

As an alternative to capture, a neutral merchant vessel or civil aircraft may, with its consent, be diverted from its declared destination. **20.24**

1. This rule is based on the San Remo Manual.[185] In some situations, a belligerent may prefer to divert vessels and aircraft from their declared destinations instead of exercising the right of visit and search. Similarly, neutral merchant vessels and civil aircraft may prefer to proceed to a new destination rather than to a belligerent port or airfield and to be subjected to visit and search. Accordingly, Section 20.24 provides for an alternative to capture by diverting a vessel or aircraft from its destination. However, since neutral merchant vessels and civil aircraft are not under an obligation to comply with a diversion order their consent is required. It may be recalled in this context that consent is not required to divert an enemy merchant vessel or civil aircraft from its declared destination.

[183] See Art. 30 of the 1923 Hague Rules.
[184] San Remo Manual, paras 146(f), 153(f); Art. 53(i) of the 1923 Hague Rules.
[185] San Remo Manual, paras 119, 126.

Chapter 21

MARITIME INTERCEPTION/ INTERDICTION OPERATIONS

1. As stated in the introduction to Chapter 20 this Section deals with maritime security operations outside the context of an international armed conflict. Accordingly, the legal bases for interference with international shipping (and aviation) recognized under the law of naval and aerial warfare are not applicable to the maritime operations discussed in this chapter.

2. Maritime security operations that are dealt with here as 'maritime interception/ interdiction operations' may take different forms and are conducted for varying purposes. For example, they may be authorized by the Security Council in response to a threat to the peace, breach of the peace, or act of aggression. Or they may be conducted with a view to the suppression of illegal acts, such as piracy or the proliferation of weapons of mass destruction by non-State actors. While the legal basis for maritime interception/interdiction operations will differ in accordance with the aims pursued, they all have in common that they are lawful only if public international law provides a—treaty or customary—rule explicitly authorizing interference with foreign vessels or aircraft.

3. In this chapter the terms 'maritime interdiction operations' and 'maritime interception operations' are seen as interchangeable terms and are used as such. The term 'interception' would seem to be preferable because, in view of the overall importance of the freedom of navigation and aviation, such operations will only in exceptional cases result in an interdiction of sea and air traffic *stricto sensu*. However, in view of the wide range of possible measures covered, even the use of the term 'interception' might be too narrow. Be that as it may, both terms have become generally accepted in operational practice and are, therefore, used in the present Handbook as well.

21.01 **Maritime Interception Operations (MIO) may range from querying the master of the vessel to stopping, boarding, inspecting, searching, and potentially even seizing the cargo or the vessel, or arresting persons on board. As a general principle, vessels in international waters are subject to the exclusive jurisdiction of their flag State. Moreover, interference with a vessel in international waters violates the sovereign rights of the flag State unless that interference is**

WOLFF HEINTSCHEL VON HEINEGG AND MARTIN D. FINK

authorized by the flag State or otherwise permitted by international law. Inside a coastal State's national waters, the coastal State exercises sovereignty, subject to the right of innocent passage and other rules of international law. Given these basic tenets of international law, commanders should be aware of the legal bases underlying the authorization of MIO when ordered by competent authorities to conduct such operations. **21.01**

1. The term maritime interception operations (MIO) is not a legal but an operational term of art. As shown by the first sentence of this Section, such operations may cover a wide range of measures. Some States also consider the surveillance and control of sea traffic, the protection of endangered vessels, or the establishment and enforcement of certain zones to fall within the framework of MIO.

2. As stated in the introduction of this chapter, it is important to emphasize that MIO are maritime operations, which are not governed by the law of international armed conflict. While interference with enemy or neutral merchant vessels and civil aircraft during an international armed conflict may in some cases operationally not be distinguishable from MIO as dealt with here, their legal basis, their range, and even the legal consequences vary considerably. As emphasized in Section 21.13, belligerent operations directed against merchant vessels and aircraft under the law of international armed conflict are to be clearly distinguished from MIO as dealt with in the present chapter. Accordingly, MIO are measures used in times of peace or crisis only. This does, however, not rule out the possibility that MIO are conducted simultaneously with an ongoing armed conflict. For example, during an international armed conflict between States A and B, the Security Council, acting under Chapter VII of the Charter, may have determined a threat to the peace and may have authorized UN Member States to prevent the flow of arms into the region. While those States acting under the authorization will conduct MIO, the States parties to the conflict may continue to take measures against foreign vessels and aircraft under the law of international armed conflict. Also, States A and B may take prize measures against foreign shipping and aviation, and simultaneously conduct counter-drug operations that are unrelated to the armed conflict.

3. Section 21.01 emphasizes the importance of the flag State principle in MIO. This is to remind naval commanders that any interference with foreign shipping will be in accordance with international law only if such interference is justified under an express source of legal authorization in public international law. Moreover, it needs to be stressed that the freedoms of navigation and aviation are far too important—for both economic and security policy reasons—to be interfered with lightly.

The flag State principle is recognized in the 1982 United Nations Convention on the Law of the Sea (UNCLOS)[1] and is to be considered customary in character. The US Supreme Court has characterized it as follows:

[1] Especially in Articles 91 (Nationality of ships), 92 (Status of ships), 94 (Duties of the flag State), and 97 (Penal jurisdiction in matters of collision or any other matter incident to navigation).

21.01 Perhaps the most venerable and universal rule of maritime law is that which gives cardinal importance to the law of the flag. Each State under international law may determine for itself the conditions on which it will grant its nationality to a merchant ship, thereby accepting responsibility for it and acquiring authority over it.[2]

Accordingly, merchant vessels are subject to the exclusive jurisdiction of the flag State.[3] In 1926, the Anglo-American Claims Commission emphasized that:

> [it] is a fundamental principle of international maritime law that, except by special convention or in time of war, interference by a cruiser with a foreign vessel pursuing a lawful avocation on the high seas is unwarranted and illegal and constitutes a violation of the sovereignty of the country whose flag the vessel flies.[4]

It follows that, in principle, MIO by which a foreign flagged vessel is stopped and boarded will constitute a violation of the flag State principle and, thus, a violation of the flag State's exclusive jurisdiction and sovereignty, *unless* such interference is 'expressly provided for in international treaties'[5] or in customary international law.

4. The aforementioned principles undoubtedly apply in the high seas and in sea areas seawards of the outer limit of the territorial sea of coastal States.[6] The fourth sentence of Section 21.01 is devoted to the status of foreign vessels in sea areas in which the coastal State enjoys territorial sovereignty, i.e. internal waters, archipelagic waters, and the territorial sea.

(a) Within their internal waters coastal States enjoy full territorial sovereignty. Without prejudice to the right of distress entry, foreign vessels are allowed to enter the internal waters of a foreign State only with that State's permission. Vessels in foreign ports or other parts of the internal waters (e.g. juridical and historic bays) are subjected to the domestic law of the coastal State. Therefore, the coastal State is entitled to apply and enforce its domestic law against foreign vessels present in that State's internal waters. An exception only applies with regard to warships and other State ships enjoying sovereign immunity.[7]

[2] US Supreme Court, *Lauritzen v Larsen* (1953) 345 US 571.

[3] It may be recalled that the PCIJ, in the *Lotus* case, stated that 'a ship on the highs seas is assimilated to the territory of the state the flag of which it flies', PCIJ, Judgment no. 9, The Case of the S.S.: 'Lotus', PCIJ Series A no. 10, at p. 25 (1927). This approach, i.e. regarding a ship as 'floating territory', has been rejected and has not become part of customary international law.

[4] Anglo-American Claims Commission, Award, *The Jessie, The Thomas F. Bayard and The Pescawha*, Nielsen's Report (1926), 479 *et seq.*

[5] Art. 92(1) UNCLOS.

[6] Arts 91 *et seq.* UNCLOS apply not only to high seas areas in the technical sense but, according to Arts 58(2) and 78(2) UNCLOS, also in the exclusive economic zone (EEZ) and in the superjacent waters over the continental shelf of foreign States. Subject to the limited rights enjoyed by coastal States the same holds true for the contiguous zone of foreign States.

[7] On the one hand, foreign warships are obliged to respect the coastal State's domestic legal order. On the other hand, an exercise of jurisdiction against a warship is prohibited. Warships in foreign internal waters may not be subjected to judicial proceedings or any enforcement measure, including foreclosure, capture, or search. The exercise of criminal jurisdiction is prohibited even if in response to criminal acts committed against the host nation or its nationals. The commander and the crew may not be prosecuted if they leave the warship for visits on land. However, if members of the crew have left the

(b) In the territorial sea and, where applicable, the archipelagic waters the territorial sovereignty of coastal (or archipelagic) States is subject to the right of innocent passage.[8] Accordingly, the coastal (archipelagic) State's right to apply and enforce its domestic law is limited by the applicable rules of UNCLOS. **21.01**

5. Without prejudice to the inherent right of self-defence, the right of coastal States to interfere within their territorial sea with foreign vessels is regulated in Articles 25, 27, and 28 UNCLOS. According to Article 27 UNCLOS the coastal State may exercise its criminal jurisdiction on board a foreign ship, i.e. it may arrest persons, conduct investigations, and temporarily detain the vessel, if crimes have been committed on board during passage. In view of the fact that coastal States are entitled to prescribe laws and regulations over, *inter alia*, customs, fiscal, immigration, and sanitary measures,[9] enforcement measures taken against vessels suspected of being engaged in criminal activities (e.g. drug smuggling) or in activities supporting—directly or indirectly—transnational terrorism or the proliferation of weapons of mass destruction, do not pose any problems. If the coastal State has enacted legislation prohibiting such activities it would be in a position to enforce these regulations against suspect vessels. It may, however, not be left out of consideration that the mere breach of the domestic criminal law of the coastal State will justify the exercise of its criminal jurisdiction only in cases where the crime has been committed on board a ship passing through the territorial sea after leaving the coastal State's internal waters.[10] If the vessel concerned has not left a port of the coastal State, criminal jurisdiction, according to Article 27(1) UNCLOS, may be exercised only if:

(a) the consequences of the crime extend to the coastal State;
(b) the crime is of a kind to disturb the peace of the country or the good order of the territorial sea;
(c) the assistance of the local authorities has been requested by the master of the ship or by a diplomatic agent or consular officer of the flag State; or
(d) such measures are necessary for the suppression of illicit traffic in narcotic drugs or psychotropic substances.

6. In the context of MIO directed against illicit activities not expressly mentioned in Article 27(1) UNCLOS (e.g. counter-proliferation and counter-terrorism operations) the coastal State will be obliged to prove that the prohibited conduct meets the conditions of either lit. (a) or lit. (b). In view of the fact that the coastal State's

ship for other than official purposes and if they have committed a criminal or other act contrary to the host nation's domestic laws they are no longer protected, unless there is a special agreement exempting them from the host nation's jurisdiction. See C.J. Colombos, *The International Law of the Sea*, 6th rev. edn (London: Longmans, 1967), 275.

[8] See Arts 17 *et seq.* (territorial sea) and 52 UNCLOS (archipelagic waters).

[9] Art. 21(1) UNCLOS. [10] Art. 27(2) UNCLOS.

21.01 enforcement jurisdiction in the territorial sea is, in principle, complete[11] and in view of the dangerous character of such activities the coastal State will in most cases be in a position to provide sufficient evidence that the said conditions are met. If the crime has been committed before entry into the territorial sea and if the vessel, proceeding from a foreign port, is only passing through the territorial sea without entering internal waters, the coastal State may not take any steps on board the ship.[12] However, this rule will in most cases not be an obstacle for MIO because terrorist or proliferation activities as well as any contribution to such activities, constitute a permanent crime, i.e. the perpetration continues during passage. Moreover, it is important to observe that according to Article 25(1) UNCLOS, the coastal State 'may take the necessary steps in its territorial sea to prevent passage which is not innocent'. According to Article 19 UNCLOS passage is not innocent if it is 'prejudicial to the peace, good order or security of the coastal State' or if the vessel is engaged in one of the activities listed in Article 19(2) UNCLOS. In case of terrorist activities, including support of transnational terrorism, it will not be difficult to conclude that the conditions laid down in Article 19(1) UNCLOS are met. This, however, seems less than clear if a vessel is suspected of being engaged in illicit proliferation activities. The transport of missiles and of WMD is not mentioned in Article 19(2) UNCLOS, which according to the US and other States, is 'an exhaustive list of activities that would render passage not innocent'.[13] Accordingly, some authors have serious doubts as to whether interdiction measures may be based upon the assumption of the non-innocent character of the transport of WMD.[14] However, this position has its merits only if the focus is laid on UNCLOS alone. It should be noted that according to Security Council Resolution 1540[15] 'proliferation of nuclear, chemical and biological weapons, as well as their means of delivery, constitutes a threat to international peace and security'. Therefore, it 'should be relatively unproblematic [...] for coastal states to justify any interference with the right of innocent passage when there is a reasonable basis for suspicion that they are involved in proliferation'.[16] Although the coastal State's reaction, according to Article 25(1) UNCLOS, will be limited to 'preventing' such innocent

[11] R.R. Churchill and A.V. Lowe, *The Law of the Sea*, 3rd edn (Manchester: Manchester University Press, 1999) at 98 *et seq*.; Ch. Schaller, *Die Unterbindung des Seetransports von Massenvernichtungswaffen, SWP-Studie* (Berlin: SWP, May 2004), 11.

[12] Art. 27(5) UNCLOS. Note, however, that this restriction does not apply to cases provided for in Part XII UNCLOS on the protection of the marine environment or with respect to violations of laws and regulations adopted in accordance with Part V UNCLOS on the EEZ.

[13] The rules of the UNCLOS on the territorial sea and on innocent passage are generally considered to be customary in character. Hence, they are binding on all States. For an appraisal of the customary character see especially the US–USSR Declaration of Jackson Hole of 23 September 1989, reprinted in 28 *ILM* 1444 (1989).

[14] B. Friedman, *The Proliferation Security Initiative: The Legal Challenge*, Bipartisan Security Group Policy Brief (Washington DC: Bipartisan Security Group, September 2003), 3.

[15] SC Res. 1540, 28 April 2004.

[16] D.H. Joyner, *International Law and the Proliferation of Weapons of Mass Destruction* (Oxford: Oxford University Press, 2009), 299–332; Joyner, 'The PSI and International Law', 10 *The Monitor* (Spring 2004), 7–9, at 8.

passage this does not mean that the suspect vessel may only be ordered to immediately leave the territorial sea. Such a restriction merely applies in cases of warships not complying with the coastal State's laws and regulations because warships, even if within a foreign territorial sea, enjoy sovereign immunity.[17] With regard to merchant vessels that do not enjoy sovereign immunity the coastal State will therefore be entitled to take all necessary steps, including the seizure of the vessel and of its cargo.[18] **21.01**

7. It is necessary to stress that the aforementioned rights of coastal States are also applicable in international straits and in archipelagic sea lanes. While coastal States may not hamper or otherwise impede the rights of transit passage or of archipelagic sea lanes passage the regime of passage through international straits and archipelagic sea lanes does not in other respects affect the legal status of the waters concerned or the exercise by the bordering States of their sovereignty or jurisdiction over such waters, the sea bed, subsoil, and the airspace above.[19] In conclusion, the international law of the sea offers a rather flexible legal framework that enables coastal States to exercise MIO, within their territorial sea areas, against foreign vessels, if certain preconditions are met. This certainly holds true with regard to measures taken against transnational terrorism or the proliferation of weapons of mass destruction by non-State actors. It needs to be emphasized, however, that the restrictions laid down in Article 27 UNCLOS must be observed scrupulously. Otherwise, the right of innocent passage would become an empty shell.

8. It must be added that MIO may also be based upon the rights coastal States enjoy within their respective contiguous zone. This, of course, presupposes that such a contiguous zone has been proclaimed by the coastal State. According to Article 33 UNCLOS:

> [the] coastal State may exercise the control necessary to:
> a) prevent infringements of its customs, fiscal, immigration or sanitary laws and regulations within its territory or territorial sea;
> b) punish infringements of the above laws and regulations committed within its territory or territorial sea.

It is important to stress that enforcement measures 'may be taken only in respect of offences committed within the territory or territorial sea of a State, not in respect of anything done within the contiguous zone itself'.[20]

9. According to the law of the sea, coastal States also enjoy the right of 'hot pursuit'.[21] Hence, foreign vessels that have violated the laws and regulations of the coastal State within that State's territory, internal waters, or territorial sea[22] may

[17] Art. 30 UNCLOS. Sovereign immunity of warships is recognized in Art. 236 UNCLOS. See also US Supreme Court, *The Case of The Schooner Exchange v McFadden & Others*, 11 US 116.

[18] M. Volz, *Extraterritoriale Terrorismusbekämpfung* (Berlin: Duncker & Humblot, 2007), 261 *et seq.*; Joyner, *International Law*, 310; Schaller, *Die Unterbindung*, 12.

[19] Arts 34(1) and 49(3) UNCLOS.

[20] Churchill and Lowe, *The Law of the Sea*, 137.

[21] Art. 111 UNCLOS.

[22] Churchill and Lowe, *The Law of the Sea*, 214.

21.01 be pursued and arrested on the high seas. It is important, however, that the coastal State, either under Article 27 or Article 33 UNCLOS, is indeed entitled to enforce its laws and regulations. According to Article 111(2) UNCLOS:

> [t]he right of hot pursuit shall apply *mutatis mutandis* to violations in the exclusive economic zone or on the continental shelf, including safety zones around continental shelf installations, of the laws and regulations of the coastal State applicable in accordance with this Convention to the exclusive economic zone or the continental shelf, including such safety zones.

An arrest after hot pursuit, however, is legal only if pursuit has commenced within the sea areas mentioned in Article 111(1) and (2) UNCLOS, and the pursuit has been continuous and in compliance with the further conditions laid down in that Article.

10. The last sentence of Section 21.01 is to remind naval commanders that any interference with foreign vessels must be based on one of the exceptional rules mentioned earlier or in the following Sections. Therefore, naval commanders must have sufficient knowledge of the respective legal basis. Moreover, if they are to conduct MIO within the territorial waters of their State, sound knowledge of the geographical limits is crucial. In case of doubt, naval commanders must do everything feasible to seek competent legal advice and/or advice from their superior officers and civil authorities.

21.02 **There are several legal bases available to conduct MIO, none of which is mutually exclusive. Depending on the circumstances, one or a combination of these bases can be used to justify permissive and non-permissive interference with suspect vessels. Possible legal bases for MIO are authorization by the UN Security Council (21.03), consent through either ad hoc (21.04–21.05) or general international agreements (21.06), international law of the sea (21.07–21.09) and self-defence (21.10).**

1. Apart from the rights coastal States enjoy within their internal waters and territorial sea areas vis-à-vis foreign vessels and based on the right of hot pursuit, several legal bases exist permitting the exercise of MIO, especially in high seas areas. In the following Sections authorization by the Security Council, consent through either ad hoc or international agreements, authorization based on the international law of the sea, and self-defence will be discussed.

2. That a specific legal basis may not apply in a MIO is without prejudice to the other legal bases provided by public international law. Hence, a boarding and search may for instance not be in compliance with the flag State's consent, but it may still be in accordance with international law under a separate legal basis, such as an authorization by the Security Council.

3. It may be added that it is an unsettled matter whether the legal bases explicitly dealt with in the present Section are to be considered exhaustive. That would, for

instance, not be the case if MIO could also be based on the right of counter-measures.[23] 21.02

One legal justification for maritime interception operations is authorization by the UN Security Council. Under Article 41 of the UN Charter the Security Council may authorize, *inter alia*, the 'complete or partial interruption of economic relations and of rail, sea, air, postal, telegraphic, radio, and other means of communication'. 21.03

1. *Authorization by the Security Council* can provide a legal basis for MIO. On a number of occasions the Security Council has authorized States to prevent the transport of, *inter alia*, arms, other military material, or oil to a certain State or region. For example, on 20 November 1965, the Security Council adopted Resolution 217 in which the Council called upon:

> all States to refrain from any action which would assist and encourage the illegal régime and, in particular, to desist from providing it with arms, equipment and military material, and to do their utmost in order to break all economic relations with Southern Rhodesia, including an embargo on oil and petroleum products.

It also called 'upon the Government of the United Kingdom to enforce urgently and with vigour all the measures it has announced, as well as those mentioned [. . .] above'. From 1966 on, the Royal Navy, on the basis of Resolution 217, conducted a MIO that became known as the 'Beira Patrol'.[24] On 25 August 1990, the Security Council, in Resolution 665, called upon:

> those Member States co-operating with the Government of Kuwait which are deploying maritime forces to the area to use such measures commensurate to the specific circumstances as may be necessary under the authority of the Security Council to halt all inward and outward maritime shipping, in order to inspect and verify their cargoes and destinations and to ensure strict implementation of the provisions related to such shipping laid down in resolution 661 (1990).

With regard to sanctions against Yugoslavia, on 25 September 1991, the Security Council, in Resolution 713, decided:

> under Chapter VII of the Charter of the United Nations, that all States shall, for the purposes of establishing peace and stability in Yugoslavia, immediately implement a general and complete embargo on all deliveries of weapons and military equipment to Yugoslavia until the Security Council decides otherwise following consultation between the Secretary-General and the Government of Yugoslavia.

[23] For a position to that effect in the context of counter-proliferation operations see W. Heintschel von Heinegg, 'The Proliferation Security Initiative–Security vs. Freedom of Navigation?' 35 *Israel Yearbook of Human Rights* (2005), 181–203, at 198 *et seq.*

[24] See R. Mobley, 'The Beira Patrol: Britain's Broken Blockade against Rhodesia', 55 *Naval War College Review* (2002), 63–84.

21.03 These sanctions were tightened by Resolution 757 of 30 May 1992. NATO ships and Maritime Patrol Aircraft (MPA) began monitoring operations in the Adriatic Sea which were undertaken in support of the UN arms embargo against all republics of the former Yugoslavia under Resolutions 713 and 757. With regard to Haiti, on 16 June 1993, the Security Council, in Resolution 841, decided:

> to prohibit any and all traffic from entering the territory or territorial sea of Haiti carrying petroleum or petroleum products, or arms and related material of all types, including weapons and ammunition, military vehicles and equipment, police equipment and spare parts for the aforementioned.

A more recent example of Security Council authorization for MIO has been the MIO off the coast of Libya. On 17 March 2011, the Security Council, in Resolution 1973:

> [c]alls upon all Member States, in particular States of the region, acting nationally or through regional organisations or arrangements, in order to ensure strict implementation of the arms embargo established by paragraphs 9 and 10 of resolution 1970 (2011), to inspect in their territory, including seaports and airports, and on the high seas, vessels and aircraft bound to or from the Libyan Arab Jamahiriya, if the State concerned has information that provides reasonable grounds to believe that the cargo contains items the supply, sale, transfer or export of which is prohibited by paragraphs 9 or 10 of resolution 1970 (2011) as modified by this resolution, including the provision of armed mercenary personnel, calls upon all flag States of such vessels and aircraft to cooperate with such inspections and authorises Member States to use all measures commensurate to the specific circumstances to carry out such inspections;

A week after the adoption of the Resolution NATO started *Operation Unified Protector* (OUP) of which naval operations to enforce the embargo were part.[25]

2. It is today generally accepted that the Security Council, in exercising its powers under Chapter VII of the Charter, enjoys a wide margin of discretion. Therefore, the Council is entitled to characterize the situation between two or more States or within a single State as a threat to the peace and to make use of the full spectrum of preventive or enforcement measures provided for by Chapter VII. *Inter alia*, the Council may authorize Member States to take all necessary measures to enforce its decisions. Such authorization will, therefore, constitute a clear legal basis for MIO. Of course, exact knowledge of the content of the relevant resolutions is crucial. Naval commanders should consult their legal advisors and must undertake everything feasible to fully understand which measures have been authorized by the Security Council.

3. It is, however, important to keep in mind that within the context of the UN collective security system an authorization may also be based upon the consent of a State. This was, for example, the case with UNIFIL,[26] and is of continued

[25] See M.D. Fink, 'UN-mandated Maritime Arms Embargo Operations in Operation Unified Protector', 50(1–2) *Revue de Droit Militaire et de Droit de la Guerre* (2011), 237–60.

[26] SC Res. 1701, 11 August 2006.

importance for the counter-piracy operations conducted off the coast of Somalia (see Section 21.08). In such situations exact knowledge of the respective governments' consent may be as important as knowledge of the relevant resolution. In a peacekeeping operation, such as UNIFIL, the forces will act on a mandate (as distinct from an authorization). Mandated operations will be executed under the authority of the UN Secretary General (or his Special Representative) and under supervision and control by Department of Peacekeeping Operations (DPKO). Peacekeeping forces must then strictly observe the rules of engagement that may have been issued by DPKO. **21.03**

As a general rule ships are subject to the jurisdiction of their flag State. As such, the flag State has the right to authorize officials of another State to board vessels flying its flag. Care shall be taken to identify and comply with the limits of the flag State's consent. Consent to board a vessel does not automatically extend to inspection or search of the vessel or to the seizure of persons or cargo. Commanders need to be aware of the exact nature and extent of flag State consent prior to conducting interceptions at sea. **21.04**

1. *Consent* by the flag State of the vessel can also serve as a legal basis for the interception, boarding, and search of foreign merchant vessels. Such consent may be given on a case-by-case basis or in a general and advance manner by a multilateral or bilateral treaty (see Section 21.06).

2. Exact knowledge of the content of the flag State's consent is of overall importance. Any measure not covered by such consent will, *prima facie*, be a violation of the flag State's sovereignty. For example, a flag State may have consented to the boarding of its merchant vessels for the sole purpose of inspecting the ship's documents. Hence, a search of the vessel and its cargo would not be covered by the flag State's consent in such a case.

21.05

(a) **Commanders, via the chain of command, may seek ad hoc consent to board a vessel from a particular State. A consensual boarding is conducted at the invitation of the master (or person in charge) of a vessel that is not otherwise subject to the jurisdiction of the boarding officer. The plenary authority of the master over all activities related to the operation of the vessel while in international waters is well established in international law and includes the authority to allow anyone to come aboard the vessel as a guest, including foreign law enforcement officials. However, some States do not recognize a master's authority to assent to a consensual boarding.**

(b) **The voluntary consent of the master permits the boarding, but it does not allow the assertion of law enforcement authority. A consensual boarding is not, therefore, an exercise of maritime law enforcement jurisdiction *per se*. The scope and duration of a consensual boarding may be subject to conditions imposed by the master and may be**

21.05 **terminated by the master at his discretion. Nevertheless, such boardings have utility in allowing rapid verification of the legitimacy of a vessel's voyage by obtaining or confirming vessel documents, cargo, and navigation records without undue delay to the boarded vessel.**

1. Lit. (a) provides that, despite the fact that some States do not recognize such consent, master's consent, according to the position taken in the present Handbook, provides a sufficient legal basis for the boarding of a foreign vessel.

2. It is made clear in lit. (b), however, that master's consent does not necessarily go beyond the boarding of the vessel concerned. Moreover, it is emphasized that master's consent may not be considered a legal basis for any form of law enforcement. Rather, it serves as a tool to verify a vessel's true character and its destination, thus enabling the intercepting forces to exclude them from further measures. It is very important to observe that the master of a foreign merchant vessel is under no obligation to consent to the boarding of his ship. Such consent is always voluntary and may be limited or terminated as the master may consider appropriate. If withdrawn, the forces are obliged to immediately leave the ship. It may be added however that, for example, during Operation Enduring Freedom most boardings have been consensual and most effective with a view to verifying the true character of the intercepted vessels.

21.06 **Flag State consent to board and search can be provided in advance by bilateral or multilateral agreements. Similar to agreements in the law enforcement realm nations may negotiate bilateral or multilateral agreements to obtain advance consent to board another nation's vessels for other than law enforcement purposes. Such agreements greatly expedite the process by which officials of one State can board suspect vessels of another State.**

1. Flag State consent to board and search foreign merchant vessels can be provided in advance using *bilateral or multilateral agreements*. States can conclude bilateral treaties permitting the States parties to board and inspect merchant vessels flying their respective flags. Such agreements greatly expedite the process by which officials from one State can board suspect vessels of another State. For a long time, those bilateral agreements related primarily to counter-drug operations. However, as part of the Proliferation Security Initiative (PSI),[27] a multinational undertaking currently supported by some 95 States and the Holy See, the US has begun to conclude bilateral agreements that enable 'warships and other vessels of the Parties, or of third States as may be agreed upon by the Parties' to board merchant vessels if there are reasonable grounds for suspicion that they are engaged in the illicit transport of weapons of mass destruction, including their delivery

[27] See Interdiction Principles for the Security Proliferation Initiative (4 September 2003), <http://www.state.gov/t/isn/c27726.htm>.

systems and related materials. States having entered into such bilateral agreements **21.06**
with the US include Panama,[28] Liberia,[29] and Cyprus,[30] i.e. more than 60 per cent of world tonnage.[31]

2. Another example of prior consent by a multilateral treaty is the 1988 Convention for the Suppression of Unlawful Acts Against the Safety of Maritime Navigation (SUA Convention), as amended by the 2005 Protocol.[32] The basis for conducting lawful boardings of suspect foreign vessels at sea has been enhanced by the provisions of the 2005 Protocol. The SUA Convention, as amended by the 2005 Protocol, *inter alia,* provides that a foreign merchant vessel encountered on the high seas and suspected of being involved in either of the offences specified in Article 3, 3*bis*, 3*ter*, or 3*quater*, may be boarded and searched with the express authorization of the flag State.[33] This is a clear recognition of the flag State principle and, initially, does not seem to enhance the possibilities of other States to interfere with foreign merchant vessels. However, Article 8*bis*(5) also provides *inter alia*:

> (d) Upon or after depositing its instrument of ratification, acceptance, approval or accession, a State Party may notify the Secretary-General that, with respect to ships flying its flag or displaying its mark of registry, the requesting Party is granted authorization to board and search the ship, its cargo and persons on board, and to question the persons on board in order to locate and examine documentation of its nationality and determine if an offence set forth in article 3, 3*bis*, 3*ter* or 3*quater* has been, is being or is about to be committed, if there is no response from the first Party within four hours of acknowledgement of receipt of a request to confirm nationality.

[28] Amendment to the Supplementary Arrangement between the Government of the United States of America and the Government of Panama to the Arrangement between the Government of the United States of America and the Government of Panama for Support and Assistance from the United States Coast Guard for National Maritime Service of the Ministry of Government and Justice, Washington, DC, 12 May 2004.

[29] Agreement between the Government of the United States of America and the Government of the Republic of Liberia Concerning Cooperation to Suppress the Proliferation of Weapons of Mass Destruction, Their Delivery Systems, and Related Materials by Sea, Washington, DC, 11 February 2004, <http://www.state.gov/t/isn/trty/32403.htm>.

[30] Agreement Between the Government of the United States of America and the Government of the Republic of Cyprus Concerning Cooperation to Suppress the Proliferation of Weapons of Mass Destruction, Their Delivery Systems, and Related Materials By Sea, Washington, DC, 25 July 2005.

[31] See M. Byers, 'Proliferation Security Initiative (PSI)', *Max Planck Encyclopedia of Public International Law*, <http://www.mpepil.com>; R. Alcaro, N. Pirozzi, and N. Ronzitti, 'The Global Initiative and Other Multilateral Initiatives and Partnerships Against Nuclear Terrorism', in N. Ronzitti (ed.), *Coordinating Global and Regional Efforts to Combat WMD Terrorism* (Rome: Istituto Affari Internazionali, 2009), 75–111, at 84–95; W. Heintschel von Heinegg, 'The Proliferation Security Initiative'.

[32] Convention for the Suppression of Unlawful Acts against the Safety of Maritime Navigation, Done at Rome, 10 March 1988 (entry into force 1 March 1992); Protocol of 1988 Relating to Fixed Platforms Located on the Continental Shelf. Protocol of 2005 to the Convention for the Suppression of Unlawful Acts against the Safety of Maritime Navigation, London, 14 October 2005; Protocol of 2005 to the Protocol for the Suppression of Unlawful Acts against the Safety of Fixed Platform Located on the Continental Shelf, London, 14 October 2005.

[33] Art. 8*bis*(5) of the SUA Convention as amended by the 2005 Protocol.

21.06 (e) Upon or after depositing its instrument of ratification, acceptance, approval or accession, a State Party may notify the Secretary-General that, with respect to ships flying its flag or displaying its mark of registry, the requesting Party is authorized to board and search a ship, its cargo and persons on board, and to question the persons on board in order to determine if an offence set forth in article 3, 3*bis*, 3*ter* or 3*quater* has been, is being or is about to be committed.

Hence, the novelty and enhancement brought about by the SUA Convention, as amended by the 2005 Protocol, is to be seen in the fact that flag States may give prior and general consent to the boarding and search of merchant vessels flying their flags. It remains to be seen whether States parties will make use of Article 8*bis*(5)(d) or (e).

21.07 **International law allows non-permissive interference with ships where there are reasonable grounds to suspect that the ship is engaged in, *inter alia*, piracy, slave trade, or unauthorized broadcasting. If a warship encounters a foreign-flagged vessel on the high seas, it may board the ship without the flag State's or master's consent if there are reasonable grounds to suspect that the ship is engaged in one of these unauthorized activities.**

1. Sections 21.07 to 21.09 are primarily based on the right of visit laid down in Article 110 UNCLOS, which applies if there are reasonable grounds for suspecting that a vessel is either engaged in any of the activities stated in Article 110 UNCLOS, or if it is without nationality or in fact has the same nationality as the intercepting warship.

2. It follows from the first sentence of Article 110(2) UNCLOS that the right of visit is limited to the verification of 'the ship's right to fly its flag'. This means that the intercepting warship is allowed to take only those measures which are necessary to verify whether the grounds for suspicion prove to be founded. The second sentence of Article 110(2) UNCLOS provides that:

> to this end, it may send a boat [or an aircraft][34] under the command of an officer to the suspected ship. If suspicion remains after the documents have been checked, it may proceed to a further examination on board the ship, which must be carried out with all possible consideration.

Unfortunately, Article 110 UNCLOS gives no further guidance as to the further measures that may be taken against a vessel if the suspicions prove to be well-founded. However, with regard to piracy, Article 105 UNCLOS provides: 'On the high seas, or in any other place outside the jurisdiction of any State, every State may seize a pirate ship or aircraft, or a ship or aircraft taken by piracy and under the control of pirates, and arrest the persons and seize the property on board.' Hence, there are good reasons to argue that those measures may also be taken against a

[34] According to Art. 110(4) UNCLOS 'these provisions apply *mutatis mutandis* to military aircraft'.

foreign vessel if the suspicions that they are engaged in or any of the other activities prove to be well-founded. 21.07

3. The boarding may only be exercised vis-à-vis ships and aircraft when there are *reasonable grounds for suspicion* that they are engaged in one of the activities. In general, it is obvious that foreign vessels can never be boarded at the discretion of the naval commander. Rather, a boarding and further measures are made dependent upon the existence of reasonable grounds for suspicion that the vessel concerned is engaged in an activity characterized as illicit, for instance under UNCLOS, an agreement, or a Security Council resolution. 'Reasonable grounds' implies, however, that the responsible naval commander may rely on information that does not amount to sufficient or clear evidence. If the information is such that every reasonable person will affirm the probability of an illicit activity, the naval commander is entitled to take measures to verify whether such a probability continues to exist.

4. If the suspicions prove to be unfounded the vessel must be allowed to proceed immediately. If the boarded vessel has not committed any act justifying the suspicions, the vessel 'shall be compensated for any loss or damage that may have been sustained'.[35] This articles may also be a reminder for naval commanders—as also stated in Section 21.01—that boarding a foreign flagged vessel and subsequently arresting persons must be seen as exceptional in public international law and should not take the decision to board all too lightly.[36] It may be added that Article 106 UNCLOS specifically states that seizures of vessels on suspicion of piracy without adequate grounds leads to liability of the State for any loss or damage done caused by the seizure.

Piracy is any illegal act of violence, or detention or any other act of depredation, committed for private ends by the crew or the passengers of a private ship, and directed on the high seas, against another ship, or against persons or property on board such ship in a place outside the jurisdiction of a state. If there are reasonable grounds for suspicion that a vessel is engaged in piracy, it may be boarded and captured. The persons on board may be arrested, the cargo may be seized. The exercise of those rights is limited to warships or other State vessels. Pirate-suspects may be prosecuted before the seizing State's courts. States should have a domestic legal framework, which allows for the prosecution of acts of piracy and which enables naval personnel to act in a law enforcement capacity. States do not have an obligation to prosecute or extradite suspect pirates. States shall, however, cooperate to the fullest possible extent in the repression 21.08

[35] Art. 110(3) UNCLOS.

[36] P. Wendel, *State Responsibility for Interferences with the Freedom of Navigation in Public International Law* (Berlin: Springer, 2007), 113.

21.08 **of piracy. In the conduct of counter-piracy operations, force may be used only to that degree, which is permissible for law enforcement activities.**

1. This Section is based on the UNCLOS provisions on piracy, which reflect customary international law.[37] The first sentence refers to the definition of piracy as defined by Article 101 UNCLOS. It emphasizes the four key conditions of an act of piracy in international law: An illegal act of violence, detention, or depredation; committed for private ends; on the high seas; and against another vessel or persons on board that vessel. The limiting geographical condition in the definition effectively limits the definition of piracy to those acts that are committed outside the territorial sea of a State.[38] It is therefore important to note that acts of armed robbery at sea or other acts of violence committed with the territorial sea (or archipelagic and internal waters) of another State do not constitute acts of piracy. Only the coastal State concerned is entitled to take measures against vessels, and persons in such crimes. Of course, the UN Security Council, the flag State, and the affected coastal State may authorize measures against acts of piracy. Whereas the condition of private ends is often argued in the context of the question whether terrorist activities may fall under piracy, in which political acts are seen as the opposite of private ends, another view is that this condition makes a distinction between private acts and acts of a State (public acts), in which the latter are vessels that are commissioned by a State.[39]

2. Article 110(1) UNCLOS states that warships may board vessels suspected of being engaged in piracy. Article 107 UNCLOS extends the authority to seize on account of piracy also to State vessels. Article 105 UNCLOS establishes universal jurisdiction on the act of piracy, against which every State may seize a pirate ship or a ship taken by pirates, arrest the persons, and seize the property on board. This article effectively deals with the exclusive jurisdiction of the flag State over a vessel to suppress acts of piracy, as consent of the flag State is not needed.

3. Article 105 also states that piracy may be prosecuted before the seizing State's courts. For States to enforce universal jurisdiction, however, they must also have domestic legislation that enables them to take measures against piracy. Important issues in the domestic legal framework to consider are criminalizing piracy under national laws, the authority to act extraterritorially against the criminal act through the use of the military, who are generally not automatically also authorized to conduct law enforcement actions. Domestic legislation and procedural systems to authorize a warship commander to act in a law enforcement capacity role should therefore also be in place. Furthermore, to better facilitate prosecution efforts for

[37] Arts 100–107, 110 UNCLOS.

[38] Article 58(2) UNCLOS makes the provisions on piracy also applicable in an EEZ.

[39] D. Guilfoyle, Treaty Jurisdiction over Pirates: A compilation of legal texts with introductory notes prepared for the 3rd meeting of Working Group 2 on legal issues of the Contact Group off the coast of Somalia, Copenhagen, 27–29 August 2009, 3.

the conviction of pirate suspects, the crews should be trained in criminal law enforcement standards and procedures, for instance with regard to evidence collecting. These issues have proven to be challenging during the counter-piracy operations off the coast of Somalia, which emphasize that successful prosecution of piracy needs both international and national legal frameworks. As the report of the Special Advisor to the Secretary General on legal issues related to piracy off the coast of Somalia noted: 'Failure to criminalize piracy in domestic laws is the first obstacle to effective prosecution.'[40] **21.08**

4. UNCLOS neither contains an obligation to prosecute, nor an obligation to extradite pirate suspects to a State that could have jurisdiction over the criminal act. It only provides a general clause that States shall cooperate with each other to the fullest extent possible to repress piracy.[41] Naval operations off the coast of Somalia have shown that such cooperation between States can range from multinational naval operations for the suppression of piracy in a region, to transfer-agreements for the prosecution of pirate suspects,[42] to vessel protection detachment (VPD) agreements to be placed on board foreign flagged vessels,[43] but also to use of foreign territory and ports to logistically enable bringing pirate suspects before a domestic court.[44] Article 105 UNCLOS, on the other hand, also poses no restriction on transfer of pirate suspects to be tried by other States, nor does it prohibit States that were not the capturing State from exercising jurisdiction. Possible legal issues that may, however, arise with regard to the transfer of pirate suspects may be found in applicable human rights law rather than in the law of the sea, such as with the *non-refoulement* principle. Counter-piracy operations are law enforcement operations that are governed by applicable human rights law. Next to legal issues that may arise out of transferring pirate suspects, the applicability of human rights law also has consequences for the procedural treatment of detained pirate suspects, such as that the individual's human rights would not be observed if the detained suspect is not brought promptly before a judge. It may be added here that detailed procedures and authorities for detaining pirate suspects may differ between the existing multinational counter-piracy operations. Specific rules of engagement on detention will apply per operation on how to proceed to detain and process suspect pirates.

[40] S/2011/30, Report of the Special Advisor to the Secretary General on legal issues related to piracy off the coast of Somalia, annexed to the letter of the UNSG to the UNSC, dated 24 January 2011, at para. 46.

[41] Art. 100 UNCLOS.

[42] See, for example, the transfer agreement between the EU and Mauritius; Agreement between the European Union and the Republic of Mauritius on the conditions of transfer of suspected pirates and associated seized property from the European Union-led naval force to the Republic of Mauritius and on the conditions of suspected pirates after transfer, 14 July 2011.

[43] Malta, for example, concluded an MOU in 2010 with the Netherlands to embark a Maltese VPD-team on board a Netherlands warship.

[44] For example, the EU concluded a status of forces agreement with Djibouti (EU Council Decision, 2009/88/CFSP, 22 December 2008) to support the EU counter-piracy efforts.

21.08 5. The legal basis of the counter-piracy operations[45] off the coast of Somalia consists of a combination of Security Council resolutions,[46] Host State consent, and the law of the sea. As regards operations in the high seas directed against pirates there was no necessity for an authorization by the Security Council since, under Articles 105 and 110, warships (and other State ships) of all States have the right to visit and search vessels and aircraft suspected of piracy, to seize the vessel (or aircraft) and to arrest the persons on board. However, as regards acts of armed robbery at sea (as distinct from piracy) or measures taken against pirates within the territory (including the territorial sea) of a third country the law of the sea provides no legal basis. Therefore, it was important that the Security Council, in paragraph 7 of Resolution 1816 (2008) decided that:

> [...] States cooperating with the TFG[47] in the fight against piracy and armed robbery at sea off the coast of Somalia, for which advance notification has been provided by the TFG to the Secretary-General, may:
>
> (a) Enter the territorial waters of Somalia for the purpose of repressing acts of piracy and armed robbery at sea, in a manner consistent with such action permitted on the high seas with respect to piracy under relevant international law; and
>
> (b) Use, within the territorial waters of Somalia, in a manner consistent with action permitted on the high seas with respect to piracy under relevant international law, all necessary means to repress acts of piracy and armed robbery.

Moreover, in paragraph 6 of Resolution 1851 (2008), the Security Council decided that:

> [...] States and regional organizations cooperating in the fight against piracy and armed robbery at sea off the coast of Somalia for which advance notification has been provided by the TFG to the Secretary-General may undertake all necessary measures that are appropriate in Somalia, for the purpose of suppressing acts of piracy and armed robbery at sea, pursuant to the request of the TFG, provided, however, that any measures undertaken pursuant to the authority of this paragraph shall be undertaken consistent with applicable international humanitarian and human rights law.

6. The last sentence of this Section emphasizes that the degree of force authorized during counter-piracy operations is the force permissible for law enforcement activities.[48] The force necessary to affect an arrest must adhere to the general conditions set out in Section 21.12. It needs to be emphasized that the reference made in the resolutions on piracy to international humanitarian law does not imply

[45] In 2015, several counter-piracy operations are active to suppress piracy off the coast of Somalia. Next to the NATO (Ocean Shield) and EU (Atalanta) naval operations against piracy, the US-led Combined Maritime Force (CMF) and several individual States also make efforts to act against piracy in this region.

[46] SC Res. 1814 (2008), 1816 (2008), 1838 (2008), 1844 (2008), 1846 (2008), 1851 (2008), 1897 (2009), 1918 (2010), 1950 (2010), 1976 (2011), 2015 (2011), 2020 (2011), 2077 (2012), 2125 (2013), and 2184 (2014).

[47] Transitional Federal Government of Somalia (TFG).

[48] T. Treves, 'Piracy, Law of the Sea, and the Use of Force: Developments off the coast of Somalia', 20(2) *EJIL* (2010), 399–414.

that that body of law is applicable to counter-piracy operations. Rather, it is to be understood either as a reminder that the fight against pirates and armed robbers at sea within the territory of Somalia may amount to an armed conflict that is governed by international humanitarian law or as an overabundance of caution by the Security Council.[49] 21.08

Vessels that are not legitimately registered in any one State are without nationality and are referred to as stateless vessels. Such vessels are not entitled to fly the flag of any State and, because they are not entitled to the protection of any State, they are subject to the jurisdiction of all States. Additionally, a ship that sails under more than one flag, using them according to convenience, may not claim any of the nationalities in question and may be assimilated to a ship without nationality. If a warship encounters a stateless vessel or a vessel that has been assimilated to a ship without nationality on the high seas, it may board and search the vessel without the consent of the master. 21.09

1. Section 21.09 is based on Articles 92(2) and 110 UNCLOS. Vessels flying the flags of two or more States, using them according to convenience, according to Article 92(2) UNCLOS, are assimilated to vessels without nationality and may therefore be visited on the basis of Article 110 UNCLOS. Accordingly, the boarding of the *So San* by a Spanish boarding team in 2002 was legal under Article 110 UNCLOS because, at the time the vessel was intercepted, it did not fly a flag.[50] Therefore, it did not matter that there were also grounds for suspicion that the *So San* was engaged in the transport of weapons of mass destruction. As a matter of fact, during the search of the *So San* SCUD missile parts were discovered. Ultimately, however, the vessel had to be released after it had become clear that the missiles, though coming from North Korea, were destined for Yemen.

States can conduct MIO pursuant to customary international law under circumstances that would permit the exercise of the inherent right of individual and collective self-defence. 21.10

1. *Self-defence* may also provide a legal basis for MIO. Section 21.10 must not be misunderstood as dealing with situations in which a warship is under attack, or imminent attack, by another vessel or aircraft. It is self-evident that, if an armed attack occurs, the warship is entitled to defend itself with all necessary and

49 See also R. Geiß and A. Petrig, *Piracy and Armed Robbery at Sea* (2011), 131, who hold that 'this reference does not provide any clear-cut determination whether international humanitarian law does indeed apply' and conclude that 'the Security Council did not declare international humanitarian law applicable to the counter-piracy operations in the Gulf of Aden region'.

50 For the facts see 'Threats and Responses: Arms Smuggling; Scud Missiles Found on Ship of North Korea', *New York Times*, 11 December 2002, at A1; P. Kerr, 'US Stops Then Releases Shipment of N. Korean Missiles', <http://www.armscontrol.org/act/2003_01-02/yemen_janfeb03.asp>.

21.10 proportionate means. Rather, Section 21.10 has to be seen in light of the recent developments of international law with regard to the threat posed by transnational terrorism. In view of the fact that the Council has recognized the right of self-defence against terrorist attacks and that all Member States have at least acquiesced in this interpretation of Article 51 of the Charter and of the customary inherent right of individual and collective self-defence,[51] this right may very well serve as an operable legal basis for MIO and other measures taken against foreign vessels and aircraft when encountered in the high seas and in international airspace.[52] Accordingly, the States contributing to Operation *Enduring Freedom* (OEF) have based their counter-terrorism operations off the Horn of Africa and around the Arabian Peninsula (and in the Mediterranean)[53] on the right of individual and collective self-defence.[54] It should, however, not be left out of consideration that some States participating in OEF do not seem to recognize that they are allowed to interfere with foreign vessels and aircraft in disregard of the right of the flag State or State of registry. In particular, they seem to hold the view that the right of self-defence does not prevail over the flag State principle. Hence, they restrict their activities to monitoring operations and to consensual boardings. This may be due to the fact that they no longer consider themselves in a self-defence situation *stricto sensu* that is characterized by the criteria of necessity and immediacy.[55] Nevertheless, according to the position taken here, MIO may still be based on the right of self-defence alone, i.e. without the necessity of obtaining prior consent of either the master or the flag State, if there are reasonable grounds for suspicion that a vessel or aircraft is contributing to terrorist activities by, e.g. transporting terrorists, weapons destined to terrorists, or other items indirectly serving terrorist aims. Denying a continuing self-defence situation of the target States of transnational terrorism would mean an illegitimate restriction of the right of self-defence because the target States would thus be obliged to wait for the next terrorist assault that could be as disastrous as the attacks of 11 September 2001.[56] It needs to be emphasized, however, that States merely agree on the principal applicability of the right of self-defence as a legal basis for MIO. There is no agreement as to the specific measures that may be taken against suspect vessels and persons onboard. The practice of those States whose navies have taken part in counter-terrorism operations at sea is quite diverse and has

[51] See Y. Dinstein, *War, Aggression and Self-Defence*, 4th edn (Cambridge: Cambridge University. Press, 2005), 175 *et seq.*; M. Scholz, *Staatliches Selbstverteidigungsrecht gegen terroristische Gewalt* (Berlin: Duncker & Humblot, 2006), 153 *et seq.*

[52] W. Heintschel von Heinegg, 'Legality of Maritime Interception Operations within the Framework of Operation Enduring Freedom', in M. Bothe, M.E. O'Connell, and N. Ronzitti (eds), *Redefining Sovereignty—The Use of Force after the Cold War* (Ardsley: Transnational Publishers, Inc., 2005), 365 *et seq.*

[53] In the Mediterranean: 'Operation Active Endeavour'.

[54] Heintschel von Heinegg, 'Legality of Maritime', 374 *et seq.*

[55] Dinstein, *War, Aggression*, 235 *et seq.*

[56] See also W. Heintschel von Heinegg, 'Current Legal Issues in Maritime Operations: Maritime Interception Operations in the Global War on Terrorism, Exclusion Zones, Hospital Ships and Maritime Neutrality', 34 *Israel Yearbook of Human Rights* (2004), 151–78.

not contributed to the emergence of agreed-upon criteria. This explains the importance of other rights of maritime interception, as explained in this chapter. 21.10

Visit and search of vessels and aircraft must be conducted in accordance with the generally accepted principles and procedures. 21.11

1. Visit and search of vessels is usually exercised as follows:

(a) If the commander determines that there are reasonable grounds for suspicion that the vessel is engaged in an activity triggering the right of interception the vessel will be contacted by radio on an internationally recognized frequency.
(b) If the vessel does not dispose of communications equipment contact must be established by use of other appropriate and available means. It is important that communication with the vessel is in a manner or language easily comprehensible by the vessel's master or crew. The vessel may be asked to provide information about its nationality, origin, destination, its cargo, or its passengers.
(c) If the response proves insufficient for ruling out the reasonable grounds for suspicion the vessel may be ordered to stop and to allow inspection of the vessel's documents on board. Depending on the respective legal basis boarding may be exercised with or without the master's consent. The boarding team may use either one of the warship's boats or a helicopter in order to reach the suspect vessel. As soon as the boarding team is on board the commanding officer will inspect the vessel's documents. If those documents are insufficient or if other grounds for suspicion continue to exist the boarding team may, if the respective legal basis so provides, search the vessel and its cargo. It is important that, during its presence on board, the boarding team acts in a courteous and professional manner.

2. It is obvious that the procedure to be applied vis-à-vis vessels is inoperable vis-à-vis aircraft, since aircraft cannot be inspected while in the air. Therefore aircraft have to be intercepted in accordance with generally established interception procedures. ICAO has published a Manual on the interception of civil aircraft[57] that may be considered as reflecting customary international law. It is necessary to stress that under Principle 2.5 lit. a) 'interception of civil aircraft will be undertaken only as a last resort'. For example, the US Federal Aviation Administration has issued the following interception procedures:

In phase 1—approach phase—the aircraft to be intercepted will be approached from the stern by two intercepting military aircraft. At night or in Instrument Meteorological Conditions (e.g. fog), a radar trail tactic will be used.

In phase 2—identification phase—the intercepted aircraft should expect to visually acquire the lead interceptor and possibly the wingman. The wingman will assume a surveillance position while the flight leader approaches the intercepted aircraft.

[57] International Civil Aviation Organization, *Manual concerning Interception of Civil Aircraft*, 2nd edn, ICAO Doc. 9433-AN/926 (1990).

21.11 In phase 3—post-identification phase—after identification of the aircraft by type, nationality, etc., the flight leader will turn away from the intercepted aircraft. The wingman will remain well clear and accomplish a rejoin with the leader.

An aircraft which is intercepted shall immediately: (a) follow the instructions given by the intercepting aircraft, interpreting and responding to the visual signals; (b) notify, if possible, the appropriate air traffic services unit.[58]

21.12 **The use of force must be strictly limited to what is necessary and proportionate.**

1. Most of the legal bases dealt with here provide no specific guidance as to the extent of force that may be used in order to enforce an MIO. However, the applicable legal basis and corresponding legal paradigm governing the operation do provide general guidance. In the context of law enforcement activities based on the law of the sea and relevant domestic law, such as counter-narcotic and anti-piracy operations, the relevant legal regime governing the use of force is that relating to law enforcement and the use of deadly force will be restricted to situations in which armed resistance is encountered or imminent threat to the lives or safety of the arresting force or vessel or to third persons or vessels is encountered. Some additional guidance relative to the use of force in a law enforcement context can be found in Article 8*bis*(9) of the SUA Convention as amended by the 2005 Protocol:

> When carrying out the authorized actions under this article, the use of force shall be avoided except when necessary to ensure the safety of its officials and persons on board, or where the officials are obstructed in the execution of the authorized actions. Any use of force pursuant to this article shall not exceed the minimum degree of force which is necessary and reasonable in the circumstances.

While limiting the use of force to what is necessary and reasonable, it is to be considered an impressive improvement that there now exists an explicit rule authorizing the use of force for the purpose of enforcing the rights recognized under the SUA Convention.

In relation to the execution of a Security Council mandate imposing an embargo or other restrictions on navigation, the use of force will be governed by the mandate and the rules of engagement relating to the execution of the mandate. In the context of MIO operations based upon the right of (national) self-defence, the principles of necessity, and proportionality relating to self-defence will be applicable and will, in most cases, be further regulated by the applicable rules of engagement.

2. It goes without saying that the principles of necessity and proportionality are relative in character. They must be judged in the light of the respective legal basis and of the aims legitimately pursued under that legal basis. In the context of MIO, those principles certainly provide a legal yardstick that differs from similar concepts

[58] US Federal Aviation Administration, National Security and Interception procedures, 5-6-2, <https://www.faa.gov/news/safety_briefing/2002/media/janfeb2002.pdf>.

under the right of self-defence and the law of armed conflict. In other words: the use of force is strictly limited to that degree that is necessary to overcome resistance against the exercise of an interception, a boarding, an inspection, or an order to proceed on a given course. Deadly force will, therefore, be the exception rather than the rule. It needs to be emphasized that this also holds true for MIO based on an authorization by the UN Security Council, e.g. establishing an embargo against a given State. The use of deadly force will be necessary and proportionate in exceptional cases only. However, in exceptional cases if resistance by a vessel or aircraft rises to the level of an armed attack the right of (unit) self-defence would become applicable—not the rules providing the legal basis for an MIO. **21.12**

3. Regularly, the naval commander will be operating under rules of engagement that will contain detailed provisions on when which kind of force may be employed in order to achieve a certain aim. There are, however, some general observations that can be made with regard to the use of force in the course of MIO. If, under the applicable legal basis, vessels are obliged to obey an order to stop in order to be subjected to visit and search, non-compliance with an order to stop may be answered by warning shots. In accordance with the principle of proportionality, the first shot may not be fired into the direction of the vessel. If the first warning shot remains unheeded the second warning shot may be fired across the vessel's bow. If the vessel continues on its course the warship is entitled to use incapacitating force, i.e. to use that degree of force that is necessary to prevent the vessel from escaping from the area. Usually, a shot into the rudder will be in compliance with the applicable law. If, under the applicable law, the intercepted vessel is obliged to tolerate visit and search any act of resistance against the boarding or search of the vessel may be overcome by physical force or by the use of non-lethal weapons.

4. It is necessary to stress that the force dealt with in Section 21.12 is that force used to enforce the rights of the intercepting warship, i.e. the rights of visit, search, and, if that is provided for by the respective legal basis, arrest or seizure. Accordingly, Section 21.12 is without prejudice to the inherent right of self-defence. In case of an armed attack, or of an imminent armed attack, against the boarding team the use of deadly force is permissible.

The provisions of the present Chapter are without prejudice to belligerent rights at sea. **21.13**

As already stated in the commentary to Section 21.01 MIO are naval operations not governed by the law of international armed conflict. Therefore, the restrictions that have to be observed when conducting MIO under the present Section do not apply under the law of armed conflict. For example, under the law of international armed conflict, enemy merchant vessels are liable to capture simply because they possess enemy nationality. No further grounds are necessary for an exercise of the belligerent right of capture.

Chapter 22

LEGAL DIMENSIONS OF SPECIAL OPERATIONS AND INFORMATION OPERATIONS

22.1 Legal Dimensions of Special Operations

22.01 **There is no legal prohibition in using special operations forces (SOF) in military operations. Importantly, there is no special law for special operations forces. SOF, like conventional forces, must fully comply with international law, and applicable domestic law, in all their operations.**

1. Most of today's military forces include special operations forces (SOF). There is no legal prohibition to using SOF in international military operations. The distinctive nature of Special Operations (SO) often requires specialized legal knowledge and experience to react and respond to the unique SOF challenges. Frequently, SOF missions are characterized as 'no failure' ones of 'last resort'. In this stressful context, vigilance must be maintained by military commanders, individual members of a force, and legal advisors to identify and resolve legal issues and operational challenges. However, despite the use of the term 'special', it is important to note that there is no special law for SOF. Like conventional military forces, SOF must comply with international law, and where applicable, national and host nation law, in all of their operations.[1]

2. SO are characterized by qualities that distinguish them from regular operations. Generally, most SO are conducted by SOF. SOF organizations usually consist of small units containing specially selected personnel that are organized, equipped, and trained to conduct high-risk, high-value special military operations to achieve strategic and operational objectives and effects. SOF achieve their missions by using special and unique operational tactics, techniques, and procedures (TTPs) often in hostile, denied, or politically or diplomatically sensitive areas during times of peace or conflict. The success or failure of SOF missions often has a direct and immediate impact on national and international interests.

[1] See G. Walsh, 'Role of the Judge Advocate in Special Operations', 4 *The Army Lawyer* (August 1989), 5.

3. SO core activities usually consist of the following which can be conducted in times of peace or conflict: Direct Action (DA), Counter-Terrorism (CT), Counter-Insurgency (COIN), Counter-proliferation (CP), Special Reconnaissance (SR), Defence, Diplomacy, and Military Assistance (DDMA), Combat Search and Rescue (CSAR) and Hostage Rescue, Close Personal Protection (CPP), Psychological Operations (PSYOPs), and Information Operations (IO). These are commonly described as follows:[2] **22.01**

(a) *Direct Action (DA).* DA operations are short duration precision attacks and other precise small-scale offensive actions conducted by SOF to seize, destroy, capture, exploit, recover, or damage designated lawful targets. Direct action differs from conventional offensive actions in the level of operational, legal and political risk, operational TTPs, and the degree of highly discriminate and precise use of force to achieve specific strategic and operational objectives and effects.
(b) *Counter-Terrorism (CT).* CT operations are offensive and defensive measures taken to prevent, deter, mitigate, pre-empt, and respond to terrorism. CT missions are usually offensive actions such as hostage rescue, recovery of sensitive material, or strikes at terrorist infrastructure.
(c) *Counter-Insurgency (COIN).* COIN operations are offensive and defensive measures taken to prevent, deter, mitigate, pre-empt, and respond to insurgency. Broadly, 'insurgency' is an organized movement aimed at the overthrow of a constituted government through the use of subversion and violence which often rises to the level of armed conflict.
(d) *Counter-proliferation (CP).* CP operations are actions to limit the possession, use, acquisition, or transit of weapons of mass destruction (WMD). It includes actions to locate, seize, capture, and recover WMD and, in some cases, prevent the unlawful use of materials.
(e) *Special Reconnaissance (SR).* SR operations are conducted to collect or verify information of strategic or operational significance. These actions complement and refine other collection methods but are normally directed upon highly significant, and often time-sensitive, areas or targets of interest.
(f) *Defence, Diplomacy, and Military Assistance (DDMA).* DDMA operations contribute to nation building through assistance to designated states through the provision of specialized military advice, training, and assistance.
(g) *Combat Search and Rescue (CSAR)* and Hostage Rescue CSAR and hostage rescue operations are conducted to recover military personnel or civilians in

[2] See Canadian Special Operations Forces Command (CANSOFCOM), *An Overview, CANSOFCOM Tasks, available at* <http://www.forces.gc.ca/en/operations-special-forces/index.page>; US Joint Chiefs of Staff Joint Publication 3-05 (16 July 2014), *Doctrine For Special Operations*, II-2–II-18; ADRP 3-05, at <http://www.dtic.mil/doctrine/new_pubs/jp3_05.pdf>; *US Army Reference Doctrine Publication Special Operations* (2012), 2-1 ff at <http://armypubs.army.mil/doctrine/DR_pubs/dr_a/pdf/adp3_05.pdf>; see NATO SOF at <http://www.nato.int/cps/en/natolive/topics_105950.htm>.

22.01 distress during times of peace, tension, or conflict. CSAR often involves the entry into hostile or denied territory, sea, or airspace.

(h) *Close Personal Protection (CPP).* CPP operations are offensive and defensive measures taken to prevent, deter, mitigate, pre-empt, and respond to threats and attacks against designated military personnel and civilians.

(i) *Psychological Operations (PSYOPs).* PSYOPs are conducted to shape and influence attitudes and behaviour affecting the achievement of political and military objectives and effects.

(j) *Information Operations (IO).* IO actions are taken to shape and influence an adversary's information and information systems while defending one's own information and information systems.[3]

It is important to note that the abovementioned types of SO can be conducted within the context of any of the legal bases for operations covered in Parts II and III of this Handbook. These categories are descriptive from the point of view of SO military doctrine and the function of the particular operation can fit into any of the legal categories in this Handbook (i.e. (peace) enforcement, self-defence, peace operations and so on). Some SO may be more likely to be used in certain legal categories than others. For example, DA, CT, and CP operations would be most likely to fall within the legal categories of either (peace) enforcement or self-defence operations. COIN operations would most likely fall within the legal categories of (peace) enforcement and intervention by invitation. Others, such as DDMA, SR, CPP, PSYOPS, and IO, could be conducted within the context of all the legal categories in the Handbook, including consensual peace operations. While SOF are often better equipped and trained to conduct the above-noted operations, they may be also conducted by conventional forces.

4. While SO are subject to the same laws as conventional operations the operational and legal challenges are different and, frequently, unique. The legal issues associated with SO are most often related to the nature of the operational risks and special requirements involved with their largely unique operations as noted earlier. Some of the SOF operational issues that often pose legal challenges are use of force/rules of engagement (ROE), targeting, intelligence gathering, use of weapons, equipment, and uniforms. These issues may arise during times of peace, tension, and conflict. Therefore, the application, as matter or law or policy, of international humanitarian law (IHL) or the law of armed conflict (LOAC) and international human rights law will always be an important consideration for decision-makers (civilian and military), military operators, and legal advisors involved in SO.

5. Frequently, SOF DA operations require the killing or capturing of a specific individual. Often the killing of such an individual is labelled an 'assassination' or a

[3] See sub-Chapter 22.2, 'Legal Dimensions of Information Operations'.

'targeted killing'.[4] If the killing is conducted in accordance with applicable law, particularly IHL, then it is not an assassination, and therefore, not prohibited.[5] 22.01

6. SOF are often concerned about being discovered or compromised by a civilian (normally a non-combatant or non-hostile) entity during SO, especially during DA, SR, and CSAR. It must be emphasized that there is no 'SOF exception' to the law in this area. Therefore, compromise alone never justifies the killing of a civilian.[6] Depending on the legal basis for the operation and the ROE, it may be permissible to capture and detain such a person, to evacuate the person, or to temporarily incapacitate the person using non-deadly force. However, if the civilian is taking a direct part in hostilities or demonstrates a hostile act or hostile intent sufficient to engage the right of self-defence, then SOF ROE would most probably permit the use of necessary and proportional force against the person.[7]

7. Another potentially challenging legal issue for SOF is the question of the use of riot control agents (RCAs—usually CS gas and pepper spray as non-deadly uses of force) during operations, particularly for CSAR and SR during armed conflict operations. Essentially, the Chemical Weapons Convention prohibits the use of RCAs as a 'method of warfare'.[8] However, it does permit the use of RCAs for law enforcement, including domestic riot control purposes.[9] Therefore, it raises the question of whether military forces can use RCAs during international armed conflict, particularly for crowd control, CSAR, and SR.[10] This is a controversial issue because the lack of an ability to use RCAs may push militaries to consider the

[4] Generally, 'assassination' means the killing or wounding of a selected non-combatant for a political or religious motive. See Canadian Forces Publication B-GJ-005-104/FP-021 *Law of Armed Conflict at the Operational and Tactical Levels, GL-2;* also Walsh, 'Role of the Judge Advocate', 8. See Chapter 17 of this Handbook for a detailed discussion on 'targeted killing'.

[5] It is not forbidden to send a detachment or individual members of the armed forces to kill, by sudden attack, a person who is a combatant or a person who has taken a direct part in hostilites unless the attack is 'treacherous', 'perfidious', or otherwise prohibited under applicable national or international law. See Canadian Forces Publication B-GJ-005-104/FP-021 *Law of Armed Conflict at the Operational and Tactical Levels*, 6-4; also Walsh, 'Role of the Judge Advocate', 8 and Chapter 17 of this Manual, 'Targeted Killings in Operational Law Perspective'.

[6] G. McLoone, 'Sledgehammers, Scalpels and Software: Special Operations and the Law of War in the 21st Century', 12 *U.S. A.F. Acad. J. Legal Stud.* (2002–2003), 130–69; Walsh, 'Role of the Judge Advocate', 4 which indicate that the killing of a civilian in a compromise circumstance would, on its face, constitute a breach and, likely, a war crime.

[7] See Chapter 24 'Force Protection, Unit Self-Defence, and Personal Self-Defence: Their Relationship to Rules of Engagement'.

[8] Arts I(5) and II(7) CWC—The use of riot control agents, including tear gas and other gases that have debilitating but non-permanent effects, as a means of warfare is prohibited.

[9] Art. II(9) CWC—Law enforcement including domestic riot control purposes.

[10] For example, US Executive Order 11850 (available at: <http://www.archives.gov/federal-register/codification/executive-order/11850.html>) renounces first use of RCA in international armed conflicts except in defensive military modes to save lives, such as: controlling riots in areas under direct and distinct US military control, to include rioting prisoners of war; dispersing civilians where the enemy uses them to mask or screen an attack; rescue missions for downed pilots/passengers and escaping POWs in remotely isolated areas; and, in our rear echelon areas outside the zone of immediate combat, to protect convoys from civil disturbances, terrorists, and paramilitary organizations.

22.01 use of deadly force to control crowds or during CSAR and SR operations. Nonetheless, caution dictates that any uses of RCAs that could be reasonably perceived as a 'method of warfare' should be avoided.

8. A similar controversy surrounds the use of soft point or hollow-point ammunition during SO in armed conflict. Such ammunition is commonly used by national law enforcement authorities, including during domestic counter-terrorist operations. However, as a starting position, the use of such ammunition by military forces in armed conflict is prohibited as it is viewed as causing 'superfluous injury' and 'unnecessary suffering'.[11] There is also some controversy regarding 'open tip' or 'matchking' ammunition. Many forces, such as the US, view the prohibition on hollow point/soft-nosed military projectiles as not prohibiting the use of full-metal jacketed projectiles that yaw or fragment, or 'open tip' rifle projectiles containing a tiny aperture to increase accuracy.[12] 'Open tip' or 'matchking' ammunition does not function like a hollow or soft point and is not designed to cause expansion. It can be lawful for use across the conflict spectrum, including SO (effective for snipers), but shall not be modified, such as through further opening the tiny aperture to increase the possibility of expansion.[13] Nonetheless, as with the use of RCAs, caution dictates that any uses of ammunition that expands, or could reasonably be perceived as expanding, against hostile entities during armed conflict must be avoided.

9. Another legal challenge for SO is avoiding 'treachery' or 'perfidy', which are prohibited acts under IHL or LOAC.[14] Generally, 'perfidious' and 'treacherous' acts are those which invite the confidence of adversaries and lead them to believe that SOF are entitled to protection or are obliged to grant protection under the IHL or LOAC with intent to betray that confidence. In other words, 'perfidy' and 'treachery' consist of unlawfully committing a hostile act under the cover of a legal

[11] Hollow point or soft point ammunition contains projectiles with either a hollow point boring into the lead core, or exposed lead core that flatten easily in the human body. They are designed to expand dramatically upon impact at all ranges. This ammunition is prohibited for use in international armed conflict against lawful enemy combatants, see IV 3 Hague Declaration Concerning Expanding Bullets (29 July 1899), 1 (Supplement) *AJIL* (1907), 157, 157–9; St Petersburg Declaration Renouncing the Use, in Time of War, of Explosive Projectiles Under 400 Grammes Weight (11 December 1868), 1 (Supplement) *AJIL* (1907), 95; and Art. 23(e) Hague Regulations (18 October 1907), 36 Stat. 2277 (1907), T.S. No. 539, 3 *Martens Nouveau Recueil* (ser. 3) 461, reprinted in 2 *AJIL* (1908), 90. See also J.-M. Henckaerts and L. Doswald-Beck, *Customary International Humanitarian Law* (Cambridge: Cambridge University Press, 2005), Rules 77 and 78.

[12] US Army JAG *Operational Law Handbook* (2014), JA 422, 34.

[13] Ibid. See also W.H. Parks, 'Memorandum for Commander, United States Army Special Operations Command—Subject: Sniper Use of Open-Tip Ammunition' (23 September 1985) and 'Memorandum for Commander, United States Army Special Operations Command—Subject: Sniper Use of Open-Tip Ammunition—Memorandum of Law' (12 October 1990), both memos on file with the author. Also, R.C. Burton, 'Recent Issues With The Use of Matchking Bullets And White Phosphorous Weapons In Iraq', 19 *Army Lawyer* (August 2006), 19–22 for discussion of the legality of open tip or matchking ammunition.

[14] Art. 23(b) Hague Regulations, Art. 37(1) AP I. See Henckaerts and Doswald-Beck, *Customary International,* Rules 62, 63, and 65.

protection. This issue often arises in the context of SOF using uniforms or camouflage, which are different from those used by conventional forces, during their operations. SOF frequently use different non-standard uniforms, camouflage patterns, or civilian clothes as legitimate ruses or means of deception during operations, including during armed conflict.[15] 22.01

10. However, SOF must be careful to avoid using uniforms, camouflage patterns, and especially civilian clothes, which fail to distinguish them from the civilian population. If they fail to so distinguish themselves they may expose themselves to being accused of committing war crimes such as perfidious acts. Moreover, they can be denied prisoner-of-war status and tried by the capturing authority as spies. This is an issue that military personnel and legal advisors must constantly monitor to ensure mission success is achieved in compliance with the law.

11. Like conventional military forces, SOF must comply with international law and applicable national and host nation law in all of their operations. As stated previously there is no 'special exception' or 'special law' for SOF. However, it must be recognized that, while conventional forces face legal and operational challenges, the distinctive nature of SO often require specialized legal knowledge and experience to react and respond to the unique challenges to SOF. Legal advisors provide SOF commanders and decision-makers with the information and legal analysis they need to help evaluate options, assess risks, and make informed decisions. Accordingly, it is critical that SOF commanders at all levels seek, and have immediate access to legal advice to assist in the planning, execution, and review of SOF missions.

22.2 Legal Dimensions of Information Operations

All information operations (IO) conducted by military forces must comply with international law, and, where applicable, domestic law. 22.02

A. Basic Overview and Terminology of IO

1. Information itself is a strategic resource vital to national security. Information and its flow are fundamental to the sovereignty of a nation. Today's societies are dependent on a sophisticated civil/military information infrastructure that underpins

[15] See W.H. Parks, 'Special Forces' Wear of Non-Standard Uniforms', 4 *Chi. J. Int'l L.* (2003), 493–560, G. McLoone, 'Sledgehammers'; Walsh, 'Role of the Judge Advocate'; R.D. Drone, 'Non-Traditional Uniforms Do Accord Prisoner of War Status For Special Operations Forces', thesis submitted to George Washington University Law School (31 August 2003), available at: <http://www.fas.org/man/eprint/drone.pdf> W.H. Ferrell III, 'No Shirt, No Shoes, No Status: Uniforms, Distinction and Special Operations in International Armed Conflict', 178 *Military Law Review* (2003), 94–140. See also Henckaerts and Doswald-Beck, *Customary International*, Rule 57: 'Ruses of war are not prohibited as long as they do not infringe a rule of international humanitarian law.'

22.02 every aspect of society in most developed countries. Accordingly, more and more complex information systems are being integrated into all aspects of today's military operations. Increasingly, command, transport, logistics, intelligence, and weapon systems rely heavily on computers, satellite communications, and a host of electronic systems. Generally, the use of such systems by the military is described as 'information operations' (IO).[16]

2. There is also an emerging concept of 'influence operations'.[17] Essentially, influence operations are similar to IO in that they are centred on affecting the perceptions and behaviours of others, usually the adversary. However, 'influence operations' tend to be focused at the strategic level by using a wide variety of capabilities in attempting to shape the perceptions and behaviours of leaders, groups, or entire populations.[18] IO function at all levels—strategic, operational, and tactical—and are focused on the use and protection of systems. Influence operations employ both military and civilian IO capabilities to achieve the desired effect. Therefore, influence operations and IO are closely related. While both concepts are still developing, IO is currently a more mature and a better understood concept. Also both concepts are heavily linked to the concept of 'cyberspace'. Generally, cyberspace has emerged as the newest domain for the conduct of military operations, including IO and influence operations. Such operations are broadly labelled 'military cyber operations'. There is much overlap in the concepts of IO and cyber operations. The focus of this Section will be on IO rather than on influence operations or cyber operations. See Chapter 23 of this Handbook for a detailed discussion of military cyber operations.

3. When IO systems are deployed on operations, they often reach back to higher levels of command and can interact with other national and international (public and private) systems. The systems are not fully reliable, and, with ever increasing use, they become vulnerable to attack and exploitation. These vulnerabilities are

[16] Many States' Armed Forces have Information Operations Doctrine and Policy which generally describe 'IO' as noted here. See United States Joint Chiefs of Staff Publication 3–13, *Information Operations* (27 November 2012), ix, available at <http://www.dtic.mil/doctrine/jel/new_pubs/jp3_13.pdf> (hereinafter US JOINT PUB. 3-13); and United Kingdom Ministry of Defence Joint Warfare Publication 3-80 *Information Operations* (June 2002), available at <http://ics.leeds.ac.uk/papers/pmt/exhibits/2270/jwp3_80.pdf>. NATO's IO doctrine is Allied Joint Publication (AJP) 3.10 at <https://info.publicintelligence.net/NATO-IO.pdf>.

[17] See e.g. UK Chiefs of Staff (2010) Joint Doctrine Publication 04 (JDP 04) Understanding, December 2010, at: <https://www.gov.uk/government/publications/jdp-04-understanding>; and P.A.L. Ducheine, 'Non-kinetic Targeting: Complementing the Kinetic Prevalence to Targeting', in Ducheine, Schmitt and Osinga (eds), *Targeting: The Challenges of Modern Warfare* (The Hague: TMC Asser Press/Springer, 2015).

[18] See B.M. Ward, 'Strategic Influence Operations - The Information Connection', US Army War College Strategy Research Project, Carlisle Barracks, Pennsylvania (7 April 2003), available at <http://www.fas.org/irp/eprint/ward.pdf>; B.D. Adams, 'Military Influence Operations: Review of Relevant Scientific Literature', Defence Research and Development Canada (DRDC) (Department of National Defence, Toronto no. CR 2007-146, November 2007), available at <http://cradpdf.drdc.gc.ca/PDFS/unc69/p528897.pdf>.

two-sided: they provide opportunities to exploit an adversary's IO systems and, simultaneously, they make a State's systems susceptible to exploitation. This results in both an offensive and a defensive aspect to IO. **22.02**

4. As the concept of IO is relatively new, and somewhat complex, it is no surprise that there are many legal issues and challenges arising in this expanding field. In order to address some of the key legal challenges, it is necessary to understand the core and related capabilities of IO which are used in times of peace, tension, and conflict. Commonly, the core capabilities are: psychological operations (PSYOPs), military deception operations (MILDECOPS), electronic warfare (EW), and computer network operations (CNO). Supporting capabilities include: operations security (OPSEC), counter-intelligence (CI), public affairs (PA), and civil-military operations (CMO).[19] These are generally described as follows:

(a) *Psychological Operations (PSYOPS).* PSYOPS are actions to convey selected information and indicators to a variety of audiences. They are primarily designed to shape and influence emotions, motives, reasoning, and ultimately, the behaviour of foreign governments, organizations, groups, and individuals. The purpose of PSYOPs is to achieve an effect which is favourable to the originator's objectives. While PSYOPs should usually deal with truthful information, during armed conflict operations international humanitarian law (IHL) or the law of armed conflict (LOAC) permits legitimate ruses or deceptions, as long as they do not amount to 'treachery' or 'perfidy'.

(b) *Military Deception Operations (MILDECOPS).* MILDECOPS are those actions at the strategic, operational, and tactical levels that are designed to mislead the adversary by manipulation, distortion, or falsification of evidence to induce the adversary to react in a manner prejudicial to that adversary's interests. There are many ways in which a force can conduct MILDECOPS. The most common examples consist of physical means (i.e. ruses such as dummy and decoy equipment and camouflage) and technical means (i.e. use and manipulation of digital photography and electronic signals). As with PSYOPs, during armed conflict operations, IHL or the LOAC permit legitimate MILDECOPS (ruses or deceptions), as long as they do not amount to 'treachery' or 'perfidy'. Normally, MILDECOPS shall not intentionally target or mislead the military forces' own government, citizens, or media.

(c) *Electronic Warfare (EW).* EW is an action that exploits the electromagnetic (EM) spectrum. EW encompasses the interception and identification of electromagnetic emissions, the employment of electromagnetic energy, including directed energy, to reduce or prevent hostile use of the electromagnetic spectrum. It also includes actions to ensure its effective use by a State's military forces.

[19] There may be some differences amongst States on IO core and supporting capabilities, but they are generally grouped as described here. See US Joint Publication 3-13, CF Info Ops Manual and UK JWP 3-80.

22.02 The three main subdivisions of EW are electronic warfare attack (EA), electronic warfare support measures (ESM), and electronic protection measures (EPM). These are generally described as follows:

(i) *Electronic Warfare Attack (EA).* EA involves the use of EM energy, directed energy, or anti-radiation weapons to attack lawful objectives (e.g. personnel, property, areas, facilities, or equipment) with the intent of degrading, neutralizing, or destroying an adversary's capabilities;
(ii) *Electronic Warfare Support Measures (ESM).* ESM consists of measures to search for, intercept, identify, and locate sources of radiated EM energy for the purpose of threat recognition, targeting, planning, and the conduct of future operations;
(iii) *Electronic Protection Measures (EPM).* EPM consists of measures to protect personnel, facilities, and equipment from any effects of the use of the EM spectrum that degrade, neutralize, or destroy a State's capabilities.

(d) *Computer Network Operations (CNOs).* CNOs are actions to disrupt, deny, degrade, deceive, exploit, or destroy information resident in any information system, or the information system itself. It also consists of the defence of a State's own electronic information and infrastructure. CNO are usually divided into computer network attack (CNA), computer network defence (CND), and computer network exploitation (CNE). CNO may also include EW:

(i) *Computer Network Attack (CNA).* CNA is action using computer networks to disrupt, deny, degrade, or destroy information resident in computers and computer networks, or the computers and the networks themselves.
(ii) *Computer Network Defence (CND).* CND is action using computer networks to protect, monitor, analyse, detect, and respond to unauthorized activity within and exploitation of a State's information systems and computer networks.
(iii) *Computer Network Exploitation (CNE).* CNE is action which enables information gathering and intelligence collection through the use of computer networks.

(e) *Operations Security (OPSEC).* OPSEC is action to ensure that military forces establish and maintain an appropriate level of security, using passive or active means, to deny the adversary knowledge of the forces' plans and capabilities.

(f) *Counterintelligence (CI).* CI is action to identify and counteract the threat to security posed by hostile entities or by individuals engaged in espionage, sabotage, subversion, or terrorism.

(g) *Public Affairs (PA).* PA is action directed at both external and internal audiences who are interested in military affairs. PA's principal focus is to inform domestic and international audiences of military operations. Transparency, credibility, and truthfulness are key elements to conducting PA, including during operations.

(h) *Civil-Military Operations (CMO).* CMO are actions to establish, maintain, influence, or shape relations between military forces, governments, non-governmental organizations, and the civilian population. CMO can be particularly effective and influential in peacetime and pre/post-conflict stability or nation-building operations when other capabilities and actions may be limited or non-existent. 22.02

It is important to note that the abovementioned types of IO can be conducted within the context of any of the legal bases for operations covered in Parts II and III of this Handbook. These categories are descriptive from the point of view of IO military doctrine and the function of the particular operation can fit into any of the legal categories in this Handbook (i.e. (peace) enforcement, self-defence, peace operations and so on). Some IO may be more likely to be used in certain legal categories than others. For example, CNA, EW, PSYOPS, CI, and MILDECOPS would be most likely to fall within the legal categories of either (peace) enforcement or self-defence operations. Others, such as PA and CMO would be conducted during consensual peace operations. However it is unlikely that IO, such as CNA, PSYOPS, and MILDECOPS, would be conducted during consensual peace operations as they would probably be perceived as conflicting with principles of neutrality and transparency.

5. Within the context of these above-noted core and related IO capabilities, military forces can conduct both 'offensive' and 'defensive' IO. Offensive IO includes actions taken to influence actual or potential adversarial decision-makers. This may be accomplished by affecting the adversary's use of or access to information and information systems.

6. Defensive IO includes action taken to protect one's own information and ensure a State's or organization's decision-makers have timely access to necessary, relevant, and accurate information. Defensive IO also ensures that information systems are protected from any hostile acts or threats.

7. Normally, the military information infrastructure is a shared or interconnected system of computers, communications, data, security, and other information systems serving national and international needs. The military system connects mission support, command and control (C2), and intelligence computers through voice, telecommunications, imagery, video, and multimedia services. It also includes C2, tactical, intelligence, and commercial systems used to transmit military information.[20]

8. IO occurs in a complex and global environment. There are no fixed boundaries in the information universe. Open and interconnected systems are merging into a rapidly expanding global information system (GIS) that includes individual national information infrastructures. The GIS incorporates all the systems of industry, government, academia, commercial networks, and switching systems. Often, military information infrastructures are embedded in the national

[20] See, for example, US Joint Pub 3-13, CF Info Ops Manual and UK JWP 3-80.

22.02 infrastructures. Accordingly, it is virtually impossible to consistently distinguish the military information infrastructures from the civilian ones.

9. There is a wide spectrum of uses for IO. In today's complex security environment, IO plays a significant and important role in conducting military operations. For example, an IO operation might include efforts to influence, manipulate, or neutralize an adversary's key leadership, strategic communications, military infrastructure, civil infrastructure (including industry, financial, and populace) along with an adversary's weapon systems. The type of IO could range from a mere temporary jamming of communications or dissemination of false information, to lethal manipulations of weapons electronics systems to massive interference with the infrastructure of a State. Therefore, a variety of key legal issues and challenges exist in the conduct of IO in times of peace, tension, and conflict.[21]

B. Conclusion

10. How current principles of international law will be applied to IO by the international community is still evolving. Much will depend on the development of State practice and how the international community responds to the particular circumstances of an IO attack, usually in the domain of cyberspace. It is probable that the international community will be more interested in the consequences or effects of Offensive IO than in the means used to create the effects. There is little doubt that Offensive IO, particularly in cyberspace, can cause significant human casualties, property, and economic damage on the same scale as kinetic uses of force.

11. IO is a complex and quickly expanding area of operations that is often related to military cyber operations and has immediate effects at the strategic, operational, and tactical levels. IO is often conducted by using special, sensitive, and unique operational tactics, techniques, and procedures (TTPs) to influence or shape the perceptions and behaviours of adversaries, leaders, groups, or entire populations during times of peace, tension, or conflict. The success or failure of IO missions often has a direct and immediate impact on national and international interests. This, when combined with the complex operational and security environment in

[21] For an overview of *jus ad bellum* (recourse to the use of State force) and *jus in bello* (largely IHL or LOAC) legal issues arising from IO see Chapter 23 'Military Cyber Operations'; M. Schmitt, 'Computer Network Attack and the Use of Force in International Law: Thoughts on a Normative Framework', 37 *The Columbia Journal of Transnational Law* (1999), 885–937; M. Schmitt, 'Wired Warfare: Computer Network Attack and *Jus in Bello*', 84(846) *International Review of the Red Cross* (June 2002), 365–98; G. Walker, 'Information Warfare and the Law of Neutrality', 33 *Vanderbilt Journal of Transnational Law* (November 2000), 1079–202; S. Shackleford, 'From Nuclear War to Net War: Analogizing Cyber Attacks in International Law', 25(3) *Berkeley Journal of International Law* (2009), 191–251; K. Dörmann, *Applicability of the Additional Protocols to Computer Network Attacks* (Geneva: ICRC, November 2004), <http://www.icrc.org/Web/eng/siteeng0.nsf/htmlall/68LG92/$File/ApplicabilityofIHLtoCNA.pdf>; and W.G. Sharp Sr., *Cyberspace and the Use of Force* (Falls Church, VA: Aegis Research Corporation, 1999).

which today's militaries operate, makes it vital for decision-makers, commanders, and legal advisors to understand the basic concepts and capabilities of IO and associated legal issues.[22] **22.02**

12. In many respects, the law, both national and international, related to IO is challenged to keep pace with evolving IO technology. For example, it can be difficult to conceptualize the application of *jus ad bellum* and *jus in bello* principles (which are largely based on hostilities using kinetic weapons) to IO (which largely is based on non-kinetic systems, see Chapter 23 'Military Cyber Operations' for more detailed discussion of such legal challenges). IO is, and will continue to be, an important component of international military operations, including UN operations. IO is clearly an area that could affect mission success and require a solid understanding of the technology and the legal framework. Accordingly, military planners and legal advisors must remain vigilant in understanding IO technology and capabilities. Moreover, they must recognize the application and interrelationship of national, Host State, and international law to the conduct of IO and must ensure that all IO comply with the law.

[22] The complexity and importance of IO were underscored with the recent establishment in 2006 of the North Atlantic Treaty Organization (NATO) Cooperative Cyber Defence Centre of Excellence (CCD COE) in Tallinn, Estonia. The CCD COE mission is to enhance the capability, cooperation, and information sharing among NATO, NATO nations, and partners in cyber defence by virtue of education, research and development, lessons learned, and consultation. The CCD COE vision is to be the main source of expertise in the field of cooperative cyber defence by accumulating, creating, and disseminating knowledge in related matters within NATO, NATO nations, and partners. CCD COE core areas of research include: Legal and Policy; Concepts and Strategy; Tactical Environment; and Critical Information Infrastructure Protection. Of note, in 2007 the CCD COE conducted an analysis of the cyber attacks against Estonia (see above in this footnote). See also the CCD COE website at <https://ccdcoe.org>.

Chapter 23

MILITARY CYBER OPERATIONS

23.01 **Military cyber operations refer to the employment of cyber capabilities with the primary purpose of achieving *military* goals in or by the use of cyberspace.**

1. Military Cyber Operations (MCO) could be briefly described as 'Cyber Operations conducted by armed forces'.[1] Yet, this rather inconclusive definition fails to address the crucial element of 'cyber operations'. Cyber operations are often referred to as cyber warfare.[2] Cyber operations have been explicitly and implicitly described by States,[3] non-governmental organizations[4] and other authors,[5] mixing cyber war

[1] See the definition of 'Military Operations' as defined in the Glossary.

[2] See (Netherlands) Advisory Council on International Affairs (AIV) and (Netherlands) Advisory Committee on Issues of Public International Law (CAVV), 'Cyber Warfare (Report no. 77/22, 2011)' (hereafter: AIV and CAVV), at <http://aiv-advice.nl/6ct/publications/advisory-reports/cyber-warfare>, 9; and Paul Cornish et al., 'On Cyber Warfare' Chatham House, at <http://www.chathamhouse.org/sites/files/chathamhouse/public/Research/International%20Security/r1110_cyberwarfare.pdf> 37. Both volumes use warfare as a term referring to the art of war, in which military operations are planned, mounted and executed. See also: M.N. Schmitt (ed.), *Tallinn Manual on the International Law applicable to Cyber Warfare: Prepared by the International Group of Experts at the Invitation of the NATO Cooperative Cyber Defence Centre of Excellence* (Cambridge: Cambridge University Press, 2013), 5 (hereafter: The Tallinn Manual), using cyber warfare in a 'purely descriptive, non-normative sense' and referring to 'cyber-to-cyber operations' only. However, cyber warfare is the narrower form of cyber operations, see M. Roscini, *Cyber Operations and the Use of Force in International Law* (Oxford: Oxford University Press, 2014), 11.

[3] e.g. Belgium, *Cyber Security Strategy* (Français-Dutch, 2012); and Italy, *National Strategic Framework for Cyberspace Security* (Presidency of the Council of Ministers (December), 2013), both using cyber war(fare). The US Department of Defense, 'Joint Publication Cyberspace Operations (JP 3-12 (R))' (Joint Chiefs of Staff, 2013) <http://www.dtic.mil/doctrine/new_pubs/jp3_12R.pdf>, v and I-1, used cyberspace operations.

[4] ICRC, International Humanitarian Law and the challenges of contemporary armed conflicts, Report prepared by the ICRC for the 31st International Conference of the Red Cross and Red Crescent (2011(31IC/11/512)), 36: 'Cyber operations can be broadly described as operations against or via a computer or a computer system through a data stream. Such operations can aim to do different things, for instance to infiltrate a system and collect, export, destroy, change, or encrypt data or to trigger, alter or otherwise manipulate processes controlled by the infiltrated computer system. By these means, a variety of "targets" in the real world can be destroyed, altered or disrupted, such as industries, infrastructures, telecommunications, or financial systems.'

[5] Tallinn Manual, 258; Markus Maybaum, 'Technical Methods, Techniques, Tools and Effects of Cyber Operations', in Katharina Ziolkowski (ed.), *Peacetime Regime for State Activities in Cyberspace International Law, International Relations and Diplomacy* (NATO CCDCOE, 2013), 104; Roscini, *Cyber Operations*, 10; Paul A.L. Ducheine, 'The Notion of Cyber Operations', in N. Tsagourias and R. Buchan (eds), *The Research Handbook on the International Law and Cyberspace* (Cheltenham: Edward Elgar, 2015), 211–32 at 213.

PAUL A.L. DUCHEINE

or warfare and cyber or cyberspace operations. These descriptions vary on a number of parameters: locus, purpose, targets, means and methods, and effects, which will be explored later on. 23.01

Following this Handbook's prevalence and focus on operations which include operations undertaken both within and outside the context of an armed conflict the notion of operations will be used here as well.[6] Though the goal of military operations may vary to a large extent and may include the 'confiscation' of information, whilst 'theft' and 'espionage' (other than intelligence gathering as part of military operations) fall outside the scope of this Handbook's description.[7] MCO could therefore be described as the employment by the armed forces of cyber capabilities with the primary purpose of achieving military goals in or by the use of cyberspace.

2. Cyberspace, although often discussed and commented upon, is as yet poorly understood.[8] The precise meaning of cyberspace is often ill defined, unclear, or lacking at all.[9] Cyberspace shares tangible elements with conventional physical domains of air, land, sea, and space,[10] but is unique as it also contains non-physical or virtual elements. When defined,[11] three approaches with corresponding layers within this space can be recognized. The first focuses on the virtual, digital, and logical layer mainly concentrating on data and software,[12] the second also recognizes a physical layer with the tangible ICT infrastructure used to communicate and connect,[13] and some also acknowledge a social layer with humans as part of cyberspace.[14] These approaches are echoed in multi-layered representations of cyberspace used by some States, universities, and authors.[15] Understanding this multi-layered system is essential for grasping the technological and

[6] See Chapter 2 'History and Development of the International Law of Military Operations'.

[7] Note however, that MCO could be planned and executed in response to such activities.

[8] Paul A.L. Ducheine and Jelle van Haaster, 'Fighting Power, Targeting and Cyber Operations', in P. Brangetto, M. Maybaum, and J. Stinissen (eds), *Proceedings of the 6th International Conference on Cyber Conflict* (CCDCOE, 2014) (hereafter referred to as Brangetto et al. in 6th CCDCOE Proceedings), 303–27, at 309.

[9] See e.g. the Tallinn Manual, in which cyberspace is not defined.

[10] US Army Training and Doctrine Command, *TRADOC Pamphlet 525-7-8 Cyberspace Operations Concept Capability Plan 2016–2028* (Issued 22 February 2010) (hereafter referred to as TRADOC), 9.

[11] See the Cyber Definitions page on: CCDCOE, 'Cyber Definitions' (2014) <https://ccdcoe.org/cyber-definitions.html>, listing 19 different definitions used by 16 States and 3 non-state actors; ITU, International Organization for Standardization and International Electrotechnical Commission (IOS-IEC), and Oxford Dictionary.

[12] D.J. Betz and T. Stevens, *Cyberspace and the State* (Adelphi Series, 2011), 36: the 'exclusive' model.

[13] Ibid. 37: the 'inclusive' model, e.g. AIV and CAVV, 12: 'the sum of all ICT equipment and services [comprising] not only [. . .] the internet but also all the networks and other digital devices that are not connected to the internet'; and Cornish et al., 'On Cyber Warfare', 1: 'the global digital communication and information transfer infrastructure'.

[14] See the definitions of cyberspace used by Hungary, India, the International Organization for Standardization and International Electrotechnical Commission, the ITU, and CCDCOE.

[15] E.g. US Department of Defense, 'Joint Publication Cyberspace', I-3; P. Rosenzweig, *Cyber Warfare—How Conflicts in Cyberspace Are Challenging America and Changing the World* (Santa Barbara: Praeger, 2013), 19; P.T. Beaudette, 'Legal Framework for Cyber Operations' (Brown University, Department of Computer Sciences) <http://cs.brown.edu/courses/cs180/lectures/Cyber_Law_for_Law_Students_120207.pdf>.

23.01

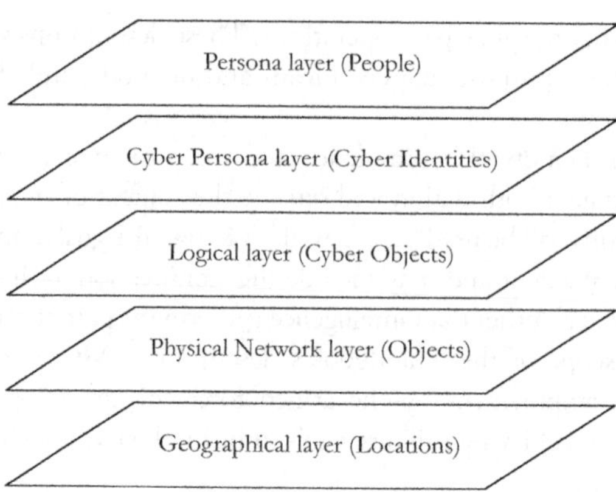

Figure 3 Cyberspace as a five layered system

military-operational drivers for the various legal issues that arise with cyber operations. These issues comprise targeting (purpose, targets, desired effects, collateral damage, means, and methods), as well as general issues such as attribution and jurisdiction.

In its most comprehensive form, cyberspace can be described by using five interrelated (sub)layers (see Figure 3).[16] At the bottom is the geographic layer, that is, the physical location of physical elements (objects and people) of the network. As a consequence, these physical elements are subject to the legal systems, such as jurisdiction, of various geographic entities, i.e. States.

Next is the physical network layer, with linked hardware and the physical infrastructure, such as computers, routers, cables, servers etc., in other words: tangible objects.

On top of these two 'real world' layers come two virtual layers. First, the logical layer comprising the operating systems, applications, other software and data, information and content.[17] These virtual elements or 'cyber objects'[18] are stored, placed, or transiting on/over the physical network infrastructure throughout its various geographical locations. Secondly, the cyber persona layer, with its email addresses, social media accounts etc., but also smart house and electric grid identities.[19] These virtual 'cyber identities'[20] enable people (in the top level persona layer) to connect to the logical layer.

16 Rosenzweig, *Cyber Warfare*, 20; D. Raymond et al. (eds), 'Key Terrain in Cyberspace: Seeking the High Ground', in P. Brangetto et al. in 6th CCDCOE Proceedings, 292, and The Netherlands (updated) Defence Cyber Strategy (2015), in *Kamerstukken II* (Parliamentary Papers) 2014–2015, 33 321, nr. 5. The US Department of Defense, 'Joint Publication Cyberspace', I-3, uses three layers with sublayers, five layers in total.

17 See H. Harrison Dinniss, 'The Nature of Objects: Targeting Networks and the challenge of defining Cyber Military Objectives', 48 *Israel Law Review* (2015, forthcoming), differentiating between content and code.

18 Ducheine and Van Haaster, 'Fighting Power', 310.

19 Rosenzweig, *Cyber Warfare*, 20.

20 Ducheine and Van Haaster, 'Fighting Power', 310.

Finally, there is the persona layer, with real people operating in the real world, using, enabling, or misusing cyberspace. **23.01**

3. Depicting cyberspace as a set of virtual and physical layers enables a proper understanding of cyber operations and their legal issues. This can be explained by looking at the operational parameters of purpose, targets, means and methods, and effects.[21] Cyber operations may serve various goals or purposes, ranging from information gathering, deception, and deterrence, to disruption and destruction.[22] They may serve offensive or defensive goals.[23]

Cyber operations differ from kinetic or information operations as they are directed against the virtual layers of cyberspace:[24] the logical network layer and the cyber persona, thus targeting and directly affecting cyber objects and/or cyber identities.[25] They may however, also produce secondary physical effects, by indirectly affecting people in the persona layer, physical objects in the physical network layer, and physical objects outside cyberspace.[26]

A number of descriptions of cyber war(fare) and cyber operations seem to focus on enemy targets only, seeking disrupting effects.[27] Others take a broader approach

[21] See Paul A.L. Ducheine, 'The Notion of Cyber Operations in International Law', in N. Tsagourias and R. Buchan (eds), *The Research Handbook on the International Law and Cyberspace* (Cheltenham: Edward Elgar Publishing, 2015), para. 6 'Operationalizing Cyber Operations'; and Brangetto et al. in 6th CCDCOE Proceedings.

[22] Roscini, *Cyber Operations*, 17; and Georg Kerschischnig, *Cyberthreats and international law* (Eleven International Publishing, 2012), 26. Also US Department of Defense, 'Joint Publication Cyberspace', vi: 'Commanders conduct cyberspace operations (CO) to retain freedom of manoeuvre in cyberspace, accomplish the joint force commander's (JFC's) objectives, deny freedom of action to adversaries, and enable other operational activities'.

[23] See e.g. Netherlands Ministry of Defence, *Defence Cyber Strategy* (2012), 5, using three goal-related categories (intelligence gathering, defence, offence) and some subcategories that are capacity and/ or effect-related (low-tech v. high tech, tactical v. strategic, see the (updated) Netherlands Defence Cyber Strategy (2015)); and US Department of Defense, 'Joint Publication Cyberspace', vii: offensive cyberspace operations, defensive cyberspace operations and 'DODIN operations' to 'design, build, configure, secure, operate, maintain, and sustain DOD communications systems and networks'.

[24] The approach taken in this chapter is that operations directed at tangible objects, people, and geographic entities (i.e. 'terrain') are covered by the chapters dealing with regular military operations.

[25] K. Mačák, 'Military Objectives 2.0: The Case for Interpreting Computer Data as Objects under International Humanitarian Law', 48(1) *Israel Law Review* (2015 forthcoming), via <http://papers.ssrn.com/sol3/papers.cfm?abstract_id=2456955>. H. Harrison Dinniss, *Cyber Warfare and the Laws of War* (Cambridge: Cambridge University Press, 2012), 185–7.

[26] As was the case in the Stuxnet situation, where the ultimate purpose was to disrupt Iran's nuclear enrichment process, see P. Shakarian, J. Shakarian, and A. Ruef, *Introduction to Cyber-Warfare: A Multidisciplinary Approach* (Amsterdam etc.: Elsevier/Syngress, 2013), 224–35. Also Scott Applegate, 'The Dawn of Kinetic Cyber', in K. Podins, J. Stinissen, and M. Maybaum (eds), *Proceedings of the 5th International Conference on Cyber Conflict (2013)* (CCDCOE, 2013).

[27] E.g. AIV and CAVV, 9: 'the conduct of military operations to disrupt, mislead, modify or destroy an opponent's computer systems or networks by means of cyber capabilities'; US Department of Defense, *Memorandum on Joint Terminology for Cyberspace Operations* (Vice Chairman of the Joint Chiefs of Staff, 2010), 8: 'Military operations conducted to deny an opposing force the effective use of cyberspace system and weapons in a conflict. It includes cyber attack, cyber defense, and cyber enabling actions.'

23.01 to potentially include neutral and/or supportive actors too thereby enlarging the potential addressees (or 'targets') for cyber operations.[28] The latter inclusion implies that the effects sought (and the goal or purpose defined) could be constructive as well. One could think of cyber operations designed to boost the cyber situational awareness of allies or coalition partners.[29] It should be noted however, that an overlap with Information Operations might occur at this stage.[30]

Agreement seems to exist on the notion that cyber capabilities, that is means and methods are used in cyber operations. Noting that cyber capabilities are those capabilities that contribute to cyber fighting power,[31] and accepting that cyberspace is described as a multi-layered cake, it is obvious that the unique character of cyber operations lies in the fact that the virtual layers of cyberspace (the logical network layer and the cyber persona layer) are addressed to generate primary effects in those layers. The means and methods used—direct access, malware, viruses, denial of service, etc.—can be described as code, software, data, administrator rights, email accounts, or in other words: cyber objects and cyber identities.[32]

23.02 Military cyber operations with extraterritorial effects are governed by international law.

1. International law applies to MCO generating effects abroad. The International Group of Expert responsible for the Tallinn Manual 'unanimously concluded that general principles of international law applied to cyberspace' and thus to cyber operations.[33] This position is shared by a number of States,[34] international organizations,[35]

[28] E.g. Belgium, 12 (French version), Italy, 13, as well as ICRC, 36.

[29] See G. Conti, J Nelson, and D. Raymond (eds), 'Towards a Cyber Common Operating Picture', K. Podins, J. Stinissen, and M. Maybaum, *Proceedings of the 5th International Conference on Cyber Conflict* (CCDCOE, 2013) 279–98; or data-mining capabilities.

[30] On the relationship between Cyber Operations (CO) and Information Operations (IO), see US Department of Defense, 'Joint Publication Cyberspace', I-5: 'CO are concerned with using cyberspace capabilities to create effects which support operations across the physical domains and cyberspace. IO is more specifically concerned with the integrated employment of information-related capabilities during military operations, in concert with other lines of operation (LOOs), to influence, disrupt, corrupt, or usurp the decision making of adversaries and potential adversaries while protecting our own.'

[31] Ducheine and Van Haaster, 'Fighting Power'.

[32] Following the Tallinn Manual's approach to exclude kinetic cyber operations against cyberspace from the definition of cyber operations: Tallinn Manual, 5. This also excludes the mere use of information and communication technology (ICT) for communication solely.

[33] Ibid. 14.

[34] See e.g. the Netherlands' Government response to the AIV-CAVV advice: *Kamerstukken II* 2011–2012, 33 000 X, nr. 79 and 99; United States of America, *International Strategy for Cyberspace: Prosperity, Security, and Openness in a Networked World* (Executive Office of the President, 2011), 9: 'Long-standing international norms guiding state behavior—in times of peace and conflict—also apply in cyberspace.' Germany (UN Doc. A/69/112, full text of the submission), 2; Republic of Korea (UN Doc. A/69/112/Add.1, full text of the submission), 1; Switzerland (A/69/112), 15.

[35] See the UN GA Res. 68/243 (2013, December 27). Also (on *jus ad bellum* and *jus in bello* in particular): NATO, *Wales Summit Declaration (Issued by the Heads of State and Government participating in the meeting of the North Atlantic Council in Wales)* (2014), para. 72.

non-governmental organizations,[36] and experts.[37] Some States however, take a more defensive stance, as they do not take the applicability of certain areas for granted.[38] **23.02**

2. The relevant fields of international law for MCO[39] can be found in the areas of sovereignty, non-intervention, respect for territorial integrity, international (law enforcement) cooperation and mutual assistance, jurisdiction, immunities, international human rights law, international economic law, including the law of intellectual property, the law governing international responsibility for breach of international obligations and international telecommunications law to name some of the most important.[40] Clearly the law governing the use of force and the law of armed conflict will be especially relevant if and when cyber operations cross the threshold of a use of force and occur within the context of an armed conflict. These two latter areas of international law, dealing with the legal bases, and the applicable legal and extra-legal regimes for cyber operations will be addressed later in the chapter.

3. The original Tallinn Manual (2013) drafted by an independent group of experts at the invitation of NATO CCDCOE in Tallinn was drafted to describe the *lex lata* with respect to cyber warfare in the traditional sense of the word 'warfare' and consequently focuses on 'the most disruptive and destructive cyber operations',[41] and thus on the *jus ad bellum* and *jus in bello*, albeit with some rules also devoted to the areas of sovereignty, jurisdiction, immunity, control, state responsibility, and

[36] E.g. ICRC, *Statement by the ICRC, General debate on all disarmament and international security agenda items*, United Nations, General Assembly, 69th session, First Committee, New York, 14 October 2014 (2014) <https://www.icrc.org/en/document/weapons-icrc-statement-united-nations-2014#.VFtD6uktDcs>.

[37] UN GA, *Group of Governmental Experts on Developments in the Field of Information and Telecommunications in the Context of International Security* (UN Doc. A/68/98 (2013), 2013, Dec 2), 2: 'The report reflects the Group's conclusion that international law and in particular the United Nations Charter, is applicable and is essential to maintaining peace and stability and promoting an open, secure, peaceful and accessible ICT environment.' See also K. Ziolkowski, 'General Principles of International Law as Applicable in Cyberspace', in Ziolkowski (ed.), *Peacetime Regime*, xiii: 'The starting point for such deliberations must be norms of international law as applicable outside the digital world'; and D. Fleck, 'Searching for International Rules Applicable to Cyber Warfare: a Critical First Assessment of the New Tallinn Manual', 18 *Journal of Conflict & Security Law* (2013), 331; Harrisson Dinniss, *Cyber Warfare*, 137–8.

[38] See, *inter alia*, the field of *jus in bello* and the position of China and Russia: M.N. Schmitt, 'The Law of Cyber Warfare: Quo Vadis?' (2014) 25 *Stanford Law and Policy Review* 269, at 271, noting that 'Russia and China did not agree to a reference to international humanitarian law'. Also A. Segal, *China, International Law and Cyber Space* (The Council of Foreign Relations, 2 October 2012).

[39] Ziolkowski, *Peacetime Regime*, 115 *et seq*. S.J. Shackelford, *Managing Cyber Attacks in International Law, Business, and Relations: In search of cyber peace* (Cambridge: Cambridge University Press, 2014), 49–50; J.-C. Woltag, *Cyber Warfare: Military cross-border computer network operations under international law* (Intersentia, 2014).

[40] On these issues see Ziolkowski (ed.), *Peacetime Regime*; R. Geiß and H. Lahmann, 'Freedom and Security in Cyberspace: Shifting the Focus away from Military Responses towards Non-Forcible Countermeasures and Collective Threat-Prevention', in Ziolkowski (ed.), *Peacetime Regime*, 621–58. The so-called Tallinn Manual 2.0 process will also address these issues in more detail.

[41] See: <http://ccdcoe.org/research.html>.

23.02 counter-measures.[42] The follow-on project, Tallinn 2.0, also covers other cyber operations and will also cover other fields of law.[43]

4. Another relevant area of law for MCO is international human rights law. As cyberspace enables and enhances communication, freedom of speech, and thought as well as education and economic growth, it evidently has boosted the enjoyment of human rights since its inception. However, because of its pervasiveness and intrusiveness, it is also true that well-intended as well as malicious cyber activities can jeopardize human rights.[44] Various State-initiated cyber activities, including MCO, can affect human rights,[45] as was clearly demonstrated by the Snowden revelations on extraterritorial surveillance activities and operations.[46] As noted by PoKempner:

> access to cyberspace, and freedom to communicate and receive information online, are enabling, lynchpin freedoms, important not just in themselves, but as necessary conditions for the realisation of a much wider set of human rights. [. . .] The proposition that human rights apply to digital events, online media and cyber technologies is also well-accepted at this point.[47]

As a result of this relationship, the UN Special Rapporteur on the promotion and protection of the right to freedom of opinion and expression, Frank La Rue, called upon States 'to ensure that Internet access is maintained at all times, including during times of political unrest'.[48] Looking at recent crises in Libya, Ukraine, and North Korea, it seems clear that this call is not always answered.[49] It may be only a matter of time before legal advisors will have to give more attention to the human rights ramifications of cyber activities including MCO.[50]

[42] For the purpose of this Handbook, the Tallinn Manual's black letter rules are taken to reflect *lex lata*, unless specifically mentioned otherwise.

[43] L. Vihul, 'The Tallinn Manual on the International Law applicable to Cyber Warfare' (*EJIL: Talk!*, 15 April 2013) <http://www.ejiltalk.org/the-tallinn-manual-on-the-international-law-applicable-to-cyber-warfare>.

[44] D. PoKempner, 'Cyberspace and State Obligations in the Area of Human Rights', in Ziolkowski (ed.), *Peacetime Regime*, 239–60.

[45] Geiß and Lahmann, 'Freedom and Security', 641, pointing at Art. 50(1)(B) of the ILC Articles on State Responsibility (ASR): 'Countermeasures shall not affect: [. . .] obligations for the protection of fundamental human rights.'

[46] Luke Harding, *The Snowden Files: The Inside Story of the World's Most Wanted Man* (Paperback edn, Vintage, 2014). See also the web-based publications (of, *inter alia*, G. Greenwald and L. Poitras) in *The Guardian*, *Der Spiegel*, and *The Intercept*; and E. Morozov, *The Net Delusion: The Dark Side of Internet Freedom* (New York: Public Affairs, 2011).

[47] PoKempner, 'Cyberspace', 239.

[48] UN Human Rights Council, *Report of the Special Rapporteur on the promotion and protection of the right to freedom of opinion and expression* (6 May 2011), 21.

[49] A. Tsotsi, 'Libya Finds New Way To Cut Off Internet' (*TechCrunch*, 4 March 2011) <http://techcrunch.com/2011/03/04/libya>; B. Scheiner, 'North Korea DDoSed Off the Internet' (*Scheiner on Security*, 23 December 2014) <https://www.schneier.com/blog/archives/2014/12/north_korea_ddo.html?utm_source=twitterfeed&utm_medium=twitter>.

[50] Taking the evolving extraterritorial application of human rights obligations as demonstrated by, *inter alia*, the European Court of Human Rights to international military operations. See Chapter 4 of this Handbook, and see e.g. ECHR, *Jaloud v The Netherlands* (Grand Chamber). Also A. Zimmermann,

5. Considering cyberspace as the multi-layered cake presented earlier implies that several of its parts and elements will be affected by the jurisdiction (in its various categories) of States.[51] This is evident as soon as people and/or physical objects that are part of (or contribute to) cyberspace are within the territory (and or the jurisdiction) of such States.[52] In addition, legal presence may also imply jurisdiction over, e.g. companies, such as Internet service providers and cloud services.[53] This is also the case over certain activities such as crimes.[54] The Tallinn Manual lists the relevant forms (and sources) of jurisdiction.[55] **23.02**

Jurisdiction over the non-physical layers of cyber space, entailing cyber identities and cyber objects, without resorting to physical or legal presence, remains a complicated issue. It is clear that cyber objects such as data, operating systems, and software in general will be present in or on the physical network layer, hence, on physical objects geo-located somewhere. However, as noted in the Tallinn Manual, the essence of e.g. cloud computing or 'Office 365', is that these cyber objects may be moved, or could be based outside the direct jurisdiction of a State.[56] For certain fields of law, it is already clear that cyber-objects such as 'avatars', an e-book and cyber identities could be relevant as 'objects' in law as they can be stolen or traded. The implications in terms of the international law of military operations, is not clear yet for all cyber objects and cyber identities.

One of the approaches in this respect is the requirement of a substantial connection with or effects upon a State's territory or nationals (alongside a number of other considerations) before a State can assert jurisdiction. This follows the leading interpretation of 'effects based' jurisdiction in the literature and case law.[57]

6. Of special importance within the various legal fields is the notion of attribution. Accurate attribution will be particularly relevant for those MCO that are planned to

'International Law and "Cyber Space"', 3(1) *ESIL Reflections* (10 January 2014) <http://www.esil-sedi.eu/node/481>: 'Another aspect of the de facto de-territorialisation of "cyber space" activities can be seen in the fact that the effects of activities in "cyber space", even when they emanate from States, take place abroad, which in many cases raises the question whether the international (be they treaty-based or of a customary nature) obligations a State has undertaken also apply in such cross-boundary and extraterritorial settings, human rights obligations being a particularly relevant issue at hand.'

[51] J. Zekoll, 'Jurisdiction in Cyberspace', in G. Handl, J. Zekoll, and P. Zumbansen (eds), *Beyond Territoriality—Transnational Legal Authority in an Age of Globalization* (Oxford: Oxford University Press, 2012); B. Pirker, 'Territorial Sovereignty and Integrity and the Challenges of Cyberspace', in Ziolkowski (ed.), *Peacetime Regime*, 194–9, 215.

[52] See Tallinn Manual, Rule 2, para. 2.

[53] Ibid. para. 3. The US used the legal presence of (international) companies in the USA to impose obligations based on the Foreign Intelligence Surveillance Act (FISA), see J. van Hoboken, A. Arnbak, and N. van Eijk, *Obscured by Clouds or How to Address Governmental Access to Cloud Data from Abroad* (SSRN-id2276103, 2013), 2.

[54] See Tallinn Manual, Rule 1, para. 12.

[55] Ibid. Rule 2, paras 6–9. The follow on project Tallinn Manual 2.0 will contain more detail in these areas.

[56] Ibid. Rule 2, paras 2–5.

[57] R. Jennings and A. Watts (eds), *Oppenheim's International Law*, Vol. I, para. 123, 9th edn (Harlow: Longman, 1992), 472–5; M.N. Shaw, *International Law*, 6th edn (Cambridge: Cambridge University Press, 2008), 688–96.

23.02 respond to prior cyber incidents and addressing the author of that incident.[58] Due to the techniques and characteristics of cyberspace, accurate attribution, however, may be complicated: 'There is a significant amount of effort required to track malicious actors, especially when dealing with more proficient adversaries.'[59] Attribution also carries different notions outside the legal realm. It also has relevance in the technical[60] and the political realm.[61] Apart from legal and technical assessment, attribution also requires political judgement if, e.g. response options are considered.[62] For instance, whether to prosecute a cyber intruder or to launch counter-measures.[63]

The standard for attribution may differ depending on the purpose of the attribution, that is, between one field of law or another.[64] From an operational law angle, attribution most often relies on standards that differ from criminal law, i.e. certainty beyond reasonable doubt.[65] Most likely, the standards required may be lower.[66] However, though a universally agreed 'law of evidence' in international law is lacking, 'decisions by most courts and tribunals point to a fairly high burden of proof to establish responsibility' when it comes to State responsibility for international wrongful acts.[67]

[58] See e.g. M.N. Schmitt and L. Vihul, 'Proxy Wars in Cyberspace', 1 *Fletcher Security Review* (2014), 55.

[59] M. Pihelgas, 'Back-Tracing and Anonymity in Cyberspace', in Ziolkowski (ed.), *Peacetime Regime*, 58.

[60] H.K. Kalutarage et al., 'Sensing for Suspicion at Scale: A Bayesian Approach for Cyber Conflict Attribution and Reasoning', in C. Czosseck, R. Ottis, and K. Ziolkowski (eds), *Proceedings of the 4th International Conference on Cyber Conflict* (CCDCOE, 2012), hereafter referred to as Czosseck in 4th CCDCOE Proceedings, 393–412; H.F. Lipson, *Tracking and Tracing Cyber-Attacks: Technical Challenges and Global Policy Issues* (2002) at <http://resources.sei.cmu.edu/library/asset-view.cfm?assetID=5831>.

[61] T. Rid and B. Buchanan, 'Attributing Cyber Attacks' 38 (1–2) *Journal of Strategic Studies* (2015), 4–37; and F. Hare, 'The Significance of Attribution to Cyberspace Coercion: A Political Perspective', in Czosseck in 4th CCDCOE Proceedings, 125–40.

[62] M.C. Libicki, *Managing September 12th in Cyberspace* (Testimony, Before the Committee on Foreign Affairs Subcommittee on Europe, Eurasia, and Emerging Threats United States House of Representatives, 21 March 2013, The RAND Corporation, 2013).

[63] E.g. Pirker, 'Territorial Sovereignty', 210; and J. Rivera and F. Hare, 'The Deployment of Attribution Agnostic Cyberdefense Constructs and Internally Based Cyberthreat Countermeasures' in Brangetto et al. in 6th CCDCOE Proceedings, 104 (Figure 4).

[64] On the lack of a general law of evidence and the relatively high burden of proof in international law, see T.D. Gill and P.A.L. Ducheine, 'Anticipatory Self-Defense in the Cyber Context', 89 *International Law Studies* (2013), 438, at 451–2 (with accompanying notes). Also N. Tsagourias, 'Cyber Attacks, Self-defence and the Problem of Attribution', 17 *Journal of Conflict & Security Law* (2012), 229–44; and J. Carr, *Responsible Attribution: A Prerequisite for Accountability* (CCDCOE Tallinn Paper no. 6, 2014); J. Klabbers, 'Responsibility of States and International Organisations in the Context of Cyber Activities with Special Reference to NATO', in Ziolkowski (ed.), *Peacetime Regime*, 504; M.N. Schmitt, 'Cyber Activities and the Law of Countermeasures' in Ziolkowski (ed.), *Peacetime Regime*, 685.

[65] Geiß and Lahmann, 'Freedom and Security', 623.

[66] See e.g. Chapters 5 and 6 (on enforcement, peace enforcement and peace operations) versus Chapter 8 (on the right of self-defence).

[67] T.D. Gill, 'Non-Intervention in the Cyber Context', in Ziolkowski (ed.), *Peacetime Regime*, 228. Also Klabbers, 'Responsibility', 490; and particularly Geiß and Lahmann, 'Freedom and Security', 624,

The sources or bases for attribution will be different as well, as forensic evidence will be complemented with other factors and parameters.[68] Cyber activities will most likely not occur in a vacuum of events, hence, other circumstances such as statements, physical behaviour, technical and logical deductions, and above all, intelligence from whatever source, will be taken into account as well. Within the specific field of the law of armed conflict attribution correlates with the question of identification of, *inter alia*, military targets. **23.02**

Extraterritorial military cyber operations below the threshold of use of force (as described in Art. 2(4) UN Charter) are, most prominently, governed by principles relating to sovereignty and non-intervention. **23.03**

1. Within the limits posed by International Law, States are permitted to conduct MCO. States conducting MCO that fall short of the use of force as defined in Article 2(4) of the UN Charter are governed by the general principles of International Law and in particular the principle of territorial sovereignty,[69] and respect for the political independence and territorial integrity, and inviolability of States.[70] Notwithstanding their 'short of force' character, cross-boundary MCO can obviously also be launched when the *jus ad bellum* offers a legal basis for forceful operations,[71] that is consent,[72] UN Security Council authorization, or self-defence in which cases these legal bases are in compliance with the rules and principles of international law (see later).[73]

2. Whereas MCO offer unique opportunities to conduct non-forceful operations they may also be undertaken outside the framework of the *jus ad bellum* (see later), provided they respect other (than the prohibition on the use of force) rules and

listing four formalized standards in this respect: 'the prima facie possibility of an asserted fact being true; a preponderance of evidence; the "clear and convincing" evidentiary standard; and proof beyond reasonable doubt.'

[68] Geiß and Lahmann, 'Freedom and Security', 637, referring to 'all-source attribution'. Also W.A. Owens, K.W. Dam, and H.S. Lin, *Technology, Policy, Law, and Ethics Regarding U.S. Acquisition and Use of Cyberattack Capabilities* (Washington: The National Academies Press, 2009), 139. For such a case, see US Federal Bureau of Investigaton, 'Update on Sony Investigation' (19 December 2014). <http://www.fbi.gov/news/pressrel/press-releases/update-on-sony-investigation>; accompanied by critique e.g. B. Jordan, 'Experts: North Korea May Not Have Hacked Sony After All' (*Defense Tech*, 20 December 2014) <http://defensetech.org/2014/12/29/experts-north-korea-may-not-have-hacked-sony-after-all/>; and F.Y. Rashid, 'The Sony Hack Question: If Not North Korea, Then Who?' (*Security Week*, 29 December 2014) <http://www.securityweek.com/sony-hack-question-if-not-north-korea-then-who>.

[69] On this principle in cyberspace: Ziolkowski, 'General Principles of International Law'; and Pirker, 'Territorial Sovereignty'. Also Tallinn Manual, Rule 4.

[70] On this principle in cyberspace: Gill, 'Non-Intervention in the Cyber Context'.

[71] *Argumentum a maiore ad minus*.

[72] See e.g. the Tallinn Manual, Rule 1, para. 8, following the notion of sovereignty, States 'may consent to cyber operations conducted from its territory or to remote cyber operations involving cyber infrastructure that is located on its territory'.

[73] See Chapters 5, 6, and 8.

23.03 principles of international law. First of all, the principle of sovereignty[74] implies that States may exercise jurisdiction in its various forms[75] over MCO provided they have a substantial connection or effect upon a State's territory.[76] As a consequence, MCO may be governed by domestic or host nation legislation. Secondly, they may be subject to rules set by treaties or international arrangement that have been concluded or ratified by the territorial State and or customary international law. Thirdly, MCO will have to respect the territorial integrity of other States. Fourth, MCO that qualify as intervention are prohibited.

3. Those parts of cyberspace that are covered by the territorial sovereignty of a territorial State enjoy protection against interference by other States.[77] What kind of interference exactly amounts to a violation of territorial sovereignty is not exactly clear-cut. Certainly, an armed attack, an otherwise unjustified use of force or coercion (see later) would constitute such a violation.[78] In addition, it is often argued that the territorial sovereignty is violated by 'any acts causing physical effects on another State's territory'.[79] However, the International Group of Experts drafting the original Tallinn Manual could not achieve 'consensus as to whether the placement of malware that causes no physical damage (as with malware used to monitor activities) constitutes a violation of sovereignty'.[80] It remains controversial whether MCO entailing non-authorized surveillance and intelligence gathering constitutes a violation of sovereignty. Some States consider this to be the case, as became evident in the wake of the so-called Snowden revelations,[81] whereas others take different views.[82]

Some authors argue that 'any activity attributable to another State, e.g. because it constitutes an exercise of that State's jurisdiction, is to be considered a violation of

[74] The Permanent Court of Arbitration laid down the basic rule in relation to territorial sovereignty as the exclusive right of a State to exercise the powers of a State within its territory, see the *Island of Palmas Case (Netherlands v USA)* 2 R.I.A.A. 829, 838–9 (PCA, 4 April 1928).

[75] Legislative, judicial, and enforcement jurisdiction: I. Brownlie, *Principles of Public International Law*, 6th edn (Oxford: Oxford University Press 2003), 162.

[76] See Tallinn Manual, Rules 2 and 3.

[77] W. Heintschel von Heinegg, 'Legal Implications of Territorial Sovereignty in Cyberspace', in Czosseck in 4th CCDCOE Proceedings, 7–20, at 11.

[78] Ibid.

[79] Ziolkowski, 'General Principles of International Law', 163 and the accompanying notes (204). Also Tallinn Manual, Rule 1, para. 6: 'A cyber operation by a State directed against cyber infrastructure located in another State may violate the latter's sovereignty. It certainly does so if it causes damage.'

[80] Tallinn Manual, Rule 1, para. 6.

[81] See e.g. Brazil's Justice Minister Jose Eduardo Cardozo, in S. Pearson, 'Brazil says US violated its sovereignty with spying programme' (*Financial Times*, 2 September 2013) <http://www.ft.com/cms/s/0/61ee909e-13f1-11e3-b0b4-00144feabdc0.html>; and the Brazilian President Dilma Rousseff, in J. Borger, 'Brazilian President: US surveillance a "breach of international law"' (*The Guardian*, 24 September 2013), <http://www.theguardian.com/world/2013/sep/24/brazil-president-un-speech-nsa-surveillance>.

[82] See by way of analogy 'Spying is a sovereign right', M. Bohm in *The Moscow Times*, 30 August 2013, referring to the practice of the United States and Russian Federation in openly acknowledging the presence of intelligence officers at each other's embassies at <http://www.themoscowtimes.com>.

the sovereignty of the territorial State',[83] and that 'due to the enormous negative effects malicious cyber activities can have on the national security of another State, which can be, although not of physical nature, though well "perceptible" (e.g. disruption of a State's—digital—stock exchange system), it can be claimed that such effects could violate the victim State's sovereignty'.[84] **23.03**

The original Tallinn Manual and the International Group of Expert specifically refer to interference with an object that enjoys sovereign immunity, stating that '[a]ny interference by a State with cyber infrastructure aboard a platform, wherever located, that enjoys sovereign immunity constitutes a violation of sovereignty'.[85] Activities causing 'damage to [tangible] objects' or which 'significantly impair its operation' such as a denial of service (DoS) operation against a State's military satellite would indeed constitute a violating of such sovereign immunity.[86]

4. The principle of non-intervention is viewed as the mirror image of the sovereignty of States.[87] MCO coercively or dictatorially interfering with the cyberspace of another State[88] qualify as an intervention, thus violating the principle of non-intervention.[89] Though the unauthorized use of force and armed attack (see later) qualify as 'intervention',[90] the focal point for the rule laid out here involves MCO short of force that are:

[83] Heintschel von Heinegg, 'Legal Implications', 11, 'Rather, any activity attributable to another State, e.g. because it constitutes an exercise of that State's jurisdiction, is to be considered a violation of the sovereignty of the territorial State', referring to Jennings and Watts (eds), *Oppenheim's International Law*, para. 123.

[84] Ziolkowski, 'General Principles of International Law', 163, referring to the US position in the United States of America (International Strategy for Cyberspace, 14), that doesn't seem to support that reading: 'However, as indicated by the US, who declared that it considered its (territorial) sovereignty as violated by "disruption of networks and systems", i.e., including intrusions without (directly or indirectly) showing a physical effect, it could be argued that physical damage is irrelevant in the cyber context.'

[85] Tallinn Manual, Rule 4, para. 4.

[86] Ibid.

[87] Jennings and Watts, *Oppenheim's International Law*, 428 *et seq*. The principle is laid down in the Friendly Relations Declaration UN GA Res. 2625 (XX): *Declaration on Principles of International Law concerning Friendly Relations and Co-operation among States in accordance with the Charter of the United Nations* (14 October 1970): 'No State or group of States has the right to intervene, directly or indirectly, for any reason whatever, in the internal or external affairs of any other State. Consequently, armed intervention and all other forms of interference or attempted threats against the personality of the State or against its political, economic and cultural elements, are in violation of international law.'

[88] Tallinn Manual, Rule 10, para. 6: 'The fact that a cyber operation does not rise to the level of a use of force does not necessarily render it lawful under international law. In particular, a cyber operation may constitute a violation of the prohibition on intervention.'

[89] Gill, 'Non-Intervention in the Cyber Context', 217. Also Chatham House, *The Principle of Non-Intervention in Contemporary International Law: Non-Interference in a State's Internal Affairs Used to be a Rule of International Law: Is It Still?* (28 February 2007).

[90] See later in the chapter, and also Tallinn Manual, Rule 10, para. 9: 'The clearest cases are those cyber operations, such as the employment of Stuxnet, that amount to a use of force. Such operations are also acts of intervention because all uses of force are coercive *per se*.'

23.03 intended to (or have the effect of) violate a State's sovereignty by preventing it from carrying out State functions, and/or preventing it from exercising activities or making choices which it is entitled to engage in or make under international law.[91]

In addition to the Stuxnet case that was qualified as the use of force and as intervention, the International Group of Experts drafting the original Tallinn Manual (IGE), submitted that attempts to achieve regime change or coercive political interference enabled by cyber capabilities could amount to intervention:[92]

Cases in point are the manipulation by cyber-means of elections or of public opinion on the eve of elections, as when online news services are altered in favour of a particular party, false news is spread, or the online services of one party are shut off.[93]

Some authors provided an indicative list of MCO, varying in form and intensity, that could amount to intervention, comprising:[94]

(a) misinformation and propaganda aimed at weakening a foreign government's legitimacy and amounting to promotion and coordinating of subversion, thus boosting civil unrest or regime change;
(b) (mis)use of social media, email, and digital (telephone) communications in spurring or supporting opposition to an unfriendly regime (especially in instable States);
(c) manipulating or influencing the outcome of digitally supported elections;
(d) the compromising of confidential governmental and other critical websites with the aim of interfering with governmental communications, manipulating key economic and financial activities; or
(e) planting malware designed to degrade or shut down essential governmental and other key services at a moment of the intervening State's choosing, resulting in the undermining of public and corporate confidence in a State's ability to secure vital interests (*inter alia*, the maintenance essential services, economic stability, and public order);
(f) massive and coordinated distributed denial of services (DDoS) operations against governmental and other key economic or financial websites, aimed at hampering or crippling governmental activity for a period of time;
(g) cyber sabotage (or cybotage) resulting in physical damage, of e.g. defence communications, a nuclear research facility, or a particular weapon system, in

[91] Gill, 'Non-Intervention in the Cyber Context', 218.

[92] Tallinn Manual, Rule 10, para. 10.

[93] Tallinn Manual, Rule 10, para. 10. Reference could arguably be made to GCHQ's programs revealed by Edward Snowden, called Underpass, Gateway, and Slipstream, in G. Greenwald, 'Hacking Online Polls and Other Ways British Spies Seek to Control the Internet' (*The Intercept*, 14 July 2014) <https://firstlook.org/theintercept/2014/07/14/manipulating-online-polls-ways-british-spies-seek-control-internet/>.

[94] Gill, 'Non-Intervention in the Cyber Context', 234. Ducheine, 'The Notion of Cyber Operations' in N. Tsagourias and R. Buchan (eds), *The Research Handbook on the International Law and Cyberspace* (Cheltenham: Edward Elgar, 2015); R. Buchan, 'Cyber Attacks: Unlawful Uses of Force or Prohibited Interventions?' 17 *Journal of Conflict & Security Law* (2012), 211.

which case it would approach or cross the threshold of a use of force and, in some cases, could potentially amount to an armed attack.[95] **23.03**

However, pure interference by means of cyber capabilities short of coercion cannot be viewed as intervention.[96] The IGE deemed 'cyber espionage and cyber exploitation operations' to lack a coercive element, besides the fact that a '[m]ere intrusion into another State's systems' was also considered as not violating the non-intervention principle per se, even when such intrusion necessitates 'the breaching of protective virtual barriers (e.g. the breaching of firewalls or the cracking of passwords)'.[97] Notwithstanding the fact that MCO of this kind do not violate the non-intervention principle, in some cases, they could nevertheless be regarded as a violation of the domestic law of the victim State, 'unfriendly', or violating sovereignty (see earlier).[98]

Referring to 'the disclosure of the massive and systematic use of, inter alia, cyber techniques to intercept, monitor, and store the email and telephone communications of private citizens, corporations, governmental and intergovernmental organs', Gill notes that these MCO do not necessarily amount to intervention,[99] 'except possibly in the situation that governmental offices or diplomatic premises are violated or diplomatically protected communications are intercepted and stored'.[100] 'As always, the decisive test remains coercion', hence, a case-by-case assessment will be required as not every form of political or economic interference enabled by MCO violates the non-intervention principle.[101]

5. Apart from the legal bases for the forceful MCO that are provided by the *jus ad bellum* (see later), and notwithstanding adherence to principles of sovereignty and non-intervention, MCO that may potentially amount to interference, a violation of sovereignty, and intervention, may nevertheless be lawful under International Law. Provided the circumstances enable that particular course of action, States could resort to cross-border cyber operations, performed or supported by armed forces, as remedies after prior wrongdoing: as a law enforcement measure, as a form of retorsion, a counter-measure, or as self-help based on a 'plea of necessity'.[102]

Cross-border law enforcement responding to illegal (cyber) activity could be undertaken with respect to the territorial sovereignty of other States with the consent of that State.[103]

[95] Gill, 'Non-Intervention in the Cyber Context', 234.

[96] Tallinn Manual, Rule 10, para. 8: 'It is clear that not all cyber interference automatically violates the international law prohibition on intervention; "interference pure and simple is not intervention"' (with reference to Jennings and Watts, *Oppenheim's International Law*, 432).

[97] Tallinn Manual, Rule 10, para. 8.

[98] Gill, 'Non-Intervention in the Cyber Context', 225.

[99] Ibid. 214 and 225. [100] Ibid. 225.

[101] Tallinn Manual, Rule 10, para. 10.

[102] See Gill, 'Non-Intervention in the Cyber Context', 228 *et seq.*; Geiß and Lahmann, 'Freedom and Security', 628 *et seq.*; Schmitt, 'Cyber Activities and the Law of Countermeasures'.

[103] Gill, 'Non-Intervention in the Cyber Context', 229.

23.03 Retorsion by using cyber capabilities could be at stake in a response to unfriendly or unlawful acts (including intervention) by other States.[104] Retorsion 'being internationally lawful acts, do not require any prior violation of international law' and (unlike reprisals or counter-measures) 'do not interfere with the target State's rights under international law'.[105] This could take the form of 'misleading a prospective intervening party by providing it with bogus or useless information or otherwise diverting cyber break-ins from their intended targets' or 'hacking back to the source of the cyber intervention and temporarily or permanently disabling, damaging or destroying the intervening party's systems which were being used to achieve or attempt a form of cyber interference rising to the level of coercive cyber intervention'.[106]

Counter-measures may be defined as 'pacific unilateral reactions which are intrinsically unlawful, which are adopted by one or more States against another State, when the former considers that the latter has committed an internationally wrongful act which could justify such a reaction'.[107] Unlike retorsion, counter-measures interfere with the target State's rights under International Law. Counter-measures are therefore subject to strict preconditions.[108] They require a prior internationally wrongful act attributable to a State; their sole purpose is to induce the wrongdoer's compliance; they are limited to non-forceful and proportionate actions only; and a prior demand to the wrongdoer is required. Finally, counter-measures are not allowed once the unlawful act has ceased.[109]

A last resort would be to initiate a MCO based on a plea of necessity.[110] Unlike counter-measures, MCO based on this plea do not require a prior internationally wrongful act to which it is responding, and the author of the original act could also be a non-State actor or an unknown entity. However, the threshold is high, as the plea requires a situation of grave and imminent peril to an essential interest.[111] Moreover, MCO out of such a plea may not exceed the threshold of the use of force.

[104] Ibid. 230 and the accompanying notes (referring to A. Norrtman, *Enforcing International Law. From Self-Help to Self-Contained Regimes* (Hampshire: Ashgate, 2005)); and T.D. Gill, 'The Forcible Protection, Affirmation and Exercise of Rights by States under Customary International Law' 23 *Netherlands Yearbook of International Law* (1992), 105.

[105] *Max Planck Encyclopedia of Public International Law* (on-line), last updated March 2011.

[106] Gill, 'Non-Intervention in the Cyber Context', 236.

[107] Geiß and Lahmann, 'Freedom and Security', 629.

[108] Schmitt, 'Cyber Activities and the Law of Countermeasures', 678. Tallinn Manual, Rule 9.

[109] Geiß and Lahmann, 'Freedom and Security', 638.

[110] M.N. Schmitt, 'Normative Voids and Asymmetry in Cyberspace' (*Just Security*, 29 December 2014), <http://justsecurity.org/18685/normative-voids-asymmetry-cyberspace>; Geiß and Lahmann, 'Freedom and Security'. Tallinn Manual, Rule 9, para. 12.

[111] Schmitt, 'Normative Voids and Asymmetry in Cyberspace'. Schmitt, 'Cyber Activities and the Law of Countermeasures', 663: 'In the cyber context, the plea of necessity is most likely relevant when cyber operations threaten the operation of critical cyber infrastructure.'

Extraterritorial military cyber operations constituting a threat or use of force are governed by Article 2(4) of the UN Charter and the recognized exceptions thereto. 23.04

1. As set out in this Handbook, military operations amounting to the use of force are governed by Article 2(4) of the UN Charter and the *jus ad bellum*, including the valid legal bases that were set out above in the sub-Chapters 5.1 and 6.1 and Chapters 8, 12, and 14.

2. The International Group of Experts drafting the original Tallinn Manual (IGE) has defined the use of force in cyberspace when 'its scale and effects are comparable to non-cyber operations rising to the level of a use of force'.[112] This description has triggered critique as it uses an effect-based approach only.[113] Some States and experts have used similar descriptions nevertheless.[114]

Armed force that has a real or potential physical impact on the target State is subject to the prohibition on the use of force.[115] Such force is not restricted to the kinetic impact of conventional weapon systems, but could also include MCO. However, MCO 'intended to economically coerce another state to engage in, or desist from, a particular course of action would not amount to a use of force; nor would financing a rebel group's cyber operations'.[116] Referring to the Stuxnet case, the IGE was unanimous in qualifying the use of Stuxnet against Iranian nuclear facilities and having resulted in physical damage to the ultra-centrigues used in those facilities, as a use of force.[117]

The IGE developed a non-exclusive list of indicative factors that would likely influence the characterization of cyber operations by States as uses of force.[118] Admittedly, these indicators and the 'scale and effects' part of the Tallinn Manual Rule 11 were taken from the definition and description of an armed attack.[119]

3. Most States and experts agree that cyber operations, although constituting a use of force, may nevertheless not rise to the level of an armed attack. This implies that

[112] Tallinn Manual, Rule 11.

[113] L.J.M. Boer, 'Restating the Law "As It Is": On The Tallinn Manual and the Use of Force in Cyberspace', 5 *Amsterdam Law Forum* (2013), 4; and L.J.M. Boer, '"Echoes of Times Past": On the Paradoxical Nature of Article 2(4)', *Journal of Conflict & Security Law* (2014), 1. M.N. Schmitt, the editor of the original Tallinn Manual, at the occasion of the Conference 'The Cyber Warfare Manual: A Detailed Assessment' (3 December 2014) at the Asser Institute in The Hague, suggested that the 'scale and effects' part in Rule 11, might not reoccur in the updated Tallinn Manual (the so-called Tallinn Manual 2.0).

[114] See e.g. AIV and CAVV, 20. The report has been endorsed in general terms by the Netherlands, see: *Kamerstukken II* 2011–2012, 33 000 X, nr. 79 and 99.

[115] AIV and CAVV, 20.

[116] Schmitt, 'The Law of Cyber Warfare: Quo Vadis?', 280, and the accompanying note 41.

[117] Tallinn Manual, Rule 10, para. 9.

[118] Tallinn Manual, Rule 11, para. 9: severity, immediacy, directness, invasiveness, measurability, military character, state involvement, and presumptive legality. See also: Gill, 'Non-Intervention in the Cyber Context', 219, n. 4.

[119] M.N. Schmitt, 'Computer Network Attacks and the Use of Force in International Law: Throughts on a Normative Framework' 37 *Columbia Journal of Transnational Law* (1999), 885.

23.04 an armed attack requires a higher threshold than the use of force.[120] It should be noted that the *jus ad bellum* is at the very heart of the original Tallinn Manual, and that Rules 10–19 of the Manual deal with these issues. Without duplicating these rules, and with reference to the chapters in this Handbook already mentioned, the legal bases for the use of cross-boundary force are reiterated here briefly.[121]

4. First of all, forceful MCO may be conducted at the invitation or with the consent of other States involved.[122] Secondly, MCO may be undertaken by States with the authorization of the UN Security Council, operating under Chapter VII of the UN Charter.[123] The International Court of Justice (ICJ) confirmed that the UN Charter provisions referring to the *jus ad bellum* 'apply to any use of force, regardless of the weapons employed', and thus also include cyber capabilities to be deployed by States on this basis in the course of operations.[124] Thirdly, States may resort to MCO (and other operations) as a measure of self-defence in the case of an armed attack either using conventional or cyber capabilities (see later).[125]

23.05 **Extraterritorial cyber activities or operations qualifying as armed attack in the sense of Article 51 of the UN Charter, taking into account the other requirements for self-defence, trigger a State's right to self-defence.**

1. A State that is the target of operations that reach the threshold of an armed attack may resort to MCO as a lawful measure of self-defence against the author(s) of that armed attack, provided it does so in conformity with the other material (necessity and proportionality)[126] and procedural requirements of exercising self-defence (reporting to the Security Council). Whether cyber activities or operations qualify as an armed attack 'depends on its scale and effects'.[127] An armed attack is generally viewed as a more serious form of the use of force.[128]

Only when 'the scale and the effects' of cyber activities and operations equate with those of conventional armed attacks, may they trigger the right to

[120] For an alternative reading: see the US position as set forth in *Developments in the Field of Information and Telecommunications in the Context of International Security: Report of the Secretary-General*, 18–19, UN Doc. A/66/152 (20 July 2010), 18.

[121] Also Roscini, *Cyber Operations*, chapter 2, and M. Waxman, 'Cyber-Attacks and the Use of Force: Back to the Future of Article 2(4)', 26 *Yale Journal of International Law* (2011), 421.

[122] See Chapters 6 'Peace Operations' and 14 'Military Intervention with the Consent or at the Invitation of a Government'. See also Tallinn Manual, Rule 1, para. 8 and Rule 13, para. 22.

[123] See Chapter 5 'Enforcement and Peace Enforcement Operations'. Also Tallinn Manual, Rule 1, para. 7, and Rules 18 and 19.

[124] ICJ, *Advisory Opinion on the Legality of the Threat or Use of Nuclear Weapons*, 1996, ICJ 226, para. 39.

[125] See Chapter 8 'Legal Basis of the Right of Self-Defence under the UN Charter and under Customary International Law' and Chapter 12 'Rescue of Nationals'. See also Tallinn Manual, Rules 13–17.

[126] See Tallinn Manual, Rule 14 on necessity and proportionality.

[127] Ibid. Rule 13. [128] Ibid. Rule 13, para. 5.

self-defence.[129] The IGE agreed on the fact that a cyber operation that 'injures or kills persons or damages or destroys property' would meet the scale and effects requirement,[130] though, as noted by Schmitt, the 'requisite degree of damage or injury remains, however, the subject of some disagreement'.[131] The Group agreed that the 2007 Estonia case did not meet the threshold of an armed attack, but failed to reach agreement on the Stuxnet case.[132] **23.05**

Like the Estonian case, non-disruptive activities such as cyber intelligence gathering, cyber theft, or periodic disruption or denial of non-essential cyber services do not qualify as armed attacks.[133]

2. Despite some States' positions, it is still unclear whether cyber activities or operations that do not generate physical damage or injury may nevertheless qualify as an armed attack when they generate 'severe non-destructive or non-injurious consequences'.[134] State practice and *opinio juris* have yet to develop further regarding this subject.

The Netherlands has, for instance, albeit in general terms,[135] accepted the conclusions delivered in a joint report by two of its advisory councils, stating that the 'disruption of the state and/or society, or a sustained attempt thereto, and not merely an impediment to or delay in the normal performance of tasks' could indeed qualify as an armed attack. A mere 'disruption of banking transactions or the hindrance of government activity', however, would not qualify as such. Notably, a cyber operation that targets 'the entire financial system or prevents the government from carrying out essential tasks' could well be equated with an armed attack.[136]

3. The majority of the IGE drafting the original Tallinn Manual agreed on the interpretation that the author of the armed attack triggering the right to self-defence could be a State as well as a non-State entity.[137] The IGE felt the need to dedicate a separate rule on the notions of imminence and immediacy.[138] The majority agreed on the notion of anticipatory self-defence, responding to an imminent armed attack

[129] Pro: Fleck, 'Searching', 336. Contra: M.E. O'Connell, 'Cyber Security without Cyber War', 17 *Journal of Conflict & Security Law* (2012), 187, at 190–1: 'Indeed, the law of self-defence should have little bearing in discussions of cyber security. Even if some cyber incidents could fit a solid definition of what constitutes an armed attack, responding to such an attack will rarely be lawful or prudent if the response is a use of force. The emphasis, therefore, in terms of legal norms and commitment of resources should be in the non-military sphere.'

[130] Tallinn Manual, Rule 13, para. 6.

[131] Schmitt, 'The Law of Cyber Warfare: Quo Vadis?', 282.

[132] Tallinn Manual, Rule 13, para. 13: 'some members of the International Group of Experts were of the view that the [Stuxnet] operations had reached the armed attack threshold [unless justifiable on the basis of anticipatory self-defence (Rule 15)]'.

[133] Tallinn Manual, Rule 13, para. 6 and Schmitt, 'The Law of Cyber Warfare: Quo Vadis?', 282.

[134] Schmitt, 'The Law of Cyber Warfare: Quo Vadis?', 283, referring to the US position (described in: UN Doc. A/66/152, 18) and the Netherlands' stance (as formulated in AIV and CAVV, 21).

[135] See *Kamerstukken II* 2011–2012, 33 000 X, nr. 79 and 99.

[136] AIV and CAVV, 21.

[137] Tallinn Manual, Rule 13, para. 17. Also Schmitt, 'The Law of Cyber Warfare: Quo Vadis?', 287 and Gill and Ducheine, 'Anticipatory Self-Defense'. 446 (both with accompanying notes).

[138] See Tallinn Manual, Rule 15.

23.05 in accordance with the *Caroline* criteria, while at the same time rejecting the so-called 'preventive claims of self-defence'.[139]

23.06 **International humanitarian law applies to military cyber operations that qualify as an international or non-international armed conflict, whether alone or alongside other military operations.**

1. As soon as MCO are conducted 'in the context' of an armed conflict, whether alongside other military operations, or as a stand-alone measure, the law of armed conflict (*jus in bello*) usually referred to as IHL is applicable and thus applies to the execution of these MCO.[140] This subdivision of international law is the main component of the original Tallinn Manual.[141] Without repeating the findings of the IGE, some controversial issues merit attention here. It is beyond doubt that State practice in this domain is developing and will develop further in the (near) future.[142] As State practice has indeed developed since the naissance of the Tallinn Manual, the following section will briefly reflect on some of the Tallinn Manual's controversial issues.

2. The IGE disagreed on the nature of the nexus requirement 'in the context' of an armed conflict. One group considers IHL to govern 'any cyber activity conducted by a party to an armed conflict against its opponent', whereas another group argues that the MCO must have been executed 'in furtherance of the hostilities, that is, in order to contribute to the originator's military effort'.[143]

3. The normal rules delineating the geographical scope of an armed conflict also apply to MCO, though establishing the exact scope may be complicated given the occurrence of so-called transnational armed conflicts, and certain restrictions may be hard to implement.[144]

4. MCO that qualify as attacks within the meaning of Article 49(1) of Additional Protocol I are governed by the rules on the conduct of hostilities, in general language, the rules on attacks.[145] The IGE deemed an MCO to qualify as an attack when such a 'cyber operation, whether offensive or defensive, [could] reasonably [be] expected to cause injury or death to persons or damage or destruction to objects'.[146] A controversial point within the group (and amongst experts, as well as States) is the issue of 'damage' in terms of (*inter alia*) non-physical nature, as in the

[139] See Tallinn Manual, Rule 15, para. 2. Also Gill and Ducheine, 'Anticipatory Self-Defense'.
[140] Tallinn Manual, Rule 20.
[141] See Rules 25–90 (making 66 out of the 95 rules). Also Harrison Dinniss, *Cyber Warfare and the Laws of War*.
[142] See for 'future' points of development (and discussion), also Schmitt, 'The Law of Cyber Warfare: Quo Vadis?'.
[143] Tallinn Manual, Rule 20, para. 5.
[144] Tallinn Manual, Rule 21.
[145] Set out in the Tallinn Manual in Rules 30–59. These Rules are sometimes referred to as 'targeting rules', although those may encompass extra-legal 'directives' as well in military operational readings.
[146] Tallinn Manual, Rule 30.

case of so-called 'loss of functionality'.[147] Two views are prevalent. Some experts take a narrow approach that limits the scope of attacks to military operations that result in physical damage or injury only. Others take a broader approach that also includes certain non-destructive operations, such as loss of functionality without causing permanent damage.[148] The IGE could only agree on a narrow reading (see earlier).[149] **23.06**

5. This narrow reading impacts other issues related to the targeting rules as well. First of all, the debate reoccurs in choosing potential targets for MCO as it influences the type of objects that qualify as 'military objectives' within the meaning of Article 52(2) AP I.[150] Apart from the question whether non-tangible elements such as 'cyber identities' (e.g. email accounts) and 'cyber objects' (i.e. data) may qualify as 'an object' within the meaning of Article 52(2) AP I,[151] the experts disagreed on the constituent elements of (i) 'effective contribution to military action', (ii) 'in the circumstances ruling at the time', and what offers a (iii) 'definite' (iv) 'military advantage'.[152] A very short reading of the debate is that 'definite', 'damage', and 'military advantage' are complicated issues in the course of MCO, and that more debate is likely to follow (or may be silenced?) as practice evolves over time.[153]

Secondly, the narrow reading also affects the collateral damage assessment that may be required during targeting, including in the course of MCO that amount to attacks (as defined in Article 49(1) AP I).[154] Here again, the effects that may (or may not) contribute to the 'military advantage anticipated' on the plus side, have to be weighed against what amounts to expected (or not) 'collateral damage' on the other side.

6. In addition to rules of international humanitarian law, other directives may be used to (further) regulate MCO, for instance, through rules of engagement.[155]

[147] Schmitt, 'The Law of Cyber Warfare: Quo Vadis?', 294.

[148] See ICRC, International Humanitarian Law and the challenges of contemporary armed conflicts, Report prepared by the ICRC for the 31st International Conference of the Red Cross and Red Crescent, 37.

[149] Tallinn Manual, Rule 30, paras 10–12.

[150] Tallinn Manual, Rule 38.

[151] See the distinction made by Harrison Dinniss, 'The Nature of Objects', differentiating between content-level data and operational-level data ('code'). Content-level data includes text, databases, archives, catalogues. Operational-level data ('code' or logical-level data or program data) enable hardware to work. When 'code' is affected by a MCO, the functionality of the system will be impaired, unlike when only content-level data is affected. She argues that only 'code' qualifies as a 'military objective'.

[152] See Tallinn Manual, Rule 38, especially, paras 13–16, focusing on the 'effective contribution to military action part of the definition' and paras 17–25, focusing on the element of 'in the circumstances ruling at the time, offers a definite military advantage'. Also: E. Talbot Jensen, 'Cyber Attacks: Proportionality and Precautions in Attack', 89 *International Law Studies* (2013), 198; Harrison Dinniss, 'The Nature of Objects'; and Mačák, 'Military Objectives 2.0'.

[153] Schmitt, 'The Law of Cyber Warfare: Quo Vadis?', 299, referring to '[t]he future ain't what it used to be'.

[154] Tallinn Manual, Rules 54–57; Jensen, 'Cyber Attacks'.

[155] See sub-Chapter 6.4 'Application of Force and Rules of Engagement in Peace Operations'; Chapter 10 'Application of Force and Rules of Engagement in Self-Defence Operations'; and Chapter 24 'Force Protection, Unit Self-Defence, and Personal Self-Defence: Their Relationship to Rules of Engagement'.

Chapter 24

FORCE PROTECTION, UNIT SELF-DEFENCE, AND PERSONAL SELF-DEFENCE

Their Relationship to Rules of Engagement

24.01 **The concept of self-defence, while always referring to the right to use force to defend against an attack, encompasses several different types and levels of this right. At the strategic level, it includes the right of national self-defence. At the operational level, it includes the concepts of extended self-defence and force protection, as well as the specific concept of self-defence in the context of UN operations. At the threshold between the operational and tactical level, the concept of self-defence includes the concept of unit self-defence. At the individual, personal level, it includes the right to personal self-defence.**

1. The philosophical and historical backgrounds of the right to self-defence are beyond the scope of this commentary, as this commentary will focus primarily on the relationship between the right of personal self-defence and rules of engagement which may be applicable to a given operation. Furthermore, as national self-defence is discussed elsewhere,[1] it will not be discussed further in this chapter.

24.02 **Extended self-defence is the right of Alliance units operating within a NATO-led operation or under NATO command to assist each other in the event of an (imminent) attack.**

1. Although self-defence and rules of engagement (ROE) are in principle mutually exclusive in the sense that ROE must not limit the right of self-defence (see Sections 5.24, 6.09, and 10.03), the NATO doctrine as regards mutual self-defence by units under NATO command and control can be found in the NATO Military Committee document on NATO Rules of Engagement (document MC 362/1).

2. Both the source, a NATO document, and the emphasis placed on the Alliance context in which extended self-defence may be exercised, illustrate that this specific

[1] See Chapter 8. See also Section 5.24 as regards the relationship between ROE and self-defence.

form of self-defence applies only to units from NATO Member States operating within the context of a NATO operation, that is, under NATO command and control. Consequently, the concept of Extended Self-Defence is unique to NATO and does not exist elsewhere. It was introduced in the first version of MC 362 (NATO Rules of Engagement) and has been a cause for some confusion. The wording of the document suggests that the concept has a significance and meaning beyond its legal limits, which can lead to the erroneous assumption that it confers upon NATO military personnel a right to use force at any time and under any circumstance. It does not and furthermore, in the instances in which it does apply, cannot extend beyond the limits of Article 51 of the Charter of the United Nations. **24.02**

3. It follows from the above that units participating in any other type of operation cannot refer to the right of extended self-defence. In non-NATO operations, the NATO membership of the parent State becomes, in effect, irrelevant as regards the lawful right to use force within the context of that operation.

The right of extended self-defence is derived from Article 5 of the North Atlantic Treaty and is a unit-level expression of the right to collective national self-defence. **24.03**

1. The NATO concept of extended self-defence is essentially a statement of solidarity within the Alliance and as such reflects the NATO principle of mutual assistance in (national) self-defence as set forth in Article 5 of the North-Atlantic Treaty. In Article 5 operations, the legal basis for mutual assistance is, of course, the exercise of the right of collective self-defence as referred to in Article 51 of the Charter of the United Nations. As a logical extension of that right, units participating in such operations have an equal corollary right to come to the aid of each other in self-defence situations.

The right for a Force other than a NATO Force to defend itself is derived from the mandate of the operation in question. This authorization can be specific, but is also inherently implicit in the existence and tasking of the Force. Without such right, a Force would be *prima facie* unable to carry out its mandate. **24.04**

1. The legal basis for the use of force to protect the military force in question depends on the type of operation and the (provisions of the) mandate on which it is based.[2] The most clear and legally solid basis for international military operations is

[2] While the term 'force protection' encompasses many measures from actual use of force to public information campaigns, it is used here in the former sense. The concept of force protection differs from unit self-defence as discussed later, but common elements exist between the various forms of self-defence available to a military force. The use of force in (mutual) defence within an operation may consequently reflect several different legal concepts regarding (mutual) self-defence. Which of these most accurately describes or supports the actions taken will depend on the context in which the actions took place and the specific circumstances thereof.

24.04 a mandate by the United Nations Security Council. Some mandating resolutions contain a specific provision authorizing the Force to protect itself.[3] When the resolution does not contain such a provision, the authority for self-defence by the military force can be inferred from the language of the resolution as a whole, especially the provisions that comprise the actual mandate itself. If those provisions authorize the Force to use 'all necessary means' to accomplish the mandate, it logically follows that the Force is thereby also authorized to use such force as may be necessary to protect itself.[4]

2. For operations not based on a mandate by the Security Council, the legal basis for the use of force is generally integrated in, or derived from, the nature of the operation itself. In the case of international armed conflicts, for example, the combatants of the parties to the conflict are authorized to participate directly in the hostilities. In operations based on less clearly defined principles or concepts of international law, such as humanitarian intervention and the general area of rescuing nationals abroad, the unclear nature of their status under international law extends to the use of force to achieve such operations as well.[5] When such operations do not escalate into an actual armed conflict,[6] the level of force used, the targeting criteria applied, the objective of the operation, and the use of force therein will all be relevant in the determination of the political and legal ramifications of the operation.[7]

24.05 **United Nations forces under United Nations command and control have the right to defend themselves against an (imminent) attack as well as against armed attempts to interfere with the execution of the mandate.**[8]

[3] For example, SC Res. 1088 (1996), para. 20.

[4] SC Res. 1386 (2001), para. 3, authorizes the International Stabilization and Assistance Force (ISAF) in Afghanistan to use all necessary means to achieve the mandate. The subsequent conclusion that ISAF is thereby entitled to use all necessary means to defend itself is based on the logic that if ISAF is not authorized to protect itself, it cannot be expected to achieve the mandate. Furthermore, the use of force in self-defence would certainly fall within the normal ambit of the term 'all necessary means' in any case.

[5] For a discussion of the legal basis for the use of military force to rescue nationals abroad, see C.H.M. Waldock, 'The Regulation of the Use of Force by Individual States in International Law', 81 *RdC* (1952-II), at 459, 467, and 503. See also Chapter 12 'Rescue of Nationals'.

[6] An example of a military operation involving the use of force abroad without escalating into an armed conflict is the rescue operation by Israeli military forces to free the hostages at Entebbe, Uganda, on 4 July 1976. NATO Operation Allied Force and the simultaneous American Operation Noble Anvil against Serbia over the situation in Kosovo in 1999 were officially based on the principle of humanitarian intervention, but were by their nature, extent, and the type of force used undeniably part of an armed conflict.

[7] An illustration of the emphasis placed by command authorities on exercising restraint in the use of force during civilian evacuation operations can be found in para 3.c on pp. 1–2 and 1–3 of the Joint Chiefs of Staff Publication on *Joint Tactics, Techniques, and Procedures for Noncombatant Evacuation Operations*, Joint Publication 3-07.5. See also Chapter 12.

[8] The legal basis for United Nations peace operations is discussed in Chapters 5 and 6. See especially Section 6.09 as regards self-defence and peace operations.

1. Two distinctions must be made regarding the term 'United Nations forces', in order to correctly define the scope of the specific right of self-defence under discussion. First, the term refers exclusively to forces operating under the direct command and control of the United Nations and does not include so-called 'coalitions of the willing', that is forces consisting of military units of States willing to carry out a United Nations mandate but under national or command and control or as part of a NATO operation. United Nations policies, regulations, and rights apply only to forces under direct command and control of the United Nations.[9] **24.05**

2. The second distinction is that the specific right of self-defence in question applies only to United Nations forces operating under a 'purely' peacekeeping mandate. This distinction will be clarified further below in Section 24.06 and its commentary.

3. 'True' UN peacekeeping forces have always only been authorized to use force in personal self-defence and are given instructions never to take the initiative in the use of (armed) force.[10] From the operation in Cyprus (UNFICYP) onward, however, 'self-defence' as applied by the United Nations includes unique elements not normally found in definitions of that term in other areas. The UN Secretary General's Aide-memoire of 10 April 1964, as well as his report of 10 September 1964, included as part of the principles on the use of force in self-defence by UNFICYP the authority to use force against 'attempts by force to prevent [the Force] from carrying out [its] responsibilities as ordered by [its] commanders'.[11] In the Report of the Secretary General on the Implementation of Security Council Resolution 340 (1973)[12] on the operation UNEF II, this extensive view on the right of self-defence was repeated, by stating that self-defence for UNEF included 'resistance to attempts by forceful means to prevent it from discharging its duties under the mandate of the Security Council'.

4. The right of UN peacekeeping forces to exercise the right of self-defence, including the use of necessary force to counter attempts by forceful means to prevent them from carrying out their mandate, is now part of the standard UN guidelines and regulations on peacekeeping.[13]

[9] The special status and legal consequences of forces under United Nations command and control played a central part in the cases before the District Court at The Hague between (relatives of) victims of the fall of the enclave in Srebrenica in 1995 and the Dutch Government. Supreme Court rulings ECLI: NL:HR:2013:BZ9225 and ECLI:NL:HR:2013:BZ9228, 6 September 2013.

[10] K.E. Cox, 'Beyond Self-Defence: United Nations Peacekeeping Operations & The Use of Force', 27(2) *Denver Journal of International Law and Policy* (1999), 239–73.

[11] Ibid. 254, and <http://www.unficyp.org/nqcontent.cfm?a_id=1565&tt=graphic&lang=l1>.

[12] UN Document S/11052/Rev.1, 27 October 1973.

[13] The UN Department of Peacekeeping Operations 1995 *General Guidelines for Peace-Keeping Operations*, para. 35: 'Since 1973, the guidelines approved by the Security Council for each peace-keeping force have stipulated that self-defence is deemed to include resistance to attempts by forceful means to prevent the peace-keeping force from discharging its duties under the mandate of the Security Council'. See also M. Bothe, 'Peace-Keeping', in B. Simma (ed.), *The Charter of the United Nations: A Commentary*, 3rd edn (Oxford: Oxford University Press, 2012), before Chapter VII, MN 126.

24.06 **United Nations self-defence against armed attempts to interfere with the execution of the mandate is not limited to operations authorized under Chapter VII of the Charter of the United Nations. In traditional peacekeeping operations, however, it may not always be expedient to exercise this aspect of the United Nations right of self-defence to its fullest extent when the agreement of the local parties is a necessity for mission accomplishment.**

1. The relationship between the right of UN forces to use force and the nature of the mandating resolution can be a source of confusion. Given the nature of Chapter VII of the United Nations Charter and consequently of any operations authorized under that Chapter, it is tempting to deduce a conditionality between the extent of the right to use force by UN forces and an authorization of the mandate under Chapter VII.

2. The legal significance of the difference between peacekeeping missions and operations carried out under a mandate authorized under Chapter VII of the Charter is that the forces in the latter operations are authorized to enforce the entire mandate at all times. Their enforcement authority is consequently not limited to defence against armed interference (reactive), but extends to enforcing any element in the resolution in order to restore or maintain international peace and security (proactive). While support by the local parties of such actions is relevant from a military operational point of view, since that defines the difference between a permissive and a hostile environment, it is not legally relevant for the authority of the UN Force to act.

3. For peacekeeping operations, however, the consent of the local parties is a *conditio sine qua non*. After all, such operations can only be set up and carried out with the (continued) consent of the (former) parties to the conflict. Consequently, while such UN forces may be authorized to act in a certain manner, it may not always be expedient to do so. The range of possible actions available to such forces may thus be limited not necessarily by legal restrictions, but by practical or operational limitations intended to enhance or display the impartial status of the Force.

4. The difficulties of reconciling the authority to use force and the need to maintain good relations with the local parties has led to suggestions that peacekeeping forces would do well to limit all use of force to 'traditional' self-defence only.[14] The Report of the Panel on United Nations Peace Operations[15] appears to support this view in paragraph 48, stating: 'The Panel concurs that consent of the local parties, impartiality and use of force only in self-defence should remain the bedrock principles of peacekeeping.' The Panel continues, however, with a slightly

[14] M. von Grüningen, 'Neutrality and Peace-Keeping' in A. Cassese, *United Nations Peace-Keeping: Legal Essays* (Alphen aan den Rijn: Sijthoff & Noordhoff, 1978), 138.

[15] UN Doc. A/55/305—S/2000/809. More commonly referred to as the 'Brahimi Report'.

more pragmatic approach: 'Experience shows, however, that in the context of modern peace operations dealing with intra-State/trans-national conflicts, consent may be manipulated in many ways by the local parties. [A party may] withdraw consent when the peacekeeping operation no longer serves its interest.' The Panel therefore recommends in paragraph 49: 'Once deployed, United Nations peacekeepers must be able to carry out their mandate professionally and successfully. This means that United Nations military units must be capable of defending themselves, other mission components and the mission mandate.' The last part of that suggestion appears to be a clear and direct reference to the specific right of self-defence for UN forces at issue. 24.06

5. It follows from the above that the right of self-defence for UN peacekeeping forces is extensive, authorizing not only the use of force in defence of personnel and equipment, but also the use of force against attempts by forceful means to prevent the units from carrying out their mission.

Unit self-defence consists of the right of a commander to take all necessary measures to defend his unit against an (imminent) attack. 24.07

1. Commanders of military units have the right to take all necessary actions to defend their unit against an attack or an imminent attack. In the United States, a commander additionally has the obligation to do so.[16] Although there is some controversy regarding the precise legal basis for this right, its existence is generally accepted.[17]

2. The right to unit self-defence is exclusive to military units, regardless of their nature. A unit can consist of an army platoon, a ship, an aircraft, or can encompass a national or international task force which is operating as a single unit.[18]

3. The use of force exercised in the context of unit self-defence must be in response to an attack or imminent attack[19] and must additionally meet the criteria of necessity and proportionality.[20] As may be stipulated in the applicable rules of engagement,[21] the right to unit self-defence is an inherent right and applies regardless of the rules of engagement or the mission at hand.

[16] The US Joint Chiefs of Staff Standing Rules of Engagement (JCS SROE), 15 January 2000, para. 5.a. of Enclosure A.

[17] J.A. Roach, 'Rules of Engagement', 36(1) *Naval War College Review* (1983), 49 and D. Stephens, 'Rules of Engagement and the Concept of Unit Self Defence', 45 *Naval Law Review* (1998), 126–51.

[18] For example, a naval task force or a fighter wing operating or manoeuvring as a single unit can be considered a unit in the sense of unit self-defence. The size or composition of the unit is not relevant, the operation as a single unit is.

[19] Roach, 'Rules of Engagement', 49.

[20] Stephens, 'Rules of Engagement'. See also JCS SROE, para. 5.f. of Enclosure A.

[21] JCS SROE, para. 6.b. of the main body and paras 2.a., 5.a., and 5.d. of Enclosure A.

24.08 **The right to unit self-defence is primarily derived from the right of national self-defence, combined with the status of military units as representatives of the sovereign rights of the State in question.**

1. Three theoretical models can be suggested as a legal source of the right of unit self-defence.

2. The first model views the unit as a collection of individuals, thus making unit self-defence a form of 'collective personal self-defence'. While it is undeniable that units consist of individuals and that individuals enjoy the right of personal self-defence, this would place unit self-defence in the realm of criminal law. Since the specific requirements demanded by the legal regime on which personal self-defence is based vary from State to State, as will be discussed later, this in itself already makes personal self-defence an unstable basis for unit self-defence by multinational units.[22] Furthermore, the legal requirements for personal self-defence are not easily reconcilable with the nature and activities of a military unit. Unit self-defence, however, is exclusive to military units and indelibly linked to the military nature of the unit. While 'collective personal self-defence' is therefore not entirely untenable as a legal basis for the concept of unit self-defence, it cannot by itself fully support all the acts which may be required in unit self-defence.

3. A second model views the right of personal self-defence as a corollary to the right to life and extends that corollary to the right of military personnel to defend themselves as a unit.[23] While this approach is laudable in terms of emphasizing both the right to life and the right to personal self-defence of military servicemen, the right of unit self-defence cannot be based on the provisions of human rights instruments. First, the human rights set forth in those instruments, such as the International Covenant on Civil and Political Rights (ICCPR), are designed as the rights of people against abuse of power by their governments. Military units, on the other hand, are representatives of those governments and carry out government orders and policy. While the individuals in those units may, in other words, have recourse to the law of human rights, it cannot be argued that the military unit as such has such recourse. Second, the right to life as enshrined in Article 6 of the ICCPR prohibits the arbitrary taking of life, not all taking of life. The right to life as set forth in Article 2 of the European Convention for the Protection of Human Rights and Fundamental Freedoms (ECHR) is a little different and, contrary to Article 6 of the ICCPR, is written more clearly to allow for lawful exceptions.

[22] The JCS SROE limit unit self-defence to the defence of the unit and other US forces in the vicinity. Multinational unit self-defence or defence of non-US units in the vicinity is consequently not an automatic prerogative for US forces under the SROE.

[23] Stephens, 'Rules of Engagement'; D. Stephens, 'Human Rights and Armed Conflict—The Advisory Opinion of the International Court of Justice in the Nuclear Weapons Case', 4 *Yale Human Rights & Development Law Journal* (2001), 1–24, <http://islandia.law.yale.edu/yhrdlj/pdf/Vol%204/Stephens.pdf>; M.D. Maxwell, 'Individual Self-Defence and the Rules of Engagement: Are the Two Mutually Exclusive?', 41(1–2) *The Military Law and the Law of War Review* (2002), 39–53.

Article 2, paragraph 2, of the ECHR states that deprivation of life is not contrary to the Convention if it is the result of minimum necessary force in defence of any person, in order to effect the arrest or prevent the escape of a person lawfully detained or in action lawfully taken to quell a riot or insurrection. While the right to personal self-defence (and defence of others) is thus included in the ECHR provision on the right to life, that does not mean that Article 2 of the ECHR creates a corollary right to use force in self-defence. This would be comparable to the freedom of speech granting a corollary right of (forced) access to the media, regardless of the wishes or discretion of editors or publishers. **24.08**

4. The final model is based on the classical view of military units as representatives of the sovereign State to which they belong and bestowing on them some of the inherent, sovereign rights enjoyed by the State. In this model, unit self-defence is a unit-level representation of the national right of self-defence.[24]

5. The model based on sovereign rights presents two main questions to be resolved. First, national self-defence is normally an area of political decision-making at the highest levels of government, involving aspects of foreign policy, national security, and possible constitutional requirements. The unit commander is not usally part of such decision-making and may not have access to all the information required for such decisions. Second, the trigger event or consideration for the use of force in self-defence at the level of national self-defence can differ from that at the level of unit self-defence (see Section 8.03 and the commentary thereto for the trigger requirement of an armed attack in the context of national self-defence under Article 51 of the Charter of the United Nations). At the unit level, different considerations apply and responses may be required even though the act being defended against may not meet the definition of 'armed attack' as applicable for national self-defence.[25] In practice, the trigger event being defended against at the unit level will be more immediate, of smaller scale than an attack on a nation as a whole, and require an immediate response.

6. The first problem already identified can be addressed by viewing unit self-defence as a tactical-level right, whereas the right of national self-defence is a strategic-level right. In downscaling from the strategic level to the tactical level, the command requirements and the extent of the response equally diminishes. In other words, a unit commander need not have the authority to order the entire military assets of his nation to respond to the attack as if the nation was under attack but merely needs to have, and has, the authority to defend his unit against the attack on his or her unit. Similarly, an attack on a unit does not ordinarily lead to an activation of all the national self-defence responses in the nation whose unit is under attack, but will usually be only a piece in a larger composition of events and circumstances that define the national security situation at the time in question.

[24] The legal basis for the right of national self-defence is discussed in Chapter 8.
[25] Stephens, 'Rules of Engagement'.

24.08 7. Consequently, while the model of unit self-defence as a tactical-level representation of the sovereign right of nations to national self-defence requires some interpretation and modification to allow for the differences in scale and command level, this model most clearly and coherently explains and supports the right of unit self-defence under international law.

24.09 **The criteria applicable to the actual exercise of unit self-defence are the *Caroline* criteria: the use of force in self-defence must be immediately and unequivocally necessary; there must be no feasible alternatives to the use of force; and the force used must be proportional to the level of the attack being defended against.**

1. The use of force in (unit) self-defence must be related to an (imminent) attack on the unit in question.[26] Furthermore, the measures taken must be necessary as well as proportionate to the attack being defended against.[27]

2. The right of unit self-defence is an inherent right and its exercise does not require authorization from higher command authority. On the other hand, given the inherent impact of the use of force by a military unit in terms of foreign relations, national security, and international peace and security, it is clear that the exercise of this right is limited to situations in which alternatives to the use of force no longer exist or would not be feasible.

24.10 **Units comprising a larger unit, such as aircraft flying together as a single flight or ships sailing together as a single naval squadron, may assist each other in the exercise of unit self-defence if they operate together as a single unit. Units which arrive at the scene of events after the attack has already commenced, such as quick reaction forces sent as reinforcements in the context of a (multinational) operation, cannot act automatically on the basis of unit self-defence but derive their authorization from either extended self-defence or the right of a Force to defend itself, as applicable.**

1. The right of unit self-defence, by its nature, is limited to military units. While units can consist of a composition of smaller units, the crucial criterion is the activity as one single unit. Consequently, the entire armed forces of a nation, even if committed to the same operation or same theatre of war, cannot be said to be a 'unit' as they will not manoeuvre or respond as one single unit.

2. Composite units of a larger unit which is exercising the right of unit self-defence can, of course, assist each other in the exercise of that right. The right adheres to the unit as a whole, meaning each constituent part of that whole shares in that right.

[26] J.A. Roach, 'Rules of Engagement'. [27] JCS SROE, para. 5.f. of Enclosure A.

3. Reinforcements arriving on the scene at a later moment in time do not meet the requirements of unit self-defence on two grounds. First, they are not part of the unit exercising the right of unit self-defence and therefore do not share in that unit's right of self-defence. Second, they arrive on the scene for the very purpose of engaging an enemy in an already existing combat situation, which is not the same legal context as defending against an attack as referred to in the right of unit self-defence. **24.10**

4. This commentary, it should be noted, does not mean that reinforcement units may not assist the units they have come to reinforce or that such units necessarily operate illegally. They simply do not operate under the right of unit self-defence and therefore the legal requirements and the legal basis for their actions, including any use of force, must be found in other principles of law.

Unit self-defence (and ultimately personal self-defence) is an inherent right and not dependent or contingent on a mandate or mission. Although restricted to situations involving an (imminent) attack on the unit invoking this right, the right is neither dependent on, nor limited by, any ROE. Nothing in any ROE limits or prohibits this inherent right. **24.11**

1. The common statement in ROE that nothing in the ROE negates or limits the inherent right of self-defence clearly does not refer unmitigated to all conceptually possible forms of self-defence. As will be discussed later in this chapter, that statement cannot apply to the NATO concept of extended self-defence or the use of force in the context of force protection measures in their entirety. Some actions will be subject to the ROE for the operation in question, and some ROE will apply to the use of force in extended self-defence or force protection. Examples include ROE restricting the use of certain specific weapons and ROE regulating the geographic limits of the operation.

2. Where the situation in a given operation deteriorates and the military force is no longer able to carry out the mandate but is occupied with saving itself, such as prior to an emergency extraction, or in situations in which individual servicemen find themselves the subject of a personal attack, such as during an off-duty activity, the use of force in self-defence becomes based on other forms of self-defence, such as unit self-defence and personal self-defence. Outside the context of an operation, unit self-defence and personal self-defence are the only bases on which the use of force in self-defence can be based.

3. Both unit self-defence and personal self-defence are inherent rights and are not linked to the mandate, objective, or mission of any operation. They are therefore not subject to restriction or regulation by ROE. Consequently, the reference to self-defence in ROE and the instruction that the ROE do not limit or restrict the right of self-defence refers to unit and personal self-defence, as a reminder that ultimately

24.11 the use of force in self-defence is justified and the ROE may not interfere with that inherent right.

4. In the context of armed conflicts, the right of unit self-defence will be mostly inapplicable or irrelevant. The use of force by military units against the enemy, including defence against acts of war by the enemy, is by its nature justified as part of the conduct of hostilities. While the use of force in such contexts must be in accordance with the applicable rules of engagement (and meet the requirements of the laws of armed conflict), its legal basis is not unit self-defence but the right of combatants to directly participate in hostilities.[28]

24.12 **Extended self-defence and self-defence in the context of force protection are indelibly linked to the nature and tasks of the Force as such and are therefore equally indelibly linked to mission accomplishment. Consequently, the use of force in such contexts may be regulated by ROE and may extend beyond mere defence against an (imminent) attack.**

1. A fundamental conceptual difference exists between the right of self-defence as an inherent right to save life and defend against an attack on the one hand, and the use of force to achieve a mandate or a military or political objective. By their natures and due to their legal bases, extended self-defence as utilized by NATO and the various forms of self-defence utilized by a military force in the context of force protection are contingent on the nature of the Force in question. In the case of extended self-defence, the Force in question is a Force consisting of units from NATO nations operating under NATO command. In the case of the use of force in force protection, the Force in question is a (multinational) force carrying out a mandate. In both cases, the right to defend that force is related to the tasks, orders, and objectives of the Force and the very existence of the Force for a given purpose or objective. Consequently, the use of force in these two forms of self-defence is related to achieving the objective or accomplishing the mission of the military force in question.

2. The use of force in the context of mission accomplishment is normally regulated by rules of engagement. The use of force in the context of extended self-defence and as part of the force protection measures which can be taken by a military (peace) force are linked to, and can be considered part of, the use of force for mission accomplishment. Consequently, the use of force in these two forms of self-defence may be subject to the ROE for the operation in question.[29]

[28] Even during armed conflict, the right of unit self-defence still exists, of course, and situations may (theoretically) arise in which it may be the basis for action by military servicemen. Any attack being defended against must in that case, in terms of intent, be something other than a direct participation in the hostilities by the attacking party (which would render it, after all, a 'normal' combatant situation) and be committed by a party other than a(n enemy) party to the armed conflict in question.

[29] Another line of reasoning that supports this statement is the observation that if the ROE were not applicable to these two forms of the use of force, and these two forms of the right to use force would

ROE relating to the concepts of hostile act and hostile intent, in the meaning as used by NATO, are intended to equalize the response abilities of units within multinational forces and enable coherent response in extended self-defence and force protection regardless of national statutes on self-defence. The same applies to the so-called 'confirmatory ROE' used within the context of EU operations. **24.13**

1. Paragraph 5.a. of the United States Joint Chiefs of Staff Standing Rules of Engagement (SROE)[30] lists, as part of the definition of the 'inherent right of self-defence', the acts against which this right may be exercised. These acts are 'hostile acts' and 'demonstrated hostile intent'. Paragraph 5.g. subsequently defines 'hostile act' as '[a]n attack or other use of force . . . '.[31] 'Hostile intent' is defined in paragraph 5.h. as '[t]he threat of imminent use of force'.

2. Within NATO, however, as became clear in the Military Committee working group which drafted the MC 362 document on NATO Rules of Engagement, many nations view the concepts of hostile act and hostile intent as referring to different situations than those triggering the right of self-defence.[32] Instead, these nations consider the use of force in the context of the concepts of hostile act and hostile intent as part of the use of force for mission accomplishment and therefore dependent on suitable ROE authorization. To these nations, self-defence is seen as the right to defend against an (imminent) attack, while a hostile act is considered an act detrimental to the objectives and purposes of the Force but not rising to the level of an actual attack. Finally, hostile intent is seen by these nations as the intent to commit a hostile act. For these nations, acting against a hostile act or a hostile intent requires ROE authorization, while for nations adhering to the US definitions such a response is based on inherent rights derived from national law or policy. The ROE regulating the use of force against hostile acts and hostile intent in the context of a

render the ROE inapplicable, the first combat engagement in the operation in question would already be enough to render the ROE for the operation nullified and would beg the question why there are ROE in the first place.

[30] Roach, 'Rules of Engagement'.

[31] A second definition of 'hostile act' given in the SROE is 'force used directly to preclude or impede the mission and/or duties of US forces, including the recovery of US personnel and vital US Government property'. This extensive definition of 'hostile act' is also included, with the addition of the 'imminent' aspect, in the definition of 'hostile intent'. It is arguable whether this particular definition finds support in legal views outside the United States.

[32] The statements regarding the negotiations in the working group referred to in the text are based on the observations of the present author as a participant of that working group. It is customary within NATO not to attribute opinions or statements of national delegates or the national positions of delegations. An exception is made here in attributing the source of the concepts of hostile act and hostile intent to the United States, as well as the specific US definition thereof, for two reasons. First, the SROE document in which these terms are defined is publicly available and is unclassified. Second, the US can be considered the source and standard for ROE analysis and development by nature of their long and varied experience in developing and applying ROE in a wide variety of situations and operations. Consequently, theories and observations on ROE doctrine are by necessity compared to the US standard.

24.13 NATO operation give those nations requiring such ROE the basis to act; while they are superfluous, but thereby not detrimental, to those nations that already claim an inherent right to act.

3. Within the context of EU operations, recognition of the differences in national legal approaches to the right of self-defence has led to the adoption in each set of EU ROE a number of so-called 'confirmatory ROE'. These ROE authorize the use of force in situations which most nations would consider self-defence situations but which for some nations may fall outside the strict legal framework of (personal) self-defence law. The use of such confirmatory ROE is therefore identical in intent to the NATO use of ROE on hostile acts and hostile intent, in that they allow a unified response to a given threat.[33] Within the EU context, the ROE for the use of force against a hostile act or hostile intent are instead viewed as 'attack' ROE.

4. While it is unfortunate that the same terms are used by different parties to define different enemy acts, and therefore refer to different legal contexts for the use of force in response, the debate on this issue within NATO has made clear the conceptual relationship between self-defence and the NATO and EU concepts of hostile act and hostile intent. This relationship exists in a temporal form and in a situational form. The temporal form is derived by evaluating the imminence of the threat to be defended against. In case of an actual attack or an imminent attack, the defence can be based on the inherent right of (personal) self-defence. Threats which are not imminent enough to justify recourse to (personal) self-defence but are hostile in nature, are classified as 'hostile acts other than actual attacks'. The use of force in defence against such acts requires ROE authorization and cannot be justified by an inherent right to use force, such as in (personal) self-defence. Finally, threats or estimates which are identified or based on intelligence information and which signal preparations by the enemy to commit hostile acts are classified as cases of 'hostile intent other than an imminent attack'. Any use of force in response to such cases similarly requires ROE authorization. When placed on a graphical representation such as a timeline, attacks and imminent attacks are located at, or very close to, the 'now' end of the timescale. Hostile intent not constituting an imminent attack exists at the far end of the timescale. Finally, hostile acts not constituting actual attacks can be placed somewhere in between the two ends of the scale, the precise location depending on the nature of the hostile act.

5. The situational form of the relationship between (personal) self-defence, hostile acts, and hostile intent consists of qualifying the threat encountered on the basis of the political or operational context in which the threat takes place. An act which can trigger a justified response on the basis of (personal) self-defence in one situation may be classified as a hostile act not constituting an actual attack in a different

[33] It should be noted that the UN, on the other hand, follows the US definitions in the sense that hostile acts are considered attacks or other use of force against a UN force and hostile intent is considered the intent to carry out a hostile act.

situation. The determination of the nature of, and therefore the required response to, enemy actions will, logically, depend on the geopolitical situation prevailing at the time, including political tension levels or operational threat estimates in the theatre of operations, prior events, or prior activities of the enemy, etc.[34] Where there is no real threatening behaviour as yet and intelligence information or the interpretation of observed activities of another party are the only sources available to evaluate the intentions of that other party, the situational form of the relationship between self-defence, hostile acts, and hostile intent becomes especially critical. 24.13

6. As national statutes differ as regards the trigger point for justified use of force in (personal) self-defence, both in terms of the degree of imminence required and in terms of the subjects of that right,[35] this point cannot be placed on any timeline or be linked to any specific trigger criterion that would satisfy the various legal or political interests of all nations. This means that an enemy act may trigger a (right to) response based on self-defence in one national contingent, while another contingent may need ROE before being considered authorized to respond. In international operations involving multinational forces, this issue needs to be addressed in the ROE in order to ensure a unified response to threats against the Force.

The right to personal self-defence is well recognized in criminal law systems around the world. It is distinct from the other forms of self-defence discussed in this chapter both in terms of legal basis and as regards the applicable legal framework. 24.14

1. The right of personal self-defence is normally associated with the field of criminal law and seen as an exception to the (limited or absolute) State monopoly on the use of force through the law enforcement and military institutions. Analysis of the laws and statutes of the United States, the Netherlands, Canada, Belgium, Germany, and France shows personal self-defence as a justification,[36] although in any case the Netherlands' criminal code also allows a form of personal self-defence as an excuse.[37]

[34] A deliberately oversimplified example may illustrate this point. The transfer of stores of ammunition and troops in one nation as observed by an allied nation will not usually raise any concern. The same activity in one nation as observed by another nation which is on the brink of war with that nation may trigger national self-defence measures in preparation or response to an imminent attack and outbreak of war.

[35] See later in the chapter as regards the commentary to Sections 23.09 and 23.11 right of personal self-defence.

[36] A justification is a form of legal defence under criminal law which admits the commission of the (criminal) act in question, but provides sufficient reason why the accused was justified to do so and should therefore be acquitted. An excuse, on the other hand, is a form of legal defence under criminal law which argues that the accused lacked the *mens rea* (intent to commit the act and knowledge that a criminal or wrongful act was being committed) to commit the criminal act as charged. J. Gardner, 'Fletcher on Offences and Defences', available at <http://users.ox.ac.uk/~lawf0081/fletcher.pdf>.

[37] Art. 41, para. 1, of the Criminal Code of the Netherlands provides the basis for the justification of self-defence, under the conditions as set forth in that Article and case law. Art. 41, para. 2, on the other hand, provides the basis for the excuse of excessive self-defence, provided the accused can prove the self-defence situation caused such mental or emotional turmoil that he no longer knew what he was doing.

24.14 2. Personal self-defence as part of the criminal law system is related to the individual as a member of society. As such, it is distinct from the other forms of self-defence as described earlier, which are related to the individual as a member of a military unit, a UN peace force, or other types of military forces. While those other types of self-defence also bestow a right upon the individual serviceman to defend himself, the right to do so in those circumstances derives from different legal bases. Consequently, the applicable rules and requirements for a legitimate recourse to self-defence differ considerably between the forms of self-defence related to the military identity of the defending party and the form discussed below, for which the military identity is (mostly) irrelevant.[38]

3. The basis for personal self-defence in criminal law sets it apart from the international law bases for the other forms of self-defence. It also makes it subject to national interpretation and thereby pluriform in its application by (members of) national contingents in multinational forces. While the interpretation and application of the other forms of self-defence are, or should be, uniform for all members of a multinational force, variations in national statutes and interpretations of personal self-defence can lead to variations in the rights to use force in self-defence among the national contingents of a multinational force.

24.15 **The central criteria for a legitimate recourse to self-defence are necessity and proportionality.**

1. The principles of necessity and proportionality are inherent in every form of self-defence, as was shown earlier. The meaning normally given to these principles in the civilian criminal law context, however, may not always correlate with the circumstances and complexities of the military operational context.

2. Proportionality in a criminal law approach to personal self-defence is commonly occupied with whether the response of the accused matched the threat posed by the other party. In such an evaluation, the use of weapons, especially firearms, is not normally considered justified except in the rare cases where such use is justified by a (real or reasonably believed) high level of (armed) threat being defended against. In the military context, however, the use of weapons and firearms is more commonplace and the minimum level of force which can be applied in response to a threat is frequently already much higher than normally encountered in a civilian situation. It should be noted, however, that the proportionality test refers to the choice of means from those available at the time. There is no legal requirement (nor any possibility) to always have all conceivable types of means available. Consequently, if the only reasonable recourse is to use force in self-defence and the minimum force available is the use of automatic weapons, for example, then the proportionality requirement

[38] The military identity may be relevant in relation to the evaluation whether proper care and diligence were applied, as discussed in Section 24.21.

may already have been met even though in non-military situations the use of automatic weapons would not as easily be considered a proportional response.[39] 24.15

3. In applying the criminal law concept of personal self-defence to military operational contexts, the necessity criterion creates more interpretative difficulties than the proportionality criterion. As self-defence allows individuals to take action normally reserved for State authorities, the law, including statutes and case law, assigns considerable importance and additional conditional elements to the test whether the use of force in self-defence was necessary. If the necessity to use force in self-defence cannot be proven, then the use of force can only be justified if it was supported by applicable ROE.

Proving necessity in the context of personal self-defence consists of two evaluations: 24.16

(a) proof of the necessity to defend, as opposed to other courses of action to reconcile the situation; and

(b) proof of the necessity to choose, within the choice of means available, the particular means employed in the actual exercise of personal self-defence.

1. In the criminal law context of personal self-defence, and contrary to the more usual military operational context, the necessity to defend oneself against an attack is not self-evident. Alternatives to self-defence, and especially alternatives to the use of force, must be taken into consideration. Furthermore, proof will normally be required why those alternatives were not considered reasonable or viable. Some specific examples of this will be discussed later.

2. Although there is a certain degree of conceptual overlap between the principles of necessity and proportionality in the context of the use of force, the two principles are not identical. In the proportionality test, the main concern is whether the means used in the exercise of the right of self-defence was commensurate with the threat being defended against. In the necessity test, the need to use force in self-defence may need to be proven or supported by evidence in addition to proving the necessity to defend oneself at all. This element of the necessity test is concerned with proving that the least destructive or damaging choice of means was used.

Proof of the necessity to defend oneself may be negated by prior provocation by the defending party. On the other hand, a provoked attack which is disproportionate to the provocation may be cause for a legitimate recourse to personal self-defence after all. 24.17

[39] The test whether a serviceman's response was proportional should not examine whether the deployment of military personnel and weapons in itself was appropriate or proportional. The decision to deploy military personnel is a political decision for which others than the serviceman exercising personal self-defence are responsible.

24.17 1. Many national criminal law statutes, laws, and case law specify that prior provocation on the part of the defending party negates that party's right to invoke the right of self-defence in subsequent criminal prosecution.[40]

2. Defining or identifying which acts constitute provocation can be challenging in the context of a military operation. In some cases, the presence of military forces can have an intrinsically provocative effect on the inhabitants and authorities of the region in question, including neighbouring States. Consequently, the negation of justified recourse to the right of self-defence by prior provocation may necessitate extensive interpretation and situational awareness on the part of the court in trials involving military personnel invoking the right of personal self-defence.

3. The NATO doctrine on rules of engagement states that in addition to regulating the use of force, ROE are also used to regulate actions which may be deemed to be provocative.[41] ROE doctrine also emphasizes that the right of self-defence applies regardless of any ROE which may be in effect. However, the relationship between provocation and the right of personal self-defence as used in the context of national criminal law makes recourse to that right to defend against the consequences of actions taken under provocative ROE legally unstable.[42] The reference to self-defence in the NATO doctrine must therefore be understood to refer, in most cases, to the other forms of self-defence discussed earlier, which find their legal bases in international law.[43]

24.18 **Proof of the necessity to defend oneself may be negated if the defending party knowingly and willingly placed himself or herself, without necessity or objectively legitimate reason, in the vicinity of the attacking party even though the capability and intent of the attacking party to carry out an attack was known beforehand.**

1. Where provocation is an active form of inciting situations that may give rise to a need for the use of force in self-defence, a passive form exists in knowingly and

[40] For example, the statutes on self-defence in Arizona (13.404), Connecticut (Section 53a, para. 19, subsection (c)), Delaware (para. 464 subsection (c)(1)), Georgia (Section 16-3-21, subsection (b)(1)) and Indiana (35-41-3-2, subsection (c)(2)) contain such specifications regarding provocation. In the Netherlands, provocation is not mentioned in the actual text of the Criminal Code but is included in the court's considerations and rulings in criminal cases involving (claims of) the right of self-defence.

[41] NATO document MC 362/1.

[42] It should be emphasized that this observation applies only to personal self-defence as part of the national criminal law system and does not necessarily apply to the other forms of self-defence as discussed in this chapter. Consequently, actions authorized by ROE and intended to be provocative may lead to situations in which extended self-defence, unit self-defence, or the use of force in the context of force protection may need to be applied in accordance with the international legal bases for those forms of self-defence. Such situations may be very difficult to reconcile with the traditional criminal law concept of personal self-defence.

[43] An exception would be a situation in which national criminal law provisions on personal self-defence are sufficiently lenient to allow for the use of force in such circumstances. Such a situation would not resolve the inherent flaw, however, in relying on national criminal law provisions aimed at the individual as a basis to use force in international military operations by military units.

willingly seeking out specific situations or deliberately placing oneself in harm's way in order that a need for the use of force in self-defence will ultimately arise. Being at fault for the situation that occurred, or intentionally causing such a situation can negate the justification of self-defence in the same way as provocation.[44] **24.18**

2. The nullifying effects of seeking out a self-defence situation on the justification of self-defence under national criminal law create complications for the application of personal self-defence in an operational environment. Placing oneself in harm's way, seeking out the enemy, and drawing fire or attack from the enemy are commonly among the tasks of servicemen in the context of a military operation or, at least, the 'ordinary course of events' of many military operational deployments. The use of force in such situations consequently cannot easily be justified on the basis of the right of personal self-defence as set forth in national criminal law but instead must be based on ROE which reflect the mandate of the operation and the authority to use force in the interest of mission accomplishment, whether it be through enforcement action or one of the forms of 'military' self-defence discussed previously, Sections 24.08–24.11.

Proof of the necessity to defend oneself may be negated if an avenue of retreat was available but not utilized. The duty to retreat is not imposed in all statutes and is limited in certain statutes. Even in such cases, however, the choice to defend rather than to break off a confrontation may be taken into account in judging the legitimacy of the recourse to personal self-defence. **24.19**

1. Some national or federal State statutes on personal self-defence require the defending party to retreat if an avenue of retreat is available, while failure to do so negates the justification of self-defence.[45] Where and when such a duty applies, it will by its very nature be difficult to reconcile with military operational intentions and duties and the mission objectives of the operation in question. Put simply, the duty to retreat as set forth in certain statutes and laws consists of the requirement to retreat if it is reasonable or safe to do so before the use of force in self-defence can be considered justified.[46]

[44] For a case law application of the interaction between intent, knowledge, and negligence or fault as regards the circumstances, see the decision by the Supreme Court of the Netherlands of 31 October 2000 (LJN AA7960).

[45] S.P. Aggergaard, 'Criminal Law—Retreat From Reason: How Minnesota's New No-Retreat Rule Confuses the Law and Cries for Alteration—State v. Glowacki', 29(2) *William Mitchell Law Review* (2002), 657–93. See also Supreme Court of the Netherlands, HR 11 June 2002 (LJN AE 1316).

[46] The Texas Penal Code, Chapter 9, para. 32, subsection (a) under (2), contains such a 'reasonable' test as part of the duty to retreat. A common exception to the duty to retreat in several state statutes on self-defence in the United States is the 'castle doctrine'. This doctrine states that the duty to retreat does not apply if the defending party was exercising the right of personal self-defence in his own home. See Aggergaard, 'Criminal Law', 665–6. It is self-evident that this doctrine has no real use in making personal self-defence any more readily suitable as a basis for the use of force in the context of achieving military objectives.

24.19 2. Where the duty to retreat is required by local law and is incompatible with the objectives or purpose of a military operation, any use of force in furtherance of those objectives or that purpose must be based on applicable ROE or the 'military' forms of self-defence discussed in Sections 24.08–24.11 and cannot be justified by recourse to the right of personal self-defence as set forth in national criminal law.

24.20 **In deciding on the choice of means, the least destructive means available and suitable must be chosen.**

1. Although the principles of necessity and proportionality are distinct and have their own criteria, the two principles are reflected jointly in the requirement, when using force to respond to a threat, to use the least destructive means available which is still suitable to answer the threat. This requirement is usually reflected in ROE in the form of an injunction to use no more force than is strictly necessary.

2. The proportionality aspect of the choice of means requires that there be a reasonable relationship between the attack being defended against and the means chosen in carrying out that defence. Put simply, the force used in defending against an attack must not be unnecessarily greater in intensity or type of force than that being defended against.

3. As was discussed briefly in Section 24.07, commentary para. 3, the injunction to use no more force than is strictly necessary does not mean that a serviceman or unit whose only recourse is the use of deadly force through the use of firearms may only defend itself if the attack matches such use of force and must suffer or tolerate any other, lesser attack. It does carry an implicit responsibility, however, to exercise due diligence and caution in evaluating whether self-defence is necessary or whether other means of resolving the situation are feasible and reasonable under the circumstances as well as evaluating whether the use of force as such is necessary.

4. The injunction to use no more force than is strictly necessary does not mean that the least destructive means in an absolute sense must be used. The choice of means must also still be suitable for the task at hand. In situations in which the choice of means is limited, this may require the use of a weapon or weapon system that would otherwise not be considered the most obvious choice. Conversely, in deployments in which non-lethal weapons are part of the available means, proper training and instruction is required to clarify the role such weapons have in relation to the ROE in order to avoid the misconception that such means must always be exhausted prior to the use of deadly force.[47]

24.21 **The level of training and expertise that may be expected of military personnel increases the level of care and diligence expected from**

[47] For conflicting views on the issue of deadly force and restrictions in ROE, see W.H. Parks, 'Deadly Force is Authorized', in Vol. 127 *US Naval Institute: Proceedings* (January 2001), 32–7, and M.S. Martins, 'Deadly Force is Authorized, But Also *Trained*', *Army Lawyer* (September–October 2001).

military personnel and may impose restrictions on the applicability of the criminal law concept of personal self-defence in an operational context. 24.21

1. Most of the tests involved in the determination as to whether the use of force in self-defence was justified involve a determination whether the action under review was commensurate with what a reasonable person would do.[48] The 'reasonable person test' in civilian criminal law settings, however, is not commonly calibrated to evaluate the actions of highly trained military personnel in operational circumstances.[49]

2. Where liability or culpability is closely related with (failure to abide by) an obligation to exercise due diligence, higher standards of diligence or a more disciplined exercise of that diligence may be required of those who exercise an occupation or function, or have received special training, that puts them in a higher or special category of being responsible for the specific actions under review. Examples would be the use of a ladder by a certified window washer, the use of a fire extinguisher by a fire-fighter, and the use of weapons by trained military personnel.

3. While the special circumstances under which military personnel must carry out their duties may result in a more ready acceptance that the use of force is concomitant to their tasks and duties, the special training and status[50] military personnel receive will commonly result in a higher standard of diligence being expected from them while carrying out their duties. What is considered reasonable for military personnel may consequently differ from what is considered reasonable for civilians who have not been trained and are reacting on a more instinctual rather than professional level.

4. Concomitant to the level of training and professionalism of the armed forces, the tenets of military discipline and the interests of mission accomplishment may require that members of a military unit abstain from exercising their (assumed) right of personal self-defence under certain circumstances. Failure to do so or the

[48] P. Kazan, 'Reasonableness, Gender Difference and Self-Defence Law', 24(3) *Manitoba Law Journal* (1997), 549–75.

[49] See especially paras 42–58 of *Bici and Bici v Ministry of Defence*, 7 April 2004, [2004] EWHC 786 (QB). A distinction is necessary between systems of military justice, especially between those in which the entire system is military in nature, such as in the United States, and those which are based on civilian justice systems or on mixed systems, such as in most Western European nations. In the US system, the 'reasonable test' can be applied more easily to evaluate military actions as the system is experienced in the application of military standards. Courts in systems which are not (exclusively) military in nature will commonly require guidance or explication by subject-matter experts to assist them in evaluating military actions.

[50] What is meant here by 'status' is not related to the legal status of forces, such as set forth in treaties, but to the position of military personnel in society as, in a classic sense, warriors and defenders of the nation. More relevant from a legal perspective is that military personnel act on government authority and are authorized to use force, both of which are commonly considered sufficient cause for careful scrutiny of any actions which result in injury, death, or damage to property.

24.21 absence of such restrictions would otherwise result in, for example, every member of a unit on patrol or on a covert mission having a personal right to open fire of his own volition on the basis of a personal threat perception, regardless or in contravention of the orders or intent of the unit commander.

24.22 **Defence of property is not recognized as part of the inherent right of personal self-defence in many national criminal law statutes. Consequently, lesser means of defending property may be required in the context of personal self-defence and the use of deadly force, such as the use of firearms, may be reserved for defence of life. It is understood, on the other hand, that a situation involving the use of lesser means to defend property may at any time escalate to a situation requiring the use of deadly force to defend life.**

1. The status of the right to personal self-defence as an exception to State monopoly on the use of force implicitly requires that the interests to be defended should be of sufficient gravity. In some national statutes, this has resulted in a limitation of the right to personal self-defence in the criminal law context to defence of life only, although commonly including the right of defence against personal injury if the injury reasonably to be expected from the attack is of sufficient gravity. In many national statutes or case law, property is not recognized as an interest of sufficient gravity to warrant the use of force in personal self-defence. Where such limits are not set forth in the statutes themselves, courts may impose such limits in case law by considering the defence of property as failing the necessity test.

2. In the military context, defence of property is commonly a critical component of the assigned duties, tasks, and responsibilities. As all ROE require a solid legal basis, the authorization to use force in the defence of property by military forces requires careful attention when such defence cannot be justified by the inherent right of personal self-defence as set forth in national criminal law. In those nations in which the defence of property is not part of the right of personal self-defence, the legal basis for ROE authorizing the use of force to defend (military) property needs to be derived from other national statutes, an international mandate, or the right of 'military' self-defence as described in Sections 24.08–24.11.

3. Where the use of force to defend property is not authorized as part of personal self-defence, lesser means of defending such property are still possible. Examples include verbal persuasion, physically obstructing access to the property, etc. In the event that such lesser means to defend property develop into an (imminent) attack on the defending personnel, the right of personal self-defence will, of course, apply and authorize the use of force to defend against such an attack. In that case, the right to personal self-defence is triggered by the threat to the personnel involved and not by the (continued) threat to the property in question.

4. The threat of theft of weapons or weapon systems carries an inherent and implicit risk of a (future) threat against life. It is arguable whether such a potential

threat can give rise to a lawful (anticipatory) recourse to the right of personal self-defence in nations in which the defence of property is not part of that right. Aspects such as the nature of the weapon or weapon system will be relevant in evaluating the validity of a claim of personal self-defence in the event of any use of force in such circumstances. **24.22**

5. Threats against property critical to the survival of a Force or individual servicemen may give rise to a lawful recourse to personal self-defence. In such events, the critical nature of the property for the survival of the personnel defending it must, of course, be proven or self-evident.[51]

Some statutes specify that personal self-defence is only authorized against an illegal or unauthorized attack. This principle prevents a claim of personal self-defence in cases involving the use of force against law-enforcement officials on official duty. 24.23

1. Most statutes or case law specify that the use of force in personal self-defence is only justified if the attack being defended against was illegal or unauthorized.

2. In the context of military operations, the limitation of the right to personal self-defence to situations involving illegal attacks renders this right mostly inapplicable or irrelevant during an armed conflict. Attacks by the military forces of the enemy under such circumstances are, after all, legal under the applicable law if they are targeted at military objects, including military personnel. The use of force in reaction to, or in defence against, such legitimate acts of war by the enemy is by its nature justified as part of the conduct of hostilities. While the use of force in such contexts must be in accordance with the applicable rules of engagement (and meets the requirements of the laws of armed conflict) it is not related to the right to personal self-defence under national criminal law.[52]

The defence of others under application of the right of personal self-defence is well recognized in most statutes. Certain logical limitations may be imposed on this aspect in case law or statutes, however, to prevent unbridled invocation of the right of personal self-defence as justification for, effectively, vigilantism. Such limitations may relate to the need for proximity between the defending party and 24.24

[51] Examples would be the water supply in a desert environment, fuel supplies in very remote locations or in arctic circumstances, etc. The (im)possibility of resupplying the unit and the (non-) availability of transportation will, of course, be factors in evaluating a claim of personal self-defence in such circumstances.

[52] Even during armed conflict, the right of personal self-defence still exists, of course, and situations may (theoretically) arise in which it may be the basis for action by military servicemen. Any attack being defended against must in that case be something other than a direct participation in hostilities by the attacking party (which would render it, after all, a combatant situation and not a criminal law self-defence situation).

24.24 **the party being aided, the necessity of providing the aid (e.g. was the party being aided actually under attack or not), etc.**

1. Many statutes regarding personal self-defence extend the aegis of this right to include the defence of others.[53] The combination of this extension of the right of personal self-defence and the legal principle that the ROE do not limit the inherent right of personal self-defence requires careful consideration in the context of military operations.

2. In theory, situations can arise in military operations in which the use of force in defence of others is justified even though the use of force or the actions required exceed or may even be specifically prohibited by the applicable ROE. For such exercise of the right to personal self-defence to be justifiable in practice will require meeting all of the criteria for personal self-defence and ruling out any of the elements which can negate the justification of personal self-defence.

3. In applying the criteria for legitimate recourse to the right of personal self-defence to the use of force in defence of others, the necessity test will also encompass testing whether it was necessary to come to the defence of those others. For example, the geographical relationship between those to be defended and those coming to their rescue may be taken into consideration to determine whether the force used was part of the right of personal self-defence or part of a military engagement in the context of operational ROE.[54] The greater the distance between those to be defended and those coming to their rescue, the less likely such actions will be justifiable as personal self-defence. Similarly, preparations for potential deployment in defence or aid of other units cannot be based on the criminal law right of personal self-defence but must be based on the applicable ROE and operational orders for the operation at hand.[55]

24.25 **The right to personal self-defence is an inherent right and therefore cannot be limited or prohibited by ROE.**

[53] In the United States, some state laws only allow the use of deadly force in this context in defence of (close) relatives or persons belonging to the household of the defending party. Examples include the Oklahoma Penal Code, Title 21, Chapter 24, Section 733 (see also *OWM v State* (1997 OK CR 49, 946 P.2d 257)) and the California Code, Section 197, subsection 3. In Canada, Section 37, para. 1, of the Criminal Code limits defence of others in the context of personal self-defence to the defence of persons under the protection of the defending party. In the Netherlands, on the other hand, Article 41 of the Criminal Code (Wetboek van Strafrecht) does not contain such restrictions and extends the right to the protection of oneself or another person ('*eigen of andermans*'). This is similar to the French Code Pénal, Article 122-5 ('*légitime défense d'elle-même ou d'autrui*') and the German Strafgesetzbuch, para. 32, subsection 2 ('*von sich oder einem anderen*').

[54] A comparable restriction can be found in the requirements for legitimate application of unit self-defence, as discussed in Section 24.07.

[55] For example, units on stand-by for close air support are not exercising the right of personal self-defence in the defence of others but are engaged in a pre-planned military task.

1. While many aspects of the law regarding the right to personal self-defence effectively render that right partly irrelevant in the context of military operations, that does not mean that the right itself is never applicable or that there is no right to defend one's life. Rather, the discussion is intended to analyse and explicate that the legal basis for the use of force to defend one's life in the context of military operations will not usually be the right to personal self-defence but will instead be based on different legal principles or other forms of the right to self-defence, as discussed in Section 24.01. **24.25**

2. As the use of force to defend one's life in military operational contexts will commonly be based on different aspects of law, the conditions and requirements which must be met will need to be identified and expressed clearly to the personnel involved. Such conditions, as well as the authority to use force, when not based on the right to personal self-defence, should be set forth in the ROE or similar guidance for the operation in question.

3. In addition to the authority to use force as set forth in the ROE, the right to personal self-defence may in certain situations, and subject to the criteria and conditions inherent in that right, be applicable to actions undertaken by military personnel. The ROE do not limit this right and should instead be considered a parallel, but preferred, authorization to use force.[56]

4. The conclusion to be drawn from this is that the right to personal self-defence is an inherent right, but should be reserved as a safety net, a measure of last resort in the event that the mission-specific authorizations to use force, as set forth in the ROE, and the 'military' types of self-defence discussed earlier are somehow insufficient to save one's life. The right to personal self-defence should not be considered an excuse to take action contrary to ROE purely as a matter of convenience, as such actions are highly unlikely to meet the strict criteria for the justified use of force in personal self-defence under applicable national criminal law.

Personal self-defence as a criminal law justification is subject to many variations in national statutes and case law interpretation of those statutes, subject to conditions which are generally incompatible with military objectives and missions and is consequently particularly flawed as a legal basis for planning or executing military operations. While the inherent right of personal self-defence may exist and be applied by individual servicemen and servicewomen within the context of a military operation on an individual and case-by-case basis, it cannot be utilized as a basis for a military operation as such. **24.26**

[56] The term 'preferred' is used, since the ROE are written specifically for the operation in question, taking into account all the various political, legal, and operational concerns, as well as the authorizations given in the mandate for the operation. The right of personal self-defence is generic and does not offer mission-specific guidance or authorizations.

24.26 1. The conceptual (legal) framework for personal self-defence is incompatible with the conceptual framework for military operations. The concept of personal self-defence is centred on exercising a personal, individual right as a means of last resort, as an exception to the monopoly of the national authorities on the use of force, and is a justification under criminal law. Military operations are centred on exercising State authority,[57] enforcing the (political) will of the government in question,[58] and are governed principally by international law. Consequently, the requirements for the justified use of force and the legal consequences of any action taken may differ significantly depending on which framework is applied.

2. Personal self-defence, as opposed to the other forms of self-defence discussed previously, attaches to each individual person regardless of whether that person is military or civilian. The right to personal self-defence as a justification under criminal law consequently is not in itself specifically or particularly designed to be applied in the circumstances of operational deployment. Those circumstances may, however, differ considerably from the civilian context on which the law pertaining to personal self-defence is ordinarily based.

3. The laws and statutes pertaining to personal self-defence differ considerably between nations and, in federal nations, even between states within a nation. This renders a uniform response by a military force against a threat posed to that force somewhat of a challenge, if not in fact an impossible expectation. Furthermore, many such laws and statutes, and the case law pertaining to them, contain provisions and conditions which are not readily reconcilable with the dictates and necessities of carrying out a military operation.

4. While there can be no doubt that the right to personal self-defence applies to military personnel just as it does to civilians, the right applies to them in their capacity as individual persons and not in their capacity as members of the armed forces or members of a military force carrying out a specific mandate. Consequently, the right to personal self-defence applies to military personnel in order that they, just as anyone else, may ultimately resort to such force as is necessary to defend their lives. It does not authorize military personnel, or anyone else, to initiate or continue (combat) operations in order to attain military or political objectives.

5. As the law on self-defence is principally designed for application in a civilian environment, particular complications may present themselves in cases involving (a claim to) the justification of personal self-defence by military personnel and especially in cases in which the facts took place in the context of a military operation. Such complications may not render recourse to the right of personal

[57] Whether a military operation represents the exercise of State rights, as opposed to purely representing a State's political will, depends on the legality of the operation under international law and is not necessarily a given fact.

[58] It should be noted that even operations authorized by the Security Council of the United Nations, while thus reflecting 'the will of the international community', still require the political will of the individual participating nations in order to exist or be carried out by the forces of those nations.

self-defence impossible in all cases, but serve to emphasize the role of that right as a last resort, in the absence or failure of all other possibilities to resolve the situation. **24.26**

6. The right of personal self-defence must be recognized and applied as what it is—a justification under criminal law allowing individuals to use necessary force to defend themselves when there are no other methods to resolve the situation. It therefore provides an unstable, or in fact untenable, basis for the planning of a military operation or planning military engagements within such an operation. Instead, such actions need to be based on properly drafted ROE, reflecting the mandate of the operation in question and taking into account the legal, political, and military operational dictates and needs regarding the operation.

Chapter 25

THE MAINTENANCE OF LAW AND ORDER IN MILITARY OPERATIONS

25.01 **In international military operations States are obliged to cooperate in the maintenance of law and order.**

1. The phrase 'maintenance of law and order' refers to a broad range of activities. In many cases the taking of positive steps to maintain law and order will involve responding to the commission of serious crimes against individuals and property, the suppression of such crimes, and the development of procedures for dealing with such crimes. However, the maintenance of law and order may not necessarily involve responding to criminal activity. A military force may, for example, need to control a public demonstration or require individuals to be disarmed. Neither of these situations may necessarily constitute crimes but may nonetheless be justified on the basis of security concerns. It is important to stress that the concept of the maintenance of law and order used here covers a broad range of activities. This range of activities may include peaceful measures such as the adoption of legislation and the development of military doctrine and training programmes extending through to operational use of lethal force to prevent serious crimes such as genocide, war crimes, and crimes against humanity. These obligations apply to States, international organizations and, in some circumstances, to non-State actors.

2. Whether specific positive steps to maintain law and order must be taken by forces involved in international military operations will depend upon a range of variable factors including: the nature of the suspected or actual activity; the source of the legal authority to undertake law and order functions; the express or implied functions mandated to the military force; force capability; and relations with the Host State or other law and order authorities. Irrespective of obligations to undertake specific maintenance of law and order functions, all forces involved in international military operations are obliged to cooperate in the maintenance of law and order responsibilities. Cooperation will often be required between forces involved in joint military operations, with forces and/or relevant national authorities of the Host State, and also with relevant international organizations, agencies, and bodies.

3. International legal obligations to cooperate in the maintenance of law and order in military operations arise from several sources including peremptory or *jus cogens* norms, customary international law, bilateral and multilateral treaties, and Security Council resolutions. The precise scope of specific obligations to maintain law and order will vary depending upon the source of the obligation. For example, the

TIMOTHY MCCORMACK AND BRUCE M. OSWALD

obligation to maintain law and order in situations of military occupation is dependent upon the authority of the legitimate power passing into the hands of the occupant. In contrast, where the Security Council mandates a force to undertake law and order functions, the fulfilment of those functions will require cooperation with the Host State. States parties to the Rome Statute have a treaty obligation to cooperate with the work of the International Criminal Court and that particular treaty obligation may well have implications for the conduct of military operations. Furthermore, States participating in joint military operations may take operational decisions to allocate specific law and order functions to one or more national contingents and other contingents will be obliged not to frustrate or obstruct the fulfilment of those functions. 25.01

4. One specific example arising from the deployment of the International Force for East Timor (INTERFET) illustrates the significance of cooperation in relation to law and order functions. The Office of the High Commissioner for Human Rights issued a *Note on Guidance for Multinational Peace-Keeping Force in East Timor on Preservation of Evidence.*[1] The High Commissioner explained that the Note was based upon a range of sources including 'relevant United Nations standards and guidelines, investigation procedures of International Tribunals, and relevant established practice' on the investigation of serious crime scenes. In particular, the Note explains that even those:

> responsible for investigating alleged human rights violations are generally instructed to leave crimes scenes untouched and not to attempt to substitute themselves for the relevant national/international authorities. This is particularly important as any action which is not professionally conducted may even tamper with criminal investigations and be ultimately detrimental to the effective prosecution of perpetrators of human rights violations.[2]

5. Military forces must plan for, train their personnel for, and devote resources to, a range of activities to ensure operational compliance with existing international legal obligations. For example, many law and order activities will require military forces to cooperate in the preservation and gathering of evidence relating to serious crimes such as genocide as well as in the development of procedures to deal with detainees.

All States are obliged to repress, and to provide penal sanctions for persons committing or ordering to be committed, serious crimes under international law. 25.02

1. There is a range of serious international crimes regulated by various international legal regimes. These crimes include war crimes, genocide, crimes against humanity, torture, piracy, and human trafficking. Maintenance of law and order obligations in

[1] For the text of the Note see Australian Defence Force Military Law Centre, *Law and Military Operations in East Timor September 1999–February 2000* (Canberra: Australian Defence Force, 2002), Annex L. See also M.J. Kelly, T.L.H. McCormack, P. Muggleton, and B.M. Oswald, 'Legal Aspects of Australia's Involvement in the International Force for East Timor', 841 *IRRC* (2001), 101–39.

[2] Australian Defence Force Military Law Centre, *Law and Military Operations in East Timor September 1999–February 2000*, Annex L.

25.02 relation to these crimes accrues pursuant to treaties, customary international law, Security Council resolutions, and the statutes and jurisprudence of international courts and tribunals.

2. In relation to war crimes, the relevant legal regime has traditionally distinguished between 'grave breaches' of the Four Geneva Conventions of 1949 and of Additional Protocol I of 1977 and other serious violations of the laws and customs of war. In relation to the grave breaches regime, all States parties to the 1949 Conventions and all States parties to Additional Protocol I have two key obligations: to enact penal sanctions for those found guilty of grave breaches; and to proactively investigate those allegedly responsible for grave breaches and either extradite or prosecute such accused. The Four Geneva Conventions (GC) require States parties to undertake these measures to repress grave breaches[3] and impose an additional obligation 'for the suppression of all acts contrary to the provisions of the... Convention'.[4] Article 85 of Additional Protocol I (AP I) states that '[t]he provisions of the Conventions relating to the repression of breaches and grave breaches... shall apply to the repression of breaches and grave breaches of this Protocol'. It provides a supplemented list of grave breaches and confirms that all grave breaches shall be regarded as war crimes.[5]

3. In the English language, the meanings of 'repress' and 'suppress' are synonymous. The text of the Conventions and Additional Protocol I does not explicitly make any distinction between the two terms. In the First Geneva Convention the words 'Repression of Abuses and Infractions' are used as headline for Articles 49–54 which, *inter alia*, comprise the criminal prosecution of grave breaches and the 'suppression of all acts contrary to the provisions of the present Convention other than grave breaches'. According to the ICRC Commentary, '[g]rave breaches must be repressed, which implies the obligation to enact legislation laying down effective penal sanctions for perpetrators of such breaches'.[6] The Commentary also states that:

> [f]or breaches of the Protocol other than grave breaches the terms are the same as those used by the Conventions:... the Parties to the Protocol undertake to suppress them, which means that any 'repression' that might be undertaken by penal or disciplinary sanctions are the responsibility of the authority on which those committing such breaches depend or the Power to which they belong.[7]

4. In this discussion the Commentary focuses upon the prosecution of grave and other breaches of Additional Protocol I and not on any intended distinction between

[3] Art. 49(2) GC I; Art. 50(2) GC II; Art. 129(2) GC III; Art. 146(2) GC IV; Art. 85(1) AP I.

[4] Art. 49(3) GC I; Art. 50(3) GC II; Art. 129(3) GC III; Art. 146(3) GC IV; Art. 85(1) AP I.

[5] For a detailed discussion about the grave breaches regime see Y. Sandoz, J.-M. Henckaerts, K. Dörmann et al., in 'Special Issue: The Grave Breaches Regime in the Geneva Conventions: A Reassessment Sixty Years On', 7 *Journal of International Criminal Justice* (2009), 653–877.

[6] Y. Sandoz, C. Swinarski, and B. Zimmermann (eds), *Commentary on the Additional Protocols of 8 June 1977 to the Geneva Conventions of 12 August 1949* (Geneva: ICRC, 1987), para. 3538.

[7] Ibid. 3539.

the two terms. However, the drafters of both the Conventions and the Protocol must have intended some distinction between the two terms since all five of these treaties suggest that the obligation in relation to grave breaches differs from the obligation in relation to all other breaches. The Commentary clearly adopts a view that 'repression' relates to ultimate penal sanctions. Perhaps then 'suppression' was intended to mean measures to stop the ongoing occurrence of the breaches. If this distinction is correct, then 'repression' could also incorporate 'suppression' but not vice versa. **25.02**

5. Assuming that the suggested distinction is correct, there are important maintenance of law and order implications for military forces. In circumstances where a party to an international armed conflict fails to act to prevent violations of international humanitarian law when it has a duty to do so, forces should take measures to stop those violations of international humanitarian law. Military forces should not ignore breaches of international humanitarian law and should cooperate to report and where possible investigate and prevent ongoing breaches. The ability of military forces to report, investigate, and prevent ongoing breaches will depend on a variety of factors including the resources available to them and their level of training. At the very least, commanders should ensure that their personnel have the appropriate resources and training to report violations of international humanitarian law. In recognition of generally accepted principles it would be reasonable to assume that any investigations carried out must be independent, impartial, timely, and effective.[8]

6. In this context military forces must also recognize that they will often be required to cooperate with other organisations such as the International Criminal Court, international humanitarian organizations such as the International Committee of the Red Cross, and the Office of the High Commissioner for Human Rights, and national law and order organizations to repress and suppress grave breaches of international humanitarian law by monitoring, reporting, and investigating allegations of such breaches. The obligation to cooperate arises from a variety of sources including treaty obligations,[9] Security Council resolutions,[10] and bilateral agreements.[11]

[8] For an articulation of some of the key procedural requirements for undertaking investigations see, for example, *Al-Skeini v Secretary of State for Defence* [2004] EWHC 2911 (Admin), para. 322.

[9] See, for for example, Additional Protocol I, which requires States party to that Protocol to provide mutual assistance in relation to criminal proceedings in respect of grave breaches (Art. 88) and in situations where there are allegations of serious violations of the Conventions or Additional Protocol I to cooperate with the UN (Art. 89); and the ICC Statute, Art. 86 which establishes a general obligation for state parties to cooperate with the ICC in its investigation and prosecution of crimes that are within the jurisdiction of the Court.

[10] See, for example, UN peacekeepers serving with the United Nations Mission in the Democratic Republic of the Congo (MONUC) who were mandated to 'cooperate with efforts to ensure that those responsible for serious violations of... international humanitarian law are brought to justice, while working closely with the relevant agencies of the United Nations'. See SC Res. 1565 (1 October 2004), para. 5(g).

[11] See, for example, the agreement between INTERFET and the Office of the High Commissioner for Human Rights to ensure that appropriate modalities were in place to report, investigate, and prevent grave breaches. See Australian Defence Force Military Law Centre, Annex L.

25.02 7. In relation to war crimes, a term which goes beyond that of grave breaches of either the Geneva Conventions or Additional Protocol I in that it comprises all serious violations of international humanitarian law, all States have a right to vest universal jurisdiction in their domestic criminal courts. The ICRC Study on *Customary International Humanitarian Law* recognizes the existence of this right[12] which is consistent with the statutes and jurisprudence of international and domestic criminal courts and tribunals.[13]

8. Pursuant to Article 89 of Additional Protocol I States parties are obliged jointly or individually to cooperate with the United Nations in accordance with their obligations under the UN Charter, in situations of serious violations (including grave breaches) of the Protocol, or of the four Geneva Conventions.

9. There are a number of other international crimes codified in specific treaty regimes the proscription of which has been widely recognized as having attained peremptory status, i.e. as norms of international law from which no derogation is permitted. These crimes have also been widely recognized as obligations owed *erga omnes*:

> that is, obligations owed towards all the other members of the international community, each of which then has a correlative right. In addition, the violation of such an obligation simultaneously constitutes a breach of the correlative right of all members of the international community and gives rise to a claim for compliance accruing to each and every member, which then has the right to insist on fulfilment of the obligation or in any case to call for the breach to be discontinued.[14]

10. The peremptory status and the *erga omnes* character of these crimes has been affirmed by the International Court of Justice, various international criminal courts and tribunals, and by the International Law Commission. The crimes in this category include, *inter alia*, genocide, torture, and piracy. In the context of the maintenance of law and order, military forces should take all reasonably available measures to prevent such crimes from occurring and to monitor, report, investigate and to assist in the prosecution of those responsible where such crimes have occurred.

11. *Genocide.* The customary international law prohibition of genocide was first codified in the Convention on the Prevention and Punishment of the Crime of

[12] J.-M. Henckaerts and L. Doswald-Beck (eds), *Customary International Humanitarian Law* (Cambridge: Cambridge University Press, 2005), Rule 157 on War Crimes.

[13] Ibid. Vol. I, 604–7, referring to the legislation of Australia, Azerbaijan, Bangladesh, Belarus, Belgium, Canada, Colombia, Costa Rica, Ecuador, El Salvador, Ethiopia, France, Germany, Luxembourg, New Zealand, Niger, Slovenia, Sweden, Switzerland, Tajikistan, United Kingdom, and United States, and to draft legislation of Lebanon, Sri Lanka, and Trinidad and Tobago. See also Art. 8(2)(b) Rome Statute of the International Criminal Court (ICC Statute) of 17 July 1998, and the implementation of that provision by various States parties into their domestic criminal law.

[14] ICTY, *Prosecutor v Furundzija*, Case no. IT-95-17/I-T, Trial Chamber Judgment of 10 December 1998, para. 151.

Genocide in 1948. That treaty definition has been replicated in the statutes of all international criminal courts and tribunals since—including in the Rome Statute for the International Criminal Court. Article 1 of the Genocide Convention obligates States parties in time of peace or in war to prevent and punish acts of genocide. The International Court of Justice has characterized the prohibition on genocide as 'assuredly' a peremptory norm of international law (*jus cogens*)[15] and also as an obligation owed *erga omnes*.[16] The Court has specifically considered the extent of the obligation in Article 1 of the Genocide Convention and found: 25.02

> that the obligation in question is one of conduct and not one of result, in the sense that a State cannot be under an obligation to succeed, whatever the circumstances, in preventing the commission of genocide: the obligation of States Parties is rather to employ all means reasonably available to them so as to prevent genocide so far as possible . . . responsibility is, however, incurred if the State manifestly failed to take all measures to prevent genocide which were in its power, and which might have contributed to preventing genocide.[17]

12. *Torture*. The customary international law prohibition of torture is located in a range of international treaties including the Geneva Conventions, the Convention Against Torture, and the Rome Statute of the International Criminal Court. In the context of the maintenance of law and order on military operations the 1984 Convention Against Torture requires that States parties 'shall take effective legislative, administrative, judicial or other measures to prevent acts of torture in any territory under its jurisdiction'.[18] Torture may never be justified in any circumstances including on the basis of conflict, internal political stability, or other public emergency.[19] Furthermore, States parties are prohibited from expelling, returning, or extraditing a person 'to another State where there are substantial grounds for believing that he would be in danger of being subjected to torture'.[20] In its judgment in the *Furundzija Case* the Trial Chamber of the ICTY found that:

> it would seem that one of the consequences of the *jus cogens* character bestowed by the international community upon the prohibition of torture is that every State is entitled to investigate, prosecute and punish or extradite individuals accused of torture, who are present in a territory under its jurisdiction. Indeed, it would be inconsistent on the one hand to prohibit torture to such an extent as to restrict the normally unfettered treaty-making power of sovereign States, and on the other hand bar States from prosecuting and punishing those torturers who have engaged in this odious practice abroad. This legal basis for States' universal jurisdiction over torture bears out and strengthens the legal foundation for such jurisdiction found by other courts in the inherently universal character of the crime. It has

[15] ICJ, *Armed Activities on the Territory of the Congo (New Application: 2002) (Democratic Republic of the Congo v Rwanda)*, Judgment on jurisdiction of 3 February 2006, ICJ Reports, 2006, 6, 32, para. 64.

[16] ICJ, *Barcelona Traction, Light and Power Company, Limited (Belgium v Spain)*, Judgment of 5 February 1970, ICJ Reports, 1970, 3, 34.

[17] ICJ, *Application of the Convention on the Prevention and Punishment of the Crime of Genocide (Bosnia and Herzegovina v Serbia and Montenegro)*, Judgment of 26 February 2007, ICJ Rep 1, 154.

[18] Art. 2(1) Convention against Torture and Other Cruel, Inhuman or Degrading Treatment or Punishment of 10 December 1984.

[19] Ibid. Art. 2(2). [20] Ibid. Art. 3(1).

25.02 been held that international crimes being universally condemned wherever they occur, every State has the right to prosecute and punish the authors of such crimes.[21]

13. *Piracy*. The customary international law prohibition of piracy is codified in the UN Convention on the Law of the Sea in 1982. Article 100 of the Convention requires that States 'shall co-operate to the fullest possible extent in the repression of piracy on the high seas or in any other place outside the jurisdiction of any State'. The Security Council in its Resolution 1816 (2008) reaffirmed that such repression included but was not limited 'to boarding, searching, and seizing vessels engaged in or suspected of engaging in acts of piracy, and to apprehend persons engaged in such acts with a view to such persons being prosecuted'.[22] The repression of piracy also extends to the sharing of information about 'acts of piracy and armed robbery... and to render assistance to vessels threatened by or under attack by pirates or armed robbers in accordance with relevant international law'.[23] The International Law Commission has reaffirmed the *jus cogens* character of this prohibition.[24] One recent example of precisely this kind of law and order function in relation to piracy has arisen in the context of the EU NAVFOR Somalia—Operation ATALANTA which is directed against piracy off the Somali Coast and is undertaken in fulfilment of the UN Security Council resolutions.[25] EU military personnel involved in the operation may arrest, detain, and transfer persons who are suspected of having committed or who have committed acts of piracy or armed robbery in the areas they are present. They can seize the vessels of the pirates or the vessels captured following an act of piracy or an armed robbery and which are in the hands of the pirates, as well as the goods on board. The suspects can be prosecuted, as appropriate, by an EU Member State or by Kenya under the agreement signed with the EU on 6 March 2009 giving the Kenyan authorities to right the prosecute.[26]

14. *Slavery*. The customary international law prohibition of slavery was first codified in the Convention to Suppress the Slave Trade and Slavery of 25 September 1926. Pursuant to Article 2 of the Convention States parties are obligated, in respect of the territories placed under their 'sovereignty, jurisdiction, protection, suzerainty or tutelage' to prevent and suppress the slave trade and to bring about, progressively and as soon as possible, the complete abolition of slavery in all its forms. In addition, pursuant to Article 4 of the Convention, States parties are obliged to 'give to one another every assistance with the object of securing the abolition of slavery and the slave trade'.

[21] *Furundzija Judgment*, para. 156.

[22] SC Res. 1816 (2 June 2008), preambular para. 3.

[23] Ibid., operative para. 3.

[24] See Report of the Study Group of the International Law Commission, *Fragmentation of International Law: Difficulties Arising from the Diversification and Expansion of International Law*, UN GAOR, 58th sess, UN Doc. A/CN.4/L.682 (2006), 166–205.

[25] See Chapter 20 'The Law of Military Operations at Sea' (specifically Sections 20.06 and 20.16) and the supporting commentary; and Chapter 21 'Maritime Interception/Interdiction Operations'.

[26] European Union, European Security and Defence Policy, *EU Naval Operation Against Piracy (EU NAVFOR Somalia—Operation ATALANTA)* (2009), <http://www.consilium.europa.eu/uedocs/cmsUpload/090325FactsheetEUNAVFOR%20Somalia-version4_EN.pdf>.

15. *Transnational Crime and Human Trafficking.* The United Nations Convention Against Transnational Crime has been developed to 'promote cooperation to prevent and combat transnational organised crime more effectively'.[27] Pursuant to Article 3 the Convention applies to the prevention, investigation, and prosecution of serious crimes,[28] participation in an organized criminal group,[29] laundering of proceeds of crime,[30] and corruption[31] where 'the offence is transnational in nature and involves an organized criminal group'. The Convention also includes a Protocol to Prevent, Suppress and Punish Trafficking in Persons, Especially Women and Children.[32] The Protocol includes measures to 'prevent such trafficking, to punish the traffickers and to protect the victims of such trafficking, including by protecting their internationally recognised human rights'.[33] A further purpose of the Protocol is to 'promote cooperation among States Parties in order to meet' the objectives of the Protocol.[34] Both the Convention and the Protocol impose maintenance of law and order obligations in circumstances where military forces are confronted with organized criminal groups involved in the proscribed crimes. A recent example of military forces being authorized to deal with transnational crimes in cooperation with national authorities involved NATO's announcement of the ISAF's increased role in countering the illegal narcotics trade in Afghanistan.[35] **25.02**

16. Other maintenance of law and order obligations include the exchange of information aimed at identifying perpetrators and victims of the proscribed crimes,[36] and to strengthen border controls to detect and to prevent human trafficking.[37] In relation to identified victims of proscribed crimes, military forces are required to take appropriate measures within their means 'to provide assistance and protection . . . in particular in cases of threat of retaliation or intimidation'.[38] States may have additional treaty obligations pursuant to relevant regional or bilateral treaties and agreements requiring them to cooperate in responding to particular criminal activities including in the context of military operations. One

[27] Art. 1 United Nations Convention against Transnational Organized Crime of 15 November 2000, 2225 UNTS 209.

[28] For definition see ibid. Art. 2(b).

[29] For a description of participation in an organized criminal group, see ibid. Art. 5.

[30] For a description of laundering the proceeds of crime, see ibid. Art. 6.

[31] For the criminalization of corruption, see ibid. Art. 8.

[32] UN GA Res. 55/25, UN GAOR, 55th session, 62nd plenary meeting, Annex II (Protocol to Prevent, Suppress and Punish Trafficking in Persons, Especially Women and Children), Agenda Item 105, preamble, UN Doc. A/RES/55/25 (8 January 2001) ('Trafficking Protocol').

[33] Ibid. [34] Ibid. Art. 2(c).

[35] See, for example, the announcement by NATO in October 2008: NATO, *NATO steps up counter-narcotics efforts in Afghanistan* (2008), <http://www.nato.int/docu/update/2008/10-october/e1010b.html>.

[36] See, generally, Arts 5–9 United Nations Convention against Transnational Organized Crime of 15 November 2000, 2225 UNTS 209.

[37] Art. 11 of the Trafficking Protocol.

[38] Art. 25 United Nations Convention against Transnational Organized Crime of 15 November 2000.

25.02 example is the Council of Europe's Convention on Action Against Trafficking in Human Beings.[39]

17. When engaged in operations where international crimes are alleged to have been committed, or are being committed, military commanders need to consider what specific powers they will authorize military personnel to exercise in relation to such crimes. For example, the commanders of European naval forces taking part in Operation ATALANTA to protect vessels from piracy and armed robbery in the Gulf of Aden and off the Somali Coast are authorized to 'employ the necessary measures, including the use of force to deter, prevent and intervene, in order to bring to an end acts of piracy and armed robbery which may be committed in the areas where they are present'.[40]

18. The ability of military forces to repress and suppress international crimes by means such as reporting on and investigation of the crimes, will depend on a variety of factors including the resources available to them and their level of training. At the very least, commanders should ensure that their personnel have the appropriate training to enable them to report such crimes. Effective training would ensure knowledge of the core elements of each category of serious international crime. Where military personnel are required to work with, or liaise with, other law enforcement organizations engaged in the prevention of such crimes it is important that they develop appropriate mechanisms to ensure that the handling and treatment of international criminals are dealt with in accordance with the law pursuant to which the accused is likely to be dealt with. Such mechanisms might include the implementation of a memorandum of understanding to deal with such matters as handing physical custody of the accused, and any evidence relating to the alleged crime, over to the law enforcement organization. Thus, in relation to dealing with those accused of conducting piracy in the Gulf of Aden, the governments of the United Kingdom and Kenya have entered into a memorandum of understanding which defines the 'modalities for transferring suspects held for conducting acts of piracy... from the custody of UK forces to Kenyan authorities'.[41]

19. When military forces are engaged with non-State entities, such as private military companies or civil defence groups,[42] in law and order operations, they

[39] Council of Europe Convention on Action against Trafficking in Human Beings of 16 May 2005, OJ [2005] L197.

[40] Operation ATALANTA. See also Chapter 20.

[41] See Wafula Okumu and Augustine Ikelegbe (eds), 'Militias, Rebels and Islamist Militants', 2010, available at <https://www.issafrica.org/uploads/MilitiasRebelsIslamistMilitantsNov2010.pdf>.

[42] The term 'civil defence groups' as used here refers to groups that are created or supported by governments to undertake law and order functions or maintain security in areas of operations where the State is either unwilling or unable to maintain law and order or security. Members of such groups are civilians who are armed and organized. They are not members of the profession or arms in the same way that a State's military are. For more detailed discussion concerning civil defence groups see e.g. Bruce 'Ossie' Oswald, 'Civil Defense Groups: Developing Accountability', Special Report 30, United States Institute of Peace (August 2014).

must undertake appropriate assessments to ensure that those entities are complying with fundamental legal obligations. 25.02

20. In a number of conflicts and post-conflict situations States have used private military and security companies, and civil defence groups to assist in maintaining law and order. For example, during the conflicts in Iraq and Afghanistan armed private military and security companies carried out a range of functions such as security to bases, guard services, convoy protection, and the operation of prison or detention facilities. In such cases the contracting State, the territorial State, the home State, and all other States have certain international law obligations.[43]

21. When local law and order authorities are unwilling or unable to maintain law and order some military forces have created or supported the existence of local civil defence groups or militia to assist in protecting the local community. For example, in Afghanistan in 2010, US Special Forces established 'local police' to provide protection to villages where either coalition forces or Afghan law and order officials were unable to operate.[44] In such situations the level of control a State has over a civil defence group will be a key element in determining the extent of that State's responsibility for the acts or omissions of that group.

In situations of military occupation the occupant is obliged to take all measures within its power to restore, and as far as possible ensure, public order and safety while respecting, unless absolutely prevented, the laws in force in the occupied country. 25.03

1. A specific obligation to restore and to maintain law and order in occupied territory arises pursuant to Article 43 of the 1907 Hague Regulations.[45] As the 'authority of the legitimate power having in fact passed into the hands of the occupant, the latter shall take all the measures in his power to restore, and ensure, as far as possible, public order and safety while respecting, unless absolutely prevented, the laws in force in the country'.[46] This specific obligation would extend to the occupying force preventing such activities as rioting, unlawful killing, violence against persons including sexual violence, looting, arson etc.

2. The International Court of Justice in the *Case Concerning Armed Activities on the Territory of the Congo* (2005) determined that the obligations arising under

[43] For a more detailed discussion of those obligations see Federal Department of Foreign Affairs, and International Committee of the Red Cross, *The Montreux Document on pertinent international legal obligations and good practices for States related to operations of private military and security companies during armed conflicts*, 17 September 2008.

[44] For a brief history of the US Special Forces programme creating and supporting civil defence groups see, for example, M. Brown, 'Village Stability Operations: An Historical Perspective from Vietnam to Afghanistan', *Small Wars Journal* (March 28, 2013).

[45] Hague Regulations (IV) respecting the Laws and Customs of War on Land, Annex to the Convention, Regulation respecting the Laws and Customs of War on Land of 18 October 1907.

[46] Ibid. Art. 43.

25.03 Article 43 of the Hague Regulations are binding on Occupying Powers as rules of customary international law. In that case, the Congo argued that Uganda had violated various international legal obligations as a result of the activities of its armed forces on Congolese territory. Specifically, the Court considered that the Uganda Peoples' Defence Forces (UPDF) 'took no action to prevent such [ethnic] conflicts in Ituri districts'.[47] The Court also relied upon findings presented to the Security Council that:

> Ugandan Army commanders already present in Ituri, instead of trying to calm the situation, preferred to benefit from the situation and support alternatively one side or the other according to their political and financial interests' and that 'UPDF troops stood by during the killings and failed to protect the civilians'.[48]

3. The obligation in Article 43 of the Hague Regulations was further developed by Geneva Convention IV of 1949 which provides in relevant part that the maintenance of law and order may include subjecting the population of the occupied territory:

> to provisions which are essential to enable the Occupying Power to fulfil its obligations . . . to maintain the orderly government of the territory, and to ensure the security of the Occupying Power, of the members and property of the occupying forces or administration, and likewise of the establishments and lines of communication used by them.[49]

This provision acknowledges the entitlement of the Force to guarantee its own security as a fundamental prerequisite to the Force's own ability to maintain law and order. Likewise the Israeli High Court of Justice in *Beit Sourik Village Council v The Government of Israel and the Commander of IDF Forces in the West Bank* (2004) stated that:

> the law of belligerent occupation recognizes the authority of the military commander to maintain security in the area and to protect the security of his country and her citizens. However, it imposes conditions on the use of this authority. This authority must be properly balanced against the rights, needs and interests of the local population.[50]

4. One particular example of the balance between the security needs of the occupying forces and the rights, needs, and interests of the local population arises in the requirements for dealing with those suspected of activities hostile to the security of the occupier. Article 5 of Geneva Convention IV stipulates that such persons shall be treated humanely and 'in case of trial, shall not be deprived of the rights of fair and regular trial prescribed by the present Convention'. A further guarantee of the rights of 'protected persons' is provided for in Article 70 of Geneva

[47] ICJ, *Armed Activities on the Territory of the Congo (Democratic Republic of the Congo v Uganda)*, Judgment of 19 December 2005, ICJ Reports, 2005, 168, 241.

[48] Ibid. [49] Art. 64 GC IV.

[50] Israeli Supreme Court, *Beit Sourik Village Council v The Government of Israel and the Commander of IDF Forces in the West Bank ('separation fence in the area of Judea and Samaria')*, 2004 HCJ 2056/04, Judgment of 30 June 2004, para. 34.

Convention IV which prohibits the Occupying Power from arresting, prosecuting, or convicting such persons 'for acts committed or for opinions expressed before the occupation, or during a temporary interruption thereof, with the exception of breaches of the laws and customs of war'. **25.03**

5. In relation to the humane treatment of protected persons, occupying powers are obliged to ensure that such persons are protected 'against all acts of violence or threats thereof and against insults and public curiosity'. Women 'shall be especially protected against any attack on their honour in particular against rape, enforced prostitution, or any form of indecent assault'. The obligations on occupying powers to treat protected persons humanely, therefore, require commanders to ensure that they uphold the highest standards of discipline on their own troops and train their personnel on the obligation of humane treatment. Concerning the obligation to protect individuals from all acts of violence or threats thereof, commanders should plan for the creation of zones of protection including non-defended localities and demilitarized zones.[51] Other strategies for the protection of individuals may include the establishment of curfews and the implementation of security patrols where law and order is threatened or has broken down.

6. In maintaining law and order in situations of military occupation, there is a general prohibition on amending the penal laws of the occupied territory.[52] This general prohibition is limited to circumstances where the penal law of the occupied territory 'constitutes a threat to its [the occupying power's] security or an obstacle to the application of the present Convention'. The requirement to respect local laws is qualified not only by the security needs of the Occupying Power but also where local laws are at variance with established international human rights law standards. The approach that maximizes the protection of the occupied population should be given priority.

7. By implication, pursuant to Article 27 of Geneva Convention IV occupying forces may need to engage in the maintenance of law and order to comply with the requirement to 'take such measures of control and security in regard to protected persons as may be necessary'.[53] This requirement may include assigning residence or interning protected persons 'for imperative reasons of security'.[54]

8. There is also an obligation that occupying military forces 'shall as far as possible support the competent national authorities of the occupied country in safeguarding and preserving its cultural property'.[55] Military forces are required to 'prohibit, prevent and, if necessary, put a stop to any form of theft, pillage, or misappropriation of, and any acts of vandalism against, cultural property'.[56]

[51] Arts 59 and 60 GC IV. [52] Art. 64 GC IV.
[53] Art. 27(4) GC IV. [54] Art. 78 GC IV.
[55] Art. 5(1) Hague Convention for the Protection of Cultural Property in the Event of Armed Conflict of 14 May 1954.
[56] Ibid. Art. 4(3).

25.03 9. The law of occupation, therefore, has a considerable impact on planning and conducting maintenance of law and order aspects of military operations. For example, commanders will need to consider the extent to which rules of engagement will need to authorize the use of force in dealing with various levels of criminals such as looters and those carrying out petty theft. Commanders will also need to identify how best to train their subordinates to understand the legal system of the occupied territory so that people are not detained arbitrarily or unlawfully. In relation to taking and dealing with internees, commanders will also need to ensure that adequate resources are devoted to accommodating any internees that might be detained for imperative reasons of security.

10. Even in situations where the law of occupation does not apply *de jure*, it may nonetheless be a useful body of law to use by analogy when maintaining law and order because its rules and principles provide useful guidance for military forces dealing with the civilian population when law and order has broken down. The International Force in Timor Leste, for example, used the law of occupation to establish its interim justice system.[57] The Law of Military Occupation did not apply to that particular operation because Indonesia had consented to the deployment of INTERFET.

25.04 **Where military operations are conducted pursuant to Security Council authorization and the Security Council mandate specifies a maintenance of law and order obligation, the military force is obliged to implement the mandate and to act consistently with it.**

1. Article 25(1) of the UN Charter requires Member States of the UN to carry out the decisions of the Security Council. Consequently, whenever the Council mandates the maintenance of law and order on peace operations, contributing States should use all means reasonably available to them to maintain law and order so far as is possible to implement the mandate. Sometimes the mandate is specific. In its authorization of the deployment of INTERFET to East Timor in 1999, for example, the Council mandated the Force:

> to restore peace and security in East Timor, to protect and support UNAMET in carrying out its tasks and, within force capabilities, to facilitate humanitarian assistance operations, and authorizes the States participating in the multinational force to take all necessary measures to fulfil this mandate.[58]

2. On other occasions the Council mandates the Force to cooperate with national authorities in the maintenance of law and order. For example, in Resolution 1794 the Council tasked MONUC to cooperate with Congolese authorities to bring 'those responsible for serious violations of human rights and international

[57] For further detail see B.M. Oswald, 'The INTERFET Detainee Management Unit in East Timor', 3 *Yearbook of International Law* (2000), 347–61.

[58] SC Res. 1264 (15 September 1999), para. 3.

humanitarian law . . . to justice'.[59] In some cases the Council has expressly mandated peacekeepers to carry out law and order functions such as 'arrest and detain' and, in the case of at least one detainee, the transfer of a detainee to another State.[60] 25.04

3. There are also other circumstances in which the Council authorizes peace operations to undertake a range of functions which, by implication, require the maintenance of law and order by peacekeepers. For example, the Council has mandated forces to 'protect civilians under imminent threat of physical violence'[61] and to 'provide security and protection of displaced persons, refugees and civilians at risk'.[62] The Security Council has also encouraged multinational forces to assist local authorities to deal with specific crimes such as drug trafficking. The International Security Force (ISAF) in Afghanistan, for example, has been encouraged to 'effectively support, within its designated responsibilities, Afghan-led sustained efforts to address, in cooperation with relevant international and regional actors, the threat posed by the illicit production, of and trafficking in drugs'.[63] There are also cases where the Council has mandated peacekeepers and other military forces to enforce embargoes or prevent the import of certain commodities.[64] In situations where elections are threatened by the breakdown of law and order the Council has authorized peacekeepers to 'contribute . . . to the security of areas where voting is to take place'.[65] In circumstances where peacekeepers use force in fulfilling their mandates they must comply with the legal parameters for the use of force.[66]

4. In such circumstances, military personnel should take all reasonable measures to fulfil their law and order functions. Such measures might include intelligence sharing and the conduct of efficient public information campaigns, training local authorities and providing resources to them to ensure that they are capable of dealing with law and order matters in accordance with generally accepted international standards, developing appropriate rules of engagement and directives so as to ensure that members of the military force know the extent of their law and order

[59] SC Res. 1794 (21 December 2007), para. 16.

[60] The Security Council authorized United Nations Operation in Somalia (II) peacekeepers to arrest and detain those responsible for carrying out the unprovoked attack against UN peacekeepers in Somalia on 5 June 1993 (see SC Res. 837 (6 June 1993), para. 5). The Council also authorized the UN Mission in Liberia to 'apprehend and detain former President Charles Taylor . . . and to transfer or facilitate his transfer to Sierra Leone for prosecution . . .' (see SC Res. 1638 (11 November 2005), para. 1). For further detail see Chapter 6 'Peace Operations', especially Section 6.14; and Chapter 26 'Operational Detention and the Treatment of Detainees'.

[61] SC Res. 1794 (21 December 2007), para. 8.

[62] SC Res. 918 (17 May 1994), para. 3(a), on the expansion of the mandate of the UN Assistance Mission for Rwanda and imposition of an arms embargo on Rwanda.

[63] SC Res. 1833 (22 September 2008), preamble.

[64] See, for example, SC Res. 2182 (24 October 2014), paras 13 and 15 concerning the enforcement of a ban on the direct and indirect importation of coal, and maintaining an arms embargo in Somalia.

[65] SC Res. 1609 (24 June 2005), para. 2(s).

[66] See Chapter 6 'Peace Operations', particularly Sections 6.3 and 6.4, and Chapters 24 'Force Protection, Unit Self-Defence, and Personal Self-Defence: Their Relationship to Rules of Engagement' and 26 'Operational Detention and the Treatment of Detainees'.

25.04 powers when dealing with the nationals of the Host State, and having sufficient resources to deal with any persons taken into custody.

5. For a number of years military peacekeepers, particularly those serving on UN peace operations, have worked in multidimensional environments where they have shared their mandate of maintaining law and order with other international actors such as UN Police and gendarmerie forces, officers from the UN Office of the High Commissioner for Human Rights, and UN rule of law specialists. Consequently, military peacekeepers are increasingly expected to adjust their interpretation of their role and functions to avoid 'mission creep' into areas beyond their expertise or resources.

6. From time to time the Security Council adopts thematic resolutions which impact upon the maintenance of law and order during military operations. For example, in Resolution 1888 (2009) dealing with Women, Peace and Security the Security Council demanded:

> that all parties to armed conflict immediately take appropriate measures to protect civilians, including women and children, from all forms of sexual violence, including measures such as, inter alia, enforcing appropriate military disciplinary measures and upholding the principle of command responsibility, training troops on the categorical prohibition of all forms of sexual violence against civilians, debunking myths that fuel sexual violence and vetting candidates for national armies and security forces to ensure the exclusion of those associated with serious violations of international humanitarian and human rights law, including sexual violence.[67]

This particular provision creates maintenance of law and order obligations on military forces to take steps including disciplinary measures and training. In addition, where military forces are responsible for training national armies and security forces there is a requirement to ensure vetting of prospective personnel to exclude those associated with serious violations of international humanitarian law.

7. In military operations established not by a Security Council resolution but pursuant to bilateral or multilateral agreements, obligations for the maintenance of law and order can be mandated specifically and by implication. The Agreement between the Solomon Islands and various Pacific Forum contributing nations to the Regional Assistance Mission to the Solomon Islands (RAMSI) specifies, for example, the following:

> The Assisting Countries may deploy a Visiting Contingent of police forces, armed forces and other personnel to Solomon Islands to assist in the provision of security and safety to persons and property; maintain supplies and services essential to the life of the Solomon Islands community; prevent and suppress violence, intimidation and crime; support and develop Solomon Islands institutions; and generally to assist in the maintenance of law and order in Solomon Islands.... Members of the Participating Armed Forces and Participating Police Force and other members of the Visiting Contingent appointed to the Solomon Islands

[67] SC Res. 1888 (30 September 2009), para. 3. See also Chapter 6 'Peace Operations', Section 6.17.

Police Force may detain and disarm any person or persons who are committing or attempting to commit offences in relation to person or property.[68] **25.04**

8. One example of assistance in the maintenance of law and order arose by implication from the Dayton Accord. The Commander of the multinational military Implementation Force (IFOR) was authorized to undertake all that was 'necessary and proper, including the use of military force, to protect IFOR and to carry out responsibilities' and this mandate was interpreted to include the disarming of individuals carrying military weapons within the agreed Zone of Separation.[69]

[68] Arts 2 and 6 Agreement between Solomon Islands, Australia, New Zealand, Fiji, Papua New Guinea, Samoa, and Tonga concerning the operation and status of the police and armed forces and other personnel deployed to Solomon Islands to assist in the restoration of law and order and security of 30 June 2003 (2003 *ATS* 17).

[69] Art. 6(5) and Art. 4(2), *General Framework Agreement for Peace in Bosnia and Herzegovina* of 14 December 1995 (35 *ILM* (1996)), 89.

Chapter 26

OPERATIONAL DETENTION AND THE TREATMENT OF DETAINEES

26.01 **Operational detention is the deprivation of physical liberty of a person in the context of a military operation, whether for reasons of security or for law enforcement purposes.**

1. *General.* The present definition of what constitutes 'operational detention' is purposively broad in order to capture military operations in their entire variety. Military operations as understood in the present context differ significantly (see typology in Sections 5.01, 6.01, and 8.01). They range from enforcement operations to traditional peacekeeping, and they include combat operations and the maintenance of law and order. The deprivation of an individual's physical liberty can occur in any of these types of military operations. The definition used in Section 26.01 extends to the deprivation of liberty of a combatant who has fallen into the power of the enemy and is therefore entitled to the status and treatment as prisoner of war,[1] as much as to the detention of an individual by military personnel of a peacekeeping operation in accordance with its mandate to assist the local government with the restoration and maintenance of the rule of law, public safety, and public order through the provision of operational support to the national police force.[2] However, the different types of military operations are relevant in as much as the reasons and legal bases for, and law applicable to, the respective deprivation of liberty will depend on the nature and mandate of the military operation and the context in which it occurs.

2. *Deprivation of Physical Liberty.* Although the definition is purposively wide, not all limitations placed upon the freedom of movement of a person amount to the actual deprivation of physical liberty. While all restrictions of the freedom of movement of a person raise international legal questions in their own right,[3] only serious measures of physical constraint amount to the deprivation of physical liberty. Whether or not that level of seriousness is being reached is a matter of degree or intensity. Criteria such as the type, effects, and manner of implementation of the measure in question are relevant in determining whether a restriction on the

[1] Cf. Art. 4 GC III, 44 AP I.

[2] See e.g. the mandate of the United Nations Stabilization Mission in Haiti as authorized under SC Res. 1542 (2004), para. 1(d).

[3] See e.g. Art. 12 ICCPR.

freedom of movement of a person does amount to a deprivation of physical liberty.[4] 26.01 Clear-cut cases of deprivation of physical liberty include the apprehension of a person, the confinement to a detention centre or military installation or police post that a person is not free to leave, or to a private house where he or she is held under guard in conditions similar to those in detention centres.[5] However, in other situations of restricted freedom of movement the determination whether or not a person is being deprived of his or her physical liberty and hence qualifies as someone who is detained in the present sense will depend on the specific context, drawing on the aforementioned criteria.

3. *Duration*. It is immaterial whether a given deprivation of physical liberty is for a limited amount of time, for instance in the context of the compulsory search of an individual at a checkpoint, or for a prolonged period in the case of a prisoner of war who can be detained until the cessation of active hostilities. The respective regulatory frameworks come into operation as soon as a person is deprived of his or her physical liberty, until that deprivation comes to an end. However, the practical operability of some aspects of these frameworks may depend on a minimum duration of the detention. For instance, access to detainees by impartial humanitarian organizations, such as the International Committee of the Red Cross, or by other visiting mechanisms (see Section 26.05) will in the majority of cases be dependent on a minimum duration of the detention and will for instance not be operable with regard to a person that has been detained for only a very short period of time at a checkpoint before being released. As an exception to the rule that the international legal framework governing operational detention will cease to apply with the end of the deprivation of physical liberty, a number of rules extend to the situation *after* the detention by one custodial authority has come to an end, such as those pertaining to the investigation of alleged violations of international law during detention and to transfers of detainees by one detaining authority to another (see Sections 26.05 and 26.06).

4. *Types of Detainees*. One can generically distinguish between different types of operational detainees on the basis of the *reason* for the detention, and on the basis of the *situation* in which the detention occurs. These distinctions are relevant in determining the specific legal regime that governs the deprivation of physical liberty of the person in question. As regards the categorization of detainees on the basis of the *reason* for which they are being detained, persons deprived of their physical liberty for reasons of security (security detainees), on the one hand, can be distinguished from those deprived of their liberty because they are suspected of or convicted for an offence and therefore being detained for reasons of law enforcement (law enforcement detainees), on the other. As regards a distinction on the basis of the *situation* in which such detentions occur, one can further differentiate

[4] See e.g. ECtHR, *Guzzardi v Italy*, Application no. 7960/77 (1977), para. 92.

[5] ECHR, *Cyprus v Turkey* (1st and 2nd Applications), Application nos 6780/74 and 6950/75, 4 EHRR 482 at 529, (1976) Com Rep.

26.01 between those detained in the course of an international armed conflict, those deprived of their liberty during a non-international armed conflict, and persons detained in situations not amounting to an armed conflict. In the case of an international armed conflict, the formal categorization of specific types of detainees under international humanitarian law is coming into operation. These formal categories are:

— prisoners of war and those detainees that are entitled to equivalent protections, namely medical personnel and chaplains;[6]
— protected persons in the sense of the Fourth Geneva Convention,[7] including those that are being interned and those arrested on suspicion of having committed a criminal offence;
— persons deprived of their liberty who do not benefit from more favourable treatment under international humanitarian law, and in particular under the regimes of the Third or the Fourth Geneva Convention, including nationals of States not parties to the armed conflict, nationals of allied States, refugees and stateless persons, mercenaries, persons who have taken a part in hostilities without being entitled to prisoner-of-war status, and protected persons subject to derogations in accordance with Article 5 of the Fourth Geneva Convention.[8]

The law of non-international armed conflicts, on the other hand, does not distinguish between different formal categories of detainees. Captured fighters (i.e. members of the armed forces of a party to a non-international armed conflict), who are detained for security reasons, may at the same time be prosecuted under national criminal law. In such a case, detainees may hence be qualified as security and law enforcement detainees simultaneously. Yet it may be unrealistic and even counterproductive in many circumstances, to give them 'the benefit of *habeas corpus* as defined by human rights'.[9] Similar problems may arise for other areas of applicable law (see Section 25.02). When persons are being detained outside the context of an armed conflict, international humanitarian law and the distinctions between the formal categories of detainees that exist in international armed conflicts are inapplicable.

26.02 **The international legal framework governing operational detention consists primarily of international humanitarian law and human rights law, as complemented by applicable Security Council resolutions, secondary UN legislation, rules of regional organizations, status-of-forces, and other bilateral agreements.**

[6] Cf. Arts 4 and 33 GC III. [7] Cf. Art. 4 GC IV.

[8] For these various categories, see Y. Sandoz et al. (eds), *Commentary on the Additional Protocols of 8 June 1977 to the Geneva Conventions of 12 August 1949* (Geneva: ICRC, 1987), Commentary to Art. 75, pp. 869–71, paras 3022–3036.

[9] M. Sassòli and L. Olson, 'The Relationship between International Humanitarian and Human Rights Law where it Matters: Admissible killing and internment of fighters in non-international armed conflicts', 90(871) *IRRC* (2008), 599–627 [627].

1. *International Humanitarian Law.* In situations amounting to an armed conflict, international humanitarian law supplies relevant rules on operational detentions, including the legal bases for such detentions, standards of treatment, and certain procedural safeguards. The latter apply in particular in international armed conflicts. **26.02**

2. *Human Rights Law.* Operational detainees find themselves 'within the jurisdiction' of the Detaining State. Accordingly, human rights law applies to the relationship between the individual detainee and the detaining authority (see Section 4.01). Human rights law primarily supplies standards of treatment and procedural guarantees.

3. *Security Council Resolutions.* Security Council resolutions, in particular those establishing peace operations, may supply the legal basis for operational detentions in general terms. However, they regularly do not provide for standards of treatment and procedural safeguards, although the Council has repeatedly stressed the need for respect for international humanitarian law and human rights in general terms in the context of situations that may involve detentions, such as measures to combat terrorism.[10]

4. *Secondary UN Legislation.* When the United Nations assumes legislative powers in the context of a transitional administration, it may adopt further legal parameters for operational detentions, as occurred in East Timor and Kosovo.[11]

5. *Rules of Regional Organizations.* Occasionally, regional organizations also adopt rules on operational detentions in the context of military operations in which they participate. An example from the European Union is a specific provision on the transfer of detainees for criminal prosecution in the context of the European Union military operation to contribute to the deterrence, prevention, and repression of acts of piracy and armed robbery off the Somali coast (EU NAVFOR Somalia).[12]

6. *Status-of-Forces Agreements.* Rules on operational detentions may also at times be found in status-of-forces agreements. For instance, the US-Iraqi Agreement on the withdrawal of US Forces from Iraq and their activities during their temporary presence regulates several aspects of operational detentions. These include the conditions under which US Forces may carry out arrests and detentions, the handing over of detainees, requests for assistance in the arrest or detention of a

[10] See e.g. SC Res. 1269 (1999), 1456 (2003), 1566 (2004), and 1624 (2005).

[11] See e.g. UNTAET Detainee Ordinance; B. Oswald, 'The INTERFET Detainee Management Unit in East Timor', 3 *YIHL* (2000), 347–61; UNMIK Regulation no. 1999/26 (22 December 1999) On the Extension of Periods of Pre-Trial Detention; UNMIK Regulation no. 2001/18 (25 August 2001) On the Establishment of Detention Review Commission for Extra-Judicial Detention Based on Executive Orders; UNMIK Regulation no. 2001/28 (11 October 2001) On the Rights of Persons Arrested by Law Enforcement Authorities.

[12] See Art. 12 of the Council Joint Action 2008/851/CFSP of 10 November 2008 on a European Union military operation to contribute to the deterrence, prevention, and repression of acts of piracy and armed robbery off the Somali coast.

26.02 person from the Iraqi authorities, the sharing of information on detainees held by US Forces, and their transfer or release.[13]

7. *Other Bilateral Agreements.* Other bilateral agreements, such as those regulating the transfer of detainees from one Detaining State or other authority to another, supply further applicable rules. A pertinent set of such agreements are those diplomatic assurances that are legally binding.[14] The substance of these assurances ranges from commitments by a Receiving State as regards standards of treatment of an individual detainee and as regards the place of detention of the detainee after having been transferred, to commitments that a particular element of the Receiving State will hold an individual, and mechanisms by which the condition of transferred detainees will be monitored.

8. *Domestic Law.* The aforementioned international legal sources governing operational detention are complemented by applicable domestic law.

26.03 **No person may be detained except on lawful grounds. Detention must cease as soon as the lawful grounds for it cease to exist. Unlawful confinement and imprisonment or other severe deprivation of physical liberty are prohibited.**

1. *Requirement of Legal Basis.* International law requires detention to be based on lawful grounds. Under human rights law, this is clear from the prohibition on arbitrary arrest or detention and of any deprivation of liberty 'except on such grounds [. . .] as are established by law'.[15] Indeed, human rights law also establishes a right to compensation for unlawful detention.[16] Customary international humanitarian law similarly prohibits the arbitrary deprivation of liberty, which is understood to require that the deprivation is only permissible on those grounds recognized by applicable law.[17] Absent permissible grounds, or once such permissible grounds have ceased to exist, the deprivation of physical liberty is unlawful and in certain instances criminalized under international law. Thus, the Fourth Geneva Convention prohibits as a grave breach of that Convention the unlawful confinement of a protected person.[18] If committed as part of a widespread or systematic

[13] See Art. 22 of the Agreement between the United States of America and the Republic of Iraq on the Withdrawal of United States Forces from Iraq and the Organization of their Activities during their Temporary Presence in Iraq, signed 17 November 2008, available at <http://www.cfr.org/publication/17880>.

[14] On the question whether diplomatic assurances are binding agreements, see e.g. A. Deeks, 'Promises not to torture', ASIL Discussion Paper (December 2008), <http://www.pegc.us/archive/Journals/deeks_refoulment_2008.pdf>, at 8–9.

[15] Cf. Art. 9(1) 2nd and 3rd sentences ICCPR. See also the very similar wording in Art. 7(2) and (3) IACHR and Art. 6 AfrCHPR. See also Art. 5(1) ECHR, containing an exhaustive list of permissible grounds for detention.

[16] Cf. Art. 9(5) ICCPR; Art. 5(5) ECHR.

[17] Cf. J.-M. Henckaerts and L. Doswald-Beck (eds), *Customary International Humanitarian Law* (Cambridge: Cambridge University Press, 2005), Vol. I (hereinafter CIHL), Rule 99.

[18] Art. 147 GC IV.

attack directed against any civilian population and with knowledge of the attack, the severe deprivation of physical liberty in violation of fundamental rules of international law, including without the required legal basis, may also amount to a crime against humanity and thus entail individual criminal responsibility under international conventional[19] and customary law.[20] Yet for security detentions during armed conflicts, the exact contours of their permissibility remain obscure to some extent due to the absence of an exact definition of what constitute 'imperative reasons of security' that justify such detentions, of practical guidelines, and of a list of specific requirements that would in all circumstances justify confinement and imprisonment.[21] **26.03**

2. *Sources of Legal Basis.* Although the following list does not purport to be exhaustive, the legal power to detain may stem from:

— *Security Council resolutions*: Security Council resolutions do not, as a rule, *expressly* stipulate a legal basis for operational detentions in so many words. However, a mandate 'to use all necessary means' to achieve the assigned tasks logically encompasses operational detention as one such means, if indeed necessary. As such a mandate is generally interpreted and applied to include the ultimate means, the use of potentially deadly force, it may logically also include the lesser means of operational detention.[22] Decisions of the Security Council are binding upon Member States,[23] and in the event of a conflict between the obligations of the Member States under the Charter and their obligations under 'any other international agreement' their obligations under the Charter shall prevail.[24] This would not apply, however, to any obligations of States under peremptory law (*jus cogens*),[25] and the general commitment under the Charter, to promote 'universal respect for, and observance of, human rights and fundamental freedoms for all without distinction as to race, sex, language, or religion'[26] is to be considered also in this context (see Section 3.03 and commentary). Furthermore, a mandate 'to use all necessary means' is regularly expressed in the form of an authorization—as opposed to an obligation. In the absence of clear provision to the contrary, the presumption must be that such an authorization by the Security Council is intended to be carried out by States

[19] Cf. Art. 7(1)(e) ICC Statute.

[20] See e.g. ICTY *Kordic and Cerkez*, (Appeals Chamber), 17 December 2004, paras 114–116.

[21] Report on an Expert Meeting on Procedural Safeguards for Security Detention in Non-International Armed Conflict, Chatham House & ICRC, London, 22–23 September 2008, 91 *IRRC* (2009), 865.

[22] Cf. ECHR Grand Chamber, *Behrami and Saramati*, Admissibility Decision, para. 124, 31 May 2007.

[23] Art. 25 UN Charter. [24] Art. 103 UN Charter.

[25] See Section 4.03; see G. Nolte, 'The Limits of the Security Council's Powers and its Functions in the International Legal System: Some Reflections', in M. Byers (ed.), *The Role of Law in International Politics* (Oxford: Oxford University Press, 2000), 315–26; E. de Wet, *The Chapter VII Powers of the United Nations Security Council* (Oxford and Portland Oregon: Hart, 2004).

[26] Cf. Art. 55(c) UN Charter.

26.03 while complying with their obligations under international law.[27] Hence, it may hardly be assumed that a Security Council mandate 'to use all necessary means' could provide a legal basis for operational detentions that would not be clearly available under other rules of law.

— *International humanitarian law*: The Third Geneva Convention provides the legal basis for the internment of prisoners of war.[28] The Fourth Geneva Convention grants States parties the legal power to detain in a number of scenarios. First, protected persons may be interned or placed in assigned residence if the security of the Detaining Power makes it absolutely necessary.[29] Such a power is also available to an Occupying Power that considers it necessary, for imperative reasons of security, to take safety measures concerning protected persons.[30] Second, an Occupying Power has the authority to detain protected persons in an area particularly exposed to the dangers of war if the security of the population or imperative military reasons so demand.[31] Third, persons may be detained for law enforcement purposes in occupied territory in the course of the Occupying Power's fulfilment of its obligation 'to restore, and ensure, as far as possible, public order and safety'.[32] The law of non-international armed conflict is less explicit in stipulating the legal basis for operational detention than the law of international armed conflicts. This has led some to suggest that no authority to detain can be derived from the law of non-international armed conflict.[33] However, it is submitted that a generic power to that effect is implicit in Common Article 3, in as much as it identifies as one category of persons taking no active part in hostilities 'those placed *hors de combat* by . . . detention'.[34] Articles 5 and 6 of Additional Protocol II also refer to 'persons deprived of their liberty for reasons related to the armed conflict, whether they are interned or detained', which makes it clear that the deprivation of physical liberty of a person is contemplated in the law applicable to non-international armed conflicts. While the applicable law does not identify the grounds on which such deprivation is permissible, it emerges from other relevant rules of international humanitarian law that these grounds include law enforcement and security.[35] As far as operational detention for law enforcement purposes is concerned, this is clear from Article 6 of AP II that applies to the prosecution and punishment of criminal offences related to the armed conflict. That operational detention for security reasons is also permissible logically

[27] Cf ECtHR, *Al-Jedda v UK*, Application no. 27021/08, Judgment of 7 July 2011, para. 105.
[28] Cf. Art. 21 GC III. [29] Art. 42 GC IV.
[30] Art. 78 GC IV. [31] Art. 49(5) GC IV.
[32] Cf. Art. 43 1907 HagueReg; Arts 64–77 GC IV.
[33] See e.g. High Court of England and Wales, per Mr Justice Leggatt, *Serdar Mohammed v Ministry of Defence* [2014] EWHC 1369 (QB) judgment of 2 May 2015, paras 239–268.
[34] In this vein, cf. amongst others US *Gherebi v Obama* 609 F. Supp. 2d at 65.
[35] See also ICRC Commentary, p. 1386 at 4568, clarifying that the terms '[persons] deprived of their liberty for reasons related to the armed conflict' in Art. 5 AP II covers both persons being penally prosecuted and those deprived of their liberty for security reasons, without being prosecuted under penal law.

follows from the fact that members of the armed forces may be directly attacked and that civilians directly participating in hostilities lose their protection from direct attack. Since such direct attacks allow for the use of potentially deadly force, the lesser means of putting such persons *hors de combat* by detention is equally lawful. **26.03**

— *Right to personal self-defence*: Subject to the respective conditions of necessity and proportionality, operational detentions can be justified by invoking the right to personal self-defence as recognized in applicable domestic and international criminal law (see also Chapter 24 'Force Protection, Unit Self-Defence and Personal Self-Defence: Their Relationship to Rules of Engagement'.

— *Prevention and suppression of breaches of international law, in particular international crimes*: The conventional and/or customary international legal right or obligation to prevent and suppress certain breaches of international law, including certain international crimes (see Sections 24.02, 24.04, and 24.07–24.10) provides a legal ground for operational detentions as a means of prevention and/or suppression. Furthermore, operational detentions may find a basis in the law governing the cooperation with international and internationalized criminal courts and tribunals.[36]

— *Agreement with the Host State; authorization under domestic law*: Bilateral or multilateral agreements between troop contributing countries (TCCs) or international organizations and Host States may equally provide the legal basis for operational detention.[37] Such agreements may also stipulate that military personnel of TCCs are allowed to detain individuals in accordance with the domestic law of the territorial State.[38]

3. *Legal Development.* As many questions pertaining to the legal basis of operational detentions, their lawful duration, the procedural safeguards afforded to detainees, and the legal regime of transfers of detainees are unclear, especially in non-international armed conflicts and in military operations below the threshold of an armed conflict,[39] the Danish Government initiated the 'Copenhagen Process on the Handling of Detainees in International Military Operations' in 2007, which culminated in the adoption of 16 Principles and Guidelines in 2012.[40] Founded on

[36] See Part 9 of the ICC Statute; Art. 29(2) ICTY Statute; Art. 28(2) ICTR Statute. On internationalized criminal courts, see G. Sluiter, 'Legal Assistance to Internationalized Criminal Courts and Tribunals', in C.P.R. Romano, A. Nollkaemper, and J.K. Kleffner (eds), *Internationalized Criminal Courts: Sierra Leone, East Timor, Kosovo, and Cambodia* (Oxford: Oxford University Press, 2004), 379–416.

[37] For relevant national legislation and State practice with respect to security-based administrative detentions see M. Hakimi, 'International Standards for Detaining Terrorism Suspects: Moving Beyond the Armed Conflict-Criminal Divide', 33(2) *The Yale Journal of International Law* (Summer 2008), 369–416.

[38] See e.g. Art. 22 of the Agreement between the United States of America and the Republic of Iraq.

[39] See e.g. M. Wood, 'Detention During International Military Operations: Article 103 of the UN Charter and the *Al-Jedda* case', 2008-3-4 *RDMilG*, 277–375; B. Oswald, 'Detention in Military Operations: Some Military, Political and Legal Aspects', 2007-3-4 *RDMilG*, 341–62.

[40] Copenhagen Principles and Guidelines on the Handling of Detainees in International Military Operations, <http://um.dk/en/-/media/UM/English-site/Documents/Politics-and-diplomacy/Copenhangen%20Process%20Principles%20and%20Guidelines.pdf>.

26.03 'the legal principles that all persons who are detained or whose liberty is being restricted must be treated humanely, that any detention must be conducted in accordance with applicable law, and on the policy principle that legal authority to detain should be exercised in a prudent manner',[41] these Principles and Guidelines address matters ranging from humane treatment, release, developing and implementing standard operating procedures and other relevant guidance regarding the handling of detainees, the use of physical force against detainees, registration of detainees and adequate conditions for detainees to contact the outside world, notification of the ICRC or other impartial humanitarian organization, periodic reviews of security detention, the processing of law enforcement detainees, the right of detainees to submit complaints regarding their treatment or conditions of detention, and the transfer of detainees. Furthermore, the ICRC is engaged in a consultation process on certain aspects of detention in non-international armed conflicts, which is envisaged to result in a report with a range of options, including recommendations, to be presented at the 2015 International Conference of the Red Cross and Red Crescent.

26.04 **Without prejudice to further rights under international humanitarian law, detainees are entitled to humane treatment and conditions of detention, without distinction of any kind. No person under detention shall be subjected to torture or to cruel, inhuman, or degrading treatment or punishment. Enforced disappearances are prohibited.**

1. *Human Rights Law.* Human rights law obliges detaining authorities to treat detainees with humanity and with respect for the inherent dignity of the human person.[42] This obligation has been interpreted to entail a positive obligation towards detainees, to ensure their freedom from:

> any hardship or constraint other than that resulting from the deprivation of liberty; respect for the dignity of such persons must be guaranteed under the same conditions as for that of free persons. Persons deprived of their liberty enjoy all the rights set forth in the Covenant, subject to the restrictions that are unavoidable in a closed environment.[43]

2. *International Humanitarian Law.* Similarly, international humanitarian law obliges the humane treatment of detainees in both international and non-international armed conflicts.[44] Indeed, the more detailed rules of international humanitarian law that address the treatment of specific categories of persons, such

[41] Ibid. p. 2 at VIII.

[42] Cf. Art. 10(1) ICCPR; Art. 5(2) IACHR. While the ECHR does not contain a similar provision that stipulates the humane treatment of the specific category of detainees, the general prohibition on torture and inhuman or degrading treatment or punishment in Art. 3 of the Convention has been applied to detainees and conditions of detention.

[43] HRC General Comment 21 concerning humane treatment of persons deprived of liberty (Art. 10), 10 April 1992, para. 3.

[44] Cf. Common Art. 3 GC I–IV; Arts 12 GC I, 12 GC II, 13 GC III, 5 and 27 GC IV, 75(1) AP I, 4(1) AP II; Rule 87 CIHL.

as the wounded, sick and shipwrecked, prisoners of war, and other persons deprived of their liberty, are specific applications of the requirement of humane treatment of civilians and persons *hors de combat*.[45] The generic entitlement to humane treatment and conditions of detention is thus without prejudice to such additional rights under international humanitarian law. **26.04**

3. *Non-discrimination*. Both human rights law and international humanitarian law prohibit discrimination of any kind between detainees as far as their entitlement to humane treatment and conditions of detention is concerned.[46]

4. *Prohibition and Definition of Torture*. The requirement that detainees be treated humanely and offered humane conditions of detention complements the prohibition of torture or other cruel, inhuman, or degrading treatment or punishment contained in international human rights law,[47] as well as international humanitarian law.[48] The 1984 UN Convention against Torture and Other Cruel, Inhuman or Degrading Treatment or Punishment defines torture as:

> any act by which severe pain or suffering, whether physical or mental, is intentionally inflicted on a person for such purposes as obtaining from him or a third person information or a confession, punishing him for an act he or a third person has committed or is suspected of having committed, or intimidating or coercing him or a third person, or for any reason based on discrimination of any kind, when such pain or suffering is inflicted by or at the instigation of or with the consent or acquiescence of a public official or other person acting in an official capacity. It does not include pain or suffering arising only from, inherent in or incidental to lawful sanctions.[49]

That conventional definition under human rights law differs from the definition of torture under international humanitarian law, in as much as the latter has been found not to require that the severe physical or mental pain or suffering be 'inflicted by or at the instigation of or with the consent or acquiescence of a public official or other person acting in an official capacity'.[50]

5. *Prohibition and Definition of Cruel, Inhuman, or Degrading Treatment or Punishment*. Cruel, inhuman, or degrading treatment or punishment is as much prohibited under international human rights law and international humanitarian law as is

[45] In this vein, see also CIHL, Vol. 1, p. 308. Particularly pertinent in this respect as regards detainees are Rules 118–128 on persons deprived of their liberty.

[46] See amongst others, Art. 2(1) ICCPR; Common Art. 3 GC I–IV; Arts 16 GC III; 13 GC IV; 75(1) AP I; 4(1) AP II; Rule 88 CIHL.

[47] Cf. Art. 7 ICCPR; Art. 1(1) CAT; 1985 Inter-American Convention to Prevent and Punish Torture; Art. 3 ECHR; Art. 5(2) IACHR; Art. 5 AfCHPR.

[48] Common Art. 3 GC I–IV; Arts 12(2) GC I; 12(2) GC II; 17(4), 87(3) and 89 GC III; 32 GC IV; 75(2) AP I; 4(2) AP II; Rule 90 CIHL.

[49] Art. 1(1) CAT.

[50] Cf. ICC Statute, Elements of Crime for the War Crime of Torture, Art. 8(2)(a)(ii)-1 and Art. 8(2)(c)(i)-4. See also amongst others the following ICTY case law: *Brdjanin*, (Trial Chamber), 1 September 2004, paras 488–489; *Kunarac, Kovac*, and *Voković* (Appeals Chamber), 12 June 2002, para. 148; *Limaj et al.* (Trial Chamber), 30 November 2005, para. 240.

26.04 torture. However, the dividing line between inhuman or degrading treatment or punishment, on the one hand, and torture on the other hand is difficult to establish. The Human Rights Committee has refused to establish sharp distinctions between the different kinds of punishment or treatment and held that the distinctions between them depend on the nature, purpose, and severity of the treatment applied.[51] The European Court of Human Rights, on the other hand, principally derives the distinction of torture from inhuman or degrading treatment only from a difference in the intensity of the suffering inflicted.[52] This again differs from the ICC Elements of Crimes, where the main difference between the war crime of torture and the war crimes of inhuman and cruel treatment is that a specific purpose for which severe physical or mental pain or suffering is being inflicted upon a person is absent from the definitional requirements for the latter.[53] It follows from the foregoing that different opinions exist about the definition of cruel, inhuman, or degrading treatment or punishment, and about its precise delimitation from torture. The differences between the two concepts have some implications for the legal consequences of a breach of the prohibition, e.g. the mandatory regime for the suppression of acts of torture as established under the 1984 CAT,[54] or for the question whether a given act violates *jus cogens* (since the prohibition of torture is widely recognized to amount to a norm of *jus cogens*,[55] while the prohibition of cruel, inhuman, or degrading treatment or punishment 'only' amounts to an 'ordinary' prohibition under international law). However, these differences in the area of legal consequences and *jus cogens* status do not alter the fact that both torture and cruel, inhuman, or degrading treatment or punishment are equally subject to a comprehensive, non-derogable[56] ban under human rights law, and under international humanitarian law.

6. *Prohibition and Definition of Enforced Disappearances.* It is prohibited to forcefully cause or bring about the disappearance of any person. Enforced disappearance is defined as:

> the arrest, detention, abduction or any other form of deprivation of liberty by agents of the State or by persons or groups of persons acting with the authorization, support or acquiescence of the State, followed by a refusal to acknowledge the deprivation of liberty or by concealment of the fate or whereabouts of the disappeared person, which place such a person outside the protection of the law.[57]

[51] HRC, General Comment no. 20, 10 March 1992, para. 4.

[52] ECtHR, *Ireland v UK*, 13 December 1977, para. 167.

[53] Cf. ICC Statute, Elements of Crime for the war crime of torture, Art. 8(2)(a)(ii)-1 and war crime of inhuman treatment, Art. 8(2)(a)(ii)-2; war crime of torture, Art. 8(2)(c)(i)-4 and war crime of cruel treatment, Art. 8(2)(c)(i)-3. For the war crime of outrages upon personal dignity, see Art. 8(2)(c)(ii) and Elements of Crime.

[54] Cf. Arts 2–15 CAT.

[55] L. Hannikainen, *Peremptory Norms (Jus Cogens) in International Law. Historical Development, Criteria, Present Status* (Helsinki: Lakimiesliiton Kustannus, 1988), 718.

[56] Cf. Art. 4(2) ICCPR.

[57] Cf. Art. 2 of the International Convention for the Protection of All Persons from Enforced Disappearance of 20 December 2006. While the 2006 Convention had not entered into force at the time of writing, its definition is very similar to the definition in Art. II of the 1994 Inter-American

Detention shall be subject to the procedures as are required by applicable law, which may include those relating to: 26.05

— being informed about the reasons for detention;

— status determination;

— challenging the lawfulness of detention and review of the lawfulness by an independent and impartial body;

— contacts with family members;

— submissions concerning treatment and conditions of detention;

— access to detainees by impartial humanitarian organizations, such as the International Committee of the Red Cross, or by other visiting mechanisms.

1. *Situations not Amounting to an Armed Conflict.* In situations that do not amount to an armed conflict and hence are exclusively governed by human rights law and domestic law, international law prescribes a number of procedural guarantees to which both security and law enforcement detainees are entitled. The first such guarantee is to be informed about the reasons for one's detention.[58] As far as law enforcement detainees are concerned, that guarantee further entails to be informed of any charges.[59] The ICCPR and regional human rights instruments also provide for the right of any detainee to have the lawfulness of his/her detention determined and for the right to be released if the detention is determined to be unlawful.[60] Except for the African Charter on Human and Peoples' Rights, which lets it suffice that the lawfulness be subject to control by any 'competent national organ', these instruments require that a 'court' determine the lawfulness of the detention.[61] Law enforcement detainees have an additional right to be brought promptly before a judge or other authorized officer, and to be tried within a reasonable time.[62] According to the ICCPR and the ECHR, the aforementioned rights are derogable in times of public emergency threatening the life of the nation. However, the IACHR and the interpretation of the ICCPR by the Human Rights Committee suggest that derogations from the right to have the lawfulness of detention reviewed are impermissible.[63]

Convention on Enforced Disappearance of Persons and also incorporates the majority of elements in the definition of enforced disappearance of persons as a crime against humanity under Art. 7(1)(i) and (2)(i) of the ICC Statute.

[58] Cf. Arts 9(2) ICCPR; 5(2) ECHR; 7(4) IACHR. See also Principle 10 of the UN Basic Principles for the Protection of All Persons under Any Form of Detention or Imprisonment, UN GA Res. A/RES/43/173 (1988).

[59] Principle 10 of the UN Basic Principles.

[60] Arts 9(4) ICCPR; 5(4) ECHR; 7(6) IACHR; 7(1)(a) AfrCHPR. The right to be released is not expressly stated in the African Charter for Human and Peoples' Rights.

[61] Ibid.

[62] Cf. Art. 9(3) ICCPR; Art. 5(3) ECHR. While the IACHR extends the right to be brought promptly before a judge to *any* person detained (Art. 7(5)), the AfrCHPR does not stipulate a right to be brought promptly before a judge.

[63] Human Rights Committee, General Comment 29, States of Emergency (Article 4), UN Doc. CCPR/C/21/Rev.1/Add.11 (2001), para. 16. Art 27(2) IACHR is slightly broader in as much as it

26.05 2. *Armed Conflicts, Law Enforcement Detainees.* During international and non-international armed conflicts, international humanitarian law provides for the aforementioned procedural guarantees in the context of law enforcement detentions.[64] A number of additional such guarantees apply.[65]

3. *Armed Conflicts, Security Detainees.* In international armed conflicts, the two specific regimes for the treatment of prisoners of war and for the treatment of civilian security internees govern procedural guarantees.[66] While conventional international humanitarian law applicable in non-international armed conflict does not provide for procedural guarantees applicable to security detention, customary international humanitarian law provides an obligation to inform a detainee of the reasons for detention and entitles detainees to challenge the lawfulness of detention.[67] In 2005, the ICRC published the *Procedural principles and safeguards for internment/administrative detention in armed conflict and other situations of violence.*[68] Based on an amalgamation of positive international humanitarian, human rights law, and considerations of 'policy and good practice',[69] it suggests the following procedural safeguards:

— the right to information about the reasons for internment/administrative detention;
— the right to be registered and held in a recognized place of internment/administrative detention;
— the right of foreign nationals in internment/administrative detention to have their national authorities informed thereof and the right to communicate with and be visited by such authorities;
— the right to challenge the lawfulness of his/her detention;
— the right to have the lawfulness of internment/administrative detention reviewed by an independent and impartial body;
— that internees/administrative detainees should be allowed to have legal assistance;
— the right to have the lawfulness of continued internment/administrative detention periodically reviewed;
— that internees/administrative detainees and their legal representative should be able to attend the proceedings in person;
— the right to have contacts with family members;

stipulates that the judicial guarantees essential for the protection of non-derogable rights are non-derogable.

64 Cf. Arts 71 GC IV; 75 AP I; 6 AP II.

65 Cf. Chapter III GC III; Art. 64–78 GC IV.

66 Cf. CIHL, Vol. 1, pp. 345–6. See generally also, Krähenmann, Sections 724–725, and Gasser and Dörmann, Sections 585–586, in D. Fleck (ed.), *The Handbook of International Humanitarian Law*, 3rd edn (Oxford: Oxford University Press, 2013).

67 CIHL, Vol. 1, pp. 349–52.

68 J. Pejić, 'Procedural Principles and Safeguards for Internment/Administrative Detention in Armed Conflict and Other Situations of Violence', 87(858) *IRRC* (2005), 375–92.

69 Ibid. 379.

— the right to medical care and attention required by the condition of the internee/administrative detainee; 26.05
— the right to make submissions relating to treatment and conditions of detention;
— that internees/administrative detainees can be accessed by the ICRC.

The ICRC procedural principles and safeguards are more exhaustive and detailed than the Copenhagen Process Principles and Guidelines[70] in a number of respects.

Without prejudice to applicable rules of international humanitarian law, a detainee may not be transferred to another detaining authority when there are substantial grounds for believing that there is a real risk that he or she will be subjected to torture, cruel, inhuman or degrading treatment, or other serious violations of human rights. 26.06

1. *International Armed Conflicts.* The Third Geneva Convention provides two conditions for any transfer of prisoners of war by the Detaining Power: the Transferee Power must be party to the Convention and the Detaining Power must have satisfied itself of the willingness and ability of the Transferee Power to apply the Convention.[71] The Fourth Geneva Convention contains an identical provision applicable to aliens that find themselves in the territory of a party to the conflict.[72] International humanitarian law also provides for a number of post-transfer responsibilities.[73]

2. *Non-International Armed Conflicts.* Persons captured in a non-international armed conflict do not enjoy prisoner-of-war status under the Third Geneva Convention. They are, however, entitled to humane treatment under human rights law and international humanitarian law, and this may limit their transfer by the Detaining Power. As far as humanitarian law is concerned, the transfer of a person by a State to another State despite the former State's knowledge that the person is likely to face inhumane treatment may incur the responsibility under international law of that State since it may be qualified as aid or assistance in the commission of an internationally wrongful act, provided that the person concerned will indeed be subjected to inhumane treatment subsequent to the transfer.[74] Moreover, a plethora of human rights instruments and jurisprudence of various human rights bodies clearly establish that the transfer of a person is prohibited if circumstances reveal substantial grounds for believing that that person would face a real risk of being subjected to torture or other forms of cruel, inhuman, or degrading treatment or punishment, and arguably also if the person would face a real risk of falling victim to other violations of certain other fundamental rights.[75] Since detainees find

[70] Copenhagen Principles and Guidelines. [71] Art. 12(2) GC III.
[72] Art. 45(3) GC IV. [73] Art. 12(3) GC III; Art 45(3) GC IV.
[74] Cf. Art. 16 ILC Articles on State Responsibility.
[75] For an overview of the pertinent human rights instruments and jurisprudence, cf. C. Droege, 'Transfers of Detainees: Legal framework, *non-refoulement* and contemporary challenges', 90 *IRRC* (2008), 669–701, at 671–3.

26.06 themselves 'within the jurisdiction' of the Detaining Power (see Section 4.01), these *non-refoulement* obligations also apply extraterritorially. This is of great practical importance, as in many military operations Sending States forces cooperate with the authorities of the Receiving State in the quest to improve security and detain individuals in the process but do not wish to detain such persons for a prolonged period of time and instead seek to transfer them to the authorities of the Receiving State. However, at the same time they must comply with their obligations under international law, in particular human rights law. Some States have sought to accommodate these two considerations of wishing to transfer and complying with their international obligations by concluding transfer agreements that contain certain assurances from the Receiving State and post-transfer mechanisms to monitor compliance with these assurances. An example is the Memorandum of Understanding between Denmark and Afghanistan concerning the transfer of persons.[76] It needs to be emphasized, however, that the decisive test for assessing the lawfulness or otherwise of a given transfer remains whether circumstances reveal substantial grounds for believing that a transferee would face a real risk of being subjected to serious violations of human rights. If the circumstances on the ground do not reflect the assurances given from the Receiving State, a transfer may nevertheless be impermissible.

3. *Situations not Amounting to an Armed Conflict*. In situations that do not amount to an armed conflict the aforementioned principle of *non-refoulement* as emanating from human rights law applies.

[76] See Memorandum of Understanding of 6 June 2006, <http://www.fmn.dk/gamlesites/Forsvars-%20og%20sikkerhedspolitik/International%20sikkerhedspolitik/Den%20Humanitære%20Folkeret/Documents/DKAFGoverdragelsesaftale.pdf://www.pegc.us/archive/Journals/deeks_refoulment_2008.pdf>; amended on 1 May 2007, <http://data.information.dk/legacy/files/fakta/amendment.pdf>.

Chapter 27

CIVIL–MILITARY COOPERATION AND HUMANITARIAN ASSISTANCE

Humanitarian assistance is aid to an affected population in order to save lives and alleviate suffering and must be provided in accordance with basic humanitarian principles of humanity, impartiality, and neutrality. Dialogue and interaction between civilian and military actors in peace operations are necessary to protect and promote humanitarian principles, avoid competition, minimize inconsistency, and when appropriate pursue common goals. 27.01

1. Over the years military units have been involved in humanitarian operations in both peacetime, providing relief during disasters, flooding, and famine, and during peacekeeping and stability operations. In today's security environment the military component seems more involved in the 'direct' provision of aid, as humanitarian actors are often faced with situations where there are no alternatives but to rely on the military, as a last resort, for safety and to access populations in need—at the serious risk of compromising their neutrality, impartiality, independence, and thus their ability or credibility to operate. While many humanitarian organizations strongly advocate for a clear distinction between humanitarian assistance and political and military action, governments and political bodies do not necessarily agree with such distinction. A 2005 Security Council Resolution[1] notably welcomed the participation of the Multinational Force in Iraq in the provision of humanitarian and reconstruction assistance.[2]

2. Another way to address security threats is the use of mixed civilian–military teams to provide aid and assist in reconstruction efforts. In order to be effective and work with complementary actors, military and humanitarian professionals at all levels should understand and apply basic principles of humanitarian assistance. Four pertinent concepts (United Nations Integrated Missions, NATO's Civil Military Coordination, EU Civil–Military Cooperation, and the concept of Provincial Reconstruction Teams) will be discussed in what follows.

[1] SC Res. 1637 (2005) of 11 November 2005, preambular para. 12.

[2] See Humanitarian Policy Group, Policy Brief, 30 March 2008 <http://www.odi.org.uk/resources/download/1089.pdf>, at 4, stating that '[h]umanitarian work should be performed by humanitarian organisations. In so far as military organisations have a role to play in supporting humanitarian work, it should, to the extent possible, not encompass direct assistance in order to retain a clear distinction between the normal functions and roles of humanitarian and military stakeholders.'

27.01 3. *UN.* The United Nations have embraced the concept of integrated missions. An integrated mission is one in which there is a shared vision among all United Nations actors, both military and civilian, as to the strategic objectives of the United Nations presence at the country level.[3] This strategy should reflect a shared understanding of the operating environment and agreement on how to maximize the effectiveness, efficiency, and impact of the United Nations' overall response. Structural or programmatic integration between United Nations actors must be driven by an assessment of whether or not it will add real value and improve the impact of the United Nations engagement. An integrated mission's structure should be derived from an in-depth appreciation of the specific country setting and an honest assessment of the United Nations' capacities to respond effectively. It should be driven by the United Nations strategy for that country and the resources available to the United Nations.[4]

4. In situations where there is little or no peace to keep, integration may create difficulties for humanitarian and development partners, particularly if they are perceived to be too closely linked to the political and security objectives of the peacekeeping mission. In the worst case, integration may endanger their operations and the lives of their personnel. Integrated planning should also bear these worst case scenarios in mind and ensure appropriate dialogue, communication, and contingency planning.[5]

5. *NATO.* The twenty-first-century strategic environment involves a myriad of ethnic, religious, ideological, and capability drivers, which require sustainable solutions in societies ravaged by conflicts, disasters, or humanitarian catastrophes. Solutions to these serious events are impossible to achieve by military means alone.[6]

NATO's contribution to a comprehensive approach, as one of its military facilitators, is a link to the civil environment, with civil–military cooperation (CIMIC) as one of the military facilitators. This enables the military to help reaching the desired end state by coordinating, synchronizing, and de-conflicting military activities with civil actors, thus linking military operations with political objectives.[7]

The influence of the vast variety of civil contributions to stabilize a dysfunctional society must continue to be considered by the military. This will enable the smooth transition from offensive/defensive operations to security/stability operations, thus reaching a status of development where Alliance forces can leave a secure area behind much sooner.[8]

The aim and purpose of CIMIC is the interaction between military and civil actors within a comprehensive environment to support the military commander's

[3] United Nations Department of Peacekeeping Operations, Department of Field Support, Peacekeeping Operations Principles and Guidelines, January 2008, 53.

[4] Ibid. 54. [5] Ibid. 54.

[6] Allied Joint Publication AJP-3.4.9 Edition A Version 1, Allied Joint Doctrine for Civil–Military Cooperation, of 8 February 2013.

[7] Ibid. p. VII. [8] Ibid. p. VII.

plan. Ideally all actors will work to a common goal, but where this is not possible this interaction will ensure that activities to support each plan are harmonized as far as possible. This will minimize interference or unintended conflict between all actors. This interaction might consist of, but is not limited to, coordination, cooperation, mutual support, coherent joint planning, and information exchange, covering the political mandate. It includes NATO military forces, governance, and civil actors.[9] **27.01**

CIMIC is applicable to all types of NATO operations. In all conceivable scenarios commanders are increasingly required to take into account political, social, economic, cultural, religious, environmental, and humanitarian factors when planning and conducting their operations. Furthermore, commanders recognize that operational areas contain the presence of a large number of civil actors with their own mandate, aims, methods, principles, structure, role, and perspectives, that might have implications for operations and vice versa. The context and profile of CIMIC will alter according to the nature of the crisis or operation.[10]

The coordination of activities with national and local governments as well as both international organizations and non-governmental organizations is the responsibility of a commander. A so-called Civil–Military Cooperation branch or staff section will be integrated in headquarters at various levels and will support the commander in achieving this. CIMIC activities form an integral part of the Joint Force Commander's plan, are conducted in support of his mission, and are related to implementing the overall strategy and achieving a stable and sustainable end-state.[11] In cooperating with a potentially wide range of civilian organizations, NATO forces will, as far as possible and within military means and capabilities, accommodate and support the activities of these organizations, provided this does not compromise the mission. CIMIC activities are carried out with a view to timely transfer of those functions to the appropriate civilian organizations or authorities.

6. The context and profile of CIMIC will alter according to the nature of the crisis or operation. In combat operations, the focus of CIMIC is likely to be narrower than in other operations. In a Crisis Response Operation, the focus of CIMIC will be broader and more complex, enabling a commander to play his part in what is likely to be a composite, multi-functional approach to a complex political emergency. The military may have been given an explicit supporting role to an overall civil authority. Nonetheless, only the commander can decide the extent to which military resources should be committed to CIMIC tasks. It is the responsibility of commanders at all levels to direct CIMIC activities, achieve the necessary unity of command and unity of effort, and to recognize the importance of integrating into the overall effort. Commanders should be aware of the impact of military operations on the civil environment and the impact of the civil environment on their operations.

[9] Ibid. para. 0202. [10] Ibid. para. 0202. [11] Ibid.

27.01 7. *European Union*. In the context of the European Security and Defence Policy (ESDP), CIMIC is mainly concerned with the enhancement of cooperation at the various civil–military interfaces in the operational context, including the relationship towards other collective actors (international, governmental, non-governmental organizations) deployed in the region concerned. EU-CIMIC focuses exclusively on civil–military relations at the operational and tactical level. Civil–military cooperation in the field has to be backed by improved political and strategic coordination between the EU's institutional actors on both the civilian and the military sides. In the official context, the efforts taken to tackle these specific institutional challenges are referred to as Civil–Military Coordination (CMCO).[12] The EU-CIMIC doctrine borrows largely from the counterpart established earlier by NATO. However, an in-depth analysis shows that in line with its comprehensive approach to security, EU-CIMIC clearly goes beyond traditional CIMIC conceptions in terms of their exclusive focus on the military support function of CIMIC.[13]

8. Since 2003, so-called Provincial Reconstruction Teams (PRTs) have attempted to combine relatively small civilian and military components on the ground in Afghanistan, to achieve results by focusing on provincial and district centres, and to support the political leadership as well as the Afghan society. In August 2009, 26 PRTs were operating in Afghanistan.[14] Although PRTs, in principle, covered a variety of short-term and mid-term development projects (rebuilding, reconstruction, infrastructure, security sector reform) they could additionally be involved in humanitarian assistance in a traditional sense, such as providing food and shelter. Although experience with PRTs points towards their considerable potential as an instrument in conflict management, the variance in lead-country funding and guidance, and the permissiveness of the PRTs' operational environment has created inconsistent PRT missions and measures of success. Many participating nations disagreed over the role the military should play within PRTs and whether civilian reconstruction and aid organizations can work in coordination with the military.[15] Some PRTs were subject to 'national caveats' enforced by the host nation's government, which limited the PRTs' operational capabilities. For example, some lead nations had restricted their PRTs from venturing beyond certain distances of their bases, while others forbade operating after dark.[16]

9. Depending on the lead nation, PRTs also varied in the size, structure, and manning of the teams. The US PRT model had a staff of 50 to 100 people, was led

[12] C. Gebhard, 'Civil–Military Coordination and Cooperation in the Context of the EU's Crisis Management', National Defence Academy Austria, Institute for Peace Support and Conflict Management, INFO AKTUELL 01/2008, Vienna, March 2008, 2.

[13] Ibid. 3.

[14] <http://www.nato.int/isaf/docu/epub/pdf/placemat.pdf>.

[15] R.M. Perito, 'The US Experience with Provincial Reconstruction Teams in Afghanistan: Lessons Identified', Special Report No. 152, US Institute of Peace, October 2005.

[16] Ibid.

by a military officer, and stressed force protection and small, quick impact reconstruction and assistance operations. The civilian staff included specialists from the State Department, the US Agency for International Development, the Department of Agriculture, the Department of Justice, and other civilian agencies.[17] The British PRT model was similar to the US model in personnel size, but stressed 'Afghan security sector reform' and the resolution of conflicts between competing warlords.[18] German PRTs had a staff of more than 300 people and were led by a senior foreign ministry official. The German model strictly separated the military and civilian functions of the teams. German PRTs had established satellite German Assistance Agency posts separate from the military base.[19] 27.01

10. PRTs were also divided based on the tasks they performed. During their deployment in Afghanistan, Italy, the Netherlands, New Zealand, and Spain have carried out Quick Impact Projects (QIPs) as their primary activity. These countries regard QIPs as a vital tool to build a relationship with locals by bringing 'peace dividends' to the local population. Hence, QIPs is considered to be a completely different endeavour from mid- and long-term development projects, which are conducted by bilateral development agencies outside the PRT framework. In addition to QIPs, PRTs led by other countries such as Canada, Germany, Hungary, Lithuania, Norway, Turkey, the UK, and the US undertook security sector reform.[20] By the end of 2014, all PRTs had been phased out and their functions handed over to the Afghan government, traditional development actors, non-governmental organizations, and the private sector.

A clear separation between the roles of the military and humanitarian actors is necessary to distinguish their respective spheres of competence and responsibility. This approach is implicit in and builds on the principles of international humanitarian law, and is crucial to maintaining the independence of humanitarian action. 27.02

1. In times of armed conflict the distinction between combatants and civilians is one of the fundamental principles protecting those that do not or no longer take part in hostilities. Proximity of humanitarian actors to soldiers may therefore expose humanitarian actors to certain risks as soldiers are considered legitimate military targets. Any coordination between humanitarian actors and a party to an armed conflict must proceed with caution, care, and sensitivity, given that the actual or perceived affiliation with a belligerent might lead to the loss of neutrality and impartiality of the humanitarian organization, which might in turn affect the security of beneficiaries as well as humanitarian staff, and jeopardize the whole

[17] Ibid.

[18] UK Embassy in Afghanistan <http://ukinafghanistan.fco.gov.uk/en>.

[19] See W.J. Durch, 'Twenty-First-Century Peace Operations', US Institute of Peace Press, 2006.

[20] See Y. Uesugi, 'Developing A Typology of Provincial Reconstruction Teams in Afghanistan: A Comparative Study of PRT Initiative by Major Lead Nations', Paper presented at the annual meeting of the ISA's 49th Annual Convention, Hilton San Francisco, 2008.

27.02 humanitarian operation in a conflict zone.[21] The attack on United Nations Headquarters Baghdad in 2003 may illustrate that while the UN mission's mandate was political and humanitarian, opponents may have perceived the mission as closely linked to the US-led coalition.

2. The emphasis on distinction should not be interpreted as a suggestion of non-coordination between humanitarian and military actors. The particular situation on the ground and the nature of the military operation in a given situation will be a determining factor on the type of coordination that may take place. Classical peacekeeping operations under Chapter VI with full consent of all parties may allow for sharing of information on ongoing operations, full integrated planning, division of tasks, and joint execution.

3. Other types of more complex peace operations involving parties that do not adhere to the peace agreement require a much less visible coordination and collaboration between humanitarian actors and peacekeepers as the latter may at times use up to deadly force against spoilers, who may simultaneously through their families benefit from humanitarian assistance. Where cooperation between the humanitarian and military actors is not appropriate, opportune, or possible, or if there are no common goals to pursue, then actors merely operate side-by-side. Such a relationship may be best described as one of co-existence, in which case civil–military coordination should focus on minimizing competition in order to enable the different actors to work in the same geographical area with minimum disruption to each other's activities.

27.03 **Civil–military coordination is a shared responsibility of the humanitarian and military actors and it may take place in various levels of intensity and form. Humanitarian workers must never present themselves or their work as part of a military operation, and military personnel must refrain from presenting themselves as civilian humanitarian workers.**

1. Depending on circumstances, coordination may take place at company, battalion, brigade, division, or corps level on a weekly or daily basis. Larger headquarters normally will have a dedicated branch dealing with civil–military matters. Officers usually have received specific training and should understand fundamental principles of humanitarian action. Humanitarian workers likewise should have basic knowledge of military operations and understand why the military wish to participate in humanitarian efforts. They also should be aware of capacities and limitations of military units.

[21] United Nations Office for the Coordination of Humanitarian Affairs and the Inter-Agency Standing Committee (IASC), 'Civil–Military Guidelines & Reference for Complex Emergencies', New York, 2008.

2. When there is a common goal and agreed strategy, and parties accept to work together, cooperation may become possible, and coordination should focus on improving the effectiveness and efficiency of the combined efforts to serve humanitarian objectives. In order to help create clarity for the civilian population in general and for the beneficiaries of assistance in particular, humanitarian workers should present themselves as such. Civilian workers wearing camouflage pattern clothes may not be helpful in that process and may become a potential target for opponents. **27.03**

In any civil–military cooperation, humanitarian actors should retain the lead role in undertaking and directing humanitarian activities. Humanitarian organizations must not implement tasks on behalf of the military nor represent or implement their policies. **27.04**

1. The independence of humanitarian action and decision making must be preserved both at the operational and policy levels at all times. Basic requisites such as freedom of movement for humanitarian staff, freedom to conduct independent assessments, freedom of selection of staff, freedom to identify beneficiaries of assistance based on their needs, or free flow of communications between humanitarian agencies as well as with the media, must not be impeded.[22]

2. Military commanders do need to recognize that prioritizing and providing humanitarian assistance is a sensitive matter as choices in time of scarcity may impact the lives of thousands. It is therefore a matter that requires specific experience and knowledge, usually not available within military organization. Humanitarian actors naturally should lead decision-making processes whereas military commanders may provide support in terms of manpower and logistic assets.

As a general rule, humanitarian convoys do not use armed or military escorts. Exceptions to the rule will be considered, as a last resort, and only when the criteria independence of humanitarian actors/agencies—need, safety, and sustainability—have been met. **27.05**

1. The military often have the capability and assets to help secure an enabling environment on the ground in which humanitarian activities can take place in relative safety. Ideally, humanitarian convoys would like to operate independently without armed escorts. The year 2013 set a new record for violence against civilian aid operations, with 251 separate attacks affecting 460 aid workers.[23] The spike in attacks in 2013 was driven mainly by escalating conflicts and deterioration of governance in Syria and South Sudan. These two countries along with Afghanistan, Pakistan, and Sudan together accounted for three-quarters of all attacks.

[22] Ibid.

[23] Aid Worker Security Report 2014, <https://aidworkersecurity.org/incidents/report>. The 2,013 victims include 155 who lost their lives. In addition, 171 were seriously wounded and 134 were kidnapped.

27.05 Military involvement may include controlling routes, patrolling in front and rear of convoys, or patrolling alongside or in between convoys. It is clear that the increase of such mixed operations has somewhat blurred the distinction on 'humanitarian space'—the necessary space demanded by humanitarians, wishing to be seen acting independently from the military.

2. The nature of the relation between one or a group of humanitarian organization(s) and the military as well as the conduct of these actors in this relationship may also have an effect on other humanitarian agencies working in the same area and even beyond, possibly affecting the perception of humanitarian action in general. For example, the use of armed escorts by one humanitarian organization may negatively influence the perception of neutrality and impartiality of other humanitarian organizations in the same area.[24] Coordination amongst humanitarian actors, preferably leading to a common approach to civil–military relations in a given complex emergency, is therefore desirable.

[24] Civil–Military Guidelines & Reference for Complex Emergencies, 17.

Chapter 28

PRIVATE CONTRACTORS AND SECURITY COMPANIES

Private contractors may be employed by a Sending State to provide logistical and technical support and security for installations and persons. They should not be employed in combat functions or engage in direct participation in hostilities in the context of an armed conflict, as such participation would entail the loss of civilian protection and could result in their being prosecuted for acts of unprivileged belligerency. 28.01

1. The use of private contractors has become widespread. Reference has been made to them already in early codification of the law of armed conflict.[1] Their use in the types of functions referred to in Section 28.01 is long-standing, non-controversial, and accepted in both treaty law and in general practice.[2] Such personnel may be contracted individually or via private companies providing the respective services. Likewise, the use of private contractors and security firms for (assistance in) the training of local military and police personnel is well accepted. However, in recent years, their use in various other types of functions has become increasingly prevalent. Expressly authorized or not by armed forces or other competent authorities, and in many instances not effectively controlled, they have provided personal protection, guarded installations, and secured transports. There is no prohibition against the use of contractors for the purpose of (assisting in) providing security against unlawful theft or assault against installations or persons. Nevertheless, care should be exercised to avoid that such activities include law enforcement functions not clearly authorized. In an armed conflict it is essential not to cross the line separating security functions and active participation in hostilities. Also related activities, such as the guarding and interrogation of prisoners of war and other detainees, etc., should not be assigned to private contractors and security firms.[3]

[1] Art. 13 Hague Regulations (HagueReg) of 1899 and 1907.

[2] See e.g. in addition to the HagueReg, Art. 4A(4) of the Third Geneva Convention which makes reference to contractors.

[3] See e.g. US Department of Defense Instruction 3020.41 USD (AT&L) of 3 October 2005 'Contractor Personnel Authorized to Accompany the US Armed Forces' and US Department of Defense Instruction 1100.22 USC (P&R) of 7 September 2006 'Guidance for Determining Workforce Mix'.

TERRY D. GILL AND DIETER FLECK

28.01 2. Notwithstanding the abovementioned statement of best practice, it is undeniable that the employment of contractors in many recent operations has included many instances in which their activities have, in fact, crossed the line to include direct combat support and other forms of activity, which until the end of the Cold War, would have been reserved for members of State armed forces. The reasons for this are various and have received considerable attention, and need not concern us here.[4] What is important from a legal perspective is what the legal ramifications of this development are. Firstly, it should be noted that such activities, when amounting to direct participation in hostilities, can result in loss of civilian protection. It can also constitute 'unprivileged belligerency' for those so involved. While unprivileged belligerency is not generally considered to constitute a war crime, it can well result in criminal prosecution under national law on the part of any State which possesses jurisdiction.[5] It also signifies that such persons would not be entitled to prisoner-of-war status or treatment. It furthermore undermines the principle of distinction and increases the risks for other civilians in proximity to the forces. This could include both contractors with more traditional non-combat functions and other civilians, such as journalists, aid workers, and officials of international organizations who happen to be in the vicinity of the forces involved. Secondly, it raises questions relating to the responsibility and accountability of such personnel for their actions, including acts which could constitute violations of either national or international law.[6] Since such personnel may not be subject to the same standards of training and discipline as members of the regular armed forces, they could deliberately, or simply due to lack of proper preparation and supervision, engage in acts which constitute violations of national and international law, undermine the legitimacy of the operation, or otherwise have a negative impact upon the success of and support for the mission. It therefore makes good sense, from both an operational and a legal perspective, to restrict contractors to clear civilian functions and to ensure that certain activities which are inherently governmental in nature will remain military, as referred to in the previous paragraph.

28.02 **In all cases in which private security companies and contractors are utilized on missions abroad, adequate provision for regulation, supervision, and accountability must be made to ensure that their activities are carried out in full conformity with applicable national and international legal standards and to ensure the existence of an adequate**

[4] See, in general, P. Singer, *Corporate Warriors: The Rise of the Privatized Military Industry* (Ithaca and London: Cornell University Press, 2003); G. Bartolini, 'PMS Contractors as "Persons who Accompany the Armed Forces"', in F. Francioni and N. Ronzitti, *War by Contract: Human Rights, Humanitarian Law, and Private Contractors* (Oxford: Oxford University Press, 2011).

[5] M. Schmitt, 'Humanitarian Law and Direct Participation in Hostilities by Private Contractors and Civilian Employees', in 5 *Chicago Journal of International Law* (2005), 511–46, at 520–1.

[6] A. McDonald, 'Ghosts in the Machine: Some Legal Issues Concerning US Military Contractors in Iraq', in M. Schmitt and J. Pejic (eds), *International Law and Armed Conflict: Exploring the Faultlines* (Leiden: Nijhoff, 2007), 357–401, at 386 *et seq.*

regulatory legal framework. This is in the interest of both Sending and Receiving States and the international community as a whole. In no case should it be possible for such activities to be carried out in the absence of such a regulatory and supervisory framework with the resulting possibility of impunity for any violations which may occur. 28.02

1. In cases where the activities of a private security company, or more particularly of an individual private contractor, are subject to the jurisdiction of either the Sending or the Receiving State (or both), there will be at least a possibility of providing for criminal jurisdiction and civil accountability and liability on the basis of recognized principles upon which jurisdiction can be based. In practice, however, this may prove to be less than adequate, unless specific legislation and arrangements for its enforcement are in place, which make it possible to conduct investigations, provide for legal cooperation and extradition or repatriation, and for adequate oversight and for redress and compensation for acts which violate existing national or international legal standards.[7] While many countries provide for extraterritorial prescriptive jurisdiction over the actions of their nationals, this may not result in adequate supervision or investigation, much less prosecution of alleged violations for any number of reasons. These could range from lack of information and evidence or lack of resources to conduct such investigations, to unwillingness or inability to initiate such action. Likewise, the Receiving State could also be unable or unwilling to proceed with investigation or prosecution due to similar or other constraints. While the Receiving State will normally possess jurisdiction over foreign civilian contractors in the absence of other arrangements (see Section 28.03) this may not always be the case. For example, civilian contractors were afforded immunity from Receiving State jurisdiction in the occupation phase of operations in Iraq[8] and there are other situations in which the Receiving State may be constrained from exercising its jurisdiction over foreign private contractors. To enhance accountability, some States have enacted specific legislation to bring the activities of contractors possessing their nationality or under their employment within the scope of national criminal law. Examples of such legislation are the adoption of the US Military Extraterritorial Jurisdiction Act (MEJA), which applies to contractors employed by the US Department of Defense (DoD). Some other States have enacted legislation which would bring certain offences, particularly those constituting war crimes or other recognized international crimes, within the scope of their jurisdiction.[9] But neither the US MEJA, nor other legislation relating

[7] Aside from criminal and civil liability under national law, this could have implications for State responsibility under international law. For a clear overview of these implications, see McDonald, 'Ghosts in the Machine', 392–8.

[8] CPA Order Number 17 (rev) CPA/ORD/27 June 2004, referred to in McDonald, 'Ghosts in the Machine', 387.

[9] Military Extraterritorial Jurisdiction Act (MEJA); 18 USC, Sections 3261–3267 (2000). An example of legislation relating to international crimes is the Netherlands 'Wet Internationale Misdrijven (WIM)' of 19 June 2003.

28.02 to international crimes, would necessarily cover all types of offences, or extend to all contractors. For example, the MEJA does not apply to contractors engaged by agencies of the US Government other than the DoD and many legislative instruments relating to international crimes, would not extend to other offences, or necessarily be applicable to non-nationals not present on the Sending State's territory.[10] Consequently, notwithstanding the existing provisions enabling either Receiving State or Sending State jurisdiction, there are numerous gaps and insufficiencies which can only be remedied by the adoption of some form of international regulation and supervision.

2. In this context, initiatives have been undertaken to provide for better international supervision of the activities of private contractors and security companies.[11] Further activities include the establishment of a working group by the UN Human Rights Council to draw up a possible legal instrument for regulating the activities of private security companies and contractors[12] and the initiation by the European Union of a research project aimed at examining the regulatory framework at national, European, and international levels, with a view to ensuring improved compliance with international humanitarian law and human rights.[13] In the absence of a binding international legal framework, the International Code of Conduct for Private Security Providers, a multi-stakeholder initiative convened by the Swiss Government, may promote best practice in the area of improving compliance with international legal standards and supporting cooperation between both Sending and Receiving States.[14] It confirms principles and standards based on human rights and international humanitarian law, and aims at improving accountability of the industry by establishing an external independent oversight mechanism.

28.03 **In the absence of a status-of-forces or similar agreement granting functional immunity, the status of private contractors is that of**

[10] The MEJA would not apply to contractors engaged by e.g. the CIA or Department of State. The Netherlands WIM only applies to non-nationals if they are present on Dutch territory or the suspected offence was directed at a Netherlands national (Art. 2, para.1 lit. a and b). It also applies to offences committed by Netherlands nationals abroad (lit. c).

[11] See Montreux Document on pertinent international legal obligations and good practices for States related to operations of private military and security companies during armed conflict of 17 September 2008, UN GA Doc. A/63/467 and UN SC Doc. S/2008/636 (6 October 2008), <https://www.icrc.org/eng/assets/files/other/icrc_002_0996.pdf>.

[12] See Report of the Special Representative of the Secretary-General on the issue of human rights and transnational corporations and other business enterprises, John Ruggie: Principles for responsible contracts: integrating the management of human rights risks into State-investor contract negotiations: guidance for negotiators, UN Doc. A/HRC/17/31/Add.3 (25 May 2011), <http://www.ohchr.org/Documents/Issues/Business/A.HRC.17.31.Add.3.pdf>.

[13] The EU 'Priv-War' Project was established within the context of the European Community's 7th Framework Programme and is coordinated through the European University Institute (Academy of European Law) in collaboration with six partner universities in France, Germany, Italy, Latvia, the Netherlands, and the UK. See <http://priv-war.eu>.

[14] See International Code of Conduct for Private Security Providers (ICoC), <http://www.geneva-academy.ch/docs/publications/briefing4_web_final.pdf >.

foreign civilian workers in the Receiving State. It should be in the interest of all parties to ensure that adequate provision is made to ensure accountability and supervision while, at the same time, allowing for the contractors and their employers to carry out the functions for which they have been engaged within the limits referred to above. 28.03

1. Private contractors and security companies are often not regulated in status-of-forces agreements (SOFAs) concluded to specify the legal status of foreign missions in a Receiving State.[15] The mere fact that they may be subsumed under the law of armed conflict as persons who accompany the armed forces does not give them special status in the Receiving State during peacetime. Different from armed forces or the police, private contractors or security companies are not organs of the Sending State and consequently they do not enjoy the sovereign immunity status of the latter within the Receiving State or any Transit State, unless such status is expressly agreed.

2. Both Sending and Receiving States will have an interest in addressing issues of private contractors and security companies in the context of SOFA negotiations. Thus, a SOFA could be used to ensure an unimpeded exercise of functions by those contractors and to assure the Receiving State that they are effectively controlled and held accountable for any wrongdoing. For the latter purpose the SOFA may provide that jurisdiction may be exercised exclusively or concurrently by one of the parties. The US–Iraqi SOFA provides that Iraq shall have the primary right to exercise jurisdiction over United States contractors and United States contractor employees.[16] Previously, Blackwater guards employed for the US Embassy in Baghdad were held to enjoy immunity from local prosecution in Iraq. Blackwater security guards who had opened fire on unarmed Iraqi civilians in 2007 were convicted of murder and manslaughter in 2014.[17]

[15] See sub-Chapter 5.2 'Status of Forces in Enforcement and Peace Enforcement Operations', sub-Chapter 6.2 'Status of Forces in Peace Operations', Chapter 9 'Status of Forces in Self-Defence Operations'.

[16] Art. 12(2) Agreement between the United States of America and the Republic of Iraq on the Withdrawal of United States Forces from Iraq and the Organization of Their Activities during their Temporary Presence in Iraq of 17 November 2008, <http://www.cfr.org/publication/17880>.

[17] *The New York Times*, 22 October 2014, <http://www.nytimes.com/2014/10/23/us/blackwater-verdict.html?ref=topics>.

Chapter 29

THE PROSECUTION OF INTERNATIONAL CRIMES IN RELATION TO THE CONDUCT OF MILITARY OPERATIONS

The purpose of this chapter is to provide an overview of international crimes which may be committed during military operations or which may occur in areas where military operations are being conducted. It is not intended to be a substitute for legal texts devoted to international criminal law.[1] It will not address the maintenance of law and order in areas under the control of international military forces, including possible investigations of human rights violations (see Chapter 24) and it will not address matters of State or organizational responsibility (see Chapter 30).

29.01 **War Crimes, crimes against humanity, and genocide are international crimes which may occur in relation to military operations. War crimes may only occur in armed conflict but crimes against humanity and genocide may occur in or outside of armed conflict. All three types of crimes may be prosecuted on the basis of universal jurisdiction, that is, they may be prosecuted by the authorities of any State regardless of where the offence is committed although, usually, the accused must be in the hands of the State authorities which commence the prosecution. In certain circumstances, persons accused of any of the three types of crimes may be prosecuted before an international tribunal.**

1. The following paragraphs will address specific issues related to each of the categories of crimes: war crimes, crimes against humanity, and genocide. All of these crimes are international crimes and may be prosecuted on the basis of the principle of universal jurisdiction. There are two versions of the universality principle: conditional and absolute. Under conditional universal jurisdiction, the more widely accepted and narrower approach, the presence of the accused on the territory of a State is a condition for the exercise of jurisdiction by that State although the alleged crime may have been committed elsewhere. Under absolute

[1] See e.g. A. Cassese, *International Criminal Law* (Oxford: Oxford University Press, 2003); R. Cryer et al., *An Introduction to International Criminal Law and Procedure* (Cambridge: Cambridge University Press, 2007); and M.C. Bassiouni, *Introduction to International Criminal Law* (New York: Transnational Publishers, 2003).

WILLIAM J. FENRICK

universal jurisdiction, the less widely accepted but broader approach, a State may prosecute persons accused of international crimes whether or not the accused is in custody or present in the territory of the State where the trial is held. Even in States which accept absolute universal jurisdiction, however, the presence of the accused on the territory is a condition for the exercise of jurisdiction unless their legal systems permit trials in absentia. 29.01

2. All of these crimes may, as a matter of public international law, be prosecuted before national tribunals. Generally speaking, however, national implementing legislation would also be required before prosecutions before national tribunals would be practicable.

3. It may also be possible to prosecute accused individuals before an international tribunal if one exists which possesses the appropriate jurisdiction. As examples of international tribunals, the International Criminal Tribunal for the former Yugoslavia (ICTY) has jurisdiction over certain offences committed in the territory of the former Yugoslavia since 1 January 1991,[2] the International Criminal Tribunal for Rwanda (ICTR) has jurisdiction over certain offences committed during 1994 in the territory of Rwanda or by Rwandan citizens in the territory of neighbouring States,[3] and the International Criminal Court (ICC) has jurisdiction over certain offences committed in the territory of States parties and in certain other circumstances since the ICC Statute came into force on 1 July 2002.[4]

War crimes are violations of the treaty or customary law applicable during armed conflict. The content of the applicable law may vary depending on the treaty obligations of parties to the relevant conflict and on the classification of the conflict as international or non-international. A reasonably comprehensive and generally usable list of war crimes is contained in Article 8 of the Statute of the International Criminal Court although the provisions of the Statute do not apply, as treaty law, to States which are not parties to the Statute. 29.02

1. War crimes are violations of the treaty or customary law applicable in armed conflict. War crimes may be committed in international or in non-international armed conflicts. Customary and treaty law obligations vary depending on the type

[2] Art. 1, Statute of the International Criminal Tribunal for the Prosecution of Persons Responsible for Serious violations of International Humanitarian Law Committed in the Territory of the former Yugoslavia, in D. Schindler and J. Toman (eds), *The Laws of Armed Conflicts*, 4th rev. and complete edn (Leiden: Martinus Nijhoff, 2004), 1285–96 at 1288.

[3] Art. 1, Statute of the International Criminal Tribunal for the Prosecution of Persons Responsible for Genocide and Other Serious violations of International Humanitarian Law Committed in the Territory of Rwanda and Rwandan Citizens Responsible for Genocide and Other Such Violations Committed in the Territory of Neighbouring State, Between 1 January 1994 and 31 December 1994 in Schindler and Toman, *The Laws of Armed Conflicts*, 1297–308 at 1300.

[4] Arts 5–21, Rome Statute of the International Criminal Court in Schindler and Toman, *The Laws of Armed Conflicts*, 1309–95 at 1315–26.

29.02 of conflict. Treaty law obligations vary depending on which States are party to the relevant treaties. As a result, it is not practicable to make a complete list of all war crimes applicable to all conflicts. A reasonably comprehensive and generally usable list of war crimes is contained in Article 8 of the ICC Statute. An additional convenient feature of the ICC Statute is that elements of crimes have been prepared for each of the offences listed in Article 8.[5] It must, however, be borne in mind that the list in Article 8 is not exhaustive and that the ICC Statute does not bind non-parties to it.

2. War crimes are certain prohibited acts committed by persons, military or civilian, linked to one side of a conflict and directed against persons or property on the other side of the conflict or neutral in the conflict. The actions of peace-keepers, for example, would not usually be regarded as war crimes, although they may be crimes, because they would not be linked to one side of the conflict in the region where they are deployed. On the other hand, war crimes could be committed against peacekeepers because they are neutrals in the conflict.

3. Examples of war crimes would be murder or ill treatment of prisoners of war or of civilians in occupied territory and plunder of public or private property. Grave breaches of the Geneva Conventions of 1949 and of AP I are war crimes. A single act by a single person, the murder of a prisoner of war by a soldier, for example, can constitute a war crime. Generally speaking, war crimes are acts related to the conflict, not ones committed in a purely private context. Finally, war crimes are acts which are regarded as, and should be, punishable by all sides in a conflict. For this reason, acts of espionage or of unlawful combatancy do not constitute war crimes.[6] Spies and unlawful combatants may well be regarded as national heroes by the party on whose behalf they are acting. They may, however, be punished for their acts under certain circumstances under national law by the party against whom they are acting.

29.03 **Crimes against humanity are various prohibited acts committed as part of a widespread or systematic attack directed against any civilian population. A reasonably comprehensive and generally usable list of crimes against humanity is contained in Article 7 of the Statute of the International Criminal Court although the provisions of the Statute do not apply, as treaty law, to States which are not parties to the Statute.**

1. The concept of crimes against humanity was developed initially to address the problem of massive mistreatment of parts of its own or allied civilian populations by a State as the potential victim group for war crimes is limited to neutral persons or

[5] Finalized Text of the Elements of Crimes, UN Doc. PCNICC/2000/1/Add.2, at 18–48.

[6] R. Baxter, 'The Duty of Obedience to the Belligerent Occupant', 27 *BYBIL* (1950), 235–66; and R. Baxter, 'So-Called "Unprivileged Belligerency": Spies, Guerillas and Saboteurs', 28 *BYBIL* (1951), 323–45.

persons linked to the other side in an armed conflict.[7] At present, crimes against humanity may be committed during or outside of armed conflict. Further, the victims of crimes against humanity may include any civilian population, including civilians on the other side or neutral civilians in an armed conflict. As a result, some persons may be the victims of either war crimes or crimes against humanity and some acts, provided they are committed in an appropriate context, may be regarded as either crimes against humanity or war crimes. As opposed to the treaty law concerning war crimes, which is quite voluminous, there is relatively little treaty law concerning crimes against humanity. Article 7 of the ICC Statute is by far the most elaborate treaty provision relating to crimes against humanity and it includes a reasonably comprehensive and generally usable list of such offences although its provisions do not apply, as treaty law, to States which are not parties to the Statute. As an additional helpful factor, element of offences have also been agreed to for each of the offences enumerated in Article 7.[8] 29.03

2. As opposed to war crimes, single acts committed outside a context of widespread or systematic acts directed against a civilian population do not constitute crimes against humanity. Crimes against humanity must be 'widespread or systematic'. The 'widespread' requirement means the prohibited act must occur within a context of massive numbers of prohibited acts being directed against the civilian population. The prohibited acts need not, however, all be of the same type. If, for example, a sexual assault occurs while a large number of civilians are being tortured, both the sexual assault and the acts of torture can constitute crimes against humanity. 'Systematic' refers to the existence of a pattern of conduct or a methodical plan. The jurisprudence of the ICTY indicates quite clearly that crimes against humanity must be either widespread or systematic but need not be both. Article 7(1) of the ICC Statute states that a crime against humanity is a proscribed act 'when committed as part of a widespread or systematic attack directed against any civilian population'. In Article 7(1)(a), however, the Statute states: '"Attack directed against any civilian population" means a course of conduct involving the multiple commission of acts . . . pursuant to or in furtherance of a State or organizational policy . . .'. In other words, as a result of its definition of 'attack', the ICC Statute requires that crimes against humanity be *both* widespread and systematic.

Genocide is one of a specific series of acts, enumerated in the 1948 UN Convention against Genocide, committed with intent to destroy, in whole or in part, a national, ethnical, racial, or religious group, as such. 29.04

1. Genocide is often regarded as the crime of crimes.[9] It may be committed during or outside of armed conflict. It involves the attempted physical destruction of a

[7] M.C. Bassiouni, *Crimes Against Humanity in International Law*, 2nd rev. edn (The Hague: Kluwer, 1999).

[8] Elements of Crimes, 9–17.

[9] W.A. Schabas, *Genocide in International Law* (Cambridge: Cambridge University Press, 2000).

29.04 national, ethnical, racial, or religious group as such by one of a variety of means as specified in the 1948 UN Convention against Genocide, including: killing members of the group; causing serious bodily or mental harm to members of the group; and deliberately inflicting on the group conditions of life calculated to bring about its physical destruction in whole or in part. Proof of the nature of the group—national, ethnical, racial, or religious—is essential. There is no such thing as genocide directed against a social class or members of a political party. Proof of the intent to destroy is also essential. From a purely legal perspective, there is no such thing as cultural genocide at the present time. Genocide is prohibited under customary international law as well as by treaty. The customary law prohibition is also restated in Article 6 of the ICC Statute. As already indicated, the ICC Statute does not apply as such to non-State parties. The agreed elements for each of the modes of committing genocide which have been prepared for use by the ICC may, however, also be useful for non-State parties.[10]

29.05 **Individuals are criminally responsible when they commit or participate in the commission of war crimes, crimes against humanity, or acts of genocide.**

1. Rule 151 of the ICRC CIHL Study contains an essentially similar provision although it does not refer to crimes against humanity or acts of genocide.[11] Generally speaking, national law provisions indicate when persons are involved in the commission of an offence to a sufficient degree that they should be held criminally responsible. Persons who actually commit an offence while possessing the requisite mental element are criminally responsible. In addition, under the Statutes of the ICTY (Article 7) and the ICTR (Article 6), persons who planned, instigated, ordered, committed, or otherwise aided and abetted in the planning, preparation, or execution of a crime are individually criminally responsible for that crime. Under the Statute of the ICC (Article 25), persons who committed a crime; ordered, solicited, or induced the commission of a crime which was committed or attempted; aided or abetted the commission or attempted commission of a crime; contributed to the commission or attempted commission of a crime by a group with a common purpose; or attempted the commission of a crime are individually criminally responsible for that crime. The existence of individual criminal responsibility is without prejudice to the possible responsibility of a State or international organization (see Chapter 30).

29.06 **Individuals have a duty to disobey a manifestly unlawful order.**

1. Rule 154 of the ICRC CIHL Study contains an essentially identical provision.[12] Individuals, particularly members of the armed forces, have a duty to obey lawful

[10] Elements of Crimes, 6–8.

[11] J.-M. Henckaerts and L. Doswald-Beck (eds), *Customary International Humanitarian Law,* vol. 1—Rules (Cambridge: Cambridge University Press, 2005), 551–5.

[12] CIHL Study, 563–5.

orders given to them by persons placed in lawful authority over them. Obedience to lawful orders is a cornerstone of effective military operations. What constitutes a manifestly unlawful order involves a degree of judgement and may depend on the education and relative sophistication of the person receiving the order. An order to commit genocide or a crime against humanity is a manifestly unlawful order by definition under ICC Statute Article 33(2).[13] As an example, under Canadian legislation passed to implement the ICC Statute, an accused cannot raise as a defence his belief that an order was not manifestly unlawful if that belief 'was based on information about a civilian population or an identifiable group of persons that encouraged, was likely to encourage or attempted to justify the commission of inhumane acts or omissions against the population or group'.[14] An order to kill or mistreat persons in the hands of a party to a conflict, such as civilians or prisoners of war would be manifestly unlawful under international law. **29.06**

2. The existence of individual criminal responsibility is without prejudice to the possible responsibility of a State or international organization (see Chapter 30).

Obeying a superior order does not relieve a subordinate of criminal responsibility if the subordinate knew that the act ordered was unlawful or should have known because of the manifestly unlawful nature of the act ordered. **29.07**

1. Rule 155 of the ICRC CIHL Study is identical to this provision.[15] As obedience to lawful orders is a cornerstone of military effectiveness, the extent to which a plea of superior orders should be a complete defence to a charge of committing an international crime has been much debated. The Statute of the International Military Tribunal at Nuremberg (IMT) provided that proof of superior orders would not constitute a defence but could be considered in mitigation of sentence (Article 8).[16] The Statutes of the ICTY (Article 7(4))[17] and the ICTR (Article 6(4))[18] contained similar provisions. On the other hand, the Principles of the Nuremberg Tribunal adopted by the International Law Commission in 1950 asserted: 'The fact that a person acted pursuant to order of his government or of a superior does not relieve him from responsibility under international law provided a moral choice was in fact possible to him.'[19] The ICC Statute adopts an approach which differs in part from that adopted in the Statutes of the IMT, ICTY, and ICTR. It provides that superior orders can constitute a defence in limited

[13] Art. 33(2) ICC Statute, 1329–30.

[14] *Crimes Against Humanity and War Crimes Act*, Statutes of Canada 2000, Chapter 24, Section 14(3).

[15] CIHL Study, 565–7.

[16] London Agreement on War Criminals 1945, in Schindler and Toman, *The Laws of Armed Conflicts*, 1253–61, at 1257.

[17] ICTY Statute, in Schindler and Toman, *The Laws of Armed Conflicts*, 1289.

[18] ICTR Statute, in Schindler and Toman, *The Laws of Armed Conflicts*, 1301.

[19] Principles of International Law Recognized in the Charter of the Nuremberg Tribunal and in the Judgment of the Tribunal, in Schindler and Toman, *The Laws of Armed Conflicts*, 1265–6.

29.07 circumstances, specifically, when a subordinate is under a legal obligation to obey the order, the subordinate does not know the order is unlawful, and the order is not manifestly unlawful (Article 33).[20] The same article goes on to indicate that orders to commit genocide or crimes against humanity are deemed to be manifestly unlawful. The provision above and Rule 155 of the ICRC CIHL Study adopt the approach taken in the ICC Statute. It must be noted that this provision gives very little scope for a successful superior orders defence.

2. Although there is very little scope for a successful superior orders defence as such, superior orders, because of their linkage to compulsion, may be linked to a duress defence with a greater likelihood of success. In the *Erdemović* case, the Appeals Chamber of the ICTY, by a split decision, rejected duress, combined with superior orders, as a complete defence to a charge including unlawful killing although it did consider duress as a mitigating factor for sentencing.[21] The drafters of the ICC Statute, however, adopted the dissenting viewpoint in *Erdemović* and provided that duress could be a complete defence even for charges including unlawful killing in certain extreme circumstances (Article 31(1)(d)).[22]

29.08 **Commanders and other superiors are criminally responsible for war crimes, crimes against humanity, or acts of genocide committed pursuant to their orders.**

1. Rule 152 of the ICRC CIHL Study is substantially identical to this provision.[23] The commander or superior must possess authority to issue binding orders to the perpetrator although there need not be a formal superior–subordinate relationship in effect. The order may be given indirectly and need not be in any particular form. There must be a causal link between the act of ordering and the physical perpetration of the crime. A commander or superior who issues an order which does not explicitly require that a crime must be committed may still be held liable for a crime if he issues an apparently lawful order which both he and the recipient understand to implicitly authorize the commission of a crime.[24]

29.09 **Commanders and other superiors are criminally responsible for war crimes, crimes against humanity, or acts of genocide committed by their subordinates if they knew, or had reason to know, that the subordinates were about to commit or were committing such crimes and did not take all necessary and reasonable measures in their power to prevent their commission, or if such crimes had been committed, to punish the persons responsible.**

[20] ICC Statute, in Schindler and Toman, *The Laws of Armed Conflicts*, 1329–30.
[21] *Prosecutor v Drazen Erdemović*, ICTY Case no. IT-96-22, Sentencing Judgment, 29 November 1996, Appeals Judgment, 7 October 1997, Revised Sentencing Judgment, 5 March 1998.
[22] ICC Statute, in Schindler and Toman, *The Laws of Armed Conflicts*, 1328–9.
[23] CIHL Study, at 556–8.
[24] *Prosecutor v Tihomir Blaskić*, ICTY Case no. IT-95-14-A Appeals Judgment 29 July 2004, para. 42.

1. This provision is essentially similar to Rule 153 in the ICRC CIHL Study.[25] Command responsibility is a doctrine in international law whereby a person in authority may, under certain circumstances, be held criminally responsible for acts committed by subordinates because of a failure to prevent them committing such acts or a failure to take all measures within his or her power to have the subordinates punished after the acts have been committed. As a practical matter, in most military or other disciplinary systems, the commander will have no direct authority to punish subordinates for major offences because of a requirement to insulate the disciplinary system from improper command influence. The best the commander can do is take all practicable measures to have the alleged offences investigated and to refer the matter to proper authorities for possible prosecution. The doctrine of command responsibility is very closely related to the concept of responsible command which appears in treaties such as HC IV[26] and GC III[27] as one of the indicators of the existence of an armed force (a disciplinary system which enables a superior to control his subordinates). As a doctrine related to criminal responsibility, command responsibility has its roots in various post-World War II war crimes cases,[28] particularly *Yamashita*,[29] *High Command*,[30] and *Hostages*.[31] The doctrine is also occasionally referred to as the doctrine of superior responsibility, as 'command' is regarded as a particularly military concept and the doctrine can, in limited circumstances, be applied to non-military superiors. **29.09**

2. Treaty law provisions related to command responsibility are also contained in Articles 86 and 87 of AP I and in Article 28 of the ICC Statute but these, of course, bind only States parties. AP I merely codifies customary law. Article 28 of the ICC Statute contains new law in that it broadens the scope of applicability of the doctrine to apply to a wider range of non-military superiors in certain circumstances.

3. The decisions of the ICTY related to command responsibility provide the best reasoned indicators of the content of the doctrine in customary law. The leading case before the ICTY is the *Celebici* Trial Judgment which was subsequently endorsed by the Appeals Chamber. It indicates that the essential elements for proof of command responsibility are: (i) individuals were about to commit or had committed an offence; (ii) a superior–subordinate relationship existed between the individuals and the superior; (iii) the superior knew or had reason to know that the

[25] CIHL Study, 558–63.

[26] Art. 1, HC IV, in Schindler and Toman, *The Laws of Armed Conflicts*, 55–87, at 66.

[27] Art. 4, GC III, in Schindler and Toman, *The Laws of Armed Conflicts*, 507–74, at 513–14.

[28] W.H. Parks, 'Command Responsibility for War Crimes', 62 *Military Law Review* (1973), 1–104.

[29] *Trial of General Tomoyuki Yamashita*, IV *Law Reports of Trials of War Criminals* (Washington, DC: US Government Printing Office, 1949), 1–96.

[30] *United States v von Leeb and others* (the *German High Command* case), 15 Annual Digest and Reports of Public International Law Cases (H. Lauterpacht, ed.), 376–98.

[31] *United States v Wilhelm List and others (The Hostages Trial)*, 8 *Law Reports of Trials of War Criminals* (Washington, DC: US Government Printing Office, 1949), 34.

29.09 offence was about to be committed or had been committed; and (iv) the superior failed to take necessary and reasonable measures to prevent the commission of the offence or to punish the perpetrators.[32]

4. In the view of the *Celebici* Trial Chamber, the doctrine applied to civilian superiors only to the extent that they exercised a degree of control over their subordinates which was similar to that of military commanders. This degree of control was referred to as 'effective control... in the sense of having the material ability to prevent and punish the commission of (the) offences'.[33] The same Chamber rejected strict liability and offered useful guidance on the meaning of 'had reason to know' as follows: '... a superior can be held criminally responsible only if some specific information was in fact available to him which would provide notice of offences committed by his subordinates'.[34]

5. The ICC Statute modifies the knowledge standard for command responsibility in that it substitutes for 'had reason to know' the following standards: (a) for military commanders or persons effectively acting as military commanders, 'owing to the circumstances at the time, should have known', and (b) for other superiors, 'consciously disregarded information which clearly indicated'.[35]

6. The liability of the commander of a multinational force for acts perpetrated by members of one or more national contingents may vary depending on the type and degree of command he exercises over the national contingents. For example, a commander exercising operational command (OPCOM) or operational control (OPCON) over forces of another country would have no basis in law for exercising disciplinary authority over these forces. It is also possible that the commander of a multinational force, because of the international obligations accepted by his or her State, will have obligations under international law which differ from those imposed on one or more national contingents. As a matter of practice, the commander must not order the national contingents to perform tasks which violate their international obligations or the obligations incurred by his or her own State.

7. It should be noted that under existing international treaties and jurisprudence, a commander or superior held criminally liable on the basis of the doctrine of command responsibility is held liable for the offence committed by his subordinates because of his failure to prevent or punish. Some may regard this approach as unduly harsh while others may regard it as merely one of the many burdens of command and one which is necessary if armed forces are to be instruments for the controlled use of force. It is probable that prosecutions for command responsibility type offences under national laws would be for separate offences such as dereliction

[32] *Prosecutor v Zejnil Delalić et al.* (*Celebici* case), ICTY Case no. IT-96-21 Trial Judgment, 16 November 1998, Appeals Judgment, 20 February 2001. Trial Judgment, para. 346.

[33] *Celebici* case, Trial Judgment, paras 377–378.

[34] *Celebici* case, Trial Judgment, para. 393.

[35] ICC Statute, Art. 28 in Schindler and Toman, *The Laws of Armed Conflicts*, 1309–95, at 1328. See also G. Mettraux, *The Law of Command Responsibility* (Oxford: Oxford University Press, 2009).

of duty or negligent performance of duty. It is interesting to note that the Canadian legislation implementing the ICC Statute provides for two additional offences: breach of responsibility by a military commander; and breach of responsibility by a superior.[36] Perhaps this approach to command responsibility will be adopted by others in future. 29.09

In order to meet their obligations to have their subordinates comply with thc law, commanders should establish a reporting mechanism so that incidents in which it appears war crimes, crimes against humanity, or acts of genocide may have been committed by members of the contingent or force are brought to their attention. An adequately staffed particular office should be designated within the contingent or force to receive the incident reports, to advise the commander of the contents of the reports, and to advise on follow-up action. 29.10

1. This provision states a suggested good practice to fulfil a legal obligation, not a legal obligation in itself. Commanders are obligated to take a variety of measures to ensure their subordinates comply with the law.[37] One particularly useful measure is the establishment of an adequate monitoring mechanism so the commander can be kept informed of whether or not subordinates are acting in accordance with legal obligations. International crimes may occur in any area where forces are deployed outside their country and the likelihood of such crimes occurring is substantially increased when armed conflict exists. It is also desirable to have the designated office receive reports of allegations of crimes being committed by the armed forces or nationals of the States in which the Force is deployed. As examples, in Bosnia during the period when the United Nations Protection Force (UNPROFOR) was deployed, at least one contingent designated its military information (military intelligence) officer to collect reports of war crimes, crimes against humanity, and acts of genocide being committed by the various parties engaged in the armed conflicts. Similarly, the European Community Monitoring Mission (ECMM) collected such reports on occasion during its deployment.[38] Although forces deployed on peacekeeping and peace support operations may have a variety of missions and mandates, commanders should never turn a blind eye to massive atrocities simply because there is no express requirement to gather information

[36] Crimes Against Humanity and War Crimes Act, ss. 7(1) and (2).

[37] Standards for investigating violations are detailed in M.N. Schmitt, 'Investigating Violations of International Law in Armed Conflict', 2 *Harvard National Security Journal* (2011), 31–84. The Public Commission to Examine the Maritime Incident of 31 May 2010 (the Turkel Commission) Second Report, *Israel's Mechanisms for Examining and Investigating Complaints and Claims of Violations of the Laws of Armed Conflict According to International Law*, February 2013 (<http://www.inss.org.il/index.aspx?id=4538&articleid=2608>) reviews the approaches currently taken under the laws of Israel, the United States, Canada, Australia, the United Kingdom, Germany, and the Netherlands.

[38] Knowledge of the ECMM and UNPROFOR examples was derived by the author during time spent as a member of the Commission of Experts established pursuant to SC Res. 780 (1992).

29.10 about or investigate atrocities. Missions and mandates almost inevitably will permit a degree of flexibility in interpretation without generating complaints about mission creep. If, for example, the stated mission of a peacekeeping force is to ensure the transit of relief supplies, commanders who deliberately ignore the fact their trucks are driving by the local equivalent of Auschwitz on a daily basis will not enhance their own image or that of peacekeeping in general.

29.11 **Commanders must direct that investigations be conducted of incidents in which it appears war crimes, crimes against humanity, or acts of genocide may have been committed by their subordinates. If the contingent or force is involved in an armed conflict, the commander may direct that investigations be conducted of incidents in which it appears that war crimes, crimes against humanity, or genocide may have been committed by persons on the opposing side. If the contingent or force is engaged in peace support operations, the commander may direct that investigations be conducted of incidents in which it appears that war crimes, crimes against humanity, or genocide may have been committed by persons in the State in which the Force is deployed unless it is prohibited by the Force mandate.**

1. Commanders have a duty to do all that is practically possible to ensure incidents in which their own subordinates are involved are properly investigated to determine what actually happened and to identify alleged perpetrators. If they do not do so they may be held liable for failure to punish under the doctrine of command responsibility.[39]

2. An effective investigation of a major atrocity incident will usually be labour intensive and will usually require the use of multi-disciplinary teams including legal, military, police, and forensic experts as well as others. Those involved in the investigative process should be properly trained to carry out complex investigations of war crimes type incidents. The lawyers must have a sound understanding of the law of armed conflict and of military operational issues. The police too must have an understanding of the relevant law and of military operational concerns. War crimes type incidents are not normal crimes and they are not usually or usefully investigated by relying on the techniques or skills which are required by police for the investigation of crimes under national law.

3. If atrocities are committed in which members of the Force are the victims, it can be expected that commanders will wish to or be directed to have investigations conducted of these incidents also. Effective investigations of these incidents will require at least as much effort as investigation of own-side atrocities because the

[39] A useful handbook for non-experts is M. Nystedt (ed.), in cooperation with C.A. Nielsen, and J.K. Kleffner, *A Handbook on Assisting International Criminal Justice* (Folke Bernadotte Academy and Swedish National Defence College, 2011).

investigation must also place the incident in the context of the other side's operations, doctrine, and command structure. Particular use must be made of the skills of intelligence officers and military analysts in conducting these investigations. 29.11

4. It is unlikely the mandates or mission statements for peace support operations will make any explicit reference to whether or not Force Commanders have the authority to conduct investigations of alleged atrocities committed by persons in the State in which the Force is deployed. This should not be used as an excuse to ignore the issue. The Force Commander will usually have a substantial amount of discretion concerning whether or not to direct that such investigations can be conducted. While UNPROFOR was deployed in the territory of the former Yugoslavia, its forces conducted at least two substantial investigations, one in Croatia concerning incidents in the Medak Pocket and one in Bosnia concerning incidents at Stupni Do.[40] If such investigations are conducted, the investigators will require an array of skills and resources similar to those required for an investigation of other-side atrocities. It should be borne in mind, however, that every effort should be made by such investigation teams to gather and preserve evidence so that it can be used in possible future court proceedings. In particular, evidence should be properly documented and secured and a chain of custody must be established and preserved. One issue for Force Commanders contemplating directing an investigation of atrocities allegedly committed by persons in the State in which the Force is deployed is that the disputing parties can and will use atrocity stories as a weapon of war. They will do their best to convey the impression that their side is the aggrieved and innocent side with an enormous victim surplus while the other side is composed for the most part of moral monsters. The Force Commander must make a particular effort to be neutral in the atrocity war as well as in the real conflict. On the occasions when UNPROFOR did conduct investigations into particular alleged atrocities, all sides did their best to swamp UNPROFOR with additional allegations of atrocities committed by the other side.

Commanders must take all practicable measures within their authority to ensure that their subordinates who appear to have committed war crimes, crimes against humanity, or genocide are tried before appropriate tribunals and, if found guilty, appropriately punished. Often, because the military justice system is insulated from command influence, a commander may do no more than direct that an investigation be undertaken and then turn the matter over to military police and judicial authorities. 29.12

1. A commander cannot be expected to do the impossible. He or she can only take measures which are within his or her powers. Lack of formal legal competence to

[40] Personal knowledge of the author derived during his time as a member of the Commission of Experts established pursuant to SC Res. 780 (1992).

29.12 take action will not be a barrier to culpability, however, if, in fact, a commander does have the power to take appropriate action.[41]

29.13 **If an international tribunal has been created by the UN Security Council to try accused for the alleged commission of war crimes, crimes against humanity, or genocide in the State in which the Force is deployed, commanders must cooperate with the tribunal. If the International Criminal Court exercises jurisdiction, commanders of forces or contingents from State parties must cooperate with the court while commanders from other States should cooperate with the court, subject to national direction. If a national court exercises jurisdiction, commanders of forces or contingents from that State must cooperate while other commanders may cooperate.**

1. All members of the United Nations are obligated to comply with decisions of the Security Council as a result of Article 25 of the UN Charter. The ICTY and ICTR were both created by the Security Council and States are obligated to cooperate with them as a result of Articles 29 and 28 of their respective statutes. Further, as a matter of comity, UN entities with separate identities, such as peacekeeping forces, are also obligated to cooperate with these tribunals. Unless specifically indicated in a mandate or mission statement, however, the degree of cooperation to be provided to a tribunal may be a matter within the discretion of the Force Commander, bearing in mind the security situation, resource availability, and the requirements of the mission. As an example, the various international forces deployed to the territory of the former Yugoslavia—UNPROFOR, Implementation Force (IFOR), and Stabilisation Force in Bosnia and Herzegovina (SFOR) at different times—always provided a degree of logistical, administrative, and security support to ICTY missions in the area. Initially, however, because of a relatively unstable security situation there was a degree of reluctance to participate in the apprehension of persons indicted for war crimes or in the enforcement of search warrants. As time passed and the security situation stabilized, SFOR provided an ever increasing degree of assistance in apprehending suspects and enforcing search warrants. If ICC staff members are implementing a mandate assigned by the Security Council, they should receive assistance similar to that provided to ICTY as a matter of comity. In other circumstances, the degree of assistance to be provided will be a matter of negotiation and may well be embodied in cooperation agreements. In all circumstances, it must be borne in mind that international tribunals do have personnel skilled in conducting investigations and prosecutions but they do not have an enforcement arm equipped with weapons. For armed assistance in carrying out their mission they must depend on local authorities or on the aid of deployed forces.[42]

41 *Celebici* case, Trial Judgment, paras 394–395.
42 Nielsen and Kleffner, *Handbook on Assisting International Criminal Justice.*

Chapter 30

INTERNATIONAL RESPONSIBILITY AND MILITARY OPERATIONS

1. One may distinguish between the international responsibility of international organizations, States, and individuals in peacekeeping operations. Whereas the international responsibility of individuals is a form of criminal responsibility, that of States and international organizations is more akin to tortious liability.[1] This chapter only deals with the latter, the former is the topic of Chapter 29.

2. International responsibility is part of the broader notion of (international) accountability. There is no generally accepted definition of 'accountability', but there is agreement that the concept is an essential part of the rule of law.[2] Accountability is a broad term that reflects a range of understandings. The core sense of the term has been described as that associated with the process of being called to account to some authority for one's actions.[3] Responsibility refers specifically to the legal element of accountability. The legal accountability of military operations under international law is governed by the rules of international responsibility.

3. The application of the rules of international responsibility to military operations is complicated by the fact that such operations often involve multiple actors. First, military operations are frequently carried out by a number of States working together rather than by a single State. Secondly, the operation may be led by an international organization but carried out by troops from different Sending States, as in the case of United Nations (UN) peace operations. Thirdly, where the UN does not lead a military operation, it may nevertheless have authorized it. Finally, the Host State of the military operation also plays a role that may impact on questions of responsibility.

[1] But note that analogies between international responsibility and responsibility under domestic law do not hold up, *inter alia*, because international responsibility does not distinguish between contractual and tortious responsibility. See J. Crawford, *State Responsibility: The General Part* (Cambridge: Cambridge University Press, 2013), 51–4.

[2] Final Report of the Committee on Accountability of International Organisations, Recommended Rules and Practices on Liability/Responsibility of International Organisations (RRPs), Section IV (peacekeeping and peace enforcement activities), in The International Law Association, *Report of the Seventy-first Conference, held in Berlin, 16–21 August 2004* (London: ILA, 2004), 164–241, at 168–70 available at <http://www.ila-hq.org/en/committees/index.cfm/cid/9>.

[3] R. Mulgan, 'Accountability: an Ever-Expanding Concept?', 78 *Public Administration* (2000), 555–74, at 555.

BORIS KONDOCH AND MARTEN ZWANENBURG

30.01 **International responsibility in the context of military operations refers to the legal consequences arising from wrongful acts committed during such operations.**

1. The basic principle underlying international responsibility is that a breach of international law entails international responsibility. The term 'international responsibility' refers to the new legal relations that arise under international law by reason of the internationally wrongful act.

2. Only actors with international legal personality can be internationally responsible. This is because only an international legal person is capable of having obligations under international law. As stated, there is no international responsibility without the breach of such an obligation. States have international legal personality as a matter of course. International organizations may have such personality.[4]

3. The principle of international responsibility forms part of international customary law, but the same is not necessarily the case for all the detailed rules surrounding responsibility. These have been the subject of work of the International Law Commission (ILC) which adopted Articles on Responsibility of States for Internationally Wrongful Acts (ARSIWA) in 2001.[5] In 2011, the ILC adopted Draft Articles on the Responsibility of International Organisations (DARIO), which are to a large extent modelled on the ARSIWA.[6]

4. Both the ARSIWA and DARIO require two elements to be satisfied for international responsibility to arise: (a) conduct consisting of an action or omission that is attributable to a State or international organization under international law that (b) constitutes a breach of an international obligation of that State or organization.

5. The law of international responsibility is not concerned with the substance of the obligations referred to under (b) (also referred to as 'primary' rules). Rather, it deals with the rules for determining whether the 'primary' obligations have been breached, and with what legal consequences (also referred to as 'secondary' rules). In principle the same general 'secondary' rules always apply to States and international

[4] That the UN has such personality was accepted by the International Court of Justice (ICJ) in the *Reparations for Injuries* case. *Reparations for Injuries Suffered in the Service of the United Nations*, Advisory Opinion of 11 April 1949, ICJ Reports, 174 at 179. Of other international organizations that lead military operations, the European Union (EU), the North Atlantic Treaty Organization (NATO), the Organization of American States (OAS), and the African Union (AU) are also generally regarded as possessing such personality.

[5] Draft Articles on Responsibility of States for Internationally Wrongful Acts, ILC, Report on the Work of its Fifty-third Session (23 April–1 June and 2 July–August 2001), GA, Official Records, Fifty-fifth Session, Supplement no. 10, UN Doc. A/56/10.

[6] Draft Articles on the Responsibility of International Organizations, Report of the International Law Commission on the work of its sixty-third session, 26 April to 3 June and 4 July to 12 August 2011, GA, Official Records, Sixty-third Session, Supplement no. 10, UN Doc. A/61/10.

organizations respectively. Although the ARSIWA and DARIO make clear that primary rules may include special rules that deviate from these general secondary rules, there are no such special rules that apply specifically to military operations. **30.01**

6. A particular challenge with regard to international organizations can be to establish their obligations under international law. They are very often not parties to multilateral treaties. While it is generally accepted that they are bound by rules of customary international law in the fields in which they operate, the precise content of these rules is sometimes difficult to establish.

7. International responsibility is to be distinguished from international liability for injurious consequences. The latter refers to situations according to which States have a duty to take reparatory and, at the same time, preventive measures vis-à-vis other States for damage caused, or likely to be caused, by activities—which are not prohibited under international law.[7] There is no general rule of liability under international law, but there are a number of specific treaty-based regimes providing for it that may be relevant for military operations. An example is the International Convention on International Liability for Damage Caused by Space Objects, which provides for a regime of strict liability.

8. The element of attribution is discussed in Sections 30.04–30.06.

A State is responsible for conduct consisting of an act or omission that is attributable to the State and that breaches an international obligation of the State. Conduct of the armed forces of a State is in principle attributable to the State as conduct of a State organ. In regard to omissions, a State is only responsible if there was a duty to act. **30.02**

1. States are legal constructs and as such cannot act in the physical world. They act through individuals and organs which engage in conduct on behalf of the State. Attribution is the legal operation which links specific conduct of such persons to a specific State for the purposes of international responsibility.

2. The main principle of attribution is that the conduct of an organ of a State is attributable to that State. The armed forces are regarded as the example par excellence of a State organ.

3. Conduct can consist of an act or omission. An omission can only lead to responsibility if there was a duty to act. Whether there was such a duty, and the precise content of any such duty, will depend on the primary rule concerned. An example that could be relevant in military operations is the obligation to investigate alleged human rights violations in territory under a State's jurisdiction.[8]

[7] A. Tanzi, 'Liability for Lawful Acts', *Max Planck Encyclopedia of Public International Law*.

[8] In 2008 the UN Committee against Torture criticized Sweden for not investigating an incident in which French soldiers who were part of the EU peace operation EUFOR Artemis in the DRC allegedly

30.03 **International organizations bear responsibility for conduct that is attributable to them and that breaches an international obligation of the organization, in principle in the same way as States.**

1. Generally speaking the same principles of responsibility that apply to States also apply to international organizations. Consequently, the same two criteria (attribution and breach of an international obligation) are relevant for establishing whether an international organization is responsible in connection with a military operation.

2. Two main avenues potentially lead to responsibility of an international organization in connection with a military operation. The first is conduct carried out by (personnel of) the operation that is attributable to an organization leading the operation. This possibility is dealt with by Section 30.04. The second possibility is responsibility of an organization for conduct not committed by (personnel of) the operation but that is connected to the operation. An example of such a situation is where an international organization circumvents one of its international obligations by authorizing Member States or another international organization to commit an act that would be internationally wrongful if committed by the former organization and the act in question is committed because of that authorization.[9]

30.04 **The question, whether the conduct of a military force led by an international organization consisting of troops contributed by States can be attributed to the international organization or to troop contributing States is determined by the question which actor exercises effective control over that conduct.**

1. Many military operations are led by an international organization but carried out by personnel placed at the disposal of that organization by States. Such personnel retains certain links to the Sending States, such as formally staying in the service of the troop Sending State and remaining subject to that State's disciplinary and criminal jurisdiction. This raises the question to which international actor the conduct of such personnel must be attributed. This question must be answered on the basis of a determination which actor exercised effective control over the conduct concerned. This rule of attribution has been laid down in Article 7 DARIO and finds broad support in legal literature. It has also been applied by national courts.[10]

tortured a prisoner in the presence of Swedish soldiers. UN Doc. CAT/C/SWE//10/5, 4 June 2008, p. 6, para. 19.

[9] See Art. 17(2) DARIO and the discussion later in the chapter.

[10] Supreme Court of the Netherlands, *The Netherlands v Mustafić and others*, Case no. 12/03329, 6 September 2013; Supreme Court of the Netherlands, *The Netherlands v Nuhanović*, Case no. 12/03324, 6 September 2013; Court of First Instance of Brussels, *Mukeshimana-Ngulinzira and others v Belgium and others*, Interlocutory Judgment of 8 December 2010.

2. Article 7 DARIO provides: **30.04**

The conduct of an organ of a State or an organ or agent of an international organization that is placed at the disposal of another international organization shall be considered under international law an act of the latter organization if the organization exercises effective control over that conduct.

Being 'placed at the disposal of' an international organization implies that an institutional link is established between the organ and the organization. In practice, this is usually achieved by the transfer of a level of command and control by the Sending State to the organization.[11] It is not necessary that the lent organ is given the status of organ of the organization.[12] The difficulty in applying this rule lies in particular in determining what constitutes effective control in a specific situation.

3. It is uncontroversial that effective control is a factual criterion. In giving substance to this standard, the ILC appears to set a relatively high threshold. On this interpretation, conduct must be under the exclusive direction and control of the international organization, rather than on instructions from the Sending State, to be attributable to the organization.

4. Whereas the ILC invites an analysis of which entity exercised effective control on a case-by-case basis, it has been argued that there may be a presumption that conduct must be attributed to the organization. Such a presumption is either created by the transfer of command and control to the organization,[13] or more generally by that fact that the organ concerned has been placed at the disposal of the organization.[14]

5. Another approach to what constitutes 'effective control' has been suggested in literature. Under this theory, 'effective control' is held by the entity that is best positioned to act effectively and within the law to prevent the abuse in question.[15] This theory appears to have inspired national courts, for example, in the Netherlands in torts cases concerning the role that Dutch peacekeepers played during the fall of Srebrenica in July 1995.[16]

[11] See e.g. T. Gill, 'Legal Aspects of Transfer of Authority in UN Peace Operations', 42 *Netherlands Yearbook of International Law* (2012), 37–68.

[12] P. Palchetti, 'International Responsibility for Conduct of UN Peacekeeping Forces: The Question of Attribution', in Koninklijke Vereniging voor Internationaal Recht, *Mededelingen van de Koninklijke Nederlandse Vereniging voor Internationaal Recht* 141 (2014), 1–29, at 15.

[13] U. Häußler, 'Human Rights Accountability of International Organizations in the Lead of International Peace Missions', in J. Wouters et al. (eds), *Accountability for Human Rights Violations by International Organizations* (Antwerp: Intersentia, 2010), 215–68.

[14] Palchetti, 'International Responsibity', 16–18; F. Salerno, 'International Responsibility for the Conduct of "Blue Helmets": Exploring the Organic Link', in M. Ragazzi (ed.), *Responsibility of International Organizations: Essays in Memory of Sir Ian Brownlie* (Leiden: Martinus Nijhoff Publishers, 2013), 414–27.

[15] T. Dannenbaum, 'Translating the Standard of Effective Control into a System of Effective Accountability: How Liability Should be Apportioned for Violations of Human Rights by Member State Troop Contingents Serving as United Nations Peacekeepers', 51 *Harvard International Law Journal* (2010), 113–92.

[16] *The Netherlands v Mustafić and others*; *the Netherlands v Nuhanović.*

30.04 6. The *Nuhanović v the Netherlands* and *Mustafić c.s. v the Netherlands* cases concerned claims by relatives of men who were killed by Bosnian Serbs troops following the fall of the enclave. The plaintiffs considered that the Dutch battalion (Dutchbat) forming part of the UN Protection Force (UNPROFOR) wrongfully evicted the men from the Dutchbat compound, and that that conduct was attributable to the Netherlands. The District Court held that the question of attribution should be decided on the basis of international law.[17] It referred to Article 6 of the ARSIWA, which the Court accepted as codifying customary international law. According to the Court, this rule of attribution also applies to the armed forces deployed by a State in order to assist another State, provided that they are placed under the 'command and control' of that other State. It then went on to apply this rule by means of analogy to the attribution of the actions of armed forces made available by States to the United Nations. Because Dutchbat had been placed under the 'operational command and control' of the UN and the Netherlands had not 'cut across' UN command and control, the Court concluded that the conduct could not be attributed to the Netherlands.

7. This conclusion was overturned on appeal.[18] The Court of Appeal also considered that the question of attribution should be decided on the basis of international law. It was of the view that for the attribution of the conduct of Dutchbat to the UN or the State, the question should be who had 'effective control' and not, as assumed by the District Court, who exercised 'command and control'. The Court referred to draft article 6 of the DARIO, which was later to be renumbered Article 7 and which uses the words 'effective control'. The Court considered that the question of who had 'effective control' over Dutchbat was essential, and to be determined as follows:

The question whether the State had 'effective control' over the conduct of Dutchbat which Nuhanovic considers to be the basis for his claim, must be answered in view of the circumstances of the case. This does not only imply that significance should be given to the question whether that conduct constituted the execution of a specific instruction, issued by the UN or the State, but also to the question whether, if there was no such specific instruction, the UN or the State had the power to prevent the conduct concerned. Moreover, the Court adopts as a starting point that the possibility that more than one party has 'effective control' is generally accepted, which means that it cannot be ruled out that the application of this criterion results in the possibility of attribution to more than one party. For this reason

[17] District Court of The Hague, *H.N. v the State of the Netherlands*, (265615/HA ZA 06-1671, LJN: BF0181), 10 September 2008; *M.M., D.M., and A.M. v the Netherlands*, (265618/HA ZA 06-1672, LJN: BF0182), 10 September 2008.

[18] The main findings of the Court of Appeal on the issue of attribution were made in interlocutory judgments: Court of Appeal of The Hague, *Hasan Nuhanović v the Netherlands* (200.020.174/01, LJN: BR5388), 5 July 2011; *Mehida Mustafić, Damir Mustafić and Alma Mustafić v the Netherlands* (200.120.173/01, LJN: BR5386), 5 July 2011. These findings were confirmed in the final judgments of the Court of Appeal: *N. v the Netherlands* (200.020.174/01, LJN: BW9015), 26 June 2012; *M. c.s. v the Netherlands* (200.020.173/01, LJN: BW9014), 26 June 2012.

the Court will only examine if the State exercised 'effective control' over the alleged conduct and will not answer the question whether the UN also had 'effective control'.[19] **30.04**

In applying this interpretation of 'effective control' to the facts of the case, the Court took a number of elements it saw as specific to the alleged conduct of Dutchbat into account. These included the fact that the context in which the alleged conduct of Dutchbat took place differed significantly from the situation in which troops placed at the disposal of the UN normally operate, Srebrenica having fallen and it being out of the question that Dutchbat or UNPROFOR in any other composition would continue or resume the mission. The Court also attached much significance to a meeting between high-ranking Dutch military officials and the UN commander, in which the Court considered a decision to evacuate Dutchbat and the refugees was taken by mutual agreement. Based, *inter alia*, on these considerations, the Court concluded that the Dutch Government could have prevented the alleged conduct if it had been aware of this conduct at the time. The State therefore possessed effective control over the alleged conduct of Dutchbat.[20]

8. The Netherlands then lodged an appeal with the Supreme Court. This court upheld the judgment of the Court of Appeal.[21] It considered that the Court of Appeal had correctly used Article 7 DARIO as the applicable standard. According to the Supreme Court, for the purpose of deciding whether the State had effective control it was not necessary for the State to have countermanded the command structure of the UN by giving instructions to Dutchbat or to have exercised operational command independently. The Court of Appeal's ruling that the State had effective control over the conduct of which Dutchbat was accused did not reveal an incorrect interpretation or application of the law on the concept of effective control.

9. The same interpretation of 'effective control' was used in the subsequent judgment of the District Court of the Hague in a third civil case against the Netherlands concerning Srebrenica.[22] In this case the Court attributed specific conduct by Dutchbat to the Netherlands on the basis of instructions given by the Dutch Minister of Defence, and on the basis of Dutchbat having acted in contravention of instructions from the UN Commander, respectively. With respect to the latter the Court held that:

[19] *Hasan Nuhanović v the Netherlands*, Court of Appeal of The Hague, 5 July 2011, LJN BR0133 (English translation BR0133), at 5.9.

[20] See for analysis of the judgments A. Nollkaemper, 'Dual Attribution: Liability of the Netherlands for Conduct of Dutchbat in Srebrenica', 9 *Journal of International Criminal Justice* (2011), 1143–57; O. Spijkers, '"The Netherlands" and the United Nations' Legal Responsibility for Srebrenica before the Dutch Courts', 50 *Military Law and the Law of War Review* (2011), 517–34.

[21] Court of Appeal, The Hague (30 March 2010), *The Association et al. v The State of the Netherlands*, LJN: BL8979.

[22] District Court of the Hague, *Stichting Mothers of Srebrenića and others* (C/09/295247/HA ZA 07-2973, ECLI:NL:RBDHA:2014:8562), 16 July 2014. The judgment was appealed by the plaintiffs and by the Netherlands.

30.04 If a military force's command and control over operational implementation of the mandate is transferred to the UN and said military force then goes on to act beyond the authority given it by the UN or on its own initiative acts against the instructions of the UN as Claimants point out said military force acts ultra vires [= beyond its legal power or authority]. Such action is attributable to the State supplying the troops because the State has a say over the mechanisms underlying said ultra vires actions, selection, training and the preparations for the mission of the troops placed at the disposal of the UN. Moreover the State supplying the troops has it in its powers to take measures to counter ultra vires actions on the part of its troops given the fact that it has a say about personal matters and disciplinary punishments.

In order to attribute ultra vires actions to the State supplying the troops there is no requirement for said state to give any instruction or order relating to ultra vires action or that this specifically influences the case in some other way. What is decisive is that the State delivering the troops retains the powers it has after transfer of command and control to the UN as well as the relevant say in respect of and with it effective control over self-willed powers acting beyond the powers the UN has granted or against the instructions of the UN concerning the actions of troops put at the UN's disposal.[23]

10. Yet another approach to attribution was taken by the European Court of Human Rights in a string of cases starting with the *Behrami* and *Saramati* cases.[24] In the case of *Saramati*, the applicant complained under Article 5 (right to liberty and security) and Article 13 (right to an effective remedy) of the Convention about his detention by KFOR. He further complained under Article 6(1) (right to a fair trial) that he did not have access to court, and, under Article 1 (obligation to respect human rights), that France, Germany, and Norway had failed to guarantee the Convention rights of individuals living in Kosovo. The case of *Behrami* concerned the death of Gadaf Behrami and the injuries of Bekir Behrami which occurred in Mitrovića. The city was at that time within the sector of Kosovo for which a multinational brigade led by France was responsible. The brigade was part of KFOR, authorized by Security Council Resolution 1244 of June 1999. The applicants alleged that the death of one brother and the serious injuries of the other brother were caused by the failure of the French KFOR troops to mark and/or defuse the undetonated cluster bombs which KFOR had known to be present on

[23] Ibid. paras 4.57–4.58.

[24] For a detailed discussion, see U. Häußler, 'Regional Human Rights v. International Peace Missions: Lessons Learned from Kosovo', *Humanitäres Völkerrecht-Informationsschriften* (2007), 238–44; H. Krieger, 'A Credibility Gap: The Behrami and Saramati Decision of the European Court of Human Rights', 13 *Journal of International Peacekeeping* (2009), 159–80, at 170–2; K.M. Larsen, 'Attribution of Conduct in Peace Operations: The "Ultimate Authority and Control" Test', 19 *EJIL* (2008), 509–31; M. Milanović and T. Papić, 'As Bad as It Gets: The European Court of Human Rights Behrami and Saramati Decision and General International Law', 58 *ICLQ* (2009), 267–96; and A. Sari, 'Jurisdiction and International Responsibility in Peace Operations: The *Behrami* and *Saramati* Cases', 8 *Human Rights Law Review* (2008), 1–20. The Venice Commission arrived at the conclusion that alleged human rights violations by KFOR were not attributable to the UN but to NATO or the Sending State. It also considered intermediate cases, see the opinion of the Venice Commission, Opinion no. 280/2004 on *Human Rights in Kosovo: Possible Establishment of Review Mechanisms*, CDL-AD (2004)033, para. 79. For a general discussion on the international responsibility of NATO, the Sending States, and the United Nations in regard to the administration of Kosovo, see K.A. Wierse, *Post-Conflict: Peace-building im Kosovo* (Köln, München: Carl Heymanns Verlag, 2008), 223–35.

the site in question. They relied on Article 2 of the ECHR (right to life). They submitted that KFOR was the responsible organization. Neither KFOR's acts nor omissions could be attributed to the UN, since KFOR was not a UN peacekeeping operation and the Security Council lacked operational control. Furthermore, the applicants maintained that KFOR troops were subject to exclusive control of their troop contributing nations (TCNs).[25] France and Norway submitted that the UN exercised effective control and KFOR exercised control over Saramati.[26] The ECtHR rejected the claim, because the UN had ultimate authority and control and therefore the individual States had no responsibility.[27] The Court concluded that issuing detention orders fell within the security mandate of KFOR and that the supervision of de-mining fell within the mandate of United Nations Interim Administration Mission in Kosovo (UNMIK). It further analysed whether the impugned action of KFOR and inaction of UNMIK could be attributed to the UN. According to the ECtHR, Chapter VII of the UN Charter provided a framework for the delegation of the Security Council powers to KFOR and powers to UNMIK. Because KFOR exercised lawfully delegated Chapter VII powers of the Security Council and UNMIK was a subsidiary organ of the UN established under Chapter VII, the impugned action and inaction were, in principle, 'attributable' to the UN which has a legal personality separate from that of its Member States and is not a contracting party to the Convention. According to the ECtHR, operations established under Chapter VII of the UN Charter were fundamental to the mission of the UN to secure international peace and security and since they relied for their effectiveness on support from Member States, the Convention could not be interpreted in a manner which would subject the acts and omissions of contracting parties which were authorized by Security Council resolutions. Furthermore, the Court held that the impugned acts and omissions of KFOR and UNMIK could not be attributed to the respondent States and, moreover, did not take place on the territory of those States or by virtue of a decision of their authorities. UNMIK was a subsidiary organ of the UN created under Chapter VII and KFOR was exercising powers lawfully delegated under Chapter VII of the Charter by the Security Council. Their actions were directly attributable to the UN and therefore, the Court decided the cases as inadmissible. **30.04**

11. The interpretation of effective control used by the ECtHR has been criticized by commentators. The ILC has also rejected it, stating: '[o]ne may note that, when applying the criterion of effective control, "operational" control would seem more significant than "ultimate" control, since the latter hardly implies a role in the act in

[25] See Final Report of the Committee on Accountability of International Organisations, Recommended Rules and Practices on Liability/Responsibility of International Organisations (RRPs), Section IV (peacekeeping and peace enforcement activities), in The International Law Association, *Report of the Seventy-first Conference, held in Berlin, 16–21 August 2004* (London: ILA, 2004), 164–241, at 168–70 available at <http://www.ila-hq.org/en/committees/index.cfm/cid/9>, paras 73–81.

[26] Ibid. paras 82–95. [27] Ibid. paras 133–140.

30.04 question.'[28] The 'ultimate authority and control test' introduced by the ECtHR is contrary to the 'effective control test' adopted by the ILC and the majority of legal scholars. It is regrettable that the Court did not explain why it did not apply the 'effective control test'. It appears that if the 'ultimate authority and control test' was to be followed, wrongful conduct could not be attributed any longer to Sending States in regard to military operations authorized by the Security Council.

12. The UN considers that peace operations under command and control are subsidiary organs of the principal organ that established the operation. As such, the UN appears to consider that the conduct of such operations is in principle attributable to the organization on the basis of their status as an organ, rather than on the basis of the 'effective control' criterion. That the UN considers peace operations as organs is supported, *inter alia*, by wording in the model SOFA between the UN and Host States.[29] According to the UN:

> A United Nations peacekeeping force established by the Security Council or the General Assembly is a subsidiary organ of the United Nations. Members of the military personnel placed by Member States under United Nations command, although remaining in their national service, are, for the duration of their assignment to the force, considered international personnel under the authority of the United Nations and subject to the instructions of the force commander. The functions of the force are exclusively international and members of the force are bound to discharge their functions with the sole interest of the United Nations in view. The peacekeeping operation as a whole is subject to the executive direction and control of the Secretary-General, under the overall direction of the Council or the Assembly, as the case may be.
>
> As a subsidiary organ of the United Nations, an act of a peacekeeping force is, in principle, imputable to the Organization, and, if committed in violation of an international obligation, entails the international responsibility of the Organization and its liability in compensation. The fact that any such act may have been performed by members of a national military contingent forming part of the peacekeeping operation does not affect the international responsibility of the United Nations *vis-à-vis* third States or individuals.[30]

13. On this basis it may be concluded that the law on attribution of conduct of military operations constituted by personnel contributed by States and led by an international organization is not settled. Although for the purposes of attribution the UN focuses on the role of its peace operations as organs of the organization, the dominant theory appears to be the one that focuses on which actor has effective control. No single authoritative interpretation of 'effective control' has crystallized until now, however. Future State practice will have to provide further clarity in this regard.

[28] ILC, Commentaries to DARIO, 23.

[29] Model Status of Forces Agreement for Peacekeeping Operations, UN Doc. A/45/594, 9 October 1990, Art. 15.

[30] UN Doc. A/CN.4/545, 25 June 2004, p. 28.

There may be dual or multiple international responsibility of an international organization and one or more states for conduct of a military operation. 30.05

1. Until now[31] either the relevant organization, e.g. the UN, or the Sending State has been held responsible for wrongful acts based on the effective control. Can in theory one or more States and/or an international organization simultaneously have 'effective control' over conduct committed in the context of a military operation? In the first place, it is clear that the higher the threshold for effective control, the more difficult it is to envisage such a situation.

2. Commentators are divided on the question whether more than one actor can exercise effective control at any one time.[32] Nor is the ILC clear: neither Article 7 DARIO nor the Commentary thereto express themselves on the question whether the ILC considers that both a State and an international organization may exercise effective control at the same time.[33] On the one hand the Commentary suggests that dual attribution on this basis is not possible when it states that 'control' concerns the issue to 'which entity—the contributing State or organization or the receiving organization—conduct has to be attributed'.[34] This suggests that it is either one actor or the other which has effective control, but not both. On the other hand, the Commentary also refers to cases in which courts in the Netherlands considered the possibility of dual attribution without rejecting that possibility.[35] The *Mustafić* and *Nuhanović* cases both concerned torts claims against the Netherlands relating to the conduct of the Dutch Battalion (Dutchbat) that was part of the UN Protection Force in Bosnia Herzegovina. The Supreme Court of the Netherlands dismissed the appeal by the Netherlands against the judgment of the Court of Appeal, which had held that the conduct at issue was attributable to the Netherlands. In doing so, it held that 'international law, in particular Article 7 DARIO in conjunction with Article 48(1) DARIO, does not exclude the possibility of dual attribution of given conduct'.[36] Article 48 DARIO explicitly refers to joint responsibility, although neither the article itself nor the Commentary make mention of such responsibility specifically in connection with Article 7.

[31] On the practice of international organizations, K. Schmalenbach, *Die Haftung Internationaler Organisationen* (Frankfurt am Main: Peter Lang, 2004), 513–75.

[32] Commentators who support such multiple attribution: H. Krieger, 'A Credibility Gap: The Behrami and Saramati Decision of the European Court of Human Rights', 13 *Journal of International Peacekeeping* (2009), 159–80, at 170–3; C. Ahlborn, 'To Share or not to Share? The Allocation of Responsibility between International Organizations and their Member States', 88 *Die Friedenswarte* (2013), 45–75.

[33] See F. Messineo, 'Attribution of Conduct', in P.A. Nollkaemper and I. Plakokefalos (eds), *Principles of Shared Responsibility in International Law: An Appraisal of the State of the Art* (Cambridge: Cambridge University Press, 2014), 60–4.

[34] ILC, DARIO Commentary, 21.

[35] ILC, DARIO Commentary, 25, n. 129.

[36] Supreme Court of the Netherlands, *The Netherlands v Mustafić and others*, Case no. 12/03329, 6 September 2013; Supreme Court of the Netherlands, *The Netherlands v Nuhanović*, Case no. 12/03324, 6 September 2013, para. 3.11.2.

30.05 3. Other possible bases for dual or multiple responsibility are referred to in Articles 14 to 18 DARIO, which concern the responsibility of an international organization in connection with the act of a State, and in Articles 58 to 62 DARIO, which deal with the responsibility of a State in connection with the internationally wrongful act of an international organization.[37] Responsibility arising from these rules is sometimes referred to as 'indirect' responsibility. Such responsibility refers not to an act committed by another State or organization, but responsibility as a result of conduct directly attributable to the State or organization.

4. For the purpose of clarity, the discussion which follows focuses on responsibility of a State in connection with internationally wrongful conduct of an international organization. Unless otherwise indicated, however, the same applies to responsibility of an international organization in connection with internationally wrongful conduct of a State.

5. Of the possible legal bases for responsibility set out in the abovementioned articles, the most directly relevant would appear to be the rule that a State is responsible if it aids or assists an international organization in the commission of an internationally wrongful act if it does so with the knowledge of the circumstances of the internationally wrongful act and the act would have been internationally wrongful if committed by the State.[38]

6. 'Aid or assistance' comprises a broad category of conduct, covering all conduct that facilitates or contributes to the commission of an internationally wrongful act. Aid or assistance only leads to responsibility if the State or organization that aids or assists does so with knowledge of the circumstances of the internationally wrongful act that it aids or assists. This should be read as containing an element of intent by the assisting State or organization, resulting in a high threshold.[39] Moreover, for international responsibility to arise, aid or assistance should contribute 'significantly' to the commission of the act.

7. A State is also responsible if it directs and controls an international organization in the commission of an internationally wrongful act. This is subject to the requirements that the State does so with knowledge of the circumstances of the internationally wrongful act, and that the act would breach an obligation of the State if committed by the State. An act by a State member of an international organization done in accordance with the rules of the organization does not as such engage the international responsibility of that State.[40] This means that in principle,

[37] See for a more detailed discussion of joint or parallel attribution of wrongful acts to an international organization and to its members: P. Klein, 'The Attribution of Acts to International Organizations', in J. Crawford, A. Pellet, and S. Olleson (eds), *The Law of International Responsibility* (Oxford: Oxford University Press, 2010), 297–315, at 306–14.

[38] Art. 58 DARIO.

[39] H.P. Aust, 'Complicity in Violations of International Humanitarian Law', in H. Krieger (ed.), *Enforcing International Humanitarian Law in Contemporary African Conflicts* (forthcoming).

[40] Art. 59(2) DARIO.

the vote by a State in the context of decision-making within the organization does not lead to its responsibility on the basis of this rule. It seems that in practice the high level of control required would be difficult to prove. **30.05**

8. Another possible basis for responsibility of a State in connection with the internationally wrongful act of an international organization was laid down in Article 61 DARIO. This article provides that:

> (1) A State member of an international organization incurs international responsibility if, by taking advantage of the fact that the organization has competence in relation to the subject-matter of one of the State's international obligations, it circumvents that obligation by causing the organization to commit an act that, if committed by the State, would have constituted a breach of the obligation.
>
> (2) Paragraph 1 applies whether or not the act in question is internationally wrongful for the international organization.

9. It may be pointed out first that unlike the rules discussed in earlier Sections, this rule is limited to Member States of an international organization. For responsibility to arise under this rule, there must be a significant link between the conduct of the circumventing Member State and that of the international organization. The act of the international organization has to be caused by the Member State.[41]

10. In addition to the causality requirement, intention on the part of the State is also a requirement, implied in the use of the term 'circumvention'. International responsibility will not arise when the act of the international organization, which would constitute a breach of an international obligation if done by the State, has to be regarded as the unintended result of the Member State's conduct.[42] This constitutes a high threshold, both in terms of substance and in terms of burden of proof for an actor invoking responsibility. The obligation has been described as a due diligence obligation on Member States not to take advantage of the competence of an international organization.[43]

11. Article 61 appears to be derived from case law of the ECtHR and the former European Commission of Human Rights. Starting with the *M. & Co. v the Federal Republic of Germany* case, they have held that the European Convention on Human Rights (ECHR) does not exclude the transfer of competences to international organizations provided that ECHR rights continue to be 'secured'.[44] Member States' responsibility therefore continues even after such a transfer.[45] The ECtHR has not yet applied this theory in a case concerning a military operation, however.

12. It is important to point out that Article 61 DARIO is controversial, because it concerns a rule of responsibility that would 'pierce the veil' of international

[41] Commentary Art. 61 DARIO, 95, para. 7. [42] Ibid. 93.

[43] C. Ryngaert and H. Buchanan, 'Member State Responsibility for the Acts of International Organizations', 7 *Utrecht Law Review* (2011), 131–46, at 144; Klein, 'The Attribution of Acts', 310.

[44] *M & Co. v Federal Republic of Germany*, Application no. 13258/87, Decision of 9 January 1990.

[45] *Matthews v United Kingdom*, Judgment of 18 February 1999, Application no. 24833/94, para. 32.

30.05 organizations by holding Member States responsible for acts of the organization.[46] Outside of the specific context of the ECHR, the rule must be regarded as a progressive development of the law rather than existing law.[47] In a sense the mirror image of Article 61, Article 17 DARIO concerns the circumvention by an international organization of its obligations through a decision binding a State or an authorization addressed to a State.

13. In the context of military operations, the possibility of responsibility for an authorization is of particular interest. The UN Security Council regularly authorizes States or other international organizations to use force in other States under Chapter VII of the UN Charter. Whether or not an authorization by the Security Council under Chapter VII of the UN Charter can actually lead to the responsibility of the UN on this basis depends on the answer to the question of which law binds the Security Council and the related question whether the Council can deviate from otherwise applicable law. This is a controversial question that is far from settled.[48]

30.06 **In general, breaches of international law committed by personnel of a military operation are not attributable to the Host State.**

1. A wrongful act committed by a member of a military operation cannot be attributed to the Host State merely because the wrongful act occurred on the territory of the Host State or the Host State gave its consent to the military operation.

There are no reported cases in which the Host State has been held liable. However, one may argue that wrongful conduct could be attributed to the Host State when there is a causal link between the wrongful act and acts or omissions by the Host State.[49] The Host State bears responsibility if it aids and assists, or directs and controls the international organization or the Sending State in the commission of an internationally wrongful act. However in these situations, the Sending State has to have had knowledge of the circumstances of the international wrongful act. Furthermore, the act has to be in violation of international law if committed by the Sending State.

[46] O. Murray, 'Piercing the Corporate Veil: The Responsibility of Member States of an International Organization', 8 *International Organizations Law Review* (2011), 291–347, at 296.

[47] See e.g. A. Gattini, 'Breach of International Obligations', in A. Nollkaemper and I. Plakokefalos (eds), *Shared Responsibility in International Law: An Appraisal of the State of the Art* (Cambridge: Cambridge University Press, 2014), 25–59, at 54.

[48] See e.g. T. Gill, 'Legal and Some Political Limitations on the Power of the UN Security Council to Exercise its Enforcement Powers under Chapter VII of the Charter', 26 *Netherlands Yearbook of International Law* (1995), 33–138.

[49] See also S.R. Lüder, *Völkerrechtliche Verantwortlichkeit bei Teilnahme an 'Peace-keeping' Missionen der Vereinten Nationen* (Berlin: Berliner Wissenschaftsverlag, 2004), 65–9 and C. Wickremasinghe and G. Verdirame, 'Responsibility and Liability of Human Rights in the Course of UN Field Operations', in C. Scott, *Torture as Tort. Comparative Perspectives on the Development of Transnational Human Rights Litigation* (Oxford: Hart Publishing, 2001), 465–89.

Valid consent, self-defence, necessity, counter-measures, distress and *force majeure* preclude wrongfulness but there is no preclusion in case of the breach of peremptory norms. Core norms of human rights and humanitarian law are considered as peremptory. 30.07

1. Certain circumstances such as valid consent, self-defence, necessity, counter-measures, and *force majeure* may provide a justification or excuse for non-performance.[50] However, there is no preclusion in case of the breach of peremptory norms.[51] Core norms of human rights and humanitarian law are considered as peremptory.[52]

International responsibility entails the obligation to cease the internationally wrongful act if it is continuing, and the obligation to make full reparation. Forms of reparation include restitution, compensation, rehabilitation, satisfaction, and guarantees of non-repetition. 30.08

1. International responsibility leads to new legal obligations arising for the responsible State or organization. The core legal consequences are the obligation to cease the internationally wrongful act if it is continuing, and the obligation to make full reparation for the injury caused by the internationally wrongful act. Such injury includes any damage, whether material or moral, caused by the internationally wrongful act. Full reparation may take the form of restitution, compensation, or satisfaction, singly or in combination, as required by the circumstances. If circumstances so require, there is also an obligation to offer appropriate assurances and guarantees of non-repetition.

2. In principle international responsibility is vis-à-vis another State or international organization, not private individuals. Traditionally the latter were not regarded as having international legal personality, and therefore they were not seen as having rights under international law. Increasingly however individuals have gained substantive rights under international law, in particular in the field of international human rights law. The breach of these rights entails responsibility and the legal consequences attached thereto. It is also increasingly recognized that individuals also have rights under international humanitarian law.[53]

3. It may be noted that a State or international organization may be responsible under (private) national law, in addition to or instead of under international law.

[50] See Arts 20–25 ARSIWA and Arts 20–25 DARIO.

[51] See Art. 26 ARSIWA and Art. 26 DARIO.

[52] See L. Hannikainen, *Peremptory Norms (jus cogens) in International Law* (Helsinki: Lakimkesliiton Kustannus, 1988); A. Orakhelashvili, *Peremptory Norms in International Law* (Oxford: Oxford University Press, 2008).

[53] S. Gorski, 'Individuals in International Law', *Max Planck Encyclopedia of Public International Law*; L. Zegveld, 'Remedies for Victims of Violations of International Humanitarian Law', 85 *International Review of the Red Cross* (2003), 497–526.

30.08 The extent to which this is possible will depend on the national legal system of the State where a claim for such responsibility is brought.

30.09 **International organizations and Sending States should provide effective remedies to victims of violations committed by military operations.**

1. Whether it is an international or a domestic obligation that has been breached by the conduct of a military operation, victims should be given an effective remedy. There is increasing support for a 'right to a remedy', in particular in the case of violations of human rights and of international humanitarian law. Nevertheless, in practice there are many obstacles to obtaining redress for violations of the law by military operations. Even in regard to violations of international humanitarian law, the exercise of international and individual responsibility is generally rudimentary.[54]

2. With regard to responsibility under international law, individuals do not have standing to invoke such responsibility, except where a specific procedure has been established to that effect. Thus, the fact that individuals have substantive rights does not automatically mean that they can enforce these rights. As was stated earlier, individuals arguably have rights under international humanitarian law. It is not generally accepted that they also have international standing to invoke a breach of those rights, however.[55]

3. Traditionally, individuals must rely on their State of nationality to espouse their claim. That State has the right to exercise 'diplomatic protection' on behalf of its nationals who have suffered damage or injury as a consequence of an internationally wrongful act. They do not have an obligation to do so, however. An example of the exercise of diplomatic protection in relation to a military operation is the case that led to the payment of lump sums by the UN to several States, nationals of which have suffered damage as a result of conduct of the UN Operation in the Congo (ONUC) in the 1960s.[56]

[54] See D. Fleck, 'Individual and State Responsibility for violations of the Ius in Bello: An Imperfect Balance', in W.H. von Heinegg and V. Epping (eds), *International Humanitarian Law Facing New Challenges* (Berlin, etc.: Springer, 2007), 171–206; D. Fleck, 'International Accountability for Violations of the Ius in Bello: The Impact of the ICRC Study on Customary International Humanitarian Law', 11 *JCSL* (2006), 179–99; M. Sassòli, 'State Responsibility for Violations of Humanitarian Law', 84 *IRRC* (2002), 401–34; L. Zegveld, 'Remedies for Violations of International Humanitarian Law', 85 *IRRC* (2003), 497 and the work of the ILA Committee on Reparations for Victims of Armed Conflict, available at <http://www.ila-hq.org/en/committees/index.cfm/cid/1018>.

[55] See e.g. the judgment of the German Constitutional Court in the 'Bridge of Varvarin' case, 13 August 2013, Case nos 2 BvR 2660/06 and 2 BvR 487/07, discussed by K. Gärditz, 108 *American Journal of International Law* (2014), 86.

[56] See M. Zwanenburg, *Accountability of Peace Support Operations* (Leiden: Martinus Nijhoff Publishers, 2005).

4. In the field of human rights, specific procedures that enable individuals to invoke international responsibility do exist. Examples are the possibility of submission of a communication to the United Nations Human Rights Committee, or of an application to the European Court of Human Rights. Such procedures have limitations however. First, they only provide for a remedy against the State party to a particular human rights treaty, and in some cases only if that State has separately accepted the possibility of individual complaints. Secondly, only some of these procedures provide for the possibility of binding judgments. International organizations are not affected by these human rights mechanisms, because they are not parties to the human rights treaties on the basis of which these mechanisms were established. More generally, international courts generally do not have jurisdiction over international organizations. **30.09**

5. With regard to responsibility under domestic law, a major obstacle to holding a State or international organization responsible is immunity from jurisdiction. In many cases a status-of-forces agreement will be concluded with the Host State of a military operation that provides that the operation and/or its personnel enjoy immunity from jurisdiction of the courts of the Host State. Such immunity may be complete or partial. International organizations often enjoy immunity from jurisdiction also in other States, either on the basis of their constituent instrument or on the basis of a treaty concluded specifically for that purpose. The United Nations in particular enjoys a large measure of immunity on the basis of Article 105 of the UN Charter and the Convention on the Privileges and Immunities of the United Nations. Attempts before national and international courts to limit this immunity, including in the context of military operations, have so far been unsuccessful.[57] As discussed in sub-Chapters 5.2 and 6.2, armed forces also enjoy immunity in foreign territory on the basis of their status as organ of their Sending State.

6. Before its own courts, a Sending State often has the possibility to invoke various procedural arguments to prevent those courts from exercising jurisdiction over the State. Examples are the doctrine of 'combat immunity' in English law and the political question doctrine.[58]

7. Nevertheless, claims arising from military operations are sometimes successful before national courts. An example is the *Bici* case, where a claim was upheld concerning damages sought from the United Kingdom Ministry of Defence in negligence and trespass to the person for injuries as a result of actions of British

[57] See e.g. Supreme Court of the Netherlands, *Mothers of Srebrenica and others v the Netherlands and the United Nations*, Judgment of 13 April 2012, Case no. 10/04437; ECtHR, *Stichting Mothers of Srebrenica and others v the Netherlands*, Decision of 11 June 2013, Application no. 65542/12.

[58] For the doctrine of combat immunity see e.g. *Smith and ors v Ministry of Defence* [2013] UKSC 41. For the political question doctrine see D. Amoroso, 'A Fresh Look at the Issue of Non-Justiciability of Defence and Foreign Affairs', 23 *Leiden Journal of International Law* (2010), 938–48; Supreme Court of the Netherlands, *Daniković et al. v the Netherlands*, 29 November 2002, NJ 2003, 35.

30.09 soldiers taking part in the UN-authorized operation in Kosovo. The case was determined according to English law.[59]

8. Partly due to the impossibility of bringing such claims to a court as a result of immunity, a mechanism is frequently set up within a military operation for receiving and settling claims arising from the operation. This mechanism may find its legal basis in a status-of-forces agreement concluded with the Host State, or it may be established without reference to such an agreement. There is no blueprint for a claims settlement procedure, and the procedures used and standards applied vary. Status-of-forces agreements concluded between the UN and Host States provide for a standing claims commission with representation from the UN and the Host State. In practice, such commissions have never been established. Instead, the UN has created local claims review boards, which are made up of personnel of the UN operation.[60] The standards developed by these boards limit the type of claims that are receivable, and also imposes strict financial and temporal limits. In operations not led by the UN, it is generally the responsibility of the individual Sending States to settle claims. States that do so often also use standards that limit the possibility of successfully submitting a claim.[61]

30.10 **The responsibility under international law of an international organization or State for wrongful acts committed during a military operation does not affect the individual criminal responsibility of the perpetrator.**

1. Individual members of a military operation bear individual criminal responsibility for serious breaches of international law (war crimes, crimes against humanity, etc.). International responsibility of States and international organizations does not preclude individual criminal responsibility, and vice versa.[62]

2. Personnel of a military operation may be criminally responsible for wrongful acts even if they are carrying out the orders of a superior. They have a duty not to comply with manifestly unlawful orders. Superiors, whether they are military commanders or civilian superiors, are responsible for orders that are in violation of international law. They are likewise responsible, if they allow their subordinates to act in violation of international law, fail to punish such violations, or do not prevent such violations if they knew, or should have known, that such a violation was being committed or was going to be committed. See in this respect Chapter 29.

3. Where personnel in a military operation commit crimes, they ought to be subject to criminal proceedings. Immunity from jurisdiction is often an obstacle

[59] See *Bici and Bici v Ministry of Defence*, 7 April 2004, [2004] EWHC 786, QB.

[60] See M. Zwanenburg, 'UN Peace Operations between Independence and Acountability', 5 *International Organizations Law Review* (2008), 23–47; Schmalenbach, *Die Haftung Internationaler Organisationen* (Frankfurt am Main: Peter Lang, 2004).

[61] See J. Prescott, 'Claims', in D. Fleck (ed.), *Handbook of the Law of Visiting Forces* (Oxford: Oxford University Press, 2011), 159.

[62] This is reflected, *inter alia*, in Article 148 of the fourth Geneva Convention.

to such proceedings before the courts of the Host State. In such cases it is all the more important that the Sending State carry out an investigation and where indicated, submit the case for the prosecution. It may be pointed out that in respect of a number of international crimes, States have an obligation to prosecute or extradite alleged perpetrators of such crimes if found on their territory. Apart from these crimes, the legal system of the State concerned will determine the applicable legal regime. It is important to underline, however, that impunity for crimes committed by members of a military operation carries the risk of seriously compromising the legitimacy of such an operation. **30.10**

PART V

SYNTHESIS AND CONCLUSION

Chapter 31

THE ROLE OF THE MILITARY LEGAL ADVISOR

I. Commentary

Each State must make legal advisors available to the staff of military commanders whose forces are likely to be deployed on military operations. 31.01

1. *Historical Background on Legal Advisors.* For centuries it was customary for military leaders, usually Heads of State, to issue instructions, sometimes called articles of war, to their armies. These included rules, based on the laws and customs of war, that would be recognizable in today's law of armed conflict treaties. One notable example is the Instructions for the Government of Armies of the United States in the Field, prepared by Dr Francis Lieber and issued to the Union forces by President Lincoln in 1863 as Army Order 100. Several other States subsequently issued manuals of their own. This practice became enshrined in Hague Convention No. IV of 1907, Article 1 of which requires States parties to issue to their armed forces instructions that were to be in conformity with the regulations, now known as The Hague Regulations, annexed to the Convention. At that stage, the treaty rules on the law of armed conflict were more limited than they are today and they could easily be issued in pamphlet form or as part of military law manuals.[1] Things became more complicated with the adoption of the 429 Articles of the Geneva Conventions of 1949 and the 130 Articles of Protocols I and II thereto, not to mention the various treaties on weapons and on international criminal law. By the time the Protocols were negotiated, it was considered that military commanders could not be expected to have a good grasp of this substantial body of law in addition to all the other required areas of military expertise and it was proposed, by the Federal Republic of Germany,[2] that there should be a requirement for lawyers to be appointed to advise military commanders about the law of armed conflict. After some discussion of the precise terms of this obligation, it was eventually accepted by the Diplomatic Conference at which Protocol I was negotiated.

[1] Before the Second World War, the United Kingdom Manual of Military Law had just one chapter devoted to the law of war. It was only after the war, and the Geneva Conventions of 1949, that the subject was dealt with in a separate volume.

[2] M. Bothe, K.J. Partsch, and W. Solf, *New Rules for the victims of Armed Conflicts* (The Hague: Martinus Nijhoff, 1982) (hereinafter, *New Rules*), 499.

A.P.V. ROGERS[†] AND DARREN STEWART

31.01 2. *Additional Protocol I.* This was, therefore, the first treaty to lay down a requirement for States to have available legal advisors to advise military commanders about the law of armed conflict. Article 82 provides:

> The High Contracting Parties[3] at all times, and the Parties to the conflict in time of armed conflict, shall ensure that legal advisors are available, when necessary, to advise military commanders at the appropriate level on the application of the Conventions and this Protocol and on the appropriate instruction to be given to the armed forces on this subject.[4]

3. *Discussion of Article 82 Requirements.* It is immediately apparent that, while it is mandatory for States parties to have legal advisors available, there is a certain amount of latitude, evidenced by words such as 'when necessary', 'at the appropriate level', and 'appropriate instruction', as to how this requirement should be interpreted and applied in practice. For example, the qualifications such legal advisors must possess are not laid down. It is not stated, for example, that they must be qualified legal practitioners.[5] It may have been taken for granted that legal advisors would be legally qualified. It was, perhaps, assumed that they would be appointed from the ranks of military lawyers.[6] However, it can be inferred that, whatever their qualifications, they must possess sufficient knowledge of the Geneva Conventions and Protocols to be able to advise commanders properly and to provide legal instruction. That would entail special training in this field of the law if necessary; certainly more than that customarily given to other military personnel. As for the appropriate level of the military command structure at which legal advisors should be appointed, that seems to be left to States to decide.[7]

De Preux expresses the view that the role of the legal advisor is to instruct personnel in the law of armed conflict, which can include involvement in the preparation of exercises; to establish procedures for consultation on legal matters and to review operational plans from a legal point of view; to give advice about the execution of the commander's legal responsibilities in attack or defence,[8] or about particular legal problems arising in the course of the conflict. He considers that, for the army, legal advisors should be posted to the highest command levels down to divisions, independent brigades, or other independent units and to the headquarters of commanders of military bases and areas, including those in occupied territory.

[3] As of 2014, 174 States are parties to Protocol I, see <https://www.icrc.org/applic/ihl/ihl.nsf/>.

[4] Although the word 'subject' is presumably a reference to the application of, and instruction in, the Conventions and Protocol, it would make more sense in practice if this were interpreted more broadly as referring to the law of armed conflict generally and, indeed, the other legal aspects of military operations.

[5] The word 'qualified', which appeared before 'legal advisers' in an earlier draft was deleted. See *New Rules*, 500.

[6] J. De Preux, in Y. Sandoz, C. Swinarski, and B. Zimmermann (eds), *Commentary on the Additional Protocols* (Geneva: International Committee of the Red Cross, 1987) (hereinafter *Commentary*), 949.

[7] 'Some may wish to appoint those advisers at all—or nearly all—levels of command, while others intend to appoint them only at the headquarters of large units and at military academies, and still others only envisage their participation in exceptional situations', see *Commentary*, 949.

[8] Protocol I, Arts 57 and 58.

He discusses the issue of to whom the legal advisor should be subordinated and the pros and cons of having as legal advisors military lawyers, other military personnel with law of armed conflict training, or civilians, but without reaching any firm conclusions, presumably on the basis that these are matters for States to decide.[9] **31.01**

It is clear from State practice that De Preux's view is shared by many of those States with large, or heavily committed, military forces. Within some military alliances, e.g. The North Atlantic Treaty Organization (NATO), such practice has been incorporated into standardization documents which give further weight to the structure De Preux outlines. The experience of the authors and many of those consulted in carrying out research for this chapter would suggest that such an approach to the provision of legal support within a military context has much to commend itself, albeit in the detailed manner described by De Preux, it is often subject to the vagaries of available resources.

Another question that arises from the text of Article 82 is who the 'parties to the conflict' might be if they are not High Contracting Parties. It seems that this is a reference to national liberation movements.[10]

4. *Customary Law Study*. Henckaerts and Doswald-Beck in their volume of rules of customary international humanitarian law, include the following rule:[11]

Rule 141. Each State must make legal advisers available, when necessary, to advise military commanders at the appropriate level on the application of international humanitarian law.

The authors of the study claim that this is a rule of customary law established by State practice. This may seem surprising since the requirement was introduced into treaty law for the first time in Protocol I of 1977, more than 30 years ago. At the time of writing, the Protocol is binding on 168 States, a substantial body of the international community, though not its totality. Some important military powers, such as the United States and Israel, that are not parties to Protocol I have nevertheless for many years appointed legal advisors in their armed forces. Whether this is done out of a sense of legal obligation or for other reasons, such as a sense of propriety, is not clear.[12]

As the authors have experienced in practice, the vast majority of western States, whether or not members of NATO, have well-developed structures for military legal advisors who are also to be found in the armed forces of, for example, Russia, India, South Africa, Brazil, China, and Thailand. Even States that are not as militarily powerful as these but that have experienced armed conflict, such as Sierra

[9] *Commentary*, 952–7.

[10] *Commentary*, 956. *New Rules*, 500. See also, Protocol I, Art. 1, para. 4. More recently this quandary could be said to equally apply to terrorist organizations and other non-government organizations in the same context as the wider question concerning compliance by those groups with IHL.

[11] J.-M. Henckaerts and L. Doswald-Beck (eds), *Customary International Humanitarian Law*, Vol. I (Cambridge: Cambridge University Press, 2005), 500.

[12] Anecdotal evidence obtained by the authors, having spoken to many US military legal advisors, suggests that this obligation outlined by Protocol I is accepted by the US as reflecting customary international law.

31.01 Leone, have military legal advisors.[13] Smaller States may not have legal advisors in their armed forces but those forces may be able to seek legal advice from, say, their respective ministries of defence or Attorney-General's department. The precise model for legal advisors tends to reflect the size and experience of the States concerned. In some cases, there is a mixture of civilian and military legal advisors and in others civilians only.

5. *Recent Developments.* Although the requirements of treaty and customary law refer to advice on international humanitarian law, there has been an increasing practical requirement in recent years for lawyers to be available to give advice to military commanders on the wider aspects of the law that relates to the conduct of military operations whether in time of armed conflict[14] or in peacetime. Apart from that, legal advice may also be needed with regard to constitutional law, criminal law, contracts law, administrative law, human rights law, and the law of international organizations. The list is not exhaustive. These areas of law can have both national and international law dimensions. Increasingly in peace support missions legal advisors from many nations find themselves employed in Rule of Law activity, supporting local institutions and often preparing the ground for follow-on civilian missions.

It is evident that there are many States which are not party to Protocol I that have, nevertheless, made very sophisticated and progressive attempts to implement the spirit of Article 82. Indeed, in the absence of significant numbers of international armed conflicts, the widespread deployment and use of military legal advisors in conflicts or security operations of an internal nature, peace operations, or operations other than war lend substantial weight to the contention that States parties now regard the deployment of such specialists as reflective at the very least of 'best practice'.

6. *Implementation in Practice: Some Examples.* For many years the United States, though not a party to Protocol I, has taken the lead with regard to 'best practice' in the appointment of legal advisors to the armed forces and the development of their role in relation to military operations. Its armed forces developed the concept of 'operational law' to cover a wider field than law of armed conflict, appointed military lawyers in large numbers, set up their own training establishments for military lawyers, involved lawyers in the drafting, development, and application of rules of engagement, and involved lawyers in targeting decisions. The US example has had a profound impact on the approach adopted by a number of its allies and others who have observed US practice. By contrast, and not dissimilar to the experience of many other countries, developments in the United Kingdom have

[13] Experience of countries such as Columbia, Uganda, and the Philippines amongst others highlight how the role of the military legal advisor will often be forged during the conduct of armed conflict including internal conflict.

[14] Including those circumstances falling short of international armed conflict and which might be categorized as peace operations.

been rather modest. Although military lawyers had, since 1948, been based at higher command level and also at independent commands overseas to give advice on military law, it was not until the troubles in Northern Ireland from 1969 onwards that military lawyers dealt increasingly with operational law matters. **31.01**

In anticipation of the ratification of Protocol I, it was decided to establish a post with responsibility for developing training programmes and training materials in the law of armed conflict for military training establishments.[15] It was also decided to deploy Army lawyers to divisions and this process started in 1981. The role of those lawyers was to advise the commanders and staff on all aspects of military law, but advice and training on the law of armed conflict tended to be confined to relatively few military exercises because of the pressure of other work.

During the conflict in the South Atlantic in 1982, the one military lawyer assigned to the United Kingdom task force dealt mainly with prisoner-of-war issues. In the early 1990s the need for trained operational lawyers became more acute with a constant need to find legal advisors to deploy to Bosnia with elements of the United Nations Protection Force. The reforms to the court-martial system precipitated by a judgment of the European Court of Human Rights[16] resulted in the centralization of court-martial work outside the chain of command, lawyers at divisions being relieved of that responsibility. Apart from Bosnia, British forces started being deployed elsewhere: in Iraq in 1991 and again in 2003, in Kosovo, Sierra Leone, and Afghanistan.[17] It became rare for existing divisional formations to be deployed, with ad hoc formations of division or brigade size being put together instead, but always with a legal team.[18]

Experience from these operational tours and acceptance of the need for further specialization has led to the establishment within the British Army of an operational law branch, with a military one-star officer head, and with responsibility to support legal advisors on operational deployments. The tasks of the branch include:

— taking the lead on operational law developments within the British Army,
— carrying out legal reviews of weaponry,
— training legal officers and the Army generally on operational law,
— supporting operations with a pool of trained and deployable legal officers,
— exercising functional control over legal officers deployed on operations,
— providing advice on all aspects of operational law,
— maintaining contacts with other bodies working in the same field of law.[19]

[15] The co-author, A.P.V. Rogers, was the incumbent of this post from 1979–1982.

[16] *Findlay v The United Kingdom* (1997) 24 EHRR 221.

[17] The co-author, D.M. Stewart, was the senior legal advisor for UK Forces in Kosovo (1999), Sierra Leone (2000), and Afghanistan (2006–7).

[18] The notable exception being the deployment of 1 (UK) Armoured Division during the invasion of Iraq in 2003.

[19] A fuller review of the developments in this section can be found in G. Risius, 'Development of Operational Law within ALS', in R. Burchill, N.D. White, and J. Morris (eds), *International Conflict and Security Law* (Cambridge, Cambridge University Press, 2005), 21–31.

31.01 It is not only service lawyers who are dealing with operational law issues. Because there is nearly always a political aspect to military operations, one has seen an increase in recent years in the involvement of civilian lawyers, who are answerable to the Ministry of Defence legal advisor, and not the heads of service legal services, and who occupy posts not only in the Ministry of Defence but also at the United Kingdom's Permanent Joint Headquarters.

Australia, too, has experienced an increase in the number of military operations since the late 1980s. That has led to an increasing role for lawyers to assist commanders in training, planning, managing, and conducting military operations. These operations have ranged from domestic operations such as counter-terrorism and border control, to international operations, such as United Nations and multinational peace operations, armed conflict, and situations of occupation.

The increase in operational tempo of the Australian Defence Force (ADF) and the corresponding interest in operational law matters shown by various government agencies and by civil society more generally has also led to an increasing emphasis on a 'whole of government approach' in addressing operational law matters. Operational law advice to the Australian Government is now provided by a range of government departments including the Department of Foreign Affairs and Trade and the Attorney-General's Department. Thus, such tasks as developing rules of engagement for ADF operations, identifying key issues that may impose criminal liability on ADF personnel, and negotiating multilateral and bilateral agreements with coalition partners are no longer solely the purview of ADF lawyers.

For developing States too, modern military operations in which their armed forces are involved—whether domestic law enforcement operations, peace operations, or armed conflict—have shown the need for the presence and participation of legal advisors who have the necessary breadth of knowledge and experience and who are able to operate in austere battlefield conditions. Many of those States are parties to Protocol I, and therefore have accepted the Article 82 obligations, but tend to rely on specialist advisors at ministry of defence or at military command headquarters, probably because of a shortage of suitable personnel who are more likely to be found in government departments, academic institutions, or in international organizations. This means, however, that legal advice may not be readily available when decisions about the actual conduct of military operations are made. To create a legal structure along the lines De Preux suggests will not only be manpower intensive but will also involve the development of the necessary capacity in terms of experience and span of knowledge. It is likely to require cultural change in the manner in which military legal advisors and their ability to contribute to command decisions are viewed in these countries.

7. *Conclusions.* It has been pointed out that the drawback of military legal advisors is that they may find it more difficult than civilians to provide independent and objective legal advice to their military superiors. The same might be said of civilian lawyers working for the government, who would face similar challenges when

advising civilian superiors or politicians.[20] While civilian lawyers in private practice would be impartial, they are unlikely to have the deep specialist knowledge required and might find it difficult to integrate into and be accepted by the armed forces. Military lawyers are likely to be subject to military discipline and required to deploy when ordered to do so; civilian lawyers sent on military operations are likely to be volunteers. **31.01**

Article 82 of Protocol I places a positive obligation on States to provide legal advisors at the appropriate level to give advice on the law of armed conflict. It makes sense if such legal advisors are able to advise on other aspects of operational law as well. Although it is left to States to decide how best to deploy such lawyers, and it must be recognized that they will be a rare commodity in some countries, best practice indicates that, to be effective, they need to be deployed not only at ministerial or high command level, but also to serve with commanders in the field. At whatever level they are deployed, they need to be integrated into the staffing structures so that they are involved, for example, in the drafting of rules of engagement. In some States the legal advisors are part of the armed forces and have military rank; in others they are civilian lawyers who work for the government, perhaps in the Ministry of Defence, the Attorney-General's office, or justice departments. It will be left to States to decide upon the best solution. That will depend very much on the history and traditions of the State concerned.

The duty of those legal advisors will be to provide advice that will enable the commander and his staff to carry out the commander's military mission in accordance with the law. The legal advisor may also be required to advise on appropriate legal training for the forces concerned. 31.02

1. When discussing the status of legal advisors, it should be borne in mind that they may have civilian or military status. In the past, lawyers who accompanied the armed forces tended to be military lawyers though in some countries they may have been civilians in peacetime with a liability to be called up for military service in time of armed conflict. Because of the political dimension to military operations, it is not uncommon for civilian personnel (including lawyers) to be deployed to the theatre of operations, though it is preferable at command levels where contact with opposing enemy forces is likely for the lawyers concerned to have military and, therefore, combatant status. Many of the answers to the questions discussed later will also vary depending on how legal officers are incorporated in the military force of the country. Are they soldiers with legal training or lawyers with military training? In the United Kingdom, for example, both types of military lawyer serve side-by-side: those who qualified as lawyers first and then received basic military training on joining the service; but also those who served in the armed forces first and then qualified as lawyers. In the United States Marine Corps,

[20] This would appear to be particularly so in the case of political appointees.

31.02 military lawyers are expected to serve in their capacity as officers in legal and non-legal roles alike.

2. *General Role of Legal Advisor.* In many States, the role of the military lawyer has probably changed considerably in the past 50 to 60 years. At first, he might have been deployed to an operational theatre after the end of active hostilities to deal, for example, with disciplinary matters or with war crimes prosecutions. Then, gradually, there came a creeping realization that military decisions may have legal consequences for the State or even for commanders personally. So it became common for lawyers to be deployed during operations to give advice, for example, on the treatment of prisoners of war, and eventually to give advice on the legal aspects of the conduct of military operations: issues such as targeting or, in internal security operations, intelligence gathering. In the same period, the law of armed conflict has become more complicated. It has also moved gradually away from a general spirit of humanitarianism to one of enforcement, with the establishment of criminal tribunals, especially the international criminal court, and its reinforcement of the doctrine of command responsibility. The legal advisor thus also plays an increasingly important role in assisting the commander in exercising this responsibility.

These developments have, in turn, led to the increasing involvement of lawyers in what might previously have been regarded as matters of policy or operational planning, mainly because the lawyers are present on the commander's staff. If the lawyer is at hand and is a trusted member of the staff, the commander might regard the lawyer as his 'man of affairs' and may well wish to make use of the skills developed as part of his legal training to help him analyse non-legal problems and suggest possible solutions.

This gradual development has accelerated in the West in the light of evolving military doctrine, particularly the 'effects based approach to operations' (EBAO). The legal advisor plays an increasingly important role in helping the commander to achieve his military mission. The importance of EBAO is to emphasize the second, third, and fourth order effects of a particular act and in turn to use these anticipated effects in order to inform decisions about military strategy.

The result for the lawyer's role is not so different from that which he has traditionally performed, namely, to consider the consequences of decisions, acts, measures, or policies. However, the significance of the EBAO approach for the legal advisor is that legal skills are now at the heart of operational or strategic thinking or planning. As a consequence, the temptation to apply these skills to other matters, such as policy advice, or to exert influence is often difficult to resist without a disciplined approach to the core function the legal advisor performs. This is a key vulnerability which requires a mature and considered response from the legal advisor so as to not compromise his position and the advice he gives.

So what is the commander's perspective of the lawyer's role? All experts consulted agreed that, ultimately, the decision-making responsibility remained with the commander. The commander was responsible for making any decisions relating

A.P.V. ROGERS[†] AND DARREN STEWART

to the conduct of the military operations that had been assigned to him by higher authority. In reaching decisions he would normally take advice from his staff, including his legal advisor. The precise staffing process, and the extent to which staff members including legal advisors would be involved, varies from State to State. In some cases, involving certain areas of expertise, commanders would delegate decision-making power to nominated subordinates who would in turn seek specialist legal advice, though the commander would continue to remain ultimately responsible for the decisions made. **31.02**

It has been suggested that in some countries, State policy is regarded as paramount and so lawyers have been kept at arm's length and not brought into the decision-making process. That isolation, and their subordination to commanders, renders them impotent and ineffective. Even in States that are open in principle to greater involvement of legal advisors, the overall attitude may be quite conservative, namely, that the role of the legal advisor is to provide legal advice only.

At the other extreme, in States adopting the EBAO approach, the commander's perspective of the legal advisor's role would probably be to enable the commander legally to create the effect he wished to achieve his military mission. That approach requires a closer integration of the legal advisor into the staffing and even decision-making process. He would provide legal advice on how to undertake military operations as effectively and efficiently as possible. His advice would thus relate to both law and policy.

Is the lawyer's perspective of his role any different from that of the commander? A legal advisor from, for example, a NATO background[21] might consider it his job to enable the commander to make informed decisions, to provide the commander with options, and to protect him from any legal consequences of his decisions. The lawyer might thus see himself as an enabler as well as an advisor, as somebody who shapes thinking.

Some of the experts consulted, however, expressed concern and doubt about whether 'enabler or shaper of thoughts' was correct and thought that allowing the lawyer too much latitude or encouraging 'creativity' on his part could land commanders and States in legal trouble.[22]

The lawyer's attitude to his role will depend, to some extent, on his own background, training, and experience. Thus, a positivist lawyer will state the law as he sees it, whereas the policy-aware lawyer will start from the perspective of how the law can best achieve the policy goal that is sought. Those in the latter category need to know, however, when no margin of interpretation is left and when there is a limit to creativity, otherwise they may be inclined to sanction law of armed conflict violations on the basis of necessity.

[21] Where policy seems to tend toward a greater involvement of the legal advisor in the decision-making process.

[22] Especially where such an approach encourages experimental or innovative interpretations of the law.

31.02 Even when adopting the positivist approach, the mere giving of legal advice may be insufficient. The legal advisor must not stand by while breaches of the law of war are planned for and executed without any attempt on his part to influence decision-making towards respect for the law of armed conflict.

Others point out that there are grey areas in the law and that it is sometimes hard to determine whether a proposed concept of operations accords with pertinent legal standards because it is not certain what those standards are. Examples include the questions of what rules of Protocol I have acquired customary international law character, whether occupation should be governed by a law enforcement model rather than an armed conflict model, or what impact human rights treaty law may have on operations. It is even more complicated in an international environment. For example, within an alliance like NATO, what some Member States consider lawful might not be so regarded by others. What was considered lawful at the planning stage might be regarded, after the event when all the facts have emerged, as unlawful—if not by the military, perhaps by the judiciary or by a non-governmental organization. In the end, the notion of 'enabling' is neither right nor wrong. Like so many notions, it can work towards ensuring lawful conduct; it can also lead to abuse.

Legal advisors should be able to identify potential legal problems and the areas where legal uncertainty exists and advise their commanders as to whether the course proposed is legal, illegal, or falls into an area of legal uncertainty. In the last case, it may be necessary to seek clarification or guidance from higher command.

In the final analysis, the lawyer is just one of many advisors whose counsel the commander will take into consideration and the final decision will rest with the commander. In this respect, the greatest contribution the legal advisor can make to ensuring legality is to see that taking the law into account becomes a normal part of the staffing process; as one expert put it: 'that legal obligations are not seen as a hindrance but as an essential component of a professional military, balancing the legitimate use of power against the terror and pain that conflict causes'.

There seems to be general agreement that, however he might see his role, the legal advisor does have the role of 'honest broker' or 'guardian of legitimacy'. Thus, the legal advisor's role includes the various elements already outlined but also includes an overriding duty to ensure that international law is complied with. As Sir Franklin Berman, a former United Kingdom Foreign and Commonwealth Office Legal Advisor, put it: 'the main role of the governmental legal adviser is to "make" his government comply with international law'. He went on to explain that:

> [i]t must be assumed to be a necessary part of the role that the international law adviser should be expected to use his gifts of exposition and persuasion to bring those with whom the power of decision lies to use this power to the right result.[23]

[23] F.D. Berman, 'The Role of the International Lawyer in the Negotiation of Treaties', in C. Wickremasinghe (ed.), *The International Lawyer as Practitioner* (London: British Institute of International and Comparative Law, 2000), 4.

A.P.V. ROGERS[†] AND DARREN STEWART

By 'the right result' we understand him to mean that there is a positive obligation on the part of the lawyer to see that the law is not violated. This, of course, will be influenced by that lawyer's training and the national perspective on what is viewed as being the current position of the law on a particular issue. 31.02

As treaty texts do not always provide answers to legal questions that arise during military operations, legal advisors will always need to be guided by the fundamental principles of customary law, for example, ensuring that a military purpose is to be achieved by the proposed action; enquiring if there is room for humanity; ensuring that civilians are not directly attacked and are protected so far as possible from the incidental effects of military action; considering the rule of proportionality; ensuring that persons who are *hors de combat* through injury, capture, or detention are invariably treated with humanity and dignity; and, in cases of doubt, adopting presumptions in favour of protection.

The legal advisor, therefore, has to understand the military mission and what the commander is trying to achieve. That will include knowledge of the military forces, their tactics and weapons, and what they can achieve. Spending time with deployed troops, perhaps even going on patrol or on other operations with them, will be time well spent in that respect. The legal advisor may well be one of the closest advisors to the commander, along with the chief of staff and the political advisor. To be effective the lawyer must be a respected member of the staff team. That respect will be earned if the legal advisor can put his advice into a military and political context and is able to think of various options for action and the advantages and consequences of each. Above all, the advice must be clear and unambiguous; if something is, or is potentially, unlawful, he should say so. If he considers that another option is preferable for legal reasons, he needs to be able to argue his case. Imagination is needed too. The lawyer might be able to think of possibilities that the commander has not considered. Flexibility is also called for: the need to assess and give legal advice on an option or scenario that arises in the course of staffing or at a briefing and which has not occurred to him before. He must be prepared to talk to others, for example, legal advisors of other coalition forces or lawyers of the host nation, in order to find solutions. If, despite all that has been said, the legal advisor is unable to dissuade the commander from taking a course of action that the legal advisor considers would be unlawful, he may consider it necessary to give the commander written legal advice to that effect. A legal chain of command (see later) might prevent such a situation arising.

3. *Who is the Client?* This is a question that somebody trained as a practising lawyer might ask, concerned about to whom he owed a duty of care and of confidentiality. So, in discussing 'client' here we are discussing the person or persons to whom those duties are owed. Of course, a legal advisor in the service of the State is in a different position from a lawyer in private practice. A civil service lawyer might regard the client as the person to whom he owed a duty of care, ultimately, as the minister in charge of his department but there might be many officials in the department to whom he gives advice. A lawyer assigned to the armed forces might see his ultimate

31.02 'client' as the chief of the defence staff, or the chief of his branch of the armed forces, rather than a politician. But he would see his immediate client as the commander of the unit or formation where he serves as well, no doubt, as members of the staff of that headquarters. A military legal advisor assigned for duty to an international military headquarters would probably see his 'client' as the allied or coalition commander, rather than his own national authorities. More immediately, the 'client' would be the person to whom advice is given.

Although the view was expressed to the authors that international law itself is the 'client' and one person consulted thought the government was the 'client', the vast majority of the experts consulted saw the commander and the chain of command as the 'client' in a qualified lawyer/client relationship. The lawyer would feel obliged to provide advice about legal options to pursue national and shared international interests. Some were uncomfortable about the use of the word 'client' at all since legal advisors were required to provide 'quality objective legal advice'. That is why the majority described the relationship as a qualified lawyer/client relationship, both because, inevitably, there were principal and secondary 'clients' and because it would be naïve to suggest that the lawyer would serve only the law and would not advocate a national or alliance interpretation of the law. However, as one expert consulted suggested, while the legal advisor should secure the best interests of his client, it must be within the four corners of the law. As another expert commented, the legal advisor also has to act within the spirit of the law and not exploit gaps and loopholes in the interests of his 'client' where such would be contrary to the spirit of the law.

Since we are discussing the role here of legal advisors to military commanders, it is not necessary to consider the role of lawyers on the staff of ministries except in those countries where those legal advisors provide advice directly to military commanders or are deployed on a temporary basis to the staff of commanders. It may be difficult to avoid divided loyalties, especially in the former case, unless it is made clear from the outset that the lawyer's function is to advise the commander; and that protecting the interests of ministers will be the function of other lawyers. It should be expected that with such a division of responsibility, there will be from time to time conflict or friction as between advisors over detail, but that this should be seen within a broader context of general agreement as to the national approach concerning the substantive *ad bellum* issues. Similarly, a complete separation of advisory and prosecutorial functions is essential to avoid conflicts of interest. Yet the need for professional support and functional control by responsible superiors in a legal chain of command is widely accepted (see Legal Chain of Command, Section 31.04).

4. *What are the Peculiarities of a Multinational Environment?* It is vital for military legal advisors on multinational operations to perceive the broader alliance approach to interpreting the mandate and the legal basis for the operation as well as having a good knowledge and understanding of the relevant instruments, regulations, guidelines, and practices of the organization concerned.

A.P.V. ROGERS† AND DARREN STEWART

That will include the differing national positions, what caveats have been entered, and in turn where potential for friction can arise. This may involve drawing conclusions from such caveats as to how a particular nation's force contribution to a mission might conduct operations assigned to it. A legal advisor can have both national and international responsibilities, depending on the nature of his post. **31.02**

5. *Duty to Advise on Appropriate Legal Training.* The legal training for military operations of members of the armed forces, and how this should be carried out, will vary from State to State. In general terms, it will fall into three stages. First, there is the basic legal training that would be carried out at national training establishments. Second, there is the general training that would be carried out at formation level and which is designed to prepare personnel for the legal issues that they might face according to the role of the formation concerned. For example, a deployable headquarters or formation might have a general role that envisages its deployment to trouble spots anywhere in the world. The type of legal training would depend on likely scenarios, such as war fighting, peace operations, nation-building, or humanitarian assistance, and would be tailored to supplementing the basic legal training by anticipating likely legal problems and preparing members of the Force or headquarters for those eventualities. Third, there is specific training, once the mission has been established, of preparing for that mission.

We are discussing here the second and third stages of legal training: that which is designed for the military operations for which the forces are likely to be deployed or for a specific mission for which they have been appointed. Of course, if basic legal training has not already been done, that would have to be carried out too.

Second and third stage legal training will probably be undertaken within the formation or headquarters concerned, so may not benefit from the infrastructure or staff of military academies or training establishments. The legal advisor will have to identify the legal training required and then, in discussion with the operational and training staff, if any, decide how best to implement that training. How this is done will depend very much on the ethos and traditions of the State and forces concerned but, in so far as one can generalize, it is better that legal training of non-commissioned ranks is carried out by their officers as part of normal military training and integrated within it, and not dealt with as a separate subject. The legal advisor can provide legal input into training or exercise scenarios, take part as an exercise controller to ensure that the legal issues are not ignored and, perhaps, provide one of his deputies to play the part of the legal advisor. For commissioned officers, that integrated approach can be supplemented by formal presentations by a legal advisor if necessary but even then, it is helpful if presentations are made jointly by operational and legal staff. The operational staff can provide realistic military scenarios; the legal advisor can provide some typical legal issues that might arise within that scenario; the class can discuss how best to deal with those issues within the law; the joint operational and legal instructors can then draw conclusions and reinforce any lessons to be learned.

31.02 Formal training of the kind described above will usually be supplemented by written instructions or pamphlets, such as rules of engagement cards, soldiers' rules cards, or the international humanitarian law pamphlets that are commonly issued nowadays.

31.03 **To enable legal advisors to fulfil their duties, they need appropriate general and specific training in advance.**

1. *General Training of Legal Advisors*. What level of knowledge, experience, and training is required? How can this be achieved? There are generally two different approaches to the appointment of legal advisors. In some States lawyers are recruited into the armed forces and then given military and military law training; in others, officers with, say, some years' military experience, are sent away to qualify as lawyers before returning to the armed forces as legal advisors. The disadvantage of the latter approach is probably cost, since the training is usually paid for by the State, and there can be wastage because the legal advisors may be tempted to seek more lucrative openings in legal practice; but there are great advantages in the integration of legal advisors into the armed forces and the authority that such legal advisors will have because of their previous military service, not to mention the contacts they will have acquired as a result.

Given the high cost of legal training, some States may be reluctant to provide legal training for persons to become specialist legal advisors. They might be more inclined to provide legal training as part of the overall training of generalist officers of the armed forces. As one expert has commented, that would be better than having no legal expertise at all at the front line. As he says: 'at least the most hard-nosed operational commander imbued with good legal training can serve as the "conscience"'.

There is an old adage, widely known in the common law world, that 'the lawyer who represents himself has a fool for a client'. There is much to be said for the considerations of impartial and objective advice which underpin the sentiments of this phrase. They should act as a salutary influence on those who would view the legal training of generalist officers alone as being a panacea for ensuring legal input into military decision-making.

It is assumed that most legal advisors will have had basic legal training in their own countries and, probably, are qualified to practise law in those countries. They will also need to have legal training in the legal aspects of military operations. That will include an understanding of the principles of international law, including subjects like law of international institutions, treaties, State responsibility, human rights, the environment, and international criminal law; and, in more detail, the law of armed conflict and the law relating to the use of force. Naval and air specialists would also need to know about the law of the sea and air and space law. A legal advisor at a joint command headquarters would probably need to have, or to have access to, expertise in all these areas of law.

A.P.V. ROGERS[†] AND DARREN STEWART

Academic legal knowledge is just the start. To be effective, a legal advisor needs to have had some years of practice as a lawyer behind him. For example, the analytical, logical, and advocacy skills associated with a criminal law practice can be useful assets for a legal advisor. Practical skills acquired during service in the armed forces prior to undertaking legal training is equally valuable, for example, as officer of the watch on board a warship or as a sub-unit commander exercising disciplinary powers. **31.03**

In addition to the right blend and balance of academic and practical legal knowledge, there needs to be military knowledge, including structures, staffing procedures, and an understanding of the military culture, ethic, and language. This would include at least a basic knowledge of the operational command process, of tactics and of weapon systems, their workings and effects. That should lead to an understanding of the limitations of what can be achieved by military force.

There needs also to be an appreciation of the need for the clarity, directness, and legal certainty that commanders would expect. Furthermore, legal advisors need to be able to operate in the uncomfortable and stressful conditions sometimes associated with military operations. This requires legal advisors who are mentally flexible but who are also able to apply common sense in fast-moving and constantly-changing conditions where little legal guidance may exist and where time for making decisions may be short or very short. Although these are really personal attributes, realistic training can help enormously to prepare people for such challenges.

One would expect general training to be carried out nationally, but multinational training can also be important, not only to prepare for the peculiarities of a multinational deployment but also in filling gaps in the skills required. For example, some States do not train for certain eventualities because their defence doctrine assigns them a low priority. In States that have a gendarmerie, there may be more emphasis on policing and police law that legal advisors from those States could put to good use in some nation-building scenarios. Legal advisors from other States might be unfamiliar with that area of law.

Apart from their formal training, legal advisors have a personal duty to keep abreast of operational law matters as well as anything specific to a pending deployment.

The key to success of the legal advisor will be the nature and breadth of his experience and of that available in his legal team. The effectiveness of legal advisors will usually depend on the extent to which they have been prepared for working in a military environment. States that have successfully integrated effective legal advisors into their armed forces can assist with training sessions for States that are about to embark on this process. Through attendance at courses, seminars, and conferences run by international organizations such as the International Institute of Humanitarian Law or the International Society for Military Law and the Law of War or by alliance bodies, such as the NATO School, or by national training centres, such as the Stockton Centre for the Study of International Law located at the United States Naval War College or the United States Army Judge Advocate General School, legal advisors can benefit from shared experiences whilst building up a useful network of international contacts.

A.P.V. ROGERS† AND DARREN STEWART

31.03 2. *Specific Training of Legal Advisors.* Over and above the general legal training just described, certain legal roles, for example, advising in the fields of intelligence, detainee handling, or targeting, may require special training. The nature of any given mission will dictate the type and nature of any theatre-specific training that should be carried out. For example, if the mission is nation rebuilding, the legal advisor's role might be to assist in ensuring that the local criminal court system is operating properly. That would require a good knowledge of the workings of courts in more than one legal system, including that of the State concerned, as well as of the norms of international criminal law. Of course, it is self-evident that those appointed to key senior appointments will by necessity require a higher level of knowledge, experience, and skill than those deploying to junior posts. In those States where operational deployments are frequent, the development of an 'operational law' speciality might help to ensure that the necessary expertise could be found.

In a multinational organization, such as NATO, it may be possible to encourage the sharing of legal training and to reach agreement about the levels of legal training that are required and about numbers of legal advisors that are needed for the various force levels that might be deployed.

31.04 **Once appointed, they need to be integrated into the staff structure but also have the right of direct access to the commander whenever they deem it legally necessary. The staff structure should be such as to ensure the legal advisors' independence from the commander with regard to the exercise of their legal functions. Legal advisors should be enabled to act within their legal chain of command.**

1. *Whereabouts Should the Legal Advisor be Placed in the Staff Structure?* The location of the legal staff within the headquarters structure seems to be the key to perceptions as to the role and importance of the legal advisor. For many years in the British Army, for example, the legal advisor was placed in the personnel branch of the headquarters, so it took a long time for officers in other staff branches, especially those dealing with operations, to realize that, first, it was open to them to consult the legal advisor on non-personnel matters and, second, that the legal advisor might have something useful to contribute to their area of expertise. In fact, if he is to able to fulfil his potential, the legal advisor must be available to the command group, working to the commander and available across all staff functions. He also requires the right of direct access to the commander when necessary. One cannot expect staff without legal training to be able to brief the commander adequately on legal matters and answer questions that the commander might have about those matters.

Given that States and alliances or regional organizations will have their own staffing structures, decisions about the appropriate location of the legal advisor should be based on two assumptions: first, that the legal advisor must have direct access to the commander when needed and, second, that the legal advisor should be available to all staff branches. In some States, this is achieved by placing the legal advisor in the chief of staff's office. Alternatively, he can be part of and be located within the command group, next to the political and other key advisors. Some multinational organizations have adopted this latter premise or concept as part of their doctrine, for example, NATO. 31.04

2. *Legal Chain of Command.* Should there be a legal chain of command? Strictly speaking, one should not speak of a chain of command, as command will remain with the commander. What is required, for a number of reasons, is a system of specialist, or technical, communication and supervision. The deployed legal advisor may need someone to turn to for help or advice when legal problems arise that are outside his experience or where he is experiencing difficulties in his relationship with the commander. That can help to guarantee the legal advisor's independence from the commander. Some technical supervision of the deployed legal advisor is also necessary because the commander and staff of the headquarters where the legal advisor serves will not, without legal training themselves, be able to judge his competence. Supervision can also ensure that a proper balance is maintained by the deployed legal advisor in establishing a close working relationship with the commander but, at the same time, maintaining his professional distance and independence. A specialist staffing process that can focus on legal matters should result in advice and clarification on legal matters becoming available more quickly, rather than being dealt with through the normal staffing process. Of course, such a process should not undermine the formal chain of command.

The nature of the military legal advisor's work demands that he understand the military strategic and operational context being considered by higher headquarters. If there is a technical line of communication, that professional advice and support can be obtained in direct communication and supervision and control is ensured.

The process is facilitated if it naturally follows that military legal advisors in superior headquarters are senior to those in subordinate headquarters and where those in superior headquarters actively take on the role of providing support through technical advice and encouragement to military legal advisors in subordinate headquarters. That would be the normal procedure in national chains of command in States that regularly deploy legal advisors on military operations.

In a multinational context, however, this will be somewhat complicated by the existence of parallel multinational and national lines of communication and an understanding of the scope of responsibility of these is often woefully absent. One could, for example, have a national brigade-sized formation deployed under the command of a regional defence organization, such as NATO, which, in turn, is carrying out a mandate of the United Nations Security Council. All of those parties might have their own interest in and attitude towards legal problems that have to be addressed. It is important, in cases such as these, for careful thought to be given to the appropriate legal lines of communication before deployment, otherwise the ad hoc arrangements that are inevitably put in place may not work efficiently.

However, some criticism of the idea of legal lines of communication has been expressed by legal advisors at a lower, for example brigade, level. Some considered that this would impede decision-making because of the failure of higher legal

31.04 authorities to respond quickly enough, doubts about whether those at higher headquarters had the relevant training or experience, difficulties over communications, the tendency for superiors to make broad policy decisions that do not fit the situation on the ground, and the tendency, if such a chain is in place, to refer everything to higher authority. If a pending decision is a real showstopper—for example, it relates to a war crime—one would refer it anyway. It would make the deployed legal advisor's position untenable if, when advising the commander, he had to act as a mouthpiece for his legal superior.

It follows, therefore, that those superior in the legal line need to have even more legal knowledge and operational experience than their subordinates if they are to be able to perform their role effectively. The legal superior needs an understanding of the position of the deployed legal advisor. A light touch is required to make the technical chain viable. The emphasis must be on a collaborative approach and a recognition that, just as in many other staff functions, horizontal and vertical liaison is required to make the headquarters function as efficiently as possible, so that legal advisors can feel comfortable about seeking counsel and advice from more senior lawyers whenever necessary. If the senior lawyers are in possession of all the relevant factual information and are unable to persuade their juniors about the correct interpretation of the law to be applied to those facts, they are always able, as a last resort, to invoke the power of command of their own commanders in order to put things right.

3. *Legal Support Staff.* It is common in civilian legal practice for staff to be engaged who specialize in dealing with legal work, being familiar with legal language, forms, procedures, and accounting practices, and so able to deal with many of the routine and administrative tasks of a legal practice and free lawyers to concentrate on work with a legal content. In some countries members of such legal support staff have additional training that permits them to carry out certain types of routine legal work. They are sometimes referred to as 'para-legals'. The question arises as to whether there is a role for such personnel in the armed forces. Of course, there will be the usual requirement for clerical or administrative support staff, whether military or civilian, but is there a need beyond that? One suggestion ventured was that such specially trained personnel could carry out legal training, especially in the requirements of the law of armed conflict, at non-commissioned officer and other rank (enlisted personnel) level because they might relate better to the audience than the legal advisor. Others commented they might do more harm than good and that it would be better for legal advisors to have better military training themselves to enable them to do the training of others effectively. In the British Army, legal training of personnel below commissioned officer rank is carried out at unit level by unit staff as part of normal military training but there would have been some input from legal officers into that training, the rationale being that such training reinforces the role of the chain of command in monitoring and ensuring compliance with basic law of armed conflict principles.

A.P.V. ROGERS[†] AND DARREN STEWART

II. Some Practical Experience

31.04

1. *Appointment and Tasks of Legal Advisor.* Ideally a formation's own legal advisor should deploy with the formation on military operations. However, the reality of military life is such that ad hoc formations are often put together for operations and the legal advisor may, therefore, be brought in from outside. To enable the headquarters staff and the legal advisor to form a good working relationship, the legal advisor should be attached six months before deployment, or at the very least, two months. The legal advisor needs to be part of the planning process from the outset.

His tasks will include the following:

First, to ensure that all personnel subordinate in the chain of command are aware of their legal responsibilities. This has to be commensurate with their level of responsibility. That includes general legal responsibilities as well as those peculiar to the mission. The preparation of pocket cards, leaflets, or pamphlets with, for example, the basic principles of the law of armed conflict or the rules for the use of lethal force, would be one way of dealing with this requirement. Or, if such materials already exist, training on their implementation may be necessary.

Second, training staff to recognize potential legal problems and seek legal advice. This involves liaison with the staff branches that are likely to be dealing with problems that may have a legal dimension, in particular those dealing with personnel, intelligence, operations, and civil–military cooperation. Even branches dealing with logistics may need some legal advice, for example, on status-of-forces agreements, taxation, and privileges and immunities.

Third, reflecting on possible problem areas and, through research, writing for publication, attendance at conferences, discussions with other lawyers and so on, trying to find solutions.

Fourth, developing doctrine, including analysis of past 'lessons learned' exercises. Maintenance of and accessibility to a lessons-learned database is crucial. This would include not only national data but also that of allies or international bodies such as NATO or the United Nations. Attendance at mission rehearsal exercises and other pre-deployment or leadership training and visits to legal offices at higher headquarters, particularly for those filling senior deployed posts such as chief or deputy legal advisor for a particular operation, would be useful forms of preparation.

Part of the problem here is that States do not learn from each other; that although there are welcome initiatives by various international bodies, seats of learning, or societies to discuss 'lessons learned', the information gathered is quite fragmented; and that when relevant institutions are established, the emphasis tends not to be on the legal aspects of military operations. What is needed is a broader legal community with shared knowledge and information which can be integrated with national training requirements.

Fifth, and most importantly, the legal advisor needs to be aware of and involved in the operational plans that are being developed by the headquarters staff and provide legal advice as appropriate.

A.P.V. ROGERS† AND DARREN STEWART

31.04 2. *Compatibility with Other Legal Functions*. One problem is that this operational role might be incompatible with other aspects of peacetime work of the legal advisor that appears more pressing. Legal advisors, when not deployed on military operations, may be required to deal with a multitude of legal matters, for example, disciplinary and court-martial cases, contracts and claims, legal assistance to service personnel about private legal problems, boards of inquiry, and other investigations, so insufficient time may be devoted to legal preparation for military operations. Either time must be set aside for this or an operational law speciality needs to be developed.

It is clear that some important skills such as applying logic, quick thinking and flexibility of approach, calmness and composure in time of stress, and advocacy of advice are important assets in an effective legal advisor both in peacetime and on operations. It is the reality for most military legal advisors that the majority of peacetime roles are non-operational in character. It follows that careful career development and the necessary pre-operational training provide the foundation for operational legal advisors. When added to 'on-the-job experience', and—for senior appointments—experience and maturity, there should be the necessary preparation for the legal advisor to work effectively on operations.

3. *Separation of Functions*. One approach would be to have an operational law speciality. Because of the increasing complexity of the law in this field, and the time it takes to develop a specialist, it is apparent that the generalist legal advisor, despite having some of the useful skills mentioned above, would probably be inadequate. The specialist approach would work only in those States where the legal services are large enough and the operational activity is sufficient to justify it. Even then, it may be difficult to achieve without there being a detrimental impact on the career development of legal advisors. Too much specialization can also be a handicap if legal advisors lose sight of general principles of law or of the consequences in another area of decisions taken in the area of specialization. So the answer to this dilemma will require the right balance to be found, involving a mixture of career development, legal supervision, and specialized training.

4. *Consistency of Legal Advice*. Military commanders require consistency of legal advice. It is no help to them if, presented with the same problem, two lawyers give different advice. There might then be a temptation for the commander to seek the legal advice that best suits his purposes. It has been wryly observed that if you put two lawyers together you get a legal argument. So how does one achieve consistency of legal advice? It is difficult enough nationally when only one legal system applies. It becomes more difficult when international law is added and even more so in a coalition of States, whose national laws and legal traditions differ and whose interpretations of international law may vary.

In a perfect world, there would be international agreement, at least within a coalition or regional defence organization, about acceptable standards, courses, or qualifications for those entrusted with operational law training or legal advice. In a less perfect world, commanders, knowing the importance of legal considerations in

A.P.V. ROGERS[†] AND DARREN STEWART

military planning and understanding the doctrine of command responsibility, would themselves see to it that mechanisms aimed at achieving legal consistency are established. However, they are likely to have more pressing priorities. In the world as it is, legal advisors will have to take the initiative here. **31.04**

The legal advisor has to understand the national positions of respective troop contributing States in order to be able to advise the Force Commander of his options with respect to force employment and those issues which are likely to be friction points for alliance cohesion. There are significant benefits if national legal advisors similarly understand the alliance or coalition context.

The legal chain of command discussed earlier can help. Even in military operations conducted by one State, clear legal annexes or explanatory memoranda in operational documentation is essential, particularly in covering issues such as the national position on the force mandate and sensitive matters, of which targeting and detention are two examples. That becomes even more important in a multinational environment where clear statements of the alliance position on legal issues would be helpful but in reality, owing to political considerations, are not always forthcoming. In the absence of such written annexes, regular meetings of legal advisors in an attempt to reach unity of opinion on difficult issues are also necessary. Legal advisors require the ability to take a detached and objective view of their own national positions so that they can explain these adequately to their coalition colleagues.

In the event of insoluble differences of opinion among legal advisors, one would expect clarification to be sought from superiors in the legal chain of command. If time and security considerations permit, opinions could also be sought from acknowledged experts.

5. *Legal Interoperability*. The point about consistency of legal advice is that it eases legal interoperability. Legal interoperability means ensuring that within a military alliance or coalition, despite different levels of ratification of international treaties and different interpretations of those treaties and of customary international law, military operations can be conducted effectively and within the law.

That involves identifying likely problem areas, understanding the various national positions, and trying to achieve a legal practice to which all can subscribe. In the event of insurmountable legal differences, procedures have to be adopted on how best to proceed.[24] As these are often seen as the primary stumbling blocks upon which alliance or coalition operations suffer setbacks (or as the military describes it, friction), this approach will go a considerable way towards building force unity and provide the commander with freedom of action. In so doing operational and tactical level solutions arrived at in theatre will tend to strip away

[24] According to Häussler, even though it will most likely be impossible to overcome policy differences at field level, military lawyers can do their part in sorting out the worst effects thereof. To that end they should liaise regularly from the earliest possible stage onward and find ways to properly factor irresolvable difference into the planning and execution of missions. See U. Häussler in 3–4 *Military Law and Law of War Review* (2005), 151.

31.04 all but the most irreconcilable legal differences. This will in turn expose, often uncomfortably so, the fact that it is differing national policy considerations, often dressed up as legal concerns, which prove most problematic to effective multinational operations rather than the law itself.

How can this be achieved? First, one has to try to arrive at a common understanding and interpretation of the applicable law, with irreconcilable differences identified. Second, one has to try and anticipate problems that may arise in the practical application of that body of law, noting where differences of interpretation and approach occur. An important element of this is in trying to learn lessons from past experience and project these forward to where potential legal problems might arise in the future. Third, it is necessary to draw up an agreed plan or set of procedures which can be implemented when the anticipated problems arise. These are referred to by the military as Standard Operating Procedures (SOPs). These SOPs will often require prior agreement by troop contributing States before being put in place. In the absence of such contingencies, legal advisors will at least need a checklist of unresolved issues and possible approaches to dealing with them. It would be most desirable if such a list were to be prepared by national authorities which could then be supplemented by 'in theatre' knowledge. Fourth, the plan or procedures must be kept up-to-date in the light of changing circumstances.

An important element in all this is to develop personal contacts with legal advisors at all levels of the command.[25] From these contacts agreements, arrangements, and procedures can be developed. Contact with outside experts, for example, from international organizations, non-governmental organizations, governmental organizations, treaty organizations and others, such as universities, may be helpful in resolving potential problems.

1. The Pre-Deployment Phase

1. *Timing*. Timing is everything. Ideally, the lawyer needs to be part of the deployable formation's staff. Integration into the staff is important—six months prior to deployment is preferable and two months workable, depending on the number of legal staff and the type of work likely to be undertaken, though it is better to send a lawyer at the last minute than none at all. The legal advisor with operational responsibilities may be regarded by the staff as a novel concept, and it may take time for them to get used to it. Several of the experts consulted stressed the importance of developing a good working relationship between the commander and his staff and legal advisor well before the deployment takes place.[26] This will enable

[25] Andres Munoz, in an email of 7 November 2007 to co-author A.P.V. Rogers.

[26] One commented that he was the legal advisor at a military base during military operations when several operational legal advisors rotated through every four months. Almost none of these gained the confidence of the commander who preferred, informally, to seek advice from him, the base legal advisor, not because his legal advice was better but because he was known and trusted.

the legal advisor's presence and availability to become known and for a sense of awareness of the legal implications of military planning to be created. 31.04

2. *Tasks.* Part of the legal advisor's integration process will involve getting to know the commander and his staff, including the political, or policy, advisor as well as the commanding officers and other key personnel of subordinate units, hoping to gain their trust in the process. Legal advisors must not only develop working relationships with key staff they are to advise, but also have an intimate understanding of the processes and operation of the headquarters they are to work in so that they know when the best opportunities arise to influence operations and staff activity by the provision of legal advice.

Working relationships will be tested under difficult, stressful circumstances and therefore must be able to sustain the stress of operational dynamics, including the tempo of operations, so that objective, clear, and pragmatic legal advice continues to be sought and listened to.

It may be helpful to make contact with relevant outside bodies, including Sending State and host nation officials and representatives of, for example, the International Committee of the Red Cross and other non-governmental organizations. The extent and nature of these contacts will not only depend upon the time available but also the level of the headquarters, as certain levels of command would not expect to have detailed dealings with non-governmental organizations. It is also likely that tactical level contact will be with field delegates who are unlikely to be identified or available for more formal contact prior to deployment.

The legal advisor will have to become familiar with the mandate for and legal background to the deployment, including status-of-forces issues. He should also deal with any of the issues mentioned in the previous section that should have been addressed as part of the peacetime preparation. This should follow from the operational planning process, which should have had legal input. The process is considerably easier when a legal advisor is on the staff of a headquarters which is deployed and therefore he can be heavily involved in the planning process prior to deployment, in effect having 'ownership' of the responsibility for legal input from an early stage. More problematic is where a legal advisor is deployed late and must therefore obtain situational awareness of the nature of the operation and of the legal issues through a combination of pre-deployment training or preparation and a detailed in-theatre handover.

In the case of multinational operations, the legal advisor will need knowledge of the broader alliance understanding of the mandate and the legal basis for the conflict, as previously discussed.

Legal advisors will also need to deal with legal issues peculiar to the deployment. These will depend on the nature of the conflict, the mandate, and nature of a particular mission. Issues that may require particular attention include the legal status of the parties to the conflict or operating in the conflict zone, detention, targeting, policing powers, and occupation law. Obviously, the legal aspects of, say, targeting, would be very different if the mission were to run a detention centre, or to

31.04 ensure security to permit nation-building, or to 'use all necessary means' to defeat an enemy in conventional warfare. Some knowledge of the local law, legal system, religion, culture, and socio-economic circumstances may be required. There may be status-of-forces issues to be resolved, such as memoranda of understanding with the local authorities about how powers conferred by a United Nations mandate can be exercised in their territory.

While legal skills are essential for the legal advisor, core military skills must also be maintained and developed. These will include general military skills such as the use of personal weapons but also the specific military skills required prior to deploying to an operational theatre, for example, ambush drills or improvised explosive device drills.

2. *Deployment*

1. *Legal Resources*. The first issue concerns manpower. Some States are better endowed with legal advisors that others. They would, therefore, expect their legal advisors to provide a wider range of expertise, covering things like contracts, claims, and military discipline as well as the legal aspects of the conduct of military operations. One would expect to find at least one legal advisor when a national or multinational contingent is operating independently, probably at brigade level. Some States may not be able to achieve this but will have, at a higher level, legal advisors who can be called upon for advice. This is often referred to as reach-back which the authors regard as an adequate, but inferior solution.

By way of example, a medium-sized State, the United Kingdom, would certainly have a legal advisor of the rank of major at brigade headquarters. He might be assisted by a legal advisor in the rank of captain, whose main responsibility would be to deal with disciplinary matters but who should also have been prepared so that he can deal with operational matters, such as shooting incident reviews, as well. It is important for the brigade legal advisor to have some years of military-related legal practice behind him including operational experience. Having a legal team of two enables the less experienced to gain experience under supervision as well as providing for greater flexibility. There is greater scope for those at higher headquarters to gain experience. Typically, a divisional headquarters would have a legal advisor in the rank of lieutenant-colonel with six to seven, more junior, legal advisors in support. That would enable the legal branch to cover a wider range of services. For example, if the Ministry of Defence, which normally deals with claims, does not deploy a claims officer to the operational theatre, the divisional legal branch might take on responsibility for that work. It should be mentioned here that in the United Kingdom the prosecution of courts-martial is now performed by a separate and independent authority, so that work would not fall to be dealt with at brigade or divisional headquarters.

In general, the rank of deployed legal advisor will correspond with the normal rank level of the staff at the headquarters in question. Where civilian legal advisors are deployed, the pool of those available may be smaller if they have to be volunteers, which might result in civilians of a higher grade than their service counterparts being deployed. To avoid tensions and improve working relations, it would be wise for them not to insist on being treated as of equivalent military rank to their civilian grade. **31.04**

One would also expect legal advisors to be supported by such administrative and clerical staff and interpreters as they need to carry out their work effectively. The presence of such staff would enable legal advisors to concentrate on legal matters.

What legal equipment is needed? Despite the trend towards paperless offices, lawyers tend still to maintain paper files and libraries of books and journals.[27] It has been pointed out that, in some States, books published abroad are expensive and hard to come by. When deploying on military operations, legal advisors may be severely restricted, because of weight and space limitations, in the books and papers that they are permitted to take with them. Experience of military operations tends to indicate, too, that the tempo is such that there is not much time for legal research. Careful decisions will have to be made about what is essential and what can be left behind. In an armed conflict situation, legal advisors will certainly need the relevant treaty texts and commentaries, national or international manuals, and the odd interpretative or practical monograph but there probably will not be space for many additional books. In other operations, key documents will include anything related to the mandate, status-of-forces issues, rules of engagement, and the like. Similarly, legal advisors who may be called upon to provide personal legal assistance to members of the armed forces, for example the preparation of wills, need to give careful thought to the extent that such a service is viable in an operational climate and what minimal books and documents will be essential for the purpose.

Fortunately, much information is now available via the Internet. For example, all the law of armed conflict treaties and commentaries are available on the website of the International Committee of the Red Cross. Assuming that military operations will be carried out in circumstances where Internet access can be assured, or there is adequate electric power, the weight and space problem is eased. In some States, legal advisors will be issued with personal laptop computers with all the necessary material, or portable hard drives, compact discs, or other external storage devices, as well as printers, mobile telephones, digital cameras, and similar equipment. Mobility is another point to be considered. The legal advisor engaged in nation-building projects may need the use of a vehicle and driver if his work requires contact with the host nation authorities and relevant United Nations authorities or non-governmental organizations. However, there may be questions of compatibility of equipment, security of information, and personnel that will have to be considered in this context. Communications are also vital. Sometimes legal advisors

[27] It is interesting to note that British experience in recent years, learnt from litigation in domestic courts and the EctHR, has highlighted the importance of operational record keeping and audit trails not only for legal advisors but more generally for deployed British forces.

31.04 do not have access to secure communications and this can be a severe handicap to the effective performance of their role.

2. *Legal Issues.* The legal issues that are likely to arise will depend on the nature of the deployment. In an armed conflict situation, one of the biggest areas of legal uncertainty relates to the status of the conflict and, therefore, about what law to apply. Thus, in order to apply the right body of law, legal advisors will ask whether the conflict is international or non-international. When does an occupation end? What is the situation if there is an occupation but also an ongoing fight with insurgents? In counter-insurgency operations, to what extent does the host government have a power of veto over planned military operations—must they be consulted? These questions are so bound up with political considerations that they can hardly be left to deployed legal advisors to resolve and should be tackled prior to deployment.

Another perennial problem area relates to the arrest, handling, treatment, and handover of detainees, who are usually nationals of or residents in the host nation, and the legal powers associated with such actions. Again, these are issues that must be clarified prior to deployment. Sometimes there are problems about transferring detainees to local prisons because of human rights concerns and also related to evidence about the handover of detainees. Memoranda of understanding covering the handover of detainees, their treatment, and rights of visiting them have proved useful.

Deployment of troops is usually done on the basis that the local courts will have no jurisdiction over them, particularly with regard to the on-duty acts of those personnel. In an armed conflict situation, that position would be maintained by force of arms if necessary. In cases where troops are deployed with the assent of the host nation, however, it is best to have memoranda of understanding with the local authorities confirming their lack of jurisdiction over members of the Sending State forces. Of course it follows that the Sending State authorities need a form of jurisdiction over the personnel concerned so that good discipline can be enforced and offenders can be brought to trial if necessary. There has been some criticism in recent years of the activities of civilian security personnel who did not seem to be subject to any form of jurisdiction to curb their activities. It is important to ensure that there are no 'legal black holes'.[28]

Very often, the Force is tasked with securing the environment so that other activities, for example, nation-rebuilding or the establishment of the rule of law, can be conducted effectively. The legal advisor can be involved in both aspects and may have to deal with rules of engagement and targeting as well as assisting the local courts to function.

[28] This suggests a clear requirement for the military legal advisor to keep abreast of 'soft law' developments such as the Montreux Document and various International Codes of Practice for PMSCs in varying forms of development and which seek to provide an industry-led self-regulatory framework in this area.

A.P.V. ROGERS† AND DARREN STEWART

One expert consulted said that the greatest challenge he faced was in connection with operations in support of establishing and maintaining the rule of law, where a lack of mission focus, preparation, training, and resources posed considerable problems. For example, assisting local courts to function may prove difficult if the different parties involved are not prepared to cooperate. In some cases, the courts function well; they just need help with equipment or with training in human rights law. It is very often a question of 'mentoring, monitoring, and training', or creating or ensuring the functioning of the judicial system. That might require the building of facilities, such as prisons or court buildings or the employment of judges. A functioning judicial system is part of ensuring security. However, the legal advisor must be attuned to the local way of doing things and has to proceed on the foundation of the laws already in place. It could be said that the military legal advisor is not best placed to support such activity, the lead properly lying with civilian authorities. However, it is equally the case, and commented upon by a number of experts, that a considerable lapse of time can occur between resolution of a conflict, or the return to a 'near' peaceful scenario, and the engagement of civilian agencies, both domestic and international. As this period is often one which presents considerable opportunities (the golden hour so to speak), there is initial activity which can be undertaken by military legal advisors that can assist in creating the conditions for future success of the civilian effort. This underscores the need both for consultation prior to deployment as discussed previously, as well as the consideration of what actions can best enable the broader civilian plan—assuming, of course, one exists.[29] **31.04**

Another expert commented that the legal advisor could perform a useful function when the armed forces are fighting irregular opponents that tend to disregard the rule of law by ensuring a timely analysis of facts and law relating to any violations so that accurate reports can be issued about them in good time. The same could, of course, be said about alleged violations by the legal advisor's own forces.

A legal advisor working in a multinational environment can have both national and international responsibilities, depending on the nature of his post. This can lead to a conflict of loyalties if, as is sometimes the case, rules of engagement are classified at national level, which does not allow them to be shared with allies, or national caveats conflict with alliance planning, or questions of State responsibility arise when things go wrong.

Some kind of legal back-up is therefore needed to support deployed legal advisors. Thus reach-back, both on a national basis and in the case of multinational operations, to those static multinational headquarters in the chain of command where these exist, is essential. This must be a formalized process and not merely a 'calling in' of favours or imposing on those perceived to be subject-matter experts.

[29] Reference to this task as a likely output has become much more commonplace in military planning. It both covers Rule of Law activity (also referred to as part of stabilization operations) and reflects the integration of military effect as part of a whole of government approach (the Comprehensive Approach).

31.04 Without adequate reach-back a sense of isolation can result in a drop in morale and also lead to a dangerous dislocation in perception between the operational or tactical level and the strategic. This applies equally to the consideration of legal issues as it does to the strictly military ones. As has already been mentioned in the discussion of the legal chain of command, reach-back is only effective if those at higher levels have the knowledge and experience to be able to help. Of course such measures depend on efficient means of communication, otherwise there will be no reach-back and no legal supervision.

3. Post-Deployment

1. At the conclusion of a tour of duty there is a strong urge to pack up and get home as quickly as possible but this must not be at the expense of ensuring that lessons learned are recorded and passed on. Failure to do so is not fair on those taking over and it can have a detrimental effect on subsequent operations.

Nor can this be left to the last moment, as important points may be forgotten. It must be done as a matter of routine during the tour of duty. That may be difficult to achieve, as dealing with day-to-day commitments may rightly seem to have a higher priority than maintaining an adequate record of lessons identified. A balanced perspective is also required to ensure that what is noted will be of benefit and is not merely a record of a particular tactic to deal with a passing problem. Capturing lessons identified is, therefore, a wearisome but necessary process. An alternative to placing an obligation on the individual to keep a continuous record might be to conduct a de-brief, which could be done out of theatre, with prepared, focused questions designed to draw out important experiences which are then recorded in a database which is kept up-to-date. Invariably the most desirable solution would be a combination of an ongoing 'in-theatre' lessons learned process, perhaps as part of an internal headquarters policy, coupled with a detailed de-brief at the end of the operational tour. If there is a formal de-briefing process, this should be conducted at a central location with returning staff before they proceed on post-operational leave.

Another possibility is for legal advisors in theatre to be required to submit periodic, say monthly, reports as one might forget important lessons when thinking back over a six-month period and there are other pressures after a tour that militate against the production of useful reports.

2. Ideally, there should be a national, or in the case of an alliance, a multinational database of lessons learned that is accessible from the field or from training establishments. It would be helpful if at least unclassified material in such a database were made available to academic institutions that specialize in war studies or operational law.[30]

[30] NATO has pursued work in this area by producing the Comprehensive Legal Overview Virtual Information System (CLOVIS) as a tool developed to increase information sharing, meet Allied Command Operations (ACO) requirements, encourage collaboration, and improve interoperability. Although this resource is only available to NATO Member State personnel or those personnel of States

3. Part of the process of passing on lessons learned is to include them in any handover briefings, whether oral or written, that are prepared for successors in post. Again a balance has to be achieved between focused communication of information and allowing the incoming military legal advisor to get on with the job. How handovers are conducted will depend on the military custom and ethos in the State concerned. Pre-deployment training and preparation should preferably be such that the handover can focus on bringing the replacement up-to-date with the current operational picture, ongoing work, and an introduction to key personalities within the headquarters, followed by a brief period of working together. In reality handovers may require other training on a spectrum from complete reading in to the conflict, legal issues, and the headquarters mission, which would be highly undesirable, to the scenario described earlier where an individual arrives well prepared. It is considered that the handover period devoted entirely to the discussion of legal issues should be from three to five days. Advance contact between the incumbent and the replacement will help shape this and where possible make the in-theatre processing and familiarization as easy as possible. **31.04**

authorized by NATO, it reflects the only truly international database of its kind the authors could identify. See article by S.L. Bumgardner, *The Transformer* 2013-01 available at: <http://www.act.nato.int/article-2013-1-7>.

Chapter 32

INTERNATIONAL LAW FOR MILITARY OPERATIONS

Conclusions and Perspectives

1. *General.* The International Law of Military Operations is relatively new and open for further development. While it encompasses 'all relevant aspects of military law that affect the conduct of operations',[1] it may still be premature to state that operational law is now 'recognized as a core legal discipline'.[2] Yet it may be acknowledged that in this emerging branch of international law, which has been shaped by the practice of many States, the role of legal scholarship was considerable from the outset and that cooperation between legal and operational experts may most effectively contribute to the rule of law in military operations. The principles and rules of this new discipline, as demonstrated in the various contributions to this Handbook, have drawn upon three classical branches of international law, i.e. the *jus ad bellum*, the *jus in bello*, and an emerging *jus post bellum*. The manner of that amalgamation and its intensity is part of a remarkable process that may itself influence the contents of those three branches of international law. The notion of operational law has undeniably already made its mark in the planning and conduct of military operations and its importance from an operational perspective has potentially far-reaching implications for both policy makers and practitioners. It is only natural that this is increasingly being realized at the level of legal scholarship as well.

2. This Handbook demonstrates the close relationship between legal theory and practice and the necessity of combining the two to ensure that operations are conducted in conformity with the law and that the law is capable of being applied in a way that takes account of operational challenges and realities. For international law to really 'matter' in the conduct of military operations, it must be capable of being applied in a way that enhances both of these goals. At the same time a theoretical classification of that new legal discipline is necessary and its wide range comprising different phases of international law application which have been kept

[1] US Army *Operational Law Handbook 2014* (Charlottesville, Virginia: The Judge Advocate General's Legal Center & School, International and Operational Law Department); US Field Manual 1-04, *Legal Support to the Operational Army* (2013), Section 1–5.

[2] US Army *Operational Law Handbook 2014*; *Legal Support to the Operational Army* (2013), Section 1–5.

DIETER FLECK AND TERRY D. GILL

apart for good reasons and will remain distinct is now more visible and open to a more comprehensive evaluation than before.

3. The *jus ad bellum* or international law on the use of force has been shaped by the prohibition of the use of force and the recognized exceptions to that core rule contained in Chapter VII of the UN Charter and the inherent right of self-defence. Its interpretation and implementation, unlike most other parts of operational law, is a matter of high-level decision-making. This of course does not exclude disputes being held at all levels on controversial aspects of certain of its rules. The ongoing discussion on such aspects may best demonstrate that international law is 'a system, a process, rather than [a simple catalogue of] rules or commands'.[3] While decisions relating to the *jus ad bellum* may belong to the realm of high policy, it makes its influence felt throughout all levels and aspects of military operations and is therefore a core component of the International Law of Military Operations.

4. The *jus in bello*, or law of war, more often referred to now as international humanitarian law applicable in armed conflict, is the most traditional and most specified of the legal disciplines to be considered in the context of military operations. The term 'humanitarian law' is very broad in that it not only focuses on the protection of the victims of armed conflict, but in fact relates to any action belligerent States may undertake during an armed conflict. Thus, it also comprises their relationship to neutral States and their operations in occupied territories after the end of active hostilities. It is due to the remarkable activities of the International Committee of the Red Cross and the International Red Cross and Red Crescent Movement that international humanitarian law was shaped, further developed, and implemented despite so many breaches. Hardly any other branch of international law can benefit today from a comparable dense discussion on the global scale, from so many *fora* provided for this discussion, and a proliferation of expertise worldwide. The relatively broad attention for these activities is part of a progressive development which includes the introduction of humanitarian principles and rules even in areas well beyond the realm of armed conflicts, i.e. beyond the specific field of application for which that body of law was originally designed. In this way, international humanitarian law has obtained a double relevance to military operations: firstly, as the applicable law relating to the conduct of hostilities and treatment of protected categories of persons and objects in situations of *de jure* armed conflict, whether international or non-international in character; secondly, as a source of guidance in crafting rules of best practice even in situations not amounting to an armed conflict.

(a) It is widely accepted today that principles and rules of international humanitarian law must also be observed in peace operations and related activities conducted

[3] R. Higgins, *Problems & Process. International Law and How We Use It* (Oxford: Clarendon Press, 1994), 10.

by the United Nations and by States.[4] While it is appropriate to positively respond to such a wider perception of and respect for international humanitarian law, certain clarifications remain necessary, to ensure a correct understanding and proper application of its rules in practice. The protection of victims of military operations is part of a balance which may require different considerations in armed conflicts than would normally be the case in peacetime. This distinction may be difficult in practice, as quite often the dividing line between peace and armed conflict is blurred. Peace enforcement operations are a case in point. The pertinent directives of the UN Secretary General on *Observance by United Nations Forces of International Humanitarian Law*[5] may be interpreted as limiting the application of international humanitarian law to situations where 'UN forces [are] engaged as combatants in an armed conflict', while it may also be held that in a more general sense not only enforcement and peace enforcement operations, but also all peace operations are affected by international humanitarian law, even if this perception is not explicitly confirmed in treaty law.[6] Similarly, the United States requires its forces to 'comply with the law of armed conflict during all armed conflicts, however such conflicts are characterized, and in all other military operations'.[7] A similar policy is observed by many other States and international organizations with a view to guiding military conduct in situations which may be difficult to define in an undisputable manner. This policy not only makes practical sense, as it avoids a 'double-book' attitude at operational level, it is also theoretically convincing, as key principles of humanitarian law, i.e. the distinction between civilian objects and military objectives, the avoidance of unnecessary suffering, and the principle of humanity, are as valid in peacetime as they are in armed conflict.

(b) The Security Council has developed an expanded role relating to international humanitarian law. In many emergency situations, both during and after armed conflicts, it has called States and non-State actors to respect its principles and rules.[8] Regional organizations have supported this trend. The well-known *European Union Guidelines on promoting compliance with international humanitarian law*[9] are designed to ensure that important aspects of this legal order are sufficiently present in political and military planning processes. Yet there is still a widespread lack of

[4] D. Fleck (ed.), *The Handbook of International Humanitarian Law*, 3rd edn (Oxford: Oxford University Press, 2013), Sections 421, 1305–9.

[5] Secretary General's Bulletin: *Observance by United Nations Forces of International Humanitarian Law*, ST/SGB/1999/13 (1999).

[6] Fleck (ed.), *Handbook of International Humanitarian Law*, Sections 1301–1352.

[7] Department of Defense, Law of War Program (DoD Directive 2311.01E, 9 May 2006), para. 4.1; US Navy, US Marine Corps, US Coast Guard, *The Commander's Handbook on the Law of Naval Operations* (NWP 1-14M, MCWP 5-12.1, COMDTPUB P5800.7A), para. 6.1.2 (June 2007).

[8] See G. Nolte, 'The Different Functions of the Security Council With Respect to Humanitarian Law', in V. Lowe, A. Roberts, J. Welsh, and D. Zaum (eds), *The United Nations Security Council and War. The Evolution of Thought and Practice since 1945* (Oxford: Oxford University Press, 2008), 519–34.

[9] *European Union Guidelines on promoting compliance with international humanitarian law,* [2005] OJ C 327/04, 1, 23 December 2005.

knowledge of existing principles and rules, and the issue of different legal approaches by States and non-State actors as to the interpretation and application of existing law remains important. New efforts are required to harmonize interpretation of pertinent obligations in multinational military operations. Differences have to be bridged for those forces which shoulder different legal obligations but are tasked to operate in concert.[10]

(c) While international humanitarian law may be seen as a guiding parameter for any use of force, irrespective of whether the situation qualifies *de jure* as an armed conflict, there are still limits for its application, as principles and rules for law enforcement operations may be different from the rules applicable to the conduct of hostilities. For law enforcement a strict rule to capture rather than kill applies, *habeas corpus* must be respected in any event, and each case of death by force must be formally investigated.[11] A more liberal approach may be taken for the conduct of hostilities, yet the principles of proportionality and necessity which have been developed in international humanitarian law are generally relevant for police operations and military operations in peacetime as much as during armed conflict, even if there may be differences in their application in a 'peace setting' as opposed to an 'armed conflict setting'.

(d) Human rights obligations also form a significant part of operational law. That significance may be seen under three different aspects.[12] Firstly, in an ideal situation there would be an express mandate by the Security Council and/or a regional organization requesting not only all parties to an armed conflict, but in particular peacekeeping forces in post-conflict situations to protect human rights.[13] Secondly, even where such commitment has not been expressly stated, peace operations are to respect the law of the Receiving State including its obligations under international law of which human rights are an important part. Finally, the human rights obligations of the Sending State apply extraterritorially for acts committed within their jurisdiction. The relationship between international humanitarian law and human rights has been shaped as part of a development,

[10] See e.g. Art. 21 Dublin Convention on Cluster Munitions of 30 May 2008.

[11] See Fleck, 'Law Enforcement and the Conduct of Hostilities: Two Supplementing or Mutually Excluding Legal Paradigms?' in A. Fischer-Lescano, H.-P. Gasser, T. Marauhn, and N. Ronzitti, *Frieden in Freiheit. Peace in Liberty. Paix en liberté* (Baden-Baden: Nomos, 2008), 391–407, at 405.

[12] See Fleck (ed.), *Handbook of International Humanitarian Law*, Section 1307; T.D. Gill, 'Some Thoughts on the Relationship Between International Humanitarian Law and International Human Rights Law: A Plea for Mutual Respect snd a Common-Sense Approach', *Yearbook of International Humanitarian Law 2013*, 251–66.

[13] In its recent practice the Security Council has confined itself to calling on all parties to the conflict to protect human rights and respect international humanitarian law, while the obligation of peace-keepers to comply with these rules themselves is obviously taken for granted, see e.g. SC Res. 1291 (2000), para. 15, with respect to the conflict in the Democratic Republic of Congo. For the interim UN authorities in Kosovo and East Timor the Security Council has included the maintenance of law and order (which should include the protection and promotion of human rights) in the respective mandates, without, however, establishing specific control mechanisms, see SC Res. 1244 (1999), para. 9, for Kosovo and SC Res. 1272 (1999), para. 2, for East Timor.

which started with the Human Rights Conference in Teheran 1968[14] and did not end with the adoption of major human rights principles in Article 75 of Protocol I Additional to the Geneva Conventions.[15] Legally speaking, this relationship may be characterized by mutual complementarity, as described by the Human Rights Committee,[16] and also by the *lex specialis* principle which, however, should not be misunderstood as applying to the general relationship between the two branches of international law as such, but rather relates to specific rights in specific circumstances. The International Court of Justice has stated in its Advisory Opinion on the *Threat or Use of Nuclear Weapons* that the 'test of what is an arbitrary deprivation of life... falls to be determined by the applicable *lex specialis*, namely, the law applicable in armed conflict that is designed to regulate the conduct of hostilities'.[17] More recently, in its Advisory Opinion on the *Wall in the Occupied Palestinian Territory*, the Court asserted that in armed conflicts some rights are governed exclusively by international humanitarian law, while others are governed exclusively by human rights, and still others are governed by both bodies of law. The Court expressly confirmed that in the latter case 'both these branches of international law, namely human rights law and, as *lex specialis*, international humanitarian law' must be considered.[18] This jurisprudence was confirmed in *Congo v. Uganda*.[19] It is of great significance for the conduct of military operations.

5. The *jus post bellum* or law applicable to the transition from armed conflict to peace is connected to the aforementioned categories of *jus ad bellum* and *jus in bello*, yet it covers a much wider range of topics, rules, and decision-makers. Focusing on peacemaking, *jus post bellum* is of a transitional nature, and it often requires a simultaneous application of peacetime law and the law of armed conflict.[20] Those applying *jus post bellum* today have to operate in a network between different legal orders and bodies of international and domestic law. They are challenged to reconcile a wide spectrum of interests and, as traditional solutions may remain

[14] Resolution XXIII Human Rights in Armed Conflict, in D. Schindler and J. Toman (eds), *The Laws of Armed Conflict*, 4th edn (Leiden: Nijhoff, 2004), 347.

[15] See M. Bothe, 'The Historical Evolution of International Humanitarian Law, International Human Rights Law, Refugee Law and International Criminal Law', in H. Fischer, U. Froissart, W. Heintschel von Heinegg, and C. Raap (eds), *Krisensicherung und Humanitärer Schutz. Crisis Management and Humanitarian Protection* (Berlin: Berliner Wissenschafts-Verlag, 2004), 37–45.

[16] General Comment No. 31, 'The Nature of the General Legal Obligation Imposed on States Parties to the Covenant', UN Doc. CCPR/C/21/Rev.1/Add. 13 (2004), <http://www.unhchr.ch/tbs/doc.nsf/(Symbol)/58f5d4646e861359c1256ff600533f5f?Opendocument>, paras 2, 10, 11; see also General Comments Nos 15, 18, and 28. All General Comments are available at <http://www.unhchr.ch/tbs/doc.nsf>.

[17] ICJ, *Legality of the Threat or Use of Nuclear Weapons*, Advisory Opinion of 8 July 1996, ICJ Reports, 1996, 226, *ILM* 35 (1996), 809, para. 25.

[18] ICJ, *Legal Consequences of the Construction of a Wall in the Occupied Palestinian Territory*, Advisory Opinion of 9 July 2004, General List no. 131, ICJ Reports, 2004, *ILM* 43 (2004), 1009 *et seq.*, paras 102–142, at 106.

[19] ICJ, *Case Concerning Armed Activities on the Territory of the Congo (Dem. Rep. Congo v. Uganda)*, 19 December 2005, para. 216.

[20] C. Stahn and J.K. Kleffner (eds), *Jus Post Bellum. Towards a Law of Transition From Conflict to Peace* (Cambridge: Cambridge University Press/T.M.C. Asser Press, 2008), 234.

exceptions, the need for compromises will be the rule. A comprehensive set of norms of *jus post bellum* cannot be developed easily. To accomplish that task, not only must an inventory of relevant treaty obligations be assessed; also the relationships between various applicable branches of law and the institutional frameworks for the law to operate are to be considered. Clear commitments to individual and collective responsibility are of particular relevance for this process, as for a stable peace justice must become visible, even if full reparation is impossible post-conflict.

6. As many military operations are conducted in the transitional phase between war and peace, the law of military operations is to a significant extent *jus post bellum*. This phase may be characterized by a lack of clear applicable rules mixed with additional requirements for enhanced civil–military cooperation in a difficult environment. Hence, specific efforts of military legal advisors are essential in this phase to identify pertinent rules and apply them in a convincing and effective manner. Sending States and international organizations should support this by providing necessary personnel support and issuing clear rules of behaviour for each mission.[21]

7. *Controversial Problems.* The present Handbook has been written in an effort to provide reliable information for practitioners and to encourage further research in the academic field. Both aims include an openness for existing controversies and for questions yet to be answered. Indeed, not all contributions are uncontroversial and some chapters have deliberately been written in an effort to carry a critical dialogue to further depths.

(a) The conceptual distinction between law enforcement and conduct of hostilities is a case in point. Discussion shows that different rules must apply in these two different modes of operation. The principles of necessity and proportionality will spell out differently for combat and police tasks. In combat, necessity is a Force enabler empowering both sides to employ the degree of force necessary within the law to achieve the goals of their respective missions and proportionality relates to the balance between military advantage and likely damage to civilians and civilian objects (and not to the use of force between combatants *inter se*), whereas in a law enforcement operation, necessity relates strictly to the question whether force may be employed to achieve a lawful purpose, in particular, in response to grave danger to the law enforcement officers themselves or to civilians, and likewise proportionality places strict limitations on the degree of force to achieve that purpose. Yet these differences will be a matter of graduation where risks for innocent persons exist, and they do not affect the applicability of the principles as such.[22] States deciding on the use of armed forces for law enforcement purposes bear a responsibility to consider the relevant legal implications and they must ensure that the personnel employed is trained in the applicable rules.

[21] The Council of the European Union *Generic Standards of Behaviour for ESDP Operations*, 8873/3/05REV 3 (18 May 2005) may be welcomed as a first step in this direction.

[22] Cf. Fleck, 'Law Enforcement and Conduct of Hostilities', 401–6.

(b) Operational detentions are in the focus of the dividing line between law enforcement and the conduct of hostilities. The principle that only prisoners of war enumerated in Article 4 of the Third Geneva Convention may be detained until the 'cessation of active hostilities'[23] and that *habeas corpus* rights must be ensured in all other situations is difficult enough to be translated to the requirements of non-international armed conflict. It is even more difficult in a peace enforcement action where a state of armed conflict does not exist or may be disputed, so that there may be ambiguity as to applicability of the law of armed conflict, including prisoner-of-war status. The executive branch must ensure that operational detentions are confined to imperative reasons of security. They must be limited in purpose, time, and procedures. Human rights must be fully respected. Parliaments and governments authorizing operational detentions are responsible for the full legality of their actions and they must exercise effective control over such activities.

(c) The legal bases for military deployment and the use of force may as such be a matter of dispute that cannot be resolved in every single case, even though one should be careful to distinguish between genuine lack of clarity as to the relevant facts and grey areas in the law on the one hand and simple violation of the law coupled with *ex parte* justifications on the other. Parties may continue to differ on the causes and modalities of their military action. It is all the more important to apply *jus in bello* rules irrespective of any consideration of *jus ad bellum* and to develop cooperative steps towards application of a *jus post bellum*. Parties may continue to differ on the causes and purposes underlying their resort to force. However, this should never result in or be used as a pretext for less than full compliance with the *jus in bello*, or prevent cooperative efforts to achieve peace and apply the *jus post bellum*, once the conflict has ended.

8. *Open Issues*. A number of issues had to be left open in this Handbook. It would go beyond its purpose to discuss the important influence national law and policy have on the conduct of any military operations. That discussion would have to be country-specific,[24] even if there will be similarities in many States, and it would transgress what is possible in a single volume. We have made one partial exception to this consideration, namely in relation to the right of personal or individual self-defence, which is largely governed by national criminal law. This was unavoidable, as this right is so closely related to military operations that its omission would have left many questions unanswered. Chapter 24 makes clear that the different 'guises' or applications of what is sometimes loosely referred to as 'self-defence' are, in fact quite distinct notions, albeit stemming from a common root. It is also clear, notwithstanding widely varying interpretations of what is allowed under personal self-defence, that it is at best a concept of limited usefulness in most situations arising in the context of military operations and should not be used out of context.

[23] Cf. Art. 118(1) GC III.

[24] For an excellent example see N.D. White, *Democracy Goes to War. British Military Deployments Under International Law* (Oxford: Oxford University Press, 2009). For a comparative study in the European region see G. Nolte (ed.), *European Military Law Systems* (Berlin: de Gruyter, 2003).

There are other topics, however, that would deserve further study in continuation of the contributions included in this Handbook:

(a) The post-conflict and peacetime application of rules of international humanitarian law should be evaluated, to specify their *lex specialis* role in relation to human rights and support their full implementation during armed conflict.

(b) The role of non-State actors in the conduct of military operations deserves further discussion. Even if they may be widely considered today as not only enjoying individual rights, but also bearing obligations under international law,[25] it may be difficult to see insurgent fighters as exercising law enforcement authority, unless they actually control territory and may thus exercise quasi-governmental authority over persons and territory in a classic civil war context. On the other hand, principles and rules of law enforcement go beyond existing human rights obligations and insurgents executing law enforcement measures should be held to respect all relevant obligations irrespective of their authority to act at all.

(c) Command and control issues will remain case-specific, and even within one single organization, like the UN, different rules may apply to regulate specific cases. Yet it is striking that rules concerning general terms and conditions, such as operational command and operational control, have not yet been formally adopted in the UN, so that the authors of sub-Chapter 6.5 had to develop their commentary on the basis of more informal internal policy. In the interest of transparency and accountability such policy should be adopted in a formal review process and duly published. Relevant international organizations should also take initiatives to ensure that reparation be made for wrongful acts committed during military operations.

(d) Economic reconstruction and military support that may be given to this end are too important in any post-conflict situation to leave them unregulated. International organizations and States involved in post-conflict reconstruction should cooperate in the development of principles and rules that help to ensure respect for self-determination, national sovereignty, and individual protection, and avoid conflicting situations for individual soldiers participating in such activities.

9. There will remain a variety of different sources of the international law relevant for military operations. For the applicable treaty law with its overlapping rules and varying States parties, interpretive efforts are required to ensure common understanding. Rules of customary law must be identified, based on the well-established components of practice and *opinio juris*. Even where the customary status of a certain rule may be disputed, its characterization as best practice, shaped by international experience, national interests, and national law, may be relevant. For all rules so identified the task of implementation and enforcement requires particular efforts to be taken, to ensure restoration of the rule of law with a clear sense of international responsibility. Lawyers at all levels are involved in this process.

[25] See A. Clapham, *Human Rights Obligations of Non-State Actors* (Oxford: Oxford University Press, 2006).

A proactive role to ensure compliance with existing rules may be key to a successful performance of military missions.

10. Aside from the three branches of international law referred to in the preceding paragraphs, it is clear that the International Law of Military Operations draws upon and is influenced by many other sub-disciplines of international law. These include, as has been shown in various chapters, the law of the sea, air law, the law of international responsibility, and international criminal law. These branches of international law provide a framework for shaping operations themselves, identifying rights and obligations of the State(s) involved and those of third States and avoiding unnecessary contention and disputes. The complexity of contemporary military operations is such that a firm understanding of how these areas of international law relate to military operations is essential from both a practical and a more theoretical perspective. Yet, in many cases, insufficient attention has been given to these implications and how the law both influences and is influenced by the conduct of military operations. The inclusion of chapters in this Handbook relating to these areas of international law will hopefully contribute to a better understanding of this mutual relationship and stimulate further clarification and development of the law, where necessary.

11. Finally, it is clear that, while no complete summary of the conclusions of a volume such as this is possible, one point in particular deserves some attention. That is the role of the (military) legal advisor who is, and should be, involved at all stages and levels of planning and conducting any military operation and in the training and instruction of the personnel who carry it out. This crucial role is twofold, firstly to ensure that commanders and sub-commanders receive the necessary legal advice to enable them to conduct their mission, and secondly, to promote and as far as possible to ensure that the operation is conducted in full compliance with the law. This task is a demanding, indispensable, and essential one and requires both a firm command of the law, operational and situational awareness, and an ability to constructively guide and advise on a wide range of issues and in varying situations. It is hoped that this Handbook will contribute to a better understanding of this task and will aid in its successful execution.

DIETER FLECK AND TERRY D. GILL

The Manual on International Law of Military Operations

PART I

GENERAL ISSUES

Chapter 1 Concept and Sources of the International Law of Military Operations

The International Law of Military Operations comprises all areas of public international law which relate to: 1.01

- **the provision of a legal basis for any type of military operation in an international context;**
- **the command and control of such operations;**
- **the deployment of forces from the State(s) participating in the operation to and within the mission area (and vice versa) through the transit of international sea and airspace, and through the territory of third States;**
- **the use and regulation of force for the conduct of hostilities and law enforcement operations, the maintenance of public order, and the treatment of persons captured or detained within the context of the conduct of the operation;**
- **the status of the forces throughout the duration of the operation; and**
- **the legal responsibility of States, of international organizations, and of individual members of the forces and all other entities participating in the operation for any violations of international law and contravention of relevant international regulations in force for the operation.**

As such, the International Law of Military Operations includes rules embedded in: 1.02

- **the UN Charter and customary international law relating to the use of force and the maintenance and restoration of international peace and security,**
- **international humanitarian law,**
- **international human rights law,**

— other areas of conventional and customary international law relevant to international military operations such as international law relative to the status of forces and the exercise of criminal jurisdiction, the international law of the sea and air law, the law of international responsibility and international criminal law, international environmental law, and the law of international organizations.

It is supplemented by national constitutions, laws, and regulations. While the conduct of hostilities in armed conflict is regulated by international humanitarian law as *lex specialis*, law enforcement operations undertaken outside the context of armed conflict must follow human rights law. Where authority is exercised over persons or territory within the context of an armed conflict, both bodies of law are applicable and should be applied in accordance with established rules of legal interpretation and methodology to ensure compliance with all applicable legal obligations and resolve any conflict between rules from different bodies of law which may arise.

1.03 Alongside rules of positive international law of either a conventional or customary nature, international military operational law is also influenced and to a significant extent regulated by rules and practices which are not of a legal nature, but which are part of the policy of States and international organizations. International cooperation has led to accepted standards and best practice, even in the absence of treaty or established customary obligations. However, while States and international organizations may adopt further going restrictions on the employment of force or allow for more favourable treatment of persons who have been detained for any lawful reason, they may never exceed what is allowed by the relevant binding international legal obligations applicable in a given situation.

1.04 In applying rules from different branches of international law, all applicable rules must be taken into account and interpreted and applied with a view to giving them the fullest possible effect. This follows both from the obligations the parties have undertaken and are bound by and from the fact that international law is an integrated system of rights and obligations which is governed by established rules of interpretation and legal methodology.

1.05 The International Law of Military Operations is therefore more than a mere collection of rules from different legal sub-disciplines. It can serve as an instrument which is aimed at harmonizing obligations arising from different legal sub-disciplines and translating such obligations from the abstract level of treaty and customary law to operational directives aimed at applying these obligations in the practical context of military operations.

Chapter 2 History and Development of the International Law of Military Operations

The International Law of Military Operations has developed in both theory and practice in response to the development of: 2.01
- **(a) the nature of warfare;**
- **(b) the use of military forces; and**
- **(c) underlying international norms.**

The International Law of Military Operations is further developing in a reactive manner challenging the military legal advisor to stay current and to anticipate future developments in law and practice. 2.02

Chapter 3 Human Rights and International Humanitarian Law: General Issues

In military operations amounting to an armed conflict, international humanitarian law applies. Human rights law is generally considered to apply to the extent that individuals are subject to the jurisdiction of a State or international organization. 3.01

When applicable simultaneously, international humanitarian law and human rights law are complementary. In case of collision between a norm of international humanitarian law and a norm of human rights law, the more specific norm prevails in principle. 3.02

In the event of a conflict between, on the one hand, applicable international humanitarian law and human rights law, and, on the other hand, obligations of States under the United Nations Charter, the latter prevails. 3.03

Chapter 4 Conceptual Distinction and Overlaps Between Law Enforcement and the Conduct of Hostilities

Forces involved in contemporary military operations are often called upon to assume functions both of law enforcement and of hostilities, each of which are governed by different legal standards. It is therefore important to distinguish between these two concepts, identify potential overlaps between them, and determine how the respective legal paradigms governing each type of operation interrelate. 4.01

4.02 **The generic concept of law enforcement can be defined for the purposes of operational law as comprising all territorial and extra-territorial measures taken by a State or other collective entity to maintain or restore public security, law and order or to otherwise exercise its authority or power over individuals, objects, or territory. The rules and principles of international law governing the conduct of law enforcement activities form the legal paradigm of law enforcement.**

4.03 **The generic concept of hostilities refers to the resort to means and methods of warfare between parties to an armed conflict. Strictly speaking, the actual 'conduct' of hostilities corresponds to the sum total of all hostile acts carried out by individuals directly participating in hostilities. The rules and principles of international law governing the conduct of hostilities form the legal paradigm of hostilities.**

4.04 **Within the context of an armed conflict, the paradigms of law enforcement and of hostilities can apply in parallel to different persons and objects at the same time and location. The legal paradigm of law enforcement continues to govern all exercise by parties to the conflict of their authority or power outside the conduct of hostilities. The resort to means and methods of warfare between parties to an armed conflict is governed by the legal paradigm of hostilities even if the ultimate purpose of its military operations is to maintain, restore, or otherwise impose public security, law, and order.**

4.05 **The legal paradigm of hostilities imposes special restrictions on certain means and methods of warfare, such as riot control agents, expanding bullets, or undercover operations and other forms of deception, although very similar means and methods are widely used by law enforcement officials in peacetime.**

PART II

MILITARY OPERATIONS WITHIN THE CONTEXT OF THE UN COLLECTIVE SECURITY SYSTEM

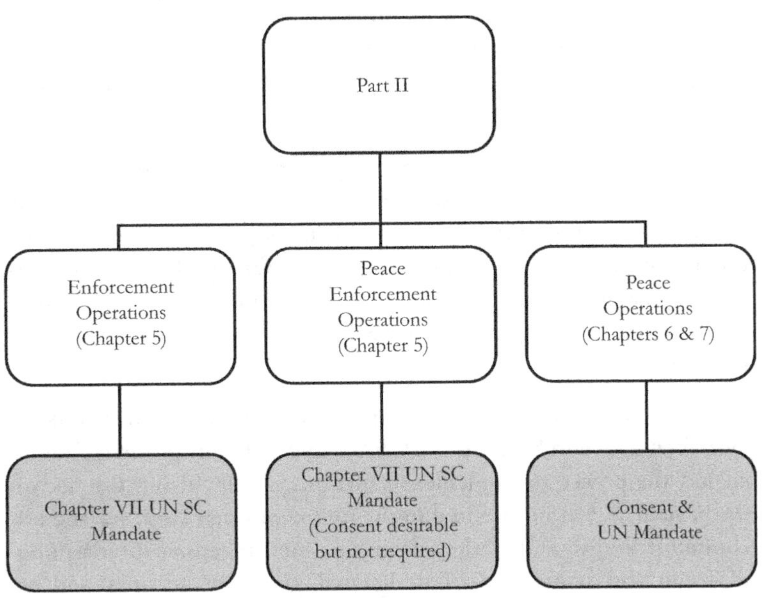

Chapter 5 Enforcement and Peace Enforcement Operations

5.1 Legal Characterization and Basis for Enforcement Operations and Peace Enforcement Operations under the Charter

Enforcement Action taken or authorized by the Security Council of a military nature can be conceptually subdivided into two broad categories: *enforcement operations*, which can be characterized as sustained full-scale combat operations directed against a State authorized by the Security Council to maintain or restore 5.01

international peace and security, and *peace enforcement operations*, which, while potentially involving combat, will not amount to full-scale warfare on a sustained basis against a State, and which fall conceptually and in terms of their objectives and the intensity of the use of force between enforcement operations and traditional peacekeeping (see Section 5.21 below).

5.02 **Both enforcement and peace enforcement operations have the overriding purpose of the maintenance or restoration of international peace and security through the employment of the degree of force which is necessary and required under the circumstances to suppress breaches of the peace and acts of aggression and/or to respond to threats to the peace. Consequently, enforcement and peace enforcement operations are by their nature proactive, coercive, and directed against a particular State or entity which has been deemed by the Security Council as a threat to or in breach of international peace and security.**

5.03 **While both enforcement operations and peace enforcement operations share certain common characteristics of not requiring the consent of the Host State and not requiring impartiality or restricting the use of force to self-defence, they can differ significantly in their objectives and in the degree, intensity, and duration of the force they are required to employ in order to carry out their respective mandates.**

5.04 **In addition to enforcement and peace enforcement operations as described above in Sections 5.01, 5.02, and 5.03, the Security Council has the power to implement sanctions not involving the use of force, such as, but not limited to the interruption of land, sea and air communications, and/or the selective or comprehensive interruption of trade and commerce in designated goods or services and to authorize the effective implementation and enforcement of such non-military sanctions. To the extent such measures of implementation called for the threat or use of limited force to ensure compliance, they would qualify as military enforcement measures for that specific purpose. Such measures will not be designated as enforcement or peace enforcement operations as described above, in order to avoid possible confusion.**

5.05 **Enforcement operations and peace enforcement operations are taken pursuant to a Security Council determination under Chapter VII of the Charter that there is a threat to international peace and security, or that a breach of international peace or act of aggression has occurred.**

In practice, the Council has taken a broad view of what constitutes a threat to the peace to include internal conflicts, large-scale violations of human rights and humanitarian law, the proliferation of weapons of mass destruction, and acts of international terrorism. The Council's authority and discretion within the context of making such determinations can be characterized as being extremely broad and in practice only limited by the Council's ability to reach such a determination and by the Purposes and Principles of the UN Charter. 5.06

While the Security Council is empowered under Article 42 of the Charter to take such action by air, sea, or land forces as may be necessary to maintain or restore international peace and security, in the absence of agreements with Member States under Article 43, which were originally intended to provide the Council with independent military capacity, the Council is in fact dependent upon the voluntary participation of Member States to carry out enforcement and peace enforcement operations. The practice of the Council is to authorize such States or international organizations as are willing to participate in a given enforcement or peace enforcement operation with the legal authority to do so by use of the phrase 'all necessary means', or similar terminology, on a case-by-case basis. 5.07

The mandate provided by the Council, including the specific authorization to use the necessary force to carry it out, is a legal requirement for the deployment of forces onto a State's territory in the absence of that State's consent and for any use of force going beyond self-defence. While a mandate from the Council authorizing deployment and the use of force will obviate the need for the consent of the State where the operation is conducted, wherever appropriate or feasible, such consent will be sought as providing a useful and desirable complement to the Council's authority to act under Chapter VII of the Charter. 5.08

While the Security Council provides the legal authority for enforcement and peace enforcement operations through the provision of a mandate and retains overall political control, the actual conduct of these operations may be delegated to the participating State(s) or international organization. 5.09

Military operations requiring and reaching the level of full-scale hostilities against a State are normally entrusted to a lead nation or nations providing the bulk of the forces employed in the operation. Forces established and controlled by the UN for the conduct of enforcement action have remained an exception. 5.10

5.11 **In situations where the Security Council has mandated a particular State, group of States, or regional or other organization to carry out an enforcement or peace enforcement operation, it will retain overall authority over and responsibility for the operation, notwithstanding any delegation of command and control which may be decided upon.**

5.2 Status of Forces in Enforcement and Peace Enforcement Operations

5.12 **Forces participating in an enforcement or peace enforcement operation enjoy immunity vis-à-vis the Receiving State and any Transit State, as a matter of customary international law. Status-of-forces agreements entered into with any Receiving State(s) or third States may specify the rights and obligations of the forces participating in the operation.**

5.13 **The responsibility of the Sending State extends to all acts performed by its forces on its behalf. This includes acts committed in excess of authority or in contravention of instructions (see below, sub-Chapter 6.2 and Chapter 30).**

5.14 **The responsibility of the United Nations Organization for acts committed in an enforcement or peace enforcement operation is limited to acts committed under UN command and control.**

5.3 Legal Parameters for the Use of Force in the Context of the UN Collective Security System

5.15 **The UN collective security system requires express authorization of any use of force other than in self-defence.**

5.16 **Such authorization should also be provided for law enforcement operations including detentions (see Chapter 25 and 26).**

5.17 **The UN Charter and customary international law prohibit the use of force in international relations outside the maintenance or restoration of international peace and security within the context of the UN collective security system or in the exercise of the right of self-defence.**

5.18 **Any force used in enforcement and peace enforcement operations, other than in self-defence, requires specific authorization provided for by the Security Council within the mandate to be worked out under the specific Operational Plan (OPLAN) and Rules of Engagement (ROE) for the operation. The OPLAN and ROE may under no circumstances exceed the level or objective of the force provided for in the mandate. In addition, the general principles of necessity and** proportionality relating to any use of force are likewise relevant to the employment of force within the context of enforcement and peace enforcement operations.

The nature and purpose of both enforcement and peace enforcement operations (referred to in Section 5.01) signifies that the use of force within the context of such operations need not be restricted to reactive and defensive responses to counter overt hostile acts or intent. On the contrary, the force necessary to carry out the mandate, within the limitations posed by mandate, articulated through the OPLAN and the ROE, and the principles of necessity and proportionality, is legally permitted. Where circumstances require, this can include the use of offensive and proactive force and threat of force necessary for mission accomplishment and to carry out the mandate. 5.19

Wherever and whenever circumstances do not require the use of force to secure the mission objectives or maintain force protection or where the use of force would be counterproductive, the principles of necessity and proportionality would prohibit the use of force. Likewise, where a lesser degree or duration of the use of force would suffice to secure the mission objectives and maintain force protection, the use of force in excess of what was required would be unnecessary and/or disproportionate, and consequently illegal. 5.20

Peace enforcement operations lie conceptually between military enforcement operations and traditional peacekeeping. While sharing the characteristics of possessing a Security Council mandate under Chapter VII of the Charter and the ability to operate proactively and coercively outside the context of self-defence, they will not involve the conduct of hostilities against a State and may or may not involve participation of the Peace Enforcement Force as a party to a non-international armed conflict in support of a government, depending on whether the material conditions for the existence of such a conflict and the participation of the Peace Enforcement Force as a party thereto are met. Consequently, force will be applied on a case-by-case basis and may not necessarily include the use of high intensity force on a protracted and systematic basis as will be the case with military enforcement operations which are synonymous with full-scale warfare. Where at all feasible, they will require the cooperation and consent of the Host State government and other relevant parties. Consequently, the use of force parameters must be strictly and judiciously tailored to what is required to achieve the mission objective and maintain such consent and cooperation without prejudice to the inherent right of self-defence. 5.21

5.4 *Force Application in Enforcement and Peace Enforcement Operations*

5.22 **Controlling the use of force by United Nations (UN) or Troop Contributing Countries (TCCs) is both an operational command responsibility and legal imperative. Rules of Engagement (ROE) are accepted by the UN and TCCs as the most common and effective framework in which to control the use of force by military forces. The ROE framework ensures that political direction and objectives as well as legal, diplomatic, policy and operational considerations are coherently conveyed in military orders or directives. This is to make sure the level of force authorized for UN or TCCs forces contributes towards mission accomplishment.**

5.23 **Generally, ROE are defined as orders or directives that are intended to ensure commanders and their subordinates use only such force or other measures as are necessary, appropriate and authorized by higher command. ROE are an essential instrument of command and control for ordering, directing and controlling the use of force during military operations. ROE are orders or directives (i.e. lawful commands) issued by a competent military authority, which define the circumstances, conditions, degree, manner and limitations within which force may be applied to achieve military objectives in furtherance of the UN mandate. Mission specific ROE are tailored to meet the requirements of each operation.**

5.24 **ROE should be established for each military operation, including enforcement and peace enforcement operations. Generally, ROE in (peace) enforcement operations are restrictive whereas in self defence they are permissive. ROE must not permit the use of force that exceeds existing legal limitations and may further limit the use of force. The right of self-defence (individual and national) must be respected (see below, Sections 6.09, 8.01-4, and 23.01). The right of self-defence is closely linked to ROE but may not necessarily be expressed as a ROE. The exercise of the use of force in personal self-defence may be the subject of further military direction (e.g. types of weapons authorized for use or hold fire orders).**

5.5 *Applicability and Application of International Humanitarian Law to Enforcement, Peace Enforcement, and Peace Operations*

5.25 **Where peace enforcement operations fall below the threshold of armed conflict, international humanitarian law will not apply; the Force will be subject to relevant international and national law, including that applicable to law enforcement operations as defined**

above (see Section 3.01). Peace enforcement operations which do not reach the threshold of an armed conflict must adhere to law enforcement principles and follow the mandate issued by the Security Council. Whenever the Force has become a party to an armed conflict or is in belligerent occupation of foreign territory, international humanitarian law applies.

In enforcement operations involving the authorized use of force against a State amounting to an armed conflict, the full body of international humanitarian law relevant to international armed conflicts will apply. The State(s) participating in the operation will be governed by the provisions of any conventions and protocols thereto in the realm of international humanitarian law to which they are a party, as well as by the rules and principles of customary international humanitarian law. 5.26

Where a UN or UN-authorized force is acting on behalf of a State engaged in a non-international armed conflict and becomes involved in the conduct of operations against a non-State actor participating in that conflict, or becomes a party to a non-international armed conflict in its own right, the international humanitarian law relating to non-international armed conflicts will apply. 5.27

Without prejudice to more restrictive applicable rules of international law, States participating in a UN or UN-authorized operation may require their forces to comply with the principles of international humanitarian law as a matter of policy, regardless of its applicability as a matter of law. 5.28

Chapter 6 Peace Operations

6.1 Characterization and Legal Basis for Peace Operations

While a strict division between peacekeeping and peace enforcement has often proven to be difficult or even impossible to achieve and maintain in practice, there are clear distinctions in legal concept and in the resulting applicable legal regime between peace enforcement falling short of traditional war-fighting operations on the one hand, and other peace operations which are essentially consensual in nature, on the other. 6.01

Enforcement operations and peace enforcement operations have their legal basis in Chapter VII of the Charter and are not subject to the consent of the Host State where they are deployed, nor to 6.02

considerations of impartiality in the conduct of their operations. (See sub-Chapters 5.1 and 5.3 above.) By contrast, peace operations other than enforcement and peace enforcement operations are subject to the consent of the Receiving State and are governed by the principles of impartiality and restricted to the use of force in self-defence. These operations will be referred to subsequently as peace operations.

6.03 **Peace operations have their legal basis in the general powers of the Security Council, of the General Assembly, and of regional organizations. The authorization of such operations with the consent of the Receiving State has emerged in UN practice as a means of support for diplomatic efforts to establish and maintain peace. Notwithstanding the absence of a specific provision in the UN Charter which refers to such operations, they have become an established and generally accepted instrument in the maintenance of peace.**

6.04 **Political control, exercised by the Security Council, by regional organizations, and by States is the predominant factor for the regulation of such operations, alongside any conditions posed by the Receiving State which have been accepted by the Security Council or other authorizing entity such as a regional organization. This regulation is further subject to the abovementioned principles of consent, impartiality, and the restriction of force to self-defence. These existing legal restraints are worked out into multinational and national rules of engagement (ROE) which often contain additional restraints of an operational or policy nature.**

6.05 **While all consent-based peace operations share the above mentioned general characteristics which define their legal status and which differentiate them from enforcement and peace enforcement operations, their mandates and objectives, the challenges they face, and their resulting practices will differ (widely) from case to case. In cases where peacekeeping forces become involved in hostilities, the principles and rules of international humanitarian law will be applicable to them for the duration of their participation as parties.**

6.2 Status of Forces in Peace Operations

6.06 **Forces participating in peace operations enjoy immunity vis-à-vis the Receiving State and any other (Transit) State as a matter of customary international law. Their rights and obligations may be specified in status-of-forces agreements (SOFAs).**

6.07 **Forces participating in peace operations shall observe their obligations under international law, in particular human rights law. They**

shall also respect the laws applicable in the Receiving State and any Transit State. Local institutions and individuals should be given appropriate access to independent review mechanisms to control and ensure these obligations.

6.3 Legal Parameters for the Use of Force within the Context of Peace Operations

The conduct of peace operations with the consent of the Receiving State excludes any use of force other than in self-defence. According to UN doctrine, this includes any force which is authorized and necessary for mission accomplishment and the protection of civilians (see Chapter 22). In cases of such authorization, self-defence may extend beyond mere reaction to direct threat of force against the peacekeeping forces and can include reactions in response to armed threats against the integrity of the mission and the protection of civilians accompanying the mission and of the civilian population of the Receiving State within the capability of the mission. 6.08

6.4 Application of Force and Rules of Engagement in Peace Operations

Rules of engagement should be established for each peace operation. They may limit the use of force, but must not exceed existing legal limitations. The inherent right of personal self-defence must be respected (see above, Section 5.24, and below, Sections 10.02–10.03). Where hostilities take place, the rules of humanitarian law will be applicable (see Section 5.25 above). 6.09

While remaining predominantly defensive in nature, the ROE allow for the potential need for offensive action if necessary, in order to ensure the implementation of the tasks assigned. The ROE contain definitions for the circumstances under which the use of force may be justified. Whenever the operational situation permits, every reasonable effort must be made to resolve any hostile confrontation by means other than the use of force. Any force used must be limited in its intensity and duration to what is strictly necessary to achieve the objective. 6.10

In some circumstances operational urgency may dictate the immediate use of deadly force. The use of force must be commensurate with the level of the threat and all necessary measures are to be taken to avoid collateral damage. During peace operations, use of force beyond personal self-defence may only be used in the circumstances as specified in the ROE. 6.11

6.12 The implementation of the ROE is a command responsibility. The ROE are normally addressed to the Force Commander, who is then responsible for issuing them to all subordinate commanders. All commanders have an obligation to seek clarification, if the authorized ROE are considered to be unclear or inappropriate for the military situation.

6.13 Rules of engagement will determine under what circumstances search, apprehension, and detention operations may take place. Minimum principles must be observed during all search procedures: the purpose of the search must be clearly stated in the orders and to the individuals to be searched; searchers are not to humiliate, nor embarrass persons being searched; the search procedure must take into account gender and be sensitive to other factors such as race, religion, etc.

6.14 Detainees must not be subjected to torture, to cruel, inhuman or degrading treatment or punishment, or to intimidation, deprivation, humiliation, mistreatment, or any form of abuse (see below, Chapter 25). Full respect is to be shown for their gender, race, and religious beliefs and for the customs and practices of the group to which they belong. Particular care is to be taken to ensure the protection and wellbeing of women and children. Detainees must be protected against all acts or threats of violence, insults, and public curiosity. Detainees are to be given rations, shelter, and access to medical care.

6.5 Authority, Command, and Control in United Nations-led Peace Operations

6.15 The Security Council provides the legal authority, high-level strategic direction, and political guidance for all UN peace operations, and it vests the operational authority for directing these operations in the Secretary General of the United Nations. The Under-Secretary General for Peacekeeping Operations (USG DPKO) has been delegated responsibility from the Secretary General for the administration of, and provision of executive direction for, all UN peace support operations.

6.16 United Nations Member States may transfer authority to the United Nations to use the operational capabilities of their national military contingents, units, and/or uniformed personnel to undertake mandated missions and tasks. Operational authority over such forces and personnel is vested in the Secretary General, under the authority of the Security Council. Contributing Member States that provide

uniformed personnel to United Nations peace operations retain full and exclusive strategic level command and control of their personnel and equipment.

The Head of Mission is the senior UN Representative and has overall authority over the activities of the United Nations in the mission area. He leads and directs the heads of all mission components and ensures unity of effort and coherence among all UN entities in the mission area. The Head of Military Component exercises operational control over all military personnel, including military observers and in the mission. The Head of Police Component exercises operational control over all members of the police component of the mission. 6.17

Chapter 7 Peace Operations Conducted by regional Organizations and Arrangements

The UN Charter does not preclude regional organizations from addressing matters of regional peace and security 'as are appropriate for regional action' (Article 52 of the UN Charter). Subject to the requirements of its constituent treaty a regional organization is competent under international law to authorize a peace operation with the consent of the Receiving State (this can be implied from Article 52). Subject to the requirements of its constituent treaty, a regional organization is competent to authorize peace enforcement and enforcement operations but only with authority from the Security Council (this is an express requirement under the terms of Article 53). 7.01

For peace operations based on consent, operating with impartiality, and restricted to defensive force, Security Council authorization need not be sought but is desirable. Regional organizations should report on the activities of any military operations undertaken under its authority to the Security Council (Article 54 of the UN Charter). 7.02

Any regional organization conducting military operations that have or exercise enforcement elements must obtain the authority of the Security Council under Chapter VIII (Article 53 of the UN Charter). 7.03

Peace operations by regional organizations should be conducted under the authority, command, and control of the regional organization. Even to the extent they are commanded by TCCs, they remain under the control of the regional organization. 7.04

7.05 **For peace operations regional organizations should seek encouragement and support by the Security Council and will require the consent of the Receiving State. Whenever a peace enforcement operation is undertaken in the absence of such consent, the operation will require the authorization of the Security Council. Such authorization can take various forms and modalities, but may not be dispensed with under any circumstances.**

PART III

MILITARY OPERATIONS WITHIN THE CONTEXT OF THE RIGHT OF SELF-DEFENCE AND OTHER POSSIBLE LEGAL BASES FOR THE USE OF FORCE

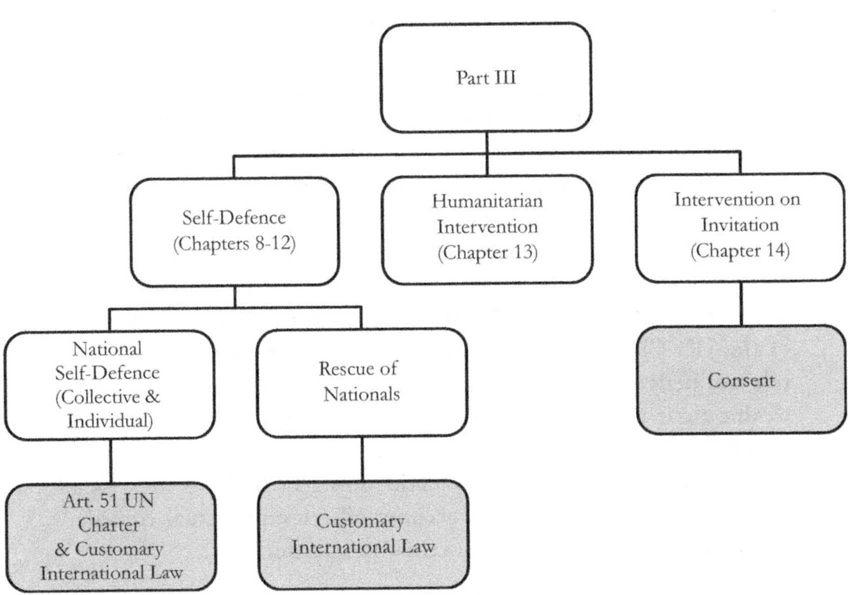

Chapter 8 Legal Basis of the Right of Self-Defence under the UN Charter and under Customary International Law

The right of self-defence is used within different contexts (i.e. national or State self-defence, unit self-defence, and individual or personal self-defence) and can relate to different applicable legal regimes (e.g. international law, national criminal law, etc.). While 8.01

these different manifestations of the right of self-defence share certain characteristics, in particular the notion that self-defence denotes the lawful use of force in response to a prior or impending illegal use of force, they are governed by different and distinct legal criteria and considerations. For the sake of clarity, the term self-defence as used in Part III of this Handbook will be used to denote the right of a State under international law to respond individually or collectively to an illegal armed attack directed against its territory, citizens, military vessels, aircraft, or installations, abroad or located in international sea or airspace, and subject to the legal criteria and conditions laid down in the UN Charter and in customary international law. These international legal criteria and conditions can be supplemented by other considerations of a policy or domestic legal nature, but those are separate and distinct and should not be confused with the legal regime governing the exercise of self-defence under international law.

8.02 The right of self-defence under international law is directed towards and possessed by States and is governed firstly by the provisions of the UN Charter relating to the use of force in general and the exercise of that right in particular. The relevant provision (Article 51) refers to the right as being 'inherent' in nature. This reference is generally accepted as a reference to the continuing relevance of customary international law which provides an additional legal basis and criteria for the exercise of this right, alongside those contained in Article 51 and other relevant provisions of the UN Charter. Consequently, the international right of self-defence has a dual legal basis: Article 51 of the UN Charter and customary international law, and both are relevant in determining the legality and the modalities of the exercise of this right. They should be applied in a complementary fashion which fully takes into account the criteria and conditions for the exercise of this right which are laid down in both of these legal sources, as well as taking into account all relevant factual considerations which are available at the time in question.

8.03 The exercise of self-defence under Article 51 of the Charter is predicated upon the occurrence of an armed attack. Under customary international law, the possibility is not ruled out that a State may respond to a clear and manifest danger of an impending armed attack when the danger of such an impending attack is supported by convincing factual evidence and no other alternatives are reasonably available. An armed attack can be carried out either directly by a foreign State's armed forces, or indirectly by a State acting through organized armed groups which are under a foreign State's control or are subject to significant involvement and influence from a foreign State. Additionally, an armed attack can be carried out by an organized armed

group which is capable of mounting an armed attack, which is comparable in its scale and effect to a conventional armed attack carried out by a State. An 'armed attack' denotes a reasonably significant use of force originating or directed from abroad, or a series of smaller related armed incidents which have the common purpose of destabilizing the victim State or exacting political concessions from it.

In addition to the occurrence of an armed attack, or the clear and manifest danger of an impending attack, the Charter requires that any action undertaken in self-defence be reported forthwith to the Security Council and gives the Council primacy in determining what further measures may be necessary in order to restore international peace and security. Under customary international law, the requirements of necessity, proportionality, and immediacy are well established as complementing the requirements provided in the Charter in relation to the exercise of self-defence. Necessity relates to the existence of an ongoing armed attack or clear threat of repeated attack within the near future, as well as the absence of feasible alternatives including measures undertaken by the Security Council which have the effect of restoring the situation pertaining prior to the attack and ending the threat of further attacks. Proportionality in this context refers to the requirement that the measures taken in self-defence must be roughly commensurate with the scale and effect of the attack and are directed towards ending the attack and neutralizing the danger of further attack. Immediacy refers to the requirement that measures of self-defence must be taken within a reasonable period, taking into account the relevant factual circumstances. 8.04

Self-defence may be exercised either individually by a State which has been subjected to an attack, or collectively by one or more States which have been subjected to an attack originating from a common source, or by one or more States which at the request of a State which has been subjected to an attack, elect to come to that State's assistance. Such a request for assistance may be based on a pre-existing commitment to provide assistance in the event of an attack, or be made on an ad hoc basis once an attack has been mounted or is imminent. 8.05

Chapter 9 Status of Forces in Self-Defence Operations

Regular armed forces participating in a self-defence operation in an international armed conflict are combatants in relation to the opposing State. They enjoy immunity in the assisted Receiving State and any Transit State as a matter of customary international law. 9.01

9.02 **Regular armed forces participating in a self-defence operation amounting to a non-international armed conflict enjoy immunity in the assisted Receiving State and any Transit State as a matter of customary international law. Armed opposition fighters in non-international armed conflicts do not enjoy the combatant privilege under international humanitarian law. However, this does not preclude agreements or unilateral conferral of such status or amnesty from prosecution under national law for participation in hostilities which does not constitute a violation of international humanitarian law.**

Chapter 10 Application of Force and Rules of Engagement in Self-defence Operations

10.01 **Controlling the use of force by military forces is both an operational command responsibility and legal imperative. Rules of Engagement (ROE) are accepted by military forces as the most common and effective framework in which to control the use of force. The ROE framework ensures that political direction and objectives as well as legal, diplomatic, policy and operational considerations are coherently conveyed in military orders or directives. This is to make sure the level of force authorized for military forces contributes towards mission accomplishment.**

10.02 **Generally, ROE are defined as orders or directives intended to ensure (see above, Sections 5.23–5.24) commanders and their subordinates do not use force or other measures beyond that authorized by higher command. ROE are an essential instrument of command and control for ordering, directing and controlling the use of force during military operations. ROE are orders or directives (i.e. lawful commands) issued by a competent military authority, which define the circumstances, conditions, degree, manner and limitations within which force may be applied to achieve military objectives in furtherance of the national or collective self-defence mission. ROE, therefore, regulate the use of force by military forces during operations in peacetime, periods of tension and armed conflicts.**

10.03 **ROE should be established for each military operation, including national or collective self-defence operations. ROE may limit the use of force, and must not permit a use of force that exceeds existing legal limitations. The right of individual (personal) self-defence must be respected in so far as it is relevant (see above, Sections 5.22 and 6.09). The right of self-defence is closely linked to ROE but may not necessarily be expressed as a ROE. The exercise of the use of force in individual self-defence may be the subject of further military direction (e.g. types of weapons authorized for use or hold fire orders).**

Chapter 11 International Humanitarian Law in Self-defence Operations

In so far as self-defence operations amount to armed conflict, international humanitarian law is fully applicable in such operations (see above, Sections 5.24–5.26). 11.01

The applicable international humanitarian law will depend on the nature of the conflict. Unless and until it is determined that the conflict is non-international, the law applicable to international armed conflict should generally apply. Once the nature of the conflict is determined, all the law relevant to that type of conflict and binding on the individual parties will apply. 11.02

Necessity cannot be used to justify actions prohibited by international humanitarian law. Military necessity is fully incorporated into international humanitarian law which reflects a balance between military and humanitarian considerations in all of its provisions. 11.03

Chapter 12 Rescue of Nationals

States may rescue their nationals when their lives or physical safety are directly threatened and the State in which this occurs is either directly responsible, or is unable or unwilling to provide security. Rescue of nationals is generally referred to as 'non-combatant evacuation' in military doctrine. 12.01

Action undertaken in this context must be directly aimed at ending the threat to the safety of the victims and evacuating them as quickly as possible from the State where they are located with the force strictly necessary to achieve these objectives. It is not prohibited under such circumstances to additionally evacuate the nationals of third States when their lives or safety are also directly threatened and circumstances allow for their evacuation along with the rescuing State's nationals, in so far as they wish to be evacuated. 12.02

Chapter 13 Humanitarian Intervention

In cases of large-scale, systematic, and acute violations of fundamental human rights, especially of the right to life, which result either from a government deliberately targeting (a significant part of) its 13.01

population, or through a general breakdown in governmental authority, the Security Council should take all necessary and feasible measures, including whenever necessary, the authorization of military enforcement measures with the purpose of ending the ongoing violations and preventing further violations, and restoring a secure and stable environment. In the event the Security Council issues a mandate under Chapter VII of the Charter to halt the violations, the operation undertaken will have a recognized legal basis and will constitute a (peace) enforcement operation within the context of the UN Collective Security System (see Chapter 5, above).

13.02 **Humanitarian intervention defined as military intervention, which is undertaken without the authorization of the UN Security Council by one or more States, or by a regional organization, with the purpose of halting or preventing large-scale systematic and acute violations of fundamental human rights of persons who are not nationals of the intervening State(s), falls outside of either of the two generally recognized exceptions to the prohibition on the use of force contained in the UN Charter and in customary international law. As such, it is in contravention of the prohibition on the use of force and the closely related principle of non-intervention and is *prima facie* illegal under contemporary international law. Nevertheless, such intervention can be legitimized and wholly or partially justified under strict legal, moral, and policy conditions, provided it meets certain requirements which have increasingly come to be recognized by a wide segment of the international community, by the public conscience, and by leading authorities and publicists. While this has not yet resulted in creating a new generally recognized exception to the prohibition on the use of force of a customary or conventional nature, it can be seen as grounds for partial or complete mitigation of responsibility for otherwise illegal conduct on the part of the intervening State(s).**

13.03 **To qualify for legitimization resulting in complete or partial mitigation of responsibility under international law humanitarian intervention must meet the requirements of necessity, proportionality, and immediacy governing the use of force and must additionally fully comply with relevant humanitarian and human rights rules and principles. It must, additionally, not pose a greater threat to international peace and security than the situation it purports to address. Legitimization and mitigation of responsibility in no way affect the legal status of the prohibition on the use of force under international law, or the primacy of the UN Security Council in the maintenance and restoration of international peace and security.**

To the extent a humanitarian intervention fully conforms to the abovementioned criteria laid down in Section 13.03 and the commentary thereto, it should qualify for far-reaching mitigation of responsibility and legitimization. To the extent it falls short of meeting these criteria, the intervention will not (fully) qualify for mitigation of responsibility and the intervention will incur any consequences determined by the Security Council, by other competent organs of the United Nations, and by the international community at large. **13.04**

Chapter 14 Military Intervention with the Consent or at the Invitation of A government

Consent of a government for a military intervention can form either a separate or an additional legal basis for the deployment of forces onto its territory and can include permission to conduct operations, either alongside and in conjunction with the consenting State's forces or independently. In the absence of any other legal basis, consent is a strict requirement for the deployment of armed forces or the conduct of any type of military operations on another State's territory. **14.01**

Any consent granted must be freely given and issued by the lawful authority of the consenting State which is recognized under international law and the national law of the consenting State as authorized to act on behalf of that State. **14.02**

To the extent the intervention has another legal basis in the form of either a Security Council mandate under Chapter VII of the Charter, or the lawful exercise of the right of self-defence, the consent of the State where the intervention is conducted would not be required from a strictly legal perspective. However, such consent would provide an additional legal basis alongside the primary one and would be welcome from a political and operational perspective. In such cases, the conduct of operations should conform to any conditions put forward by the consenting State's government in so far as these do not clash with the legal requirements and conditions which form part of the primary legal basis for the intervention. In the event of any conflict between the two, the requirements and conditions relating to the primary legal basis will prevail.[1] **14.03**

[1] On the basis of, *inter alia*, Articles 103 and 24 of the Charter in relation to a Security Council mandate and the right of a State to defend itself within the terms of the Charter and customary law relating to self-defence with regard to the concurrent applicability of consent and self-defence; see para. 3 of the commentary to this Section below, for further elaboration.

PART IV

CAPITA SELECTA OF INTERNATIONAL MILITARY OPERATIONAL LAW

Chapter 15 Command and Control in Military operations

Generally, in multinational and coalition force operations, including UN (peace) enforcement operations, command authority, in the form of operational command (OPCOM) or operational control (OPCON), over military members and units will be assigned from Sending States or troop contributing countries (TCCs) to a multinational allied or coalition force. However, Sending States or TCCs will normally retain full command over their units and members when they are assigned to a coalition or allied force. 15.01

Many key operational and legal issues arise from command and control (C2) matters, particularly when military forces are involved in multinational coalition or allied operations. When working in a coalition or allied force operation, it is important to be aware of the command structure and terminology of the coalition or allied forces. While military forces may use the same terms, such as 'full command', 'operational command', 'operational control', and 'tactical control', these may have different meanings. This could have significant operational and legal consequences, particularly in areas such as issuing orders and taskings (especially as related to command responsibility); requesting, authorizing, and implementing ROE; identifying decision-making authority in targeting, disciplinary, and policing jurisdiction; identifying signing authority for agreements, contracts, leases, and Memoranda of Understanding (MOUs); and controlling movement of personnel and equipment. 15.02

Chapter 16 Targeting in Operational Law

The general rules governing targeting apply equally in land, air, sea, space, and cyberspace. Specialized rules may apply in particular types of operations, such as peace operations or naval warfare. 16.01

16.02 **The parties to the conflict must distinguish between civilians and combatants. Attacks must not be directed against civilians unless, and for such time as, they directly participate in hostilities. Acts or threats of violence the primary purpose of which is to spread terror among the civilian population are prohibited.**

16.03 **Parties to a conflict must distinguish between civilian objects and military objectives. Attacks may only be directed against military objectives. Military objectives are those objects which by their nature, location, purpose, or use make an effective contribution to military action and whose partial or total destruction, capture, or neutralization, in the circumstances ruling at the time, offers a definite military advantage. Civilian objects are all objects that are not military objectives.**

16.04 **Indiscriminate attacks are prohibited. Indiscriminate attacks are those which are not directed at a specific military objective, employ a method or means of combat which cannot be directed at a specific military objective, or employ a method or means of combat the effects of which cannot be limited as required by international humanitarian law, and consequently are of a nature to strike military objectives and civilians or civilian objects without distinction.**

16.05 **Attacks that treat as a single military objective a number of clearly separated and distinct military objectives located in a city, town, village, or other area containing a similar concentration of civilians or civilian objects are prohibited.**

16.06 **Ordering or executing an attack which may be expected to cause incidental loss of civilian life, injury to civilians, damage to civilian objects, or a combination thereof, which would be excessive in relation to the concrete and direct military advantage anticipated is prohibited.**

16.07 **Constant care is required to spare the civilian population, civilians, and civilian objects. All feasible precautions must be taken to avoid, and in any event to minimize, incidental injury to civilians or collateral damage to civilian objects. In particular, an attacker must do everything feasible to confirm that targets are in fact military objectives and to assess the proportionality of a planned attack. When the available options yield a similar military advantage, methods and means of warfare, as well as targets, must be selected with a view to minimizing incidental injury to civilians and collateral damage to civilian objects.**

16.08 **Persons performing certain functions enjoy special protection under international humanitarian law. Medical, religious, civil defence, and**

humanitarian relief personnel may not be attacked unless they commit, outside their humanitarian functions, acts harmful to the enemy. Civilian journalists performing professional functions may not be attacked unless they directly participate in hostilities. Forces participating in a UN mission may not be attacked so long as they are entitled to protection, in the circumstances, as civilians.

Certain objects and facilities enjoy special protection under international humanitarian law. They may not be attacked unless they become military objectives. These include medical facilities and units; areas specially established as civilian protective zones and for the care of wounded and sick; humanitarian relief facilities, supplies, and transports; peacekeeping equipment and facilities; cultural property; works and installations containing dangerous forces, such as dams, dykes, and nuclear electrical generating stations; the natural environment; and objects indispensable to the survival of the civilian population. Designated protective emblems are used to make certain of these objects and facilities. **16.09**

Combatants who are *hors de combat* because they have surrendered, are prisoners, or are wounded or shipwrecked may not be attacked. Persons parachuting from an aircraft in distress may not be attacked during their descent and must be afforded an opportunity to surrender upon landing. Parlementaires may not be attacked while performing their functions. **16.10**

Perfidious attacks are prohibited. In a perfidious attack, the attacker feigns protected status in order to kill, injure, or capture the enemy. Examples include feigning: an intent to negotiate under a flag of truce or of surrender; incapacitation by wounds or sickness; civilian, non-combatant status; or protected status by the use of signs, emblems, or uniforms of the United Nations or of neutral or other States not parties to the conflict. **16.11**

An attack involving use of means and methods of warfare which are of a nature to cause superfluous injury or unnecessary suffering or which are by nature indiscriminate is prohibited. **16.12**

The rules governing targeting apply to the employment of all weapons and weapon systems, including unmanned, autonomous and cyber weapon systems, during an armed conflict. **16.13**

The use of poison, chemical, or biological weapons is generally prohibited, although riot-control agents and herbicides may be used in certain limited circumstances. Small arms projectiles that are designed to explode within the human body, certain types of booby-traps, laser weapons designed to blind, and weapons the **16.14**

primary effect of which is to injure by fragments that escape detection by X-ray are prohibited, as are, during periods of international armed conflict, bullets that flatten upon impact. Specific treaty prohibitions or limitations apply, for States party to the instruments, to the use of anti-personnel land mines, incendiary weapons, and cluster munitions. There is no absolute obligation to use precision weapons. Rather, their use is governed by the feasible precautions in attack requirements (see Section 16.07).

16.15 **Parties to a conflict who are subject to attack shall, to the extent feasible, endeavour to remove civilians and other protected persons and objects under their control from the vicinity of military objectives, avoid locating military objectives within or near protected persons or objects, and take other measures that are necessary to protect civilians and civilian objects under their control against the dangers resulting from military operations.**

16.16 **Except as noted, the basic international humanitarian law rules of targeting set forth above apply equally in both international and non-international armed conflict.**

Chapter 17 Targeted Killings in Operational Law Perspective

17.01 **For the purposes of this Handbook, the term 'targeted killing' refers to military operations involving the use of lethal force with the aim of killing individually selected persons who are not in the physical custody of those targeting them.**

17.02 **The international lawfulness of targeted killing is regulated primarily by human rights law and, in situations of armed conflict, international humanitarian law. To the extent that targeted killings attributable to a State also interfere with the sovereignty of another State, their international lawfulness additionally depends on international law governing the use of inter-State force.**

17.03 **Outside the conduct of hostilities in armed conflict, a targeted killing can be permissible only in very exceptional circumstances, namely where it, cumulatively: (a) aims at preventing an unlawful attack by the targeted person on human life; (b) is absolutely necessary for the achievement of this purpose; (c) is the result of an operation which is planned, prepared and conducted so as to minimize, to the greatest extent possible, the recourse to lethal force. States have a duty to regulate the use of lethal force by their agents in accordance with these standards.**

In a situation of armed conflict, a targeted killing can be permissible only where it cumulatively: (a) is directed against a person subject to lawful attack; (b) is planned and conducted so as to avoid erroneous targeting, as well as to avoid, and in any event to minimize, incidental civilian harm; (c) is not expected to cause incidental civilian harm that would be excessive in relation to the concrete and direct military advantage anticipated; (d) is suspended when the targeted person surrenders or otherwise falls *hors de combat*; and (e) is not otherwise conducted by resort to prohibited means or methods of warfare. Even where not expressly prohibited under the above standards, targeted killings may not be resorted to where the threat posed by the targeted person can manifestly be neutralized through capture or other non-lethal means without additional risk to the operating forces or the civilian population. 17.04

Chapter 18 Weapons Under the Law of Military Operations

18.1 The Conventional and Customary Principles of Weapons Law Applying in Armed Conflict

The right to choose methods or means of warfare is not unlimited. 18.01

(a) It is prohibited to employ weapons, projectiles and material and methods of warfare of a nature to cause superfluous injury or unnecessary suffering.

(b) It is prohibited to employ weapons that are of a nature to be indiscriminate.

(c) Customary law requires all States to have due regard to the natural environment and provides that, as a civilian object, the natural environment may not be made the object of attack and may not be subjected to wanton destruction.

(d) It is prohibited to use the following weapons or weapon technologies:

(1) poison or poisoned weapons;

(2) asphyxiating, poisonous or other gases, all analogous liquids, materials or devices and bacteriological methods of warfare;

(3) the use of expanding bullets in armed conflict;

(4) exploding bullets intended for anti-personnel use;

(5) certain conventional weapons prohibited under CCW Protocols to which the relevant State is party;

(6) for States party to the Ottawa Convention, anti-personnel mines;
(7) chemical weapons;
(8) riot control agents, if used as a method of warfare;
(9) bacteriological or biological weapons; and
(10) for States party to the Cluster Munitions Convention, cluster munitions.

(e) The use of certain weapons is subject to treaty law restrictions.

18.02 **The application of weapons law does not discriminate between weapons exclusively on the basis of their intended non-lethal character.**

18.03 **International law neither specifically prohibits nor explicitly permits the use of, or a threat to use, nuclear weapons. Any use, or threat to use, nuclear weapons is unlawful unless it complies with the general principles of international law, including the law applicable to armed conflict.**

18.04 **All States are required legally to review new weapons to determine whether their employment would in some or all circumstances breach the rules of international law applicable to that State.**

18.05 **There are similarities and differences in the weapons law rules that apply respectively to international and non-international armed conflicts.**

18.2 Rules Applying in Situations Other than Armed Conflict

18.06 **Domestic and human rights law determine the weapons that may lawfully be used, and the weapon options that should be available, in dealing with law enforcement situations both inside and outside the territory of the user irrespective of whether in the context of an armed conflict or otherwise.**

Chapter 19 Air Law and Military Operations

19.01 **Airspace is classified as either national or international. National airspace lies over the land, internal waters, archipelagic waters, and territorial seas of a State. International airspace is that over contiguous zones, exclusive economic zones, the high seas, and territory not subject to the sovereignty of any nation, such as Antarctica and the Arctic.**

Airspace extends vertically to space. Although not authoritatively defined in international law, space is generally understood as beginning at the point at which artificial satellites can be placed in orbit without free-falling to earth. 19.02

Each State enjoys complete and exclusive sovereignty over its national airspace and may deny entry to it, subject to the right of transit passage through international straits and archipelagic sea lane passage. There is no right of innocent passage through the airspace above the territorial sea. Except as agreed to by treaty, the aircraft of all nations are free to operate in international airspace. All States enjoy equal access to space; no State may exercise sovereignty over space or claim its exclusive use. 19.03

When necessitated by *force majeure* or distress, foreign aircraft may enter a State's national airspace; in such cases, every effort must be made to coordinate entry with the concerned authorities. Foreign aircraft may also enter national airspace in 'assistance entry' to render emergency assistance to those in distress at sea. They must depart upon request once the coastal State is providing rescue services. The right of assistance entry only applies in situations where the location of the distress is known; there is no right to enter national airspace to conduct a search absent the consent of the coastal State. 19.04

States may declare a temporary closure or warning area on or over the high seas to conduct hazardous activities such as missile testing, gunnery exercises, and space vehicle recovery operations. Although ships and aircraft are not required to remain outside a declared closure or warning area, they must not directly interfere with activities within them; by entering the area, such ships and aircraft place themselves at risk from the hazardous activities. 19.05

Some States have established Air Defence Identification Zones (ADIZ) in international airspace adjacent to their national airspace. In an ADIZ, a foreign aircraft can be required to identify itself and provide position reports as a condition for entry into national airspace. 19.06

In peacetime, no-fly zones, or other restrictions on flight, may be established by UN Security Council resolution(s). The relevant mandates govern permissible enforcement activities within the zone. In the absence of a Security Council mandate, such zones are unlawful except within an establishing State's national airspace. 19.07

Most States are a party to the 1944 Convention on International Civil Aviation (Chicago Convention). The Convention established the International Civil Aviation Organization (ICAO) to enhance 19.08

flight safety by developing international air navigation principles and procedures. In particular, ICAO has established Flight Information Regions (FIR) in national and international airspace to provide flight information and alerting services. The Convention does not apply to 'State aircraft' (including military aircraft). Although such aircraft may follow ICAO flight procedures as a matter of policy, certain operational missions (such as classified missions, politically sensitive missions, or routine aircraft carrier operations) may require non-compliance with them. In such cases, the aircraft involved must fly pursuant to the 'due regard' standard.

19.09 **The legal rights and obligations of aircraft, and the duties owed them by others, depend in great part on their status. There are two broad categories of aircraft, 'State' and 'civil'. Although the term 'State' aircraft is not defined in international law, it is understood to mean any aircraft owned or used by a State for exclusively non-commercial purposes. The category includes military, police, and customs aircraft. All other aircraft are 'civil' aircraft. For the purposes of international humanitarian law, it is necessary to further subdivide aircraft into 'cartel aircraft', 'civilian aircraft' (including the subcategory 'civilian airliners'), 'medical aircraft', and 'military aircraft'.**

19.10 **Aircraft must have a national identity, unless representing an intergovernmental organization, such as the United Nations, vested with an international legal personality.**

19.11 **Military aircraft are those operated under the command of members of the armed forces and marked as such, as well as unmanned aerial vehicles operated by the military. As 'State aircraft', they enjoy sovereign immunity from foreign search and inspection and foreign officials may not board them without the aircraft commander's authorization. However, if the aircraft commander fails to certify compliance with local customs, immigration, or quarantine requirements, the aircraft may be directed to leave immediately.**

19.12 **Civilian aircraft flying in the vicinity of ongoing military operations should file flight plans with the relevant air traffic control service that include such information as route, registration, destination, passengers, cargo, and identification codes and modes. They may not leave a designated air traffic service route or deviate from their flight plan without air traffic control clearance. In the case of unforeseen situations involving safety of the aircraft or its occupants, such aircraft must immediately notify civil and military authorities.**

19.13 **All States providing air traffic control service should establish procedures that permit military forces to be aware of designated routes** assigned to, or flight plans filed by, civilian aircraft in the area of military operations. Supplemental data should include, but not necessarily be limited to, communication channels frequencies, identification modes and codes, flight destination, and passengers and cargo.

Only military aircraft may engage in attacks. All enemy military aircraft constitute military objectives, unless they enjoy specific protection. Other enemy aircraft may acquire the status of military objectives through their use or purpose (see Section 16.03). 19.14

During armed conflict, the establishment of an exclusion or no-fly zone is governed by international humanitarian law and other applicable rules of international law. The extent, location, and duration of the zone, and enforcement measures, are limited to those required by military necessity or the need to safeguard protected persons and objects. A zone may not include neutral airspace. The party establishing such a zone must provide full notification of its establishment, location, duration, and conditions. Aircraft, other than enemy belligerent aircraft, approaching the zone must be appropriately notified and warned away. 19.15

During armed conflict, aircraft and their crews are entitled to surrender. However, as there is no accepted means for doing so, a military force accepting surrender of an aircraft may establish reasonable procedures for doing so. Non-compliance may subject the aircraft to attack. Aircrew of the surrendering aircraft should do everything possible to communicate their intention to surrender. 19.16

Persons parachuting from an aircraft in distress may not be attacked during their descent. They should be given an opportunity to surrender upon landing. Those who continue fighting (for example, by firing a weapon) may be attacked in the air or upon landing. Airborne troops, including Special Forces and others who intend to perform military activities upon reaching the ground, may be attacked while in the air. 19.17

As a general rule, medical aircraft may not be attacked. 19.18

Medical aircraft performing military activities harmful to the enemy become military objectives subject to attack. 19.19

Aircraft conducting military search-and-rescue operations do not enjoy special protection, unless pursuant to prior consent of the enemy. 19.20

Aircraft involved in civil defence functions, humanitarian relief, or UN activities (other than those which qualify them as a party to an 19.21

armed conflict) are entitled to special protection. In particular, a party to the conflict should agree to relief flights to aid a civilian population under its control if in need of food, medical supplies, and other items indispensable to its survival. The party may set reasonable conditions, such as search of aircraft involved, incident to the delivery of the items. Relief efforts must be conducted impartially. Occupiers of an occupied territory are required to agree to humanitarian relief activities in such circumstances.

19.22 **Civilian airliners are entitled to special protection, as well as the general protections to which civilian objects are entitled by international humanitarian law. Absent reliable information to the contrary, civilian airliners are presumed to be carrying civilian passengers.**

19.23 **Belligerent military aircraft may intercept and inspect civilian aircraft to determine their identity, cargo, and nature of use.**

19.24 **Parties to a conflict may agree to grant aircraft safe conduct. However, such aircraft lose protection if they seriously violate the terms of the agreement or act in a manner that makes them a military objective.**

19.25 **Neutral airspace is inviolable, except for the right of transit passage through an international strait or archipelagic sea lanes passage. Belligerents are prohibited from conducting any military activities in neutral territory, including airspace. Neutrals may not permit such use and must use all means available, including the use of force if necessary, to preclude it. If possible, offending belligerent military or auxiliary aircraft should be forced to land and the aircraft and crew interned for the remainder of the armed conflict. Should a serious violation of the neutral's territory nevertheless continue because of the inability or unwillingness of the neutral to end it, the opposing belligerent may, in the absence of non-forceful alternatives, use such force as is required to terminate its opponent's unlawful activities.**

19.26 **Neutral aircraft may not be attacked unless they become military objectives.**

19.27 **A State remains responsible for the actions of its aircraft engaged in coalition operations, regardless of the nationality of the commander or any other command and control relationships.**

Chapter 20 The Law of Military Operations at Sea

20.1 *The Area of Naval Operations and Navigational Rights*

Without prejudice to the powers of the UN Security Council under Chapter VII of the UN Charter or to special agreements, the area of naval operations is to be determined in accordance with the international law of the sea. 20.01

Belligerent measures may be taken in the following sea areas: 20.02
— belligerent internal waters,
— where applicable, belligerent archipelagic waters,
— belligerent territorial seas, and
— sea areas where the high seas freedoms apply.

Belligerent measures are strictly forbidden in those sea areas in which third/neutral States enjoy territorial sovereignty. In sea areas in which third/neutral States enjoy sovereign rights—EEZ, continental shelf, fishery zones—belligerent measures are not prohibited. However, due regard must be paid to the sovereign rights enjoyed by the (neutral) coastal States. 20.03

In the high seas due regard must be given to the high seas freedoms enjoyed by third/neutral States. 20.04

Vis-à-vis third States belligerents may suspend the right of innocent passage. However, the rights of transit passage and, where applicable, of archipelagic sea lanes passage may neither be suspended nor impeded. 20.05

In any case, due regard should be given to rare and fragile marine ecosystems. 20.06

20.2 *Warships and Other Platforms*

'Warship' means a ship belonging to the armed forces of a State bearing the external marks distinguishing such ships of its nationality, under the command of an officer duly commissioned by the government of a State and whose name appears in the appropriate service list or its equivalent, and manned by a crew which is under regular armed forces discipline. 20.07

'Military aircraft' means an aircraft operated by commissioned units of the armed forces of a State having the military marks of that State, commanded by a member of the armed forces, and manned by a crew subject to regular armed forces discipline. 20.08

20.09 **Only warships and military aircraft are entitled to perform belligerent acts at sea.**

20.10 **Warships and military aircraft enjoy sovereign immunity. This also applies to unmanned (surface, subsurface, or aerial) vehicles whether operating autonomously or not.**

20.3 General Principles of the Law of Naval Warfare

20.11 **In naval warfare, the general rules of the law of armed conflict apply.**

20.4 Specially Protected Enemy Vessels and Aircraft

20.12 **The following classes of enemy vessels are exempt from attack:**
— hospital ships; small craft used for coastal rescue operations and other medical transports;
— vessels granted safe conduct by agreement between the belligerents;
— vessels engaged in transporting cultural property under special protection;
— passenger vessels when engaged only in carrying civilian passengers;
— vessels charged with religious, non-military scientific, or philanthropic missions, and vessels collecting scientific data of likely military applications are not protected;
— small coastal fishing vessels and small boats engaged in local coastal trade, but they are subject to the regulations of a belligerent naval commander operating in the area and to inspection;
— vessels designed or adapted exclusively for responding to pollution incidents in the marine environment;
— vessels which have surrendered;
— life rafts and life boats.

20.13 **The following classes of enemy aircraft are exempt from attack:**
— medical aircraft;
— aircraft granted safe conduct by agreement between the belligerents; and
— civil airliners.

20.14 **Vessels and aircraft listed in Sections 20.12 and 20.13**
— must be innocently employed in their normal role;
— must submit to identification and inspection when required; and
— must not intentionally hamper the movement of combatants and obey orders to stop or move out of the way when required.

20.5 *Legitimate Military Targets at Sea*

In so far as objects are concerned, military objectives are limited to those objects which by their nature, location, purpose, or use make an effective contribution to military action and whose total or partial destruction, capture, or neutralization, in the circumstances ruling at the time, offers a definite military advantage. 20.15

20.6 *Methods and Means of Naval Warfare*

Means of naval warfare, such as missiles, torpedoes, and mines, shall be used in conformity with the principles of target discrimination and the prohibition on unnecessary suffering and superfluous injury. 20.16

(a) Blockade is a method of naval warfare aimed at preventing all vessels and/or aircraft from entering or exiting specified ports, airfields, or coastal areas belonging to, occupied by, or under the control of an enemy nation. 20.17

(b) A blockade must be effective. It may be enforced and maintained by a combination of legitimate methods and means of warfare. A blockade must not bar access to ports and coasts of third/neutral States.

(c) Due regard must be paid to the humanitarian needs of the civilian population of the blockaded area.

Special zones may be established for the purpose of, *inter alia*: 20.18
— defending objects and installations of high military value;
— containing the geographic area of military operations;
— subjecting civil navigation and/or aviation to restrictions or contraband control; or
— safeguarding:
- **protected persons,**
- **works and installations containing dangerous forces,**
- **objects and installations for the medical treatment of wounded and sick civilians or combatants, or**
- **objects protected under the law of armed conflict such as cultural property.**

(a) Should a belligerent party establish a special ('no-fly') zone outside its territory, in principle, the same rules of the law of armed conflict will apply both inside and outside the exclusion ('no-fly') zone. 20.19

(b) The extent, location, and duration of the ('no-fly') zone and the measures imposed shall not exceed what is reasonably required by military necessity or by the need to safeguard protected persons and objects.

(c) The commencement, duration, location, and extent of the ('no-fly') zone, as well as the restrictions imposed, shall be appropriately notified to all concerned.

(d) In principle, the establishment of a ('no-fly') zone may not affect neutral territory or airspace.

20.20 **The right to establish and maintain special ('no-fly') zones is without prejudice to the customary right of a belligerent to control merchant shipping and civil aviation in the immediate vicinity of military operations.**

20.7 Economic Warfare at Sea

20.21 **Belligerent warships and military aircraft have a right to visit and search merchant vessels and civil aircraft where there are reasonable grounds for suspicion that they are subject to capture.**

20.22 **Specially protected enemy merchant vessels and civil aircraft may not be captured, unless they:**

- **are not employed in their normal role;**
- **commit acts harmful to the enemy;**
- **do not immediately submit to identification and inspection when required; or**
- **intentionally hamper the movement.**

20.23 **Neutral merchant vessels and civil aircraft are subject to capture if they:**

- **are carrying contraband;**
- **are on a voyage especially undertaken with a view to the transport of individual passengers who are embodied in the armed forces of the enemy;**
- **are operating directly under enemy control, orders, charter, employment, or direction;**
- **present irregular or fraudulent documents, lack necessary documents, or destroy, deface or conceal documents;**
- **are violating regulations established by a belligerent within the immediate area of military operations; or**
- **are breaching or attempting to breach a blockade.**

20.24 **As an alternative to capture, a neutral merchant vessel or civil aircraft may, with its consent, be diverted from its declared destination.**

Chapter 21 Maritime Interception/interdiction Operations

Maritime Interception Operations (MIO) may range from querying the master of the vessel to stopping, boarding, inspecting, searching, and potentially even seizing the cargo or, the vessel, or arresting persons on board. As a general principle, vessels in international waters are subject to the exclusive jurisdiction of their flag State. Moreover, interference with a vessel in international waters violates the sovereign rights of the flag State unless that interference is authorized by the flag State or otherwise permitted by international law. Inside a coastal State's national waters, the coastal State exercises sovereignty, subject to the right of innocent passage and other rules of international law. Given these basic tenets of international law, commanders should be aware of the legal bases underlying the authorization of MIO when ordered by competent authorities to conduct such operations. 21.01

There are several legal bases available to conduct MIO, none of which is mutually exclusive. Depending on the circumstances, one or a combination of these bases can be used to justify permissive and non-permissive interference with suspect vessels. Possible legal bases for MIO are authorization by the UN Security Council (21.03), consent through either ad hoc (21.04-21.05) or general international agreements (21.06), international law of the sea (21.07-21.09) and self-defence (21.10). 21.02

One legal justification for maritime interception operations is authorization by the UN Security Council. Under Article 41 of the UN Charter of the United Nations the Security Council may authorize, *inter alia*, the 'complete or partial interruption of economic relations and of rail, sea, air, postal, telegraphic, radio, and other means of communication . . .'. 21.03

As a general rule ships are subject to the jurisdiction of their flag State. As such, the flag State has the right to authorize officials of another State to board vessels flying its flag. Care shall be taken to identify and comply with the limits of the flag State's consent. Consent to board a vessel does not automatically extend to inspection or search of the vessel or to the seizure of persons or cargo. Commanders need to be aware of the exact nature and extent of flag State consent prior to conducting interceptions at sea. 21.04

a) **Commanders, via the chain of command, may seek ad hoc consent to board a vessel from a particular State. A consensual boarding is conducted at the invitation of the master (or person in** 21.05

charge) of a vessel that is not otherwise subject to the jurisdiction of the boarding officer. The plenary authority of the master over all activities related to the operation of the vessel while in international waters is well established in international law and includes the authority to allow anyone to come aboard the vessel as a guest, including foreign law enforcement officials. However, some States do not recognize a master's authority to assent to a consensual boarding.

b) The voluntary consent of the master permits the boarding, but it does not allow the assertion of law enforcement authority. A consensual boarding is not, therefore, an exercise of maritime law enforcement jurisdiction per se. The scope and duration of a consensual boarding may be subject to conditions imposed by the master and may be terminated by the master at his discretion. Nevertheless, such boardings have utility in allowing rapid verification of the legitimacy of a vessel's voyage by obtaining or confirming vessel documents, cargo, and navigation records without undue delay to the boarded vessel.

21.06 Flag State consent to board and search can be provided in advance by bilateral or multilateral agreements. Similar to agreements in the law enforcement realm nations may negotiate bilateral or multilateral agreements to obtain advance consent to board another nation's vessels for other than law enforcement purposes. Such agreements greatly expedite the process by which officials of one State can board suspect vessels of another State.

21.07 International law allows non-permissive interference with ships where there are reasonable grounds to suspect that the ship is engaged in, *inter alia*, piracy, slave trade, or unauthorized broadcasting. If a warship encounters a foreign-flagged vessel on the high seas, it may board the ship without the flag State's or master's consent if there are reasonable grounds to suspect that the ship is engaged in one of these unauthorized activities.

21.08 Piracy is any illegal act of violence, or detention or any other act of depredation, committed for private ends by the crew or the passengers of a private ship, and directed on the high seas, against another ship, or against persons or property on board such ship in a place outside the jurisdiction of a state. If there are reasonable grounds for suspicion that a vessel is engaged in piracy, it may be boarded and captured. The persons on board may be arrested, the cargo may be seized. The exercise of those rights is limited to warships or other State vessels. Pirate-suspects may be prosecuted before the seizing State's courts. States should have a domestic legal framework, which

allows for the prosecution of acts of piracy and which enables naval personnel to act in a law enforcement capacity. States do not have an obligation to prosecute or extradite suspect pirates. States shall, however, cooperate to the fullest possible extent in the repression of piracy. In the conduct of counter-piracy operations, force may be used only to that degree, which is permissible for law enforcement activities.

Vessels that are not legitimately registered in any one State are without nationality and are referred to as stateless vessels. Such vessels are not entitled to fly the flag of any State and, because they are not entitled to the protection of any State, they are subject to the jurisdiction of all States. Additionally, a ship that sails under more than one flag, using them according to convenience, may not claim any of the nationalities in question and may be assimilated to a ship without nationality. If a warship encounters a stateless vessel or a vessel that has been assimilated to a ship without nationality on the high seas, it may board and search the vessel without the consent of the master. 21.09

States can conduct MIO pursuant to customary international law under circumstances that would permit the exercise of the inherent right of individual and collective self-defence. 21.10

Visit and search of vessels and aircraft must be conducted in accordance with the generally accepted principles and procedures. 21.11

The use of force must be strictly limited to what is necessary and proportionate. 21.12

The provisions of the present Chapter are without prejudice to belligerent rights at sea. 21.13

Chapter 22 Legal Dimensions of Special Operations and Information Operations

22.1 Legal Dimensions of Special Operations

There is no legal prohibition in using special operations forces (SOF) in military operations. Importantly, there is no special law for special operations forces. SOF, like conventional forces, must fully comply with international law, and applicable domestic law, in all their operations. 22.01

22.2 Legal Dimensions of Information Operations

22.02 **All information operations (IO) conducted by military forces must comply with international law, and, where applicable, domestic law.**

Chapter 23 Military Cyber Operations

23.01 **Military cyber operations refer to the employment of cyber capabilities with the primary purpose of achieving *military* goals in or by the use of cyberspace.**

23.02 **Military cyber operations with extraterritorial effects are governed by international law.**

23.03 **Extraterritorial military cyber operations below the threshold of use of force (as described in Art. 2(4) UN Charter) are, most prominently, governed by principles relating to sovereignty and non-intervention.**

23.04 **Extraterritorial military cyber operations constituting a threat or use of force are governed by Article 2(4) of the UN Charter and the recognized exceptions thereto.**

23.05 **Extraterritorial cyber activities or operations qualifying as armed attack in the sense of Article 51 of the UN Charter, taking into account the other requirements for self-defence, trigger a State's right to self-defence.**

23.06 **International humanitarian law applies to military cyber operations that qualify as an international or non-international armed conflict, whether alone or alongside other military operations.**

Chapter 24 Force Protection, Unit Self-defence and Personal Self-defence: their Relationship to Rules of Engagement

24.01 **The concept of self-defence, while always referring to the right to use force to defend against an attack, encompasses several different types and levels of this right. At the strategic level, it includes the right of national self-defence. At the operational level, it includes the concepts of extended self-defence and force protection, as well as the specific concept of self-defence in the context of UN operations.**

At the threshold between the operational and tactical level, the concept of self-defence includes the concept of unit self-defence. At the individual, personal level, it includes the right to personal self-defence.

Extended self-defence is the right of Alliance units operating within a NATO-led operation or under NATO command to assist each other in the event of an (imminent) attack. 24.02

The right of extended self-defence is derived from Article 5 of the North Atlantic Treaty and is a unit-level expression of the right to collective national self-defence. 24.03

The right for a Force other than a NATO Force to defend itself is derived from the mandate of the operation in question. This authorization can be specific, but is also inherently implicit in the existence and tasking of the Force. Without such right, a Force would be *prima facie* unable to carry out its mandate. 24.04

United Nations forces under United Nations command and control have the right to defend themselves against an (imminent) attack as well as against armed attempts to interfere with the execution of the mandate.[2] 24.05

United Nations self-defence against armed attempts to interfere with the execution of the mandate is not limited to operations authorized under Chapter VII of the Charter of the United Nations. In traditional peacekeeping operations, however, it may not always be expedient to exercise this aspect of the United Nations right of self-defence to its fullest extent when the agreement of the local parties is a necessity for mission accomplishment. 24.06

Unit self-defence consists of the right of a commander to take all necessary measures to defend his unit against an (imminent) attack. 24.07

The right to unit self-defence is primarily derived from the right of national self-defence, combined with the status of military units as representatives of the sovereign rights of the State in question. 24.08

The criteria applicable to the actual exercise of unit self-defence are the *Caroline* criteria: the use of force in self-defence must be immediately and unequivocally necessary; there must be no feasible alternatives to the use of force; and the force used must be proportional to the level of the attack being defended against. 24.09

[2] The legal basis for United Nations peace operations is discussed in Chapters 5 and 6. See especially Rule 6.09 as regards self-defence and peace operations.

24.10 **Units comprising a larger unit, such as aircraft flying together as a single flight or ships sailing together as a single naval squadron, may assist each other in the exercise of unit self-defence if they operate together as a single unit. Units which arrive at the scene of events after the attack has already commenced, such as quick reaction forces sent as reinforcements in the context of a (multinational) operation, cannot act automatically on the basis of unit self-defence but derive their authorization from either extended self-defence or the right of a Force to defend itself, as applicable.**

24.11 **Unit self-defence (and ultimately personal self-defence) is an inherent right and not dependent or contingent on a mandate or mission. Although restricted to situations involving an (imminent) attack on the unit invoking this right, the right is neither dependent on, nor limited by, any ROE. Nothing in any ROE limits or prohibits this inherent right.**

24.12 **Extended self-defence and self-defence in the context of force protection are indelibly linked to the nature and tasks of the Force as such and are therefore equally indelibly linked to mission accomplishment. Consequently, the use of force in such contexts may be regulated by ROE and may extend beyond mere defence against an (imminent) attack.**

24.13 **ROE relating to the concepts of hostile act and hostile intent, in the meaning as used by NATO, are intended to equalize the response abilities of units within multinational forces and enable coherent response in extended self-defence and force protection regardless of national statutes on self-defence. The same applies to the so-called 'confirmatory ROE' used within the context of EU operations.**

24.14 **The right to personal self-defence is well recognized in criminal law systems around the world. It is distinct from the other forms of self-defence discussed in this chapter both in terms of legal basis and as regards the applicable legal framework.**

24.15 **The central criteria for a legitimate recourse to self-defence are necessity and proportionality.**

24.16 **Proving necessity in the context of personal self-defence consists of two evaluations:**

(a) proof of the necessity to defend, as opposed to other courses of action to reconcile the situation; and

(b) proof of the necessity to choose, within the choice of means available, the particular means employed in the actual exercise of personal self-defence.

Proof of the necessity to defend oneself may be negated by prior provocation by the defending party. On the other hand, a provoked attack which is disproportionate to the provocation may be cause for a legitimate recourse to personal self-defence after all. 24.17

Proof of the necessity to defend oneself may be negated if the defending party knowingly and willingly placed himself or herself, without necessity or objectively legitimate reason, in the vicinity of the attacking party even though the capability and intent of the attacking party to carry out an attack was known beforehand. 24.18

Proof of the necessity to defend oneself may be negated if an avenue of retreat was available but not utilized. The duty to retreat is not imposed in all statutes and is limited in certain statutes. Even in such cases, however, the choice to defend rather than to break off a confrontation may be taken into account in judging the legitimacy of the recourse to personal self-defence. 24.19

In deciding on the choice of means, the least destructive means available and suitable must be chosen. 24.20

The level of training and expertise that may be expected of military personnel increases the level of care and diligence expected from military personnel and may impose restrictions on the applicability of the criminal law concept of personal self-defence in an operational context. 24.21

Defence of property is not recognized as part of the inherent right of personal self-defence in many national criminal law statutes. Consequently, lesser means of defending property may be required in the context of personal self-defence and the use of deadly force, such as the use of firearms, may be reserved for defence of life. It is understood, on the other hand, that a situation involving the use of lesser means to defend property may at any time escalate to a situation requiring the use of deadly force to defend life. 24.22

Some statutes specify that personal self-defence is only authorized against an illegal or unauthorized attack. This principle prevents a claim of personal self-defence in cases involving the use of force against law-enforcement officials on official duty. 24.23

The defence of others under application of the right of personal self-defence is well recognized in most statutes. Certain logical limitations may be imposed on this aspect in case law or statutes, however, to prevent unbridled invocation of the right of personal self-defence as justification for, effectively, vigilantism. Such limitations may relate to the need for proximity between the defending party and 24.24

the party being aided, the necessity of providing the aid (e.g. was the party being aided actually under attack or not), etc.

24.25 **The right to personal self-defence is an inherent right and therefore cannot be limited or prohibited by ROE.**

24.26 **Personal self-defence as a criminal law justification is subject to many variations in national statutes and case law interpretation of those statutes, subject to conditions which are generally incompatible with military objectives and missions and is consequently particularly flawed as a legal basis for planning or executing military operations. While the inherent right of personal self-defence may exist and be applied by individual servicemen and servicewomen within the context of a military operation on an individual and case-by-case basis, it cannot be utilized as a basis for a military operation as such.**

Chapter 25 The Maintenance of Law and Order in Military Operations

25.01 **In international military operations States are obliged to cooperate in the maintenance of law and order.**

25.02 **All States are obliged to repress, and to provide penal sanctions for persons committing or ordering to be committed, serious crimes under international law.**

25.03 **In situations of military occupation the occupant is obliged to take all measures within its power to restore, and as far as possible ensure, public order and safety while respecting, unless absolutely prevented, the laws in force in the occupied country.**

25.04 **Where military operations are conducted pursuant to Security Council authorization and the Security Council mandate specifies a maintenance of law and order obligation, the military force is obliged to implement the mandate and to act consistently with it.**

Chapter 26 Operational Detention and the Treatment of Detainees

26.01 **Operational detention is the deprivation of physical liberty of a person in the context of a military operation, whether for reasons of security or for law enforcement purposes.**

The international legal framework governing operational detention consists primarily of international humanitarian law and human rights law, as complemented by applicable Security Council resolutions, secondary UN legislation, rules of regional organizations, status-of-forces, and other bilateral agreements. 26.02

No person may be detained except on lawful grounds. Detention must cease as soon as the lawful grounds for it cease to exist. Unlawful confinement and imprisonment or other severe deprivation of physical liberty are prohibited. 26.03

Without prejudice to further rights under international humanitarian law, detainees are entitled to humane treatment and conditions of detention, without distinction of any kind. No person under detention shall be subjected to torture or to cruel, inhuman, or degrading treatment or punishment. Enforced disappearances are prohibited. 26.04

Detention shall be subject to the procedures as are required by applicable law, which may include those relating to: 26.05

- **being informed about the reasons for detention;**
- **status determination;**
- **challenging the lawfulness of detention and review of the lawfulness by an independent and impartial body;**
- **contacts with family members;**
- **submissions concerning treatment and conditions of detention;**
- **access to detainees by impartial humanitarian organizations, such as the International Committee of the Red Cross, or by other visiting mechanisms.**

Without prejudice to applicable rules of international humanitarian law, a detainee may not be transferred to another detaining authority when there are substantial grounds for believing that there is a real risk that he or she will be subjected to torture, cruel, inhuman or degrading treatment, or other serious violations of human rights. 26.06

Chapter 27 Civil–Military Cooperation and Humanitarian Assistance

Humanitarian assistance is aid to an affected population in order to save lives and alleviate suffering and must be provided in accordance with basic humanitarian principles of humanity, impartiality, and neutrality. Dialogue and interaction between civilian and military actors in peace operations are necessary to protect and promote 27.01

humanitarian principles, avoid competition, minimize inconsistency, and when appropriate pursue common goals.

27.02 **A clear separation between the roles of the military and humanitarian actors is necessary to distinguish their respective spheres of competence and responsibility. This approach is implicit in and builds on the principles of international humanitarian law, and is crucial to maintaining the independence of humanitarian action.**

27.03 **Civil–military coordination is a shared responsibility of the humanitarian and military actors and it may take place in various levels of intensity and form. Humanitarian workers must never present themselves or their work as part of a military operation, and military personnel must refrain from presenting themselves as civilian humanitarian workers.**

27.04 **In any civil–military cooperation, humanitarian actors should retain the lead role in undertaking and directing humanitarian activities. Humanitarian organizations must not implement tasks on behalf of the military nor represent or implement their policies.**

27.05 **As a general rule, humanitarian convoys do not use armed or military escorts. Exceptions to the rule will be considered, as a last resort, and only when the criteria independence of humanitarian actors/agencies—need, safety, and sustainability—have been met.**

Chapter 28 Private Contractors and Security Companies

28.01 **Private contractors may be employed by a Sending State to provide logistical and technical support and security for installations and persons. They should not be employed in combat functions or engage in direct participation in hostilities in the context of an armed conflict, as such participation would entail the loss of civilian protection and could result in their being prosecuted for acts of unprivileged belligerency.**

28.02 **In all cases in which private security companies and contractors are utilized on missions abroad, adequate provision for regulation, supervision, and accountability must be made to ensure that their activities are carried out in full conformity with applicable national and international legal standards and to ensure the existence of an adequate regulatory legal framework. This is in the interest of both Sending and Receiving States and the international community as a whole. In no case should it be possible for such activities to be carried** out in the absence of such a regulatory and supervisory framework with the resulting possibility of impunity for any violations which may occur.

In the absence of a status-of-forces or similar agreement granting functional immunity, the status of private contractors is that of foreign civilian workers in the Receiving State. It should be in the interest of all parties to ensure that adequate provision is made to ensure accountability and supervision while, at the same time, allowing for the contractors and their employers to carry out the functions for which they have been engaged within the limits referred to above. 28.03

Chapter 29 The Prosecution of International Crimes in Relation to the Conduct of Military Operations

War Crimes, crimes against humanity, and genocide are international crimes which may occur in relation to military operations. War crimes may only occur in armed conflict but crimes against humanity and genocide may occur in or outside of armed conflict. All three types of crimes may be prosecuted on the basis of universal jurisdiction, that is, they may be prosecuted by the authorities of any State regardless of where the offence is committed although, usually, the accused must be in the hands of the State authorities which commence the prosecution. In certain circumstances, persons accused of any of the three types of crimes may be prosecuted before an international tribunal. 29.01

War crimes are violations of the treaty or customary law applicable during armed conflict. The content of the applicable law may vary depending on the treaty obligations of parties to the relevant conflict and on the classification of the conflict as international or non-international. A reasonably comprehensive and generally usable list of war crimes is contained in Article 8 of the Statute of the International Criminal Court although the provisions of the Statute do not apply, as treaty law, to States which are not parties to the Statute. 29.02

Crimes against humanity are various prohibited acts committed as part of a widespread or systematic attack directed against any civilian population. A reasonably comprehensive and generally usable list of crimes against humanity is contained in Article 7 of the Statute of the International Criminal Court although the provisions of the Statute do not apply, as treaty law, to States which are not parties to the Statute. 29.03

29.04 **Genocide is one of a specific series of acts, enumerated in the 1948 UN Convention against Genocide, committed with intent to destroy, in whole or in part, a national, ethnical, racial, or religious group, as such.**

29.05 **Individuals are criminally responsible when they commit or participate in the commission of war crimes, crimes against humanity, or acts of genocide.**

29.06 **Individuals have a duty to disobey a manifestly unlawful order.**

29.07 **Obeying a superior order does not relieve a subordinate of criminal responsibility if the subordinate knew that the act ordered was unlawful or should have known because of the manifestly unlawful nature of the act ordered.**

29.08 **Commanders and other superiors are criminally responsible for war crimes, crimes against humanity, or acts of genocide committed pursuant to their orders.**

29.09 **Commanders and other superiors are criminally responsible for war crimes, crimes against humanity, or acts of genocide committed by their subordinates if they knew, or had reason to know, that the subordinates were about to commit or were committing such crimes and did not take all necessary and reasonable measures in their power to prevent their commission, or if such crimes had been committed, to punish the persons responsible.**

29.10 **In order to meet their obligations to have their subordinates comply with the law, commanders should establish a reporting mechanism so that incidents in which it appears war crimes, crimes against humanity, or acts of genocide may have been committed by members of the contingent or force are brought to their attention. An adequately staffed particular office should be designated within the contingent or force to receive the incident reports, to advise the commander of the contents of the reports, and to advise on follow-up action.**

29.11 **Commanders must direct that investigations be conducted of incidents in which it appears war crimes, crimes against humanity, or acts of genocide may have been committed by their subordinates. If the contingent or force is involved in an armed conflict, the commander may direct that investigations be conducted of incidents in which it appears that war crimes, crimes against humanity, or genocide may have been committed by persons on the opposing side. If the contingent or force is engaged in peace support operations, the commander may direct that investigations be conducted of incidents**

in which it appears that war crimes, crimes against humanity, or genocide may have been committed by persons in the State in which the Force is deployed unless it is prohibited by the Force mandate.

Commanders must take all practicable measures within their authority to ensure that their subordinates who appear to have committed war crimes, crimes against humanity, or genocide are tried before appropriate tribunals and, if found guilty, appropriately punished. Often, because the military justice system is insulated from command influence, a commander may do no more than direct that an investigation be undertaken and then turn the matter over to military police and judicial authorities. **29.12**

If an international tribunal has been created by the UN Security Council to try accused for the alleged commission of war crimes, crimes against humanity, or genocide in the State in which the Force is deployed, commanders must cooperate with the tribunal. If the International Criminal Court exercises jurisdiction, commanders of forces or contingents from State parties must cooperate with the court while commanders from other States should cooperate with the court, subject to national direction. If a national court exercises jurisdiction, commanders of forces or contingents from that State must cooperate while other commanders may cooperate. **29.13**

Chapter 30 International Responsibility and Military Operations

International responsibility in the context of military operations refers to the legal consequences arising from wrongful acts committed during such operations. **30.01**

A State is responsible for conduct [of/in relation to a military operation] consisting of an act or omission that is attributable to the State and that breaches an international obligation of the State. Conduct of the armed forces of a State is in principle attributable to the State as conduct of a State organ. In regard to omissions, a State is only responsible if there was a duty to act. **30.02**

International organizations bear responsibility for conduct that is attributable to them and that breaches an international obligation of the organization, in principle in the same way as States. **30.03**

The question, whether the conduct of a military force led by an international organization consisting of troops contributed by States **30.04**

can be attributed to the international organization or to troop contributing States is determined by the question which actor exercises effective control over that conduct.

30.05 **There may be dual or multiple international responsibility of an international organization and one or more states for conduct of a military operation.**

30.06 **In general, breaches of international law committed by personnel of a military operation are not attributable to the Host State.**

30.07 **Valid consent, self-defence, necessity, counter-measures, distress and *force majeure* preclude wrongfulness but there is no preclusion in case of the breach of peremptory norms. Core norms of human rights and humanitarian law are considered as peremptory.**

30.08 **International responsibility entails the obligation to cease the internationally wrongful act if it is continuing, and the obligation to make full reparation. Forms of reparation include restitution, compensation, rehabilitation, satisfaction, and guarantees of non-repetition.**

30.09 **International organizations and Sending States should provide effective remedies to victims of violations committed by military operations.**

30.10 **The responsibility under international law of an international organization or State for wrongful acts committed during a military operation does not affect the individual criminal responsibility of the perpetrator.**

PART V

SYNTHESIS AND CONCLUSION

Chapter 31 The Role of the Military Legal Advisor

Each State must make legal advisors available to the staff of military commanders whose forces are likely to be deployed on military operations. 31.01

The duty of those legal advisors will be to provide advice that will enable the commander and his staff to carry out the commander's military mission in accordance with the law. The legal advisor may also be required to advise on appropriate legal training for the forces concerned. 31.02

To enable legal advisors to fulfil their duties, they need appropriate general and specific training in advance. 31.03

Once appointed, they need to be integrated into the staff structure but also have the right of direct access to the commander whenever they deem it legally necessary. The staff structure should be such as to ensure the legal advisors' independence from the commander with regard to the exercise of their legal functions. Legal advisors should be enabled to act within their legal chain of command. 31.04

Glossary of Terms

The terms listed here are used as designated below for the purposes of this Handbook. Definitions marked with '*' are based on NATO terminology.[1]

1. Accountability

State of being responsible or answerable.[2] The concept of accountability is broader than the principles of responsibility and liability for internationally wrongful acts and rests upon the notion that the lawful application of power imports accountability for its exercise. Such accountability will necessarily range across legal, political, administrative, and financial forms and essentially create a regulatory and behavioural framework.[3]

2. Administrative control (ADCON)

Direction or exercise of authority over subordinate or other organizations in respect to administrative matters such as personnel management, supply, services, and other matters not included in the operational missions of the subordinate or other organizations.*

3. Aircraft, civil; see: **Civil aircraft**

4. Aircraft, medical; see: **Medical aircraft**

5. Aircraft, military; see: **Military aircraft**

6. Aircraft, State; see: **State aircraft**

7. Air Defence Identification Zone (ADIZ)

Zone in international airspace adjacent to the national airspace, where a foreign aircraft can be required to identify itself and provide position reports as a condition for entry into national airspace.

1 NATO Glossary of Terms and Definitions, (AAP-06 2014), available at <http://nso.nato.int/nso/zPublic/ap/aap6/AAP-6.pdf>.

2 Black, H.C. and B.A. Garner, *Black's Law Dictionary*, 8th edn (St Paul, MN: West Group, 2004).

3 Shaw, M., *International Law*, 6th edn (Cambridge: Cambridge University Press, 2008), 1317–18.

8. Airspace

The space in the air directly above an area of the earth's surface, especially as used for the operation of aircraft. Airspace is classified as national or international. See: **International airspace; National airspace.**

9. Armed attack (in the context of self-defence)

(1) Significant direct use of force—or a series of smaller related armed incidents from one source with a common purpose—by a State's regular armed forces or by a non-State actor across an international border, or (2) the sending by or on behalf of a State of armed bands, groups, irregulars, or mercenaries which carry out acts of armed force against another State of such gravity as to amount to (*inter alia*) an actual armed attack conducted by regular forces, or (3) the substantial involvement therein. Note a broader definition of 'attack', comprising any act of violence against the adversary, whether in offence or defence, is used in international humanitarian law (Art. 49, para. 1, AP I).

10. Armed conflict

The resort to armed force between States or protracted armed violence between governmental authorities and organized armed groups or between such groups within a State.[4] Ref.: **International armed conflict; War; Non-international armed conflict.**

11. Attributability

Capability of being legally responsible for conduct of behaviour.[5] Syn.: imputability.

12. Belligerent measures

The use of methods and means of (naval) warfare against the enemy or against persons and objects qualifying as legitimate military targets/objectives as well as prize measures against neutral vessels and aircraft.

13. Caveat/restriction

In NATO operations, any limitation, restriction, or constraint by a nation on its military forces or civilian elements under NATO command and control or otherwise available to NATO, that does not permit NATO commanders to deploy and employ these assets fully in line with the approved operation plan. Note A caveat may apply, *inter alia*, to freedom of movement within the joint operations area and/or to compliance with the approved rules of engagement.*

[4] ICTY, *The Prosecutor v Tadić*, IT-94-1-A, Decision on the Defence Motion for Interlocutory Appeal on Jurisdiction, 2 October 1995, para. 70.

[5] Derived from 'attribution' and 'attribute', ref.: *Oxford English Dictionary Online* at <http://dictionary.oed.com>.

14. Civil aircraft

All non-State aircraft (i.e. non military, police, customs). Ref.: **State aircraft.**

15. Civil–military Cooperation (CIMIC)

The coordination and cooperation, in support of the mission, between a commander and civil actors, including the national population and local authorities, as well as international, national, and non-governmental organizations and agencies.*

16. Combined operation; see: Multinational operation

17. Command; see: Command and control

18. Command and control

Command: To exercise command, i.e. the authority vested in an individual of the armed forces for the direction, coordination, and control of military forces. Note: The term 'command' as used internationally, implies a lesser degree of authority than when it is used in a purely national sense. No NATO or coalition commander has full command over the forces assigned to him since, in assigning forces to NATO, nations will delegate only operational command or operational control.*

Control: That authority exercised by a commander over part of the activities of subordinate organizations, or other organizations not normally under his command, which encompasses the responsibility for implementing orders or directives. All or part of this authority may be transferred or delegated.* Syn.: Command & Control, C2. Ref.: **Administrative control (ADCON); Full command; Operational command (OPCOM); Operational control (OPCON); Tactical control (TACON).**

19. Command, full; see: Full command

20. Command, operational; see: Operational command (OPCOM)

21. Command responsibility

Criminal responsibility of military commanders or other (i.e. civil) superiors for war crimes, crimes against humanity, or acts of genocide committed by their subordinates if they knew, or had reason to know, that the subordinates were about to commit or were committing such crimes and did not take all necessary and reasonable measures in their power to prevent their commission, or if such crimes had been committed, to punish the persons responsible. Syn.: Superior responsibility.

22. Conduct of hostilities

The collective resort to means and methods of warfare between parties to an armed conflict. The conduct of hostilities is a term of art in international humanitarian law relating especially to the actual carrying out of attacks (either offensively or defensively) and implies the application of means and methods of combat.

23. Consent

Expression (by a government or other entity such as a rebel or insurgent movement) indicating concisely its legal and its operational significance in the context of (peace) enforcement or peace operations or as a separate legal basis for deployment of troops on a State's territory.

24. Control; see: **Command and control**

25. Control, administrative—(ADCON); see: **Administrative control (ADCON)**

26. Control, operational—(OPCON); see: **Operational control (OPCON)**

27. Control, tactical—(TACON); see: **Tactical control (TACON)**

28. Crime against humanity

Various prohibited acts—inside or outside armed conflict—committed as part of a widespread or systematic attack directed against any civilian population. Ref.: **International crimes.**

29. Cyber operations; see: **Military cyber operations**

30. Deployment

The movement of forces within areas of operations; or the positioning of forces into a formation for battle; or the relocation of forces to desired areas of operations.*

31. Detainee(s)

A person who is detained, i.e. deprived of his/her physical liberty in the context of a military operation, whether for reasons of security or for law enforcement purposes, except as a result of conviction for an offence. Ref.: **Operational detention.**

32. Detention(s); see: **Operational detention**

33. Enforcement action

Action taken pursuant to Chapter VII of the UN Charter, taken or authorized by the UN Security Council in the context of maintenance or restoration of international peace and security. Enforcement action can be divided into measures of military nature and those not involving the use of force. Enforcement action of a military character can be further subdivided into (1) enforcement operations and (2) peace enforcement operations. Syn.: enforcement measures. Ref.: **Enforcement operation(s); Peace enforcement operation(s).**

34. Enforcement measures; see: Enforcement action

35. Enforcement operation(s)

Military enforcement action pursuant to Chapter VII of the UN Charter, which can be characterized as sustained full-scale combat operations authorized by the Security Council to maintain or restore international peace and security. Syn.: enforcement. Ref.: **Enforcement action; Peace enforcement operation(s).**

36. Extended self-defence

The right derived from Art. 5 NATO Treaty, of Alliance units operating within a NATO-led operation or under NATO command to assist each other in the event of an (imminent) attack. It does not and cannot extend beyond the limits of Art. 51 of the Charter of the United Nations. Ref.: **Unit self-defence.**

37. Force protection

All measures and means to minimize the vulnerability of personnel, facilities, equipment, and operations to any threat and in all situations, to preserve freedom of action and the operational effectiveness of the Force.*

38. Full command

The military authority and responsibility of a commander to issue orders to subordinates. It covers every aspect of military operations and administration and exists only within national services.*

39. Functional immunity

Exemption from the territorial jurisdiction of another State, derived from the general principle of State immunity, but limited to the performance of official acts. While a foreign force may not be considered free to disregard the constitutional, penal, or other law of a Receiving State, the latter is bound not to exercise jurisdiction where this would affect the performance of official duties of the foreign force. See **Immunity.**

40. Genocide

One of a specific series of acts, enumerated in the 1948 UN Convention against Genocide, committed with intent to destroy, within or outside armed conflict, in whole or in part, a national, ethnical, racial, or religious group. Ref.: **International crimes.**

41. Hostilities; see: **Conduct of hostilities**

42. Human rights law; see: **International human rights law (HRL)**

43. Humanitarian assistance

Humanitarian assistance is aid to an affected population in order to save lives and alleviate suffering and provided in accordance with basic humanitarian principles of humanity, impartiality, and neutrality.

44. Humanitarian intervention

Military intervention, which is undertaken without the authorization of the UN Security Council by one or more States, or by a regional organization, with the purpose of halting or preventing large-scale systematic and acute violations of fundamental human rights of persons who are not nationals of the intervening State(s), which can be legitimized and wholly or partially justified under strict legal, moral, and policy conditions.

45. Humanitarian law; see: **International humanitarian law (IHL)**

46. Immunity

Exemption from the territorial jurisdiction of another State, derived from the duty of every sovereign State to respect the independence and dignity of every other sovereign State. See **Functional immunity**.

47. Individual self-defence; see: **Personal self-defence**

48. Information operations

The integrated employment of the core capabilities of Information-Related Capabilities (tools, techniques, or activities using data, information, or knowledge to create effects and operationally desirable conditions within the physical, informational, and cognitive dimensions of the information environment, *inter alia*, electronic warfare, computer network operations, psychological operations, military deception, and operations security), in concert with other lines of operations to influence, disrupt, corrupt, or usurp (potential) adversarial human and automated decision-making while protecting our own. *Also called IO.[6]

[6] US Department of Defense, Joint Publication 3-13, Information Operations (20 November 2014), ix and I-4, <http://www.dtic.mil/doctrine/new_pubs/jp3_13.pdf>.

49. International airspace

The airspace above contiguous zones, exclusive economic zones, the high seas, and territory not subject to the sovereignty of any State, such as Antarctica and the Arctic. Ref.: **Airspace.**

50. International armed conflict

Armed conflict as defined by Common Article 2 of the Geneva Conventions (1949) or Article 1(4) of Additional Protocol I to the Geneva Conventions (1977). Ref.: **Armed conflict; War; Non-international armed conflict.**

51. International crimes

War crimes, crimes against humanity, and genocide. Ref.: **War crime; Crime against humanity.**

52. International human rights law (HRL)

Part of treaty-based and customary public international law, designed to promote and protect human rights. It defines the rights of individuals and obligations of State parties and provides for procedures of (judicial) supervision and accountability. In the context of military operations it can complement international humanitarian law and can be applicable in so far as jurisdiction exists over territory or individuals.

53. International humanitarian law (IHL)

The part of public international law that applies to armed conflict. IHL is the legal corpus comprised of the Geneva Conventions and the Hague Conventions, as well as subsequent treaties, case law, and customary international law. It defines the conduct and responsibilities of belligerent nations, neutral nations, non-State actors, and individuals engaged in armed conflict of either an international or non-international character.

Syn.: humanitarian law, Law of Armed Conflict (LOAC), international humanitarian law of armed conflict, Law(s) (and Customs) of War.

54. International law of military operations (ILMO)

All areas of public international law which relate to military operations in the international context. ILMO comprises *inter alia jus ad bellum* (legal basis for international military operations); command and control of such operations; status of forces; deployment and transit of forces; the use and regulation of force and the treatment of detainees; the legal responsibility of States, of international organizations, and of individual members of the forces and all other entities participating in the operation.

55. International responsibility

Legal consequences based on Public International Law, arising from wrongful acts committed. International responsibility is part of the broader concept of international accountability and reparation for wrongful acts.

56. Law enforcement

All territorial and extraterritorial measures taken by a State under its domestic or under international law to maintain or re-establish public security, law, and order or to otherwise exercise its authority or power over individuals, objects, or territory.

57. Law of armed conflict; see: **International humanitarian law (IHL)**

58. Law(s) (and customs) of war; see: **International humanitarian law (IHL)**

59. Legal advisor (Legad)

Qualified lawyer or officer specialized in Military Law, providing legal advice to commanders and headquarters/military units/armed forces. Syn.: Military legal advisors.

60. Maritime interception operation(s) (MIO)

An operation—ranging from querying the master of the vessel to stopping, boarding, inspecting, searching, and potentially even seizing the cargo or the vessel—conducted to enforce prohibition on the maritime movement of specified persons or material within a defined geographic area. Syn.: Maritime interdiction operation (MIO).*

61. Maritime interdiction operation(s) (MIO); see: **Maritime interception operation(s) (MIO)**

62. Medical aircraft

(As used in IHL) An aircraft as defined in Art. 8(f) and (j) of Additional Protocol I to the Geneva Conventions, which is exclusively assigned to medical transportation which is under the control of the competent authorities of a party to an armed conflict.

63. Military aircraft

Aircraft operated under the command of members of the armed forces and marked as such, as well as unmanned aerial vehicles operated by the military. Ref.: **State aircraft**.

64. Military cyber operations

The employment of cyber capabilities with the primary purpose of achieving *military* goals in or by the use of cyberspace.

65. Military enforcement action; see: **Enforcement action**

66. Military legal advisors; see: **Legal advisor (Legad)**

67. Military operation(s)

Operation(s)—i.e. sequence(s) of coordinated actions with a defined purpose—conducted by armed forces.*

68. Multinational operation

Military operation in which contingents of more than one State participate. Syn.: Combined operation.

69. National airspace

National airspace lies over the land, internal waters, archipelagic waters, and territorial seas of a State. Ref.: **Airspace**; **International airspace**.

70. No-fly zone

Part of airspace where the use of airspace is restricted or prohibited; or geographic area over which aircraft are not permitted to fly. Syn.: Exclusion zone.

71. Non-combatant evacuation operation (NEO); see: **Rescue of nationals**

72. Non-international armed conflict

An armed conflict not of an international character. Ref.: **Armed conflict**; **International armed conflict**; **War**.

73. Operation; see: **Military operations**

74. Operational command (OPCOM)

The authority granted to a commander to assign missions or tasks to subordinate commanders, to deploy units, to reassign forces, and to retain or delegate operational and/or tactical control as the commander deems necessary. Note: It does not include responsibility for administration.*

75. Operational control (OPCON)

The authority delegated to a commander to direct forces assigned so that the commander may accomplish specific missions or tasks which are usually limited by function, time, or location; to deploy units concerned; and to retain or assign tactical control of those units. It does not include authority to assign separate employment of components of the units concerned. Neither does it, of itself, include administrative or logistic control.*

76. Operational detention

The deprivation of physical liberty of a person in the context of a military operation, whether for reasons of security or for law enforcement purposes, except as a result of conviction for an offence.

77. Operational plan (OPLAN)

A plan for a single or series of connected [military] operations to be carried out simultaneously or in succession. It is usually based upon stated assumptions and is in the form of directive employed by higher authority to permit subordinate commanders to prepare supporting plans and orders. The designation 'plan' is usually used instead of 'order' in preparing for operations well in advance. An operation plan may be put into effect at a prescribed time, or on signal, and then becomes the operation order.*

78. Peace enforcement operation(s)

Military enforcement action pursuant to Chapter VII of the UN Charter, authorized by the Security Council to maintain or restore international peace and security, which—while potentially involving combat—will not normally entail the use of full-scale combat on a sustained basis against a State, and which fall conceptually and in terms of their objectives and the intensity of the use of force between enforcement operations and traditional peacekeeping. Syn.: peace enforcement. Ref.: **Enforcement action**; **Enforcement operation(s)**.

79. Peacekeeper(s)

Military conducting peace operations. Ref.: **Peace operation(s)**.

80. Peacekeeping

The execution of peace operations. Ref.: **Peace operation(s)**.

81. Peace operation(s)

Military operations—enforcement and peace enforcement operations excluded—to establish or maintain peace, which have their legal basis in the general powers of the

Security Council, of the General Assembly, and of regional organizations, and which require the consent of the Receiving State(s). Peace operations are governed further by the underlying principles of consent of all relevant parties, impartiality, and use of force restricted to defence of the peacekeepers and their mandate. Syn.: Peace support or Peacekeeping operations.

82. Personal self-defence

An individual's inherent right to defend itself against an (imminent) attack. Syn.: Individual self-defence.

83. Reparation

Adequate, effective, and prompt action intended to promote justice by redressing gross violations of international human rights law or serious violations of international humanitarian law. Reparation should be proportional to the gravity of the violations and the harm suffered. Forms of reparation include restitution, compensation, rehabilitation, satisfaction, and guarantees of non-repetition.

84. Rescue of nationals

A military operation aimed at protecting and evacuating nationals of a State or a group of States when their lives or physical safety are directly threatened in a foreign country. Syn.: Non-combatant evacuation operation (NEO).

85. Responsibility; see: **International responsibility**

86. Rules of engagement (ROE)

ROE are orders or directives (i.e. lawful commands) issued by a competent military authority, which define the circumstances, conditions, degree, manner, and limitations within which force may be applied to achieve military objectives in furtherance of the UN mandate. ROE are intended to ensure commanders and their subordinates use only such force or other measures as are necessary, appropriate, and authorized by higher command. ROE are an essential instrument of command and control for ordering, directing, and controlling the use of force during military operations.

87. Search, visit and; see: **Visit and search**

88. Self-defence

(i.e. National or State Self-Defence, as used in Part III) The inherent right of a State under international law to respond individually or collectively to an illegal armed attack directed against its territory, citizens, military vessels, aircraft, or installations, abroad or located in international sea or airspace, and subject to the legal criteria and conditions laid down in the UN Charter and in customary international law. Ref.: **Extended self-defence; Unit self-defence.**

89. Sexual exploitation and abuse (SEA)

(i.e. in the context of Peace Operations) An abuse of a position of vulnerability, encompassing a differential in power or an abuse of trust for sexual purposes. Any form of sexual violence, intimidation, or abuse directed against the civilian population by any group or individual, or by members of a peacekeeping force.

90. Space

Outer space as the area beyond airspace.

91. Special forces (SF); see: Special operations forces (SOF)

92. Special operations

Military activities conducted by specially designated, organized, trained, and equipped forces using operational techniques and modes of employment not standard to conventional forces. These activities are conducted across the full range of military operations independently or in coordination with operations of conventional forces to achieve political, military, psychological, and economic objectives. Politico-military considerations may require clandestine, covert, or discreet techniques and the acceptance of a degree of physical and political risk not associated with conventional operations.* Ref.: **Special operations forces (SOF).**

93. Special operations forces (SOF)

Armed forces conducting special operations. See: **Special operations.**

94. State aircraft

All aircraft 'belonging' to a State (i.e. non-civil aircraft), *inter alia*, military, police, and customs aircraft. See: **Civil aircraft, Military aircraft.**

95. Status of forces

A term of art referring to matters pertaining to immunity from, and respect for, the law of the Receiving State, Transit States, and any third States. Status-of-forces rules include provisions on jurisdiction, entry and exit modalities, force protection, freedom of movement, weapons and ammunition, communications, host nation support, tax and duty exemptions, and other issues relevant for an unimpeded performance of the particular mission. Regulation of such matters in status-of-forces agreements (SOFA) does not affect issues of combatant status under international humanitarian law of regular armed forces engaged in hostilities, neither should it prejudge legal issues of protection of civilians in an armed conflict.

96. Superior responsibility; see: **Command responsibility**

97. Tactical control (TACON)

The detailed and, usually, local direction and control of movements or manoeuvres necessary to accomplish missions or tasks assigned.*

98. Targeted killing

Military operations involving the use of lethal force with the aim of killing individually selected persons who are not in the physical custody of those targeting them.

99. Targeting

The military process of selecting and prioritizing targets and matching the appropriate response to them, taking into account operational requirements and capabilities.*

100. Troop contributing country (TCC)

State contributing to a multinational military operation with armed forces. Syn.: Troop contributing nation (TCN).

101. Troop contributing nation (TCN); see: **Troop contributing country (TCC)**

102. UN Collective Security System

The maintenance and/or restoration of international peace and security through collective measures authorized or conducted by the United Nations. The collective security system encompasses measures of both an enforcement and of a non-enforcement character and is regulated by the relevant provisions of the UN Charter and by the general powers of the UN Organization in this context, as well as by other relevant rules and principles of international law.

103. Unit self-defence

Unit self-defence consists of the right derived from the State's inherent right of Self-Defence, of a commander of a military unit to take all necessary measures to defend his unit against an (imminent) attack. Ref.: **Extended self-defence**.

104. United Nations self-defence

(i.e. in the context of peace operations) The right of UN forces under United Nations command and control to defend themselves against an (imminent) attack as well as against armed attempts to interfere with the execution of the mandate.

105. Visit and search

The rights of visit and search are to enable belligerents in the context of naval warfare to verify the true character of neutral merchant vessels and civil aircraft or whether they are employed in their innocent role. The exercise of the right of visit and search is subject to reasonable grounds of suspicion that they are engaged in activities rendering them liable to capture.

106. War; see: **Armed conflict**

107. War crime

Violations of the treaty or customary law applicable during armed conflict. Ref.: **International crimes.**

108. Warship

A ship belonging to the armed forces of a State bearing the external marks distinguishing such ship of its nationality, under the command of an officer duly commissioned by the government of a State and whose name appears in the appropriate service list or its equivalent, and manned by a crew which is under regular armed forces discipline.

Index

Note: please see under entries for individual countries for specific topics relating to that country

Printed and bound by CPI Group (UK) Ltd, Croydon, CR0 4YY